Lecture Notes in Computer Science 2888

Edited by G. Goos, J. Hartmanis, and J. van Leeuwen

Springer-Verlag Berlin Heidelberg GmbH

Robert Meersman   Zahir Tari
Douglas C. Schmidt et al. (Eds.)

On The Move to Meaningful Internet Systems 2003: CoopIS, DOA, and ODBASE

OTM Confederated International Conferences
CoopIS, DOA, and ODBASE 2003
Catania, Sicily, Italy, November 3-7, 2003
Proceedings

 Springer

Series Editors

Gerhard Goos, Karlsruhe University, Germany
Juris Hartmanis, Cornell University, NY, USA
Jan van Leeuwen, Utrecht University, The Netherlands

Volume Editors

Robert Meersman
STAR Lab, Vrije Universiteit Brussel
Pleinlaan 2, Gebouw G-10, 1050 Brussels, Belgium
E-mail: Robert.Meersman@vub.ac.be

Zahir Tari
RMIT University
School of Computer Scienc and Information Technology
GPO Box 2476V, Melbourne, Victoria 3001, Australia
E-mail: zahirt@cs.rmit.edu.au

Douglas C. Schmidt
University of California at Irvine
Electrical and Computer Engineering Department
Irvine, CA 92697-2625, USA
E-mail: schmidt@uci.edu

Cataloging-in-Publication Data applied for

A catalog record for this book is available from the Library of Congress.

Bibliographic information published by Die Deutsche Bibliothek
Die Deutsche Bibliothek lists this publication in the Deutsche Nationalbibliografie;
detailed bibliographic data is available in the Internet at <http://dnb.ddb.de>.

CR Subject Classification (1998): H.2, H.3, H.4, C.2, H.5, I.2, D.2.12, K.4

ISBN 978-3-540-20498-5   ISBN 978-3-540-39964-3 (eBook)
DOI 10.1007/978-3-540-39964-3

Springer-Verlag is a part of Springer Science+Business Media

springeronline.com

© Springer-Verlag Berlin Heidelberg 2003
Originally published by Springer-Verlag Berlin Heidelberg in 2003

Typesetting: Camera-ready by author, data conversion by PTP-Berlin, Protago-TeX-Production GmbH
Printed on acid-free paper   SPIN: 10970614   06/3142   5 4 3 2 1 0

DOA 2003

Bernd Krämer
Maarten van Steen
Steve Vinoski

ODBASE 2003

Roger (Buzz) King
Maria Orlowska
Rudi Studer

CoopIS 2003

Elisa Bertino
Dennis McLeod

OTM 2003 General Co-chair's Message

We as General Chairs are rather proud to announce that the conference series we started in Irvine last year proved to be a concept that continues to attract a representative selection of today's research in distributed, heterogeneous yet collaborative systems, of which the Internet and the WWW are its prime examples.

Indeed, as large, complex and networked intelligent information systems become the focus and norm for computing, software issues as well as methodological and theoretical issues covering a wide range of topics, such as data and Web semantics, distributed objects, Web services, databases, workflow, cooperation, ubiquity, interoperability, and mobility for the development of Internet- and Intranet-based systems in organizations and for e-business, need to be addressed in a fundamental way. The second, 2003 edition of the "On The Move" (OTM) federated conference event provided an opportunity for researchers and practitioners to understand and publish these developments within their respective as well as within their broader contexts. It co-located the three related, complementary and successful conference series: DOA (Distributed Objects and Applications), covering the relevant infrastructure-enabling technologies, ODBASE (Ontologies, DataBases and Applications of SEmantics) covering Web semantics, XML databases and ontologies, and CoopIS (Cooperative Information Systems) covering the application of these technologies in an enterprise context through, for example, workflow systems and knowledge management. Each of these three conferences treated its topics within a framework of theory, conceptual design and development, and applications, in particular case studies and industrial solutions.

In 2003 we also invited a number of workshop proposals to complement the more archival nature of the main conferences with research results in a number of selected and more avant garde areas related to the general topic of distributed computing. For instance, the so-called Semantic Web has given rise to several novel research areas combining linguistics, information systems technology, and artificial intelligence, such as the modeling of (legal) regulatory systems and the ubiquitous nature of their usage. One such event was continued from last year, a so-called "Industry Program" workshop soliciting relevant case studies and best practice results from industry in the areas covered by On The Move 2003.

All three conferences and the associated workshops therefore shared the distributed aspects of modern computing systems, and the resulting application pull created by the Internet and the so-called Semantic Web. For DOA 2003, the primary emphasis stayed on the distributed object infrastructure; for ODBASE 2003, it became the knowledge bases and methods required for enabling the use of formal semantics; and for CoopIS 2003, the main topic was the interaction of such technologies and methods with management issues, such as occur in networked organizations. These subject areas naturally overlap and many submissions in fact also treat an envisaged mutual impact among them. As for the 2002 edition in Irvine, the organizers wanted to stimulate this cross-pollination with a program of shared famous keynote speakers (this year we got Sycara, Goble, Soley and Mylopoulos!), and encouraged multiple attendance by providing authors with free access to another conference or workshop of their choice.

We received an even larger number of submissions than last year for the three conferences (360 in total) and the workshops (170 in total). Not only can we therefore again claim a measurable success in attracting a representative volume of scientific papers, but such a harvest allowed the program committees of course to compose a high-quality cross-section of worldwide research in the areas covered. In spite of the increased number of submissions, the Program Chairs of the three main conferences decided to accept only approximately the same number of papers for presentation and publication as in 2002 (i.e., around 1 paper out of every 4–5 submitted). For the workshops, the acceptance rate was about 1 in 2. Also for this reason, we decided to separate the proceedings into two volumes with their own titles, and we are grateful to Springer-Verlag for their collaboration in producing these two books. The reviewing process by the respective program committees was very professional and each paper in the main conferences was reviewed by at least three referees. The On The Move federated event organizers therefore also decided to make both (sizeable) books of proceedings available to all participants of the conferences and workshops. Even though this meant that participants had extra weight to carry home.

The General Chairs are especially grateful to all the many people directly or indirectly involved in the setup of these federated conferences, and who in so doing made then a success. In particular we thank our eight conference PC co-chairs (DOA 2003, Bernd Krämer, Maarten van Steen, and Steve Vinoski; ODBASE 2003, Roger (Buzz) King, Maria Orlowska, and Rudi Studer; CoopIS 2003, Elisa Bertino and Dennis McLeod) and our 13 workshop PC co-chairs (Angelo Corsaro, Corrado Santoro, Priya Narasimhan, Ron Cytron, Ernesto Damiani, Brian Blake, Giacomo Cabri, Mustafa Jarrar, Anne Salaun, Elizabeth Chang, William Gardner, Tharam Dillon, and Michael Brodie), our publicity chair (Guillaume Pierre) and our publication chair (Kwong Lai), who together with their many PC members did a superb and professional job in selecting the best papers from the large harvest of submissions.

We do hope that again the results of this federated scientific event may contribute to your work and that we may see you all again, as well as many others, for next year's edition!

August 2003   Robert Meersman, Vrije Universiteit Brussel, Belgium
                                       Zahir Tari, RMIT University, Australia
                     Douglas Schmidt, University of California at Irvine, USA

Organizing Committee

The OTM (On The Move) 2003 Federated Conferences, which involve CoopIS (Cooperative Information Systems), DOA (Distributed Objects and Applications) and ODBASE (Ontologies, Databases and Applications of Semantics) 2003, are proudly supported by RMIT University (School of Computer Science and Information Technology) and Vrije Universiteit Brussel (Department of Computer Science).

Executive Committee

OTM 2003 General Co-chairs	Robert Meersman (Vrije Universiteit Brussel, Belgium), Douglas Schmidt (UCI, USA) and Zahir Tari (RMIT University, Australia)
CoopIS 2003 PC Co-chairs	Elisa Bertino (University of Milan, Italy) and Dennis McLeod (University of Southern California, USA)
DOA 2003 PC Co-chairs	Bernd Krämer (FernUniversität in Hagen, Germany), Maarten van Steen (Vrije Universiteit of Amsterdam, The Netherlands) and Steve Vinoksi (Iona, USA)
ODBASE 2003 PC Co-chairs	Roger (Buzz) King (University of California, USA), Maria Orlowska (University of Queensland, Australia) and Rudi Studer (University of Karlsruhe, Germany)
Publication Chair	Kwong Yuen Lai (RMIT University, Australia)
Local Organizing Chair	Corrado Santoro (University of Catania, Italy)
Publicity Chair	Guillaume Pierre (Vrije Universiteit of Amsterdam, The Netherlands)

CoopIS 2003 Program Committe

Dave Abel	Anne Doucet	Yahiko Kambayashi
Naveen Ashish	Marie-Christine Fauvet	Latifur Khan
Karin Becker	Klaus Dittrich	Roger (Buzz) King
Klemens Boehm	Elena Ferrari	Steven Laufmann
Mic Bowman	Timothy Finin	Qing Li
Omran Bukhres	Avigdor Gal	Cha-Hwa Lin
Tiziana Catarci	Mohand-Said Hacid	Toshiyuki Masui
Ming-Syan Chen	Joachim Hammer	Claudia Medeiros
Umesh Dayal	Arthur ter Hofstede	Ben Chin Ooi
Alex Delis	Michael Huhns	Christine Parent

Evaggelia Pitoura
Allessandro Provetti
Tore Risch
Marek Rusinkiewicz
Felix Saltor
Cyrus Shahabi

Antonio Si
Susan Urban
Athena Vakali
W.M.P. van der Aalst
Kyu-Young Whang
Mike Wooldridge

Jian Yang
Kokou Yetongnon
Arkady Zaslavsky
Roger Zimmermann

DOA 2003 Program Committee

Gul Agha
Matthias Anlauff
Egidio Astesiano
Ozalp Babaoglu
Jean Bacon
Mark Baker
Sean Baker
Roberto Baldoni
Guruduth Banavar
Judith Bishop
Gordon Blair
Michel Chaudron
Shing-Chi Cheung
Francisco (Paco) Curbera
Wolfgang Emmerich
Pascal Felber
Mohand-Said Hacid
Daniel Hagimont
Franz Hauck
Arno Jacobsen
Mehdi Jazayeri

Fabio Kon
Doug Lea
Hong Va Leong
Peter Loehr
Joe Loyall
Frank Manola
Keith Moore
Priya Narasimhan
Andry Rakotonirainy
Heinz-Walter Schmidt
Richard Soley
Jean-Bernard Stefani
Joe Sventek
Stefan Tai
Guatam Thaker
Nalini Venkatasubramanian
Norbert Voelker
Andrew Watson
Doug Wells
Shalini Yajnik

ODBASE 2003 Program Committee

Aberer, Karl
Bussler, Christoph
Carlis, John
Catarci, Tiziana
Chen, Arbee
Colomb, Bob
Dayal, Umeshwar
Decker, Stefan
Delis, Alex
Drew, Pamela

Euzenat, Jérôme
Fensel, Dieter
Gal, Avigdor
Gil, Yolanda
Goble, Carole
Green, Peter
Guarino, Nicola
Kashyap, Vipul
Klas, Wolfgang
Lenzerini, Maurizio

Lee, Dik
Li, Qing
Liu, Chengfei
Liu, Ling
Ling, Tok Wang
Maedche, Alexander
Mark, Leo
Marjanovic, Oliviera
McLeod, Dennis
Mendelzon, Alberto
Missikoff, Michele
Mylopoulos, John

Navathe, Sham
Neuhold, Erich
Papazoglou, Mike
Rosemann, Michael
Sadiq, Shazia
Sadiq, Wasim
Schulz, Karsten
Sheth, Amit
Sycara, Katia
Sure, York
Zeleznikow, John

Table of Contents

Cooperative Information Systems (CoopIS) 2003 International Conference

Agent Systems and Applications

Cooperation and Evolution in Innovative Applications

Peer-to-Peer Systems

Processing, Availability, and Archival for Cooperative Systems

Trust Management

Advances in Workflow Systems

Information Dissemination Systems

Data Management on the Web

Ontologies, Databases, and Applications of Semantics (ODBASE) 2003 International Conference

Keynotes

Web Services

The Semantic Web

Data Mining and Classification

Ontology Management and Applications

Temporal and Spatial Data

Data Semantics and Metadata

Distributed Objects and Applications (DOA) 2003 International Conference

Keynote

Real-Time

Ubiquitous Systems

Adaptibility and Mobility

Systems Engineering

Software Engineering

Transactions

Author Index

Clustering Schemaless XML Documents

Yun Shen and Bing Wang

Department of Computer Science, University of Hull
HULL, HU6 7RX, UK
{Y.Shen,B.Wang}@dcs.hull.ac.uk

Abstract. This paper addresses the issue of semantically clustering the increasing number of the schemaless XML documents. In our approach, each document in a document collection is firstly represented by a **macro-path** sequence. Secondly, the similarity matrix for a document collection is constructed by computing the similarity value among these macro-path sequences. Finally, the desired clusters are constructed by utilizing the hierarchical clustering technique. Experimental results are also shown in this paper.

1 Introduction

Nowadays, a subset of the Web formed by the XML [2] documents, hereafter called the XML web [1], is growing into a large XML data repository. However, in [1], it shows that only 48% of the documents contain the links to the specific schemas. Consequently, integrating the enormous schemaless and semantically different documents to realize a Web database is an astonishing task.

The above integrating task can be relieved by utilizing document clustering technique [4], [5], which assembles together the related documents. It implies that relevant documents which are highly similar to each other are classified in the same cluster, and a very large XML data collection can thus be automatically divided into smaller subsections. The benefits of document clustering are obvious.

- Efforts in integrating XML documents with different structures and semantics can be alleviated because reconciling analogous and relatively small document set is easier.
- Ranges of queries (mining operations) can be dramatically decreased to applicable documents (areas of interest) after relevant documents are aggregated together.

However, XML has no formal semantic, which implies that a suitable definition must be provided. Moreover, it is difficult to define and compute the similarity among the schemaless XML documents when the semantics are concerned. To tackle the problems, an efficient clustering technique is proposed to group these schemaless XML documents on the basis of a competent document decomposition mechanism.

R. Meersman et al. (Eds.): CoopIS/DOA/ODBASE 2003, LNCS 2888, pp. 767–784, 2003.

The remainder of the paper is organized as follows. Section 2 surveys on related work; Section 3 presents preliminaries for this paper, and gives a specific definition on the semantic of an XML document; Section 4 explains the algorithms of computing the similarity between the macro-paths; Section 5 introduces the algorithms of computing the similarity matrix for an XML document collection and the hierarchical clustering technique; Section 6 presents some experimental results. Finally, section 7 gives a conclusion and proposes our future work on clustering XML schema definition(XSD) [3] files and a proposed commercial implementation for BPML [16].

2   Related Work

Clustering XML related documents is a potential research topic in integrating a large XML document collection. Several research approaches [7], [8], [9], [6], [10] had tackled the issue. However, the deficiencies in these efforts are not trivial.

In [7], Antoine Doucet et al. address the problem of clustering a homogenous collection of text-based XML documents. In this approach each document is represented by an n-dimensional vector, which is generated by using three different feature (defined as most significant words in the document) sets in an XML document: 1) text features only; 2) tag features only; 3) text and tags. Secondly, the document vectors are filled with normalized frequency and inverted document frequency measures. Finally, k-means clustering algorithm is utilized to cluster these documents. This approach is purely text-based and ignores the structural information in XML documents. Thus the semantic information of an XML document is completely ignored.

In [8], Jong Yoon et al. describe a bitmap indexing technique to cluster the XML documents. In this approach, an XML document is firstly defined as a sequence of ePaths with associated element contents. Secondly, a bitmap index is constructed from all the ePaths in the documents. Finally, a bitcube is assembled when element contents of the ePaths are integrated into the bitmap index. Similarity and popularity operations are defined to compute the similarity among these documents. Statistical analysis is also provided. Though Bitcube can support clustering XML documents, it contains many unnecessary zero bits, especially for the word dimension. The size of Bitcube impedes both its extensibility and computational efficiency.

In [9], Sergio Flesca et al. propose a technique for detecting the similarity in the structure of XML documents. This approach represents the structure of an XML document as a time series. Each impulse in the time series corresponds to a certain tag in the document. The similarity between documents is computed by analyzing the frequencies of the consonant Fourier transform. Though this approach can approximately determine the similarity between XML documents, it can not detect isomorphic tree structures and in particular the semantics are not preserved due to its encoding mechanism.

Xyleme [6] is a dynamic warehouse for XML data of the Web. Its data integration method is mainly on the basis of natural language and machine learning techniques. Firstly, DTDs are classified into domains based on a statistical analysis of the ontology similarities between words in different DTDs. Secondly, an abstract DTD for a specific domain is manually constructed. Finally, the semantic connections (mappings) between elements in the abstract DTD and elements in concrete ones are generated. However, its semantic preservation is mainly relied on human interaction. Thus its accuracy and extensibility are degraded with the increasing number of DTDs.

Recently, Mong Li Lee et al. introduce XClust [10] to cluster DTDs for a data integration system. The approach models a DTD as a tree T(V, E) where V is a set of nodes and E is a set of edges. To facilitate schema matching, the author proposes a set of transformation rules to determine the degree of similarity of two elements that have AND-OR nodes. Finally a similarity matrix among DTDs is computed and a hierarchical clustering technique is utilized to group DTDs into clusters. This approach considers not only the linguistic and structural information of DTD elements but also the context of a DTD element. However, the computational complexity of XClust is astonishing and its loss of semantic information is inevitable due to its transformation rules. Also XClust is for DTDs only. Furthermore, to adapt XClust for the schemaless documents is not trivial due to its computational complexity.

In [1], the author concludes that only 48% XML documents in the web contain the links to the schemas. This implies a huge amount of XML documents are schemaless. Thus providing an efficient mechanism to cluster these schemaless XML documents is very necessary. The proposed technique should:

- Find a balance between efficiency and accuracy.
- Preserve the semantics defined in the XML documents when clustering.

However, the above approaches we surveyed so far do not match the requirements of due to their computational complexity and loss of semantic information. To overcome these deficiencies, an efficient clustering technique is proposed to semantically assemble the schemaless XML documents. In this approach, each document is firstly decomposed into an macro-path sequence in which the semantic and structural information are maximally preserved. Secondly, the similarity matrix of the document collections is constructed by computing the similarity value among these macro-path sequences. Finally, the hierarchical clustering technique is used to group these documents on the basis of the generated similarity matrix. The proposed method can enable the data mining systems access the data that satisfies the desired similarity to a template. Also the proposed macro-path methodology can later be adapted to support efficient indexing and querying XML data in a large data collection.

3   Preliminaries

3.1   Data Model

Conventional tree-structured data model T(V, E)[13] is extended to define XML documents. The specifications are listed below.

```
<book>
  <preface number = "0">
    <author key = "CS-01-03">
      <name>John Philips</name>
      <name>William Moore</name>
    </author>
  </preface>
  <chapter number = "1">
    <content> ... </content>
  </chapter>
  <chapter number = "2">
    <author key = "IR-88-01" refno = "interal-021">
      <name>Frank allen</name>
    </author>
    <content>...</content>
  </chapter>
</book>
```

Fig. 1. An XML document

- V is a set of nodes and E is a set of edges.
- There is a root node r.
- The character data(value) of an element (an attribute) is separated with its tag name(name-value pair) and is independently modelled as a *text* node.
- Associated with each edge $e \in E$ there is an ordered pair of nodes $v \in V$, the source node s(v) and the target node t(v).
- A path is a sequence of v_1, v_2, v_3, ..., v_n of nodes such that $t(v_i) = s(v_{i+1})$, $1 \le i \le n - 1$. The number of nodes in this path, d, is its length. There exists one and only one path from node v_i to node v_j for every v_i, v_j, $v_i \neq v_j$.

To summarize, the data model is a rooted, directed, and node-labelled tree. The order between siblings is ignored due to our observation that the order will cause semantic information loss when computing the similarity value between two documents(Section 4). An XML document is listed in Fig. 1 and its relative data tree is shown in Fig. 2. In the rest of this paper, an XML document is denoted as D_T.

3.2   Macro-Path(mPath)

Currently, there is no formal semantic for an XML document. In this paper, the semantic expressed in an XML document is proposed to be related to:

- Synonyms (including the abbreviation form) of the word set used in the document.
- Structural information of an XML document.
- Topological information of an XML document when modelled as a tree.

However, directly computing the degrees of the similarity among the trees is not feasible due to the computational complexity. It implies that an efficient decomposition mechanism for an XML data tree must be provided when computing

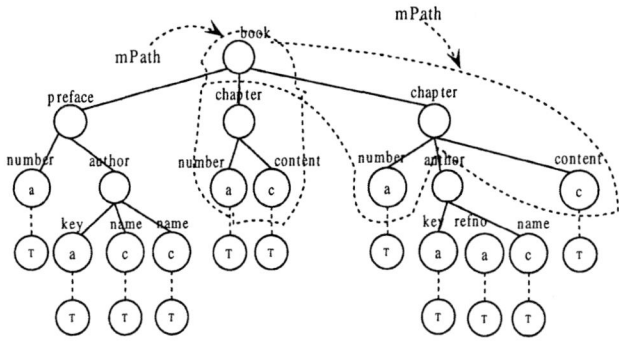

Fig. 2. An XML data tree

the similarity between documents while preserving the semantics of the XML documents. The mechanism should,

- Maintain the linguistic information in an XML document.
- Maximally prevent the semantic information loss.
- Efficiently support a set of algorithms possessing a competent computational complexity when clustering a large amount of documents.

To match the above three requirements, an efficient decomposition mechanism, called macro-path, is proposed to support clustering a large schemaless XML document collection. Before we formally define macro-path (mPath), we firstly give three relative definitions. In the rest of the paper, $\sum_{D_T}$ denotes the set of tag and attribute names in a document D_T.

Definition 1 Path Sequence. Given a node v_i in an XML document tree D_T, the path sequence $Path_{Seq}^{D_T}$ of node v_i is defined as an ordered sequence of tag names from root to node v_i, denoted as

$$p_{v_i}^{D_T} = \{v_0, v_1, ..., v_m\}, v_k \in \sum_{D_T}, k \in [1...m]$$

Given the node v_l and the node v_p, we say v_l is *nested* in v_p when l<p $\wedge v_l$, $v_p \in p_{v_i}^{D_T}$. Due to the order, $p_{v_i}^{D_T}$ describes the structural information on how a node v_i is nested in an XML document.

Example 1. Consider, for example, in Fig. 2. The $Path_{Seq}^{D_T}$ of node "author" in the second chapter is {book, chapter, author}. It means the node "author" is nested in a node "chapter", which is further nested in a node "book".

Definition 2 Attribute Sequence. Given a node v_i in an XML document tree D_T, the attribute sequence $Attr_{Seq}^{D_T}$ of node v_i is defined as a sequence of its attribute names, denoted as

$$a_{v_i}^{D_T} = \{a_0, a_1, ..., a_l\}, a_k \in \sum_{D_T}, k \in [1...l]$$

mPath$_1$	({book, preface}, {number}, {})
mPath$_2$	({book, preface, authors}, {key}, {name, name})
mPath$_3$	({book, preface}, {number}, {})
mPath$_4$	({book, chapter}, {number}, {content})
mPath$_5$	({book, chapter}, {number}, {content})
mPath$_6$	({book, chapter, author}, {key, refno}, {name})

Fig. 3. mPath list

Example 2. Consider, for example, in Fig. 2. The $Attr_{Seq}^{D_T}$ of node "author" in the second chapter is {key, refno}. It means the node "author" have two attributes, called "key" and "refno" respectively. Contrasting to the path sequence, the order among the attribute sequence is ignored.

Definition 3 Content Sequence. Given a node v_i in an XML document tree D_T, the content sequence $Cont_{Seq}^{D_T}$ of node v_i is defined as a sequence of the tag names of its direct descendants, whose direct descendants are content in our data model, denoted as

$$c_{v_i}^{D_T} = \{c_0, c_1, ..., c_r\}, c_k \in \sum_{D_T}, k \in [1...r]$$

Example 3. Consider, for example, in Fig. 2. The $Cont_{Seq}^{D_T}$ of node "author" in the preface is {name, name}. The duplicate element names are not omitted.

Definition 4 Macro-path (mPath). Given a node v_i in an XML document tree D_T, an mPath of node v_i is defined as a 3-tuple $(p_{v_i}^{D_T}, a_{v_i}^{D_T}, c_{v_i}^{D_T})$, $|p_{v_i}^{D_T}| \neq 0$. An XML document is later decomposed into a mPath sequence, denoted as

$$D_T = \{mPath_0^{D_T}, mPath_1^{D_T}, ..., mPath_t^{D_T}\}$$

When an XML document consists of only a root node, t=0. The order in D_T is also ignored to support the isomorphic tree similarity and the tree inclusion similarity(section 4).

Example 4. Consider, for example, in Fig. 2. The mPath of node "author" in the second chapter is ({book, chapter, author}, {key, refno}, {name}). The mPath of node "preface" is ({book, preface}, {number}, {}). The complete list of mPaths for Fig. 2 is shown in Fig. 3.

$a_{v_i}^{D_T}$ and $c_{v_i}^{D_T}$ describe the content of a node v_i in an XML document. By combining with $p_{v_i}^{D_T}$, they consist of the semantic information of v_i in the document. We observe that the nodes without any direct attribute nodes or content nodes are mostly utilized to clarify the structure of an XML document. Their semantic information is less important comparing with the nodes having attributes or content. When we decompose an XML document into mPath sequence, we only preserve the significant semantic information in the document. As a consequence, an mPath is generated only when a certain node v_i has attributes or content nodes. It implies that $Attr_{Seq}^{D_T}$ or $Cont_{Seq}^{D_T}$ may be empty when a node

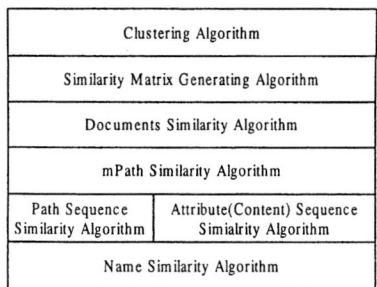

Clustering Algorithm	
Similarity Matrix Generating Algorithm	
Documents Similarity Algorithm	
mPath Similarity Algorithm	
Path Sequence Similarity Algorithm	Attribute(Content) Sequence Simialrity Algorithm
Name Similarity Algorithm	

Fig. 4. Relationship of the algorithms

does not have any attributes or content nodes. The nodes without any attribute nodes or content nodes are not eligible for mPath generating. Thus the semantic information in these nodes are lost. However, in the next section, we can see that the semantic loss of these nodes can be recaptured when computing the path similarity.

4   Macro-Path Similarity

After an XML document is decomposed into an mPath sequence, the document similarity problem is further turned into an mPath similarity problem. It is formally defined below:

Given two mPaths, $mPath_i^{D_{T_m}} = (\ Path_{Seq_i}^{D_{T_m}},\ Attr_{Seq_i}^{D_{T_m}},\ Cont_{Seq_i}^{D_{T_m}})$ and $mPath_j^{D_{T_l}} = (Path_{Seq_j}^{D_{T_l}},\ Attr_{Seq_j}^{D_{T_l}},\ Cont_{Seq_j}^{D_{T_l}})$ The similarity between $mPath_i^{D_{T_m}}$ and $mPath_j^{D_{T_l}}$ is defined as:

$$mPathSimilarity(mPath_i^{D_{T_m}}, mPath_j^{D_{T_l}}) =$$
$$Weight(PathSimilarity(Path_{Seq_i}^{D_{T_m}}, Path_{Seq_j}^{D_{T_l}}),$$
$$AttrSimilarity(Attr_{Seq_i}^{D_{T_m}}, Attr_{Seq_j}^{D_{T_l}}),$$
$$ContSimilarity(Cont_{Seq_i}^{D_{T_m}}, Cont_{Seq_j}^{D_{T_l}})) \tag{1}$$

To efficiently compute the similarity between two mPaths, the algorithms should,

- Compute the linguistic similarity between the tag names. This characteristic targets to the linguistical accuracy of clustering.
- Preserve the semantics of the mPaths. This characteristic targets to the semantical correctness of clustering.
- Provide a resourceful computational complexity. This characteristic targets to the computational efficiency of clustering.

To meet the above requirements, two algorithms are presented in this paper. One is to compute the similarity value between $Path_{Seq}$ and another is to uniformly compute the similarity value between two $Attr_{Seq}(Cont_{Seq})$. A weight mechanism is proposed to flexibly combine these similarity values.

4.1   Name Similarity

We firstly describe measure of computing the name similarity between tag names. This measure is mainly focused on the linguistic similarity between words which are used to defined element tag names (attribute names). This kind of similarity has been broadly utilized in many applications, such as information retrieval, information extraction, text classification, word sense disambiguation, example-based machine translation, etc. In this paper we adapt the algorithm proposed by Mong Li Lee et al. in [10]. The WordNet [12] API which returns the synonym set is utilized. The algorithm is given in Algo. NAMESIMILARITY and Algo. ONTOLOGYSIMILARITY. The name similarity value is denoted as θ_{name} in the rest of the paper. The computational complexity is with the number of synonym of a certain word.

Algorithm NAMESIMILARITY
Input: e_1, e_2: the names of two elements. β: the base ontology similarity value, the default value is 0.9. δ: the search depth, the default maximum value is 4.
Output: θ_{name}: the name similarity value
1.   **if** $e_1 = e_2$
2.   **then return** 1.0
3.   **else** $Set_{Syn} \leftarrow$ the synonym set of e_2
4.   ($*$ A recursive function is called $*$)
5. $\theta_{name} \leftarrow$ ONTOLOGYSIMILARITY(e_1, Set_{Syn}, 1, β)
6.   **return** θ_{name}

Algorithm ONTOLOGYSIMILARITY
Input: e_1: an element name. Set_{syn}: a synonym set. δ: the search depth, the default maximum value is 4. β: the base ontology similarity value, the default value is 0.9
Output: $\theta_{ontology}$: the ontology similarity value
1.   **if** $delta <= 4$
2.   **if** $e_1 \in Set_{Syn}$
3.   **then return** β^{δ}
4.   **else**
5. $Set_{Syn_{new}} \leftarrow \emptyset$
6.   **for** each $s_i \in Set_{Syn}$
7.   **do** $Set_{s_i} \leftarrow$ the synonym set of s_i
8. $Set_{Syn_{new}} \leftarrow Set_{Syn_{new}} \cup Set_{s_i}$
9.   OntologySimilarity(e_1, $Set_{Syn_{new}}$, $\delta + 1$, β)
10. **return** 0

Consider, for example, in our algorithm,   NAMESIMILARITY(writer, author) returns 0.9 if β in Algo. NAMESIMILARITY is set to 0.9,
NAMESIMILARITY(chapter, part) returns 0.81, and NAMESIMILARITY(name,
order) returns 0.

4.2   Path Similarity

We now introduce our path similarity measure. This measure is carried out by
the fact that a path sequence describes the detail information on how an element
is nested in an XML document due to its order (Definition 1). The structural
similarity between two nodes are therefore captured when computing the path
sequence similarity. In this paper, it is connected with,

- The name similarity value θ_{name} between two tag names. If θ_{name} is greater
  than the threshold value (τ_{name}), we say a *matching point* is reached. If not,
  we say a *gap* is obtained.
- The path alignment, which is connected with the gaps between continuous
  matching points.

To match the above two requirements, a complete algorithm for path similarity
is given in Algo. PATHSIMILARITY. The computational complexity is O(mn),
where m and n stand for the individual lengths of two path sequences.

Algorithm PATHSIMILARITY
Input: $Path_{Seq_i}, Path_{Seq_j}$: the path sequences. *penalty*: a penalty value for mis-
matching of tag names. τ_{name}: the threshold value, default value is 0.6.
Output: θ_{path}: the path sequence similarity value
1. $m \leftarrow LEN(Path_{Seq_i})$
2. $n \leftarrow LEN(Path_{Seq_j})$
3.   Initialize an m-by-n array $S_{m \times n}$ to zero
4. $r, t \leftarrow 0$
5.   **for** $r \leftarrow 1$ **to** m
6.   **for** $t \leftarrow 1$ **to** n
7.   **do** S(r, t) $\leftarrow MAX$(S(r-1, t) + penalty, S(r, t-1)) + penalty,
                       S(r-1, t-1) + SELECT($Path_{Seq_i}(r), Path_{Seq_j}(t), \tau_{name}$))
8. $\theta_{path} \leftarrow S(m, n)/MAX(m, n)$
9.   **return** θ_{path}

Algorithm SELECT
Input: e_1, e_2: element names. τ_{name}: the threshold value, default value is 0.6.
Output: value: selected name similarity value
1.   **if** ((value $\leftarrow$ NAMESIMILARITY(e_1, e_2, δ, β))$> \tau_{name}$)
2.   **then return** value
3.   **else   return** 0

Alignment	Similarity
m₁: **book**/**chapter**/**auhtor** **book**/**chapter**/**content**	0.67
m₂: **book**/**chapter**/**auhtor** **book**/**preface**/**author**	0.6

Fig. 5. Path alignment weight

Consider for example, in Fig. 5. Though the two path sequences have the same matching points, however, m_1 is better that m_2 for there is no gap between matching points in m_1 while there exists one gap in m_2. Thus our algorithm has a subtle weight mechanism not only for the name similarity but also for the structural similarity when comparing two path sequences. Moreover, though the nodes without any attribute nodes or content nodes are not eligible for mPath generating, their semantics are thus partly recaptured when computing the path similarity because they are encoded within the path sequences.

4.3   Attribute(Content) Similarity

We then consider the similarity between attribute(content) sequences. This mechanism is motivated by the fact that edit distance is not sufficient to detect the similarity between attributes(Content). For example, given two XML fragments, <PDATE DAY = "02" MONTH = "feb" YEAR = "1998"/> ($PDATE_1$) and <PDATE MONTH = "may" DAY = "12" YEAR = "2003"/> ($PDATE_2$). They are different localizations of an certain XML document on pay date and contain the same semantic information. But if edit distance algorithm [9] is utilized to compute the similarity, the semantic information is ignored. To maximally prevent semantic information loss, an efficient algorithm is proposed in Algo. ACSIMILARITY. The computational complexity is O(mn), where m and m stand for the individual length of two attribute/content sequences.

Algorithm ACSIMILARITY
Input: seq_i, seq_j: attribute(content) sequences
Output: θ_{ac}: attribute(content) similarity value
1. $m \leftarrow LEN(seq_i)$
2. $n \leftarrow LEN(seq_j)$
3.   **for** r $\leftarrow$ 1 **to** m
4.   **do for** t $\leftarrow$ 1 **to** n
5.   **do if** ((value $\leftarrow$ NAMESIMILARITY($seq_i(r)$, $seq_j(t)$)) > τ_{name})
6. $count \leftarrow count + 1$
7. $\theta_{ac} \leftarrow \theta_{ac} + value$
8. $para \leftarrow MAX(count, m, n)$
9.   **return** $\theta_{ac}/para$

Consider, for example. Given two attribute sequence, $attr_1 = \{writer, essay\}$, $attr_2 = \{author, article\}$ and τ_{name} 0.6,   ACSIMILARITY$(attr_1, attr_2) =$ 0.9. Consider again the above two pay date fragments, $Attr_{PDATE_1} = \{$DAY, MONTH, YEAR$\}$ and $Attr_{PDATE_2} = \{$DAY, MONTH, YEAR$\}$. ACSIMILARITY$(Attr_{PDATE_1}, Attr_{PDATE_2}) = 1.0$ when τ_{name} is set to 0.6.

4.4   mPath Similarity

We finally inspect the mPath similarity on the basis of the above two algorithms. This technique is motivated by the fact that most important semantic information in an XML document is reflected by the nodes that have either attribute nodes or content nodes. Definition 4 shows that the semantic information of a certain node v_i is preserved in its mPath $(p_{v_i}^{DT}, a_{v_i}^{DT}, c_{v_i}^{DT})$. When generating the final result, a weight mechanism is proposed to combine the path similarity and the attribute(content) similarity to obtain the final result. In this paper we use w_p, w_a, and w_c to respectively represent the weight values for $Path_{Seq}$, $Attr_{Seq}$, and $Cont_{Seq}$ where $w_p, w_a, w_c \in [0,1] \wedge w_p \geq w_a \geq w_c$. By using the weight mechanism, we can flexibly adjust how the three sequences are combined. The complete algorithm is given in Algo. MPATHSIMILARITY.

Algorithm MPATHSIMILARITY
Input: $mPath_i$, $mPath_j$: two macro-paths. w_p, w_a, w_c: weight value
Output: θ_{mpath}: mPath similarity value
1. $\theta_{path} \leftarrow$ PATHSIMILARITY$(Path_{Seq_i}, Path_{Seq_j})$
2.   **if** $Attr_{Seq_i} = \emptyset$ **or** $Attr_{Seq_j} = \emptyset$
3.   **then** $\theta_{atti} \leftarrow -0.1$
4.   **else** $\theta_{atti} \leftarrow$ ACSIMILARITY$(Attr_{Seq_i}, Attr_{Seq_j})$
5.   **if** $Cont_{Seq_i} = \emptyset$ **or** $Cont_{Seq_j} = \emptyset$
6.   **then** $\theta_{cont} \leftarrow -0.1$
7.   **else** $\theta_{atti} \leftarrow$ ACSIMILARITY$(cont_{Seq_i}, Cont_{Seq_j})$
8. $\theta_{mpath} \leftarrow (w_p \times \theta_{path} + w_a \times \theta_{attr} + w_c \times \theta_{cont})$
9.   **return** θ_{mpath}

Example 5. Consider, for example, Given two mPaths

$$mPath_1 = (\{book, chapter\}, \{number\}, \{content\}) \in D_{T_m}$$

and

$$mPath_2 = (\{book, chapter\}, \{number\}) \in D_{T_l}$$

If given $w_p = 1.0$, $w_a = 0.9$, $w_c = 0.8$, mPathSimilarity($mPath_1$, $mPath_2$) $= (w_p \times$ PathSimilarity($\{$book, chapter$\}$, $\{$book, chapter$\}$) $+ w_a \times$ ACSimilarity($\{$number$\}$, $\{$number$\}$) $+ w_c \times$ ACSimilarity($\{$content$\}$, $\{\}$))/3 = (1.0$\times$ 1.0 + 0.9$\times$ 1.0 + 0.8$\times$ (-0.1))/3 = 0.64.

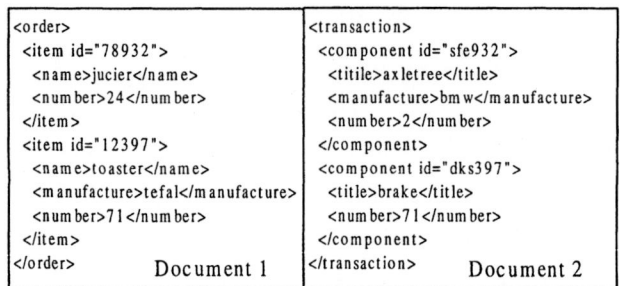

Fig. 6. Two sample XML documents

5   Clustering Schemaless XML Documents

5.1   Document Similarity

Given two XML documents, $Doc_r = (mPath_{r1}, mPath_{r2}, ..., mPath_{rm})$ and $Doc_t = (mPath_{t1}, mPath_{t2}, ..., mPath_{tn})$ The similarity between Doc_r and Doc_t) is formally defined as:

$$DocSimilarity(Doc_r, Doc_t) = \sum_{1 \leq i \leq m, 1 \leq j \leq n} select(mPathSimilarity(mPath_{ri}, mPath_{tj})) \qquad (2)$$

The approximate tree inclusion and the isomorphic tree similarity are also supported in our algorithm. A complete algorithm is listed in Algo. DOCSIMILARITY. The computational complexity is O(mn), where m and n stand for the number of mPaths in two documents after the decomposition.

Algorithm DOCSIMILARITY

Input: doc_i, doc_j: two XML documents. τ_{mpath}: mPath threshold value. $\tau_{inclusion}$: tree inclusion threshold value, default value is 0.9. *range*: tree inclusion range, its default value is 0.05

Output: θ_{doc}: document similarity value

1. $m \leftarrow LEN(doc_i)$
2. $n \leftarrow LEN(doc_j)$
3. $count \leftarrow 0$
4.   (* The following three variables are for tree inclusion detecting purpose *)
5. $uniset \leftarrow \emptyset$
6. $unicount, \theta_{inclusion} \leftarrow 0$
7.   **for** r ← 1 **to** m
8.   **do** $flag \leftarrow$ **false**
9.   **for** t ← 1 **to** n
10.   **do if** ((value ← MPATHSIMILARITY$(doc_i(r), doc_j(t))) > \tau_{mpath}$)
11.   **then if** (flag = false) **and not** (t ∈ uniset) **and** value ≥ $\tau_{inclusion}$

12.   **then** $\theta_{inclusion} \leftarrow \theta_{inclusion} + value$
13. $unicount \leftarrow unicount + 1$
14. $uniset \leftarrow uniset \cup \{t\}$
15. $flag \leftarrow$ **true**
16. $\theta_{doc} \leftarrow \theta_{doc} + value$
17. $count \leftarrow count + 1$
18. $k \leftarrow MIN(m,n)$
19.   **if** $unicount \in [(1 - range) \times k, (1 + range) \times k]$
20.   **return** $\tau_{inclusion}/unicount$
21. $\theta_{doc} \leftarrow \theta_{doc}/MAX(count, m, n)$
22.   **return** θ_{doc}

Example 6. Consider, for example, in Fig. 6. We give two sample documents:

$$Doc_1 = \{mPath_{11}, mPath_{12}\}(D_{T_1})$$

and

$$Doc_2 = \{mPath_{21}, mPath_{22}\}(D_{T_2})$$

Let $mPath_{11} = (\{order, item\}, \{id\}, \{name, number\})$, $mPath_{12} = (\{order, item\}, \{id\}, \{name, number,\}, \{ manufacture\})$, $mPath_{21} = (\{transaction, component\}, \{id\}, \{title, number, manufacture\})$, $mPath_{22} = (\{transaction, component\}, \{id\}, \{title, number\})$ and given $w_p = 1.0$, $w_a = 0.9$, $w_c = 0.8$ and $\tau_{mpath} = 0.72$, $\tau_{name} = 0.6$, $\tau_{inclusion} = 0.9$. DocSimilarity(Doc_1,Doc_2) is (0.688 + 0.73 + 0.778 + 0.688)/4 = 0.721. Moreover, we can discern that D_{T_1} and D_{T_2} are isomorphic trees when comparing their data trees. Thus we can also see that mPath easily detect the similarity between them.

5.2   Clustering XML Document Collection

Given an XML document collection,$D=\{Doc_1, Doc_2, ..., Doc_n\}$ and the similarity matrix $M_{n \times n}=\{m_{ij}|m_{ij} = $ DocSimilarity$(Doc_i, Doc_j), 1 \leq i, j \leq n\}$ The XML documents which are,

- From the same area of interest and
- Having similar semantics and structures

should be clustered together by analyzing the similarity matrix M. Once these documents are grouped together, the beneficiary is obvious: the range of a certain query (mining operation) can be dramatically decreased only to applicable documents (areas of interest), the speed of data retrieving (mining) can be increased [11]. The algorithm is given in Algo. SIMILARITYMATRIX

Algorithm SIMILARITYMATRIX
Input: D: an XML document collection
Output: M: similarity matrix
1. $n \leftarrow LEN(D)$
2.   **for** $i \leftarrow 1$ **to** n - 1

3.   **do for** j $\leftarrow$ i $+$ 1 **to** n
4.   **do** ($*$ doc_i, $doc_j \in D$ $*$)
5. $M(i,j) = $ DocSimilarity(doc_i, doc_j)
6. **return** M

After the similarity matrix of the XML document collection is generated, hierarchical clustering technique [15] is utilized to group these XML documents on the basis of the matrix. In a hierarchical classification, the data are not partitioned into a particular number of clusters at single step. Instead the classification consists of a series of partitions which may run from a single cluster containing all individuals, to n clusters each containing a single individual. However, in this paper, we are not interested in the complete hierarchy but only in one certain partitions obtained from it. Therefore, intensive experiments are performed to select the best partition which appropriately decides on the number of clusters for our data while minimizing the percentage of wrong clustering.

6   Experimental Results

In order to evaluate the performance of the mPath decomposition and clustering, intensive experiments are performed. 100 XML documents are collected from the Internet and 100 schemaless documents are generated by our own program. The above real world documents and synthesized documents are then randomly mixed to set up a general data environment. On the basis of the data sets, the efficiency of mPath decomposition and the clustering accuracy are experimented. The computing environment is a celeron 400MHZ machine with 128MB memory and libxml[14] library.

6.1   mPath Decomposition

In this experiment, the execution time of the mPath decomposition when storing an XML document into a local storage system is investigated. Four different data sets are initialized and each data set contains 80, 120, 150 or 200 documents. Two criteria are essential to evaluate the performance of mPath decomposition: the reasonable computing time concerning the resource provided and the number of mPaths with respect to the number of individual nodes in a document. Two experimental results are assessed: 1) the mPath decomposition time; and 2) the entire storage time. The experimental result on mPath decomposition is listed in table. 1 and the entire storage time is in Fig. 7. We find out that the storage time increases slightly when mPath decomposition is involved but is still within the acceptable range.

We next evaluate the relationship between the number of mPaths and the number of nodes in an XML document. An mPath is treated as a unit when computing in our clustering algorithm. Thus, efficiently generating a number of mPaths with respect to the number of nodes is vital to the accuracy and efficiency of clustering. The experimental result is shown in Fig. 8. We find out that the number of mPaths is less than 30% of the number of nodes in an XML document. Consequently, the efficiency of computing is guaranteed.

Table 1. mPath Decomposition Time

Number of Documents	Size in Total(KB)	Time(ms)
80	14,238	2,444
120	23,924	4,928
150	36,321	7,261
200	59,114	26,548

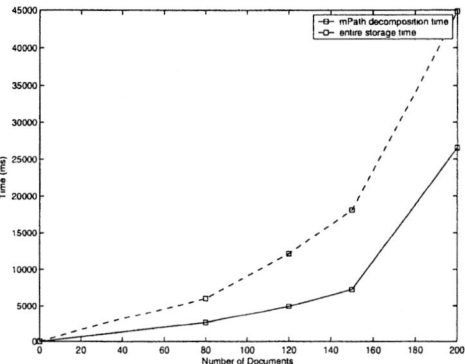

Fig. 7. Entire Storage Time

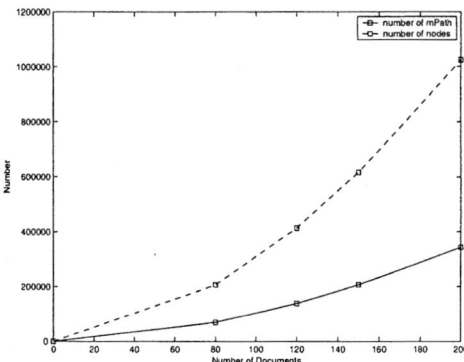

Fig. 8. The number of mPaths with respect to the number of nodes in XML documents

6.2 Clustering Efficiency

In this experiment, we investigate the accuracy of clustering schemaless XML documents. Firstly, the documents are manually classified into l clusters. Secondly, our algorithms are executed to automatically group the documents. Finally, by specifying the various cut-off values, the different number of clusters is generated. By comparing with the manual results, the accuracy of our algorithms can thus be defined. Figure 9 and Fig. 10 respectively are the preliminary

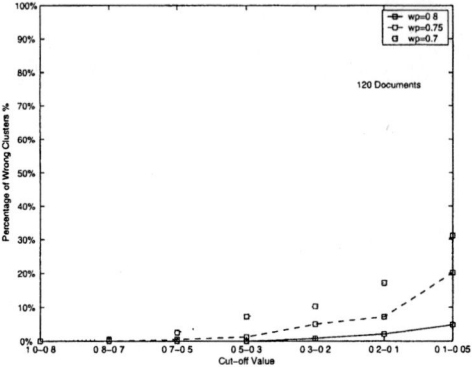

Fig. 9. Clustering 120 Documents

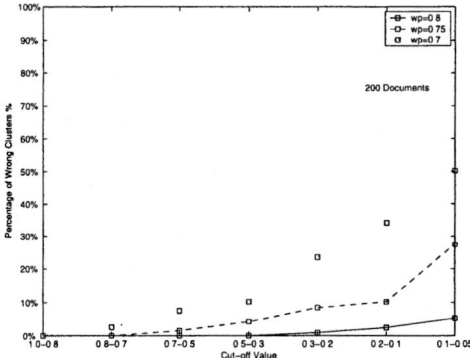

Fig. 10. Clustering 200 Documents

results for 120 and 200 documents. Three various values for w_c are experimented in each data set.

We find out that in Fig. 9 and Fig. 10, the accuracy of clustering degrades when the number of documents in a collection increases. However, this problem can be partly solved when a statistical pre-processing mechanism is applied. For example, we can pre-divide a large document collection into small groups based on a statistical analysis of the words used in a certain domain. Also the accuracy of clustering degrades when the value of w_c is decreased. This shows that the direct descendant is an important part of a node's semantics which mPath well preserves and our weight mechanism maximally preserves the semantic information within an XML document.

7   Conclusion and Future Work

In this paper we propose an efficient clustering technique to group the schemaless XML documents. The main contributions of our approach are:

- An efficient decomposition mechanism for a schemaless XML document. An XML document is represented by an mPath sequence after the decomposition.
- A set of competent algorithms for computing the similarity between documents. These algorithms rely on the mPath sequences while maximally preserving the linguistic, structural and semantic information in the sequences when clustering.
- An approximate mechanism for computing the tree inclusion and the isomorphic tree similarity.

On the basis of the algorithms, the XML schema definition(XSD) files can be clustered in our future work. This future work is motivated by the fact that an schema definition file is a schemaless file cause there dos not exist a "schema" for a schema. There are, however, several difficult issues that must be addressed before this is practical. Moreover, by utilizing path join and join predicates [11], a framework for grouping, indexing and querying a large schemaless XML document collection can be further constructed. This framework can apply for the future data storage, analysis and computing systems. Additionally, the Business Process Modeling Language (BPML) [16], targeting to the strict separation of control and data flow, enables a way to "reengineer reengineering". This takes what was good about reengineering "the creativity, the insight" but eradicates the pain of discontinuity and new process introduction. By utilizing our approach, all applications and procedures in format of BPML can thus automatically exposed and classified, forming a potentially rich palette of reusable business processes.

References

1. Mignet, L., Barbosa, D., Veltri, P.: The XML web: a first study. In the proceedings of the twelfth international conference on World Wide Web,500–510, 2003.
2. W3C:Extensible Markup Language.http://www.w3.org/XML/, 1999.
3. W3C: XML Schema. http://www.w3.org/XML/Schema, 2001.
4. Anderberg, M.R.: Clustering analysis for Applications. Academic Press, New York, 1973.
5. Baeza-Yates, R.: Modern Information Retrieval. ACM Press, New York, 1999.
6. Lucie Xyleme: A dynamic warehouse for XML Data of the Web. IEEE Data Engineering Bullet, 24, 2, 40–47, 1991.
7. Doucet, A., Ahonen-Myka, H.: Naive clustering of a large XML document collection. In the proceedings of the First Annual Workshop of the Initiative for the Evaluation of XML retrieval (INEX), 2002.
8. Yoon, J.P., Raghavan, V., Chakilam, V., Kerschberg, L.: BitCube: A Three-Dimensional Bitmap Indexing for XML Documents. Journal of Intelligent Information Systems, 17, 2–3, 241–254, 2001.
9. Flesca, S., Manco, G., Masciari E., Pontieri L., Pugliese, A.: Detecting Structural Similarities between XML Documents. Fifth International Workshop on the Web and Databases (WebDB 2002), 2002.

10. Lee, M.L., and Yang, L.H., Hsu, W., Yang, X.: XClust: clustering XML schemas for effective integration. In the proceedings of the eleventh international conference on Information and knowledge management, 292–299, 2002.
11. Shen, Y., Wang, B.: Path Join For Retrieving Data From XML Documents. Technical Report 02–03, 2003.
12. Fellbaum, C.: WordNet: An Electronic Lexical Database. MIT Press, 1998.
13. Abiteboul, S., Buneman, P., Suciu, D.: Data On The Web: From relations to Semistructured Data and XML. Morgan Kaufmann Publishers, San Francisco, California, 2000.
14. The XML C parser and toolkit for Gnome. http://xmlsoft.org/
15. Jain, A.K., Murty, M.N., Flynn, P.J.: Data clustering: a review. ACM Computing Surveys, vol.31, 1999.
16. The Business Process Management Initiative (BPMI): http://www.bpmi.org/. 2002

Automatic Expansion of Manual Email Classifications Based on Text Analysis

Enrico Giacoletto and Karl Aberer

School of Computer and Communication Science, EPFL
CH-1015 Lausanne, Switzerland
{enrico.giacolettoroggio,karl.aberer}@epfl.ch

Abstract. The organization of documents is a task that we face as computer users daily. This is particularly true for management of email. Typically email documents are organized in directory structures, which reflect the users' ontology with respect to his daily communication needs. Since users' activities are continuously changing this may render email classifications increasingly inaccurate and manual maintenance is a painstaking task. In this paper we present an approach for integrating user-defined folder structures with classification schemes that have been automatically derived from the email content. This allows to automating the process of evolving and optimizing directory structures without sacrificing knowledge captured in manually created folder structures. A prototype demonstrating the feasibility and utility of our approach has been developed and evaluated. With our approach we address both an important practical problem and provide a relevant study on the application of various techniques for maintaining application specific ontologies.

1 Introduction

The organization of documents is a task that we face as computer users daily. This is particularly true for the management of emails, still the main application of the Internet. Whittaker [19] has written one of the first papers on the issue of email organization. He introduced the concept of "email overload" and discussed – among other issues - why users file their e-mails in folder structures. He identifies a number of reasons: users believe that they will need the emails in the future, users want to clean their inbox but still keep the emails, and users want to postpone the decision about an action to be taken in order to determine the value of the information contained in the emails. He also pointed out that it seems plausible that grouping related emails is considered useful in preserving meaningful context for historical communications and activities and is not simply a strategy to support information search.

Typically email documents are organized in directory structures, where folders and subfolders are used to categorize emails according to various criteria, such as projects, personal relationships, and organizational structures. Therefore these directories reflect the users' ontology with respect to his daily communication needs. Since the communciation is related to continuously changing activities and users cannot foresee

R. Meersman et al. (Eds.): CoopIS/DOA/ODBASE 2003, LNCS 2888, pp. 785–802, 2003.

all kinds of messages arriving in the future this user ontology is anything but stable and can become disorganized quickly. We all know from our daily experience how painful the manual maintenance of email folder structures can be. The user must carefully examine all emails to determine the best possible reorganization according to his current needs. He may want to split folders that have become overpopulated. Or he may want to group all the emails concerning one topic that are scattered over several folders, since at the time of creating the folder structure the emergence of such a topic could not be foreseen. In addition the resulting folder structures are typically far from being optimal, leaving many useless, under-populated folders.

Current email software supports users in automatically classifying emails based on simple criteria, such as sender, time etc., into pre-existing folder structures [1, 2]. However, this does not alleviate the user from first provisioning the necessary folder structures. Also classification of documents based on basic email attributes taken from the header, does not take advantage of the content of the documents during classification. Recent research on ontology development is considering the use of data and text mining techniques in order to derive classification schemes for large document collections [17]. Such an approach appears also to be attractive for addressing the problem of creating email folder structures. However, plainly applying mining tools to email databases in order to create classification schemes, e.g. by applying text clustering techniques [16], does not take into account existing knowledge on the application domain and would render specific knowledge of users in terms of pre-existing folder structure useless.

Therefore we propose in this paper a more differentiated approach. We want to integrate user-defined folder structures with classification schemes that have been automatically derived from the email content. This approach is similar to work that is currently performed in ontology evolution [17], but the profile of the target users is fundamentally different. Whereas in ontology evolution we may expect experts to modify existing ontologies to be shared among large communities in a very controlled and fine-granular manner, probably supported by mining techniques, email users are normally not experts on ontology evolution and integration. Therefore our goal is to automate the process of integrating classification schemes derived by mining techniques with user-defined classifications as far as possible. By analyzing the content of existing email databases we provide classification schemes that are specifically well adapted to the current content of the emails, whereas by retaining the user-provided existing classification by a folder structure we tailor the classification schemes towards the user needs and expectations. This will allow to substantially streamlining the classification schemes being derived from the user and extracted classifications.

The approach we present is based on existing techniques for text content analysis, feature-based clustering and schema integration. The key insight that we want to emphasize is that only by tailoring and combining such techniques in a way that optimally exploits existing knowledge about the structure of the domain it will be possible to have a practical solution for automated ontology generation and evolution. In this sense we not only provide a working solution to a practical problem everyone is facing today, but also a case study on the feasibility and challenges of creating application and personalized ontologies in general.

We will give first in Section 2 an overview of our approach, before we dwelve into the technical details of each of its aspects. In Section 3 we will introduce the various methods for feature extraction we developed. These are essential as they take specifically advantage of the application domain. In Section 4 we introduce our method for creating folder structures automatically based on feature clustering. In Section 5 we present the algorithm used for integrating computer-generated folder structures with user folder structures. We may view this as a solution to a specific instance of a schema integration problem. In Section 6 we discuss the graphical user interface that has been developed to allow the user to postprocess the automatically generated folder structures. In Section 7 we report on initial evaluation results obtained by providing our solution to real users. In Section 8 we give a short overview on some related work and conclude the paper in Section 9.

2 Overview of the Approach

With our approach we try to combine the best of two worlds: the capability of users to intelligently classify their email and the power of computers to perform computationally intensive content analysis to discover possibly useful content-based classification schemes. An overview of the approach is given in Fig. 1.

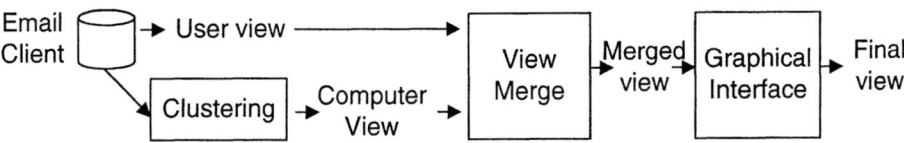

Fig. 1. Proposed solution schema to reorganize user data

Given an email database we assume that a user has already created some existing folder structure which we will call the *user view*. In practice, after some time, this view does no longer match the requirements of the user. Therefore by applying content analysis to the email database we create a new view by providing a computer generated classification of the email data, which we call the *computer view*. The automatic generation of the computer view may be adapted to the needs of the user by controlling which information is considered in the classification process, e.g. topics, dates or headers of emails. The two views may be incompatible. Therefore we need a mechanism to integrate the two views. This is done in a merge step and is a core element of our approach. The view merge algorithm identifies folders with overlapping contents and tries thus to identify semantically identical or related folders. The resulting view is called *merged view*. In general, the merged view will have no longer a tree structure, but be a general lattice, even if both input views had the structure of a tree. The merged view is guaranteed to contain all structural elements of the original user view and to cover the complete email database.

The resulting merged view may still not meet all expectations of the user. Therefore in a final step the user can use a graphical user interface to refine the merged view and thus to produce the final view. This final feedback given by the user is important as only the user can decide what he ultimately wants. The graphical user interface displays the merged view to the user and lets him modify it in accordance with his needs. One issue this graphical user interface has to address is the ability to deal with lattice structures, rather than trees, as the merged view is in general a lattice. As the merge algorithm summarizes the information of the user and the computer view, for the user it is always possible to retrieve his original view and to remove all the computer's suggestions. He cannot loose work he already invested into classifying emails. In the following we will discuss in more detail the approach taken to realize each of the steps described.

3 Feature Extraction

The automated classification of emails consists of the two steps of feature extraction and classification, which are standard for any content analysis process. Each email has header fields and a body. Among the header fields "To", "Cc", "From", "Date" and "Subject" are taken into account to characterize emails. In the feature extraction process we try to focus already on those features that will be most relevant for the subsequent classification process. Therefore we use different heuristics resulting in the following four feature categories which we have identified as being most relevant for semantically meaningful email classification: one that deals with persons, one that deals with groups of persons exchanging emails over a limited time frame, a so-called email thread, one that deals with subject lines that are related and one that deals with email bodies related over a limited time frame. Each email will be either associated with a specific feature or not. For example, the features from person category will consist of the different persons occurring frequently in emails, and emails will either be related to one of those persons or not. This very selective approach to extracting features is essential in order to optimize the classification schemes that are obtained in the subsequent classification process.

The set of features belonging to each of these feature categories are extracted from the email collection using different methods. We describe these methods in the following shortly.

- *Extraction of person features:* The identification of person features is based on the email address. An email address can contain two fields: the email address itself and the optional name. We use the optional name in order to identify whether the same person uses different email addresses. From this we can create a table relating email addresses with their corresponding person names and thus identify emails belonging to the same person, even if different email addresses were used. Only person names that occur frequently will be used as an email feature.

- *Extraction of email threads:* An email conversation thread consists of a series of replies to a message and the replies to those replies. This is very commonly occuring in email conversations. A thread can also capture complex discussion processes among a group of people whose members may change over time. For extracting threads we examine each email in the database to see if any were sent after the currently examined email involving the sender of the email at the base of the search. There is a time distance limit between every email in a thread list. Only a maximal number of days between two emails are allowed within the same thread. In order to be considered as email feature, a thread must contain more than a minimal number of emails.

- *Extraction of subjects:* Each email has a subject line. Sometimes it is empty, contains a trivial greeting such as "hello" or simply a "Re:". An email subject containing a greeting is polite, but not very useful in our case. For this reason, we maintain a huge list of "stop words". These words will not be accepted as features. This list contains French, English, German and Italian words, but it can be adapted to other language(s) being used. A list of all the remaining words encountered in subject lines is created to create the features.

- *Extraction of topics from email bodies:* The extraction of topics from email bodies is based on pairwise evaluation of similarity of the textual content of the email body using a TF-IDF based similarity measure. In order to extract the relevant words from an email body, first text that is not relevant for the evaluation of content–based similarity, like signatures, html tags, webmail signatures and email headers of replies is removed in a pre-processing step. Stopwords for each of the four languages French, English, German and Italian are removed as well. The stopword list was created by using the one found on the Porter's algorithm web page [10] and the one from [14]. Once all useless words have been removed, the person names and email adresses found in the email body, that have been earlier extracted from the email headers, are removed since person features are covered separately. For the remaining text word vectors are created.

In order to dramatically reduce the effort in identifying related clusters of emails by computing the complete email similarity matrix we exploit a specific characteristic of email texts. The temporal order of writing of emails is known and emails that are temporally distant are less likely related. This idea has been first exploited in [18] for news articles. There exists a great similarity between newspaper articles and emails since both are chronologically ordered documents. The method proposed in [18] allows the identification of email threads in $O(n)$ time.

A collection of emails is represented as an ordered set $E = \{e_1, e_2, ..., e_n\}$. The sequence 1, 2,..., n corresponds to the passage of time. Email e_i is older than e_{i+1}. Emails sent on the same day receive an arbitrary order.

The function $sim(e_i, e_j)$ calculates the word-based similarity between an email e_i and an email e_j from the set $comp_{e_i}$, where $comp_{e_i}$ is the set of emails of size k considered for comparison.

$$sim(e_i, e_j) = \frac{\sum_{kw} w_{kw}^{e_i} w_{kw}^{e_j}}{\sqrt{\sum_{kw} (w_{kw}^{e_i})^2} \sqrt{\sum_{kw} (w_{kw}^{e_j})^2}} \qquad (1)$$

Here, $w_{kw}^{e_i}$ is the weight given to keyword kw in email e_i.

$$w_{kw}^{e_i} = \frac{C_{e_i}(kw)}{C_{e_i}} \log \frac{k}{N_k(kw)} g_{kw}^{e_i}, \qquad (2)$$

where $C_{e_i}(kw)$ is the frequency of word kw in e_i, C_{e_i} is the number of words in e_i and $N_k(kw)$ is the number of emails in $comp_{e_i}$ that contain the word kw. $g_{kw}^{e_i} = 1,5$ if $kw \in differential(e_i)$ and $g_{kw}^{e_i} = 1$ otherwise. The function $differential(e_i)$ returns the set of keywords that appear in e_i but do not appear in $comp_{e_i}$.

The original method in [18] was modified in the way of how $comp_{e_i}$ is determined. Rather than considering the k last news articles, as in the original method, we consider all emails from from the last d days. Taking into account for comparison all emails written in the last d days (e.g. $d = 28$) affects the complexity of the algorithm, since the number of emails compared becomes variable. But from the perspective of email analysis it appears more logical to compare an email with all the emails written in a certain period, than with a fixed number of earlier emails. The execution time has not been a practical problem, since the number of emails considered remains much smaller than the size of the email database. As a further optimization the feature extraction algorithm determines in which language every email is written and only emails written in the same language are compared. This can reduce considerably the computation cost for users who receive emails written in different languages.

Email threads correspond then to sequences of emails that are linked by a similarity value $sim(e_i, e_j)$ for $i < j$ that is larger than a given threshold. Each email thread represents a feature.

Once all the features have been determined we eliminate all features and emails that are not useful. A feature appearing only once in an email is not relevant and therefore will be removed. Emails that do not have enough features will also not be taken into account in the following. They would generate non-relevant folders and hurt the result quality. The outlier removal before the start of the clustering and classification process substantially simplifies the subsequent processing.

4 Automatic Folder Generation

A clustering program, Cluto [4], is used to create clusters of emails using the features that have been extracted from the emails. This program takes as input a sparse matrix file whose rows are the data points (in our case email identifiers) and whose columns are the features. The Cluto toolkit was chosen because of its simplicity of use and its flexibility and the fact that it is freely available for research purposes.

The user can choose the number of levels the computer view folder structure should have and the minimal number of folders he wants at each level. The number of clusters per level is (naturally) monotonically increasing with the level of the tree. The clustering tool will then generate at each level in separate runs the required number of clusters. This approach exploits the fact that the clustering tool is using bisective K-Means and is thus creating clusters by successive (binary) splitting of the data sets. More precisely the tool proceeds by first splitting the data sets into two subsets with the closest features, then selecting one of the sets created in this way for further splitting, and so on till the desired number of clusters is reached. So if, for example, a clustering for the first level of the folder hierarchy has been created, a second execution of the clustering will again first create the same clusters and then continue to refine these clusters further, thus creating *the second level partitioning*. We give a simple example illustrating of how the construction of the folder structure works in Fig. 2.

email ID   clusters level 1   clusters level 2

email ID	clusters level 1	clusters level 2
1	1	1
2	1	1
3	1	2
4	2	3
5	2	3

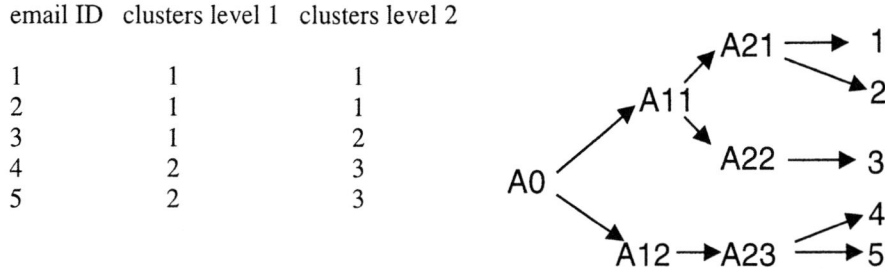

Fig. 2. Creation of folder structure through clustering

The optimal number of clusters to be generated is difficult to determine since it depends both on the available data and the user intentions. If the clustering program generates too many folders, the potential problem is that the subsequent merge algorithm, which will be described in the next section, will create too many folders in the merged view and related emails run the risk of being scattered over multiple folders. Also result visualization and comprehension becomes difficult. If the clustering program does not generate a sufficient number of folders some folders will contain emails on different topics that do not belong together.

The following approach has been used to achieve an optimal number of folders and still to allow the user to specify a minimal number of folders to be generated. The minimal number of folders required by the user is the number of clusters that the clustering program Cluto will have to find among for the email collection. These email clusters will become folders. There is no warranty that all the emails in a folder are related, as we want them to be. For this reason there is a further step, called group outlier removal, which will check every folder and determine if all its emails are related. If not, it will create new folders until all the emails contained in one folder are related. This approach will produce the minimal number of folders needed to generate a meaningful view.

We considered two methods to detect outlier emails within a generated folder. In the first approach we try to identify a representative email that shares with each other email in that folder at least one feature. We may consider this as testing whether the cluster contains a central element. In the second approach we test whether each email in the folder shares at least one feature with some other email in the folder. We may consider this as testing whether the cluster is connected. In both cases we exclude features related to the user's email address, as they would in general relate all emails of a folder. The first approach generates more folders and decreases the chances that one folder contains more than one topic. For this reason this is the method we have chosen for our implementation. Figure 3 illustrates the group outlier removal process. Group outlier removal proved to be very effective in order to dramatically improve the quality of the merged views.

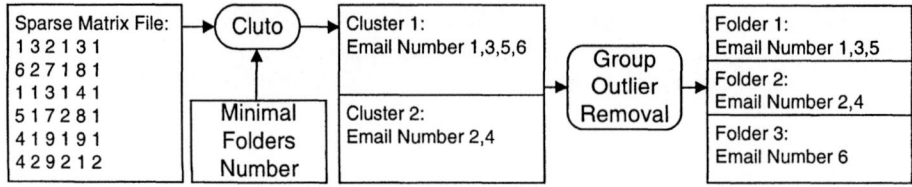

Fig. 3. Email 6 is an outlier in folder 1 as it cannot share a common feature with a central email (e.g. 1, 3). The group outlier removal creates a separate folder for it, if it is based on the first method presented

5 Folder Merge Algorithm

The folder merge algorithm takes two trees as input (the user view and the computer view) and produces a directed graph called merged view. First the merge algorithms needs to be able to determine when two folders are to be considered and thus should be merged. For this we introduce a similarity measure for folders. Then we discuss the different operations that can be performed to merge folders depending on their similarity. Finally we present the global algorithm and its properties. Note that even though we present this algorithm for the context of email folders it is generally applicable to any hierarchical schema used for data classifications.

5.1 Folder Similarity Measure

We view a folder structure as a tree where internal nodes correspond to folders and leaf nodes correspond to emails. For a folder A we denote by $leaf(A)$ the set of all direct and indirect leaves that it contains. Then the Shared Leaves Ration (SLR) is the measure used to determine the similarity of the content of two folders. This measure will be used to identify which folders should be compared and what actions are taken based on the comparison. The Shared Leaves Ratio comparing folders A and B is defined as

$$SLR_A(B) = \frac{\left| leaf(A) \cap leaf(B) \right|}{\left| leaf(A) \right|} \tag{3}$$

It is important to note that SLR is a non-symmetric relationship. If

$$\left| leaf(A) \right| \leq \left| leaf(B) \right|$$

then

$$SLR_B(A) \leq SLR_A(B)$$

with equality only if

$$\left| leaf(A) \right| = \left| leaf(B) \right|.$$

5.2 Basic Operations

Different merge operations can be applied after two folders from the user and the computer view have been compared. We introduce first the basic merge operations and then the merge algorithm that applies these operations in a proper order to merge two folder structures.

Basic operations always involve a folder A from one of the two input trees. The list G_A contains all the folders C such that folder C and A have some leaves in common (i.e. contain some common emails). If G_A is non empty, the merge algorithm will try to combine folders contained in list G_A with the folder A, otherwise folder A will no be modified and be considered as merged. The merge algorithm will be designed such that it always guarantees that the condition $|leaf(A)| \leq |leaf(C)|$ is satisfied (see algorithm *FolderSelection* in Section 5.3). Therefore when introducing the basic operations we will assume that this condition holds.

Specialization
If, after comparison, it turns out that a folder C in G_A is contained in A then C can appear as a subfolder of A in the merged folder structure. This situation occurs if

$$SLR_A(C) = 1, C \in G_A \qquad (4)$$

An example of specialization is given in Fig. 4. Creating subfolders through specialization is particularly interesting for partitioning large folders in the original folder structure into smaller folders.

Fig. 4. Result of the specialize operation

Specialization with a Shared Folder
This operation is executed when folder A and a folder C in G_A have only some leaves in common, but neither is contained in the other. This operation creates a new folder to contain the common emails. The new folder becomes a subfolder of both folders A and C and thus in general the folder structure generated by the merge algorithm will be a directed graph. This operation occurs if:

$$0 < SLR_A(C) < 1, C \in G_A \qquad (5)$$

An example of specialization is given in Fig. 5.

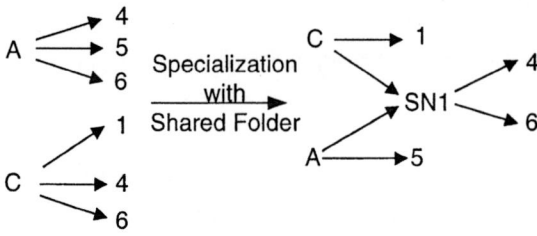

Fig. 5. Result of the specialization with shared folder operation

This operation is useful in dealing with emails that belong to more than one topic. It is also useful to correct classification errors. It happens quite often that an email is classified into a wrong folder. Such an email will appear in the wrong folder in the user view, but it will be regrouped with related emails in the computer view. After performing this operation, the problematic email will appear both in the wrong and right folder. Later, this email will attract the user's attention when he is inspecting the folder structure with the graphical user interface and he will be able to decide what to do. Either he or the computer did a classification mistake and the email should appear in only one folder, or it is of interest to have the email in two folders, because it is related to more than one topic.

If G_A contains more than one folder, folder A shares leaves with more than one folder C. In this case, the basic operation of specialization with a shared folder is executed once with every folder in G_A, but folder A is inserted only once into the merged graph.

Insertion of the Folder in the Merged Graph
If none of the two basic specialization operations can be executed, i.e. if G_A is empty, the folder A is inserted in the merged graph without modifications. The leaves of folder A are as well inserted into the merged graph.

5.3 Merge Algorithm

We give a general overview of the merge algorithm that relies on the basic operations. For initialization the computer and user view are merged into a common tree. This step is performed by merging the two root nodes of the two trees into a common root node resulting in the unified input tree.

After initialization the merge algorithm can be divided into three steps which are repeatedly executed as illustrated in Fig. 6. The first step called *TreeTraverseStrategy* ensures that the unified input tree is traversed in the correct order. It maintains a folder list called *PossibleBaseFolder*, which contains the list of folders whose sons must be merged. *PossibleBaseFolder* is a FIFO queue that determines the folder *currentRoot*. Initially *PossibleBaseFolder* contains the common root node of the unified tree. This folder is passed to the next step of the algorithm.

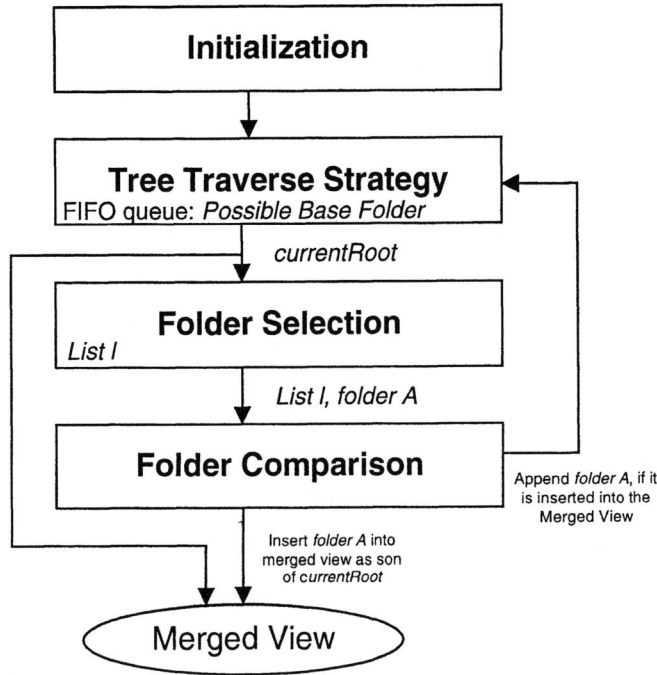

Fig. 6. Merge algorithm structure

The second step called *FolderSelection* determines a folder list *l*. This list contains the sons of the folder *currentRoot*. Once the list is determined, it is sorted in increasing order according to the number of leaves each folder contains. The first element of this list will then successively be removed from list *l* and passed to the next step of the algorithm, along with the remaining list *l*. The folder passed successively to the next step of the algorithm part will be called folder *A*.

```
FolderSelection(currentRoot)
        l = { A | A is a son of currentRoot};
        Sort l in increasing order according to |leaf(A)|;
        while l not empty
           A := first element of l;
           Drop first element of l;
           FolderComparison(l, A)
        endwhile;
```

The third and last step, called *FolderComparison*, derives the list G_A from *l*. This is done by calculating the *SLR* of all vertices in list *l* with folder *A* and including those folders in *l* that have a *SLR* greater than 0 into G_A. If G_A is empty, the folder will be inserted into the merged graph directly. If there is an element in G_A that satisfies the condition for the specialization or specialization with a shared folder operation, then the operation is executed. Every time when the algorithm adds a folder to the merged view by executing a basic operation, this folder is also added to the FIFO queue

PossibleBaseFolder. The detailed folder comparison algorithm is given in the following

```
FolderComparison(l, A)
    Calculate SLR_A(C) for each folder C ∈ l;

    CloseFolders = { C | C ∈ l, SLR_A(C) > 0 };
    Sort CloseFolders in decreasing order according to SLR_A(C);
    ClosestFolder = first element of CloseFolders;
    nrSharedLeaves = |leaf(A) ∩ leaf(ClosestFolder)|;
    if SLR_A(ClosestFolder) > inclusionThreshold
        then   specialize(A, closestFolder)
        elseif SLR_A(ClosestFolder) > 0 and

                nrSharedLeaves ≥ nrSharedLeavesThreshold

        then specializeWSharedFolder(A, CloseFolders);
                insertFolderIntoMergedGraph(A, currentRoot)
        else insertFolderIntoMergedGraph(A, currentRoot);
```

The algorithm terminates when *PossibleBaseFolder* is empty while executing *TreeTraversalStrategy*. This algorithm does not loose any information that is contained in the user view. All folders from the user view will be retained in the merged view. Also no emails can be lost since all emails contained in a folder of the user view will show up as elements of the respective folder retained in the merged view.

We demonstrate the execution of the merge algorithm by a simple example. Let the following two folder structures be given as input.

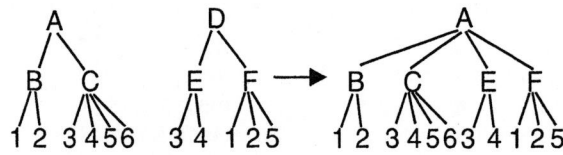

The first step is to create a unified tree with a common root. At the beginning *CurrentRoot* is set to *{A} PossibleBaseFolder* is empty. The folder selection algorithm produces initially a list *l = {B, E, F, C}*. Processing folder *B* produces the first graph in the following figure. The following steps are related to processing the remaining elements in *A*.

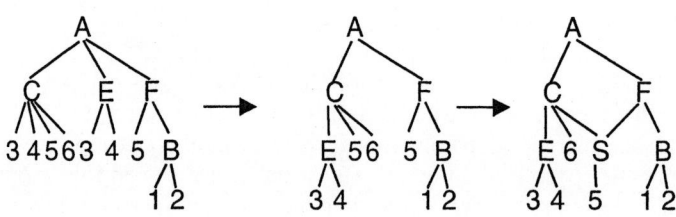

Once the merge algorithm termiantes, the output must still be post processed. Folders with no leaves and containing only a single *folder will be removed, unless* these folders are not user folders.

5.4 Label Creation

During the merge processes new folders are created by the algorithm. For these folders new labels have to be created. Creating intelligible labels is an extremely important and equally difficult problem. The labels are generated using the features of the emails in the folder. We chose to use both person and subject related features. We developed several rules to generate from terms found in the emails labels enriched by additional information extracted from the structure of the email. The following rules were applied to that respect:

- email f *name* a *subject*: a folder with this label contains essentially emails from a person with *name*. The most frequent terms related to a subject are indicated.
- a *subject*: a folder with this label contains emails essentially related to a specific subject, which is the most frequently observed feature.
- g-email(*number of person in the email-list*) *name1 name2 email-list* a *subject words*: a folder with this label contains essentially emails which had always the same recipient list *email-list*. The first two members of the email list are mentioned.
- e received w *name* a *words*: a folder with this label contains essentially emails that have been received from a person with *name*. Frequently emails of this type are sent via a distribution list.
- discussion w *name* a *subject*: a folder with this label contains emails where a discussion is carried on with person *name*. The person whose name is included into the label is involved as person feature in most of the folders or emails, both in the from field and in the recipient list.

6 Graphical User Interface

In general, the merge algorithm results in a directed graph. This graph contains new access points to email either created through folders integrated from the computer view or created through the specialization with new folder operation. Since the resulting folder structure is a directed graph it cannot be directly displayed with standard tools for tree-like directory structures. A special user interface was thus developed to allow the user to visualize the generated folder structure, and more importantly to manipulate it according to his needs. The user interface also allows to filtering the merged view in order to focus the users' attention on specific aspects of the folder structure. Thus the user interface provides a tool that allows the user to efficiently transform the merged view into the desired final user view.

The graphical user interface for postprocessing the merged view is an essential part of the solution we propose. Ultimately, only the user is able to decide whether certain folders created by the preceding process are semantically meaningful. All the steps for the automatic reorganization of folder structures presented earlier are designed in order to produce potentially useful results, but the final decision about their utility has to be left to the user.

The most challenging requirement when designing the graphical user interface was to provide the user the possibility to explore the different parents of a folder and at the same time exhibit the structure of the original user view. In order to help the user to navigate easily in the result, tools have been added that aid in quickly understanding the automatically created folder structure and accepting or rejecting changes swiftly. For doing that two modes of browsing are supported, namely browsing vertically along the paths of the tree hierarchy and browsing horizontally among the different fathers of a shared folder. Folders from the merged view which should be examined by the user are specially marked (with the letter "M" as it is shown in Fig. 7). Marked folders that have been examined and processed by the user are unmarked.

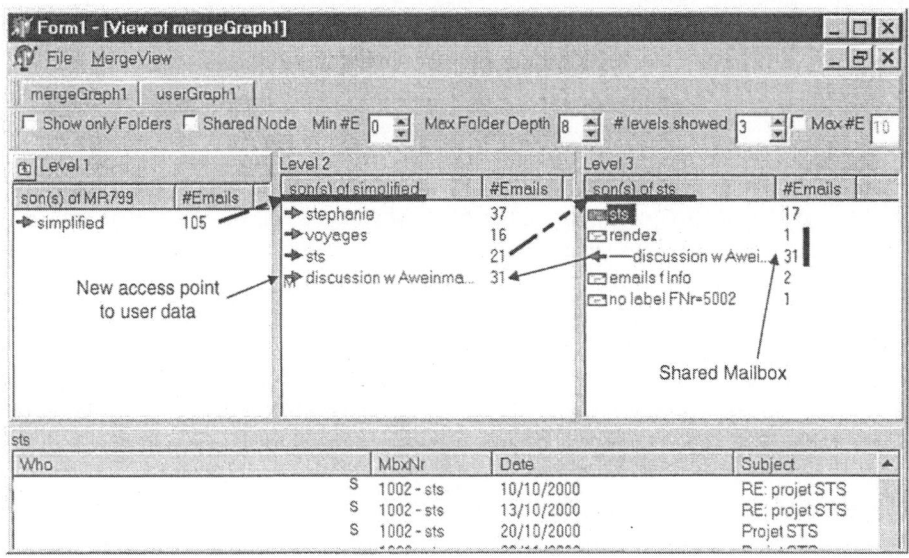

Fig. 7. This is a screenshot of the implementation of the graphical user interface. It shows how folder structures are displayed and how the different characteristics described in this section are implemented. The letter "M" near the folder "discussion w Aweinma…" indicates to the user that he should start to examine the merged view by looking at this folder and thus to focus his attention.

With respect to editing of the folder structures the following rules have to be observed. (1) It is only possible to remove a folder if it has no parents left and (2) if a folder that is shared among multiple folders is removed, it is only removed from one of the parent folders. The second rule allows to reorganizing shared folders such that a more tree-like structure can be achieved. With respect to filtering the user can specify to see only folders that contain a maximal or minimal number of emails. This is useful to eliminate potentially useless folders and thus to reduce the complexity of the folder structure.

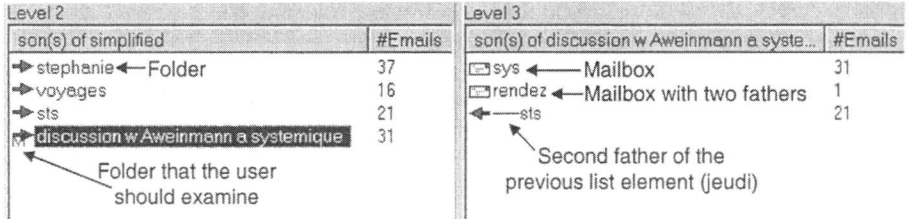

Fig. 8. This figure shows how the graphical user interface displays folders having more than one parent

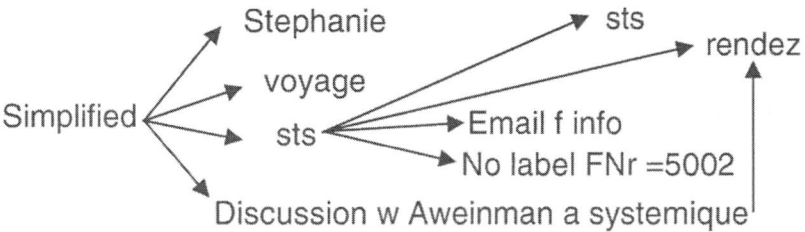

Fig. 9. This figure shows the folder structure of the merged view displayed in Fig. 8. It is interesting to observe of how the folder "rendez", that has two parents, is displayed.

7   Evaluation

The approach described in this paper has been fully implemented. To connect the various steps of the overall process, including feature extraction from emails, processing by the clustering tool and display at the graphical user interface a set of perl scripts was used that communicate through files. The graphical user interface has been implemented in Delphi. For mailboxes the Eudora format has been used.

For evaluation different user tests have been performed. Two types of questions have been addressed in the evaluation: the evaluation of the quality of the merged view and the evaluation of the usability of the graphical user interface. A secondary issue that we evaluated was the computational performance of the implementation of the algorithms. The results of the usability test were reflected in several redesigns of the graphical user interface. In the following we focus on the test concerning the generation and quality of the merged view. We report the results from one representative test.

A user provided his mailbox containing 3466 emails organized into 4 folders. The user then requested the tool to produce a merged view on two levels with 5 folders on the first level and 20 folders on the second level. It took approximately 26 minutes to produce the merged view on a Pentium PC with 700Mhz. After the creation of the merged view the user inspected 15 of the new folders. 11 out of the 15 folders were judged to be meaningful since they concerned a specific topic. The user remembered that sometime he classified his emails without much consideration, but he was astonished to see how many topics were spread over different mailboxes. Most of the time topics were split among two folders, but one topic even had been split among three folders. The 4 folders that were considered meaningless had two kinds of problems. The most frequent problem (also in other experiments) has been folders containing unrelated emails. This typically results from using person-related features from the email. This indicates a possible improvement in the feature extraction process. The second problem was related to the intelligibility of the produced folder structure. As it turns out it is difficult for a user to well understand the folder structure, in particular in the presence of shared folders, when the depth of the folder structure is more than one.

From this and the other tests made (a total of 9) we can thus draw the following conclusions. The different tests show that a majority of the folders and mailboxes produced by the proposed solution are meaningful. An average of 50 to 70% of meaningful folders is achieved when the number of clusters from which the computer view is generated is reasonable. It is difficult to say in general what a reasonable value would be as this parameter depends on the characteristics of the user mailbox and the number of preexisting folders. But experience showed that this parameter should be chosen such that the number of folders in the computer view should be approximately the number of folders in the user view, unless the user view does not contain too many small folders that the user wants to group together. Increasing the minimal number of folders to be generated increases the probability of creating meaningful folders, but it decreases the probability of finding all the emails related to a topic in the same folder. Once a user has made the necessary effort to understand the graphical user interface, the comprehension of a merged view of depth one is straightforward. Some parts of the merged view become difficult to understand if the depth of the user or the computer view is greater than one. There are two possible solutions to improve the result intelligibility. Either the display at the graphical used interface is changed or the merge algorithm is modified such that complex folder structures are avoided while maintaining the user information retention property.

8   Related Work

The application of text classification techniques to email documents has been widely studied in the literature. We do not give a complete overview on this field, but just mention some typical examples. We can characterize this work along two dimensions: the techniques used and the specific application targeted. As for the techniques that have been considered in the literature we find rule induction [1], word-based TF-IDF weighting [15], naïve Baysian text classification [8, 11, 12], and hierarchical clustering [6], the latter being the method also we were using. In most cases emails are considered as unstructured text, not taking advantage of the specific email structure during feature extraction. A notable exception is [6], who use similar feature extraction methods as we do. As for the scope of the different approaches they are more limited than our approach, as they focus on a specific task. The following standard tasks can be identified:

- automatic creation of folder structures, e.g. [6]
- automatic classification by filtering of email messages, e.g. [12]
- filtering of email messages into user defined folders, e.g. [1]
- spam detection, e.g. [8]

None of these approaches aims at reorganizing user-defined folder structures as we do. Either no user-defined folders are used at all and classifications are automatically generated only, or the preexisting folder structure is the target of an email filtering method. On the other hand these works provide a rich set of methods that could be used as alternative methods to the one we have applied in the computer view generation. Our focus was not so much to make use of sophisticated text classification techniques, but to use existing techniques in a way that took most advantage of the specific problem structure at hand.

The merge technique that we applied is essentially based on ideas that have already been introduced in the very first works on database schema integration [7]. The approach of integrating techniques for document analysis, for schema integration and user interfaces can be seen in line with current developments on ontology engineering tools [3]. Similarly as our work, these tools have been recently extended by introducing document analysis methods, as in [5], to enable semi-automatic development of ontologies.

9 Conclusions

In this paper we have introduced an approach to evolve user-defined email folder structures taking advantage of text content analysis techniques. One challenge was to completely preserve existing knowledge of users while at the same time apply modifications obtained from email content analysis. In this sense the method bridges the gap on earlier work on email filtering (relying on user-defined folder structures only) and email classification (relying on computer generated folder structures only). Another challenge was to address all the phases of the process starting from email classification, to folder merging and interactive postprocessing of the result by the user, while taking in each phase advantage of the specific knowledge available on the email domain. The approach has been implemented and evaluated.

The approach is besides addressing an important practical problem also a relevant study on the application and combination of various techniques for creating and maintaining user/application specific ontologies. Many of the observations and techniques would naturally generalize to onotology management in more general settings.

References

1. Cohen, W. W.: Fast Effective Rule Induction. Proceedings of the Twelfth International Conference on Machine Learning (ICML), Tahoe City, CA, USA, July 9–12, 1995, Morgan Kaufmann, pp. 115–123, 1995.
2. Crawford, E., Kay, J., McCreath, E.: IEMS – The Intelligent Email Sorter, Proceedings of the Nineteenth International Conference (ICML 2002), University of New South Wales, Sydney, Australia, July 8–12, 2002, Morgan Kaufmna, pp. 83–90, 2002.
3. Duineveld, A. J., Stoter, R., Weiden, M. R., Kenepa, B., Benjamins, V. R.: Wondertools? A comparative study of ontological engineering tools, Proceedings of the Twelfth Workshop on Knowledge Acquisition, Modeling and Management, Voyager Inn, Banff, Alberta, Canada, October 16–21, 1999.

4. Karypis, G.: Cluto A Clustering Toolkit manual, University of Minnesota, Department of Computer Science Minneapolis, MN 55455, related papers are available at http://www.cs.umn.edu/~karypis.
5. Maedche, A., Staab, S.: Semi-automatic Engineering of Ontologies from Text. Proceedings of the Twelfth International Conference on Software Engineering and Knowledge Engineering (SEKE), Chicago, July 6–8, 2000.
6. Manco, G., Masciari, E., Ruffolo, M., Tagarelli, A.: Towards an Adaptive Mail Classifier, Proceedings of Tecniche di Intelligenza Artificiale per la ricerca di informazione sul Web (AIIA), Siena, Italy, Septemmber 11–13, 2002.
7. Motro, A., Buneman, P.: Constructing Superviews, Proceedings of the 1981 ACM SIGMOD International Conference on Management of Data, Ann Arbor, Michigan, April 29–May 1, 1981, ACM, New York, pp. 56–64, 1981.
8. Pantel, P. Lin, D.: SpamCop – A Spam Classification & Organization Program. AAAI-98 Workshop on Learning for Text Categorization, pp. 95–98, 1998.
9. Pazzani, M.J.; Representation of electronic mail filtering profiles: a user study. Proceedings of the 2000 International Conference on Intelligent User Interfaces, January 9–12, 2000, New Orleans, LA, USA, ACM, New York, pp. 202–206, 2000.
10. Porter, M.: Porter's algorithm implementation official page, http://www.tartarus.org/~martin/porterstemmer/
11. Provost, J.: Naïve-Bayes vs. Rule-Learning in Classification of Email. The University of Texas at Austin, Artificial Intelligence Lab. Technical Report AI-TR-99-284, 1999.
12. Rennie, J.: ifile: An Application of Machine Learning to Mail Filtering. Proceedings of the KDD-2000 Workshop on Text Mining, Boston, USA, August 20, 2000.
13. Rohall, S: Reinventing Email. CSCW 2002 Workshop: Redesigning Email for the 21st Century, 2002.
14. Savoy J.: Report on CLEF-2001 Experiments. In C. Peters (Ed.), Results of the CLEF-2001, cross-language system evaluation campaign, (pp. 11–19). Sophia-Antipolis: ERCIM, http://www.unine.ch/info/clef, 2001,
15. Segal, R., Kephart, M.: MailCat: An intelligent assistant for organizing e-mail. Proceedings of the Third Annual Conference on Autonomous Agents, May 1–5, 1999, Seattle, WA, USA. ACM, pp. 276–282, 1999.
16. Steinbach, M., Karypis, G., Kumar, V.: A Comparison of Document Clustering Techniques, Proceedings of the KDD-2000 Workshop on Text Mining, Boston, USA, August 20, 2000.
17. Sure, Y., Angele, J., Staab, S.: OntoEdit: Guiding Ontology Development by Methodology and Inferencing. Proceedings of the Confederated International Conferences DOA, CoopIS and ODBASE 2002 Irvine, California, USA, October 30–November 1, 2002, LNCS 2519, Springer, pp. 1205–1222, 2002.
18. Uramoto, N., Takeda, K.: A Method for Relating Multiple Newspaper Articles by Using Graphs, and Its Application to Webcasting. Proceedings of the 36th Annual Meeting of the Association for Computational Linguistics and 17th International Conference on Computational Linguistics, August 10–14, 1998, Université de Montréal, Quebec, Canada. ACL / Morgan Kaufmann, pp. 1307–13, 1998.
19. Whittaker, S., Sidner, C.: Email Overload: exploring personal information management of email. Proceedings of the Conference on Human Factors in Computing Systems (CHI'96), April 13–18, 1996, Vancouver, British Columbia, Canada, pp. 276–283, 1996.

Mining for Lexons: Applying Unsupervised Learning Methods to Create Ontology Bases

Marie-Laure Reinberger[1], Peter Spyns[2], Walter Daelemans[1], and Robert Meersman[2]

[1] CNTS - University of Antwerp,
Universiteitsplein 1, B-2610 Wilrijk - Belgium,
{reinberg,daelem}@uia.ua.ac.be
[2] STAR Lab - Vrije Universiteit Brussel,
Pleinlaan 2 Gebouw G-10, B-1050 Brussel - Belgium
{Peter.Spyns,Robert.Meersman}@vub.ac.be

Abstract. Ontologies in current computer science parlance are computer based resources that represent agreed domain semantics. This paper first introduces ontologies in general and subsequently, in particular, shortly outlines the DOGMA ontology engineering approach that separates "atomic" conceptual relations from "predicative" domain rules. In the main part of the paper, we describe and experimentally evaluate work in progress on a potential method to automatically derive the atomic conceptual relations mentioned above from a corpus of English medical texts. Preliminary outcomes are presented based on the clustering of nouns and compound nouns according to co-occurrence frequencies in the subject-verb-object syntactic context.

Keywords: knowledge representation, machine learning, text mining, ontology, semantic web, clustering, selectional restriction, co-composition.

1 Introduction and General Background

1.1 The Semantic Web

Internet technology has made IT users aware of both new opportunities as well as actual needs for large scale interoperation of distributed, heterogeneous, and autonomous information systems. Additionally the vastness of the amount of information already on-line, or to be interfaced with the WWW, makes it unfeasible to depend merely on human users to correctly and comprehensively identify, access, filter and process the information relevant for the purpose of applications over a given domain. Be they called software agents, web services, or otherwise, this is increasingly becoming the task of computer programs equipped with *domain knowledge* . Presently however there is an absence of usable formal, standardised and shared domain knowledge of what the information stored inside these systems and exchanged through their interfaces actually means. Nevertheless this is a prerequisite for agents and services (or even for human users) wishing to access the information but who, obviously, were never involved when these systems were created. The pervasive and explosive proliferation of computerised information systems (databases, intranets, communication systems, or other) quite simply makes this into the key problem of the application layer of the current internet and

R. Meersman et al. (Eds.): CoopIS/DOA/ODBASE 2003, LNCS 2888, pp. 803–819, 2003.

its semantic web successor. The equally obvious key to the solution of this problem therefore lies in a better understanding, control and management of the semantics of information in a general sense.

1.2 Ontologies

The semantic principles and technology underlying such solutions are emerging in the form of *ontologies*, i.e. practically usable computer-based repositories of formal and agreed semantics about application domains [35]. Ultimately these ontologies will coalesce, more or less tightly, into a vast knowledge resource about the entire "information universe" that is the web. In the present parlance [17], a computer-implemented ontology roughly is constituted of :

1. a computer-based lexicon, thesaurus, glossary, or other type of controlled and structured vocabulary of linguistic terms; the terms in those vocabularies are assumed to refer in well-defined ways to concepts.
2. an extension with explicit "knowledge" about a given domain, under the form of relationships between concepts, often including a taxonomy of those concepts.
3. an extension with a set of general rules and constraints supporting reasoning about the concepts. [1]

Roughly speaking, in the realm of information systems a (first order) formal semantics of an application may be defined by a *formal interpretation*, viz. mapping, of some given computer representation of that application (in a suitable computer language) in terms of a given world domain, or rather some suitably elementary and agreed conceptualisation of it. This common classic formalism, also the most amenable to ontologies, is called declarative or Tarski semantics [34] and may be found in various places in the database and AI literature, in Reiter's seminal paper [31] linking the two fields through first order logic, or in the textbook by Genesereth & Nilsson [14].

Essentially this approach replaces "the world" (the domain) by a *conceptualisation*, a mathematical object that typically consists of very elementary constructs such as a set of objects and a set of (mathematical) relations. Conceptualisations theoretically are language-, context-, and usage independent formalisations of this world, or domain of discourse. A formal ontology on the other hand is a formal rendering of such a conceptualisation through e.g. an ontology language [35]. For a proper understanding, the actual notion of ontology should therefore be seen as separate from this conceptualisation of the "world" [17]. Note that this distinction is not always made in parts of the recent literature on ontologies.

1.3 Mining for DOGMA Terms and Lexons

The *DOGMA* (Developing Ontology-Guided Mediation for Agents) ontology engineering approach of VUB STAR Lab is based on the three rather evident observations that:

1. agreements become easier if the items involved are simpler

---

[1] This latter item falls outside the scope of this paper.

2. most relevant human knowledge is massively available in natural language in text documents and other "lexical" sources such as databases

3. conceptualisations -and hence ontologies- should be as independent as possible of intended application and design(er) context, and of the language used to reach the agreement

A DOGMA inspired ontology [2] is based on the principle of a double articulation: an ontology is decomposed into an ontology base, which holds (multiple) intuitive conceptualisation(s) of a domain, and a layer of ontological commitments, where each commitment holds a set of domain rules.

The *ontology base* consists of sets of intuitively "plausible" domain fact types, represented and organised as sets of context-specific binary conceptual relations, called *lexons*. They are formally described as $< \gamma, \lambda : term_1, role, co - role, term_2 >$, where γ is a context identifier, used to group lexons that are intuitively "related" in an intended conceptualisation of a domain for a specific natural language λ. Informally we say that a lexon is a fact that may hold for some application, expressing in that case that within the context γ the $term_1$ may plausibly have $term_2$ occur in an associating $role$ (with $co - role$ as its inverse) with it. Lexons are independent of specific applications and should cover relatively broad domains. For each context γ and term $term$ for a natural language λ, the triplet $(\gamma, \lambda, term)$ is assumed to refer to a unique concept *concept*. Formulated alternatively, a *concept* is lexicalised for a natural language λ by a specific $term$ depending on a specific context γ of use. More details on the DOGMA engineering approach (e.g., the commitment layer) can be found in [19,33].

The main research hypothesis is that lexons, representing the "basic facts" expressed in natural language about a domain can be extracted from textual sources. Other potential sources are database schemas or semi-structured data (e.g. XML files). (Semi-)automatic mining for lexons to populate the ontology base would allow to short-circuit the knowledge acquisition bottle-neck (human knowledge elicitation and acquisition implies a high cost in terms of time and resources). We have opted for extraction techniques based on unsupervised learning methods since these do not require specific external domain knowledge such as thesauri and/or tagged corpora [3]. As a consequence, the portability of these techniques to new domains is much better [27]:p.61].

A first step in order to mine for DOGMA lexons is the discovery and grouping of relevant terms. A domain expert will then distill concepts from the set of terms and determine which relationships hold between the various newly discovered concepts. Note that the terms and lexons operate on the language level, while concepts and conceptual relationships are considered to be, at least in principle, language independent. By doing so, the domain expert - together with the help of an ontology modeller - shapes the conceptualisation of a domain as it is encoded in the textual sources (taking synonymy into account). The second step will most probably be repeated several times before an adequate and shared (formal) domain model is agreed upon.

---

[2] An overview of other ontology representation techniques can be found in [32].

[3] Except the training corpus for the general purpose shallow parser - see below.

1.4 Selectional Restrictions and Co-composition

A lot of information about the meaning of words can be inferred from the contexts in which they occur [20]. For example, information about the functionality and properties of the concepts associated with a word can be inferred from the way nouns and verbs are combined. Of course, a fine-grained representation of the meaning of a word cannot be reached without the use of large amounts of syntactically analysed data about their use. The use of powerful and robust language processing tools such as shallow parsers allows us to parse large text collections (available in massive quantities) and thereby provide potentially relevant information for extracting semantic knowledge.

The linguistic assumptions underlying this approach are (i) the principle of selectional restrictions (syntactic structures provide relevant information about semantic content), and (ii) the notion of co-composition [28] (if two elements are composed into an expression, each of them imposes semantic constraints on the other). The fact that heads of phrases with a subject relation to the same verb share a semantic feature would be an application of the principle of *selectional restrictions*. The fact that the heads of phrases in a subject or object relation with a verb constrain that verb and vice versa would be an illustration of *co-composition*. In other words, each word in a noun-verb relation participates in building the meaning of the other word in this context [11,12]. If we consider the expression "write a book" for example, it appears that the verb "to write" triggers the informative feature of "book", more than on its physical feature. We make use of both principles in our use of clustering to extract semantic knowledge from syntactically analysed corpora.

2   Objectives

Our purpose is to build a repository of lexical semantic information from text, ensuring evolvability and adaptability. This repository can be considered as a complex semantic network. An important point is that we assume that the method of extraction and the organisation of this semantic information should depend not only on the available material, but also on the intended use of the knowledge structure. There are different ways of organising it, depending on its future use and on the specificity of the domain. In this paper, we deal with the medical domain, but one of our future objectives is to test our methods and tools on different specific domains.

In the remainder of this paper, we will shortly introduce in the next section (Material and Methods) the shallow parser to extract subject-verb-object structures and the English medical corpora used (section 3.1), the clustering methods applied to the task (section 3.2), and an evaluation of their accuracy (section 3.3) using WordNet [24] as a gold standard. Section 4 describes the various experiments in detail. We have tested similarity based clustering algorithms, applying some variations to the set of data and to the algorithm in order to compare and improve the quality of the clusters: soft (section 4.1) and hard clustering (section 4.2) are compared (section 4.3 and 4.4) and merged (section 4.5). Particular attention is paid to compound nouns (section 4.6). The results are briefly discussed and related to other on-going work in this area (section 5). Some ideas about future work are also presented before concluding this paper (section 6).

3   Material and Methods

3.1   Shallow Parsing

In a specific domain, an important quantity of semantic information is carried by the nouns. At the same time, the noun-verb relations provide relevant information about the nouns, due to the semantic restrictions they impose. In order to extract this information automatically from our corpus, we used the memory-based shallow parser which is being developed at CNTS Antwerp and ILK Tilburg [4,5,9] [4]. This shallow parser takes plain text as input, performs tokenisation, POS tagging, phrase boundary detection, and finally finds grammatical relations such as subject-verb and object-verb relations, which are particularly useful for us. The software was developed to be efficient and robust enough to allow shallow parsing of large amounts of text from various domains.

The choice of the specific medical domain has been made since large amounts of data are freely available. In particular, we decided to use Medline, the abstracts of which can be retrieved using the internal search engine. We have focused on a medical subject that was specific but common enough to build a moderately big corpus. Hence, this corpus is composed of the Medline abstracts retrieved under the queries "hepatitis A" and "hepatitis B". It contains about 4 million words. The shallow parser was used to provide a linguistic analysis of each sentence of this corpus, allowing us to retrieve semantic information of various kinds.

3.2   Clustering

Different methods can be used for the extraction of semantic information from parsed text. Pattern matching [2] has proved to be a efficient way to extract semantic relations, but this method involves the predefined choice of the semantic relations that will be extracted. We rely on a large amount of data to get results using clustering algorithms on syntactic contexts in order to also extract previously unexpected relations.

Clustering requires a minimal amount of "manual semantic pre-processing" by the user. Clustering on nouns can be performed by using different syntactic contexts, for example noun+modifier relations [7] or dependency triples [20]. As we have mentioned above, the shallow parser detects the subject-verb-object structures. This gives us the possibility to focus on the noun-verb relations with the noun appearing as the head of the subject or the object phrase, but also on the relation noun-verb-noun, where the verb features a link between the two head nouns. From now on, we will refer to the nouns appearing as the head of the subject or object phrase as "nouns".

The first step of the similarity-based clustering algorithm we are using consists of processing the parsed text to retrieve the co-occurring noun-verb-noun relations, and remembering whether the noun appeared in a subject or in an object position. This step is performed with the use of a stop list that skips all pairs containing the verbs *to be* or *to have*. We want to point out that we are not implying by doing so that those two verbs do not provide relevant information. They simply are too frequent and have such a broad range of meanings that we cannot, with this method and at this stage of the

---

[4] See http://ilk.kub.nl for a demo version.

experiments, take them into account. The words are then lemmatised, before we select from the resulting list the most frequent relations. Those relations are organised in classes before the processing of a clustering algorithm. We will describe in the next section the evaluation method that we have used.

3.3   Evaluation

Evaluation of extracted clusters is problematic, as we do not have any reference or model for the clusters that we want to build. At the same time, we wanted an automatic evaluation method. We chose to use WordNet, which is freely available. As WordNet is not devoted to a particular domain, it can be used for the different corpora we are experimenting with. WordNet has been used by [20] for the evaluation of an automatically constructed thesaurus. Wordnet was transformed into the same format as the thesaurus, and a comparison was carried out between the entries of the thesaurus and the entries of the transformed WordNet, allowing a global evaluation of the constructed thesaurus.

We want to validate the relations between words that are established through our clustering process on medical text, but as WordNet does not contain all information related to the medical domain, it will provide us with only a sample of the correct associations. The semantic information provided by WordNet is only used in the evaluation process. We do not intent to correct or enlarge the clusters with this information, as we wish to stay as much as possible within the paradigm of purely unsupervised learning.

From the list of all nouns appearing in the clusters, we have kept the sublist that belongs to WordNet (WN words). Then, we have used this list to build the list containing all the pairs of nouns connected in WordNet through a relation of synonymy, hypernymy, hyponymy, meronymy or holonymy. Here are some examples of the relations found in WordNet:

> hepatitis - disease (hypernymic relation)
> blood - cells (meronymic relation)
> aim - purpose (synonym)

This list of pairs (WN pairs) allows us to compute a recall value R, with:
R = # WN pairs in the clusters / # WN pairs

Computing a precision value was more difficult as Wordnet is not complete or even representative for the medical domain. Our clusters depend on subject-verb and object-verb relations, and consequently some of them will stand for functional relations. One cluster for example will contain the list of elements that can be "gathered" or "collected", namely "blood", "sample" and "specimen". Another cluster will link "infection" and "disease" as object of the verbs "to cause" and "to induce". "Syringe" and "equipment" appear in the same cluster, gathered by the verbs "to share" and "to reuse". Those relations do not appear in WordNet. Therefore, the precision values we give must be considered as a "lower bound precision" or "minimum precision" mP. It is computed by dividing the number of correct WordNet pairs found in the clusters by the total number of pairs of words (formed with WordNet words) in the clusters:
mP=# WN pairs in the clusters / # pairs

In order to balance this minimum precision, we have made an attempt to build a more exhaustive set of relations, in order to extrapolate a more realistic precision value.

We have worked on a sample of words W and clusters C, associated to a set of WordNet pairs WnP. They correspond to a minimum precision mP=(# WnP in C) / (# pairs in C). We have derived manually all possible pairs, including functional relations like the ones mentioned above. We obtain an augmented set of pairs AugP, that allows us to find the new set of correct pairs in the set of clusters C and a new precision:

newP = (# AugP in C) / (# pairs in C)

We have used the ratios obtained with this sample to compute a new value that we will call extrapolated precision (eP) for the various clustering experiments. To do this, we assume that WnP/AugP is a constant value, and that:

(# WnP in C)/WnP = (# AugP in C)/AugP

This extrapolated precision will allow us to propose an estimation for the real precision. In the next sections, we will give a description of the different steps of our experiment and of the evaluation of the different results.

4   Description of the Experiments

The first step of the experiment was to measure if and to what extent the information provided by the shallow parser is relevant for the extraction of semantic relations. Even if the syntactic analysis supplies useful information, it requires some processing time as well, and this cost is only motivated if it improves the semantic analysis. In order to evaluate this, we carried out a comparative study on the results of the clustering applied to raw text and parsed text. We have compared the results using three different clustering algorithms: a soft (or disjunctive) similarity-based clustering algorithm, a hard bottom-up hierarchical similarity-based clustering algorithm, and a non-hierarchical clustering algorithm (AutoClass [8]). We have applied the hard clustering algorithms to two different corpora: our Medline corpus and the Wall Street Journal (WSJ) corpus (1M words). We refer here to "soft clustering" as clustering algorithms that allow an element to appear in more than one cluster, contrary to "hard clustering" where an element can appear in one and only one cluster. We will give a description of the clustering algorithms we have been using before commenting on the results.

4.1   Soft Clustering

The bottom-up soft clustering we have performed gives us the possibility to take into account the ambiguity of the words [10] by allowing a word to belong to different clusters. The soft similarity-based clustering algorithm applied on parsed text starts with the processing the parsed text to retrieve the co-occurring noun-verb pairs, and remembering whether the noun appeared in a subject or in an object position. We then select from the list we get the most frequent co-occurrences: the 100 most frequent noun-verb relations with the nouns appearing in the subject group, and the 100 most frequent relations where the noun is part of the object group. What we obtain is a list of verbs, each verb associated with a list of nouns that co-occur with it, either as subjects only or as objects only. Here is an extract of the list ("_o" (resp "_s") indicates that the list of nouns appears as object (resp. subject)):

acquire_o: hepatitis infection virus disease
compensate_o: liver cirrhosis disease
decompensate_o: liver cirrhosis disease
decrease_s: rates prevalence serum incidence proportion number percentage
estimate_o: prevalence incidence risk number
transmit_o: hepatitis infection disease

It appears, for example, that the same set of nouns occur as object of the verbs "compensate" and "decompensate", or that "acquire" and "transmit" present a very similar set of nouns occurring as object. Some cases are more interesting, for example the fact that the set of nouns appearing as the subject of "decrease" present strong similarities with the set of nouns appearing as object of "estimate".

The next step consists of clustering these classes of nouns according to their similarity. The similarity measure takes into account the number of common elements and the number of elements that differ between two classes. Each class is compared to all other classes of nouns. For each pair of classes C1-C2, the program counts the number of nouns common to both classes (sim), the number of nouns only present in C1 (dif1) and the number of nouns only present in C2 (dif2). If sim, dif1 and dif2 respect some predefined values the matching is considered to be possible. After the initial class has been compared to all other classes, all the possible matchings are compared and the one producing the largest new class is kept (in case of ties, the first one is kept). Each time a new cluster is created, the 2 classes involved are removed from the processed list. The whole process is iterated as long as at least one new matching occurs, resulting in the creation of a new cluster.

4.2   Hard Clustering

The hard clustering experiments have been performed on the most frequent vectors associating nouns to their co-occurring verbs. On raw text, we have extracted 2-grams, 3-grams and 4-grams and built vectors representing co-occurring words. The input of the bottom-up similarity-based algorithm is a list of nouns (or words), each of them associated to its list of co-occurring verbs (or words). Contrarily to the soft clustering algorithm, the nouns (words) are clustered according to the similarity between the classes of verbs. The similarity measure, as for the soft clustering algorithm, takes into account the number of common elements and the number of elements that differ between two classes of verbs. The classes are compared two by two and the process is iterated as long as a cluster can be modified. When no change is possible, the similarity measure is lowered and the process is iterated again until we obtain one cluster containing all the nouns. The resulting tree is cut according to the percentage of nouns that have been clustered. A cluster is valid when at least two nouns are in it.

The second hard clustering algorithm we have used is a non-hierarchical hard clustering algorithm called AutoClass. AutoClass is fed with ordered vectors of attribute values and finds the most probable set of class descriptions by performing successive reallocations, given the data and prior expectations. We have selected AutoClass among

Table 1. Recall (R), minimum precision (mP) and extrapolated precision (eP) values for the hard clustering similarity-based algorithm on parsed text and on plain text (n-grams). The experiment has been carried out for about 150 words, 90% of them are clustered and the set of clusters contains 250 pair relations

	% of words clustered	R	mP	eP	Nb of pairs
SP	90%	15%	13%	33%	250
3-grams	90%	10%	13%	23%	250

Table 2. Comparison of 2 hard clustering algorithm: the hierarchical similarity based algorithm vs. the non-hierarchical AutoClass algorithm, on 2 corpora

	Sim. based			AutoClass		
	R	mP	eP	R	mP	eP
WSJ corpus						
n-grams	7%	10%	16%	8%	7%	10%
SP	11%	12%	19%	6%	10%	15%
MEDLINE corpus						
n-grams	10%	13%	23%	30%	2%	4%
SP	15%	13%	33%	11%	8%	12%

other existing clustering algorithms for this comparative experiment as it showed good results on our data. For raw text, the best results have been observed on 3-grams.[5]

4.3   Comparison

The comparative study parsed text/raw text showed very different results for the soft and for the hard clustering. Concerning the soft clustering, we have observed a better recall on parsed text, but a better precision on raw text. This part of the experiment is described in detail in [29].

For the hard clustering, Table 1 shows better results on parsed text for the Medline corpus. But the comparative study we have carried out with two hard clustering algorithms (similarity-based and AutoClass) and two corpora (Medline and WSJ) shows less clear results on the WSJ corpus, and with AutoClass (Table 2). Further experiments are necessary in order to check to what extent the size and the specificity of the corpus influence the results.

4.4   Performing Hard and Soft Clustering

Next we discuss the performance of the similarity-based hard and soft clustering algorithms applied only to parsed text. The soft clustering has been performed on two different sets of data. The first set consisted in the 200 vectors associating a noun to its co-occurring verbs and corresponding to the most frequent co-occurrences (poor verbal information). In the second set, each of the 200 nouns was associated to the list of verbs

---

[5] The results of this study have been presented at CLIN-02 [30].

Cluster 1: aim objective purpose study
Cluster 2: immunization vaccine vaccination

Fig. 1. Examples of soft clusters

Cluster 1: month year
Cluster 2: children infant
Cluster 3: concentration number incidence use prevalence level rate
Cluster 4: course therapy transplantation treatment immunization

Fig. 2. Examples of hard clusters

frequently co-occurring, and consisted therefore of 200 couples noun-list of verbs (rich verbal information). The purpose was to vary the amount of verbal information, in order to decide whether considering more verbal information would improve the results or increase the noise.

This soft clustering algorithm tends to produce too many clusters, especially too many large clusters (although we get good small clusters as well, see Fig. 1), and it is difficult to sort them. Restricting the similarity conditions reduces the number of "bad" clusters as well as the number of "good" clusters. The evaluation shows that good information is found in the small clusters, and that we obtain the best results with rich verbal information (with poor verbal information, we have observed, for the same number of words clustered, a lower recall and a lower precision) and by dismissing the biggest clusters. The results, using rich verbal information, are displayed in Table 3.

The experiment on hard clustering has been carried out with poor verbal information. When we compare with the soft clustering results, we notice an important decrease of the number of clusters, and a reduction of the average size of the clusters (see Fig. 2). Inconveniences are that we miss every case of polysemy, that we cannot get an exhaustive set of the possible relations between the nouns, and that the recall is very low. Nevertheless, a positive aspect lies in the fact that here, in accordance with the co-composition hypothesis, the nouns are clustered according to the semantic information contained in the sets of verbs, whereas for the soft clustering, only the initial classes of nouns are built using verbal information.

The modification of the similarity measure produced only minor changes for this experiment in the results, and the ratio between recall and precision was steady. We give a summary of the results in Table 4. Both methods (soft and hard) present a balance between advantages and shortcomings and produce good clusters and we would like to keep the best clusters resulting from each method. That lead us to the idea of merging, or combining the two sets of results.

4.5   Merging Soft and Hard Clustering

To summarise the results described above, we can say that the soft clustering provides too many clusters and too many large clusters, and the hard clustering does not build enough clusters, hence not enough relations. But both sets of results present as well strong similarities, and numerous clusters are formed whatever algorithm used.

Table 3. Number of clusters, % of those words clustered, average size of the clusters, recall, min. and ext. precision values for the different soft clustering experiments (rich verbal information), for about 150 words. E1.1 is the initial experiment. E2.1 has been carried out easing the similarity measure but discarding big clusters. E1.2 and E2.2 are based resp. on E1.1 and E2.1, the small clusters (2 elements) being discarded

	Nb of cl.	% wds in cl.	Size cl.	R	mP	eP
E1.1	120	94%	8.87	75%	4%	10%
E2.1	155	91%	5.39	74%	6%	15%
E1.2	28	64%	10.71	57%	7%	18%
E2.2	32	66%	9.81	65%	8%	19%

Table 4. Best recall, min. and ext.precision values for the hard clustering experiment (about 160 words clustered)

	Nb of cl.	% wds in cl.	Size cl.	R	mP	eP
Hd cl.	45	90%	4	15%	13%	33%

In consequence, our next attempt has been to try to combine the results of both algorithms (soft and hard). More precisely, we assume that the relations between nouns that are produced with both methods are more reliable, and we have filtered the soft clustering results, using the hard clustering results. By doing this, we keep the possibility for a noun to belong to more than one cluster, which represents the situation that a noun can share relations of different kinds, and also represents the polysemic properties of some nouns. We have used the similarity measure described for the previous clustering algorithms, and we have compared each hard cluster with every soft cluster, considering the number of common elements and the number of differing elements to decide if the soft cluster would be kept or not.

We give below some concrete examples of this operation of merging. We indicate successively in the examples below the hard cluster in which the word appears, followed by extracts of some soft clusters in which it appears, and finally the clusters obtained by combining both results.

Merging clusters, Example 1: "Disease"
1. Hard clustering:
- disease transmission
2. Soft clustering: 8 clusters, including:
- drug disease treatment clinic
- prevalence infection correlation disease...
- ...
3. Merging: 2 clusters
- hepatitis infection disease case syndrome
- disease liver cirrhosis carcinoma vaccine HCC HBV virus history method model

Table 5. Recall, min. and ext. precision values for the different clustering experiments, considering 150-200 words (summary)

	R	mP	eP	Nb of pairs
Random	4%	2%	10%	(250)
Hard cl.	15%	13%	33%	250
Soft cl.	74%	6%	15%	8000
Merging	62%	12%	31%	1100

In the hard clustering results, the noun "disease" appears in a two-element cluster, the second element being "transmission". This is very poor if we consider the importance of this word and the various relations it shares. Alternatively, "disease" appears in 8 different soft clusters, some of them containing about 20 words and including non relevant relations. After combination, "disease" is associated to 2 clusters. These 2 clusters belong to the 8 soft clusters set containing "disease". They have been kept because they hold relations that appear as well in a hard cluster. One of them contains general words (case, syndrome, infection) and the other more specific information related to "disease"(cirrhosis, carcinoma, virus...)

Merging clusters, Example 2: Chemotherapy
1. Hard clustering:
- therapy transplantation immunization treatment
2. Soft clustering:
- hepatitis blood factor HBV doses chemotherapy treatment vaccine vaccines vaccination injection drug immunization
- liver chemotherapy treatment transplantation
3. Merging:
- liver transplantation chemotherapy treatment

The noun "chemotherapy" does not appear in a hard cluster, and appears in 2 soft clusters, including a big cluster (13 words). But as a hard cluster links "transplantation" and "treatment", the merging operation keeps the soft cluster that associates "chemotherapy" to "liver", "treatment" and "transplantation".

The operation of merging has also revealed reliable two-element clusters composed of strongly related words, such as "hepatitis infection" or "hepatitis virus" for example. The best results for the merging have been obtained by sorting the soft clusters obtained with rich verbal information with the hard clusters. Comparative results are displayed in Table 5.

The merging of soft and hard clustering has improved the results of the soft and hard clustering experiments. But we have only considered in this first step the clustering of head nouns, without taking into account the numerous compound nouns that are used in the medical domain.

In the last section of this paper, we will describe the first set of clustering experiments we have carried out on compound nouns.

Table 6. Recall and precision values for the clustering experiments on compound nouns

	Tot. nb of words	Nb of WN words	R	mP	eP
Sbj	252	45	24%	12%	65%
Obj	241	71	22%	11%	49%

4.6   Turning to Compound Nouns...

Compound nouns are an important source of semantic information, especially in the medical domain. As we process in an unsupervised way, we do not know which association of nouns is a compound noun, but the syntactic analysis allows us to detect associations "noun noun" and "adjective noun" frequently occurring in the subject and object phrases. Not all of them fit with the formal definition of a "compound nouns". However, we have performed the clustering on all the frequently occurring associations, and we will refer from now on to those expressions as "compounds". We have chosen to perform a hard clustering on the compounds for two reasons. As we have shown it above, the hard clustering takes into account the notion of co-composition (by clustering nouns through the semantic verbal information), which could allow us in a next step to build semantic relations between classes of nouns and verbs. The second reason is based on the fact that a noun can appear in different compounds, each of them standing for a different semantic feature of this noun. In consequence, this noun can appear in different clusters. At the same time, we have modified the similarity measure in order to take into account more sparse data.

The first results show an improvement when we compare them to the previous clustering on nouns, especially in the quality of "large" clusters (more than 10 words). For comparison, we have clustered the compounds appearing in the subject phrase, and the compounds appearing in the object phrase separately. It seems that the clustering of compounds belonging to the object phrase is more efficient than the clustering of compounds appearing in the subject phrase. That appears to be the case especially for the extrapolated precision value. We can advance two hypotheses for this difference in the results. On the one hand, the high proportion of passive sentences limits the number of subject-verb structures found by the shallow parser. On the other hand, a higher proportion of the compounds occurring in the object phrases are domain-specific. At this point of our study, we have only evaluated the results using WordNet. The examples below show clusters containing sparse data that were not taken into account before. Those clusters could be validated by WordNet:

  - face mask, mask, glove, protective eyewear
  - woodchuck, mouse, animal, chimpanzee

We observe (Table 6) a low recall in the results if we compare it to the recall values of the soft clustering experiments described above, but still this recall is better than the one obtained in the hard clustering experiment. We must signal here that the proportion of words and consequently the proportion of relations we can evaluate is inferior to the proportion evaluated in the previous experiments, due to the high percentage of compounds that do not belong to WordNet. Actually, a third of the compounds appearing in the objects clusters has been evaluated, but only a fifth of the nouns appearing in the subjects (which means that the evaluation concerning the subjects cannot be considered as reliable). The evaluation with WordNet allows us to compare the results with the previous clustering experiments, but we are planning to perform now a more reliable evaluation using UMLS (Unified Medical Language System [18]). We hope to get a better and more reliable evaluation by making use of this specific ontology, as we can spot the presence of many clusters that WordNet could not evaluate but the content of which looks "interesting". Here are some of them, whose content has been validated using UMLS:

- immunoadsorbent, immunoassay, immunospot, immunosorbent, immunosorbent assay
- passive haemagglutination, transcriptase activity, transcriptase inhibitor, transcription, transcriptase, transcriptase polymerase chain reaction, transcription-polymerase chain reaction, transcription polymerase chain reaction
- blood sample, information, sample, sera, blood specimen, serum sample, specimen

5   Discussion and Related Work

Unsupervised clustering allows us to build semantic classes. The main difficulty lies in the labelling of the relations for the construction of a semantic network. The ongoing work consists in part in improving the performance of the shallow parser by increasing its lexicon and training it on passive sentences taken from our corpus, and in part in refining the clustering and using UMLS for the evaluation. At the same time, we work on using the verbal information to connect clusters of nouns-subject and clusters of noun-objects, and we turn as well to pattern matching in order to label semantic relations.

Related work in the medical area happens in the context of the MuchMore project [27]. However, the UMLS is used as an external knowledge repository to discover additional terms on basis of attested relations between terms appearing in a text. Relations themselves are not the focus of the research. Earlier work on creating medical ontologies from French text corpora has been reported on by [25]. Instead of using shallow parsing techniques, "full parse" trees are decomposed into elementary dependency trees. The aim is to group bags of terms or words according to semantic axes. Another attempt involving clustering on specific domains, including the medical domain, is described in [3]. Term extraction is performed on a POS-tagged corpus and followed by a clustering operation that gathers terms according to their common components, in order to build a terminology. An expert provides some help in the process, and performs the evaluation.

Some work of the same kind has been done for other specific domains, for example the terrorist attacks domain in French, as described in [10]. Nouns are gathered in classes and clustered according to their semantic similarity. Here as well, an expert participates in the process, sorting the information after each step of clustering, in order to obtain classes of nouns and frames of sub-categorization for verbs. Unsupervised clustering has been performed as well on general domains. In [20], a thesaurus is built by performing clustering according to a similarity measure after having retrieved triples from a parsed corpus. Here, a big corpus (64M words) was used, and only very frequently occurring terms were considered. A domain independent recent work is presented in [21]. But here again, external knowledge (a semantic dictionary that relates terms to concepts and an external taxonomy) is used. This method allows to calculate whether a relation should involve a particular concept or rather one of its ancestor nodes. A very recent overview of ontology learning methods and techniques is provided by [15].

Unsupervised clustering is difficult to perform. Often, external help is required (expert, existing taxonomy...). However, using more data seems to increase the quality of the clusters ([20]). Clustering does not provide you with the relations between terms, hence the fact that it is more often used for terminology and thesaurus building than for ontology building.

Performing an automatic evaluation is another problem, and evaluation frequently implies a manual operation by an expert [3,10], or by the researchers themselves [16]. An automatic evaluation is nevertheless performed in [20], by comparison with existing thesauri like WordNet and Roget.

6 Future Work and Conclusion

Note that the terms and lexons operate on the language level, while concepts and conceptual relationships are considered to be, at least in principle, language independent. The next step of this research could consist on one side in adding more medical information, especially a kind of information that would enrich the corpus and the semantic relations, and could consist for example of more basic medical facts than the ones encountered in Medline abstracts. However, care has to be taken to maintain the general purpose and flexibility of the method, by avoiding to rely too heavily on external knowledge sources (taxonomy, semantic lexicon, semantic corpus annotations, ...). Therefore, we are planning similar experiments for other specific domains, as the comparison with the Wall Street Journal corpus seems to show that different data can have an effect on the semantic extraction operations. Although it is too early for solid conclusions, we feel that the method presented in this paper merits further investigations, especially regarding the discovery of semantic relations. Only then, genuine lexons, as defined according to the DOGMA approach, could be automatically mined from text corpora. This would constitute a major breakthrough in the field of ontological engineering.

Acknowledgments. Most part of this research was carried out in the context of the Onto-Basis project (GBOU 2001 #10069), sponsored by the IWT (Institute for the Promotion of Innovation by Science and Technology in Flanders).

References

1. Agirre E. and Martinez D., Learning class-to-class selectional preferences. In *Proceedings CoNLL-01*, 2001.
2. Berland M. and Charniak E., Finding parts in very large corpora. In *Proc. of ACL-99*, 1999.
3. Bourigault D. and Jacquemin C., Term extraction + term clustering: An integrated platform for computer-aided terminology. In *Proceedings of EACL-99*, 1999.
4. Buchholz S., *Memory-Based Grammatical Relation Finding*. 1999.

5. Buchholz S., Veenstra J., and Daelemans W., Cascaded grammatical relation assignment. PrintPartners Ipskamp, 2002.
6. Caraballo S., Automatic construction of a hypernym-labeled noun hierarchy from text. In *Proceedings of ACL-99*, 1999.
7. Caraballo S. and Charniak E., Determining the specificity of nouns from text. In *Proceedings of SIGDAT-99*, 1999.
8. Cheeseman P. and Stutz J., Bayesian classification (autoclass): Theory and results. In *Advances in Knowledge Discovery and Data Mining*, pages 153–180. 1996.
9. Daelemans W., Buchholz S., and Veenstra J., Memory-based shallow parsing. In *Proceedings of CoNLL-99*, 1999.
10. Faure D. and Nédellec C., Knowledge acquisition of predicate argument structures from technical texts using machine learning: The system Asium. In *Proc. of EKAW-99*, 1999.
11. Gamallo P., Agustini A., and Lopes G., Selection restrictions acquisition from corpora. In *Proceedings EPIA-01*. Springer-Verlag, 2001.
12. Gamallo P., Alexandre Agustini A., and Lopes G., Using co-composition for acquiring syntactic and semantic subcategorisation. In *Proceedings of the Workshop SIGLEX-02 (ACL-02)*, 2002.
13. Gamallo P., Gasperin C., Agustini A., and Lopes G., Syntactic-based methods for measuring word similarity. In *Proceedings TSD-01*. Springer, 2001.
14. Genesereth M. and Nilsson N., *Logical Foundations of Artificial Intelligence*. Morgan Kaufmann, 1987.
15. Gómez-Pérez A. and Manzano-Macho D., (eds.)., A survey of ontology learning methods and techniques. OntoWeb Deliverable #D1.5, Univ. Politécnica de Madrid, 2003.
16. Grishman R. and John Sterling J., Generalizing automatically generated selectional patterns. In *Proceedings of COLING-94*, 1994.
17. Guarino N. and Giaretta P., Ontologies and knowledge bases: Towards a terminological clarification. In Mars N., editor, *Towards Very Large Knowledge Bases: Knowledge Building and Knowledge Sharing*, pages 25–32, Amsterdam, 1995. IOS Press.
18. Humphreys B. and Lindberg D., The unified medical language system project: a distributed experiment in improving access to biomedical information. In Lun K.C., (ed.), *Proc. of the 7th World Congress on Medical Informatics (MEDINFO92)*, pp. 1496–1500, 1992.
19. Jarrar M. and Meersman R., Formal ontology engineering in the dogma approach. In Meersman R., Tari Z., and al., (eds.), *On the Move to Meaningful Internet Systems 2002: CoopIS, DOA, and ODBASE; Confederated International Conferences CoopIS, DOA, and ODBASE 2002 Proceedings*, LNCS 2519, pp. 1238–1254. Springer, 2002.
20. Lin D., Automatic retrieval and clustering of similar words. In *Proceedings of COLING-ACL-98*, 1998.
21. Maedche A. and Staab S., Discovering conceptual relations from text. Technical Report 399, Institute AIFB, Karlsruhe University, 2000.
22. Maedche A. and Staab S., Ontology learning for the semantic web. *IEEE Intelligent Systems*, 16, 2001.
23. McCarthy D., Carroll J., and Preiss J., Disambiguating noun and verb senses using automatically acquired selectional preferences. SENSEVAL-2, 2001.
24. Miller G., Wordnet: a lexical database for english. *Comm. of the ACM*, 38(11):39–41, 1995.
25. Nazarenko A., Zweigenbaum P., Bouaud J., and Habert B., Corpus-based identification and refinement of semantic classes. In R. Masys, editor, *Proceeding of the AMIA Annual Fall Symposium - JAMIA Supplement*, pages 585–589. AMIA, 1997.
26. Pantel P. and Lin D., Discovering word senses from text. In *Proceedings of ACM SIGKDD-02*, 2002.
27. Peeters S. and Kaufner S., State of the art in crosslingual information access for medical information. Technical report, CSLI, 2001.

28. Pustejovsky J., *The Generative Lexicon*. MIT Press, 1995.
29. Reinberger M.-L., and Daelemans W., Is shallow parsing useful for the unsupervised learning of semantic clusters? In *Proceedings CICLing03*. Springer-Verlag, 2003.
30. Reinberger M.-L., Decadt B., and Daelemans W., On the relevance of performing shallow parsing before clustering. Computational Linguistics in the Netherlands 2002 (CLIN02), Groningen, The Netherlands, 2002.
31. Reiter R., *Readings in AI and Databases*, chapter Towards a Logical Reconstruction of Relational Database Theory. Morgan Kaufman, 1988.
32. Ribière M. and Charlton P., Ontology overview motorola labs. Technical report, Networking and Applications Lab – Centre de Recherche de Motorola Paris, 2000.
33. Spyns P., Meersman R., and Jarrar M., Data modelling versus ontology engineering. *SIGMOD Record Special Issue*, 31 (4), 2002.
34. Tarski A., *Problems in the philosophy of language*, chapter The semantic concept of truth. Holt, Rinehart & Winston, New York, 1969.
35. Ushold M. and Gruninger M., Ontologies: Principles, methods and applications. *The Knowledge Engineering Review*, 11(2):93–155, 1996.

The OntoWordNet Project: Extension and Axiomatization of Conceptual Relations in WordNet

Aldo Gangemi[1], Roberto Navigli[2], and Paola Velardi[2]

[1] Laboratory for Applied Ontology, ISTC-CNR,
viale Marx 15, 00137 Roma, Italy
gangemi@ip.rm.cnr.it
[2] Dipartimento di Informatica, University of Roma "La Sapienza"
via Salaria 113, 00198 Roma, Italy
{navigli,velardi}@dsi.uniroma1.it

Abstract. In this paper we present a progress report of the OntoWordNet project, a research program aimed at achieving a formal specification of WordNet. Within this program, we developed a hybrid bottom-up top-down methodology to automatically extract association relations from WordNet, and to interpret those associations in terms of a set of conceptual relations, formally defined in the DOLCE foundational ontology. Preliminary results provide us with the conviction that a research program aiming to obtain a consistent, modularized, and axiomatized ontology from WordNet can be completed in acceptable time with the support of semi-automatic techniques.

1 Introduction

The number of applications where WordNet (WN) is being used as an ontology rather than as a mere lexical resource seems to be ever growing. Indeed, WordNet contains a good coverage of both the lexical and conceptual palettes of the English language. However, WordNet is serviceable as an ontology (in the sense of a *theory* expressed in some *logical language*) if some of its lexical links are interpreted according to a formal semantics that tells us something about the way we use a lexical item in some context for some purpose. In other words, we need a *formal specification of the conceptualizations that are expressed by means of WordNet's synsets*[1]. A formal specification requires a clear semantics for the primitives used to export WordNet information into an ontology, and a methodology that explains how WordNet information can be bootstrapped, mapped, refined, and modularized.

The formal specification of WordNet is the objective of the so-called OntoWordNet research program, started two years ago at the ISTC-CNR, and now being extended with other partners, since collaborations have been established with the universities of Princeton, Berlin and Roma. The program is detailed in section 2, where we outline the main objectives and current achievements.

---

[1] Concept names in WordNet are called *synsets*, since the naming policy for a concept is a set of synonym words, e.g. for sense 1 of car: { car, auto, automobile, machine, motorcar }.

R. Meersman et al. (Eds.): CoopIS/DOA/ODBASE 2003, LNCS 2888, pp. 820–838, 2003.

In this paper we describe a joint ongoing work of ISTC-CNR and the University of Roma that has produced a methodology and some preliminary results for adding *axioms* (DAML+OIL "restrictions") to the concepts derived from WordNet synsets. The methodology is hybrid because it employs both top-down techniques and tools from formal ontology, and bottom-up techniques from computational linguistics and machine learning. Section 3 presents a detailed description of the methodology.

The preliminary results, presented in section 4, seem very encouraging, and provide us with the conviction that a research program aiming to obtain a consistent, modularized, and axiomatized ontology from WordNet can be completed in acceptable time with the support of semi-automatic techniques.

2 Objectives of the OntoWordNet Research Program

The OntoWordNet project aims at producing a formal specification of WordNet as an axiomatic theory (an *ontology*). To this end, WordNet is reorganized and enriched in order to adhere to the following commitments:

- *Logical commitment.* WordNet synsets are transformed into logical types, with a formal semantics for lexical relations. The WordNet lexicon is also separated from the logical namespace.
- *Ontological commitment.* WordNet is transformed into a general-purpose ontology library, with explicit categorial criteria, based on formal ontological distinctions (Gangemi et al. 2001). For example, the distinctions enable a clear separation between (kinds of) concept-synsets, relation-synsets, meta-property-synsets, and enable the instantiation of individual-synsets. Moreover, such formal ontological principles facilitate the axiomatic enrichment of the ontology library.
- *Contextual commitment.* WordNet is modularized according to knowledge-oriented domains of interest. The modules constitute a partial order.
- *Semiotic commitment.* WordNet lexicon is linked to text-oriented (or speech act-oriented) domains of interest, with lexical items ordered by preference, frequency, combinatorial relevance, etc.

In (Gangemi et al 2001,2002) these commitments are discussed in detail and working hypotheses and first achievements are presented. This paper is concerned mainly with the ontological commitments.

WordNet's *ontological commitments* are more demanding to be explicitated, but many results are already available. For example, an incremental methodology has been adopted, in order to revise or to reorganize WordNet synset taxonomies and relations (see also paragraph 3.2.1). Substantial work has been done on the refinement of the *hyponym/hyperonym* relations, which have being investigated since several years. The hyperonymy relation in WN is basically interpreted as *formal subsumption*, although hyperonymy for concepts referring to individuals (geographical names, characters, some techniques, etc.) is interpreted as *instantiation*. This will be referred as *assumption A1* ("hyperonymy as synset subsumption").

WordNet *synonymy* is a relation between words, not concepts, therefore we should assume that the synonymy relation (*synsets* in WordNet) is an *equivalence class* of words (or phrases), sharing the same *meaning* within an ontology. Consequently, two words are synonyms when their intended meaning in WordNet is the same. This will be referred to as *assumption A2* ("synset as meaning equivalence class").

However, we have no formal definition of words in WordNet that allows us to create equivalence classes (synsets) analytically (i.e., to state *semantic equivalences*). Instead, we have pre-formal synsets that have been validated by lexicographers with an intuition that *could* be formalized as semantic equivalence. Part of this intuition is conveyed by textual definitions (called *glosses*). This will be referred as *assumption A3* ("glosses as axiomatizations"). We are trying to formalize such intuition.

A related assumption that we make is that words in glosses are used in a way consistent to the WordNet synsets. This will be referred as *assumption A4* ("glosses are synset-consistent"). A4 lets us assume also that the informal theory underlying synsets, hyperonymy relations, and glosses, can be formalized against a finite signature (the set of WN synsets), and a set of axioms derived from the associations (*A-links*) between any synset S and the synsets that can be associated to the words used in the gloss of S. This is dependent on A3 and A4, and may be referred as *assumption A5* ("*A-links* as conceptual relations").

3 Semi-automatic Axiomatization of WordNet

The task of axiomatizing WordNet, starting from assumptions A1-A5 outlined in the previous section, requires that the informal definition in a synset gloss be transformed in a logical form. To this end, first, words in a gloss must be disambiguated, i.e. replaced by their appropriate synsets. This first step provides us with pairs of generic semantic associations (A-links) between a synset and the synsets of its gloss. Secondly, A-links must be interpreted in terms of more precise, formally defined semantic relations. The inventory of semantic relations is selected or specialized from the foundational ontology DOLCE, as detailed later, since in WordNet only a limited set of relations are used, that are partly ontological, partly lexical in nature. For example, part_of (*meronymy* in WordNet) and kind_of (*hyponymy* in WordNet) are typical semantic relations, while *antonymy* (e.g. *liberal* and *conservative*) and *pertonymy* (e.g *slow* and *slowly*) are lexical relations. Furthermore, WordNet relations are not axiomatized, nor are they used in a fully consistent way.

To summarize, the objective of the method described in this section is to:

- automatically extract a number of semantic relations implicitly encoded in WordNet, i.e. the relations holding between a synset and the synsets in its gloss.
- (semi)-automatically interpret and axiomatize these relations.

For example, sense 1 of *driver* has the following gloss "the operator of a motor vehicle". The appropriate sense of *operator* is #2: *operator, manipulator* ("an agent that operates some apparatus or machine"), while motor vehicle is monosemous: *motor vehicle, automotive vehicle* ("a self-propelled wheeled vehicle that does not run on rails").

After automatic sense disambiguation, we (hopefully) learn that there exists an A-link between driver#1 and operator#2, and between *driver#1* and *motor vehicle#1*.

Subsequently, given a set of axiomatized semantic relations in DOLCE, we must select the relation that best fits the semantic restrictions on the relation universes (domain and co-domain, or range). For example, given an A-link between *driver#1* and *motor vehicle#1*, the best fitting relation is *agentive-co-participation* (Fig. 1), whose definition is:

$$AG\_CO\_PCP(x,y) =_{df} CO\_PCP(x,y) \land \text{Agentive\_Physical\_Object}(x) \land$$
$$\land \text{Non\_Agentive\_Functional\_Object}(y)$$

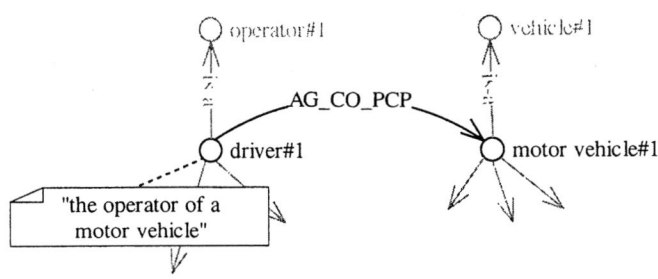

Fig. 1. An example of semantic relation

The definition says that *agentive co-participation* is a relation of mutual participation (participation of two objects in the same event), with the domain restricted to "Agentive_Physical_Object" and the range restricted to "Non_Agentive_Functional_Object".

Domain and range in a conceptual relation definition are established in terms of the DOLCE ontology. Consequently, another necessary step of our method is to re-link at least some of the higher level nodes in WordNet with the DOLCE upper ontology.

In the following sub-sections we detail the procedures for gloss disambiguation, WordNet re-linking, and selection of conceptual relations.

3.1 Bottom-Up Learning of Association Links

The first step is a bottom-up procedure that analyses the NL definitions (glosses) in WordNet and creates the A-links.

For each gloss (i.e., linguistic concept definition), we perform the following automatic tasks:

a) POS-tagging of glosses (using the ARIOSTO NL processor) and extraction of *relevant* words;

b) Disambiguation of glosses by the algorithm described hereafter;

c) Creation of explicit "association" links (A-links) from synsets found in glosses to synsets to which glosses belong.

3.1.1 Description of the Gloss Disambiguation Algorithm

We developed a greedy algorithm for gloss disambiguation that relies on a set of heuristic rules and is based on multiple, incremental iterations. The algorithm takes as input the synset S whose gloss G we want to disambiguate.

Two sets are used, P and D. D is a set of disambiguated synsets, initially including only the synset S. P is a set of terms to be disambiguated, initially containing all the terms from gloss G and from the glosses {G'} of the direct hyperonyms of S. As clarified later, adding {G'} provides a richer context for semantic disambiguation. The term list is obtained using our NL processor to lemmatize words, and then removing irrelevant words. We use standard information retrieval techniques (e.g stop words) to identify irrelevant terms.

When, at each iteration of the algorithm, we disambiguate some of the terms in P, we remove them from P and add their interpretation (i.e. synsets) to the set D. Thus, at each step, we can distinguish between *pending* and *disambiguated* terms (respectively the sets P and D). Notice again that P is a set of terms, while D contains synsets.

Step a) Find monosemous terms
The first step of the algorithm is to remove monosemous terms from P (those with a unique synset) and include their unique interpretation in the set D.

Step b) Disambiguate polysemous terms
Then, the core iterative section of the algorithm starts. The objective is to detect *semantic relations* between some of the synsets in D and some of the synsets associated to the terms in P. Let S' be a synset in D (an already chosen interpretation of term t') and S'' one of the synsets of a polysemous term $t'' \in P$ (i.e., t'' is still ambiguous). If a semantic relation is found between S' and S'', then S'' is added to D and t'' is removed from P.

To detect semantic relations between S' and S'', we apply a set of heuristics grouped in two classes, *Path* and *Context*, described in what follows. Some of these heuristics have been suggested in (Milhalcea, 2001),

Path heuristics
The heuristics in class Path seek for *semantic patterns* between the node S' and the node S'' in the WordNet semantic network. A *pattern* is a chain of nodes (synsets) and arcs (directed semantic relations), where S' and S'' are at the extremes.

Formally, we define $S' \xrightarrow{R}^n S''$ as $S' \xrightarrow{R} S_1 \xrightarrow{R} ... \xrightarrow{R} S_n \equiv S''$, that is a chain of n instances of the relation R. We also define $\xrightarrow{R_1,R_2}$ as $\xrightarrow{R_1} \cup \xrightarrow{R_2}$.

The symbols: $\xrightarrow{@}, \xrightarrow{\sim}, \xrightarrow{\#}, \xrightarrow{\%}, \xrightarrow{\&}$ respectively represent the following semantic relations coded in WordNet 1.6: *hyperonimy* (kind_of), *hyponymy* (has kind) *meronymy* (part_of), *holonymy* (has_part), and *similarity*. Similarity is a generic relation including near synonyms, adjectival clusters and antonyms. Finally, the *gloss* relation $S \xrightarrow{gloss} T$ indicates that the gloss of S includes a term t, and T is one of the synsets of t.

The following is an example of heuristics that we use to identify semantic paths ($S' \in D$, $S'' \in Synsets(t'')$, $t'' \in P$):

Hyperonymy/Meronymy path: if $S' \xrightarrow{@,\#}{}^n S''$ choose S'' as the right sense of t'' (e.g.,

$archipelago\#1 \xrightarrow{\#} island\#1$);

Context heuristics

The Context heuristics use several available computational linguistic resources to detect co-occurrence patterns in sentences and contextual clues to determine a semantic proximity between S' and S''. The following heuristics are defined:

Semantic co-occurrences: word pairs may help in the disambiguation task if they always co-occur with the same senses within a tagged corpus. We use three resources in order to look for co-occurrences, namely:

- o   the *SemCor corpus*, a corpus where each word in a sentence is assigned a sense selected from the WordNet sense inventory for that word
- o   the *LDC corpus*, a corpus where each document is a collection of sentences having a certain word in common. The corpus provides a sense tag for each occurrence of the word within the document.
- o   *gloss examples:* in WordNet, besides glosses, examples are sometimes provided containing synsets rather than words. From these examples, as for the LDC Corpus, a co-occurrence information can be extracted.
- o   As we said above, only the SemCor corpus provides a sense for each word in a pair of adjacent words occurring in the corpus, while LDC and gloss examples provide the right sense only for one of the terms.

In either case, we can use this information to choose the synset S'' as the interpretation of t'' if the pair t' t'' occurs in the gloss and there is an agreement among (at least two of) the three resources about the disambiguation of the pair t' t''. For example:

*[...] Multnomah County may be short of general assistance money in its budget to handle an unusually high **summer#1 month#1**'s need [...].*
*Later#1, Eckenfelder increased#2 the efficiency#1 of treatment#1 to between 75 and 85 percent#1 in the **summer#1 months#1**.*
are sentences respectively from the LDC Corpus and SemCor. Since there is a full agreement between the resources, one can easily disambiguate *summer* and *months* in the gloss of *summer_camp#1*: "*a site where care and activities are provided for children during the **summer months***".

Common domain labels: Domain labels are the result of a semiautomatic methodology described in (Magnini and Cavaglia, 2000) for assigning domain labels (e.g. *tourism, zoology, sport..*) to WordNet synsets[2]. This information can be exploited to disambiguate those terms with the same domain labels of the start synset S.

---

[2] Domain labels have been kindly made available by the IRST to our institution for research purposes.

Step c) Update *D* and *P*

During each iteration, the algorithm applies all the available heuristics in the attempt of disambiguating some of the terms in *P*, using all the available synsets in *D*. The heuristics are applied in a fixed order reflecting their importance, that has been experimentally determined. For example, Context heuristics are applied after Path heuristics 1-5. At the end of each iterative step, new synsets are added to *D*, and the correspondent terms are deleted from *P*. The next iteration makes use of these new synsets in order to possibly disambiguate other terms in *P*. Eventually, either *P* becomes empty, or no new semantic relations can be found.

When the algorithm terminates, $D \setminus \{ S \}$ can be considered a first approximation of a *semantic definition of S*. For mere gloss disambiguation purposes, the tagged terms in the hyperonyms' gloss are discarded, so that the resulting set (*GlossSynsets*) now contains only interpretations of terms extracted from the gloss of *S*. At this stage, we can only say that there is a semantic relation (A-link) between *S* and each of the synsets in *GlossSynsets* .

A second, more precise approximation of a sound ontological definition for *S* is obtained by determining the nature of the A-links connecting *S* with each concept in $D \setminus \{ S \}$. This is an ongoing task and is discussed in Section 4.

3.1.2 A Running Example

In the following, we present a sample execution of the algorithm on sense 1 of *retrospective*. Its gloss defines the concept as "*an exhibition of a representative selection of an artist's life work*", while its hyperonym, *art exhibition#1*, is defined as "*an exhibition of art objects (paintings or statues)*". Initially we have:

D = { retrospective#1 }
P = { work, object, exhibition, life, statue, artist, selection, representative, painting, art }

The application of the monosemy step a) gives the following result:

D = { retrospective#1, statue#1, artist#1 }
P = { work, object, exhibition, life, selection, representative, painting, art }

because statue and artist are monosemous terms in WordNet. During the first iteration, the algorithm finds three matching paths:

$$retrospective\#1 \xrightarrow{@}^{2} exhibition\#2, \quad statue\#1 \xrightarrow{@}^{3} art\#1 \ and \ statue\#1 \xrightarrow{@}^{6} object\#1$$

this leads to:

D = { retrospective#1, statue#1, artist#1, exhibition#2, object#1, art#1 }
P = { work, life, selection, representative, painting }

During the second iteration, an hyponymy/holonymy path is found:

$$art\#1 \xrightarrow{\sim}^{2} painting\#1 \ (painting \ is \ a \ kind \ of \ art)$$
D = { retrospective#1, statue#1, artist#1, exhibition#2, object#1, art#1, painting#1 }
P = { work, life, selection, representative }

Since no new paths are found, the third iteration makes use of the LDC Corpus to find the co-occurrence *"artist life"*, with sense 12 of *life (biography, life history)*:

D = { retrospective#1, statue#1, artist#1, exhibition#2, object#1, art#1, painting#1, life#12 }
P = { work, selection, representative }

Notice that, during an iteration, the context heuristics are used only if the path heuristics fail.

The algorithm stops because there are no additional matches. The chosen senses concerning terms contained in the hyperonym's gloss were of help during disambiguation, but are now discarded. Thus we have:

GlossSynsets(retrospective#1) = { artist#1, exhibition#2, life#12 }

Figure 2 shows in dark gray the A-links between *retrospective#1* and the synset of its glosses, while in the light gray area are shown the synsets of the hyperonyms.

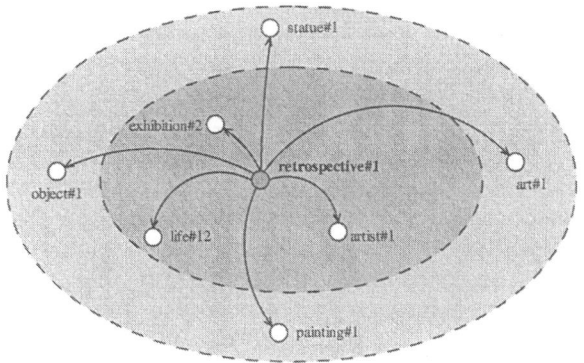

Fig. 2. A first approximation of a semantic definition of retrospective#1.

3.2 Top-Down Learning: Formal Ontologies and WordNet "Sweetening"

In the top-down phase, the A-links extracted in the bottom-up phase are refined. A-links provide just a *clue* of relatedness between a synset and another synset extracted from the gloss analysis, but this relatedness must be explicit, in order to understand if it is a hyperonymy relation, or some other conceptual relation (e.g. part, participation, location, etc.).

First of all, we need a shared set of conceptual relations to be considered as candidates for A-links explicitation, otherwise the result is not easily reusable. Secondly, these relations must be formally defined. In fact, as already pointed out at the beginning of section 3, not only are A-links vague, but they also lack a formal semantics: for example, if we decide (which seems reasonable) to represent associations as binary relations –like DAML+OIL "properties"– is an association symmetric? Does it hold for every instance, or only for some of the instances of the classes derived from the associated synsets? Is it just a constraint on the applicability of a relation to that pair of classes? Is the relation set a flat list, or there is a taxonomic ordering?

To answer such questions, the shared set of relations should be defined in a logical language using a formal semantics.

Since WordNet is a general-purpose resource, the formal shared set of relations should also be general enough, based on *domain-independent* principles, but still flexible, in order to be easily maintained and negotiated.

3.2.1 The DOLCE Descriptive Ontology

A proposal in this direction is provided by the WonderWeb[3] project Foundational Ontology Library (WFOL), which will contain a library including both compatible and alternative modules including domain-independent concepts and relations. A recently defined module that accomplishes the abovementioned requirements is DOLCE (Descriptive Ontology for Linguistic and Cognitive Engineering).

DOLCE is expressed in an S5 modal logic (Masolo et al. 2002), and has counterparts in computational logics, such as KIF, LOOM, RACER, DAML+OIL, and OWL. The non-KIF counterparts implement a reduced axiomatization of DOLCE, called DOLCE-Lite. DOLCE-Lite has been extended with some *generic plugins* for representing information, communication, plans, ordinary places, and with some *domain plugins* for representing e.g. legal, tourism, biomedical notions. The combination of DOLCE-Lite and the existing plugins is called DOLCE-Lite+. The current version 3.6 of DOLCE-Lite+ without domain plugins contains more than 300 concepts and about 150 relations (see http://www.loa-cnr.it for DOLCE versioning).

DOLCE assumes that its categories (top classes) constitute an *extensionally* closed set on any possible *particular* entity, i.e., entities that cannot be further instantiated within the assumptions of the theory (cf. Masolo et al. 2002, Gangemi et al. 2001). Of course, DOLCE does not assume an *intensionally* closed set, thus allowing for alternative ontologies to co-exist. Such assumptions will be referred to as *A6_D* ("extensional total coverage of DOLCE"). Consequently, we also assume that WN globally can be tentatively considered a (extensional) subset of DOLCE, after its formalization. Since we cannot practically obtain a complete formalization of WN, we will be content with incrementally approximating it.

A trivial formalization of WN might consist in declaring formal subsumptions for all *unique beginners* (top level synsets) under DOLCE categories, but this proved to be impossible, since the intension of unique beginners, once they are formalized as classes, is not consistent with the intension of DOLCE categories. Then we started (Gangemi et al. 2002) deepening our analysis of WN synsets, in order to find synsets that could be subsumed by a DOLCE category without being inconsistent.

In our previous OntoWordNet work, WordNet 1.6 has been analyzed, and 809 synsets have been relinked to DOLCE-Lite+ in order to harmonize ("sweeten") WN taxonomies with DOLCE-Lite+. A working hypothesis (*A7_D*) has been that the taxonomy branches of the relinked synsets are ontologically consistent with the DOLCE-Lite+ concepts, to which the relinking is targeted. After some additional work, the current linking of 809 synsets seems acceptable, but it needs refinement,

---

[3] http://wonderweb.semanticweb.org

since some subsumptions are debatable, and it must be considered that some extensions of DOLCE-Lite+ are still unstable.

3.2.2 Disambiguation of Association Links

Assumptions A4 and A5 (section 2), together with A6_D (in previous sub-section), make it possible to exploit the axiomatized relations in DOLCE-Lite+. Such relations are formally characterized by means of *ground axioms* (e.g. symmetry, transitivity, etc.), *argument restrictions* (qualification of their *universe*), *existential axioms, links to other primitives, theorems*, etc. (Masolo et al. 2002).

By looking at the A-links, a human expert can easily decide which relation from DOLCE-Lite+ is applicable in order to disambiguate the A-link, for example, from:

1. A-link(*car#1, engine#1*)

we may be able to infer that cars have engines as components:

$$\forall x.\ \text{Car}(x) \rightarrow \exists y.\ \text{Engine}(y) \wedge \text{Component}(x,y)$$

or that from

2. A-link(*art_exhibition#1, painting#1*)

we can infer that exhibitions as collections have paintings as members:

$$\forall x.\ \text{Art\_exhibition}(x) \rightarrow \exists y.\ \text{Painting}(y) \wedge \text{Member}(x,y)$$

But this is an intellectual technique. We are instead interested, at least for the sake of bootstrapping a preliminary axiomatization of synsets, in a (semi) *automatic classification technique*. From this viewpoint, the only available structure is represented by the concepts to which the A-links apply. Such synsets can be assumed as the *argument restrictions* of a conceptual relation implicit in the association. For example, given (A-link(S_1, S_2)), where S_1, S_2 are synsets, we can introduce the argument restrictions for a conceptual relation $R^{a\text{-link}}_i(x,y) \rightarrow S_1(x) \wedge S_2(y)$. Then, from A5 and its depend-on assumptions, we have a good heuristics for concluding that $S_1(x) \rightarrow \exists y.\ R^{a\text{-link}}_i(x,y) \wedge S_2(y)$. In other words, we formalize the association existing between a synset and another synset used in its gloss. This leaves us with the question of what is the intension of $R^{a\text{-link}}_i(x,y)$, beyond its argument restrictions: e.g. what does it mean to be a relation between *art exhibitions* and *paintings*? And are we allowed to use this heuristics to conclude that art exhibitions are related to at least one painting?

Assuming A6_D, we can claim that some $R_i(x,y)$ from DOLCE-Lite+ subsumes $R^{a\text{-link}}_i(x,y)$. Since the relations from DOLCE-Lite+ have a total extensional coverage on any domain, we can expect that at least one relation from DOLCE has a universe subsuming that of $R^{a\text{-link}}_i(x,y)$. For example: Member(x,y) from DOLCE-Lite+ can subsume $R^{a\text{-link}}_i(x,y)$ when Art_exhibition(x) and Painting(y), since the domain and range of "Member" subsume "Art_exhibition" and "Painting" respectively.

These subsumptions are easily derivable by using a description-logic classifier (e.g. LOOM, MacGregor, 1993, or RACER, Moeller, 2001) that computes the applicable relations from DOLCE-Lite+ to the training set of A-links.

For example, an "ABox" query like the following can do the job in LOOM:

<u>ABox-1</u>
(retrieve (?x ?R ?y) (and (get-role-types ?x ?R ?y) (min-cardinality ?x ?R 1) (A-link ?x ?y)))

i.e., provided that A-links have been defined on DOLCE-Lite+ classes (i.e. that WN synsets ?x ?y are subsumed by DOLCE-Lite+ classes), the relation "get-role-types" will hold for all the relations in DOLCE-Lite+ that are applicable to those classes, with a cardinality≥1. For example, given the previous example (2) of A-link, the classifier uses some of the DOLCE-Lite+ axioms to suggest the right conceptual relation. In fact, the WordNet synset *art_exhibition#1* is a (indirect) sub-class of the DOLCE class "unitary collection", a category for which the following axiom holds:

$$\forall x. \text{ Unitary\_Collection}(x) \rightarrow \exists y. \text{ Physical\_Object}(y) \land \text{Member}(x,y)$$

Furthermore, since *painting#1* is a (indirect) sub-class of "physical object", and the axiom holds with a cardinality≥1, the correct relation and axiom are guessed.

In other cases, ABox-1 does not retrieve an existing appropriate relation. For example, given:

3. A-link(*boat#1*,*travel#1*)

with *boat#1* subsumed by Physical_Object and *travel#1* subsumed by Situation in DOLCE+WordNet, and the relation "Setting" holding between physical objects and situations, we have no axiom like the following in DOLCE-Lite+:

$$* \ \forall x. \text{ Physical\_Object}(x) \rightarrow \exists y. \text{ Situation}(y) \land \text{Setting}(x,y)$$

then the relation $R^{\text{a-link}}_i$ formalizing the A-link between *boat* and *travel* cannot be automatically classified and proposed as subsumed by the relation "Setting" in DOLCE-Lite+. In other words, in general *it is not true* that "for any physical object there is at least a situation as its possible *"setting"*: we can figure out physical objects in general, without setting them anywhere, at least within the scope of a computational ontology.

The above examples show that axioms representing generally acceptable intuitions in a foundational ontology may prove inadequate in a given application domain, where certain axiomatizations need an ad-hoc refinement.

The solution presented here exploits a partition of argument restrictions for the gloss axiomatization task. For this solution, we need a partition Π of relation universes, according to the 25 valid pairs of argument restrictions that can be generated out of the five top categories of DOLCE-Lite+ (*Object*, *Event*, *Quality*, *Region*, and *Situation*), which on their turn constitute a partition on the domain of entities for DOLCE-Lite+. This enables us to assign one of the 25 relations to the A-link whose members are subsumed by the domain and range of that relation. For example, from:

$(\text{Boat}(x) \rightarrow \text{Object}(x))$, and $(\text{Travel}(y) \rightarrow \text{Situation}(y))$, we can infer that some $R_{<\text{Object,Situation}>}$ holds for the pair $\{x,y\}$.

However, in DOLCE-Lite+, existing relations are based on primitives adapted from the literature, covering some basic intuitions and that are axiomatized accordingly. Therefore, the current set of DOLCE-Lite+ relations $\Pi\delta$ is not isomorphic with Π, while the same extensional coverage is supported. For example, the DOLCE-Lite+ relation "part" corresponds to a *subset* of the union of *all* the argument pairs in Π that include only the same category (e.g., <Event, Event>). $\Pi\delta$ is inadequate to perform an automatic learning of conceptual relations, because we cannot distinguish between "part" and other relations with the same universe (e.g. "connection"). Similarly, we cannot distinguish between different pairs of argument restrictions *within* the "part" universe (e.g. <Event, Event> vs. <Object, Object>).

The choice of axioms in DOLCE-Lite+ is motivated by the necessity of *grounding* the primitive relations in human intuition, for example in so-called *cognitive schemata* that are established during the first steps of an organism's life by interacting with its environment and using its specific abilities to react to the stimuli, constraints, and affordances provided by the context (Johnson 1987). In fact, without that grounding, the meaning of relations cannot be figured out at all (even though they are correct from a logical viewpoint).

There is also another reason for the inadequacy of $\Pi\delta$. A conceptual relation in DOLCE-Lite+ can be "mediated", e.g. defined through a *composition* (called also *chaining*, or *joining* in the database domain). For example, two objects can be related because they participate in a same event, for example, *engine* and *driver* can "co-participate" because they both *participate in driving*.

In brief: we cannot use $\Pi\delta$, since it does not discriminate at the necessary level of detail, and because it is not a partition at all, if we take into account mediated relations. On the other hand, we cannot use Π, because it is cognitively inadequate.

Consequently, we have evolved a special partition $\Pi\delta+$ that keeps both worlds: a real partition, and cognitive adequacy. $\Pi\delta+$ denotes a partition with a precise mapping to $\Pi\delta$. In appendix 2, the current state of $\Pi\delta+$ is shown.

For example, by using $\Pi\delta+$, the proposed relation for the *car/engine* example is *(Physical-)Mereotopological-Association* (PMA), defined as the union of some DOLCE-Lite+ primitive relations: part, connection, localization, constituency, etc., holding only within the *physical object* category. In fact, many possible relational paths can be walked from an instance of *physical object* to another, and only a wide-scope relation can cover them all. Formally:

$$PMA(x,y) =_{df} (Part(x,y) \vee Overlaps(x,y) \vee Strong\text{-}Connection(x,y) \vee$$
$$\vee Weak\text{-}Connection(x,y) \vee Successor(x,y) \vee Constituent(x,y) \vee$$
$$\vee Approximate\text{-}Location(x,y)) \wedge$$
$$\wedge Physical\_Object(x) \wedge Physical\_Object(y)$$

Starting from $\Pi\delta+$, other relations have been defined for subsets of the domains and ranges of the relations in $\Pi\delta+$.

By means of $\Pi\delta+$, the query function ABox-1 can be adjusted as follows:

ABox-2
(retrieve (?x ?r ?y)
    (and (A-Link ?x ?y) (Superrelations ?x Physical_Object) (Superrelations ?y
        Physical_Object)
    (not (and (Superrelations?x Unitary_Collection) (Superrelations?y
        Physical_Object)))

```
(not (and (Superrelations?x Amount_of_Matter) (Superrelations?y
    Physical_Body)))
(not (subject ?x dolce)) (not (subject ?y dolce))
(not (Superrelations ?x ?y)) (not (Superrelations ?y ?x))
(min-cardinality ?x ?r 1)))
```

The query approximately reads "if two synsets subsumed by *physical object* (provided that the first is not an amount of matter or a collection, and that they are not related by hyperonymy), are linked by an A-link, tell me what relations in DOLCE+WordNet are applicable between those synsets with a cardinality of at least 1".

In this way, we are able to learn all the relations that are applicable to the classes ?x and ?y involved in the A-Link tuples. For example, applied to the synset *car#1* that has an A-link to the synset *engine#1*, the query returns:

$$R_{PMA}(car\#1, engine\#1)$$

that, on the basis of known assumptions, is used to propose an axiom on *car#1*, stating that cars have a "physical mereotopological association" with an *engine*, because a DOLCE-Lite+ ancestor of both *car#1* and *engine#1* ("*physical object*") defines the universe of the relation PMA with a cardinality of at least 1 on the range. This heuristics supports the logical axiom:

$$\forall x.\ Car(x) \rightarrow \exists y.\ Engine(y) \wedge PMA(x,y)$$

Notice that at this level of generality, the classifier cannot infer the "component" relation that we intellectually guessed at the beginning of section 3.2. A more specific relation can be approximated, if we define more specialised relations and axioms. For example, a "functional co-participation" can be defined with a universe of only "functional objects", which are lower in the DOLCE-Lite+ taxonomy, but still higher than the pair of synsets associated by the A-link. Functional co-participation ("FCP") is defined by composing two participation relations with a common event (in the example, a common event could be "car running"):

$$FCP(x,y) =_{df} \exists z.\ Participant\_in(x,z) \wedge Participant(y,z) \wedge Event(z)$$

FCP is closer to the "component" intuition. The last can be precisely inferred if we feed the classifier with "core" domain relations. For example, we may define a domain relation holding for vehicles and functional objects, provided that the functional object plays the role of system component for vehicles:

$$vehicles \hat{\ } Component(x,y) =_{df} FCP(x,y) \wedge Vehicle(x) \wedge Functional\_Object(y) \wedge$$
$$\wedge \exists z.\ Plays(y,z) \wedge Vehicle\_System\_Component(z)$$

In other words, by increasing the specificity of the domain (tourism in the examples discussed so far), we may assume that relations should be specified accordingly. As discussed in this section, this process is triggered by the observation of some A-link, and proceeds semi-automatically until a reasonable coverage is reached.

4   Experimental Results and Discussion

The gloss disambiguation algorithm and the A-link interpretation methods have been evaluated on two sets of glosses: a first set of 100 general-purpose glosses[4] and a second set of 305 glosses from a tourism domain. This allows us to evaluate the method both on a restricted domain and a non-specialized task.

For each term in a gloss, the appropriate WordNet sense has been manually assigned by two annotators, for over 1000 words.

To assess the performance of the gloss disambiguation algorithm we used two common evaluation measures: *recall* and *precision*. Recall provides the percentage of right senses with respect to the overall number of terms contained in the examined glosses. In fact, when the disambiguation algorithm terminates, the list P may still include terms for which no relation with the synsets in D could be found. Precision measures the percentage of right senses with respect to the retrieved gloss senses. A baseline precision is also computed, using the "first sense choice" heuristic. In WordNet, synsets are ordered by probability of use, i.e. the first synset is the most likely sense. For a fair comparison, the baseline is computed only on the words for which the algorithm could retrieve a synset.

Table 1 gives an overview of the results. Table 1a provides an overall evaluation of the algorithm, while table 1b computes precision and recall grouped by morphological category. The precision is quite high (well over 90% for both general and domain glosses) but the recall is around 40%. Remarkably, the achieved improvement in precision with respect to the baseline is much higher for general glosses than for domain glosses. This is motivated by the fact that general glosses include words that are more ambiguous than those in domain glosses. Therefore, the general gloss baseline is quite low. This means also that the disambiguation task is far more complex in the case of general glosses, where our algorithm shows particularly good performance.

An analysis of performance by morphological category (Table 1b) shows that noun disambiguation has much higher recall and precision. This is motivated by the fact that, in WordNet, noun definitions are richer than for verbs and adjectives. The WordNet hierarchy for verbs is known as being more problematic with respect to nouns. In the future, we plan to integrate in our algorithm verb information from FRAMENET[5], a lexico-semantic knowledge base providing rich information especially for verbs.

In Table 2 we summarize the efficacy of the A-link semi-automatic axiomatization, after the partly manual creation of a domain view $\Pi\delta+$ as discussed in section 3.2.

As a preventive measure, we have excluded the A-links that include either an adjective or a verb, since these synsets have not been integrated yet with DOLCE-Lite+. Another measure excluded the A-links that imply a subsumption (sub-class) link, since these are already formalized. This filter has been implemented as a simple ABox query that uses relations that range on classes:

---

[4] The 100 generic glosses have been randomly selected among the 809 glosses used to re-link WordNet to DOLCE-Lite+.

[5] http://www.icsi.berkeley.edu/~framenet/

Table 1. a) performance of the gloss disambiguation algorithm; b) performance by morphological category

Domains	# glosses	# words	# disamb. words	# of which ok	Recall	Precision	Baseline Precision
Tourism	305	1345	636	591	47,28%	92,92%	82,55%
Generic	100	421	173	166	41,09%	95,95%	67,05%

Domains	noun recall	noun precision	adj recall	adj precision	verb recall	verb precision	# tot nouns	# tot adj	# tot verbs
Tourism	64,52%	92,86%	28,72%	89,29%	9,18%	77,78%	868	195	294
Generic	58,27%	95,95%	28,38%	95,24%	5,32%	80%	254	74	94

ABox-3
(retrieve (?x ?y) (and (A-Link ?x ?y) (Superrelations ?x ?y)))

These measures reduced the amount of A-Links from the experimental set to 582 (435+147). We have used these tuples to run the revised query ABox-2.

The revised query produced 711 (569+142) candidate axioms by using all the pruned relations defined for the experiment in $\Pi\delta$+. Table 3 shows the resulting axioms ordered by generality of the relation universes (domain and range).

The most relevant results (see Table 4 for relation data) are:

One third of the A-Links from the tourism domain are actually subsumption links, while only 20% from the mixed generic set is a subsumption. This could be explained by the fact that glosses for generic synsets are less informative, or because generic words are not defined, in WN, in terms of more generic ones.

The correct subset of axioms learnt for the tourism domain is about 4 to 6% larger than for the generic one with reference to the whole sets.

Table 2. Axiomatizations for the A-links. "Best arrangement" data refer to results in Table 3

Domains	Synsets	A-links	Noun-only	Subsumptions	Filtered A-links	Axioms generated	Correct
Tourism	305	725	644	209	435	569	511
Generic	100	212	187	40	147	142	121

Table 3. Axiomatizations ordered by generality

	Tourism	Tourism correct	Generic	Generic correct
Total amount of axioms	569	511 (89.80%)	142	121 (85.21%)
Axioms with generic universes	540	490 (90.74%)	139	121 (87.05%)
Axioms with some specific universes	545	507 (93.02%)	136	118 (86.76%)
Axioms with only topmost universes	375	356 (94.93%)	110	98 (89.09%)

Table 4. An excerpt of the experimental set of relations $\Pi\delta+$. Argument restrictions into brackets, with assignment numerosity (correct ones in italics).

Relation taxonomy	Tourism	Tou. corr.	Generic	Gen. corr.
Conceptual_Relation (Entity, Entity)	*top: correct by A5*			
: Descriptive_Association (Object, S-Description)	7	*6*	5	*4*
: Functional_Association (Object, Functional-Role)	72	*68*	22	*19*
: : Functional_Role_Co_Participation (F-Role,F-Role)	21	*21*	13	*12*
: Physical_Location_Of (Geographical-Entity, Physical-Object)	2	*2*	2	*2*
: Mereotopological_Association (Physical-Object, Physical-Object)	140	*140*	29	*29*
: : Functional_CoParticipation (Functional-Object, Functional-Object)	98	*94*	1	*1*
: : Has_Member (Collection, Object)	4	*4*		
: : Provides (Functional-Object, Functional-Matter)	22	*17*	3	*0*
: : Biological_Part_Of (Biological-Object, Organism)			4	*4*
: : Has_Material_Constituent (Physical-Object, Amount-Of-Matter)	24	*4*	6	*3*
: : Used_By_Co_Pcp (Functional-Object, Agentive-Physical-Object)	7	*4*		
: : Member_Of (Object, Collection)	1	*0*		
: Participant (Event, Object)	14	*14*		
: : Agentive_Participant (Event, Agentive-Object)	3	*3*		
: Participant_In (Object, Event)	14	*13*	6	*6*
: Setting_For (Situation, Entity)	18	*17*		
: Setting (Entity, Situation)	21	*21*	8	*7*

We have tried to use some relations that are in principle "less precise". For example, a universe composed of *physical objects* and *amounts of matter* has a basic intuition of "constituency", and the relation *has_n_constituent* has been defined to such purpose. This relation has proved very inefficient though: in the generic set, only 50% of learnt axioms are correct, while in the tourism domain, only 16% are correct. We could expect that domains like *earth science* and *physics* can be more appropriate for constituency relations. For this reason, we have included a relation with a functional flavor in the experimental set of relations (including $\Pi\delta+$ and its specializations), called "provides", and defined on *functional objects* and *functional matters* (this universe is a meaningful subset of the previous one). This relation proved quite efficient in the tourism domain, just as expected, with about 78% of correct axioms, while it is useless in the generic set, with 0%. This is an example of "provides" axioms: $\forall x.$ Brasserie$(x) \rightarrow \exists y.$ Beer$(y) \wedge$ Provides(x,y).

This, and similar examples, confirm our expectations about the importance of developing dedicated sets of relations for different domains or tasks.

In 8 cases, the axioms were not definable with a cardinality≥ 1, although they could be used in more restricted domains or for subclasses of the universe.

Some indirect A-links can be investigated as well (though our first strategy has been to disregard indirect links, as explained in section 3.1). For example in the *retrospective#1* example of Fig. 2, two synsets (*painting#1* and *statue#1*) are learnt as "indirect" synsets (they are learnt from the glosses relative to the hyperonyms of *retrospective#1*). But paintings and statues are not always found in exhibitions, then we are not allowed to infer an axiom with cardinality ≥ 1. In these cases, the algorithm could be refined to propose an axiom that includes a common parent to both *painting#1* and *statue#1*, i.e. *art#1*, which incidentally is another "indirect" A-link to *retrospective#1*. In Fig. 3 the refined A-links for *retrospective#1* are shown: a *retrospective* in WordNet 1.6 has the intended meaning of a (unitary) collection in DOLCE-Lite+, which is a kind of non-agentive functional object. This lets the classifier infer:

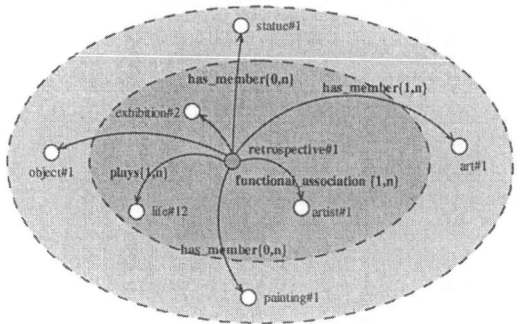

Fig. 3. Interpretation of A-links for retrospective#1

– a "functional association" to *artist#1*, because an artist is a functional role;
– a more precise "plays" relation to *life#12*, since an artistic biography is a functional role as well, and a collection of art works plays just the role of an artistic biography; a subsumption of *retrospective#1* by *exhibition#2*;
– three "has_member" relationships to the indirect A-links: *art#1*, *painting#1*, and *statue#1*. These are correct, since a collection can have functional objects (art works) as members. But while the first has a meaningful cardinality 1 to n, the others have a logically irrelevant cardinality of 0 to n.

5   Conclusions

In this paper we have presented some preliminary results of OntoWordNet, a large-scale project aiming at the "ontologization" of WordNet. We presented a two step methodology: during the first, automatic phase, natural language word sense glosses in WordNet are parsed, generating a first, approximate definition of WN concepts (originally called synsets). In this definition, generic associations (A-links) are established between a concept and the concepts that co-occur in its gloss.

In a second phase, the foundational top ontology DOLCE (in the *DOLCE-Lite+* version), including few hundreds formally defined concepts and conceptual relations, is used to interpret A-links in terms of axiomatised conceptual relations. This is a partly automatic technique that involves generating solutions on the basis of the available axioms, and then creating a specialized partition of the axioms (the set $\Pi\delta+$ and its specializations) in order to capture more domain-specific phenomena.

Overall, the experiments that we conducted show that a high performance may be obtained through the use of automatic techniques, significantly reducing the manual effort that would be necessary to pursue the objective of the OntoWordNet project.

References

(Basili et al. 1996) Basili R., Pazienza M.T. and Velardi P. *An Empirical Symbolic Approach to Natural Language Processing*, Artificial Intelligence, n. 85, (1996).

(Berners-Lee, 1998) Berners-Lee T., Semantic Web Road map, http://www.w3.org/DesignIssues/Semantic.html, 1998.

(Fellbaum 1995) Fellbaum, C. *WordNet: an electronic lexical database*, Cambridge, MIT press, (1995).

(Gangemi et al. 2001) Gangemi, A., Guarino, N., Masolo, C., and Oltramari, A. 2001. Understanding top-level ontological distinctions. In *Proceedings of IJCAI-01 Workshop on Ontologies and Information Sharing*. Seattle, USA, AAAI Press: 26–33. http://SunSITE.Informatik.RWTHAachen. DE/Publications/CEUR-WS/Vol-47/

(Gangemi et al. 2002) Gangemi A., Guarino N. Masolo C. Oltramari A., Schneider L. "Sweetening Ontologies with DOLCE", Proc. Of EKAW02 http://citeseer.nj.nec.com/cache/papers/cs/26864/http

(Harabagiu and Moldovan 1999) Harabagiu S. and Moldovan D. *Enriching the WordNet Taxonomy with Contextual Knowledge Acquired from Text*. AAAI/MIT Press, (1999).

(Karkaletsis V. Cucchiarelli A Paliouras G. Spyropolous C. Velardi P. "Automatic adaptation of Proper Noun Dictionaries through cooperation of machine learning and probabilistic methods" 23rd annual ACM-SIGIR, Athens, June 2000.

(Johnson 1987) Johnson, Mark. 1987. *The Body in the Mind*. Chicago: University of Chicago Press.

(Mac Gregor, 1993) MacGregor, R. M. 1993. Using a Description Classifier to Enhance Deductive Inference. In *Proceedings of Seventh IEEE Conference on AI Applications*: 141–147.

(Masolo et al. 2002) Claudio Masolo, Stefano Borgo, Aldo Gangemi, Nicola Guarino, Alessandro Oltramari, and Luc Schneider. The WonderWeb Library of Foundational Ontologies. WonderWeb Deliverable 17, 2002.

(Magnini and Caviglia 2000) Magnini, B. and Cavaglia, G.: Integrating Subject Field Codes into WordNet. Proceedings of the 2nd International Conference on Language resources and Evaluation, LREC2000, Atenas .

(Miller et al. 1993) G. A. Miller, R. Beckwith, C. Fellbaum, D. Gross & K. Miller; "Introduction to WordNet: An On-Line Lexical Database"; http://www.cosgi.princeton.edu/~wn; August 1993.

(Mihalcea and Moldovan, 2001) Milhalcea, R. and Moldovan. D. *eXtended WordNet: progress report*. NAACL 2001 Workshop on WordNet and Other Lexical Resources, Pittsbourgh, June (2001).

(Moeller, 2001) Volker Haarslev, Ralf Möller Description of the RACER System and its Applications Proceedings International Workshop on Description Logics (DL-2001), Stanford, USA, 1.-3. August 2001

(Morin, 1999) Morin E., *Automatic Acquisition of semantic relations between terms from technical corpora*, Proc. of 5th International Congress on Terminology and Knowledge extraction, TKE-99, (1999).

(Navigli et al. 2003) R. Navigli, P. Velardi and A. Gangemi, *Ontology Learning and its Application to Automated Terminology Translation*, IEEE Intelligent Systems, vol. 18, n.1, pp. 22–31, January 2003

(Searle, 1985) Searle, J.R and Vanderveken, D. *Foundations of Illocutionary Logics*, Cambridge UP, (1985).

(Smith and Welty, 2001) Smith, B. and Welty, C. *Ontology: towards a new synthesis*, Formal Ontology in Information Systems, ACM Press, (2001).

(Vossen 2001) Vossen P. *Extending, Trimming and Fusing WordNet for technical Documents*, NAACL 2001 workshop on WordNet and Other Lexical Resources, Pittsburgh, July (2001).

Web Sites

DAML+OIL	http://www.daml.org/2001/03/daml+oil-index
LDC	corpus http://www.ldc.upenn.edu/
FRAMENET	http://www.icsi.berkeley.edu/~framenet/
WordNet 1.6	http://www.cogsci.princeton.edu/~wn/w3wn.html
Semcor	http://engr.smu.edu/~rada/semcor/
WonderWeb	http://wonderweb.semanticweb.org

Ontology Based Query Processing in Database Management Systems

Chokri Ben Necib and Johann-Christoph Freytag

Department of Computer Science
Humboldt-Universität zu Berlin, Germany
{necib,freytag}@dbis.informatik.hu-berlin.de

Abstract. The use of semantic knowledge in its various forms has become an important aspect in managing data in database and information systems. In the form of integrity constraints, it has been used intensively in query optimization for some time. Similarly, data integration techniques have utilized semantic knowledge to handle heterogeneity for query processing on distributed information sources in a graceful manner. Recently, ontologies have become a "buzz word" for the semantic web and semantic data processing. In fact, they play a central role in facilitating the exchange of data between the several sources. In this paper, we present a new approach using ontology knowledge for query processing within a single relational database to extend the result of a query in a semantically meaningful way. We describe how an ontology can be effectively exploited to rewrite a user query into another query such that the new query provides additional meaningful results that satisfy the intention of the user. We outline a set of query transformation rules and describe by using a semantic Model the necessary criteria to prove their validity.

Keywords: Databases, Ontologies, Semantic Knowledge, Query Processing

1 Introduction

Semantic knowledge in its various forms including meta-models and integrity constraints is becoming an important aspect in managing data in database management and information systems: Semantic query optimization techniques have emerged in the 90s to complement the traditional approaches to reducing processing costs and to overcoming the heterogeneity problem in a distributed processing environment [7,12,3,1]. Here, semantic rules about the data such as integrity constraints are the basis for reformulating user queries into more efficient, but semantically equivalent queries, which return the same answer in less time or with less resources. There are also several mechanisms in knowledge databases that use semantic knowledge from a set of intentional knowledge including deduction rules, generalized rules and concept hierarchies in order to provide an "intelligent answer" for queries. "Intelligently answering" a query

R. Meersman et al. (Eds.): CoopIS/DOA/ODBASE 2003, LNCS 2888, pp. 839–857, 2003.

refers to providing the user with intentional answers in addition to the data (facts) as answers. These answers include some generalized, neighborhood or associated information that characterizes the data results [10]. Moreover, the intentional knowledge is stored in the database; thus the user can retrieve this additional knowledge as well.

In recent years, semantic knowledge in the form of *ontologies* has proven to be a powerful support for the techniques used for managing data. Ontologies promise solutions to the problems of semantic interoperability and data heterogeneity in querying distributed databases. An ontology might be used to capture the semantic content of each source and unify the semantic relationships between their data structures such as the attribute properties and relation names. Thus, users should not care about where and how the data are organized in the sources. For this reason, systems like OBSERVER [16] and TAMBIS [20] allow users to formulate their queries over an ontology without directly accessing the data sources. Since the ontology defines the set of terms to be used in a query, the users must be familiar with the content of the ontology. However, using a large ontology to navigate and to select appropriate terms causes many difficulties. In our approach, the user does not have to deal with the ontology directly; he can formulate his queries over the database as usual. In this case, it is the responsibility of the query processor to reformulate the query using the ontology associated with that database.

On the other hand, ontologies might enhance the functionality of the search engines on the web by adding semantics to the information content of web pages. Ontologies are used to define the meaning of the terms emerging on the web pages and these can be used to make inferences to get more information related to the objects of interest [2].

In this paper, we present a new approach using ontologies for query processing within a single relational database management system. We assume that a preexisting ontology is associated with a database and provides the context of its objects. We show how an ontology can be exploited effectively to reformulate a user query such that the resulting query provides additional meaningful results meeting the intention of the user. A query can be defined by a set of projections over the objects satisfying a set of conditions. These conditions are defined by a set of terms and determine the answer. If a user wants to retrieve information from a database about a certain object, he might use terms, which do not exactly match the database values (due to the mismatch between the user's and the database designer's world views). However, there might be values in the database that are syntactically different from one another but semantically equivalent to the user terms and that express the same intention of the user. Wee address this issue as a semantic problem rather than as a pattern matching problem. We define two terms as semantically equivalent if they have the same meaning, i.e. they define the same concept with respect to the ontology. For example, if two terms are synonyms, they are semantically equivalent. As a result, if we consider semantics in query processing, the number of results for the transformed query might increase or decrease. In both cases the user receives an answer that is further satisfying his expectations. For example, if two terms are synonyms, they are semantically equivalent. As a result, if we consider semantics in query processing, the number of results for the transformed query might increase or decrease. In both cases the user receives an answer that is further satisfying his expectations. For example, let us assume that a user intends to query a database of products to get some information about the product "computer". Thus, the user will not obtain all the related instances from the database unless he know in advance that the database contains additional values that are semantically synonyms for "computer" such as "calculator" or "data processor". By considering these terms in the query the user will get more results from the database.

We use an ontology as a semantic layer over a database to describe the semantic relationships between the database values in order to transform user queries to other meaningful queries. To this end, a set of transformation rules must be developed taking into account possible mappings between the database and the ontology content. We assume the preexistence of an ontology associated with the database; but we point out its main features to fit the semantics of the database and assert the validity of such rules. Therefore, we develop a semantic model and basic criteria like correctness and completeness.

Our approach can be appropriate for the databases where some attributes are enumerated from a list of terms. For example, in product databases, the product items are described according to a collection of standard terms [19]. These terms are organized in taxonomies.

The remainder of this paper is organized as follows. In section 2 we discuss some preliminaries. In section 3, we present the problem by means of an example. In section 4, we illustrate our approach. In section 5, we describe a semantic model to validate this approach ,and in section 6 we reach our conclusion.

2   Preliminaries

2.1   Ontology

Nowadays, the term *"Ontology"* or *"ontologies"* is intensively used in artificial intelligence and information systems areas. However, there is no clear definition of what an ontology is. Often, we find in the literature definitions that are general or tailored according to the domain where the application is developed. The term *"Ontology"* is sometime used as a synonym for other terms such as *"Controlled Vocabulary"*, or *"Taxonomy"*, or *"Knowledge Base"*. This is due to the overlapping of some common features of these concepts. Since it is not the goal of this paper to discuss the definition of an ontology, we first give our own definition of this notion and then a short comparison with other similar notions. Readers, who are interested in the different meanings of "Ontology" are referred to [8,9,17,4].

Informally, we define an ontology as an intentional description of what's known about the essence of the entities in a particular domain of interest using abstractions, also called *concepts* and their *relationships* . Basically, the hierarchical organization associated to the concepts through the inheritance ("ISA") relationship constitutes the backbone of an ontology. Other kinds of relationship like the aggregation ("PartOf") or Synonym ("SynOf") or application specific relationships might exist.

The term "Controlled Vocabularies" (CVs) is commonly used in the field of linguistics, to mean a set of standardized terms with commonly agreed semantics for a specific domain within user communicate [14]. A special kind of a controlled vocabulary is a *thesaurus* . A common feature of an ontology and a thesaurus is that they contain a large set of special terms concerning a certain domain and provide a clear understanding of their meanings. Furthermore, both an ontology and a thesaurus use relationships among the terms to represent these meanings. However, most of the relationships used in a thesaurus are different from those used in an ontology. In addition, they are usually ambiguous and less specified. For example, the relationships Broader Term (BT) and Narrower Term (NT) indicating that a term has broader meaning than another term and vise versa, indicate sometimes the specialization and the part-whole aspects at the same time [21]. Moreover, such inverse relationships are not explicitly represented in an ontology. Finally, a thesaurus deals with terms whereas an ontology deals with concepts but uses terms to represent these concepts. In general, a concept is not a word and it is not specific to a given natural language [13]. Thesaurus are dependent upon a specific natural language (or multiple language in case of Multilanguage thesaurus).

The term "Taxonomy" refers the classification of entities, whether they are terms or objects, in a hierarchical structure according to the sub/super class paradigm. Thus, there is only one type of relationship relating these entities, namely the ISA-relationship. For this reason, if we reduce the types of relationships in an ontology to only the ISA-types to represent concepts, the ontology will be equivalent to a taxonomy.

Moreover, the use of the term "Ontology" can be confused with the use of the term "Knowledge Base". A knowledge base for the AI-community consists of two parts: A terminology Box, called *"T-Box"* and an assertions Box, called *"A-Box"* . The T-Box comprises a set of concepts and their definitions. It includes usually a taxonomy of terms related to each other with ISA-relationships. The A-Box comprises a set of instances of these concepts, called the universe of discourse, and a set of assertions between them. The common feature of Ontologies and knowledge bases is that both represent knowledge. However, knowledge bases provide in addition instances, for which knowledge is applied and inferred. Thus, if we reduce a knowledge base to the T-Box, we can say that the an ontology is equivalent to the resulting knowledge base.

"What does an ontology look like?" and "How can it be created?" still remain struggling topics for researchers but what they all agree upon is that an ontology must play the following role: An ontology must provide knowledge in the form of concise and unambiguous concepts and their meanings. This knowledge can be shared and reused from different agents i.e. human or/and machines.

2.2 Graphical Representation of an Ontology

In this section, we introduce a graph based representation of an ontology and set the associated graph operations. We agree that The graphical representation is more appropriate than the text based one found in the literature [13]. This representation conveys the properties of an ontology in a simple, clear and structured model.

Formal representation. Formally, we define an ontology as a set $\zeta = \{c_1, \ldots, c_n\}$ and a set $\Re = \{"\texttt{ISA}", "\texttt{SynOf}", "\texttt{PartOf}"\}$ where $c_i \in \zeta$ is a concept name, and $r_i \in \Re$ is the type of the binary relation relating two concepts (c_i and r_i are non-null strings). Other domain specific types can also exist. In the literature, the word "concept" is frequently used as a synonym for the word "concept name". Hence, for the design of an ontology only one term is chosen as a name for a particular concept [24]. Further, we consider that the terms "concept" and "concept name" have the same meaning.

We represent an ontology as a directed graph $G(V, E)$ (DAG) where V is a finite set of vertices and E is a finite set of edges: Each vertex of V is labeled with a concept and each edge of E represents the relation between two concepts. Formally, the label of a node $n \in V$ is defined by a function $N(n) = c_i \in \zeta$ that maps n to a string from ζ. The label of an edge $e \in E$ is given by a function $T(e)$ that maps e to a string from $\Re$.

Finally, an ontology is given by the set $O = \{G(V, E), \zeta, \Re, N, T\}$.

Figure 1 gives an example of a graph representation of a selected portion from the ontology "Product". A part of this ontology is adopted from an ontology described in [11].

Graph operations. In order to navigate the ontology graph, we define the following primitive operations: ISAChild, PartOfChild, ISAParent, and PartOfParent and two sets of concepts: $DESC$ and $SYNs$. We need these operations and sets to identify nodes in the graph, which hold concepts that are of interest for a query manipulation.

Given two nodes $n_1 = node(c_1)$ and $n_2 = node(c_2)$

- $n_2 = \text{ISAChild}(n_1)$ iff $n_2 = child(n_1)$ and $T[(n_1, n_2)] = "\texttt{ISA}"$
- $n_2 = \text{PartOfChild}(n_1)$ iff $n_2 = child(n_1)$ and $T[(n_1, n_2)] = "\texttt{PartOf}"$
- $n_2 = \text{ISAParent}(n_1)$ iff $n_2 = parent(n_1)$ and $T[(n_1, n_2)] = "\texttt{ISA}"$,
- $n_2 = \text{PartOfParent}(n1_1)$ iff $n_2 = parent(n_1)$ and $T[(n1, n_2)] = "\texttt{PartOf}"$
- $n_2 = \text{SynOf}(n_1)$ iff $T[(n_1, n_2)] = "\texttt{SynOf}"$
- $DESC(r, c) = \{s \in \zeta \mid \forall e \in E \wedge e \in P(node(c) - node(s)) \wedge T(e) = r\}$
- $SYNs(c) = \{s \in \zeta \mid \forall e \in E \wedge e \in P(node(c) - node(s)) \wedge T(e) = "\texttt{SynOf}"\}$

Informally, $DESC(r, c)$ gives the set of all concepts in O obtained by retrieving recursively all the labels of the children nodes related with the node of c by following only the links of type r. Similarly, $SYNs(c)$ gives the set of all synonyms of c in O. We denote by $P(n_1 - n_2)$ the directed path between two nodes n_1 and n_2.

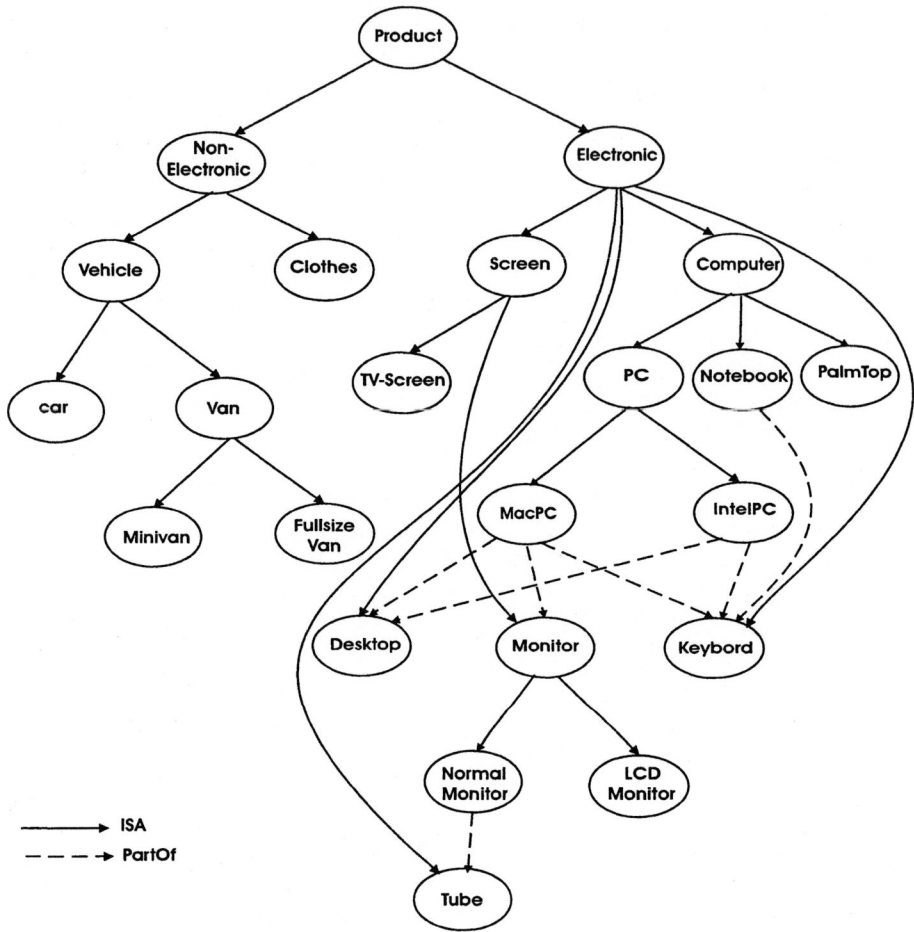

Fig. 1. Product Ontology

3   Motivation and Problem Statement

Data semantics, as defined in [22], is *the meaning of data and the reflection of the real world.* Since designers perceive the real world differently, there exist more than a single way to represent the existing objects and their relationships. The real world objects might have complex structures and dynamic behaviors. Thus, capturing the semantics completely from the real world seems to be impossible i.e. there does not exist any model which can define all the aspects of the real world objects. For example, relational database systems overcome the limitations of the relation model by adding a set of integrity constraints to maintain data that is consistent and to provide support for semantic rules such as cardinality, containment, and type hierarchies [18].

We believe that a new generation of DBMSs requires additional semantic supports for a flexible and efficient data management. This includes facilities for data integration, query optimization and meaningful query processing. The later problem is addressed in our paper. The basic idea, is to give the DBMS the ability to deal with the queries both at the semantic as well as the syntactic level. In fact, if a user attempts to retrieve information about objects from the database, the answer to his query might not meet his expectations. This might be one to the following reasons:

First, there might be semantic ambiguities between the terms used in the query and the database values that represent these objects (vocabulary problems). In fact, the user's perception of real world objects might not match exactly that of the database designer. Second, there might be different ways to formulate the query using semantic equivalent terms. We define two sets of terms to be equivalent if their relevant concepts and relationships in the ontology identify the same concept. There might be several such sets. We will specify this definition in our future work. Therefore, when the user formulate his query, he might use terms cover partially these semantics. Third, some results in the answer might not be related to the same context associated with the query. The context must be defined by the user.

Now, we give an example that can illustrate these reasons and our ideas throughout the paper:

We consider the ontology 'Product' given in figure 1, denoted by O_1. This ontology describes several products. We assume that we have a simple relational database, denoted by DB_1, including two relations called 'Article' and 'Component'. The relation Article contains a set of items described by the attributes 'name', 'model' and 'price'. The relation component contains the parts belonging to each item. The relational schema of DB_1 is the following:

ARTICLE(AID, Name, Model, Price)
AID: Article identifier
Name: Name of the article
Model: Model of the article
Price: Price of the article
PrimaryKey(AID)

COMPONENT (S-Part-ID, M-Part-ID)
M-Part-ID: Main part identifier
S-Part-ID: Second part identifier
Foreign-Key(M-Part-ID) TO ARTICLE
Foreign-Key(S-Part-ID) TO ARTICLE
Primary-Key(S-Part-ID)

Suppose, at present, that DB_1 contains the following instances as shown in the tables 1 and 2.

When a user want to retrieve information about computers from DB_1, he may submit a query that looks like

```
Q1: SELECT * FROM article WHERE name ='computer'.
```

In this query, the user intention concerns the object "computer". However, according to the ontology O_1, the concept "computer" is synonymous with the concepts "data processor" and "calculator". Furthermore, it has a broader meaning than the specialized concepts "notebook" and "palmtop". Intuitively, the ISA-relationship implies a strong similarity between the general concept and its sub-concepts. Since the ISA-relationship is transitive, the same argument can be

Table 1. Article relation

A-ID	Name	Model	Price
123	Computer	IBM	3000 $
124	IntelPc	Toshiba	5000 $
125	Notebook	Dell	4000 $
127	PC	Compaq	2500 $
128	Product	HP	3000 $
129	Monitor	Elsa	1000 $
135	Keyboard	ITT	80 $
136	Desktop	IBM	1000 $
140	MacPc	Mac	2000 $
141	Calculator	Siemens	1500 $

Table 2. Component relation

S-Part-ID	M-Part-ID
123	129
123	135
123	136
124	129
124	135
124	136
125	135
127	129
127	135
127	136
128	129
128	135
128	136
140	129
140	135
140	136
141	135

applied to further specialization i.e. "MacPC" and "IntelPC" . The database designer might use any of the specialized terms to specify the article "computer". If the user does not know these semantics in advance, he will not obtain all the relevant instances from DB_1. Thus, a meaningful processing of Q_1 has to transform the user query by adding these terms to the query condition. As consequence, the result of the transformed query might be greater than the result of the previous query and satisfy more of the user's needs. Note that without a semantic support, like the ontology, it is hard for the DBMS query processor to solve such vocabulary ambiguities. In this case, the ontology provides additional meanings for the database values related to a certain attribute name. These meanings are expressed through the relationships between the corresponding concepts. Now, suppose the user wants to get information about the article "PC". His query may look like

```
Q2: SELECT * FROM article WHERE name = 'PC'.
```

In this query, the user's intention concerns the object "PC". According to the ontology O_1 the concept "PC" is specialized into the concepts "MacPC" and "IntelPC". In addition, following the PartOf-links, a "PC" has three parts: a "desktop" , a "monitor" and " a "keyboard". If we assume, that all the PC-objects in the database must be composed exactly of these parts and that there do not exist any other objects composed of these, then we can find another way to characterize the same object "PC" by means of its components. With regard to the definition mentioned earlier, we can say that the terms "desktop", "monitor" and "keyboard" can build a new query condition which is semantically equivalent to the condition of Q_2. Therefore, it is not surprising that the tuples 123 and 128 with attribute names "computer" and "product" meet fully the intention of the user. When a user poses a Q_2-query to the database DB_1, these tuples will certainly be missed. The DBMS query processor has to extend the user query considering these semantics in addition to those suggested for the previous query Q_1. Note that in this case the number of tuples in the answer result will also increase. These examples clearly show which problems we are intended to solve:

"How can database queries be transformed using an ontology?"
"How can these transformations be validated?"
"How should the ontology look with respect to the database?"

Formally, the problem can be stated as follows:
Given a database DB, an ontology O and a user query Q, how to find a rewriting Q' of Q by using O, such that Q' returns to the user possibly more or fewer meaningful results than Q.

4 Ontology Based Query Processing

We address the problem above and choose the Domain relational calculus (DRC) formalism to represent user queries of the form $Q = \{s \mid \psi(s)\}$, where s is a tuple variable and $\psi(s)$ is a formula built from atoms and collection of operators to be defined shortly:
The atoms of formulas $\psi(s)$ are of three types: $u \in R$, $v \,\theta\, w$, and $u \,\theta\, t$, where R is a relation name and u, v and w are tuple variables, and t is a constant. θ is an arithmetic comparison operator ($=$, $<$ and so on). An occurrence of a variable in a formula can be bound or free. Formulas and variables in Q can be also defined recursively using the logic operators "$\wedge$" and "$\vee$ (see [23])

Our approach consists of three phases: preprocessing, execution and post-processing phase.

In the preprocessing phase, we transform a user query into another one based on new terms extracted from the ontology associated with this database. To this end, a set of transformation rules and of mapping functions must exist. The mapping functions have to map database types such as relation names, attribute names and data values to the concepts in the ontology. The transformation rules must contribute to:

- Expand the queries by changing their select condition α using terms synonymous with t and the terms specifying its concept. To achieve this purpose, the ontology must have the capabilities of reasoning over the synonym and hyponym relations, and
- Substitute the query conditions with other conditions that are semantically equivalent. Building such rules with respect to the database and the ontology is not an easy task.

However, the rules should not be developed according to ideal alone but they must lead to results closer to the user expectations. In addition, we need a semantic model that can reflect semantics of the transformations made at the syntax level. This might assert the validity of these rules. In the next section we propose this model. In the execution phase, the transformed query is processed using available query strategies of the system and the result is checked. If the result is empty, we perform the third phase. In the post-processing phase, we attempt to generate a more generalized answer to the query. That is, for each mapped attribute in the query condition three steps are performed:

(1) We substitute its value with the term of the corresponding parent concept by ascension of the ontology relations one level
(2) We execute the query again. If the answer set is still empty then we continue the substitution process in step 1 using much higher level concepts.
(3) We repeat step 2 until we find tuples in the answer set or no substitution is possible i.e. we achieve the root concept node.

5   Semantic Model

Given an ontology $O = \{G(V, E), \zeta, \Re, N, T\}$ and a database DB. Let U be a set of the attributes $A_1, \ldots, A_n$ where each attribute domain, $dom(A_i)$, is considered finite. The database schema is defined as a set of relation schema $R_1, \ldots, R_m$ where the attributes of each relation schema belong to U. The set of attributes that are primary keys is denoted by $PRIMKEY(U)$. Let also $U(R_i)$ be the set of attributes of U that define the schema of R_i. In addition, let M_1 be defined as the function that represents the mapping of the relation names into the concepts in O, called *relation-concepts*; let M_2 be the function that represents the mapping of attribute names into the concepts in O, called *attribute-concepts*, and let M_3 be the function that represents the mapping of the attribute values into concepts in O, called *value-concepts*.

We propose a semantic model that enables us to validate the syntactic transformations of the database queries proposed earlier. This model is defined as a particular ontology, denoted O^*, which is an extension of the original ontology

O. Additional concepts and relationships are introduced as specified below. Note that there is no single consensual methodology for the ontology design [15]. Thus, we would not restrict our ontology development to particular guidelines for the building of the ontology. In fact, the purpose of this work is not to discuss how to develop or integrate an ontology. These issues alone are challenging problems for the researcher. For more interests to these topics, readers are recommended to refer to [6,24].

Additional Concepts

For each relation R of the database new concepts are created to represent the relation name, its attributes (expect the primary key attribute) and their domain attribute values unless such concepts already exist in O. In this case, we adopt the following naming conventions for the concepts:

(1) No single term can name two different concepts.
(2) The name of an attribute-concept is prefixed by the name of its relation concept.

These conventions are defined not only to make the extension of the ontology easier, but also to help avoid ambiguities in distinguishing concepts. We define the Id-concepts as the set of value-concepts that represent the values of the primary-key attributes. We denote by ID the set of nodes labeled by Id-concepts. We denote also the new set of relation-concepts, attribute-concepts, and value-concepts as C_{RN}, C_A and C_V respectively.

Additional Relationships

Because new concepts might be created as described above, one needs to link them with the existing concepts and/or with each other. To this end, additional binary relationships holding new semantics are introduced. The types of these relationships are defined as:

- ValueOf: This is the type of the relationship that relates each value-concept to the attribute-concept.
  Formally, $\forall A_i \in U \setminus PRIMKEY(U)$, $\forall w \in dom(Ai)$, $T(node(M_3(w))$, $node(M_2(A_i))) = $ "ValueOf". Note that the ValueOf-relationship has nothing to do with Id-concepts.
- HasA: This is the type of the relationship between the relation-concepts and the attribute-concepts.
  Formally, $\forall A_i \in R_i$, $R_i \in DB$, $T(node(M_1(R_i)), node(M_2(A_i))) = $ "HasA".
- InstanceOf: This is the type of the relationship that relates the Id-concepts to their corresponding relation-concepts so that $\forall A_i \in PRIMKEY(U)$, $A_i \in R_i$ and $id \in dom(A_i)$, $T(node(M_3(id)), node(M_1(R_i))) = $ "InstanceOf".
- TupleVal: TupleVal is defined as the type of relationship relating the concepts associated with the attribute values of each tuple. This relationship

is represented in the graph of O^* as a directed arc going out from the Id-concept node to other value-concept nodes associated to each attribute value of a given tuple.

Formally, given a tuple $\mu \in R_i$, $\mu : U \rightarrow dom(U)$, $\forall A_i \in U(R_i)$, and $ID \in PRIMKEY(R_i)$, $T(node(M_3(\mu(ID))), node(M_3(\mu(A_i)))) = $ "TupleVal".

Summary

O^* is defined as $O^* = \{G^*(V, E), \zeta^*, \Re^*, N, T\}$, where $\zeta^* = \zeta \cup C_{RN} \cup C_A \cup C_V$, and $\Re^* = \Re \cup \{$"ValueOf", "HasA", "InstanceOf", "TupleVal"$\}$

Figure 2 describes the semantic model for the product ontology. For the sake of a good visibility, we reduce the graph to some nodes and edges.

Definitions

For the ease of semantic reasoning on the concepts in the ontology graph of O^*, we introduce the graph operator: $SelectRel$. This operator will be used in the following sections.

SelectRel Operator:

This operator returns all edge types of the path between two value-concept nodes in G^* that are connected with two other id-nodes via edges of type "TupleVal".

Semantically, if two id-nodes are adjacent (there is a common edge of type "TupleVal") then the semantic relationship between the represented concepts can be deduced from the result of the SelectRel operation on these nodes. We assume that the PartOf-relationship semantically dominates the "ISA" one. This means that, if a path between two nodes consists of edges of types "ISA" and "PartOf" then the semantic relationship between the concepts, which label these nodes, is of type "PartOf". For example, if the semantic relationship between two database instances is of part-whole type then there exist in O^* a "PartOf"-relationship between two value-concepts, which are related to id-concepts of the tuple- identifier. In other word, the part-whole semantic between two database tuples will be reflected in the semantic model through relevant concept-values. Thus, if we want to know which semantics relate the tuple 123 and the tuple 123, we have to operate SelectRel on their corresponding id-nodes. As a result, we get two types of relations "ISA" and "PartOf". Due to the assumption above, we conclude that the object identified by 129 is part of that object identified by 123.

Formally, let id_1, $id_2 \in ID(G^*)$

$SelectRel(G^*, id_1, id_2) = \{R_i \in R \mid R_i = T(x, y) \wedge \exists n_1, n_2 \in V(G^*) \wedge T(id_1, n_1) = $ "TupleVal" $\wedge T(id_2, n_2) = $ "TupleVal" $\wedge [(x, y) \in P(n_1 - n_2) \vee (x, y) \in P(ISAChild(n_1) - ISAChild(n_2))]\}$.

We denote by $|SelectRel_{PartOf}(G^*, id_1, id_2)|$ the number of "PartOf"-labels returned by the $SlectRel$ operator.

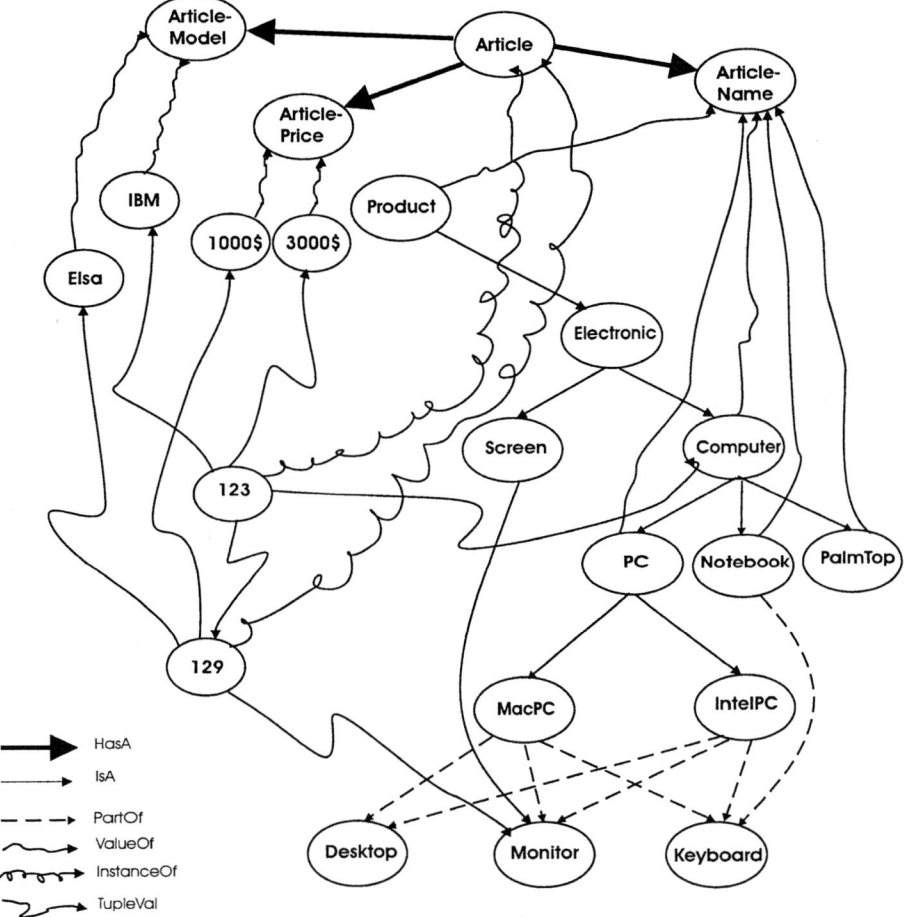

Fig. 2. A portion of the Semantic Model for Product Ontology

5.1   Logical Interpretation of the Model

In this section, we want to express the semantic model in a logical framework using the First Order Language (FOL) [5]. The later representation will be useful for formulating the criteria related to our semantic model. From a logical point of view, O^* is a theory Γ, which consists of an Interpretation I and a set of well formed formulas. I is defined by the set of individuals Δ, called universe of discourse, and an interpretation function $\cdot^I$.

Formally, Γ:

$$I = (\Delta, \cdot^I)$$
$$\Delta = \zeta^*$$

$$ISA^I = \{(a, b) \in \Delta^2 | T(node(a), node(b)) = \text{"ISA"}\}$$
$$SYN^I = \{(a, b) \in \Delta^2 | T(node(a), node(b)) = \text{"SynOf"}\}$$

$PARTOF^I = \{(a,b) \in \Delta^2 | T(node(a), node(b)) = "PartOf"\}$
$HASA^I = \{(a,b) \in \Delta^2 | T(node(a), node(b)) = "HasA"\}$
$VALUEOF^I = \{(a,b) \in \Delta^2 | T(node(a), node(b)) = "ValueOf"\}$
$INSTANCEOF^I = \{(a,b) \in \Delta^2 | T(node(a), node(b)) = "InstanceOf"\}$
$TUPLEVAL^I = \{(a,b) \in \Delta^2 | T(node(a), node(b)) = "TupleVal"\}$
$WHOLE^I = \{a \in \Delta | \forall b_1 b_2 c.\ ISA(a,b_1) \wedge ISA(a,b_2) \wedge PARTOF(b1,c) \rightarrow PARTOF(b2,c)\}$
$HASPART^I = \{a \in \Delta | \forall b \exists p.\ ISA(a,b) \rightarrow PARTOF(b,p)\}$
$Key^I = \{a \in \Delta | \exists b.T(node(a), node(b)) = "instanceOf"\}$

$\forall x.\ ISA(x,x)$
$\forall x.\ SYN(x,x)$
$\forall x.\ PARTOF(x,x)$
$\forall xyz.\ ISA(x,y) \wedge ISA(x,z) \rightarrow ISA(x,z)$
$\forall x.y\ SYN(x,y) \leftrightarrow SYN(y,x)$
$\forall xyz.\ SYN(x,y) \wedge SYN(x,z) \rightarrow SYN(x,z)$
$\forall xyz.\ SYN(x,y) \wedge SYN(x,z) \rightarrow SYN(x,z)$
$\forall xyz.\ PARTOF(x,y) \wedge PARTOF(x,z) \rightarrow PARTOF(x,z)$
$\forall xy\ \exists z.\ TUPLEVAL(x,y) \rightarrow INSTANCEOF(x,z)$
$\forall xy\ \exists z.\ VALUEOF(x,y) \rightarrow HASA(z,y)$
$\forall xyz.\ VALUEOF(y,z) \wedge ISA(x,y) \rightarrow VALUEOF(x,z)$
$\forall xyz.\ VALUEOF(y,z) \wedge SYN(x,y) \rightarrow VALUEOF(x,z)$
$\forall xyz.\ \exists\ w.\ INSTANCEOF(x,y) \wedge HASA(y,z) \rightarrow TUPLEVAL(x,w) \wedge VALUEOF(w,z)$
$\forall xyz.\ ISA(x,y) \wedge SYN(y,z) \leftrightarrow ISA(x,z)$
$\forall xyz.\ ISA(x,z) \wedge SYN(x,y) \leftrightarrow ISA(y,z)$
$\forall xyz.\ PARTOF(x,y) \wedge SYN(x,z) \leftrightarrow PARTOF(z,y)$
$\forall xyz.\ PARTOF(x,y) \wedge SYN(y,z) \leftrightarrow PARTOF(x,z)$
$\forall xyz.\ PARTOF(x,y) \wedge ISA(y,z) \leftrightarrow PARTOF(x,z)$
$\forall xyz.\ WHOLE(x) \wedge ISA(x,y) \wedge PARTOF(y,z) \leftrightarrow PARTOF(x,z)$
$\forall xy\ COMMONPART(x,y) \leftrightarrow \forall z_1 z_2 ISA(x,z_1) \wedge ISA(x,z_2) \wedge WHOLE(z_1) \wedge WHOLE(z_2) \wedge PARTOF(z_1,y) \wedge PARTOF(z_2,y)$

5.2   Correctness and Completeness Criteria

We define two criteria, *correctness* and *completeness*, for the validation of the transformation rules. The basic idea underlying these criteria is that, if we reflect any syntax transformation of the query on the semantic level it must be correct i.e. it will not violate the semantic model. Symmetrically, the semantic model is defined as complete if the mapping of concepts, which represent the result of the transformed query, are reflected by the database i.e. the corresponding values in the database are stored consistently.

To define formally these criteria, we need the following preliminary definitions:

Definition 1: An attribute A of U is said to be *covered* by O, if each value of its domain is represented by a concept in O.
Formally, $\forall x \in dom(A), \exists c \in \zeta \mid M_3(x) = c$

Definition 2: A relation R is said to be *partially covered* by O, if there exist an attribute A of R which is covered by O.

Definition 3: Two id-concepts id_1 and id_2 are said to be *semantically dependent* if and only if $SelectRel(G^*, node(id_1), node(id_2)) \neq \emptyset$

Correctness Criterion

Formally, An extended ontology O^* is said to be a correct model for a relation R if and only if:
$\forall id_1, id_2 \in dom(ID)$, $ID \in PRIMKEY(R)$, and $ic_1 = M_3(id_1)$ and $ic_2 = M_3(id_2)$

(1) IF $T(node(ic_1), node(ic_2)) = $ "TupleVal"
    THEN ic_1 and ic_2 are semantically dependent,
    and
(2) IF $|SelectRel_{PartOf}(G^*, node(ic_1), node(ic_2))| \neq \emptyset$
    THEN $|SelectRel_{PartOf}(G^*, node(ic_1), node(ic_2))| = 1$

The intuition behind the first condition, is that if two database tuples are related to each other, then there exist in O^* at least one semantic relationship between the two value-concepts associated to two attribute values of the tuples. For example, if we examine the semantic model of the product ontology (see figure 2), then we deduce that the relation between the tuples 123 and 129 (see relation component) is reflected by the semantic relationship of the concepts "computer" and "monitor". That is, the object 129 is part of the object 123.

The intuition behind the second condition, is that only a PartOf-relation level is allowed for all the database instances i.e. if item A is part of item B and item B is part of item C than the database does not store explicitly the relation: Item A is part of item C.

Completeness Criterion

The extended ontology O^* is *complete* if and only if:

(1) $\forall id_1 a_v p.\ Key(id_1) \wedge TUPLEVAL(id, a_v) \wedge WHOLE(a_v) \wedge PARTOF(a_v, p)$
    $\rightarrow \exists id_2 Key(id_2) \wedge TUPLEVAL(id1, id_2) \wedge TUPLEVAL(id_2, p)$,
    and
(2) $\forall id_1 a_v p\ \ \exists id_2\ \ Key(id_1) \wedge TUPLEVAL(id, a_v) \wedge HASPART(a_v) \wedge COMMONPART(a_v, p) \rightarrow Key(id_2) \wedge TUPLEVAL(id_1, id_2) \wedge TUPLEVAL(id_2, p)$

are satisfied.

Axiom (1) denotes that each decomposition of a concept in the ontology must reflect the same decomposition for the associated values in the database instance. In this case, the decomposition is said to be mandatory for the database instances. For example, each instance of the Database DB1 where the article name is "PC" should have a "desktop", "monitor" and "keyboard" instance. In addition, the condition asserts when the PartOf-relationship is transitive with respect to the ISA-relationship. A concept, say B, is a part of a concept, say A, if B is a part of all the sub-concepts of A. For example, the concept "monitor" is a part of the concept "PC" because it's a part of both concepts "MacPC" and "IntelPC", which are sub-concepts of "PC".

Axiom (2) denotes that if all the sub-concepts of a concept, say A, have a common part concept, say P, then each database instance reflecting A must be minimally related to an instance, which reflects P. For example, suppose that the concept "palmtop" does not exit in the ontology "Product". Thus, for each tuple of the database where the article name is "computer" must be related to another tuple where the article name is "keyboard".

Summary

Based on the criteria above a database instance is *consistent* with respect to an ontology O if

(1) O^* is a correct model for the database, and
(2) O^* is a complete model for the database.

5.3   Example of a Transformation Rule

Now, we present a possible transformation rule and illustrate its validation using our proposed semantic model. This will help illustrating the basic ideas of our approach in this paper.

Intuitively, this rule derive terms from the ontology, which are synonymous with terms used in the query conditions and other terms that specialize them. The query example Q_1 in the section 3 is related to this rule.

Formally, let D be the set of domain attributes of a database, $t_0 \in D$, and $c_0 \in O$.

IF $Q = \{(x_1, \ldots, x_n) \mid (x_1, \ldots, x_n) \in R \wedge x_i \theta t_0\}$ and $M_3(t_0) = c_0$

THEN $Q' = \{(x_1, \ldots, x_n) \mid (x_1, \ldots, x_n) \in R \wedge [(x_i \theta t_0) \vee (x_i \theta t_1) \vee \ldots \vee (x_i \theta t_m)]\}$ where $t_k \in I_0 \cup I_1, 1 \leq k \leq m = |I_0 \cup I_1|$

$I_0 = \{t \in D \mid M_3(t) \in DESC_{isA}(c_0)\}$, and
$I_1 = \{t \in D \mid M_3(t) \in SYNs(c), \ c \in I_0\}$

We note that this rule might increase the result set, say S_Q, provided by Q. This augmentation is not arbitrary but it is proved by the semantic model O^* associated with the database: According to O^*, the tuple identifier of S_Q are represented by id-concepts, which are linked with value-concepts, and the relation-concept through TupleVal and InstanceOf-relationship, respectively. Formally, this set is given by the following:

$\Omega_{BT} = \{x \mid W(x)\}$

$\qquad = \{x \mid TUPLEVAL(x, A_V) \wedge INSTANCEOF(x, R_N) \rightarrow$

$\qquad\qquad VALUEOF(A_V, A_N)\},$

where x is a variable and A_V, A_N, and R_N are constants. O^* interprets the rule as the existence of additional value-concepts, which are semantically related to those representing terms in the condition of the query Q. We call the id-concepts, which are related to the later ones *virtual tuple-concepts* and the semantic relationship between them *DrivedTupleVal*. Formally, this type of relationship can be expressed by a predicate $DRIVEDTUPLEVAL$ as follows:

$W'(x)$: $\forall x$ $\exists$ z $DRIVEDTUPLEVAL(x, y)$ $\rightarrow$ $TUPLEVAL(x, z) \wedge$ $[ISA(A_V, z) \vee SYN(A_V, z)]$.

We denote by Ω_{VT}, the set of virtual tuple-concepts and express it as follows:

$\Omega_{VT} = \{x \mid \exists z \, DRIVEDTUPLEVAL(x, z)\}$.

As a result, if we unify the sets Ω_{BT} with Ω_{VT}, we get then a set of individuals from Δ, which represents id-concepts of the result of the query Q'. We denote this set by Ω.

Formally,

$\Omega = \Omega_{BT} \cup \Omega_{VT}$
Ω = $\{x$ | $\exists$ z $TUPLEVAL(x, z) \wedge INSTANCEOF(x, R_N)$ $\rightarrow$ $VALUEOF(z, A_N)$ $\wedge$ $[ISA(A_V, z)$ $\vee$ $SYN(A_V, z)]\}$.

6 Conclusion and Outlook

Today, Database management systems face challenging problems in dealing with the huge amount of data and the variety of its format. Thus, current database systems not only need additional supports for manipulating data but also for understanding its meaning. Semantic knowledge in its various forms become a necessary tool for enhancing the usefulness and flexibility of data management, especially in integrating data from multiple sources and in optimizing the queries. In fact, this makes the database aware of the semantics of its stored values and thus provides better ways to answer a query request. Conventional database querying does not always provide answers to users, which fully meet their expectations. One of the reasons, is that the query is treated at only the syntactical level.

In this paper, we have presented an approach for the query processing that processes the query at both the syntactical and the semantical level. Our approach allows to generate answers, which contain enough informative and meaningful results for the user. We use the ontology as a semantic tool for processing data in a single database management system. We have showed how can we capture semantics between database objects and use them for reformulating the user queries. We have outlined the basic features of the rules that allow these reformulations. Then we presented a semantic model and the basic criteria to validate any transformations made at the syntactical level.

Our approach can be appropriate for the databases where some attributes are enumerated from a list of terms. For example, in product databases, the product items are described according to a collection of standard terms [19].

Currently, we are developing a set of transformation rules for use in relational database systems. Although these rules might not be ideal, we hope that they can bring more insight into the nature of query answers. We believe that using ontologies for managing data will provide meaningful information to answer a database query.

In the future, we will investigate how to use ontologies to generate knowledge answers which are compact and intuitive for the user and describe the characteristics of the query results.

References

1. K. Aberer and G. Fischer. Semantic query optimization for methods in object-oriented database systems. In *IEEE International Conference Data Engineering*, pages 70–79, 1995.
2. T. Berners-Lee, J. Hendler, and O. Lassila. The semantic web, a new form of web content that is meaningful to computers will unleash a revolution of new possibilities. In *Scientific American*, 2001.
3. U. Chakravarthy, J. Grant, and J. Minker. Logic-based approach to semantic query optimization. In *ACM Transactions on DatabaseSystems*, pages 162–207, 1990.
4. B. Chandrasekaran, J.R. Josephson, and V.R. Benjamins. What are ontologies, and why do we need them? In *IEEE Intelligent Systems*, pages 20–26, 1999.
5. E. Franconi. Description logics. Course at the International Doctoral school of Technology and Science at the Aalborg University, Denmark, 2002.
6. A. Gomez-Perez, M. Fernandez-López, and O. Corcho. *Ontological Engineering*. Springer Verlag, London Ltd, 2003. To be published.
7. J. Grant, J. Gryz, , J. Minker, and L. Raschid. Semantic query optimization for object databases. ICDE, November 1997.
8. T.R Gruber. A translation approach to portable ontology specifications. In *Knowledge Acquisition (5) No. 2, USA*, pages 199–220, 1993.
9. N. Guarino and P. Giaretta. Ontologies and knowledge bases: towards a terminological clarification. In *Knowledge Building Knowledge Sharing,ION Press*, pages 25–32, 1995.
10. J. W. Han, Y. Huang, N. Cercone, and Y. J. Fu. Intelligent query answering by knowledge discovery techniques. In *IEEE Trans*, pages 373–390, 1996.
11. AA. Kayed and R.M. Colomb. Extracting ontological concepts for tendering conceptual structures. *Data and Knowledge Engineering*, 41(1–4), 2001.
12. L.V.S. Lakshmanan and R. Missaoui. On semantic query optimization in deductive databases. In *IEEE International Conference on Data Engineering*, pages 368–375, 1992.
13. D.B. Lenat and R.V. Guha. *Building Large Knowledge-Based Systems: Representation and Inference in the CYC Project*. Addison-Wesley, Reading, Massachusetts, 1990.

14. L. Liu, M. Halper, J. Geller, and Y. Perl. Controlled vocabularies in OODBs: Modeling issues and implementation. In *istributed and Parallel Databases*, pages 37–65, 1999.
15. F. Lopez. Overview of methodologies for building ontologies. In *the IJCAI-99 Workshop on Ontologies and Problem-Solving Methods: Lessons Learned and Future Trends.Intelligent Systems*, pages 26–34, 2001.
16. E. Mena, V. Kashyap, A. Sheth, and A. Illarramendi. OBSERVER: An approach for query processing in global information systems based on interoperation across pre-existing ontologies. *Conference on Cooperative Information Systems*, 41:14–25, 1996.
17. N.F. Noy and C. D. Hafner. The state of the art in ontology design. *AI Magazine*, 3(18):53–74, 1997.
18. C.W. Olofson. Addressing the semantic gap in databases: Lazy software and the associative model of data. Bulletin), 2002.
19. B. Omelayenko. Integrating vocabularies: Discovering and representing vocabulary maps. *The Semantic Web-ISWC 2002, First International Semantic Web Conference, Sardinia, Italy*, pages 206–220, 2002.
20. N.W. Paton, R. Stevens, P. Baker, C.A. Goble, S. Bechhofer, and A. Brass. Query processing in the TAMBIS bioinformatics source integration system. *Statistical and Scientific Database Management*, pages 138–147, 1999.
21. H.S. Pinto and J. P. Martins. A methodology for ontology integration. In *the First International Conference on Knowledge Capture (K-CAP)*, pages 368–375, 2001.
22. A. Sheth. Data semantics: what, where and how. Technical Report Preprint CS-01-99, TR-CS-95-003, LSDIS Lab, Dept. of CS, Univ. of GA, 1995.
23. J.D. Ullman. *Principles of Database and Knowledge-Base Systems*. Computer Science Press, 1988.
24. M: Uschold and M: Grüninger. Ontologies: principles, methods, and applications. *Knowledge Engineering Review*, 11(2):93–155, 1996.

OntoManager – A System for the Usage-Based Ontology Management

Ljiljana Stojanovic[1], Nenad Stojanovic[2], Jorge Gonzalez[3*], and Rudi Studer[1,2]

[1] FZI - Research Center for Information Technologies at the University of Karlsruhe,
Haid-und-Neu-Str. 10-14, 76131 Karlsruhe, Germany
{Ljiljana.Stojanovic,studer}@fzi.de
[2] Institute AIFB, University of Karlsruhe,
76128 Karlsruhe, Germany
{studer,nst}@aifb.uni-karlsruhe.de
[3] SAP AG,
69190 Waldorf, Germany
jorge.gonzalez@sap.com

Abstract. In this paper, we propose an approach for guiding ontology managers through the modification of an ontology with respect to users' needs. It is based on the analysis of end-users' interactions with the ontology-based applications, which are tracked into the usage-log. Several measures taking into account the ontology hierarchy are defined. Their application on the usage log results in the set of the recommendations for the ontology improvement. The approach has been implemented in the system called OntoManager. The evaluation study shows the benefits of supporting ontology management by our approach.

1 Introduction

An application has to be modified in order to reflect changes in the real world, changes in user's requirements, drawbacks in the initial design, to incorporate additional functionality or to allow for incremental improvement [1]. Some requests for the adaptation might be specified explicitly, such as the need for a new type of a product due to a change in the business strategy. Other changes are implicit and might be discovered from the usage of this application. For example, if none of the users was interested in the information about a product in an on-line catalog, then, probably, this product should be excluded from the list of products offered by that application. These "discovered" changes are very important for optimising performance of an application, e.g. by reducing the hierarchies of products that have to be browsed. Moreover, they enable a continual adaptation of the application to the implicit changes in the business environment.

The usage analysis that leads to the change discovery is a very complex activity, as are all the methods for learning from the data [2]. Firstly, it is difficult to find meaningful usage patterns. For example, is it useful for an application to discover that

---

* This research was carried out while the author was with the Institute AIFB, University of Karlsruhe

R. Meersman et al. (Eds.): CoopIS/DOA/ODBASE 2003, LNCS 2888, pp. 858–875, 2003.
© Springer-Verlag Berlin Heidelberg 2003

much more users are interested[1] in the topic *"industrial project"* than in the topic *"research"*? Secondly, when a meaningful usage pattern is found, the open issue is how to translate it into a change that leads to the improvement of an application. For example, how to interpret the information that a lot of users are interested in *"industrial"* and *"basic research projects"*, but none of them are interested in the third type of the projects – *"applied research projects"*.

Since in an ontology-based application an ontology serves as a conceptual model of the domain [3], the interpretation of these usage patterns on the level of the ontology alleviates the process of discovering useful changes in the application. The pattern mentioned above firstly can be treated as useless for discovering changes if there is no relation between the concepts[2] *"industrial project"* and *"research"* in the underlying ontology. Moreover, the structure of an ontology can be used as the background knowledge for generating useful changes. For example, in the case that the *"industrial"*, *"basic research"* and *"applied research project"* are three subconcepts of the concept *"Project"* in the domain ontology, in order to tailor the concepts to the users' needs, the pattern mentioned secondly could lead to either deleting the "unused" concept *"applied research project"* or its merging with one of the two other concepts (i.e. *"industrial research"* or *"basic research"*). Such an interpretation requires the familiarity with the ontology model definition, the ontology itself, as well as the experience in modifying the ontologies. Moreover, the increasing complexity of ontologies demands a correspondingly larger human effort for its management. It is clear that the manual effort can be time consuming and error-prone. Finally, this process requires highly skilled personnel which makes it costly.

In this paper, we present an approach for efficient management of an ontology-based application based on the usage of the underlying ontology. The focal point of the approach is the continual adaptation of the ontology to the users' needs. As illustrated above, by analysing the usage data with respect to the ontology, more meaningful changes can be discovered. Moreover, since the content and layout (structure) of an ontology-based application are based on the underlying ontology [3], by changing the ontology according to the users' needs, the application itself is tailored to the users' needs.

The basic requirement for such a management system is that it has to be simple, correct and usable for ontology managers[3]. Thus, it must provide capabilities for automatic identification of problems in the ontology based on its usage in the underlying application, and ranking them according to the importance for the users. When such problems arise, a management system must assist the ontology manager in identifying the sources of the problem as well as in analysing and defining solutions for resolving them. Finally, the system should help in determining the ways for applying the proposed solutions.

We have developed such an approach and implemented it in the **OntoManager** tool. It concerns the truthfulness of an ontology with respect to its problem domain - does the ontology represent a piece of reality and the users' requirements correctly? Indeed, it helps to find the "weak places" in the ontology regarding the users' needs,

---

[1] The interest for a topic might be measured by the number of queries for the corresponding topic.

[2] A topic is treated as a concept.

[3] An ontology manager is a person responsible for administrating ontology-based applications and doesn't need to be an experienced ontology engineer.

ensures that generated recommendations for the ontology improvement reflect the users' needs, and promotes the accountability of managers. In this way, the *OntoManager* provides an easy-to-use management system for ontologists, domain experts, and business analysts, since they are able to use it productively, with a minimum of the training. We present an evaluation study, which demonstrates the benefits of this system. As known to the authors, none of the existing ontology management systems offer support for (semi-)automatic ontology improvement in response to the users' needs analysis.

This paper is organised as follows: Section 2 describes an approach for guiding ontology managers through the modification of an ontology with respect to users' needs. In section 3, we elaborate the modules of the *OntoManager* enabling the integration, visualisation and analysis of the users' needs regarding the domain ontology. As a proof of the concept, section 4 contains a short evaluation study of the usability of our system. After a discussion of related work, concluding remarks outline some future work.

2   Usage-Driven Hierarchy Pruning

2.1 Task Description

Our goal is to help an ontology manager in the continual improvement of the ontology. This support can be split into two phases:

(i) to help the ontology manager find the changes that should be performed and
(ii) to help her in performing such changes.

The first phase is focused on discovering some anomalies in the ontology design, whose repairing improves the usability of the ontology. It results in a set of ontology changes. Since a change can be resolved in different ways (e.g. the removal of the concept in the middle of the concept hierarchy can cause the removal of its subconcepts or their reconnection to the parent concept or to the root of the hierarchy), the second phase guides a user how to do that, by setting up the evolution strategies. The changes are realized using ontology evolution functionalities described in [5]. We omit here the description of the second phase.

The main problem we faced in developing an ontology is the creation of a hierarchy of concepts [3], since a hierarchy, depending on the users' needs, can be defined from various points of view and on the different levels of the granularity. It is clear that the initial hierarchy has to be pruned, in order to fulfil the user's needs. Moreover, the users' needs can change over time, and the hierarchy should reflect such a migration. The usage of the hierarchy is the best way to estimate how a hierarchy corresponds to the needs of the users. Consider the example shown in Fig. 1.

Let us assume that in the initial hierarchy (developed by using one of above-mentioned approaches), the concept X has ten subconcepts (c_1, c_2,...,c_{10}), i.e. an ontology manager has found that these ten concepts correspond to the users' needs in the best way. However, the usage of this hierarchy in a longer period of time showed that about 95% of the users are interested in just three subconcepts (i.e. 95=40+32+23) out of these ten. It means that 95% of the users obtain 70% (i.e. 7 of 10 subconcepts) useless information via browsing this hierarchy, since they find seven subconcepts irrelevant. Consequently, this 95% of the users invest more time for performing a task than needed, since irrelevant information can get their attention. Moreover, there are more chances to make an accidental error (e.g. an accidental click on the wrong link), since the probability of selecting irrelevant information is greater.

In order to make this hierarchy more suitable to the users' needs, two ways of "restructuring" the initial hierarchy would be useful:

1. *expansion* – to put down in the hierarchy all seven "irrelevant" subconcepts, while grouping them into a new subconcept g (see in Fig. 1c);
2. *reduction* – to remove all seven "irrelevant" concepts, while redistributing their instances into remaining subconcepts or the parent concept (see in Fig. 1d).

Through the expansion, the needs of the 5% of the users are preserved by the newly introduced concept and the remaining 95% of the users benefit from the more compact structure. By the reduction, the new structure corresponds completely to the needs of 95% of the users. The needs of 5% of the users are implicitly satisfied. Moreover, the usability of the ontology increased, since the instances which were hidden in the „irrelevant" subconcepts are now visible for additional 95% of the users. Consequently, these users might find them useful, although in the initial classification they are a priori considered as irrelevant (i.e. these instances were not considered at all). Note that the Pareto diagram[4] shown in Fig. 1b enables the automatic discovery of the minimal subset of the subconcepts which covers the needs of most of the users.

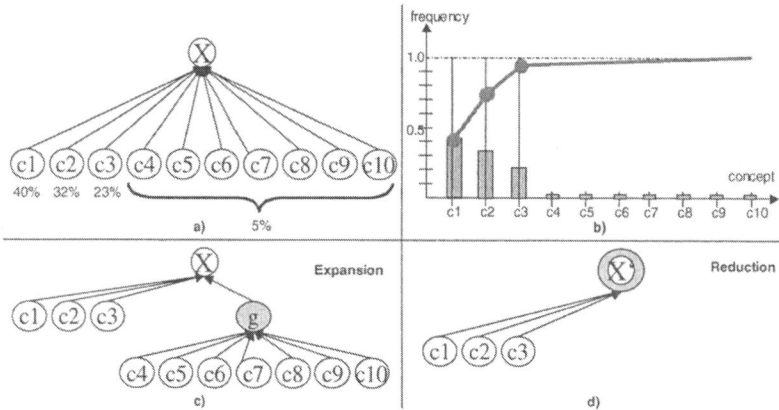

Fig. 1. An example of the non-uniformity in the usage of the children. (a) the problem; (b) the Pareto diagram of the problem; (c) the resulting ontology after its extension and (d) the resulting ontology after its reduction.

The problem of post-pruning a hierarchy in order to increase its usability is explored in the research related to modelling the user interface. The past work [11] showed the importance of a balanced hierarchy for the efficient search through hierarchies of menus. Indeed, even though the generally accepted guidelines for the menu design favour breadth over depth [12], the problem with the breadth hierarchy in large-scale systems is that the number of items at each level may be overwhelming.

---

[4] According to the Pareto principle, by analysing 20% of most frequently used data 80% problems in the ontology can be eliminated.

Hence, a depth hierarchy that limits the number of items at each level may be more effective. This is the so-called breadth/depth trade-off [13].

Moreover, organising unstructured business data in useful hierarchies has recently got more attention in the industry. Although there are some methods for an automatic hierarchy generation, such a hierarchy has to be manually pruned, in order to ensure the usability of the hierarchy. The main criterion is the "coherence" of the hierarchy [14] (some kind of the uniform distribution of documents in all parts of the hierarchy), which ensures that the hierarchy is closely tailored to the needs of the intended user.

In the rest of this section, we describe how to fine-tune a hierarchy according to the users' needs.

2.2 Tailoring a Hierarchy to the Needs of Its Users

Since in this subsection we consider the concept hierarchy as a graph, we use the terms 'node' and 'link' as synonyms for a concept and a *direct hierarchy*[5] relation, respectively. Moreover, the *parent* and the *child* of a *direct hierarchy* relation correspond to the source and the destination node of a link in a graph.

From the structural point of view, there are four basic anomalies that can be accounted in a hierarchy: (i) a node is missing, (ii) a node is not necessary, (iii) a link is missing, (iv) a link is not necessary. All other anomalies (e.g. wrong position of a node in a hierarchy) can be described as a composition of four basic ones. These anomalies correspond to the four basic changes, which an ontology manager can perform on a hierarchy: (1) adding a concept, (2) deleting an existing concept, (3) adding a direct hierarchy relation and (4) deleting a direct hierarchy relation.

From a user's point of view, two problems can arise while using a hierarchy:
- *Problem1*: too many outgoing links from a node;
- *Problem2*: too few outgoing links from a node.

Regarding the first problem, the user has to check/consider too many irrelevant links for her information needs, in order to find the most relevant link she should follow. For the explanation about possibilities to resolve this problem see Fig. 1. Regarding the second problem, the user misses some relevant links required to fulfil her information need. Consequently, some new links, which correspond to the users' need, have to be added. Another solution for resolving that problem can be the addition of some new nodes and their linkage to the given node.

However, the discovery of places in the hierarchy, which correspond to the *Problem1* or the *Problem2*, is difficult, since we do not expect the explicit feedback from users about the usefulness/relevance of some links. On the other hand, it is difficult to define automatically an "optimal" number of outgoing links for a node, since from the user's point of view it is possible that two nodes in a hierarchy have quite different "optimal" number of outgoing links (e.g. 3 vs. 10). A criterion to define this optimality is the usage of these links. Our approach tries to discover such a links' usefulness by analysing the users' behaviours on these links, i.e. by using the so-called users' implicit relevance feedback [15]. Additionally, the usage of a link has to be considered in the context of the neighbouring links (i.e. the links which have a

---

[5] A set of the direct hierarchy relations is obtained by excluding the transitive closure from a concept hierarchy.

common node with the given link). Indeed, the consideration of a link in isolation (from the neighbouring links) can lead to the discovery of "wrong" changes. For example, based on the information that a link is visited 1000 times (which is more than the average visiting), one can imply the need to split the information conveyed through this link, i.e. to split the **destination** node of that link into several nodes. However, in case all of its sibling-links (links which have the same source node) are uniformly visited, then the "right" change would be to split the **source** node by introducing an additional layer of nodes between it and all the existing destination nodes. The interpretation is that the source node models too many users' needs and has to be refined through more levels of granularity. The process of analysing the usage of a link in the context of its neighbouring' links is called *the discovery of problems*.

Another difficulty is the mapping of the resolutions of the *Problem1* and the *Problem2* into the set of elementary changes (1)-(4), since a problem in a hierarchy can be resolved in different ways. This process is called *the generation of changes*. It depends on the specificity of the discovered problem and the intention of the ontology manager. She can always choose between the possibilities to reduce or to expand the hierarchy, based on her need, as described in the subsection 2.1 (see Fig. 1).

To cope with these two issues (*the discovery of problems* and *the generation of changes*), we use two basic measures obtained from the Semantic Log [875]:

– *Usage(p, c)* - the number of browsing the link between nodes (concepts) p and c;
– *Querying(n)* - the number of querying for the node n.

Moreover, the total[6] usage of the node c through the browsing of the concept hierarchy can be defined as:

$$- TotalUsage(c) = \sum_{\forall x \ dh(x,c) \in DH} Usage(x,c), \text{ where } DH \text{ is a set of direct hierarchy relations.}$$

It is the sum of the usage of a node through all incoming links into this node. Note that in order to avoid the division with 0, we set up the default values for *Usage(p,c)* and *Querying(n)* to 1.

Additionally, we define four measures for estimating the uniformity (balance) of the usage of a link regarding the link's neighbourhood:

$$- \ SiblingUniformity(p,c) = \frac{Usage(p,c)}{\frac{1}{\left|\{x \mid dh(p,x) \in DH\}\right|} \sum_{\forall ci \ dh(p,ci) \in DH} Usage(p,ci)},$$

The ratio between the usage of a link and the average usage of all links which have the common source node with that link (the so called sibling links);

$$- \ ChildrenUniformity(p) = \frac{\sum_{\forall ci \ dh(p,ci) \in DH} Usage(p,ci)}{TotalUsage(p)}$$

The ratio between the sum of the usage of all the links whose source node is the given node and the total usage of that node;

$$- \ ParentUniformity(p,c) = \frac{Usage(p,c)}{\frac{1}{\left|\{x \mid dh(x,c) \in DH\}\right|} \sum_{\forall pi \ dh(pi,c) \in DH} Usage(pi,c)}$$

---

[6] Note that multiple inheritance is allowed. Consequently, a concept can have more than one *parent*.

The ratio between the usage of a link and the average usage of all links which have the common destination node with that link;

$$- UpDown(\,p,c\,) = \frac{Usage(\,p,c\,)}{Usage(\,c,p\,)}$$

The ratio between the usage of a link in two opposite directions, i.e. in browsing down and browsing up through a hierarchy.

The extreme values of these measures indicate the existence of a problem in the hierarchy, i.e. they are used for *the discovery of problems*. The interpretation of these extremes with respects to the users' needs and according to the intention of an ontology manager (to expand or to reduce the hierarchy) leads to *the generation of changes*. Table 1 shows the summary of typical problems in using a hierarchy, discovered and resolved by our approach. The threshold values for all parameters are set either automatically (i.e. statistically) or manually by the ontology manager.

Table 1. The interpretation of the extreme values of the proposed measures

1. SiblingUniformity (SU)		
Discovery of problems		
Problem[7]	Value	Interpretation
Problem1	below the threshold	If the SU(p,x) is low then the link p-x might be irrelevant.
Generation of changes		
Example	Reduction	Extension
Users who browse down the node p, use the link p–x very rarely.	The link p–x is deleted.	The set of destination nodes with low SU, c_{i+1}, ...,x, is grouped in newly added node g.
2. SiblingUniformity (SU)		
Discovery of problems		
Problem	Value	Interpretation
Problem2	above the threshold	If the SU(p,x) is huge then the link p-x might cover many different users' needs.
Generation of changes		
Example	Reduction	Extension
Users who browse down the node p, use the link p–x very often.	Since this link conveys much relevant information, it has to be kept.	The destination node x is split in several new nodes. The special case is when it is split into so many nodes as it has child-nodes. In that case the node is **replaced** with its child-nodes.

---

[7] This column correspond to the type problems in using a hierarchy from the user's point of view (i.e. the *Problem1* and the *Problem2*).

3. ChildrenUniformity (CU)

Discovery of problems

Problem	Value	Interpretation
Problem1	below the threshold	If the CU(x) is low then all outgoing links from the node x might be irrelevant.

Generation of changes

Example	Reduction	Extension
Users who "visit" the node x, browse down the node x very rarely.	All outgoing links from x are deleted.	The new layer of nodes is introduced by grouping the child-nodes according to a criterion defined by ontology manager.

4. ChildrenUniformity (CU)

Discovery of problems

Problem	Value	Interpretation
Problem2	below the threshold	If the CU(x) is low then it seems that some relevant outgoing links from x are missing.

Generation of changes

Example	Reduction	Extension
A lot of users stop the browsing in the node x. Probably they miss some relevant links to browse further.	-	A new node n is introduced and connected to the node x.

5. ParentUniformity (PU)

Discovery of problems

Problem	Value	Interpretation
Problem1	below the threshold	If the PU(x,c) is low then the link x-c might be irrelevant.

Generation of changes

Example	Reduction	Extension
The link x-c is used very rarely	The link x-c is deleted.	The set of source nodes with low PU, p_{i+1}, ..., x, is grouped in a newly added node g.

6. ParentUniformity (PU)

Discovery of problems

Problem	Value	Interpretation
Problem2	above the threshold	If the PU(x, c) is huge then the link x-c might cover many different users' needs.

Generation of changes

Example	Reduction	Extension
The link x-p is used very often.	Since this link conveys much relevant information, it has to be kept.	The source node is split in several new nodes.

7. UpDown (UD)		
Discovery of problems		
Problem	Value	Interpretation
Problem1	above the threshold	If the UD(p, x) is huge then the node x might be inappropriate, since almost all visits to x finish by browsing back to node p.
Generation of changes		
Example	Reduction	Extension
Almost every user who browsed down the link p-x, browsed afterwards back (up) that link.	The link p-x is deleted.	It is possible that the node x is proper, but its child-nodes are inappropriate – that is the reason to browse back. It is up to ontology manager to perform such an analysis.
8. Querying(Q)		
Discovery of problems		
Problem	Value	Interpretation
Problem1	above the threshold	If the Q(x) is huge then the node x might be very relevant as a starting point in browsing
Generation of changes		
Example	Reduction	Extension
A lot of users made the query about the content of the node x.	-	A link between the root of the hierarchy and the node x is added.

Due to the lack of space, we here give the interpretation of the first case shown in Table 1 only, i.e. *SiblingUniformity*. The reduction is done by deleting a link that is very rarely browsed, since we assume that the frequency of usage is related to the relevance of that link for the users. By deleting such a link, we enable the focus of the users on relevant links only. Note that the removal of a link does not necessary cause the removal of the destination node. It is up to the ontology evolution system [16] to decide about it with respect to the consistency of the ontology. On the other hand, if the ontology manager wants to make this hierarchy more suitable for users by **keeping** the rarely browsed links, then she has to expand the hierarchy by introducing a new node that groups all less relevant links. In that way, all links are kept, but the users have the focus on the most important ones only. However, this expansion (as all others) requires more efforts of ontology managers, since they have to define the meaning of the new node and to select nodes to be grouped. Similar interpretations can be done for all other cases. Note that $0 < ChildrenUniformity(p) \leq 1$, where the value 1 corresponds to the "ideal" browsing down a node (i.e. all arrivals in a node are continued down the hierarchy). Therefore, the max extreme of the *ChildrenUniformity* is not considered for the problem discovery.

The process of discovering changes is performed in two ways: either the system recommends the "problematic" parts of the hierarchy automatically, or the ontology manager selects a part of the ontology, which she wants to update, and interprets the presented parameters on her own. In the automatic discovery, the threshold value can be tuned according to the needs of the ontology manager.

Table 2 shows the dependencies between elementary ontology changes related to a hierarchy with the extreme values of the proposed measures, used for the discovery of changes. Note that grouping or the splitting of a node or a link represents a composite ontology change that is realized as a sequence of elementary ontology changes, i.e. (1)-(4). We show only the requested changes. However, the ontology evolution system can induce additional changes [5], in order to keep the consistency of the ontology.

Table 2. Dependency between the discovery of problems (columns) and the generation of changes (rows)

	min SU		max SU		min CU		min PU		max PU		max UD		max Q	
	red.	exp.	red.	exp.	red.	exp.	red.	exp.	red.	exp.	red.	exp.	red.	exp.
add concept			x		x		x		x		x			
delete concept											x			
add dh relation			x		x		x		x				x	
delete dh relation	x				x		x				x			

3 OntoManager

The *OntoManager* has been designed to provide the methods and tools that support the ontology managers in managing and optimising the ontology according to the users' needs. This system incorporates mechanisms that assess how the ontology (and by extension the application) is performing based on different criteria, and then enable to take action to optimise it.

One of the key tasks is to check how the ontology fulfils the perceived needs of the users. In that way, we obtain an in-depth view of the users' perspective on the ontology and the ontology-based application, since on the top of this ontology the application is going to be conducted. The technique that can be used to evaluate/estimate the users' needs depends on the information source. By tracking users' interactions with the application in a log file, it is possible to collect useful information that can be used to assess what the main interests of the users are. In this way, we avoid asking the users explicitly, since they tend to be reluctant to provide the feedback via filling questionnaires or forms.

The *OntoManager* has two inputs: the domain ontology that is the backbone of the whole system and the Semantic Log defined in [18]. The output of the system is a set of the required changes. Conceptually, the *OntoManager* consists of three modules:

- The Data Integration Module that aggregates, transforms and correlates the usage data;
- The Visualisation Module that makes the integrated usage data more useful for human beings by presenting the data in a comprehensible visual form;
- The Analysis Module that provides guidance for adapting the ontology with respect to the users' needs.

Subsequently, we describe these three modules in detail.

3.1 Data Integration Module

The *Data Integration Module* has three main functionalities:
- to *collect* data from different, possibly distributed logs in case an ontology-based application is deployed on several web servers;
- to *pre-process* data by transforming disparate data into meaningful information. This phase also covers the cleaning and validation of the data for achieving the required quality;
- to *organise* them in a way that enables a fast and efficient access to the data.

In order to integrate data from various servers, we replicate the *Semantic Logs* of all these servers into a "common" log, so called *OntoLog*. Since all logs are based on the *Log Ontology* [18] and they reference the same domain ontology, the semantic heterogeneity problem doesn't occur. Another possibility for the integration was to integrate the logs virtually (on-the-fly) by accessing them in the time of processing. Such a solution would enable the immediate visibility (actuality) of log data in the *OntoManager*, but it requires extensive distribute processing and, thus, it is slow and expensive. Since the analyses we want to perform are statistic-based, the actuality of the data is not so critical. However, the update of the *OntoLog* is performed periodically (currently once per week).

Moreover, during this phase, the data is also pre-processed, in order to make it better suited for the further analysis. We perform two types of data pre-processing:
- **Data abstraction** - Since the interaction of the users with the portal is mainly done on the level of ontology instances, the Semantic Logs (and consequently the *OntoLog*) mainly contain the information about the usage of ontology instances. For example, if a user has seen more details about the project "*SemIPort*", the log file recorded this information explicitly. However, the goal of our system is to improve the ontology and not its knowledge base. Thus, all log entries regarding ontology instances have to be transformed into corresponding ontology concepts. Regarding the previous example, all the appearances of the instance "*SemIPort*" in the *OntoLog* have to be replaced with the concept "*Project*";
- **Extracting links** - the most important information for the analyses we want to perform is the frequency of browsing relations between two concepts (see subsection 2.2). Since the *OntoLog* does not contain explicit information about the source and target of a browsing event, we extract it in this pre-processing phase by analysing successive events.

Finally, the integrated and pre-processed data has to be analysed, in order to enable the ontology manager to manage the ontology efficiently. However, with increasing frequency of the application usage, the log might contain a large quantity of data. Thus, it has to be reengineered, to enable ontology managers to perform sophisticated data analysis through a fast access to a variety of possible views of the underlying information. Further, in order to get a fast response, it would be useful to pre-calculate at least some of the information that will be needed for analysis. Since OLAP techniques [8] typically handle huge volumes of data that is interrelated in complex ways, and enable the pre-calculation of everything that may be needed, we decided to transfer the log into *OLAP cubes*. In this way, the *OntoLog* only contains the pre-processed information about the users' interactions, which are needed to improve the ontology, whereas the *OLAP cubes* enable the analysis of this information at an aggregate level.

Indeed, an OLAP cube as a part of the ***OntoManager*** performs various in-advance analyses, in order to speed up the decision making process. The most important data (see subsection 2.2) is the number of browsing[8] the *direct hierarchy relation* between two concepts c1 and c2 (denoted as Usage(c1,c2)) and the number of querying[9] for a concept c (denoted as Querying(c)). By processing the *OntoLog,* these values increase.

Due to the lack of space, we omit here the detailed description of the OLAP cube. In the current implementation, the OLAP cube is queried via a web service. An advantage of using web service is that it enables having a thin client that can access the OLAP data in a remote server without threatening the security of the server.

3.2   The Visualisation Module

Since "information visualisation is the use of computer-supported, interactive, visual representation of abstract data to amplify cognition" [9], the graphical representations of the ontology-usage data can help the ontology manager adapt an ontology with respect to the users' needs.

In order to achieve that, the *Visualization Module* combines graphically (transparently and intuitively) the integrated ontology usage data with the ontology itself. Besides, it enables the representation of different aspects of the underlying information. Finally, it allows for easy and flexible presentations of the same information in different ways. By showing different aspects of the underlying information and in different ways (from one or more perspectives), the visualisation mechanisms offer support for analysis tasks.

The presentation of the results of analysis in the form of tables, histograms, charts or other easily comprehensive ways can increase the understanding of the usability of the ontology entities. On the other way, the requirements put on visualisation can considerably vary with different analytical tasks. Thus, the *Visualisation Module* presents information in several different ways:

- **Graph-based representation** of the ontology (see the left part of the screenshot shown in Fig. 2), where nodes correspond to the concepts in the ontology, and links correspond to the direct hierarchy. It enables:
  - easy manipulation with large ontologies. A lot of visual features are implemented in the current version: focus on the part of the ontology (zoom, anti-zoom), rotating the nodes and lines around a selected node, adapting the number of hierarchical levels in the ontology presented on the screen (locality), tracking the path followed to reach the current selected node, the existence of back and forward button to repeat actions;
  - efficient inspection of various "problems" which can be found in an ontology, i.e. not-used concept, very sought concepts. In this version, a suitable colouring is performed as an indicator of the frequency of using an ontology concept and its relations;

---

[8] Browsing is treated as a click on the hyperlink between two concepts that are in a direct hierarchy relation.
[9] The number of queries related to a concept.

- **Table-based presentation** of the results (see the right part of the screenshot represented in Fig. 2). It enables a comprehensible two-dimensional view on the data, and supports very fast sorting of data;
- **Bar-based presentation** (e.g. histogram, Pareto diagram, etc.) that shows several measures at the same time by means of a vertical bar. For example, Pareto diagram (see Fig. 1b) enables a very easy detection of the most important concepts, e.g. concepts that take the most of the users' attention.

The application of these visual metaphors supports discovering patterns, trends in the ontology usage data, and, consequently, leads to the new insights into the ontology. Indeed, this module digests the result of the data integration modules and produces the summary reports easily readable by the ontology managers. The added value of our visualisation lies in its **expressivity**. For example, it is very easy to detect unused concepts. In addition, the correlation between two concepts is immediately apparent. The Pareto diagram can show which concepts take the useful information and which can be treated as useless.

Figure 2 illustrates some of the above-mentioned functionalities of the *OntoManager*. The content is taken from our evaluation study. This screenshot presents the inspection of the concept "*Project*" (cf. 1) and its subconcepts "*EUProject*", "*RegionalProject*" and "*NationalProject*". The upper left part shows the hyperlinked path of the concept (i.e. tracking). On the left panel, a graphical representation of the ontology is presented, enabling an ontology manager to traverse/navigate the ontology by clicking on the nodes. When the information about the usage of the selected concept is required, a query is submitted to the OLAP via a right-click button menu. The information about the number of visitors, visits and times that the sub-concepts have been accessed is presented in the right-most panels. The ontology manager can select between querying and navigation data. The label colour of the nodes will then change according to some user-defined rules (darker colour indicates more visits in Fig. 2). The coupling between the structure of the ontology and the aggregated data enables visual highlighting when an entity has not been accessed at all (e.g. "*RegionalProject*" (cf. 2 in Fig. 2)).

3.3 The Analysis Module

Whereas the Visualisation Module provides the ontology managers with convenient representations of underlying data, the *Analysis Module* suggests them how to improve the ontology. The basic assumption of our system is that evolution of an ontology should be guided by the real interest of the users. Thus, the ontology should be re-engineered considering this feedback, e.g. adding more granularity to most sought-after concepts by splitting them or grouping less accessed concepts. The theoretical background of this module, i.e. how a hierarchy can be tailored to the users' needs, is described in section 2.2.

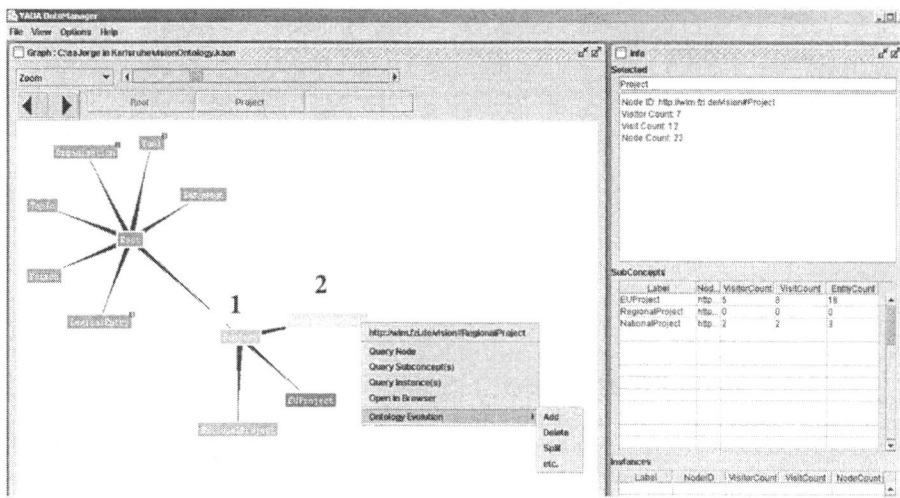

Fig. 2. The Visualisation Module in the OntoManager

4 Evaluation

As a test bed for the presented research, we use the VISION Portal (www.km-vision.org), a semantics-driven portal that allows browsing and querying of the state-of-the-art information (persons, projects, software, etc.) related to the knowledge management. It is developed in the scope of the EU-funded VISION project, which should provide a strategic roadmap towards the next-generation organisational knowledge management. The backbone of the system is the VISION ontology, which consists of more than 300 concepts, 50 relations and about 900 information resources (the web page of concrete persons, projects, etc.). Each of the information resources is related to a concrete instance in the ontology (e.g. to the project "*SemIPort*"). All users' interactions with the VISION Portal in the last five months are tracked into its Semantic Log.

In the VISION ontology there are several *direct hierarchies* (the hierarchy of persons, projects and organisations), as well as a non-taxonomic hierarchy "*hasTopic*", expressing the hierarchy of research areas. Since this "*hasTopic*" hierarchy is huge (the number of the concepts: 223, the average depth: 5, the average number of direct hierarchy of a concept: 3) and very often browsed, it is very suitable for the evaluation of our approach.

We made some changes in the "*hasTopic*" hierarchy, which corrupt the uniformity of its usage, expecting from users to reverse them by using the **OntoManager**. Indeed, we induced 35 changes in the hierarchy, as follows:

C1. the addition of five new concepts and their linkage into the hierarchy with a low usage;

C2. the addition of five "*hasTopic*" relations, with a low usage, between existing concepts;

C3. the extension of three leaf concepts (i.e. concepts without children) with three new subconcepts for each leaf concept;

Table 3. The result of the evaluation

Corruption	Useful parameter for the change discovery	Correctness (total for all four users)	Time (average time for a recovery)
C1	min *SiblingUniformity*	15/20	120 sec
C2	min *ParentUniformity*	18/20	90 sec
C3	min *ChildrenUniformity*	11/12	50 sec
C4	max *SiblingUniformity*	8/12	180 sec
C5	min *ChildrenUniformity*	6/20	420 sec

C4.   the merging of two children into a concept at three different positions in the concept hierarchy;

C5.   the deletion of five "*hasTopic*" relations.

Four subjects who had small experience in ontology editing by using traditional ontology editors participated in the experiment. The task was to improve the "corrupted" ontology by using the *OntoManager*, i.e. to refine the given ontology by balancing its usage.

We measured the correctness of the final hierarchy and the time spent in the modification process. The "gold standard" was the initial ontology, i.e. they should discover all corruptions we made in the ontology. Since there are no available tools for the usage-based ontology management, we evaluate only the usability of the *OntoManager*, without comparing it to other methods. Moreover, the manual discovery and resolving of the implied changes was impossible, due to a huge number of entries in the Semantic Log of the VISION Portal and the complexity of the "*hasTopic*" hierarchy. The results of the evaluation are presented in the Table 3. Note that the correctness is defined as the ratio between the number of discovered changes and the number of corruptions in the initial hierarchy.

Discussion:

1. The discovery of irrelevant concepts is well supported in our approach. However, the discovery depends on the "uniformity" of the usage of the neighbourhood concepts. For example, in the case C1 there is a corruption, which was not found by any user. That corruption corresponds to the case that a low-used concept was introduced in the low-used neighbourhood and, therefore, could not be discovered as a problem.

2. Our approach enables a very efficient discovery of the irrelevant links, since it compares the usage of a link with three types of neighbours: parents, child-nodes and siblings. It seems to be sufficient information for the discovery of irrelevances.

3. The irrelevant sub-hierarchies can be found easily by considering the CU parameter.

4. The discovery of links, which can be split into several links, is well supported in our approach. If these links convey much more information than sibling-nodes, then they can be recognised in the *OntoManager* very easily. However, similar to the case C1, for C4 there is a corruption, which was not found by any user, since it was "hidden" in the huge usage of the sibling links.

5. The discovery of missing links/concepts is the most challenging problem. As we explained in Fig. 1, it requires much more effort of an ontology manager to prove possible hypotheses about adding a new concept. However, the suggestions made by the *OntoManager*, based on the parameter *ChildrenUniformity*, seem to be useful.

Since there is no gold standard for the time, we do not discuss these values in detail. The duration of tasks corresponds to the level of the difficulty of the corresponding task. Moreover, all participants denoted them as the huge improvement with respect to the manual change discovery.

5 Related Work

In [16] we made a comprehensive evaluation of most frequently used tools[10] for editing ontologies, Protege, OilEd and OntoEdit, by comparing them regarding several criteria, including their support for the continual ontology improvement. None of them provides support neither for the integration of the usage data into the ontology evolution process nor for the discovery of changes in an ontology, which are crucial facilities of the *OntoManager*. Therefore, these capabilities of the *OntoManager* are novel in comparison to the existing ontology editors.

Moreover, the *OntoManager* is a tool for a comprehensive management of the ontology-based applications, which incorporates the collection, the integration and the analysis of the data needed for the management. In that way, the *OntoManager* is a unique tool, since, as known to the authors, such a management tool for ontology-based applications does not exist. However, there are management systems for other types of the applications, which can be related to our work. For example, an approach for managing changes in a knowledge management (KM) system is given in [17]. The authors consider two types of changes: (i) functional changes that are about new KM-systems in the organization, new versions of a KM-system and new features in one KM-system and (ii) structural changes that deal with new business models, new subsidiaries and new competencies in the organisation. The results of that study show that managing the evolution of KM-systems on an ad hoc basis can lead to unnecessary complexity and KM-systems failures. Both types of changes can be treated as the explicit changes, which can be very efficiently resolved in our system. However, contrary to the *OntoManager*, this approach does not consider implicit changes, which can be derived from the usage of the system.

Regarding the creation of a hierarchy, there are three approaches: top-down, bottom-up and middle-out, which start the creation of a hierarchy from the top, bottom, or middle of the hierarchy, respectively [10]. These approaches have different strengths and weaknesses. The top-down approach is better at producing crisp top-level distinctions, but it can miss important low-level topics. Conversely, the bottom-up approach is better at defining all the significant low-level topics, but it can produce obscure high-level topics. The middle-out approach enables the development of the hierarchy in both directions (i.e. top-down and bottom-up). The problem is how to find the right level of the granularity. Our approach supports the middle-out approach by determining the granularity of the hierarchy based on its usage.

Regarding the proposed measures (SU, CU, PU, etc.) this work can be seen as an extension of our previous work [18], where we consider only the querying activities. We defined several measures based on the frequency of the querying for the ontology concepts. These measures took into account the usage of each ontology concept in

---

[10] http://protege.stanford.edu/;
http://oiled.man.ac.uk/; http://www.ontoprise.de/com/co_produ_tool3.htm

isolation, i.e. independently of the usage of other ontology concepts. The information about the ontology structure (e.g. whether a concept is a leaf in a concept hierarchy or has subconcepts) is captured very roughly through the *clarity factor* [18]. Here, we take into account the browsing activities as well, which are predominant activities in a portal. Since the browsing is related to a concept hierarchy, the proposed measures consider the concept in the context that is defined through its neighbourhood (i.e. its parents, children and siblings). Moreover, in this work we integrated these measures into the management system based on the MAPE model [4].

6 Conclusion

The possibility to cope with the implicit changes discovered from the users' behaviour seems to be the most important characteristic of an application, which aspires to be useful. Indeed, it enables the continual adaptation of an application to the changes in the users' needs, without demanding the users to provide an explicit feedback about the usability of the application. The most common attribute for discovering changes is the usage of some structures (buttons, options in the menu, etc.), whose analysis enables their fine-tuning to the users' needs.

In an ontology-based application, the domain ontology is used as a conceptual backbone for structuring the domain information provided in the application. Consequently, the data about the usage of the application can be analysed using the ontology as the background knowledge, which alleviates the process of discovering useful changes in the application. The discovered changes lead to the improvement of the ontology, but in the end effect, since the content and layout (structure) of an ontology-based application are based on the underlying ontology, by changing the ontology according to the users' needs, the application itself is tailored to the users' needs.

In this paper, we presented an integrated approach for the usage-based management of the ontology-based applications, which covers capturing and structuring the users' activities with the application, their integration and filtering, then the visualisation of the usage data in the context of the underlying ontology and, finally, the automatic discovery of changes and their systematic resolution by ensuring the consistency of the resulting ontology. The special focus of this paper was on the measures to discover some anomalies in modelling the hierarchies of concepts in an ontology, and the methods to tune these hierarchies to the real users' needs. The approach has been implemented in the system called OntoManager, a user-friendly platform that integrates the results from the analysis of the usage data with the tools that guide the process of modifying the ontology. The evaluation study shows the benefits of supporting the ontology management by our approach. Since the hierarchy-based organisation of (business-) data is a very efficient solution for the improvement of the searching for information, and is more and more applied in the e-business environment, our approach seems to be a very useful method for tailoring these manually or semi-automatically produced classifications (like UNSPSC – http://eccma.org/unspsc/) to the real needs of their end users.

Acknowledgement. The research presented in this paper would not have been possible without our colleagues and students at the Institute AIFB and the FZI, University of Karlsruhe. Research for this paper was partially financed by BMBF in the project "SemIPort" (08C5939) and by EU in the IST-2000-28293 project "Ontologging".

References

[1] A. Maedche, B. Motik, L. Stojanovic, R. Studer, R. Volz, *Ontologies for Enterprise Knowledge Management*, IEEE Intelligent System, pp. 26–34, March/April 2003.

[2] I. Witten, E. Frank, *Data Mining: Practical Machine Learning Tools and Techniques with Java Implementations*, Morgan Kaufmann, 1999.

[3] N. Stojanovic, A. Maedche, S. Staab, R. Studer, Y. Sure, *SEAL – A Framework for Developing SEmantic PortALs*, ACM K-CAP 2001, Vancouver, 2001.

[4] J. Kephart, D. Chess, *The Vision of Autonomic Computing*, IEEE Computer, January 2003., pp. 41–50.

[5] L. Stojanovic, A. Maedche, B. Motik, N. Stojanovic, *User-driven Ontology Evolution Management*, Proceedings of the 13th European Conference on Knowledge Engineering and Knowledge Management EKAW'02, Madrid, 2002.

[6] N. Stojanovic, L. Stojanovic, J. Gonzalez, *On Enhancing Searching for Information in an Information Portal by Tracking Users' Activities*, First International Workshop on Mining for Enhanced Web Search (MEWS 2002), held in conjunction with WISE 2002, Singapore, 2002.

[7] N. Stojanovic, *On the Query Refinement in the Ontology-based Searching for Information*, the 15th Conf. On Advanced Information Systems Engineering, CAiSE'03, Austria, 2003.

[8] R. Kimball, R. Merz, *The Data Webhouse Toolkit: Building the Web-Enabled Data Warehouse*, John Wiley & Sons, 2000.

[9] S. Card, J. Mackinlay, B. Shneiderman, *Readings in Information Visualization: Using Vision to Think*, Morgan Kaufmann, 1999.

[10] M. Uschold and M. Gruninger, *Ontologies: Principles, methods, and applications*, Knowledge Engineering Review, vol. 11, no. 2, pp. 93–155, 1996.

[11] R. Botafogo, E. Rivlin, and B. Shneiderman. *Structural Analysis of Hypertexts: Identifying Hierarchies and Useful Metrics*, ACM Transactions on Office Information Systems, 10(2):142–180, 1992.

[12] J. I. Kiger, *The Depth/Breadth Trade-Off in the Design of Menu-Driven User Interfaces*, Int J of ManMachine Studies, 20(2), pp. 201–213., 1984.

[13] K. Norman, *The Psychology of Menu Selection: Designing Cognitive Control of the Human/Computer Interface*. Ablex Publishing Corporation., 1991.

[14] V. Ramana, *The Importance of Hierarchy Building in Managing Unstructured Data*, Special Supplement to KM World, March 2002

[15] G. Salton, C. Buckley, *Improving retrieval performance by relevance feedback,*. Journal of the American Society for Information Science. 41(4): 288–297, 1990.

[16] L. Stojanovic, B. Motik, *Ontology Evolution within Ontology Editors*, EKAW'02/EON Workshop, Madrid, 2002.

[17] C. Hardless, R. Lindgren, U. Nulden, K., Pessi, *The Evolution of knowledge management system need to be managed*, http://www.viktoria.informatik.gu.se/groups/KnowledgeManagement/Documents/kmman.pdf, 2000.

[18] N. Stojanovic, L. Stojanovic, *Usage-oriented Evolution of Ontology-based Knowledge Management Systems*, Proceedings of the 1st Int'l Conf. on Ontologies, Databases and Application of Semantics, Irvine, CA, 2002.

Breaking the Deadlock

Fabio Rinaldi, Kaarel Kaljurand, James Dowdall, and Michael Hess

Institute of Computational Linguistics,
University of Zürich,
Winterthurerstrasse 190, CH-8057 Zürich,
Switzerland
rinaldi@cl.unizh.ch

Abstract. Many of the proposed approaches to the semantic web have a substantial drawback. They are all based on the idea that web pages (or more generally, resources), will contain semantic annotations that would allow remote agents to access them. However the problem of creating these annotations is seldom addressed. Manual creation of the annotations is not a feasible option, except in a few experimental cases.

We propose an approach based on Language Processing techniques that addresses this issue, at least for textual resources (which still constitute the vast majority of the material available on the web). Documents are analized fully automatically and converted into a semantic annotation, which can then be stored together with the original documents. It is this annotation that constitutes the machine understandable resource that remote agents can query. A semi-automatic approach is also considered, in which the system suggests candidate annotations and the user simply has to approve or reject them. Advantages and drawbacks of both approaches are discussed.

1 Introduction

The major purpose of activities in the Semantic Web area is to help users better locate, organize, and process content, irrespective of its physical location and of the way it is presented. Adding machine-understandable semantics to web resources will make them processable by software agents, and ultimately make them more useful to all of us.

There is a wealth of research efforts focusing on the foundations of the semantic web [8], and in particular on the problem of how to represent the semantic information carried by web resources (be they structured databases or unstructured natural language documents, or a combination of both). The XML-based Resources Description Framework [14] is the standardized Semantic Web language, however it is really meant for use by computers, not humans. The same applies to all the extensions that have been proposed, such as RDF Schema [2], which provides a basic type system for use in RDF models, or DAML+OIL [4], which provides a language with well-defined semantics for the specification of Ontologies.

However, there seems to be significantly less interest in the problem of how to help users in the transition from conventional web pages to richly annotated semantic web resources. The major barrier to a wider adoption of the Semantic Web proposals is a classic deadlock problem [11]. On the one hand, significant additional effort is required

R. Meersman et al. (Eds.): CoopIS/DOA/ODBASE 2003, LNCS 2888, pp. 876–888, 2003.

to add semantic annotations to existing (or newly created) web resources, and people are not willing to pay this price until they can see a clear benefit for it. On the other hand, software agents that can reap the benefit of richer annotations will not be useful (and thus there will be fewer incentives to develop them) until a "critical mass" of semantically annotated web resources has been achieved.

Current efforts to tackle this problem seem to focus on the development of user-friendly editors for semantic annotations: details of XML/RDF should be hidden behind GUI authoring tools. Users do not need (and do not want) to get in contact with XML/RDF. However this approach defeats the purpose of the Semantic Web vision: to make the web more effective for users by making it machine-understandable. Instead it makes it less effective for users: by forcing them to add machine-level markup (albeit shielded by an effective GUI). Unless the users can see the real benefit, they will not be motivated to adopt such editors and be prepared to pay the price (in terms of additional effort that might be required).

The benefits of the semantic web should come for free to most of the users: semantic markup should be a by-product of normal computer use. There is a real need to lower the barrier of entry: the vast majority of the users cannot be expected to understand and use formal ontologies. In order to achieve interoperability between software agents, a lot of human understandability has been sacrificed: precise ontologies and formally defined semantics are foreign concepts to the average users.

As a very large proportion of existing web resources are represented by human-readable documentation, we believe that a possible way to break the deadlock mentioned above is to start using available information extraction tools to enrich the documents with automatically generated annotations. In this paper we propose an approach based on natural language processing (NLP) techniques, geared towards the creation of semantic annotations, starting from the available textual documents.

One of the motivations behind the semantic web movement was that computers are not powerful enough to process (and understand) natural language. Therefore machine understandable information should be added to web resources. This is still true: it would be unfeasible to process the enormous amounts of textual resources that are added to the web every day (let alone process all the existing web content). However, it is technically possible (and practically conceivable) to have specialised editors that process (in a transparent fashion) textual resources as the users publish them on the web, and add semantic annotations automatically extracted from the documents. In other words, the idea is to move the problem from the consumer of the information to the producer.

As Natural Language is the information access most users are comfortable with, we will also discuss possible ways to access the information encoded in the semantic annotations. Given a user question phrased in natural language, existing tools can convert it into the same kind of annotations as those stored in the documents. A new type of software agent (or search engine) might then be capable of retrieving those web pages whose annotations match those derived from the user question.

The approach presented in this paper is based on our previous work in the area of Question Answering, resulting in the ExtrAns system [22]. Specific research in the area of Question Answering has been promoted in the last few years in particular by the Question Answering track of the Text REtrieval Conference (TREC-QA) competitions [26].

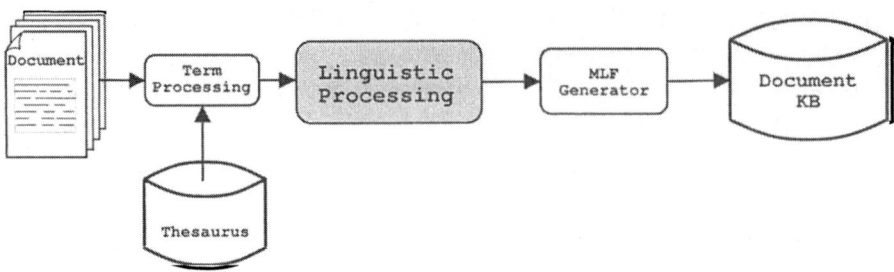

Fig. 1. Offline analysis of documents

ExtrAns uses a combination of robust natural language processing technology and dedicated terminology processing [19,20] to create a Knowledge Base, containing a semantic representation for the propositional content of the documents [23]. Our research group has been working in the area of Question Answering for a few years, targeting different domains, such as the Aircraft Maintenance Manual (AMM) of a large aircraft [22] or a computer manual [15].

In a recently started EU project ("Parmenides") focusing on the integration of Information Extraction and Data Mining techniques, we aim at exploiting the work done in the ExtrAns system by moving from the system-specific semantic representation (Minimal Logical Forms) to a semantic representation based on W3C standards, like RDF. A secondary aim might be to explore possible synergies with the standardization effort of the ISO TC37/SC4 committe in the domain of linguistic annotations [21].

We will first briefly describe our past work resulting in the ExtrAns system (section 2), then describe the annotations that we aim at generating automatically in the Parmenides project (section 3). The following section (4) will describe in detail the approach that we propose in order to automatically create semantic annotation for textual web resources. Finally, in section (5) we explore advantages and disadvantages of the proposed methodologies, and describe our current work and suggestions for future development.

2   ExtrAns

In this section we briefly describe the linguistic processing performed in the ExtrAns systems, extended details can be found in [22]. An initial phase of syntactic analysis, based on the Link Grammar parser [24] is followed by a transformation of the dependency-based syntactic structures generated by the parser into a semantic representation based on Minimal Logical Forms, or MLFs [15]. As the name suggests, the MLF of a sentence does not attempt to encode the full semantics of the sentence. Currently the MLFs encode the semantic dependencies between the open-class words of the sentences (nouns, verbs, adjectives, and adverbs) plus prepositional phrases. The notation used has been designed to incrementally incorporate additional information if needed. Thus, other modules of the NLP system can add new information without having to remove old information.

We have chosen a computationally intensive approach, which allows a deeper linguistic analysis to be performed, at the cost of higher processing time. Such costs are negligible in the case of a single sentence (like a user query) but become rapidly impractical in the case of the analysis of a large document set. The approach we take is to analyse all the documents in an off-line stage (see Fig. 1) and store a representation of their contents (the MLFs) in a Knowledge Base. In an on-line phase, the MLF which results from the analysis of the user query is matched in the KB against the stored representations, locating those MLFs that best answer the query. At this point the system can locate in the original documents the sentences from which the MLFs where generated (see Fig. 2).

One of the most serious problems that we have encountered in processing technical documentation is the syntactic ambiguity generated by multi-word units, in particular technical terms. Any generic parser, unless developed specifically for the domain at hand, will have serious problems dealing with them. On the one hand, it is likely that they contain tokens that do not correspond to any word in the parser's lexicon, on the other, their syntactic structure is highly ambiguous (alternative internal structures, as well as possible undesired combinations with neighbouring tokens). In fact, it is possible to show that, when all the terminology of the domain is available, a much more efficient approach is to pack the multi-word units into single lexical tokens prior to syntactical analysis [5]. In our case, such an approach brings a reduction in the complexity of parsing of almost 50%.

During the process described above, terms are gathered into WordNet style synsets and organized into a taxonomy. During the analysis of documents and queries, if a term belonging to a synset is identified, it is replaced by its synset identifier, which then allows retrieval using any other term in the same synset. This amounts to an implicit 'terminological normalization' for the domain, where the synset identifier can be taken as a reference to the 'concept' that each of the terms in the synset describe [10]. In this way any term contained in a user query is automatically mapped to all its variants.

When an answer cannot be located with the approach described so far, the system is capable of 'relaxing' the query, gradually expanding the set of acceptable answers. A first step consists of including hyponyms and hyperonyms of terms in the query. If the query extended with this ontological information fails to find an exact answer, the system returns the sentence (or set of sentences) whose MLF is semantically closest with the MLF of the question. Semantic closeness is measured here in terms of overlap of logical forms; the use of flat expressions for the MLFs allows for a quick computation of this overlap after unifying the variables of the question with those of the answer candidate. The current algorithm for approximate matching compares pairs of MLF predicates and returns 0 or 1 on the basis of whether the predicates unify or not. An alternative that is worth exploring is the use of ontological information to compute a measure based on the ontological distance between words, i.e. by exploring its shared information content [18].

3   Parmenides Annotations

It is by now widely accepted that some W3C standards (such as XML and RDF) provide a convenient and practical framework for the creation of field-specific markup languages (e.g. MathML, VoiceXML). However XML provides only a common "alphabet" for interchange among tools, the steps that need to be taken before there is any real sharing

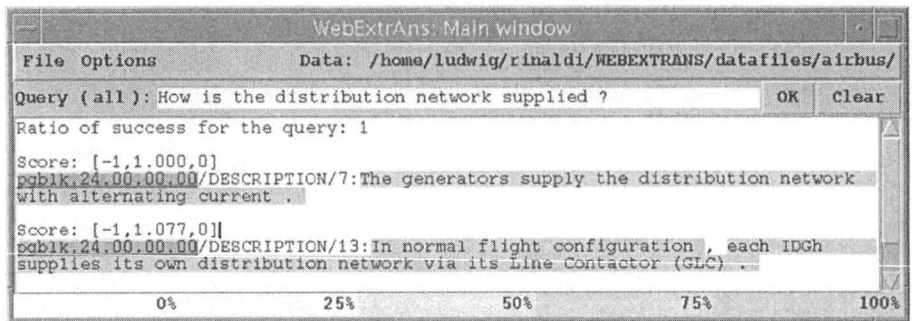

Fig. 2. Example of interaction with the system

are still many (just as many human languages share the same alphabets, that does not mean that they can be mutually intelligible). A minimal approach is to create a common data model.

The existence of a common standard brings many other advantages, like the ability to automatically compare the results of different tools which provide the same functionality, from the very basic (e.g. tokenization) to the most complex (e.g. discourse representation). Some of the NIST-supported competitive evaluations (e.g. MUC) greatly benefited from the existence of scoring tools, which could automatically compare the results of each participant against a gold standard. Another clear benefit of agreed standards is that they will increase interoperability among different tools. It is not enough to have publicly available APIs to ensure that different tools can be integrated. In fact, if their representation languages (their "data vocabulary") are too divergent, no integration will be possible (or at least it will require a considerable mapping effort).

In this section we will briefly describe the XML-based annotation scheme proposed for the Parmenides project (for more details see [21]). In general terms the project is concerned with organisational knowledge management, specifically, by developing an ontology driven systematic approach to integrating the entire process of information gathering, processing and analysis. The annotation scheme is intended to work as the projects' *lingua franca*: all the modules will be required to accept as input and generate as output documents conformant to the (agreed) annotation scheme. The specification will be used to create data-level compatibility among all the tools involved in the project.

Each tool might choose to use or ignore part of the information defined by the markup: some information might not yet be available at a given stage of processing or might not be required by the next module. Facilities will be provided for filtering annotations according to a simple configuration file. This is in fact one of the advantages of using XML: many readily available off-the-shelf tools can be used for parsing and filtering the XML annotations, according to the needs of each module.

Parmenides aims at using consolidated Information Extraction techniques, such as Named Entity Extraction, and therefore this work builds upon well-known approaches, such as the Named Entity annotation scheme from MUC7 [3]. Other sources that have been considered include the GENIA tagset [7], TEI [25] and the GDA tagset [12]. Crucially, attention will also be paid to temporal annotations, with the aim of using extracted temporal information for detection of trends (using Data Mining techniques).

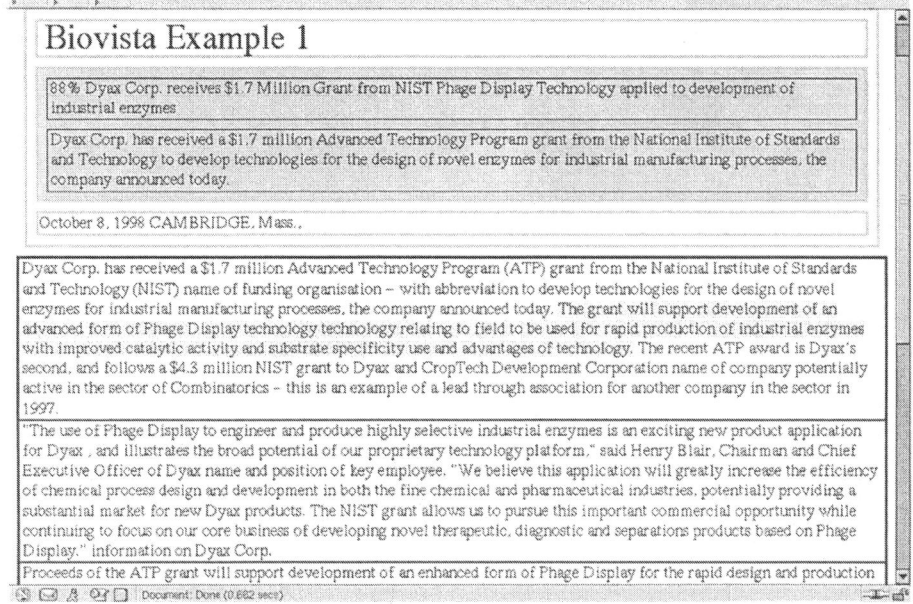

Fig. 3. Visualization of Structural Annotations

Therefore we have investigated all the recently developed approaches to such a problem, and have decided for the adoption of the TERQAS tagset [9,17]. The domain of interests (e.g. Biotechnology) are also expected to be terminology-rich and therefore require proper treatment of terminology.

There are currently three methods of viewing the document which offer differing ways to visualize the annotations. These are all based on transformation of the same XML source document, using XSLT and CSS (and some Javascript for visualization of attributes).

The set of Parmenides annotations is organized into three levels:

- **Structural Annotations**
- **Lexical Annotations**
- **Semantic Annotations**

Structural annotations are used to define the physical structure of the document, it's organization into head and body, into sections, paragraphs and sentences. Lexical annotations identify lexical units that have some relevance for the Parmenides project. Semantic annotations are meant to represent the propositional content of the document (the "meaning"). While structural annotations apply to large text spans, lexical annotations aplly to smaller text spans (sub-sentence) and semantic annotations are not directly associated to a specific text span, however, they are linked to text units by co-referential identifiers. All annotations are required to have an unique ID and thus will be individually addressable, this allows semantic annotations to point to the lexical annotations

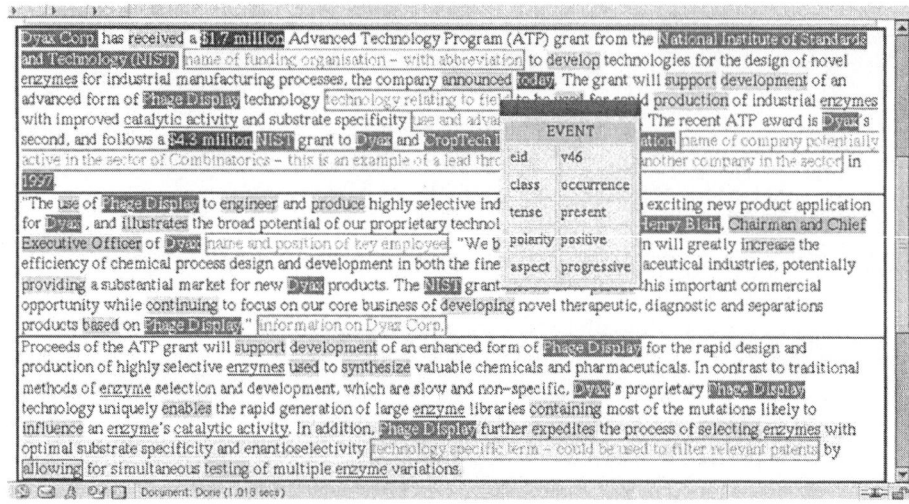

Fig. 4. Visualization of Lexical Annotations and their attributes

to which they correspond. Semantic Annotations themselves are given a unique ID, and therefore can be elements of more complex annotations.

The structure of the documents will be marked using an intuitively appropriate scheme based on the TEI recomendations [25]. Broadly speaking, structural annotations are concerned with the organization of documents into sub-units, such as section, title, paragraphs and sentences. Figure (3) demonstrates the annotation visualization tool displaying the documents structure (using nested boxes).

Lexical Annotations are used to mark any text unit (smaller than a sentence), which can be of interest in Parmenides. They include (but are not limited to): Named Entities in the classical MUC sense, new domain-specific Named Entities, Terms, Temporal Expressions, Events. When visualizating the set of Lexical Tags in a given annotated document, clicking on specific tags displays the attribute values (see Fig. (4)).

The relations that exist between lexical entities are expressed through the semantic annotations. So lexically identified people can be linked to their organisation and job title, if this information is contained in the document (see Fig. (6)).

4   From Documents to Semantic Annotations

In this section we will describe the approach taken in the Parmenides project towards the automatic creation of Semantic Annotation starting from existing documents (see Fig. 5). Documents are assumed to be gathered from a variety of sources, and thus will present different formats. The first step of processing is going to be a conversion from the source-specific document format to the agreed Parmenides format. This conversion is based on a set of source-specific wrappers [13], which transforms the original document into the XML structural annotations previously described.

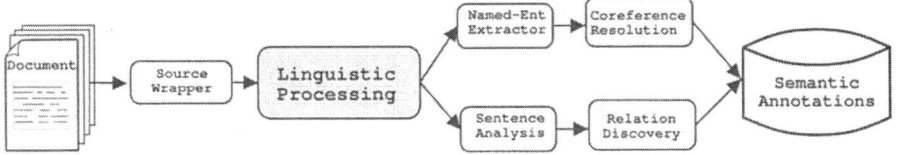

Fig. 5. From Documents to Semantic Annotations

The next step of processing involves addition of basic linguistic information: documents are tokenized, morphologically analyzed and tagged. At this stage sentence boundaries are also detected. This phase completes the creation of the structural annotation, going down to the lowest levels: the sentence and the token. An example of the resulting annotation can be seen below:

```
<tok id="t15" pos="CD" lem="@card@">
100
</tok>
<tok id="t16" pos="NNS" lem="calorie">
calories
</tok>
```

A Named Entity Extractor [1] is then used to detect persons, organizations, locations and numerical amounts. Together with a terminology extraction tool [6] this module creates the base Lexical Annotations.

At this stage however many different references to the same conceptual objects are not resolved. For instance different occurrences of the string "Dyax" will be considered as different lexical entities. The same problem would happen with cases like "Bill Clinton", "Clinton", "The former president of the United States". An anaphora resolution module [16] is thus used to detect coreferent lexical entities. Simple string based match might suffice in some cases of named entities, however in more complex cases complex pronominal resolution algorithms are needed. This results in a set of equivalence classes (which contain coreferent lexical entities). Each class is then mapped into conceptual entities. The result of this process is illustrated in the upper half of Fig. 6.

A more thorough linguistic analysis is now needed to obtain relations among the entities discovered in the previous stage. First, each sentences is parsed using the Link Grammar parser, this is followed by a step of disambiguation and another step of (pronominal) anaphora resolution, as described in detail in section 2. The result of this phase of analysis is a representations of the propositional content of the sentences, as minimal logical forms.

From the minimal logical forms, it is possible to detect relations, on the basis of axioms associated to lexical items, for instance the sentence "A works for B" gives rise to the logical form `work(A,B)`, while the sentence "A is employed by B" gives rise to the logical form `employ(B,A)`. Specific axioms associated to the lexical entries for "work" and "employ" allow to obtain the following mappings:

```
work(A,B)   -> worksFor(A,B)
employ(B,A) -> worksFor(A,B)
```

Now what is left to do is only to transform the results obtained into a standard formalism. The Conceptual Entities obtained after co-reference resolution can be mapped directly into RDF resources, as illustrated below.

```
<Organization rdf:ID="obj1"
      xmlns:rdf="http://www.w3.org/1999/02/22-rdf-syntax-ns#"
      xmlns="http://www.parmenides.org/ontology/organization#"
      xml:base="http://www.parmenides.org/docbase/pardoc12566">
   <name>Dyax Corp</name>
   <activity>Biotechnology</activity>
</Organization>

<Organization rdf:ID="obj2"
      xmlns:rdf="http://www.w3.org/1999/02/22-rdf-syntax-ns#"
      xmlns="http://www.parmenides.org/ontology/organization#"
      xml:base="http://www.parmenides.org/docbase/pardoc12566">
   <name>NIST</name>
   <activity>Government Agency</activity>
</Organization>
```

Relations can then be added to them as attributes, for instance to the RDF resource for "obj5" (Charles R. Wescott), it is possible to add the attribute "worksFor", as illustrate below.

```
<Person rdf:ID="obj5"
     xmlns:rdf="http://www.w3.org/1999/02/22-rdf-syntax-ns#"
     xmlns="http://www.parmenides.org/ontology/person#"
     xml:base="http://www.parmenides.org/docbase/pardoc12566">
  <name>Charles R. Wescott</name>
  <role>Senior Scientist</role>
  <worksFor rdf:resource=
    "http://www.parmenides.org/docbase/pardoc12566#obj1"/>
</Person>
```

The RDF annotations obtained with the process described above can be added automatically to documents being published on the web (in a totally transparent fashion). In this way, they will become immediately accessible to automated software agents, which will be able to make more meaningful access to the document to which they are associated.

5   Current and Future Work

The method described in the previous section can work in an unsupervised manner, and help populate the semantic web with initial RDF resources. However, the NLP tools that are used to create them, might introduce various elements of errors, thus potentially decreasing the value of the resulting annotations. Missing annotations might be considered an acceptable price to pay, however conceptually wrong annotations might introduce dangerous contradictory information. In any case, the annotations, even if not

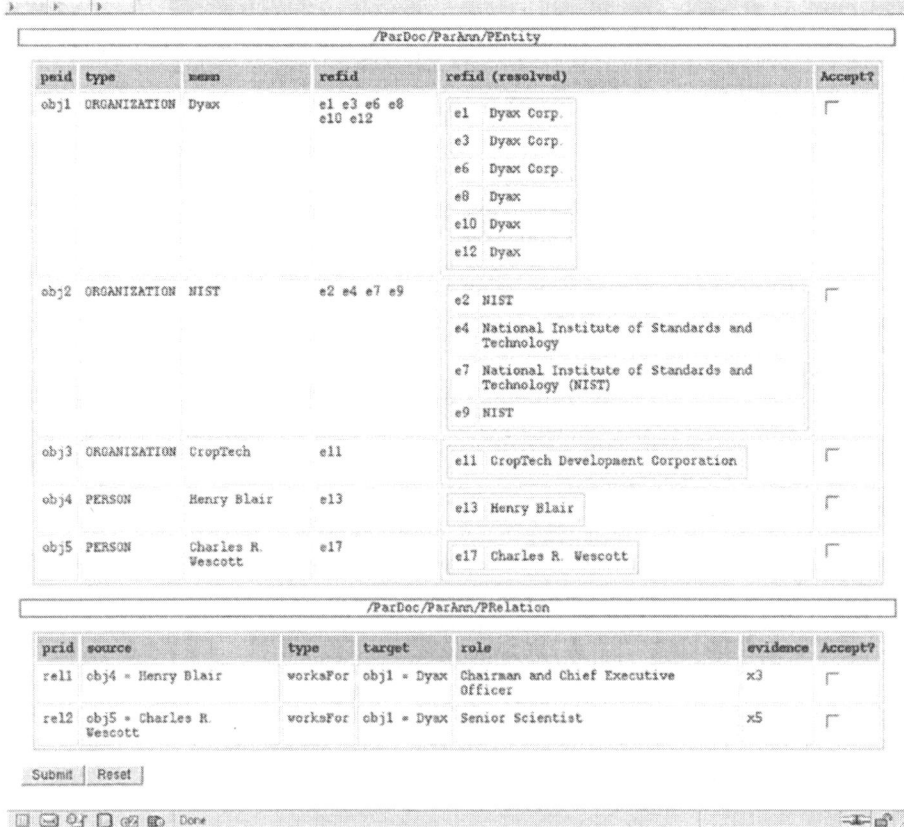

Fig. 6. Visualization of Semantic Annotations

always 100% reliable, might help in creating the "critical mass" that is so desperately needed in order to kick-start practical deployment of Semantic Web formalism and tools.

We are also considering a partially revised approach, in which a user can approve or reject the annotations suggested by the system. We have developed a simple graphical interface (based on XSLT transformations of the original XML documents and annotations), that allow a user to inspect the proposed resources and either accept or reject them. Consider again Fig. 6, what so far we have not explained is that this representation is also a web form, where the user can accept or reject individual objects and relations suggested by the system. The input from the user is processed by a conventional form processing script, which will then add to the published document only the annotations approved by the user. We think this approach would be particularly helpful in avoiding the introduction of contradictory or false knowledge, without posing too great a burden on the user.

A further (planned) development, would allow detailed editing of the resources within the same browser page. Clearly the users can in any case inspect the annotations with a conventional XML editor, but we believe that such an approach would not be feasible for large quantities of documents or for non-experienced users. We would fall back in the loop that we described at the beginning of the paper. A simple user-friendly interface like the one shown in the figure (possibly extended with more powerful editing capabilities) might provide a significant boost in allowing users to create RDF resources in a semi-automated fashion.

An aspect that we have not explored so far (but which is within our future targets) is the generalisation of resources from one document to a collection. All the resources described with the methodology illustrated in this paper are document specific, thus when we talk of *"Dyax"*, we should really say, the company *"Dyax as mentioned in the Parmenides document 12566"*, which might not be the same as the company *"Dyax"* mentioned in another document. So the complete reference to a particular instance of Dyax could be:

http://www.parmenides.org/docbase/pardoc12566#obj1

An aggregator tool should be able to detect the existence of the same company within different documents, and thus create a new, document-independent resource, to which all the individual mentions of "Dyax" in different documents point to, such as:

http://www.parmenides.org/organization#Dyax

Finally, a very natural extension of the work described here is the use of NL also for querying. This is in the spirit of our original ExtrAns system (as described in section 2), which was developed specifically for that purpose. Although this is not a direct target of the Parmenides project, we believe that the very same techniques can be extended to the Semantic Web area. We are actively looking for a chance to explore this very intriguing idea.

6   Conclusion

Despite the still experimental level of the current implementation, we are confident that the ideas described in this paper provide a powerful (and extremely useful) contribution to the future developments of the Semantic Web.

We are certain that we will witness in the near future a deeper convergence of the Semantic Web and the Natural Language Processing communities, towards the common goal of easing the information access bottleneck to web resources.

Acknowledgments. The originalExtrAns project (1996-2000) was funded by the Swiss National Science Foundation (contracts 1214-45448.95 and 1213-53704.98). Later work on the AMM manual (2000-2002) was privately funded by the Gebert Rüf Foundation (contract GRS-043/98). The Parmenides project is funded by the European Commission (contract No. IST-2001-39023) and by the Swiss Federal Office for Education and Science (BBW/ OFES).

The authors wish to thank all the Parmenides partners for helpful comments and insights. Special thanks to Biovista (http://www.biovista.com/) for their contribution to this work in supplying sample data and domain specific knowledge relating to corporate intelligence in biotechnology. Any remaining errors are the sole responsibility of the listed authors.

References

1. William J Black, Fabio Rinaldi, and David Mowatt. FACILE: Description of the NE system used for MUC-7. In *Proceedings of the 7th Message Understanding Conference*, 1998.
2. Dan Brickley and R.V. Guha. RDF vocabulary description language 1.0: RDF Schema. Technical report, W3C working draft, World Wide Web Consortium, April 2002. A reference for RDFS.
3. Nancy Chinchor. MUC-7 Named Entity Task Definition, Version 3.5, 1997. http://www.itl.nist.gov/iaui/894.02/related_projects/muc/proceedings/ne_task.html.
4. DAML+OIL, 2001. http://www.daml.org/.
5. James Dowdall, Michael Hess, Neeme Kahusk, Kaarel Kaljurand, Mare Koit, Fabio Rinaldi, and Kadri Vider. Technical terminology as a critical resource. In *International Conference on Language Resources and Evaluations (LREC-2002), Las Palmas*, pages 1897–1903, 29–31 May 2002. [1]
6. Katerina T Frantzi and Sophia Ananiadou. The C/NC value domain inpedented method for multi-word term extraction. *Journal of Natural Language Processing*, 6(3):145–180, 1999.
7. GENIA. Genia project home page, 2003. http://www-tsujii.is.s.u-tokyo.ac.jp/~genia.
8. Nicola Guarino. Formal ontologies in information systems. In N. Guarino, editor, *Proceedings of FOIS'98*, pages 3–15, Trento, June 1998. IOS Presss, Amsterdam.
9. Bob Ingria and James Pustejovsky. TimeML Specification 1.0 (internal version 3.0.9), July 2002. http://www.cs.brandeis.edu/%7Ejamesp/arda/time/documentation/TimeML-Draft3.0.9.html.
10. Kyo Kageura. *The Dynamics of Terminology, A descriptive theory of term formation and terminological growth*. Terminology and Lexicography, Research and Practice. John Benjamins Publishing, 2002.
11. Boris Katz, Jimmy Lin, and Dennis Quan. Natural language annotations for the semantic web. In *Proceedings of the International Conference on Ontologies, Databases, and Application of Semantics (ODBASE2002)*, October 2002.
12. Hasida Kôiti. The GDA Tag Set. http://www.i-content.org/GDA/tagset.html.
13. Nicholas Kushmerick, Daniel S. Weld, and Robert B. Doorenbos. Wrapper induction for information extraction. In *Intl. Joint Conference on Artificial Intelligence (IJCAI97)*, pages 729–737, 1997.
14. Ora Lassila and Ralph R. Swick. Resource description framework (RDF) model and syntax specification. Technical report, W3C, 1999. http://www.w3.org/TR/1999/REC-rdf-syntax-19990222.
15. Diego Mollá, Rolf Schwitter, Michael Hess, and Rachel Fournier. ExtrAns, an answer extraction system. *T.A.L. special issue on Information Retrieval oriented Natural Language Processing*, pages 495–522, 2000. [1]
16. Diego Mollá, Rolf Schwitter, Fabio Rinaldi, James Dowdall, and Michael Hess. Anaphora resolution in Extrans. In *The 2003 International Symposium on Reference Resolution and Its Applications to Question Answering and Summarization*, Venice, June 2003. [1]
17. James Pustejovsky, Roser Sauri, Andrea Setzer, Robert Gaizauskas, and Bob Ingria. TimeML Annotation Guideline 1.00 (internal version 0.4.0), July 2002. http://www.cs.brandeis.edu/ jamesp/arda/time/documentation/TimeML-Draft3.0.9.html.
18. Philip Resnik. Semantic similarity in a taxonomy: An information-based measure and its application to problems of ambiguity in natural language. *Journal of Artificial Intelligence Research*, 11:95–130, 1998.
19. Fabio Rinaldi, James Dowdall, Michael Hess, Kaarel Kaljurand, and Magnus Karlsson. The Role of Technical Terminology in Question Answering. In *Proceedings of TIA-2003, Terminologie et Intelligence Artificielle*, pages 156–165, Strasbourg, April 2003. [1]

---

[1] Available at http://www.cl.unizh.ch/CLpublications.html

20. Fabio Rinaldi, James Dowdall, Michael Hess, Kaarel Kaljurand, Mare Koit, Kadri Vider, and Neeme Kahusk. Terminology as Knowledge in Answer Extraction. In *Proceedings of the 6th International Conference on Terminology and Knowledge Engineering (TKE02)*, pages 107–113, Nancy, 28–30 August 2002. [1]

21. Fabio Rinaldi, James Dowdall, Michael Hess, Kaarel Kaljurand, Andreas Persidis, Babis Theodoulidis, Bill Black, John McNaught, Haralampos Karanikas, Argyris Vasilakopoulos, Kelly Zervanou, Luc Bernard, Gian Piero Zarri, Hilbert Bruins Slot, Chris van der Touw, Margaret Daniel-King, Nancy Underwood, Agnes Lisowska, Lonneke van der Plas, Veronique Sauron, Myra Spiliopoulou, Marko Brunzel, Jeremy Ellman, Giorgos Orphanos, Thomas Mavroudakis, and Spiros Taraviras. Parmenides: an opportunity for ISO TC37 SC4? In *The ACL-2003 workshop on Linguistic Annotation, July 2003, Sapporo, Japan.*, 2003. [1]

22. Fabio Rinaldi, James Dowdall, Michael Hess, Diego Mollá, and Rolf Schwitter. Towards Answer Extraction: an application to Technical Domains. In *ECAI2002, European Conference on Artificial Intelligence, Lyon*, pages 460–464, 21–26 July 2002. [1]

23. Fabio Rinaldi, James Dowdall, Michael Hess, Diego Mollá, Rolf Schwitter, and Kaarel Kaljurand. Knowledge-Based Question Answering. In *Proceedings of KES-2003, Knowledge-Based Intelligent Information and Engineering Systems*, Oxford, September 2003. Accepted for publication.[1]

24. Daniel D. Sleator and Davy Temperley. Parsing English with a link grammar. In *Proc. Third International Workshop on Parsing Technologies*, pages 277–292, 1993.

25. TEI Consortium. The text encoding initiative, 2003. http://www.tei-c.org/.

26. Ellen M. Voorhees. The TREC question answering track. *Natural Language Engineering*, 7(4):361–378, 2001.

Using Ontologies in the Development of an Innovating System for Elderly People Tele-assistance*

Miren I. Bagüés, Jesus Bermúdez, Arantza Illarramendi,
Alberto Tablado, and Alfredo Goñi

University of the Basque Country (UPV/EHU)
LSI Department. Donostia-San Sebastián. Spain
jipileca@si.ehu.es
http://siul02.si.ehu.es/

Abstract. We have used most recent advances in the fields of artificial intelligence (knowledge representation), mobile computing and networking to develop the AINGERU system that provides a new kind of tele-assistance service for elderly people. The new features incorporated over the traditional tele-assistance are: high quality monitoring, anywhere and anytime. In this paper we focus on the high quality aspect and, more precisely, we present the role that two specific ontologies play and the advantages that they provide to the system. One ontology describes domain knowledge and the other one describes the operational model of the system.

1 Introduction

Nowadays, ontologies are used in many application domains and their usefulness is widely accepted. The goal of this paper is to present the interest of using two specific ontologies that describe knowledge of different nature, within an application called AINGERU. This system uses agent technology, semantic web technology and Personal Digital Assistant (PDA) with wireless communications, to provide high quality assistance to elderly people, giving them more freedom and protection.

Many recent surveys agree with the following statement: "the population of the first world is aging". Traditional Social Services could well be overwhelmed within 30 years. Another important issue is that elderly people are becoming more and more independent. As medical science advances, people can live alone with better health up to a very advanced age. Therefore, in order to let elderly people live in their own homes leading their normal life, while, at the same time taking care of them, special purpose services are required. Up to now, most of tele assistance services offered are based on specific hardware (e.g. [1,2,3]), but all of them are constrained by their limited coverage and functionality. Due to this, they do not fulfill the aim of a *high-quality*, *anywhere* and *anytime* assistance.

Nevertheless, apart from supporting the functionalities provided by present tele assistance services, AINGERU also: offers an *active assistance* by using agents that

---

* This work was mainly supported by the University of the Basque Country and Diputación Foral de Gipuzkoa.

R. Meersman et al. (Eds.): CoopIS/DOA/ODBASE 2003, LNCS 2888, pp. 889–905, 2003.

behave in face of anomalous situations; offers an *anywhere* and *anytime* assistance by using wireless communications and PDAs; and, allows to *monitor vital signs* by using sensors that capture the values of those signus and feed a decision support system that analyzes them and generates an alarm when necessary.

The main elements that enable AINGERU to offer those functionalities are:

- A set of PDAs, one for each user, which can be carried everywhere by these users and which support wireless communication with other devices such as sensors and computer servers.
- A set of computers located at different centers that mainly take part of a sanitary network.
- A set of specialized agents that work autonomously accomplishing tasks that have been assigned to them and that are parts of the global application. For example, an agent called Localization Agent is in charge of knowing where the user is at every moment, while other agents could ask him this information whenever needed.
- Two logic-based ontologies that allow reasoning on them, and web services that support enquires about user data stored at the PDA.

Although in the following section we show some features of the agents and PDAs, the main focus of this paper is on the two above-mentioned ontologies. Notice that the development and use of these two ontologies is a novelty that AINGERU brings with respect to other tele assistance services. Both ontologies are described using semantic web technology [1].

The purpose of the first ontology, called *MedOnt*, is to describe the different situations in which a medical alarm has to be activated. Hence, in this ontology not only are the different symptoms that a user can have described, with respect to Vital Constants that several sensors can monitor, but also the usual illnesses that elderly people suffer from. Moreover, this ontology can be customized for every user. That is, this ontology can be easily adapted to different users depending on their own situation. This ontology is being developed by experts (so far we only have a small prototype).

The purpose of the second ontology, called *OperOnt,* is to describe the operational model of AINGERU. For example, in this ontology we describe messages for the communication among agents in AINGERU. The concepts in this ontology are defined independently from any agent system implementation, so that it helps interoperability among agents without pre-defined agreements. At the same time, the *OperOnt* ontology describes contextual information that several agents are able to share. This ontology is easily extensible as the functionality of AINGERU increases.

The main advantages of using the above-mentioned ontologies in our AINGERU system are:

- The ontologies allow sharing knowledge (in our case, medical and operational) with other systems, so they favor the interoperability of AINGERU with other systems.

---

[1] Right now DAML+OIL [4] is used to describe the ontologies, but there is a direct translation to OWL [5], the W3C web ontology language.

- The *OperOnt* ontology allows the interoperation of independently generated agents without pre-establishing specific protocols. The communication among agents is at the semantic level.
- Reasoning with the *MedOnt* ontology allows the system to activate alarms for many different situations that can happen to the users.

In the rest of this paper, first we briefly describe the global framework of AINGERU. Then, we show the features of the *MedOnt* and *OperOnt* ontologies. We continue presenting a trace of the system at work and some related works. We finish with some conclusions.

2 Global Architecture of AINGERU

The goal of this section is to present the main features of the AINGERU architecture, which appears in Fig.1, from two different perspectives. First, from the physical perspective, i.e., the components that take part in the architecture and the type of communication among them. Next from the software perspective, i.e., the main software elements – specialist agents, ontologies, reasoner and web services– that operate to accomplish the pursued goal of AINGERU.

2.1 Physical Perspective of AINGERU

As can be observed in Fig. 1, there are five different types of components, namely: PDAs, Control Center, Care Center, Health Center and Technical Center. AINGERU supports the distributed nature of the application domain.

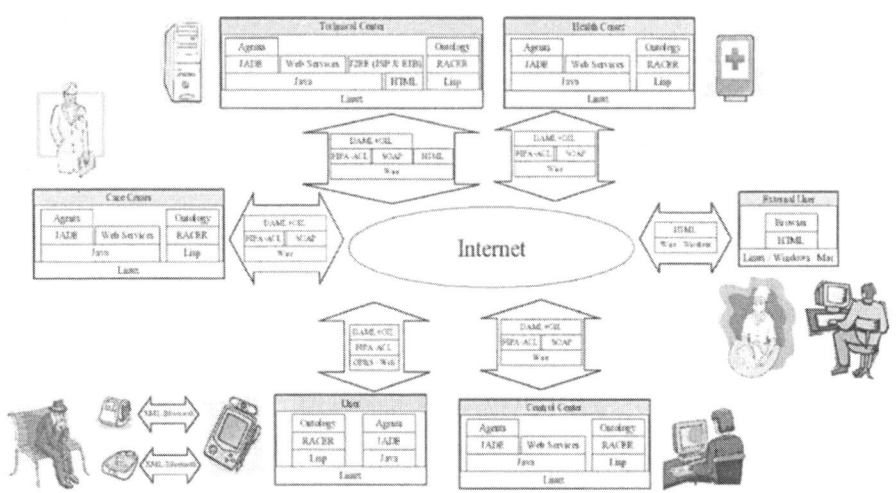

Fig. 1. Global architecture of AINGERU

Fig. 2. One of the interfaces of the AINGERU system

Personal Digital Assistant PDA

Each person monitored by AINGERU carries a PDA. The PDA is a central element in AINGERU architecture and its main goal is twofold, first to monitor the user and then, when special circumstances require it, to be the link between the person and the center (Control Center) that is also responsible for monitoring her/him. Due to its reduced size a PDA can be carried anywhere. Moreover, the technical features that PDAs nowadays support, allow us to run the software application of AINGERU in them. In the following paragraphs we mention three basic functionalities of PDAs: manual activation of an alarm, automatic activation of an alarm and agenda services.

Manual activation of an alarm. Devices nowadays (those mentioned in the introduction) allow people to activate an alarm from their home, mainly by pressing a button. AINGERU also supports this functionality by providing the user with the interface shown in Fig. 2. When the user feels bad, or something is happening in his environment and he wants to notify it, he presses the button that appears in the interface and an alarm is activated in the Control Center. Notice that in the case of AINGERU this functionality is not constrained to users' homes, as it occurs nowadays.

Automatic activation of an alarm. Aside from the previous basic functionality an added value which AINGERU contributes to is the possibility of controlling in situ the vital constants of a person in order to monitor risk situations. The PDA receives data sent by sensors (even by wireless sensors) related to pulse, mobility, etc., and analyzes them in order to activate an alarm when an anomalous situation is being detected.

Agenda services. Apart from the two mentioned functionalities, the users' PDA provides them with classical agenda services such as remembering when they have to visit the doctor, when they have to take their medicines, which appointments they have, etc.

Control Center

Control Centers are the centers in charge of monitoring people. Each Control Center hosts a computer called Control Center. The number of Control Centers depend on how many users must be monitored. The main goal of a Control Center is to react in the presence of user alarms and to take the adequate actions.

Care Center
Care Centers are the public health centers for primary assistance. Each Care Center hosts one or more computers. Part of the AINGERU application must run in one of those computers (called Care Center) in order to provide AINGERU users with new functionalities such as: accessibility of physicians to data stored in the user PDA, direct insertion of medical appointments in the PDA, etc.

Health Center
Health Centers correspond to hospitals. In the presence of an alarm, the Control Center could decide that the user must be moved to a hospital. In that case, the Control Center would send information about the user to the hospital so they could be prepared when receiving the user. For this reason, part of the AINGERU application must also run at one Health Center computer (called Health Center) without interfering with existing applications.

Technical Center
The goal of this center is the development and support of the AINGERU application. It hosts a computer called Technical Center. It is in charge of providing the PDA users with new software releases, new services, and so on.

Concerning communication aspects among the components, in Fig. 1 we can observe the different levels that are used. At the physical level the wired or wireless communication appears. At the transport level, FIPA is used for inter agent communications and SOAP for web services. At the application level, agents and web services communicate through ontologies described in DAML+OIL.

2.2 Software Perspective of AINGERU

In Fig. 1 we can observe the main software elements that take part of AINGERU: ontologies, web services and agents. In this subsection we briefly present web services and agents because ontologies are explained in more detail in the following sections.

Web Services
In AINGERU we have developed web services that export part of agent knowledge and allow desktop applications to dive into the agency world. This possibility, not taken into account in the tele-assistance applications nowadays, is very interesting, and opens new opportunities for future extensions of AINGERU. Examples of these web services are:

- *Vital Constants:* A web service exported by the Care Center. It provides information about user vital constants in real-time. Authorized agents (physicians, for example) can obtain data about the current values of the sensors that monitor the user.
- *Location:* A web service exported by the Technical Center. It provides information about the location of the user. Location information is managed by the Location Agent residing in the User Agency within the PDA.

- *Appointments:* Web services exported by the Care Center and Technical Center. They manage the user's appointments (with physicians, with relatives, etc). The User Agency will alert the user on time.
- *Medical Records:* Web service exported by the Care Center. It allows physicians to obtain medical records of the users.

These services can be invoked via SOAP. But we have also developed an HTML front-end to those web services. This facility will allow that anybody that has a web browser installed on their computers to access those web services.

Agents

We decided to use agent technology in AINGERU because features that agents provide are vital in our context. Among those features we point out the following: agents are autonomous, reactive and can be mobile. The autonomy feature allows us to distribute the global functionality of the AINGERU system among different agents, each agent being responsible for performing a specific task and controlling its reactions independently of others. The reactiveness feature allows the development of an active assistance which responds to changes in the user health conditions. Last but not least, mobility allows agents to travel from the user's PDA to Care Center, Health Center or Control Center computers and vice versa, in order to perform certain tasks locally, saving wireless communications costs.

Furthermore, a set of agents can cooperate to accomplish a task, and this task can be a step to achieve a goal. For example, two agents can cooperate to check a person's pulse: the *Bluetooth Agent*, which knows how to deal with bluetooth wireless technology, and the *Pulse Agent*, which manages specific knowledge related to pulse. Moreover, checking the pulse may be only a step in vital constants control.

Among the different agents that we have developed in AINGERU, we only mention here the details of two of them: *Majordomo* and *Conditions Checker* (see [6] for more information).

The *Majordomo Agent* is located at the user's PDA and its goal is to be the link between the user and the AINGERU system. It shows information on the screen or tells it through the speaker, and it gets user's response by handwriting recognition on screen, speech recognition or pressing buttons on the interface. This agent can be customized for different users.

The *Condition Checker Agent* is also located at the user's PDA and its goal is to monitor user health values. To accomplish its goal this agent makes use of the *MedOnt* ontology explained in section 3. The behavior of this agent is as follows: when it receives data, captured by sensors, it pushes those values into the reasoning system as values filling properties associated to concepts in the *MedOnt* ontology and observes the inferences made by the reasoner. If an instance is recognized into the Alarm concept the Condition Checker Agent activates an alarm and sends it to the Control Center. This agent, the *MedOnt* ontology and its supporting reasoner, constitute the Decision Support System that permits AINGERU to provide its users with a high quality tele-assistance service.

After trying out some implementations for agents, we selected the JADE system because it was the one that most accurately fulfilled our requirements. Key features that affected our decision are:

- Standards-compliant: JADE is compliant with the latest FIPA standards [7]. We use FIPA as a transport level standard protocol. Above *that*, *agents communicate at a semantic level provided by the* OperOnt *ontology*.
- Lightweight: because some agencies will be running in PDAs, we need a platform that is not very heavyweighted. JADE has versions that can run on J2ME/MIDP complaint devices, like phones and watches.
- Generality: it allows us to use different transport drivers to carry messages among agencies. For example, there are drivers that use CORBA, HTTP or even SMTP (mail protocol).
- Security: in addition to establishing secure channels based on SSL communications, JADE allows to sign messages by binding an identity to every message. This prevents unauthorized agents killing other agents. Furthermore, message integrity is assured, preventing message tampering.

There are other systems that also promote applying agents in Health Care [8,9,10,11]. However, as far as we know, they are still in their initial development and they do not put special emphasis on combining the agent technology with the use of PDAs.

3   Medical Ontology (*MedOnt*)

As we have mentioned in the introduction, our AINGERU system, apart from allowing anywhere and anytime monitoring, has the goal of providing a high quality monitoring. This means that AINGERU not only will generate an alarm when the user requires it, but also when the system autonomously detects anomalous situations. Thus, its behavior is reactive when the user's health is in danger. In our opinion this last feature is a step forward in the field of tele-assistance applications.

In order to accomplish the goal of detecting anomalous situations, two components are necessary: first, sensors that capture users' health values such as temperature, pulse, etc. and then, a knowledge based system that analyzes the captured values. Nowadays there is a tremendous interest, from the research point of view as well as from the commercial point of view, in developing wireless intelligent sensors that capture biological signal data and transmit these data using bluetooth technology. Aspects relative to these sensors are beyond the scope of this paper, but we believe that they will be added to the AINGERU system in the near future.

Concerning the development of the knowledge based system to represent data sent by the sensors, we think that the ontology based approach, following the direction promoted by the Semantic Web vision, is far more adequate than a rule based representation approach. After all, the latter presents the following disadvantages: it tends to be less open, it is biased towards case by case analysis, and its validity is more difficult to reason about. By contrast, the ontology based approach consists of describing concepts, at a semantic level using well founded operators. In our case, concepts describe states of illnesses that elderly people can suffer as well as states generated by the values captured by the sensors. With respect to our *MedOnt* ontology we follow the approach of GALEN [12] (which, in turn, is directly related to the well-known SNOMED [13] medical terminology) although we do not use the GALEN Representation and Integration Language (GRAIL) [14]. We decided to use

DAML+OIL (an ontology representation language from the Semantic Web forum, with a direct translation to the recently launched OWL) to take advantage of semantic web technology and its richer primitives for concept descriptions. Furthermore, DAML+OIL allows the description of some datatypes, so we are able to deal with properties with integer values and with structured values such as HL7 [15] rows. Moreover, for the reasoning process we selected the RACER [16] system, which implements a highly optimized tableau calculus for a very expressive description logic that covers all the DAML+OIL primitives we need; in particular, it deals with reasoning about individuals of concepts, which is crucial in our framework.

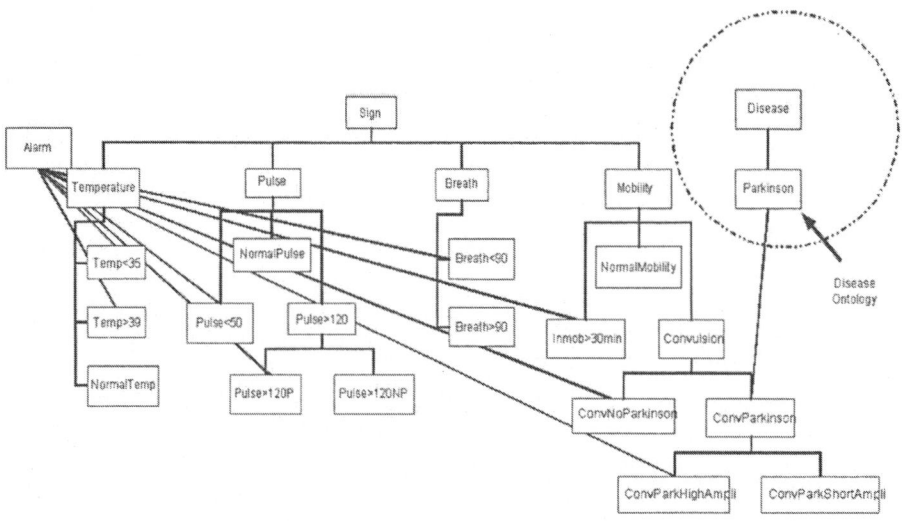

Fig. 3. Graphic representation of a fragment of the *MedOnt* ontology

The *MedOnt* ontology is being built by physicians who are experts in the care of elderly people. So far, to build the AINGERU prototype, we deal with a "toy" *MedOnt* ontology that we have built with the collaboration of physicians (see Fig. 3 and Fig. 5). For example, in this ontology we can observe the Pulse<50 concept that describes the bradycardia situation and which is related to the Pulse signs. Concepts in this ontology fragment are described according to the values captured by different sensors (temperature, pulse, etc.). There are concepts describing normal situations such as NormalPulse, and others describing anomalous situations, such as Pulse>120P, that are recognized as (*subsumed by*) an Alarm situation.

In Fig. 4 the AlertJohn concept illustrates the desirable customization of the *MedOnt* ontology loaded into each user's PDA (AlertJohn for the user John). The AlertJohn concept is a kind of Alarm that describes all the potential anomalous situations of the user of this particular PDA. We consider customization a very interesting feature because every single person has peculiarities added to general symptoms; for example, the state of John who suffers Bradycardia is not in an alarm situation if the pulse is below 50 but above 40: AlertJohn is, in fact, activated if the pulse is below 40. Notice that in the customization process the concept Pulse<50 has been removed.

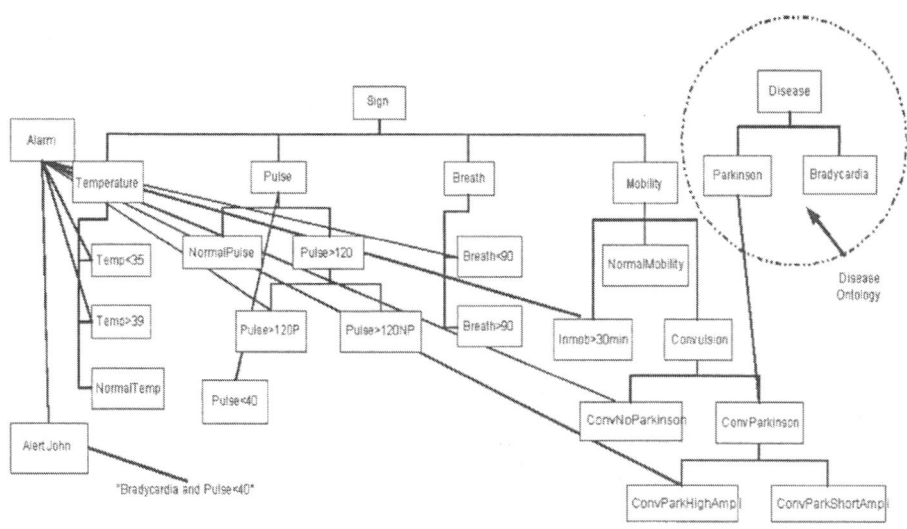

Fig. 4. Graphic Representation of a fragment of a Personalized *MedOnt*

There are also some concepts in the *MedOnt* ontology that describe states combining Signs detected by sensors with a state of disease. For example, the concept Convulsion describes the state when the Mobility Sensor reports shaking over a certain threshold and ConvParkinson describes the state of the kind of Convulsion of a person who suffers from Parkinson's disease. Notice that ConvParkinson is not considered a state of alarm. By contrast, ConvNo Parkinson describes a kind of Convulsion of people not suffering from Parkinson's disease, and this concept is considered a kind of Alarm because the person is possibly suffering from an epilepsy episode.

```
<daml:Class rdf:about="file:/C:/Aingeru/OntoMed.daml#Breath">
  <rdfs:subClassOf>
    <daml:Class rdf:about="file:/C:/Aingeru/OntoMed.daml#Sign"/>
  </rdfs:subClassOf>
</daml:Class>
<daml:Class rdf:about="file:/C:/Aingeru/OntoMed.daml#Breath&lt;90">
  <rdfs:subClassOf>
    <daml:Class rdf:about="file:/C:/Aingeru/OntoMed.daml#Breath"/>
  </rdfs:subClassOf>
  <rdfs:subClassOf>
    <daml:Class rdf:about="file:/C:/Aingeru/OntoMed.daml#Alarm"/>
  </rdfs:subClassOf>
  <rdfs:subClassOf>
    <daml:Restriction>
      <daml:onProperty rdf:resource="file:/C:/Aingeru/OntoMed daml#value"/>
      <daml:toClass rdf:resource="http://siul02.si.ehu es/Aingeru/Schemas#BreathMin90"/>
    </daml:Restriction>
  </rdfs:subClassOf>
</daml:Class>
```

Fig. 5. Definition of a fragment of the *MedOnt* ontology in DAML+OIL

Nevertheless, we want to stress that *MedOnt* is only a toy ontology and in the near future we hope to develop a real one that allows making smart reasonings, such as the one described in the following abstract example.

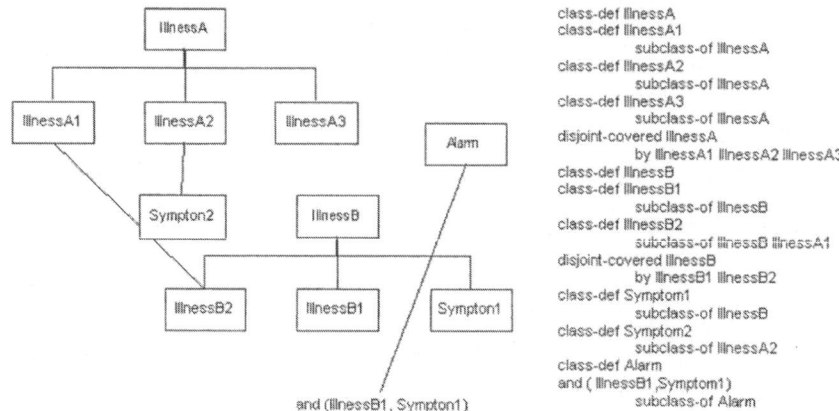

Fig. 6. Graphic representation of a fragment of an ontology and its specification using an abstract syntax

Assume a conceptualization as shown in Fig. 6, describing different kinds of illnesses and their relationships. Assume that there are also two symptoms - Symptom1 and Symptom2- whose conceptualization –accorded by the ontology designers- classifies them as subsumees of IllnessB and IllnessA2, respectively (i.e., it is admitted by ontology designers that if Symptom1 is recognized about a person, then that person suffers from IllnessB, and similarly for Symptom2 and IllnessA2). In addition, it is described as an Alarm when a person suffers from IllnessB1 and Symptom1.

Now, assume that it is recognized that a person suffers from Symptom1 and Symptom2. Then, the reasoning mechanism will infer that this person is in an Alarm situation. The inferencing process works this way: Symptom1 implies that the person suffers from IllnessB, although what specific subclass is still uncertain -IllnessB1 or IllnessB2-. On the other hand, Symptom2 implies IllnessA2. Moreover, IllnessA1 is discarded due to the specification of the IllnessA concept as the pairwise disjoint union of the IllnessA1, IllnessA2 and IllnessA3 concepts (notice the disjoint-covered operator in Fig. 6). Then, IllnessB2 -being subclass of IllnessA1- must be also discarded. Finally, it is inferred that IllnessB must specifically be an IllnessB1 and, consequently, there is an Alarm.

This is the kind of reasoning provided by the description logic underlying DAML+OIL.

4 Operational Ontology (*OperOnt*)

As mentioned in section 2.2, agents play a very important role in the AINGERU system. Those agents are implemented using the JADE agent system; nevertheless, taking into account that interoperability with other systems is a goal for AINGERU, we have defined an ontology, called *OperOnt*, for the description of concepts that allow the operation of agents at a semantic level. That means that the ontology includes descriptions of agents, messages, and subjects of the messages.

Communication among agents takes place by sending messages. A message has properties. For example a `BluetoothSensorQuery` message has the following properties: `OperOnt:subject`, `OperOnt:priority`, `OperOnt:ident`, `OperOnt:sender`, `OperOnt:receiver` and `OperOnt:sendingNumber`

The concepts and properties in *OperOnt* offer a well founded common understanding of terms for the interaction of agents. This approach favors, on the one hand, interoperation since new agents wishing to interact with the system only need to browse the corresponding ontology, and on the other hand, evolution because properties of messages can be modified without altering the agents that work with those messages.

For example, if an agent wants Bluetooth Sensor information, it only has to create an instance of the `Query` concept filled with the property `OperOnt:subject=` "BluetoothSensor", and push it into the reasoning system. The reasoning system will infer that the message to be sent is a `BluetoothSensorQuery` and will inform the agent about the properties the message must fulfill. Similarly, if an agent receives a `MedicalAppointmentModify` message it will push it into the reasoning system, which will infer that somebody is making a `Request` (see Fig. 9) to modify a `Medical Appointment`, as well as which properties the message has.

The *OperOnt* ontology is basically divided into three interrelated areas (in URL http://siul02.si.ehu.es/Aingeru/OperOnt.owl can be seen the specification of this ontology): (i) The actors who interact using messages, (ii) the subjects of the messages, and (iii) the functionality of the messages. Next we will outline each area, but we want to stress that there are axioms in the ontology that describe their interrelationships. Furthermore, it is worth mentioning that the formalism used in this approach together with the semantic web technology enable the proper integration of new areas into this ontology.

4.1 Actors

We divide this area (see Fig. 7) into human agents, software agents and AINGERU web services. Human agents are classified into two groups: on one hand AINGERU users and in the other hand all those that form part of the system (sanitary and non-sanitary).

Software agents are described taking into account their location and their goals (for instance, whether they work in a PDA or in a computer, if they are attending a sensor or interacting with an ontology, and so on). Web services are described on the basis of their functionality.

4.2 Subject of the Messages

This area describes concepts about the subject or the topic on which the message is centered (see Fig. 8). For example, `InputOutput`, `Location`, `Urgency`, `Emergency`, `Sensor`, `HospitalSubject`, `Appointment` and `Medicine` describe different kinds of subject.

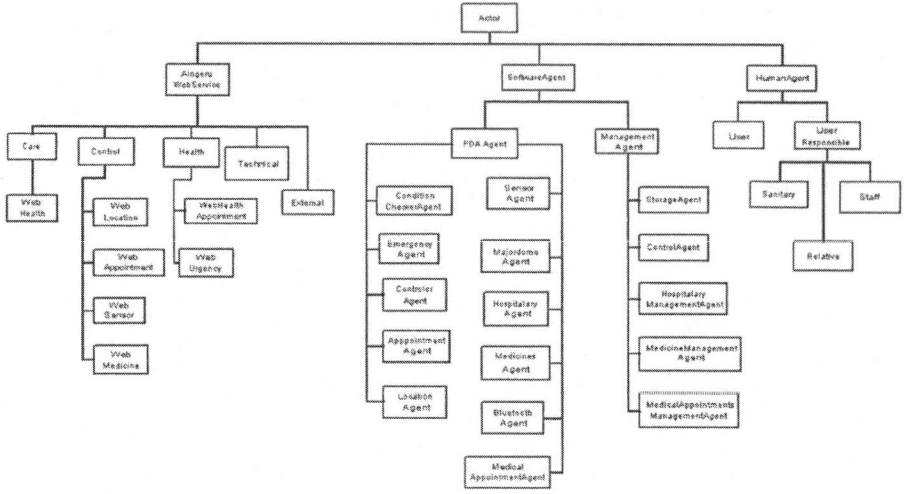

Fig. 7. Actors area

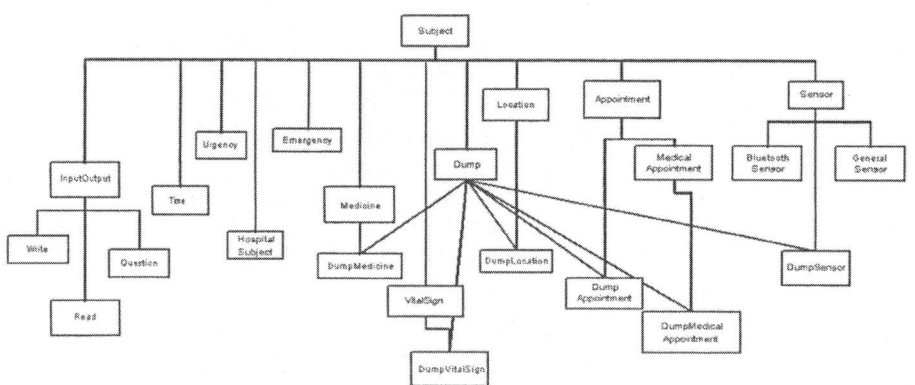

Fig. 8. Subjects area

More specialized subjects are defined taking into account their context (for example origin, destination, etc.). For instance, GeneralSensor is related to sensors that the user carries, BluetoothSensor is related to the bluetooth transmission performed by the sensors and DumpSensor is related to historical information saved in sensor agents.

This conceptualization describes subjects of messages in order to interpret their contents properly.

4.3 Functionality of the Messages

Considering the standards-compliant principle in AINGERU, we have included descriptions of messages according to their functionality in FIPA protocols (see Fig. 9).

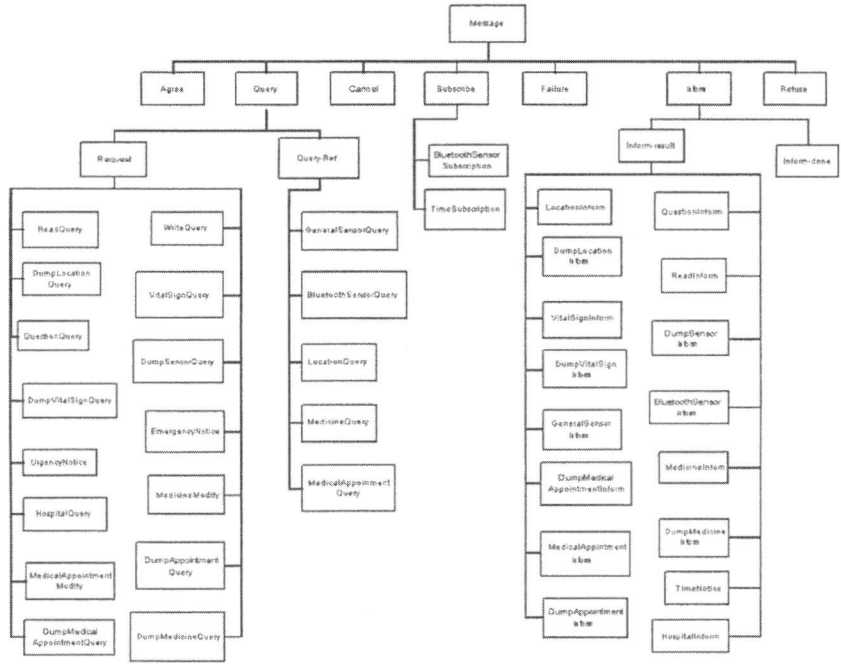

Fig. 9. Functionality of the messages area

Message descriptions are based on three FIPA[2] protocols: FIPA Request Interaction Protocol, FIPA Subscribe Interaction Protocol and FIPA Query Interaction Protocol. Types of messages that appear in *OperOnt* are: Agree, Cancel, Failure, Refuse, Query, Subscribe and Inform.

Another feature that differentiates messages is the particular subject of the message content. For example, if we have two messages whose functionality is Query-ref, they are different kinds of messages if they differ in the kind of subject they request (for instance, if one requests a Location, and the other requests some Medicine).

With these examples we also show the relationships among concepts presented in different areas. Typically, conceptualization in one area is used as qualification for concepts in another area, i.e., different concepts in one area serve as a domain or a range for properties in the other.

5   Trace of AINGERU at Work

For the construction of the AINGERU system we have used an object oriented development process based on UML (Unified Modelling Language) [17]. In this section we show a trace of AINGERU system at work, corresponding to the use case

---

[2] At the current state of AINGERU we use those three protocols. However, more could be considered if necessary.

represented in Fig. 10. This use case considers the situation in which the alarm is activated automatically.

The *Condition Checker Agent* periodically receives information from different Sensor Agents that exist in the PDA (every Sensor Agent controls the information obtained by one of the sensors that the user carries). When the *Condition Checker Agent* receives this information (for example pulse of 125), it pushes s <MedOnt:value> 125 into the reasoning system and observes the inferences made by it. If s is recognized as an instance of the Alarm concept, the *Condition Checker Agent* asserts the following statements to create a new message:

m : OperOnt:Query[3]; ur : OperOnt:Urgency;
m <OperOnt:subject> ur;

Then the reasoning system will infer that m is an instance of the OperOnt:AlarmNotice concept.

m : OperOnt:AlarmNotice;

Next the *Condition Checker Agent* ask the Knowledge Base System to retrieve the properties associated to OperOnt:AlarmNotice (in our case this is done using RICE [18]). It will receive the following list of properties:

{OperOnt:ident; OperOnt:subject; OperOnt:theSender; OperOnt:theReceiver; OperOnt:tryNumber}

With this information the *Condition Checker Agent* can create the AlarmNotice message to be sent to the *Emergency Agent*.

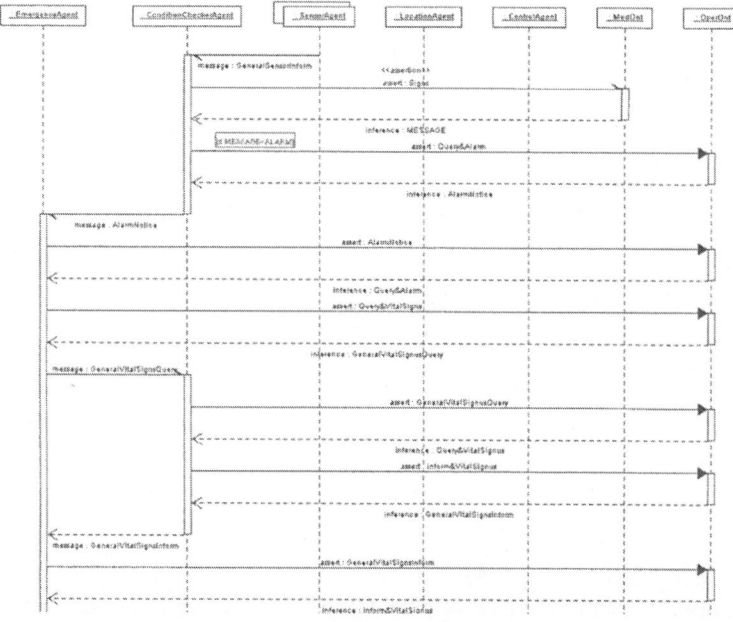

Fig. 10. UML Sequence Diagram of some steps of the use case "Automatic Alarm Activation"

---

[3]. We use abstract syntax.

```
<OperOnt:EmergencyNotice>
    <OperOnt:ident>
        M1234-A
    </OperOnt:ident>
    <OperOnt:theSender>
        <OperOnt:EmergencyAgent />
    </OperOnt:theSender>
    <OperOnt:theReceiver>
        <OperOnt:ControlAgent />
    </OperOnt:theReceiver>
    <OperOnt:tryNumber>
        1
    </OperOnt:tryNumber>
    <OperOnt:subject>
        <OperOnt:TheVitalSignus>
            MSH|^~\&|EMERGENCY AGENT||CONTROL AGENT|200229091030|| ORF^R04|RCVP001|P|2.3.1<cr>
            MSA|AA| PCVP001 <cr>
            QRD|200229091030|R|||QCV0001|||20|RD|123456789|RES<cr>
            QRF|EMERGENCY AGENT||200229091030<cr>
            PID|1|||1234234-N||RODRIGUEZ^JUAN|JIMENEZ||M|||943565656 <cr>
            OBR|4|P8756^OE|N2345^NR|3000.02^VITAL SIGNS|||200229091028|||SENS_PULSO^SENS_COR |N<cr>
            OBX|1|ST|8462-4^INTRAVASCULAR DIASTOLIC.PRES:^LN|||90|mm(hg)|60-90|||F<cr>
            OBX|2|ST|8479-8^INTRAVASCULAR SYSTOLIC.PRES:^LN|||120|mm(hg)|100-160|||F<cr>
            OBX|3|ST|8478-0^INTRAVASCULAR MEAN:PRES:^LN|||100|mm(hg)|80-120|||F<cr>
            OBX|4|ST|8867-4^HEART BEAT:NRAT:^LN|||125|/min|60-100|HH|||F<cr>
        </OperOnt:TheVitalSignus>
        <OperOnt:EmergencyType>
            Medical Emergency
        </OperOnt:EmergencyType>
        <OperOnt:TheLocation>
            43"18'26",-2"0'41"
        </OperOnt:TheLocation>
    </OperOnt:subject>
</OperOnt:EmergencyNotice>
```

Fig. 11. EmergencyNotice message in DAML+OIL

Then, the *Emergency Agent* asks the *Condition Checker Agent* for all the vital constants, and the *Location Agent* for the location of the user.

As soon as the *Emergency Agent* receives all the information, it creates the `EmergencyNotice` message (following the above-mentioned steps for creating the message using the *OperOnt* ontology). This message appears in Fig. 11.

Finally, the message in Fig. 11 is sent to the *Control Agent* (located at the Control Center). Then, the Control Center decides what to do depending on the information received. Moreover, as it is a medical emergency (since the alarm has been activated by the *Condition Checker Agent*) an ambulance will be sent to wherever the user is.

6   Related Works

Works related to AINGERU may be classified into two major groups: works whose aim is to build tele-assistance applications for elderly people, and works that advocate for the use of ontologies in the Pervasive Ubiquitous Computing Environments.

We also classify tele-assistance applications in two groups. In the first group we include those systems that provide limited coverage, such as existing tele-alarms. The main features of these systems are the following: they use wired phone communications to contact Social Services, their coverage is restricted usually to the user's home and their activation is triggered by the user, generally using a button. Therefore, they do not support *anywhere* and *anytime* assistance. In the second group we include more advanced systems. The coverage provided by these systems is broader: they use PDAs and take advantage of wireless communication. They provide *anywhere* and *anytime* assistance, but they are not *reactive*. PDAs are used as intermediary elements and their goal is merely reduced to the transmition of data from sensors to a central computer where data analysis is made. They do not take advantage of the ability of the PDAs to carry out a certain pre-analysis before sending data to the central computer. Notice that wireless communications are slow, expensive and unstable so, analysis made in the PDA can save costs and detect anomalies earlier. Examples in this group are doc@HOME [1] , Sensatex [19] , SILC [2] or TeleMediCare [3]. AINGERU goes one step further by providing not only anywhere and anytime assistance using wireless communication, but also a high quality assistance, mainly due to the use of agents and semantic web technology.

With respect to the use of ontologies in a pervasive computing environment, we point out two works [20,21]. The first paper [20] presents the features of the CoBrA ontology described in OWL, that models the basic concepts of people, agents, places and presentation events in intelligent meeting room environments. Two main features differentiate our work from their approach: first, in our work the reasoning is made at the mobile device, while in their case it is made at the stationary servers. While it is true that doing the reasoning process at the PDA has not been an easy task, we have verified its feasibility and in our opinion the advantages that provide the local reasoning justify its use. The second difference corresponds to *OperOnt* ontology. In CoBrA ontology they do not consider the type of terms and the goal pursued by our *OperOnt* ontology. In the second paper [21], they show how the use of ontologies can help overcome three major issues that confront the development and deployment of Pervasive Computing Environments (discovery and matchmaking, inter-operability between different entities and context-awareness). Although we agree with most of their conclusions, our work is centered in one specific application domain.

7 Conclusions

To develop new social and sanitary programs, as well as new software and hardware systems that help elderly people to increase their quality of life, is a challenge nowadays posed in developed countries.

In this paper we have presented our system, called AINGERU, that gives one step forward in that direction of improving the quality of life, by allowing the monitoring of people anywhere and anytime. Moreover, this monitoring is reactive, i.e., not only is an alarm activated when the user requires it, but also when the system detects an anomalous situation. In order to perform the detection process, the system makes an extensive use of an application domain ontology, *MedOnt*, that describes states outlined by vital constant values that must be monitored, as well as diseases that elderly people can suffer from. Another contribution of the system is the development and management of an operational ontology, *OperOnt,* that permits agents that take part in the system to communicate at a semantic level.

References

[1]   doc@HOME, The bridge to care. http://www.docobo.com, (2003, July).
[2]   Supporting Independently Living Citizens.
       http://www.fortec.tuwien.ac.at/silcweb/SILC.htm, (2002, July).

[3]   The TelemediCare project. http://www.telemedicare.net, (2003, July).
[4]   Connolly,D., Van Harmelen, F., Horrocks, I., McGuinness, D.L., Patel-Schneider, P.F., Stein, L.A. : DAML+OIL (March 2001) Reference Description. http://www.w3.org/TR/daml+oil-reference (2003, July).
[5]   OWL Web Ontology Language Guide. http://www.w3.org/2001/sw/WebOnt/guide-src/Guide.html. (2003, July).
[6]   Tablado, A., Illarramendi, A., Bermúdez, J., Goñi, A.: "Intelligent monitoring of elderly people". in *4th Annual IEEE Conference on Information Technology Applications in Biomedicine*, 2003, pp. 78–81.
[7]   FIPA. Foundation for Intelligent Physical Agents. http://www.fipa.org/specifications/index.html. (2003, July).
[8]   Mouratidis, H., Manson, G., Giorgini, P., and Philp, I.: "Modelling an agent-based integrated health and social care information system for older people". In *15th European Conference on Artificial Intelligence*, 22 July 2002.
[9]   Mabry, S. L., Kollmansberger, S. J., Etters, T., and Jones, K. L.: "IM-Agents for patient monitoring and diagnostics". In *15th European Conference on Artificial Intelligence*, 22 July 2002.
[10]   Moreno, A. and Isern, D.: Offering agent-based medical services within the AgentCities project. In *15th European Conference on Artificial Intelligence*, 22 July 2002.
[11]   Camarinha-Matos, L. M. and Afsarmanesh, H.: Virtual Communities and Elderly Support. *Advances in Automation, Multimedia and Video System, and Modern Computer Science*, pages 279–284, September 2001.
[12]   OpenGALEN: Making the impossible very difficult. http://www.opengalen.org/. (2003, July).
[13]   SNOMED International. http://www.snomed.org/. (2003, July).
[14]   Rector, A. , Bechhofer, S. et. al.: "The GRAIL concept modelling language for medical terminology" Artificial Intelligence in Medicine, 9: 139–171 ,1997.
[15]   HL7 Version 2.3 Implementation Guide. http://www.hl7.org/Special/IG/final.pdf (2003, July).
[16]   Haarslev, V., Möller, R.: RACER: Renamed ABox and Concept Expression Reasoner. http://www.fh-wedel.de/~mo/racer/ (2003, July).
[17]   UML Resource page. http://www.omg.org/uml/ (2003, July).
[18]   Cornet, R. RICE: Racer Interactive Client Environment http://www.b1g-systems.com/ronald/rice/ (2003, July)
[19]   Sensatex. http://www.sensatex.com. (2003,July).
[20]   Chen, H., Finin, T. and Joshi, A.: An Ontology for Context-Aware Pervasive Computing Environments. Eighteenth International Joint Conference on Artificial Intelligence Workshop on Information Integration on the Web(IIWeb-03) August 9–10, 2003 Acapulco Mexico.
[21]   Ranganathan, A., McGrath, R. E., Campbell, R. H., Mickunas, M. D.: Ontologies in a Pervasive Computing Environment. Eighteenth International Joint Conference On Artificial Intelligence Workshop on Information Integration on the Web(IIWeb-03) August 9–10, 2003 Acapulco Mexico.

A Fuzzy Model for Representing Uncertain, Subjective, and Vague Temporal Knowledge in Ontologies*

Gábor Nagypál and Boris Motik

FZI Research Center for Information Technologies
at the University of Karlsruhe
Haid-und-Neu-Str. 10-14
76131 Karlsruhe, Germany
{nagypal,motik}@fzi.de
http://www.fzi.de

Abstract. Time modeling is a crucial feature in many application domains. However, temporal information often is not crisp, but is uncertain, subjective and vague. This is particularly true when representing historical information, as historical accounts are inherently imprecise. Similarly, we conjecture that in the Semantic Web representing uncertain temporal information will be a common requirement. Hence, existing approaches for temporal modeling based on crisp representation of time cannot be applied to these advanced modeling tasks. To overcome these difficulties, in this paper we present fuzzy interval-based temporal model capable of representing imprecise temporal knowledge. Our approach naturally subsumes existing crisp temporal models, i.e. crisp temporal relationships are intuitively represented in our system. Apart from presenting the fuzzy temporal model, we discuss how this model is integrated with the ontology model to allow annotating ontology definitions with time specifications.

1 Introduction

Time modeling is a crucial feature in many application domains, such as medicine, history, criminal and financial applications. Its importance is shown by the numerous works in the area of temporal databases [1,2] and temporal reasoning [3]. Our experience from the EU-IST sponsored VICODI project[1] supports this claim fully. The main aim of this project is to develop an ontology of European history used for semantical indexing of historical documents. The goal of the VICODI system is to demonstrate benefits of semantics by improving searching and navigation in historical databases. We note that the system is not intended to be used by the general public, but is aimed at power-users,

---

* This work was partially supported by the EU in the framework of the VICODI project (EU-IST-2001-37534)
[1] http://www.vicodi.org/

R. Meersman et al. (Eds.): CoopIS/DOA/ODBASE 2003, LNCS 2888, pp. 906–923, 2003.
© Springer-Verlag Berlin Heidelberg 2003

such as historians and librarians. Therefore, the expressivity and accuracy of the modeling capabilities are crucial to the success of the project.

It is quite obvious that time modeling is a fundamental issue for modeling historical information, since almost every historical statement is time dependent. Moreover, we identified several specific features that make capturing this information a challenge. For one, time information in history is often uncertain or ill-defined. It is usually extracted from historical documents written in an imprecise and inherently vague style. Even worse, important documents are often missing or contain contradictory information, so temporal information about historical events is uncertain. Apart from the uncertainty of temporal information, historical events are often abstract, so their definition is inherently subjective. For example, we have found it impossible to precisely define the time span of the 'Middle Ages'.

To the best knowledge of authors, there is no existing approach for temporal modeling which is capable of capturing such uncertain, subjective and vague temporal information. The vast majority of related work concentrates on modeling crisp and definite temporal information (for which we use synonyms 'traditional' or 'classical' in this paper). Moreover, existing approaches for modeling imprecise temporal information focus on handling either uncertainty or subjectivity, but not both. Therefore, we decided to propose a new model capable of fulfilling our requirements. We designed our model based on a rigorous requirements analysis. Although this analysis is driven by our application scenario, we believe that the temporal model is general enough to be applied in other settings demanding advanced temporal modeling as well. Also, temporal model alone is not worth much – a mechanism for embedding it into an ontology model is needed. Hence, in this paper we present an approach for integrating two orthogonal models, namely the temporal and the ontology model, into a unified modeling framework.

This paper is organized as follows. Section 2 introduces the requirements posed by temporal knowledge in history. Section 3 formally introduces our temporal model. Section 4 shows how to extend the classical temporal interval relations introduced by J. F. Allen [4] to our model. Section 5 discusses various properties of the new temporal model, and Section 6 discusses how to integrate the temporal model in ontologies. Section 7 analyzes related work and Section 8 concludes the paper and provides some outlook about future work.

2   Requirements

In this section we discuss requirements we gathered in the course of the VICODI project, based on which we design our temporal model. Although these requirements come from the domain of modeling historical information, they are still valid in many other application settings.

2.1   Unique Features of Historical Temporal Knowledge

History, as a human science, is different from natural sciences, mainly because information sources are historical documents written by people using vague natural languages, using vague and subjective concepts, such as 'revolution' or 'golden age'. Therefore, the concepts found in these sources, as well as their temporal specifications, are often imprecise.

Based on the accounts of history experts in the VICODI project, debate and disagreement over temporal specifications in history is rather the norm than an exception. This makes modelling this type of knowledge extremely difficult. In this subsection we discuss the nature of these challenges and give some examples.

Uncertainty. Sometimes information about a historical event can only be deduced from documents reporting about related events. Often several documents state contradictory facts about some event. As an example consider Stalin's birthdate. Officially for the USSR it is 21 December 1879 but according to church records his birth was registered in 6 December 1878. Historians are in disagreement over which time specification is the right one.

In such a case we say that the temporal specification of the event is uncertain. In natural language such uncertain temporal specifications are often written informally as ? - 1640 (meaning that the beginning time of the event is unknown) or as ca. 1801 (meaning circa, or around this year).

Subjectivity. Many historical events are not exactly defined, but are subjective. For example, the 'early renaissance', 'Russian revolution' or 'industrial revolution' do not have a clear definition, so it is impossible to clearly state exactly when these events occurred. In this case it is intuitive for historians to talk about 'beginning or end phases', 'process, development and core periods' or of 'transition periods', which clearly indicates that the traditional model of having temporal intervals with definite start and end points does not meet the reality in this case.

Vagueness. Historical time specifications are given at different granularity (years, months, days) and are often defined fuzzily (early morning, spring etc.). Hence, the temporal specification is not known precisely, but is vague. The reader may also note that any temporal specification made in a natural language will become vague if we refine the granularity of temporal axis sufficiently.

There are also events exhibiting a combination of the afore mentioned properties, so the temporal model should be capable of representing all of them in a unified manner.

2.2   Temporal Relations

Since the goal of the VICODI project is to allow creating powerful temporal queries, expressive relations among temporal primitives are of paramount importance. The model should at least be able to represent the temporal interval relations defined by Allen in [4]. Apart from these relations, we have found out that the relation **intersects**, checking whether two time intervals have a common point, is crucial in the historical context. Hence, Table 1 summarizes all of the operations required. For an interval i, i^- denotes the starting point of the interval, and i^+ denotes the ending point of the interval.

It is a natural requirement that our temporal model should, if applied to traditional temporal specifications, yield the same results as in classical temporal models. With other words, our approach should naturally subsume the classical case.

2.3   Temporal Specifications versus General Theory of Time

Our requirements differ from those found usually in temporal reasoning literature (eg. [5,6,7,8]). Our goal is not to develop a general axiomatization of time using which one can reason about time. For example, in temporal logic one can axiomatize that event A occurred before event B, and event B occurred before event C. Then one can derive that A occurred before C, even without knowing the exact time when either of the events occurred.

In our application field we are dealing primarily with concrete temporal specifications, which may be imprecise, but still use absolute dates. In such setting, axiomatizing total order of the time dimension is not necessary, since it follows naturally from the total order of dates. We have found out that many application domains share this fundamental feature: rather than requiring a general theory of time allowing arbitrary inferences, they deal with numerous concrete temporal facts associated domain entities. In such setting a general theory of time is an overkill, requiring inferencing capabilities of significant computational complexity. We can replace these with more efficient mechanisms, implemented outside the logical framework.

3   Fuzzy Temporal Model

3.1   Basic Decisions

Intervals or Points? The most fundamental question in any temporal model is the choice of the basic temporal primitive. Literature mentions two usual primitives [3,9]: time instants (or time points, chronons) and time intervals. A temporal model can be based on either or on both of them. In literature there there is an ongoing debate about which primitive is more appropriate, with no clear winner. While in the temporal database research community the time instant is more commonly used [2], in the artificial intelligence community time interval or mixed approaches are more popular [3]. In [3] it has been argued that the choice of the basic primitive mostly depends on the application requirements. We believe that time intervals are closer to human intuitive perception of time. Instants can always be viewed as time intervals if the granularity of time dimension is sufficiently increased. Further, intervals lend themselves to intuitive generalization to the fuzzy case.

Continuous vs. Discrete Temporal Model. Although there are some good arguments in the temporal database literature (e.g. [10]) for using a discrete time model, most of the approaches in AI use the continuous model, as it fits well with the choice of intervals as the basic primitive. Under a continuous temporal model, each natural language 'time point' translates to an interval in the temporal model, which is not necessarily the case for the discrete model. Therefore, we choose the unbounded, continuous time line $\mathcal{T}$ as the basis for defining time intervals, which is isomorphic to the set of real numbers, i.e. there exists a natural total ordering among elements of $\mathcal{T}$. Elements of $\mathcal{T}$ are termed as 'time points' in this paper. To anchor this abstract time line to a real calendar system, we choose the zero time point t_0 to match to the zero point of the Gregorian calendar, measured by the Greenwich Mean Time (GMT).

3.2   Time Intervals as Fuzzy Sets

We base the rest of this paper extensively on fuzzy set theory [11]. In Appendix we give a brief overview of fuzzy set theory, along with the pointers to relevant introductory literature.

In the following presentation, we assume that we need to represent a crisp interval i when a historical event happens. We denote with i^- its crisp starting point and with i^+ its crisp ending point. As discussed in Section 2.1, although the interval is crisp (after all, historical events really did occur at some precise time), the interval's start and ending points may not be known precisely. We call such an interval *imprecise* and model it by means of a fuzzy set $\tilde{I}$, defined by its membership function $\tilde{I} : \mathcal{T} \to [0,1]$. $\tilde{I}(t)$ represents our confidence level that t is in i. If $\tilde{I}(t) = 0$, we are completely confident that t is not in i; if $\tilde{I}(t) = 1$, we are completely confident that t is in i. We term such a fuzzy set representing an abstract interval as a *fuzzy interval*. We denote the set of all fuzzy intervals as $\mathcal{I}$.

Fuzzy intervals are capable of representing imprecision caused by all of the three special properties of historical knowledge (vagueness, uncertainty or subjectivity) in a unifying way. Indeed, the possibility to express partial confidence of the membership of some time point t in i allows us the express the imprecision of the accounts about the interval i, regardless of the actual nature of imprecision.

We do not pose any constraints on the fuzzy intervals except from the requirement that they should be convex, thus reflecting our requirement that the abstract interval i which is represented by the fuzzy interval should be continuous. Although some events occur at time intervals which are not continuous (e.g. 'Poland exists as a country'), they can be represented as a set of subevents denoting continuous parts of the original event (e.g. 'Poland exists for the first time', 'Poland is divided among the Russian Empire, the Habsburg Empire and Prussia/Germany' and 'Poland exists again').

In the case of convex fuzzy sets, their support and core are continuous. Further, all time points of i must be in the support of $\tilde{I}$ (denoted as $S_{\tilde{I}}$). I.e., if $t \notin S_{\tilde{I}}$, then we are certain that $t \notin i$. We also assume that all of the time points in the core of $\tilde{I}$ (denoted as $C_{\tilde{I}}$) are really members of i. I.e., if $t \in C_{\tilde{I}}$, then we are certain that $t \in i$. This can also be written as $C_{\tilde{I}} \subseteq i \subseteq S_{\tilde{I}}$.

4 Fuzzy Temporal Relations

In this section we show how to realize relations from Table 1 in our fuzzy model. We start with the observation that, since our intervals are not crisp, our relations will also not be crisp. After all, since the intervals are not exact, we cannot exactly determine whether one interval precedes the other one. Hence, given two imprecise crisp intervals i and j and a crisp temporal relation θ, the fuzzy temporal relation $\tilde{\theta}$ will take fuzzy sets $\tilde{I}$ and $\tilde{J}$ and produce a number $c \in [0,1]$, giving the confidence that the classical temporal θ relation holds between i and j.

Extending classical temporal relations to fuzzy sets is not easy, since classical relations in Table 1 are defined using interval endpoints. However, for fuzzy intervals the notion of endpoints is meaningless. Therefore, we define fuzzy temporal relations in an alternative way, compatible with the crisp case. We do this in several steps: first we reformulate the definition of crisp temporal relations based on the set operations on intervals, thus eliminating references to interval endpoints. In doing so, we introduce several auxiliary unary operators on intervals (e.g. 'before extension'), representing intervals with particular relationship to the original interval (e.g. interval additionally including the time before the interval). After that we extend the definitions of temporal relations to the fuzzy case by providing a fuzzy counterpart of auxiliary operators and reusing the usual fuzzy set operations.

4.1 Defining Crisp Temporal Relations Using Set Operations

The basic idea for eliminating references to interval endpoints is the following. Firstly, if $t_1 < t_2$, then the interval between t_1 and t_2 is not equal to the empty set. This we can be written as

$$t_1 < t_2 \quad \Leftrightarrow \quad (t_1, t_2) \neq \emptyset \tag{1}$$

Secondly, if $t_1 = t_2$, then we have to make sure that both intervals (t_1, t_2) and (t_2, t_1) are empty sets, thus expressing that neither t_1 is after t_2 or vice versa. This we can be written as

$$t_1 = t_2 \quad \Leftrightarrow \quad (t_1, t_2) = \emptyset \ \wedge \ (t_2, t_1) = \emptyset \tag{2}$$

Further, we define several auxiliary unary operators on intervals. The role of these operators is to construct the intervals commonly used in definitions of temporal relations. The following eight operators $<-, \leq-, >-, \geq-, <+, \leq+, >+, \geq+$ take an interval and construct an interval containing all of the time points which are (strictly) before or (strictly) after the starting or ending point of the original interval. E.g. $<-(i) = (-\infty, i^-)$. The definition of these operators is given in Table 2.

Now we are ready to redefine the temporal relations using the ideas presented in (1) and (2) and the unary operators from Table 2. We explain how this is done for the starts relation, since its definition uses both endpoint equality and inequality. Other relations are defined similarly and are given in Table 3. We did not redefine the after, overlapped-by, contains, met-by, started-by and finished-by relations, as they are simply the inverse of other relations.

We start the redefinition of the **starts** relation by repeating the definition from Table 1:

$$i \, \mathtt{starts} \, j \; \equiv \; i^- = j^- \; \wedge \; i^+ < j^+ \tag{3}$$

The constraint $i^- = j^-$ can be expressed as (cf. (2))

$$i^- = j^- \; \Leftrightarrow \; (i^-, j^-) = \emptyset \; \wedge \; (j^-, i^-) = \emptyset \tag{4}$$

which can be written with the help of auxiliary unary operators as

$$>\!\!-(i) \cap <\!\!-(j) = \emptyset \; \wedge \; >\!\!-(j) \cap <\!\!-(i) = \emptyset \tag{5}$$

because we know that

$$(t_1, t_2) = (t_1, +\infty) \cap (-\infty, t_2) \tag{6}$$

This last step is needed to eliminate all references to interval endpoints in the definition.

Similarly, the constraint $i^+ < j^+$ can be expressed using (1) and (6) as

$$i^+ < j^+ \; \Leftrightarrow \; >\!\!+(i) \cap <\!\!+(j) \neq \emptyset \tag{7}$$

Hence, the **starts** relation can be defined by means of set operations on intervals as

$$i \, \mathtt{starts} \, j \; \equiv \; \begin{aligned} &>\!\!-(i) \cap <\!\!-(j) = \emptyset \; \wedge \\ &>\!\!-(j) \cap <\!\!-(i) = \emptyset \; \wedge \\ &>\!\!+(i) \cap <\!\!+(j) \neq \emptyset \end{aligned} \tag{8}$$

Finally, we note that the **intersects** relation has not been derived from the definition in Table 1. Instead, simply the fact was used that it expresses the constraint that the intersection of i and j is not empty.

4.2   Extending Auxiliary Interval Operators to Fuzzy Intervals

In this section we extend the auxiliary interval operators to operate on fuzzy intervals. We denote the extended operators with the same symbols, i.e. as $<\!\!-, \leq\!\!-, >\!\!-, \geq\!\!-, <\!\!+, \leq\!\!+, >\!\!+, \geq\!\!+$, exactly as in the crisp case. Each operator $\tilde{\theta}$ will be function $\tilde{\theta} : \mathcal{I} \to \mathcal{I}$, i.e it will take a fuzzy interval and yield another fuzzy interval. The semantics of $\tilde{\theta}(\tilde{I})$ should be understood as follows: $\tilde{\theta}(\tilde{I})(t)$ gives our confidence that t is in $\theta(i)$. For example, $<\!\!-(\tilde{I})(t)$ represents our confidence that t is in $<\!\!-(i)$. In order to make our notation simpler, we will sometimes write $\tilde{\theta}(\tilde{I})$ as $\tilde{I}_{\tilde{\theta}}$.

In the rest of this section we will show how to extend the operators $\geq\!\!-$ and $<\!\!-$ to the fuzzy case. The other operators can be extended in a similar manner, and their definitions are shown in Table 4.

The operator $\geq\!\!-$ should, for some fuzzy interval $\tilde{I}$ representing interval i, give a fuzzy interval $\tilde{I}_{\geq\!\!-}$, representing the interval $\geq\!\!-(i)$. Let $s_{\tilde{I}}^-$ and $s_{\tilde{I}}^+$ denote the starting and ending points of $S_{\tilde{I}}$ (i.e. of the the support of $\tilde{I}$). By assumptions from Section 3.2, we known that $i \subseteq S_{\tilde{I}}$. Therefore, $\tilde{I}_{\geq\!\!-}(t)$ should be 0 for each $t < s_{\tilde{I}}^-$, and should be 1 for each $t > s_{\tilde{I}}^+$, as we know that each time point

Table 1. Required Temporal Relations

Interval Relation	Definition
i before j	$i^+ < j^-$
i after j	j before i
i overlaps j	$i^- < j^- \wedge i^+ > j^-$ $\wedge i^+ < j^+$
i overlapped-by j	j overlaps i
i during j	$i^- > j^- \wedge i^+ < j^+$
i contains j	j during i
i meets j	$i^+ = j^-$
i met-by j	j meets i
i starts j	$i^- = j^- \wedge i^+ < j^+$
i started-by j	j starts i
i finishes j	$j^- < i^- \wedge i^+ = j^+$
i finished-by j	j finishes i
i equals j	$i^- = j^- \wedge i^+ = j^+$
i intersects j	$i^+ > j^- \wedge i^- < j^+$

Table 2. Auxiliary Unary Operators on Intervals

Operator	Result
$<-$	$<-(i) = (-\infty, i^-)$
$\leq-$	$\leq-(i) = (-\infty, i^-]$
$>-$	$>-(i) = (i^-, +\infty)$
$\geq-$	$\geq-(i) = [i^-, +\infty)$
$<+$	$<+(i) = (-\infty, i^+)$
$\leq+$	$\leq+(i) = (-\infty, i^+]$
$>+$	$>+(i) = (i^+, +\infty)$
$\geq+$	$\geq-(i) = [i^+, +\infty)$

Table 3. Transcribed Temporal Relations

Temporal Relation	Definition
i before j	$>+(i) \cap <-(j) \neq \emptyset$
i overlaps j	$>-(i) \cap <-(j) \neq \emptyset \wedge$ $<+(i) \cap >-(j) \neq \emptyset \wedge$ $>+(i) \cap <+(j) \neq \emptyset$
i during j	$<-(i) \cap >-(j) \neq \emptyset \wedge$ $>+(i) \cap <+(j) \neq \emptyset$
i meets j	$>+(i) \cap <-(j) = \emptyset \wedge$ $<+(i) \cap >-(j) = \emptyset$
i starts j	$>-(i) \cap <-(j) = \emptyset \wedge$ $<-(i) \cap >-(j) = \emptyset \wedge$ $>+(i) \cap <+(j) \neq \emptyset$
i finishes j	$<-(i) \cap >-(j) \neq \emptyset \wedge$ $>+(i) \cap <+(j) = \emptyset \wedge$ $<+(i) \cap >+(j) = \emptyset$
i equals j	$>-(i) \cap <-(j) = \emptyset \wedge$ $<-(i) \cap >-(j) = \emptyset \wedge$ $>+(i) \cap <+(j) = \emptyset \wedge$ $<+(i) \cap >+(j) = \emptyset$
i intersects j	$i \cap j \neq \emptyset$

before $s_{\tilde{I}}^-$ are before i^-, and we know that each time point after $s_{\tilde{I}}^+$ is after i^+ and therefore also after i^-. For a $t \in S_{\tilde{I}}$, we can tell that our confidence that $t \in \geq-(i)$ should be as big as our confidence that $s \in \geq-(i)$ for any $s \leq t$. Therefore we define the operator $\geq- : \tilde{I} \to \tilde{I}$ as follows:

$$\tilde{I}_{\geq-}(t) = \begin{cases} 0 & \text{if } t < S_{\tilde{I}}^- \\ \sup_{s \leq t} \tilde{I}(s) & \text{if } t \in S_{\tilde{I}} \\ 1 & \text{if } t > S_{\tilde{I}}^+ \end{cases} \tag{9}$$

The definition of the operator $<-$ is easy if we already defined the $\geq-$ operator. We note that, if $t \in <-(i)$, then $t \notin \geq-(i)$. Therefore we simply define the $\tilde{I}_{<-}$ fuzzy interval as the fuzzy complement of the $\tilde{I}_{\geq-}$ fuzzy interval:

$$\tilde{I}_{<-}(t) = \tilde{I}_{\geq-}^C(t) = 1 - \tilde{I}_{\geq-}(t) \tag{10}$$

The results of applying the $\geq-$ and $<-$ operators on a fuzzy interval are shown in Figure 1.

4.3   Constraints Using Comparison with Empty Set

Before we can finally extend the definitions of the temporal relations to fuzzy intervals, we must extended constraints of the form $a \cap b \neq \emptyset$ and $a \cap b = \emptyset$ to fuzzy intervals. We use the following intuition: the value $\sup_t \tilde{I}(t)$ (i.e. the maximum confidence of membership of any time point in the interval) gives the confidence that some t is in i, i.e. our confidence that i is not empty.

Since fuzzy intersection is expressed using min operator (cf. Appendix), our confidence that $a \cap b \neq \emptyset$ can be represented as

$$\sup_t \min(\tilde{A}(t), \tilde{B}(t)) \tag{11}$$

Since $a \cap b = \emptyset$ is simply the negation of $a \cap b \neq \emptyset$, our confidence in that this constraint is fulfilled is given as

$$1 - \sup_t \min(\tilde{A}(t), \tilde{B}(t)) = \inf_t \max(\tilde{A}^C(t), \tilde{B}^C(t)) \tag{12}$$

4.4   Temporal Relations on Fuzzy Intervals

Now we are ready to extend the definition of the temporal relations to fuzzy intervals based on the transformed definitions from Table 3. We define a fuzzy temporal relation γ as a function $\gamma : \tilde{I} \times \tilde{I} \to [0, 1]$. In another words, a temporal relation takes two fuzzy intervals and gives the confidence that the crisp temporal relation holds between the abstract intervals represented by the respective fuzzy intervals. We denote the fuzzy temporal relations with big letters to distinguish them from their crisp counterparts.

We discuss the definition of relation $\text{STARTS}(\tilde{I}, \tilde{J})$. Other relations can be defined in a similar way, and they are shown in Table 5. We start from the definition of the crisp relation starts, which was defined in Section 4.1 as

$$i \,\text{starts}\, j \;\equiv\; \begin{array}{l} >-(i) \cap <-(j) = \emptyset \;\wedge \\ >-(j) \cap <-(i) = \emptyset \;\wedge \\ >+(i) \cap <+(j) \neq \emptyset \end{array} \tag{13}$$

After applying the rules for transcribing the constraints (cf. subsection 4.3) we get:

Table 4. Auxiliary Operators on Fuzzy Intervals

$\tilde{\theta}$	$\tilde{\theta}(\tilde{I})(t)$	
$<-$	$1 - \tilde{I}_{\geq -}(t)$	
$\leq-$	$1 - \tilde{I}_{> -}(t)$	
$>-$	0	if $t < S_{\tilde{I}}^-$
	$\sup_{s<t} \tilde{I}(s)$	if $t \in S_{\tilde{I}}$
	1	if $t > S_{\tilde{I}}^+$
$\geq-$	0	if $t < S_{\tilde{I}}^-$
	$\sup_{s\leq t} \tilde{I}(s)$	if $t \in S_{\tilde{I}}$
	1	if $t > S_{\tilde{I}}^+$
$<+$	0	if $t < S_{\tilde{I}}^-$
	$\sup_{s>t} \tilde{I}(s)$	if $t \in S_{\tilde{I}}$
	1	if $t > S_{\tilde{I}}^+$
$\leq+$	0	if $t < S_{\tilde{I}}^-$
	$\sup_{s\geq t} \tilde{I}(s)$	if $t \in S_{\tilde{I}}$
	1	if $t > S_{\tilde{I}}^+$
$>+$	$1 - \tilde{I}_{\leq -}(t)$	
$\geq+$	$1 - \tilde{I}_{< -}(t)$	

Table 5. Temporal Relations on Fuzzy Intervals

Relation	Definition
$\mathtt{BEFORE}(\tilde{I},\tilde{J})$	$\sup_t \min(\tilde{I}_{>+}(t), \tilde{J}_{<-}(t))$
$\mathtt{OVERLAPS}(\tilde{I},\tilde{J})$	$\min(\ \sup_t \min(\tilde{I}_{>-}(t), \tilde{J}_{<-}(t))\ ,$ $\sup_t \min(\tilde{I}_{<+}(t), \tilde{J}_{>-}(t))\ ,$ $\sup_t \min(\tilde{I}_{>+}(t), \tilde{J}_{<+}(t))\ )$
$\mathtt{DURING}(\tilde{I},\tilde{J})$	$\min(\ \sup_t \min(\tilde{I}_{<-}(t), \tilde{J}_{>-}(t))\ ,$ $\sup_t \min(\tilde{I}_{>+}(t), \tilde{J}_{<+}(t))\ )$
$\mathtt{MEETS}(\tilde{I},\tilde{J})$	$\min(\ \inf_t \max(\tilde{I}_{\leq+}(t), \tilde{J}_{\geq-}(t))\ ,$ $\inf_t \max(\tilde{I}_{\geq+}(t), \tilde{J}_{\leq-}(t))\ )$
$\mathtt{STARTS}(\tilde{I},\tilde{J})$	$\min(\ \inf_t \max(\tilde{I}_{\leq-}(t), \tilde{J}_{\geq-}(t))\ ,$ $\inf_t \max(\tilde{I}_{\geq-}(t), \tilde{J}_{\leq-}(t))\ ,$ $\sup_t \min(\tilde{I}_{>+}(t), \tilde{J}_{<+}(t))\ )$
$\mathtt{FINISHES}(\tilde{I},\tilde{J})$	$\min(\ \inf_t \max(\tilde{I}_{\leq+}(t), \tilde{J}_{\geq+}(t))\ ,$ $\inf_t \max(\tilde{I}_{\geq+}(t), \tilde{J}_{\leq+}(t))\ ,$ $\sup_t \min(\tilde{I}_{>-}(t), \tilde{J}_{<-}(t))\ )$
$\mathtt{EQUALS}(\tilde{I},\tilde{J})$	$\min(\ \inf_t \max(\tilde{I}_{\leq+}(t), \tilde{J}_{\geq+}(t))\ ,$ $\inf_t \max(\tilde{I}_{\geq+}(t), \tilde{J}_{\leq+}(t))\ ,$ $\inf_t \max(\tilde{I}_{\leq-}(t), \tilde{J}_{\geq-}(t))\ ,$ $\inf_t \max(\tilde{I}_{\geq-}(t), \tilde{J}_{\leq-}(t))\ )$
$\mathtt{INTERSECTS}(\tilde{I},\tilde{J})$	$\sup_t \min(\tilde{I}(t), \tilde{J}(t))$

$$\mathtt{STARTS}(\tilde{I}, \tilde{J}) = \min(\\ \inf_t \max(\tilde{I}_{\leq-}(t), \tilde{J}_{\geq-}(t)), \\ \inf_t \max(\tilde{I}_{\geq-}(t), \tilde{J}_{\leq-}(t)), \\ \sup_t \min(\tilde{I}_{>+}(t), \tilde{J}_{<+}(t))) \tag{14}$$

5   Discussion

In this section we discuss the model and relations presented in Sections 3 and 4 and demonstrate how they fulfill the requirements from Section 2.

Representing Imprecise Information. As discussed briefly in Section 3.2, fuzzy intervals are capable of representing all three causes of impreciseness in history. They represent the net confidence of the history expert about the statement $t \in i$, where the lack of confidence can be caused by any combination of vagueness, uncertainty and subjectivity.

Of course, in a realistic application scenario historical experts will not specify fuzzy intervals by encoding their confidence about each $t \in \mathcal{T}$, but will apply some heuristics on their intuitive temporal knowledge. Finding the best heuristics in the specific cases is subject of further research. As an example, we show a possible interpretation of the intervals 'late twenties – early thirties', '320? B.C. – 280 B.C.' and 'Russian Revolution happens' in Figure 1, each of them showing one of the special characteristics of historical knowledge.

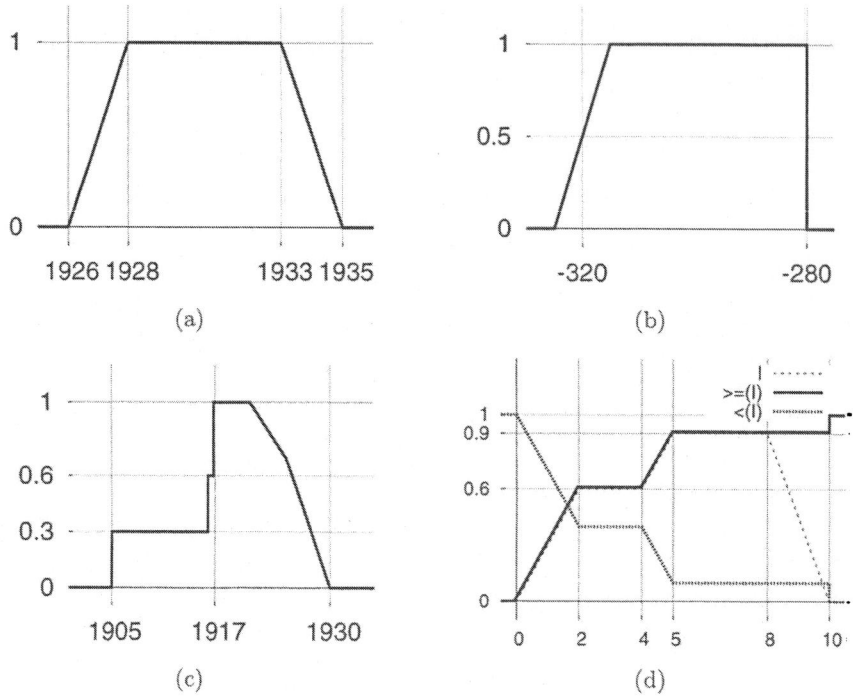

Fig. 1. Fuzzy intervals (a) 'late twenties' – 'early thirties' (b) 320? B.C. – 280 B.C.
(c) Russian Revolution happens (d) $\tilde{I}_{\geq-}$ and $\tilde{I}_{<-}$

Compatibility with Crisp Case. It is easy to see that fuzzy relations are natural
extensions of the classical ones, as they give the same results on crisp intervals
as the classical ones. This is because we defined the fuzzy relations based on
the original definitions of the classical relations. Hence, the requirements on the
compatibility with the crisp case is fulfilled completely.

Intuitiveness of Fuzzy Relations. We believe that our fuzzy relations yield intuitive result, where 'intuitive' for us means that the relation gives 1 as result if
we are completely certain that the classical relation exists between the classical
abstract intervals represented by the fuzzy intervals, and 0 if we are certain that
this is impossible. A result between 0 and 1 is given if neither of these possibili-
ties are sure. E.g. in case of the BEFORE($\tilde{I},\tilde{J}$), it should yield 0 if $S_{\tilde{I}}$ before $S_{\tilde{J}}$
holds (i.e. we are sure that i before j holds) and it should yield 1 if $C_{\tilde{I}}$ before
$C_{\tilde{J}}$ does not hold (i.e. we are sure that i before j does not hold). Intuitiveness
can similarly be checked for other fuzzy relations as well.

6   Connecting Temporal and Ontology Models

In this section we discuss how the temporal model described previously is used in
ontology modeling. Our approach for integrating temporal and ontology models

is general and not tied to any particular model. However, to make the discussion more concrete, we briefly describe the designated *ontology* model first, after which we show how model integration is actually done.

6.1 Target Ontology Model

Out target ontology model is that of KAON[2] – an ontology management framework developed by FZI and AIFB at University of Karlsruhe. The model [12] is based on RDF(S) [13], allowing modeling of concepts, properties, instances and relations between instances. It extends RDF(S) with several useful features, such as symmetric, transitive and inverse properties. Unlike RDF(S), however, KAON does not support reification of statements, due to the fact that formal semantics of the KAON language is much more similar to OWL [14] (actually, KAON ontology model is currently being extended with OWL primitives using results from logic programming [15]). As it is the case in all description logics based languages, formal semantics of OWL is based on the usual first-order theory. However, contrary to OWL, KAON semantics is based on HiLog [16], providing a clean mechanism for second-order flavor of the ontology language. For example, in KAON it is possible to interpret a symbol as a concept or as an instance, depending on the symbol's context. In KAON information about concepts and instances is structured in OI-models (ontology-instance models). Figure 2 shows a fragment of the VICODI OI-model.

6.2 Integrating Temporal and Ontology Model

Our approach for integrating the temporal model into ontological definitions follows a pattern of modular semantics, which we believe will gain importance in the near future as the complexity of domains being modeled increases. This pattern is based on the observation that particular formalism may be good for some modeling tasks, but totally inappropriate for other ones. Trying to apply the most general formalism (e.g. first-order logic) to all modeling tasks usually results in cumbersome systems with inadequate performance. Rather, a more promising approach is to combine various formalisms in a modular way, thus harvesting the best of each of them. In this paper we apply this principle to time modeling. However, we could imagine a spatial algebra being orthogonally added to the temporal and description logics formalisms in a similar manner.

Our approach may schematically be described as in Figure 3. On the left-hand side of the figure is the ontology model with its HiLog semantics, whereas on the right-hand side is the fuzzy temporal model with the semantics as described in Sections 3 and 4. These two heterogeneous semantics are orthogonal and need to be integrated at the syntactical and at the semantic level.

Integration at the syntactical level defines how to physically connect elements from one model with another. We have found out that data types provide an excellent mechanism for this purpose. Many ontology languages (e.g. OWL) offer the capability of modeling atomic objects whose semantics is out

---

[2] http://kaon.semanticweb.org/

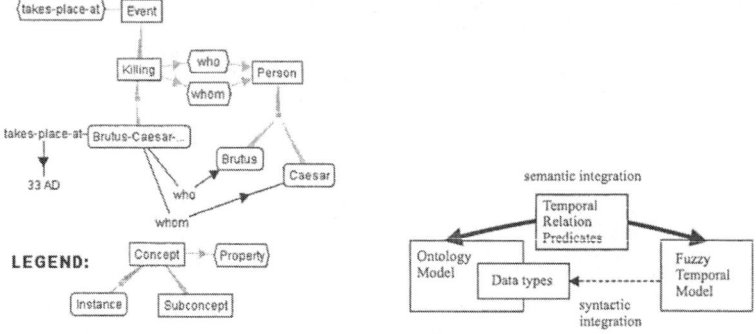

Fig. 2. Fragment of VICODI OI-model

Fig. 3. Integrating Ontology and Fuzzy Temporal Models

of scope of the logical theory. In semantic interpretation of the ontology, instances of data types are interpreted as members of some concrete domain (often denoted as Δ_D). On the other hand, ontology instances are interpreted as members of the abstract domain (often denoted as Δ^I). The concrete and abstract domains must be disjoint, thus causing the semantics of data types and of the ontology model to be separated. In our case, we introduced a separate TEMPORALSPECIFICATION data type which is responsible for representing temporal information. Currently, TEMPORALSPECIFICATION has only one sub-data type called FUZZYTIMEINTERVAL.

Integration at the semantic level defines how properties of one model semantically relate to the other model. In our case this means we need to specify how the temporal relations from Section 4 is represented in the first-order setting. This is done by introducing for each temporal relation from Table 5 a many-sorted predicate reflecting the logical properties of the relation. One can think of these predicates as built-ins: the arguments of the predicate are fuzzy intervals whose content is opaque to the logic infrastructure. The predicates serve as a gate between the two worlds, providing an abstract interface to the interval model. One must observe that the semantics of the predicates is not axiomatized in first-order logic, but reasoning may still be performed on the arguments and results of the predicates. Each predicate has an additional argument receiving the fuzzy value of the relation. For example, if fuzzy interval $\tilde{I}$ is before interval $\tilde{J}$ with confidence level 0.8, then the first-order formula BEFORE($\tilde{I},\tilde{J}$,0.8) is true. Note that constraints on the confidence level can be expressed by using variables:

$$\text{BEFORE}(\tilde{I}, \tilde{J}, X) \ \wedge \ X > 0.8 \tag{15}$$

6.3 Annotating Ontology Definitions with Temporal Specifications

The previous subsection discussed how to integrate ontology and temporal model at the generic level. However, an important question remains open: how to attach the temporal specifications to the ontology definitions? For example, how to represent the fact that French Revolution lasted from 1789 to 1794? Before answering this question, we examine the types of ontology definitions to which temporal specifications could be applicable at all.

Annotating Ontology Elements Themselves. At the first glance, it seems to be useful annotating ontology definitions, such as concept or property declarations, themselves, with time information in which the concept or property definition exists. For example, one might be tempted to state that the concept EUCOUNTRY exists only after 1992. Before this date it does not make much sense to talk about EU countries anyway. Another useful example is annotating the subconcept relationship with time information, thus allowing representation of classification which varies over time. Although useful at the first glance, such annotations are extremely difficult to manage in a logical setting. Concept and property declarations are semantically represented as predicates. In a first-order theory one cannot attach additional information to predicates – one would need a full second-order language where predicates can be treated as instances of meta-predicates. Second-order logic is extremely difficult to manage, and introducing such features in HiLog or first-order logic is extremely messy, so we decided not to support such annotations. Further, ontology axioms stating that A is a subclass of B are tantamount to first-order formulas $\forall x(A(x) \rightarrow B(x))$. Annotating formulas is not possible in any logic and the semantic interpretation of such annotations has not been proposed yet.

After some considerations, one may see that such annotations often do not make sense. One may argue that the concept of EU countries existed before 1992, it just did not have any instances. Therefore, this is in practice not really a limitation. Thus, we have dismissed temporal annotations for ontology definitions, but we allow temporal annotations for instances and relationships among them.

Semantics of Temporal Specifications. When building ontologies containing temporal information, a fundamental question about the meaning of temporal specifications for ontology entities arises. Most approaches in temporal databases [10] use only one type of time. Namely, each tuple in the database is annotated with the validity time, thus specifying the period when the information represented by the tuple is valid in the real world. In temporal reasoning the usual approach is to associate an additional temporal argument with each predicate [3].

We argue that such approaches are too simple for many applications, as they allow specifying only one type of time. For example, one may say that ALLAN TURING LIVED from 23 June 1912 until 7 June 1954, which certainly may be represented as his validity time. On the other hand, one may associate with him additionally the interval from 1931 until 1935, which represents the time when he studied at King's College. Hence, we see that different types of time information are needed for expressive ontology modeling. If needed, one may additionally axiomatize the LIVED relation as validity time, but this is, according to our opinion, domain-specific.

Annotating Relationships between Instances. A unique feature of ontologies containing temporal information is that temporal information is not only associated to instances (e.g. PERSON WAS-BORN-AT certain time), but also to relationships between instances (e.g. BRUTUS KILLS CAESAR with annotation that this event TAKES-PLACE-AT certain time). Capturing this type of information presents new challenges to our approach for integrating temporal and ontology models. In particular, our ontology model allows connecting two instances through a property instance (i.e. at the logical level all relationships between instances are represented as two-place predicates). This restriction is fundamental to our ontology model, since it is known that ontology languages with predicates of arbitrary arity may easily become undecidable.

We could solve this problem using reification approaches of RDFS. However, as we explained in subsection 6.1, the semantics of statement sets reification is not clean in RDFS and does not match well with the usual first-order semantics. Therefore, we solve the problem by reifying relationships annotated by temporal specifications into first-class objects. In another words, the example problem presented above is solved by introducing the concept KILLING as a subconcept of the EVENT concept, with properties WHO, WHOM and TAKES-PLACE-AT. This solution is presented in Figure 2.

Although cumbersome at the first glance, this approach has an advantage that all time information is represented in a uniform way through a taxonomy of temporal properties. In this way selecting all events taking place at certain point in time becomes very easy.

7   Related Work

There is a significant amount of approaches for representing temporal information in the areas of temporal reasoning and temporal databases. Most of these, however, consider only classical time intervals (or time points) and do not deal with any form of imprecisions.

There are some approaches, however, which provide some solutions for handling uncertain temporal information. Most of them model uncertainty with possibility or probability distributions on interval endpoints.

In the area of temporal databases [2], the approaches [17,18] define the probability distribution of each endpoint of crisp time intervals. However, it is generally debated whether probability distributions are appropriate for representing subjective information at all, as objective statistics, that probability distributions are based on, are often missing when defining subjective information [19].

Because of that, most approaches in temporal reasoning for modeling subjective temporal knowledge use probability distributions expressed as fuzzy sets to represent uncertainty. Dubois and Prade [5] propose an approach where endpoints of a fuzzy interval are modeled as fuzzy numbers. Further, they use possibility theory [20,19] to calculate time points which are possibly or necessarily between the two fuzzy endpoints. They also provide fuzzy extensions of Allen's interval algebra and some basic inference mechanisms.

Kurutach [21] also proposes using fuzzy numbers representing interval endpoints similarly to Dubois and Prade. Moreover, he imposes constraints on the length of intervals. Godo and Vila [7] propose using fuzzy sets constraining the length of the time period between intervals. Although this approach is adequate for some problems in the health-care domain, we found it quite inadequate for modeling historical imprecise intervals as it is not possible to specify absolute dates for intervals.

Almost all of the approaches for representing uncertain intervals is based on the notion of uncertain interval endpoints. However, as it was discussed in Section 2.1 it is not always intuitive to assume that there is a (possibly ill-known) definite starting and ending point for an interval. There are some events, where it makes sense of speaking of 'transition periods' in addition of a 'core period'. E.g. consider the case of the Russian revolution, whose interval is shown in Figure 1. In this case the transtition periods are much longer as the core period of the event. Using an endpoint-based approach one has to decide which one of the possible endpoints to take, which means loosing information. With our approach it is possible to model not only the core period of an event, but also transtition, development etc. periods, which are only partially relevant for a specific event. This is posisble because we define intervals directly, without referencing the endpoints.

An interesting approach for representing uncertainty about time-dependent events which follows a different idea as the works introduced so far is that of Dutta's [6]. He uses the set of known intervals as the universe for fuzzy sets. A fuzzy set representing an event e shows the possibility for each interval i that that event occurs in it. Although this approach is different from the other described approaches in the sense that it is capable of representing fuzzily defined events, it views intervals themselves only as abstract, crisp entities without any further temporal specification, therefore it is not applicable in our application scenario.

8   Conclusion and Outlook

In this paper we presented a fuzzy temporal model that is capable to represent all aspects of historical temporal knowledge in a common formal framework. Although the model's design was based on the requirements from the application domain of history, it can also be used in other application domains that require representing uncertain, subjective and vague temporal knowledge (such as health-care). Apart from defining the temporal model based on fuzzy sets, we also generalized Allen's temporal relations on intervals. We did this by providing a definition of crisp interval relations based on set theory and then generalized them to the fuzzy case.

Our temporal model is intended for use in ontology modeling. Hence, we provided an approach for integrating temporal and ontology models. The approach follows the modular semantics pattern, which tries to keep the semantics of each model separate and to provide clean interfaces between them.

We are presently working on a methodology for capturing fuzzy temporal knowledge from experts. There are specifically two challenges we plan to address. Firstly, we want to provide an easy, intuitive strategy for capturing temporal specifications without the need to specify fuzzy intervals directly. In this way we hope to make our system usable by non-IT experts. Secondly, a conversion mechanism between different temporal granularities is needed since temporal granularity of historical facts usually differs (e.g. some accounts are specified in years and some in days).

We are also examining the different properties of our new fuzzy temporal relations (like transitivity) which work will allow us to make basic inferences even in case of fuzzy intervals (e.g. $\text{BEFORE}(\tilde{I}, \tilde{J}) = 0.8 \land \text{BEFORE}(\tilde{J}, \tilde{K}) = 0.7 \Rightarrow \text{BEFORE}(\tilde{I}, \tilde{K}) \geq 0.7$).

References

1. Jensen, C.S., Dyreson, C.E., Böhlen, M., Clifford, J., Elmasri, R., Gadia, S.K., Grandi, F., Hayes, P., Jajodia, S., Käfer, W., Kline, N., Lorentzos, N., Mitsopoulos, Y., Montanari, A., Nonen, D., Peressi, E., Pernici, B., Roddick, J.F., Sarda, N.L., Scalas, M.R., Segev, A., Snodgrass, R.T., Soo, M.D., Tansel, A., Tiberio, P., Wiederhold, G.: The consensus glossary of temporal database concepts – february 1998 version. Lecture Notes in Computer Science **1399** (1998) 367–405
2. Etzion, O., Jajodia, S., Sripada, S., eds.: Temporal databases: research and practice. In Etzion, O., Jajodia, S., Sripada, S., eds.: Temporal databases: research and practice. Volume 1399 of Lecture Notes in Computer Science., New York, NY, USA, Springer-Verlag Inc. (1998)
3. Vila, L.: A survey on temporal reasoning in artificial intelligence. AICOM (Artificial Intelligence Communications) **7** (1994) 4–28
4. Allen, J.F.: Maintaining knowledge about temporal intervals. Communications of the ACM **26** (1983) 832–843
5. Dubois, D., Prade, H.: Processing fuzzy temporal knowledge. IEEE Transactions of Systems, Man and Cybernetics **19** (1989) 729–744
6. Dutta, S.: An event-based fuzzy temporal logic. In: Proc. 18th IEEE Intl. Symp. on Multiple-Valued Logic, Palma de Mallorca, Spain (1988) 64–71
7. Godo, L., Vila, L.: Possibilistic temporal reasoning based on fuzzy temporal constraints. In Mellish, C., ed.: IJCAI'95: Proceedings International Joint Conference on Artificial Intelligence, Montreal (1995)
8. DARPA Agent Markup Language project: DAML-Time Homepage. (2002) Accessible from the URL http://www.cs.rochester.edu/~ferguson/daml/.
9. Chomicki, J.: Temporal query languages: A survey. In Gabbay, D.M., Ohlbach, H.J., eds.: Proceedings of the 1st International Conference on Temporal Logic. Volume 827 of LNAI., Berlin, Springer (1994) 506–534
10. McKenzie, E., Snodgrass, R.: An evaluation of relational algebras incorporating the time dimension in databases. ACM Computing Surveys **23** (1991) 501–543
11. Zadeh, L.A.: Fuzzy sets. Information and Control **8** (1965) 338–353
12. Motik, B., Maedche, A., Volz, R.: A conceptual modeling approach for semantics-driven enterprise applications. In: Proc. 1st Int'l Conf. on Ontologies, Databases and Application of Semantics (ODBASE-2002). (2002)
13. Brickley, D., Guha, R.: RDF Vocabulary Description Language 1.0: RDF Schema. W3C. (2000) Accessible from the URL http://www.w3.org/TR/rdf-schema.
14. Patel-Schneider, P.F., Hayes, P., Horrocks, I., van Harmelen, F.: Web Ontology Language (OWL) Abstract Syntax and Semantics. W3C. (2002) Accessible from the URL http://www.w3.org/TR/owl-semantics/.
15. Grossof, B., Horrocks, I., Volz, R., Decker, S.: Description logic programs: Combining logic programs with description logic. In: Proceedings of WWW 2003, Budapest, Hungary (2003)

16. Chen, W., Kifer, M., Warren, D.S.: Hilog: A foundation for higher-order logic programming. Journal of Logic Programming **15** (1993) 183–230
17. Dekhtyar, A., Ross, R., Subrahmanian, V.S.: Probabilistic temporal databases, I: algebra. ACM Transactions on Database Systems (TODS) **26** (2001) 41–95
18. Dyreson, C.E., Snodgrass, R.T.: Supporting valid-time indeterminacy. ACM Transactions on Database Systems **23** (1998) 1–57
19. Dubois, D., Prade, H.: Possibility Theory: An Approach to Computerized Processing of Uncertainty. Plenum Press, New York (1986)
20. Zadeh, L.: Fuzzy sets as a basis for possibility. Fuzzy Sets and Systems **1** (1978) 3–28
21. Kurutach, W.: Modelling fuzzy interval-based temporal information: a temporal database perspective. In: Proceedings of 1995 IEEE International Conference on Fuzzy Systems, Yokohama, Japan (1995) 741–748
22. Dubois, D., Prade, H.: Fundamentals of Fuzzy Sets. Volume 7 of The handbooks of fuzzy sets series; FSHS 7. Kluwer Academic Publishers (2000)
23. Nguyen, H.T., Walker, E.A.: A First Course in Fuzzy Logic. CRC Press, New York (1997)

Appendix: Fuzzy Set Basics

In this appendix we briefly recapitulate the fundamental notions about the fuzzy sets and fuzzy logic. Further details can be found in any textbook of fuzzy sets or fuzzy logic (e.g. [22,23]).

Fuzzy sets generalize the notion of classical sets (also called as crisp sets as a counterpart of fuzzy). A subset A of the set $\mathcal{U}$ (the universe of discourse) can be specified using the *characteristic function* $A : \mathcal{U} \to \{0,1\}$. $A(x) = 1$ if $x \in A$ and $A(x) = 0$ if $x \notin A$. Similarly, a *fuzzy subset* $\tilde{A}$ of $\mathcal{U}$ can be characterized with a *membership function* $\tilde{A} : \mathcal{U} \to [0,1]$. For each $x \in \mathcal{U}$ $\tilde{A}(x)$ represents the membership grade of x in $\tilde{A}$. Hence, x can be a member of a $\tilde{A}$ partially. We call fuzzy subsets (of $\mathcal{U}$) simply as fuzzy sets from now on and assume that the universe of discourse is understood from the context.

Similarly as in the crisp case, logical connectives $\wedge$, $\vee$ and $\neg$ may in the fuzzy case be identified with the set operations $\cap, \cup$ and $\tilde{A}^C$ (the former is the fuzzy complement of $\tilde{A}$). The usual definition of the fuzzy set operations (which we will also use in this paper) are the following:

$$(\tilde{A} \cap \tilde{B})(x) = \min(\tilde{A}(x), \tilde{B}(x)) \tag{16}$$
$$(\tilde{A} \cup \tilde{B})(x) = \max(\tilde{A}(x), \tilde{B}(x)) \tag{17}$$
$$\tilde{A}^C(x) = 1 - \tilde{A}(x) \tag{18}$$

The *core* of $\tilde{A}$ is the crisp set $C_{\tilde{A}} = \{x \in \mathcal{U} : \tilde{A}(x) = 1\}$, i.e. the set of elements which completely belong to $\tilde{A}$ and the *support* of $\tilde{A}$ is the crisp set $S_{\tilde{A}} = \{x \in \mathcal{U} : \tilde{A}(x) > 0\}$, i.e. the set of elements which somewhat belong to $\tilde{A}$.

A fuzzy set $\tilde{A}$ is called convex if the following holds:

$$\forall x \forall x_1 \forall x_2 \ x \in [x_1, x_2] \Rightarrow \tilde{A}(x) \geq \min(\tilde{A}(x_1), \tilde{A}(x_2)) \tag{19}$$

Semantics and Modeling of Spatiotemporal Changes

Peiquan Jin, Lihua Yue, and Yuchang Gong

Department of Computer Science and Technology,
University of Science and Technology of China,
230027, Hefei, China
{jpq,llyue,gcgong}@ustc.edu.cn
http://staff.ustc.edu.cn/~jpq

Abstract. Typical spatiotemporal information systems, such as traffic management and land management, need to trace the spatiotemporal changes of objects. Different applications have different requirements on describing spatiotemporal changes. It is necessary to make a systematic research on spatiotemporal changes in order to design a general spatiotemporal data model for different spatiotemporal applications. Based on the semantics of objects and spatiotemporal changes in the real world, this paper proposes a systematic classification on spatiotemporal changes of objects and a new approach to describe spatiotemporal changes, which is based on object identity and descriptor. The new approach uses object-level spatiotemporal changes and attribute-level spatiotemporal changes to describe the evolving history of objects. It overcomes the shortcomings of previous approaches, which are lacking in completeness and systematization on representing spatiotemporal changes, and can describe spatiotemporal changes completely.

1 Introduction

The representation and querying method of spatiotemporal changes is the basis of a spatiotemporal data model. Typical spatiotemporal database applications such as land management and traffic management require the DBMS to trace and query the changing history of objects in a specific period, e.g. to find the trajectory of a car in a traffic management system. To answer queries about spatiotemporal changes effectively, a systematic research on the semantics of spatiotemporal changes is necessary, which includes the types of spatiotemporal changes and the approach to describe spatiotemporal changes. Then it is possible to design a general spatiotemporal data model that can represent object and spatiotemporal changes effectively.

The research on spatiotemporal changes is derived from the research of temporal databases. G. Langran [7] and A. Renolen [10] investigated the temporal aspects of GIS from cartography, and others from data model. Basic spatiotemporal changes include the appearance, disappearance, split and transformation of objects [2,3] but other types of spatiotemporal changes are omitted and no systematic and complete research so far has been undertaken. K. Hornsby and M. Egenhofer [6] proposed an identity-based description of spatiotemporal changes. According to this approach, two states of objects, existence and non-existence, were used to represent changes with

R. Meersman et al. (Eds.): CoopIS/DOA/ODBASE 2003, LNCS 2888, pp. 924–933, 2003.
© Springer-Verlag Berlin Heidelberg 2003

identities. But changes that do not result in changes of identities cannot be represented. History graph is another approach to represent spatiotemporal changes [10]. It used version state and transition state to represent changes. Though history graph can model discrete changes, it lacked the ability to model continuous changes of objects.

In order to model spatiotemporal changes, a lot of researchers suggested to explicitly store spatiotemporal changes in a spatiotemporal data model [1,2,3,4,5,6,9]. According to this view, each change is related to a specific event, so spatiotemporal changes can be represented by an explicit event list. Previous models such as the snapshot model and spatiotemporal composite model did not store changes explicitly but store versions in different instant, and spatiotemporal changes were got by comparing different versions [11]. These models provided weak support for spatiotemporal changes, e.g. changes involving several objects such as split and mergence were not supported. Besides, the efficiency of change queries was also poor. On the other hand, storing all the changes explicitly causes additional costs, because not only the relationships among objects but also the relationships among the versions of each object should be stored when each change occurs. In fact, we need to answer such query as "How did field A change into field B?" but need not to answer "How did the owner of field A change from Mary to Rose?", i.e. changes among different objects should be explicitly stored but internal changes of an object need not to be explicitly stored.

The purpose of this paper is to investigate the types of spatiotemporal changes and the approach to describing spatiotemporal changes. The semantics of spatiotemporal changes are studied and a systematic classification on spatiotemporal changes is proposed. We also present a new approach to the representation of spatiotemporal changes, which is complete and systematic. This approach is based on object identity and descriptor, and spatiotemporal changes are described through object-level spatiotemporal changes and attribute-level spatiotemporal changes. The former is represented by history topology, while the latter is described by descriptors. We prove that the approach introduced can completely describe spatiotemporal changes. Compared with previous work, our research is more systematic and complete, and forms the foundation of spatiotemporal data models.

The remainder of this paper is structured as follows: Section 2 proposes a systematic classification on spatiotemporal changes. Section 3 introduces the new approach to describing spatiotemporal changes. Section 4 discusses how attribute-level changes are described using descriptors. Section 5 focuses on describing object-level changes based on history topology. Section 6 discusses the formal definition of spatiotemporal object as well as spatiotemporal changes. And conclusion and future work are presented in Section 7.

2   The Types of Spatiotemporal Changes

One limitation that researchers of spatiotemporal database and temporal GIS seem to impose on their models is that objects can only be created, changed and eventually removed. However this is a too simplistic view in a spatial context. Spatial objects may also split into two or more objects, and two or more objects may also be merged into one single object. There are different kinds of changes existed in the real world, and current spatiotemporal data models are usually short in supporting different types of changes completely. This is mainly because of the insufficient cognition to the real world.

According to the object-oriented view, the objects in the real world are identified through identifiers, and the state of an object is represented by its internal attributes, which are spatial attribute and non-spatial attributes. The former describe the position and region occupied by an object, and the latter are those attributes that are related to the applications an object is involved in, which are called thematic attributes. So according to the structure of an object, the spatiotemporal changes of objects can be divided into two categories, which are changes of object identities and changes of internal attributes. And the changes of internal attributes can be further classified into changes of spatial attribute and changes of thematic attributes.

On the other hand, spatiotemporal changes can be classified into continuous changes and discrete changes, as many papers have proposed before [2,3,10]. Thus, a spatiotemporal change of an object now could be any one among the following six types (see table 1).

Table 1. Types of spatiotemporal changes

	Change of Spatial Attributes	Change of Thematic Attributes	Change of Object Identity
Continuous Change	Continuous Spatial Change	Continuous Attribute Change	Continuous Identity Change
Discrete Change	Discrete Spatial Change	Discrete Attribute Change	Discrete Identity Change

On the above six types of spatiotemporal changes, continuous identity change is not existed in the real world, because a change of object identity always happens right away. So in fact there are only five types of spatiotemporal changes meaningful in the real world, which are:

(1) *Continuous spatial change*: the spatial attributes of an object change continuously with time, such as spread of fire, flowing of flood and moving of a car. These changes are always related to a period of time.

(2) *Discrete spatial change*: the spatial attributes keep static in a period and suddenly change to another value. A typical example is the change of a field's boundary. Discrete spatial change always happens in a specific instant.

(3) *Continuous attribute change*: the thematic attributes of an object change continuously with time, such as changes of soil type.

(4) *Discrete attribute change*: the thematic attributes are basically static, but which are changed into another values suddenly. E.g. the change of the ownership of a field.

(5) *Discrete identity change*: sudden changes that result in change of object identity, such as split of a field or mergence of two fields into one field.

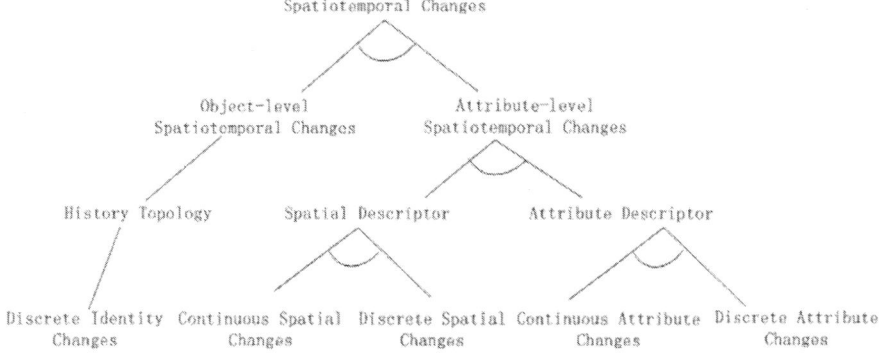

Fig. 1. The framework for modeling spatiotemporal changes

3 Modeling Spatiotemporal Changes

The framework for modeling spatiotemporal changes is showed in Fig. 1 as an *And/Or Tree*. Spatiotemporal changes are represented by object-level spatiotemporal changes that result in changes of object identities and attribute-level spatiotemporal changes that do not change any objects' identities but only the internal attributes of an object. Attribute-level spatiotemporal changes are spatial attribute changes or thematic attribute changes, which are described by spatial descriptor and attribute descriptor, while object-level spatiotemporal changes are discrete identity changes, which are represented by history topology. The modeling of spatiotemporal changes as showed in Fig.1 is complete, i.e. any spatiotemporal changes can be described through object-level spatiotemporal changes and attribute-level spatiotemporal changes. The proof is given as follows:

Proof:
Step1: Since an object is structured as identity, spatial attribute and thematic attributes, the state of an object at any time can be determined by its identity, spatial attribute and thematic attributes. Suppose that during a given period $[t_s, t_e]$ an object's state is changed, this change can only occur in its identity, its spatial attribute or its thematic attributes. So in order to describe the spatiotemporal changes of an object in $[t_s, t_e]$, we only need to represent those changes that occur in the object identity, the spatial attribute and the thematic attributes. That means the following equation is true:

$$\xi_o[t_s, t_e] \; \underline{\underline{\Delta}} \; \eta_o(t_d) \; \cup \; \omega_o[t_s, t_e] \; \cup \; \mu_o[t_s, t_e] \tag{1}$$

Here, $\xi_o[t_s, t_e]$ is the spatiotemporal change of object O during $[t_s, t_e]$. $\eta_o(t_d)$ is the identity change happened at td. $\omega_o[t_s, t_e]$ is the spatial change during $[t_s, t_e]$, and $\mu_o[t_s, t_e]$ is the thematic change.

Step 2: The identity change $\eta_o(t_d)$ can only occur at the instant t_s or t_e+1. This is because if it occur at t_i and $t_s < t_i \leq t_e$, then:

a) If in $[t_s, t_{i-1}]$ the object identity is O, and after t_i the origin object has been another object identified by P, then the changes happened in $(t_i, t_e]$ can be described in the object P, which is $\xi_P[t_i, t_e]$. Then we can get the following result:

$$\xi_o[t_s, .t_e] = \xi_o[t_s, .t_{i-1}] \cup \xi_P[t_i, t_e], \text{where:}$$

$$\xi_o[t_s, .t_{i-1}] \triangleq \eta_o(t_i) \cup \omega_o[t_s, .t_{i-1}] \cup \mu_o[t_s, .t_{i-1}] \text{ and}$$

$$\xi_P[t_i, .t_e] \triangleq \eta_P(t_i) \cup \omega_P[t_i, .t_e] \cup \mu_P[t_i, .t_e]$$

b) If in $[t_s, t_{i-1}]$ the object identity is P, and after t_i it is O. Then the changes happened in $(t_i, t_e]$ can be described in the object P, which is $\xi_P[t_s, t_{i-1}]$. Thus:

$$\xi_o[t_s, .t_e] = \xi_P[t_s, .t_{i-1}] \cup \xi_o[t_i, .t_e], \text{where:}$$

$$\xi_P[t_s, .t_{i-1}] \triangleq \eta_P(t_i) \cup \omega_P[t_s, .t_{i-1}] \cup \mu_P[t_s, .t_{i-1}] \text{ and}$$

$$\xi_o[t_i, .t_e] \triangleq \eta_o(t_i) \cup \omega_o[t_i, .t_e] \cup \mu_o[t_i, .t_e]$$

The above discussion shows that if the identity change of object O occurs at t_i and $t_s < t_i \leq t_e$, then the spatiotemporal change of O can be decomposed into two objects, each of which satisfies: for each $\eta_o(t_d)$, $t_d = t_s$ or $t_d = t_{e+1}$.

Step 3: The spatial change $\omega_o[t_s, t_e]$ can be treated as following progress:

a) $t \leftarrow t_s$; $\omega_o = \Phi$;

b)   *Loop while* $t \leq t_e$
        If there exists a maximal $t_j \geq t$ and the spatial attribute of O remains
        unchanged in $[t, t_j]$ *Then*
        $k \leftarrow$ discrete spatial change of O in $[t, t_j]$;
        Else If there exists a maximal $t_j \geq t$ and in $[t, t_j]$ the spatial attribute changes
        continuously with time *Then*
        $k \leftarrow$ continuous spatial change of O in $[t, t_j]$;
        End If
        Append k to ω_o;

        $t \leftarrow t_{j+1}$;
        End Loop

c)   *Return* ω_o;

Finally, $\omega_o[t_s, t_e]$ is represented as a list of discrete spatial changes and continuous spatial changes.

Step 4: The processing of thematic attributes change is similar to spatial attribute.

So the spatiotemporal changes in a period can always be described by the above five types of spatiotemporal changes.   □

4   Modeling Attribute-Level Spatiotemporal Changes Using Descriptors

Attribute-level spatiotemporal changes are those changes occur internally in a single object and do not change any object identities. We use spatial descriptor and attribute descriptor to describe attribute-level spatiotemporal changes. In this section, we only discuss the spatial descriptor. The description of attribute descriptor is much like spatial descriptor.

Spatial descriptor represents spatial attribute changes of an object. Its description is based on two states: continuous spatial existence state and discrete spatial existence state.

Definition 1. continuous spatial existence state: Given a period $[t_s, t_e]$, if the spatial attribute of an object O can be represented as a continuous function on time, denoted as $\psi(t)$, where $t_s \leq t_i \leq t_e$, and the previous instant of t_s and the next instant of t_e both do not satisfy $\psi(t)$, then the state of the object O in $[t_s, t_e]$ is called continuous spatial existence state, denoted as $E_c(O, [t_s, t_e]) = <S_o, \psi(t), [t_s, t_e]>$, where S_o is O's spatial attribute at t_s. The instant t_s is called the start instant of E_c, while t_e is the end instant of E_c.

Definition 2. discrete spatial existence state: Given a period $[t_s, t_e]$, if the spatial attribute of an object O keeps static during $[t_s, t_e]$, and the spatial attribute at the previous instant of t_s and at the next instant of t_e are neither the same as that in$[t_s, t_e]$, then the state of the object O in $[t_s, t_e]$, is called discrete spatial existence state, denoted as $E_d(O, [t_s, t_e]) = <S_o, [t_s, t_e]>$, where S_o is O's spatial attribute in $[t_s, t_e]$. The instant t_s is called the start instant of E_d, while t_e is the end instant of E_d.

Definition 3. spatial descriptor: The spatial descriptor SD(O) of an object O in $[t_0, t_n]$ is a series of spatial existence states $< E_0, E_1, E_2, ..., E_m >$, where for each $0 \leq i \leq m$, E_i is either a continuous spatial existence state or a discrete spatial existence state. The start instant of E_i is denoted as t_s^i and the end instant of E_i is t_e^i. And SD(O) satisfies: $t_s^0 = t_0$ and $t_e^m = t_n$ and $t_s^{i+1} = t_e^i + 1$.

Fig. 2 is an example about spatial changes: the object O's spatial attribute S_o keeps static in $[t_0, t_1]$, and expands to S_o^1 at t_2, and then contracts to S_o^2 at t_4, and then continuously changes to t_5, and then deforms into S_o^3 at t_6, and then moves to a new position at t_8, and then rotates at t_{10}, and this state keeps till t_{11}. The following is the corresponding description of the spatial descriptor of the object O:

SD(O) = $<(S_o, [t_0, t_1]), (S_o^1, [t_2, t_3]), (S_o^2, (1, 3+t, 1, 3+t), [t_4, t_5]), (S_o^3, [t_6, t_7]), (S_o^4, [t_8, t_9]), (S_o^5, [t_{10}, t_{11}])>$

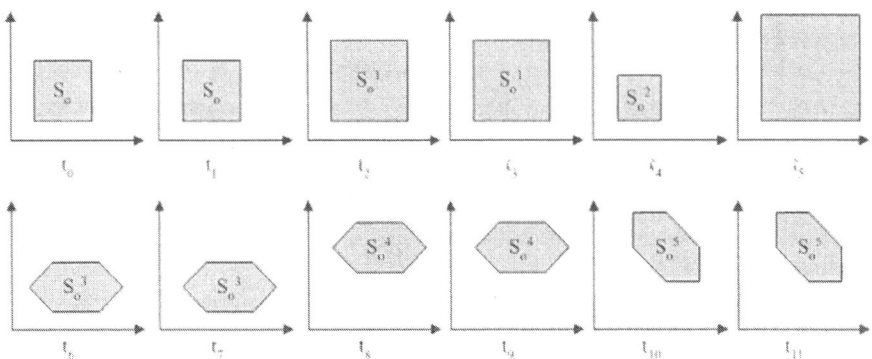

Fig. 2. Spatial changes occur in $[t_0, t_{11}]$

The special case is the continuous spatial change occurs from t_4 to t_5. This is described through a continuous spatial existence state, and we have used parametric rectangle [8] to represent the continuous change. Parametric rectangle represents an object as a set of parametric rectangles, and each parametric rectangle is constructed using a constraint expression on X and Y dimension. In our example, the spatial attribute of the object O from t_4 to t_5 is expressed by the constraint expression: $1 \leq x \leq 3 + t$ and $1 \leq y \leq 3 + t$ and $t_4 \leq t \leq t_5$. It has been proved that each 2D object can be represented as a set of parametric rectangles [8], so it is feasible to represent continuous changes of 2D spatial attribute using this technique.

The querying of spatial changes can be obtained by defining query operations on spatial descriptor. The two basic operations are:

(1) $When_s(O, t)$: Object $\times$ time $\rightarrow S_o$: return the state of spatial attribute at instant t.

(2) $History_s(O, t_s, t_e)$: Object $\times$ time $\times$ time $\rightarrow SD(O)$: return the state of spatial attribute in period $[t_s, t_e]$. The result is a spatial descriptor.

5   Modeling Object-Level Spatiotemporal Changes Using History Topology

The object-level spatiotemporal changes describe changes that are related to several objects, i.e. changes that result in changes of object identities. As described in Fig. 1, we use discrete identity change to represent object-level spatiotemporal change, and history topology to represent discrete identity change. A history topology relates an object with its ancestors and offspring. The ancestors indicate where the object comes from and how it becomes being, and the offspring show what the object changes into at the end and why the change occurs. Representing discrete identity changes on the basis of history topology is direct: when the identity of an object changes, the history topology of this object is immediately updated in order to record this identity change.

But in real applications there exist many kinds of identity changes, e.g. an object may split into several sub-objects, according to which should all the objects' history topologies be updated simultaneously. So in order to describe history topology more appropriately, a classification of discrete identity changes is necessary. Four types of discrete identity changes are listed as below:

(1) *Creation*: A creation of an object means that a new object becomes being and its ancestors and offspring are both empty.

(2) *Elimination*: An elimination of an object means the object is removed from the real world permanently. The ancestors of the object remain untouched, while the offspring are empty.

(3) *Split*: That means an object is splited into several new objects. The offspring of the origin object now should contain all the sub-objects, while its ancestors remain untouched. The ancestors of each sub-object should point to the origin object and the offspring are empty.

(4) *Mergence*: Several objects are merged and form a new object. The offspring of each origin object now should be the new object, and the ancestors of the new object are all the origin objects.

In fact, it is not enough only to record the ancestor and offspring objects of an object. E.g. if an object was created at instant t and then was eliminated later, we cannot acquire these two identity changes if we only record the ancestor and offspring objects because they were both empty for either change. We use an explicit changing type to solve this problem, i.e. to add an explicit type of discrete identity change into history topology when updating history topology. This differs from the implicit description of attribute-level spatiotemporal changes. The explicit identity changes make it feasible to answer such queries like 'Was the object O merged into another object in $[t_1, t_2]$?' and 'From which object did the object O derive?'.

For defining the structure of history topology, we first give the definition about history topology state of an object.

Definition 4. history topology state: If an object O's identity changes at instant t, i.e. discrete identity change occurs, then the state of O at t is called a history topology state, denoted as $E_n(O_p, O_n, CT, t)$, where O_p is the set of object identities of O's parents and O_n is the set of object identities of O's children, CT is the type of change, it could be creation, elimination, mergence or split. The instant t is called the history topology instant of E_n.

The parents of O denote those objects that produce O, while the children of O indicate those objects that are produced from O.

Definition 5. history topology: The history topology HT(O) of an object O in $[t_0, t_n]$ is a series of history topology states $< E_0, E_1, E_2, ..., E_m >$, where for each $0 \leq i \leq m$, E_i is a history topology state. The history topology instant of E_i is denoted as t_h^i and satisfies: $t_0 \leq t_h^i \leq t_h^{i+1} \leq t_n$, $1 \leq i \leq m - 1$.

Fig. 3 is an example that shows the changing history of a field. This is very typical in land management system. In Fig. 3, a field O_1 was created at t_1 and saved in database, at t_2 O_1 splited into O_2 and O_3, and at t_3 the field O_3 further splited into O_4 and O_5, and at t_4 O_2 and O_4 were merged and became a new field O_6, and at t_5 O_5 was eliminated from the database. These changes are represented using history topology as following:

$HT(O_1) = <(\Phi, \Phi, Creation, t_1), (\Phi, \{O_2, O_3\}, Split, t_2)>$
$HT(O_2) = <(\{O_1\}, \Phi, Split, t_2), (\Phi, \{O_6\}, Mergence, t_4)>$
$HT(O_3) = <(\{O_1\}, \Phi, Split, t_2), (\Phi, \{O_4, O_5\}, Split, t_3)>$
$HT(O_4) = <(\{O_3\}, \Phi, Split, t_3), (\Phi, \{O_6\}, Mergence, t_4)>$
$HT(O_5) = <(\{O_3\}, \Phi, Split, t_3), (\Phi, \Phi, Elimination, t_5)>$
$HT(O_6) = <(\{O_4, O_5\}, \Phi, Mergence, t_4)>$

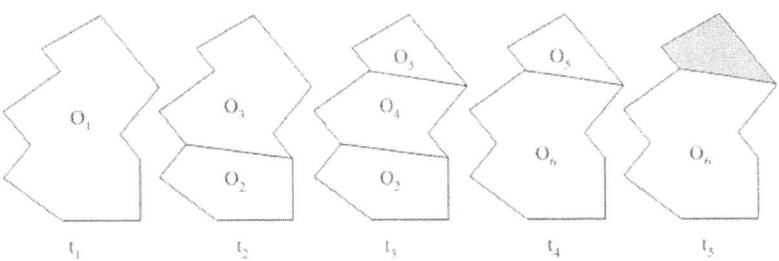

Fig. 3. The changing history of a field

Query operations on history topology are defined for querying discrete identity changes. Two basic operations are:

(1) $When_h(O, t)$: Object × time → E_h: Returns the history topology state at instant t.

(2) $History_h(Object, t_s, t_e)$ Object × time × time → HT(O): Returns the changing history of an object identity during $[t_s, te]$. The result is a list of history topology state.

6 Spatiotemporal Object and Spatiotemporal Changes

Based on the discussion of spatiotemporal changes above, a spatiotemporal object can be represented as a quadruple.

Definition 6. spatiotemporal object: A spatiotemporal object is a quadruple O = < OID, SD, AD*, HT>, where OID is the object identity, SD is the spatial descriptor of the object O, AD* is the attribute descriptor, and HT is the history topology.

According to object-orient theory, the attributes of an object describe characteristics of the object. And the characteristics of a geospatial object include spatial attribute and thematic attributes. In traditional GIS and spatial applications, those attributes are all static and it accords with the perspective of people's looking on a static geospatial object. But in spatiotemporal applications and temporal GIS, geospatial objects are dynamic, i.e. their spatial attributes and thematic attributes both change with time. So change is an intrinsic characteristic of spatiotemporal object. And thus a spatiotemporal object should not only contain its spatial attribute and thematic attributes but also contain the evolvement of those attributes with time. Furthermore, changes are always related to some characteristics of the spatiotemporal object, which maybe the spatial attribute, or the thematic attributes, or the whole object. So, description of changes cannot depart from the attributes of object, they should be integrated. And this is why we define a spatiotemporal object as the above quadruple.

According to the definition of spatiotemporal object, we can formally define the spatiotemporal changes and the query on spatiotemporal changes.

Definition 7. spatiotemporal change: The spatiotemporal changes of an object O are the set of SD, AD* and HT, where SD is spatial descriptor, AD* is attribute descriptor, and HT is history topology.

Definition 8. query on spatiotemporal changes: The query on spatiotemporal changes of an object O is a combination of the query on spatial descriptor SD, attribute descriptor AD* and history topology HT.

7 Conclusions

Typical spatiotemporal database applications need to trace and query spatiotemporal changes of objects. An effective representation of spatiotemporal changes is the essence of the research on spatiotemporal database and spatiotemporal data model. Based on the semantics of objects and changes in the real world, we proposes a systematic classification on spatiotemporal changes of objects, and a new approach to describe spatiotemporal changes is presented, which is based on object-level spatiotemporal changes and attribute-level spatiotemporal changes. The attribute-level spatiotemporal changes are described through spatial descriptor and attribute descriptor(s), and they mainly aim at the internal changes of single object. History topology is presented as an effective tool to represent the object-level spatiotemporal changes, and it aims at those changes that are related with single objects. The description of spatiotemporal changes based on descriptor and history topology forms a formal basis for a change-based spatiotemporal data model, which will be further studied in the future.

References

1. Jun, C., J., Jiang, J.: An Event-Based Approach to Spatio-temporal Data Modeling in Land Subdivision Systems, GeoInformatica, 4(2000) 387–402
2. Claramunt, C., Thériault, M.: Managing Time in GIS: An Event-Oriented Approach. In: Clifford, J., Tuzhilin, A. (eds.): Recent Advances in Temporal Databases, Springer-Verlag, Berlin Heidelberg (1995) 23–42
3. Claramunt, C., Thériault, M.: Toward Semantics for Modeling Spatio-temporal Processes within GIS. In: Kraak, M., Molenaar, M. (eds.): Proceedings of 7th International Symposium on Spatial Data Handling, Taylor & Francis Ltd. , Delft, NL (1996) 47–63
4. Hornsby, K., Egenhofer, M.: Qualitative Representation of Change. In: Hirtle, S., Frank, A. (eds.): Spatial Information Theory – A Theoretical Basis for GIS, Lecture Notes in Computer Science 1329, Springer Verlag, Berlin Heidelberg, Laurel Highlands (1997) 15–33
5. Hornsby, K., Egenhofer, M.: Identity-Based Change Operations for Composite Objects. In: Poiker, T., Chrisman, N. (eds.): Proceedings of 8th International Symposium on Spatial Data Handling, International Geographical Union, Vancouver, Canada (1998) 202–213
6. Hornsby, K., Egenhofer, M.: Identity-Based Change: A Foundation for Spatio-temporal Knowledge Representation, International Journal of Geographical Information Science, 3(2000) 207–224
7. Langran, G.: Time in Geographic Information Systems, Taylor & Francis Ltd., Bristol (1992)
8. Mengchu, C.: Parametric Rectangles: A Model for Spatiotemporal Databases, PhD. dissertation, The University of Nebraska – Lincoln, Lincoln, U.S.A (2000)
9. Peuquet, D., Duan, N.: An Event-Based Spatiotemporal Data Model (ESTDM) for Temporal Analysis of Geographical Data, International Journal of Geographical Information Systems, 1(1995) 7–24
10. Renolen, A.: History Graphs: Conceptual Modeling of Spatiotemporal Data. In Proceedings of GIS Frontiers in Business and Science, International Cartographic Association, Brno, Czech Republic (1996)
11. Yuan, M.: Temporal GIS and Spatio-temporal Modeling, In: http://www.ncgia.ucsb.edu/conf/SANTAA-FE-CD-ROM/ssf-papers/yuan-may/may.html

Maintaining Ontologies for Geographical Information Retrieval on the Web

Christopher B. Jones, Alia I. Abdelmoty, and Gaihua Fu

Department of Computer Science, Cardiff University, Wales, UK
{c.b.jones,a.i.abdelmoty,gaihua.fu}@cs.cf.ac.uk

Abstract. A geo-ontology has a key role to play in the development of a spatially-aware search engine, with regard to providing support for query disambiguation, query term expansion, relevance ranking and web resource annotation. This paper reviews these functions, discusses the user requirements which influence the design of the ontology, with regard to different types of query and fundamental spatial concepts, before presenting a base model for a geographical ontology which will provide a foundation for subsequent implementation as well as experimentation with alternative ontology models. The report also reviews various ontology languages available for expressing ontologies and give examples for encoding the geo-ontology in them.

1 Introduction

This paper is concerned with intelligent web-based information retrieval of geographical information. The assumption is that people may wish to find information about something that relates to somewhere. The most common way to refer to a location is to use place names, which may be qualified by spatial relationships (such as in or near). In order to assist in recognising place names and spatial relationships when they are employed in a search engine query it is proposed to employ an ontology which encodes geographical terminology and the semantic relationships between geographical terms. The idea is that the geographical ontology, henceforth denoted geo-ontology, will enable the search engine to detect that the query refers to a geographic location and to perform a search which will result in the retrieval and relevance ranking of web resources that refer both exactly and approximately to the specified location [Ala01]. This will entail retrieval of resources that refer to alternative versions of a specified place name as well as to places that are spatially associated with it or through relations such as those of containment and adjacency. It is also proposed that an ontology should be used to assist in a process of metadata extraction whereby the geographical context of resources is determined for the purpose of search engine indexing as well as providing the potential to annotate a resource to improve its future geographical visibility.

In this paper, issues and considerations related to the design and maintenance of such an ontology are explored. In section 2, the role of the Place ontology as a component of a spatially aware search engine is described. An overview of related

R. Meersman et al. (Eds.): CoopIS/DOA/ODBASE 2003, LNCS 2888, pp. 934–951, 2003.
© Springer-Verlag Berlin Heidelberg 2003

research is given in section 3. Design issues and implementation considerations are discussed in section 4. This is followed by a proposal for a conceptual design of the ontology in section 5. Some operations on the ontology are also described. In section 6, possible tools for encoding and maintaining the ontology are reviewed and one tool namely, DAML + OIL is used for demonstration.

2   Roles of the Geo-ontology

The main distinguishing factor of the Spatially-Aware Search Engine envisioned in this paper, hence forth, denoted SPIRIT, is its search for information about a Place. Hence, queries to SPIRIT are characterised by their need to identify, either precisely or vaguely, a Place, which may be an extended region in space. A query to SPIRIT will be associated with a geographical context. The search engine needs to match the geographic content of the query with that of the available resources and the most relevant resources would then be returned. Definitions of the concepts of geographical content and geometric footprint associated with queries and documents are first introduced, and then the roles of geo-ontology in SPIRIT are discussed.

2.1   Basic Definitions

A reference to a geographic Place could be by its name and/or by its location. A location is either absolute or relative. The type of the Place is also an important identifier which facilitates the disambiguation of Places with similar names. Hence, a Place reference, denoted, Pl-Ref, can be either absolute or relative. An absolute place reference can be defined as a tuple of place name, place type and location (location is denoted here as Place Footprint, or Pl-FP): Pl-Ref-Abs = <Pl-name, Pl-type, Pl-FP> where Pl-FP refers to the actual position of the Place in space which may be faithful or approximate. On the other hand, a Place may be defined through its spatial relationship(s) to other Places. Hence, a relative Place reference could be defined as follows: Pl-Rlv = <Spatial Relation, Pl-name, Pl-type, Pl-FP>. Note that, in the latter case, the resulting Pl-FP would normally be computed using the spatial relationship in the expression. An example of an absolute Place reference is: <Eiffel Tower, Monument, $\{< x, y >\}$ >. An example of relative Place reference is: <In, Zurich, City, $\{< x, y >\}$ >.

A query to SPIRIT will contain one or more references to Pl-Ref. The same is true for web resources to be searched by SPIRIT. The process of query interpretation would result in the identification of the geographic content of the query as defined by the Pl-Ref(s) it is referring to, and similarly the process of (semantic and spatial) metadata extraction in web documents would result in the identification of the geographic content of the document as defined by its contained Pl-Ref(s).

Hence, the geographic content of a query, denoted, $Query_{GC}$ is defined as a set of Place reference expressions, namely, $Query_{GC} = \{\text{Pl-Ref}\}$. The geometric

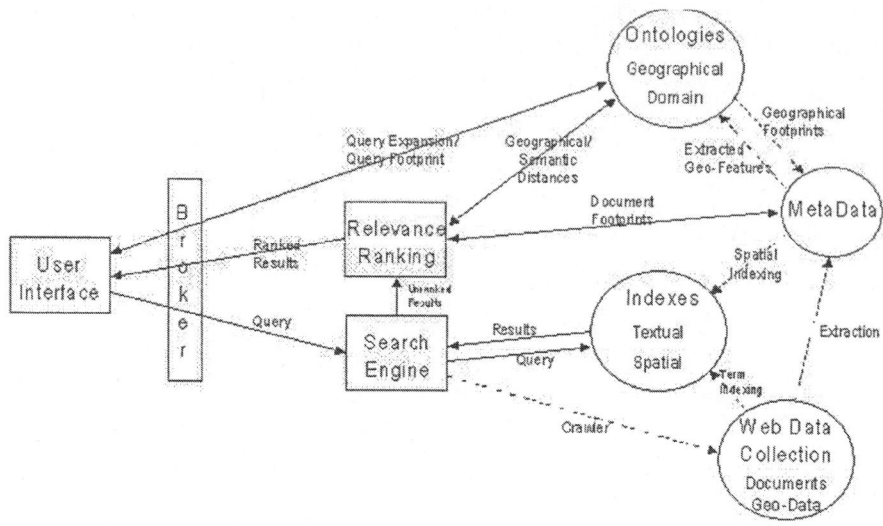

Fig. 1. The role of the geo-ontology as a component of a spatially-aware search engine

footprint of a query could be defined as a function of the footprints of its associated Pl-Ref(s), namely, $Query_{FP} = \{FP(Query_{GC})\}$. Similarly, the geographic content of a document, denoted, Doc_{GC} is defined as a set of Place reference expressions associated with the resource, namely, $Doc_{GC} = \{Pl\text{-Ref}\}$. The geometric footprint of a document could be defined as a function of the footprints of its associated Pl-Ref(s), namely, $Doc_{FP} = FP(Doc_{GC})$.

There are four main areas of application of the geo-ontology in a search engine which are 1) user's query interpretation 2) system query formulation 3) metadata extraction; 4) relevance ranking. These are described below. Figure 1 gives an overview of a possible architecture for SPIRIT and illustrates the central role of the geo-ontology.

User query interpretation. When a place name is employed in a user query, a geo-ontology will serve several purposes. It will facilitate disambiguation of the place name in the event of there being more than one place with the given name. It will also enable graphical feedback of the $Query_{FP}$. The user could then be given the option of accepting or revising the interpretation of the extent of the location. The ontology will also be able to generate alternative names, including historical variants, which the user could accept or reject according to their interests.

Domain-specific ontologies could be used to expand non-geographical terms to include synonyms. In the event of the subject (i.e. the something element) of a query being itself a place type then the place type ontology could also be used to generate similar terms for purposes of query expansion.

Metadata extraction. Ontologies could be used to identify the presence of place names, spatial qualifiers and domain-specific terminology in a free text document. If the geographical terminology was regarded as characterising the geographical context of the document, then the footprints of the respective places could be used to generate a document footprint or set of footprints that were associated with the document. This footprint metadata could be stored in the search engine database, or as metadata that could be attached to the original document using an annotation tool. The metadata might also include the textual place names extracted from the document in combination with the concept terms (or subjects) that were associated with them.

System query formulation. The geo-ontology could be used to generate alternative names and spatially associated names (according to spatial relationships such as inside, near or north of), which could in principle be included in a query expression to a text-based query processor. Alternatively, or as well, the ontology could be used to generate $Query_{FP(s)}$, as indicated above, which may be used to access a spatially indexed database of web document metadata. Thus all documents whose own footprint intersected the query footprint could be retrieved prior to being filtered according to the textual query terms. Equally it could be that text-indexed search preceded spatial filtering (again based on the query footprint).

Relevance ranking. A geographical ontology will provide the potential for geographical relevance ranking that might be combined with non-geographical ranking. The footprints associated with documents could be used to measure the distance between the document and the query footprint in geographic coordinate space. In the case of queries that used a directional qualifier the document footprint could be used to assess geometric similarity with the interpretation of the user's query footprint, according to whether it was near its core or its periphery. It would also be possible to use other aspects of the structure of geographic space for purposes of ranking. Thus for example the similarity of the query footprint and the document footprint might be regarded as a function of the parent (containing or overlapping) regions that they had in common, and those that were non-common [Ala01].

3   Related Research and Resources

The most often cited geographical thesaurus is the Getty Information Institute's Thesaurus of Geographic Names (TGN) [Get02] which is a specialisation of the general thesaurus model. For each place name the TGN maintains a unique id, a set of place types taken from the Art and Architecture Thesaurus (AAT), alternative versions of the name, its containing administrative region, a footprint in the form of a point in latitude and longitude, and notes on the sources of information. Gazetteers also constitute geographic vocabularies but some of them are very limited with regard to their semantic richness. Typically a gazetteer may encode just a single name, a single place type, a point-based footprint and a parent administrative area. As such they constitute fairly crude terminological ontologies. A recent development in the realm of gazetteers is the Alexandria Digital Library (ADL) gazetteer content standard [ADL02] which supports many types of place name metadata that may be represented either as core or optional information. This provides for a relatively rich description of place, but unlike a thesaural model there is no requirement to encode hierarchical relationships.

Recently the Open GIS Consortium has been developing a Web Gazetteer Service standard for distributed access to gazetteers. Its gazetteer model is based on location instances as defined in ISO DIS 19112 [Iso02], which are related to each other via thesaural hierarchical relationships to parent and child location instances.

In [MSS01], experiments are reported on user cognition of basic concepts in a geographic ontology, which revealed a difference in the interpretation of synonymous concepts of geographic feature and geographic object. In [CEFM01], a study of ontological specification of remotely sensed images is reported, which highlights the requirements for geographic image ontologies and proposes a representation framework for modelling them.

In adopting the term geographical ontology it is intended that more formal ontology models are designed, with a view to exploiting the automatic reasoning that it will facilitate. This move toward formalisation is reflected later in this paper in the use of the ontology language DAML/OIL [Hor00] to encode the specified ontology design. The language, and its successor OWL [W3c02], is associated with various editing and reasoning tools that can be used in defining and maintaining the ontology. An interesting issue in the design of the geoontology is to determine the most appropriate set of spatial relationships that might be encoded between places and the appropriate balance between the use of pre-computed spatial relationships between places and the on-line computation of relationships using the geometric footprint. With regard to some of the prominent existing geographical ontologies, the TGN design is limited by the use of only a point form footprint and the restriction to only hierarchical relations between places. The OGC Web Gazetteer Service model is also limited by the use of only hierarchical thesaural relationships between locations. The ADL may hold the potential for forming the basis of a more versatile geographical ontology, provided appropriate relationships between places are defined and used in addition to those specified in the published documentation. In all cases there is considerable scope to experiment with computational geometric and spatial reasoning techniques to exploit the stored place name information for purposes of effective information retrieval.

The focus of this work concerns the modelling of geographic place. An aspect of this process is the modelling of place types. There is also an interest in modelling the terminology of one or more application areas or domains that we may use for evaluation. Here we are referring to the something aspect of a query. It is expected that the modelling of place types and domain-specific terminology can be accomplished using conventional thesaural methods, i.e. without the need to introduce specialised types of relationships and category attributes. Thus equivalent terms or synonyms are represented via USE and USE-FOR relations. Hierarchical relations whether generic (is-a) or meronymic (part-of) are represented with Broader Term (BT) and Narrower Term (NT) relations, though it is appropriate to distinguish between these hierarchical types. If required, other associations between terms that belong to different classification groups or facets can be represented with Related Term (RT) relationships.

4 Design Issues and Considerations

In this section, factors are identified which should be taken into account in designing the geo-ontology. A typology of possible queries that may be issued to the extended search engine is identified. This is followed by a discussion on design issues related to the various elements of a query and other specific maintenance issues.

4.1 A Typology of Possible Queries

In this section, the possible types of queries that an geographically aware search engine is expected to handle are identified. In what follows, a set of atomic query expressions is first identified which can then be used to build more complex queries and scenarios. A basic query expression will consist of a reference to:

- A Place Name, or,
- An aspatial Entity with a Relationship to a Place Name[1], or,
- An aspatial Entity with a Spatial Relationship to a Place Name, or,
- A Place Name with a Spatial Relationship to a Place Name, or,
- A Place Type with a Spatial Relationship to a Place Name, or,
- A Place Type with a Spatial Relationship to a Place Type.

A Place Name is an actual name of a geographic object, e.g. Hannover. Aspatial entities are general non-geographic objects, which may correspond to a physical or an abstract theme, subject or activity, e.g. a person, a publisher, a holiday, etc. A Relationship is an instance of an aspatial, semantic, relationship which may exist between concepts in a conceptual data model, in particular, the is-related-to relationship. A Spatial Relationship is an instance of a relationship between any types of objects in space, e.g. inside, contains and near-to. A Place Type corresponds to a class of Place Names, e.g. City, Town, River and Restaurant. In what follows, Pl-name is used to denote a Place Name, SRel is used to denote a Spatial Relation, Pl-type is used to denote a Place Type, and AS-entity is used to denote an aspatial entity and AS-Rel is used to denote a non-spatial (semantic) relation. The set of basic types of queries is listed in table 1.

The above are atomic query expressions that may be used to generate more complex query expressions using binary logic operators and spatial operators.

---

[1] An aspatial Entity is a non-geographic entity

Table 1. A list of possible basic query types to be handled by SPIRIT

Query Type	Example
Find <Pl-name>	Zurich
Find <Pl-name SRel Pl-name>	City Hall IN Paris
	Barry NEAR Cardiff
Find <AS-entity AS-Rel Pl-name>	Books on-the-subject-of (About) Taipei
Find <AS-entity SRel Pl-name>	Scottish Dance groups based IN or NEAR
	Edinburgh
Find <Pl-type SRel Pl-name>	Hotels NEAR Paris
	Big Cities IN Japan
	Rented accommodation NEAR Brussels
Find <AS-entity SRel Pl-type>	Database conferences NEAR Sunny Beaches
Find <AS-entity AS-Rel Pl-type>	Presidents of countries
	Books on the subject of rivers
Find <Pl-type SRel Pl-type>	Hotels NEAR Airports
	Airports NEAR Big Cities

Hence, in processing the complex queries, atomic expressions are first extracted that correspond to one of the forms above. The following are examples of such queries. In what follows, Op is used to denote a logical operator, e.g. AND, OR, NOT.

```
 - Find <(Pl-name Op Pl-name) SRel Pl-name>
   Atomic expressions:
       Find <Pl-name SRel Pl-name> OP Find <Pl-name SRel Pl-name>
   Example:
       Shoreditch and Stratford IN London
 - Find <Pl-type SRel Pl-type SRel Pl-name>
   Atomic expressions:
       Find <Pl-type SRel Pl-name> OP <Pl-type SRel Pl-name>
   Examples:
       Hotels NEAR Airports AND IN Washington
       Hotels IN Munich AND Hotels within a short walk from
       Munich's Main Station.
```

4.2 Design Considerations Regarding the Primary Query Elements

From the above, it can be seen that the main query constructs are: a Place Name, an aspatial Entity, a Place Type, a Relation and a Spatial Relation. In this section, an investigation of the issues related to the above constructs is presented.

Place Name. A place name is used to reference a particular geographic object. There may exist different names and variations of names for the same geographic object, e.g. Treforest and Trefforest. The ontology is expected to store as many as possible Place names and known alternatives, including historic names. Ideally, Place names in different languages should also be stored. Places may be referred to that may have no formal definition, such as the south of France, the Midlands or the Rocky Mountains. There are two ways to define such imprecise regions. The Places, and their associated locations, may be pre-recognised and stored explicitly in the ontology, or an interactive dialogue with the user needs to be carried out at the interface to clarify the location and/or extent of those objects. Indeed, both scenarios may be used together to confirm the correspondence between the stored and intended definitions.

Place Location. The ontology must associate a geometric footprint with all the stored geographic objects. The footprint may be approximate, e.g. a representative (centre) point or a bounding box, or more detailed, e.g. approximate shapes, or exact, i.e. a faithful representation of the object geometry. This decision has direct storage implications and the benefits and limitations of the choice need to be carefully studied. Also, more than one type of geometry may be associated with the same object. For example, a region may be associated with both a representative point and a polygon, which may itself be an approximation of the actual shape.

Place Address. The use of an address is a common form of reference to the location of a geographic object. A street name is considered to be a type of Place name as defined above. A postcode or zip-code is normally a part of an address used commonly to group sets of individual addresses or places. The codes may also serve as a constraint on query location during query interpretation and expansion.

Spatial Relations. It is desirable that an ontology of spatial relations be defined in the system to allow for the interpretation of terms given at the interface. The ontology of relations should cater for the different types of spatial relations possible, namely, topological, proximal, directional and size in both quantitative and qualitative expressions. A number of explicit types of spatial relationships between geographic objects may be stored in the ontology facilitating the interpretation and expansion of query expressions by direct matching and reasoning over spatial relations.

Coordinate systems. In view of the objective of a global geographical ontology it would appear desirable to employ a single geometric coordinate system that is global in coverage. The obvious choice is therefore the use of latitude and longitude ("geographical" as opposed to "grid") coordinates. In practice latitude and longitude are not unique as they are based on a specific geodetic datum, which denotes the dimensions of a spheroid that is used to approximate the shape of the Earth. Assuming that the geo-ontology employs geographical coordinates on a specified datum, then all geometric calculations such as distance, orientation and area could be performed directly on the surface of the spheroid.

An alternative approach would be to store coordinates on the various local grid systems (e.g. the UK National Grid) used by the national mapping agencies or other data providers. This might be more efficient relative to spherical (geographical) coordinates for calculations that were confined to the geographic zone of the respective grid system, but would cause problems whenever inter-zone calculations were required (these could be done via intermediate coordinate transformations). In conclusion the simplest approach to adopt in the first place appears to be to use geographical coordinates on a specified datum. Alternative approaches could then be considered at the implementation stage.

Time. A characteristic of all geographical places is that they are embedded not just in space but also in time. Settlements and other topographic features have some time of origin (though it may not always be known) and in some cases dissolution. The names of many places have changed over time and geopolitical and natural environmental boundaries are subject to appearance, disappearance or re-location over time. Full support for spatio-temporal information is highly desirable in a geographical ontology for purposes of information retrieval, but it is also demanding. On the assumption that some of the data resources for the ontology may have some temporal data relating for example to the date of establishment or duration of a place name it seems appropriate to support the storage of such data with a view to developing procedures for their exploitation. It should be noted that the introduction of support for time would extend the typology of possible queries presented in section 4.1.

Language. The importance of multi-lingual support for geographical information retrieval is highly desirable. Some limited support for encoding alternative language versions of names is relatively simple to provide in the ontology design. Full support for a multi-lingual search engine is beyond the scope of this research.

Semantic and Geometric Generalisation. It is well known that geographic data may be represented at multiple levels of generalisation. One aspect of generalisation concerns the level of detail with which a specific object is represented. Thus the areal extent of a settlement could be represented for example by a polygonal boundary with detailed sinuosity, representing a large proportion of the humanly perceptible detail. Alternatively it could be represented by a coarsely simplified polygon, a bounding rectangle or simply a representative point or centroid. These types of generalisation are examples of geometric generalisation. For reasons of data availability and usefulness, it would be impractical and also unnecessary to encode all geographic data in a geo-ontology at the highest levels of geometric detail. However, in order for the geo-ontology to fulfill its roles, it is desirable that it can encode geographic data, especially the geometric data, with sufficient geometric detail. For example, encoding the footprint with a single coordinate point might be adequate for a feature which is of type village, of relatively small areal extent, but might not be sufficient for a feature which is of type country, especially when the query expansion, relevance ranking and spatial index are considered. The same argument applies in the case of the semantic level of detail, e.g. geographical information may be recorded in high level classes, e.g. countries, cities, primary roads, etc. as well as lower levels of detail, e.g. counties and towns, side streets, etc. For the ontology to be useful, it should be able to encode geographic data at multiple levels of semantic generalisation.

Explicit vs implicit maintenance of spatial data. It has been noted above that there are several types of spatial information, ranging from coordinate-based geometry, in the form of points, lines, areas and volumes, to the spatial relationships categorised as topology, proximity, orientation and size. The question arises as to what is an appropriate balance between explicit storage of spatial information and the use of online procedures to derive or deduce information from what is stored.

Because of the high storage costs of detailed geometry and the associated computational costs, there is an argument for explicit storage of topological relationships between neighbouring objects. Topological relationships between non-neighbouring objects can often be deduced reliably with spatial reasoning rules. From a computational point of view there might be a case for explicit storage of proximal, orientation and size relationships, at least between neighbouring objects. Clearly this would result in a significant storage overhead. It is also the case however that logical deduction of these relationships (apart from size) between non-neighbouring objects cannot be performed reliably, due to the often imprecise nature of the relations. The cost of explicit storage of all possible such relationships would be combinatorially explosive. Following the above considerations it appears reasonable therefore to decide initially to store geometry at variable levels of detail in addition to storing topological relationships between neighbouring spatial objects. The balance between online computation and explicit storage of other spatial relations and of more detailed geometry will be examined in future work.

4.3   Checking and Maintaining the Integrity of the Geo-ontology

Maintaining the consistency and the integrity of the geo-ontology is essential for supporting the correct functionality of the search engine and for ensuring the viability and the quality of the search results produced. Maintenance tools are therefore needed for the initial set-up and building of the geo-ontolgy. Also, the ontology is expected to be updated and extended frequently, as new classes of geographic objects and new instances of geographic features are identified. Hence, such maintenance tools must be supported as an integral part of the whole system. Examples of possible maintenance tasks needed when building the ontology base are:

- Ensuring that all mandatory relationships are satisfied, e.g. that every geographic feature belongs to at least one geographic type and has at least one footprint.
- If a feature is involved in a containment relationship or an overlap relationship, where it is the parent, then it must have at least one extended footprint, i.e. a polyline or a polygon.
- A polygon footprint with more than two points, must have at least four points, with the first point being equal to the last point.
- For two features in a containment relationship, the bounding box of the child must be enclosed in the bounding box of the parent.
- For two features in an overlap relationship, the bounding boxes of both must intersect.

Note that the assertion of spatial relationships between geographic features needs to be based on detailed geometric representations, as far as possible, even if such representations are not stored subsequently. Although this may be an expensive process initially, it will be limited, as explicit encoding of spatial relations will be limited to parent-child relationships, and also constrained by feature types. Maintenance tools are needed for checking the consistency of stored spatial relations. Such tools can make use of spatial reasoning techniques, e.g. composition tables [Ege89,BA01], to implement rules for constraining the propagation and derivation of such relationships. Spatial reasoning techniques exploit the inherent properties of relations, such as transitivity and symmetry. Examples of rules for topological relationships include:

- $contain(x, y), contain(y, z) \rightarrow contain(x, z)$
- $inside(x, y), meet(y, z) \rightarrow disjoint(x, z)$
- $meet(x, y), inside(y, z) \rightarrow inside(x, z)$ or $covered - by(x, z)$ or $overlap(x, z)$
  Knowledge of size relationships can further enhance the reasoning process; for example, the last rule can be modified with the knowledge that the size of x is larger than the size of z as follows:
- $meet(x, y), inside(y, z), larger(x, z) \rightarrow overlap(x, z)$

5   Conceptual Design of the Geo-ontology

The geo-ontology proposed here is composed of three components , namely, a geographic feature ontology, a geographic type ontology and a spatial relation ontology. A feature type is associated with a feature type name, and a resource from which the feature type is derived. Feature types can be related by normal thesaural relationships. The base schema for the geographic feature ontology is illustrated in Fig. 2. For each geographic feature, it encodes

1. One and only one Feature-ID, which uniquely identifies a geographical feature
2. One and only one Standard-Name, which specifies a name by which a geographical feature is best known. A name is associated with the date when it was used and the language in which it is specified, as well as a resource which contributes the information.

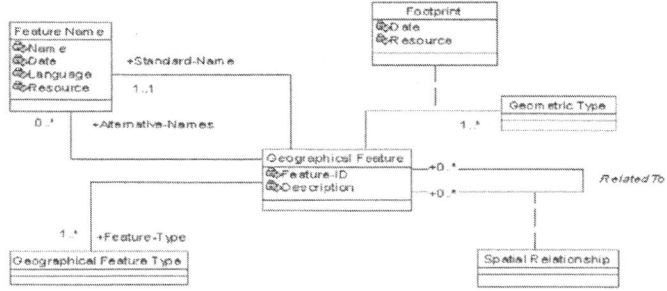

Fig. 2. Base Schema of the geographic feature ontology

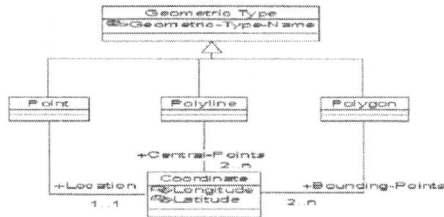

Fig. 3. Basic types of footprints in the geo-ontology

Table 2. Synonymous spatial relationship terms

Spatial Relation	Synonym
Beside	(alongside, next-to)
Near	(close, next-to)
Overlap	(intersect, cross)
Inside	(in, contained-in, within)
Disjoint	(outside, not-connected)
Touch	(adjacent, on the boundary of, next, side by side, close, abutting, adjoining, bordering, contiguous, neighbouring) [wordnet]

3. Zero or more Alternative-Names.
4. One or more Feature-Types as defined in geographical feature type ontology.
5. One or more spatial Footprint. Basic footprints to be supported are points, polylines or polygons, as shown in Fig. 3.
6. Description, a short narrative description of the geographical feature.
7. Zero or more Spatial Relationships, representing how geographical features are related. An ontology of spatial relationships is supported as shown in Fig. 4. Some explicit spatial relationship types may also be supported, e.g. adjacency and containment as shown in the figure. Some examples of synonymous terms to be encoded in the ontology are shown table 2.

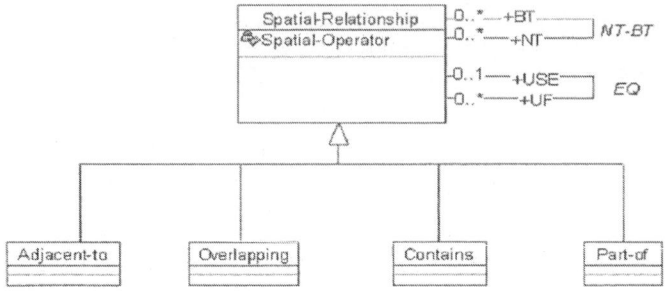

Fig. 4. Ontology of Spatial Relationships

5.1 Spatial Ontology Access Operations

A set of operations on the geo-ontology are defined to facilitate the manipulation and derivation of the stored information. A sample of the set of basic operations is given below.

getFeature(L1, L2). This operation retrieves geographic features using a constraint L1 and returns a set of properties of the feature L2. For example, getFeature(<Feature-Type.Name=city>, <Footprint>) will displays the footprints of features of which the feature type is of city, and getFeature(<Standard-Name.Name=Bremen>, <Identifier, Feature-Type>) displays the Identifiers and the Feature-Types of the feature of which the standard name is Bremen.

getFeatureType(L1). This operation retrieves geographic feature types using an optional constraint L1. For example, getFeatureType(<Feature-Type.NT= city>) displays the feature types of which the narrow term is city, and getFeatureType(<Feature-Type.USE=city>) displays the feature types of which city is used as the preferred term.

getHierarchy (L1, L2, L3). This operation retrieves features in containment hierarchies. This is achieved by transitive traversal of the part-of or contains relationships of the concerned feature to derive the parent or children of that feature. For example, getHierarchy (<high>, <Feature-ID=01079>, <level=3>) retrieves the 3rd level parents of the feature whose identifier is 01079.

6 Tools for Encoding the Geo-ontology

Various ontology-representation languages exist and can be used for modelling the geo-ontology. They differ in the degree of formality, ranging from semi-informal, e.g the text version of "enterprise ontologies" [UK89], to semi-formal languages, e.g. KIF [GF92]. A language for encoding the geo-ontology should aim to satisfy the following.

- Be compatible with existing Web standards, such as XML, RDF, RDFS, in order to facilitate information exchange with other components of the search engine;
- Have adequate expressive power to represent the geo-ontology, and be flexible enough to allow the extension of the ontology schema;
- Be formally specified to facilitate automated reasoning to support query expansion tasks;
- Have sufficient tools to support the updating and maintenance of the ontology.

In the rest of this section, a variety of ontology languages are reviewed and their suitability for encoding the geo-ontology is discussed. Various languages have been used in the literature for specifying ontologies. Some languages are based on XML, such as XOL [KCT99], SHOE [LH00], OML citeKent-26, RDF [LW99] etc, some are based on Description Logics (DLs), e.g. KIF[GF92], CycL[cyc02], CLASSIC [BBMR89], and some are built based on both of XML and DLs, e.g. OIL [Hor00], DAML+OIL, OWL [W3c02].

6.1   DL-Based Ontology Languages

Description logics (DLs) are knowledge representation languages for expressing knowledge about concepts and concept hierarchies. They can be seen as sub-languages of predicate logic. The basic building blocks of DLs are concepts, roles and individuals. Concepts describe the common properties of a collection of individuals and can be considered as unary predicates which are interpreted as sets of objects. Roles are interpreted as binary relations between objects. Each DL language defines also a number of language constructs (such as intersection, union, role quantification, etc.) that can be used to define new concepts and roles. For instance, the following DL expression, based on the language CLASSIC [BBMR89], represents the constraints on the geographic feature; "every geographic feature can have one and only one identifier, at least one feature name, and at least one footprint which is one of the following types: point, polyline and polygon".

```
feature

⊒

(AND  (AT-LEAST, 1, identifier)
                (AT-MOST, 1, identifier)
                (AT-LEAST, 1, name)
                (ATLEAST, 1, footprint)
                (ALL footprint  (ONEOF  point, polyline,
                                              polygon)))
```

The potential of DLs lies in their expressiveness and their associated decidable and efficient inference procedures. Limitations of DL languages include their incompatibility with existing web languages, which makes it hard for ontologies represented in them to be shared and exchanged. Also, the tools developed for DLs often do not integrate well with existing web tools, which makes it difficult to import, export and access the ontologies specified in them.

6.2   XML-Based Ontology Languages

Notable examples include RDF [LW99], RDFS [BR99], XOL [KCT99], SHOE [LH00] etc. They restrict XML by providing a set of primitives to express knowledge in a standardized manner to facilitate machine-understanding. A relevant language of this group is GML (Geographical Markup Language) [OGC02], which is proposed by OGC for specifying geographic information, including both spatial and non-spatial properties of geographical features. The basic idea of GML is to provide an open, vendor-neutral framework for the definition of geospatial application schema. It supports the description of geographic data by providing a set of base types and structures and allowing an application to declare the actual feature types and property types of interest by extending basic types in GML. For example, the following code defines a geographic feature type Mountain, which extends base feature type AbstractFeatureType provided by GML, and a specific property elevation is defined for it.

```
<complexType name="Mountain">
    <complexContent>
        <extension base="gml:AbstractFeatureType">
            <sequence>
                <element name="elevation" type="Real"/>
            </sequence>
        </extension>
    </complexContent>
</complexType>
```

Using the above definition, we can encode information for Everest as follows:

```
<Mountain>
    <gml:description>World's highest mountain </gml:description>
    <gml:name>Everest</gml:name>
    <elevation>8850</elevation>
</Mountain>
```

Unlike DLs, the XML-based languages are relatively compatible with existing Web standards since many of them are designed to facilitate machine-understandable web representation. However, the main limitation of this group of languages is the lack of supporting tools necessary for the maintenance of the geo-ontology.

6.3   DL+XML-Based Ontology Languages

Another stream of ontology languages are built on top of both XML and DLs, and thus they are compatible with existing Web standards and at the same time retain the formal semantics and reasoning services provided by DLs. Examples of such languages include OIL [Hor00], DAML-ONT [DAR02], DAML+OIL and OWL [W3c02].

DAML-ONT is developed by the DARPA project [DAR02] and it inherits many aspects from OIL, and the capabilities of the two languages are relatively similar. DAML+OIL layers on top of RDFS and combines the efforts from OIL

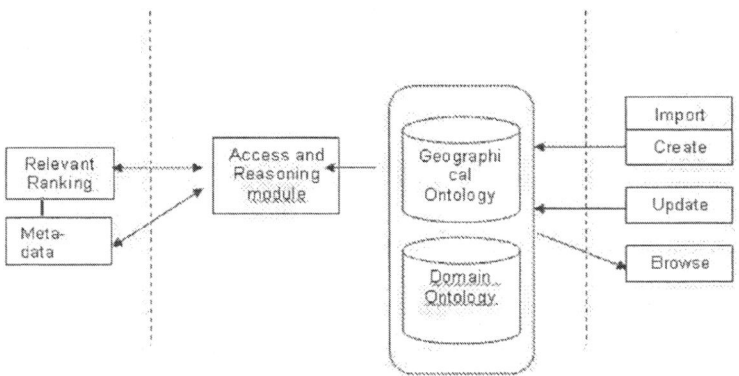

Fig. 5. SPIRIT ontology implementation architecture

and DAML-ONT. It Inherits many ontological primitives from RDFS, e.g. subclass, range, domain, and adds a much richer set of primitives from OIL and DAML-ONT, e.g. transitivity, cardinality, and it allows assertion of axioms. For example, we can specify in DAML+OIL the axiom "A big city is a city which has a population greater than 5 million" as the follows:

```
<daml:Class rdf:ID="BigCity">
   <rdfs:label> Big City</rdfs:label>
   <rdfs:subClassOf  rdfs:resource=#City>
   <rdfs:subClassOf
        <daml:Restriction >
               <daml:onProperty rdf:resource="#population"/>
               <daml:hasClass  rdf:resource=#over5m/>
        </daml:Restriction>
   </rdfs:subClassOf>
</daml:Class>
```

Derived from DAML+OIL, OWL is released by W3C as a semantic markup language for publishing and sharing ontologies on the WWW. It aims to overcome various problems with DAML+OIL, for example, problems with syntax and semantics, mainly related to relationship with RDF.

Ontology Implementation. Figure 5 sketches the different components required for implementing the geo-ontology within SPIRIT. As shown in the figure, the ontology repository consists of a geo-ontology and a domain specific ontology. A module for accessing and reasoning over the ontology is built on top and acts as an interface to the other components of SPIRIT. Maintenance tools for importing, creating, updating and browsing the ontology are also required.

7   Conclusions and Future Work

This paper identifies and describes the central role of a geographic ontology in the development of a spatially-aware web search engine. The functionality associated with it is directly associated with the three areas of the user interface, metadata extraction and relevance ranking. The ontology may be used to disambiguate the place name expression in user queries and subsequently generate alternative place names and associated place names for query expansion. The geo-ontology could also be used to identify the presence of place names, spatial qualifiers and domain-specific terminology in a free text document which may be used to annotate those documents in the web repository. Geographical relevance ranking in the search engine needs to use the geo-ontology for the derivation of footprints and for the application of similarity measures over the query footprints and the footprints associated with the web resources. The paper also introduces a typology of queries over places and place types which the search engine is expected to handle. Various requirements which influence the design of the geo-ontology are reviewed. Maintenance issues for ensuring the consistency of the ontology are also discussed. A base ontology model is then proposed for the geographic ontology which aims to provide a foundation for subsequent implementation and experimentation. The paper also reviews various ontology languages available for expressing ontologies, namely, DLs, XML-based languages, and the combination of both, and gives examples of their use for encoding the geo-ontology.

Acknowledgment. This work is done within the scope of the SPIRIT project. The project is funded by EC Framework V IST programme under the Semantic Web Technologies action line, for which their support is gratefully acknowledged.

References

[ADL02]   ADL Gazetteer Content Standard
            http://alexandria.sdc.ucsb.edu/ lhill/adlgaz/, 2002.
[Ala01]   Alani, H. and Tudhope, D. and Jones, C.B. Geographical information
            retrieval with ontologies of place. In *Spatial Information Theory Founda-
            tions of Geographic Information Science, COSIT 2001*, volume Lecture
            Notes in Computer Science 2205, pages 323–335, 2001.
[BA01]   El-Geresy. B.A. and A.I. Abdelmoty. Towards a general theory for qual-
            itative space. In *Proceedings of the Thirteenth Int. Conf. On Tools with
            Artificial Intelligence*, pages 111–120, 2001.
[BBMR89]   A. Borgida, R.J. Brachman, D.L. McGuinness, and A.L. Resnick. Classic:
            A structural data model for objects. In *SIGMOD Conference*, pages 58–
            67, 1989.
[BR99]   D. Brickley and Guha R.V. Resource description framework (rdf) schema
            specification – www.w3.org/tr/pr-rdf-schema, 1999.
[CEFM01]   G. Camara, M.J. Egenhofer, F. Fonseca, and A.M. Monteiro. What's
            in an image? In *COSIT'01. Lecture Notes in Computer Science*, volume
            2205, pages 474–487, 2001.

[cyc02]   Cycorp, the syntax of cycl – http://www.cyc.com/cycl.html, 2002.

[DAR02]   Darpa, the darpa agent markup language homepage
             http://www.daml.org/, 2002.

[Ege89]   M.J. Egenhofer. A formal definition of binary topological relationships.
             In *International Conference on Foundations of Data Organization and
             Algorithms*, pages 457–472, 1989.

[Get02]   Getty, getty thesaurus of geographic names
             http://www.getty.edu/research/tools/vocabulary/tgn/, 2002.

[GF92]   M.R. Genesereth and R.E Fikes. *Knowledge Interchange Format, version
             3.0 reference manual*, 1992.

[Hor00]   I. Horrocks. OIL in a Nutshell. In *ECAI Workshop on Application of
             Ontologies and PSMs*, 2000.

[Iso02]   Iso19112, geographic information – spatial referencing by geographic
             identifiers, 2002.

[KCT99]   R. Karp, V. Chaudhri, and J. Thomere. Xol: An xml-based ontology
             exchange language – www.ai.sri.com/ pkarp/xol, 1999.

[LH00]   S. Luke and J. Heflin. Shoe 1.01 proposed specification –
             www.daml.org/ 2000/12/reference.html,
             www.cs.umd.edu/projects/plus/shoe/spec1., 2000.

[LW99]   O. Lassila and R. Webick. Resource description framework (rdf) model
             and syntax specification – www.w3.org/tr/pr-rdf-syntax, 1999.

[MSS01]   D.M. Mark, A. Skupin, and A. Smith. Ontological distinctions in the
             geographic domain. In *COSIT'01. Lecture Notes in Computer Science*,
             volume 2205, pages 488–502. Springer Verlag, 2001.

[OGC02]   Opengis geography markup language (gml) implementation specification
             – http://www.opengis.org/techno/implementation.htm, 2002.

[UK89]   M. Uschold and M. King. The Enterprise Ontology. *Knowledge Engi-
             neering Review*, 13(1):31–89, 1989.

[W3c02]   W3c, owl web ontology language – http://xml.coverpages.org/owl.html,
             2002.

Ontology Translation on the Semantic Web[*]

Dejing Dou, Drew McDermott, and Peishen Qi

Yale Computer Science Department
New Haven, CT 06520, USA
{dejing.dou,drew.mcdermott,peishen.qi}@yale.edu

Abstract. Ontologies as means for formally specifying the vocabulary and relationship of concepts are seen playing a key role on the Semantic Web. However, the Web's distributed nature makes ontology translation one of the most difficult problems that web-based agents must cope with when they share information. Ontology translation is required when translating datasets, generating ontology extensions and querying through different ontologies. OntoMerge, an online system by ontology merging and automated reasoning, can implement ontology translation with inputs and outputs in DAML+OIL or other web languages. The merge of two related ontologies is obtained by taking the union of the concepts and the axioms defining them. We add *bridging axioms* not only as "bridges" between concepts in two related ontologies but also to make this merge into a new ontology for further merging with other ontologies. Our uniform internal representation, *Web-PDDL*, is a strong typed first-order logic language for web application, used to separate ontology translation into syntactic translation and semantic translation. Syntactic translation is done by an automatic translator between Web-PDDL and DAML+OIL or other web languages. Semantic translation is implemented using an inference engine (*OntoEngine*) which processes assertions and queries in Web-PDDL syntax, running in either a data-driven (forward chaining) or demand-driven (backward chaining) way.

1   Introduction

One major goal of the Semantic Web is that web-based agents can process and "understand" data rather than merely display them as at present [21]. Ontologies, which are defined as the formal specification of a vocabulary of concepts and axioms relating them, are seen playing a key role in describing the "semantics" of the data.

More and more ontologies are being developed and many of them describe similar domains. The distributed nature of the Web allows web-based agents to use different ontologies. In this section, we first describe the syntactic and semantic differences between ontologies on similar domains. We then define ontology translation problem in three categories: datasets translation, ontology extension

---

[*] This research was supported by DARPA as DAML program.

R. Meersman et al. (Eds.): CoopIS/DOA/ODBASE 2003, LNCS 2888, pp. 952–969, 2003.
© Springer-Verlag Berlin Heidelberg 2003

generation and querying through different ontologies. We will also distinguish ontology translation from ontology mapping and talk about some previous related work.

We call our new approach *ontology translation by ontology merging and automated reasoning*. Our focus is on formal inference from facts expressed in one ontology to facts expressed in another. We will have little to say about eliminating syntactic differences, and instead will generally assume that the facts to be translated will be in the same logical notation after translation as before; only the vocabulary will change. The *merge* of two related ontologies is obtained by taking the union of the terms and the axioms defining them, using XML namespaces to avoid name clashes. *Bridging axioms* are then added to relate the concepts in one ontology to the concepts in the other through the terms in the merge. Devising and maintaining a merged ontology must involve the contribution from human experts, both domain experts and "knowledge engineers". Once the merged ontology is obtained, ontology translation can proceed without further human intervention. The inference mechanism we use, a theorem prover optimized for the ontology-translation task, is called *OntoEngine*. We use it for dataset translation (section 2), ontology-extension generation(section 3), and query handling through ontologies (section 4). We also will discuss related work and our future plans for about semi-automatic tools for ontology merging in section 5.

1.1   The Differences between Ontologies on Similar Domains

The differences between two ontologies on similar domains can include syntactic and semantic differences, both of which we must deal with. Although current web-agent languages, including DAML+OIL [1], OWL [9] and WSDL [7], all have XML encodings, they are basically different syntactically.

The semantic differences can be caused by many factors. One simple case is different taxonomic structures of concepts. For example, one genealogy ontology uses two properties - firstname and lastname - to represent a person's name but another genealogy ontology might use only one property fullname to represent it. The following gives another example of simple semantic differences, which is between two bibliography ontologies in the DAML ontology library [2]. One ontology was developed at Yale, and we give it the prefix yale_bib [14]; the other was developed at CMU and gets the prefix cmu_bib [13]. While they are both obviously derived from the Bibtex terminology, different decisions were made when ontology experts developed them.

EXAMPLE 1.1.1. Both ontologies have a class called Article. In the yale_bib ontology, Article is a class which is disjoint with other classes such as Inproceedings and Incollection. Therefore, in the yale_bib ontology, Article only includes those articles which were published in a journal. But in the cmu_bib ontology, Article includes all articles which were published in a journal, proceedings or collection. There are no Inproceedings and Incollection classes in the cmu_bib ontology.

Even if the concepts from two ontologies share the same class or property name, it is still possible that they have quite different meanings. The following example is about the booktitle property in the yale_bib ontology and cmu_bib ontology:

EXAMPLE 1.1.2. In the cmu_bib ontology, booktitle's domain is the Book class and it's range is String. It means a Book has some string as its title. In the yale_bib ontology, booktitle's domain is Publication and its range is Literal which can be taken the same class as String. However, yale_bib's booktitle means that there is an Inproceedings or Incollection in some Proceedings or Collection and it is this Proceedings or Collection that has the string as its title.

Another reason for complicated semantic differences is that they can be inherited from those between basic concepts, such as time, space etc.

EXAMPLE 1.1.3. There are several ontologies about time, such as DAML Time [4] and the time ontology in OpenCyc [5]. Those time ontologies have semantic differences among their concepts, such as events. Some special events, such as birth, marriage and death in two genealogy ontologies can be created based on the event concepts of two different time ontologies. The semantic differences between the concepts of birth in different genealogy ontologies can be inherited from the semantic differences of events between the time ontologies.

1.2   Three Kinds of Ontology Translation Problems

Overcoming syntactic and semantic differences between ontologies is one of the most difficult problems that web-based agents must cope with. In general, we call it the *ontology translation problem*. It includes syntactic translation and semantic translation.

Ontology translation for datasets can be defined as the translation of a "dataset" from one ontology to another. We use the term *dataset* to mean a set of facts expressed in a particular ontology [31]. The translation problem arises when web-based agents try to exchange their datasets but they use different ontologies to describe them.

EXAMPLE 1.2.1. Suppose there is a web-based agent which uses the cmu_bib ontology to collect and process the bibliography information of researchers in the area of computer science. A web-based agent at Yale can provide such information of professors in the CS department of Yale. And its datasets are written in DAML+OIL using the yale_bib ontology. Although the CMU agent might be able to handle the DAML+OIL syntax, it still can't completely process these datasets because of the semantic differences between the two ontologies. The CMU agent needs an ontology translation service to translate those datasets into the cmu_bib ontology first.

We also found ontology translation is required when generating ontology extensions and querying through different ontologies. The problem of *ontology extension generation* is defined thus: given two related ontologies O_1 and O_2 and an extension (subontology) O_{1s} of O_1, construct the "corresponding" extension O_{2s}. The ontology experts are developing more and more similar subontologies extended from existing ontology(s) manually. This work is tedious at the Web scale and we need some tools to make it easier.

EXAMPLE 1.2.2. DAML-S [3] is a general ontology describing web services in the application level and WSDL Schema [8] is another general ontology describing web services in the communication level about messages and protocols. Ontology experts have manually developed some subontologies extended from DAML-S, such as a book seller web service called Congo and an air ticket reservation web service called BravoAir. To make a web service really work, we need to describe it on the communication level. In other words, we need the corresponding subontologies extended from WSDL Schema for Congo and BravoAir. This process is also called "grounding" in [20]. It is possible to get the grounding of Congo or BravoAir by " "translating" Congo or BravoAir from DAML-S to the corresponding subontology of WSDL Schema.

In our view, the most obvious feature of querying on the Semantic Web is: the knowledge to be used to answer a query may be in multiple knowledge bases, and these knowledge bases may describe their content using different ontologies from the ontology that the querying agent uses. On the Semantic Web model, the querying agent doesn't need to specify which knowledge base(s) can answer it's query, it also doesn't need to know what ontologies the answering knowledge base(s) uses. Without ontology translation, querying across these knowledge bases with different ontologies is very difficult.

EXAMPLE 1.2.3. Suppose a web agent wants to find the marriage date of Henry_VI, once a King of England. It need not know which knowledge base can answer its question, and can construct a query using the concepts in the drc_ged [15] genealogy ontology. One web knowledge base storing the information about the individuals and families of European royalty should be able to answer this question, but it uses a different bbn_ged [16] genealogy ontology and only can answer a query in that ontology. The two genealogy ontologies surely will have some semantic differences between them. Ontology translation is required for the agent to get its query answered.

1.3   Ontology Translation Is Different from Ontology Mapping

It's important to distinguish ontology translation from *ontology mapping*, which is the process of finding correspondence (mappings) between the concepts of two ontologies. If two concepts correspond, they mean the same thing, or closely related things. The mappings should be expressed by some mapping rules which explain how those concepts correspond. Obviously, ontology translation needs to know the mappings of two ontologies first, then it can use the mapping rules. The mappings are generated either by ontology experts or by some automatic tools. Automating the process of ontology mapping is an active area of research [33,34, 24,29]. In our view, automatic ontology mapping can save time and give suggestions to ontology experts. But without ontology experts' involvements [31], an ontology translation system can not directly use the mapping rules generated by automatic mapping tools if it doesn't expect any wrong translation. There are mainly two reasons. First, automatic mapping tool can't generate 100% accurate mappings and the result need ontology experts' manually correction. Second, although existing automatic mapping tools can express simple semantic difference between two concepts using "subclassOf," "subpropertyOf" or "equivalent" relationships, they are not very useful for complicated semantic differences because only ontology experts can figure them out. Ontology experts need a more expressive formal representation language to express the complicated mapping rules. In this paper, we usually presuppose that there is a way to find the correspondence of two ontologies with the help of ontology experts and some automatic mapping tools. We will focus on how to express complicated mapping rules and how to implement ontology translation itself.

1.4   Previous Work

Previous work on ontology translation for datasets has made use of two strategies. One is to translate a dataset in any source ontology to a dataset in one big, centralized ontology that serves as an interlingua which can be translated into a dataset in any target ontology. Ontolingua [28] is a typical example for this strategy, but this strategy can't really work well unless a global ontology can cover all existing ontologies, and we can get agreement by all ontology experts to write translators between their own ontologies and this global ontology. Even if in principle such harmony can be attained, in practice keeping all ontologies – including the new ones that come along every day – consistent with the One True Theory is very difficult. If someone creates a simple, lightweight ontology for a particular domain, he may be interested in translating it to neighboring domains, but can't be bothered to think about how it fits into a grand unified theory of knowledge representation. The other strategy is to do ontology translation directly from a dataset in a (source) ontology to a dataset in another (target) ontology, on a dataset-by-dataset basis, without the use of any kind of interlingua. OntoMorph [23] is a typical example of this strategy. For practical purposes this sort of program can be very useful, but it tends to rely on special properties of the datasets to be translated, and doesn't address the question of producing a general-purpose translator that handles any source dataset.

Previous work on ontology translation for query handling is closely related to database mediators [34]. This kind of work always more focuses on the different taxonomic structures of ontologies because the features of databases. In the Semantic Model, the difference between the ontologies describing web knowledge resources will be more complicated.

2   Deductive Ontology Translation between Datasets

In this section we briefly summarize our new approach for ontology translation, and how OntoMerge translates datasets on the Semantic Web. A more detailed account on the forward chaining algorithm for our generalized modus ponens reasoner appears in [25].

2.1 Separate Syntactic and Semantic Translation

Past work [28,23] on ontology translation has addressed both syntactic and semantic-issues, but tends to focus more on syntactic translation [23] because it is easier to automate. Semantic translation is more difficult because creating mapping rules often requires subtle judgments about the relationships between meanings of concepts in one ontology and their meanings another. It can't be fully automated.

We break ontology translation into three parts: syntactic translation from the source notation in a web language to an internal representation, semantic translation by inference using the internal notation, and syntactic translation from the internal representation to the target web language. All syntactic issues are dealt with in the first and third phases, using a translator, *PDDAML* [17] for translating between our internal representation and DAML+OIL [1]. If a new web language becomes more popular for the Semantic Web, we only need extend PDDAML to handle it (e.g. PDDAML also can handle OWL now). This allows us to focus on semantic translation from one ontology to another.

Our internal representation language is *Web-PDDL* [32], a strongly typed first order logic language with Lisp-like syntax. It extends the Planning Domain Definition Language (PDDL) [30] with XML namespaces and more flexible notations for axioms. Web-PDDL can be used to represent ontologies, datasets and queries. Here is an example, part of the yale_bib ontology written in Web-PDDL.

```
(define (domain yale_bib-ont)
    (:extends (uri "http://www.w3.org/2000/01/rdf-schema#" :prefix rdfs))
    (:types Publication - Obj
            Article Book Incollection Inproceedings - Publication
            Literal - @rdfs:Literal)
    (:predicates (author p - Publication a - Literal)
                 .....))
```

The :extends declaration expresses that this domain (i.e., ontology) is extended from one or more other ontologies identified by the URIs. To avoid symbol clashes, symbols imported from other ontologies are given prefixes, such as @rdfs:Literal. These correspond to XML namespaces, and when Web-PDDL is translated to RDF [32], that's exactly what they become. Types start with capital letters. A constant or variable is declared to be of a type T by writing "x - T". Assertions are written in the usual Lisp style: (author pub20 "Tom Jefferson"), for instance. Compared with other web languages, such as DAML+OIL, Web-PDDL can express more complicated axioms about the relationships between the concepts of different ontologies, such as the axioms with functions. Some example bridging axioms in Web-PDDL are in the following sections.

2.2 Ontology Merging and Automated Reasoning

The problem for translating datasets can be expressed abstractly thus: given a set of facts in one vocabulary (the *source*), infer the largest possible set of consequences in another (the *target*). We break this process into two phases:

1. *Inference:* working in a *merged ontology* that combines all the symbols and axioms from both the source and target, draw inferences from source facts.
2. *Projection:* Retain conclusions that are expressed purely in the target vocabulary.

For the foreseeable future the merged ontology has to be constructed by human experts. If necessary, when the source and target ontologies are very large, automatic mapping tools can give some suggestions to human experts. As we have said, the merged ontology contains all the symbols and facts from both the source and target ontologies, but in addition it must contain *bridging axioms* that relate symbols in one ontology to symbols in the other. The merged ontology itself is a new ontology and it can be used for further merging with other ontologies.

In *Example* 1.2.1, suppose the source ontology is yale_bib and the target ontology is cmu_bib. Considering the semantic difference mentioned in Example 1.1.2, the fact "The publication BretonZucker96 appeared in the Proceedings of IEEE Conf. on Computer Vision and Pattern Recognition" is expressed in the yale_bib ontology thus:

```
(:objects ... BretonZucker96 - InProceedings)
(:facts ... (booktitle BretonZucker96 "Proceedings of  CVPR'96"))
```

In the cmu_bib ontology, the same fact should be expressed thus:

```
(:objects ... BretonZucker96 - Article proc38 - Proceedings)
(facts ... (inProceedings BretonZucker96 proc38)
          (booktitle proc38 "Proceedings of  CVPR'96") ...)
```

In the merged ontology, we must be careful to distinguish the two senses of (booktitle *a s*), which in the source means "Publication *a* appeared in a book with title *s*" and in the target means "The title of book *a* is *s*". Namespace prefixes suffice for that job. The more interesting task is to relate the two senses, which we accomplish with the bridging axioms

```
(forall (a - Article tl - String)
        (iff (@yale_bib:booktitle a tl) (booktitle a tl)))

(forall (a - @yale_bib:Inproceedings tl - String)
        (iff (booktitle a tl)
             (exists (p - Proceedings)
                (and (contain p a)
                     (@cmu_bib:inProceedings a p)
                     (@cmu_bib:booktitle p tl)))))
```

The symbols without a prefix are native to the merged ontology. Note that the bridging axioms can be used to go from either ontology to the other.

The second axiom uses an existential quantifier. When used from left to right, the rule causes the inference engine to introduce a new constant (proc38) to designate the proceedings that the article (BretonZucker96) appears in. Such *skolem terms* [36] are necessary whenever the translation requires talking about an object that can't be identified with any existing object.

We also introduced term-generating functions into the merged ontologies. These functions can give finer controls over term generation than skolemization would give and improve the accuracy of the inference. We use the prefix @control as a convention our inference engine requires for the term-generating functions. So the second axiom can be rewritten as:

```
(forall (a - @yale_bib:Inproceedings tl - String)
        (if (booktitle a tl)
            (and (contains (@control:aProc a) - Proceedings a)
                 (@cmu_bib:inProceedings a (@control:aProc a))
                 (@cmu_bib:booktitle (@control:aProc a) tl)))))
```

Our decision to use theorem proving for translation may cause some concern, given that in general a theorem prover can run for a long time and conclude nothing useful. However, in our experience, the sorts of inferences we need to make are focused on the following areas:

- Forward chaining from source to target ontologies.
- Backward chaining from queries in one ontology to datasets in another.
- Introduction of skolem terms and term-generating functions as explained above.
- Use of equalities to substitute existing constant terms for skolem terms.

Our theorem prover, called "OntoEngine", is specialized for these sorts of inference. To avoid infinite loops, we set a limit to the complexity of terms that OntoEngine generates; and, of course, the deductive engine stops when it reaches conclusions (or, in the case of backward chaining, goals) in the target ontology. In addition, OntoEngine has a good type checking system making use of strong typed feature of Web-PDDL.

Instead of full-fledged resolution, OntoEngine uses chaining through implications with specified directions. That means it is not *complete* in the logical sense; we trade completeness for efficiency. In any case, the kind of completeness that might seem appropriate for ontology translation is that anything that can be expressed in the source ontology can be translated into the target ontology; call this *translation completeness*. Even a logically complete theorem prover would in general fail to achieve translation completeness because the source ontology and target ontology might not totally overlap.

2.3   OntoMerge and Experiments for Translating Datasets

On the Semantic Web model, the knowledge is mostly represented in XML-based web languages. We have set up an online ontology-translation system called OntoMerge. OntoMerge serves as a semi-automated nexus for agents and humans to find ways of coping with notational differences, both syntactic and semantic, between ontologies. OntoMerge wraps OntoEngine with PDDAML, which implement the syntactic translation for the input and output DAML files. The architecture of OntoMerge for translating datasets is shown in Figure 1.

When receiving an input dataset to translate, OntoEngine needs a merged ontology that covers the source and target ontologies. If no such merged ontology

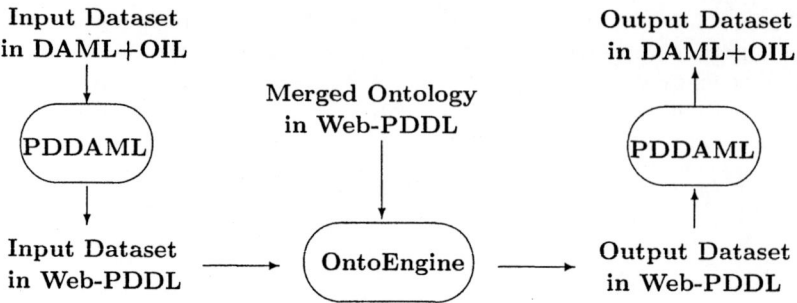

Fig. 1. The OntoMerge Architecture for Translating Datasets

is available, all OntoEngine can do is to record the need for a new merger. (If enough such requests come in, the ontology experts may wake up and get to work.) Assuming that a merged ontology exists, located typically at some URL, OntoEngine tries to load it in. Then it loads the dataset (facts) in and does forward chaining with the bridging axioms, until no new facts in the target ontology are generated.

OntoMerge has worked well so far, although our experience is inevitably limited by the demand for our services. In addition to the small example from the dataset[1] using the yale_bib ontology to the equivalent dataset using the cmu_bib ontology, we have also run it on some big ones.

Experiment 1: OntoMerge translates a dataset[2] with 7564 facts about the geography of Afghanistan using more than 10 ontologies into a dataset in the map ontology [11]. 4611 facts are related to the geographic features of Afghanistan described by the geonames ontology [12] and its airports described by the airport ontology [10]. Some facts about an airport of Afghanistan are:

```
(@rdfs:label @af:OAJL "JALALABAD")
(@airport:icaoCode @af:OAJL "OAJL")
(@airport:location @af:OAJL "Jalalabad, Afghanistan")
(@airport:latitude @af:OAJL 34.399166666666666)
(@airport:longitude @af:OAJL 70.49944444444445)
```

Actually either of these two ontologies just partly overlaps with the map ontology. The main semantic difference between their overlapping with the map ontology is: in the map ontology, any location in a map is a point whether it is an airport or other kind of geographic feature such as a bridge. But in the airport and geonames ontologies, an airport is a special location which is different from a bridge, and it's not a point. We have merged the geonames ontology and the airport ontology with the map ontology. One of bridging axioms in the merge of the airport ontology and the map ontology is given below:

```
(forall (x - Airport y z  - Object)
    (if (and (@airport:latitude x y) (@airport:longitude x z))
```

---

[1] http://cs-www.cs.yale.edu/homes/dvm/daml/datasets/yale_bib_dataset.daml
[2] http://www.daml.org/2001/06/map/af-full.daml

```
(and (location (@control:aPoint x) - Point
               (@control:aLocation x) - Location)
     (latitude (@control:aLocation x) y)
     (longitude (@control:aLocation x) z))))
```

After OntoEngine loads the two merged ontologies and all 7564 facts in, those 4611 facts in the airport and geonames ontologies are translated to 4014 facts in the map ontology by inference. The translated dataset for the above airport like:

```
(@map:label Point31 "JALALABAD")
(@map:label Point31 "OAJL")
(@map:label Point31 "Jalalabad, Afghanistan")
(@map:location Point31 Location32)
(@map:latitude Location32 34.399166666666666)
(@map:longitude Location32 70.49944444444445)
```

As part of DAML Experiment 2002, the result can be used by a map agent (BBN's OpenMap) to generate a map image about the airports and geographic features of Afghanistan. The semantic translation (inference) process by Onto-Engine, which contains 21232 reasoning steps, only takes 18 seconds (including the time for loading the input dataset and merged ontologies) on our PC in PIII 800MHZ with 256M RAM.

Experiment 2: OntoEngine translates a bigger dataset[3] with 21164 facts (on 3010 individuals and 1422 families of European royalty) in the bbn_ged genealogy ontology [16] to 26956 facts in the drc_ged genealogy ontology [15]. Here are some facts in the bbn_ged ontology about a King of France :

```
(@bbn_ged:name @royal92:@I1248@ "Francis_II")
(@bbn_ged:sex @royal92:@I1248@ "M")
(@bbn_ged:spouseIn @royal92:@I1248@ @royal92:@F456@)
(@bbn_ged:marriage @royal92:@F456 @royal92:event3138)
(@bbn_ged:date @royal92:event3138 "24 APR 1558")
(@bbn_ged:place @royal92:event3138 "Paris,France")
```

Although these two genealogy ontology are very similar and overlap a lot but there are still some differences. For example, in the drc_ged ontology, there are two properties wife and husband, but the most related concept in the bbn_ged ontology is the spouseIn property. As our general understanding, if a person is a male (his sex is "M") and he is spouseIn some family which is related to some marriage event, he will be the husband of that family. We have written the bridging axioms for the bbn_ged and drc_ged ontologies to express such semantic differences. The one for the above example is given below.

```
(forall (f - Family h - Individual m - Marriage)
    (if (and (@bbn_ged:sex h "M") (@bbn_ged:spouseIn h f)
             (@bbn_ged:marriage f m))
        (husband f h)))
```

This merged genealogy ontology works well for semantic translation. After loading the input dataset and merged ontology, OntoEngine runs 85555 reasoning

---

[3] http://www.daml.org/2001/01/gedcom/royal92.daml

steps to generate all the 26956 facts. The whole process takes 59 seconds. The translated dataset for King Francis_II in the drc_ged ontology is:

```
(@drc_ged:name @royal92:@I1248@ "Francis_II")
(@drc_ged:sex @royal92:@I1248@ "M")
(@drc_ged:husband @royal92:@F456 @royal92:@I1248@)
(@drc_ged:marriage @royal92:@F456 @royal92:event3138)
(@drc_ged:date @royal92:event3138 "24 APR 1558")
(@drc_ged:location @royal92:event3138 "Paris,France")
```

Prospective users should check out the OntoMerge website[4]. We have put all URLs of existing merged ontologies there. OntoMerge is designed to solicit descriptions of ontology-translation problems, even when OntoMerge can't solve them. However, according to our experience, we believe that in most cases we can develop and debug a merged ontology within days that will translate any dataset from one of the ontologies in the merged set to another. It's not difficult for a researcher who has first order logic background to write bridging axioms in Web-PDDL by themselves. We encourage other people to develop their own merged ontology to solve ontology translation problems they encounter.

3   Ontology Extension Generation

As we have said, manually developing subontologies extended from existing ontology(s) is tedious at the Web scale. Tools are needed to make it easier because the number of subontologies is usually much larger. In this section, we will introduce our approach to generate ontology extensions automatically by ontology translation.

One scenario is that ontology experts have some subontologies of the existing ontology(s), and they want to generate the corresponding subontologies of other related existing ontology(s). If they know the relationships between those existing ontologies, some ontology translation tools can automate this process. Another scenario is that ontology experts often need to update some existing ontologies when new knowledge or new requirement comes up. This work has to be done manually, but how about updating their subontologies? Since they know the relationships between the old and updated ontologies, new subontologies can be generated automatically.

In *Example* 1.2.2, if ontology experts can merge DAML-S and WSDL Schema first, they can translate Congo or BravoAir into their groundings. The advantage is they only need to get one merged ontology for DAML-S and WSDL Schema. Further translation from the sub web service ontologies of DAML-S to their groundings on WSDL Schema can be implemented automatically.

The structure for OntoMerge to generate ontology extensions is similar to that shown in Figure 1. The difference is the input and output are not datasets but subontologies. For *Example* 1.2.2, we have experimented with the following idea, which works in simple cases: Take a property in the Congo ontology:

---

[4] http://cs-www.cs.yale.edu/homes/dvm/daml/ontology-translation.html

```
 (deliveryAddress sp1 - SpecifyDeliveryDetails st2 - @xsd:string)
```

where SpecifyDeliveryDetails is a subtype of @DAML-S:Process. Create an instance of it, with anonymous skolem constants for the variable:

```
(deliveryAddress SDD-1 str-2)
;;SDD-1 and str-2 are skolem constants of types SpecifyDeliveryDetails
;;and @xsd:string respectively
```

Hypothetically assume that this fact is true, and draw conclusions using forward chaining. This inference process use facts like these form and the axioms in Congo ontology and the bridging axioms in the merged ontology for DAML-S and WSDL Schema like:

```
(forall (ob1 ob2)
   (if (deliveryAddress ob1 ob2) (@process:input ob1 ob2)))
;;the above axiom is from the Congo ontology to express that
;;deliveryAddress is a sub property of @process:input in DAML-S.

(forall (x - @DAML-S:Process)
        (exists (sg - ServiceGrounding) (ground sg x)))

(forall (p - Process sg - ServiceGrounding ob1 - String)
    (if (and (ground sg p) (@process:input p ob1))
        (exists (ms - Message pa - Part pm - Param)
            (and (@wsdl:input p pm) (paramMessage pm ms)
                 (part ms pa) (partElement pa ob1)))))
;;these two axioms are from merged ontology for DAML-S and WSDL Schema.
```

OntoEngine can generate the translated facts in Web-PDDL:

```
(@wsdl:input SDD-1 Param374)
(@wsdl:operation PortType367 SDD-1)
(@wsdl:partElement Part376 str-2)
(@wsdl:part Message375 Part376)
(@wsdl:paramMessage Param374 Message375)
```

where Param374 and such are further skolem terms produced by instantiating existential quantifiers during inference.

All of the conclusions are expressed in the WSDL Schema ontology. The first three mention the two skolem constants in the original assumption. These are plausible candidates for capturing the entire meaning of the deliveryAddress predicate as far as WSDL Schema is concerned. So to generate the new extension WSDL_congo, simply create new predicates for each of these conclusions and make them subproperties of the predicates in the conclusions:

```
(define (domain WSDL_congo)
   (:extends (uri "http://schemas.xmlsoap.org/wsdl/"))
   (:types SpecifyDeliveryDetails - Operation ....)
   (:predicates
      (deliveryAddress_input arg1 - SpecifyDeliveryDetails arg2 - Param)
      (deliveryAddress_operation arg1 - PortType
```

```
                                arg2 - SpecifyDeliveryDetails)
        (deliveryAddress_partElement arg1 - Part arg2 - @xsd:string)
    ...
```

The corresponding axioms for subproperty relationships are:

```
    (forall (ob1 ob2) (if (deliveryAddress_input ob1 ob2)
                          (@wsdl:input ob1 ob2)))
    (forall (ob1 ob2) (if (deliveryAddress_operation ob1 ob2)
                          (@wsdl:operation ob1 ob2)))
    (forall (ob1 ob2) (if (deliveryAddress_partElement ob1 ob2)
                          (@wsdl:partElement ob1 ob2)))
```

The output subontology is a grounding of Congo in WSDL Schema and it can be represented in WSDL after feeding it into a translator between Web-PDDL and WSDL. That translator has been embedded in PDDAML.

Our automatically generated WSDL_congo is very similar to the manually produced grounding by the DAML-S group[5]. It is encouraging but this particular technique has taken us only so far. The main gap is that it can translate the types, predicates and only those axioms about subproperties of one ontology extension O_{1s} to corresponding of O_{2s}. It works well for some sub-ontologies, such as Congo and BravoAir, because most axioms in them are those about subproperties. But we can expect there are more general axioms in other sub-ontologies, how to derive general axioms from one subontology to the other by inference will be one of our future work.

4   Querying through Different Ontologies

Forward-chaining deduction is a data-driven inference and it works well for translating datasets and ontology extension generation. We also embed a backward chaining reasoner into OntoEngine and get it run in demand-driven way. To test our backward chaining reasoner, we can extend OntoMerge to handle querying problem through different ontologies, as we have mentioned in *Example* 1.2.3.

There are some query languages for the Semantic Web. One of them is DQL [6]. We suppose some web-based agents use DQL and we have extended our PDDAML to handle syntax translation between DQL query and Web-PDDL.

To extend OntoMerge to handle querying problem through different ontologies, we embedded some tools for query selection and query reformulation. One input query can be the conjunction of some subqueries and each of them may be answered by different knowledge bases. We might not be able to "translate" the whole input query in one ontology to the query in another. We have experimented with the following idea for *Example* 1.2.3. And besides that question, the query agent also wants to know the name of the king's wife who married him on that date. It constructs the query in DQL query triples using the drc_ged ontology. Due to the limit of space, we only give out the corresponding query in Web-PDDL. The @xsd prefix is for XML Schema Datatype.

---

[5] http://www.daml.org/services/daml-s/0.7/CongoGrounding.wsdl

```
(:query (freevars (?k ?q - Individual ?f - Family ?m - Marriage
                ?n - @xsd:string ?d - @xsd:date)
        (and (@drc_ged:name ?k "Henry_VI") (@drc_ged:husband ?f ?k)
             (@drc_ged:wife ?f ?q) (@drc_ged:name ?q ?n)
             (@drc_ged:marriage ?f ?m) (@drc_ged:date ?m ?d))))
```

It is the conjunction of some subqueries in Web-PDDL. The required answer must give the bindings for variables ?d and ?n.

In the Semantic Web model, if that agent asks help from OntoMerge, it might have tried some web knowledge bases using the drc_ged ontology but got no answer. Now the ontology translation is necessary. When activated, OntoMerge will search its library of merged ontologies to see if any merged ontology includes the drc_ged ontology as its component. If yes, it means OntoMerge might be able to help answer the query with those web resources described by the other component ontologies of the merged one. So far, there is a merged ontology for the drc_ged and bbn_ged ontologies in the library of OntoMerge . So OntoMerge would ask some broker agent to find some web knowledge bases using the bbn_ged ontology. In this experiment, we just assume one such web knowledge base exists and it can answer queries described by the bbn_ged ontology.

The whole process is described as follows. OntoMerge calls the query selection tool to select one subquery. Here, the tool will first select (@drc_ged:name ?k "Henry_VI") because it only has one variable. OntoEngine then does backward chaining for this subquery and "translate" it into a query in the bbn_ged ontology, (@bbn_ged:name ?k "Henry_VI"). The new one is sent to the web knowledge base described by the bbn_ged ontology, which returns the binding {?k/@royal92:@I1217@} (@royal92:@I1217@ is an Individual in the web knowledge base). With this binding, OntoMerge call the query reformulation tool to reform the rest subqueries and get another selection:
(@drc_ged:husband ?f @royal92:@I1217@). After backward chaining and querying, the next binding we get is {?f/ @royal92:@F448@}, which leads to a new subquery

```
(and (@drc_ged:wife @royal92:@F448@ ?q)
     (@drc_ged:marriage @royal92:@F448@ ?m))
```

and its corresponding one in the bbn_ged ontology:

```
(and (@bbn_ged:sex ?q "F") (@bbn_ged:spouseIn ?q @royal92:@F448@)
     (@bbn_ged:marriage @royal92:@F448@ ?m))
```

The bindings this time are {?q/@royal92:@I1218@}, and {?m/@royal92:event3732}. Repeat the similar process and the final query in the bbn_ged ontology is

```
(and (@bbn_ged:name @royal92:@I1218@ ?n)
     (@bbn_ged:date @royal92:event3732 ?d))
```

The ultimate result is {?n/"Margaret of_Anjou"} and {?d/"22 APR 1445"}.

This example is quite simple because the bindings all happen to come from one knowledge base. We just use it to test our backward chaining reasoner in OntoEngine.

A full treatment of answering query by backward chaining across ontologies would raise the issue of *query optimization*, which we have not focused much on yet, although there are some query selection and reformulation tools in OntoMerge. There is a lot of work in this area, and we will cite just two references: [26,19]. We intend to more focus on overcoming the complicated semantic differences when querying across different ontologies.

In addition, answering query by backward chaining may be necessary in the middle of forward chaining. For example, when OntoEngine is unifying the fact $(P\ c1)$ with $(P\ ?x)$ in the axiom:

$$(P\ ?x) \wedge (member\ ?x\ [c1, c2, c3]) \Rightarrow (Q\ ?x)$$

it can't conclude $(Q\ c1)$ unless it can verify that $c1$ is a member of the list [c1,c2,c3], and the only way to implement this deduction is by answering that query by backward chaining.

5   Related Work

So far, our discussion has focused more on how to express the semantic differences between two ontologies in a merged ontology, and how to implement ontology translation by inference. Although we think the process of ontology merging needs human experts' involvements and can't be fully automated for the foreseeable future, it will be helpful to develop some semi-automatic tools for ontology merging.

Our ontology merging is rather different from what some other people have emphasized in talking about ontology combination because we focus more on bridging axioms for inference. The PROMPT [35] and Chimaera [33] systems focus on ontology editing for merging two similar ontologies. They try to do ontology matching semi-automatically according to name similarity and taxonomic structure. The matching provides user with some suggestions for further refinement. Some recent work, such as GLUE [24], has used machine learning and exploit information in the data instances to generate mapping rules of two ontologies. GLUE still only generates simple mapping rules about "subclassOf," "superclassOf," and "equivalent" relationships. Ontology experts can check the accuracy of these simple mapping rules and write the remaining, more complicated, mapping rules by themselves.

We are not the only ones who have realized that deductive rules are an important component of inference and translation systems. The emerging standard is RuleML [22], which can be characterized as an XML serialization of logic-programming rules. While we use heuristics similar to those embodied in logic programming, we believe that ontology translation requires equality substitution and a more systematic treatment of existential quantifiers than logic programming can provide. A recent paper [27] on the relation between rules and description logics attempts to restrict rules even further. Our approach is to "layer" logic on top of RDF in a way that leaves it completely independent of the constraints of description logics [32].

The idea of building up merged ontologies incrementally, starting with local mergers, has been explored in a recent paper [18], in which bridging rules are assumed to map database relations by permuting and projecting columns. These rules are simpler than ours, but in return the authors get some very interesting algorithms for combining local ontology mappings into more global views.

6 Conclusions

The distributed nature of the Web makes ontology translation one of the most difficult problems web-based must cope with. We described our new approach to implement ontology translation on the Semantic Web. Here are the main points we tried to make:

1. *Ontology translation* is required when translating datasets, generating ontology extensions, or querying through different ontologies. It must be distinguished from ontology mapping, which is the process of finding likely correspondences between symbols in two different ontologies. This sort of mapping can be a prelude to translation, but it is likely to be necessary for the foreseeable future for a human expert to produce useful translation rules from proposed correspondences.
2. Ontology translation can be thought of in terms of *ontology merging*. The merge of two related ontologies is obtained by taking the union of the terms and the axioms defining them, then adding bridging axioms that relate the terms in one ontology to those in the other through the terms in the merge.
3. If all ontologies, datasets and queries can be expressed in terms of the same internal representation, semantic translation can be implemented by automatic reasoning. We believe the reasoning required can be thought of as simple typed, first-order inference, easily implemented using a language such as Web-PDDL for expressing type relationships and axioms.

We set up an online ontology translation server, OntoMerge, to apply and validate our method. We have evaluated our approach by the experiments for large web knowledge resources and its performance is good so far. We also discuss the efficiency and completeness of our inference system. We hope the existence of OntoMerge will get more people interested in the hard problem of generating useful translation rules.

Our results so far open up all sorts of avenues of further research, especially in the area of automating the production of bridging axioms. Although these can be quite complicated, many of them fall into standard classes. We are working on tools that allow domain experts to build most such axioms themselves, through a set of dialogues about the form of the relation between concepts in one ontology and concepts in the other. We also will develop tools to check the consistency of the generated bridging axioms. These long-range goal is to allow domain experts to generate their own merged ontologies without being familiar with the technicalities of Web-PDDL.

References

1. http://www.daml.org/2001/03/daml+oil-index.html.
2. http://www.daml.org/ontologies/
3. http://www.daml.org/services/.
4. http://www.ai.sri.com/daml/ontologies/time/Time.daml.
5. http://opencyc.sourceforge.net/daml/cyc.daml.
6. http://www.daml.org/2003/04/dql/.
7. http://www.w3c.org/TR/wsdl.
8. http://schemas.xmlsoap.org/wsdl/.
9. http://www.w3.org/TR/webont-req/.
10. http://www.daml.org/2001/10/html/airport-ont.daml.
11. http://www.daml.org/2001/06/map/map-ont.daml.
12. http://www.daml.org/2002/04/geonames/geonames-ont.daml.
13. http://www.daml.ri.cmu.edu/ont/homework/atlas-publications.daml.
14. http://www.cs.yale.edu/homes/dvm/daml/ontologies/daml/yale_bib.daml.
15. http://orlando.drc.com/daml/Ontology/Genealogy/3.1/Gentology-ont.daml.
16. http://www.daml.org/2001/01/gedcom/gedcom.daml
17. http://www.cs.yale.edu/homes/dvm/daml/pddl_daml_translator.html.
18. K. Aberer, P. Cudré-Mauroux, and M. Hauswirth. The chatty web: emergent semantics through gossiping. In *Proc. International World Wide Web Conference*, 2003.
19. S.Adali, K.Candan, Y.Papakonstantinou, and V. Subrahmanian. Query Caching and Optimization in Distributed Mediator Systems. In *Proc. ACM SIGMOD Conf. on Management of Data*, pages 137–148, 1996.
20. D.-S. C. A. Ankolekar, M. Burstein, J. R. Hobbs, O. Lassila, D. Martin, D. Mc-Dermott, S. A. McIlraith, S. Narayanan, M. Paolucci, T. Payne, and K. Sycara. Daml-s: Web service description for the semantic web. In *Proceedings of International Semantic Web Conference 2002*, pages 348–363, 2002.
21. T.Berners-Lee, J.Hendler, and O.Lassila. The Semantic Web. *Scientific American*, 284(5):34–43, 2001.
22. H. Boley, B. Grosof, M. Sintek, S. Tabet, and G. Wagner. RuleML Design, September 2002. http://www.dfki.uni-kl.de/ruleml/indesign.html.
23. H. Chalupsky. Ontomorph: A translation system for symbolic logic. In *Proc. Int'l. Con. on Principles of Knowledge Representation and Reasoning*, pages 471–482, San Francisco, 2000. Morgan Kaufmann.
24. A. Doan, J. Madhavan, P. Domingos, and A. Halevy. Learning to map between ontologies on the semantic web. In *Proceedings of the World-Wide Web Conference (WWW-2002)*, 2002.
25. D. Dou, D. McDermott, and P. Qi. Ontology Transaltion by Ontology Merging and Automated Reasoning. In *Proceedings of EKAW02 Workshop on Ontologies for Multi-Agent Systems*, 2002. Available at http://cs-www.cs.yale.edu/homes/dvm/papers/DouMcDermottQi02.ps
26. M. R. Genesereth, A. Keller, and O. Duschka. Infomaster: An information integration system. In *Proc 97 ACM SIGMOD International Conference on Management of Data*, pages 539–542, 1997.
27. B. N. Grosof, I. Horrocks, R. Volz, and S. Decker. Description logic programs: Combining logic programs with description logic. In *Proc. International World Wide Web Conference*, 2003.

28. T. Gruber. Ontolingua: A Translation Approach to Providing Portable Ontology Specifications. *Knowledge Acquisition*, 5(2):199–200, 1993.

29. J. Madhavan, P. A. Bernstein, P. Domingos, and A. Halevy. Representing and Reasoning about Mappings between Domain Models. In *Proc. AAAI 2002*, 2002.

30. D. McDermott. The Planning Domain Definition Language Manual. Technical Report 1165, Yale Computer Science, 1998. (CVC Report 98-003).

31. D. McDermott, M. Burstein, and D. Smith. Overcoming ontology mismatches in transactions with self-describing agents. In *Proc. Semantic Web Working Symposium*, pages 285–302, 2001.

32. D. McDermott and D. Dou. Representing Disjunction and Quantifiers in Rdf. In *Proceedings of International Semantic Web Conference 2002*, pages 250–263, 2002.

33. D. L. McGuinness, R. Fikes, J. Rice, and S. Wilder. An Environment for Merging and Testing Large Ontologies. In *Proceedings of the Seventh International Conference on Principles of Knowledge Representation and Reasoning (KR2000)*, 2000.

34. P. Mitra, G. Wiederhold, and M. Kersten. A graph-oriented model for articulation of ontology interdependencies. In *Proceedings of Conference on Extending Database Technology (EDBT 2000)*, 2000.

35. N. F. Noy and M. A. Musen. Prompt: Algorithm and tool for automated ontology merging and alignment. In *Proceedings of the Seventeenth National Conference on Artificial Intelligence (AAAI-2000)*, 2000.

36. S. Russell and P. Norvig. *Artificial Intelligence: A Modern Approach*. Prentice-Hall, Inc, 1995.

The Semantics of the Compound Term Composition Algebra

Yannis Tzitzikas[1]*, Anastasia Analyti[2], and Nicolas Spyratos[3]

[1] Istituto di Scienza e Tecnologie dell' Informazione, ISTI-CNR, Italy
tzitzik@isti.cnr.it
[2] Institute of Computer Science, ICS-FORTH, Greece
analyti@csi.forth.gr
[3] Laboratoire de Recherche en Informatique, Universite de Paris-Sud, France
spyratos@lri.fr

Abstract. In [11], we proposed an algebra with four algebraic operators, whose composition can be used to generate valid compound terms in a given faceted taxonomy in an efficient and flexible manner. The positive operations allow the derivation of valid compound terms through the declaration of a small set of valid compound terms. The negative operations allow the derivation of valid compound terms through the declaration of a small set of invalid compound terms. Here, we formally define the model-theoretic semantics of the operations and the closed-world assumptions adopted in each operation. We prove that our algebra is monotonic with respect to both valid and invalid compound terms, meaning that the valid and invalid compound terms of a subexpression are not invalidated by a larger expression. The importance of this property is demonstrated through an example. We also show that our algebra cannot be directly represented in Description Logics. A metasystem on top of Description Logics is designed to implement our algebra.

Keywords: Faceted Taxonomies, Semantics, Description Logics.

1 Introduction

A faceted taxonomy is a set of taxonomies, each describing a given domain from a different aspect, or facet [9]. The indexing of domain objects is done through conjunctive combinations of terms from the facets, called compound terms. For example, assume that the domain of interest is a set of hotel Web pages in Greece, and suppose that we want to provide access to these pages according to the *Location* of the hotels and the *Sports* facilities they offer. Figure 1 shows these two facets. Each object is described using a *compound term*. For example, a hotel in Crete providing sea ski and wind-surfing facilities would be described by the compound term $\{Crete, SeaSki, Windsurfing\}$.

---

* Work done during the postdoctoral studies of the author at CNR-ISTI as an ERCIM fellow. The first part of this work was done when the author was at ICS-FORTH.

R. Meersman et al. (Eds.): CoopIS/DOA/ODBASE 2003, LNCS 2888, pp. 970–985, 2003.

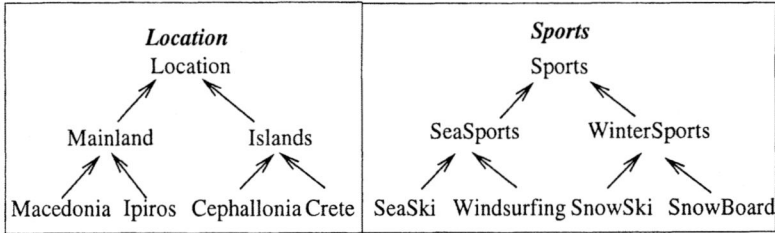

Fig. 1. Two facets

Faceted taxonomies carry a number of well known advantages over single hierarchies in terms of building and maintaining them, as well as using them in multicriteria indexing. A drawback, however, is the cost of avoiding *invalid* combinations, i.e. compound terms that do not apply to any object in the domain. For example, the compound term $\{Crete, SnowBoard\}$ is an invalid compound term, as there no hotels in Crete offering snow-board facilities.

In [11], we proposed an algebra whose operators (two positive and two negative) allow the efficient and flexible specification of valid compound terms, thus alleviating the main drawback of faceted taxonomies. Following this approach, given a faceted taxonomy, one can use an *algebraic expression* to define the desired set of compound terms. In each algebraic operation, the designer has to declare either a small set of valid compound terms from which other valid compound terms are inferred, or a small set of invalid compound terms from which other invalid compound terms are inferred. Then, a closed-world assumption is adopted for the rest of the compound terms in the range of the operation. For example, if a user declares in a positive operation that the compound term $\{Crete, SeaSki\}$ is valid then it is inferred that the compound term $\{Crete, SeaSports\}$ is also valid. If a user declares in a negative operation that the compound term $\{Crete, WinterSports\}$ is invalid then it is inferred that the compound term $\{Crete, SnowBoard\}$ is also invalid. In our example, this means that the designer can specify all valid compound terms of the faceted taxonomy by providing a relatively small number of (valid or invalid) compound terms. This is an important feature as it minimizes the effort needed by the designer. Only the expression that defines the compound terminology has to be stored, as an inference mechanism with polynomial time complexity (given in [11]) can check whether a compound term belongs to the compound terminology of the expression.

The proposed algebra can be used in order to construct taxonomies or thesauri (e.g. for Web catalogues like Yahoo! or ODP) which unlike existing thesauri, do not present the problem of missing terms or missing relationships.

In this paper, we emphasize on the semantics of the algebra. Specifically, we formally define the model-theoretic semantics of the operations and the closed-world assumptions adopted in each operation. First, intermediate semantics are defined for the particular operations, and then intermediate semantics are synthesized to define the semantics of the complete algebraic operation. Based on these, we define the models of an algebraic expression, and we prove that every *well-formed* algebraic expression is satisfiable. We also prove that our algebra is monotonic with respect to both valid and invalid compound terms, meaning that the valid and invalid compound terms of a subexpression are not invalidated by a larger expression. The importance of this property is demonstrated through an example.

In addition in this paper, we show that our algebra cannot be directly represented in Description Logics. A metasystem on top of Description Logics is designed to implement our algebra.

The remaining of this paper is organized as follows: Section 2 describes the algebra, and justifies the definition of a well-formed algebraic expression based on the monotonicity property. Section 3 gives a semantic interpretation of the algebra. Section 4 compares our approach with Description Logics. Finally, Section 5 concludes the paper.

2   The Compound Term Composition Algebra

In this section, we present in brief the *compound term composition algebra*, defined in [11]. For more explanations, and examples the reader should refer to that article.

A *terminology* is a finite set of names, called *terms*. A *taxonomy* is a pair $(\mathcal{T}, \leq)$, where $\mathcal{T}$ is a *terminology* and $\leq$ is a reflexive and transitive relation over $\mathcal{T}$, called *subsumption*.

A *compound term* over $\mathcal{T}$ is any subset of $\mathcal{T}$. For example, the following sets of terms are compound terms over the terminology *Sports* of Figure 1: $s_1 = \{SeaSki, Windsurfing\}$, $s_2 = \{SeaSports\}$, and $s_3 = \emptyset$.

A *compound terminology* S over $\mathcal{T}$ is any set of compound terms that contains the compound term $\emptyset$.

The set of all compound terms over $\mathcal{T}$ can be ordered using the *compound ordering* over $\mathcal{T}$, defined as: $s \preceq s'$ iff $\forall t' \in s' \; \exists t \in s$ such that $t \leq t'$.

That is, $s \preceq s'$ iff s contains a narrower term for every term of s'. In addition, s may contain terms not present in s'. Roughly, $s \preceq s'$ means that s carries more specific information than s'. For example, $\{SeaSki, Windsurfing\} \preceq \{SeaSports\} \preceq \emptyset$.

We say that two compound terms s, s' are *equivalent* iff $s \preceq s'$ and $s' \preceq s$. For example, $\{SeaSki, SeaSports\}$ and $\{SeaSki\}$ are equivalent. Intuitively, equivalent compound terms carry the same information.

Definition 1. A *compound taxonomy* over $\mathcal{T}$ is a pair $C = (S, \preceq)$, where S is a compound terminology over $\mathcal{T}$, and $\preceq$ is the compound ordering over $\mathcal{T}$ restricted to S.

Let $P(\mathcal{T})$ be the set of all compound terms over $\mathcal{T}$ (i.e. the powerset of $\mathcal{T}$). Clearly, $(P(\mathcal{T}), \preceq)$ is a compound taxonomy over $\mathcal{T}$.

Let s be a compound term. The broader and the narrower compound terms of s are defined as follows: $\text{Br}(s) = \{s' \in P(\mathcal{T}) \mid s \preceq s'\}$ and $\text{Nr}(s) = \{s' \in P(\mathcal{T}) \mid s' \preceq s\}$.

Let S be a compound terminology over $\mathcal{T}$. The broader and the narrower compound terms of S are defined as follows: $Br(S) = \cup\{Br(s) \mid s \in S\}$ and $Nr(S) = \cup\{Nr(s) \mid s \in S\}$.

We say that a compound term s is *valid* (resp. *invalid*), if there is at least one (resp. no) object of the underlying domain indexed by all terms in s. We assume that every term of $\mathcal{T}$ is valid. However, a compound term over $\mathcal{T}$ may be invalid. Obviously, if s is a valid compound term, all compound terms in $Br(s)$ are valid. Additionally, if s is an invalid compound term, all compound terms in $Nr(s)$ are invalid. The formal definition of validity is given in Section 3.

One way of designing a taxonomy is by identifying a number of different aspects of the domain of interest and then designing one taxonomy per aspect. As a result we obtain a set of taxonomies called *facets*. Given a set of facets we can define a *faceted taxonomy*.

Definition 2. Let $\{F_1, ..., F_k\}$ be a finite set of taxonomies, where $F_i = (\mathcal{T}_i, \leq_i)$, and assume that the terminologies $\mathcal{T}_1, ... , \mathcal{T}_k$ are pairwise disjoint. Then the pair $\mathcal{F} = (\mathcal{T}, \leq)$, where $\mathcal{T} = \bigcup_{i=1}^{k} \mathcal{T}_i$ and $\leq = \bigcup_{i=1}^{k} \leq_i$, is a taxonomy which we shall call the *faceted taxonomy generated* by $\{F_1, ..., F_k\}$. We shall call the taxonomies $F_1, ..., F_k$ the *facets* of $\mathcal{F}$.

Clearly, all definitions introduced so far apply also to $(\mathcal{T}, \leq)$. For example, the set $S = \{\{Greece\}, \{Sports\}, \{SeaSports\}, \{Greece, Sports\}, \{Greece, SeaSports\}, \emptyset\}$, is a compound terminology over the terminology $\mathcal{T}$ of the faceted taxonomy shown in Figure 1. Additionally, the pair $(S, \preceq)$ is a compound taxonomy over $\mathcal{T}$.

Let $\mathcal{F} = (\mathcal{T}, \leq)$ be the faceted taxonomy generated by a given set of facets $\{F_1, ..., F_k\}$. The problem is that $\mathcal{F}$ does not itself specify which compound terms, i.e. which elements of $P(\mathcal{T})$, are valid and which are not. To alleviate this problem, we introduce an algebra for defining a compound terminology over $\mathcal{T}$ (i.e. a subset of $P(\mathcal{T})$) which consists of the valid compound terms.

To begin with we associate the terminology $\mathcal{T}_i$ of every facet with a compound terminology T_i that we call the *basic compound terminology* of $\mathcal{T}_i$. Specifically,

$$T_i = \cup\{\ Br(\{t\}) \mid t \in \mathcal{T}_i\}$$

As every term t of a facet is considered valid, all compound terms in $Br(\{t\})$ are valid. Thus, T_i is the set of compound terms over $\mathcal{T}_i$ that are initially known to be valid. We use the basic compound terminologies as the "building blocks" of our algebra[1].

For defining the desired compound taxonomy the designer has to formulate an algebraic expression e, using the operations *plus-product*, *minus-product*, *plus-self-product*, *minus-self-product*, and initial operands the basic compound terminologies $\{T_1, .., T_k\}$.

Let S be the set of compound terminologies over $\mathcal{T}$. First, we define the auxiliary n-ary operation $\oplus$ over S, called *product*. This operation results in

---

[1] Note that each basic compound terminology is a compound terminology over $\mathcal{T}$.

an "unqualified" compound terminology whose compound terms are all possible combinations of compound terms from its arguments. Specifically, let $S_1, ..., S_n$ be compound terminologies, we define:

$$S_1 \oplus ... \oplus S_n = \{s_1 \cup ... \cup s_n \mid s_i \in S_i\}$$

2.1 Algebraic Operations

In this subsection, we describe each algebraic operation, in brief. Examples of the operations are given in [11]. The definitions of the operations are semantically justified in Section 3.

We introduce two "variations" of the $\oplus$ operation, namely the *plus-product* and the *minus-product*. Each of these two operations has an extra parameter denoted by P or N, respectively. The set P is a set of compound terms that are certainly valid. On the other hand, the set N is a set of compound terms that are certainly invalid. These parameters are declared by domain experts that perform the indexing and allow to infer all compound terms that are valid or invalid.

To proceed we need to distinguish what we shall call *genuine compound terms*. Intuitively, a genuine compound term combines non-empty compound terms from more than one compound terminologies.

Definition 3. The set of *genuine* compound terms over a set of compound terminologies $S_1, ..., S_n$, denoted by $G_{S_1,...,S_n}$, is defined as follows:

$$G_{S_1,...,S_n} = S_1 \oplus ... \oplus S_n - \bigcup_{i=1}^{n} S_i$$

For example if $S_1 = \{\{Greece\}, \{Islands\}, \emptyset\}$, $S_2 = \{\{Sports\}, \{WinterSports\}, \emptyset\}$, and $S_3 = \{\{Pensions\}, \{Hotels\}, \emptyset\}$ then

$$\{Greece, WinterSports, Hotels\} \in G_{S_1,S_2,S_3},$$
$$\{WinterSports, Hotels\} \in G_{S_1,S_2,S_3} \text{ , but}$$
$$\{Hotels\} \notin G_{S_1,S_2,S_3}$$

Assume that the compound terms of $S_1, ..., S_n$ are valid. We are interested in characterizing the validity of all combinations of compound terms of $S_1, ..., S_n$. As we already know the validity of the compound terms of $S_1, ..., S_n$, we are basically interested in characterizing the validity of the compound terms in $G_{S_1,...,S_n}$. This is done through the following operations, plus-product and minus-product.

We now define the *plus-product* operation, $\oplus_P$, an n-ary operation over $\mathcal{S}$ ($\oplus_P : \mathcal{S} \times ... \times \mathcal{S} \to \mathcal{S}$), where the parameter P is a set of valid compound terms from the product of the input compound terminologies. Specifically, the set P is a subset of $G_{S_1,...,S_n}$, as we assume that all compound terms in the input parameters are valid.

Definition 4. Let $S_1, ..., S_n$ be compound terminologies and $P \subseteq G_{S_1,...,S_n}$. The *plus-product* of $S_1, ..., S_n$ with respect to P, denoted by $\oplus_P(S_1, ..., S_n)$, is defined as follows:

$$\oplus_P(S_1, ...S_n) = S_1 \cup ... \cup S_n \cup Br(P)$$

This operation results in a compound terminology consisting of the compound terms of the initial compound terminologies, *plus* the compound terms which are broader than an element of P. This is because, if a compound term p is valid then all compound terms in $Br(p)$ are also valid.

For any parameter P, it holds: $\bigcup_{i=1}^{n} S_i \subseteq \oplus_P(S_1, ..., S_n) \subseteq S_1 \oplus ... \oplus S_n$.

Now we define the *minus-product* operation, $\ominus_N$, an n-ary operation over S ($\ominus_N : S \times ... \times S \rightarrow S$), where the parameter N is a set of invalid compound terms from the product of the input compound terminologies. Specifically, the set N is a subset of $G_{S_1,...,S_n}$, as we assume that all compound terms in the input operands are valid.

Definition 5. Let $S_1, ..., S_n$ be compound taxonomies and $N \subseteq G_{S_1,...,S_n}$. The *minus-product* of $S_1, ..., S_n$ with respect to N, denoted by $\ominus_N(S_1, ..., S_n)$, is defined as follows:

$$\ominus_N(S_1, ...S_n) = S_1 \oplus ... \oplus S_n - Nr(N)$$

This operation results in a compound terminology consisting of all compound terms in the product of the initial compound terminologies, *minus* all compound terms which are narrower than an element of N. This is because, if a compound term n is invalid then every compound term in $Nr(n)$ is invalid.

For any parameter N, it holds: $\bigcup_{i=1}^{n} S_i \subseteq \ominus_N(S_1, ..., S_n) \subseteq S_1 \oplus ... \oplus S_n$.

The operators introduced so far allow defining a compound terminology which consists of compound terms that contain at most one compound term from each basic compound terminology. However, a valid compound term may contain any set of terms of the same facet (multiple classification). To capture such cases, we define the *self-product*, $\overset{*}{\oplus}$, a unary operation which gives all possible compound terms of one facet. Subsequently, we shall modify this operation with the parameters P and N.

Let BS be the set of basic compound terminologies, that is $BS = \{T_1, ..., T_k\}$. The *self-product* of T_i is defined as: $\overset{*}{\oplus}(T_i) = P(\mathcal{T}_i)$.

The notion of genuine compound terms is also necessary here. The set of *genuine* compound terms over T_i is defined as: $G_{T_i} = \overset{*}{\oplus}(T_i) - T_i$.

Now we define the *plus-self-product* operation, $\overset{*}{\oplus}_P$, a unary operation ($\overset{*}{\oplus}_P$: $BS \rightarrow S$) where the parameter P is a set of compound terms that are certainly valid. The set P is a subset of G_{T_i}.

Definition 6. Let T_i be a basic compound terminology and $P \subseteq G_{T_i}$. The *plus-self-product* of T_i with respect to P, denoted by $\overset{*}{\oplus}_P (T_i)$, is defined as follows:

$$\overset{*}{\oplus}_P (T_i) = T_i \cup Br(P)$$

This operation results in a compound terminology consisting of the compound terms of the initial basic compound terminology, *plus* all compound terms which are broader than an element of P.

For any parameter P, it holds: $T_i \subseteq \overset{*}{\oplus}_P (T_i) \subseteq \overset{*}{\oplus} (T_i)$

The following definition introduces the *minus-self-product* operation, $\overset{*}{\ominus}_N$, a unary operation ($\overset{*}{\ominus}_N$: $\mathcal{BS} \to \mathcal{S}$) where the parameter N is a set of compound terms that are certainly invalid. The set N is a subset of G_{T_i}.

Definition 7. Let T_i be a basic compound terminology and $N \subseteq G_{T_i}$. The *minus-self-product* of T_i with respect to N, denoted by $\overset{*}{\ominus}_N (T_i)$, is defined as follows:

$$\overset{*}{\ominus}_N (T_i) = \overset{*}{\oplus} (T_i) - Nr(N)$$

This operation results in a compound terminology consisting of all compound terms in the self-product of T_i, *minus* the compound terms which are narrower than an element in N.

For any parameter N it holds: $T_i \subseteq \overset{*}{\ominus}_N (T_i) \subseteq \overset{*}{\oplus} T_i$

2.2   Algebraic Expressions

For defining the desired compound taxonomy, the designer has to formulate an expression e, where an expression is defined as follows:

Definition 8. An expression over a set of facets $\{F_1, ..., F_k\}$ is defined according to the following grammar:

$$e ::= \oplus_P(e, ..., e) \mid \ominus_N (e, ..., e) \mid \overset{*}{\oplus}_P T_i \mid \overset{*}{\ominus}_N T_i \mid T_i$$

The outcome of the evaluation of an expression e is denoted by S_e and is called the *compound terminology* of e. In addition, $(S_e, \preceq)$ is called the *compound taxonomy* of e.

As we will see in Section 3, all compound terms in S_e are *valid*, and the rest in $P(\mathcal{T}_e) - S_e$ are *invalid*, where $\mathcal{T}_e$ is the union of the terminologies of the facets appearing in e.

We are interested only in *well-formed* expressions, defined as follows:

Definition 9. An expression e is *well-formed* iff:

(i) *each basic compound terminology T_i appears at most once in e,*
(ii) *each parameter P that appears in e, is a subset of the associated set of genuine compound terms, and*

(iii) each parameter N that appears in e, is also a subset of the associated set of genuine compound terms.

For example, the expression $(T_1 \oplus_P T_2) \ominus_N T_1$ is not well-formed, as T_1 appears twice in the expression.

Constraints (i), (ii), and (iii) ensure that the evaluation of an expression is monotonic, meaning that the valid and invalid compound terms of an expression e increase as the length of e increases[2] (in other words, there are no conflicts). For example, if we omit constraint (i) then an invalid compound term according to an expression $T_1 \oplus_P T_2$ could be valid according to a larger expression $(T_1 \oplus_P T_2) \ominus_{P'} T_1$. If we omit constraint (ii) then an invalid compound term according to an expression $T_1 \oplus_{P_1} T_2$ could be valid according to a larger expression $(T_1 \oplus_{P_1} T_2) \oplus_{P_2} T_3$. Additionally, if we omit constraint (iii) then a valid compound term according to an expression $T_1 \oplus_P T_2$ could be invalid according to a larger expression $(T_1 \oplus_P T_2) \ominus_N T_3$.

This monotonic behaviour in the evaluation of a well-formed expression results in a number of useful properties. Specifically, due to their monotonicity, well-formed expressions can be formulated in a systematic, gradual manner (intermediate results of subexpressions are not invalidated by larger expressions). A comprehensive example of the algebra that also demonstrates the benefits of monotonicity can be found in [11].

In the rest of the paper, we assume that expressions are well-formed. In [11], we presented the algorithm $IsValid(e, s)$ that checks the validity of a compound term according to a (well-formed) expression e, and the algorithm $wellFormed(e)$ that checks if an expression e is well-formed. Both algorithms have polynomial time complexity.

3   Semantic Interpretation

At first we shall give a model-theoretic interpretation to faceted taxonomies and to compound taxonomies. Using this framework, we shall formally define the validity of a compound term. In the sequent, we will define the models of the compound taxonomies that *satisfy* a (well-formed) algebraic expression. At that point, it will become evident that the algebraic operations and their parameters actually pose constraints to the models of the compound taxonomy $(P(\mathcal{T}), \preceq)$. Moreover, we will show that the operations as defined in Section 2, are also justified by the semantic interpretation of this section.

We conceptualize the world as a set of objects, that is, we assume an arbitrary domain of discourse and a corresponding set of objects Obj. A typical example of such a domain is a set of Web pages. The only constraint that we impose on the set Obj is that it must be a denumerable set.

The set of objects described by a term is the *interpretation* of that term.

---

[2] Proof of this property is given in Section 3.

Definition 10. Given a terminology $\mathcal{T}$, we call *interpretation* of $\mathcal{T}$ over *Obj* any function $I : \mathcal{T} \rightarrow 2^{Obj}$.

Intuitively, the interpretation $I(t)$ of a term t is the set of objects to which the term t is correctly applied. In our discussion the set *Obj* will be usually understood from the context. So, we shall often say simply "an interpretation" instead of "an interpretation over *Obj*". Interpretation, as defined above, assigns to a term denotational or extensional meaning ([14]).

Now, any interpretation I of $\mathcal{T}$ can be extended to an interpretation $\hat{I}$ of $P(\mathcal{T})$ as follows:

$$\hat{I}(\{t_1, ..., t_n\}) = I(t_1) \cap I(t_2) \cap ... \cap I(t_n)$$

Definition 11. Let $(\mathcal{T}, \leq)$ be a taxonomy. An interpretation I of $\mathcal{T}$ is a *model* of $(\mathcal{T}, \leq)$,
if for each $t, t' \in \mathcal{T}$:   if $t \leq t'$ then $I(t) \subseteq I(t')$.

Proposition 1. Let S be a compound taxonomy over a taxonomy $\mathcal{T}$, and let s and s' be two elements of S. It holds:

$$s \preceq s' \text{ iff } \hat{I}(s) \subseteq \hat{I}(s') \text{ in every model } I \text{ of } (\mathcal{T}, \leq)$$

We can see that the compound ordering $\preceq$ is also justified semantically (it coincides with extensional subsumption).

Definition 12. Let $(\mathcal{T}, \leq)$ be a taxonomy. An interpretation $\hat{I}$ of $P(\mathcal{T})$ is a *model* of $(P(\mathcal{T}), \preceq)$,
if for each $s, s' \in P(\mathcal{T})$:   if $s \preceq s'$ then $\hat{I}(s) \subseteq \hat{I}(s')$.

From the above, it easily follows that:

an interpretation I is a model of $(\mathcal{T}, \leq)$ iff $\hat{I}$ is a model of $(P(\mathcal{T}), \preceq)$

For brevity hereafter we shall denote by I both I and $\hat{I}$. Additionally, in the following, by model I we refer to a model I of $(\mathcal{T}, \leq)$.

Let us now define compound term validity according to an expression e. For simplicity, we consider only expressions of the form $e \oplus_P e'$ and $e \ominus_N e'$.

Before we define recursively the valid and invalid compound terms of $e \; op \; e'$, we define the *valid genuine compound terms* of $e \; op \; e'$ (denoted by $VG(e \; op \; e')$) and the *invalid genuine compound terms* of $e \; op \; e'$ (denoted by $IG(e \; op \; e')$). That is, we first define the validity of the genuine compound terms associated with each operation.

Below we define the valid genuine compound terms of $e \oplus_P e'$:

$$VG(e \oplus_P e') = \{ \, s \in G_{S_e, S_{e'}} \mid I(s) \neq \emptyset \text{ in every model } I \text{ such that:}$$

$$I(s') \neq \emptyset, \forall s' \in P \}$$

Now we adopt a closed-world assumption for the invalid genuine compound terms, specifically we assume that all elements of $G_{S_e,S_{e'}} \setminus VG(e \oplus_P e')$ are invalid. Thus we write:

$$IG(e \oplus_P e') = G_{S_e,S_{e'}} \setminus VG(e \oplus_P e')$$

The following proposition holds:

Proposition 2. $VG(e \oplus_P e') = Br(P) \cap G_{S_e,S_{e'}}$

Below we define the invalid genuine compound terms of $e \ominus_N e'$:

$$IG(e \ominus_N e') = \{ s \in G_{S_e,S_{e'}} \mid I(s) = \emptyset \text{ in every model } I \text{ such that:}$$

$$I(s') = \emptyset, \forall s' \in N\}$$

Now we again adopt a closed-world assumption for the valid genuine compound terms, specifically we assume that all elements of $G_{S_e,S_{e'}} \setminus IG(e \ominus_N e')$ are valid. Thus we write:

$$VG(e \ominus_N e') = G_{S_e,S_{e'}} \setminus IG(e \ominus_N e')$$

The following proposition holds:

Proposition 3. $IG(e \ominus_N e') = Nr(N)$

Clearly, for any operation e *op* e', the sets $VG(e$ *op* $e')$ and $IG(e$ *op* $e')$ *partition* the set $G_{S_e,S_{e'}}$.

One can easily see that the semantic interpretation that is given in this section, justifies the way that the algebraic operations were defined in Section 2. Indeed, it holds:

$$VG(e \oplus_P e') = (S_e \oplus_P S_{e'}) \cap G_{S_e,S_{e'}}$$
$$VG(e \ominus_N e') = (S_e \ominus_N S_{e'}) \cap G_{S_e,S_{e'}}$$

Until now, for every operation e *op* e' we partitioned the set $G_{S_e,S_{e'}}$ to the sets $VG(e$ *op* $e')$ and $IG(e$ *op* $e')$. Let $\mathcal{T}_e$ denote the union of the terminologies of the facets that appear in e. We will show how for a given expression e we can partition the elements of $P(\mathcal{T}_e)$ into the set of *valid compound terms*, denoted by $VC(e)$, and the set of *invalid compound terms*, denoted by $IC(e)$. We define:

$$VC(T_i) = T_i, \text{ for } i = 1,...k$$
$$VC(e \text{ op } e') = VG(e \text{ op } e') \cup VC(e) \cup VC(e')$$
$$IC(e) = P(\mathcal{T}_e) \setminus VC(e)$$

Clearly, the sets $VC(e)$ and $IC(e)$ constitute a partition of $P(\mathcal{T}_e)$.

Definition 13. Let e be an expression, and let I be a model of $(\mathcal{T}, \leq)$. We say that I *satisfies* e if

    (1) $\forall s \in VC(e)$, $I(s) \neq \emptyset$,

    (2) $\forall s \in IC(e)$, $I(s) = \emptyset$.

The following proposition expresses that every expression e is satisfiable.

Proposition 4. Let e be an expression. There always exists a model I of $(\mathcal{T}, \leq)$ that satisfies e.

The following proposition expresses that the compound taxonomy S_e of an algebraic expression e (as computed from our operations) consists of exactly those compound terms which are valid according to the semantic interpretation that we described in this section.

Proposition 5. Let e be an expression. It holds:

$$VC(e) = S_e \text{ and } IC(e) = P(\mathcal{T}_e) \setminus S_e$$

The following proposition gives a very important property of our theory, that is, intermediate results of subexpressions are not invalidated by larger expressions. Thus, expressions can be formed in a constructive, gradual manner, allowing use of intermediate results.

Proposition 6. Let e be an expression and e' be a subexpression of e. Then, it holds

$$VC(e') \subseteq VC(e) \text{ and } IC(e') \subseteq IC(e)$$

To see the significance of this proposition, let $\{F_1, ..., F_k\}$ be the facets of a faceted taxonomy and let e' be an expression that defines the current desired compound taxonomy. Assume that now the designer adds some new facets of interest. Then, he has only to extend (and not to rewrite) e' with a subexpression e'' such that the new expression, $e = e' \ op \ e''$, defines the new desired compound taxonomy.

The following proposition expresses that the valid and invalid genuine compound terms of a subexpression of an expression e are indeed valid and invalid compound terms, respectively.

Proposition 7. Let e be an expression and $e_1 \ op \ e_2$ be a subexpression of e. Then, it holds

$$VG(e_1 \ op \ e_2) \subseteq VC(e) \text{ and } IG(e_1 \ op \ e_2) \subseteq IC(e)$$

From the above proposition and propositions 2 and 3, it easily follows that for any parameter P and N of e, it holds: $P \subseteq VC(e)$ and $N \subseteq IC(e)$.

In Section 2, we informally indicated that if a compound term s is valid then every compound term in $\text{Br}(s)$ is also valid. Additionally, if a compound term s is invalid then every compound term in $\text{Nr}(s)$ is also invalid. This property is formally proved in the following proposition.

Proposition 8. Let e be an expression. It holds:

$$Br(VC(e)) = VC(e) \text{ and } Nr(IC(e)) = IC(e)$$

The semantic interpretation that we described can be extended in a straightforward manner, so as to also capture the plus-self-product operation and the minus-self-product operation.

4   Comparison with Description Logics

Below we investigate whether we can represent the compound taxonomies defined by our algebra, in Description Logics [2]. Recall that any Description Logic (DL) is a fragment of First Order Logic (FOL). In particular, any (basic) DL is a subset of $\mathcal{L}_3$ i.e. the function-free FOL using at most *three* variable names.

In DL, a knowledge base, also referred as a DL theory is formed by two components: the *intensional* one, called TBox, and the *extensional* one, called ABox. The former contains the definitions of predicates, while the latter contains the assertions over constants.

One can easily see that a faceted taxonomy $F = (\mathcal{T}, \leq)$ can be expressed as a TBox containing one primitive concept t for each term $t \in \mathcal{T}$, and one expression $t \overset{.}{\leq} t'$ for each relationship $t \leq t'$. Let K_F denote the TBox that is derived in this way.

Table 1 describes a method for deriving a TBox K_e for a (well-formed) expression e of our algebra[3]. Note that a compound term $s = \{t_1, ..., t_n\}$ is written as a DL expression $d_s = t_1 \sqcap ... \sqcap t_n$. In the case of a plus-product operation we derive a new concept $x \overset{.}{\leq} t_1 \sqcap ... \sqcap t_n$ for each element $\{t_1, ..., t_n\} \in P$, while in the case of a minus-product operation we derive an expression $t_1 \sqcap ... \sqcap t_n \overset{.}{\leq} \perp$ for each element $\{t_1, ..., t_n\} \in N$.

Table 1. Using DL for representing the compound terminology of an expression

e	K_e
$e_1 \oplus_P e_2$	$K_{e_1} \cup K_{e_2} \cup$
	$\{ x \overset{.}{\leq} t_1 \sqcap ... \sqcap t_n \mid \{t_1, ..., t_n\} \in P\}$
$e_1 \ominus_N e_2$	$K_{e_1} \cup K_{e_2} \cup$
	$\{ t_1 \sqcap ... \sqcap t_n \overset{.}{\leq} \perp \mid \{t_1, ..., t_n\} \in N\}$
$\overset{*}{\oplus}_P (T_i)$	$K_{T_i} \cup \{ x \overset{.}{\leq} t_1 \sqcap ... \sqcap t_n \mid \{t_1, ..., t_n\} \in P\}$
$\overset{*}{\ominus}_N (T_i)$	$K_{T_i} \cup \{ t_1 \sqcap ... \sqcap t_n \overset{.}{\leq} \perp \mid \{t_1, ..., t_n\} \in N\}$
T_i	$\{ t \overset{.}{\leq} t' \mid \text{ for each } t, t' \in T_i, \text{ s.t } t \leq t'\}$

---

[3] It is important that the expression e be well-formed. Otherwise, the TBOX may be inconsistent.

Now, Table 2 sketches how we can check whether a compound term $s = \{t_1, ..., t_n\}$ belongs to the compound terminology S_e of an expression e by using K_e and the inference mechanisms of DL. In this table we consider that $s_1 = \{t \in s \mid F(t) \in F(e_1)\}$ and $s_2 = \{t \in s \mid F(t) \in F(e_2)\}$.

Table 2. Using DL for checking the validity of a compound term

Our approach	A DL-based approach
$IsValid(e_1 \oplus_P e_2, s)$=TRUE	$(K_{e_1 \oplus_P e_2} \models d_s) \vee$ $IsValid(e_1, s) \vee$ $IsValid(e_2, s)$
$IsValid(e_1 \ominus_N e_2, s)$=TRUE	$(K_{e_1 \ominus_N e_2} \not\models d_s \equiv \bot) \wedge$ $IsValid(e_1, s_1) \wedge$ $IsValid(e_2, s_2)$
$IsValid(\overset{*}{\oplus}_P (T_i), s)$=TRUE	$K_{\overset{*}{\oplus}_P(T_i)} \models d_s$
$IsValid(\overset{*}{\ominus}_N (T_i), s)$=TRUE	$K_{\overset{*}{\ominus}_N(T_i)} \not\models d_s \equiv \bot$

It is evident that we *cannot* check the validity of a compound term s according to an expression e by just using the classical satisfiability check of DL, that is by just checking if $K_e \models d_s$. However, if we would like to use a DL-based system for implementing our algebra then we should write (on top of DL) a *metasystem* that parses the expression e and recursively calls the inference mechanisms of DL as described in Table 2. The recursive calls are based on our theory, and are exactly those of algorithm $IsValid(e, s)$ (given in [11]). Indeed the only difference of the DL metasystem with algorithm $IsValid(e, s)$ is that the DL checks: $K_{e_1 \oplus_P e_2} \models d_s$ and $K_{\overset{*}{\oplus}_P(T_i)} \models d_s$ are replaced by: $\exists p \in P$ such that $p \preceq s$. Similarly, the DL checks: $K_{e_1 \ominus_N e_2} \not\models d_s \equiv \bot$ and $K_{\overset{*}{\ominus}_N(T_i)} \not\models d_s \equiv \bot$ are replaced by: $\not\exists n \in N$ such that $s \preceq n$. In addition, our theory is needed to guarantee that expressions are well-formed and thus, there are no inconsistencies. We do not describe here this metasystem in detail as this would not offer anything new in our discussion.

Alternatively, if we want to use the classical satisfiability check of Description Logics, then we cannot create the TBox by the method described in Table 1. Instead, we have to create a TBox that contains many more expressions, by translating each plus-product operation as described in Table 1, and by translating each minus-product operation $e_1 \ominus_N e_2$ to the following set of expressions:

$$K_{e_1} \cup K_{e_2} \cup \{ x \doteq t_1 \sqcap ... \sqcap t_n \mid \text{ for each } \{t_1, ..., t_n\} \notin S_{e_1} \oplus S_{e_2} - Nr(N)\}$$

If we derive a TBox K_e of an expression e in this way, then it will hold $IsValid(e, s)$=TRUE iff $K_e \models s$. However, in this approach, it is necessary to pre-compute all S_{e_1} and S_{e_2}, which practically makes the approach useless. Moreover, K_e will be a very big TBox.

From the above discussion it is evident that if we want to check the validity of compound terms using the classical satisfiability check of DL, then we cannot represent our algebraic expressions in DL in a straightforward manner. This is due to the closed-world assumptions inherent to our operations.

5   Concluding Remarks

In [11], we proposed an algebra for specifying the valid compound terms of a faceted taxonomy. Although faceted classification was suggested quite long ago (by Ranganathan in the 1920s [9], the associated issues have not received adequate attention by the computer science community. However, there are several works about facet analysis (e.g. see [3], [13],[5]). Facets have also been studied in library and information science (for a review see [6]). For instance, thesauri ([4]) may have facets that group the terms of the thesaurus in classes. Ruben Prieto-Diaz ([7,8]) has proposed "faceted classification" for a reusable software library. The contribution of our compound term composition algebra lies in enriching a faceted scheme with a rigorous method for specifying valid combinations of terms. This method can be used in order to construct taxonomies or thesauri which unlike existing thesauri, do not present the problems of missing terms or missing relationships (for more about this problem see [1]).

In this paper, we defined the semantics of the algebraic operations. Specifically, we justified the definition of the algebraic operations, based on the model-theoretic definition of the valid and invalid genuine compound terms. Having defined the valid (resp. invalid) genuine compound terms of a positive (resp. negative) operation, the invalid (resp. valid) genuine compound terms are computed based on a closed-world assumption. The valid compound terms according to an expression e is the union of the valid genuine compound terms of all operations of e.

Additionally, we defined the models of an algebraic expression. Intuitively, a model of an algebraic expression, is an intepretation which is non-empty for each valid compound term, and empty for each invalid compound term. We proved that every well-formed algebraic expression is satisfiable. Moreover, we proved that well-formed algebraic expressions are monotonic, which ensures that results of subexpressions are not invalidated by larger expressions.

We also showed that we cannot directly represent the compound taxonomies defined by our algebra directly in Description Logics, and a metasystem was designed on top of Description Logics to implement our algebra.

Our algebra can be used in any application that indexes objects using a faceted taxonomy. For example, it can be used for designing taxonomies for products, for fields of knowledge (e.g. for indexing the books of a library), etc. As we can infer the valid compound terms in a faceted taxonomy, we are able to generate navigation trees *on the fly*, having only valid compound terms as nodes. The algorithm for deriving navigation trees on the fly is given in [11].

Our algebra can also be used for *configuration management*. Consider a product (e.g. a software module) whose functionality, or configuration, is determined by a number of parameters, where each parameter is associated with a finite number of values. However, some configurations may either make no sense, or not supported, or they may be "dangerous". For this purpose, the designer of the product can use an expression in order to specify all valid configurations. In this way, the user of the product can select one configuration from the valid ones. The advantage of using our approach is that the space needed for storing the valid configurations is low. This is quite important, as all information about configuration management has to be stored in the product itself, e.g. in the software module.

Interest in faceted taxonomies is also indicated by the development of XFML, Core-eXchangeable Faceted Metadata Language (http://xfml.org). XFML is a model to express topics organized in facets, and allows you to assign topics to any page on the web. XFML lets you publish this information in an open, XML based format. It can be easily seen that our algebra can also be applied in this context in order to prescribe the set of valid compound terms. This can prevent some of the indexing errors that may occur in an open and collaborative environment like the Web.

Currently, our algebra is been used for building the taxonomy of a tourist portal. The results that the designers report to us, concerning flexibility and ease of use, are so far very encouraging.

Finally, we have to note that the advantages of the compound faceted taxonomies that we propose (compactness, conceptual clarity, scalability, valid compound terms) can facilitate several other associated tasks. Specifically, they can certainly facilitate the design of *mediators* over several taxonomy-based sources (using the approach presented in [12]), and the *personalization* of Web catalogs (using the approach presented in [10]).

As future work, we plan to study how updates on the faceted taxonomy, or changes to the desired compound terminology should update the expression that defines the compound terminology. This process can be automated. This is very important in practice, as it adds flexibility to the design process: the designer during the formulation of the expression e can update the faceted taxonomy, without having to bother that e will become obsolete. Additionally, the designer can add or delete compound terms from the desired compound terminology without having to worry that e will no longer reflect his/her desire.

In addition, we are going to study in depth, methodologies for the formulation of algebraic expressions that reflect the desire of the designer. Specifically, how the four operations of our algebra should be combined, so as the number of compound terms of the associated parameters P, N is minimal, and designer effort is minimized.

Acknowledgements. The first author wants to thank Tonia Dellaporta for inspiring him.

References

1. Peter Clark, John Thompson, Heather Holmback, and Lisbeth Duncan. "Exploiting a Thesaurus-based Semantic Net for Knowledge-based Search". In *Procs of 12th Conf. on Innovative Applications of AI (AAAI/IAAI'00)*, pages 988–995, 2000.
2. F.M. Donini, M. Lenzerini, D. Nardi, and A. Schaerf. "Reasoning in Description Logics". In Gerhard Brewka, editor, *Principles of Knowledge Representation*, chapter 1, pages 191–236. CSLI Publications, 1996.
3. Elizabeth B. Duncan. "A Faceted Approach to Hypertext". In Ray McAleese, editor, *HYPERTEXT: theory into practice, BSP*, 1989.
4. International Organization For Standardization. "Documentation – Guidelines for the establishment and development of monolingual thesauri", 1986. Ref. No ISO 2788-1986.
5. P. H. Lindsay and D. A. Norman. *Human Information Processing*. Academic press, New York, 1977.
6. Amanda Maple. "Faceted Access: A Review of the Literature", 1995. http://theme.music.indiana.edu/tech_s/mla/facacc.rev.
7. Ruben Prieto-Diaz. "Classification of Reusable Modules". In *Software Reusability. Volume I*, chapter 4, pages 99–123. acm press, 1989.
8. Ruben Prieto-Diaz. "Implementing Faceted Classification for Software Reuse". *Communications of the ACM*, 34(5):88–97, 1991.
9. S. R. Ranganathan. "The Colon Classification". In Susan Artandi, editor, *Vol IV of the Rutgers Series on Systems for the Intellectual Organization of Information*. New Brunswick, NJ: Graduate School of Library Science, Rutgers University, 1965.
10. Nicolas Spyratos, Yannis Tzitzikas, and Vassilis Christophides. "On Personalizing the Catalogs of Web Portals". In *15th International FLAIRS Conference, FLAIRS'02*, pages 430–434, Pensacola, Florida, May 2002.
11. Yannis Tzitzikas, Anastasia Analyti, Nicolas Spyratos, and Panos Constantopoulos. "An Algebraic Approach for Specifying Compound Terms in Faceted Taxonomies". In *13th European-Japanese Conference on Information Modelling and Knowledge Bases*, Kitakyushu, Japan, June 2003.
12. Yannis Tzitzikas, Nicolas Spyratos, and Panos Constantopoulos. "Mediators over Ontology-based Information Sources". In *Proceedings of the 2nd International Conference on Web Information Systems Engineering, WISE 2001*, pages 31–40, Kyoto, Japan, December 2001.
13. B. C. Vickery. "Knowledge Representation: A Brief Review". *Journal of Documentation*, 42(3):145–159, 1986.
14. W. A. Woods. "Understanding Subsumption and Taxonomy". In *Principles of Semantic Networks*, chapter 1. Morgan Kaufmann Publishers, 1991.

KNN Model-Based Approach in Classification

Gongde Guo[1], Hui Wang [1], David Bell [2], Yaxin Bi [2], and Kieran Greer [1]

[1] School of Computing and Mathematics, University of Ulster
Newtownabbey, BT37 0QB, Northern Ireland, UK
{G.Guo,H.Wang,Krc.Greer}@ulst.ac.uk
[2] School of Computer Science, Queen's University Belfast
Belfast, BT7 1NN, UK
{DA.Bell,Y.Bi}@qub.ac.uk

Abstract. The k-Nearest-Neighbours (kNN) is a simple but effective method for classification. The major drawbacks with respect to kNN are (1) its low efficiency - being a lazy learning method prohibits it in many applications such as dynamic web mining for a large repository, and (2) its dependency on the selection of a "good value" for k. In this paper, we propose a novel kNN type method for classification that is aimed at overcoming these shortcomings. Our method constructs a kNN model for the data, which replaces the data to serve as the basis of classification. The value of k is automatically determined, is varied for different data, and is optimal in terms of classification accuracy. The construction of the model reduces the dependency on k and makes classification faster. Experiments were carried out on some public datasets collected from the UCI machine learning repository in order to test our method. The experimental results show that the kNN based model compares well with C5.0 and kNN in terms of classification accuracy, but is more efficient than the standard kNN.

1 Introduction

The k-Nearest-Neighbours (kNN) is a non-parametric classification method, which is simple but effective in many cases [1]. For a data record t to be classified, its k nearest neighbours are retrieved, and this forms a *neighbourhood of t*. Majority voting among the data records in the neighbourhood is usually used to decide the classification for t with or without consideration of distance-based weighting. However, to apply kNN we need to choose an appropriate value for k, and the success of classification is very much dependent on this value. In a sense, the kNN method is biased by k. There are many ways of choosing the k value, but a simple one is to run the algorithm many times with different k values and choose the one with the best performance.

In order for kNN to be less dependent on the choice of k, Wang [2] proposed to look at multiple sets of nearest neighbours rather than just one set of k-nearest neighbours. The proposed formalism is based on contextual probability, and the idea is to aggregate the support of multiple sets of nearest neighbours for various classes to give a more reliable support value, which better reveals the true class of t. However, in its basic form the method is relatively slow, which needs $O(n^2)$ to classify a new instance, though it is indeed less dependent on k and is able to achieve classification performance close to that for the best k.

R. Meersman et al. (Eds.): CoopIS/DOA/ODBASE 2003, LNCS 2888, pp. 986–996, 2003.
© Springer-Verlag Berlin Heidelberg 2003

*k*NN has a high cost of classifying new instances. This is single-handedly due to the fact that nearly all computation takes place at classification time rather than when the training examples are first encountered. Though *k*NN has been applied to text categorization since the early days of its research [3] and is shown to be one of the most effective methods on Reuters corpus of newswire stories – a benchmark corpus in text categorization. Its efficiency as being a lazy learning method without pre-modelling prohibits it from being applied to areas where dynamic classification is needed for large repository. There are techniques [10, 11] that are used to significantly reduce the computation required at query time, such as indexing training examples, but it is out of our concerns in this paper.

We attempt to solve these problems and present in this paper a *k*NN type classification method called *k*NNModel. The method constructs a model from the data and classifies new data using the model. The model is a set of representatives of the training data, as regions in the data space.

The rest of the paper is organised as follows. Section 2 discusses related research in this area. Section 3 introduces the basic idea of the proposed modelling and classification algorithm, where the modelling and classification processes are illustrated by an example with the help of some graphs. The experimental results are described and discussed in Section 4. Section 5 ends the paper with a discussion on existing problems and addresses further research directions.

2   Related Work

This work is a subsequent research based on our previous research on data reduction (DR) [4]. The advantage of DR is that raw data and reduced data can be both represented by hyper relations. The collection of hyper relations can be made into a complete Boolean algebra in a natural way, and so for any collection of hyper tuples its unique least upper bound (lub) can be found, as a reduction. The experimental result shows that DR can obtain relatively higher reduction rate whilst preserving its classification accuracy. However, it is relatively slow in its basic form of model construction, since much time is spent in trying probable merge.

As the *k*-Nearest-Neighbours classifier requires storing the whole training set and may be too costly when this set is large, many researchers have attempted to get rid of the redundancy of the training set to alleviate this problem [5,6,7,8]. Hart [5] proposed a computationally simple local search method as Condensed Nearest Neighbour (CNN) by minimizing the number of stored patterns and storing only a subset of the training set for classification. The basic idea is that patterns in the training set may be very similar and some do not add extra information and thus may be discarded. Gate [6] proposed the Reduced Nearest Neighbour (RNN) rule that aims to further reduce the stored subset after having applied CNN. It simply removes those elements from the subset which will not cause an error. Alpaydin [7] investigated some voting schemes over multiple learners in order to improve classification accuracy, and Kubat *et al* [8] addressed an approach that selects three very small groups of examples such that, when used as 1-NN subclassifiers, each tends to error in a different part of the instance space. Simple voting then corrects many failures of individual subclassifiers. The experimental results of those methods conducted on some public datasets are reported in [9].

The proposed kNN model-based approach is different from the DR and other condensed nearest neighbour methods. It constructs a model by finding a set of representatives with some extra information from the training data based on similarity principle. The created representatives can be seen as regions in the data space and will be used for further classification.

3 Modeling and Classification Algorithm

3.1 Basic Idea of kNNModel

kNN is a case-based learning method, which keeps all the training data for classification. Being a lazy learning method prohibits it in many applications such as dynamic web mining for a large repository. One way to improve its efficiency is to find some representatives to represent the whole training data for classification, viz. building an inductive learning model from the training dataset and using this model (representatives) for classification. There are many existing algorithms such as decision trees or neural networks initially designed to build such a model. One of the evaluation standards for different algorithms is their performance. As kNN is a simple but effective method for classification and it is convincing as one of the most effective methods on Reuters corpus of newswire stories in text categorization, it motivates us to build a model for kNN to improve its efficiency whilst preserving its classification accuracy as well.

Looking at Fig. 1, a training dataset including 36 data points with two classes {square, circle} is distributed in 2-dimensional data space.

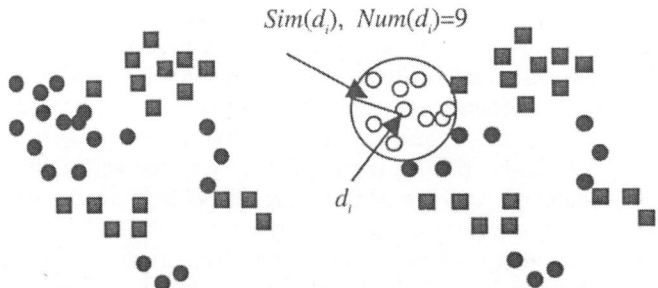

$Sim(d_i)$, $Num(d_i)=9$

d_i

Fig. 1. The distribution of data points. **Fig. 2.** The first obtained representative.

If we use Euclidean distance as our similarity measure, it is clear that many data points with the same class label are close to each other according to distance measure in many local areas. In each local region, the central data point d_i looking at Fig. 2 for example, with some extra information such as $Num(d_i)$ - the number of data points inside the local region and $Sim(d_i)$ - the similarity of the most distant data point inside the local region to d_i, might be an ideal representative of this local region. If we take these representatives as a model to represent the whole training dataset, it will significantly reduce the number of data points for classification, thereby to improve its efficiency. Obviously, if a new data point is covered by a representative it will be classified by the class label of this representative. If not, we calculate the distance of the new data point to each representative's nearest boundary and take each representative's nearest boundary as a data point, then classify the new data point in the spirit of KNN.

In model construction process, each data point has its largest local neighbourhood which covers the maximal number of data points with the same class label. Based on these local neighbourhoods, the largest local neighbourhood (called largest global neighbourhood) can be obtained in each cycle. This largest global neighbourhood can be seen as a representative to represent all the data points covered by it. For data points not covered by any representatives, we repeat the above operation until all the data points have been covered by chosen representatives. Obviously, we needn't choose a specific k for our method in the model construction process, the number of data points covered by a representative can be seen as an optimal k but it is different in different representatives. The k is generated automatically in the model construction process. Further, using a list of chosen representatives as a model for classification not only reduces the number of data for classification, also significantly improves its efficiency. From this point of view, our proposed method overcomes the two shortcomings inherited in the kNN method.

3.2   Modeling and Classification Algorithm

Let D be a collection of n class-known data tuples $\{d_1, d_2,..., d_n\}$. $d_i \in D$ could be a document represented in a form of space vector $d_i = <w_{i1}, w_{i2}, ..., w_{im}>$, where w_{ij} could be the normalised TF-IDF weighting representation in text categorization as an example. For the reason of generalisation from now on, we use the term 'data tuple' to represent all kinds of data in different applications in this paper in order to avoid limiting our algorithm to specific applications. Also the term 'similarity measure' could be any similarity measure such as Euclidean distance or Cosine similarity only if it is suitable for a concrete application. For simplicity, from now on, we use Euclidean distance as default similarity measure to describe following algorithms.

The detailed model construction algorithm is described as follows:

(1) Select a similarity measure and create a similarity matrix from the given training dataset.
(2) Set to 'ungrouped' the tag of all data tuples.
(3) For each 'ungrouped' data tuple, find its largest local neighbourhood which covers the largest number of neighbours with the same category.
(4) Find the data tuple d_i with a largest global neighbourhood N_i among all the local neighbourhoods, create a representative $<Cls(d_i), Sim(d_i), Num(d_i), Rep(d_i)>$ into M to represent all the data tuples covered by N_i, and then set to 'grouped' the tag of all the data tuples covered by N_i.
(5) Repeat step 3 and step 4 until all the data tuples in the training dataset have been set to 'grouped'.
(6) Model M consists of all the representatives collected from the above learning process.

In the above algorithm, M represents the created model. The representative $<Cls(d_i), Sim(d_i), Num(d_i), Rep(d_i)>$ respectively represents the class label of d_i, the lowest similarity to d_i among the data tuples covered by N_i; the number of data tuples covered by N_i, and a representation of d_i itself. In step (4), if there are more than one neighbourhoods having the same maximal number of neighbours, we choose the one with minimal value of $Sim(d_i)$, viz. the one with highest density, as representative.

The classification algorithm is described as follows:

(1) For a new data tuple d_t to be classified, calculate its similarity to all representatives in the model M.

(2) If d_t is covered only by one representative $<Cls(d_j), Sim(d_j), Num(d_j), Rep(d_j)>$, viz the Euclidean distance of d_t to d_j is smaller than $Sim(d_j)$, d_t is classified as the category of d_j.

(3) If d_t is covered by at least two representatives with different category, classify d_t as the category of the representative with largest $Num(d_j)$, viz. the neighbourhood covers the largest number of data tuples in the training dataset.

(4) If no representative in the model M covers d_t, classify d_t as the category of a representative which boundary is closest to d_t.

The Euclidean distance of d_t to a representative d_i's nearest boundary equals to the difference of the Euclidean distance of d_t to d_i minus $Sim(d_i)$.

To improve the classification accuracy for kNNModel, we implemented two different pruning methods in our kNNModel. One method is by removing the representatives from the model M that only covers a few data tuples and the relevant data tuples covered by these representatives from the training dataset, and then constructing the model again from the revised training dataset. The second method is by modifying the step 3 in the model construction algorithm to allow each largest local neighbourhood cover r (called error tolerant degree) data tuples with different categories to the majority category in this neighbourhood. This modification integrates the pruning work into the process of model construction. Experimental results will be reported in the next section.

3.3   An Example of Model Construction and Classification Process

To grasp the idea here, the best way is by means of an example, so we graphically illustrate the model construction and classification process.

A training dataset including 36 data tuples is divided into two classes denoted as square and circle. The distribution of data tuples in 2-dimensional data space is shown in Fig. 3.

In Fig. 4, the fine line circle covers 9 ($Num(d_i)=9$) data tuples with the same class label of d_i – circle (in this example, we use the first pruning method, viz. we assign 0 to r). The representative covers the maximal number of neighbours with the same class label at the first cycle. The $Sim(d_i)$ represents the Euclidean distance of d_i to the most distant data tuple from d_i in N_i.

After the first cycle, we obtain the first representative $<Cls(d_i), Sim(d_i), Num(d_i), Rep(d_i)>$, add it into the model M, and then turn to the next cycle. At the end of the second cycle we add another representative $<Cls(d_j), Sim(d_j), Num(d_j), Rep(d_j)>$ into the model M shown in Fig. 5. Repeat this process until all the data tuples in the training dataset have been set to 'grouped' (represented by a empty circle or square).

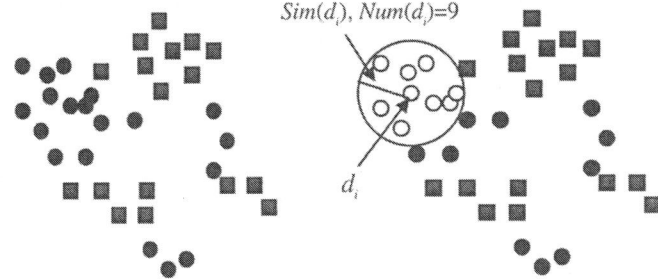

Fig. 3. The distribution of data tuples. **Fig. 4.** The first obtained representative.

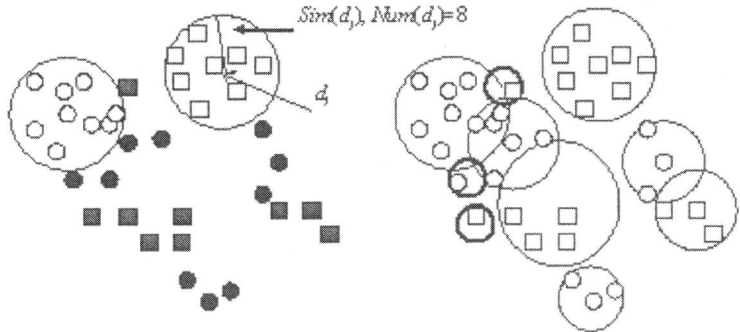

Fig. 5. The second obtained representative. **Fig. 6.** The model before pruning.

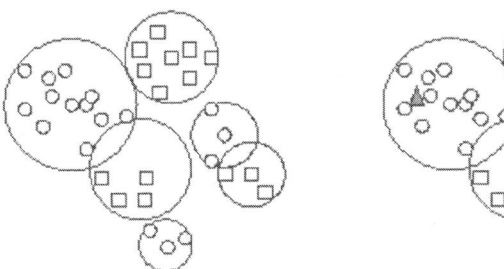

Fig. 7. The model after pruning. **Fig. 8.** The distribution of test data tuples.

At the end, ten representatives shown in Fig. 6 are obtained from the training dataset and stored in the model M, where seven in ten representatives cover more than 2 data tuples denoted by a fine line circle and the other three representatives, each of them covers only one data tuple denoted by a bold line circle.

In this situation, pruning work can be done by removing the representatives from the model M which only cover a few data tuples (for example, $Num(d_i)<2$). All the data tuples covered by these representatives will be removed as well from the training dataset. After that, we construct the model again from the revised training dataset. After pruning and model construction, we obtain the final model M, looking at Fig. 7 for a graphical illustration.

In Figure 8, there are four triangles which represent the test data tuples. According to the classification algorithm described before, these four test data tuples are classified as a label of circle, square, circle, square from left to right respectively.

If we use the second pruning method and assign 1 to r, the model construction process is shown as follows:

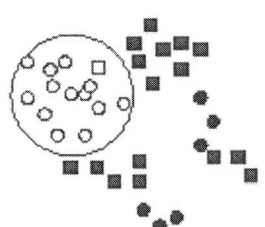

Fig. 9. The first representative.

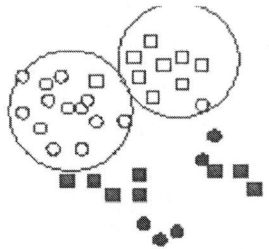

Fig. 10. The second representative.

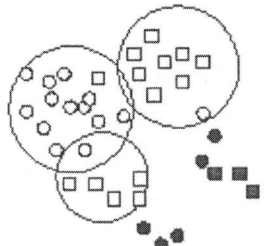

Fig. 11. The third representative.

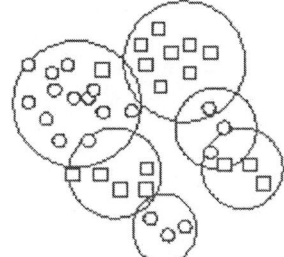

Fig. 12. The final model.

4 Experiment and Evaluation

Experiment using the 5-fold cross validation method has been carried out to evaluate the prediction accuracy of kNNModel, and to compare the experimental results with C5.0 and kNN as our benchmarks. The C5.0 is implemented in the Clementine' software package.

Six public datasets were chosen from the UCI machine learning repository. Some information about these datasets is listed in Table 1.

In Table 1, the meaning of the title in each column is follows: NA-Number of attributes, NN-Number of Nominal attributes, NO-Number of Ordinal attributes, NB-Number of Binary attributes, NE-Number of Examples, CD-Class Distribution.

The comparison of C5.0, kNN, and kNNModel in testing accuracy using the 5-fold cross validation method is listed in Table 2. The data reduction rate in the final model of the kNNModel is listed in Table 3. As we use Euclidean distance as a similarity measure in the experiment for kNN and kNNModel, six datasets were pre-processed including normalization and feature selection before conducting the classification. In experiments, we assign 1 to r and use information gain as our feature selection measure.

Table 1. Some information about the datasets

Dataset	NA	NN	NO	NB	NE	CD
Glass	9	0	9	0	214	70:17:76:0:13:9:29
Iris	4	0	4	0	150	50:50:50
Heart	13	3	7	3	270	120:150
Wine	13	0	13	0	178	59:71:48
Diabetes	8	0	8	0	768	268:500
Aust	14	4	6	4	690	383:307

Table 2. A comparison of C5.0, kNN, and kNNModel

Dataset	C5.0	Classification Accuracy (%)							
		kNNModel (r = 1)					kNN		
		N>1	N>2	N>3	N>4	N>5	K=1	K=3	K=5
Glass	66.3	70.95	70.95	70.00	68.57	67.62	67.14	70.48	68.10
Iris	92.0	96.00	96.00	96.00	96.00	96.00	95.33	94.67	95.33
Heart	75.6	80.37	80.37	80.74	80.37	81.11	75.93	80.74	82.96
Wine	92.1	96.00	96.00	96.00	96.00	96.00	96.57	95.43	94.86
Diabetes	76.6	73.59	73.59	73.86	74.25	75.42	68.24	73.59	74.38
Aust	85.5	85.65	85.65	85.07	84.93	84.93	82.17	86.23	86.38
Average	81.35	83.76	83.76	83.61	83.35	83.51	80.90	83.52	83.67

Table 3. The number of representatives and the average reduction rate in the final model

Dataset	The number of representatives in the model					kNN
	KNNModel (r = 1)					
	N>1	N>2	N>3	N>4	N>5	
Glass	31	31	24	18	13	214
Iris	5	5	4	4	4	150
Heart	26	26	22	21	19	270
Wine	8	8	8	7	7	178
Diabetes	106	106	94	78	59	768
Aust	54	54	49	44	41	690
	The average reduction rate (%) of kNNModel					
	89.87	89.87	91.15	92.42	93.70	0

Note that in Table 2 and Table 3, $N>i$ means each representative in the final model of the kNNModel at least covers $i+1$ data tuples of the training dataset. It is not an integrant parameter. It can be removed from the kNNModel algorithm by pruning process. The experimental results of different N listed here are to demonstrate the relationship between classification accuracy and reduction rate of the kNNModel algorithm.

We also carried out an experiment by assigning different value to r and N to find the best classification accuracy for knnModel, and to see the influence of the r and N play to knnModel's classification accuracy. In experiment, r and N varied from 1 to 10. The best classification accuracy of kNNModel for each dataset is obtained and listed in table 4. It shows us that the best accuracy for each dataset can be obtained via tuning r and N with rather small value. The best accuracy of knnModel outperforms C5.0 and KNN for all datasets with an exception of 1-NN on Wine.

Table 4. The influence of r and N to kNNModel

Dataset	C5.0	Classification Accuracy (%)					
		kNNModel			kNN		
		Best Accuracy	r	N	K=1	K=3	K=5
Glass	66.3	70.95	1	1	67.14	70.48	68.10
Iris	92.0	96.00	1	1	95.33	94.67	95.33
Heart	75.6	83.70	3	3	75.93	80.74	82.96
Wine	92.1	96.00	1	1	96.57	95.43	94.86
Diabetes	76.6	77.12	5	3	68.24	73.59	74.38
Aust	85.5	87.10	2	1	82.17	86.23	86.38
Average	81.35	85.15			80.90	83.52	83.67

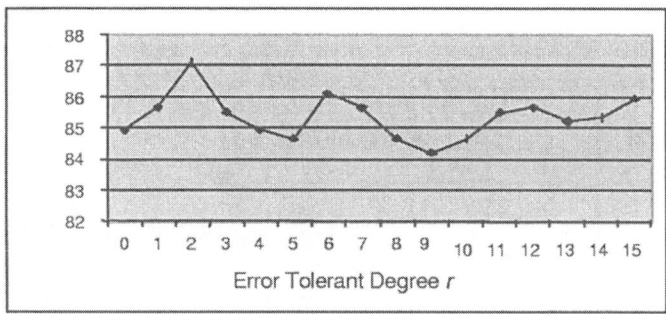

Fig.13. The accuracy of knnModel testing on Aust dataset with different r

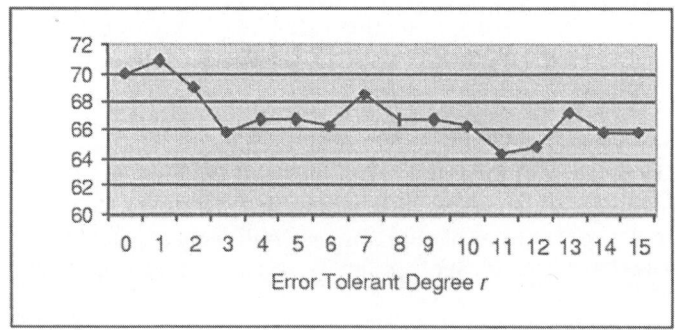

Fig.14. The accuracy of knnModel testing on Glass dataset with different r

Table 5. A comparison of C5.0, kNN, and kNNModel with model pruning

Dataset	C5.0	kNNModel (r=0)		kNN	
		CA%	RR%	CA%	RR%
Glass	66.3	68.57	82.71	68.57	0
Iris	92.0	95.33	95.33	95.11	0
Heart	75.6	80.74	89.26	79.88	0
Wine	92.1	95.43	94.94	95.62	0
Diabetes	76.6	74.77	86.32	72.07	0
Aust	85.5	86.09	93.91	84.93	0
Average	81.35	83.49	90.41	82.70	0

With N=1, the influence of different r (0~15) plays to the classification accuracy of knnModel is shown in Figure 13 and Figure 14 when do test on Aust and Diabetes datasets.

The experimental results of the kNNModel without N on six datasets are listed in Table 5.

In table 5, CA means classification accuracy, RR means reduction rate. For kNN, the CA is the average classification accuracy of k=1, 3, 5.

From the experimental results, it is clear that the average classification accuracy of our proposed kNNModel method on six datasets is better than C5.0 in 5-fold cross validation and is comparable to kNN. But the kNNModel significantly improves the efficiency of kNN by keeping only a few representatives for classification. The experimental results show that the average reduction rate is 90.41%.

5 Conclusions

In this paper we have presented a novel solution for dealing with the shortcomings of kNN. To overcome the problems of low effeciency and dependency on k, we select a few representatives from training dataset with some extra information to represent the whole training dataset. In the selection of each representative we use the optimal but different k decided by dataset itself to eliminate the dependency on k without user's intervention. Experimental results carried out on six public datasets show that the kNNModel is a quite competitive method for classification. Its average classification accuracy on six public datasets is comparable with C5.0 and kNN. Also the kNNModel significantly reduces the number of the data tuples in the final model for clasification with a 90.41% reduction rate on average. It could be a good replacement for kNN in many applications such as dynamic web mining for a large repository. Further research is required into how to improve the classification accuracy of marginal data which fall outside the regions of representatives.

Acknowledgements. This work was partly supported by the European Commission project ICONS, project no. IST-2001-32429.

References

1. D. Hand, H. Mannila, P. Smyth.: Principles of Data Mining. The MIT Press. (2001)
2. H. Wang.: Nearest Neighbours without k: A Classification Formalism based on Probability, technical report, Faculty of Informatics, University of Ulster, N.Ireland, UK (2002)
3. F.Sebastiani.: Machine Learning in Automated Text Categorization. In ACM Computing Surveys, Vol. 34, No. 1, March (2002) pp. 1–47.
4. H. Wang, I. Duntsch, D. Bell.: Data Reduction Based on Hyper Relations. In proceedings of KDD98, New York, pages 349–353 (1998)
5. P. Hart.: The Condensed Nearest Neighbour Rule, IEEE Transactions on Information Theory, 14, 515–516, (1968)
6. G. Gates.: The Reduced Nearest Neighbour Rule. IEEE Transactions on Information Theory, 18, 431–433, (1972)
7. E. Alpaydin.: Voting Over Multiple Condensed Nearest Neoghbors. Artificial Intelligence Review 11:115-132, (1997) ©1997 Kluwer Academic Publishers.
8. M. Kubat, M. Jr.: Voting Nearest-Neighbour Subclassifiers. Proceedings of the 17th International Conference on Machine Learning, ICML-2000, pp. 503–510, Stanford, CA, June 29–July 2, (2000)
9. D. R. Wilson, T. R. Martinez.: Reduction Techniques for Exemplar-Based Learning Algorithms. Machine learning, 38–3, pp. 257–286, (2000)
10. T. Mitchell.: Machine Learning. MITPress and McGraw-Hill (1997)
11. C.M.Bishop.: Neural Networks for Pattern Recognition. Oxford University Press, UK (1995)

Learning to Invoke Web Forms

Nicholas Kushmerick

Computer Science Department, University College Dublin, Ireland
nick@ucd.ie

Abstract. Emerging Web standards promise a network of heterogeneous yet interoperable Web Services. Web Services would greatly simplify the development of many kinds of data integration systems, information agents and knowledge management applications. Unfortunately, this vision requires that services provide substantial quantities of explicit semantic metadata "glue". As a step to automatically generating such metadata, we present an algorithm that learns to attach semantic labels to Web forms, and evaluate our approach on a large collection real Web data. The key idea is to cast Web form classification as Bayesian learning and inference over a generative model of the Web form design process.

1 Introduction

Emerging Web standards such as UDDI [uddi.org], SOAP [w3.org/TR/soap], WSDL [w3.org/TR/wsdl] and DAML-S [www.daml.org/services] promise an ocean of Web Services, networked components that can be invoked remotely using standard XML-based protocols. For example, major e-commerce companies such as Amazon and Google export Web Services that provide direct access to their content databases.

The key to automatically invoking and composing Web Services is to associate machine-understandable semantic metadata with each service. While the details are beyond the scope of this paper, the various Web standards involve metadata at various levels of abstraction, from high-level advertisements that facilitate discovering relevant services, to low-level input/output specifications of particular operations.

A central challenge to the Web Services initiative is the lack of tools to generate the necessary metadata (semi-)automatically. In this paper we explore the use of machine learning techniques to automatically create such metadata from training data. Such an approach complements existing uses of machine learning to facilitate the Semantic Web, such as for information extraction [6, 13,9,2] and for mapping between heterogeneous data schemata [3].

The various metadata standards are evolving rapidly, and it would be premature to commit to any particular standard. Our strategy is therefore to abstract away from such details by investigating the following core problem. To automatically invoke a particular Web Service, metadata is needed to indicate the overall "domain" of the service, as well as the intended semantic meaning of each input. For example, to invoke a Web Service that queries an airline's timetable, the

R. Meersman et al. (Eds.): CoopIS/DOA/ODBASE 2003, LNCS 2888, pp. 997–1013, 2003.

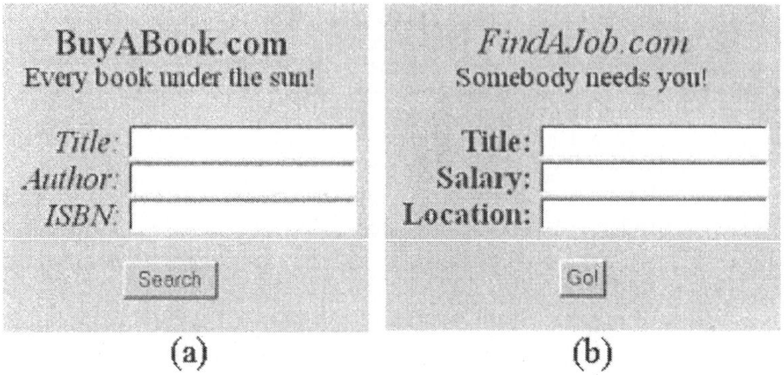

Fig. 1. Two HTML forms. An information agent that invokes these forms must automatically discover that the fields labelled 'Title' have completely different semantic interpretations

service must be annotated with metadata indicating that the operation does indeed relate to airline timetable querying, and each parameter must be annotated with the kind of data that should be supplied (departure data, time and airport, destination airport, return date, number of passengers, etc). More precisely, we focus on the problem of automatically classifying a Web Service into a taxonomy of service domains, and for labelling the service's input parameters with nodes from a taxonomy of datatypes.

A significant impediment to such research is actually obtaining an interesting collection of real Web Services: the promised ocean is just a small puddle today. Consequently, we focus on more restricted a but widely available alternative: the HTML forms available in Web pages. For example, consider the forms in Fig. 1. Suppose a Web form classifier has been trained on two kinds of forms: forms for finding a book, and for finding a job. Then we want the classifier to assign (a) to the former class, and (b) to the latter.

One simple approach would be to use traditional text classification algorithms over a bag of words harvested from the form's HTML. However, to enable interoperability, the form classifier must also label the individual fields of the forms, and for this task the simple bag-of-terms performs poorly. Note that the Title field is ambiguous: in one case it refers to a book title, and a job title in the other.

Rather than classifying each field independently, our algorithm exploits the evidence from all fields simultaneously. For example, in Fig. 1(a) our algorithm would reason as follows: the Author and ISBN terms adjacent to two of the fields provide strong bottom-up evidence that the form relates to finding a book; this tentative classification then provides top-down evidence that the Title field relates to book titles rather than job titles. By casting the Web form classification problem in Bayesian terms, we can leverage such bidirectional reasoning capability of the inference algorithms that have been developed by the Bayesian network community [15].

While our goal is to learn metadata for the Web Services standards, we believe that focusing on HTML forms is a valuable intermediate step. First, many existing information agents harvest Web content through HTML forms. Second, as the Web Services standards gain traction, there will be an increasing need for tools to migrate legacy HTML interfaces to the Web Services standards.

Finally and most importantly, both technologies have the same need for machine-understandable semantic metadata. For example, an HTML form might contain a fragment such as

```
ISBN: <input name=isbn><br>
Title: <input name=bktitle>
```

while a WSDL description of the same inputs to a Web Service might be:

```
<message name=BookSearchInput>
  <part name=title type=string/>
  <part name=ISBN  type=string/>
</message>
```

Unlike HTML, WSDL is synactically unambiguous in that identifiers and other textual clues are bound directly to relevant fields. But a deeper semantic challenge remains: the service can not be invoked automatically without additional metadata of the form "the first field expects the book's ISBN number; the second expects the book title", where "ISBN number" and "book title" are defined by some global taxonomy or ontology. For example, how can an automatic agent know that the first input corresponds to a parameter

```
<part name=bkname type=string/>
```

of another service? The standard Web Services answer to this semantic challenge is the use of yet more hand-crafted higher-level metadata such as DAML-S statements. Indeed, the relationship between our work and the emerging Web Standards is that we seek an algorithm that generates DAML-S-like statements from WSDL descriptions.

As suggested above, our algorithm uses only the evidence available in the form's HTML representation. In particular, we ignore additional sources of evidence, such as samples of the input data passed to a service, and the output data returned by the service. While such evidence may be beneficial, we ignore it to satisfy an important constraint: we permit processing only at the client side. That is, unlike some related approaches (e.g., [18,16]), we do not permit our algorithm to invoke a form while learning its semantics. The client-side-only constraint is important for several reasons. First, we want to avoid overloading the server with sample queries during learning. Second, such queries may have dangerous side-effects (e.g., modifying a database). Finally, generating such queries requires a supply of sample data values for each field, so we would just be swapping one difficult learning task for another.

Beyond our primary goal of automatically creating Web Services metadata, our techniques are relevant to several other applications. For example, our algorithm is could be used by: browsing assistants that automatically pre-populate

Web forms before they are rendered; tools to automatically re-render Web forms for small-display portable devices [8]; and spiders that automatically submit form queries in order to index the so-called "hidden Web" [18,11].

The remainder of this paper is organized as follows. We first formalize the Web form classification problem (Sec. 2), and then describe our Bayesian approach to solving this problem (Sec. 3). We then describe an empirical evaluation of our approach (Secs. 4–5). We conclude with a summary of our approach, and a discussion of related work and open issues (Sec. 6).

2   Problem Formulation

We formalize Web form classification as follows. Like any supervised learning task, we assume a set of instances, which are labelled to form a set of training data. In our case, instances correspond to Web forms, and labels correspond to taxonomic metadata attached to forms and their fields.

Web form instances are structured objects: a form comprises one or more fields, and each field in turn comprises one or more terms. More precisely, a *form* F_i is a sequence of *fields*, written $F_i = [f_i^1, f_i^2, \ldots]$, and each field f_i^j is a bag of *terms*, written $f_i^j = [t_i^j(1), t_i^j(2), \ldots]$. Terms represent words, tags, attributes, or other tokens in the HTML document. For example, Fig. 1(a) would be encoded as a form $F_1 = [f_1^1, f_2^1, f_3^1]$. If form F_1 is rendered from the following HTML:

```
<FORM action=/search.cgi>
  <P align=center>
    <B><BIG>BuyABook.com</BIG></B><BR>
    <SMALL>Every book under the sun!</SMALL></P>
  <P align=right>
    <I>Title:</I> <INPUT type=text name=ttl><BR>
    <I>Author:</I> <INPUT type=text name=auth><BR>
    <I>ISBN:</I> <INPUT type=text name=isbn></P>
  <P align=center>
    <INPUT type=submit value=Search></P>
</FORM>
```

then, as described in Sec. 4, the form's inputs would be encoded as follows:

$$f_1^1 = [\text{buyabook}, \text{com}, \text{every}, \text{book}, \text{under}, \text{the}, \text{sun}, \text{title}, \text{ttl}],$$
$$f_2^1 = [\text{author}, \text{auth}], \text{ and}$$
$$f_3^1 = [\text{isbn}, \text{isbn}].$$

The goal of our algorithm is to classify a form and its fields according to some preexisting taxonomy. Specifically, we assume two taxonomies for attaching semantic metadata to forms and fields. First, we assume a *domain* taxonomy $\mathcal{D}$. Domains capture the overall purpose of a form, such as "searching for a book", "finding a job", "querying a airline timetable", etc. We use SMALLCAPS to indicate domains, so we might have

$$\mathcal{D} = \{\text{SEARCHBOOK}, \text{FINDJOB}, \text{QUERYFLIGHT}, \ldots\}.$$

Second, we assume a *datatype* taxonomy $\mathcal{T}$. Datatypes do not relate to low-level encoding issues such as "string" or "integer", but rather to the required semantic category of a field's data, such as "book title", "salary", "destination airport", etc. SansSerif style indicates datatypes, so we might have

$$\mathcal{T} = \{\mathsf{BookTitle}, \mathsf{Salary}, \mathsf{DestAirport}, \ldots\}.$$

The Web form learning problem is as follows. The input is a set of labelled forms and fields; that is, a set $\{F_1, F_2, \ldots\}$ of forms together with a domain $D_i \in \mathcal{D}$ for each form F_i, and a datatype $T_i^j \in \mathcal{T}$ for each field $f_i^j \in F_i$. The output is a form classifier; that is, a function that maps an unlabelled form F_i, to a predicted domain $D_i \in \mathcal{D}$, and a predicted datatype $T_i^j \in \mathcal{T}$ for each field $f_i^j \in F_i$. Note that, in accordance with the client-side-only principle described earlier, the learned classifier is not permitted to probe the form being processed with sample queries, though it would be interesting to measure the benefit provided by such additional evidence.

3   Form Classification as Bayesian Inference

Our solution to the Web form classification is based on a stochastic generative model of a hypothetical "Web service designer" creating a Web page to host a particular service. Learning is thus a matter of estimating the model's parameters, and classification involves Bayesian inference over the model given evidence observed in a form.

Our strategy is to use a standard naive Bayes approach to determine the datatype of each field based on its terms, while at the same time computing the domain of the form as whole based on the datatypes of its fields. The key novelty of our approach is that these classifications are not made by greedily maximizing the likelihood of each prediction in isolation. Rather, by casting our problem as Bayesian inference, the classifications are solved in an "holistic" fashion that maximizes the likelihood of all predictions simultaneously.

3.1   Generative Model

We assume the following three-step generative model of a hypothetical Web service designer.

(1) Domain selection. First, the designer selects a domain $D_i \in \mathcal{D}$ according to some probability distribution $\Pr[D_i]$. For example, in our Web form data described in Sec. 4, forms for finding books were quite frequent relative to forms for finding colleges, so

$$\Pr[\text{SEARCHBOOK}] \gg \Pr[\text{FINDCOLLEGE}].$$

(2) **Datatype selection.** Second, the designer selects datatypes $T_i^j \in \mathcal{T}$ appropriate to D_i, by selecting according to some distribution $\Pr[T_i^j | D_i]$. For example, presumably

$$\Pr[\text{BookTitle}|\text{SEARCHBOOK}] \gg \Pr[\text{DestAirport}|\text{SEARCHBOOK}],$$

because services for finding books usually involve a book's title, but rarely involve airports. On the other hand,

$$\Pr[\text{BookTitle}|\text{QUERYFLIGHT}] \ll \Pr[\text{DestAirport}|\text{QUERYFLIGHT}].$$

Note that the selected datatypes T_i^j are assumed to be independent given the "parent" domain D_i.

(3) **Term emission.** Finally, the designer writes the Web page that implements the form by coding each field in turn. To code each field, the designer selects terms in a datatype-specific fashion. More precisely, for each selected datatype T_i^j, the designer uses terms $t_i^j(k)$ drawn according to some distribution $\Pr[t_i^j(k)|T_i^j]$. For example, presumably

$$\Pr[\text{title}|\text{BookTitle}] \gg \Pr[\text{city}|\text{BookTitle}],$$

because the term `title` is much more likely than `city` to occur in a field requesting a book title. On the other hand, presumably

$$\Pr[\text{title}|\text{DestAirport}] \ll \Pr[\text{city}|\text{DestAirport}].$$

Note that this generative model assumes independence of the selected terms $t_i^j(k)$ given the datatype that generates them.

This generative model obviously greatly simplifies the Web form design process. For example, it assumes that datatypes and terms are independent given their parents, and that all terms are associated with fields (rather than, for example, a label like "Use this form to query our flight timetable" that describes the form as a whole). The model also ignores the number of fields in a form and terms in a field. Our experiments below suggest that this simple model works well in practice, and we are exploring more sophisticated models.

3.2   Parameter Estimation

The learning task is to estimate the parameters of the stochastic generative model from a set of training data. The training data comprises a set of N Web forms $\mathcal{F} = \{F_1, \ldots, F_N\}$, where for each form F_i the learning algorithm is given the domain $D_i \in \mathcal{D}$ and the datatypes T_i^j of the fields $f_i^j \in F_i$. Note that, like any approach employing a generative model with latent variables, the learning algorithm can observe only the third step of the generative process (ie, only the HTML terms can be observed, not the designer's underlying intentions).

The parameters to be estimated are the domain probabilities $\hat{\Pr}[D]$ for $D \in \mathcal{D}$, the conditional datatype probabilities $\hat{\Pr}[T|D]$ for $D \in \mathcal{D}$ and $T \in \mathcal{T}$, and the conditional term probabilities $\hat{\Pr}[t|T]$ for term t and $T \in \mathcal{T}$. We estimate these parameters based on their frequency in the training data:

$$\hat{\Pr}[D] = N_{\mathcal{F}}(D)/N,$$
$$\hat{\Pr}[T|D] = M_{\mathcal{F}}(T, D)/M_{\mathcal{F}}(D), \text{ and}$$
$$\hat{\Pr}[t|T] = W_{\mathcal{F}}(t, T)/W_{\mathcal{F}}(T),$$

where $N_{\mathcal{F}}(D)$ is the number of forms in the training set $\mathcal{F}$ with domain D; $M_{\mathcal{F}}(D)$ is the total number of fields in all forms of domain D; $M_{\mathcal{F}}(T, D)$ is the number of fields of datatype T in all forms of domain D; $W_{\mathcal{F}}(T)$ is the total number of terms of all fields of datatype T; and $W_{\mathcal{F}}(t, T)$ is the number of occurrences of term t in all fields of datatype t. Following standard practice, we employ the Laplacean prior (ie, all counts are incremented by one, so events that did not occur in the training data have a small positive probability).

3.3   Classification

Web form classification involves converting a form into a Bayesian network. The network is a tree that reflects the generative model: there is a root node representing the form's domain, children representing the datatype of each field, and grandchildren encoding the terms used to code each field. Evidence from the term nodes is propagated to the domain and datatype nodes using standard inference algorithms [15], resulting in posterior probabilities for the form's domain and datatypes.

In more detail, a Web form to be classified is converted into a three-layer tree-structured Bayesian network as follows. The first (root) layer contains just a single node **domain** that takes on values from the set of domains $\mathcal{D}$. The second layer consists of one child **datatype**$_i$ of **domain** for each field in the form being classified, where each **datatype**$_i$ take on values from the datatype set $\mathcal{T}$.

The third (leaf) layer comprises a set of children $\{\mathbf{term}_i^1, \ldots, \mathbf{term}_i^K\}$ for each **datatype**$_i$ node, where K is the number of terms in the field. The term nodes take on values from the vocabulary set $\mathcal{V}$, defined as the set of all terms that have occurred in the training data.

Fig. 2 illustrates the network that would be constructed for a form with three fields and K terms for each field. (Each field contains the same number K of terms/field for simplicity; in fact, the number of term nodes reflects the actual number of terms in the parent field.)

The conditional probability tables associated with each node correspond directly to the learned parameters mentioned earlier. That is, $\Pr[\mathbf{domain} = D] \equiv \hat{\Pr}(D)$, $\Pr[\mathbf{datatype}_i = T|\mathbf{domain} = D] \equiv \hat{\Pr}(T|D)$, and $\Pr[\mathbf{term}_i^k = t|\mathbf{datatype}_i = T] \equiv \hat{\Pr}(t|T)$. Note that the conditional probability tables are identical for all datatype nodes, and for all term nodes.

Given such a Bayesian network, classifying a form $F_i = [f_i^1, f_i^2, \ldots]$ involves "observing" the terms in each field (ie, setting the probability $\Pr[\mathbf{term}_i^k = t_i^j(k)] \equiv 1$ for each term $t_i^j(k) \in f_i^j$), and then computing the maximum-likelihood form domain and field datatypes consistent with that evidence.

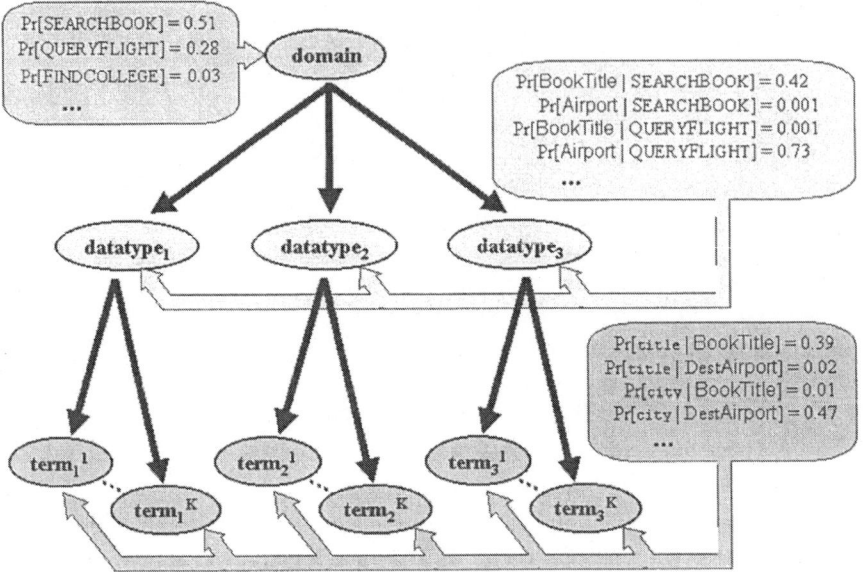

Fig. 2. The three-layer tree-structured Bayesian network used to classify a form containing three fields

4   Evaluation

We have evaluated our approach using a collection of 129 Web forms comprising 656 fields in total, for an average of 5.1 fields/form. As shown in Fig. 3, the domain taxonomy $\mathcal{D}$ used in our experiments contains 6 domains, and the datatype taxonomy $\mathcal{T}$ comprises 71 datatypes. The data-set is available to the research community; contact the author for details.

The forms were manually gathered by first selecting a domain, and then browsing Web forms indices such as InvisibleWeb.com for relevant forms. Each form was then inspected by hand to assign a domain to the form as a whole, and a datatype to each field. The collection certainly does not represent a random sample of the Web, but to avoid bias it was created by two undergraduate assistants who were not familiar with the goals of this research.

After the forms were gathered, they were segmented into fields. We discuss the details below. For now, it suffices to say that we use HTML tags such as `<input>` and `<textarea>` to identify the fields that will appear to the user when the page is rendered.

After a form has been segmented into fields, certain irrelevant fields (submit and reset buttons, hidden fields, etc.) are discarded during the labelling process. The remaining fields are then assigned a datatype. Recall that datatypes correspond not to low-level encoding details, but to semantic categories such as Airline or NUnder65.

Domain taxonomy $\mathcal{D}$ and number of forms for each domain

SEARCHBOOK (44) FINDCOLLEGE (2) SEARCHCOLLEGEBOOK (17)
QUERYFLIGHT (34) FINDJOB (23)   FINDSTOCKQUOTE (9)

Datatype taxonomy $\mathcal{T}$

Address	Airline	Airport	Author	BookCode
BookCondition	BookDetails	BookEdition	BookFormat	BookSearchType
BookSubject	BookTitle	NChildren	City	Class
College	CollegeSubject	CompanyName	Country	Currency
Date	DateDepart	DateReturn	DestCity	Duration
Email	EmployeeLevel	FaxNum	FlightTimeType	ISBN
JobCategory	JobDetails	JobExperience	JobLevel	JobSkills
JobTitle	JobType	Language	Location	LocationType
Month	NAdults	NInfants	NSeated	OriginCity
PersonAge	PersonName	PersonTitle	Price	Publisher
RegPhoneNum	RegPhoneArea	RegPhoneLocal	ReturnType	Salary
SMSNum	TickerSym	Time	TimeDepart	TimePeriod
TimeReturn	TravelType	USState	ZIP	

Fig. 3. The domain and datatype taxonomies used in the experiments

The research assistants continually refined the datatype set $\mathcal{T}$ as additional forms were examined. For example, after processing several SEARCHBOOK services, it became apparent that some forms support querying by ISBN number while others use alternative identifier codes, and so a BookCode datatype was created. The assistants were instructed to devise as parsimonious a datatype set as possible, and to revisit previously inspected forms to ensure consistency. We do not argue that we have identified the definitive or optimal domain and datatype taxonomies for these services, but merely that we have simulated a realistic scenario involving a reasonably large number of heterogeneous services and data.

A final subtlety is that some fields are not easily interpreted as "data", but rather indicate minor modifications to either the way the query is interpreted, or the output presentation. For example, some QUERYFLIGHT services have a "I'm flexible" check-box indicating that the stated departure time should be used as a loose filter, and there is a "help" option on one search services that augments the requested data with suggestions for query refinement. Rather than allow a proliferation of such extremely rare field datatypes, we discarded such fields on a case-by-case basis; a total of 12.1% of the fields were discarded in this way.

As described in Sec. 1, the primary challenge is to cope with the inherent semantic ambiguity of Web services. However, HTML forms also suffer from syntactic ambiguity, because HTML does not require any explicit binding between form fields and the labels that human users will see in their proximity. Thus the final data-preparation step is to heuristically convert an HTML fragment into the appropriate "form = sequence of fields; field = bag of terms" representation. The HTML is first parsed into a sequence of tokens. Some of these tokens are HTML field tags (eg, `<input>`, `<select>`, `<textarea>`). The form is segmented into fields by simply associating the remaining tokens with the nearest field. For example, "`<form> a <input name=f1> b c <textarea name=f2> d </form>`" would be segmented as "`a <input name=f1> b`" and "`c <textarea name=f2> d`".

The intent is that this segmentation process will associate with each field a bag of terms that provides evidence of the field's datatype. For example, our classification algorithm will learn to distinguish labels like "Book title" that are associated with BookTitle fields, from labels like "Title (Dr, Ms, ...)" that indicate PersonTitle. (We note that this simple approach can be fooled by sophisticated Web programming techniques. In the worst case, dynamic HTML technologies may mean that a label that appears near a fields does not exist in the HTML source at all!)

Finally, we convert HTML fragments like "`Enter name: <input name=name1 type=text size=20> <br>`" that correspond to a particular field, into the field's bag of terms representation. We process each fragment as follows.

First, we discard HTML tags, retaining the values of a set of "interesting" attributes, such as an `<input>` tag's `name` attribute. The result is "`Enter name: name1`".

Next, we tokenize the string at punctuation and space characters, convert all characters to lower case, apply Porter's stemming algorithm, discard stop words, and insert a special symbol encoding the field's HTML type (text, select, radiobutton, etc). This yields the token sequence [enter, name, name1, **TypeText**];

Finally, we apply a set of term normalizations, such as replacing terms comprising just a single digit (letter) with a special symbol **SingleDigit** (**SingleLetter**), and deleting leading/trailing numbers. In this example the final result is the sequence [enter, name, name, **TypeText**].

To illustrate the challenging nature of Web form classification, we conclude with the actual bags of terms generated by our pre-processing algorithm for a seven-field QUERYFLIGHT form at www.nwa.com:

> OriginCity: **TypeText**, origin, citi, destin, text;
> DestCity: **TypeText**, date, depart, citd, text;
> DateDepart: **TypeText**, departur, date, depart, time, text;
> TimeDepart: **TypeSelect**, afternoon, date, return, morn, time, even;
> DateReturn: **TypeText**, date, return, time, text;
> TimeReturn: **TypeSelect**, afternoon, morn, time, even;
> NAdults: **TypeSelect**, adult, cadu, passeng, number, **SingleDigit**.

These bags of words can be compared with those in Fig. 4, which shows the terms most frequently associated with each datatype (ie, emitted in step 3 of the generative model), as well as the datatypes most frequently associated with each domain (ie, selected in step 2 of the generative process).

SEARCHBOOK	BookDetails, Author, BookTitle
SEARCHCOLLEGEBOOK	BookDetails, Author, BookTitle
FINDJOB	JobCategory, JobDetails, USState

FINDCOLLEGE	College
QUERYFLIGHT	DateDepart, DateReturn, DestCity
FINDSTOCKQUOTE	TickerSym, CompanyName

Address	address, streetaddress, TypeTextarea	Airline	airlin, franc, lufthansa
Airport	birmingham, airport, manchest	Author	author, last, cat
BookCode	our, item, txtsku	BookCondition	class, sale
BookDetails	keyword, titl, author	BookEdition	geologi, learn, program
BookFormat	hardcov, paperback, bind	BookSearchType	titl, author, isbn
BookSubject	subject, scienc, romanc	BookTitle	titl, franc, part
City	state, input, south	Class	class, economi, coach
College	univers, school, long	CollegeSubject	cours, math, write
CompanyName	compani, omit, technic	Country	countri, canada, unit
Currency	franc, lira, rand	Date	dateyear
DateDepart	depart, mai, june	DateReturn	mai, june, juli
DestCity	vega, la, angel	Duration	night, vant, airport
Email	email, address, mail	EmployeeLevel	manag, emlevel, top
FaxNum	fax	FlightTimeType	arriv, departur, tm
ISBN	isbn, can, identifi	JobCategory	sale, insur, market
JobDetails	keyword, kei, word	JobExperience	checkbox, minimum, internship
JobLevel	not, junior, experi	JobSkills	oracl, term, pnet
JobTitle	txt, titl, frm	JobType	contract, type, temp
Language	languag, spanish	Location	true, franc, south
LocationType	statewid, bodytx, nation	Month	oct, month, nov
NAdults	adult, passeng, ag	NChildren	children, child, ag
NInfants	infant, under, passeng	NSeated	passeng, pax, ticket
OriginCity	angel, lo, san	PersonAge	ag, young, subject
PersonName	last, initi, surnam	PersonTitle	mr, miss, titl
Price	price, min, rang	Publisher	publish, inspir, omnibu
RegPhoneNum	phone, even, contact	RegPhoneArea	area, phone
RegPhoneLocal	area, phone	ReturnType	wai, trip, round
Salary	salari, less, negoti	SMSNum	info, sm, opensm
TickerSym	symbol, quot, ticker	Time	even, tm, pm
TimeDepart	pm, am, even	TimePeriod	month, dai, week
TimeReturn	pm, am, even	TravelType	checkbox, TypeCheckbox, flight
USState	state, missouri, alaska	ZIP	zip, zipcod, frmsize

Fig. 4. The datatypes most frequently associated with each domain, and the terms most frequently associated with each datatype

5   Results

We now describe several experiments designed to measure the effectiveness of our form classification algorithm.

5.1   Comparison to Baseline

We begin by comparing our approach to two simple bag of terms baselines. For domain classification, the baseline uses a single bag of all terms in the entire form. For datatype classification, the baseline approach is the naive Bayes algorithm over its bag of terms.

We measure performance using the standard F1 metric (the harmonic mean of macro-averaged precision and recall [10]), and we adopt the standard leave-one-out methodology.

For domain prediction, our algorithm has an F1 score of 0.87 while the baseline scores 0.82. For datatype prediction, our algorithm has an F1 score of 0.43 while the baseline scores 0.38. We conclude that our "holistic" approach to form and field prediction is more accurate than a greedy baseline approach of making each prediction independently.

While our approach is far from perfect, we observe that form classification is extremely challenging, due both to noise in the underlying HTML, and the fact that our domain and datatype taxonomies contain many classes compared to traditional (usually binary!) text classification tasks.

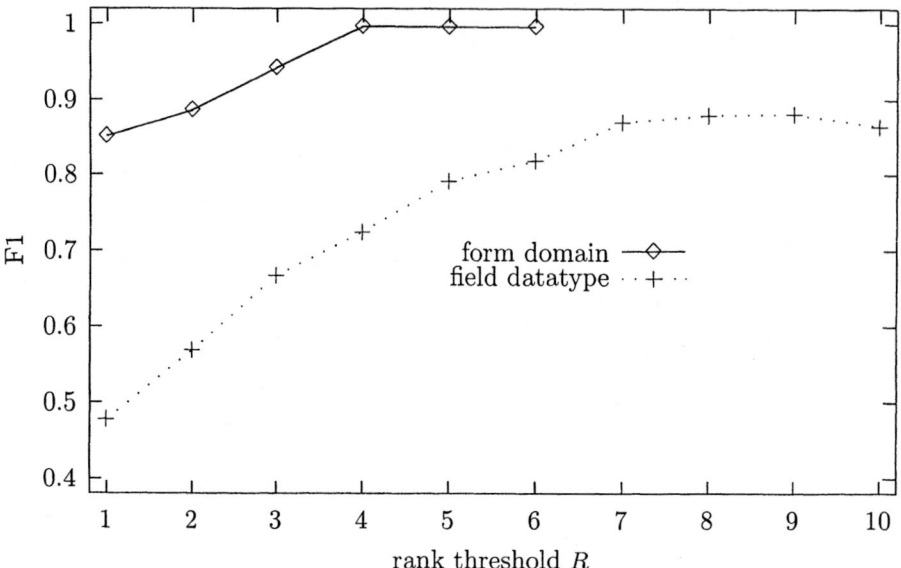

Fig. 5. F1 as a function of rank threshold R

5.2   Semi-automated Classification

While fully-automated form classification is our ultimate goal, an imperfect form classifier can still be useful in interactive, partially-automated scenarios in which a human gives "hints" in the form of the domain or datatypes of a form to be labelled, and the classifier labels the remaining elements.

Our first experiment measures the improvement in datatype prediction if the human provides the form's domain. In this case our algorithm has an F1 score of 0.51, compared to 0.43 mentioned earlier. On the other hand, we can measure the improvement in domain prediction given the "hint" of the fields' datatypes. In this case our algorithm has an F1 score of 0.92, compared to 0.87 reported earlier.

Our second investigation of semi-automated prediction involves the idea of ranking the predictions rather than requiring that the algorithm makes just one prediction. In many semi-automated scenarios, the fact that the second- or third-ranked prediction is correct can still be useful even if the first is wrong. To formalize this notion, we calculate F1 based on treating the algorithm as correct if the true class is in the top R predictions as ranked by posterior probability. Fig. 5 shows the F1 score for predicting both domains and datatypes, as a function of R. $R = 1$ corresponds to the cases described so far. We can see that relaxing R even slightly results in a dramatic increase in F1 score.

So far we have assumed unstructured datatype and domain taxonomies. However, domains and datatypes exhibit a natural hierarchical structure (eg, "forms for finding something" vs. "forms for buying something"; or "fields related to book information" vs. "fields related to personal details"). It seems reasonable that in partially-automated settings, predicting a similar but wrong class is more useful than a dissimilar class.

To explore this issue, our research assistants converted their domain and datatype taxonomies into trees, creating additional abstract nodes to obtain reasonable and compact hierarchies. We used distance in these trees to measure the "quality" of a prediction, instead of a binary "right/wrong". For domain predictions, our algorithm's prediction is on average 0.40 edges away from the correct class, while the baseline algorithm's predicions are 0.55 edges away. For datatype prediction, our algorithm's average distance is 2.08 edges while the baseline algorithm averages 2.51. As above, we conclude that our algorithm outperforms the baseline.

5.3   Scalability

Our next experiments evaluate how accurate our predictions are as a function of the inherent "complexity" of the forms. For example, our approach is not feasible if it is accurate only for forms with a very small number of fields.

Our first experiment measures accuracy as a function of the size of the domain taxonomy $\mathcal{D}$. To simulate varying the number of domains, we discarded either one or $|\mathcal{D}| - 1 = 5$ of the domains, and repeated our experiments. Retaining all domains corresponds to a complex set of heterogenous services; discarding all but one assumes that all forms serve the same domain. Fig. 6 shows that, as expected, the accuracy of domain prediction falls somewhat with the number of domains, while datatype prediction accuracy shows no clear trend. We conclude that our datatype prediction scales well with the degree of domain heterogeneity, while domain prediction is less robust.

Our second experiment measures F1 as a function of the number of fields. We repeated our experiments on only forms with 1–2 fields, and again for 3–5 , 6–10, and 10 or more fields. Fig. 7 demonstrates that datatype prediction F1 score increases for larger forms. These data show that numerous sources of possibly noisy evidence can be corroborated to produce accurate predictions. For domain prediction, there is also a large increase in F1 for larger forms, though the predictions eventually deteriorate for very large forms.

5.4   Datatype Duplication

Our final experiment explores the observation that, for many forms, there is at most one field for any given datatype. For example, a BOOKSEARCH form is unlikely to ask for the Author twice. To explore this constraint, we extended our classification algorithm so that it predicts the most-likely datatypes, such that no datatype is predicted more than once per form.

To ensure a fair comparison, we ignored forms that violate this regularity. Our original algorithm has a F1 score of 0.42 on this set of forms, and the revised classification algorithm that avoids duplicate predictions has an F1 score of 0.49.

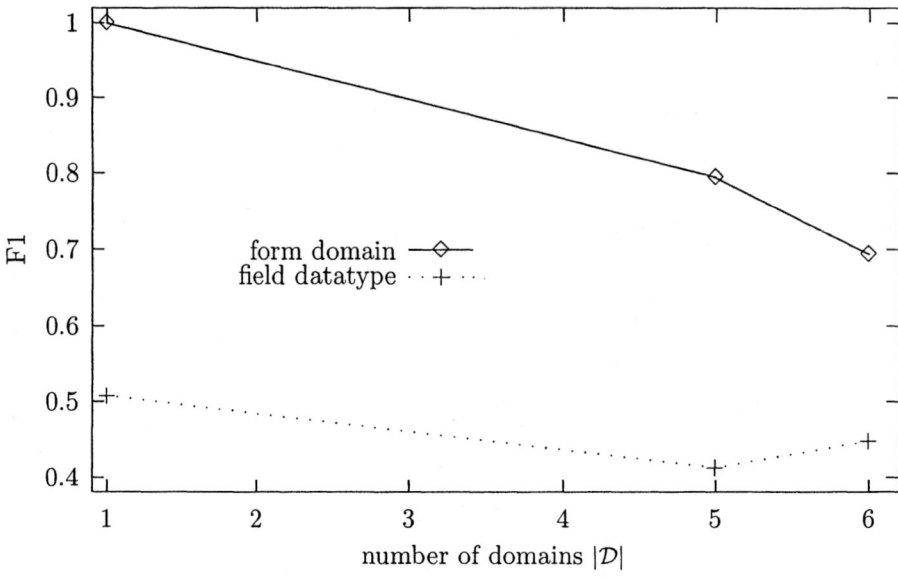

Fig. 6. F1 as a function of number of domains $|\mathcal{D}|$

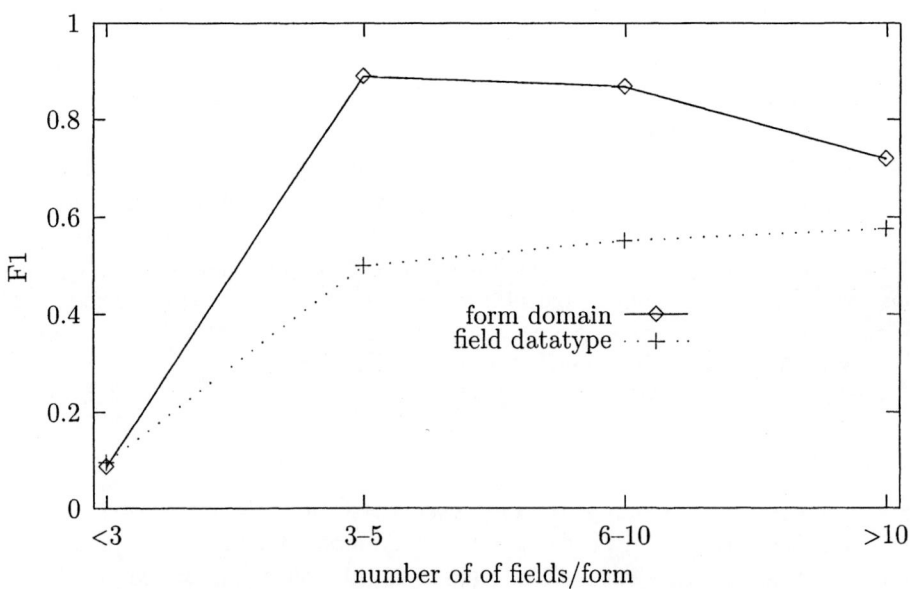

Fig. 7. F1 as a function of number of fields per form

We conclude that exploiting this constraint boosts prediction accuracy. We conjecture that other datatype regularities could lead to additional improvements. For example, association rules could be mined from the training data to learn which datatypes tend to co-occur.

6   Discussion

The emerging Web Service protocols represent exciting new directions for the Web, but interoperability requires that each service be described by a large amount of semantic metadata "glue". We have presented a learning framework for automatically generating such metadata from labelled examples, and evaluated our approach on a collection of Web forms. While our experiments involved forms, we believe our results are relevant to the emerging Web Services vision.

The most relevant recent work is on indexing the so-called "hidden Web" [18]. Raghavan and Garcia-Molina focus on a similar form and field classification task, but they evaluate their algorithm given knowledge of the form's domain (ie, in our notation, they assume $|\mathcal{D}| = 1$). Perkowitz and Etzioni also address a similar problem, and present an active learning algorithm that probes the service with sample queries in order to efficiently converge to a correct interpretation [16].

We use a simple proximity-based algorithm for segmenting HTML forms into fields. More sophisticated rendering-based approaches have been tried [8], but we defer to future work a systematic evaluation of the benefit of sophisticated heuristics over our simple approach.

Our overall motivation, and specifically our focus on Web forms, is consistent with the extensive investigation of software or information agents (eg, the seminal ShopBot agent [4]), and more recent data integration research (e.g., [7]). As far as we are aware, these agents all rely either on manual form annotation, or on hand-crafted task-specific form classification rules

Probabilistic models involving unobserved latent random variables have been used in numerous diverse settings, such as classifying structured XML documents [19], information retrieval [1] and collaborative recommendation [17].

An interesting aspect of Web form classification is that it involves simultaneously predicting multiple features of some complex object. By casting our problem in a probabilistic framework, our algorithm leverages numerous sources of weak evidence to obtain a globally optimal set of predictions. We conjecture that this idea could be extended to other tasks, such as information extraction (using retrieved data to bias the retrieval of additional data; see [14]) or personalization (recommending multiple items "simultaneously").

One important direction of future work concerns the hierarchical structure of the domain and datatype taxonomies. We have explored using such structure in our evaluation, but it may be useful to integrate these hierarchies into the classification process itself [12]. A second open issue is whether the EM algorithm would be effective in enabling semi-supervised learning.

Finally, as depicted in Fig. 8, we are currently applying these ideas to Web Services, not just Web forms [5]. The primary complication is that while a form

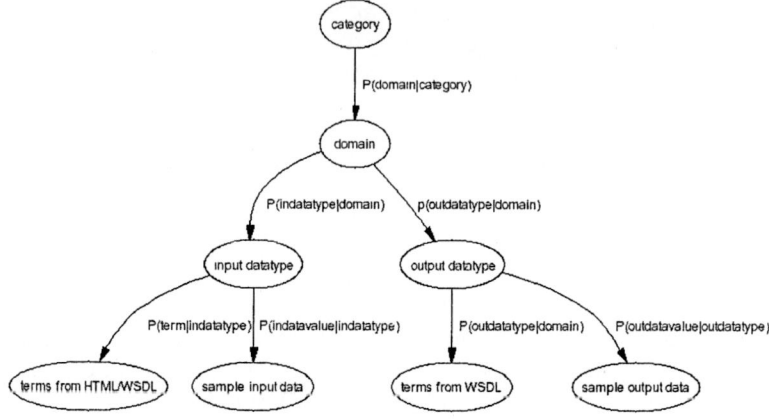

Fig. 8. We are currently extending our algorithm to incorporate additional sources of evidence that relate to the various Web Services standards

corresponds to a single operation, a Web Service may contain several distinct operations. We therefore have introduced a new category-level taxonomy that captures the overall function of a group of related operations. For example, an airline might have a Web Service in the "Travel" category that exports operations related to timetable querying, ticket reservation, frequent flyer account maintenance, etc. As noted earlier, our algorithm currently ignores two valuable sources of evidence: the data passed to a service in previous invocations, and the output data returned from the service. While the client-side-only principle described in Sec. 1 precludes access to such evidence in general, we are currrently extending our ideas to exploit this evidence in order to measure the actual benefit.

Acknowledgments. This research was supported by grants SFI/01/F.1/C015 from Science Foundation Ireland, and grants N00014-00-1-0021 and N00014-03-1-0274 from the US Office of Naval Research. We thank Kathryn Wilkinson and Ruichao Wang for creating the form database, and Andreas Heß for helpful discussions.

References

1. A. Berger, R. Caruana, D. Cohn, D. Freitag, and V. Mittal. Bridging the lexical chasm: statistical approaches to answer-finding. In *Proc. Int. Conf. Research and Development in Information Retrieval*, pages 192–199, 2000.
2. F. Ciravegna. Adaptive information extraction from text by rule induction and generalization. In *Proc. 17th Int. Conf. Artificial Intelligence*, pages 1251–1256, 2001.
3. A. Doan, P. Domingos, and A. Halevy. Reconciling schemas of disparate data sources: A machine-learning approach. In *Proc. SIGMOD Conference*, 2001.

4. R. Doorenbos, O. Etzioni, and D. Weld. A scalable comparison-shopping agent for the World-Wide Web. In *Proc. Int. Conf. Autonomous Agents*, pages 39–48, 1997.

5. A. Heß and N. Kushmerick. Learning to attach semantic metadata to Web Services. In *Proc. Int. Semantic Web Conf.*, 2003.

6. C. Hsu and M. Dung. Generating finite-state transducers for semistructured data extraction from the web. *J. Information Systems*, 23(8):521–538, 1998.

7. Z. Ives, A. Levy, D. Weld, D. Florescu, and M. Friedman. Adaptive query processing for Internet applications. *IEEE Data Engineering Bulletin*, 23(2), 2000.

8. O. Kaljuvee, O. Buyukkokten, H. Garcia-Molina, and A. Paepcke. Efficient Web form entry on PDAs. *Proc. 10th World Wide Web Conference*, pages 663–672, 5 2001.

9. N. Kushmerick. Wrapper induction: Efficiency and expressiveness. *Artificial Intelligence*, 118(1–2):15–68, 2000.

10. D. Lewis. Evaluating text categorization. In *Proc. Speech and Natural Language Workshop*, pages 312–318, 1991.

11. S. Liddle, D. Embley, D. Scott, and S. Yau. Extracting data behing Web forms. In *Proc. Int. Conf. Very Large Databases*, 2002.

12. A. McCallum, R. Rosenfeld, T. Mitchell, and A. Ng. Improving text classification by shrinkage in a hierarchy of classes. In *Proc 15th Int. Conf. Machine Learning*, pages 359–367, 1998.

13. I. Muslea, S. Minton, and C. Knoblock. A Hierachical Approach to Wrapper Induction. In *Proc. 3rd Int. Conf. Autonomous Agents*, pages 190–197, 1999.

14. U. Nahm and R. Mooney. A mutually beneficial integration of data mining and information extraction. In *Proc. 17th Nat. Conf. Artificial Intelligence*, pages 627–632, 2000.

15. J. Pearl. *Probablistic Reasoning in Intelligent Systems*. Morgan Kaufmann, 1988.

16. M. Perkowitz and O. Etzioni. Category translation: Learning to understand information on the Internet. In *Proc. 14th Int. Conf. Artificial Intelligence*, pages 930–938, 1995.

17. A. Popescul, L. Ungar, D. Pennock, and S. Lawrence. Probabilistic models for unified collaborative and content-based recommendation in sparse-data environments. In *Proc. 17th Conf. Uncertainty in Artificial Intelligence*, pages 437–444, 2001.

18. S. Raghavan and H. Garcia-Molina. Crawling the hidden Web. In *Proc. 27th Int. Conf. Very Large Databases*, pages 129–138, 2001.

19. J. Yi and N. Sundaresan. A classifier for semi-structured documents. In *Proc. Conf. Knowledge Discovery in Data*, pages 190–197, 2000.

A Proposal for Management of RDF and RDF Schema Metadata in MOF

Hélio Lopes dos Santos, Roberto Souto Maior de Barros, and Décio Fonseca

Universidade Federal de Pernambuco - UFPE
{hls,Roberto,df}@cin.ufpe.br

Abstract. This paper proposes two MOF metamodels to support the representation and management of RDF and RDF Schema metadata. A metamodel is a set of related metadata used to build models. The MOF defines an abstract language and a framework to support the specification, implementation and management of platform independent metamodels. RDF and RDF Schema are standards for the web, and are used for describing, reusing and interchanging metadata. This approach takes advantage of the flexibility of the W3C standards and of the interoperability of the OMG ones to support metadata management. The proposed metamodels may be used by any application that needs to resent RDF and RDF Schema metadata.

Keywords: MOF, RDF, RDF Schema, metadata, metamodel.

1 Introduction

In the last few years, with the increasing importance of information systems, metadata has become a key issue in management of the life cycle of these systems. Many recent efforts, both in academic areas and in industry, have concentrated in research related to metadata. These studies try to define methodologies and standards for the construction and interoperability of information systems based on metadata [HJE2001, CWM2001].

Nowadays, metadata are used in many areas, like Data warehouse, electronic libraries, software engineering and integration of heterogeneous applications. With the Internet, new applications have surged, together with new standards for representation [AHAY2001]. These new standards include XML (*Extensible Markup Language*), DTD (*Document Type Definition*), XML Schema, RDF (*Resource Description Framework*), RDF Schema, XSLT (*Extensible Stylesheet Language Transformation*), and others. Each of these standards has been developed for specific classes of applications. For example, DTD and XML Schema are standards for data structure description; RDF is used for describing resources as Web pages and XSLT is used in XML documents transformation. These are semi-structured and flexible standards created to be used in the Web, which are supported by tools and may be used as metadata description, storage and interchange formats [ABK2000].

The OMG (*Object Management Group*) supports another set of standards, as, for instance, MOF (*Meta Object Facility*) [MOF1999] and XMI (*XML Metadata*

R. Meersman et al. (Eds.): CoopIS/DOA/ODBASE 2003, LNCS 2888, pp. 1014–1031, 2003.

Interchange) [XMI2000], which have been built to support metadata modeling, management and interchanging, in the context of information systems. One of the key aspects of these standards is to allow for interoperability among software tools that share metadata.

This paper proposes metadata integration through the design and implementation of MOF metamodels, which represent the RDF and RDF Schema standards. This approach takes advantage of the flexibility of W3C standards and of the interoperability of the OMG ones to support metadata management.

One of the advantages of this approach is to use a common set of interfaces to access and manage metadata written in RDF and RDF Schema. Nowadays, the interfaces to access RDF and RDF Schema metadata are defined and implemented by each vendor, through parsers. The parser Jena[1] is an example that manipulates RDF documents.   Modeling the RDF and RDF Schema in MOF means generating interfaces to access metadata written in these standards. At this point, there are MOF mappings to IDL CORBA [MOF1999] e JMI (*Java Metadata Interface*) [JMI2002].

Another benefit is to use XMI as the unique standard to represent metadata. XMI is a standard supported by several tools in many areas such as development of information systems, for instance *Netbeans*[2]; systems specification and modeling, for instance, Rational Rose[3]; Data warehouse, such as DB2 Warehouse Manager[4]; metadata repositories, such as, MDR (*Metadata Repository*) [MDR2002] and dMOF [DMOF2001].

The following Sections present related work, the MOF standard and its architecture and the standard for its mapping to Java and CORBA interfaces. Then, we present the metamodels for RDF and RDF Schema, the interfaces generated from these metamodels and a case study using these interfaces. Afterwards, we compare MOF to RDF. Finally we present our conclusions and propose future work.

2 Related Work

In general, research topics have used metamodels related to specific applications. This paper proposes two metamodels, which will support the representation and management of RDF and RDF Schema metadata in MOF repositories. Then, any application which needs to represent metadata using RDF and RDF Schema may use the metamodels.

Other metamodels based in MOF are UML (*Unified Modeling Language*) [UML2001] for systems modeling and CWM (*Common Warehouse Metamodel*) [CWM2001], which proposes a set of metamodels to represent Data warehouse metadata. Another important work by Sun Microsystems is a metamodel to Java [DEMA2002], which proposes a way of managing Java Code in MOF repositories.

---

1 http://jena.sourceforge.net/

2 http://www.netbeans.org/

3 http://www.rational.com/

4 http://www-3.ibm.com/software/data/db2/datawarehouse/

3   MOF – Meta Object Facility

The MOF is an abstract language and a framework to specify, build and manage platform independent metamodels. Examples include the UML, CWM and MOF metamodels. MOF also supports a set of rules to implement repositories, which deal with metadata described by the metamodels. Theses rules define a standard mapping between the MOF metamodels and a set of APIs to manage metadata, instances of the metamodels. For instance, the *MOF -> IDL* (*Interface Definition Language*) mapping is applied to MOF metamodels (UML, CWM) to generate CORBA API´s that manage the corresponding metadata, instance of metamodel. The *MOF -> Java* mapping is similar and generates Java API´s using the JMI (*Java Metadata Interface*) standard. This work uses JMI.

The MOF specification is composed of:

- A formal definition of the MOF meta-metamodel, an abstract language to define metamodels;
- Rules to map MOF metamodels to an implementation technology such as CORBA or Java; and
- The XMI standard to interchanging metadata and metamodels among tools using XML. XMI defines rules to map MOF metamodels and metadata to XML documents.

3.1   OMG Metadata Architecture

The MOF is an extensible framework, i.e., new metadata standards may be added to it. It is based on a four-layer architecture, called the OMG Metadata Architecture [MOF1999, MDA2001], which is presented in Table 1.

Table 1. OMG Metadata Architecture

MOF Level	Used terms	Examples
M3	Meta-Metamodel	MOF Model
M2	Metamodel, Meta-Metadata	UML and CWM Metamodel
M1	Models, Metadata	UML Models – class diagrams, Relation schemas, instance of CWM Metamodel of the M2 layer
M0	Data, Objects	Data warehouse data

The instance of one layer is modeled by an instance of the next layer. So, the M0 layer, where there are data, is modeled using UML models (such as class diagrams), which are stored in layer M1. Accordingly, M1 is modeled by the UML metamodel, layer 2, and uses constructors such as classes and relationships. This metamodel is an instance of the MOF model (also called meta-metamodel). Another example, a CWM model in layer M1 is an instance of the CWM metamodel of M2. Extensibility is achieved through the possibility of adding classes that are instances of classes of the immediately superior layer.

3.2   The MOF Model

The MOF model, which is in the M3 layer, is presented in this subsection.

The MOF model is its own metamodel, i.e., MOF is described in terms of itself. The MOF specification describes itself using natural language and using UML (*Unified Modeling Language*) [UML2001], tables and OCL (*Object Constraint Language*) expressions. UML is used because of its graphical representation of the models, which makes it easier to read. It does not define the semantics of the MOF model, which is completely defined in the MOF specification and does not depend on any other model. The MOF does not specify which language is to be used to define constraints of the metamodels, even though it uses OCL as standard.

The MOF is an OO (*Object Oriented*) model and includes a set of modeling elements that are used to build the metamodels and rules to use them. Examples of these elements are classes, associations, packages, data types, etc.

3.3   Meta-objects

The interfaces created by the mapping MOF-> *Specific platform* share a common set of four kinds of meta-objects: *instance, class proxy, association* and *package*.

Package – An instance of the *Package* class. A meta-object package represents a container of other kinds of meta-objects.

Class Proxy – Each class in layer M2 has a corresponding class proxy. There is a proxy object to each class of layer M2. This kind of meta-object produces meta-objects of type instance.

Instance – The instances of classes in layer M2, i.e., of the metamodels, are represented by meta-objects of type instance. A meta-object instance manipulates the states of the attributes and references of the classes in layer M2.

Association – Theses objects manipulate the collection of links corresponding to the associations of layer M2. They are static objects and its containers are meta-objects package. The interfaces of the association objects are operations to retrieve a link in the set of links, to add, change, and remove links in the set of links, and to retrieve the set of links.

The MOF -> CORBA IDL/Java Mapping

The MOF -> CORBA IDL mapping is part of the MOF specification. The MOF->Java mapping was defined by the Java Community and was called JMI (*Java Metadata Interface*) [JMI2002]. The general rules of the mapping are basically the same for any platform.

The output of these mappings is a set of interfaces to support creating, changing and querying metadata, instances of the MOF metamodels. For examples, should the interfaces be created using the MOF->CORBA IDL mapping, the user may use CORBA clients to access the interface; should it be JMI, the user may use Java clients.

This subsection describes the inheritance standard of the interfaces mapped from the MOF metamodels. The Figure 1 shows an example of MOF metamodel written in UML, which has two packages P1 and P2. P1 has the C1 and C2 classes, C2 is subclass of C1, and A is an association between C1 and C2. P2 is a sub-package of P1.

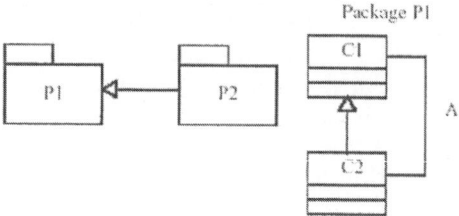

Fig. 1. Example of a MOF metamodel

The Figure 2 presents the UML diagram that shows the inheritance graph generated from the MOF->Java mapping. The root of the graph is a set of interfaces, which are part of the MOF reflexive package. The interfaces generated from the metamodels inherit, directly or indirectly, from the reflexive interfaces.

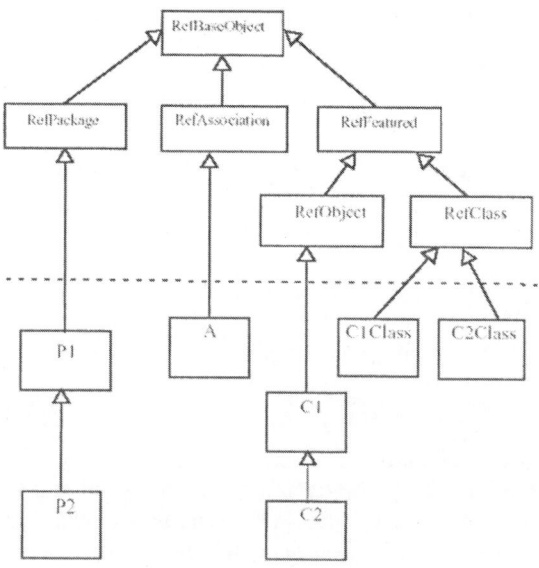

Fig. 2. Example of a MOF Metamodel mapped to Java interfaces

The mapping rules say that, for each package and each association of the metamodel, a *package* interface and an *association* interface are created, respectively. For each class of the metamodel, a *proxy* interface and an *instance* interface are created. The inheritance standard is based on the following rules:

- A meta-object *instance* without a super type inherits from *RefObject*; all other meta-object *instances* extend their super types;
- A meta-object *package* without a super type inherits from *RefPackage*; all other meta-object *packages* extend their super types;
- The meta-object *class proxies* extend *RefClass;* and
- The meta-object *associations* extend *RefAssociation.*

In the examples of Figure 2, two *package* interfaces were created from P1 and P2. The P1 package, which does not have a super type, inherited from *RefPackage*, whereas P2, which does, inherited from P1. The interface for the association between the C1 and C2 classes of the metamodel was created as well. For each class of the metamodel the mapping created two classes: one for the *instance* and another for the *proxy class*. The C1Class and C2Class interfaces represent the *proxy* interfaces created from the classes C1 and C2 of the metamodel, respectively: they inherit from *RefClass* directly. The C1 and C2 interfaces are the interfaces to the meta-objects *instance*. Only the C1 interface inherited from *RefObject*, because it does not have a super type.

4   The RDF and RDF Schema Metamodels

The modeling and implementation of these metamodels used a set of tools and a sequence of steps, which are described below and presented in Figure 3:

- Definition of the metamodels using UML -> because there are no tools to support MOF modeling, we used UML as the standard to represent the metamodels.
- Generation of XMI documents from the metamodels. We used a *Plug-in*[5] of the *Rational Rose* tool, which exports a model of classes to XMI MOF.
- Changing manually the XMI documents. This is necessary because we cannot represent in UML everything that is expressed in MOF. These changes allow for a more adequate XMI representation of the metamodel.
- The XMI metamodels are imported to the MOF repository. This was implemented using the MDR[6] (*Metadata Repository*) tool. It is part of the *Netbeans*[7] tool and implements the MOF standard. At this point, the metamodel is an instance of the MOF metamodel.
- The Java interfaces referring to the XMI metamodel are then created and compiled, following the JMI mapping of MOF metamodels to Java interfaces.
- Interfaces created are then installed as a module of the *Netbeans* tool.
- Implementation of classes to transform metadata written in the specific standards (i.e. RDF and RDF Schema) to their corresponding MOF metamodels.

Any tool that implements the MOF specification may be used in the implementation of the metamodels. We chose the MDR tool because it is open-source and generates JMI interfaces. Moreover it has a browser that shows all objects of the MOF

---

[5] http://www.rational.com/download/

[6] http://mdr.netbeans.org

[7] www.netbeans.org

repository using a graphical interface. Besides, Java is a popular programming language in academic institutions.

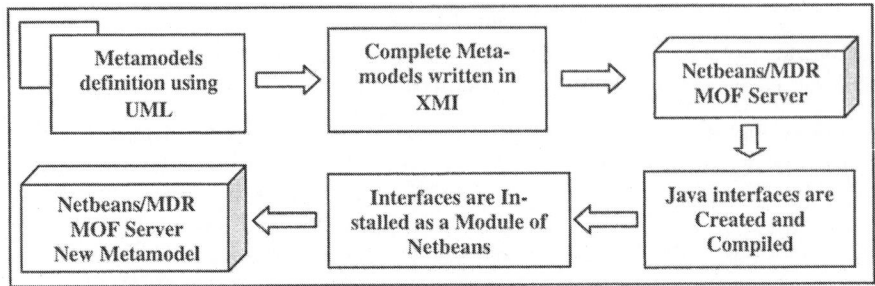

Fig. 3. Steps to model and implement MOF metamodels using MDR

4.1 RDF – Resource Description Framework

The RDF was designed by W3C to describe, interchange and reuse metadata. It is based in Web technology and may be used to describe any subject areas including: electronic resources, Web sites, electronic commerce, groupware, etc [LASW1999, HJE2001, BRAY1998].

RDF binds together two important concepts: metadata and knowledge representation. It describes the relationships among objects, called resources. A resource is any entity that can be identified by an URI (*Uniform Resource Identifier*) [WURI2000]. Examples of resources include Web pages, XML documents, elements of an XML document, a relation of a database, etc.

The description of the relationships among the resources is described using a formal model, which is based in standards for knowledge representation such as semantic nets and in graph theory. They take the form of declarations and sentences and are coded in XML [HJE2001]. RDF has three parts: the data model, the RDF Schema, and the XML codification.

The RDF data model is a graph, where each object (resource) is a node and the arcs between two nodes are properties. This data model allows for the metadata to be interpreted by programs. It is the kernel of the RDF standard. The RDF data are statements coded in XML. This makes them readable both by humans and programs [HJE2001].

4.2 The RDF Metamodel

With the RDF metamodel, users can manage RDF metadata in a MOF repository. This metamodel is presented in Figure 4. Notice that abstract classes are represented in gray.

The most generic class of the metamodel is *RDFResource*. It has an attribute *uri*, which uniquely identifies each resource of the metamodel. Each instance of the metamodel is a resource. The *RDFLiteral* and *RDFNonLiteral* represent literal and non-literal resources, respectively. *RDFLiteral* has an attribute *literaltype* of type

EnumerationType, which represents the type of the literal. Only the basic types such as integer, string, Boolean and decimal have been modeled.

The *RDFDocument* class represents a RDF document. It has some attributes of the RDF document such as version, description, dates of creation and last change, etc. For each RDF document stored in the repository there is a root object, instance of *RDFDocument*.

Classes *RDFContainer, RDFSeq, RDFBag* and *RDFAlt* represent the RDF containers, which offer the means to manipulate collections of resources. The class *RDFContainer* is abstract and is a super class of the others. Class *RDFSeq* refers to sequences of resources, *RDFBag* refers to collections of unordered resources and *RDFAlt* refers to sets of resources.

The *RDFStatement* class refers to RDF Statements, whereas *RDFProperty* refers to properties in the relationships among RDF resources. *RDFNameSpace* represent the namespaces used in the RDF document. Namespaces are used to make it possible for the statements to refer to a particular RDF vocabulary. In practice, each RDF document makes a reference to at least one namespace, the RDF namespace.

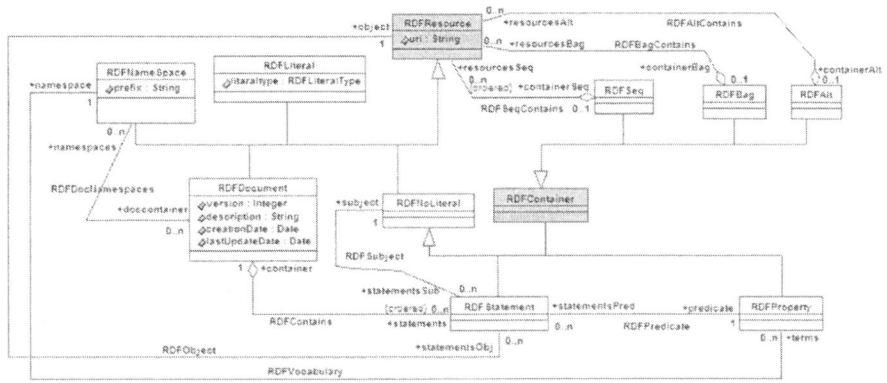

Fig. 4. The RDF Metamodel – RDFMetamodel

Some of the associations are: *RDFDocNamespace*, which associates RDF documents to the namespaces they use; *RDFContains* which associates statements to their container document; *RDFVocabulary* which associates a namespace to its terms. *RDFSubject, RDFObject* and *RDFPredicate* associate a statement to a non-literal resource, a resource, and a property, respectively.

RDFSeqContains, RDFBagContains and *RDFAltContains* associate the different kinds of containers to their resources. Table 2 presents the mapping of the RDF containers to the RDF metamodel.

After creating interfaces using the *MOF-> Java* mapping and JMI, we implemented classes to map RDF documents to RDF metamodel and vice-versa. To export a document, it is necessary to find the document in the MOF repository, browse its statements using the *RDFContains* association and map them to XML.

Table 2. Mapping RDF *containers* to RDFMetamodel

Attributes/MOF Values	Is_ordered	Is_unique	JMI Interfaces
Seq	True	False	*java.util.List*
Bag	False	False	*java.util.Collection*
Alt	False	True	*java.util.Collection*

4.3   RDF Schema

RDF provides a generic model to describe resources, which are any objects identified by an URI. These resources have properties, which are other resources. A set of properties and types of resources is called a vocabulary or ontology [BRGU2000, HJE2001]. RDF uses theses vocabularies but it is not possible to define them using only RDF. To do this, the W3C created RDF Schema. It adds to RDF the power to define vocabularies.

RDF Schema has some basic types and makes it possible to create other types. It uses the RDF data model to define relationships among concepts. RDF Schema makes RDF extensible, making it possible to build vocabularies to specific domain and to share them with other applications.

RDF Schema has a basic vocabulary, which is used to create other vocabularies. It is organized in classes, properties and constraints. Classes allow for the extensibility and reuse, through multiple inheritance. Properties are used to describe relationships among resources, which may be classes and properties – RDF Schema permits relationships among properties.

4.4   The RDF Schema Metamodel

Figure 5 shows the UML representation of the RDF Schema metamodel. The most generic class of this metamodel is *RDFSResource*, which represents a resource in RDF Schema. A resource is any entity, which may be identified by an URI. This class has two attributes: *uri*, the resource URI, and *comment*, for comments about the resource. *RDFSClass* represents classes. A class in RDF Schema is similar to a class in programming languages.

The *RDFSProperty* class refers to properties, and *RDFSDocument* represents the RDF Schema document. Each RDF Schema document has an object, instance of this class. The *RDFSLabel* class refers to labels in RDF Schema. Each resource has one or more labels, which is the way resources are represented in a given language (English, Portuguese, etc). The *RDFSNamespace* class refers to namespace in RDF Schema.

RDF Schema properties have been mapped to MOF associations. For example, *RDFSType* refers to the *type* property and says that a resource, instance of *RDFSResource*, is a member of an instance of *RDFSClass*. Other examples include: *RDFSSubClassOf*, *RDFSSubPropertyOf* and *RDFSIsDefinedBy*. It is important to notice that RDF Schema supports multiple inheritance. *RDFSDocNamespace* associates RDF documents to the namespaces they use and *RDFContains* associates RDF documents to the resource they contain.

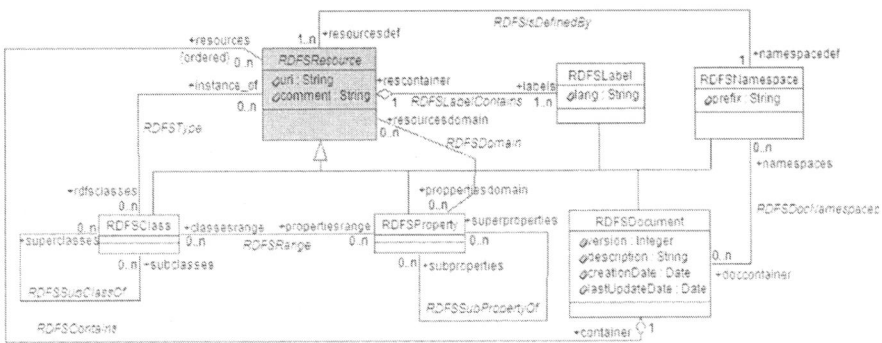

Fig. 5. The RDF Schema metamodel – RDFSMetamodel

After the creation of the *RDFSMetamodel,* the *MOF->Java* mapping was used to create a set of interfaces that make it possible for users to write Java programs that create RDF Schema vocabularies in the MOF repository.

4.5   The Interfaces Created from RDF and RDF Schema Metamodels

Metadata may be written in the repository in two different ways: importing metadata described in XMI documents, or using the interfaces created from the metamodels. These interfaces make it possible to create, update and access instances of the metamodels (i.e. metadata) using Java programs.

Following the steps described in the beginning of Section named "The RDF and RDF Schema Metamodels", we created XMI documents corresponding to the metamodels and, after that, they were imported to the MOF repository using the MDR tool.

As explained before, the MOF specification defines a set of rules to generate interfaces from a specific metamodel. One of the rules says that, for each class of the metamodel, two interfaces are created, for the meta-objects *instance* and *class proxy,* respectively.

Report 1 – The Rdfsnamespace interface of RDFS metamodel

```
Public interface Rdfsnamespace extends
                                    rdfsmetamodel.Rdfsresource{
        public java.lang.String getPrefix();
        public void setPrefix(java.lang.String newValue);
        public rdfsmetamodel.Rdfsdocument getDoccontainer();
        public void  setDoccontainer
                       (rdfsmetamodel.Rdfsdocument newValue);
        public java.util.Collection getResourcesdef();}
```

Report 1 presents the *Rdfsnamespace* interface created from the RDFS metamodel. It defines methods to access and manipulate the state of attributes and references of the *RDFSNamespace* class of RDFS metamodel.

Report 2 presents two proxy interfaces: one to *RDFSResource* and the other to *RDFSNamespace*. The proxy interfaces define operations that create instances of their corresponding classes (if it is not an abstract class).

Report 2 –RdfsresourceClass and RdfsnamespaceClass interfaces of RDFS metamodel

```
public interface RdfsresourceClass extends
                            javax.jmi.reflect.RefClass {    }
public interface RdfsnamespaceClass extends
                            javax.jmi.reflect.RefClass {
    public Rdfsnamespace createRdfsnamespace();
    public Rdfsnamespace createRdfsnamespace(java.lang.String
        uri, java.lang.String comment, java.lang.String prefix);
}
```

For each association in the metamodel, an interface and a set of methots to access, change, and insert instances of the associations are created. Theses instances refer to connections among objects, instances of the classes of the metamodel. The RDFS metamodel has an association called *RDFSContains* that says an object of type *RDFSDocument* may have other resources of type *RDFSResource*. Report 3 shows the *Rdfscontains* interface.

Report 3 –The Rdfscontains interface of RDFS metamodel

```
public interface Rdfscontains extends
                        javax.jmi.reflect.RefAssociation {
    public boolean exists(rdfsmetamodel.Rdfsresource resources,
                        rdfsmetamodel.Rdfsdocument container);
    public java.util.List getResources
                        (rdfsmetamodel.Rdfsdocument container);
    public rdfsmetamodel.Rdfsdocument getContainer
                        (rdfsmetamodel.Rdfsresource resources);
    public boolean add(rdfsmetamodel.Rdfsresource resources,
                        rdfsmetamodel.Rdfsdocument container);
    public boolean remove(rdfsmetamodel.Rdfsresource resources,
                        rdfsmetamodel.Rdfsdocument container);
}
```

For each package of the metamodel an interface containing methods to access all proxy objects referring to all classes and associations of the metamodel is created. Report 4 presents the *RdfsmetamodelPackage* interface, which is the unique package present in the RDFS metamodel.

After the interfaces are created, they must be compiled and installed as a module of the *Netbeans* tool. In some other MOF repositories, it is only necessary to compile the interfaces before they are used in client tools. Next section illustrates the use of the metamodels through the interfaces.

Report 4 –RdfsmetamodelPackage interface of RDFS metamodel

```
public         interface         RdfsmetamodelPackage         extends
javax.jmi.reflect.RefPackage {
  public rdfsmetamodel.RdfsclassClass getRdfsclass();
```

```
public rdfsmetamodel.RdfspropertyClass getRdfsproperty();
public rdfsmetamodel.RdfsdocumentClass getRdfsdocument();
public rdfsmetamodel.RdfsresourceClass getRdfsresource();
public rdfsmetamodel.RdfsnamespaceClass getRdfsnamespace();
public rdfsmetamodel.RdfslabelClass getRdfslabel();
public rdfsmetamodel.Rdfstype getRdfstype();
public rdfsmetamodel.RdfssubClassOf getRdfssubClassOf();
public rdfsmetamodel.RdfssubPropertyOf
                                getRdfssubPropertyOf();
public rdfsmetamodel.RdfsdocNamespaces getRdfsdocNamespaces();
public rdfsmetamodel.RdfslabelContains getRdfslabelContains();
public rdfsmetamodel.RdfsisDefinedBy getRdfsisDefinedBy();
public rdfsmetamodel.Rdfsrange getRdfsrange();
public rdfsmetamodel.Rdfsdomain getRdfsdomain();
public rdfsmetamodel.Rdfscontains getRdfscontains();
}
```

5   Case Study

After the metamodel is installed, the user can write client programs that connect to the MOF repository, get a package of the metamodel and use it to create metadata as instances of the metamodel.

RDF Schema is described in its own terms. So, it is possible to use the RDFS metamodel to store the RDF Schema. It is possible to create RDF Schema documents using the java interfaces created with the *MOF->Java* mapping from RDFS metamodel.

Report 5 – Java Code to create RDFS documents in the MOF repository

```
1 - MDRepository repository =
                 MDRManager.getDefault().getDefaultRepository();
2 - RdfsmetamodelPackage extent =
      (RdfsmetamodelPackage)repository.getExtent("rdfsmetamodel");
3 - if (extent !=null)    {
4 -       repository.beginTrans(true);
5 - Rdfsdocument docroot =
      factorydoc.createRdfsdocument("www.cin.ufpe.br/~hls/rdfs.rdf",
      "RDFS Definition", 1, "RDF Schema Definition in RDF Schema",
                              "01/11/2002","01/11/2002");
}
```

Report 5 presents part of a Java Code to access the RDFS repository implemented by package RDFSMetamodel. The Line 1 of program *MDRManager .getDefault() .getDefaultRepository()* returns the standard repository. It is always going to be the MOF metamodel. Then, it is necessary to search the repository for the appropriate proxy package. The method *repository.getExtent("rdfsmetamodel"),* in line 2, searches for a specific proxy package inside the MOF repository. It receives the package name as parameter and returns a *RefPackage* object. Should the search be successful, next step is to use the package to manage metadata written in RDF Schema.

To create an object in the metamodel, it is necessary to get the reference to the proxy interface of this object. For example, to create a new RDF Schema document it is necessary to get *RdfsdocumentClass*, which is obtained using the method *getRdfsdocument()* of *RdfsmetamodelPackage* package.

RDF Schema uses namespace to make it easier the identification of the resources described in the document. So, it is necessary to create the namespace objects of the document. The kernel of RDF Schema vocabulary is defined in the URI *http://www.w3.org/2000/01/rdf-schema#*, informally called *rdfs*. The kernel of RDF vocabulary is defined in the URI *http://www.w3.org/1999/02/22-rdf-syntax-ns#*, informally called *rdf*.

Both namespaces *rdfs* and *rdf* are used in RDFS documents. The namespace objects of the RDFS metamodel are instances of class *RDFSNamespace*. Report 6 presents the Java Code that creates these objects, as well as the association to the document object. To create a namespace object it is necessary to have its URI as well as the comment, which is inherited from *RDFSResource*.

Report 6 – Creating namespace objects in the repository

```
Rdfsnamespace rdf = factorynamespace.createRdfsnamespace(
                 "http://www.w3.org/1999/02/22-rdf-syntax-ns#",
                                    "rdf namespace","rdf");
Rdfsnamespace rdfs = factorynamespace.createRdfsnamespace(
     "http://www.w3.org/2000/01/rdf-schema#","rdfs namespace",
                                                      "rdfs");
factorydocnamespaces.add(rdf,docroot);
factorydocnamespaces.add(rdfs,docroot);
```

5.1   Creating the Resource Class

After creating the documents and namespaces, it is possible to create the resources defined in the schema. These resources are classes, properties and constraints. The first resource to be created is the class Resource. It is also necessary to connect the resource to the appropriate namespace and RDFS document, which is done by proxy associations *RdfsisDefinedBy* and *Rdfscontains* of the metamodel.

Report 7 presents the Java code that creates the Resource class of RDF Schema, as well as classes *Class* and *Property*.

RDFS also has other classes, which must be created similarly. Some of them are part of the RDF specification, i.e. they are defined in the RDF namespace, and others are part of RDFS.

Report 7 – Creating the Resource class of RDF Schema

```
Rdfsclass resource =
                 factoryclass.createRdfsclass("#Resource","");
factorylabelcontains.add(factorylabel.createRdfslabel(
                         "Resource","","en"),resource);
factorylabelcontains.add(factorylabel.createRdfslabel("Recurso",
                              "","pt"),resource);
```

```
factoryIsDef.add(rdfs,resource);
factorycontains.add(resource,docroot)
Rdfsclass classe = factoryclass.createRdfsclass("#Class","");
factorysubClassof.add(classe,resource);
Rdfsclass property =
                 factoryclass.createRdfsclass("#Property","");
factoryIsDef.add(rdf, property);
factorycontains.add(property,docroot);
```

5.2   Creating Constraints

The RDF standard permits writing statements that restrict the value of some properties and classes. RDF Schema has a way of specifying that a resource is a constraint, namely the classes *ConstraintResource* and *ConstraintProperty*, and properties *range* and *domain*. Report 8 presents the Java code to create these classes and properties. In addition to creating properties and associating them to a namespace and a document, it is necessary to specify that they are instances of class *ConstraintProperty* and to define some constraints about them. For example, the constraints defined about *rdfs:range and rdfs:domain* are:

• The *rdfs:domain* of the *rdfs:range* property is the class *rdf:Property*, instance of *Rdfsclass*. This means that the property rdfs:*range* is applicable to resources of type *rdf:property*;

• The *rdfs:range* of the *rdfs:range* property is the class *rdfs:Class*, instance of *Rdfsclass*.

• The *rdfs:domain* of the *rdfs:domain* property is the class *rdf:Property,* instance of *Rdfsproperty* class. This means that resources of type *rdf:Property* are the possible values of property *rdfs:domain*.

• The *rdfs:range* of the *rdfs:domain* property is the class *rdfs:Class*, instance of *Rdfsclass*.

Report 8 – Creating the constraints classes of RDF Schema

```
Rdfsclass constraintresource =
      factoryclass.createRdfsclass("#ConstraintResource","");
factorysubClassof.add(constraintresource,resource);
Rdfsclass constraintproperty =
      factoryclass.createRdfsclass("#ConstraintProperty","");
factorysubClassof.add(constraintproperty,constraintresource);
Rdfsproperty prange =
                 factoryproperty.createRdfsproperty("#range","");
Rdfsproperty pdomain =
                 factoryproperty.createRdfsproperty("#domain","");
```

The RDF Schema constraints are created through the proxy association *Rdfsrange* and *Rdfsdomain* of the metamodel, as presented in Report 9.

Report 9 – Creating constraints in the repository

```
factorytype.add(prange,constraintproperty);
factorytype.add(pdomain,constraintproperty);
```

```
factorydomain.add(property,prange);
factoryrange.add(classe,prange);
factorydomain.add(property,pdomain);
factoryrange.add(classe,pdomain);
```

5.3   Creating Properties

In addition to the classes already defined, RDF Schema has a set of properties which define the relationship among these classes. These properties are instances of class *Rdfsproperty*.

Report 10 presents the Java code used to create these properties in the MOF repository. Some are defined in the RDF standard, others in RDF Schema. However, they are all used in the RDF Schema document.

Report 10 – Creating properties in the repository

```
Rdfsproperty ptype =
              factoryproperty.createRdfsproperty("#type","");
Rdfsproperty psubclassof =
           factoryproperty.createRdfsproperty("#subClassOf","");
Rdfsproperty psubpropertyof =
         factoryproperty.createRdfsproperty("#subPropertyOf","");
```

5.4   Creating Constraints about Classes and Properties

RDF Schema constraints are used to restrict the use of properties, including RDF Schema properties.

Figure 6 presents the constraints model applied to RDF Schema properties. Report 11 presents the Java code used to create these constraints in the MOF repository.

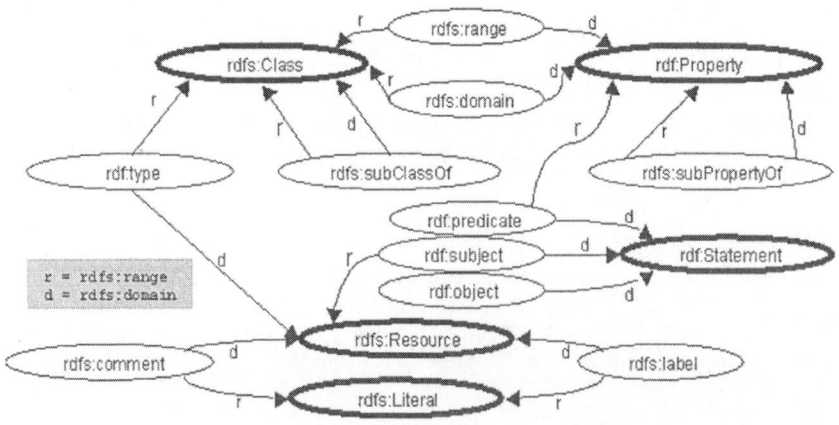

Fig. 6. The RDF Schema Constraints Model [BRGU2000]

Report 11 – Creating RDF Schema constraints model

```
factoryrange.add(classe,ptype);
factorydomain.add(resource,ptype);
factoryrange.add(classe,psubclassof);
factorydomain.add(classe,psubclassof);
factoryrange.add(property,psubpropertyof);
factorydomain.add(property,psubpropertyof);
factoryrange.add(literal,pcomment);
factorydomain.add(resource,pcomment);
factoryrange.add(literal,plabel);
factorydomain.add(resource,plabel);
factoryrange.add(resource,psubject);
factorydomain.add(statement,psubject);
factoryrange.add(property,ppredicate);
factorydomain.add(statement,ppredicate);
factorydomain.add(statement,pobject);
```

In addition to import metadata as XMI documents and to the interfaces generated from the metamodels, users may need to import metadata that are in RDF documents. This is interesting, because users may have tools that already export metadata using these standards. Thus, it would only be necessary to import them to the MOF repository. To achieve this, it is necessary to implement the mapping from the metadata (written in RDF or RDF Schema) to their corresponding metamodels. This is yet another way of interchanging metadata of these metamodels.

6 MOF versus RDF

This section compares MOF to RDF, showing how they relate to each other. Both MOF and RDF are frameworks to model and describe metadata. MOF was specified by OMG and focus in the context of information systems, whereas RDF was specified by W3C and is related to the Web. The main differences and similarities of these two frameworks are listed below:

- Standard for interchanging metadata: MOF metamodels are written in XML using the XMI standard. RDF metadata are also written in XML syntax.
- Extensibility and reuse: MOF is extensible, new MOF metamodels may be created (CWM, UML, RDF, RDF Schema). RDF is also extensible because of RDF Schema. Both of them use inheritance to achieve extensibility. MOF uses package whereas RDF uses namespace to achieve reuse.
- Interoperability: MOF achieves interoperability in two different ways: using software interfaces, where other tools manage the metadata, and through interchanging metadata written in XMI. In RDF, it is only achieved through interchanging models written in XML syntax.
- Object-orientation: MOF é strictly object-oriented, having classes, associations and inheritance. Although RDF is also object-oriented, it is not equivalent to the usual concepts used in programming language. In RDF, properties are defined in terms of the objects, rather than the objects being defined in terms of properties and methods.

It has similarities to knowledge representation on systems such as *Frames* [HJE2001].

• Architecture: MOF has a four-layer architecture suggested by the OMG, where each layer is an instance of the previous one. RDF does not define layers. RDF Schema is the only metamodel available to the users to build any number of models and using any number of layers.

• Objects and resources: In MOF, metadata are represented by object and each object has a unique ID in the repository. In RDF, objects are represented by resources and each resource has an URI (*Uniform Resource Identifiers*), which is unique in the Web.

• Constraints model: Both MOF and RDF have a way of expressing constraints. In MOF, there is the constraint class where the user may write constraints using OCL or other language. These constraints may refer to any component of the metamodel. RDF uses RDF Schema properties range and domain to specify constraints.

7 Conclusion and Future Work

This paper presented the project and implementation of two MOF metamodels to the RDF and RDF Schema standards. It simplifies material from a M.Sc. Dissertation [SAN2003], which also proposed metamodels to XML, DTD and XSLT.

RDF and RDF Schema are semi-structured, platform independent standards appropriate to represent metadata from any sources and closely related to the Web.

From these metamodels, XMI documents have been created. Any MOF repository may support these documents and thus starts to support the management of metadata written in the metamodels.

In addition to the metamodels, instances of them (metadata) may also be imported and exported by any MOF repository. We have also presented a case study showing how the interfaces of these metamodels may be used by other tools to manage RDF and RDF Schema metadata.

As future work, we anticipate that the support to namespaces may be improved, which is important to the identification of RDF Schema vocabularies. The implemented metamodels support namespaces, but there is no consistency to the definitions in the namespace. This could be implemented using OCL or XOCL constraints [RRB2003].

References

[ABK2000]   R. Anderson, M. Birbeck, M. Kay, S. Livingstone, B. Loesgen, D. Martin, A. Mohr, N. Ozu, B. Peat, J. Pinnock, P. Stark, K. Williams. "Professional XML". 2000. Wrox Press.

[AHAY2001]   AHMED, Kal; AYERS, Danny; et al. "Professional XML Metadata". 2001. UK. Wrox Press Ltda.

[BRAY1998]   BRAY, Tim. "RDF and Metadata".
             http://www.xml.com/pub/a/98/06/rdf.html. June, 1998.

[BRGU2000]   BRICKLEY, Dan; GUHA, R.V. "Resource Description Framework (RDF) Schema Specification 1.0 - W3C Candidate Recommendation". In http://www.w3.org/TR/rdf-schema. March, 2000.

[CWM2001]   Common Warehouse Metamodel Specification, Volumes 1 & 2. http://www.omg.org/. See also http://www.cwmforum.org/. February, 2001.

[DEMA2002]   DEDIC, Svata; MATULA, Martin. "Metamodel for the Java language". In: http://java.netbeans.org/models/java/java-model.html. 2002.

[DMOF2001]   "DMof – An OMG Meta Object Facility Implementation". In http://www.dstc.edu.au/Products/CORBA/MOF/. June, 2001.

[HJE2001]   HJELM, Johan. "Creating the Semantic Web with RDF". 2001. New York. John Willey & Sons, Inc.

[JMI2002]   Java Metadata Interface, JSR-40 Home Page: http://java.sun.com/aboutJava/communityprocess/jsr/jsr_040_jolap.html. March, 2002.

[LASW1999]   LASSILA, Ora; SWICK, Ralph R. "Resource Description Framework (RDF) Model and Syntax Specification". In http://www.w3.org/TR/1999/REC-rdf-syntax-19990222/. February, 1999.

[MDA2001]   OMG Architecture Board MDA Drafting Team, "Model-Driven Architecture: A Technical Perspective", ftp://ftp.omg.org/pub/docs/ab/01-02-01.pdf. February, 2001.

[MDR2002]   Sun Microsystems. "Metadata Repository Home" http://mdr.netbeans.org/. 2002.

[MOF1999]   OMG Meta Object Facility Specification, Version 1.3. http://www.dstc.edu.au/Research/Projects/MOF/rtf/. http://www.omg.org/. September, 1999.

[RRB2003]   RAMALHO, Franklin; ROBIN, Jacques; BARROS, Roberto, S. M. "XOCL – An XML language for specifying logical constraints in object oriented models". 7th Brazilian Symposium on Programming Languages. May, 2003.

[SAN2003]   SANTOS, Hélio Lopes. "A metadata solution based on MOF and XML". M.Sc. Dissertation - Centro de Informática/UFPE. March, 2003. In Portuguese.

[UML2001]   OMG Unified Modeling Language Specification, Version 1.4. http://cgi.omg.org/docs/formal/01-09-67.pdf. September, 2001.

[XMI2000]   Object Management Group, XML Metadata Interchange Specification, Version 1.1, http://www.omg.org/. June, 2000.

[WURI2000]   W3C. "Uniform Resource Identifier (URI) Activity Statement". in: http://www.w3.org/Addressing/Activity. July, 2000.

Extending OO Metamodels towards Dynamic Object Roles[1]

Andrzej Jodłowski[1], Piotr Habela[2], Jacek Płodzien[1,3], and Kazimierz Subieta[1,2]

[1] Institute of Computer Science PAS, Warsaw, Poland
[2] Polish-Japanese Institute of Information Technology, Warsaw, Poland
habela@pjwstk.edu.pl
[3] Warsaw School of Economics, Warsaw, Poland
{andrzejj,jpl,subieta}@ipipan.waw.pl

Abstract. This paper discusses some of the implications of introducing the dynamic object role concept into object-oriented metamodels on both implementational and conceptual modeling levels in a coordinated way. The notion is expected to become one of the most fundamental constructs of an object data model and our research concerning object query languages allows us to state that it can be cleanly incorporated into existing object models. On the other hand the total cost of introducing the new notion needs to be considered. Thus, in this paper we look for a lightweight way of introducing object roles, depending as far as possible on already existing and popular concepts. Looking at the issue from the object database point of view, we discuss the necessary extensions and emphasize the importance of direct support of implemented notions from the means of conceptual modeling.

1 Introduction

Dynamic roles are a powerful mean of conceptual modeling that seems to fit especially well the object data model, by making it truly capable of expressing the interrelationships among real world entities. The notion is well known from numerous papers and a general agreement concerning its main conceptual features seems to exist. However, it still has not gained the level of acceptance that would allow standardization and a broader application.

Our research concerning the dynamic object roles [7, 15], allowed us to better understand a number of significant advantages of the new construct over the traditional means of modeling. We have also proposed the way of implementing the support for roles in object-oriented database management systems (ODBMS) and query language. However, despite the promising features, the popularization of the dynamic roles seems to be difficult due to their impact on an object data model. Both the power of this notion as well as the problems with it come from the fact it is neither just modeling feature nor just a programming construct. Instead, similarly like several other object-oriented concepts, it influences both modeling and implementation areas,

---

[1] Supported by the European Commission 5th Framework project ICONS (Intelligent Content Management System); no. IST-2001-32429.

R. Meersman et al. (Eds.): CoopIS/DOA/ODBASE 2003, LNCS 2888, pp. 1032–1047, 2003.
© Springer-Verlag Berlin Heidelberg 2003

which need to be considered together in order to make the notion truly productive. For those reasons, in this paper we look for the necessary data model and implementational environment extensions, taking into consideration the cost of their introduction and thus trying to align them as far as possible with already popular solutions. To establish a uniform view of the notion in both abovementioned areas, we attempt to model it as an explicit part of a common object-oriented metamodel.

One of the impediments is the additional complexity of a data model introduced by the new notion. Even today's object oriented metamodels on both modeling and implementation levels (see e.g. [12, 3]) are already very complex, and the cost of more powerful abstractions impacts the related tools, especially the DBMSs. All concepts of a chosen data model have to be implemented in DBMSs, effectively managed by their mechanisms and well understood by developers and administrators. Thus, any extension to such data model leads to a question if its benefits justify the additional complexity. For those reasons, a number of modeling notions that proved to be relatively complex while less essential (like e.g. n-ary associations) are not supported by implementation tools. This in turn makes them being rather seldom used by analysts and designers, who prefer constructs that can be more directly mapped into implemented structures.

The dynamic object role notion does not fall into this category. The first observation is that, if introduced, this would be a fundamental notion of a data model [13] rather than an extension or variation of some existing one. Secondly, as will be shown, it allows to cleanly solve a number of problems that occur with traditional approaches. Despite the notion is well motivated, the overall productivity of the proposed solution is strongly dependent on the way it is realized both in modeling and (especially) implementation. Thus, our assumptions are following:

- In order to benefit from already widely used solutions, it is desirable to introduce the notion with minimum extensions and impact on the existing concepts. For example, the amount of necessary changes and extensions of the UML metamodel can give an idea on the cost of particular proposal.
- The related implemented well-formedness rules (e.g. within a database schema) should provide some protection against programmers' errors, but on the other hand should not restrict the potential flexibility of the dynamic roles.
- The ability of the notion to support issues other than those of conceptual modeling, e.g. separation of concerns or metadata management, needs to be investigated.

The paper is organized as follows. In order to explain the starting point and justify the assumptions presented here, section 2 briefly presents the motivation behind introducing the dynamic object role as an explicit new notion (thus suggesting the necessary features) and provides a very brief summary of our approach to dynamic roles within an ODBMS, which has been discussed in [7]. Section 3 enumerates commonly used constructs that bear semblance of dynamic roles, providing the background of our discussion. Section 4 contains our proposals and considerations concerning extensions to the modeling language, ODBMS data definition language, database schema and query language. Section 5 concludes.

2 Dynamic Object Roles – Basic Assumptions

This section, based on our previous research, is introduced to explain the context of this work. The first subsection enumerates the main features of the notion, while the following section discusses the issues of modeling that may benefit from applying it. The third subsection summarizes our approach to the development of an ODBMS, including a pragmatically complete query language to manipulate its contents. Those two elements, that is, a modeling language and an ODBMS constitute a fairy complete framework, which allows us to analyze the total impact of the introduction of dynamic object roles.

2.1 Motivation behind the Dynamic Role Notion

The situation where some entity can possess a number of different roles is ubiquitous in modeling. Although in some problem domains this may be not distinct (as they address only a certain aspect of a particular object's existence), in fact many occurrences of specialization relationship among classes constitute a (perhaps acceptable) simplification of the dependency that is in fact a dynamic role. For example, an information system of some university could model the class *Student* as the specialization of the class *Person*. Such a solution is practical only under the following conditions:

- Only one aspect of that person's existence (in this case – being a student) is within the domain of interest of the system. The other aspects (e.g. student's employment) do not need to be modeled.
- The system is not required to model a given person's data before or after the period of his/her being a student. That is, an object's migration from the *Student* class to some other class does not have to be supported.

If a certain object is described by several statically determined aspects (e.g. a vehicle classified according to its environment, powering system, purpose etc.), the traditional multiple inheritance can be used. However, with a larger number of such "dimensions" this approach results in a large number of rather artificial classes, some of which are not populated. Moreover, potential property name conflicts need to be faced. Thus, even in case of a truly static classification, the use of multiple inheritance can be problematic. If a system has to handle dynamically assignable roles (e.g. an *employee* role of person, a *project leader* role of an employee), then inheritance is not applicable: traditionally, association or aggregation is used to connect (a "base") object with objects describing its roles. This provides the necessary flexibility, however it is unnatural as a role is inherently dependent on its base object's identity and often also on its properties (including possible overriding). Thus the relationship of being a role lies somewhere between association and inheritance, while it is not satisfactorily describable by either of them.

In addition to the above problems relevant to conceptual modeling, the dynamic role notion can be also promising for some patterns and solutions at the design and implementation level. To sum up, the concept realizes the following features:

- Provides the expressive power of multiple inheritance, while avoiding name conflicts and combinatorial increase of the number of subclasses.
- Supports multiple-aspect classification and its maintenance by cleanly isolating code and data related with particular aspects.
- Allows for repeating classification (by having two or more roles of the same type).
- Covers the *variant* (or *union*) concept (known from e.g. C++ and CORBA): it can be achieved by modeling each variant branch as a role.
- Can realize object migration in a very flexible way: object's properties can be changed partly or completely (as if it were re-created under another class), while maintaining its identity.
- Provides a mean to realize the separation of concerns postulate in the spirit of AOP (Aspect-Oriented Programming). Each aspect can be encapsulated as a separate role, which would provide appropriate data and e.g. active rules.
- Similarly, it provides a convenient way to attach additional metadata to objects.

Thus, also a number of tasks that are more of technical than purely conceptual nature can be elegantly handled by roles.

2.2 Modeling with Dynamic Roles: Practical Applications

The need for the dynamic object roles is most distinct in complex systems, whose subjects have to be described in several different contexts. Another important reason is the need for dealing with complex lifecycles of objects. Although in that case using associations provides the necessary flexibility, this causes additional fragmentation and complicates data access.

An interesting and very distinct example motivating the use of dynamic object roles we have encountered in our work was a project for a Polish governmental institution dealing with regulations and investigations of the capital market. The investigations concerned various forms of data mining, making summary reports and checking legality of investors' operations on the market. Typical entities identified in the business domain were the following: person, broker, investment advisor, organizational unit, company, stock instrument, share, stock session, stock transaction, stock order, brokering house, document, legal regulation, and so on. The following characteristics of the system made it difficult to model using traditional notions (see also [15]):

- Some objects have many specializations at the same time. (e.g. a person being an employee and a broker simultaneously).
- Some objects have many specializations of the same type (e.g. a person being a member of many boards of directors at the same time).
- Some objects have specializations that depend on time. For instance, a person who was a broker a year ago, may currently be the director of a company. Furthermore, a person can be a broker several times, at different times and brokering houses.

The issue is not limited to people-related information. Similar problems, mostly related to recording historical information,[2] have also occurred with entities such as institutions, companies and documents.

The above example may suggest the dynamic roles are especially applicable to the systems covering broad problem domains. However, taking into account that a database may serve several different applications, the need to model different roles of particular subject seems to occur quite frequently.

2.3   Assumed Implementation Model

In this subsection we attempt to summarize our approach to the development of an ODBMS, focusing on the features making it different from the popular solutions in the spirit of the ODMG standard [3]. The main concern of that research is the development of a full-fledged object-oriented query language equipped with imperative constructs, which makes it a sufficient mean of programming ODBMS-based applications. For this reason we do not consider integrating the roles with general-purpose programming languages. This solution allows to avoid the so-called "impedance mismatch" between a programming language and a query language. Another benefit is the ability to define a cleaner object model, independent on the design of those languages.

The following features of the proposed query language are important for its ability to incorporate the dynamic role notion:

- Any object (including sub-objects serving as attributes) is bound in a query by its instance name. The notion of *extent* is not used. A role, represented as an object can be treated analogously.
- The behavior of language's operators and their scoping rules are precisely defined using the notion of environment stack. Particularly, the features of the static generalization hierarchy like inheritance and overriding can be easily described this way. The same mechanism can be useful for dynamic inheritance provided by roles.
- The presence of transitive closure operators makes it easier to process multi-level hierarchies, dynamic roles can form.

The language assumes a generic[3] object store model, having the following properties (see Fig. 1):

- Any object has its own (not unique) name, a unique identifier and contents. Moreover (not shown in Fig. 1) it needs to indicate its type (if necessary, accompanied by class).
- An object contents can be either a collection of other (nested) objects, a primitive value (e.g. string, number, image) or a reference to an object.

---

[2] Despite this observation we do not assume the temporal information should be a predefined property of every object role, since the feature is rather domain-specific and can be explicitly modeled where necessary.

[3] It forms a base that does not prescribe any particular object model. Thus, appropriate metamodel needs to be defined over it. Important design decisions concerning e.g. the class mechanism and the features of dynamic roles have to be made there.

- The instance name of every "root" object is added to the environment, so it can be bound analogously like a global variable and thus may serve as a starting point for querying.

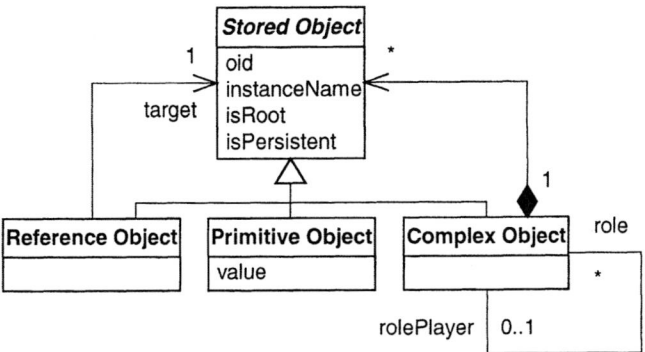

Fig. 1. A conceptual view of an object store model extended to support dynamic roles

As can be seen, to support dynamic roles, this model requires a new separate kind of relationship between objects, which can be called "is-a-role-of". A more detailed discussion of the store model and language semantics extensions for dynamic roles can be found in [7]. While in such a model many important details remain open, we decided to hold the following assumptions:

- The "is-a-role-of" relationship can connect only complex objects. It can form pure hierarchies only (each role can have further own roles, but no cycles are allowed).
- Every role belongs to exactly one object. As a result it can *inherit dynamically* and *dynamically override* the base object's properties, but it occurs only when the access is performed through this role. In other words, the query execution environment can differ, depending on the name of a base object or a name of one of its roles was used.
- The requirement for a role to be connected with its base object brings appropriate referential integrity constraints for copying and deletion operators.
- Since each role has its own unique identifier, it can be the target of reference from other object or an operation parameter.

This model served as a base for the implementation of our prototype system, consisting of an object store, schema repository and a query language interpreter.

3 Popular Solutions Related to the Dynamic Role Mechanism

Since we intend to fit the notion into traditional object data models, this section provides an overview of popular solutions related to the dynamic object role concept. On the other hand, the summary of the research concerning the dynamic object roles has been intentionally skipped here.

The case of a dynamic object role in modeling can be described as a single object having different sets of properties connected with particular aspects of its existence. As mentioned, in case of a multiple yet static classification, the most straightforward of traditional approaches to address it would be a multiple inheritance. At the same time however, this solution bears the largest number of problems and limitations:

- Possibility of name conflicts among inherited features.
- Inability to dynamically reclassify object.
- Inability to describe more than one role of the same type (e.g. instance of a class *Employee* or *Student-Employee* can not store information on a person's employment in two different companies).
- Combinatorial growth of the number of classes.

Note that in absence of multiple inheritance the situation is even worse, since code reuse is limited. That is, it becomes necessary to create unrelated "copy & paste" class definitions, instead of the natural code reuse through class specializations.

The above remarks confirm that mixing different aspects of a given object's description into a single class is not a proper approach. The conceptual modeling notions offer in this case more flexibility. The UML (Unified Modeling Language) [12] allows for specifying different specialization hierarchies for each criteria and even marking some of them dynamic. Such multidimensional classification results in a much clearer model. However, this part of the UML specification is not very detailed and, what is the most important, implementation tools do not support such features, thus the model loses its clarity during implementation.

Another notion bearing some of the desired features are Java's inner classes. Such a class is defined within the scope of its outer (base) class and its instances possess links to their base objects (being the instances of the outer class). Thus such an inner class can access properties of its base class in a way similar as if it were a subclass. Instances of an inner class can be referenced either from inside of a base class's object (that is, being its attributes) or anywhere outside its base object (in the latter case making it unaware of its dependent instances). Thus the following properties, resembling the dynamic object role concept, can be noted:

- Inner class can encapsulate some distinguished parts of object properties.
- Inner class's methods have access to the state and behavior of the base object as if they were defined in the outer class or its subclass.
- Arbitrary number of inner class instances connected with a given object can be created or removed during runtime.
- Instances of inner class connected with a given object of outer class are separated from each other, so no name conflict can occur.

As can be seen, the construct has many interesting features and can be useful in partitioning and encapsulating object's properties. However, this notion is quite far from widely agreed features of dynamic object roles in the following terms:

- There are no means of reassigning an inner class object to be connected with another outer class's instance.
- Creating an inner class definition requires access to the code of the outer (base) class. This breaks the "Open-Closed" principle [10] concerning class design.

- Private properties of an outer class are accessible to inner class's methods, which is probably undesirable in case of an object role.
- The inner class's access to the properties of outer class does not provide the former with interface of the outer class. Thus there is no substitutability between outer and inner class's instances.

Despite those limitations, the notion of Java's inner class seems to be the nearest to the dynamic object role concept from among of the broadly known solutions.

Other interesting features come from the AOP [9] language extensions. Its mission is to deal with so-called *crosscutting concerns*, being the features of software, which are difficult or impossible to modularize using classes, methods or procedures. They are often related with various kinds of non-functional requirements, like e.g. persistence, security, synchronization, real-time constraints or logging, whose implementation is usually scattered among different fragments of code, which makes it less readable and complicates its maintenance. The solution offered by the AOP is an abstraction called *aspect*, used to modularize a given concern in a way that does not affect the base code. This provides a kind of additional design "dimension", which becomes integrated into the application during the compilation phase, by a mechanism called *aspect weaver*. Particularly, the well known Java-based implementation of the AOP paradigm, called AspectJ [1], provides two general means of isolating such properties:

- **"Pointcut" and "Advice" Declarations** modify certain elements of program's control flow by augmenting or bypassing the statements of specified kind.
- **Class Structure Modification Using *Introduction*.** This mechanism allows for modifying definition of a given class, both in terms of behavior (new or overridden methods) as well as the structure (additional attributes). This includes possibility to modify inheritance hierarchy by making existing class extend other class or to implement a certain interface. All these changes can be achieved by declarations located outside the considered class.

The latter feature allows to isolate properties introduced to a class design on behalf of certain aspect or role of object's existence. However, it is necessary to note that this mechanism is purely static and, although very powerful and advantageous in terms of maintenance, it is not suitable for implementing dynamic object roles. Its capabilities in this area seem to be analogous to static multiple inheritance.

Although the modeling languages tend to be richer in terms of provided notions than implementational tools, the UML does not support a notion similar to the dynamic object role. It uses the term "role" in several other meaning; most commonly to describe an object's participation in association link or its position within a *collaboration* of objects. The necessary semantics of dynamic object role can be neither expressed precisely nor conveniently without extending the language.

As can be seen, despite there are a number of already adapted similar solutions, the notion of dynamic object role is not satisfactorily addressed, which is the case both in modeling and implementation. It is currently implemented and even modeled in an indirect and rather low-level way (see e.g. [5]).

Considering the fundamental importance of that notion, it is possible to conclude that the dynamic roles should be introduced as a separate new construct both into modeling and into implementation languages and the DBMS area.

4 Extending the Framework to Incorporate Roles

In this section we discuss the features of a modeling language, metadata management and a query language, necessary to support roles. The following issues are considered:

- Augmenting the conceptual view of ODBMS metamodel with the role-specific elements and necessary constraints. This directly concerns the shape of a data definition language and indirectly – also the features of a query language.
- Providing conceptually compatible support from the side of a modeling notation.
- Identifying new patterns that can be realized using the introduced notion.

4.1 Augmenting the DBMS Metamodel with the Role Notion

It is necessary to note that the issue of an ODBMS metamodel brings a number of specific problems that do not occur e.g. in modeling languages' metamodels and thus the metadata structure like this suggested in the ODMG standard [3] may need to be significantly redesigned to successfully meet all the requirements related to a database schema (see [6] for detailed discussion). However, the problem does not impact the conceptual view of the core elements of the object data model, so we can assume the ODMG and UML metamodels with their popular understanding of the notions of class, association, attribute, operation etc. to be an appropriate starting point for our discussion.

As mentioned, it is usually assumed that roles should be able to complement all kinds of properties the base object possesses (e.g. attributes, association links, behavior (operations), as well as the ability to have their own roles). This requires supporting them with a specification similar to that of a regular object. That is, an interface specifying role properties and a class implementing them are necessary. Additionally, the role type definition brings an additional constraint: role needs to be connected with its base (also called "player"), which can be a regular object or another role. Moreover, if a role is treated as a property a base object is aware of, a role multiplicity (like in case of attribute or association link), as well as applicability to exactly one base class (the latter constraint is called "player qualification" in [16]) can be considered. Following this path requires very little change to existing metamodels. Taking the UML metamodel as an example of the mainstream object data model, we would suggest the following extension as shown in Fig. 2:[4] *RoleClass* becomes a special kind of *Class*, distinguished by the fact that its instances cannot be instantiated in separation from their base objects.

An important question concerning constraints imposed on the dynamic object role construct is if a schema really should specify (and allow) exactly one class as a type of a base object for each role specification. This constraint seems to be justified by the following reasons:

---

[4] Analogous properties were introduced in the data definition language (DDL) of our prototype implementation. The only difference was, that following the ODMG terminology the base for our extension was the notion of *Interface*, not *Class*.

- A role is indeed usually defined to extend the properties of exactly one object type. If there are more related types, they should have something in common, so their generalization could be used as a role's base.
- Operations provided by a role interface can have their implementation dependent on particular properties (operations, attributes and association links) of the base object.
- Since a reference to a role is intended to support its base object's features, assuring that such inheritance will took a place requires appropriate type constraint.

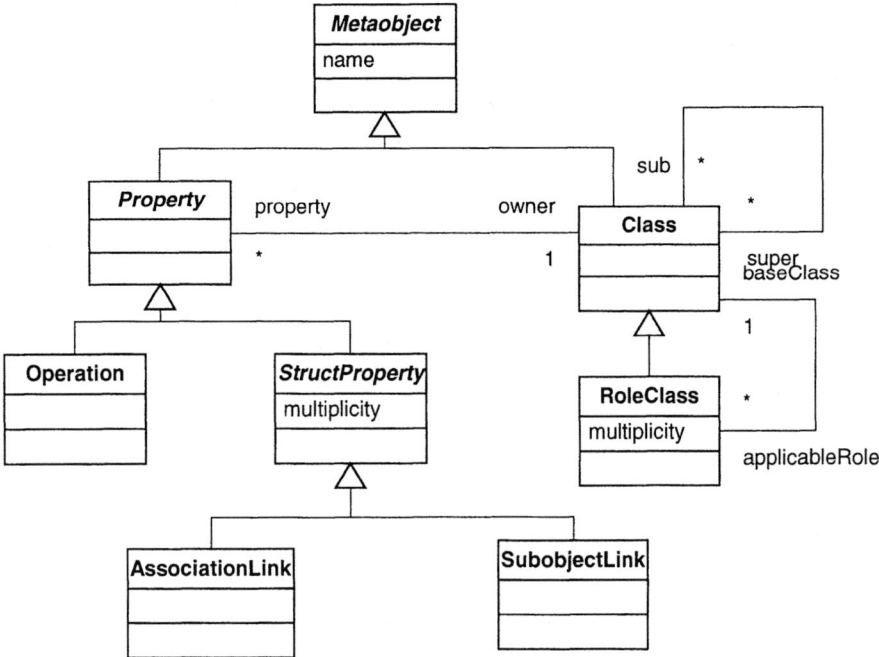

Fig. 2. Role concept incorporated into the conceptual metamodel (fragment). Note in this view a structural similarity of traditional static inheritance (sub-super relationship between classes) and dynamic inheritance (realized by a role).

On the other hand, also more "loosely" connected roles can be considered. Such roles would make no assumptions on their base objects' types and serve as "handles" or "labels" for a number of otherwise unrelated objects. This brings another question: assuming we would allow defining roles that make no assumptions on their base objects' properties, is the base class specification necessary for them? Summing up, this would lead towards much less restrictive typing constraints concerning the roles or to the need to distinguish two flavors of object roles.

Fortunately, we can achieve a satisfactory flexibility of the introduced notion while keeping the seemingly restrictive constraint of only one base class allowed, thanks to the following solutions:

- A single-rooted class hierarchy can be assumed (as e.g. in case of Java language, where all classes inherit from a predefined class *Object*). In that case all universally applicable roles can be specified as the roles of such root class.
- If some role can be applied to several specific base classes having no direct generalization, the properties of such role can be grouped within an abstract class, and specific role classes for each base can be defined as specialization of this abstract class (see Fig. 3; notation is described in the next subsection).

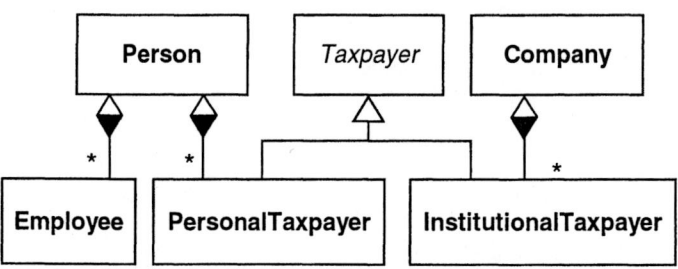

Fig. 3. Dynamic role dependency mixed with static inheritance (the details of notation are described in the next sub-section)

As the example (Fig. 3) suggests, the dynamic inheritance realized by roles can be freely combined with static inheritance. Two intuitive constraints seem to be necessary though:

- The combination of static and dynamic inheritance should not form cycles. Although there could be some interesting and perhaps useful effects of such structure, it does not seem worth of additional complexity and possible confusions.
- A regular class cannot be a specialization of role class. That is, the restriction of not having independent instances (assumed for a role class) is a constraint that should be inherited.[5]

4.2   Supporting the Role Notion in a Modeling Language

This task could be relatively easy, assuming the extensions for ODBMS and modeling language metamodel are coordinated. A natural choice for supporting notation here is the UML and the extension of its metamodel can be performed exactly as suggested in the above subsection. In that case we can benefit greatly from the postulate of possibly lightweight extension: since the *RoleClass* specializes UML's *Class* concept, we can reuse the class notation for role-classes and object notation for roles (Fig. 4). No special symbol for a *RoleClass* is necessary, since the presence of role dependency relationship distinguishes it from a regular class.[6] We only need to introduce a unique

---

[5] For example, if *Employee* is a role of *Person* and *Employee* is specialized into *Clerk*, then the *Clerk* class can only be instantiated as a role of some person, not as an independent object.

[6] The only problem with *role class* identification occurs if a given diagram does not show all the classes and skips some role's base class. In such case we suggest marking the role class with the "is-a-role-of" relationship symbol with ellipsis on its "base" end.

symbol to indicate the "is-a-role-of" relationship at the object level and "role depend-ency" (shows a given role's applicability to objects of *particular class*) at the class level. Similarly like in case of UML's *aggregation* or *composition* we can use the same symbol on both levels.

The symbol of the "is-a-role-of" relationship was intentionally chosen to resemble both generalization (triangular arrow) and composition (filled diamond) [8] notation of UML, since the role relationship is characterized by the mix of their properties:

- The way of overriding or augmenting the base object's properties by its role bears semblance to static inheritance and is similarly realized within the stack semantics [7].
- The requirement for role to be connected to exactly one player as well as the tran-sitiveness of the "is-a-role-of" relationship, and e.g. the deletion propagation from player to its roles, make the relationship similar to UML's *composition* with multi-plicity fixed to "exactly one". Thus, we need only one multiplicity specification for each role dependency, namely the one referring to the multiplicity attribute of *RoleClass*.

Another benefit of maintaining a straightforward mapping between the UML metamodel and the conceptual view of an ODBMS metamodel would be easier inte-gration of the latter with the UML-inspired Meta Object Facility (MOF) model, being the central element of the Model Driven Architecture (MDA) initiative [11].

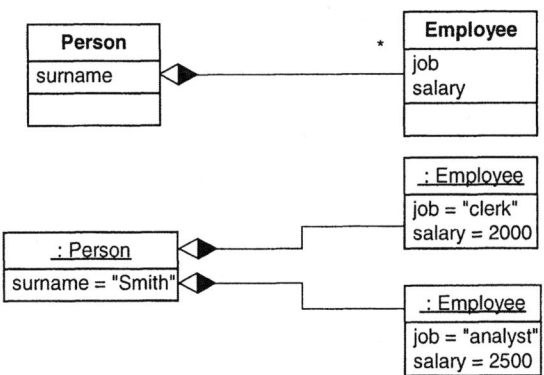

Fig. 4. Examples of applying the proposed extended UML notation to model dynamic object roles on the class level (role dependency relationship) and the object level (the "is-a-role-of" relationship)

4.3   Dynamic Roles: The Impact of a Data Model Extension

When considering the design of the role mechanism and weighting the related costs, it is worth to remind a very important idea of programming languages, known as "the principle of correspondence" [2]. It can be described as follows: any new feature in-troduced to the data model, requires considering its influence on binding mechanisms and its composition with other constructs of the language. This remark makes it clear, that extending today's already complex object models can be very costly. On the other hand, it can be significantly reduced thanks to the "reuse" of already present features. For those reasons we choose to make possibly small extensions to existing traditional metamodel.

The benefits of such approach could already be observed in case of the modeling language. As shown in the above subsection, we were able to achieve the necessary expressive power by introducing only one new symbol, taking advantage of some similarities with already present relationships (namely – generalization and composition). Although a number of additional properties can be considered (e.g. mutual exclusion of some roles connected to the same object), they do not seem to be worth the additional complexity. Analogous situation occurs for the DDL, since in our approach its statements need to have similar information content.

The similarities of the "is-a-role-of" relationship with the notions of generalization, association or UML's composition are very useful, however following them too closely may be misleading. We have identified the following differences:

- In contrast to associations the "is-a-role-of" relationships may not form cycles.
- Also the "role dependency" relationships may form cycles neither alone nor in combination with the static generalization. Such a structure is problematic and does not seem to be useful.
- Despite the inheritance of base object's properties, substitutability between a role and its base object does not occur. An attribute of a base object may be overridden by an attribute or link of the same name but of different type, defined in a role class.
- Method polymorphism is not extended over the dynamic inheritance provided by object roles. In other words, if an object is bound by its own name, its behavior is not influenced by the properties of its roles.

Although the abovementioned rules apply only to rather very specific situations, the difference between static "generalization-specialization" and roles needs to be well understood. As the example below (Fig. 5) illustrates, the "is-a-role-of" relationship indeed does not imply the properties of the "is-a" relationship. Note that if an instance of the presented structure is accessed through the role *Employee*, the result is not compatible with the *Person* class. The result would then include the *job* attribute being the structure *JobDescription* (e.g. some detailed job description used in a given company) instead of the *String* type value expected for a *Person*. On the other hand, if an object having a role *Employee* is accessed directly (that is, using the "Person" name), calling *calculateTax()* method on it would execute the code defined in the class *Person* (any roles attached to that object would be then ignored).

All those rules need to be explicitly defined as the constraints in the metamodel.

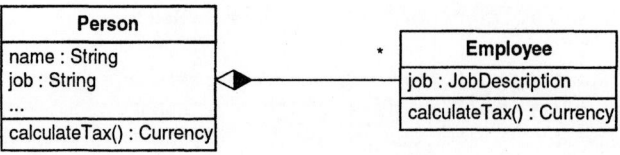

Fig. 5. A role dependency showing the difference between static inheritance related with specialization and dynamic inheritance provided by dynamic roles

Concerning the query language, we found it necessary to introduce or modify the following operators:

- The role-casting operator is necessary to make explicit conversions between a role and its base object, between base object and its role or among different roles of the same object.[7] For example (using a popular cast operator syntax) a query selecting all the persons having both *Student* and *Employee* roles could be formulated as follows. First the *Student* roles that coexist in the same tree with *Employee* roles are selected; then, the *Person* objects owning those roles are extracted:[8]

  (Person) ((Student) Employee)

- The "has role" operator, checking if a given object has at least one role of provided name.
- The "roles" operator, returning references to all direct roles of a given object.
- Other important language operators include adding and dropping a role.
- Copying and deleting objects that have roles should be propagated to their roles, to protect referential integrity.

4.4   Other Applications of the Role Construct

Finally, it is desirable to investigate all the possible combinations of newly introduced notion with already present constructs in order to identify possibly useful patterns. Here we can briefly present two interesting applications mentioned in section 2.

One example can be the issue of ontology, that is, the description of local resources required in integration of distributed systems and for mobile agent software. Particularly, the assumed interpretation of local data, which is hardwired into local system's software needs to become explicit to make the system's resources meaningful for external parties. Such descriptive elements, referred to as metadata, can be domain-specific (like e.g. the measure used to express the sizes of clothes) or may rather constitute a very general resource description, as it is the case for the Dublin Core Metadata Element Set (DCMES) [4]. This is an example of context-specific information, which may be unnecessary for local applications but critical for others. Moreover, it may be necessary to isolate the existing local applications form the impact of introducing of such descriptions. This would make the object roles an optimum choice. Note also that significant part of such metadata (especially this defined by DCMES) is rather instance-specific (e.g. resource's creator, source, language) and therefore can be stored with no redundancy within dynamic object roles, which would separate and partition it according to the needs of particular data access context.

Another application of dynamic object roles, located rather outside the conceptual modeling area, is the realization of AOP mechanism within a DBMS environment. Although a DBMS fixes a number of non-functional aspects that remain open in general-purpose programming languages, the aspect paradigm remains relevant here, and dynamic object roles seem to be well suited to provide a base for it. If the repertoire of properties traditionally defined within a class was augmented with the notion of

---

[7] Since we allow object to possess more than one role of a given name, the operator would return several role references for such object.

[8] The operator is assumed to collect results from all levels of role hierarchy (thus accessing also indirect roles).

active rule, the role-classes using this feature may be used as a very flexible mean to implement aspects.

5 Conclusions and Future Work

The dynamic object role is an example of a prominent notion, which is very likely to augment the currently used modeling and implementation languages. Although it bears semblance to several broadly used notions, the role concept is unique and thus requires dedicated solutions to support it in modeling and software development. Since it constitutes an extension of a core data model, a number of different areas have to be considered. Among them are the following:

- conceptual modeling, including a graphical notation;
- consistent and preferably limited change to an original metamodel definition;
- DBMS query language constructs;
- database object store model;
- possible usage of newly introduced concept in modeling and extending different kinds of metadata.

Introduced notion needs to take into account and adjust to pre-existing solutions, however only as far as such compliance does not appear to be a limiting factor. In this paper the intended shape of the considered dynamic object role concept respecting the abovementioned assumptions has been outlined. We suggest a modest extension to DBMS and modeling language metamodels, which introduces a special kind of dependency between the class describing a role and the class describing its player (being another role or a regular object). This dependency (constituting a specific mix or inheritance and composition features) restricts applicability of particular role to appropriate type (class) of its player. Taking into account the overall overhead of introducing the new construct, we intentionally follow a rather lightweight approach to define it.

The prototype of basic DBMS functionality with roles has been developed to verify our object store model proposal and appropriate stack-based approach [14] extensions. Since no typing constraints have been implemented so far, we are now going to experiment with the solutions discussed here. We are also going to further investigate the use of the role mechanism as a base to implement aspects in an ODBMS environment as well as the use of roles to encapsulate metainformation necessary for distributed databases.

References

1.   The AspectJ project homepage. http://aspectj.org
2.   M. Atkinson, R. Morrison. Orthogonally Persistent Object Systems. The VLDB Journal, 4(3), 1995, pp. 319–401.
3.   R. G. G. Cattell, D. K. Barry: The Object Data Standard: ODMG 3.0. Morgan Kaufmann 2000.
4.   Dublin Core Metadata Element Set, Version 1.1. http://dublincore.org/documents/

5.   M. Fowler. Dealing with Roles. http://www.martinfowler.com/ (an update to: Analysis Patterns: Reusable Object Models. Addison-Wesley 1996).
6.   P. Habela, M. Roantree, K. Subieta: Flattening the Metamodel for Object Databases. Advances in Databases and Information Systems, 6th East European Conference, ADBIS 2002, Bratislava, Slovakia, September 8–11, 2002, Proceedings. Lecture Notes in Computer Science 2435 Springer 2002.
7.   A. Jodłowski, P. Habela, J. Płodzie , K. Subieta: Objects and Roles in the Stack-Based Approach. DEXA 2002: 514–523.
8.   A. Jodłowski, J. Płodzie , E. Stemposz, K. Subieta: Introducing Dynamic Object Roles into the UML Class Diagram, materiały konferencji IASTED International Conference on Software Engineering and Applications (SEA), ACTA Press, ss. 629–634, Cambridge, MA, USA, 2002.
9.   G. Kiczales, J. Lamping, A. Mendhekar, Ch. Maeda, C. Videira Lopes, J.-M. Loingtier, J. Irwin: Aspect-Oriented Programming. ECOOP 1997: 220–242.
10. R. C. Martin. Design Principles and Design Patterns. http://www.objectmentor.com/
11. Object Management Group: Meta Object Facility (MOF) Specification. Version 1.4, April 2002 [http://www.omg.org].
12. Object Management Group: Unified Modeling Language (UML) Specification. Version 1.4, September 2001 [http://www.omg.org].
13. F. Steimann: On the representation of roles in object-oriented and conceptual modelling. DKE 35(1): 83–106 (2000).
14. K. Subieta, C. Beeri, F. Matthes, J. W. Schmidt: A Stack-Based Approach to Query Languages. East/West Database Workshop 1994: 159–180
15. K. Subieta, A. Jodłowski, P. Habela, J. Płodzien: Conceptual Modeling with Dynamic Object Roles. In: "Technologies Supporting Business Solutions" (ed. R. Corchuelo, A. Ruiz-Cortés, R. Wrembel), the ACTP Series, Nova Science Books and Journals, New York, USA.
16. R. K. Wong, H. L. Chau, F. H. Lochovsky. A Data Model and Semantics of Objects with Dynamic Roles. Proc. of Intl. Conf. on Data Engineering, 1997

Model Driven Architecture: Three Years On

Richard Soley

Object Management Group, Inc.
soley@omg.org
www.omg.org/~soley/

Abstract. Software is expensive to build, and more expensive to maintain and integrate; worse, the moment it's created it's a legacy that must be integrated with everything else that comes afterward. Getting past this problem once and for all will require some way to move up a level to designs that allow implementation on many platforms, as implementation infrastructure changes. Modeling is an obvious way to move to a meta-design level, but nearly all modeling methods have previously been focused primarily on the requirements analysis and software design stages of development-the tip of the iceberg. Model Driven Architecture (MDA) extends models to system implementation, long-term maintenance and most importantly integration of applications.

The initial vision statement for the OMG's MDA Initiative was released in September 2000, with that vision becoming the OMG's primary architecture six months later. Three years on, where does the Intiative stand? Dr. Soley will address :

- how models can encapsulate design to support development, re-implementation on changing infrastructure and integration with other corporate assets
- how Model Driven Architecture standards support integrating corporate assets case studies of system implementations based on MDA that are deployed and working
- how well the MDA Initiative is standing up to scrutiny after its first three years.

Biography

Dr. Richard Mark Soley is Chairman and Chief Executive Officer of the Object Management Group, Inc. (OMG).

As Chairman and CEO, Dr. Soley is ultimately responsible for all of the business of OMG. Since he also was the original Technical Director of the OMG, he serves as a valuable resource for a broad range of topics: from predictions and trends in the industry to the nuts and bolts of CORBA implementations and the OMG technology adoption process.

Previously, Dr. Soley was a cofounder and former Chairman/CEO of A. I. Architects, Inc., maker of the 386 HummingBoard and other PC and workstation hardware and software. Prior to that, he consulted for various technology

R. Meersman et al. (Eds.): CoopIS/DOA/ODBASE 2003, LNCS 2888, pp. 1048–1049, 2003.

companies and venture firms on matters pertaining to software investment opportunities. Dr. Soley has also consulted for IBM, Motorola, PictureTel, Texas Instruments, Gold Hill Computer and others.

A native of Baltimore, Maryland, U.S.A., Dr. Soley holds the bachelor's, master's and doctoral degrees in Computer Science and Engineering from the Massachusetts Institute of Technology.

DOA 2003 PC Co-chairs' Message

This year's DOA demonstrated again that distributed-object technology and its applications are important issues for many academic and industrial researchers. This year, we received over 100 submissions, of which 28 have been accepted for inclusion in the proceedings as full papers, with an additional 7 being presented as posters. Highlighting the truly international nature of the event, the submissions originated from 22 countries.

An interesting observation is that distributed object technology continues to cover a wide range of application areas and to absorb novel technology trends. We received papers concerning systems issues such as dynamic code loading, whereas other addressed the applicability of objects to Grid computing. In between were papers on Web applications, middleware adaptation and reflection, software engineering, and ubiquitous computing, just to name a few. Indeed, distributed objects are everywhere!

The members of the program committee have been pressed hard to provide detailed review reports and to stick to deadlines. Although it is becoming quite common to extend deadlines to increase the number of submissions, for DOA we decided to implement our original plan, knowing that we were facing vacations and hard deadlines for camera-ready copies. The two-phase approach of submitting abstracts first, a week later followed by the full paper seemed to work quite well. It gave us, as co-chairs, the opportunity to let PC members bid for papers, and do the actual paper assignment during the first week. By-and-large, together we managed to process all papers within our original time slot. We applaud the members of the PC for doing a great job and doing it on time.

We also extend a special thanks to the general organization of OTM. In contrast to many other conferences, we as co-chairs could stick to processing content and not be bothered with various organizational details. These were all very well dealt with and made our job a pleasant one.

We are certain that you will enjoy and learn many new things from this year's contributions to DOA. If you acquire new insights and motivation from our program, or if you extend your network of peers, we will consider the effort to be worthwhile. Combining high-quality content, enthusiastic participation, and a wonderful venue are the mere ingredients needed for a successful conference. We feel confident that DOA 2003 will indeed be such an event.

August 2003   Bernd Kraemer, Fern Universitat in Hagen, Germany
Maarten van Steen, Vrije Universiteit of Amsterdam, The Netherlands
Steve Vinoski, Iona, USA
(DOA 2003 Program Committee Co-chairs)

R. Meersman and Z. Tari (Eds.): OTM Workshops 2003, LNCS 2889, p. 1050, 2003.
© Springer-Verlag Berlin Heidelberg 2003

Monitoring the Distributed Virtual Orchestra with a CORBA Based Object Oriented Real-Time Data Distribution Service

Hans-Nikolas Locher[1], Nicolas Bouillot[1], Erwan Becquet[1], François Déchelle[2], and Eric Gressier-Soudan[1]

[1] CEDRIC Laboratory, CNAM, 292 rue St Martin, 75003 Paris, France
{locher_h,bouillot,becquet,gressier}@cnam.fr
[2] IRCAM, 1 place Stravinsky, 75004 Paris, France
dechelle@ircam.fr

Abstract. This paper presents a CORBA based object oriented real-time data distribution service and its use to monitor our distributed virtual orchestra over a campus LAN. This service offers two types of data management policies: periodic exchanges and condition based exchanges. The distributed virtual orchestra uses the jMax engine to generate automatically sounds (virtual player), play and transform the music from real musicians (real player). Each player is connected to a PC and sends its high quality audio stream through the network. Real players hear each other, including the sounds from virtual players, and are self-synchronized. The jMax engine is modeled by a virtual sound automaton remotely monitored through our real-time data distribution service. The monitoring service is effective and has been used for jMax management during musical performance. Future works deal with a CORBA-CCM based monitoring service.

1 Introduction

The project described in this paper is a cooperation between the "Free software and software engineering" team at IRCAM and the distributed system for multimedia research team from CNAM-CEDRIC. The aim of the global project is to provide means to musicians to play across the Internet in real-time. The full Internet is too wide, currently internetworking is limited to LANs and MAN; nation wide Internet will be tried in a second phase. Musicians exchange high quality audio streams (sampled at 44100 or 48000 Hz, encoded on 16 bits or 24 bits at least).

The overall application is monitored using an object oriented real-time data distribution service based on CORBA. As far as we know, there is no equivalent project at this time. Two enhancements will be added in a next phase. To provide a virtual concert, the public will be able to receive the concert through Internet over an ADSL network. To allow the public to hear the concert, a sound engineer will collect audio streams to perform a spatial and a traditional mixing. Spatial mixing consists in placing sources on a three dimensional space. In this way, the

R. Meersman et al. (Eds.): CoopIS/DOA/ODBASE 2003, LNCS 2888, pp. 1051–1062, 2003.

sound is multi-channel. Mixing will be done by remote control of audio devices or by sound processing after reception. The monitoring service is then a key feature of our project.

The paper is organized as follow. Section two describes the distributed virtual orchestra application: jMax, self-synchronization and network multicast. Section three presents the monitoring service. Section four describes the results obtained. The last section concludes and presents future works.

2   The Distributed Virtual Orchestra Application

The distributed virtual orchestra application is divided in four parts: JMax, self-synchronization, multicast communications and monitoring [1]. This section presents the first three. Next section deals with monitoring. The first three parts are work in progress while the current version of the monitoring service is stable and effective. We plan to evaluate the advantages of a new generation based on CCM (CORBA Component Model) [2] for this application.

2.1   jMax, a Software Sound Processor

jMax is a visual programming environment dedicated to interactive real-time music and multimedia applications [3]. jMax's visual programming paradigm exists in a large number of audio and music software: the user builds "patches" by connecting modules together with "patch cords". Via the connections, control messages or signals are sent between the modules; these modules represent processing units, data containers or system I/O like for audio and MIDI. Modules can be either primitives or patchers themselves, thus giving to patches a hierarchical structure. Some objects have graphical interactive behavior and are used to display computed values or to change parameters.

jMax adopts, for portability and modularity, a client/server architecture that separates the graphical user interface from the real-time sound processing engine [3]. This engine, called FTS (for 'Faster Than Sound'), is implemented in C and the graphical user interface is written in Java. The communication between the graphical user interface and FTS uses a very simple ad-hoc message passing protocol that is handled by a client library available in several implementations (C++, Java and Python). jMax runs on Linux, MacOS X and Windows.

The FTS engine is organized around a simple object system [3]. The operators that appear in a patch are objects in the meaning of OOP: the connections end-points are message emission and reception ports; message reception triggers the call of a method of the receiving object. A message source can be a client application (for instance a user action in the graphical user interface), an input object (for instance MIDI input from an external keyboard) or timed-tagged messages. The core of the FTS execution engine is a scheduler that activates at each tick (a time "quantum") the execution of these messages sources plus the computation of signal objects (objects that process or generates streams of audio samples) that is optimized by a pre-compilation of the patch producing a flat list of function calls, each function operating on vectors of samples.

2.2   The Distributed Self-Synchronization of Audio Streams

In the context of live music, the interaction between musicians is achieved by the predetermined various visual signs and conventions. When musicians play across a network, it is mandatory to add a mechanism that helps consistent listening and maintains a constant latency. Let us recall that some musicians are able to read a partition with several tempo in advance from the time they are just playing. Then, playing/hearing late is not an impossible task for musicians but latency should be kept constant, compensating the jitter introduced by the network, and be as small as possible.

In order to provide a consistent listening, we synchronize streams before playing them out, as fully described in [4]. For a stream, audio samples are stamped. All musicians produce sound samples at the same rate, and consume the sound samples of the other musicians. Samples are consumed in the same order everywhere, like if they were all in the same place. All consumers can compute the delta between the stamps of samples issued from the different producers. After exchanging these values, each consumer can adjust the playout of each stream, according to the consumer with the largest latency. At this point, all musicians hear the same music with a constant late and can play in a synchronized way. The algorithm needs the exchange of n*n messages if n is the number of musicians. The complexity of the self-synchronization algorithm is $\Theta(n^3)$.

Self-synchronization was deployed in the prototypes of the distributed virtual orchestra. Audio stream, sampled at 44100Hz, are transmitted via the *rtpout* object and received with the *rtpin* object developed in jMax. The RTP [5] protocol carries the audio streams, and we get feedback with RTCP (the control protocol associated to RTP).

In the first tested configuration, two remote musicians played with a third host sending on a 100Mb/s LAN sound computed by jMax. Over the LAN, we had no packet losses and got a 16ms average latency. It showed that it is possible (considering delays) to play music on a LAN as musicians were together. The reason is that the human ear does not perceive shifts lower than 20ms. The second configuration dealt with four jMax engines exchanging audio streams through a multicast tunnel as described in 1. The latency was in this case greater than 20ms.

It was predictable because one of the computer was interacting across the Multicast tunnel. The self-synchronization of audio streams behaved correctly. Due to datagram losses, "clicks" occurred. We can point out the fact that a skew exists between the clocks of the different sound cards [6], which would causes losses too. Currently, there is no mechanism to compensate losses such as forward error correction, sample substitution or clocks synchronisation. We will next evaluate various strategies such as those shown in [7] for datagram losses and in [6] for clocks.

2.3   Multicast Networking

The whole set of musicians naturally maps on an IP multicast group and then can use the same IP multicast address. All the musicians of the orchestra transmit and receive audio streams on the same IP multicast address. We have seen that it allows also to implement self-synchronization. But IP multicast implies UDP and there is no reliability nor ordering of datagrams that contain sound samples; RTP/RTCP bring the information needed to order samples.

The first key issue was to choose an IP multicast routing protocol for the project. The use of PCs running Linux eased some decisions. For LAN and campus communications, we were completely free of our choices. We also took into account other requirements. Knowing that campus routers were not able to support native IP multicast, the elected multicast routing protocol should run on Linux hosts and should use tunnels in a first approach. According to the way the group spans over a MAN, the group is naturally sparse. This eliminated routing protocols like DVMRP (mrouted) and also PIM-DM or MOSPF.

These requirements led to the PIM-SM family. It is also one of the multicast routing protocol considered by the ISPs in the context of native multicast deployment. Linux runs PIM-SDM. PIM-SDM can adapt the shared routing tree to the topology of multicast sources and leaves. This feature is mandatory when we will consider the public where final users will be able to connect and disconnect more dynamically than musicians.

To provide a first level of prototyping independently of ISPs, GRE tunnels carry IP multicast datagrams. We tried different experiments: LAN based, campus based, MAN based very recently. Figure 1 gives an overview of the different multicast network configurations we used. The LAN based experiment involved two musicians, and one virtual player on the same LAN. Latency was too short to be noticeable and to influence musicians' play. The next experiment involved four virtual players, latency is noticeable in this case. Also during the test with the multicast tunnel, the application measured 2,2% of losses in the tunnel. The losses appears at the beginning, when the tunnel is first used; this remains to be characterized and explained. Next experiments will include native IP multicast,

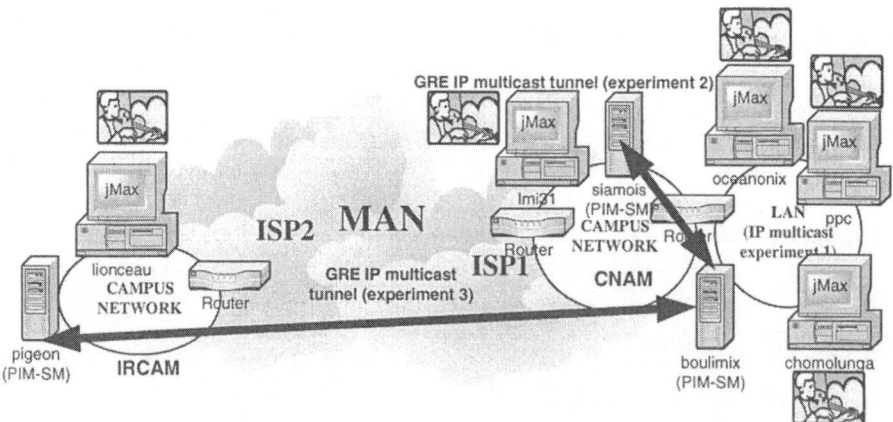

Fig. 1. IP Multicast networks overview

QoS and IPV6. IRCAM network is migrating toward IPV6. Current investigations deal with QoS management and priority inheritance across the network; this feature uses iproute2 and tc [8].

3   Main Features of the Real-Time Object Oriented Distribution Data Service

3.1   Functional Description of the Real-Time Data Distribution Service

Our real-time object oriented data distribution service inherits its definition from the IEC TASE.2 standard [9]. The IEC TASE.2 application protocol is specified to run over a full 7 layer OSI stack. The main interesting properties for our concern are the virtual device abstraction, the data management model and the corresponding services. It defines a client role, the remote monitor, and a server role, the monitored device. As an application protocol, it can be extracted form the ISO stack as a functional specification of a real-time data exchange service as described in [10] [11].

Nine functional blocks divide TASE.2 functions. As far as we are concerned, our work currently deals with blocks 1, 2. Block 1 defines a minimal set of services related to data management and periodic data exchanges. Block 2 extends block 1, it provides an exception semantic or condition-based exchanges often referred as Report By Exception semantic.

Two types of interactions are defined. "Operations" are initiated by clients toward a server, and correspond to a classical reliable method invocation (they usually return a result). "Actions" are initiated by servers and correspond to publish-subscribe interactions. Actions can be periodic or condition based. An important characteristic of the TASE.2 interaction model is that data exchanges between a client and a server are only possible through a binding, an "association" in the OSI world, that must be explicitly created during an initialization phase. This association is a kind of "communication object" used to encapsulate security and temporal Quality of Service parameters.

A key abstraction in the TASE.2 standard is the Virtual Control Center (VCC), it becomes the virtual device for our needs in the remote monitoring of jMax engines. The virtual device models a set of real resources. The way the model is mapped into the real device is not described by the standard, it is let to the implementor. The way the virtual device is mapped into jMax is described further in the paper.

TASE.2 defines "Data Value" objects and "Data Set" objects managed by the server and subscribed clients. Data Value management and Data Set management functions [9] deal with the lookup of existing Data Values and Data Sets, their creation, their destruction, etc. Data values reference in practice specific information, input measurements (which can contain status information, analog values, and attributes). Measurements can have attributes like timestamp, quality class, change of value counter... Data Set Transfer Sets describe the way Transfer Reports must be pushed toward the client and contain for each case,

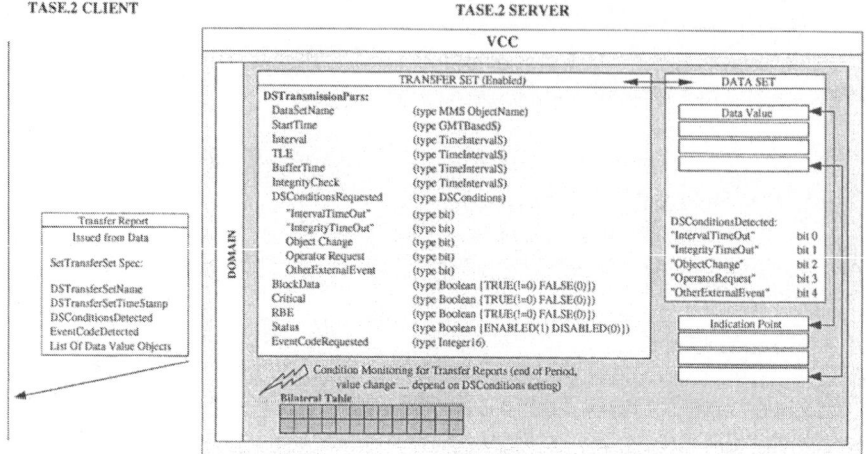

Fig. 2. Overview of Variable Management

parameters defining under which conditions data values related to data sets are transmitted. Figure 2 gives an overview of data management in TASE.2. The remote control and monitoring of jMax devices use all these abstractions and their corresponding services.

From the computing viewpoint the interaction model provided by TASE.2 matches the client/server model. The mapping of TASE.2 abstractions and services over CORBA is described in the next section. However, TASE.2 could be extended in a way that a producer provides the same data toward n subscribers if a multicast protocol was used. In a same way a client could trigger more than one server. Such extensions does not exist in the TASE.2 standard but are defined in the Utility Communication Architecture (UCA), a work close to TASE.2. Such extended facilities could be very useful to monitor the distributed virtual orchestra. The ORB we used did not implemented such features. With such facility, we could have used Transfer Reports to carry sound samples.

3.2   A CORBA Based Object Oriented Real-Time Data Distribution Service

To provide an object oriented real time data distribution service, we decided to adapt the TASE.2 services described previously over CORBA. The translation from an ISO stack toward CORBA is quite natural. CORBA, and its Common Services can advantageously replace the ISO environment and bring a distributed system approach. Confirmed services (from the TASE.2 client to the TASE.2 server) become synchronous method invocations. Unconfirmed services (from the TASE.2 server to the TASE.2 client) become one-way method invocations or synchronous method invocations without result parameters (in our case, the two choices are allowed, it depends of specified QoS parameters).

We called OpenTAZ[12] the prototype of our CORBA based object oriented real-time data distribution service. The design of OpenTAZ uses the RM-ODP/

ReTINA approach to model object interactions. Interactions between TASE.2 clients and servers (virtual device) are quite complex: all data exchanges necessarily use an explicit association created before use in response to a client request. Data exchanges correspond to operations (originating from the client) or actions (originating from the virtual device). Consequently, all TASE.2 entities are both client and server from a CORBA point of view. The so-called virtual device object declares an "Association Management interface" that is used to request the creation or the destruction of an association. An association between a client and a virtual device results in the creation of four interfaces: an "Operation interface", an "Association Management interface" and an "Association Control Interface" on the virtual device side, and, an "Action interface" on the client side.

The CORBA server object on the server side supports the virtual device interface described before, it implements operations. The corresponding methods are classical invocation methods, thus they return results. The other TASE.2 objects are supported by the virtual device as objects implemented with the programming language, C++ in our case. The virtual device interface inherits from all basic objects interface. Local communications between the virtual device and the physical resources manager use a specific adapter described later. They are implemented as efficiently as possible. The CORBA server object on the Client side supports the Transfer Report Services. The corresponding methods are classical invocation methods without result parameters.

An overview of the different kinds of supported interfaces is given in figure 3 hereafter (VCC is the Virtual Control Center and the lines are CORBA interfaces).

A generic real-time object oriented data distribution service is specified using the CORBA IDL2 (which is the most popular one). The result is a technology neutral specification of a part of the TASE.2 standard via a set of interfaces and data types. This specification is freely available [12]. Figure 4 presents a short piece of the IDL specification. It deals with the Data Value object method interface.

A C++ prototype of OpenTAZ has been built for a proof of concept [12] using MICO. Figure 5 gives an overview of the OpenTAZ design in the context of the distributed virtual orchestra.

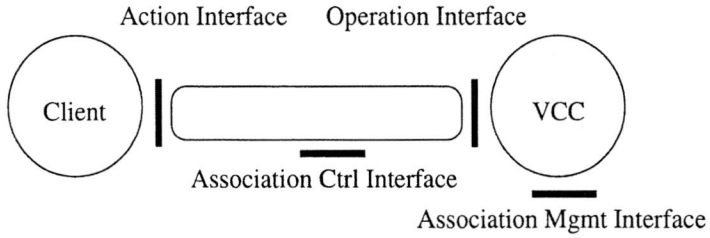

Fig. 3. The OpenTAZ binding object

```
typedef string DataNameType;
typedef sequence<DataNameType> DataNameSeqType;

exception UnknownDataNameType {};

interface DataValueManagement
{
    DataType getDataValue{in DataNameType name} raises (UnknownDataNameType);
    void setDataValue(in DataNameType name,in DataType value) raises (UnknownDataNameType);
    DataNameSeqType getDataValueNames();
    DataType getValueType(in DataNameType name) raises (UnknownDataNameType);
};
```

Fig. 4. The DataValue Management IDL Specification

4   Results

4.1   Compliance to OMG's Data Distribution Service for Real-Time Systems Request for Proposal

The Data Distribution Service for Real-Time Systems RFP[13] defines three level of compliance. We are interested in minimal compliance (L0). The service must be Publish-Subscribe oriented. It should provide a data model and basic properties.

OpenTAZ answers these requirements and a little bit more mainly because of the structure of IEC-TASE.2, especially functional blocks one (periodic exchanges) and two (condition based exchanges):

- DataSetTransferSets and TransferReports make OpenTAZ publish-subscribe oriented
- TASE.2 provides a hierarchical data model based on DataValues, DataSets and Virtual Device. Virtual Devices can model general devices. It gathers resources: DataSetTransferSets, DataSets and DataValues. DataSets gather DataValues. DataValues refer to physical measurements that can be simple

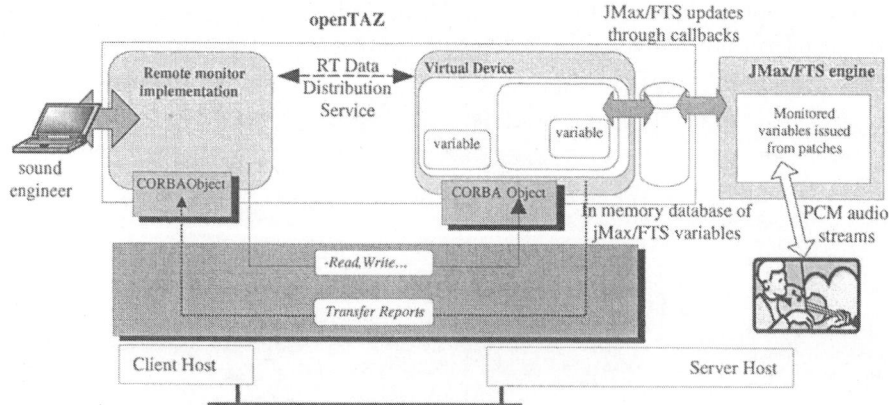

Fig. 5. OpenTAZ prototype overview for the distributed virtual orchestra monitoring

or very complex, remember Figure 1 and Table 1, but it can be extended to other kinds of data

- the COV attribute (Change of value) that counts how many times a value has been updated within the server between two successive TransferReports related to the same DataValue could achieve the atomicity requirements of the full compliance level (L2)
- QoS properties associated to data exchanges are specified in DataSetTransferSet entities within the server and are configured by the client using management method interfaces. These QoS properties are a first contribution to the partial compliance level (L1).
- the organization of the different services in four interfaces is convenient and makes a clear separation between management, relationship and data exchange
- finally, as far as we know OpenTAZ natively addresses the needs of Utility Domain Task Force, it can address also easily the needs of the Manufacturing Domain Task Force. Moreover, our experience shows that the monitoring of multimedia applications can be addressed too.

More compliance with the RFP (L1 and L2) needs to build a true distributed real- time shared memory of objects (data values or data sets) where OpenTAZ would be used to update shadow objects accessed locally by application objects. This feature is provided by the brand new OpenTAZ-CCM prototype [2] based on CCM from CORBA 3.0.

OpenTAZ should use a multicast based CORBA built over UDP and RTP/RTCP (Real-Time Protocol/Real-Time Control Protocol), RTP provides time-stamping and sequential numbers of messages whilst RTCP provides means to monitor a RTP relationship. Multicast is mandatory to update replicas of the same objects in different subscribers. Generally, ownership of an object is related to the most recent writer, here, the publisher (ownership is not considered to change on remote set operations by subscribers). Publishers could change, then consistency between publisher and subscribers can be very simple; the application reads the last received value in the shadow objects with its time-stamp and its attributes. More sophisticated real-time consistency management models like temporal causal consistency [14] could be implemented.

Our proposal fills the gap between an ISO based message oriented real-time data distribution service specified by the Utility domain, namely TASE.2, and the distributed object oriented approach of OMG. This opportunity is pointed out by the UCA specification [15] (p9). It means that we may provide the Data Distribution Service of OMG using OpenTAZ, with slight modifications on the OpenTAZ intertaces. However, it is still work in progress. As far as we know, this has not been explicitly provided anywhere else than in our proposal. We are also able, with our IDL specification of TASE.2 services, to provide a WSDL specification for free, using an IDL to WSDL translator, preparing web services based design easily.

4.2   Monitoring the Distributed Virtual Orchestra

Interaction between musicians crosses the network but are controlled by jMax and each jMax engine is remotely controlled through OpenTAZ. Interface between jMax and OpenTAZ is based on callbacks, messages, threads, and a socket. A measurement database that contains the real values from the current execution of jMax is provided in the OpenTAZ address space. Communications between the two softwares are multi-threaded.

Performance evaluation of OpenTAZ has been made, figure 6 gives an overview of results. Dark lines figure the OpenTAZ behavior. Light lines figure a CCM flavor of OpenTAZ, it will be useful in the conclusion section. The main operations we used are get (read) and set (write). Operations take around 200 microseconds. We cannot explain why the associate operation is faster with the OpenTAZ-CCM version. As it is a complexe operation in this version, the difference beetwen the two versions is probably not caused by CORBA-CCM.

The monitoring service is effective. It has been used for different purposes: jMax engine activation for each entity (real player and virtual player), sound level, both rtpin and rtpout objects initialization and the "bang" of the orchestra. This bang is the start of the application with transmission and reception of sound samples, but remains different from activation.

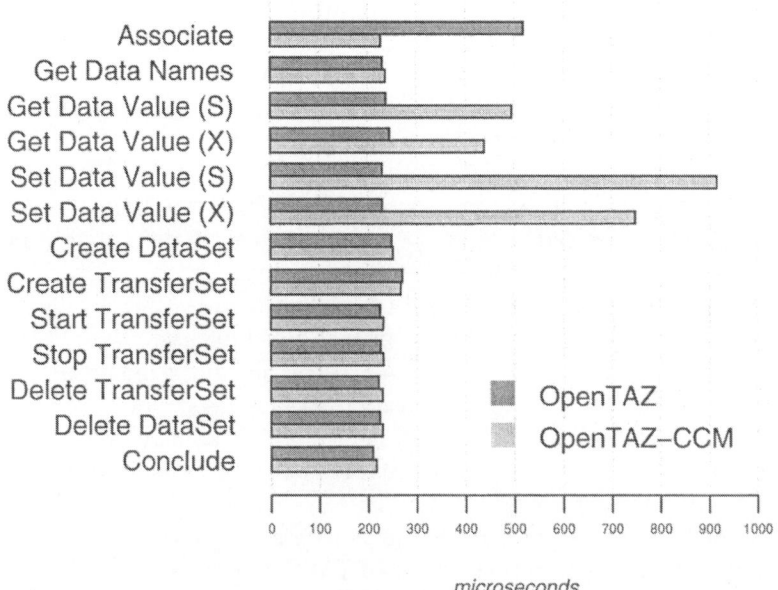

Fig. 6. OpenTAZ performance results

5   Conclusion and Future Works

The monitoring service is a useful tool. We plan to extend its use as the support of the metronome function, to learn the latency in the network and to initialize the parameters of the self-synchronization algorithm.

Moreover, enhancements involve the use of a real-time extension of Linux. Currently, we have selected the Jaluna-2 kernel (Linux extended with C5, a flavor of ChorusOS from Sun) [16]. In this context we have to decouple jMax, the GUI from FTS (the sound engine). This suggests a new global approach for the design of the monitoring service and for jMax based on software components. jMax Java GUI and FTS are plugged together using sockets. The use of CCM is not a hard problem: FTS could become a legacy component whilst jMax could use the Java ORB and IIOP to interact with the FTS CCM component.

As a side effect, our work matches partially the Data Distribution Service for Real-Time Systems RFP from OMG (L0 compliance) but we may provide the Data Distribution Service of OMG with only some adaptations on the OpenTAZ interfaces.

Component based engineering suits to system services design. It provides modular design and re-usability more easily. It could be relevant to use CCM for the distributed virtual orchestra project. The problem is performances. In [2], a CCM based prototype has been developed. Figure 6 shows performance licks for the read/write operations between OpenTAZ-CCM and the former Open-TAZ. Implementation of CCM platforms should be improved before deploying OpenTAZ-CCM for the monitoring service. However, we believe that it could become a clever solution to distribute jMax GUI over Linux, FTS an OpenTAZ-CCM over C5. Our next monitoring service works will deal fully with the component based version.

References

1. Bonafous, R., Bouillot, N., Locher, H.N., Berthelin, J., Déchelle, F., Gressier-Soudan, E.: The distributed virtual orchestra project. In: proposed to 4th IFIP International Conference on Distributed Applications and Interoperable Systems. (2003)
2. Becquet, E., Locher, H.N., Gressier-Soudan, E.: Component based industrial messaging service design for utilities. In: 9th IEEE International Conference on Emerging Technologies and Factory Automation, Lisbon (2003)
3. Déchelle, F., Borghesi, R., De Cecco, M., Maggi, E., Rovan, B., Schnell, N.: jMax: an environment for real-time musical applications. In: Computer Music Journal. Volume 23-3. (1999) 50–58
4. Bouillot, N.: Un algorithme d'auto synchronisation distribuée de flux audio dans le concert virtuel réparti. Conférence Française sur les Systèmes d'Exploitation (2003) CFSE 3. la Colle sur Loup, France.
5. Schulzrinne, Casner, Frederick, Jacobson: RTP: A transport protocol for real-time applications. RFC 1889 (1998)
6. Fober, D., Orlarey, Y., Letz, S.: Clock skew compensation over a high latency network. In ICMA, ed.: Proceedings of the International Computer Music Conference. (2002) 548–552

7. Perkins, C., Hodson, O., Hardman, V.: A survey of packet-loss recovery techniques for streaming audio. IEEE Network Magazine (1998)
8. Simon, E., Gressier-Soudan, E., Berthelin, J.: Avoid lan switches – ip routers provide a better alternative for a real-time communication system. In: 2nd International Workshop on Real-time Lans in the Internet Age, Porto, Portugal (2003)
9. KEMA-ECC: ICCP User Guide, Mineapolis, USA. Final Draft edn. (1996)
10. Guyonnet, G., Gressier-Soudan, E., Weis, F.: Cool-mms: a corba approach to iso-mms. In: ECOOP'97. Workshop: CORBA: Implementation, Use and Evaluation, Jyväskylä. Finland (1997)
11. Gressier-Soudan, E.: Prototyping a corba based mms -industrial communications with corba. In: OMG Technical Meeting, Burlingame, California USA, OMG (2000) ftp://ftp.omg.org/pub/doc/mfg/00-09-16.pdf.
12. Becquet, E.: OpenTAZ project page on savannah. http://savannah.nongnu.org/projects/opentaz (2003) URL.
13. OMG: Data distribution service for real-time systems rfp. v 1.0. orbos. Technical report, OMG (2001)
14. Cornilleau, T., Gressier-Soudan, E.: Rt-objects based on temporal causal consistency: A new approach for fieldbus systems. In: ECOOP'97. Workshop: Real Time Objects, Jyväskylä. Finland (1997)
15. EPRI: Utility communications architecture version 2.0, introduction to uca version 2.0, editorial draft 1.0. Technical report (1998)
16. Jaluna: Jaluna home page. http://www.jaluna.com (2003)

Designing Telerobotic Systems as Distributed CORBA-Based Applications

Michele Amoretti, Stefano Bottazzi, Monica Reggiani, and Stefano Caselli

RIMLab – Robotics and Intelligent Machines Laboratory
Dipartimento di Ingegneria dell'Informazione, University of Parma
Parco Area delle Scienze, 181A – 43100 Parma, Italy
{amoretti,bottazzi,reggiani,caselli}@ce.unipr.it
http://rimlab.ce.unipr.it

Abstract. Virtual laboratories and on-line robots are examples of distributed telerobotic systems based on emerging Internet technologies. Building these applications from scratch is a very demanding effort because they must satisfy a wide set of requirements, arising from both the distributed systems domain, e.g. location transparency and multiplatform interoperability, and the telerobotic domain, e.g. guaranteed quality of service, real-time operation, dynamic reconfigurability, concurrent or collaborative interaction among distributed sites. For these systems exploitation of an Object Oriented standard middleware like CORBA should be very effective, thanks to its well known features and services and its recent enhancements (Real-Time CORBA, AMI).
In this paper we summarize our experience in the development of a software framework for telerobotics based on Real-Time CORBA. The framework takes advantage from CORBA services to allow implementation of advanced teleoperation systems, thereby avoiding proprietary or ad-hoc solutions for communication and priority management. In order to enable distributed collaboration and virtual laboratories, it also supports concurrent control and data distribution with multiple Clients. The framework has been evaluated in a real scenario, building a distributed telerobotic application which allows control of a robot arm and several sensors by multiple Clients.

1 Introduction

Internet technology is rapidly evolving, providing access to timely data from news, sports, and financial sources, live video for teleconferencing, and so on. Once we are comfortable with live viewing, the next step is to reach out and touch, by controlling a physical device.

For many years, the pleasure of operating a robot has been limited to trained specialists. Ideally, the Internet opens the door to a much wider audience, but even if many networked robot systems have been developed, these are usually uncommunicative between each other. The main cause is that each system, in terms of software architecture, is implemented for itself and from scratch, without using a standard base.

R. Meersman et al. (Eds.): CoopIS/DOA/ODBASE 2003, LNCS 2888, pp. 1063–1080, 2003.

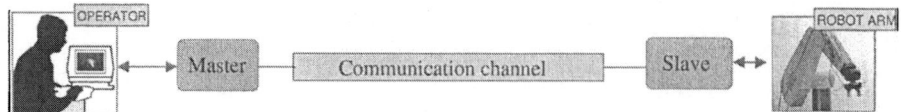

Fig. 1. Traditional model of a teleoperated system.

Considering robots (but also sensors, controllers) as objects [1], and networked robots as distributed objects [2] has been the first step towards the idea of open, reusable and scalable software architectures for teleoperation. Distributed object computing is one of the latest research and development topics in computer science and software industry. There are few de facto standards for inter-object communication, e.g. DCOM (Distributed Component Object Model), Java RMI and CORBA (Common Object Request Broker Architecture). By adhering to these standards, development time can be shortened and newly developed components can easily be connected with existing resources.

The vehicle for our research in "distributed robotics" is a CORBA-based software framework we have developed to simplify the implementation of flexible, portable, extensible and reusable telerobotic applications, and whose initial features have been described in [3]. Departing from other works [2, 4, 5, 6], we exploited advanced CORBA features to address real-time requirements, concurrency in resource access and in task execution, and data distribution.

In this paper, we discuss the requirements of modern telerobotic systems (Section 2) and the available alternatives in terms of middleware software (Section 3). We next illustrate our enhanced CORBA-based framework (Section 4), describe a distributed application based on the framework (Section 5), and report the experimental results obtained by testing different communication models (Section 6). Finally, we describe some prior work in the field (Section 7), and draw some conclusions (Section 8).

2   Requirements for Robotic Teleoperation Systems

With a brief and intuitive definition, robotic teleoperation allows an operator at one location to perform a physical task at some other location by means of a robotic device [7]. Regardless of the robot autonomy degree and of the distance between sites, a teleoperation system always has three specific components: a command and sensorial interface at the "master" station, used by the human operator to control the task, a "slave" robotic device, which performs actions at the remote site following operator's instructions, and a communication channel between sites. This is the traditional approach to robot teleoperation [7, 8], graphically described in Figure 1.

Telerobotic systems have been typically designed for critical scenarios that are too dangerous, uncomfortable, or expensive for humans to perform. Some applications are assembly, maintenance or exploration in hazardous environments

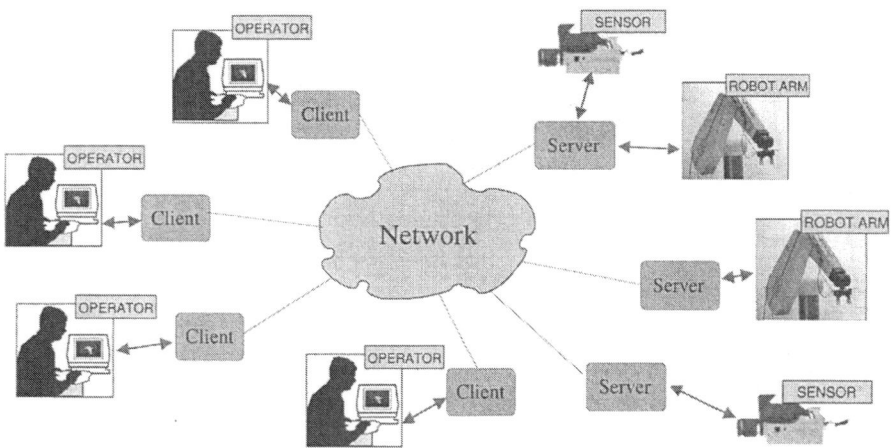

Fig. 2. An advanced teleoperation scenario.

like underwater, space, nuclear or chemical plant, remote presence, power line maintenance.

In recent years distributed computing systems and the Internet have opened new, broad application perspectives to robot teleoperation systems. Examples of novel applications are tele-teaching/tele-learning, virtual laboratories, remote and on-line equipment maintenance, and projects requiring collaboration among remote users, experts, and devices [2, 9, 10, 11, 12, 13, 14, 15].

Although the conventional architecture of Figure 1 still has a fundamental role in a high level description of a telerobotic system, it seems unsuitable for coping with these novel paradigms, which provide new interesting opportunities but also propose alternative challenges.

Modern telerobotic systems (Figure 2) tend to be very dynamic, with users and physical resources, like sensor and robot controllers, which need to be connected/disconnected at run-time to the system (e.g. students or researchers from geographically distributed sites that want to access equipments which are only part-time available, in a virtual laboratory), resulting in changes in the number and location of peers (applications which can act as a Client, as a Server, or both) and in the need of preserving performance of services also with dynamically variable system load.

Operators may have different access levels (from simple sensor monitoring to system supervision), peers must be light-weight and runnable on several platforms (from desktop workstation to embedded system), without increasing applications complexity. Support for different robot programming methods (on-line, off-line, hybrid) should be provided, along with transparency (i.e., all accessible applications must appear as if they were local). Peers directly interfaced with sensors and devices prevalently act as Servers; to execute multiple commands at the same time (from one or several Clients) they should offer a high degree of internal concurrency. Increasing the number of Clients should not affect system performance (i.e. scalability). Real-time features are needed to preserve QoS and reliability. There is also the need to distribute increasing quantities of sensory data to a potentially large number of Clients during system operation. In a telerobotic task, the timely availability of adequate sensory data to emulate the operator's physical presence at the remote site is particularly crucial [7, 16].

Furthermore, new telerobotic applications often become viable in the context of an existing infrastructure or a constrained budget, which leads to the development of heterogeneous systems built by integrating a mix of new and legacy equipment, based on hardware acquired from multiple vendors, running different operating systems and programmed in a variety of languages. The expensive development of a new application can thus be avoided relying on previous experience or, even better, on a common framework.

3   Middleware Software

In the previous section, a list of features and requirements for advanced telerobotic systems has been reported. Building such type of teleoperation architecture from scratch for heterogeneous and dynamic systems is often too demanding, due to economic and time constraints. Following a trend in modern distributed systems design, open, reconfigurable, and scalable architectures can be built using standard middleware software for distributed object computing. Available solutions include JavaSoft's Java Remote Method Invocation (Java RMI), Microsoft's Distributed Component Object Model (DCOM) and OMG's Common Object Request Broker Architecture (CORBA).

Sun's Java RMI (http://java.sun.com/products/jdk/rmi) provides a simple and fast model for distributed object architecture. It extends the well-known remote invocation model to allow the shipment of objects: data and methods are packaged and shipped across the network to a recipient that must be able to unpackage and interpret the message. The main drawback of the RMI approach is that the whole application must be written in Java. This constraint is troublesome in common heterogeneous environments of robotic applications, often incorporating legacy and specialized hardware and software components.

Microsoft's DCOM (http://www.microsoft.com/com/tech/DCOM.asp) supports distributed object computing allowing transparent access to remote objects. While DCOM overcomes RMI reliance on Java using an Object Description Language to achieve language-independence, it still has limitations concerning legacy code and scalability of applications. Developer's options are indeed restricted because DCOM is a proprietary solution mainly working on Microsoft operating systems.

When language, vendor, and operating system independence is a goal, CORBA (http://www.corba.org) is a mature solution that provides similar mechanisms for transparently accessing remote distributed objects while overcoming the interoperability problems of Java RMI and DCOM. Moreover, its advanced and recent features (Real-Time CORBA, AMI) provide functionalities almost essential in telerobotic applications. At the moment, CORBA seems the logical choice for building complex distributed telerobotic applications.

4   A Framework for Teleoperation Based on CORBA

A middleware such as CORBA offers a set of facilities and tools for connecting objects across heterogeneous computational nodes, thereby simplifying the development of distributed applications. In spite of this fact, development of a telerobotic application remains a fairly demanding task.

We have developed a framework which aims to provide a flexible and effective infrastructure for advanced telerobotic systems. The framework offers handles for implementation of multithreaded Servers, with concurrency mechanisms to simplify sharing of CPU among computation and communication activities, for management of client requests with order preservation and for adaptation of reactions to different requests depending on their urgency. Servers operate in real-time to allow implementation of the appropriate control laws with guaranteed operation. Furthermore, the framework provides synchronization mechanisms for exclusive allocation of non-sharable resources, and three methods of data distribution among peers.

A telerobotic system built with the framework exhibits location transparency, easily achieved through the CORBA middleware. Furthermore, the portability of the framework to various operating systems allows reusability of the same code in several Client stations and reallocation of sensoriality among heterogeneous Server stations. The class diagram in Figure 3 shows the structure of the framework, which is designed to cope with a wide range of situations, providing abstract classes for robots (mobile or not) and sensors. A concrete class implementation requires only adding code for the specific device or controller, whereas the functionalities for communications, concurrency, real-time are shared among all classes and based on CORBA.

In the following subsections we discuss the CORBA features exploited and their usefulness in the telerobotic application domain.

4.1   Real-Time Features

A telerobotic system should provide the operator with the guarantee of correct execution priorities of application tasks at the Server. The **Real-Time CORBA** specification [17] provides the developer with handles for resource management and predictability.

The heterogeneity of nodes, in distributed applications, precludes the use of a common priority scale, forcing users of earlier CORBA versions to concern about low-level details of threads on different OSes. The Real-Time CORBA **priority mapping** mechanism converts CORBA priority levels, assigned to CORBA operations, to OS native priority levels (and vice versa).

Teleoperation applications also require task execution at the right priority on the Server side. RT CORBA defines two invocation models: SERVER_DECLARED, in which objects are created with assigned execution priority, and CLIENT_PROPAGATED, in which the Client establishes the priority of the methods it invokes, and this priority is honored by the Server.

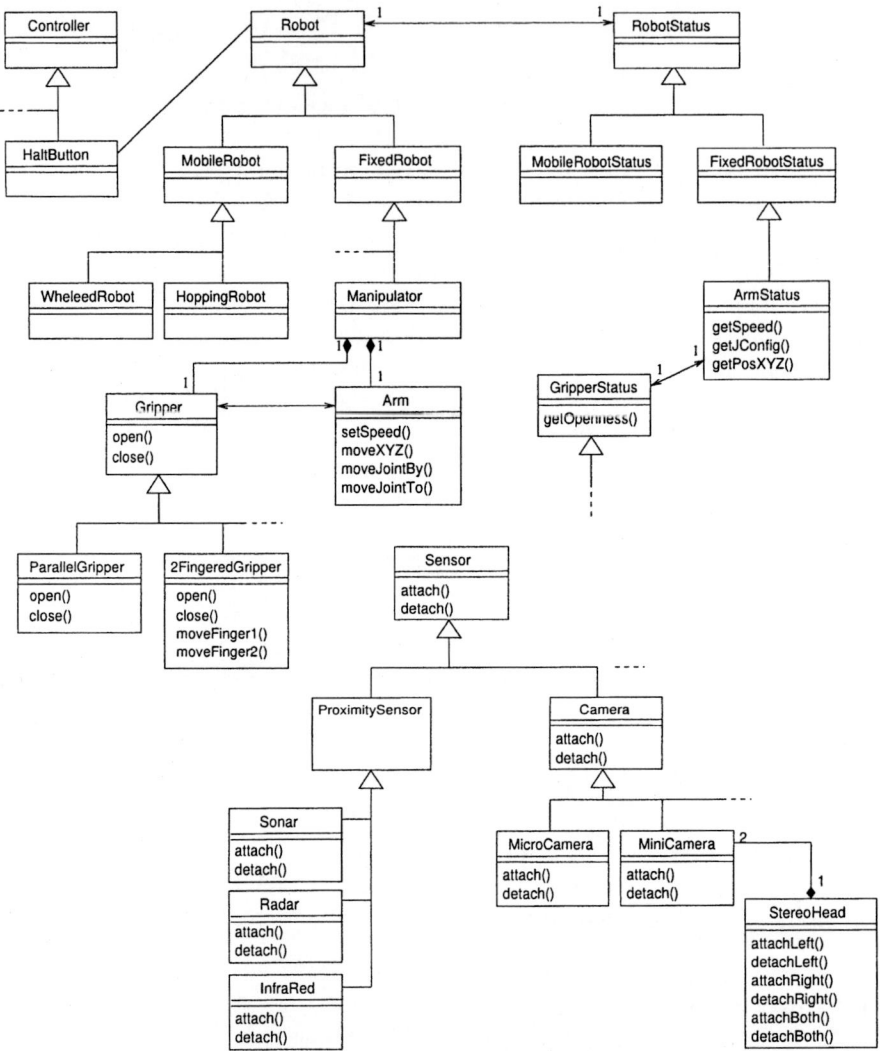

Fig. 3. Class hierarchy of the framework.

Control of several robots and sensors teleoperated from multiple remote Clients requires a multithreaded Server allowing concurrency among actions. Moreover, the Server should be able to discriminate among services, granting privilege to critical tasks (emergency stop, reading of safety sensors), and should avoid priority inversion, with low-priority tasks blocking high-priority ones.

To support programming of multithreaded Servers, RT CORBA provides **Thread Pool**, a mechanism enabling preallocation of Server resources. With the Thread Pool mechanism, a group of threads is statically created by CORBA at the Server at start-up time. These threads are always ready to be bound to requested methods, while a fixed cap is set for dynamic threads, which are created only once static threads are exhausted. Thread Pool avoids the overhead of thread creation/destruction at run-time and helps in guaranteeing performance by constraining the maximum number of threads at each host.

Under the extreme condition where the whole set of threads has been bound to low-level requests, the Server could miss the deadlines of high-priority actions, a situation clearly unacceptable in a robot teleoperation system. To avoid depletion of threads by low-priority requests, a Thread Pool can be further partitioned in **Lanes** of different priority. This partitioning sets the maximum concurrency degree of the Server and the amount of work that can be done at a certain priority. Partitioning in Lanes and related parameters cannot be modified at run-time; the only freedom is reserved to higher priority methods which can "borrow" threads from lower level Lanes once their Lane is exhausted.

4.2   Concurrency in Action Execution

Standard service requests in CORBA systems rely on the Synchronous Method Invocation (SMI) model, that blocks the Client until the Server notifies the end of the requested activity. This approach is acceptable for simple teleoperation applications consisting in the stepping of one action at a time, possibly in stop-and-go mode, whereas SMI is clearly unsuited for more advanced telerobotic scenarios where the user can invoke execution of multiple concurrent actions. Examples of such tasks are coordinated operation of multiple arms or concurrent sensing and manipulation. Non-blocking invocations with earlier CORBA versions either relied on methods not guaranteeing the delivery of the request or on techniques requiring significant programming efforts and known to be error prone [18].

A more efficient way to perform non-blocking invocations is provided by the CORBA Messaging specification [19], through the **Asynchronous Method Invocation (AMI)** model, with either a Polling or a Callback approach. AMI allows a CORBA-based system to efficiently activate multiple concurrent actions at a remote teleoperated site. Moreover, as AMI and SMI share the same object interface, Clients can choose between synchronous or asynchronous calls while Server implementation is not affected.

In robotic applications, a set of parallel actions must often begin at the "same" time, as their coordinated execution is required to ensure logical correctness or safety. This is the rationale for the introduction of a *waiting rendezvous* strategy [20] in the framework. Proper thread synchronization in the server is required to achieve this capability. The basic CORBA synchronization mechanism is the **Mutex** interface, whereas CORBA lacks higher level mechanisms, such as condition variables, semaphores, and barriers. Hence we have developed an action synchronization mechanism on top of the Mutex. An instruction termed `cobegin(n)` prefixes the invocation of parallel actions in a Server, acting as a barrier for the next n method invocations, whose execution, therefore, does not start until all calls have reached the server. We remark that the `cobegin(n)` method is not mandatory for parallel execution of actions. Without `cobegin(n)` the server schedules AMI requests as soon as they arrive.

4.3   Managing Multiple Clients

A fundamental challenge in advanced teleoperated systems is to manage input from all operators while generating a single and coherent control sequence for each robot, allowing collaborative and coordinated teamwork [21].

The basic functionality provided by the framework ensures atomicity of calls to library functions devoted to the interaction with the robot controller, regardless of its thread-safeness. Potential conflicts arising from multiple Clients are avoided forcing an exclusive access to library functions through the RTCORBA:: Mutex construct, implementing the mutual exclusion lock. The server side is solely responsible for the implementation of this functionality since Mutexes are introduced only in the servant code.

In addition to ensuring single command consistency and atomicity, the framework implements concurrent access control at session level, guaranteeing a full robot control without undesiderable interferences from other operators.

The implementation of the coordination scheme allowing multiple clients to control a single robot through a coherent and logically safe pattern of interaction is based on the CORBA **Concurrency Control Service** [22]. The Concurrency Service defined in the CORBA specification allows several Clients to coordinate their access to a shared resource so that the resource consistent state is not compromised when accessed by concurrent Clients. This service does not define what a resource is. It is up to the developer to define resources and identify situations where concurrent access to the resources leads to a conflict.

The coordination mechanism provided by the Concurrency Service is the lock. Each shared resource should be associated with a lock, and a Client must get the appropriate lock to access a shared resource. Several lock modes (read, write, upgrade, intention read, intention write) are defined, allowing different resolution of conflict among concurrent Clients. The specification defines two types of Client for the Concurrency Service: a transactional Client, which can acquire a lock on behalf of a transaction, and a non-transactional Client, which can acquire a lock on behalf of the current thread. Our framework adopts a non-transactional style, since most available RT CORBA implementations do not support transactional Clients yet.

In a scenario where several users compete to control a single robot and/or access data from multiple sensors, exclusive control of the robot must be granted to only one user in a given interval of time, while simultaneous read of sensor data should be allowed to other users as well. The scheme in Figure 4 shows how the framework copes with this requirement using the Concurrency Service. For each robot a Robot and a RobotStatus objects are created. The RobotStatus class maintains information about a robotic device while the Robot class controls movements and sets parameters. Then, for each Robot object, a CORBA:: CosConcurrencyControl:: LockSet object is created and registered in the Naming Service.

At the Client side a RobotWrapper object contains all the references to CORBA objects and interacts with the Concurrency Control Service to enforce the correct concurrent access. As shown in Figure 5 (scenario 1), the Client invok-

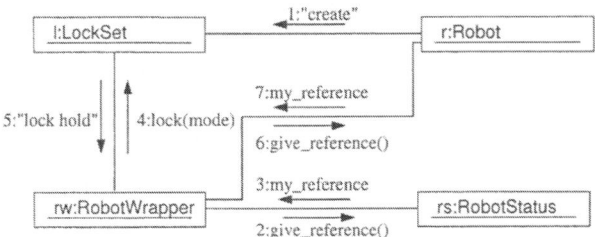

Fig. 4. Collaboration diagram describing a Client (whose core is an object of the RobotWrapper Class) that asks a lock before it is able to control a **Robot** object.

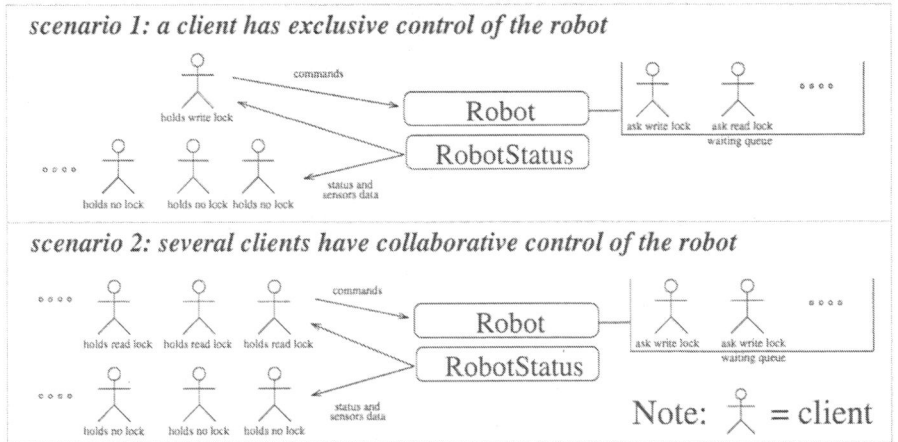

Fig. 5. Two scenarios of concurrent access to a single robot device from several Clients.

ing commands on the Robot object holds a write lock ensuring exclusive control. Indeed, as the write lock conflicts with any other locks, a Client requesting a lock on the same resource will be suspended waiting its release. Clients invoking methods on the RobotStatus object, instead, are not required to hold locks as the class has only "accessor" methods.

To preserve generality and cover a wider domain of applications [21], an alternative scenario can be outlined, where a group of users want to control a single robot in a collaborative way (e.g. a "primary" operator with some "backup" operators), while preventing further operators from obtaining exclusive control of the robot. In this scenario (Figure 5, scenario 2), a collaborating Client holds a read lock. Since the read lock conflicts only with write and intention write locks, it allows sharing of robot control with other Clients holding read locks, whereas Client requesting exclusive control through a write lock are suspended in the waiting queue.

4.4   Data Distribution

Telerobotic applications often require that large amounts of sensory data be returned to remote clients. Implementing data distribution according to the Client/Server communication model has several drawbacks, such as the inactivity of the Client while waiting for a response and the saturations effects on both the network and the Server for required polling operations. A more suitable solution for interactions among peers is the *Publisher/Subscriber* communication model [23]. Whenever a Publisher (e.g. a sensor) changes state, it sends a notification to all its Subscribers. Subscribers, in turn, retrieve the changed data at their discretion.

In this section two variants of the Publisher/Subscriber communication model defined by CORBA specification are investigated, along with a Callback-based technique. In these solutions, the peers involved in the communication do not exhibit the Client/Server relationship anymore, therefore a more suitable terminology defines *Supplier* the peer producing the data, and *Consumer* anyone who receives them.

Distributed Callbacks. Our first approach for a data distribution subsystem, avoiding polling operations and minimizing network saturation, was based on Distributed Callbacks [24]. As the Observer pattern suggests, we defined two CORBA classes for each available sensor: the Subject at the Supplier side and the Observer at the Consumer side (Figure 6). To receive data from a sensor, the Consumer calls a method attach (AMI) on the remote Subject object, passing a reference to an Observer object. Each sensor holds a list of all Observer objects that have been attached. When new sensor data are ready, they are sent by the Supplier application to all the "attached" Observer objects, by invocation of the appropriate method.

Though this approach avoids Client active waiting and network saturation, the efficiency of the Supplier is greatly affected by the number of Consumers. When multiple Consumers are attached, the Supplier is supposed to persistently

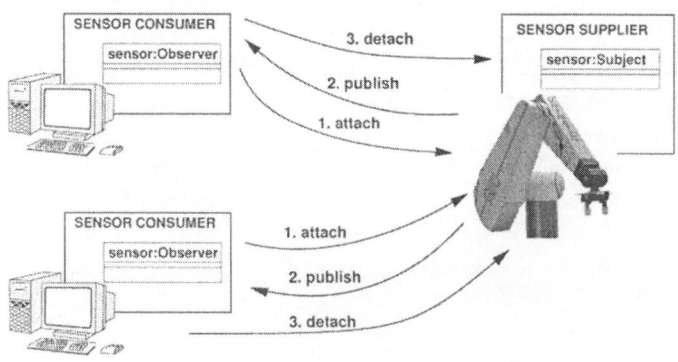

Fig. 6. Distributed callback for data distribution.

store their references and send a separate message to each in turn according to their preferences (each Consumer should be able to define the desired data receiving rate to avoid unnecessary data submission). Therefore, due to the high memory and computation requirements, scalability is bounded to a relatively small number of Consumers.

Event Service. To relieve the Supplier of administrative duties related to Consumers management, we implemented a second version of the data distribution subsystem based on the CORBA Event Service [25]. The general idea of the Event Service is to decouple Suppliers and Consumers using an *Event Channel* that acts as a Proxy Consumer for the real Suppliers and as a Proxy Supplier towards the real Consumers. This implementation also allows a transparent implementation of the broadcast of sensor data to multiple Consumers.

The CORBA specification proposes four different models interleaving active and passive roles of Suppliers and Consumers. For robotic applications the only reasonable model seems to be the Canonical Push Model, where an active Supplier pushes an event towards passive Consumers registered with the Event Channel.

Despite the benefits introduced by the adoption of an Event Channel, there are several matters of discussion. First of all, to avoid compile-time knowledge of the actual type of the "event", sensor data must be communicated as an Interface Definition Language (IDL) any type, that can contain any OMG IDL data type. The communication is therefore type-unsafe and Consumers are charged with the duty of converting the any type toward the data type they need. Moreover, the Event Service specification lacks event filtering features: everything is conveyed through the Event Channel, that in turn sends everything to any connected Consumer. Once again, the load of a missing property is laid on the Consumers that are forced to filter the whole data, looking for the ones they really need. Finally, the Event Service specification does not consider QoS properties related to priority, reliability, and ordering. Attempting to ensure these properties in an application results in proprietary solutions that prevent ORB interoperability.

Notification Service. Our third solution for the data distributed subsystem is based on the CORBA Notification Service [26], recently introduced in the CORBA specification to overcome the previously listed deficiencies of the Event Service.

The Notification Service is defined as a superset of the Event Service, enhancing most of its components. Notable improvements with respect to the Event Service include filtering and QoS management. Through the use of filter objects, encapsulating one or more constraints, each Consumer subscribes to the precise set of events it is interested in. Two filter types are defined: forwarding filter, which decides whether the event can continue toward the next component, and mapping filter, which defines event priority and lifetime. Moreover, QoS properties for reliability, priority, ordering, and timeliness can be associated to a Channel, to a Proxy, or to a single event.

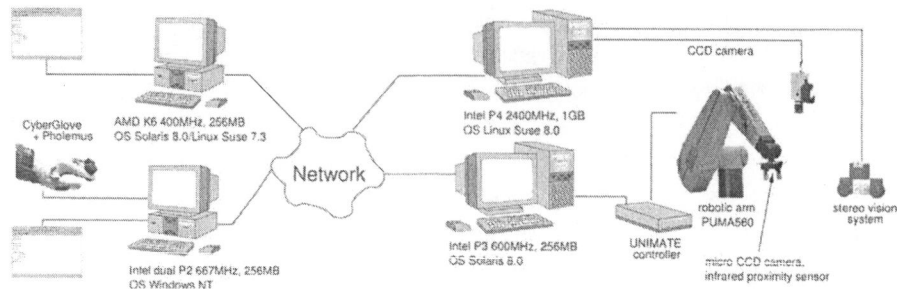

Fig. 7. The experimental testbed.

5 Building a Telerobotic Application Based on the Framework

We have developed a telerobotic application as a case study to evaluate the framework described in section 4. The application is shown in Figure 7. An operator, provided with direct continuous teleoperated control of the remote device, is required to perform a peg-in-hole task. This is a representative assembly task problem, and is often exploited for benchmarking teleoperation architectures.

The remote manipulator is an Unimation Puma 560, interfaced to a Pentium based workstation with Solaris OS running the RCI/RCCL robot programming and controlling environment. The sensory system comprises a black and white camera and an IR proximity sensor mounted near the gripper of the manipulator, a video camera mounted on the ceiling shooting the testbed area, and a stereo vision system in front of the task site. All workstations are connected in a LAN with a Fast Ethernet switch, which does not introduce substantial delay (latency is less than $100\mu s$). On the software side, the implementation is written in C++ and based on The ACE ORB (TAO) [27], a freely available, open-source, and standard-compliant real-time implementation of CORBA. Each Client station runs a Client Application allowing to graphically choose the required services among those available in the system. A more advanced station is also provided with a multimodal user interface including a virtual reality glove and a six d.o.f. tracker of the operator's wrist.

Client. The *Client Application* is built upon CORBA services providing transparency about location and implementation of the available components. The user can search for components (CORBA objects) looking for a Naming Service, that will locate requested objects based on their name and return the reference to the remote object stored under that name. The teleoperation application includes several heterogeneous sensors whose data must be broadcasted to the Client stations and quickly returned to the user.

For definition of application tasks, the operator can choose between two alternatives: submitting a sequence of single commands, or developing a program in a C-like high level language that will then be interpreted. To support invocation of concurrent actions at the server and achieve temporal continuity in command execution by the robot, the developed application takes advantage of asynchronous calls (see section 4.2).

Server. The *Server Application* manages the Puma manipulator and several sensors according to Client requests, whose order and urgency should be preserved. The server has been implemented as a multi-threaded architecture using the Thread Pool mechanism (see section 4.1). This feature allows management of the high number of requests that could be received from multiple Clients concurrently monitoring and controlling the task.

For safety reason an "Emergency Button" object is implemented in the Server to immediately stop the system in emergency situations. To this purpose, the Thread Pool with Lanes mechanism preserves server reactivity to high priority calls, avoiding priority inversion and thread exhaustion by low priority requests.

6   Empirical Performance Assessment

Several variants of the application have been implemented to test the correctness of the framework and identify the relevant parameters for the robot server. Three Lanes (low, medium, and high priority) have been defined for the Thread Pool in the Server application that controls the manipulator and the sensors which are directly related to the manipulator. Low and medium priority Lanes supply threads for the execution of actions composing the goal task. The high-priority Lane supplies threads for emergency actions, so as to guarantee their immediate dispatch. The scheduling algorithm is a Priority Level Round Robin (SCHED_RR), which is available in any POSIX-compliant operating system.

Many experiments involving simulated workload have been carried out to evaluate the correctness and robustness of the Server, which has been tested with a variety of sets of concurrent actions, with different priority levels and synchronization. A goal of these experiments was to verify the effectiveness of cobegin(n) to avoid priority inversion in the execution of parallel actions. One of the experiments is described in Figure 8 (left), showing the precedence relations, duration and priority of each method call. The correct outcome of this experiment requires that the four concurrent methods be executed according to their priority. Figure 8 (right) compares two experimental executions of the task. Without cobegin(n) (top diagram), the medium priority action (ID 4), whose request is the first reaching the server, is executed before the high priority action (ID 1). With cobegin(n) (bottom diagram), the priority of threads is always guaranteed and no priority inversion occurs.

6.1   Data Distribution

The communication models described in Section 4.4 have been integrated in the proposed CORBA-based framework for telerobotic systems. The experiments reported in the following only assess the relative performance in terms of latency

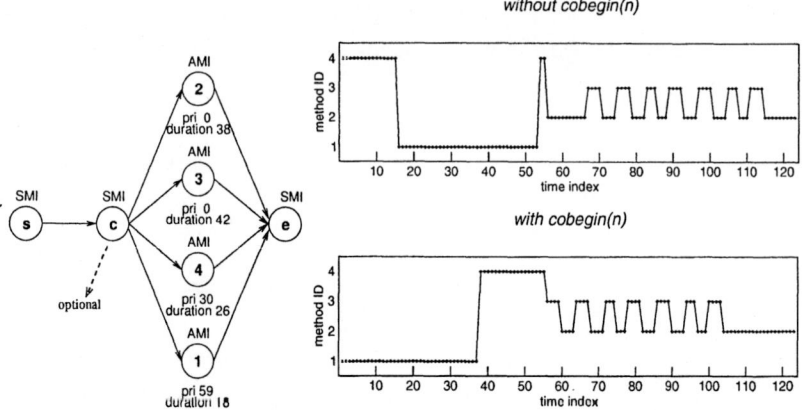

Fig. 8. (left) Precedence graph of a concurrent task, consisting of an initial action `s=start()`, an optional `c=cobegin()`, followed by four concurrent actions with different priority and duration. (right) Experimental results of concurrent actions without (top) and with (bottom) `cobegin(n)`.

and scalability of the three proposed data distribution mechanisms. All experiments reported in this section follow the Push Model: a Supplier generates data and sends them to the Event Channel, when available, or directly to Consumer processes. A single Supplier and one ore more Consumers, all requiring the same sensory data, are considered. Both Supplier and Consumer(s) are located on the same host, whereas the Event Channel can be on a different host.

Two host machines exploited in the experiments are listed in Table 1 along with their features. The hosts are connected via a Fast Ethernet switch. Aside from our tests, the network had no significant traffic nor was any other processing taking place on these hosts.

In the first set of experiments a 64 Byte packet is pushed by the Supplier to a single Consumer. Consumer activity is limited to the update of the latency value so far. Table 2 reports latency minimum, average, and standard deviation (jitter) values on a set of 50,000 samples considering alternative allocations of Event Channel, Supplier, and Consumer. Allocation of the Event Channel only affects implementations based on Event or Notification Services. Of course, due to the single Consumer type of experiment, the Distributed Callback approach exhibits a lower latency than Event and Notification Services implementations (whose additional features are not utilized). The added latency of Event and

Table 1. Experimental Setup: Host features.

Host name	Hardware configuration	Operating system
Trovatore (faster machine)	PIV 2.4GHz, 512MB RAM	SuSE Linux 8
Malcom (slower machine)	Athlon 800MHz, 256MB RAM	Mandrake Linux 9.1

Table 2. Latency (ms) with a 64 Byte packet with three configurations of Supplier(S), Consumer (C), and Event Channel (EC).

Implem.	EC,S,C on faster machine			EC on slower machine, S,C on faster machine			EC on faster machine, S,C on slower machine		
	t_{min}	t_{avg}	jitter	t_{min}	t_{avg}	jitter	t_{min}	t_{avg}	jitter
Distr. Call.	0.12	0.38	0.58	0.11	0.14	0.11	0.23	0.30	0.44
Event Serv.	0.33	0.62	0.54	0.42	1.05	0.33	0.53	1.17	0.70
Notif. Serv.	0.40	0.72	0.58	0.50	1.41	0.20	0.61	1.26	0.26

Table 3. Average interarrival time (ms) with a 64 Byte packet, increasing the number of Consumers (N) for two configurations of Supplier (S), Consumers (C), and Event Channel (EC).

Implem.	EC,S,C on faster machine						EC on faster, S,C on slower machine					
	N=1	N=3	N=10	N=50	N=70	N=100	N=1	N=3	N=10	N=50	N=70	N=100
Distr. Call.	0.73	0.98	3.76	37.76	45.53	82.77	0.66	2.23	7.64	51.90	85.90	144.1
Event Serv.	1.25	1.48	4.52	38.00	41.94	71.46	1.68	2.96	7.11	33.59	49.42	77.6
Notif. Serv.	1.38	1.67	5.15	40.60	45.18	76.34	1.82	3.23	7.75	36.47	53.09	84.32

Notification Services is small when the Event Channel is located in the same host as the Supplier and Consumer. When the Channel is located on another machine the performance of CORBA services decreases, since data are sent forth and back to the Channel host through the network.

The next set of experiments measures the average time interval between two successive 64 Byte packet receptions (interarrival time) increasing the number of Consumers from 1 to 100. Results (in ms) for selected Consumer configurations are reported in Table 3. At the beginning of the range investigated, the Callback implementation has slightly better performance than Event Channel-based ones, because it requires data to cross a lower number of hops. However, Event Service and Notification Service implementations have better scalability when the Event Channel is located on a fast machine: they achieve a performance comparable to the Callback implementation starting from 10 Consumers, and significantly better performance starting from 70 Consumers.

To summarize, for robot Servers performing several complex tasks (e.g., sensor data acquisition and distribution, motion planning, actuator control) and dealing with a large number of attached Clients, the Event Channel represents an effective tool to maintain the overall workload under control. When Clients have different QoS needs and at the expense of a slight overhead, the Notification Service is the most appropriate solution, thanks to its configurability options not available in Callback and Event Service implementations.

7 Related Work

Our work relates to the area of internet-based telerobotics, whose aim is to build flexible, cheap, dynamic, heterogeneous distributed telerobotic systems and applications. A broad perspective on these applications is given in the collection [14]. The main issue in many of these projects is the interaction with web users who, lacking technical skills, require easy-to-use command interfaces.

Other research views Internet-based telerobotics as *distributed robotic systems* [11], addressing the issues arising in the implementation of Client/Server systems. A few papers exploit the interoperability and location transparency provided by CORBA to ease system implementation in applications such as a distributed laboratory [28], a supervisory control scheme [29], or an Internet telerobotic system conceived to provide assistance to aged and disabled people [30].

Two recent papers are more directly concerned with the implementation of systems supporting distributed telerobotic applications. Hirukawa and Hara [9] propose a framework based on OO programming for robot control, whereas Dalton and Taylor [11] advocate nonblocking asynchronous communications, viewed as essential to build a distributed robotic systems. Since this feature was not available in the CORBA implementation they relied upon, the architectural framework in [11] exploited non-standard middleware. We believe that with the current CORBA and RT CORBA specifications, including the AMI invocation model and other advanced features, this choice is no longer justified.

Our research departs from this prior art in several respects. To our knowledge, we have developed the first telerobotic framework based on COTS middleware not merely for interoperability or location transparency, but taking full advantage of its multithreading and real-time features. No previous work in the area has used the Asynchronous Method Invocation model, even though an asynchronous interface is deemed an essential feature [11]. Now that RT CORBA technology has matured, it can be leveraged upon to develop reliable COTS-based telerobotic systems with strict control over computational resources.

8   Conclusions and Future Work

The viability and cost effectiveness of new telerobotic applications such as virtual laboratories, networked and on-line robots can be widely enhanced exploiting COTS-based software components. Moreover, systems implementing those applications pose also demanding challenges: they should be dynamically reconfigurable and highly scalable to deal with a potentially large number of peers, they should provide real-time features, guaranteed performance and efficient concurrency mechanisms, both locally and in a distributed environment. CORBA middleware, especially with its recent extensions, seems well suited for the needs of distributed telerobotic systems. In this paper we have summarized our experience in the development of a software framework for telerobotics based on Real-Time CORBA, ensuring proper real-time operation of the server and managing concurrent control and data distribution with multiple Clients.

The results obtained show that CORBA brings a number of remarkable advantages in the telerobotic domain, enabling portable, highly reconfigurable applications with support for concurrency and real-time features. Furthermore,

CORBA standard services for naming resolution, data distribution, and concurrency control avoid the need for ad-hoc solutions, which are often error-prone and require significant development efforts.

The major drawbacks encountered in our experience are some overhead in communications, the limited synchronization mechanims available, and, more important, the fact that none of the CORBA ORBs available offers a full implementation of the CORBA standard, i.e. covering aspects such as dynamic scheduling, fault-tolerance, fully compliant CORBA services.

We now plan to investigate additional techniques for distributing data with minimal overhead, for managing authentication of operators and for secure access to the telerobotic system. Further tests and software design efforts are also required for public distribution of the framework.

Acknowledgment. This research is partially supported by MIUR (Italian Ministry of Education, University and Research) under project RoboCare (A Multi-Agent System with Intelligent Fixed and Mobile Robotic Components).

References

1. C. Zielinski, "Object-Oriented Robot Programming," *Robotica*, vol. 15, no. 1, Jan. 1997.
2. T. Hori, H. Hirukawa, T. Suehiro, and S. Hirai, "Networked Robots as Distributed Objects," in *IEEE/ASME Int. Conf. on Advanced Intelligent Mechatronics*, 1999.
3. S. Bottazzi, S. Caselli, M. Reggiani, and M. Amoretti, "A Software Framework based on Real-Time CORBA for Telerobotic Systems," in *IEEE Int'l Conf. Intelligent Robots and Systems*, 2002.
4. S. Jia, Y. Hada, Y. Gang, and K. Takase, "Distributed Telecare Robotic Systems Using CORBA as a Communication Architecture," in *IEEE Int. Conf. Robotics and Automation*, 2002.
5. T. Ortmaier, D. Reintsema, U. Seibold, U. Hagn, and G. Hirzinger, "The DLR Minimally Invasive Robotics Surgery Scenario," in *Work. Advances in Interactive Multimodal Telepresence Systems*, 2001.
6. C. Preusche, J. Hoogen, D. Reintsema, G. Schmidt, and G. Hirzinger, "Flexible Multimodal Telepresent Assembly using a Generic Interconnection Framework," in *IEEE Int. Conf. Robotics and Automation*, 2002.
7. C. Sayers, *Remote Control Robotics*. Springer, 1999.
8. T. B. Sheridan, *Telerobotics, Automation, and Human Supervisory control*. Cambridge, MA: MIT Press, 1992.
9. H. Hirukawa and I. Hara, "Web-Top Robotics," *IEEE Robotics & Automation Magazine*, vol. 7, no. 2, pp. 40–45, June 2000.
10. K. Goldberg, S. Gentner, C. Sutter, and J. Wiegley, "The Mercury Project: A Feasibility Study for Internet Robots," *IEEE Robotics & Automation Magazine*, vol. 7, no. 1, pp. 35–39, Mar. 2000.
11. B. Dalton and K. Taylor, "Distributed Robotics over the Internet," *IEEE Robotics & Automation Magazine*, vol. 7, no. 2, pp. 22–27, June 2000.
12. H. Hirukawa, I. Hara, and T. Hori, "Online robots," in *Beyond Webcams: an introduction to online robots*, K. Goldberg and R. Siegwart, Eds. The MIT Press, 2001.

13. *WS2001: International Workshop on Tele-Education in Mechatronics Based on Virtual Laboratories*, Weingarten, Germany, July 2001.
14. K. Goldberg and R. Siegwart, Eds., *Beyond Webcams: an Introduction to Online Robots.* The MIT Press, 2001.
15. P. Backes, K. Tso, and G. Tharp, "Mars Pathfinder Mission Internet-Based Operations using WITS," in *IEEE Int. Conf. Robotics and Automation*, 1998.
16. Y. Tsumaki, T. Goshozono, K. Abe, M. Uchiyama, R. Koeppe, and G. Hirzinger, "Verification of an Advanced Space Teleoperation System using Internet," in *IEEE/RSJ Int'l Conf. on Intelligent Robots and Systems*, 2000.
17. *Real-Time CORBA Revision 1.1*, Object Management Group, Aug. 2002.
18. A. Arulanthu, C. O'Ryan, D. Schmidt, M. Kircher, and J. Parsons, "The Design and Performance of a Scalable ORB Architecture for CORBA Asynchronous Messaging," in *Proc. of the Middleware 2001 Conference ACM/IFIP*, 2000.
19. *The Common Object Request Broker: Architecture and Specification Revision 3.0*, Object Management Group, Dec. 2002.
20. B. Douglass, *Doing Hard Time: Developing Real-Time Systems with UML, Objects, Frameworks, and Patterns.* Addison-Wesley, 1999.
21. N. Chong, T.Kotoku, K. Ohba, K. Komoriya, N. Matsuhira, and K.Tanie, "Remote coordinated controls in multiple telerobot cooperation," in *IEEE Internatial Conference on Robotics and Automation*, 2000.
22. Object Management Group, "Concurrency Service Specification," http://www.omg.org/technology/documents/formal/concurrency_service.htm, Apr. 2000.
23. F. Buschmann, R. Meunier, H. Rohnert, P. Sommerlad, and M. Stal, *A System of Patterns.* Wiley and Sons, 1996.
24. M. Henning and S. Vinoski, *Advanced CORBA Programming with C++.* Addison-Wesley, 1999.
25. Object Management Group, "Event service specification, v. 1.1," http://www.omg.org/technology/documents/formal/event_service.htm, Mar. 2001.
26. ——, "Notification service specification, v. 1.0.1," http://www.omg.org/technology/documents/formal/notification_service.htm, Aug. 2002.
27. Distributed Object Computing (DOC) Group, "Real-time CORBA with TAO (The ACE ORB)," http://www.ece.uci.edu/~schmidt/TAO.html.
28. C. Paolini and M. Vuskovic, "Integration of a Robotics Laboratory using CORBA," in *IEEE Int. Conf. Systems, Man, and Cybernetics*, 1997.
29. R. Burchard and J. Feddema, "Generic Robotic and Motion Control API Based on GISC-Kit Technology and CORBA Communications," in *IEEE International Conference on Robotics and Automation*, 1997.
30. S. Jia and K. Takase, "An Internet Robotic System based Common Object Request Broker Architecture," in *IEEE Int. Conf. Robotics and Automation*, 2001.

Implementation Experience with OMG's SCIOP Mapping

Gautam Thaker, Patrick Lardieri, Chuck Winters, Ed Mulholland, Jason Cohen,
Keith O'Hara, and Gaurav Naik

Lockheed Martin Advanced Technology Laboratories
3 Executive Campus, 6th Floor
Cherry Hill, NJ 08002
{gthaker,plardier,cwinters,emulholl,jcohen,kohara,gnaik}
@atl.lmco.com

Abstract. Longevity of distributed computing middleware standards, such as
CORBA, depend on their ability to support a range of applications by providing low overhead access in a uniform manner to a large variety of platforms
and network capabilities. OMG's recent adaptation of Stream Control Transmission Protocol (SCTP) mapping is another instance of this trend. Applications can obtain all the benefits of this emerging protocol via a standard compliant, distributed object model. This paper reports on integration of SCTP with
Adaptive Communications Framework (ACE) [2] and The Ace ORB (TAO).
[3] By exploiting network path multiplexing capability of SCTP we demonstrate that CORBA applications can bound the *maximum* latencies they suffer
under stressful network failures to under 50 msec.

1 Introduction

Middleware and network infrastructure that support many distributed, real-time, embedded systems, such as command and control systems aboard naval ships, must
support stringent quality of service (QoS) requirements. These QoS requirements
generally span a broad spectrum, from timeliness to fault tolerance to security. Here
we report on our ongoing efforts to significantly enhance network link failure tolerance for Distributed, Real-time, Embedded (DRE) systems by exploiting the emerging Stream Control Transmission Protocol (SCTP), a new transport protocol standard
from IETF [1]. SCTP provides numerous new capabilities that promise to provide
significant QoS application benefits. Ideally these new capabilities become available
to applications as familiar abstractions offered by object oriented middleware frameworks and standards. We report on integration of SCTP with Adaptive Communications Framework (ACE) [2] and The Ace ORB (TAO) [3]. This integration was
greatly facilitated by design of ACE and TAO that anticipate addition of such newer
protocols under existing abstractions. The end result is that applications achieve
tightly bounded latency values even in presence of repeated network failures and

R. Meersman et al. (Eds.): CoopIS/DOA/ODBASE 2003, LNCS 2888, pp. 1081–1091, 2003.

restorations. Furthermore, where SCTP protocol is available ACE/TAO applications need not even be recompiled to obtain these benefits.

2 Summary of SCTP and SCIOP

Stream Control Transmission Protocol was originally developed in the telecommunications industry and has become a full IETF standard. SCTP, like TCP, is a connection oriented, transport layer protocol. However, SCTP differs in following ways from TCP:

- Network path multiplexing. Rather than forming a connection, SCTP forms an association between two processes. An association may consist of multiple, distinct network paths and multiplexing of traffic among these paths is automatically handled by SCTP.
- Reliability and ordering parameter configuration. Unlike TCP, SCTP provides fine grained control over reliability and ordering parameters. Among the parameters that are directly controllable are retransmission timeouts, acknowledgement delays, heartbeat intervals, maximum number of retransmissions, as well as others. Used carefully these have the potential to permit much greater control over network behavior, something that is of fundamental importance in DRE systems.
- Message (as well as byte stream) service. Unlike TCP that is strictly byte oriented and leaves it up to higher levels to provide message framing, SCTP natively supports messages.
- Connection multiplexing (multiple streams). Multiple streams can be multiplexed over a single association. This can be used to overcome familiar "head of queue blocking" problems.
- Security enhancements for better denial of service protection. SCTP uses a 4-way (rather than TCP's 3-way) handshake in connection establishment that is not susceptible to traditional DoS attacks.
- Support for very large windows for high bandwidth-delay product links.

Currently numerous implementations of SCTP are available on Linux, Sun, and various BSD variant operating systems. We have concentrated on Linux based implementations for our project due to its greater rate of development in support of real-time issues. On Linux there are at least two kernel level implementations available; one from OpenSS7 as a patch against 2.4.18 kernel and another from LKSCTP project that is integrated in 2.5.x developmental series and is thus in the 2.6-test kernels. Of these we have focused our efforts on OpenSS7's implementation since it seemed to have better support for multi-homing, both at the time we started our project in March 2002 and as of this writing, February 2003. In addition, OpenSS7's implementation closely follows existing BSD style socket API and this has facilitated its rapid integration into ACE. Nevertheless, we support both these implementations under ACE and TAO.[1]

---

[1] OpenSS7 support was released in ACE 5.3.3 and TAO 1.3.3. LKSCTP is in the CVS repository and will be released with ACE 5.3.4 and TAO 1.3.4.

The overwhelming success of IP protocol can be attributed to its ability to support a large number of applications and services above the network layer and simultaneously support a large number of different data links and physical lower layers. In the field of distributed object computing, CORBA has the potential to provide a similar capability by supporting many applications and services on a wide array of network transport protocols. OMG's adaptation of GIOP SCTP protocol mapping (known as SCIOP) [6] continues this trend. In addition to defining client and server roles in forming an association, the SCIOP specification defines the SCTP Inter ORB Reference (SCIOR) profile and enumerates the protocol properties that must be configurable from a CORBA application in a conformant implementation.

3   DRE Application System Model

Naval shipboard command and control systems are our motivation for this work. The computing environment of these ships consist of several hundred compute nodes richly interconnected by high performance switches. Reliability and damage tolerance requirements dictate that compute nodes are spatially distributed and are interconnected by multiple, independent network paths. Figure 1 shows a logical diagram of such a system. To keep the figure readable, only a few nodes are shown and only two of the nodes are shown to be multi-homed; however, in actual system most nodes will have two to four redundant network connections. We wish to use SCTP's support for network path multiplexing to exploit this rich interconnect redundancy and to provide the application with a high degree of network path loss tolerance.

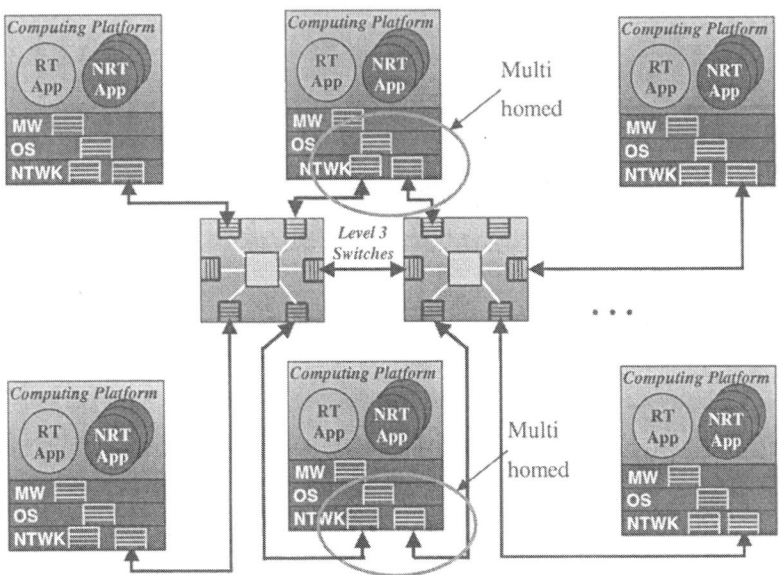

Fig. 1. Expected Shipboard Deployment of Interconnect Computer Nodes

4 SCTP Support in ACE

SCTP supports two types of network service: SOCK_STREAM and SOCK_ SEQPACKET. To integrate SCTP's SOCK_STREAM transport service into ACE we made a small modification to the current SOCK_STREAM wrapper facade. We added a protocol parameter to one constructor and one connect method of the ACE_SOCK_Connector class. After this modification the ACE SOCK_STREAM wrapper facade worked properly over both TCP and SCTP.

To integrate SCTP's SOCK_SEQPACKET transport service into ACE we created a new wrapper facade, SOCK_SEQPACK. We closely emulated the current SOCK_STREAM wrapper facade to develop our new SOCK_SEQPACK wrapper facade. Figure 2 depicts the classes that implement this new wrapper facade. Also indicated are those methods that have a substantial change from their SOCK_STREAM wrapper façade counterparts.

To enable the user to fully exploit the network path multiplexing features of SCTP we created a new subclass of ACE_INET_Addr called ACE_INET_Multi-homed_Addr. This class enables applications to specify restricted subsets of network interfaces for inclusion on SCTP associations on the client and server side. This is also depicted in Figure 2.

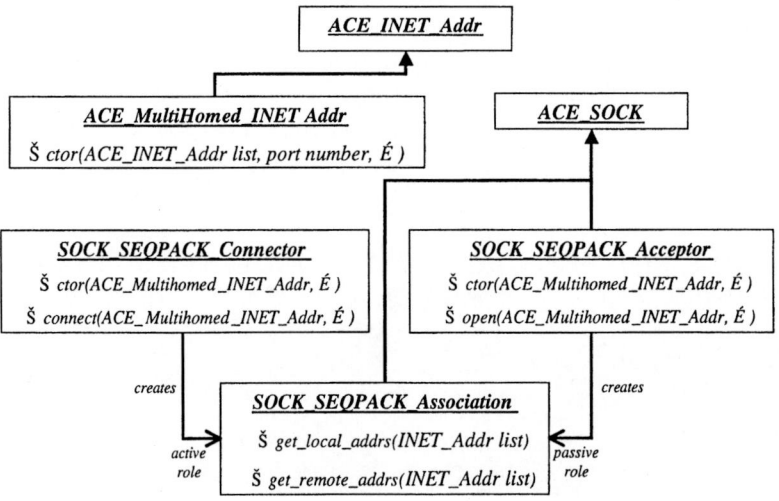

Fig. 2. Wrapper-Façade Implemented on OpenSS7 API and LKSCTP, which is Supported by Current ACE::OS Methods

All SCTP options can be read and written from the current socket options methods provided by ACE_SOCK. Finally, although Figure 2 shows that our SOCK_ SEQPACK wrapper facade support SCTP stream multiplexing capability, this has not been implemented in ACE or exploited in TAO. The SCIOP mapping [6] suggests that streams *may* be used by RTCORBA for transport level priority banding. Todate we have not completed the necessary design and implementation work to exploit SCTP streams.

After completion of support for OpenSS7's implementation of SCTP on the Linux platform another implementation with slightly different API and semantics emerged. This was the LKSCTP implementation that is in the 2.5.x series Linux kernel. While OpenSS7 supports both SOCK_STREAM and SOCK_SEQPACKET as connection oriented service, under LKSCTP only SOCK_STREAM is connection oriented. Thus, when ACE is built for LKSCTP the SOCK_SEQPACKET wrapper façade is mapped to SOCK_STREAM. The result is that all differences between these two implementations are abstracted and hidden under ACE wrapper façade classes and applications (including TAO) run without any changes.

5 SCTP Support in TAO

The Object Management Group has standardized a GIOP protocol mapping for SCTP that is referred to as SCIOP. The original RFP was issued in September 2000 and after the customary process of independent submissions and consolidation, a unified submission was adopted. Our approach for integration of SCTP in TAO closely followed our approach with ACE—reusing possible exiting patterns in TAO as we had done at the ACE level. We have emulated the use of TAO's pluggable protocol frameware [5] for IIOP to develop SCIOP.

OMG's proposed standard also includes a format for SCIOR (SCTP Inter-operable Object Reference). We have also enhanced TAO to generate proper SCIORs. We have modified the TAO program, catior, which deciphers IORs and pretty prints them, to also properly handle SCIORs. Compared to IIOP, the principal difference is that rather than having a single IP address and a port, an address list and a port are encoded in the IOR.

6 Performance Test Methodology

Our adaptation of SCTP to ACE and TAO must demonstrate real QoS benefits to applications to warrant its use. Towards this end we undertook extensive performance evaluation. Our test methodology is based on defining metrics that we use to judge the efficacy of our approach and implementation. Thus, we focused on the following parameters:
- Maximum and Mean end-to-end latencies under:
  — Normal (no failures) condition.
  — In presence of following types of network failures
    (1) Random 1%-5% packets losses.
    (2) Single link failure.
    (3) Repeated, rapid link failures and restorations.

Goal: 50 msec maximum latency under all test conditions. (This metric for SCTP is compared with the same tests performed with TCP.)

Our objective is to achieve this performance goal with minimal to no application level impact. Indeed, due to TAO's ability to dynamically load protocol factories, the application does not even have to be recompiled to receive these benefits.

7 Test Measurements

Figure 3 shows the testbed we used for evaluating our SCTP implementations in both ACE and TAO. For random packet losses we deploy a custom Linux kernel module that provides uniformly distributed, random packet drops. Typically we test with a 1% packet loss, which represents a high loss channel, but we have also tested with packet loss rates as high as 5%. For single link failures we simply disconnect the RJ-45 ethernet connector at the network interface card. For repeated, rapid link failures and restorations we have constructed a Network Failure Test Appliance shown in the Figure 3. This appliance uses a programmable IC and four solid state relays to achieve any desired pattern of link failures and restorations. Tests that we conduct with the Network Failure Test Appliance represent conditions that are more severe than are likely to be encountered in practice.

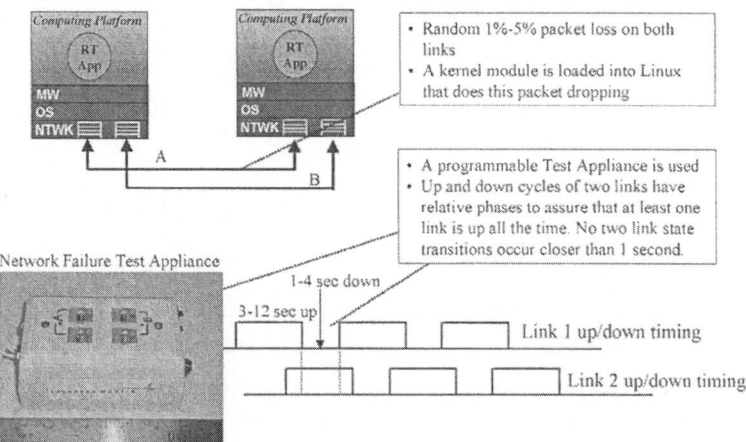

Fig. 3. Experimental Testbed for Failure Testing

Table 1 details the experiments in our test plan. As shown, while we have successfully concluded most of the tests, additional work remains for some of the tests where we note "Issues." Specific cases are further discussed below. There are a total of six test cases, two at the socket level, two at the ACE level and two at the TAO level.[2] First we examine the mean roundtrip latency values on our testbed for all six cases.

---

[2] At each level there are two tests, one based on TCP and one based on SCTP.

This is shown in Figure 4. Due to current instability in the SCTP stack for message sizes greater than 1 MTU we have limited most of our tests to messages of 1024 bytes or less. At all three levels, for small message sizes, our SCTP-based test is between 60-70 microseconds slower than the corresponding test using TCP. The fact that this difference remains unchanged as we move up the levels of abstractions tells us that our SCTP adaptations at the ACE and TAO levels are as efficient as existing TCP based adaptations.

Table 1. Current Status of Experiments

	No Failure	Induced Packet Loss (1%)*	Single Link Failure	Repeated Link Failure
TCP (SOCK_STREAM)	Done/OK	Done/OK	Done/OK	Done. OpenSS7 is OK. LKSCTP has some issues
STCP (SOCK_SEQPACK)	Done/OK	Done/OK	Done/OK	
ACE_SOCK_STREAM (TCP)	Done/OK	Done/OK	Done/OK	
ACE_SOCK_SEQPACK (SCTP)	Done/OK	Done/OK	Done/OK	
TAO_IIOP	Done/OK	Done/OK	Done/OK	
TAO_SCIOP	Done/OK	Done/OK	Done/OK	

*1% packet loss is imposed on both links

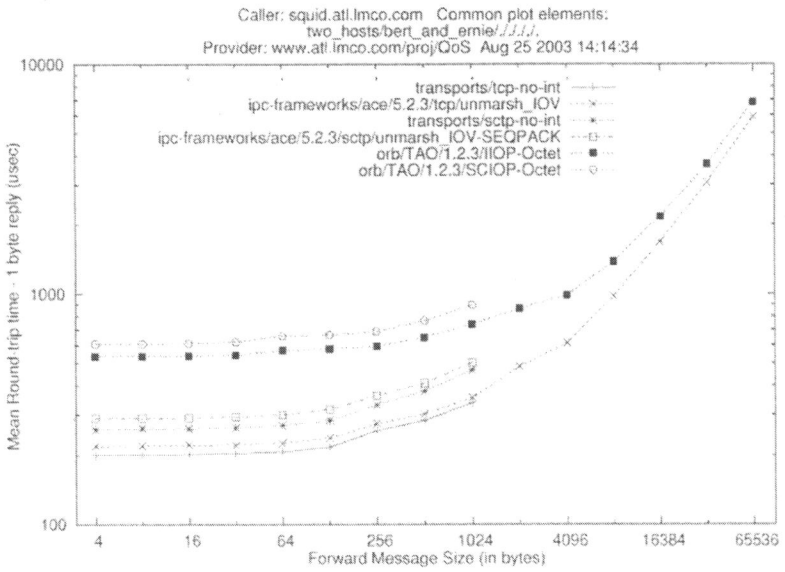

Fig. 4. Mean Roundtrip Latencies

Next, we examine the mean and maximum latencies when the 1% random packet loss module is enabled and compare this to the base case when there are no packet losses. Figures 5, 6, and 7 show these results for socket, ACE and ORB levels, respectively. In these graphs for each message size (shown on the x-axis) we show vertical lines that note the [min, max] latency range. In addition, a small symbol marks the mean value of observed data. Note that the y-axis is in logarithmic scale. In all tests the sample size is 1,000,000 roundtrip invocations.

The results show that under base tests where there are no packet losses, we experience only modest maximum latency of less than 1 msec. However, when 1% random losses are introduced, maximum latencies for TCP increases by about three orders of magnitude to well over 1 second.[3] However, SCTP maximum latencies do not increase beyond 30 msec which, we note, is below our original goal of keeping such latencies below 50 msec. This pattern of results is observed across the socket (Figure 5), ACE (Figure 6), or ORB (Figure 7) levels, which confirms that the maximum latency values are entirely controlled by the transport (and OS) issues.

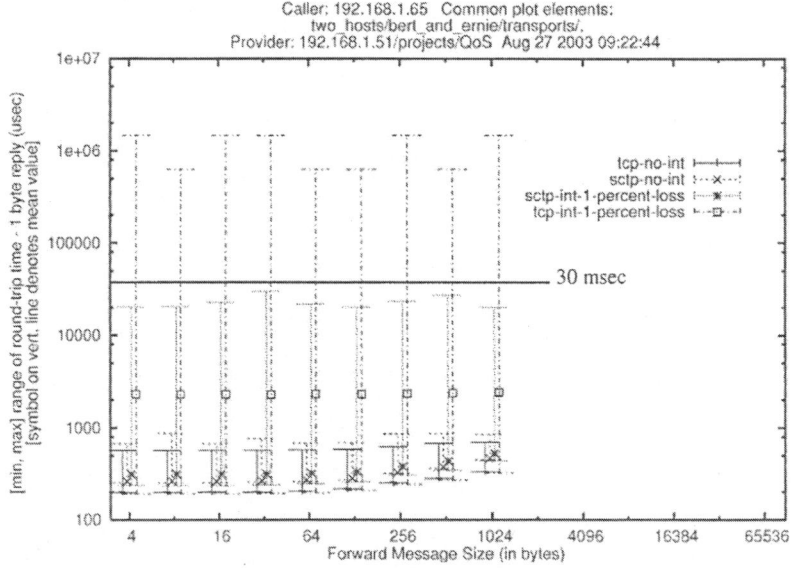

Fig. 5. Comparing TCP and SCTP at Socket Level

Finally we discuss the repeated, rapid link failures and restoration test case. We program the Network Failure Test Appliance to follow a pattern of 4 seconds down and 12 seconds up. The two links, A and B (see Figure 3), follow this pattern with an 8 second phase offset. This assures that at least one link is up all the time and that no two link state transitions occur closer than 4 seconds apart. This test, as expected, puts severe stress on the system. We conducted approximately 1,200 experiments with each experiment consisting of 10,000 roundtrip invocations. Maximum latency for each experiment is show in Figure 8. Following our observations with the 1% packet loss tests we would expect to record no maximum values greater than 30 msec. In-

---

[3] Due to extensively studied and well documented nature of TCP protocol this result is not surprising. Our goal is to compare how SCTP fares in comparison.

deed, most samples fall at or below 30 msec. Thus, even under unrealistically severe patterns of network path failure and restoration, we observe a nicely bounded application performance.

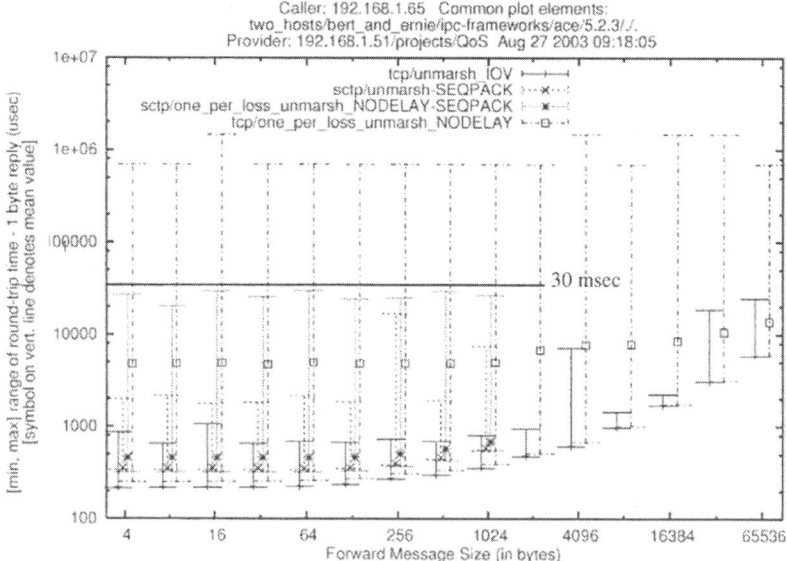

Fig. 6. Comparing TCP (SOCK_STREAM) and SCTP (SOCK_SEQPACK) at ACE Level

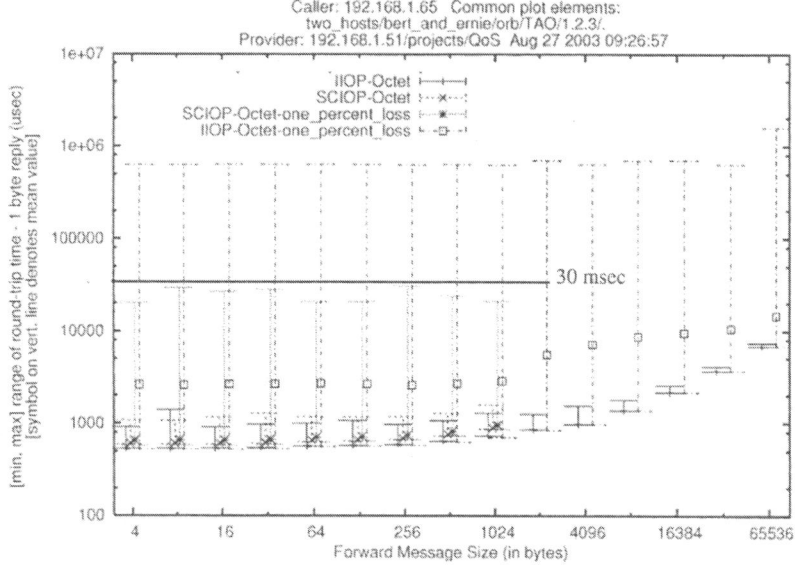

Fig. 7. Comparing TCP (IIOP) and SCTP (SCIOP) at ORB Level

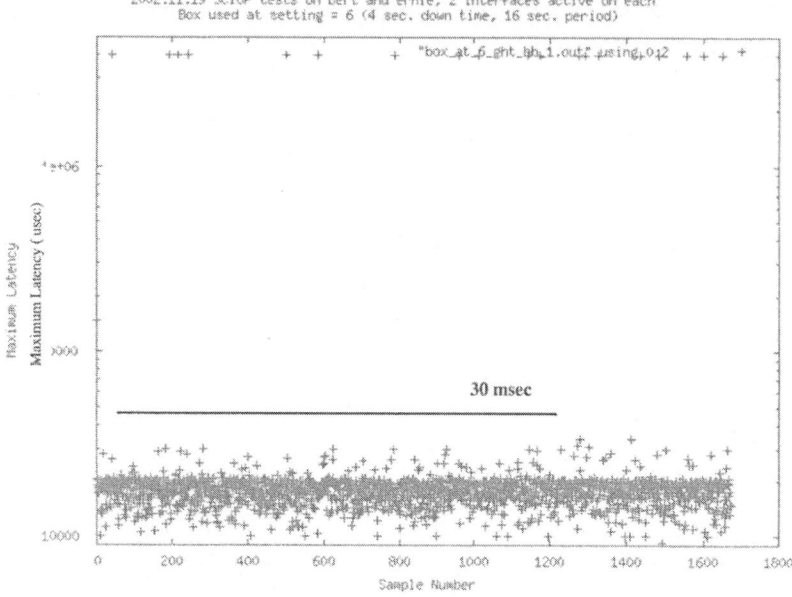

Fig. 8. Repeated Link Failure Test

8 Summary

We have successfully integrated SCTP in ACE and TAO by exploiting existing, well documented patterns and frameworks. Resulting systems show significantly improved ability to tolerate network link failures.

Table 2. Protocol Parameer Settings

Parameter	IETF	Openss7	LKSCTP
assoc_max_retrans	10	25	25
heartbeat_ivtl	30	1	1
init_retries	8	25	25
max_path_retrans	5	0	1
rto_initial	30s	0ms	1s
rto_max	60s	0ms	1s
rto_min	1s	0ms	1s

As of this writing we are experiencing significant stability and performance problems with the LKSCTP protocol stack. We are working with the developer community to overcome these difficulties. There is every reason to believe that both the OpenSS7 and LKSCTP stack will provide similar performance over the long run as they are on the same kernel. Table 2 summarizes the key protocol property settings. The IETF column has the recommended default values. These are too conservative for LAN environment for shipboard command and control. The other two columns show the aggressive settings that we use. Note that LKSCTP *does not permit RTO* (retransmission timeout) to be less than 1 second, which is too coarse for our requirements.[4] (Value of 0 msec under OpenSS7 reverts to a minimum of "1 tick" or 10 msec in 2.4.18 Linux kernel).

9 Future Work

Future work includes completing support for SCTP streams and proper integration of differentiated services with streams support. We are also working on providing support for SCIOP protocol properties. For experiments described in this paper we set various protocol properties by the /proc file system. Another possibility is to enhance some of the CORBA services, such as Audio/Video streams or RT/FT event channel, to exploit SCTP.

Acknowledgments. Primary sponsor for this projects was the U.S. Defense Advanced Research Projects Agency under the Program Composition for Embedded Systems Project, Contract #F33615-01-C-1847.
In addition, we would like to acknowledge detailed comments and suggestions from the reviewers, especially reviewer number three.

References

1. Stewart,, R., et al. "Stream Control Transmission Protocol," RFC 2960, October 2000
2. Schmidt, D.C., Huston, S.D., "Mastering Complexity with ACE and Patterns." Addison Wesley Professional, C++ Network Programming, Vol. 1–2
3. Schmidt, D.C., Levine D., and Mungee, S., "The Design and Performance of Real-Time Object Request Brokers," Computer Communications, Vol. 21, No. 4, April 1998
4. Schmidt, D.C., "Acceptor and Connector: Design Patterns for Initializing Communication Services," Pattern Languages of Program Design (R. Martin, F. Buschmann, and D. Riehle, eds.), Reading, MA: Addison-Wesley, 1997
5. O'Ryan, C., Kuhns, F., Schmidt, D.C., Othman, O., and Parsons, J., "The Design and Performance of a Pluggable Protocols Framework for Real-time Distributed Object Computing Middleware," Proceedings of the IFIP/ACM Middleware 2000 Conference, Pallisades, New York, April 3–7, 2000
6. Borland Software Corp., Nokia, Objective Interface Systems, Inc. GIOPSCTP Protocol Mapping, mars/03-05-01 and mars/03-05-02 Object Management Group, May 2003 http://doc.omg.org/mars/03-05-01, http://doc.omg.org/mars/03-05-02

---

[4] LKSCTP community is in he process of moving to msec granularity RTO values.

Enhancing Real-Time CORBA Predictability and Performance

Arvind S. Krishna[1], Douglas C. Schmidt[1], Krishna Raman[2], and
Raymond Klefstad[2]

[1] Electrical Engineering & Computer Science
Vanderbilt University, TN 37209, USA
{arvindk,schmidt}@dre.vanderbilt.edu
[2] Electrical Engineering & Computer Science
University of California, Irvine, CA 92697, USA
{kraman,klefstad}@uci.edu

Abstract. Distributed real-time and embedded (DRE) applications
possess stringent quality of service (QoS) requirements, such as low latency, bounded jitter, and high throughput. An increasing number of
DRE applications are developed using QoS-enabled middleware, such as
Real-time CORBA and the Real-time Specification for Java (RTSJ), to
ensure predictable end-to-end QoS. Real-time CORBA is an open middleware standard that allows DRE applications to allocate, schedule, and
control the QoS of CPU, memory, and networking resources. The RTSJ
provides extensions to Java that enable it to be used as the basis for
Real-time CORBA middleware and applications.

This paper provides two contributions to the study of QoS-enabled middleware for DRE applications. We first outline key Real-time CORBA
implementation challenges within the ORB Core and the Portable Object
Adapter. We then describe how these challenges have been addressed in
ZEN, which is an implementation of Real-time CORBA that runs atop
RTSJ platforms. Our results show that the judicious application of optimization strategies can enable RTSJ-based Real-time CORBA ORBs to
achieve effective QoS support for a range of DRE applications.

1 Introduction

Motivation. Over the past decade, distributed computing middleware, such as
CORBA [1], Java RMI [2], and SOAP/.NET [3], have emerged to reduce the
complexity of distributed systems. This type of middleware simplifies the development of distributed systems by off-loading many tedious and error-prone aspects of distributed computing from application developers to middleware developers. In this context, middleware offers several benefits, in particular hardware-,
language-, and OS-independence.

The benefits of middleware are also desirable for distributed real-time and
embedded (DRE) systems. Examples of DRE systems include telecommunication networks (*e.g.*, wireless phone services), tele-medicine (*e.g.*, robotic surgery),
process automation (*e.g.*, hot rolling mills), and defense applications (*e.g.*, total

R. Meersman et al. (Eds.): CoopIS/DOA/ODBASE 2003, LNCS 2888, pp. 1092–1109, 2003.
© Springer-Verlag Berlin Heidelberg 2003

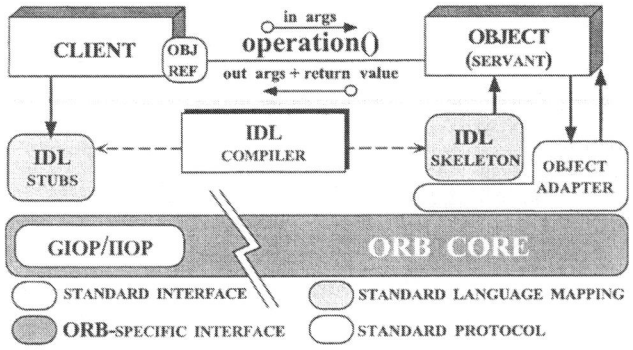

Fig. 1. Key Elements in the CORBA Reference Model

ship computing environments). DRE systems possess stringent quality of service (QoS) constraints, such as bandwidth, latency, jitter, and dependability requirements. The Real-time CORBA specification [4] was standardized by the OMG to support the QoS needs of certain classes of DRE systems, *i.e.*, those that rely on fixed-priority scheduling. Specifically, Real-time CORBA provides standard features that allow DRE applications to configure and control the following system resources:

- **Processor resources** via thread pools, priority mechanisms, intra-process mutexes, and a global scheduling service for real-time applications with fixed priorities,
- **Communication resources** via protocol properties and explicit bindings to server objects using priority bands and private connections, and
- **Memory resources** via buffering requests in queues and bounding the size of thread pools.

Optimizing Real-Time CORBA Object Request Brokers. CORBA middleware applications run atop an Object Request Broker (ORB), which allows clients to invoke operations on distributed objects without concern for object location, programming language, OS platform, communication protocols and interconnects, and hardware [5]. Figure 1 illustrates the key elements in the CORBA reference model [6] that collaborate to provide this degree of portability, interoperability, and transparency.[1] The Portable Object Adapter (POA) is the CORBA component that enables server developers to manage object implementations (known as "servants") portably across ORB implementations. The features offered by a POA can be customized via *policies* that are supplied at POA creation time [7]. These policies enable the POA to activate objects on demand or to generate persistent object references that remain active after the termination of their originating server process.

---

[1] This overview only focuses on the CORBA elements relevant to this paper. For a complete synopsis of CORBA's elements see [6].

At the heart of a CORBA implementation is the *ORB Core* and the *POA*. The ORB Core is the element in standard CORBA that handles connection and memory management, data transfer, endpoint demultiplexing, and concurrency control for client and server applications. The POA handles object activation/deactivation and request demultiplexing. When a client invokes an operation on a target object, the ORB Core works with the POA to deliver the request to the object and returns the response if the operation is has two-way semantics.

Our prior work on CORBA has explored many dimensions of ORB and POA design and performance, including scalable event processing; request demultiplexing; I/O subsystem and protocol integration; connection management, explicit binding, and real-time threading architectures, asynchronous and synchronous concurrent request processing, and IDL stub/skeleton optimizations. This paper explores a previous unexamined dimension of QoS enabled middleware design: *integration of ORB and POA optimization techniques with the Real-Time Specification for Java (RTSJ) to increase Real-time CORBA predictability, performance, and scalability.*

The vehicle used to showcase these optimizations is ZEN [8]. ZEN is an open-source[2] Real-time CORBA ORB designed using key concurrency and networked middleware patterns [9,10,11] and implemented using implementations of the Real-time Specification of Java (RTSJ) [12]. The design of ZEN was inspired by many of the patterns, techniques, and lessons learned when developing The ACE ORB (TAO). [13], which is an open-source[3] Real-time CORBA ORB implemented using C++, with enhancements designed to ensure efficient, predictable, and scalable QoS behavior for high-performance and real-time applications.

Paper Organization. The remainder of this paper is organized as follows: Section 2 presents key challenges within the ORB Core layer, focusing on buffer management and object location techniques, and explains how these challenges have been addressed in ZEN; Section 3 describes Real-time CORBA predictability challenges within the POA layer and describes how ZEN addresses these challenges; Section 4 compares our work on ZEN with related research efforts; and Section 5 presents concluding remarks and outlines our future work.

2   Optimizing ZEN's ORB Core

Optimizing the ORB Core to support DRE applications poses several challenges to ORB implementors. This section outlines some of the key challenges present in this layer and describes the optimizations we have applied in ZEN to ensure the predictability and efficiency required by DRE applications. These optimizations include minimizing memory management operations using efficient buffer management algorithms and transparently collocating clients and servants that are present in the same address space.

---

[2] ZEN can be downloaded from www.zen.uci.edu.
[3] TAO can be downloaded from deuce.doc.wustl.edu/Download.html.

2.1   Buffer Management Optimizations

Context. The ORB Core uses memory buffers to store GIOP messages before sending and after receiving the messages across a transport. These buffers are serially reusable, which means that only one thread can use a given buffer at any time, though after its completion the same buffer may be reused by another thread.

Problem. A naive Java implementation for ORB buffers would use operator `new` to allocate each one, thereby allowing the Java garbage collector to reclaim them for later use. Continued allocation/deallocation of these buffers would eventually lead to an invocation of the garbage collector, which is undesirable in DRE applications since it may incur unbounded jitter [14].

Solution → Buffer Management Optimizations. One solution to the problem of unbounded jitter is to pre-allocate buffer pools at ORB initialization time. A simple pool manager can allocate from the pool and return unneeded buffers to the pool after they are no longer needed. Application developers and/or system integrators can be given configuration control over buffer size and pool size. We can provide alternative dynamic storage management algorithms, such as first fit, random fit [15], and best fit [16].

Applying the Solution in ZEN. ZEN supports the following buffer management strategies:

- **Linked List** strategy, in which a simple list is used to maintain all allocated buffers. The first fit algorithm is used to locate the most appropriate buffer. This strategy is suitable when buffer sizes are comparable. When buffer sizes vary, however, the search time considerably degrades as the list is not ordered. For example, the worst case behavior for this strategy is $O(n)$ when all buffers in the list are smaller than the required size.
- **Multi-level buckets** strategy in which, the buffers are divided into partitions *i.e.*, buckets based using a partition strategy that is typically a factor of the block size. To locate a buffer of given size, the most appropriate bucket is first determined, then the first fit strategy is used to return the most appropriate buffer. A default bucket is used for significantly large/small buffer sizes. This strategy is an improvement over the linked list scheme and has constant time lookup time for the non-default case. The default bucket has a behavior similar to the linked list scheme.
- **Buffer Pools** strategy in which the ORB maintains a pre-allocated pool of buffers of a fixed size. These individual buffers may be chained to hold larger messages and are written using gather-write I/O system calls. This strategy has a constant buffer lookup time, but incurs the overhead of managing multiple buffers. Moreover, earlier versions of Java (*i.e.*, up to JDK 1.3) did not provide gather-write facility requiring multiple I/O calls to read/write the buffer to the stream. ZEN provides this facility via Java's new I/O (`nio`) [17] package.

In ZEN, the abstract `ByteBufferManager` class manages the various buffer management schemes. The read/write helper methods defined on the buffer manager are used to marshal/demarshal GIOP messages, which are represented in ZEN as instances of `CDRInputStream` and `CDROutputStream` classes. ZEN provides two buffer manager implementations:

- The `VectoredByteBufferManager` implements the Buffer Pool optimization strategy explained above. This manager can only be supported with a JDK version 1.4 or later that provides gather-write I/O system calls.
- The `NonVectoredByteBufferManager` implements the multi-level bucket buffer management strategy.

The application developer can chooses either one of the buffer managers by setting the `zen.cdr.bufferManagerStrategy` property in the properties file. ZEN uses the Strategy pattern [18] to transparently plug in concrete buffer managers implementations. Moreover, this pluggable approach enables other buffer manager implementations to be provided, as long as they inherit from the `BufferManager` base class. Each of ZEN's concrete buffer manager classes are associated with a buffer allocator that controls how buffers are allocated and deallocated. The `ByteBufferAllocator` class shown in Figure 2 is the base class for all concrete buffer allocators. ZEN, provides the following concrete allocation schemes:

- `DynamicByteBufferAllocator`, where buffers are allocated/deallocated for each GIOP message sent/received.
- `CachedByteBufferAllocator`, where all the allocated buffers are cached and new buffers are created only if necessary. The `CacheNIOByteBufferAllocator` class deals with caching buffers in the Java `nio` package.
- `DynamicNIOByteBufferAllocator` deals with nio buffers, but buffers are allocated for each request.

In ZEN, buffer allocators can be configured by setting the `zen.cdr.bufferAllocationStrategy` in the properties file. Similar to buffer managers, concrete buffer allocators implementations are plugged in using the Strategy pattern.

DRE applications often send small messages, whereas enterprise application may need to send larger messages. It is therefore important to configure the minimum block size (unit of allocation) to minimize fragmentation. ZEN allows the end-user to configure the block size using the `zen.giop.messageBlock`

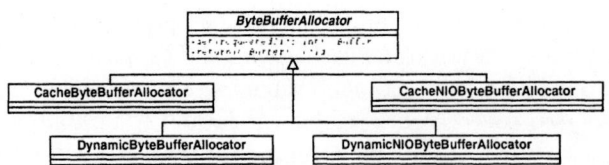

Fig. 2. ZEN Buffer Allocators Class Diagram

Table 1. ZEN's Buffer Management Summary

	Vectored	NonVectored
cached	non-compatible	compatible
cached-nio	compatible	non-compatible
dynamic	non-compatible	compatible
dynamic-nio	compatible	non-compatible

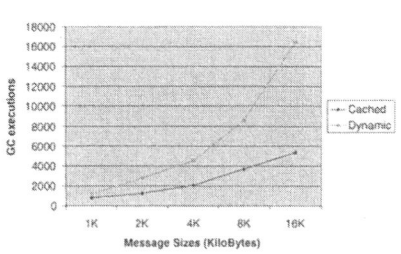

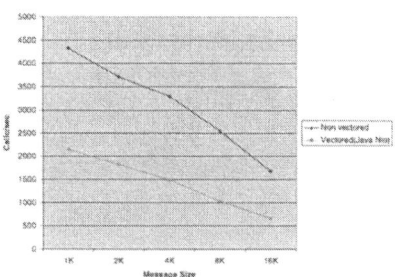

Fig. 3. Cached versus Dynamic GC analysis

Fig. 4. Vectored versus Non-Vectored Throughput Analysis

property defined in the properties file. This variable should be set with a value corresponding to the message sizes that the system expects. The default value for this property is set to 1,024 bytes in ZEN. Combining buffer manager and allocators yields the different alternatives summarized in Table 1. As shown in the table, only certain combinations are possible.

Empirical Results. We compared the performance of ZEN's buffer management optimizations. The following experiments were conducted:

- **Garbage collection analysis** compared the reduction in the number of garbage collection sweep by using caching with dynamic allocations. Our motivation was to observe if the buffer optimizations reduce garbage collection, and in turn increase predictability.
- **Throughput analysis** compared difference in throughput between `Vectored` and `NonVectored` buffer management strategies. Our motivation was to compare Buffer Pool and Multi-level bucket schemes in ZEN.

Since the RTSJ does not yet support java's nio package, these experiments were conducted using JDK 1.4.2. The testbed used was an Intel Pentium IV 1800 Mhz processor with 512 MB of main memory running Linux OS 2.4.21-0.11. We also used ZEN version 0.8 for these experiments.

- **Garbage collection analysis.** In this experiment the message sizes of the GIOP request sent by the client were increased by a factor of 2 starting with 1KB and continuing to 16KB. In each case, the number of GC executions at the server was measured for a total of 10,000 iterations.

Figure 3 shows that buffer caching significantly reduces the number of GC sweeps. For both cases, GC executions increased with increasing buffer sizes. However, with caching the increase is gradual, whereas the increase for dynamic allocation is sharper. For example, in the case when message size is 16KB, the number of GC sweeps for dynamic case is greater by a factor ~3, whereas for 1K it is greater only by a factor of ~1.5. These results show that use of ZEN's buffer management algorithms reduce GC executions significantly.

– **Throughput analysis.** For this experiment throughput was defined as the number of events processed/sec at the server. In this experiment the message sizes of the GIOP request sent by the client was increased by a factor of 2, starting with 1KB and continuing to 16KB. In each case, throughput at the server was measured for a total of 10,000 iterations.

As shown in Figure 4, for both strategies throughput decreases with increase in buffer size. The Vectored strategy, however, incurred greater overhead than the Non-Vectored strategy. This result was not expected since (1) the vectored strategy does not incur any data copying overhead as buffers are chained and (2) the Non-Vectored strategy incurs significant resizing overhead leading to greater data copying. Researchers [19] at University of Maryland also observed decreased throughput when using java's `nio` package. Their experiments showed that to speed up performance, nio's `ByteBuffers` should be converted into normal `byte[]` arrays for processing and should be used while writing to the network. We plan to implement this optimization in ZEN shortly.

2.2   Collocation Optimizations

Context. In addition to separating interfaces from implementations, a key strength of CORBA is its decoupling of servant implementations from how the servants are configured into server processes. CORBA is often used to communicate between remote objects. There are configurations, however, where a client and servant must be collocated in the same address space.

Problem. When the client and server are collocated in the same address space, there should be no overhead from marshaling and demarshaling data or transmitting requests and replies over a "loop back" transport device. A naive implementation of CORBA would incur these overheads, thereby reducing performance and increasing jitter.

Solution → Collocation Optimization. Clients can obtain an object reference in several ways, *e.g.*, from a CORBA Naming Service or Trading Service. Likewise, clients can use the `string_to_object` operation to convert a stringified Interoperable Object Reference (IOR) into an object reference. To ensure locality transparency, an ORB's collocation strategy must determine if the object is collocated within the same ORB and/or process. If so, it should optimize the request processing strategy by not incurring the overheads mentioned above.

Applying the solution in ZEN. ZEN supports the following two levels of collocation optimizations:

1. **Per-process collocation**, where the client and server ORBs are present in the same address space.
2. **Per-ORB collocation**, where the client and server ORBs are the same. This scheme is more fine-grained than per-process collocation, as the information relating to the target POA servant is directly available to the client. Moreover, this scheme also localizes the side-effects of collocation, such as priority inversions [20] within a single ORB.

For these two levels of collocation, the following two strategies can be applied:

1. **Standard collocation** where the ZEN Thru_POA collocation strategy uses "collocation-safe stubs." As indicated by this strategy's name, all invocations go through the POA, *i.e.*, the steps for processing the request are the same as that of a remote request. This strategy ensures that all standard POA services (such as POA_Current) and various locks within the ORB Core and the POA are honored. Thru_POA is the default collocation strategy in ZEN.
2. **Direct collocation** where the collocation strategy forwards all requests directly to the servant, thereby bypassing the POA. Since the Thru_POA strategy adheres to all CORBA semantics for request processing, it incurs a considerable amount of overhead that may not be acceptable for DRE applications. In contrast, the direct strategy directly delivers a request to the servant, thereby avoiding marshaling overhead and context setup overhead (initializing current services in the POA and the ORB). This extension is not compliant with the CORBA specification, however, and is provided as an extension for DRE applications having stringent latency requirements.

Irrespective of the combination used, the following three steps are involved in processing collocated requests:

1. Determining Collocation. To determine if an object reference is collocated, ZEN's ORB Core maintains a *collocation table* that maps ORB endpoints to ORB object references. For IIOP, the endpoints are specified using hostname and port number tuples.

Multiple ORBs can reside in the same server process and each of these ORBs may support multiple transport endpoints. Rather than having one table per protocol, all endpoint structures in ZEN inherit from the Address class. By overriding the hashCode() and equals() methods for each type of endpoint, a single table can maintain information about all ORBs and their respective endpoints.

2. Resolving Locality. Figure 5 shows how ZEN determines if an object is collocated. The client application uses the ORB to resolve the reference obtained ((1)). The ORB consults its registry and resolves locality based on the level of locality configured in the client ORB (**2**). If local, the collocated POA is determined using the ServerRequestHandler (**3**). The ORB then creates a special collocated CORBA object (**4**). The client application narrows this generic

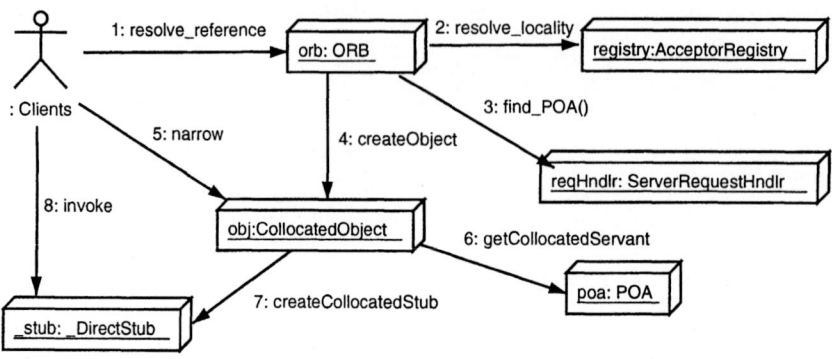

Fig. 5. Finding a Collocated Object in ZEN

object **(5)**, which obtains the collocated servant from the POA **(6)**. If a servant is found, a special `DirectStub` is created for servant-based operations **(7,8)**, otherwise the appropriate exception is raised.

3. Performing Object Invocations. ZEN has two strategies for performing object invocations after it resolves locality. These two schemes – `Thru_POA` and `Direct` collocation optimization – are discussed below:

- **Thru_POA collocation optimization.** This strategy uses a collocation safe stub to handle operation invocations on a collocated object. Invoking an operation via a collocation safe stub ensures the following checks are performed: (1) applicable client policies are used, (2) the server ORB (same/different than the client ORB) has not been shutdown, (3) the thread-safety of all ORB and POA operations, (4) the POA managing the servant still exists, (5) the POA Manager of this POA is queried to check if invocations are allowed, (6) the servant for the collocated object is still active, (7) the POA Current's context is set up for this upcall, and (8) all POA policies (*e.g.*, the *ThreadPolicy*, *LifespanPolicy*, and *ServantRetentionPolicy*) are respected.

- **Direct collocation optimization.** To minimize the overhead of the standard collocation strategy describes above, it is possible to implement collocation to forward all requests directly to the servant class, thereby bypassing the POA. When implemented correctly, the performance of ZEN's `Direct` collocation strategy should be competitive to that of invoking a virtual method call on the servant. This strategy is not compliant with the CORBA standard, however, since: (1) the POA Current is not set up, (2) interceptors are not enabled, (3) the POA manager state is ignored, (4) not all POA policies are not considered (*e.g.*, the *ThreadPolicy* and *RequestProcessing* policies are circumvented, and (5) the ORB's status is not checked.

Empirical Results. The performance of the collocation strategies described above was compared with that of no collocation, *i.e.*, where client and server communicate via the loopback device. The level of collocation was set to the the per-ORB

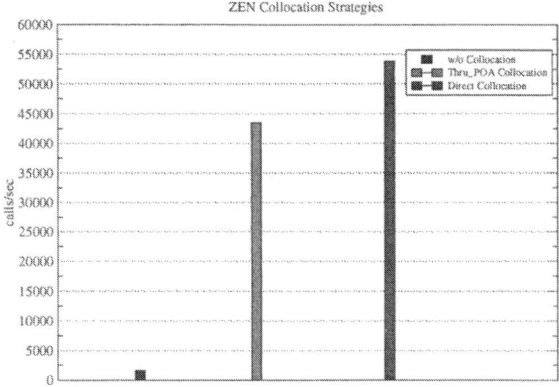

Fig. 6. Performance of ZEN's Collocation Strategies

strategy for this experiment. The measurements were performed on an Intel Pentium III 864 Mhz processor with 256 MB of main memory. For these experiments, ZEN version 0.8 was compiled using the GNU `gcj` compiler version 3.2.1 and executed using jRate [7] 0.3a on Linux 2.4.7-timesys-3.1.214 kernel.

Figure 6 shows the performance of the individual collocation strategies in ZEN.

With no collocation, ZEN performs 1,675 call/sec. With the `Thru_POA` collocation optimization, the performance is greatly improved to about 43,000 calls/sec. The `Direct` collocation strategy gives the best performance of around 53,000 calls/sec. These metrics show that `Direct` collocation would be more suitable for real-time systems that require high throughput and low latency. The standard collocation strategy is still twenty five times faster than the non-collocated request processing strategy.

3   Optimizing ZEN's Portable Object Adapter

The CORBA Portable Object Adapter (POA) is the principal component involved in request processing. Our prior work with ZEN's POA focused on designing predictable and scalable request demultiplexing techniques [21]. This section describes solutions to Real-time CORBA predictability scalability challenges in this layer, focusing on servant lookup and object key processing techniques.

3.1   Optimizing Servant Lookups

Context. By default, a POA contains an Active Object Map (AOM), which is used by the POA to map the object id in a client request to the corresponding servant that implements the request. Operations defined on a POA can be classified according to whether they operate on

- An *object id* in the request header, *e.g.*, a client request that is dispatched by the POA to a servant, or

– A *servant* outside the context of a client request, *e.g.*, the _this() method used in conjunction with the IMPLICIT_ACTIVATION POA policy, which causes the POA to activate the servant if it is not active already.

Problem. For operations based on object ids, ZEN implements an *active demultiplexing strategy* [21]. This strategy ensures constant $O(1)$ lookup in the average and worst cases, regardless of the number of servants in the POA's AOM. Unfortunately, for operations based on servants, a reverse index into the AOM is required. A naive way to implement this reverse index would use linear search, even when the active demultiplexing strategy is used for the object id lookup. Linear search becomes prohibitively expensive as the number of servants increases.

Solution → *Strategize the active object map.* To avoid the overhead of linear search, a *reverse lookup map* can be used for the operations based on servants. This type of map uses dynamic hashing to associate a servant with its object id in $O(1)$ average-case time. A disadvantage of adding a reverse lookup map to the POA is the increased overhead of maintaining an additional map in the POA. Two updates are then required for every object activation and deactivation:
– One for the active demultiplexing map and
– One for the reverse lookup map.
This additional processing, however, does not affect the run-time critical path of the lookup operations based on object ids. Moreover, a reverse map is needed only if the POA has the UNIQUE_ID value for the *IdUniqueness* policy, which guarantees a *one-to-one* association between the servant and its object id.

Applying the solution in ZEN. The reverse lookup operations require a *one-to-one* association between the servant and its object id. Hence, either a SingleMap or a DualMap (which is a single map combined with a reverse map) is used, depending on the designated *IdUniqueness* policy value. This strategization minimizes the footprint of ZEN's POA by eliminating a reverse map when it is not needed.

Though the performance of dynamic hashing degrades as the number of collisions increase, no servant-based operations occur in the request processing path, *i.e.*, critical path. For all operations present in the critical path, the strategies used in ZEN ensure $O(1)$ lookup time in the worst case.

Empirical results. To evaluate the performance of ZEN's servant lookup optimizations described above, we measured the time required to complete a servant-based operation (servant_to_id()) with and without a reverse map. The number of active servants was varied from 1 to 1,000 in increments of 250.

• *Hardware and software testbed.* Experiments were performed on an Intel Pentium III1 864 Mhz processor with 256 MB of main memory. For these experiments, ZEN version 0.8 was compiled using the GNU gcj [22] compiler version 3.2.1 and executed using jRate 0.3a on Linux 2.4.7-timesys-3.1.214 kernel. A sample size of 50,000 data points was used to generate the results.

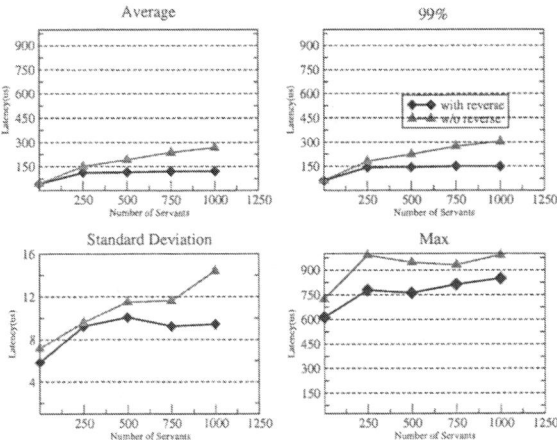

Fig. 7. Performance Comparison With/Without a Reverse Lookup Map

- *Analysis of results.* We now analyze the results of benchmarks that measure the average latency, the dispersion, and worst case behavior for the various POA demultiplexing test cases.

  - **Average measures.** Figure 7 shows how the latency increases sharply as the number of active servants in the POA increases when ZEN's reverse lookup feature is disabled. The latency becomes $\sim$266μsecs when the POA has 1,000 active servants. With the reverse lookup map enabled, however, the latency increases gradually as the number of active servants increases, with an average time of $\sim$110μsecs.

  - **Dispersion measures.** The dispersion is tighter when a reverse lookup map is used, while increasing linearly for the no reverse map case. This result shows that there is greater predictability when the reverse map is used than when no reverse map is used. Dispersion does increase, however, even with reverse maps ($\sim$4.5 for the 1 case to $\sim$8.5 for the 250 case) due to collisions that occur in the AOM.

  - **Worst case measures.** The worst case measures follow a trend similar to the average values with latency increasing with number of servants when no reverse lookup map is used. The use of a reverse map bounds the worst case measure.

  In contrast to the linear search case (where latency grows with increase in servant loads), the empirical results in Figure 7 show that the use of reverse map bounds the average latency. Moreover, dispersion and worst case measures are tighter and flatter for the reverse map, which indicates better predictability for servant lookup operations. With an increase in the load on the AOM, however, the performance of dynamic hashing does degrade, as indicated by the increase in dispersion and worst case measures.

3.2   Optimizing Object Key Generation and Processing

Context. An object key contains the information necessary to process a client request. Since the POA is in the critical path of request processing, object key parsing must be efficient.

Problem. The presence and absence of POA policies affect the structure of object keys generated by a POA. For example, the standard CORBA *Lifespan* policy stipulates that transient objects cannot outlive the POA that created them. To enforce this constraint, ZEN includes a time stamp to differentiate between instances of the same transient POA. In contrast, a persistent key needs no time stamp, since its lifetime is independent of the lifetime of the POA that created its associated object.

Similarly, dynamic activation of transient POAs is not permitted. Object keys of transient POAs therefore need not include the POA path name. Conversely, a persistent POA would have the complete path name for dynamic POA activation. Using a single parsing strategy for all generated object keys would thus be inefficient, increasing the time required for request processing.

Solution → Strategize object key formats. The structure and sizes of the object keys generated vary depending on the *Lifespan* and *IdAssignment* policy values. The efficiency of object key parsing therefore depends on the object key structure. To ensure efficient parsing, generated object keys should have different formats that enhance the predictability in the layout of the individual pieces within the object key. For example, an object key corresponding to the transient and system id policies has a predictable size for the following reasons:

1. Since the POA is transient, the POA path name may be omitted because dynamic activation is not possible.
2. The size of the object id is known *a priori*, since the strategy used for generating the id is known (*e.g.*, it is the size of an `int` or a `long`).

When the persistent and user id policies are in place, however, the size of the object key is less predictable for the following reasons:

1. Since dynamic activations are permitted, the complete POA path name is added to the object key. The size of this component depends on the depth of the POA hierarchy, which can be nested arbitrarily deeply.
2. The object id size is also variable, since server applications may assign ids in whatever fashion they choose.

Applying the solution in ZEN. The following are the four object key formats supported by ZEN, based on the combination of the two different policy values (*Lifespan* and *IdAssignment*) associated with a POA:

- [*TypeTS*] – transient and system id,
- [*TypeTU*] – transient and user id,
- [*TypePS*] – persistent and system id and
- [*TypePU*] – persistent and user id.

ZEN uses active demultiplexing [23] for POA and servant level demultiplexing. Thus, the POA and object ids in the object keys are encoded as the Asynchronous Completion Token [10] (ACT) pattern, which efficiently demultiplexes and processes the response of asynchronous operations. The use of this pattern ensures $O(1)$ lookup time irrespective of the POA organization. The POA operations `create_reference()` and `create_reference_with_id()` create references that do not activate an object in the POA for the servant. Object keys that correspond to these references do not have the ACTs encoded in their object keys. In ZEN, the efficiency of object key parsing stems from the following **hit** and **miss** penalties (which are similar to a memory cache hit and miss):

- A *hit* occurs when the ACTs at the POA and servant levels lead to the required request processors. A *hit penalty* is the processing overhead required to service the request when a *hit* occurs. In a type PU object key, for example, if the POA and the servant ACT hint yield a hit, the length of the POA path name must be processed to compute the start index of the object id. In a type TS object key, this penalty is zero.
- A *miss* occurs when the ACTs at the POA and servant level do not lead to the required request processors. A *miss penalty* is the processing overhead required to service the request when a miss occurs. For example, in a type TS object key, if the ACT hint to locate the POA fails, an OBJECT_NOT_EXIST exception is returned to the client, since dynamic activations are not supported. The additional processing time required for a miss is therefore zero.

Empirical Results. To evaluate ZEN's object key processing techniques described above, we conducted the following experiment:

• *Hardware and software test bed.* Experiments were performed on an Intel Pentium III1 864 Mhz processor with 256 MB of main memory. For these experiments, ZEN version 0.8 was compiled using the GNU `gcj` [22] compiler version 3.2.1 and executed using jRate 0.3a on Linux 2.4.7-timesys-3.1.214 kernel. A sample size of 50,000 data points was used to generate the results.

To evaluate ZEN's object key processing techniques, we compared the hit penalties associated with parsing object key types TS and PU. As the TS object key suffers no hit penalty, while a PU object key type incurs the overhead of reading the POA path name, this experiment measured the time required to parse the object id embedded in the object key. Further, as the length of path name depends on the nesting of the POA hierarchy, the nesting of the POA hierarchy was increased from 1 to 100 in increments of 25, and the resulting object id parsing time was measured.

• *Analysis of results.* We now analyze the results of benchmarks that measure the average latency, the dispersion, and worst case behavior for the object id lookup operation.

- **Average measures.** Figure 8 shows that the average latency for TS object key is constant across the POA hierarchy (~ 1.97 μsecs). However, latency for

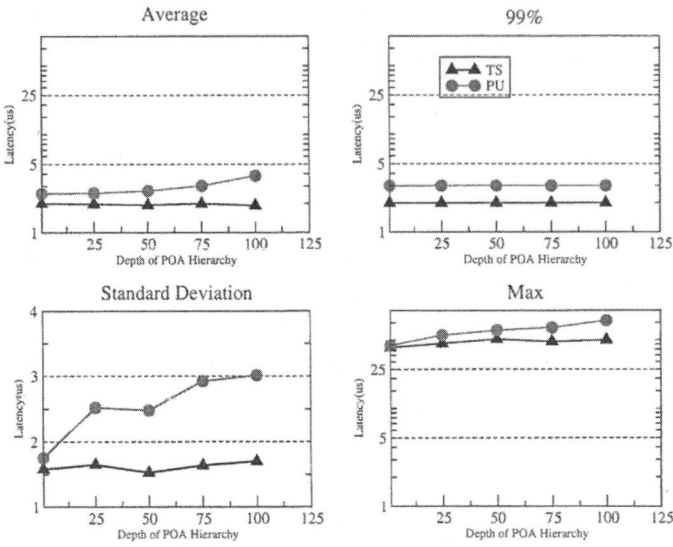

Fig. 8. Predictability analysis for TS & PU Object Keys

PU object key gradually increases with the nesting of the POA hierarchy. For example, latency varies from ∼ 1.9 μsecs (depth = 1) to ∼ 3.2 μsecs (depth = 100). The increase stems from reading the POA pathname, which increases in length with an increase in the depth of the POA hierarchy.

– **Dispersion measures.** The dispersion is flatter for TS than for PU. Dispersion measures for TS are constant across the depth of the hierarchy. However, the dispersion for PU increases with the nesting of the POA hierarchy, ∼ 2.01 (depth =1) to ∼ 3 (depth =100). This increase in the dispersion measures shows that there is a loss in the predictability for the PU object key with an increase in the nesting.

– **Worst case measures.** Both the 99% bound and the worst case measures for TS are tighter than PU for all cases. Worst case measures for PU increase with the nesting of the hierarchy.

The efficiency and predictability of object key parsing in ZEN corresponds directly to the hit and miss penalties associated with each object key structures. Since type TS and TU structures offer greater predictability in parsing, hit and miss penalties are zero. For a type PS key, the hit penalty is 0, but a miss penalty is incurred for parsing of the POA path name. A type PU key has the greatest hit and miss penalties and consequently the greatest unpredictability. The predictability in object key size therefore degrades from TS to PU.

4   Related Work

In recent years, a considerable amount of research has focused on enhancing the predictability of middleware for DRE applications. In this section, we summarize key efforts related to our work on ZEN.

TAO. TAO is an open-source, high-performance real-time ORB written in C++. It had the first implementation of the POA specification [24]. The design of the POA is based on patterns [10] that have been adopted and enhanced [11] in ZEN. TAO also provides a complete implementation of the Real-time CORBA specification, which has provided invaluable insights that we have applied to ZEN's Real-time CORBA implementation using RTSJ and jRate.

Time-Triggered Message-Triggered Objects (TMO) project [25] at the University of California, Irvine, supports the integrated design of distributed OO systems and real-time simulators of their operating environments. The TMO model provides structured timing semantics for distributed real-time object-oriented applications by extending conventional invocation semantics for object methods, *i.e.*, CORBA operations, to include (1) invocation of time-triggered operations based on system times and (2) invocation and time bounded execution of conventional message-triggered operations.

jRate and TimeSys RTSJ Reference Implementation (RI). TimeSys has developed the official RTSJ Reference Implementation (RI) [26], which is a fully compliant implementation of Java that provides all the mandatory features in the RTSJ.[4] jRate [7,27] is an open-source RTSJ-based real-time Java implementation developed at Washington University, St. Louis. jRate extends the open-source GNU Compiler for Java (GCJ) runtime system [22] to provide an ahead-of-time compiled platform. The Java and RTSJ services, such as garbage collection, real-time threads, and scheduling, are accessible via the GCJ and jRate runtime systems, respectively.

5   Concluding Remarks

Distributed real-time and embedded (DRE) systems are growing in number and importance as software is increasingly used to automate and integrate information systems with physical systems. In general, DRE middleware (1) off-loads the tedious and error-prone aspects of distributed computing from application developers to middleware developers, (2) provides standards that ultimately reduce development time, and (3) enhances extensibility for future application needs.

This paper presented the optimizations applied in ZEN to implement Real-time CORBA. To achieve effective end-to-end real-time predictability within the ORB Core and the POA, the paper focused on applying optimization principles

---

[4] As soon as we receive the commercial TimeSys RTSJ implementation, we plan to port ZEN to it and rerun our benchmarks using it.

to ensure predictability including its memory management, collocation, servant lookups and object key processing schemes. These optimizations are applied at the algorithmic and data structural level, they are independent of the RTSJ implementation.

Acknowledgments. We would like to acknowledge the efforts of the other members of the Distributed Object Computing (DOC) research group at UC Irvine who are contributing to the design and implementation of ZEN. Special thanks to Carlos 'O Ryan, Ossama Othman, and Angelo Corsaro for contributing to ZEN's initial design.

References

1. Object Management Group, *The Common Object Request Broker: Architecture and Specification, Revision 2.6*, Dec. 2001.
2. A. Wollrath, R. Riggs, and J. Waldo, "A Distributed Object Model for the Java System," *USENIX Computing Systems*, vol. 9, November/December 1996.
3. J. Snell and K. MacLeod, *Programming Web Applications with SOAP*. O'Reilly, 2001.
4. Object Management Group, *Real-time CORBA Specification*, OMG Document formal/02-08-02 ed., Aug. 2002.
5. M. Henning and S. Vinoski, *Advanced CORBA Programming with C++*. Reading, MA: Addison-Wesley, 1999.
6. Object Management Group, *The Common Object Request Broker: Architecture and Specification*, 3.0.2 ed., Dec. 2002.
7. A. Corsaro and D. C. Schmidt, "The Design and Performance of the jRate Real-Time Java Implementation," in *On the Move to Meaningful Internet Systems 2002: CoopIS, DOA, and ODBASE* (R. Meersman and Z. Tari, eds.), (Berlin), pp. 900–921, Lecture Notes in Computer Science 2519, Springer Verlag, 2002.
8. R. Klefstad, D. C. Schmidt, and C. O'Ryan, "The Design of a Real-time CORBA ORB using Real-time Java," in *Proceedings of the International Symposium on Object-Oriented Real-time Distributed Computing*, IEEE, Apr. 2002.
9. F. Buschmann, R. Meunier, H. Rohnert, P. Sommerlad, and M. Stal, *Pattern-Oriented Software Architecture–A System of Patterns*. New York: Wiley & Sons, 1996.
10. D. C. Schmidt, M. Stal, H. Rohnert, and F. Buschmann, *Pattern-Oriented Software Architecture: Patterns for Concurrent and Networked Objects, Volume 2*. New York: Wiley & Sons, 2000.
11. A. Corsaro, D. C. Schmidt, R. Klefstad, and C. O'Ryan, "Virtual Component: a Design Pattern for Memory-Constrained Embedded Applications," in *Proceedings of the 9th Annual Conference on the Pattern Languages of Programs*, (Monticello, Illinois), Sept. 2002.
12. Bollella, Gosling, Brosgol, Dibble, Furr, Hardin, and Turnbull, *The Real-Time Specification for Java*. Addison-Wesley, 2000.
13. D. C. Schmidt, D. L. Levine, and S. Mungee, "The Design and Performance of Real-Time Object Request Brokers," *Computer Communications*, vol. 21, pp. 294–324, Apr. 1998.

14. S. Grarup and J. Seligmann, "Incremental garbage collection," Tech. Rep. Student Thesis, Department of Computer Science, Aarhus University, Aug. 1993.

15. S. Albers and M. Mitzenmacher, "Average case analyses of first fit and random fit bin packing," in *9th Annual ACM Symposium on Discrete Algorithms*, May 1998.

16. E. Coffman, D. Johnson, P. Shor, and R. Weber, "Markov chains, computer proofs and average-case analysis of best fit bin packing," in *Proceedings of the 25th Annual ACM Symposium on Theory of Computing*, (New York, USA), Aug. 1993.

17. R. Hutchins, *Java NIO*. O'Reilly & Associates, 2002.

18. E. Gamma, R. Helm, R. Johnson, and J. Vlissides, *Design Patterns: Elements of Reusable Object-Oriented Software*. Reading, MA: Addison-Wesley, 1995.

19. W. Pugh and J. Spacco, "Mpjava: High-performance message passing in java using java.nio," in *MASLAP'03 Mid-Atlantic Student Worskshop on Programming Language and Systems*, Apr. 2003.

20. D. C. Schmidt, S. Mungee, S. Flores-Gaitan, and A. Gokhale, "Software Architectures for Reducing Priority Inversion and Non-determinism in Real-time Object Request Brokers," *Journal of Real-time Systems, special issue on Real-time Computing in the Age of the Web and the Internet*, vol. 21, no. 2, 2001.

21. A. Krishna, D. C. Schmidt, R. Klefstad, and A. Corsaro, "Towards predictable real-time Java object request brokers," in *Proceedings of the 9th Real-time/Embedded Technology and Applications Symposium (RTAS)*, (Washington, DC), IEEE, May 2003.

22. GNU is Not Unix, "GCJ: The GNU Compiler for Java."
http://gcc.gnu.org/java, 2002.

23. A. Gokhale and D. C. Schmidt, "Measuring and Optimizing CORBA Latency and Scalability Over High-speed Networks," *Transactions on Computing*, vol. 47, no. 4, 1998.

24. I. Pyarali and D. C. Schmidt, "An Overview of the CORBA Portable Object Adapter," *ACM StandardView*, vol. 6, Mar. 1998.

25. K. H. K. Kim, "Object Structures for Real-Time Systems and Simulators," *IEEE Computer*, pp. 62–70, Aug. 1997.

26. TimeSys, "Real-Time Specification for Java Reference Implementation."
www.timesys.com/rtj, 2001.

27. A. Corsaro and D. C. Schmidt, "Evaluating Real-Time Java Features and Performance for Real-time Embedded Systems," in *Proceedings of the 8th IEEE Real-Time Technology and Applications Symposium*, (San Jose), IEEE, Sept. 2002.

Jini Supporting Ubiquitous and Pervasive Computing*

Kasper Hallenborg and Bent Bruun Kristensen

Maersk Mc-Kinney Moller Institute
University of Southern Denmark
Odense M, 5230, Denmark
{khp,bbk}@mip.sdu.dk

Abstract. The overall purpose of this article is partly to give a brief overview of the TangO conceptual model, partly to explore the Jini technology as a means for support of pervasive systems in general and the TangO conceptual model in particular, and to emphasize the advantages and weaknesses of the Jini technology for ubiquitous computing. We will validate our survey of the Jini Technology against the TangO model in general, and through an implementation of a Pervasive Shopping Mall in particular.

1 Introduction

During the last centuries our everyday life has gradually become more and more globalized; we have reached a state where physical borders and distances only have weak impact on our collaborations and interactions. In the information ages we experienced new means of accessing an infinitive amount of information through the internet, and we are no longer constrained by technological issues for these matters on stationary PC's. But, the age of pervasive computing, we are about to enter, raises new challenges for researchers. Small intelligent devices will ubiquitously be deployed in our environment. These artifacts will even initiate interactions between humans and computers, which depend on the current context and preferences of the human. Interactions can happen anywhere and anytime, as it is clearly stated by Mark Weiser in 1991,

> In the 21st century the technology revolution will move into the everyday, the small and the invisible...

As previous evolutions this will not happen overnight. One of the greatest challenges for ubiquitous computing (UbiComp) is the infrastructure for connecting devices and retrieving reliant and relevant contextual information. There seams to be an endless number of applications for this area, because we more or

---

* This research was supported in part by Danish National Centre for IT Research, CfPC-Project No. 212, Flexible Inter Processing (FLIP) and The A. P. Møller and Chastine Mc-Kinney Møller Foundation.

R. Meersman et al. (Eds.): CoopIS/DOA/ODBASE 2003, LNCS 2888, pp. 1110–1132, 2003.
© Springer-Verlag Berlin Heidelberg 2003

less could replace human activities with these intelligent devices, but social issues must be addressed in order to create useful and usable applications. No matter how simple the task seams to be, we will discover that an enormous amount of information must be taken into account, and it is very hard to predict and adapt to individual behaviors of the user. Devices will be smaller and more powerful; eventually they will disappear, as stated by Mark Weiser

> The most profound technologies are those that disappear. They weave them-selves into the fabric of everyday life until they are indistinguishable from it.

These are the challenges for research and development in pervasive computing.

An important issue for deploying artifacts into a pervasive world is to have an architecture supporting spontaneous collaboration among these devices. In this paper we will briefly describe a conceptual model (TangO) for modelling artifacts of the pervasive world. We will investigate the Jini technology from Sun to clarify if Jini offers the required supporting architecture for a pervasive system in terms of the TangO model. After examining the features and details of Jini, we will relate the capabilities of Jini against those required by the TangO model in general. Further we will describe an implementation of a Pervasive Shopping Mall, which we have designed and implemented to get some practical experience with the Jini technology. The system provides various functionality to customers in a mall, such a maps, guidance, event-notification and pop-up commercial when shops of interests are being approached.

2   Tango Conceptual Model

We need a way to model these applications and scenarios of the pervasive world, in order to get a common vocabulary for talking about these systems. The TangO conceptual model [12] is an approach for such a modelling tool.

2.1   Abstraction and Spaces

According to [12] we interact with artifacts in physical, informational, and conceptual form and we classify the artifacts as either tangible objects, habitats, or associations as illustrated by figure 1.

Tangible Object: an artifact that has been modelled and designed for the pervasive world, incorporating design factors from each of the spaces.

Habitat: a logical context in which tangible objects exist and interact.

Association: a relation by which tangible objects and habitats collaborate in a given way at a given time — the actual collaboration is not predetermined by properties of objects and habitats.

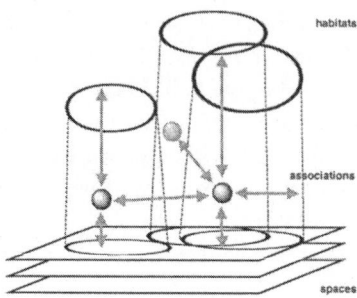

Fig. 1. Illustration of tangible objects, habitats, and associations in physical, informational, and conceptual spaces.

We elaborate on the understanding of the TangO conceptual model by discussing tangible objects, habitats, and associations at an abstract level, and exemplify these concepts by the example at the intuitive level. In relation to our example a mall will work as a habitat for the shops and persons, which are seen as tangible objects. The advertising activities are seen as examples on associations.

The conceptual aspect of for example an advertisement includes in our understanding usually a good offer, usually a time limited offer, often quantity limited, and we know that the (underlying) intention probably is to tempt us to come to the shop and in addition or instead buy something not planned and at standard price. The physical aspects of the advertisement include big boards at the shop announcing the offer (especially the price) as well as advertisements from newspapers. The informational aspect of advertisement includes the view from a printing house with properties such as size, format, contents, dates etc. The spaces are not discussed further in this article.

2.2   Tangible Object, Habitat, and Association

We distinguish between descriptions and instances of each of the concepts tangible object, habitat, and association. By a description we establish a denotation for the mall habitat, whereas the individual malls are instances of the description.

Instances of any of the concepts may be created (and deleted) dynamically. Instances of habitats enable tangible objects to move in (or out) of a habitat. The existence of tangible objects enables the instantiation of associations between individual formations of tangible objects. In our example a new mall may be established, shops may be organized within the mall, customers may visit the mall, and advertisements may be announced from shops to customers. Only tangible objects of type shop can be established in the mall — tangible objects of type persons can only visit the mall. We return to how to use the qualification of a tangible object to protect and control the possibilities of the functionality in a later section.

2.3 Habitat: Basics

We distinguish between physical and logical habitats (and mixtures of these). Both kinds of habitats may be limited in time, but only physical habitats have spatial limitations. The mall (and the shops in the mall) usually has opening hours and both have physical boundaries. We return to the problems with physical boundaries in a later section.

Habitats may be related either by being at same level or by one habitat being local to another. The mall may have a cinema as one of its facilities. The cinema may be seen as a habitat itself local to the mall habitat — and the various theaters within the cinema may in turn be considered local habitats of the cinema. We return to the problems with visibility of local habitats in a later section.

As mentioned habitats may be created and added to our system. As part of the creation various relations to existing habitats may be created as well. Habitats may also be removed from the system — in this case attention must be given to local habitats and to inhabiting tangible objects.

2.4 Tangible Object: Basics

Tangible objects exist in habitats. A tangible object may be in several habitats at the same time — in which case such habitats are seen as overlapping (a trivial case of this is the local/enclosing habitat — when a person is in the cinema that person is also in the mall). In certain food courts at malls the restaurants often share a common eating area. This may be seen as an example of overlapping habitats — for each restaurant we see the eating area as an integrated part of the restaurant habitat.

The collection of tangible objects inhabiting a habitat at a given time has an implicit relation between them. Because they are in the same habitat the (collection of) tangible objects are visible for each other. A tangible object may not want to utilize the relation or it may even refuse to be utilized through the relation, but potentially the collection of tangible objects is related. The shops of a mall probably utilize knowledge of each other's existence in the mall. A person entering a mall may want to utilize the mall to get in contact with relatives also in the mall — or may choose to obtain anonymity for other visitors in the mall.

A tangible object may be created and removed. Both operations have explicit potential consequences for tangible objects inhabiting the same habitats. When a shop is established in a mall the existing shops will observe its arrival. Tangible objects may dynamically enter and leave habitats — again with consequences for other related tangible objects. When a person leaves the mall the advertisements from the shops in the mall cannot reach the person anymore — and the person is outside the possibilities for the person search facility. We return to the problems of the legibility of a tangible object to enter (or leave) a habitat in a later section. We return to the problem with tangible objects being open to the public or anonymous in a later section.

2.5   Association: Basics

Associations exist between tangible objects. An association can be temporary or permanent. An example of a temporary association is the advertisement from a shop to a person — the advertisement lasts until either it expires or the person leaves the mall.

Different kinds of associations exist. An association can be a simple relationship between tangible objects (possibly only supporting mutual knowledge of each other) or it can provide collaboration between collections of tangible objects. The simple relationship may be seen as a more general association with respect to for example collaboration as a more special type. The shops of the mall may only have knowledge of each other but no collaboration, whereas the interaction between several persons in the mall who utilize the search person facility is an example of an association of the collaborative kind.

Associations can be established between tangible objects within the same or in distinct habitats (in the last case some alternative knowledge of its other is necessary, while there is an implicit knowledge available in the first case). The tangible objects must be potential visible to each other. Associations can be preserved in the case where a tangible object leaves a habitat — alternatively, it may have consequences dependent on the nature of the association. When a person leaves a mall that person can probably not be available for the search facility of that mall anymore. On the other hand if the person has established a permanent customer association to shops in the mall such associations are typically preserved no matter if the person is actually in the mall or not.

The creation or deletion of an association has explicit consequences for the associated tangible objects. If a search facility association is established between certain persons visiting a mall (assuming that the persons agree to take part in it) the persons may be involved in interaction and collaboration with various other persons potentially leading to physical or informational contact between typically familiar persons.

3   Jini Technology

Jini™technology is a Java™-based architecture for spontaneous networking. Participants in a Jini community require no previously knowledge of each other, and can take full advantages of the dynamic class loading and type-checking of the Java language, which requires a Java virtual machine (JVM) for all participants. Surrogate architectures connecting device and applications, which is incapable of joining the Jini community, is a way to work around these limitations.

A Jini community is established around one or more Lookup Services, which organize the services deployed in the community and respond to requests from clients. The Lookup service is itself a Jini service, acting as a bootstrapping service. References to these Lookup Services are obtained either by unicast or multicast discovery protocols defined by Jini.

Service providers deploys their services to the Jini Community by registering the services in Lookup Services, and obtains an unique `ServiceID` in return, which must be used for all future registrations to the same or other Lookup Services, to eliminate multiple responses to requesting clients. A service is a serialized Java object which resides in the Lookup Service after registration. Typically, the service object is just a proxy object, using the RMI protocol for remote invocations of a backend service object located in the Service Provider.

The clients requests services from discovered Lookup Services by sending a `ServiceTemplate`, which defines the services of interest. The service template can contain any combinations of a unique service id, class types of the requested service, or a set of attributes, which have been registered with the service.

The main idea of Jini for supporting "spontaneous networking" is achieved by a leasing principle, which means that services are leased into the community. When a service provider registers a service in the Lookup Service it obtains a lease, which must be renewed before it expires, otherwise the Lookup Service automatically deregister the service. Clients can register for changes in the Jini community, such as new, discarded, or changed services, using remote event registrations. By the same principle clients and service providers can register for events of new or discarded Lookup Services. Even event-registrations are leased in the community, so automatic cleanup can be initiated for non-responding clients. These are the real benefits of Jini, and enables opportunity to create a self-maintaining ubiquitous environment.

3.1   Jini Protocol Services

Jini is basically build on three basic protocols, the discovery protocol for finding Lookup Services, which could be either unicast or multicast discoveries. The join protocol for joining services to the Jini community, and the lookup protocol for requesting services. The reference Jini API implemented by Sun has a number of helper classes abstracting the underlying protocols.

LookupDiscoveryManager, which manages the discovery protocol, for both clients and service providers. It automatically keeps track of all Lookup Services in the community, and event notifications will be delegated to listeners through this object. The `LookupDiscoveryManager` manages both multicast and unicast discoveries, by setting group names and locators, respectively, which can be modified dynamically during the lifecycle of the object. Simpler managers for either just multicast or unicast discoveries in also part of the `net.jini.discovery` package.

JoinManager, which manages the deployment of a service for the service provider. It maintains the renewal of service registrations based on a default or given `LeaseRenewalManager`, and communicates with the Jini community through the delegated discovery manager. The manager automatically deploys the service into known Lookup Services or future discovered Lookup Services. The attributes describing the service can dynamically be modified through the `JoinManager`, which keeps the consistence for a multi-deployed service up to date.

ServiceDiscoveryManager, which manages service discoveries for clients. It collaborates with a sets of discovered Lookup Services through a given or default discovery manager, just like the `JoinManager`. The client could either poll the `lookup` method for requested services, or register for events, when services matching a given `ServiceTemplate` are discovered, discarded, or changed. The event listeners cannot be registered directly in the `Service-DiscoveryManager`, but in a `LookupCache`, which is created and kept up-to-date through the `ServiceDiscoveryManager`.

The helper classes reduces the complexity of Jini applications and removes the focus from the fundamental protocols, but users must still be familiar with Jini principle and understand some of the basic aspects of the attributes, locators, groups, events, and leases for taking full advantages of the helper classes. The hard part of using Jini for a distributed system, it not due the understanding of the principles of Jini, but more the complicated scripts for compiling and running the applications. Usually, some development time must be reserved for struggling with codebase, policy parameters, setting up HTTP servers for code retrieval, and combining the relevant class files into downloadable jar files.

4   Jini Features

In this section we will describe some of the features and capabilities of using Jini for supporting various general architectural aspects and concepts of pervasive and ubiquitous computing. Some techniques are well supported, while others either need some additional adjustments or workarounds, or are not supported at all. Because Ubicomp systems are so different in nature, it is hard to describe the features in terms of real systems, but examples will be given, and the descriptions is more an evaluation of the Jini Technology. In the next section some of the features and Jini in general, will be evaluated in terms of the TangO conceptual model.

4.1   Services and Discoveries

As stated previously, Jini is based on a *Service* and *Discovery* architectural approach, which have become quiet popular as web-services and internet applications have invaded our everyday life. The basic idea is that some system, a server, a device or whatever offers a service, which can be requested by clients. The clients locate these services by discoveries, either through one or more central servers (the approach taken by Jini) or directly from the service provider. Some approaches, like JXTA [21], just offers a set of protocols and all communications is done through XML messages. Compared to Jini, full implementations are provided by the reference implementation for establishing and handling communication. The communication is done by RMI, thus it requires no parsing of XML messages, but alternative implementations of the Jini protocols could use almost any communication methods. The list of service-based architectures is long, including SOAP [23], Sun Web Services [16], J2EE [15], Brazil [14], ECA, WSDL, KnowNow [11], and a lot of other standards specifies parts of such an architecture, like describing services by XML documents, but the protocols and communications principles for discovering and requesting these services, must be provided by a another standard. Jini includes it all, protocols for communications, means for describing services and an advanced event-system for asynchronous notifications of clients in the community. Thus, compared to many of the other architectures Jini offers a fairly complex architectural backbone for spontaneous collaborations between peer-to-peer clients. More standards will appear, but the concepts of services and discoveries seams to survive, not just for the near future, which is a positive argument for using Jini, but the strong trends for sending everything by XML, may leave Jini as a stand alone product, which is hard to integrate with other systems or require extra experiences from the programmers. Of course Jini implementations could use or shift towards more XML-based protocols, but it might violate some of the original ideas of Jini, and for performance reason some of the other standards might be more appropriate.

4.2 Experience Required

Jini is more or less defined by a set of Java APIs, thus programming with Jini should be quiet easy for Java programmers. But, some experience and detailed knowledge of the Jini protocols and ideas are required for taking full advantage of the Jini technology. Set up a simple system, deploying a service, and looking it up from a client is quiet easy, and experienced Java programmers would be able to create a simple Jini service and client in less than an hour. The hard part of using Jini for such simple systems is not writing the actual code but setting up the Jini system. One of the strong arguments for using Jini is for creating self-maintaining and re-configurable devices, which can handle changing network connectivity. But, setting up the Jini system in the right way, actually requires some detailed knowledge of classpaths, codebases, HTTP repositories and security policies, and could easily require several hours of work, even for an experienced programmer. Providing the right stub and class files for clients through HTTP servers and codebases, usually requires several tests before everything is running smoothly. The good thing is, that a Lookup service never have to be restarted when first loaded, at least theoretically, thus when the system is set up it could run forever. Then the programmer could care less about these setting, and only additional HTTP servers may be required by new service providers, or perhaps multiple activation daemons, when running Jini in a distributed environment.

Creating well-behaved services requires more than just a quick survey of the API documentation. Deploying a new instance of a service when recovering from a network failure or system breakdown, seams to work fine from the service providers perspective, but for clients in the community, who are looking for services of such a type, should not be notified about the appearance of a new service, when it comes alive again. The service has previously been discovered as a new service, and the client might already have lost interest for this particular service. The problem is that Jini services joining the community are assigned a unique service-id, which is transparent for all lookup services, where the services are deployed. Thus, after a system failure in the service provider, the service is restarted but the service-id is lost. It is avoided by setting a persistent-storage for all services, to which service-id and other configuration settings are stored. When restarting the service, settings from the storage could be retrieved and used in the join process. It is just one example, where the programmer has to know some details of the Jini protocols, in order to create a well-behaved service, because these ideas are not supported by the Jini API or utility classes. One way to work around these problems of using Jini is by relying on a service toolkit, which extends the Jini concept by more user-friendly interfaces, and hides some of the details of the low-level Jini protocols, by providing a set of utility and helper class for Jini system. Such a toolkit is described in [9].

4.3   Spontaneous Networking

One of the fundamental ideas behind Jini is support for spontaneous networking, where network resources are not assumed to be reliable. The Jini system is a self-maintaining environment, where all peers could be notified about changes in the Jini community, such as deployment of new services or discarding existing ones. So a service or a resource is only trusted for a given lease duration, which is granted by the Jini community for any type of registration, such as service or event registrations. If a lease has not been renewed before it expires, the Jini community removes the registered service and free any resources related to that registration. This is a very strong mean for handling network systems with a high failure rate, or scenarios with a high number of spontaneous and dynamic arrivals and departures of collaborators of the network. It requires a minimum or almost none control and checking of the participating artifacts regarding their current state and connectivity to the network, but is not a bullet-proof technique. Network failures could still happen within a lease period, resulting in dangling references. For a service, which is transferred as a serialized object to the lookup service, full access to service will continue even after the lease has expired, thus only the conceptual aspect of a service from a connected service provider is violated. If the deployed service object is just a proxy for a backend service, the client have to check for RemoteExceptions in any interactions with the service objects, which removes some of the transparent and high-level support for spontaneous networking, but the alternatives would require unlimited amount of performance.

Any peer, who intentionally leaves the community before the end of the lease periods, should cancel all registrations to the community and discard deployed services. Then event notifications will be sent from the community to listening peers, which could have interest in such changes or even abort interaction with a service from a provider. The event system is an important piece of the spontaneous networking paradigm, because clients could listen for almost any type of changes, deployment or discarding of a particular service in the community. The event system is also efficient, because deployment of a new service requires no scanning of participants or initial negotiations before collaborations can be established. Jini offers little or no support for automating the process, clients must register for all events of interests and add appropriated listeners. A toolkit, like the one mentioned above, could enhance the interface to this event system, and provide a basic setup of registrations and listeners.

4.4   Serialized or Backend

The lookup service in a Jini community is the central repository for all services. More than one lookup service can exist within the same community, and the set of joined services do not have to be distinct. The utility classes of the reference implementation handles multiple joins as a single service completely transparent for the client, which is one of the strong arguments for the unique service-id mentioned above. A service object in a lookup service could be a full-blown service represented by a serialized object, or just a proxy object to a backend service residing in the service provider.

A simple and full service is just a serialized Java object residing in the lookup service, which is completely independent of the JVM of the original service provider. This type of service is useful for providing static information or simple functional results. Providers have to be careful about using this type of service, because contextual information will be dependant and retrieved from the client not the provider. Any information send to the service object will never leave the client's JVM, thus it will have no impact on returned service objects for future requests to the lookup service, because the service is not transferred back to the lookup service after end of use. Such services is useful for instance to describe artifacts in a pervasive system, each device could provide a descriptive service, exposing any information, which could be useful and are allowed to be retrieved by any other artifact in the community. It could even be limited to a selected group of participants, by joining the service to a specific group in the lookup service, but the default Jini system, do not prohibit any client from joining any group.

The alternative to the simple service object is a proxy object to a backend service. Typically, the service is implemented as an extension of the `Unicast-RemoteObject`, which is a server object from the Java RMI library. Stub objects to the service will be registered in the lookup service representing a remote interface through which the clients can interact with the backend service. In other words will the stub object act as a proxy object to the backend service, but the client cannot tell the difference. By this mean we can make the service behavior dependant upon the current state of the provider, not the client, and even contextual information can be retrieved from the provider. This type of service is even more constructive than the simple, because all the simple services could be implemented by this mean as well (properly not that efficient), but there is a huge set of complex service, which could not be implemented by the simple service. Consider a moving artifact with some sort of positioning device, like a GPS receiver, it could provide a service giving proximity information to a certain object (could be an argument to a service method), which have to rely on sensor data of the provider. Alternatively, the provider could redeploy or update the service, whenever the context information is updated, which would scale very badly for most applications, but that is a trade-off between "polling" the service and change the service according to the current situation, which is left as a typical design decision to the programmer.

4.5   Event System

One of the most important features of Jini is the event system, which is built on the same well-known principles from the GUI libraries of Java (AWT and Swing); the main difference is the distributed aspect. Some additional concerns have to be taken into account for a remote event model, compared to an event system in a single JVM. Within a single JVM we can assume a generated event always will be delivered, otherwise it would be most likely that the entire JVM has crashed, but in a distributed system failure could happen in the communication or the listener could have crashed or been temperately disconnected. Even the sequence of the event notifications cannot be assumed to be received by the same order of generation. Furthermore the latency for an event send from the generator to the listener must be considered in the design phase of the system.

These problems makes it somewhat harder to work with events in a distributed system, than within a single JVM, but Jini comes with a utility packages (mercury), which is best described as an event-mailbox.

4.6   Administrating Services

Jini offers the opportunity that service providers can make their service administrable. Basically, it means that any client can modify the configuration of a deployed service, not the actual service object itself unless the service allows it, but settings like the attributes for the service, joined groups of the community, or even destroy the service. For a service to be administrable it must implement the Administrable interface, which defines a getAdmin method. By invocation of this method, the service object returns an object implementing the administrable methods for the service. The Jini API defines 3 general interfaces for administrable services, named JoinAdmin, DestroyAdmin and StorageLocationAdmin.

Through the first interface you can modify the set of lookup services to which the service is deployed, either by groups (multicast) or specific URLs (unicast), and the attributes set with the service. The DestroyAdmin allows you to destroy a service and notify the community from a client. The last one let you retrieve or specify a new storage location for services with persistent storage.

It is still up to the service provider to decide whether a service should be administrable from clients or not, it depends on whether the service object implements the Administrable interface or not. The service provider itself could still administrate the service without implementing the interface, but clients, who have to lookup the service through a lookup service, would only have access to methods defined by the service provider, and the Administrable interface is a reasonable way to handle these ideas.

The only problem with administrating services in Jini is security and authentication of the client, but this goes for every part of Jini. It seams that according to the fundamental ideas of Jini, every participant of the community could be trusted. The lookup service does not care about which client request which services, as long as the service is available, a lease will be granted for the client. The only way to differentiate between the clients, is by grouping services in the lookup service, but there is no way of restricting which clients have access to which groups.

Truthfully, most of these problems can be handled by extending the basic reference implementations from Sun, but then Jini fails as a complete and easy architecture for pervasive and ubiquitous computing.

4.7   Landlord Leases

The default lease principle of Jini described above could be manipulated in several ways. The Jini utility packages includes an API for customized lease handling, known as the `Landlord` lease system. Basically the `Landlord` system provides a set of interfaces and a paradigm of programming custom leases in Jini, but you have to do all the work by yourself. You must implement the `Landlord` interface for your lease grantor, which includes methods for renewing and cancellation of leases. How you will give access to the resources hold under lease, you have to decide by yourself, no methods has been specified, because it depends on the logical context and content of the lease grantor, as for the core Jini classes where `register` and `notify` are the names of the methods for registering services and event notifications respectively. Whenever you will grant a lease to a client, a new instance of the `LandlordLease` is created through the `LandlordLeaseFactory`, which is an inner class of the `LandlordLease` class, and takes a requested lease duration, a cookie for the resource, and a reference to the landlord object as arguments. The last part is important, because your landlord will be a remote object to your `LandlordLeases`, which are returned to the clients. By this mean `LandlordLeases` could be managed by the default `LeaseRenewalManager` of Jini, because when the manager wants the lease to be renewed the lease setup a RMI callback to the landlord, and asks for a new lease duration.

You decide the leasing policy in terms of the methods for renewing and cancellation of lease, and the method for getting the lease in the first place.

4.8   User Interfaces

Jini specifies no way of providing user interfaces for services; a client must rely on the interface specified by the service provider. This might be good enough for a number of smart Jini-enabled devices collaborating in a Jini community, where they are completely aware of each other and the services provided, but as soon as humans are participating in the community through PCs, PDAs, etc. and wants to interact with services, or the details of the service interface are unknown to the clients, more advanced user interfaces are required.

Graphical User Interfaces (GUIs) is currently the way to support the most flexible interactions between humans and computers, thus the requirement for providing GUIs for services can not be left out of a successful architecture for pervasive computing. There are a number of ways to provide UIs for services, but several issues have to be taken into consideration, because in order to support a number of different client platforms, the service object must provide different GUIs, like for PDAs, Swing or AWT based, etc.

A project named *ServiceUI* [1] has been started in the Jini Community [17], which hopefully will become part of the Jini specification in the future. The basic idea behind the ServiceUI project is that UIs should be provided as attributes to the service being deployed. Another problem of working with GUIs is static references to the GUI environment of the instantiator of the GUI object, which means that the service provider cannot instantiate the GUI as serialized objects and provide them for the clients, because for most GUI libraries like Swing and AWT, the GUI object will then hold references to the memory space of the service provider. To work around this, the GUI objects provided as attributes to the service, must be GUI factories, so the real GUI will be instantiated by the client using the factory methods. The ServiceUI API defines a wrapper entry for these factories, known as the UIDescriptor

```
public class UIDescriptor extends AbstractEntry {
  public String role;
  public String toolkit;
  public Set attributes;
  public MarshalledObject factory;

  public UIDescriptor();
  public UIDescriptor(String role, String toolkit,
    Set Attributes, MarshalledObject factory);

  public final Object getUIFactory(ClassLoader
    parentLoader) throws IOException,
      ClassNotFoundException;
}
```

where the toolkit indicates the required GUI library on the client, such as javax.swing or java.awt. The role specifies the purpose of the GUI, three types have been defined in the ServiceUI API; MainUI, AdminUI, and AboutUI. The set of attributes could contain any information used to describe the GUI. The factory member holds the factory object for the GUI as a marshalled object appropriate for serialization. Currently, eight standard factory classes have been defined in the ServiceUI API; DialogFactory, FrameFactory, JComponentFactory, JDialogFactory, JFrameFactory, JWindowFactory, PanelFactory, and WindowFactory, all representing the corresponding classes from the java.awt and javax.swing packages. Specialization still has to be performed in order to specialize for GUIs with other constraints, such as GUIs for PDAs, or they could be classified by the attributes.

4.9   Describing Services by Attributes

In order to extend the search possibilities for services deployed in the community, services could have a list of attributes attached to the services. By this mean the clients do not have to know either the class-type or the `serviceID` of the service. The lookup process is initiated by the client setting up a `ServiceTemplate`, which partly consist of attributes to be matched by the services of interest. Attributes must implement the Jini `Entry` interface, but are typically specializations of the `AbstractEntry` class, which implement basic object methods. An entry A matches an entry B if it is the same or a subclass of B, and all their common public and non-primitive fields are equal. Jini comes with a set of standard entry types for describing standard information, such as service info, status, name, address, and location.

Because attributes could be manipulated through the administrative interface, we must be able to control, whether an attribute could be changed by anyone or not. This is handled by the `ServiceControlled` interface, which is implemented by 3 of the standard entries (`ServiceInfo`, `Status`, `ServiceType`). When the client have received an administrative proxy object, like `JoinAdmin`, for the join process of a service provider, it will implement methods such as `addAttributes` and `modifyAttributes`. The administrative object will forward these messages to the `JoinManager` of the service, which have two versions of these methods. A strict version editing the attributes straight forward as expected, and a safe version with a flag indicating if services should be checked to determine if they are service controlled. If the administrative object forwards these messages through a checked safe version, then clients, who are attempting to manipulate service controlled entries will receive a `SecurityException`.

If services are discovered through the `ServiceDiscoveryManager` helper classes, a `ServiceItemFilter` could be used in the lookup process in addition to the `ServiceTemplate`. This interface defines a `check` method taking service items found by the standard lookup process as argument, and any additional checking of the service or attributes could be performed by customized implementations of this method, such as checking if a given value in an attributes is within an interval of accepted values, because traditional entry matching just compare entries by equality.

4.10   Java Spaces, Support of Transactions

In addition to the infrastructure support, Jini offers a tuple space like service, known as *JavaSpaces*. As previous tuple spaces, such as the Linda System [8], JavaSpaces works as a distributed shared memory, but in contrast to tuples in the Linda System, JavaSpaces can store real Java objects, and be used to anything from a shared blackboard to a transaction model. The `malaho` service included in the Jini utility packages is a transaction manager for distributed clients. The approach for using transactions is rather simple, because basically you create a transaction object using the factory methods of the `TransactionFactory` class; either a standard or a nested transaction. Once the transaction has been created, clients can start grouping operations into the transaction. Currently, JavaSpaces is the only service in Jini supporting transactions, and the three basic operations on the space (*read*, *take*, and *write*) take a transaction object as argument. All operations grouped into a transaction using these methods will be executed when the transaction is being committed, and changes made to the space will first take effect if all operations are committed.

Until the transaction have been committed, only clients holding the transaction object could read the space as it would look after committing the transaction, this is useful if a set of objects wants to hide information for all participants of the community. If they share a transaction object, the information could be put onto the space by one of the transaction holders and read by another. Eventually, the information could be securely removed from the space before the transaction will be committed, and other clients will never notice the content of the space has changed.

As pervasive systems emerge into our everyday, many of these services, which are ubiquitously deployed in our environment, will be provided by companies and charged by use. Thus, transactions will be required in order to confirm if a user have received a service or not.

4.11   Jini on Constrained Devices

The reference implementation of Jini provided by Sun is based on RMI from Java 2, which makes the real requirement of running Jini a JVM capable of running java code from the JDK 1.2. Thus, currently it is not possible to run Jini on PDA's using only reference implementations from Sun, because the latest implementation of the PersonalJava run-time environment for the Pocket PCs supports only JDK 1.1.8. The J2ME implementations for Palm computers are even more constrained than PersonalJava.

One way to run Jini on a Pocket PC, would be to the wipe out the Pocket PC operating system and install Linux onto the device, which includes a full JDK 1.4 (Blackdown). Several other approaches are possible as well, because PsiNaptic [18] have made their own implementation (JMatos) of the Jini protocols, which can collaborate with a standard Jini community. Recently, they have even enabled very constrained devices without a JVM or Java to participant in a Jini community and provide services to the community.

Another approach is the SavaJE [19] operating system for ARM processors in particular, which supports a full JDK 1.4.1, making it fully capable of running Jini.

5   Taking Jini for a Tango

Previously, we have shown that creating a direct mapping between the TangO conceptual model and the Jini technology is clearly a hard job [10]. The different requirements for the TangO concepts in various applications make it impossible to make a simple and general solution fitting every purpose. Thus, it would be more interesting to investigate if Jini is useful and useable for implementing applications in respect to the TangO model. We will address the problems and concerns which have to be taking into account, when Jini is used as a networking architecture for such applications. The question is not whether it is possible to use Jini for such applications, because various workarounds and adapters can be added in standard Java code, but in stead we will examine if Jini is appropriate and do not violate the conceptual ideas of the model. Because the TangO model is closely connected to ubiquitous and pervasive systems in general, the outcome will clarify and expose the strengths and weaknesses of Jini supporting such systems as well.

5.1   Fundamental Behavior of Habitats and Tangible Objects

Some of the most fundamental and important properties of artifacts in the pervasive world, is to dynamically move around and collaborate with a variety of other participants. In terms of the TangO model, we have various tangible objects which dynamically move from habitat to habitat and establish associations with other inhabitants. We could even have nested habitats, such as a local habitat limited by physical borders within a larger habitat, or logically as a more narrow classification of a wide collection of inhabitants. The number of levels in this hierarchy of nested habitats could be infinitive, but typically the most constrained habitats would have higher precedence, and only those have to be considered. Habitats with lower priority would just define some level of default behavior or functionality of the inhabitants.

The basic functionality of moving in and out of habitats, establishing and breaking of associations between the habitat and the tangible object or among the tangible objects, is properly supported by Jini through the infrastructure for spontaneous networking. An advanced event system could be set up by the programmer in order to achieve the required model of the pervasive world with collaborative behavior. The challenge is collaborate within nested habitats. One way to achieve this by the help of Jini would be through groups in the community. Each lookup service is registered for one or more groups, into which the services can be registered. A client specifies the groups of interest in the multicast discovery protocol, thus we can selectively choose among a set of coordinated or nested habitats, but the clients have to be familiar with these group names, for instance through a service retrieval when entering the larger habitat. There is no built-in support for prioritizing the visible groups in a community, so the clients must chose the appropriate service or behavior using its own set of rules. This is a natural approach when thinking of human behavior, but it requires some amount of intelligence for complex systems. In many situations, when the tangible objects are augmentations of the real world, and closes the gap between a human user and the virtual world, a list of options could be presented to the user, and let the human do simple considerations. Jini could easily be extended with various tools supporting such ideas, but it would require some amount of work to do it in an intelligent way.

The other part of merging or adjusting behavior from two or more habitats is badly supported by the core implementation of Jini. Basically, it is the same problem, because if the functionality of a local habitat has to be adjusted or take advantage of functionality from the surrounding habitat, the habitat has to lookup the services and interprets them itself, and afterwards modifies its own behavior. Alternatively, the clients must merge these services from different habitats to gain something useful and appropriate, but it depends seriously on the problem of the current situation. Again helper classes and tools would be useful to assist the programmer with these decision rules.

5.2   The World of Associations

It is clearly hard to concretizing associations closer than those conceptual ideas presented in section 2. An association could be any kind of dependency or collaboration among participants. These associations are so different from system to system that is would be hard to systemize the development process, but the creation and establishment of associations are well supported by the Jini infrastructure. The event system would be handy to trigger the creations of new associations among participants in a habitat, or between the habitat and inhabitating tangible objects. Usually associations define some form of peer-to-peer communication between clients, which is easily achieved using backend services in Jini, but in some situations more than two participants must share a common communication media and collaborate all together. One participant could act as a master and manage and route the information to the others, but the approach suffers from the risk of a sudden failure of the master, due to network problems, system failures, etc. The JavaSpaces service available in the Jini system could be helpful in this situation, where all participants could communication through the space acting as an advanced blackboard for writing information and objects to other participants. This information could even be hidden for other participants by the help of transactions, but transactions could also be useful to secure individual parts of the collaborations.

As anything, which is serializable, could be send as information or services through the Jini community, then almost anything programmable in Java could be used to construct associations, thus the programming model for association is as rich as we can get it, and should not cost us any trouble, just hard work for the programmer, because it would be hard to generalize from these associations. A toolkit could still offer some helper classes to setup the event system for creating and establishing the associations, and support the collaborative behavior between participants, so development and programming of these associations could be done on a more abstract level.

5.3   Describing Unknown Services to Tangible Objects

Tangible objects would typically be introduced into new and unknown habitats when they move around in the pervasive world. They would have no idea of the functionality provided by the current habitat. They would try to retrieve these services and adjust or embed them into their current behavior, using the most profound and advanced intelligence of the artifact. Thus, the tangible objects require some form of dynamical adaptation and retrieval capabilities of unknown behavior at run-time.

The hard part of using Jini to deploy services in a generic programming environment, is to describe the services in an appropriate way. These descriptions must be given in terms of attributes, but then these special attributes must be known by all clients and the service provider. Whereas dynamic class loading and codebases makes it possible for a client to retrieve services, which implementation is completely unknown beforehand. This is challenging in the perspective of pervasive computing, where artifacts could be introduced to a new habitat, and are completely unaware of the functionality provided by the habitat. One way, would be to define a few general service types, which only have the purpose of transferring the real service with the whole functionality to the client, using dynamic class loading, codebases, and everything needed to setup the tangible object for the current habitat. Of course this mean raises the questions of vulnerability and privacy of the artifact, and the only means for preventing such attacks are security policies and trusted signed jar-files in codebases. Several attempts have tried to run Jini on top of an encrypted RMI, or similar protocols, but it requires a lot of customization.

Another approach, which could be appropriate in some situations, is adapters or converting of services. In [22] it is described how a special service could be deployed in the Jini community with the sole purpose of converting services to an appropriate form. Basically, the service listens for services of known types that it has converters for. Whenever a service of type A is discovered, the service instantiates a new service of type B using the internal converter or adapter from type A to type B, and deploy the service into the community. When the original service is removed from the community, the converter service also takes care of cleaning up and removing the converted instances. It could be a useful mean for closing the gap between known and unknown services, by converting service to a more general form, known by more or all tangible objects.

5.4   Authentication, Admission, and Security

When tangible objects move between habitats or retrieve functionality from the habitat, it all happen transparent to issues of privacy and security, not to speak about the constraints on being part of a habitat. From a conceptual point of view it is easy to limit the functionality to a selected group of artifacts, or decide if a tangible object is inhabitating a habitat or not. We have terms of security, privacy polices, user authentication, etc. to describe the allowances of the artifact, but from a programmer's point of view these concepts are not achieved that easy.

Jini have little or no support for these problems, and it is up to the developer to customize the services and clients to achieve the necessary results. The default implementation of Jini from Sun works on standard RMI, thus there is no encryption or security whatsoever, but experiments and third party implementations have tried to cover this area, and could be used if necessary, because the Jini specification is open to almost any underlying protocols.

Jini have no support for user authentication either, which could be useful by the lease grantor, in order to restrict the number of clients to a given service. The argument for not building authentication support into the lookup service, was that is would be fairly easy for hackers to sniff the authentication information, when no encryption is used and then pretend to be the user itself. Another problem of using authentication is that clients typically would trust lookup services, if they have logged in by a username and password. But, if a hacker has come across this information, he could setup a bugous lookup service, and Jini viruses could be born as services in this lookup service. Truthfully, some of these problems could be prevented by the sake of security policies and signed jar-files in codebases, as mentioned previously, but the problem of granting a lease for a service to a client is not just about identifying the user or not, it is also about context. Physical habitats are typically limited by physical borders, and it would clearly violate the concept of a habitat if the services are provided to any interested clients, which on their own decide if they are inhabitants or not. We cannot trust clients on such issues and grants for accepted clients only, would be a more natural approach too. The default lease grantor of a Jini community, the lookup service, has no restrictions for granting the lease. Any service provider registering a new service into the community will receive a lease registering for a given lease duration, and clients requesting services from the lookup service will achieve full access to all services of a requested group. As described in the previous section the landlord leases is a way to implement custom lease grantors, but it suffers from some limitation in relation to decide whether a tangible object is in a habitat or not. For instance no information about the context of the client could be provided, when the lease have to be renewed. Thus, for a physical habitat, where crossing of borders determine if you are in or out, the landlord have to contact the clients and retrieve the necessary contextual information, which is inappropriate in stead of just providing the information in the lease renewing process, and makes the clients more complex in order to allow such a communication, but it gives a simple and general approach for the landlord system. Extending the default `LandlordLease` class is a technique to workaround this problem, but again you have to set up everything by yourself.

Logical habitat could give a problem too, because we want to use the multicast discovery process of Jini in order not to set up any network addresses and configurations, but it would only work across a limiting number of gateways and not through firewalls. For a logical habitat the inhabitating artifacts could theoretically be spread all over the world, which seriously would disqualify the use of multicast protocols. To work around this problem, the client of a logical habitat must extract the URL of the lookup service representing the habitat, and use unicast discovery to reach this lookup service, when it is outside the reach of a multicast approach.

6   Pervasive Shopping Mall

We have experimented with the implementation of a pervasive shopping mall, to get some practical experience with Jini for a scenario, which easily could be described in terms of the TangO conceptual model. We have tried to come up with some features for such a system, and the number of applications to support customers and staff members of the mall are endless, thus we haven chosen to implement just a few of these features, which were challenging to the Jini architecture. The system have never been tested in a real setup, which have not been the intension either, it has the sole purpose of experimenting and focusing on Jini as a supporting architecture. Thus, we allowed to use simplified techniques like GPS receivers to achieve the position information, which would not have worked in a real indoor shopping mall environment, but for a test case it does not matter.

6.1   Functionality of the System

The main focus of the system was to provide support and information for customers in the mall. They could be provided with a map of the mall, showing their current location and properly highlight target stores. Shops could provide commercial to the customers, so when customers are in proximity of the shops, these ads will pop up on their screen if they accepted it by categories of interest. A number of other thoughts could be implemented as well, such as information about public transportation when you are close to an exit, announcement of special events in the mall, or even a friend-searching facility, which discover friends and relatives in the area, or a more general approach, which locate other people fulfilling some customized criteria. Such a feature might be restricted to a local habitat, such as a cafe-area or enabled when the same two people have stayed in the same narrow area and have been in proximity of each other for a while.

6.2   For the TangO Point of View

In terms of the TangO model, we could clearly identify some of the concepts in the mall example. The mall itself is a true definition of a habitat, not just for the customers acting as tangible objects within the mall, but also for the shops, which themselves are physical artifacts in the mall, but they are also informational artifacts to the mall, in relation to setting up the functionality of the mall, such as a map.

6.3   Implementation of the System

The implementation of the system is build using the toolkit described in [9], which defines simple but general conceptual objects for the Jini community. The mall is the primary service provider in the system, which provides the functionality of the habitat. By the service made available to the customers of the mall, the customers could retrieve a GUI including a map and a message panel, where notification from shops and the mall would be announced according to the selected interests. The GUI is showed in figure 2. We have experimented with the ServiceUI API for transferring GUIs in the Jini Community, which also gave a convenient approach for announcing the functionality to the customer, even when they were unaware of the services provided. We just looked for services with an `MainUI` GUI object as an attribute.

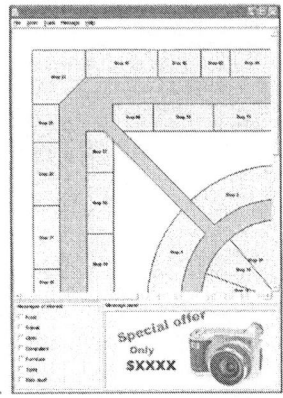

Fig. 2. Illustration of GUI downloaded by clients. Picture taken from hp.dk

When the customer retrieves and initiates the UI hiding the low-level details of the functionality, they select the type of input for their current location, which could be either a GPS sensor on a specified COM port, or a selected file containing GPS sentences, which is intended for an indoor demo mode of the application. Coordinates from the GPS sensor is converted to Cartesian coordinates and related to the coordinates for the center of the mall, which can be inputted in the mall administrative window. The customer registers for messages and commercials through the GUI, and the event system of Jini makes it simpel to display new such services discovered or changed.

Similar could the shops retrieve a map for selecting the spot in the mall, they want to rent. Afterwards they can start deploying commercials to the jini community in terms of serialized java object, because there is no backend functionality of a commercials. Both simpel text strings, styled documents and pictures are understood by the GUI of the customer.

7 Conclusion

We have investigated the Jini technology in order to validate the infrastructural and architectural support for pervasive computing. In the examination of the features of Jini we have leant against the TangO conceptual model for describing the result in relation to general concepts of pervasive computing, and not just to focus on simple examples. We have experimented with the practical implications of using Jini, by implementing a pervasive shopping mall, for the sole purpose of testing the technology.

In general we are satified we the concepts and ideas of the Jini Technology, but we clearly see the need for extension and helpful tools. So the quick answer to the question of Jini has the quality of an architecture for the future of networking is yes, but it requires an additional toolkit on top of Jini, not just to provide extra functionality, but also to abstract from the technical details of using Jini.

We will continue working on such a toolkit, which will be further described in [9].

References

1. The serviceui project. http://www.artima.com/jini/serviceui/index.html.
2. Centre for it research (cit), centre for pervasive computing - cfpc. http://www.CfPC.dk, February 2002.
3. D. Amor. *Internet Future Strategies: How Pervasive Computing Services Will Change the World*. Prentice Hall PTR, July 2001.
4. J. Burkhardt, H. Henn, S. Hepper, T. Schaeck, and K. Rindtorff. *Pervasive Computing: Technology and Architecture of Mobile Internet Applications*. Addison Wesley Professional, October 2001.
5. W. K. Edwards. *Core Jini*. Prentice Hall PTR, 2 edition, 2001.
6. M. E. Fayad, D. C. Schmidt, and R. E. Johnson. *Building Application Frameworks: Object-Oriented Foundations of Framework Design*. Wiley, 1999.
7. R. Flenner. *Jini and JavaSpaces Application Development*. Sams Publishing, 2002.
8. D. Gelernter. Linda system. http://www.cs.yale.edu/Linda/linda.html.
9. K. Hallenborg and B. B. Kristensen. Jitterbug: Jini toolkit supporting ubiquitous computing.
10. K. Hallenborg and B. B. Kristensen. Pervasive computing: Mapping tango model onto jini technology. In *The 6th World Multiconference on Systemics, Cybernetics and Informatics*, volume XI, pages 205–212, Orlando, Florida, USA, July 2002. International Institute of Informatics and Systemics.
11. KnowNow. Knownow project. http://www.knownow.com/.
12. D. C.-M. May, B. B. Kristensen, and P. Nowack. Tango: Modeling in style. In *Proceedings of the Second International Conference on Generative Systems in the Electronic Arts (Second Iteration - Emergence)*, Melbourne, Australia, 2001.
13. L. Merk, M. S. Nicklous, and T. Stober. *Pervasive Computing Handbook*. Springer Verlag, January 2001.
14. S. Microsystems. Brazil project. http://research.sun.com/brazil/.
15. S. Microsystems. Java 2 platform, enterprise edition. http://java.sun.com/j2ee/.
16. S. Microsystems. Java web services. http://java.sun.com/webservices/.
17. S. Microsystems. Jini community. http://www.jini.org/.
18. PsiNatic. Jmatos. http://www.psinaptic.com/.
19. SavaJe. Savaje os 2.0. http://www.savaje.com/.
20. Sun Microsystems. *Jini Technology Core Platform Specification*, 1.2 edition, December 2001.
21. SunSource.net. Project jxta. http://www.jxta.org/.

22. J. Vayssière. Transparent dissemination of adapters in jini. In Z. T. Gordon Blair, Douglas Schmidt, editor, *Proceedings of DOA'01, the third International Symposium on Distributed Objects & Applications*, pages 95–104, Rome, Italy, September 2001. IEEE Computer Society.

23. W3C. Simple object access protocol (soap). http://www.w3.org/TR/SOAP/, May 2000.

24. H. Wong. *Developing Jini Applications Using J2ME*. Addison Wesley, 2002.

Capturing, Analysing, and Managing ECG Sensor Data in Handheld Devices[1]

J. Rodríguez, Alfredo Goñi, and Arantza Illarramendi

University of the Basque Country (UPV/EHU)
LSI Department. Donostia-San Sebastián. Spain
http://siul02.si.ehu.es

Abstract. The new advances in sensor technology, PDAs and wireless communication favour the development of monitoring systems. In this context we have developed MOLEC, a system that monitors people that suffer from heart arrhythmias. It carries out three tasks: a) it *captures* the digital data sent by different sensors and transforms them into a concrete format; b) it *analyses* the ECG data sent by the PDA sensors to locally detect anomalous situations as soon as possible; c) it *manages* ECG data in the following way: 1) normal ECG data are stored in files and are sent compressed to a hospital, within a certain time granularity; and 2) when anomalous ECG data are identified an alarm is sent to the hospital; and also these anomalous ECG are stored at the PDA database. Data in that database can be queried, locally or remotely, in order to know different aspects that can be related to anomalous situations.

1 Introduction

Innovation in the fields of PDA, wireless communication and vital parameter sensors enables the development of revolutionary monitoring systems, which strikingly improve the lifestyle of patients, offering them security even outside the hospital. Focusing on electrocardiogram (ECG) sensors, it is important to see that the new ECG monitoring systems outperform traditional holters.

The use of a holter consists in placing electrodes (leads) on the patients' chests; these leads are attached to the holter. After the patient is sent home and goes back to normal life, a tape records a continuous ECG for 24 or 48 hours. One or two days later, the holter is removed and the tape is analysed. The physician will see each of the patients' heart beats and if abnormal beats or heart arrhythmias occur during that period, they are identified by the physician [1]. Although this solution presents the advantage that patients can continue living a normal life in their houses, it also presents a serious drawback: if the patient suffers from a serious rhythm irregularity, the holter only records it, i.e. it does not react to it.

---

[1] This work was mainly supported by the University of the Basque Country, Diputación Foral de Gipuzkoa and the CICYT: Comisión Interministerial de Ciencias y Tecnología, Spain [TIC2001-0660].

R. Meersman et al. (Eds.): CoopIS/DOA/ODBASE 2003, LNCS 2888, pp. 1133–1150, 2003.
© Springer-Verlag Berlin Heidelberg 2003

In order to overcome the previous restriction, some new proposals have appeared that not only record ECGs but also react in some concrete situations. We classify these proposals in two major groups: commercial systems and research projects.

In the first group we include those commercial systems that use a mobile telephone unit or a PDA (Personal Digital Assistant) to acquire the ECG signal. Three or four metal electrodes are situated on the back of the standard cellular phone, which record the heart event. Then, the data are transmitted to the cardiac monitor centre situated at a hospital (e.g. Vitaphone [2]). Another alternative is to use PDAs. Companies like Ventracor [3] from Australia or Cardio Control [4] from the Netherlands have developed systems capable of storing ECGs directly in the PDA. Additional features like GSM/GPRS transmission to an analyzing unit are also being developed.

In the second group there are several research projects like @Home [5], Tele-MediCare [6], or PhMon [7], whose aims are to build platforms for real time remote monitoring. These systems include wireless bio-sensors that measure vital parameters such as heart rate, blood pressure, insulin level, etc. The health monitoring system, carried by the patients, controls these sensors. The patient data recorded are sent to the hospital, where they are analysed.

All the previous systems are continuously sending ECGs to a hospital through a wireless communication network, where they are analysed. In spite of the advantages these kinds of systems provide in relation to holters, they still present main problems related to the fact that the analysis is not performed in the place where the signal is acquired. Therefore, there is a *loss of efficiency* in the use of the wireless network because normal ECGs are also sent (and wireless communications imply a high cost); and, in the case of the wireless network is not available (e.g. in a tunnel, in an elevator, etc.) at some moment, there might be a loss of ECG signal with the corresponding risk of *not detecting some anomalies*. Our proposal is to analyse the signal locally at the PDA.

In this paper we present a system called MOLEC: a PDA-based monitoring system that records user ECG signals in order to find arrhythmias, and in case of detecting them, it sends them to a hospital so that cardiologists can determine what to do with the user. The MOLEC system is separated into two subsystems, one situated at the hospital and another one situated in the PDA carried by the user.

MOLEC has been designed using a modular approach and applying distributed-object technology. Each one of the three main modules of the system is related to one task carried out during the monitoring process: to capture, to analyse and to manage ECG sensor data. Hence, the aims of the *Data Pre-processing Module* are to capture the data sent by the sensors, and to process them in order to generate a sequence of beats and associated information needed by the Decision Support Module. The *Decision Support Module* classifies the beats and the rhythms found in the ECG with the aim of finding abnormal situations. As for the third and last module, the *Database and Communication Module*, its task is to efficiently manage the data coming from the two previous modules.

Moreover, MOLEC system implies a great advance in the process of on-line monitoring of heart diseases, because it provides: 1) *efficiency:* premature detection of abnormalities by the monitoring system and optimization of wireless communications; 2) *local analysis:* even if wireless communication were unavailable, the signal could be analysed locally at the PDA; 3) *openness:* it can be integrated in hospitals that manage clinical data through the HL7 standard [9] (a representation of clinical documents); 4) *accessibility:* data recorded in the system can always be queried whether locally or remotely; 5) *simplicity*: making technical issues transparent to the users from the point of view of software and hardware components; 6) *adaptability*: possibility of working with different kinds of ECG sensors

In the rest of the paper, first we briefly explain the framework of the system and in sections 3, 4 and 5 we present the modules mentioned previously in more detail. At the end of the paper we show our conclusions.

2 Framework of the MOLEC System

As we have mentioned in the introduction, the goal of the MOLEC system is to facilitate the monitoring of the heart diseases. The following elements help in pursuing this goal: 1) the *ECG Sensors* carried by a patient, in order to register heart signals; 2) the *Sensor-PDA-Holter*, a mobile device carried by the user that acquires, processes and transmits ECG signals; 3) the *MOLEC Hospital*, which receives possible abnormalities sent by the Sensor-PDA-Holter and results of queries made by physician(see figure 1).

From left to right, figure 1 show: 1) The *ECG Sensors* acquire the electric impulse of the heart. These sensors are the 'intelligent' chips that communicate with the PDA through the bluetooth protocol. 2) We call the user mobile device the *Sensor-PDA-Holter* because it acquires the data signal in a PDA and works like a traditional holter. Besides, it detects abnormalities and notifies the hospital very quickly. The modules of the Sensor-PDA-Holter are the *Data Pre-processing Module*, the *Decision Support System Module* and the *Database and Communication Module*. 3) The *MOLEC Hospital* is a system that provides the Sensor-PDA-Holter with the user data in order to customise it. It also receives the user's possible abnormalities. Hospitals would have to incorporate the MOLEC Hospital system into their administration system.

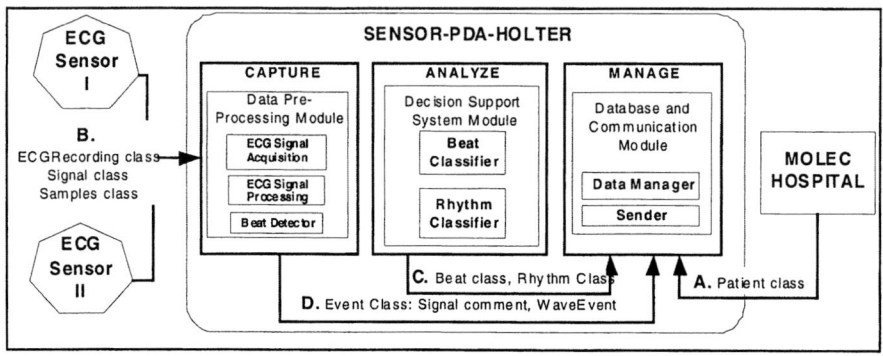

Fig. 1. MOLEC system

The data flows (see labels A, B, C and D in figure 1) represent the data exchanged among the previous modules. These data are objects of classes that express the data requirements needed to build a system that records ECG signals of users, processes them in order to identify the different beats, classifies each beat and also classifies the different beat rhythms with the aim of finding cardiac arrhythmias. These classes correspond to persistent classes that we implement by using database technology. They are also shown in the conceptual schema in figure 2.

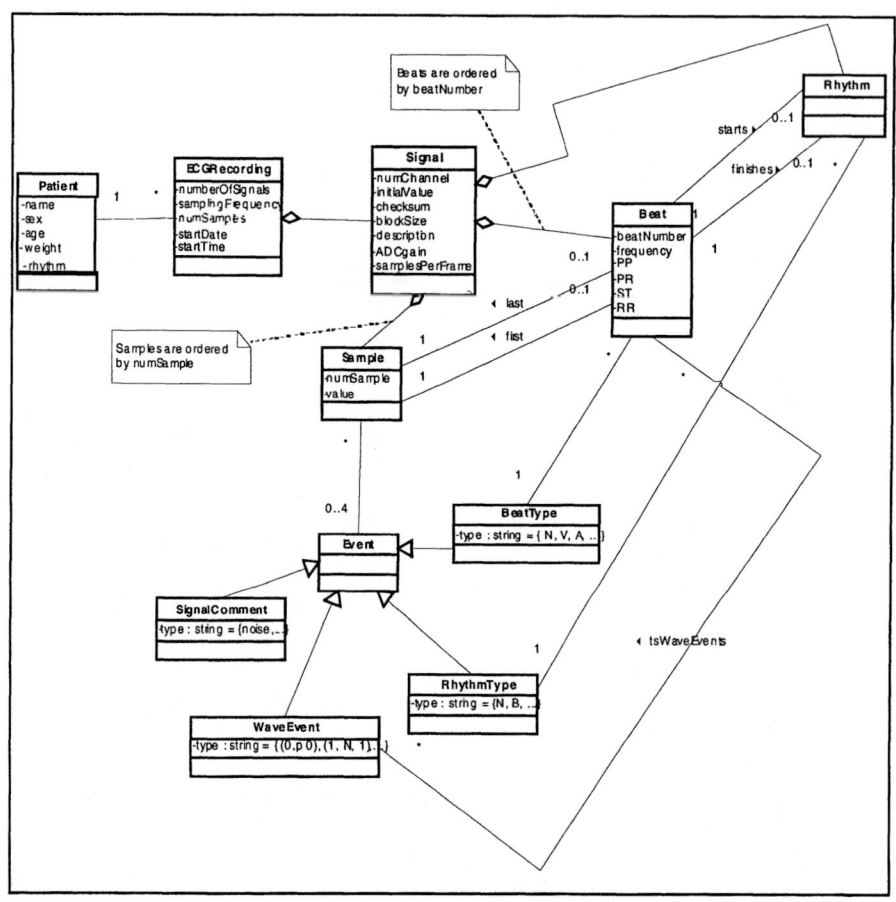

Fig. 2. Conceptual schema of MOLEC

In the following paragraphs, we explain the different classes present in figure 2 associated with the data flows that are used by the three modules that run at the PDA (i.e. Data Pre-processing Module, Decision Support Module and Database and Communication Module).

Data flow between MOLEC Hospital and Sensor-PDA-Holter (see label A in figure 1). The *Patient class* allows to store required data about users: name, sex, weight, age and typical heart parameters. These data must be stored in the hospital node, but, in every PDA, only the data corresponding to its user must be present. Those data are used to customize the PDA.

Data flow between ECG Sensor and Sensor-PDA-Holter (see label B in figure 1). The *ECGRecording class* stores different ECG recordings, each one belonging to a single user and with a sampling frequency, start time, start date, and number of samples. Each recording can consist of several signals (simultaneous recordings made in different channels). Each one of the signals is represented by a *Signal class* object. Each signal is seen as a sequence of samples, as a sequence of beats and as a sequence of rhythms. Each *Sample class* object has its sequence number and is associated with the signal object to which it belongs. These sample objects are obtained from the sensor and constitute the digital ECG signal.

Data flow inside Sensor-PDA-Holter (see labels C and D in figure 1). A sample object can be associated with four different events that are represented in the *Event class*. They are: 1) a *SignalComment class* object (for example, one that indicates if there is noise in the signal); 2) a *WaveEvent class* object (e.g. one that corresponds to a peak or to the limits of the P, QRS or T waves and also contains information about the type of T wave); 3) a *Rhythm class* object that indicates that a rhythm starts at that point of the signal; and 4) a *BeatType class* object that represents the type of beat at that point. All these event, beat and rhythm objects are obtained and attached to the sample events during the ECG signal processing by the beat detector, beat classifier and rhythm classifier. All the data corresponding to current ECG recordings are stored in the PDA; later, data can be stored in the hospital database if the physician wants to.

The rest of this article explains in detail the relationships between these classes and the PDA modules: Data Pre-Processing Module (section 3), Decision Support System Module (section 4) and Database and Communication Module (section 5).

3   Data Pre-processing Module

The data pre-processing module includes all steps necessary for a later correct analysis of the beats in the decision support system. These required steps include the acquisition of biological signals and the identification of each beat and its different parts.

The data pre-processing module (see Figure 3) consists of three submodules: 1) the *ECG Signal Acquisition*, which acquires the beat sequence from the ECG sensors and obtains the digital signals in a specific format; 2) the *ECG Signal Processing*, which receives digital signal segments and analyses them in order to determine the sequence of data that we call 'wave events' (the peaks and limits of P, QRS and T waves which are represented as points in figure 3); 3) the *Beat Detector* receives the wave events and identifies the RR, PR and QT intervals, the duration of the P, QRS complex and T waves, their frequency, and also determines the ST and PQ segments.

These three submodules convert the biological signal into a beat sequence with some important data such as wave events, intervals and frequencies, which will be used by the decision support module. We present each one of these submodules in the following subsections.

3.1   ECG Signal Acquisition

The ECG signal acquisition module, located at the PDA, manages the communication between the ECG sensors and the PDA. The electric impulses of the heart are obtained by the sensors and sent to the PDA. The information sent from the sensor to the PDA is a digital signal that has been transformed from biological signals. In order to completely understand this module, it is necessary to explain how an ECG sensor works, and how the data are translated to any format accepted by PhysioNet [11], in such a way that different ECG sensors may be adapted to MOLEC. In the following subsections we explain the submodules included in the ECG signal acquisition: the *ECG Sensor* and the *Sensor Data Adapter*.

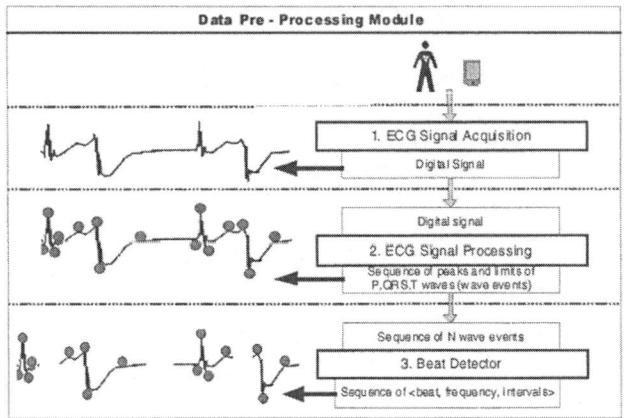

Fig. 3. Data pre-processing module

3.1.1   ECG Sensor. The electric impulse of the heart is acquired by the ECG sensors of the patient. These sensors are the intelligent chips that communicate with the PDA through the bluetooth protocol. The information to be sent is a digital signal that has been transformed from the analog signal.

Unfortunately, nowadays ECG sensor providers only sell their products with proprietary electrocardio analyser software. Therefore, in order to deal only with sensors, we have built an ECG sensor emulator that sends ECG data stored in a free downloadable database. The simulation process consists of dividing the data contained in the MIT-BIH database into bit sequences and sending those sequences periodically (see figure 4).

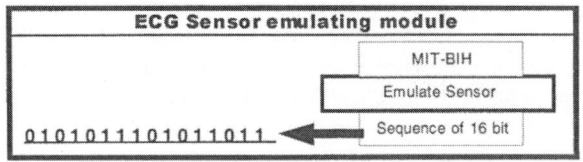

Fig. 4. ECG sensor emulating module

Through the development of this module, we have been able to provide the other modules with ECG signals, and to create a communication platform between the PDA and the sensors. Nowadays, there are some projects under development that try to build ECG wireless sensors, but they are not commercially available yet. We believe that with the architecture that we propose it would be possible to adapt our system in order to work with real ECG data sent by sensors.

3.1.2   Sensor Data Adapter and Visualisation. This module is located in the PDA and receives the signals sent by the ECG sensor. Next, the module translates the signal into a standard format that the whole system understands (Signal Class). The signal can be visualised on the MOLEC PDA screen (see figure 5) and is analysed in the next module, the ECG Signal Processing.

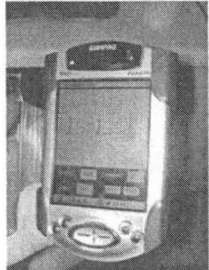

Fig. 5. ECG visualisation in Sensor-PDA-Holter of MOLEC

3.2   ECG Signal Processing

The ECG signal processing receives the digital signals and characterises the sequence of P, QRS and T waves associated with each beat. In order to read the ECG it is necessary to know the beginning, end, and the peaks of the waves that occur in a beat, because the absence, the format, the duration and other considerations allow some abnormalities to be identified.

0:00.819	279	(	beginning by P wave	0	0	0	0 corresponds
0:00.861	298	P	wave P	0	0	0	with the P
0:00.916	320	}	end P	0	0	0	wave
0:00.972	353	(	beginning by QRS	0	0	1	1 corresponds
0:01.025	370	N	wave QRS	0	0	0	with the
0:00.069	407	)	end QRS	0	0	1	QRS wave
0:01.219	424	(	beginning by T wave	0	0	2	corresponds with the T wave
0:01.300	455	t	wave T1	0	0	4	negative-positive
0:01.433	503	t	wave T2	0	0	4	negative-positive
0:01.488	523	}	end T	0	0	2	corresponds with the T wave

Fig. 6. The limits and peaks of a beat

In order to detect the limits and the peaks of the wave, we use ECGPUWAVE tool[2] [13], which is provided by PhysioNet, and implements the algorithm of on-line detection developed by Pan & Tompkins [14]. Its function is to identify the limits of the P, QRS and T waves in real time. This tool has been tested on different ECG databases: the CSE database [15], the MIT-BIH database [8] and the ST-T database [12].

---

[2] Although ECGGPUWAVE was developed for a larger computer than a PDA, it runs in our prototype of MOLEC, that is implemented in a iPAQ 3970 with Bluetooth and with 48MB ROM, 64MB RAM, Linux Familiar 0.7, Java virtual machine 1.3.1 and MYSQL version 9.38.

ECGPUWAVE works with data in a specific format where the input data are a sequence of digital signals and the output data is displayed in the next figure.

In figure 6, the first column represents exactly when the signals were acquired. The second column is relative time in relation to acquisition frequency (e.g. 360 Hz). We refer to this in the rest of the paper as 'time unit' (t.u.). The last column represents the beginning and the end of P, QRS and T waves with open and closed parentheses respectively. These parentheses are associated with the following annotations (see the last column): 0 corresponds with the P wave, 1 with the QRS wave, and 2 with the T wave. The letters P and T denote the peaks of the P and T waves. The letter N denotes the peak of the QRS complex. The classification of the T wave is shown in the last column where 0 is normal, 1 inverted, 2 positive, 3 negative, 4 negative-positive and 5 positive-negative. To identify the limits and peaks of the beats, it is necessary to send this sequence of wave events to the Beat Detector.

3.3   Beat Detector

The beat detector receives the wave events and invokes specific automata that we have developed with the purpose of building up the beats. This purpose is achieved by scanning the wave events one by one and building up each beat. A beat usually begins with a P wave followed by a QRS complex and finishes with a T wave, but some of them may be missing and others may be repeated, especially when there are heart diseases. One typical format of the beat is shown in table 1.

Table 1. Two beats detected by the automata

ID	format	(	p	)	{	QRS	}	[	t1	t2	N_t	]
1	(p){N}[tt]	279	298	320	352	370	402	424	455	503	4	523
2	{N}[t]	-1	-1	-1	562	598	605	627	658	-1	0	712

In this table we see all events that could be present in one beat (row one), but the format of the beat could be any combination of these wave events (row two, in which the absence of the P wave is indicated by -1). In other words, the detection of the beat is not a trivial process (especially when abnormal beats occur in the user due to missing and/or repetition of waves that may correspond to different beats). Hence, the automata implement all combinations of those wave events and decide which is a beat and which is not a beat.

After, identifying the format of the beat, it is necessary to determine the ST and PQ segments and to calculate the RR, PR and QT intervals, as well as the duration of the P, QRS complex and T waves and the heart frequency. These values are necessary to identify the different anomalous behaviours that could be present in the user. In figure 7 we show the signal corresponding to row 1 in table 1. The portion of the ECG between the QRS complex and the T wave is called the "ST segment" and the portion between the P wave and the QRS complex is called the "PQ segment". The portion of the beat between the P wave and the beginning of the QRS complex is called the "PR interval" and the portion between the QRS complex and the end of the T wave is called the "T interval". The distance from a QRS complex to the next QRS complex is called the "RR interval".

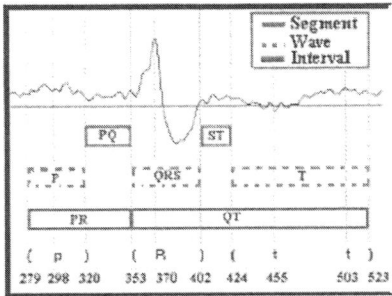

Fig. 7. Waves, segment, interval, limits and peak usually found in a beat

The duration of the waves is obtained by subtracting the end of a wave from its beginning. Looking at figure 7, it may be seen that the P wave of the beat began in time unit 279 and ended in time unit 320, i.e. it was 320-279 t.u. long. Do not forget that special values must be given when P waves, for example, have not been identified by the ECGUPWAVE tool (see table 1, row 2).

As mentioned above, this set of intervals, segments, waves, peaks, limits and format is necessary to classify one beat, so enabling the work of the next module, the Decision Support System.

4   Decision Support System Module

The decision support system is the module whose goal is twofold: to classify each beat and to classify each rhythm. The decision support module (see figure 8) receives a sequence of beats, their frequency and their intervals and classifies them as cardiac rhythms.

This module consists of two submodules: 1) the *Beat Classifier*, that classifies each beat thanks to a set of rules that we have defined with that purpose; 2) the *Rhythm Classifier*, which groups sequences of four beats and identifies the rhythm by using rules that we have defined and which reflect the properties of rhythms described in specialised literature [1]. The purpose of the decision support system is to classify each beat and rhythm in order to detect some abnormality. We present each one of these submodules in the following paragraphs.

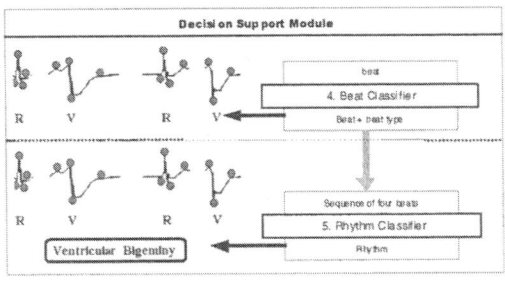

Fig. 8. Decision support system

4.1 Beat Classifier

The beat classifier receives the information related to the beats and applies a set of rules to classify them. In particular, we focus on methods that correctly classify the beat and rhythm types that PhysioNet provides.

PhysioNet contains a set of databases. One of them is the MIT-BIH database which contains 4,000 30-minute registers. However, we only have used the free 48 registers available (enumerated from 100-124 and from 200-234, with some missing in between). The first interval is a representation of typical clinical cases; in the second one, we find several complex anomalies like ventricular, supraventricular and nodal rhythms.

These registers are collected from men and woman between the ages of 23 and 89. The same instruments are used in all registers, which are first acquired analogically, and later transformed into digital signals, with a frequency of 360 Hz, using 11 bits and a resolution of approximately 5 mV. After the registers were collected, two independent cardiologists classified them, using tables 2 and 5, that show the different types of beats and rhythms, respectively.

Table 2. Table of beat type

F	Fusion of ventricular and normal beat	N	Normal beat
L	Left bundle branch block beat	E	Ventricular escape beat
R	Right bundle branch block beat	|	Isolated QRS-like artifact
j	Nodal (junctional) escape beat	"	Miss beat
f	Fusion of paced and normal beat	!	Ventricular flutter wave
A	Atrial premature beat	J	Nodal premature beat
a	Aberrated atrial premature beat	e	Atrial escape beat
V	Premature ventricular contraction	/	Paced beat
S	Supraventricular premature beat		

The process that we follow to find a set of rules that classify the beats is beyond of the scope of this article (see [10] for more details), but we can mention that a prototypical rule (table 3) is the following: a beat is normal if its R wave is between 0 and 26 time units, its frequency is between 0 and 63.16 t.u. and, finally, its RR interval is between 191 and 374 t.u. Once the beats are classified, it is necessary to classify the rhythms. The rhythms are classified using a set of beats and its components (segments, waves, frequency and intervals).

Table 3. Rule used to identify a normal beat

if wave_R >0 && wave_R <= 26 && freq > 0 && freq <= 63.16
&& intRR > 191 && intRR <= 374   **Type_Beat** = Normal Beat

4.2 Rhythm Classifier

The rhythm classifier makes groups of two to four beats and classifies the different rhythms. For this purpose the classifier uses a set of rules that reflect the properties of rhythms described in specialised literature [1]. We have extracted these rules, codified them in a programming language and tested them. One of those rules is shown in table 4. The parameters of the right (starting with "pf") are obtained from the users' data.

Table 4 represents the normal sinusual rhythm. It is the only rhythm that the system does not notify to the hospital because it is a desired rhythm. The meaning of this rule is the following: if the current beat and the previous one have their frequencies and PR intervals between the "pf" minimum and "pf" maximum and the R wave is smaller than the "pf" R maximum, then an only then is the rhythm normal sinusual rhythm. All these "pf" maximum and "pf" minimum values have been previously established by a physician.

Table 4. Rule used to identify a normal sinus rhythm

If (frequency_curr > pf_min_frec_normal && frequency_curr < pf_max_frec_normal && interval_PR_curr > pf_min_intervalPR_normal && interval_PR_curr < pf_max_intervalPR_normal && wave_R_curr < pf_max_R_normal && frequency_prev > pf_min_frec_normal && frequency_prev < pf_max_frec_normal && interval_PR_prev > pf_min_intervalPR_normal && wave_R_prev < pf_min_R_normal && interval_PR_prev < pf_max_intervalPR_normal) **Rhythm** = N (Normal Sinus Rhythm)

The classified rhythms correspond to the annotations found in PhysioNet (see table 5). All the rhythms are arrhythmias except normal rhythm N.

Table 5. Table of rhythm type

N	Normal sinus rhythm	VFL	Ventricular flutter
PREX	Pre-excitation (WPW)	AB	Atrial bigeminy
SBR	Sinus bradycardia	VT	Ventricular tachycardia
NOD	Nodal (A-V junctional) rhythm	B	Ventricular bigeminy
P	Paced rhythm	T	Ventricular trigeminy
IVR	Idioventricular rhythm	AFL	Atrial flutter
AFIB	Atrial fibrillation	BII	II heart block
SVTA	Supraventricular tachyarrhythmia		

Finally, beats and rhythms need to be stored by a Database and Communication Module. We explain this module in the following section.

5 Database and Communication Module

The database and communication module is the part of MOLEC that is in charge of storing the information generated by the Data Pre-processing and Decision Support modules and offers a set of services to the hospital. In our system, the PDAs work autonomously, receiving data from sensors, recording the data and analysing them in order to find anomalies. The PDAs are also able to send those anomalies, to receive queries formulated at the hospital about the signals, and to send the corresponding answers to the hospital.

The main goals of this module are: 1) to efficiently manage the restricted memory resources available in the PDA, at least when compared to the great capacity of ECG sensors to generate data ; 2) to reduce the quantity of data to be transmitted between the PDA and the hospital, taking into account that the wireless communication link used is usually more expensive than a wired one; and 3) to allow physicians in the hospital to formulate the kind of queries that they usually ask about ECG signals.

Flat files have been traditionally used to store recorded physiological signals. These data storage formats are not very interesting if high level queries want to be formulated, e.g. to find the number of isolated beats of type X in the current signal, or to find the number of sequences of Y consecutive beats of type X. However, these flat files are very appropriate if the goal is to reduce the quantity of data to be stored and/or transmitted, because they can be easily reduced to half their size after applying compression techniques. But these kinds of compression techniques have not been applied to classical signal files because they do not use an indirect model to analyse ECG signals: there is no computational node that processes and analyses the signal between the sensors and the host. Taking into account that, in our case, we do have an indirect model, it is possible to take advantage of it and to apply compression techniques. Therefore, we have applied common techniques in database and file technology in order to reach the previous goals: we use a relational database management system to store the data and to answer the queries made by the system (3rd goal mentioned above); and we also apply compression techniques to store the data that are not going to be queried (1st and 2nd goals mentioned above). At this point, we assume that physicians only make queries about abnormal beats and rhythms.

In figure 9, we show the database and communication module that consists of two submodules: 1) The *Data Manager Module*, which stores the data of the system; 2) the *Sender*, which communicates the PDA and MOLEC Hospital and builds the message in HL7 format [9]. HL7 is the first health care data-interchange standard.

5.1   Data Manager

The Data Manager submodule receives the data from the Data Pre-processing module and Decision Support module and processes them according to the following criteria: all normal beats and rhythms are stored *compressed in files*; and all abnormal beats and rhythms are stored in a *relational database*. The following paragraphs explain these criteria, whose aim is to optimize the use of PDA memory and the use of the wireless network.

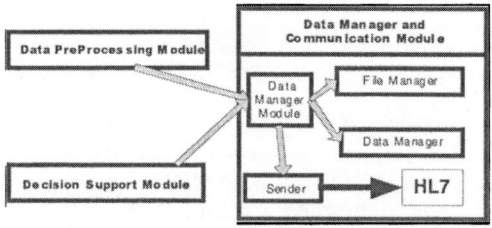

Fig. 9. Database and communication module

5.1.1.   Process Followed by the Data Manager. The Data Pre-processing and the Decision Support Modules exchange messages though their interfaces with the Data Manager module, which interprets and manages these messages. The Data Manager receives a message every time a new beat is detected. Afterwards, it also receives the beat type and the current rhythm type, and decides how to store these data. To make this decision, the system implements the state transition diagram shown in figure 10.

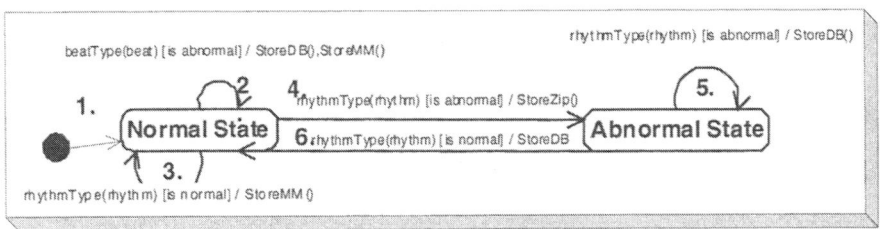

Fig. 10. State transition diagram

From left to right, figure 11 shows that: 1) the initial state is a normal rhythm; 2) if the system is in a normal state, but an abnormal beat (isolated beat) has been detected, it will be stored in the database (DB) and in a data structure in the main memory (MM). The system remains in a normal state; 3) if the system is in a normal state and a new normal rhythm has been detected, the state remains normal and the new data is stored in MM; 4) if the system is in a normal state, but an abnormal rhythm has been detected, the system retrieves from MM all data registered and creates a compressed file with them. The state of the system changes from normal to abnormal[3]; 5) if the system is in an abnormal state and a new abnormal rhythm is detected, the abnormal beat is stored in DB. The system remains in an abnormal state; 6) if the system is in an abnormal state, but a new normal rhythm is detected, the last abnormal rhythm is stored in DB, and the state of the system changes from abnormal to normal. The following subsection focuses on data compression. Afterwards, another subsection concentrates on the database and reports.

5.1.2   Compressed Data. As mentioned in this article, the digital signals emitted by the sensors are captured by MOLEC, in order to process them and determine possible abnormalities. Once the beats and the rhythms are analysed, it is possible to classify them in two great groups: *normal beats and rhythms* and *abnormal beats and rhythms.*

In figure 11, the proportion of normal and abnormal beats and rhythms corresponding to the recordings available in PhysioNet can be seen. Each one of the horizontal bars corresponds to a single patient: normal beats and rhythms are in grey, whereas abnormal ones in black. Abnormal rhythms and beats last an average of 6 minutes; some registers show no abnormal data (like register 100), and others are completely abnormal (like register 209). As for normal rhythms and beats, they last an average of 24 minutes.

---

[3] At this point, an alarm would be sent to the hospital system in order to indicate that a new abnormal rhythm has been identified.

In table 6, we can see the required memory size to store an ECG signal of some duration (Time column), depending on whether it is stored as: 1) a flat file used by
PhysioNet and MIT-BIH (.DAT column); 2) the same compressed flat file (.DAT.ZIP
column); 3) in a relational database (DB column). Notice that storing 6 minutes of
abnormal signals in the database (1.6M) plus 24 minutes of normal signals compressed in a .dat.zip file (958K) is very similar to storing all 30 minutes in the .dat file
(2.42M).

On the other hand, various ECG compression methods have already been developed. The most precise methods are less suitable because compression ratio is very
poor, although the reconstruction has a high quality. Moreover, different compression
methods yield different results, regarding that the compression ratio (2-30) and PRD
(percent mean-square difference normalised by the original data) is just 0-30%.
Hence, we only mention that we use ZIP compression, but a better one could be applied in our system if an appropriate tool for un/compressing were available.

Using our criteria, if the signal contains many *normal* beats and rhythms, the
quantity of required memory is reduced to the half because zip compression is used;
and if the signal contains many *abnormal* beats and rhythms, even more space could
be required because that data would be stored at the PDA database (in order to be able
to answer the kind of queries presented in the next subsection). Moreover, if more
memory were needed at the PDA, part of the signal could be sent compressed to the
hospital and uncompressed there. Physicians can query the PDA database about abnormal beats and rhythms from the hospital, or they can request to download in the
hospital system the data from the PDA database.

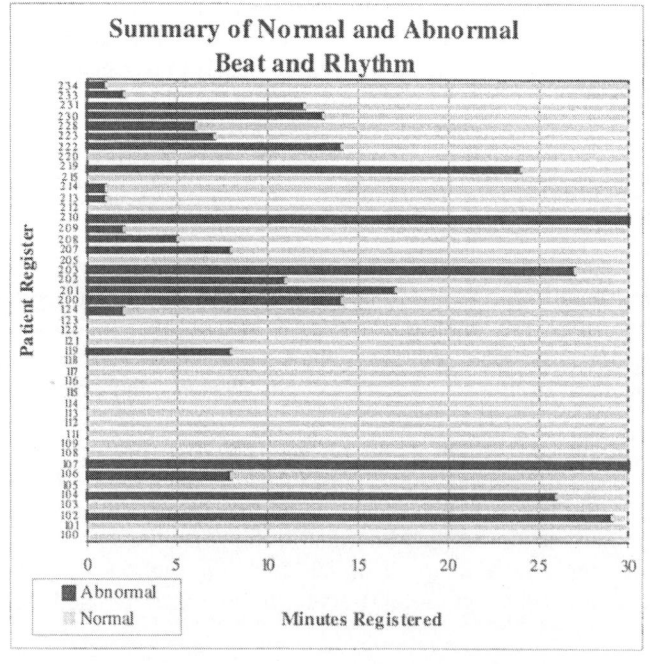

Fig. 11. Summary of recordings of MIT-BIH database

Table 6. Summary of the store types

Time	.DAT	.DAT.ZIP	DB	Time	.DAT	.DAT.ZIP	DB
2 sec	2.81 KB	1.55 KB	10 KB	6 Min	506.25K	236.64K	1.60 MB
10Min	843.75KB	398 KB	2.67 MB	24Min	1.98M	958.23K	6.42 MB
30 Min	2.42 M	1.17 M	8.3 MB				

5.1.3   Database Reports. Specialised literature [1] associates the functionality of holters with a set of reports, which enables physicians to analyse the data easily and quickly. In the following, we present some types of reports[4] usually offered by commercial products that show information about: 1) *automatic arrhythmia detection and identification* and 2) *ECG parameters*. In this subsection we present some SQL queries that would allow the system to generate the kind of reports previously mentioned. Notice that making these queries by using a database management system is much simpler than using flat files.

a) Automatic Arrhythmia Detection and Identification
These type of reports can be generated by writing queries that retrieve the different episodes of all abnormal rhythms, the frequency and the amount of beats involved. An example of an SQL query that obtains a summary of the cardiac rhythm levels (maximum, minimum, average) is shown in table 7. The columns indicate the rhythm type, the corresponding minimum and maximum rhythms, the average and the amount of beats involved. The last value is obtained by a "join" between the rhythm and beat tables. For this query, it would be interesting to define attribute RhythType as a clustering index, but that would require some reorganisation of the database.

Table 7. Levels of rhythm

SELECT	RhythmType as Type, min(freq) as min,
	max(freq) as max, avg(freq) as avg, count(*)
FROM	Rhythm r, Beat b
WHERE	b.BeatNumber between r.firstBeatNumber
	and r.lastBeatNumber and freq > 0
GROUP BY (RhythmType);	

Type	min	max	avg	count	Type	min	max	avg	count
B	30.17	251.16	79.012	140	IVR	22.57	72.73	59.34	105
N	30.55	260.24	68.73	1467	SVTA	95.15	134.16	121.02	104
VFL	42.27	675.00	143.06	169	VT	74.48	183.05	103.97	4

b) ECG Parameters
Afterwards, we offer a detail of abnormal beats because the physician is interested in retrieving the number of sequences of consecutive n beats of type A, for n=1, 2, ... m: number of isolated type A beats, number of couples of type A beats, and so on. This query is important because, this way, the physician can know the origin of the injured heart, depending on the beat type. The query can be repeated for supraven-

---

[4] There are other reports like analysis of ST segments evolution that we do not present due to lack of space.

tricular episodes (corresponding to beat types S, F, a and J) and ventricular episodes (corresponding to beat types V, ! and E).

In table 8, we present the SQL query and the obtained answer for the query corresponding to beat type A. The first column shows the length of the sequence, the second column is the number of sequences and the third one is the type of beat. Notice that this query consists of an autojoin in Beat table and of aggregation operators like "group by" and "count", that require some work. Hence, for this type of query it is interesting to define a clustering index of BeatNumber for Beat table. This is possible because consecutive numbers have been assigned to the beats.

Table 8. Detail of abnormal beats

SELECT   b.length, count(*), b.beatType
FROM   Beat b, Beat c, ECGRecording e
WHERE b.beatType like '%A%' and c.beatType not like '%A%'
         and c.BeatNumber = b.BeatNumber +1 and c.ECGRecordID = e.id
         and b.ECGRecordID = e.id and e.Name = 207 and
GROUP BY (b.length);

Length	count	Type	length	count	Type	length	count	Type
1	1	A	2	1	A	104	1	A

The previous queries can be formulated locally or remotely. If it is necessary to send information, the sender submodule sends a message to the hospital. This is explained in greater detail in the following subsection.

5.2   Sender

This module can send fragments of the user ECG signal to the hospital, as well as the reports solicited to MOLEC as seen in the previous section. A common standard is used to transmit medical data: HL7 [9]. An HL7 representation of clinical documents is called Clinical Document Architecture (CDA). The CDA is a document that specifies the syntax and semantics of a clinical document. It can include text, image, sounds and other multimedia content.

Table 9. Example of the message in HL7

MSH	|^~&| SVL || SVC || 19900324101215 || ORU^W01| 19264|P|2.3 <cr>
PID	| 1 | 4567890 | 4567890 | | Doe^John^Q^Jr^Mr <cr>
OBR	| 1 | 5678^SVC | 1234^SVL | 5^one-channel waveform recording^L <cr>
OBX	| 1 | CD|5&CHN^^L | 1| 1^ONE^0.5&mv^^200^-2048&2047 |||||| F<cr>
OBX	| 2 | TS| 5&TIM^^L | 1| 19900324081237.525 F<cr>
OBX	| 3 | NA5&WAV^^L | 1| 0^1^2^3^4^5^6^7^8^7^5^4^3^2^1^0^1^F<cr>
OBX	| 4 | CE|5&ANO^^L | 1| ^Beat Market |||||| F || 19900324081237.525 <cr>

An HL7 message is composed of various segments (see table 9). The *Message Header* segment (MSH) describes the message, including the sender, the receiver, the subject and a message ID. The *Patient Identification* (PID) identifies the user whose data is being transferred and the *Observation/Result segment* (OBX) carries the data related to measured values. In the message of table 9, each waveform channel in a recording contains the channel definition (CHN), timing (TIM), the digital time series data (WAV) and the annotation (ANO).

When the message is received by the hospital, the physician reads the report and confirms the result obtained by MOLEC. Notice that there are tools that can show the data represented in HL7 messages to physicians.

6 Conclusions

Within the development of new technology that monitors people suffering from different illnesses, MOLEC is highly innovative because it provides the following advantages: 1) *Accessibility*: data recorded in MOLEC can be queried any time, locally or remotely. 2) *Promptness*: MOLEC detects anomalous rhythms, anywhere and anytime, as soon as they are produced, and sends the corresponding alarm to the hospital. Time can very often be vital in anomalous situations. 3) *Efficiency*: MOLEC optimises the use of wireless communications and PDA resources. 4) *Local analysis:* even if the wireless communication were unavailable, the signal could be analysed locally at the PDA. 5) *Openness*: MOLEC can deal with different kinds of sensors and PDAs, and it can cooperate with other systems that follow standards such as HL7 for clinical data communication. 6) *Simplicity*: making technical issues transparent to the users from the point of view of software and hardware components.

Acknowledgment. We want to thank Igor Beaumont, Lacramiora Dranca and Iñaki Inza for their help in the implementation of MOLEC and in the use of the classification tools.

References

1. Despopoulos, A.., Silbernagl, S.: Texto y Atlas de Fisiología. ISBN: 84-8174-040-3.
2. Daja, N., Relgin, I., Reljin B.,: Telemonitoring in Cardiology –ECG transmission by Mobile Phone. Annals of the Academy of Studenica 4, 2001.
3. Ventracor Limited. http://www.ventracor.co, 2003.
4. Cardio Control. http://www.cardiocontrol.com/cardio.htm, 2003
5. I. Sachpazidis. @Home: A modular telemedicine system. Mobile Computing in Medicine, Proceedings of the 2. Workshop on mobile computing. Heidelberg, Germany, April 2002.
6. Dimitri Konstansas Val Jones, Rainer Hersog. MobiHealth- innovative 2.5/3G mobile services and applications for healthcare. Workshop on Standardization in E-Health. Geneva, Italy. May 2003.
7. Kunze, C., Großmann, U., Stork, W., Müller-Glaser, K.D.,: Application of Ubiquitous Computing in Personal Health Monitoring Systems. 36. annual meeting of the German Society for Biomedical Engineering, 2002.
8. MIT-DB Database Distribution. http://ecg.mit.edu/, 2003.
9. Health Level 7 (HL7): An application protocol for electronic data exchange in healthcare environments. http://www.hl7.org/ , 2003.
10. Rodríguez, J., Goñi A., Illarramendi, A.: Classifying ECGs in an On-Line Monitoring System. Submitted for Publication, 2003.

11. Physionet: "The research resource for complex physiologic signals".
    http://www.physionet.org/, 2003.
12. CSE Database. France: http://www.iath.virginia.edu/~spw4s/CSE/CSE_database.frame.html,
    2003
13. Jané, P., Blasi, A., García, J., Laguna, P.: Evaluation of an Automatic Threshold Based
    Detector of Waveform Limits in Holter ECG with the QT database". Computers in Cardi-
    ology 1997, vol. 24, pp. 295–298.
14. Pan, J., Tompkin, W. J.: A real-time QRS detection algorithm". IEEE Trans. Biomed. Eng.
    BME-32: 230–236, 1985.
15. European ST-T Database: http://www.physionet.org/physiobank/database/edb/, 2003.

Definition of a User Environment in a Ubiquitous System

Dulcineia Carvalho, Roy Campbell, Geneva Belford, and Dennis Mickunas

Department of Computer Science
University of Illinois at Urbana-Champaign, Urbana, IL 61801
{dcarvalh,roy,belford,mickunas}@cs.uiuc.edu

Abstract. Currently, users interact with computer systems at the level of applications or devices. In the reality of ubiquitous computing it is neither acceptable nor scalable to expect that users keep track of all their activities, explicitly migrate them, and configure resources as they need them. We conceptualize a *user environment* as an aggregation of the whole activity of a user in a ubiquitous system. In this paper we define a *user environment* in a ubiquitous system. We also propose a software architecture that maintains *user environments*, deploys and adjusts them to underlying computing spaces, as necessary.

Keywords: Ubiquitous computing, user environments, distributed objects.

1 Introduction

Computation is intrinsic to our daily lives. Ubiquitous computing makes computing power present at all times and all places in a non-intrusive and convenient way. Ubiquitous systems are heterogeneous hardware and software systems, that potentially span various administrative or geographic domains. In these systems we are faced with the reality of users that are increasingly mobile and require access to multiple services and platforms at different times and places.

We want to convey to a user the view and experience of a ubiquitous system as a continuum of spaces from which he can access services and interact with other users using a variety of devices. In the process, a continuous workplace for the user is seamlessly created in the system. This is the idea behind the concept of a *user environment.*

Current systems do not support the abstraction of global activity of a user. A mobile user today has to manually migrate his computing activity from one place to another, and has to manually select and configure any resources he needs to use. In this paper we introduce and define the concept of a *user environment* as a feasible approach to maintaining the activity of mobile users across the spaces of a ubiquitous system.

We define a *user environment* as a collection of distributed objects that collectively represent a *structured, consistent and globally available* image of the activity of a user in a ubiquitous system. We suggest that if we keep track of the

R. Meersman et al. (Eds.): CoopIS/DOA/ODBASE 2003, LNCS 2888, pp. 1151–1169, 2003.

activity of a user in a ubiquitous system, then as the user moves from location to location, we can move his activity with him. If the *activity of a user* in the system is associated with the user at all times and is made available to the user at all spaces, then a mobile user can seamlessly perform his activity as he desires. Particularly, upon arrival at a space, a user can continue any session of work that he currently has in any space of the ubiquitous system, or he can start a new session of work. We aim at making the changes in the activity of a user entailed by such movements as seamless as possible to the user. A user that moves from his office to a conference room in a ubiquitous system should seamlessly access the work left at his office and continue such work if he so desires.

In this paper we present a software architecture that realizes the concept of a *user environment* that is always present with the user, and that mimics as closely as possible the user preferences. Such an architecture requires three main capabilities. First, it has to represent and maintain a user environment in a ubiquitous system. Second, it has to deploy a user environment, making it available across the spaces of a ubiquitous system. Finally, it has to match a user environment to the characteristics of a computing space and to the preferences of a user.

2   What Is a User Environment?

We consider that a user in a ubiquitous system is defined by his identity and roles he plays, any features that he personally requires or suggests, the status of the activities he is performing, the entities with which he is interacting, the physical domains he is visiting.

We believe that if one aggregates all of these attributes that characterize a user in an entity that is structured and manageable, consistent and globally accessible in the system, then one is able to continuously associate a user with the window of his activity in the system that is relevant to him at any given time. Informally, a *user environment* is a set of distributed objects that collectively completely characterize the activity of a user in a ubiquitous system. A user environment is then an abstraction that captures the essence of a user in a ubiquitous system and consists of:
− environment identification
− user profile
− user location
− user activity

Environment identification is a unique string that identifies the environment in the system. Next each of the other elements are defined in detail.

2.1   User Profile

Each user has a profile that specifies his personal features and preferences. The profile of a user in the system consists of

- the identification of the user
- the roles played by the user
- the preferences of the user.

Profile of a user is a concept that is relevant to a particular setting. A user has a global profile that is an aggregation of all of his partial profiles, each of which is tied to a particular role or location. So, statically, the profile of a user is determined by the role of a user. Dynamically, in the context of a user environment instantiated in a certain location, the profile depends on the actual characteristics of the space. Therefore, dynamically, the profile is a function of the user role(s) and characteristics of the space where the user is currently located.

User Identification consists of a name, a password and possibly anthropometric signs such as a photo, a fingerprint scan and a retina scan.

User Roles are the roles the user is allowed to play. Each role may have its own profile specificities.

User Preferences are the characteristics that the user assumes or the features that a user requires in a particular computational setting. User preferences detail default components, preferred devices, as well as resource requirements for the user in a particular setting. User preferences are specialized by role played and by location.

2.2 User Location

User location specifies the geographical whereabouts of a user, i.e., the physical coordinates of a user. A user in a ubiquitous system, given his mobile nature, has two significant location attributes, *current location* and *home location*.

Home Location. At a given instant, the home location is defined as the location where the root of the global environment of a user sits.

In case of the existence of several replicas of the root environment of a user, the location of any of them can become a home location. When a root environment is replicated, all the replicas are maintained consistent. So, the location of any of them may be the home location.

Home location of a user is an analog to a permanent residence of a person. A user can always fall back to his home location to save or retrieve state of his user environment.

Current Location is the address of the space where the user is currently located.

2.3 User Activity

In a ubiquitous system, a user works in a particular space using applications via devices in that space, and moves from space to space, sometimes carrying his own computing devices. We define *global activity of a user* in a ubiquitous system as the set of all the applications running or suspended on behalf of a user, and the resources used by those applications, including the devices where the applications are running. In a ubiquitous system, the activity of a user may span several platforms and different protection domains, may require to be postponable, and may have to be as mobile as the user. The notion of process is no longer sufficient to seamlessly represent such activity.

Instead, we propose to aggregate the whole activity of a user in a ubiquitous system into an image that is *structured, consistent and globally available*. We establish that the *activity* of a user is organized in *sessions*.

A *session* is a set of components and devices that have been grouped together as a unit by a user, using a criterion such as application semantics, location or convenience. Typically, when a user enters a space he works on a session of his in that space. The session that a user is currently accessing is instantiated in the *current environment* of that user. A session consists of :

- state
- components, and for each component:
  - location(s)
  - devices
  - resources and statistics - including files
  - configuration parameters
  - state,
- devices, and for each device:
  - location
  - configuration parameters
  - state.

The state of a session can be running or it can be temporarily suspended to be resumed later. A session is expressed by the rule:

$$user\_session = state.components.devices \qquad (1)$$

2.4   Global Environment of a User

In general, users have more than one session of work, each of which is instantiated at a user environment. The *global environment* of a user in a ubiquitous system is a composite of all the current environments of that user in the system, each corresponding to a session that the user has in the system. There is a one-to-one relationship between a user and his global environment. The purpose of coalescing all the activity of a user in a *user global environment* is to make it more manageable, consistent and better accessible to the user.

The *global environment* of a user is organized as a hierarchy because, in general, the sessions of a user are related physically or logically. For instance, the sessions of work of a user in a building are physically related. The sessions of work that a user devotes to the same project are related logically, even though they might not be physically close to one another. The related sessions of work tend to use common or related resources. Operations in environments tend to be applied to clusters of related sessions.

The elements of the *global environment* of a user are distributed across the spaces of a ubiquitous system. In general, the *global environment* of a user forms a direct acyclic graph, and is represented in its simplest form as a rooted tree. In the global environment of a user there is a special element called the *root environment*. The *root environment* is an entry point for a *user current environment* and a *user profile* in the system. The global environment of a user is accessible from the *root environment*. The *root environment* of a user is located at the home location of a user. A session of work in a space is instantiated at a *leaf environment* in that space. *Node environments* are structure builders of the *global environment* of a user. The point of aggregation of an individual environment depends on the user intentions, and on implicit placement performed by the computing spaces traversed by the user. Structural elements relevant to the *global environment* are *parents*, *children* and *siblings* environments.

A *user environment* wraps a session of work of a user with the user preferences and the structural elements required to maintain the global structure of a *user environment*. The global activity of a user, that is, the aggregation of all sessions of a user, is accessible by navigating the sessions of a user global environment.

Figure 1 depicts the global environment of a user called Carlos. Carlos, who is a student at the University of Illinois, has currently four sessions of work in the system: two at school and two at his house. Each session of work is instantiated at a leaf environment. His sessions of work at school and at his house

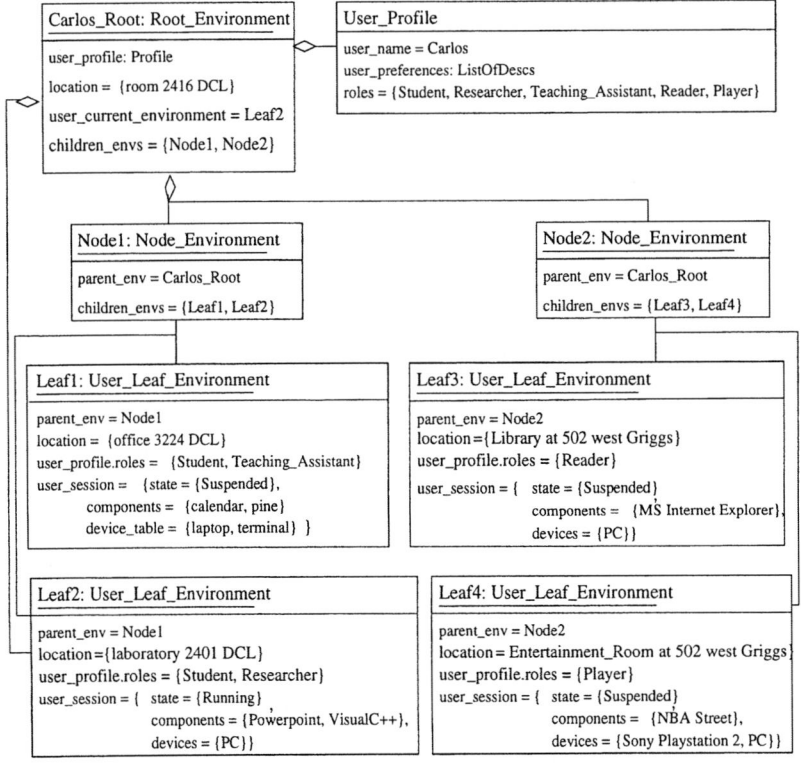

Fig. 1. Global Environment of User Carlos

are aggregated at node environments *Node1* and *Node2*, respectively. *Node1* and *Node2* are children of his root environment, *Carlos_Root*. *Carlos_root* is physically placed at the home location of Carlos, the room 2416 DCL. The root has the global profile of Carlos as one of his attributes. The root has a direct reference to the current environment of Carlos which is his leaf environment at the laboratory 2401 DCL. His session of work there, *Leaf2*, is *running*. He is working on a PC and has two applications running: a slides editor and Visual C++ Developer Studio. He is currently playing the roles of a *Student* and of a *Researcher*. All his other sessions of work are *suspended*.

A user environment can be distributed. A *distributed environment* is used to instantiate a distributed session. A distributed session is logically composed of several individual sessions communicating and interacting with one another. Each session of a distributed session is instantiated at a *peer environment*. A *distributed environment* is an association of *peer environments*.

2.5   Additional Elements of User Environment

To more completely define a user environment, we address structural elements, security elements, and event elements.

Structural Elements. These elements are necessary to maintain the composite structure of a user environment.
   – parent(s) environments
   – siblings - are environments which share at least one parent
   – peers - are member environments in a distributed environment
   – children environments - these are the node environments or sub-environments of an environment
   – root environment
   Parents, children, and *siblings* yield the hierarchical structure of an environment. *Peers* reflect the distributed nature of an environment.

Any environment points to its parents, its children and its peers at any given time. Its siblings are reachable through its parent. In addition any environment of a user points to the *root* of the environment tree of that user.

Security Elements. In a secure system, in all exchanges between users, the identity of the participants has to be verified. In user environments it is done using credentials. A credential is a data structure consisting of encryption keys and timed tickets. We define *peer users* as *users* who interact among themselves in an activity.
   – User credentials - A user is interested in a number of credentials for different purposes: his own *authentication* and *access control* credentials, as well as the access control credentials of his *peer users*. In a *user environment* all the credentials relevant to a user are kept in a credentials table.

User Environment State. The state of an environment can be *running* or *suspended* depending on whether or not the corresponding session is active. When the environment is in a suspended state then the value of the attributes of the environment are saved in the global environment structure of that particular user. When the environment is in a running state then the value of the attributes of the environment are instantiated.

User Environment Location is the physical location of an environment.

User Environment Events. The nature of user activity may require certain bookkeeping of events. Users not only move from one place to another but also can be temporarily unaccessible, or can explicitly suspend their activity and resume it later. To accommodate these requirements, a user environment needs to keep track of all the events and messages generated by or targeted to environment components. Events considered in this category are:
- user relevant events - generated by or targeted to a user
- component/device relevant events - generated by or targeted to a component/device in a session owned by a user.

Each user environment has an event table that keeps a log of the state of such events: processed, delayed, canceled or postponed.

2.6   Context of a User

As a user navigates a ubiquitous system, he interacts with the active spaces that he traverses through his sessions of work. Once in a space, a user can work on a new session or on an existing session. A *user environment* is instantiated in a space, to provide a workplace for a user and is configured according to the user preferences. One can see this workplace created for the user as a *user context* in a space. The instantiation of an environment at a particular location drives the context of that location to match the user preferences and the session requirements. One can conclude that a user brings *user context* into a space, which in turn may lead to changes in the space state.

3   Formal Definition of a User Environment

As described in section 2 a user environment is a set of objects that globally characterize the activity of a user in a ubiquitous system. The activity of a user is organized in sessions of work. At a certain time and location a user typically accesses a session of his activity.

Operationally, a *user environment* is a function that continuously spatially and temporally pairs a user with his activity. Hence, a *user environment* maintains the state of the activity of a user deploys it as the user moves and instantiates the relevant session of his activity in an actual computing space. One can say that, *user activity* is a function whose domain is the tuple (*user_id, location, time*), and whose range is the set of all the sessions in a ubiquitous system. For a given user, with a certain *user_id*, the range of the function *user_activity* is all the sessions of work of that user.

$$user\_activity : user\_id * location * time-> session \qquad (2)$$

An environment of a user in a particular location and at a particular time corresponds to an instantiation of a session qualified by the preferences of the user profile in that location and at that time.

It has been said in section 2 that a *user's environment* consists of a user's *profile*, *location* and *activity*. As discussed in 2.1 and 2.3, both the activity and the profile of a user are organized so that each element is relevant to a particular location of a user's work. Similarly, a user *environment* is organized so that each individual environment is relevant to a specific location of a user's work. Consequently, structurally, the *global environment* of a user is a rooted tree, with *node environments* and *leaf environments*, as indicated in rules 3 through 7.

$$global\_user\_environment = root\_environment \qquad (3)$$

$$\begin{aligned} root\_environment = User\_Location.User\_Profile.Current\_Environment. \\ (node\_environment)^* \end{aligned} \qquad (4)$$

The *root_environment* is located at a user's home location. *User_Profile* and *Current_Environment* of a user are directly accessible from the *root_environment*. *Current_Environment* of a user is the environment that a user is currently accessing. The user current active role(s), current location(s) and current activity are reachable from the *Current_Environment*.

Node environments allow the formation of hierarchies of environments.

$$node\_environment = Parent\_Env.(child\_environment)^*|Nil \qquad (5)$$

$$child\_environment = leaf\_environment|(node\_environment)^*|Nil \qquad (6)$$

Leaf environments are terminal environments and instantiation points for the sessions of work of a user.

$$leaf\_environment = User\_Profile.User\_Session \qquad (7)$$

The global activity of a user is accessible by navigating all the sessions which are instantiated at the leaves of a user global environment.

3.1 UML [6] Class Definition of a User Environment

With the additional elements of the definition of a user environment, introduced in section 2.5, the complete formal definition of a user environment becomes:

$$\begin{aligned} user\_environment = Env\_Id.Env\_State.Env\_Location.User\_Profile.User\_Location. \\ User\_Session.Parent\_Env.Children\_Envs.Peer\_Envs. \\ Root\_Env.Credentials\_Table.Events\_Table \end{aligned} \qquad (8)$$

One can conclude from above, however, that a user environment can be one of three kinds: root_environment, node_environment or leaf_environment. A user environment is thus a generalization of root_environment, node_environment or

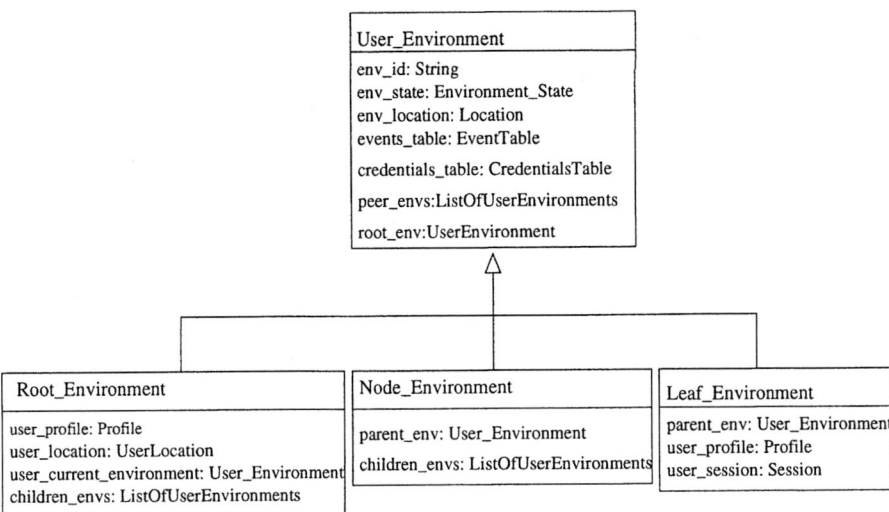

Fig. 2. UML class definition of User Environment

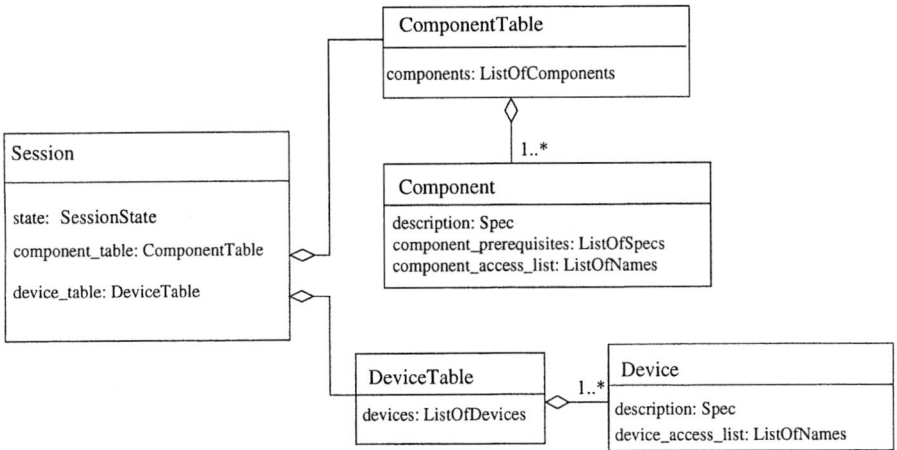

Fig. 3. UML class definition of a Session of a User Environment

leaf_environment, as depicted in figure 2. The attributes *Env_Id, Env_State, Env_Location, Peer_Envs, Root_Env, Credentials_Table* and *Events_Table* are common to all kinds of environments.

The UML class definition of a session of a user environment follows from rule 1 of section 2.3 and is depicted in figure 3.

4   Architecture of the Environment Framework

It is a fact that at times it is cumbersome for a user to move his activity from one location to another. It requires some skills of administration, configuration and adjustment on the part of a user who many times lacks them or cannot afford to deal with them. In the current state of art of computing systems, a user is tied to a computing environment that, in turn, is tied to a piece of hardware. If the user moves to another platform, explicit configurations, deployment and adjustment have to be made by the user.

One wants to convey to a user a view of a ubiquitous system as a continuum of platforms, and make him slightly aware of the existence of these platforms, not limited by them. A *user environment* is made present everywhere by a software infrastructure called *Environment Management* that is described in this section. *Environment Management* has servers for administration, migration, configuration and adjustment of a user environment in each computing space that a user visits.

Environment Management, designed to be transparent to the user, is depicted in figure 4.

The driving principles of the design of this architecture are:
- a *user* now depends only on his *environment*, and is decoupled from specific hardware platforms;
- a *user environment* is a first-class class object: it is named, it can be saved and retrieved, it can be migrated and it can be tuned to user preferences and physical space configurations;

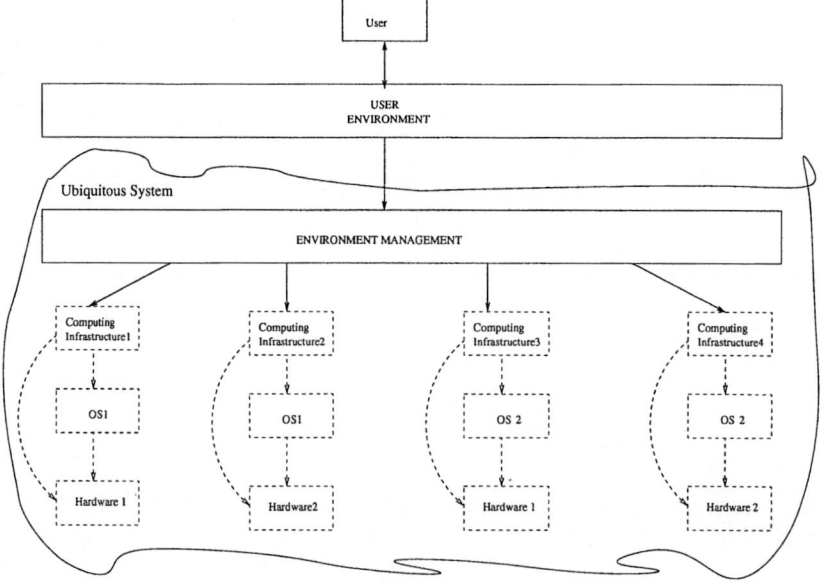

Fig. 4. Environment Management Layer in a Ubiquitous System

- a *physical space* has an environment manager that attends to users interacting with that space;
- *environment management* is a distributed software system, with one manager per space. *Environment managers* in each space cooperate with one another to support mobility of a *user environment.*

A direct result of the above principles is the architecture depicted in Figure 5.

It is a design decision to allocate an *environment manager* per space and make it attend all the users visiting that space. A *user environment* may have none of its elements active at a particular time. What is always active in each space is an *environment manager*, that attends to all users who visit that space. Upon notification of user arrival to a space, the environment manager starts a user environment for that user in that space. In doing so, an *environment manager* may ask the collaboration of other *environment manager(s)*. Consequently, in a multispace an *environment manager* has a protocol for interaction with other environment managers as indicated in Figure 6.

A different design approach would be to place one *user environment* per user in each space, and upgrade the functionality of a user environment with migration and tuning. Our design decision is based on two reasons:

Separation of Concerns. A *user environment* deals with user preferences, and user activity on a per user basis. *Environment management*, in contrast, deals with administration, mobility, tuning for all user environments.

Scalability. Having one *user environment* per user always running in every space is less scalable than one *manager* per space for all users. This is particularly true under the assumption that the number of users is at least an order of magnitude greater than the number of spaces in a ubiquitous system.

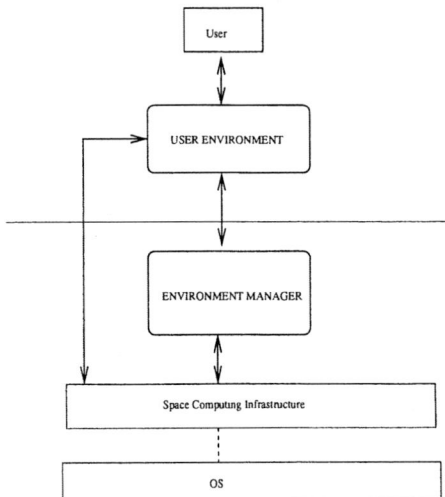

Fig. 5. Architecture for User Environments in a Space

5 Inside an Environment Manager

We consider that a ubiquitous system is an aggregation of spaces, each space being a group of hosts and devices located in a physical area, and providing services to users. While navigating a ubiquitous system, users bring along their own environment - their work and their preferences. A ubiquitous system has to pair a user with his environment, or at least the relevant part of his environment at a certain time and place. To this end and as depicted in Figure 7, an *environment manager* is conceived as a service running in each space of a ubiquitous system and providing the functionalities of:

- factory of environments - creates and removes user environments,
- migrator of environments - relocates user environments from one space to another. The migrator saves the state of an environment, ships the state to a new location, and does bookkeeping of environment state in the transient phase.
- resolver of environments - adjusts user environments to the characteristics of a space. The resolver inspects a user environment description and matches it with the characteristics of a space. A user environment description has preferences of a user and session attributes consisting of components and devices descriptions and pre-requisites.
- repository of environments - stores global user environments and searches for the environment of a user.

5.1 Organization of Environment Managers

The Environment Management Service is a distributed service that maintains the current environments of users in the system. The environment of a particular

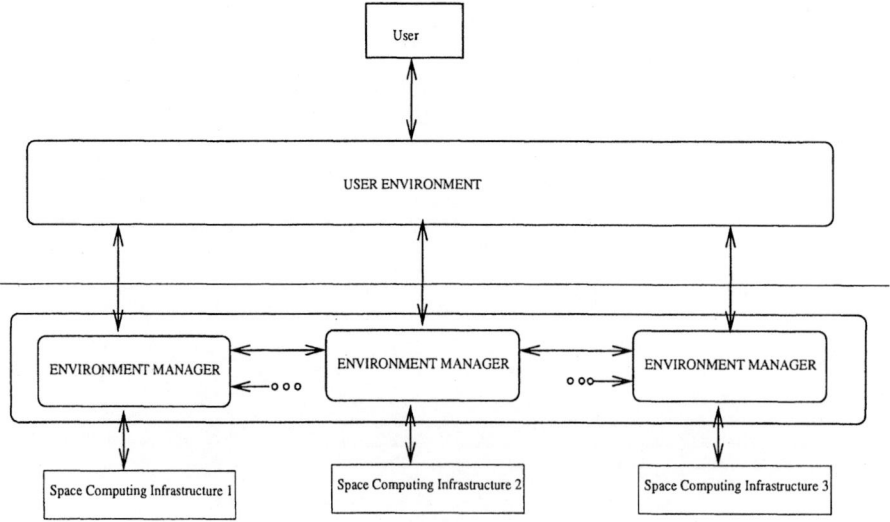

Fig. 6. Environment Managers in a Multispace System

user is a composite structure that is potentially distributed in the ubiquitous system. A function of the Environment Management Service is to make a user environment accessible where it is required in the scope of the system. Therefore, the Environment Management Service is required to be highly available in the ubiquitous system.

Environment Managers typically run one per space. The environment managers of all the spaces collectively form a distributed service that continually pairs a user with his environments throughout a ubiquitous system. In this section I discuss the organization of this distributed environment service.

A natural way of organizing the environment managers is to follow the physical organization of the underlying computing spaces. The physical spaces are normally hierarchically organized. So, the environment managers will be hierarchically organized. To accomplish this, it is required that when an environment manager is installed in a new space, its parent in the hierarchy of environment managers has to be set. An example of this hierarchy of environment managers is shown in Figure 8.

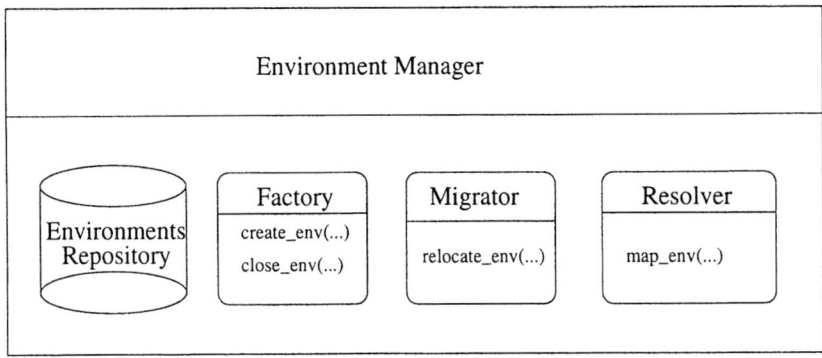

Fig. 7. Environment Manager

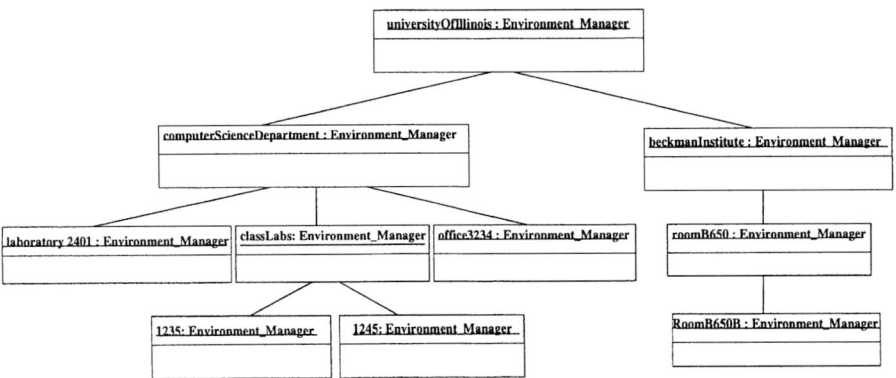

Fig. 8. Hierarchical Geographical Organization of Environment Managers

As a consequence of this organization an environment manager includes in its definition two additional structural attributes *parent_managers* and *children_managers*, as depicted in figure 9.

Alternatives to this geographical-hierarchical organization include:
- a direct acyclic graph;
- a fat balanced tree, so that the traffic in each branch is the same, and the links are increasingly thicker towards the root;
- architectures less hierarchical and more robust to partition, such as a mesh or a hypercube.

For now, we elect to use a geographical hierarchical topology. It might be interesting to evaluate the impact of different topologies on the performance of the system, that is, on how fast and how well the system adapts to changes in the location and preferences of a user.

Distributed Environment Managers Protocol. Managers cooperate to make the global environment of a user continuously available in the ubiquitous system. To accomplish that, the peer environment managers in the spaces involved may have to interact to perform operations such as:
- migration of an environment through the migrator;
- instantiation of a peer environment in a distributed environment through the factory;
- search for a particular environment and
- query environments given a certain predicate through the repositories.

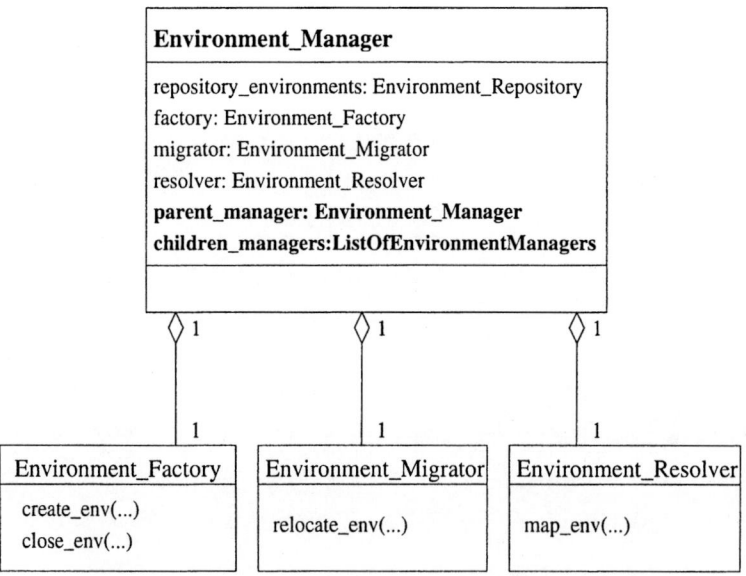

Fig. 9. Class definition of Environment Manager Revisited

The inter-manager protocol is in fact a suite of protocols consisting of the manager-manager protocol and peer-to-peer protocols of its components - factory, migrator, resolver, repository. The manager-manager protocol is used to locate the peer environment manager in the remote space. The other protocols are used to accomplish operations such as migration, remote instantiation, search and query.

An operation is typically originated by the user, or by the user environment and a request is made to one of the manager components - factory, migrator, resolver or repository. The environment manager in that space then locates its peer manager, given any attribute that identifies it, such as a name, a location of space, or a certain predicate. Given the hierarchical organization of environment managers, this operation of search follows algorithms for tree traversal in the structure of environment managers. Once the peer environment manager is located, inter-component protocols are followed to complete the operation. For instance, the migration of an environment is initiated by a user that arrives at a space, but has left his session of work in another space. So, the migrator in the current space is called to interact with the migrator in the remote space to get the user environment. The migrator in turn resorts to the local manager to locate the manager of the remote space using the manager-manager protocol. After that, the migrators in the two spaces complete the migration operation.

5.2   Repository of User Environments

A user has a home location, defined as the physical location of the space where the root of his global environment sits. Administratively, in a ubiquitous system, a home location of a user is first set when a user is inserted in the system by a system administrator, human or automated. For the purpose of this research, let us assume that a home location is determined by an administrative entity.

What is relevant to this research, is that the environment manager at the home location of a user is the repository of the environment of this user. It stores the root environment and possibly caches any subset of the global environment of a user. As discussed before, the state of any session of work of a user is reachable from the root environment of that user.

The home location of a user may change. An administrative entity may explicitly move it to another space, and this is outside the scope of our work. Implicitly, monitoring algorithms can determine the frequency of accesses of a user environment on a per location basis and set the home location as the most frequently accessed location or use any other criteria for improvement. This will be addressed as part of the evaluation of the environment architecture.

A user can have any number of environments in the system, each of them corresponding to a session in a particular space. A particular environment of a user is initially stored at the Environment Manager of the space where it is first created. When an environment is migrated to another location, as a result of user mobility, then a replica of itself is kept at the original space for a certain period of time. The duration of this period is a parameter to be tuned in system evaluations.

The reason to leave a replica of the environment behind is that if the user returns to this location he will mostly likely work on an environment very similar to this one. So, when that happens it will suffice to migrate the differential state of this environment.

All these environments are tied together in the composite global environment of a user that is maintained in the following way:

- the root environment of a user is stored at the Environment Manager of the home location of a user.
- any other environment is stored at the Environment Manager of the space where it is created, or it has been more recently accessed.

An environment manager at a particular space stores:

- user environments that are active in that space
- user environments that were created in that space, and were not yet migrated nor destroyed.

6   Related Work

The challenges of ubiquitous computing have prompted research in areas such as operating systems, user interfaces, networks, wireless, displays, among others. We approach the problem from the perspective of operating systems, addressing specifically the problem of adaptation of computer systems to human activity and to the human environment. This defines our vision of the user environment in a ubiquitous system.

We here discuss a representative subset of the work done in this area of Ubiquitous Computing: the ICrafter [7] for interactive spaces at Stanford University, the i-LAND project [9] at GMD-IPSI, the Smart-Its project [4] at Lancaster University and partners, the MIT Intelligent Room [2] and the Aura project [3] at Carnegie-Mellon University.

ICrafter is a framework for services and their user interfaces for the class of ubiquitous computing environments called interactive workspaces. Interactive workspace is a rich space consisting of interconnected computers where people gather to do naturally collaborative activities such as design reviews and brainstorms [7]. The key objective of ICrafter is to let the users interact with services in their environments using different modalities and input devices. ICrafter attacks the problem in three different ways. First, it supports user interface selection, generation and adaptation. Second, it allows user interfaces to be associated with service patterns for on-the-fly aggregation of services. Third, it facilitates the design of portable service user interfaces that still reflect the current workspace. We understand that the ICrafter approach is on services and the user interfaces to these services, particularly the selection of the better suited interfaces in a particular local environment. The emphasis of our research is on portable and mobile user environments. In our design the activity of a user is supported in the ubiquitous system over time and across space boundaries. Moreover, the activity of the user has to be tuned both to the particular characteristics of the user and to the physical environment.

i-LAND is the ubiquitous computing environment at GMD-IPSI and is based on a software architecture called BEACH that provides functionality for synchronous cooperation and interaction of roomware components, defined as room elements with integrated information technology [9]. This infrastructure provides both flexibility and extensibility for different devices that are part of a ubiquitous computing environment. It offers a user interface that includes devices with no mouse or keyboard, requiring new forms of human- and team-computer interaction. It allows synchronous collaboration through shared documents concurrently accessible via multiple interaction devices. i-LAND approaches the problem of ubiquitous computing from the device and synchronous collaboration perspective, while our emphasis aims at maintaining mobile user environments, and at reflectively adapting user and physical environments.

Smart-Its [4] argues that when everything is connected to everything what will matter most for the emergence of successful applications will be not the quantity but the quality and usefulness of connections. They define artifacts as objects of our daily life augmented with information technology. The base artifact relationship is the artifacts' context and they propose context proximity for selection of artifact communication. Smart-Its concerns are on device contexts and device interconnections, and about empowering users with the possibility of controlling the exchange of information between those devices. The user environment we propose is concerned about maintaining a usable and efficient workspace for a user by continually maintaining a composite of user contexts in the ubiquitous system. Each context can be assigned to a working session of a user, and in that instance the context will be mapped to the physical environment of the space where the session takes place.

The MIT Intelligent Room [2] focuses in creating an interactive room in which a Java based AI agent infrastructure controls the components of a room to anticipate and respond the needs of the users of the room. Their main goal is to make the room more intelligent with components such as cameras with recognition and tracking agents, and voice recognition agents that will anticipate user intentions. Our approach is to maintain a mobile workplace for a user that accompanies the user where he goes, and that is matched to the infrastructure available in the spaces that the user visits.

Project Aura [3] also focus on user mobility. Their definition of environment is equivalent to our notion of space. In their approach, a user task is a coalition of abstract services that are configured by Aura in a way that is appropriate for the environment. They define a software infrastructure to execute these tasks while trying to adapt them to changes in the environment. We emphasize the notion of a user global environment that subsumes all the sessions of work of the user in the several spaces of the system. A user environment is instantiated in a space, to provide a workplace for a user and is configured according to the user preferences to match the space availability. This workplace, which also includes user preferences, credentials and events, can be seen as a user context in that space. Our architecture supports multiple users with multiple sessions of work. It also supports the notion of a distributed user environment to instantiate a distributed session.

The related area of Human Computer Interfaces [1] and [5] is concerned with creating tools that promote a better interaction between the user and the devices that he is using, interfaces that will better conserve user attention. While our work will definitely benefit from incorporation with HCI, our concerns are different. We aim at providing a user with a mobile workplace that is deployed with the user and that is matched to characteristics of the spaces traversed.

7   Conclusions

The aim of our research is to create an environment able to provide a view of the global activity of a mobile user in a ubiquitous system, while dynamically tuning the activity of the user to the characteristics of the computing spaces the user is accessing and/or traversing.

In this paper we introduce the concept of a user environment as a set of distributed objects that continuously represent the activity of a mobile user in a ubiquitous system. A user in the system has a distributed execution environment that consists of several sessions running on different platforms or temporarily suspended to be resumed later. Each session is kept as an environment that contains the interacting components, and the profile of the user in that session. There is a one-to-one relationship between a user and his global environment, a composite of all of his current environments in the system. The mobility of a user brings up issues of deploying his activity and matching it with the traversed computing spaces.

So, we propose a software architecture to support user environments in a ubiquitous system that allows:

- representation and maintenance of a user environment in a ubiquitous system.
- deployment of the user environment, across the spaces of a ubiquitous system.
- adjustment of the user environment to the computing space, as well as to the user preferences.

The current phase of our work is the implementation and evaluation of this software architecture in *Gaia* [8], an infrastructure for ubiquitous computing developed at the University of Illinois.

We intend with this work to take one more step in the path of making the user the main focus of a ubiquitous system, rather than the devices and platforms that the user is accessing. The software architecture proposed aims at placing the *environment* of a user at his fingertips: a user can access any portion of his *environment* anywhere in the system at all times. A user, therefore, has the illusion of carrying his environment with him as he navigates the ubiquitous system.

References

1. B. Bailey, J. Konstan, and J. Carlis. Supporting multimedia designers: Towards more effective design tools. In *Proceedings of Multimedia Modeling*, pages 267–286, 2001.

2. M. Cohen. A prototype intelligent environment. In *Cooperative Buildings Integrating Information, Organization and Architecture First International Workshop CoBuild'98*, Darmstadt, Germany, 1998. Springer-Verlag.

3. D. Garlan, D. P. Siewiorek, A. Smailagic, and P. Steenkiste. Project aura: Towards distraction-free pervasive computing. In *IEEE Pervasive Computing*, April-June 2002.

4. L. E. Holmquist, F. Mattern, B. Schiele, P. Alahuhta, M. Beigl, and H.-W. Gellersen. Smart-its friends: A technique for users to easily establish connections between smart artefacts. In *UBICOMP 2001*, 2001.

5. M. T. J. Lin and J. A. Landsay. A visual sketching language for sketching large and complex interactive designs. In *Proceedings of CHI'02*, pages 307–314, 2002.

6. M. Page-Jones. *Fundamentals of Object-Oriented Design in UML*. Addison-Wesley, 1999.

7. S. Ponnekanti, B. Lee, A. Fox, P. Hanrahan, and T. Winograd. Icrafter : A service framework for ubiquitous computing environments. In *UBICOMP 2001*, 2001.

8. M. Román, C. Hess, R. Cerqueira, A. Ranganathan, R. H. Campbell, and K. Nahrstedt. Gaia: A middleware infrastructure to enable active spaces. In *IEEE Pervasive Computing*, Oct–Dec 2002.

9. P. Tandler. Software infrastructure for ubiquitous computing environments supporting synchronous collaboration with multiple single- and multi-user devices. In *UBICOMP 2001*, 2001.

ReMMoC: A Reflective Middleware to Support Mobile Client Interoperability

Paul Grace[1], Gordon S. Blair[1], and Sam Samuel[2]

[1] Distributed Multimedia Research Group, Computing Department, Lancaster
University, Lancaster, LA1 4YR, UK
{gracep,gordon}@comp.lancs.ac.uk
[2] Global Wireless Systems Research, Bell Laboratories, Lucent Technologies,
Quadrant, Stonehill Green, Westlea, Swindon, SN5 7DJ, UK
lsamuel@lucent.com

Abstract. Mobile client applications must discover and interoperate
with application services available to them at their present location. However, these services will be developed upon a range of middleware types
(e.g. RMI and publish-subscribe) and advertised using different service
discovery protocols (e.g. UPnP and SLP) unknown to the application
developer. Therefore, a middleware platform supporting mobile client
applications should ideally adapt its behaviour to interoperate with any
type of discovered service. Furthermore, these applications should be developed independently from particular middleware implementations, as
the interaction type is unknown until run-time. This paper presents ReM-
MoC, a reflective middleware platform that dynamically adapts both
its binding and discovery protocol to allow interoperation with heterogeneous services. Furthermore, we present the ReMMoC programming
model, which is based upon the Web Services concept of abstract services. We evaluate this work in terms of supporting mobile application
development and the memory footprint cost of utilising reflection to create a mobile middleware platform.

1 Introduction

Mobile computing is characterised by users carrying portable devices that allow communication between people and continuous access to networked services
independent of their physical location. The popularity of this field, driven by
new wireless network and mobile device technologies, has produced a variety
of innovative application types (e.g. context aware applications, m-commerce,
ad-hoc communities, mobile gaming and many others). To support these, new
middleware is emerging that addresses the problems of weak connection, limited
device resources and fluctuating network QoS inherent to the domain. These solutions range from extensions to well-established middleware for fixed networks
[1,2,3] and middleware designed explicitly to support mobile applications [4,5,
6]. However, the different solutions introduce the problem of middleware heterogeneity [7]. These platforms offer different communication paradigms, including: remote method invocation, publish-subscribe, message-oriented and tuple

R. Meersman et al. (Eds.): CoopIS/DOA/ODBASE 2003, LNCS 2888, pp. 1170–1187, 2003.
© Springer-Verlag Berlin Heidelberg 2003

spaces. Furthermore, implementations of individual paradigms vary e.g. SOAP and IIOP for remote method invocation. Therefore, mobile clients implemented upon one middleware type (e.g. SOAP) will not interoperate with discovered services implemented upon different platforms (e.g. IIOP or Publish-Subscribe). As an example, a tourist guide client implemented using publish-subscribe can only interoperate with matching tourist information publishers. Furthermore, tourist guide services at a different location implemented using an alternative middleware (e.g. a SOAP service), would require a separate client application and middleware implementation.

Similarly, services are advertised using one of the contrasting service discovery protocols. At present, there are four main service discovery technologies: Jini, Service Location Protocol (SLP), Universal Plug and Play (UPnP) and Salutation. In addition, new technologies are emerging to better support the discovery of services in mobile environments (e.g. JESA [8] & Centaurus [9]) and across wireless ad-hoc network types (e.g. SDP in Bluetooth and Salutation Lite). Utilising only one of these technologies to discover services will mean that services advertised by the other types will be missed. For example, a set of devices within a room (e.g. lights, video, CD player) advertising their services using UPnP cannot be used by a mobile device looking for services using SLP. This problem is likely to become significantly worse in the future with the advent of ubiquitous computing, enabled by emerging technologies to discover and interact with the services an embedded device offers.

We argue that adaptive middleware is required to support the interoperation of mobile clients with heterogeneous services. Using this approach, the middleware should alter its behaviour dynamically to: i) find the required mobile services irrespective of the service discovery protocol and ii) interoperate with services implemented by different middleware types. We advocate reflection and component technology as well suited techniques to develop middleware with these capabilities. Reflection is a principled method that supports introspection and adaptation to produce configurable and reconfigurable middleware.

For an application to dynamically operate using different middleware implementations it must be programmed independently from them. Hence, an abstract definition of the application service's functionality is required. The mobile client application, which requests this service, can then be developed using this "interface" in the style of IDL programming. A request of the abstract service is mapped at run-time to the corresponding concrete request of the middleware implementation. The emerging Web Services Architecture includes a Web Services Description Language (WSDL) that provides this format of abstract and concrete service definition. We propose that WSDL offers a suitable programming model for such a reflective middleware.

In this paper, we document the design and implementation of a reflective middleware platform, named ReMMoC (Reflective Middleware for Mobile Computing), which combines reflective middleware and the WSDL programming model to provide a solution to the problem of interoperation from mobile clients. Section 2 presents a typical mobile scenario to illustrate the heterogeneous properties of the mobile environment. The concepts of reflection, component technologies and component frameworks used by ReMMoC are then described in section 3. An overview of ReMMoC is presented in section 4 and a description of the mapping of middleware paradigms to WSDL is given in section 5. Section 6 evaluates the performance of ReMMoC in supporting a typical mobile application and related work in the field of mobile middleware is identified in section 7. Finally, overall conclusions and future work are described in section 8.

2   Mobile Scenario

In this section we present a mobile computing scenario to illustrate middleware heterogeneity that exists in the mobile domain. In the example, three application services are available to mobile users at two locations. Instances of each service are implemented using different types of middleware and advertised using contrasting service discovery protocols. Application 1 is a mobile sport news application, whereby news stories of interest are presented to the user based on their current location. Application 2 is a jukebox application that allows users to select and play music on an audio output device at that location. Finally, application 3 is a chat application that allows two mobile users to communicate with one another.

Figure 1 illustrates two locations (a coffee bar and a public house) in the session of a mobile user and the mobile services that can be interacted with. At each location the same application services are available to the user, but their middleware implementations differ. For example, the Sport News service is implemented as a publish-subscribe channel at the coffee bar and as a SOAP service in the public house. If fixed middleware were to be used, then two separate applications and middleware implementations would be needed on the device. Similarly, the chat applications and jukebox services are implemented using different middleware types. However, this is not the only type of heterogeneity in the scenario, the services themselves must first be discovered by the mobile ap-

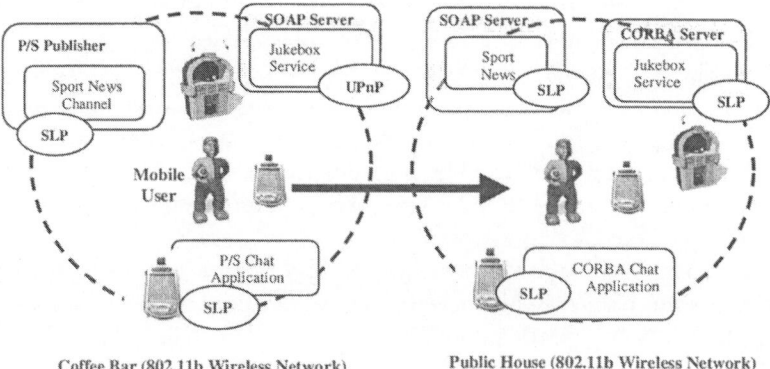

Fig. 1. An mobile computing scenario, populated with heterogeneous middleware.

plication before interaction can occur. Nevertheless, in this setting the service discovery technologies are different, i.e. the services available at the public house are discoverable using SLP and the services at the coffee bar can be found using both UPnP and SLP. If the mobile user utilises only one service discovery protocol then they may miss some available resources and in the worst-case scenario find none.

Given scenarios of this type, the authors argue that a mobile middleware platform should be reconfigurable to interact with different middleware types and utilise different service discovery protocols. In turn, this will allow the development of mobile applications independently of fixed platform types whose properties are unknown to the application programmer at design time.

3   Component Model

3.1   Background on OpenCOM

OpenCOM [10] is a lightweight, efficient and reflective component model, built atop a subset of Microsoft's COM. Higher level features of COM, including distribution, persistence, transactions and security are not used, whilst core aspects including the binary level interoperability standard, Microsoft's IDL, COM's globally unique identifiers and the IUnknown interface are the basis of the implementation. The fundamental concepts of OpenCOM are interfaces, receptacles and connections (bindings between interface and receptacles). An interface expresses a unit of service provision and a receptacle describes a unit of service requirement. OpenCOM deploys a standard runtime substrate that manages the creation and deletion of components, and acts upon requests to connect and disconnect components. Furthermore, a system graph of the components currently in use is maintained to support the introspection of a platform's structure (using the IMetaArchitecture interface).

This component model is used to construct families of middleware. More specifically, each middleware is constructed as a set of configurable component frameworks (more detail on the component framework concept is provided in section 3.2) and reflection is used to discover the current structure and behaviour, and to enable selected changes at run-time. The end result is flexible middleware that can be specialised to domains including multimedia and real-time systems, or in our case mobile computing.

3.2   OpenCOM Component Frameworks

A component framework (CF) is defined as a collection of rules and contracts that govern the interaction of a set of components [12]. The motivation behind component frameworks is to constrain the design space and the scope for evolution. A component framework in OpenCOM is itself an OpenCOM component that maintains internal structure (a configuration of components) to implement its service functionality. The design of these component frameworks is based

upon the concepts of composite components proposed by OpenORB [11]. Therefore, component frameworks can be composed, replaced and connected together
in the same manner as components. To provide this capability, each OpenCOM
CF implements the base interfaces of an OpenCOM component (IMetaInterface,
ILifeCycle, IConnections) in addition to its own interfaces and receptacles. The
interfaces and receptacles of internal components can be exposed to create these.
The architecture of a component framework is shown in figure 2.

To inspect component configurations, the OpenCOM runtime IMetaArchitecture interface examines the external structure of a component or CF (i.e. what
it is connected to). However, it does not inspect or dynamically adapt the internal structure of a component framework. Therefore, every CF implements the
ICFMetaArchitecture interface; this provides operations to inspect the internal
structure and change the component configuration. To implement this interface
a graph of local components is maintained, which is simply a view of a subset
of the OpenCOM runtime system graph to avoid replicating data.

A component framework constrains the configuration of components to a
valid implementation within its domain. To enforce this policy, each component
framework implements a receptacle called IAccept. When a change to the existing implementation has been made, a call to the IAccept interface is performed.
This executes a check of the component architecture; if the Accept component
verifies the architecture then the platform can continue its operation, otherwise, an exception is generated and the framework rolls back to the previous
configuration. The complexity of checking depends upon the implementation of
the Accept component, which can be dynamically changed. The implementation
may have no checking (no component connected), simply check against a list
of configurations (described in XML) or alternatively incorporate architectural
style rules proposed by [28].

Finally, if a change to the configuration is attempted while one or more
service calls of the component framework are executing then the results of these
invocations would be compromised or lost. Therefore, each framework utilises a

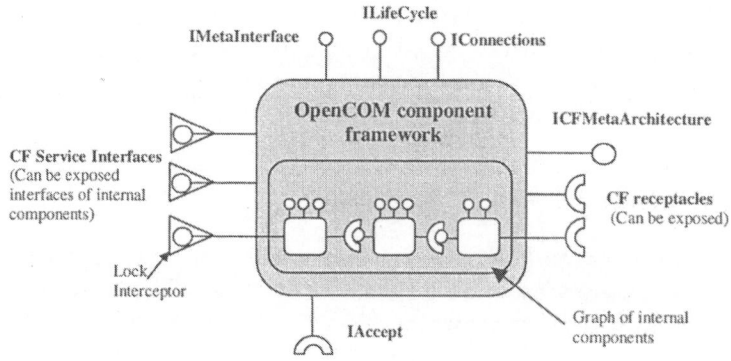

Fig. 2. An OpenCOM component framework.

readers/writers lock to access the local CF graph. Standard interface calls access the lock as a reader (there can be multiple concurrent readers) and every call to alter the CF configuration, accesses the lock as a writer (a single writer accesses the lock when there are no readers). The algorithm to implement this property is a standard readers/writers solution with priority for readers. To enforce this, every exposed interface automatically has an interceptor, to access and release the lock, attached.

4 The Design and Implementation of ReMMoC

4.1 Overview

This section describes ReMMoC, a configurable and reconfigurable reflective middleware that supports mobile application development and overcomes the heterogeneous properties of the mobile environment. ReMMoC uses OpenCOM as its underlying component technology and it is built as a set of component frameworks. Using many component frameworks (e.g. as found in OpenORB) increases the size of the middleware implementation; extra management functionality for managing reconfiguration exhausts the constrained resources of a mobile device. Therefore, ReMMoC consists of only two component frameworks: (1) a binding framework for interoperation with mobile services implemented upon different middleware types, and (2) a service discovery framework for discovering services advertised by a range of service discovery protocols. These two frameworks are illustrated in figure 3. The binding framework is configured by plugging in different binding type implementations e.g. IIOP Client, Publisher, SOAP client etc. and the service discovery framework is similarly configured by plugging in different service discovery protocols (A detailed description of the frameworks is given in the following sections). Adding more component frameworks for other non-functional properties such as security and resource management can extend the platform at a later stage. The ReMMoC component, seen in figure 3, performs reconfiguration management and provides a generic API to develop mobile applications upon (see section 5.3).

4.2 The Binding Component Framework

The primary function of the binding framework is to interoperate with heterogeneous mobile services. Therefore, over time it may be configured as an IIOP client configuration and make a number of IIOP requests, or change to a subscribe configuration and wait to receive events of interest. Different middleware paradigms, synchronous or asynchronous (e.g. tuple spaces, media streams, RPC, publish-subscribe or messaging), can be plugged into the binding framework if they have been implemented using OpenCOM components.

Within the binding framework changes are made at two distinct levels. Firstly, each binding type implementation can be replaced; e.g. a SOAP client is replaced by a publish-subscribe subscriber (illustrated in figure 4). This dynamic reconfiguration is performed by receiving information from the service discovery

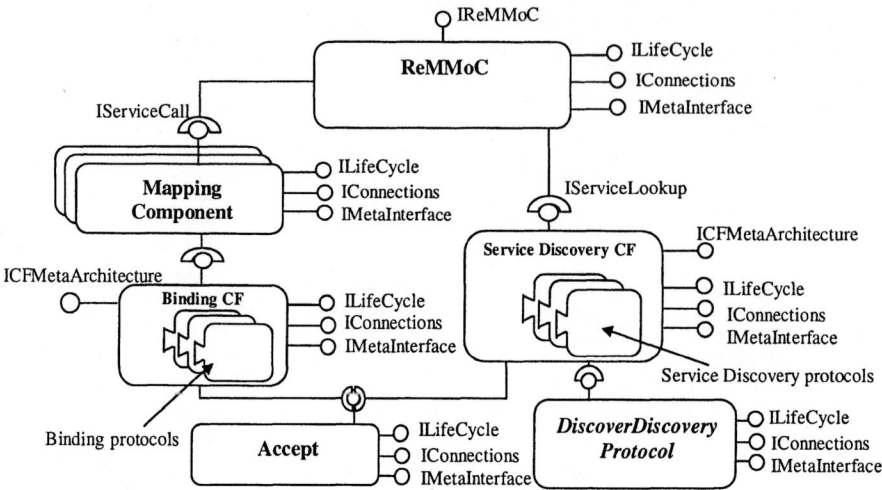

Fig. 3. Overview of the ReMMoC platform.

framework describing the type of binding; an XML description of the component configuration for this binding is then parsed to create the new configuration. Hence, new binding protocols can be dynamically added to the framework at a future date. Multiple personalities can also be created, e.g. a publish-subscribe publisher and SOAP client together; their implementation is simply a configuration of components, but more than one interface is exposed by the framework. Secondly, fine-grained changes to each configuration can be made in light of environmental context changes, such as those involving quality of service, or changes in the application's requirements. For example, an application may require IIOP server side functionality, in addition to the existing client side; therefore components implementing server side functionality are added. In order to test and evaluate the binding framework, we have implemented IIOP client and server, SOAP client and Publish-Subscribe personalities.

4.3   The Service Discovery Framework

The Service Discovery framework allows services that have been advertised by different service discovery protocols to be found. The framework is configured to discover protocols currently in use in the environment. For example, if SLP is in use, the framework configures itself to an SLP Lookup personality. However, if SLP and UPnP are found then the framework's configuration will include component implementations to discover both. Like the Binding CF, fine-grained component changes can be made. For example, in SLP you may wish to perform lookup using just the multicast protocol if no directory agent is present, but at a later stage if a directory agent is discovered the configuration can be changed to direct requests to it.

The service discovery framework offers a set of generic service discovery methods through the IServiceLookup Interface. This includes a generic service lookup

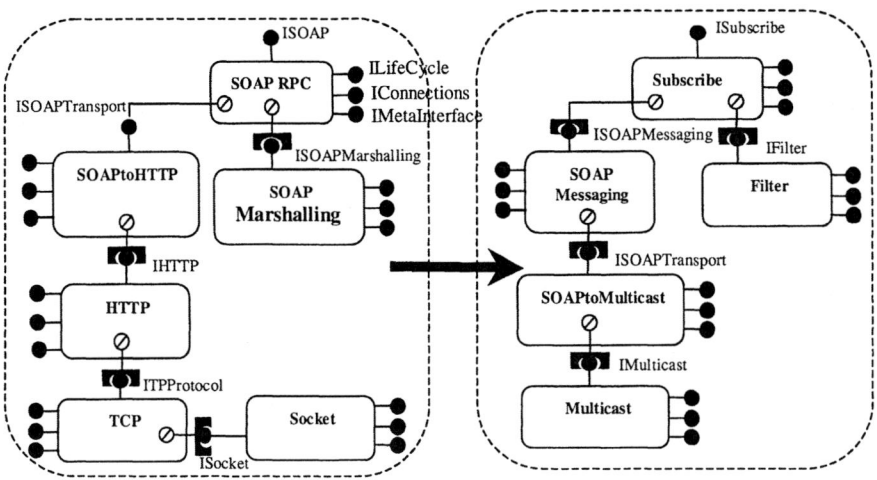

Fig. 4. A dynamic reconfiguration from a SOAP client to a subscriber implementation.

operation that returns the information from different service discovery protocol searches in a generic format. For example, a lookup of a weather service across two discovery configurations, e.g. UPnP and SLP, returns a list of matched services from both types. It is this information (the description of the service returned by the lookup protocol) that is used to configure the binding framework.

Initially, the discovery protocol(s) that are currently in use at a location must be determined. The DiscoverDiscoveryProtocol component, which is plugged into the framework, tests if individual service discovery protocols are in use, either upon a synchronous request or by continuously monitoring the environment and generating an event on detection. Continuous monitoring will quickly use up resources (e.g. battery power); therefore in some cases synchronous checking may be appropriate. The service discovery framework utilises this behaviour to automatically reconfigure itself. Other methods for discovering discovery protocols, not currently included in the implementation, may utilise the device's context information, e.g. if the device is currently using a Bluetooth connection then an SDP personality is configured. Furthermore, the middleware may use prior knowledge to select an appropriate protocol, i.e. the platform stores context information per location that details which service discovery protocols were used at that point previously.

We have implemented the service discovery framework with two service lookup protocol implementations: SLP and UPnP, allowing us to demonstrate how to overcome the problems of the availability of multiple service discovery protocols. However, as with the binding framework, it is feasible for new discovery protocols to be dynamically integrated into the framework at a later date. This requires a new version of the DiscoverDiscoveryProtocol component, which can detect the new protocol, to be plugged into the framework.

5 The ReMMoC Programming Model

5.1 Background on Web Services

The web services architecture [13] consists of three key roles: a service provider, a service requestor and the discovery agency, which the requestor uses to find the service description. Each service is described in WSDL [14]; this is an XML format for documenting the exchange of messages (containing typed data items) between the service requestor and service provider. The key property of WSDL is that it separates the abstract description of service functionality from the concrete details of the service implementation. Hence, the aim of Web Services is to allow different service providers to implement an abstract service description upon their chosen concrete middleware binding. For example, a news service may be implemented using SOAP by one vendor while another may use publish-subscribe.

In our context, WSDL offers the ability to develop mobile clients, based upon agreed abstract service descriptions, thus hiding the developer from the problem of middleware heterogeneity encountered across different locations. Hence this offers an attractive solution to ReMMoC, with the added benefit that WSDL is a recognised international standard. However, the approach does not offer any support to the dynamic adaptation of the underlying concrete implementations as required by our platform. We return to this in section 5.3. Firstly, we illustrate in the next section the mapping of abstract WSDL descriptions to different bindings e.g. RMI and publish-subscribe. This shows that WSDL can be mapped to the diverse paradigms that are encountered within mobile environments.

5.2 Mapping Abstract Services to Concrete Binding Types

In this section we demonstrate how the abstract operations of WSDL can be mapped to two contrasting binding types exposed by a reflective middleware (RMI and publish-subscribe). The following four abstract operations can be described in WSDL. (1) Request-Response (input, output), a service receives a request of its functionality and responds to it. (2) Solicit-Response (output, input), a service provider acts as a service requestor. (3) One-Way (input), a service receives a notification message. (4) Notification (output), a service outputs a notification message.

Figure 5 illustrates how abstract messages (input and output) that constitute each WSDL operation map to the RMI and publish-subscribe communication paradigms. The service requestor is the mobile client. We assume that each paradigm understands the set of types used by the abstract definition. In RMI, the input/output messages of Request-Response and Solicit-Response operations can be mapped directly to the corresponding synchronous RMI messages of SOAP and IIOP. The operation name maps to the method name, the input message to the input parameter list and the output message to the output parameter list. Similarly, Notification and One-Way operations can be mapped as one-way messages e.g. one-way IIOP invocations and asynchronous SOAP messages.

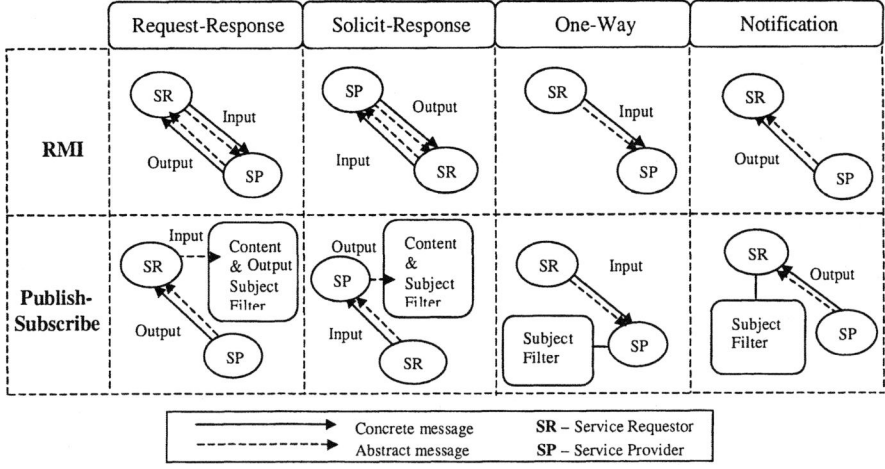

Fig. 5. Mapping WSDL operations to different middleware paradigms.

Publish-Subscribe however is an alternative communication paradigm whereby there is no direct message exchange between service requestor and provider. The service provider publishes events and a service requestor must filter to receive appropriate events. Therefore unlike RMI, the mapping of WSDL to publish-subscribe is not a direct correlation. The request-response operation is a request of a service based upon the input message. The input message can be used to filter published messages and receive the correct event, whose content maps to the output message. The operation name maps to the event subject, while the input message maps to the content filter attributes. Similarly, for Solicit-response the service filters to receive events from other services. For One-way operations and Notifications, services subscribe and publish events based upon subject filtering only, with the content of the concrete message mapping to the abstract message.

5.3   The ReMMoC API

The ReMMoC programming model is based upon the concept of WSDL described abstract services. Application developers must utilise these WSDL definitions in the style of IDL programming. To maintain a consistent information flow to the application an event-based programming model, that overrides the different computational models of each paradigm, is offered. Each abstract service operation is carried out and its result is returned as an event. For example, if that operation is executed by an RMI invocation or an event subscription the result is always an event. Similarly, service lookup operations return results as events. Figure 6 documents the API of ReMMoC, which consists of operations to: lookup services, lookup then invoke abstract WSDL operations, invoke operations on known services, or create and host service provider operations.

```
interface ReMMoC_ICF : IUnknown {
    HRESULT WSDLGet (WSDLService* ServiceDescription, char* XML);

    HRESULT FindandInvokeOperation (WSDLService ServiceDescription, char*
                    OperationName, int Iterations, ReMMoCOPHandler Handler);

    HRESULT InvokeOperation (WSDLService ServiceDescription, ServiceReturnEvent
        ReturnedLookupEvent, char* OperationName, int Iterations, ReMMoCOPHandler  Handler);

    HRESULT CreateOperation (WSDLService ServiceDescription, ServiceReturnEvent
        ReturnedLookupEvent, char* OperationName, int Iterations, ReMMoCOPHandler Handler);

    HRESULT AddMessageValue(WSDLService *ServiceDescription, char* OperationName,
                char* ElementName, ReMMoC_TYPE type, char* direction,  VARIANT value);

    HRESULT GetMessageValue(WSDLService *ServiceDescription, char* OperationName,
                char* ElementName, ReMMoC_TYPE type, char* direction,  VARIANT value);
}
```

Fig. 6. Interface definition for the ReMMoC API.

ReMMoC maps these API calls to the binding framework through the use of a reconfigurable mapping component, illustrated in figure 3. For example, an IIOP mapping component maps abstract WSDL operation calls to IIOP invocations through the interface exposed by the binding framework; it can be replaced by a subscribe mapping component that maps to subscribe requests. These components carry out the mapping of abstract to concrete operations described in section 5.2.

6   Evaluation

6.1   The Cost of Reflection

At present mobile devices have a limited amount of system memory, which can quickly be consumed by user's applications; therefore it is important to minimise the amount of memory needed to store a middleware implementation. Utilising reflection to change between protocols allows only the minimum required number of components to be stored on the device, rather than store complete multi-middleware implementations. In the future, storing components on the device is likely to be less of a problem as mobile devices with much higher memory capacity become available. However, components will still need to be transmitted across the network (for example, when the platform discovers it needs components not currently on the device). Therefore, the implementation of middleware personalities still needs to be minimised. We have implemented the components used to build the ReMMoC platform with the aim of reducing the storage space they occupy. Figure 7 documents the static memory footprint sizes of the separate parts of the platform i.e. configurations for the two frameworks (IIOP client, SOAP client etc.). Four measurements were taken for each personality: the ARM and x86 implementations for reflective and non-reflective personalities.

Function	Reflective		Non-Reflective	
	ARM (Bytes)	x86 (Bytes)	ARM (Bytes)	x86 (Bytes)
Platform Core				
OpenCOM	28160	18432	n/a	n/a
Binding CF	16896	11776	n/a	n/a
Service Discovery CF	19968	16384	n/a	n/a
Binding Configurations				
IIOP Client	96768	79872	56320	38912
IIOP Server	99840	82432	58880	40960
IIOP Client & Server	140288	114688	82944	56832
SOAP client	97792	80896	64512	47104
Publish	92160	74752	65024	49152
Subscribe	85504	71168	58368	46080
Publish & Subscribe	105984	86016	74752	56320
Service Discovery Configurations				
SLP Lookup	85504	68608	53248	36352
SLP Register	80896	65536	48128	33792
SLP Lookup & Register	103936	83456	65024	45056
UPnP Lookup	80384	64724	56320	39424

Fig. 7. Size of component configurations in ReMMoC.

The non-reflective personality is the basic component implementation, whereas a reflective personality maintains meta-information about the structure of each component and supports the subsequent introspection of this data.

The results in figure 7 illustrate that the configurations are suited to mobile devices, as minimum configurations of the binding framework and service discovery framework are less than 100Kbytes. For example, the reflective ARM measurements of IIOP client, SOAP client, subscribe, UPnP lookup and SLP lookup are each individually less than 100Kbytes. These are comparable to related systems; for example, the non-reflective ARM IIOP client implementation (55K) compares with the 29K SH3 CORBA client personality of the Universal Interoperable Core (UIC) implementation [7] and the 48K non-pluggable GIOP client Zen implementation [15], which have similar capabilities. The difference between the ReMMoC and the UIC value can be attributed to a different processor, as illustrated by ARM personalities being larger than x86 (RISC versus CISC) and using a COM based implementation.

The table also illustrates the cost in terms of extra memory requirements of the reflective personalities as opposed to their non-reflective counterparts. For the implemented configurations (ARM) this ranges between an extra 23.5K and 56K. The storage of a type library and an additional 20 lines of C++ code for each component in the configuration, accounts for the extra memory cost. The size of each type library is dependent on the complexity of interface descriptions used on that component; hence, the cost per component varies. Our results show that configurations can be created that fit on devices with limited capacity and still retain the dynamic inspection and reconfiguration properties described in the previous sections.

6.2   Operating in a Mobile Scenario

To illustrate that ReMMoC performs its primary function of discovering and interoperating with heterogeneous services, we evaluated the platform using the scenario in section 2. The test environment included Compaq iPaq h3870 Pocket PCs running the Windows CE 3.0 operating system and fitted with wireless LAN cards. With the exception of the chat services, the remainder executed on desktop machines; SOAP services were developed upon the Apache SOAP 2.0 implementation and the IIOP services were developed using ORBacus 4.05. We successfully created three applications that operated in both locations, irrespective of the underlying middleware implementations. These examples proved it was possible to discover services across different discovery platforms and interoperate with them through the appropriate binding. We briefly describe how ReMMoC dynamically changes to support the sport news application.

In the first location, the sport news service was implemented using a publish channel and advertised using SLP, in the second location the service was implemented as a SOAP service and registered with UPnP. In location one, the service discovery framework detects SLP and configures itself to an SLP lookup personality. When a lookup of the sport news service is executed a single result is returned. The returned information is used by ReMMoC to configure the binding framework to a subscribe personality. The subscribe mapping component is connected to the binding framework, which then creates a filter to receive requested events. In the same lifecycle of the application, the user moves to the second location and UPnP is detected; therefore the discovery framework changes from SLP to UPnP. This time the discovery operation detects the service is implemented by a SOAP binding. Therefore, the binding framework changes from subscribe to a SOAP client. The SOAP mapping component is connected and the abstract operations are communicated as SOAP invocations.

7   Related Work

7.1   Asynchronous Mobile Middleware

The properties of wireless networks means that mobile devices may become disconnected involuntarily, or otherwise choose to become disconnected to save resources such as battery power. Furthermore, error rates are high and packets are lost. These characteristics have proven a driving factor in the initial development of middleware platforms for this domain. For example, the Rover platform [16] was one of the very first to address this issue; the toolkit provides queued remote procedure calls that allows an application to continue making invocations asynchronously while disconnected from the network. Other asynchronous styles include publish-subscribe systems and tuple spaces. Within a publish-subscribe system, interaction takes the form of event notification; namely, consumers register for the events they are interested in and are informed when they occur. Logically, the two parties do not have to be connected simultaneously to interact. Examples of these are Elvin [17], Siena [18] and the Cambridge Event

Architecture [19]. However, these platforms were designed for fixed networks and do not take into account the dynamic connection of mobile hosts. This has enforced the emergence of some preliminary solutions. For example, Elvin has been extended to incorporate proxy servers to support the persistency of events, so that clients who disconnect repeatedly do not lose events; but it requires that clients connect to the same proxy, which cannot be guaranteed in mobile networks. An alternative is JEDI [20], which includes a dynamic tree of dispatchers (the client can reconnect to any) for ensuring publish-subscribe information is retained as members connect and reconnect. Nevertheless, both of these rely on centralised entities holding event information, which cannot be guaranteed within ad-hoc wireless networks. Consequently, STEAM [5] is a scalable, publish-subscribe system designed to operate in ad-hoc networks; the platform is based upon the concepts of group communication with publishers and subscribers belonging to the same group. The communication is scaled by the proximity of publisher to subscriber; any subscribers out of range do not receive the events.

The tuple space is an alternative asynchronous communication model that is effectively a shared distributed memory spread across all participating hosts that processes can concurrently access; hence communication is decoupled in time and space. The L^{2}imbo platform [21] is based upon the classic tuple space architecture but includes a number of extensions for operation within a mobile environment. Multiple tuple spaces can be created and used, removing the need for all operations to go through a central global tuple; this is an important factor in an environment where communication links are unreliable. Furthermore, QoS attributes can be added to a tuple, including delivery deadline allowing the system to re-order to make the best use of network connectivity. Alternative technologies are JavaSpaces [22] and Lime [6], however, none of these adapt their behaviour like L^{2}imbo, to support context changes.

7.2   Adaptive Middleware

Established middleware technologies and those described in the previous section offer a fixed black-box implementation whose underlying structure and behaviour is hidden from the programmer and cannot be altered at run-time to cope with changes that occur in the mobile environment. Therefore, future middleware platforms, for domains such as multimedia and mobile computing, should be configurable to match the requirements of a given application domain and dynamically reconfigurable to enable the platform to respond to changes in its environment [11].

Recently, a group of reflective middleware technologies have emerged to meet these requirements: OpenORB [11], DynamicTAO [23], Multe-ORB [24] and OpenCORBA [25]. A reflective system is one that provides a representation of its own behaviour that is amenable to inspection and adaptation, and is causally connected to the underlying behaviour it describes. The key to the approach is to offer a meta-interface supporting the inspection and adaptation of the underlying structure. However, these existing systems are built for application domains, such as multimedia and real-time; they do not address the issue of middleware heterogeneity in mobile computing. Consequently, [7] identifies that the key property in supporting mobile computing is the ability to seamlessly interoperate with the range of ubiquitous devices that are encountered by the mobile device as it changes location. Therefore, the Universal Interoperable Core [7] has been developed; this reflective middleware is loosely based on the reconfiguration techniques of DynamicTAO. The platform can change between different middleware personalities e.g. a SOAP client, a CORBA server and a SOAP server. The implementation of UIC concentrates on synchronous middleware styles and does not implement all paradigm types that could be encountered in a ubiquitous environment, i.e. it is likely that asynchronous platforms would be as prominent given their suitability to the environment, nor does it address the issue of heterogeneous discovery protocols.

Furthermore, middleware and applications need to be aware of context information to support adaptation. Work at University College London [4] examines the use of reflection in managing a repository of application meta-data that stores each application's requirements for adaptation. They then use reflection to inspect and adapt this so that behaviour can be altered dynamically. They also look at managing the conflicting requests for adaptation based on the amount of differing context information available [26].

7.3   Others

Alternatively, other projects have extended traditional platforms to make them effective over wireless networks. For example, ALICE [27] presents a layered architecture for managing the movement of mobile hosts and ensures that CORBA connections remain established transparently. Alternatively, DOLMEN [3] offers a special Light-Weight Inter-ORB Protocol for object communication over a wireless link. RAPP [2] allows proxies to be inserted between distributed CORBA objects to manage poor levels of network service and disconnection. Finally, [1] implements a session layer that allows CORBA invocations to be made over the Wireless Application Protocol.

The memory footprint size of a middleware implementation is often large, especially that of traditional types like CORBA, RMI and DCOM. This becomes a critical problem in the domain of mobile computing where mobile and embedded devices have a small, fixed amount of ROM and RAM available. Therefore, middleware platforms designed for mobile devices must ensure they minimise the amount of memory they utilise. OrbacusE and e*ORB are examples of commercially available CORBA ORBs optimised for memory size and performance. Nevertheless, these remain static over time and cannot alter their behaviour and performance when the available resources change. Consequently, Zen [15] is a real-time CORBA ORB that reduces the memory footprint by allowing the selection of a minimal subset of ORB capabilities used by an application, this can then be altered dynamically when the applications requirements change. However, due to middleware heterogeneity in the mobile environment, utilising multiple minimum footprint platforms is unsuitable. An improved solution is the Universal Interoperable Core [7], which is an example of a platform whose configuration can be dynamically altered over time to offer different functionality, while minimising the memory resources used.

8   Concluding Remarks and Future Work

Research into mobile middleware has addressed specific concerns such as poor network QoS, weak connection and limited device resources. We argue however that the crucial problem of cascading levels of heterogeneity has been largely ignored. We have proposed that a middleware for mobile computing must provide support to applications for discovering and interoperating with heterogeneous services in the mobile environment. We identify that a marriage of web services with reflective middleware offers a solution to mobile client interoperability. This paper presents ReMMoC, a configurable and dynamically reconfigurable middleware platform that supports interoperation in heterogeneous mobile environments. The use of component frameworks within this design offers a technique to ensure that only valid component implementations are utilised in the platform's operation. The functionality of this platform has been illustrated in a real world mobile scenario. Finally, a middleware platform for mobile and embedded devices must minimise its memory size, so memory resources are not exhausted and its components can be passed easily across networks.

ReMMoC was designed specifically for the mobile environment and has been fully developed and tested using simple applications e.g. chat, news and stock quote clients across IIOP, SOAP and Publish-Subscribe bindings. We also recognise that the properties of our platform are usable in domains other than mobile computing, hence ongoing work includes an evaluation of this method on larger, complex applications (e.g. Grid computing, ubiquitous computing and intelligent home environments) and across a range of further middleware bindings including data sharing and tuple spaces.

The evaluation of memory use has illustrated that single middleware personalities can exist on mobile devices. However, each device cannot store every possible middleware component that may be needed. Therefore, a method for dynamically downloading components when needed is required. Furthermore, techniques to ensure the component is available to start-up before it needs to be used, e.g. predictive caching based upon context information is an interesting option.

Finally, the work does not address a number of key issues in distributed systems development that are important within this application domain. Firstly, security needs to be added to the system in order to deal with access control of services. Furthermore, resource management to control use of memory, CPU and battery power is important. Also, the use of context information for driving underlying adaptation needs to be considered, i.e. how best to integrate this information with the middleware and how to deal with conflicting requests. We envisage that these orthogonal aspects will be integrated into the platform through the development of additional component frameworks.

References

1. Reinstorf, T., Ruggaber, R., Seitz, J., Zitterbart, M.: A WAP-Based Session Layer Supporting Distributed Application in Nomadic Environments. In Proceedings of Middleware 2001, Heidelberg, Germany, November 2001.
2. Seitz, J., Davies, N., Ebner, M., Friday, A.: A CORBA-based Proxy Architecture for Mobile Multimedia Applications. In Proceedings of the 2nd International Conference on Management of Multimedia Networks and Services, Versailles, France, November 1998.
3. Liljeberg, M., Raatikainen, K., et al.: Using CORBA to Support Terminal Mobility. In Proceedings of TINA 1997.
4. Capra, L., Emmerich, W., Mascolo, C.: Reflective Middleware Solutions for Context-Aware Applications. In Proceedings of REFLECTION 2001, Kyoto, Japan, September 2001.
5. Meier, R., Cahill, V.: STEAM: Event-Based Middleware for Wireless Ad Hoc Networks. In Proceedings of the International Workshop on Distributed Event-Based Systems, Vienna, Austria, 2002.
6. Murphy, A., Picco, G., Roman, G.: LIME: A Middleware for logical and Physical Mobility. In Proceedings of the 21st International Conference on Distributed Computing Systems, Arizona, USA, May 2001.
7. Roman, M., Kon, F., Campbell, R. H.: Reflective Middleware: From Your Desk to Your Hand. IEEE Distributed Systems Online, 2(5), 2001.
8. Preuss, S.: JESA Service Discovery Protocol. In Proceedings of Networking 2002, pp. 1196–1201, Pisa, Italy, May 2002.
9. Kagal, L., Korolev, V., Chen, H., et al.: Centaurus: A framework for intelligent services in a mobile environment. In Proceedings of the International Workshop on Smart Appliances and Wearable Computing (IWSAWC), April 2001.
10. Clarke, M., Blair, G., Coulson, G., Parlavantzas, N.: An Efficient Component Model for the Construction of Adaptive Middleware. In Proceedings of Middleware 2001, Heidelberg, Germany. November, 2001.
11. Blair, G. et al.: "The design and implementation of Open ORB 2". IEEE Distributed Systems Online, 2(6) , Sept 2001.
12. Szyperski, C.: Component Software: Beyond Object-Oriented Programming. Addison Wesley, 1998.
13. W3C.: Web Services Architecture. W3C Working Draft, http://www.w3.org/TR/ws-arch/, November, 2002.
14. W3C.: Web Services Description Language (WSDL) Version 1.2. W3C Working Draft, http://www.w3.org/TR/wsdl12/, March, 2003.
15. Klefstad, R., Rao, S., Schmidt, D.: Design and Performance of a Dynamically Configurable, Messaging Protocols Framework for Real-time CORBA. In Proceedings of Distributed Object and Component-based Software Systems, Big Island of Hawaii, January, 2003.
16. Joseph, A., deLespinasse, A., Tauber, J., Gifford, D., Kaashoek, M.: Rover: A Toolkit for Mobile Information Access. In Proceedings of the 15th Symposium on Operating Systems Principles, Colorado, U.S., pp. 156–171, December 1995.
17. Segall, B., Arnold, D.: Elvin has left the building: a publish/subscribe notification service with quenching. In Proceedings of AUUG97, September 1997.
18. Carzaniga, A., Rosenblum, D., Wolf, A.: Design and Evaluation of a Wide-Area Event Notification Service. ACM Transactions on Computer Systems, 19(3), pp. 332–383, 2001.

19. Bacon, J., Moody, K., Bates, J., et al.: Generic Support for Distributed Applications. IEEE Computer, pp. 68–76, March 2000.
20. Cugola, G., Di Nitto, E., Fuggetta, A.: The JEDI event-based infrastructure and its application to the development of the OPSS WFMS. IEEE Transactions on Software Engineering, 9(27), pp. 827–850, September 2001.
21. Davies, N., Friday, A., Wade, S., Blair, G. S.: Limbo: A Distributed Systems Platform for Mobile Computing" ACM Mobile Networks and Applications (MONET), 3(2), pp. 143–156, August 1998.
22. Waldo, J.: Javaspaces specification 1.0. Sun Microsystems Technical report, March 1998.
23. Kon, F., Roman, M., Liu, P., et al.: Monitoring, Security, and Dynamic Configuration with the dynamicTAO Reflective ORB. In Proceedings of Middleware 2000, New York, USA, April 2000.
24. Kristensen, T., Plagemann, T.: Enabling Flexible QoS Support in the Object Request Broker COOL. Proceedings of International Workshop on Distributed Real-Time Systems, April 2000.
25. Ledoux, T.: OpenCorba: a Reflective Open Broker. In 2nd International Conference on Reflection and Meta-level Architectures, St. Malo, France, July 1999.
26. Capra, L., Emmerich, W., Mascolo, C.: A Micro-Economic Approach to Conflict Resolution in Mobile Computing. In Proceedings of the 10th International Symposium on the Foundations of Software Engineering, South Carolina, USA, November, 2002.
27. Haahr, M., Cunningham, R., Cahill, V.: Towards a Generic Architecture for Mobile Object-Oriented Applications. SerP 2000: Workshop on Service Portability, San Francisco, December 2000.
28. Moreira, R., Blair, G., Carrapatoso, G.: Reflective Component-Based & Architecture Aware Framework to Manage Architecture Composition. In 3rd International Symposium on Distributed Objects & Applications. Rome, Italy, September, 2001.

A Dynamic Distribution and Load Balancing Experiment with Synchronous Programming-Based Mobile Objects

Bruno Dillenseger[1] and Laurent Hazard[2]

France Télécom R&D, DTL/ASR
[1] 28 chemin du Vieux Chêne, BP 98, 38243 Meylan cedex, France
[2] 38-40 rue du Général Leclerc, 92794 Issy - Moulineaux cedex 9, France
{bruno.dillenseger,laurent.hazard}@francetelecom.com

Abstract. Transparently changing the distribution of objects in a distributed system (application, service) at runtime is a way to improve service continuity and performance. For instance, it enables to transparently shutdown execution nodes for necessary maintenance operations. Moreover, optimizing service execution resources consumption, while improving service response time, is a key to both client and service provider satisfaction. However, previous work on load balancing has globally shown practical difficulties in getting effective such an approach. In the context of advanced telecommunication service execution environments, this paper proposes to revisit preemptive dynamic load balancing, by showing an experiment based on the combination between synchronous programming-based reactive objects, a flexible object request broker and a mobile agent framework. We present a full Java-based architecture, including a service example, and we show how peculiarities of synchronous programming give a chance to support low-cost preemptive mobility (also known as strong mobility), and to easily give a relevant computer-independent load indicator.

1 Introduction

Offering object mobility and load balancing features in a distributed system is a way to enhance service continuity and high availability. There exist a number of projects and systems supporting such features, at various levels: operating system, middleware such as CORBA, J2EE or mobile agent platforms. However, there are a great variety of transparency and efficiency levels among these systems.

Transparently moving a process or servant object requires the ability to freeze its execution state, to transport it, to rebuild it in another execution environment and to resume it. In the mobile computation community, Fugetta *et al* [10] call it *strong mobility*. Generally being regarded as too complex and costly, a less transparent, weakened form of mobility is typically preferred instead (*weak mobility*). Maintaining communication links is another issue raised by mobility, for which transparency support also has a cost. Nevertheless, we believe that movable processes or servant objects can provide a convenient and economically inexpensive way (compared to redundancy-based approaches) to allow execution nodes maintenance at runtime. Our concern is that transparency to mobility can be more or less complex, costly or effi-

R. Meersman et al. (Eds.): CoopIS/DOA/ODBASE 2003, LNCS 2888, pp. 1188–1207, 2003.
© Springer-Verlag Berlin Heidelberg 2003

cient, depending on the programming and communication model offered to the programmer, as well as the final execution model.

Many load balancing systems do not exploit mobility because of these complexity and cost issues [14]. In such systems, the assignment of processes or servant objects to execution nodes is computed only once, either before runtime (*static load balancing*), or at runtime whenever a new process is created (*dynamic load balancing*), and no process shall move once started (*non-preemptive load balancing*). However, some systems do exploit process mobility to implement *preemptive dynamic load balancing*, where each process may be hosted by several consecutive execution nodes during its lifetime, in order to optimize computing resources usage and processes response time. Regardless of the process mobility-related issues, search for efficient dynamic load balancing faces the inherent complexity of defining and finely tuning a number of policies and parameters.

Our approach takes advantage of some peculiarities of the synchronous programming model, in order to:
− provide a transparent and low-cost mobility of servant objects in a distributed system;
− easily obtain a relevant, reliable load indicator, regardless of the execution nodes heterogeneity;
− improve scalability in terms of number of simultaneously running servant objects.

Section 2 presents our mobile reactive object platform − Moorea − based on the integration of a reactive object platform, a flexible ORB and a mobile agent framework. Then, section 3 presents a prototype of telecommunication service execution environment. In section 4, we detail the two-step construction of a preemptive dynamic distribution and load balancing architecture, on top of our service execution environment. Section 5 presents experimental results based on the service example. Then, we discuss this work and position it to other related work in section 6. Finally, section 7 concludes on the utilization of synchronous programming for load balancing,

2   Moorea Reactive Mobile Objects

2.1   Moorea Overview

Moorea ("MObile Objects, REactive Agents") was born from research work in the field of mobile agent platforms. Interest in mobile agent technology mainly arises from its ability to handle in a unified way a variety of issues [11], such as code deployment, autonomous adaptive routing, network bandwidth saving, or disconnected operations. The aim of Moorea is to show that a mobile agent platform may offer to the programmer a convenient programming and communication model, while providing well-defined, transparent and low-cost mobility, and enhancing scalability in terms of number of simultaneously running agents.

Moorea is a pure Java reactive mobile agent platform. A growing number of telecommunication research and development projects exploit Java technology for several reasons: hardware and operating system heterogeneity support, security features, wide availability, advanced standard libraries. Today, Java-enabled routers and mobile phones are available from equipment vendors, based on initiatives such as the JavaPhone API [23], JAIN [22], or Java 2 Micro Edition. In the field of telecommunication service execution environments, Java enables the use of standard, low-cost computers as execution nodes, running any common operating system with no (big) portability issues. Moreover, thanks to language concepts and properties, as well as its wide developer community, development costs are generally considered as lower in Java than with other specialized environments.

Moorea's architecture combines:

- a reactive object model – *Rhum* – and its associated reactive execution kernel *Junior* [13],
- with a Java mobile object framework (*MobiliTools/SMI* [6] [24]) implementing OMG's Mobile Agent Facility specification [15],
- on top of a flexible Object Request Broker (*Jonathan* [26]) offering both a Java-RMI and a CORBA so-called "personalities", extended with transparency to mobility support.

This combination turns Rhum's distributed reactive objects into mobile agents. For this reason, we will use the term "Moorea agent" as a synonym of, and shortcut for, "Moorea mobile reactive object". Moorea's architecture has been described in [7] and, with more details, in [8]. We hereafter recall some key aspects.

2.2 Key Concepts and Features

2.2.1 Reactive Objects and Events

Moorea's agent model is based on Rhum's distributed reactive object model [5]. The basic processing procedures and internal data of an agent is embedded in a reactive object that controls its *behavior*. A behavior describes the agent's activity, specified in the Rhum language, which offers high-level constructs to define parallel branches, conditions, synchronization on events (triggering, preemption), loops, etc.. Agents are *reactive* in that the execution of the behavior may both depend on (or *react to*) and generate *events*.

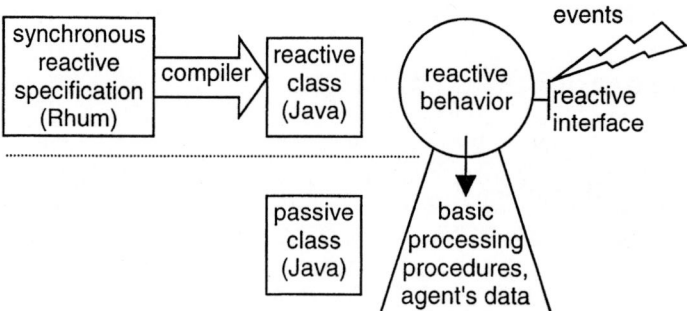

Fig. 1. The behavior specification is compiled into a composition of elementary reactive instruction objects defined as low-level reactive constructs (and along with other reactive objects such as events, execution engines, etc) in the Junior reactive kernel library. Moorea agents interact with other entities in their environment (agents, infrastructure) through their reactive interface : each method exported in this interface is mapped to a specific reactive event (i.e. each invocation triggers the corresponding event).

Agents are created, hosted and executed by *agencies*. Events are generated by agents or by their host agency. Events may hold values, and may be either locally visible by all the agents in a given agency, or specifically sent to a given agent, whatever local or remote. The exact semantics of events is given in section 2.2.2. Agents are designated through their *reference*, which may be used for managing them or for sending them events (e.g. through calls to their reactive interface).

Each agency contains an engine to locally manage instants, events and reactions. Agencies are independent *reactive domains* (for efficiency reasons, sequences of instants of distinct agencies are fully independent).

2.2.2   Focus on Synchronous Programming Model

Derived from Esterel [2], synchronous language Rhum slightly modifies its semantics to avoid causality problems and to allow dynamic program composition. However, the synchronous execution principle remains: in such an execution model, time is sliced into logical instants, which define the lifetime of an event and the reaction semantics (Fig. 2):

1. an event is present during an instant if and only if it is generated during this instant;
2. reactions to an event are triggered in the same instant;
3. an event may trigger reactions only once per instant, whatever the number of times the event has been generated during this instant.

An instant ends once all reactions are terminated or stopped. A reaction stops by waiting an event that is not present in the instant, or by explicitly waiting next instant (the reactive engine is in charge of detecting instant termination).

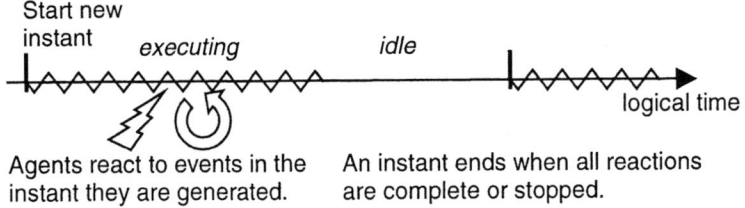

Fig. 2. A synchronous execution is split in instants where agents react to and generate events.

2.2.3   Scalability Aspects

The execution model is based on a sequential reaction to events (i.e. with no actual parallelism). This model both saves processing time (no preemptive scheduling and no context switching) and avoids complex code related to concurrency and consistency management. This model thus enforces good scalability, in terms of number of agents per agency. A scalability comparison of Rhum with thread-based agents is given in [8]. The results show that a growing number of reactive agents does not increase infrastructure overhead, which allows to run a greater number of agents. At the present time, we can run up to 10^6 reactive agents on a single PC.

2.2.4   Transparency to Mobility for Execution

Moorea agents' behavior is represented by a reactive program, whose execution is split into instants. The beginning of an instant is triggered by the reactive domain, and the end of an instant is reached when no agent reacts any more. At the end of an instant, the state of agents is coherent, stable, well defined and easy (not costly) to transport. Moorea takes advantage of this property, by actually performing moves once the end of instant is reached. A moving agent is frozen and transported with its behavior and full state, and then resumed in the new reactive domain (i.e. agency), in a new instant.

Note that the combination of mobility and reactive model considerably limits mobility overhead. This approach must be compared to thread-based mobile agents, whose mobility is either disturbing (the execution state is reset to some default state after move), or complex and costly (mobility includes execution stacks). On the contrary, Moorea's agent model allows a low-cost serialization and transport of agents' execution state (an agent behavior is equivalent to a state machine). Moreover, the synchronous reactive model offers clear mobility semantics, which is not always the case of thread-based mobile agents (sometimes unclearly) introducing various side effects to the programming semantics. Besides, the programmer is relieved from concurrency management burden, as well as inconsistency and deadlock threats when programming the passive objects[1], regardless of formal parallelism between and within behaviors (see 2.2.2 and sequential reaction principle in 2.2.3).

2.2.5   Transparency to Mobility for Communication

Since Moorea reactive model tightly couples activity with communication, transparent mobility must also consider events. While environment events remain purely local, targeted events should always follow the target agent, without being lost, even during the agent transportation timeframe. This transparency support is provided within the stubs of the distributed objects, at the underlying middleware's level (i.e. Jonathan and its RMI personality Jeremie, and Rhum) [18]. These stubs are not fully specific to Moorea, and have been reused to support object mobility in Jonathan's CORBA personality (David).

Roughly, transparency is achieved by a smart combination of two well-known techniques, namely *message forwarding* (from to the previous to the next known location) and *naming service* (or registry, to get the latest known location of a named object). The advanced features are:

– optimized forwarding chains, always reduced to a single indirection;
– limited usage of the naming service (thanks to forwarding) and possibility to have several naming services, to avoid a bottleneck effect;
– possibility to shutdown an agency without losing contact with the agents that have escaped from it.

---

[1] Of course, such troubles may occur at higher level due to incorrect behavior definitions.

3   Application to a Telecommunication Service Execution Environment

3.1   Requirements of Telecommunication Service Execution Environments

In the ATHOS ITEA European project, Moorea has been integrated into a telecommunication service creation and execution environment. This European project aimed at defining a relevant architecture for such an environment, in order to develop and run services on a bunch of computers linked to telecommunication networks through telephony legacy protocol stacks.

This context brings several requirements. First of all, *distribution* is regarded as necessary, for the execution environment has to be highly *scalable* to support a great variety of services (from tens to hundreds) and to handle thousands (or more) of simultaneously active instances of these services. Moreover, the execution environment must be able to be continuously running for a long period of time (at least for months). This requirement implies the ability to *dynamically reconfigure* the execution environment for maintenance issues (e.g. add, reboot or shutdown a node) and to dynamically update software.

3.2   Moorea in the ATHOS Architecture

The ATHOS architecture is based on the concept of Enhanced Call Server (ECS, see Fig. 3). The ECS is connected to the Internet and the telephony networks so as to offer convergent services. The logic of each service for each subscriber is executed by a Moorea agent, running on an arbitrary computer of a local network dedicated to service logic execution. Inside the ECS, a Moorea gateway handles a mapping between telephonic events and reactive events, as well as subscribers' service instances and associated service logic agents. More details are given in [7].

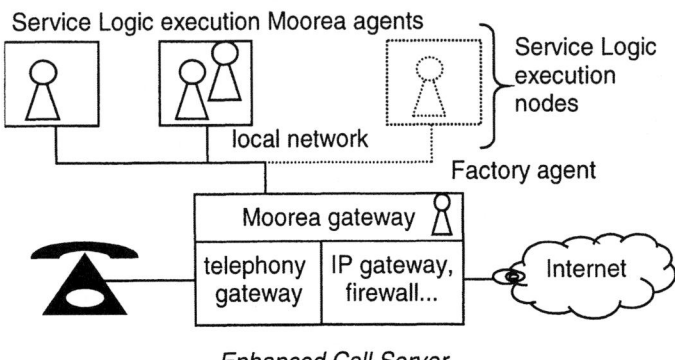

Enhanced Call Server

Fig. 3. The ATHOS Enhanced Call Server architecture makes it possible to build advanced services, accessing both the Internet and the telephony networks, using common computing technologies (typically a bunch of Ethernet-networked PCs with usual operating systems Linux or Windows).

The Moorea gateway contains a reactive domain, with a Factory agent in charge of creating and recycling service logic agents among the service logic execution nodes.

3.3   Example: A Simple Email Waiting Indicator Service

Our dynamic distribution and load balancing experiment is based on an Email Waiting Indicator (EWI) service demonstration; developed on the ECS architecture. This service consists in providing a phone subscriber with information about his pending electronic messages. Once the service is subscribed and the information about the email account is provided (typically the IP address of the POP3 server, identifier and password), the user may enable and disable the service by dialing special codes on its phone. When the service is enabled and the user unhooks his/her phone, s/he gets the information about pending messages (e.g. special tone or voice message). These telephony events (dial codes, off-hook) are handled by the ECS, which performs the appropriate action.

4   A Preemptive Dynamic Distribution and Load Balancing Experiment

4.1   Motivations

As stated in section 1, our primary concern is that any distributed system is likely to undergo maintenance actions requiring to shutdown execution nodes. This is a problem regarding service availability and system administration since such actions may require whole or part (typically depending on the architecture and the underlying middleware) of a distributed application to be cleanly stopped and then possibly redeployed on new nodes and restarted.

Fault tolerance-dedicated replication architectures are effective but expensive solutions to this problem, since they require redundant hardware while increasing overall complexity in terms of development, deployment and maintenance. Although they certainly are unavoidable technologies for critical services, there may be a category of applications requiring high availability but for which rare unexpected crashes are acceptable, because they can be quickly and automatically restarted without any heavy recovery task. This may be typically the case for our EWI service, according to a given service level agreement. In the context of an e-commerce web site, for instance, if it happens once or twice a year to have a number of sessions brutally abort, it may neither disappoint visitors too much nor be too prejudicial to the site's owner, as long as critical tasks (database, billing) are safely handled by a fault-tolerant subsystem.

Moreover, it can be imagined that a dynamically distributable bunch of servers (like our service execution environment) will undergo less interruptions due to unexpected crashes than a static system where any node is likely to require maintenance (from a simple reboot to a full replacement). Indeed, moving servant objects from one node to other available nodes makes it possible to perform preventive reboots as well as hardware or software maintenance tasks on any node at any time without interrupting the running sessions.

Finally, by adding dynamic load balancing techniques, we aim at smoothing service response time and optimizing computing resources usage.

4.2 Architecture for Preemptive Dynamic Distribution

4.2.1 An Agency Controller Agent

In this first step, we want to be able to shutdown a service execution node without disturbing running services, and see them automatically dispatched to the other nodes. In the other way round, we want to be able to add new execution nodes at runtime, and see new services automatically be created on these new nodes. We introduce a *Controller agent* in each service logic agency, in charge of:

– declaring the new agency to the Factory agent at creation, so that it has a chance to host service logic agents;
– creating new service logic agents on demand from the Factory agent;
– welcoming moving agents (typically escaping from a terminating agency);
– manage the clean shutdown of an agency.

A number of event-based protocols are necessary to implement these features. The declaration protocol is a straightforward "hello protocol", consisting in sending to the Factory agent an event holding the reference to the new agency's Controller agent. Thanks to this declaration event, the Factory agent knows the Controller agent of every available agency. When a new service logic agent is necessary, the Factory randomly chooses a target agency for the agent creation.

Protocols for a clean agency shutdown are of more interest: on the one hand, the Controller manages the correct dispatching of local service logic agents to other agencies. On the other hand, the Controller must reject both arriving agents and service logic creation requests. This behavior could be implemented in a centralized way, with a kind of a master controller handling agency shutdown and agent creation requests. But we preferred a distributed approach, making it possible to independently shutdown agencies at any time without any central control. We use the combination of three protocols:

– a service logic agent creation protocol,
– a welcome protocol for moving agents,
– and an agency shutdown protocol.

4.2.2 Protocols for Clean Agency Shutdown

The first protocol shown in Fig. 4(a) controls the service logic agent creation. A Controller agent must reject creation requests when its agency is shutting down. Otherwise, there would be a risk of prolongation, and it would make no sense since the new agent should immediately move to another agency. For the same reason, the welcome protocol shown in Fig. 4(b) prevents remote agents to come to a shutting down agency. Before moving, agents send a request to the target agency's Controller. Then, either the Controller accepts the request and moves the agent in, or it rejects the request if its agency is shutting down. In both a rejected move or rejected creation, the agent or the Factory tries another target agency.

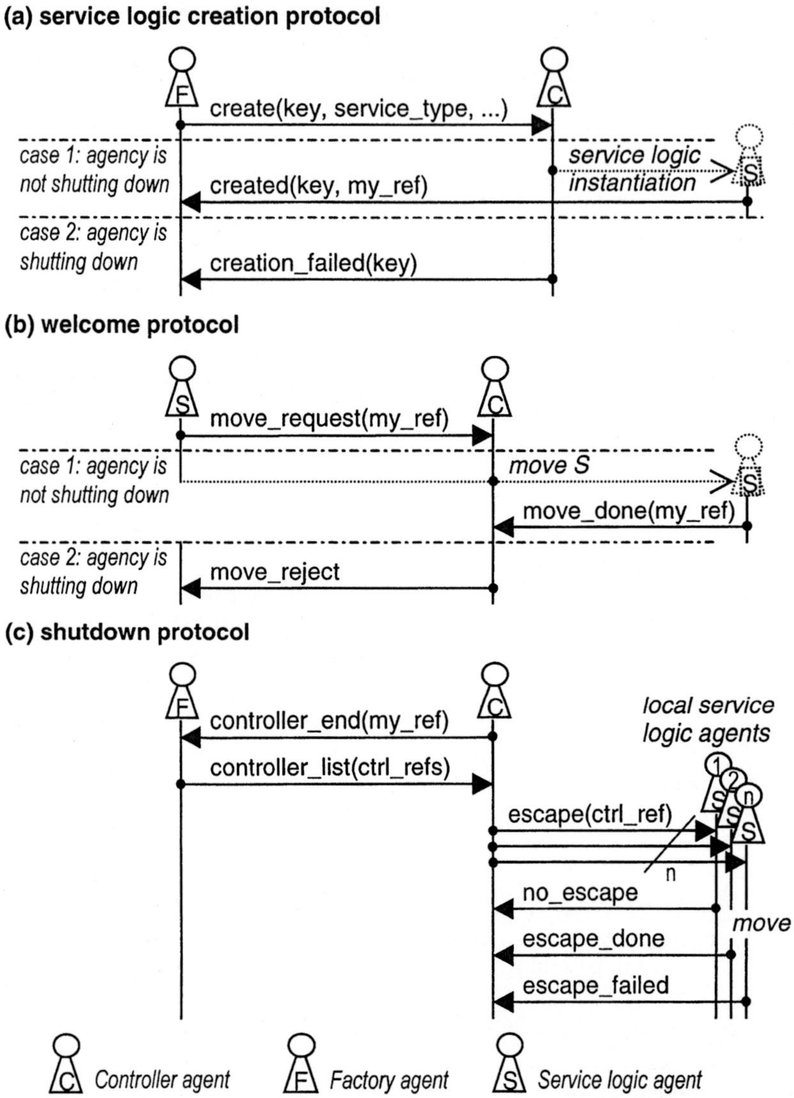

(a) service logic creation protocol

(b) welcome protocol

(c) shutdown protocol

Fig. 4. Three protocols must be defined to cleanly handle an agency shutdown: (a) service logic agent creation protocol; (b) service logic agent welcome protocol; (c) shutdown protocol.

The shutdown protocol is described by Fig. 4(b). First of all, the Controller warns the Factory that the agency is about to terminate, and, as a result, that it should not be regarded as a candidate for agent creation. The Factory replies by returning a fresh list of available agencies, that could welcome agents escaping from the shutting down agency[2]. Then, the Controller sends an event to each local service logic agent, giving

---

[2] Note that, for concurrency reasons, there is still a risk that a few creation or move requests reach the Controller however. This is the reason why the creation control and welcome protocols are useful.

the Controller reference of a target agency (picked in a round-Robin manner from the agency list). Finally, for each agent, three situations may occur:
– it successfully escapes to another agency;
– it does not want to move – it is just going to stay until its termination;
– it fails to escape (e.g. because the target agency is shutting down).
The Controller waits for all the replies from the agents, and the full protocol is repeated as long as escape failures occur.

4.3   Extension for Load Balancing

4.3.1   Architecture and Algorithm
One of our main concerns in this work is to provide flexible, dynamically adaptable, self-organizing, distributed tools. We want it to be possible to add the load balancing feature without changing anything in the service execution environment architecture. To allow a high flexibility level, load balancing may be added, stopped, or even changed at runtime.

The architecture simply consists in adding a *Balancer agent* at any time in the service execution environment. As shown by Fig. 5, the Balancer gets a fresh list of agencies and starts visiting every agency. Whenever and wherever necessary, i.e. at first visit or in case of probe update, the Balancer creates a Probe agent whose role is to observe the computing load of its host agency. The simple Probe we are using in this experiment computes an average instant duration for all instants spent between two consecutive Balancer visits, excluding the longest instant. Once all agencies have been visited, the Balancer performs a load balancing action, based on the minimum value and the maximum value of load indicators given by the probes.

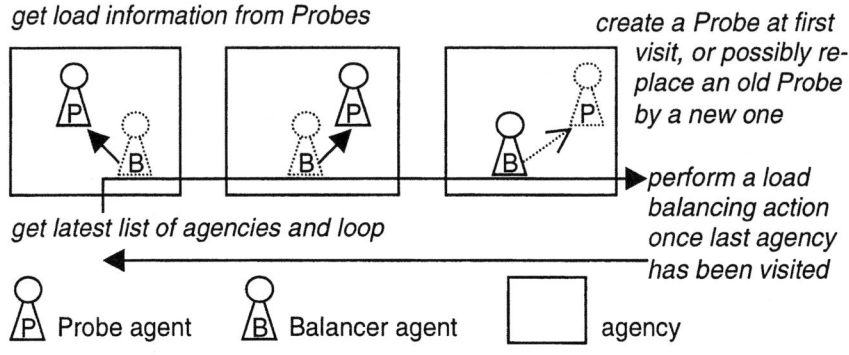

Fig. 5. The load balancing architecture is based on a single Balancer mobile agent and one Probe agent per agency. The Balancer is continuously moving from agency to agency while Probe agents observe their agency's computing load.

As a first experiment, we implemented a simple action consisting in moving a Service Logic agent from the agency with the heaviest load to the less loaded agency. The Balancer sends an event to the Probe in the agency with the heaviest load, to tell it to move an agent to the less loaded agency (whose Controller's reference is passed as an event argument). The Probe arbitrarily selects an agent and moves it as requested by the Balancer.

In our design, the Balancer must be unique in the system in order to avoid confusion in load balancing decisions and actions. For this reason, the introduction of a Balancer agent is made through a unique Management agent, running in the gateway. Before creating a new Balancer, it checks whether a Balancer is already running, and if so, it kills it.

4.3.2   Load Indicator

Relying on a relevant and reliable load indicator is a critical issue for load balancing efficiency. Our service execution environment is based on Java, and is running on any kind of computer, with arbitrary operating systems. Typical load indicators such as used and available memory, CPU usage percentage, network bandwidth usage, disk transfer rates, number of processes, etc., are not easy to get in our environment[3]. Moreover, some of them would be hard to compare from one computer to the other. For instance, how to compare CPU usage between computers with different CPU types, frequencies and numbers?

Instead of these typical indicators, our idea is to make an opportunistic utilization of the properties of synchronous programming execution model. As explained in section 2.2.2, the execution of reactive objects is cadenced by a single thread through a succession of instants. The duration of each instant is the sum of the execution times consumed by all reactive objects during the logical instant. As a result, the more agents and the more time-consuming they are, the longer the instants are, and then, finally, the slower their execution is. The key argument in favor of instant duration as a load indicator is that it is fully independent from the computing environment (such as CPU speed and memory size), and then, it can be reliably compared through our whole system. For instance, a long instant may result from an overloaded CPU or from process swapping or Java garbage collection, denoting low memory conditions.

To be more rigorous, it must be underlined that the reliability of this indicator depends on the regular distribution of reactive behaviors among the agencies. The amount of time consumed during an instant by a single reactive object depends on the way it has been programmed (how often does its behavior stop waiting next instant, how much time do its passive methods take?), as well as its runtime conditions. These concerns may be regarded as statistically neutral if a sufficient number of instances of the same service is homogeneously deployed among the agencies. If the service execution environment runs several service types (which is actually the target), the instances of each service should be homogeneously distributed among the agencies.

At each instant, the Probe object gets the duration of the previous instant by invoking a specific method on its host agency.

---

[3] Unless we implement native code for all operating systems, called through the Java Native Interface, which we would like to avoid as far as possible.

5   Experimental Results with EWI Service Prototype

5.1   Agency Shutdown and Agent Redistribution

5.1.1   Testbed

This first experiment aims at observing the behavior of our service logic execution environment when shutting an agency down. The experiment consists in 2 agencies running on 2 computers (named gvu and gvenu), and a load injector simulating 100 users performing 1000 service calls in a 400 seconds timeframe. The load injector creates one thread per simulated user in a best effort manner (i.e. as quickly as possible). Then, each thread performs periodic service calls accordingly to the call rate specification.

Let T_0 be the origin time of the experiment. At this time, agency gvu is available but no service logic agent is running. Then, the load injector is run, resulting in the creation of 100 service logic agents in gvu. The schedule is:

1. at T_0+70 seconds, the first service invocation occurs;
2. once the 100th service logic agent is created, we start an agency on gvenu;
3. at T_0+170 seconds, agency gvu is starting a shutdown process, resulting in making every local agent escape to agency gvenu;
4. at T_0+470 seconds, simulated users in the load injector stop making requests.

This scenario is run using the following computing environment:

Network	switched 100Mb/s Ethernet
Moorea's support services, Moorea gateway, load injector	Sun Blade 1000, 1Gb RAM, 1 CPU UltraSparcIII 750MHz, Solaris 8 operating system
agency gvu	PC, 192Mb RAM, 1 PentiumII CPU 333MHz, 512kB cache, Linux operating system
agency gvenu	

5.1.2   Results and Comments

The first remark is that every service invocation has been successful, even after agency shutdown, and that no error occurred, which shows a first level of robustness. The second remark is that performance is not really good. On the one hand, agency shutdown results in a great response time increase (the longest response time is almost 24 seconds). On the other hand, the process of closing an agency is too long (10 minutes to make 100 agents escape), because agents are moving too slowly.

The overall system behavior is shown by figures Fig. 6 and Fig.7. In order to extract trends, we are presenting moving average values, calculated on 50 points. We first observe a peak of response time, starting at T_0+170 seconds, which is the moment when agency gvu is terminating. Then, we notice that response times give a kind of a square periodic curve. If we look at the instant duration in both agencies, we see that those response time squares can be related to instant duration variations.

The aspect of instant duration curve results from the combination of the occurrence of garbage collection resulting in dispersed, very long instants, and the moving average calculus. Very long instant may also result from a conjunction of many polling actions (cf. EWI service logic agents behavior). Such conjunctions of polling actions may result from the distribution in time of initial service logic agent creation, which depends on the load injector, the initial agency and the Moorea gateway.

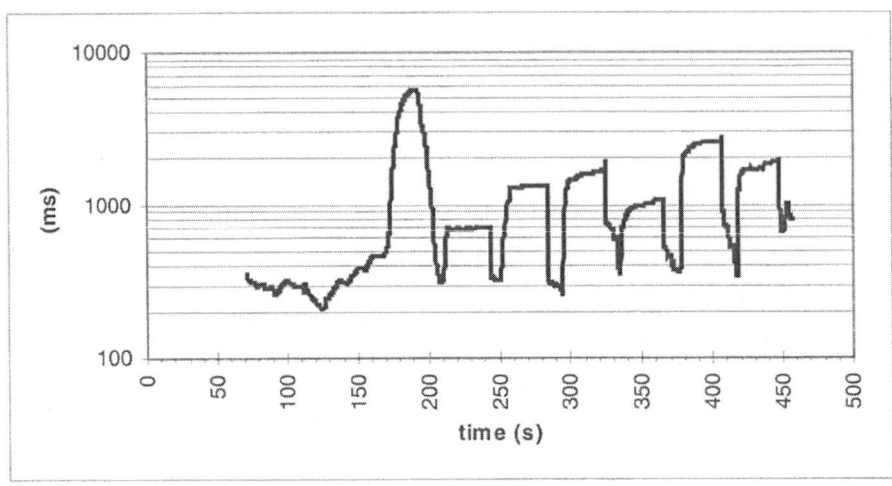

Fig. 6. Moving average on 50 points of service response time.

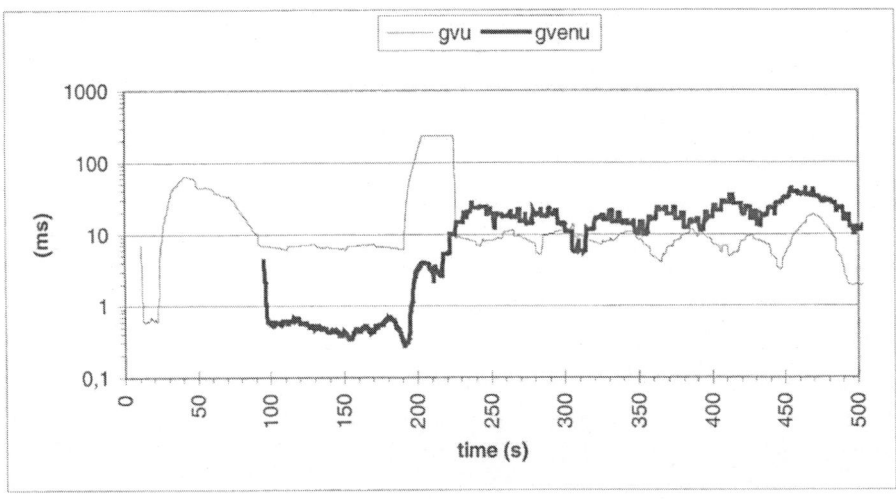

Fig. 7. Moving average on 50 points of instant duration in both gvu and gvenu.

5.1.3   Conclusion

The positive conclusion of this observation is that instant duration and response time are actually bound. The negative conclusion is that some work remains to improve the system performance, but this is not really a surprise to us. Although we were aiming at scalability through the use of synchronous programming, the implementation of Moorea does not really care about performance, simply because this platform is more like a feasibility experiment. For example, a solution had to be found to adapt the event-based one-way communication style of synchronous programming to the method call-based programming style of SMI mobility framework. This two-way adaptation is implemented in a very basic, sequential, slow way. For instance, getting a list of agencies or moving an agent can take a lot of time, waiting for previous calls to complete before actually starting.

5.2   Load Balancing Experiment

5.2.1   Testbed

The experiment consists in observing the impact of the Balancer agent on the overall system behavior. The computing environment remains the same (see 5.1.1), except that we changed the EWI service logic agent polling period from 10 minutes to one minute, in order to create more load. The scenario is the following:

1. at T_0, an agency is created on gvu;
2. at T_0+1', the load injector is run to simulate 200 users performing 6000 service calls during a 40 minutes timeframe. Calls actually begin at $T_0+2'30''$, and complete at $T_0+43'20''$;
3. at $T_0+14'30''$, an agency is created on gvenu;
4. at T_0+15', a Balancer agent is created.

5.2.2   Results and Comments

0, 0 and 0 give experimental results, still using moving average values (except for the number of agents) to help extract trends.

As far as response time is concerned, 0 shows that the introduction of the Balancer agent at T_0+900'' does not disturb the service response time. Then, we see that the response time tends to decrease, which shows that our load balancing architecture and policies are successful, and that the mobility of the Balancer does not result in observable performance degradation.

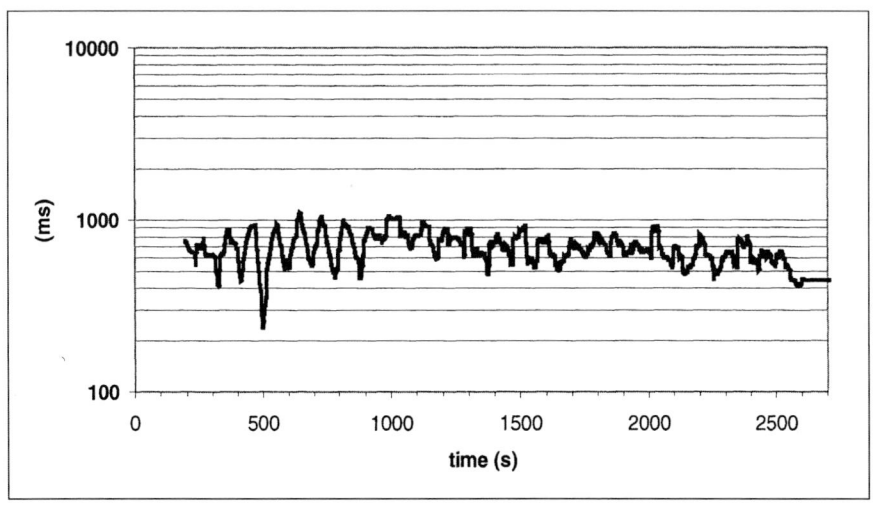

Fig. 8. Moving average on 100 points of service response time

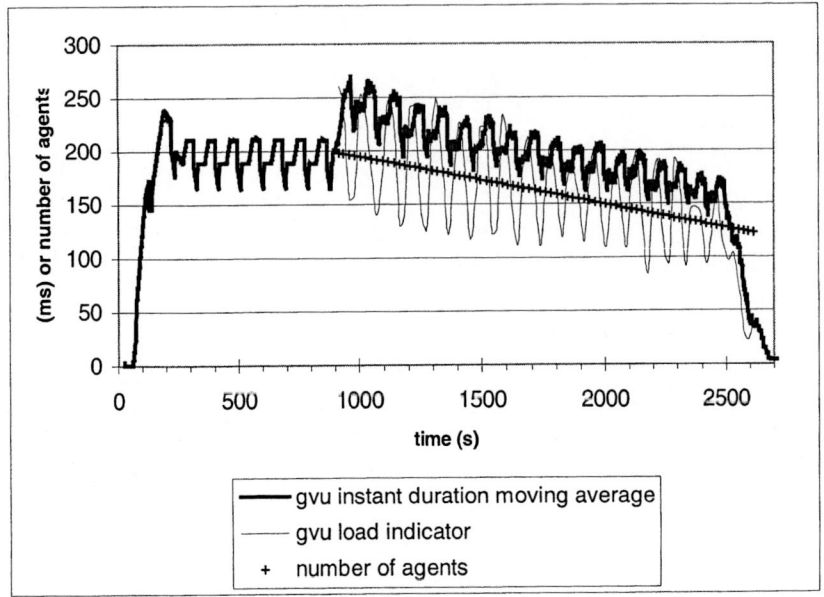

Fig. 9. Load of agency gvu.

0 shows the impact of the Balancer on the first agency gvu. At $T_0+900"$, we first see a slight increase of instant duration (about 50ms), and then a regular decrease down to 150ms. In the second agency (gvenu, 0), significant load is appearing and regularly increasing. In both agencies, the load indicator computed by the Probe agent (see 4.3.1) follows the same trends with greater oscillations. The load indicator is actually a sort of a corrected moving average. Finally, at $T_0+2600"$, service calls stop, and both load indicator and instant duration almost become zero.

Of course, the number of (active) service logic agents seems to give also a good load indicator, and follows more or less the same trends. However, it seems that the slope is a bit smaller for the number of agents, reflecting a scalability factor. Another issue about the number of agents is that it is meaningful only in the case of identical agents (same behavior, same parameters), while the service execution environment is supposed to run an arbitrary variety of services, with different parameters (e.g. different polling periods for the EWI service).

As a last observation, we note that the load balancing process is rather slow (minutes to move agents). Besides platform global performance considerations, other policies could be imagined to enhanced efficiency. For instance, several agents could be moved at once, depending on the load difference between agencies and the total number of agents, and more than two agencies could be involved in the redistribution of agents. Besides, the Probe could acquire knowledge on the local agents' execution profiles, in order to make smart choices about the agents to be moved. However, getting such information would probably require to enhance the service logic execution agencies. Moreover, a great care should be taken not to introduce a serious overload, nor to be prejudicial to scalability. As a first experiment, we consider that our simple approach offers better analysis opportunities.

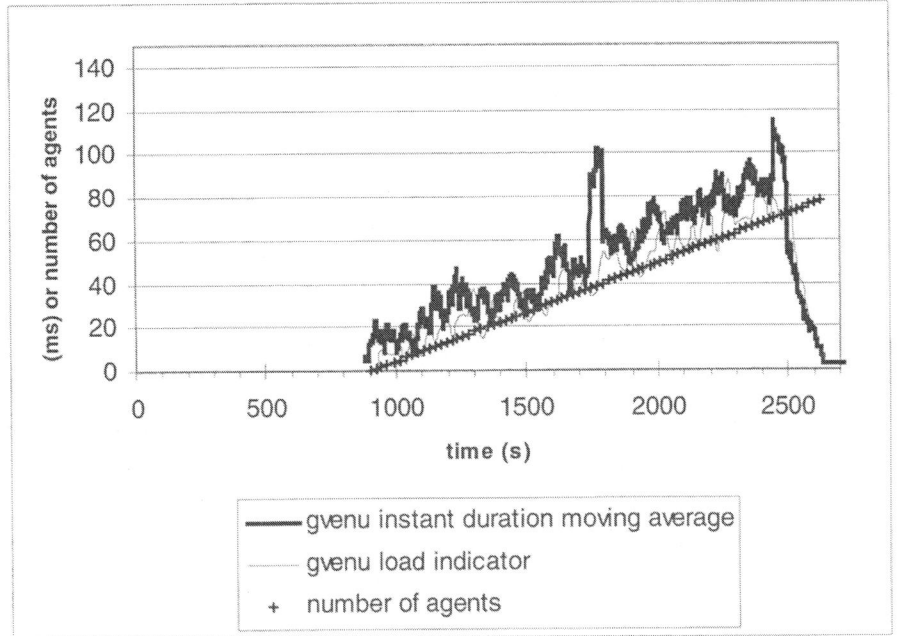

Fig. 10. Load of agency gvenu.

5.2.3   Conclusion

This experiment shows that an actual improvement in service response time can be withdrawn from our preemptive load balancing. This promising result opens a way to other experiments with improved load balancing policies, for a greater number of agents and a variety of services, and during a longer timeframe. But a preliminary work about performance improvement is certainly necessary.

6   Discussion and Related Work

6.1   About Weak and Strong Mobility

6.1.1   Thread or Process-Based Activities

Strong mobility [10] is often regarded as too costly and not really necessary. This point of view is related to considerations about the acceptable execution grain that cannot be interrupted by a move. For instance, typical RPC servers are only active when they are processing an invocation, and the response time per invocation is generally short (less than a couple of seconds in typical cases, sometimes up to a minute or so for heavily loaded transactional systems). In such situations, it is acceptable to wait for running invocations to complete before shutting down a node, while new invocations are stopped until the server has been restarted at another node. For example, [16] shows such a mechanism for CORBA objects through the implementation of the lifecycle specification.

Today, a great number of middleware environments running on common operating systems support such a *weak mobility*. For instance, just mention most of mobile agent platforms such as Aglets [21], Voyager [29] and ProActive [27]. Nevertheless, a few platforms do support strong mobility, such as Dartmouth College's AgentTcl/D'agent [11] and General Magic's Telescript [20]. In Java environment, a number of experiments have been carried out to implement movable threads, in a variety of ways:

- special Java Virtual Machine like Aroma [17]. Performance and specific JVM are the main limitations;
- code instrumentation through pre-processing or post-compilation techniques (byte-code injection). Both approaches impact on code size and performance. For example, [19] shows a 35% growth of code, and up to 27 % slow down.

Because object and activity thread are orthogonal concepts, these approaches must enforce some programming restrictions or special models with regard to the general Java programming model. As a matter of fact, strong mobility must take care of both objects and threads, which may not cross and refer each other in an unorganized, uncontrolled way.

6.1.2   Higher-Level Activity Definition

Implementing strong mobility is certainly less complex and costly if the programming and runtime environments use a higher-level activity description. The Bond agent system [4] follows such an approach: agent activity is controlled by a multi-plane state machine, generated from a description in a dedicated language named "Blue-Print". The basic processing procedures are implemented by a set of "strategies" objects, equivalent for Moorea's passive object. Mobility grain is the execution of a "strategy", which may be coded in a variety of programming languages.

Moorea's approach is quite similar. The activity of reactive objects is coded with Rhum synchronous programming language, using high-level constructs such as parallelism, synchronization, event waiting. Such a program could be transformed into automata (like Esterel compilers implicitly do). Mobility grain is bound to the notion of instant: an object move is effective only at the end of an instant, once all objects are inactive[4]. After a move, a reactive object transparently resumes its activity in a new instant, at a new location. This semantics is clear - and "natural" in some way - whatever the behavior complexity and the number of active loops or parallel branches. As a consequence of this approach, strong mobility support is provided at low cost, by avoiding to freeze and transport "expensive" items like running threads.

Below this suitability for mobility, synchronous execution also enables easy and reliable parallel programming, by preventing from handling monitors, semaphores, locks, etc., for managing synchronization and concurrency issues. Moreover, synchronous programming can be considered as a way to implement cooperative scheduling, which is typically less costly than preemptive scheduling (see scalability results in [8] comparing Rhum and threads). Finally, it opens the way to simulating and testing, and even probably to proving execution properties [3].

---

[4] I.e. when every reactive object is waiting for an absent event or for next instant, see 2.2.2.

6.2   About Dynamic Load Balancing

Dynamic load balancing aims at optimizing computing resources usage and system response time, by placing processes in a multi-processor environment during runtime, accordingly to observed load conditions. [14] details several key issues to be addressed to build a dynamic load balancing architecture. Typical architectures rely on a number of policies, that may be implemented in a distributed or centralized manner:

- the *infor*mation policy rules which, how and when load information is collected (selection of load indicators, periodic or event-driven, automatic or on-demand...);
- the transfer policy determines whether it is suitable for a node to participate to a process transfer or not (e.g. if its load is lower or greater than given thresholds);
- the location policy rules the choice of the node which may run a new process, as well as the node that may let a process go in case of preemptive load balancing;
- specifically in case of preemptive load balancing, we need to define also an election *policy* to rule the choice of the process to be migrated.

Our information policy is based on the instant duration observation. This policy is implemented in a distributed manner via the Probe agents which may be introduced, updated or terminated whenever at runtime. The other policies are implemented by the Balancer agent[5]. While a fully distributed approach would require to solve the consensus issue through the agencies, our approach combines logical centralization (a single agent makes decisions) and physical distribution.

Of course, the definition of these policies is critical. For instance, the information policy must be reactive enough so that a faithful picture of the system load can be obtained, without flooding the system with a huge information flow. The choice of system-wide comparable and reliable load indicators (such as CPU or memory usage) is also hard to make, especially in the case of heterogeneous nodes. Depending on the processes execution profiles in terms of computing resources consumption, the value of those indicators are likely to quickly change. The election policy is also critical. For instance, migrating a process that is about to terminate uselessly lowers its response time while wasting computing resources.

As a paradox, the complexity of load balancing policies can cause performance degradation, especially in the case of preemptive load balancing, as mentioned in [14], because of the process migration cost. However, some experiments showed that actual performance benefits could be obtained from preemptive load balancing, especially by carefully examining and exploiting the process lifetime distribution [12]. Our experiments tend to confirm that actual benefit can be withdrawn from preemptive load balancing based on a synchronous programming model.

Dynamic load balancing environments can be found at various levels: process placement, either within a multi-processor computer or through a distributed operating system, or servant object placement in distributed middleware. For instance, major J2EE platforms perform non-preemptive dynamic load balancing on clustered servers. A few operating systems, like Sprite [9] [28] or MOSIX [1] [25] do support preemptive dynamic load balancing.

---

[5] The Factory agent also contributes to the location policy, in a fully independent manner, through a random-based distribution of new service logic agents.

7   Conclusion

Preemptive dynamic load balancing raises a number of key issues. Among them, the questions of efficient and transparent process mobility on the one hand, and meaningful load indicator availability on the other hand, are particularly critical. We propose a specific solution to both questions by taking advantage of synchronous programming peculiarities. This programming and execution model simplifies and decreases the cost of process mobility, while providing a relevant load indicator through the measure of its elementary execution *instants*.

These ideas are experimented in the context of a telecommunication service execution distributed environment prototype, based on a mobile agent platform in Java featuring a synchronous reactive agent model. Our service logic execution environment may be considered as a dynamic cluster without redundancy, aiming at supporting high service availability and continuity, but not fault tolerance. Despite a performance limitation, the first experiment shows the ability of transparently adding and suppressing execution node to the service execution environment. The second experiment shows a preemptive load balancing architecture based on a load balancing agent moving from execution node to execution node, and deploying load probing agents in the whole execution environment. A simple load balancing policy based on the observation of synchronous instant duration in every execution node results in an effective service response time improvement.

Although the implementation-related limitations of the underlying mobile agent platform prevent from getting satisfactory pure performance results, we show the attractiveness of the synchronous reactive model for preemptive load balancing. Further work could consist in building a mobile synchronous reactive object environment in lower software layers, including the operating system, to actually address pure performance issues. Then, some work could be carried out on load balancing policies.

Acknowledgement. ATHOS project partners, and in particular Italtel for the ECS architecture, Anne-Marie Tagant for Moorea (hope/sure you are enjoying retirement), Huan Tran Viet for mobility support in Jonathan (hope you're doing well back to your country).

References

[1]   Barak, A., Shai, G., Wheeler, R. G.: The MOSIX Distributed Operating System - Load Balancing for Unix. Lecture Notes in Computer Science 672, Springer-Verlag, 1993, pp. 135–178.

[2]   Berry G., Gonthier G.: The Esterel Synchronous Language - Design, Semantics, Implementation. Science of Computer Programming, 19(2), 1992.

[3]   Bertin V., Poize M., Pulou J., Sifakis J.: Towards Validated Real-Rime Software. Proc. 12th Euromicro Conference on Real-Time Systems, Stockholm, June 2000.

[4]   Bölöni L., Jun K., Palacz K., Sion R., Marinescu D.: The Bond Agent System and Applications. Proc. ASA/MA, Lecture Notes in Computer Science 1882, Springer, September 2000, pp. 99–112.

[5]   Boussinot, F, Doumenc, G., Stefani, J.-B.: Reactive Objects. Annales des Télécommunications No 51, 1996, pp. 9–18.

[6]   Dillenseger B.: MobiliTools - An OMG standards-based toolbox for agent mobility and interoperability. Proc. 6th IFIP Conference on Intelligence in Networks (SmartNet 2000), Vienna, September 2000, Kluwer Academic Publishers, pp. 353–366.

[7]   Dillenseger B., Tagant A.-M., Hazard L.: Programming and Executing Telecommunication Service Logic with Moorea Reactive Mobile Agents. 4th International Workshop on Mobile Agents for Telecommunication Applications, Barcelona (Spain), October 2002, Lecture Notes in Computer Science 2521, Springer, pp. 48–57.

[8]   Dillenseger B., Tagant A.-M., Hazard L., Tran Viet H.: Les agents mobiles réactifs Mooréa - une approche réactive pour la transparence à la mobilité et le passage à l'échelle. RSTI-TSI 21/2002, Agents et codes mobiles, Lavoisier-Hermès ed. p. 1–26.

[9]   Douglis, F., Ousterhout, J.: Transparent process migration – Design alternatives and the Sprite implementation", Software Practice and. Experience 21/8, aug. 1991, pp. 757–785.

[10] Fugetta A., Picco G.-P., Vigna G.: Understanding Code Mobility. IEEE Transactions on Software Engineering, vol. 24, No 5, 1998, pp.342–361.

[11] Gray D., Kotz D., Nog S., Rus D., Cybenko G.: Mobile Agents: the next generation in distributed computing. Proc. 2nd Aizu Int. Symposium on Parallel Algorithms and Architectures Synthesis, Fukushima (Japan), IEEE Computer Society Press, 1997, p. 8–24.

[12] Harchor-Balter, M., Downey, A. B.: Exploiting Process Lifetime Distributions for Dynamic Load Balancing. ACM Transactions on Computer Systems, Vol. 15, No. 3, August 1997, pp. 253–285.

[13] Hazard L., Susini J.-F., Boussinot F.: The Junior reactive kernel. Rapport de recherche Inria 3732, 1999.

[14] Kameda, H., Li, J., Kim, C., Zhang, Y.: Optimal Load Balancing in Distributed Computer Systems. Springer-Verlag 1997.

[15] Object Management Group: Mobile Agent System Interoperability Facilities. TC document orbos/97-10-05, 1997. Revised in Mobile Agent Faciles, formal/2000-01-02.

[16] Peter, Y., Guyennet, H.: An Implementation of the LifeCycle Service - Object Mobility in CORBA. Conference on Parallel Computing Techniques (PaCT-99), Springer-Verlag LNCS 1662, St Petersbourg (Russia), 1999.

[17] Suri, N., Bradshaw, J., Breedy, M., Groth, P., Hill, G., Jeffers, R.: Strong-mobility and fine-grained resource control in NOMADS. Proc. ASA/MA, Lecture Notes in Computer Science 1882, Springer, September 2000, pp. 29–43.

[18] Tran Viet H.: Gestion de la mobilité dans l'ORB flexible Jonathan. Ph.D. dissertation, Université Joseph Fourier, Grenoble (France), April 2002.

[19] Truyen E., Robben B., Vanhaute B., Coninx T., Joosen W., Verbaeten P.: Portable support for transparent thread migration in Java. Proc. ASA/MA, Lecture Notes in Computer Science 1882, Springer, September 2000, p. 29–43.

[20] White J.: Telescript technology: the foundation for the electronic market place: General Magic White Paper, General Magic, 1994.

Web References

[21] Aglets - http://www.trl.ibm.com/aglets/index_e.htm

[22] JAIN - http://java.sun.com/products/jain/overview.html

[23] Javaphone API - http://java.sun.com/products/javaphone/

[24] MobiliTools - http://mobilitools.forge.objectweb.org/

[25] MOSIX - http://www.mosix.org/

[26] ObjectWeb Initiative - http://www.objectweb.org/

[27] ProActive - http://www-sop.inria.fr/oasis/ProActive/

[28] Sprite - http://www.cs.berkeley.edu/projects/sprite.papers.html

[29] Voyager - http://www.recursionsw.com/products/voyager/

An Adaptive Transactional System – Framework and Service Synchronization

Randi Karlsen

Computer science department, University of Tromsø, 9037 Tromsø, Norway
randi@cs.uit.no

Abstract. The characteristics of advanced applications vary a lot and the transaction concept must adapt to fulfil the varying transactional requirements. However, current transaction services do not support the required flexibility in a principled way. We believe that the need for transaction service flexibility can be supported through reflection, where the system is capable of inspecting and changing its own behaviour. The first part of this paper describes a framework for such a reflective transactional system, in which different transaction services can be deployed and modified, and from where a suitable transaction service can be chosen for the execution of a transaction.

As concurrent transactions may request different transaction services, the framework allows concurrently active transaction services within the same environment. To ensure correctness when heterogeneous transaction services are concurrently active, a transaction service manager within this framework, provides, among other tasks, transaction service synchronization. The second part of the paper concentrates on service synchronization, and presents algorithms that demonstrate how correctness can be guaranteed when incompatible services are requested.

1 Introduction

Transaction processing techniques play a major role in preserving correctness in important areas of computing, from hospital information systems to trading systems. Transactions guarantee data consistency, handle failure recovery and control concurrency, and are thus appropriate building blocks for structuring reliable systems [1]. The reliability provided through transactional guarantees are required in many types of advanced applications, found in for instance workflow systems, mobile systems and web services based systems.

The characteristics of advanced applications vary a lot and the transaction concept must adapt to fulfil the varying transactional requirements. Required execution guarantees are not limited to traditional ACID properties, and may include for instance timely constraints, execution flexibility and mobile transaction executions. Requirements may not only vary between applications but also between transactions within an application, depending on properties of the transactional task, user preferences and available system resources. Transactional

R. Meersman et al. (Eds.): CoopIS/DOA/ODBASE 2003, LNCS 2888, pp. 1208–1225, 2003.

requirements may also change during the lifetime of an application, and the required transaction service will consequently not be *fully known at application* design time.

Examples of applications where dynamically changing transactional requirements may be needed can be found in for instance medical information systems. In these systems patient journals and different kinds of medical information are stored over a number of sites. Users may execute simple transactions where a single patient journal is read or updated, more complex transactions using data from different sources, or transactions requiring long-running computations. In an emergency situation the user may want data as fast as possible, and will typically bind timely constraints to the transaction, or may be satisfied with incomplete or temporarily inconsistent data. The user may for instance need information about which of the nearest hospitals has enough health care personnel available to treat an injured patient. Here the information does not need to be exactly correct, but rather give a correct indication of the facts. Mobile transactions may be needed if a community nurse working in home based care wants to access patient information on her mobile device while on her way to the next patient. This may generate a transaction that starts execution at one site, and because of mobility, finishes at another site. Transactions may also require real-time access to multimedia information such as radiographs or spoken reports. Traditionally, accessing multimedia data involves quality of service guarantees, such as timeliness, throughput, media quality, and synchronization.

In addition to application specific requirements such as time and reliability, transaction executions may be effected by limited and varying system resources. Wireless networks suffer from limited bandwidth, limited battery life and connectivity is not longer a valid assumption. Availability of other resources, such as memory, disk-capacity and CPU time, may also vary over time and may require transaction executions to adapt. In component based applications, where each component has its own transaction management logic, transaction executions in the composite system is also effected by properties of underlying transactional systems (for instance ability to participate in a two-phase commit protocol).

To support the potential variety of transactional requirements, the transaction service should be highly adaptable, supporting different types of requirements. The service should allow different transactional properties to be available, new properties to be added, and transactions to be executed according to the most suited set of properties. This kind of adaptation is not supported by traditional transaction services, which are specified as closed services offering a predefined set of properties. Traditional services offer no or very limited possibilities for heterogeneous transaction executions, and can not recognize new transactional properties.

We believe that the need for transaction service flexibility can be supported through reflection [2,3], which enables inspection and modification of system structure and behaviour. In this paper, we present a framework for such a reflective transactional system, called *Transaction service execution environment (TSenvironment)*, in which different transaction services can be deployed and modified, and from where suitable transaction services can be chosen and concurrently used according to the needs of the transactions. As component technology [4] has emerged as promising for constructing configurable software systems, we have chosen a component-based approach when describing this framework.

In order to guarantee consistent use of transaction services within the framework, a *transaction service manager* will, among other tasks, be responsible for synchronizing activation of services. This paper will, in addition to describing the TSenvironment, present some algorithms that demonstrates synchronization of transaction services.

This work is part of the Arctic Beans Project [5], which is funded by The Research Council of Norway. The primary goal of the Arctic Beans project is to provide a more open and flexible enterprise component technology, with support for configurability and re-configurability, based on the principles of reflection.

The rest of this paper is organized as follows. Section 2 presents a framework for an adaptive transactional system and describes related work. Section 3 introduces a transaction service model, while section 4 presents three transaction service synchronization algorithms. Section 5 concludes.

2   Framework for an Adaptive Transactional System

2.1   Towards a Reflective Transactional System

Transaction services have traditionally been specified as closed services, offering a predefined set of transactional properties. This means that application designers and users do not know any details about the internal of the service and can not influence the service to provide a new or modified set of properties. Traditional transaction services are therefore unable to support a variety of transactional properties as described above. We believe that a highly adaptable transaction service can be achieved through the use of reflection [2,3], which is a technique for inspecting and modifying the current structure and behaviour of a system.

A *reflective system* is divided into two levels, a base level and a meta level. The base level is the part of the system that performs processing for the application (for instance controls transaction executions). The meta-level contains meta-objects that encapsulate self-representation and reflective computation for the system. The services provided by the meta-level interface, often referred to as the meta-object protocol (MOP), allow inspection and modification of system behaviour and structure [6].

We envision an environment where a variety of transactional services are available, where new or modified services offering different properties may be included when needed, and where a transaction execution request is accompanied by an indication of the required service. As transactional systems normally have a number of concurrently executing transactions, one transaction may require a new or modified transaction service, while other transactions still need the original service. Also, as two transactions may require different types of modifications, a number of different transactional properties may be requested concurrently. This diversity of transactional needs leads us to specify a reflective transactional system as a framework, the TSenvironment, in which different transaction services can be deployed, and from where a suitable transaction service can be chosen.

The TSenvironment can be seen as a transactional system offering different sets of transaction properties, $\mathcal{P} = P_1, \ldots, P_n$, where P_i represents the properties of transaction service TS_i. A transaction will request a transaction service in the TSenvironment according to the needs of the application and/or properties of the underlying system. Also, concurrent transactions may be managed by different transaction services. Reflection will enable the internals of the TSenvironment to be inspected and modified, so that new transaction services can be deployed and made available as tools to control transaction executions. Inspection of a specific transaction service TS_i within the TSenvironment will also be possible. We do however model a modification of TS_i as a new service TS_{i+1} independently deployed in the TSenvironment. The original service TS_i is kept unchanged so that it can continue to manage active transactions and serve new transactions requiring the properties offered by TS_i.

2.2   Architecture for an Adaptive Transaction Service Environment

The TSenvironment includes a number of transaction services, that may be concurrently used according to the needs of the executing transaction, and a transaction service manager. The *transaction service manager (TSmanager)* controls transaction service deployment and modification, and guarantees consistent use of different transaction services. A *transaction service* is seen as a self-contained software component that is independently developed and delivered to a TSenvironment. A transaction service component may be composed of a number of smaller components representing well defined tasks within a transaction service, for instance recovery, lock and resource management. The TSenvironment architecture, also described in [7], is depicted in figure 1.

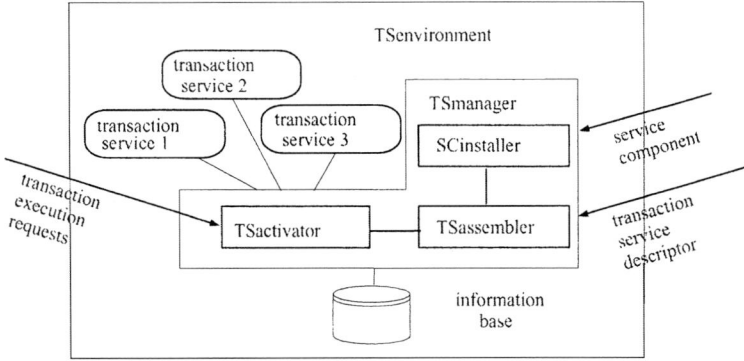

Fig. 1. Architecture for the TSenvironment

Component Deployment

The TSmanager handles deployment of components, both transaction service components and task components, through a *Service Component Installer (SCinstaller)* that receives components and registers them in the TSenvironment. The SCinstaller also stores information about the components as provided in accompanying component descriptors. The component designer provides the component descriptor that holds all relevant information about the component, for instance transaction management properties and conditions for using the component. The SCinstaller also handles revocation of components that are no longer needed in the TSenvironment.

Service Assembly

A component deployed in the TSenvironment is either a transaction service or a task that must be assembled with other tasks to form a complete service. In the last case the *Transaction Service Assembler (TSassembler)* constructs the transaction service based on information from the service descriptor. The service descriptor, provided by a transaction service designer, must include information on the transactional properties guaranteed by the service, which components the service is composed of, and additional software needed for binding the components together. The service designer must also give guarantees concerning correctness of the described transaction service. When a transaction service is available, the TSassembler registers the service in the TSenvironment together with information concerning use of the service (for instance transactional properties).

Service Activation

Traditionally, the request for transaction execution is handled by a transaction service directly. In our environment, a transaction execution request is first handled by the *Transaction Service Activator (TSactivator)*, which *i)* determines the proper transaction service to use, and *ii)* activates the transaction service when use of the service does not violate correctness. These tasks, which are described in the following, are handled by two different components in the TS-activator, the *Transaction Service Detector (TSdetector)* and the *Transaction Service Synchronizer (TSsynchronizer)*, and are seen in figure 2.

Before executing a new transaction, the appropriate transaction service must be determined. The choice of service depend on the input from different sources, such as required transactional properties as seen from the user, available systems resources, and properties of underlying systems. Based on this information, the TSdetector will determine, either automatically or with help from the user, a suitable transaction service from the pool of available services.

The task of the TSsynchronizer is to control that concurrent use of heterogeneous transaction services does not cause inconsistencies. If incompatible transaction services are used concurrently, transaction executions may interfere with each other so that the required transactional properties can no longer be guaranteed. When a requested transaction service safely can start executing, the responsibility for managing the transaction is handed over to the transaction service. The task of the TSsynchronizer is further described in section 4, which presents some algorithms for transaction service synchronization.

2.3   Related Work

While the concept of reflection was originally introduced in the area of programming language design [3], it is now a concept used in different areas to make systems flexible. Reflection is for instance used in operating systems [8], distributed systems [9], middleware [10], and now also in transactional systems [11, 12].

In [11] a Reflective Transaction Framework is described, that implements extended transaction models on top of TP-monitors. The framework uses transaction adapters on the meta level to extend TP-monitor behaviour. The adapters, which include the transaction management logic for an extended model, are given the control over transaction processing at certain transactional events.

[12] describes how Reflective Java can be used to implement a flexible transaction service. It allows application developers to provide application-specific information to a container so that this can be used to customize the transaction service. The framework enables a container to change its functionality by plugging/unplugging its metaobjects, and thus be customized to meet new application requirements or changing environment conditions.

Besides the related work on reflective transaction services, our work also relates to research on dynamic combination and configuration of transactional and middleware systems. The work of [13,14,15,16] recognizes the diversity of systems and their different transactional requirements, and describes approaches to how these diverse needs can be supported. In [13] a formal method to synthesis transactional middleware is specified. The work describes an approach that takes transactional requirements for a given system as input, selects available service components and composes a transactional middleware customized to the needs of the system. [14] argue the necessity to allow both design time and runtime specification of transaction models. Transaction model elements are organized

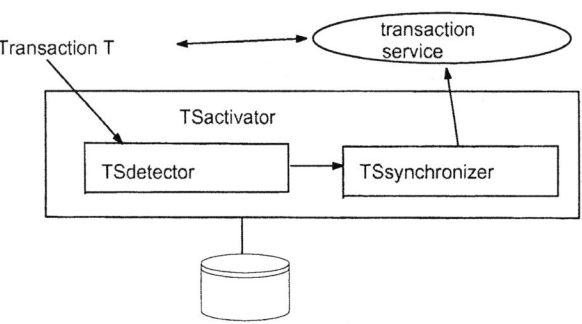

Fig. 2. Transaction service activation manager

such that parts of the specification can be done before transactions are executed, while the remaining parts can be specified during runtime. Runtime specification of transaction executions are done by users. [15] proposes an extension of the transaction concepts in EJB, called Bourgogne transactions, that adds a set of advanced transactional properties allowing some flexibility in transaction executions. In [16] the ACTA framework is used as a tool to support the development and analysis of new extended transaction models. However, implementing a model specified in ACTA is up to the developer.

Our work on a reflective transactional system contrasts previous work on two matters: Firstly, we focus on how to guarantee correctness for the reflective transactional system. The close relationship between different transaction service modules (for instance recovery-, lock- and resource managers), makes it necessary to re-evaluate correctness of the transaction service if the internals of the service is manipulated. Secondly, we allow an application to have a number of concurrently active transaction services, and must guarantee consistent use of possibly incompatible services.

3   Transaction Service Model

3.1   Transaction Services

The TSenvironment may include a number of transaction services, each represented as a component, possibly constructed of components. A transaction service is designed outside the TSenvironment by some transaction service designer, and is a self-contained service managing transactions according to a set of guaranteed transactional properties. The service designer provides either a complete implementation of the service or a description of how to construct the service based on known components.

An important characteristic of a transaction service TS_i is the *set of transactional properties* P_i guaranteed by TS_i. For a traditional transaction service this would typically be the ACID properties. An advanced service would guarantee different properties, such as semantic atomicity or semantic consistency, or an extended set of properties. See [1] for a description of different types of transaction models.

Another characteristic of TS_i, is the *set of components*, C_i, of which the service is composed. All required components in C_i are identified by the service designer, which also designs an *infrastructure* (or framework) for the components and describe how they are assembled to a transaction service. An infrastructure could typically be software provided by the service designer that facilitates the combination of the components into the desired service.

Each transaction service has an associated *transaction service descriptor* that includes all relevant information about the service. The descriptor serves as an agreement that defines the behaviour of the transaction service and describes how to interact with it. The service descriptor includes information on *i)* how *transaction management* is performed, such as transactional properties, underlying transaction model and transaction management protocols, *ii) composition* of the transaction service, i.e. components and infrastructure for composing the service are identified, *iii) conditions* for using the service and *compatibility* to other transaction services.

As a transaction service is designed to guarantee correct transaction executions, is it of vital importance that the transaction service itself performs correctly. The designer of transaction service TS_i will thus be responsible for guaranteeing the correctness of TS_i.

We define transaction service correctness as follows:

Transaction Service Correctness: A transaction service TS_i with announced properties P_i is correct if every transaction managed by TS_i is given transactional properties P_i.

Properties of a transaction service can be modified by adding and/or removing components. This will in effect give a new transaction service with new properties. Service correctness must be guaranteed for each modification. As an example, assume a correct transaction service TS_i designed of components C_i. After a modification, transaction service TS_j with properties P_j may be composed of a subset of C_i, i.e. $C_j \subset C_i$. TS_j is a correct service providing that correctness of TS_j is guaranteed according to properties P_j. A correct service is in the following also denoted a *complete service*.

A *task component* typically implements a well defined part of a transaction service, such as commit or recovery management. Components are deployed in the TSenvironment, and have an associated descriptor that include all relevant information about the component. A task component may potentially be used in a number of services. If a component in the TSenvironment is not part of a complete transaction service, the transaction management provided by the component is not available for use by any transaction.

3.2   Distributed Transaction Service Architecture

Applications often require concurrent access to distributed data shared among multiple nodes. Global transactions may thus execute over a number of nodes, accessing data from different resources. A transaction service should maintain integrity of data in situations where a number of nodes are issuing concurrent global transactions.

A typical transaction service architecture includes a transaction manager (TM) and a resource manager (RM) for each data source. TMs manage global transactions, coordinate the decision to commit or abort them, and coordinate failure recovery. The TM will, with help from RMs in different nodes, preserve transaction properties. An RM manages persistent and stable data storage system of a single node, and participates in commit and recovery protocols.

This basic architecture represents the essential features in several transaction models and services, including the X/OPEN Distributed Transaction Processing Model from the Open Group [17], OTS (Object Transaction Service) from OMG [18], and JTS (Java Transaction Service) [19]. The architecture describes a traditional transaction processing environment where only a single set of transactional properties is available. To allow an adaptable transactional system supporting a variety of transactional properties, a modified architecture is needed to allow concurrently active transaction services.

In a new, flexible transaction service architecture, each node may have a number of TMs, one for each available transaction service. Each node may also have a number of RMs, that can manage the resource differently.

A transaction service TS_i includes a transaction manager TM_i and a number of matching RMs. We say that a resource manager RM_j matches TM_i if it can participate in TM_i's commit and abort protocols, and if TM_i and RM_j together preserve the transactional properties of TS_i. We assume that one RM may support different TMs, and that one TM may well be supported by different RMs. Generally, a transaction service can be described by the tuple $TS_i = (TM_i, \{RM_1, \ldots, RM_n\})$, where TM_i is the TM managing transactions according to rules in TS_i, and $\{RM_1, \ldots, RM_n\}$ are different matching RMs.

To execute a global transaction T from node N using transaction service TS_i, node N must have transaction manager TM_i available and every subordinate node must have a matching RM. When activating service TS_i for the execution of T, this implies activating TS_i at a number of nodes, both node N, that initiate and coordinate the execution of T, and every subordinate node on which sub-transactions of T will be executed.

3.3   Transaction Service Compatibility

A TSenvironment may have a number of available transaction services, which are either active or inactive. An *active service* is currently in use by at least one transaction. An *inactive service* represents a transaction service that is available, but is currently not managing any transaction. The TSsynchronizer is responsible for controlling activation of transaction services.

To enable transaction service synchronization, the TSenvironment holds information about *transaction service compatibility*. Two services, TS_i and TS_j, are *incompatible* if the service properties of either one of them can not be guaranteed if they are both active at the same time. *Compatible* transaction services do not interfere with each other and can thus be concurrently active. The TSsynchronizer controls activation of transaction services so that incompatible services do not cause inconsistencies.

Determining transaction service compatibility requires detailed knowledge of transaction services and is therefore the task of transaction service designers. To automatically reason about service compatibility, properties for determining compatibility must be identified and the service designer must include all necessary information in the service descriptor. If uncertainty exist about service compatibility, one could either consult a human transaction service designer or assume incompatibility.

In the following examples we briefly describe different types of transaction services and indicate how services are related with regard to compatibility. This does, however, only give an indication of the facts. To determine compatibility for two specific services, the rules (or protocols) for transaction management in both services must be thoroughly compared. If conflicting rules are used, the services are incompatible.

ACID Transactions: Assume a TSenvironment with a set of available transaction services $\mathcal{TS} = \{TS_1, \ldots, TS_n\}$, where TS_1 is a transaction service, as described in [20], guaranteeing ACID properties and using a two-phase commit protocol to reach an agreement with underlying systems. TS_2 is a service following an advanced transaction model, such as [21], allowing sub-transactions to commit independently and partial results of the transaction to be exposed. According to the rules in TS_1, exposing partial results of a transaction may cause inconsistencies and is therefore disallowed. Since TS_1 and TS_2 follow conflicting rules for transaction executions, TS_1 and TS_2 are incompatible and can not be concurrently active.

Flexible Transactions: A third transaction service, TS_3, supports flexible transaction executions by allowing execution of alternative sub-transactions in case of primary sub-transaction failure [22]. This service represents an extension of TS_2, and the transaction management rules of TS_3 and TS_2 are not conflicting. TS_2 and TS_3 are thus compatible and can be concurrently active, while TS_1 and TS_3 are incompatible.

Mobile Transactions: A mobile transaction service, TS_4, such as Kangaroo transactions [23], will typically divide the network into different zones, each with one base station controlling transaction executions. Transaction management is propagated from base station to base station as the device initiating the transaction moves. A mobile transaction manager in each base station provides mobility. The global database system is not aware of the mobile transaction managers and the mobility. A mobile transaction service as sketched here may not conflict with TS_2 and TS_3, while TS_1 is a conflicting service.

Real-Time Constraints: Transactions with real-time constraints may in some services be assigned priorities, such as 'earliest deadline first' or 'minimum slack first' [24], and are scheduled according to their priority. Using for instance the 'earliest deadline first' rule for some transactions, while other transactions follow a different strategy, may not give the intended real-time support. A real-time transaction service, TS_5, will thus be incompatible with services without real-time guarantees, such as TS_1 or TS_2. Two real-time transaction services using different priority rules may also be incompatible.

4   Services Synchronization

When allowing concurrent use of different and possibly incompatible services, service synchronization is needed to guarantee consistency. We will in this section present three simple transaction service synchronization algorithms that may be used by the TSsynchronizer to control activation of transaction services. When designing these algorithms we assume centralized control over service activation. In a distributed environment this means that the TSsynchronizer is allowed to control activation of transaction services for a collection of cooperating nodes.

This approach may be useful in environments where the nodes are, at least to some extent, controlled by a central authority, for instance nodes within a company or organization.

4.1 Basic Transaction Service Synchronization Algorithm

The *Basic transaction service synchronization (BasicTSS) algorithm* controls activation of a transaction service requested by a single transaction. Assuming transaction T requires service TS_i, the algorithm controls service activation according to the following rules: If transaction service TS_i is already active or if TS_i is not incompatible with currently active transactions, TS_i is activated (if necessary) and immediately given responsibility over T. Execution of T can then be started and managed according to the rules in TS_i. If incompatible services are currently active, activation of TS_i, and consequently also execution of T, is postponed until TS_i can safely execute.

The BasicTSS algorithm uses a set, *ActiveTS*, that includes every currently active transaction service; and a function, $InCompatible(TS_i, ActiveTS)$, that checks compatibility between transaction service TS_i and the services in *ActiveTS*. The function returns a set of active services all incompatible with TS_i. If TS_i is compatible with every active service, the set is empty.

```
Synch_Trans_Service(TS_i, T):
  If TS_i ∈ ActiveTS Then
    Execute_Transaction(T, TS_i)
  Else If TS_i ∉ ActiveTS AND InCompatible(TS_i,ActiveTS) = ∅ Then
    ActiveTS = ActiveTS ⋃ TS_i
    Execute_Transaction(T, TS_i)
  Else If TS_i ∉ ActiveTS AND InCompatible(TS_i,ActiveTS) ≠ ∅ Then
    Wait until InCompatible(TS_i,ActiveTS) = ∅
    ActiveTS = ActiveTS ⋃ TS_i
    Execute_Transaction(T, TS_i)

Execute_Transaction(T, TS_i):
  UseOfService(TS_i) = UseOfService(TS_i) + 1
  Control of T is given to TS_i
```

To keep track of currently active transaction services, the BasicTSS algorithm register for each transaction service, the number of transactions currently controlled by this service. The algorithm use simply a $UseOfService$ count for each service. $UseOfService$ is increased by one for each transaction passed to the service for execution. When a transaction terminates, $UseOfService$ is decreased by one. When $UseOfService$ for a service TS_i equals 0, TS_i is returned to an inactive state.

```
at Termination of T:
  UseOfService(TS_i) = UseOfService(TS_i) - 1
  If UseOfService(TS_i) = 0 Then
    ActiveTS = ActiveTS - TS_i
```

A problem with this approach is that a transaction T requesting a service incompatible with the currently active services, can be forced to wait for a very long time. Every transaction using active services will be allowed to proceed and may prolong the waiting time for T. Assume transaction T requesting service TS_i where $InCompatible(TS_i, ActiveTS) = A$, i.e. A is a set of transaction service incompatible with TS_i. The BasicTSS algorithm let T wait until the services in A are no longer active, i.e. until every transaction controlled by services in A has completed and the services are returned to an inactive state. However, while T is waiting, new transactions requesting services in A may be started and are allowed to execute. The waiting time for T may therefore be prolonged as new transactions are started, and T may in extreme cases never be allowed to start. One solution to the above problem is described in the following algorithm, where the TSsynchronizer guarantees that a requested transaction service will be activated.

4.2   Alternate Transaction Service Synchronization Algorithm

The *Alternate transaction service synchronization (AlternateTSS) algorithm* is a modification of the BasicTSS algorithm, which guarantees that requested transaction services will be activated. To describe this approach, we continue the above example where transaction T requests service TS_i which is incompatible with active services, i.e. $InCompatible(TS_i, ActiveTS) = A$. To guarantee that T will be executed, the AlternateTSS algorithm blocks the transaction services in A for new transactions. This means that new transactions requesting services in A must wait, while currently executing transactions controlled by services in A are allowed to complete. We say that the services in A are *suspended*. When a suspended transaction service TS is returned to an inactive state, the algorithm will activate every service waiting for TS to finish. Suspension on TS will not end until every service waiting for TS has been activated.

The AlternateTSS algorithm uses the boolean *Suspend(TS)* to indicate suspension of a service TS; and a set, *RequestedTS*, to hold every service for which activation is requested but incompatible services are still active. When a new service TS_i is included in the set *RequestedTS*, it also suspends every service in $InCompatible(TS_i, ActiveTS)$. TS_i will be activated when $InCompatible(TS_i, ActiveTS) = \emptyset$. The modified *Synch_Trans_Service* module will postpone execution of every transaction requesting a suspended service.

If a transaction can not be immediately activated, it is put in a waiting queue for the required service, i.e. transaction T requesting use of TS_i enters the queue $WaitingQ(TS_i)$. When TS_i is activated, the service is given control over every transaction in $WaitingQ(TS_i)$. When activating a service TS, the algorithm checks whether TS is incompatible with any requested service, i.e. services in *RequestedTS*. If incompatibility is found, TS is suspended after receiving management responsibility over every transaction in $WaitingQ(TS_i)$. This check is done in the module *Check_Suspension(TS)*.

```
Synch_Trans_Service(TSᵢ,T):
  If Suspend(TSᵢ) Then
    Add T to WaitingQ(TSᵢ)
  Else If TSᵢ ∈ ActiveTS Then
    Execute_Transaction(T,TSᵢ)
  Else If TSᵢ ∉ ActiveTS AND InCompatible(TSᵢ,ActiveTS) = ∅ Then
    ActiveTS = ActiveTS ⋃ TSᵢ
    Execute_Transaction(T,TSᵢ)
  Else If TSᵢ ∉ ActiveTS AND InCompatible(TSᵢ,ActiveTS) ≠ ∅ Then
    Add T to WaitingQ(TSᵢ)
    If TSᵢ ∉ RequestedTS Then
      Request_Use_Of_Service(TSᵢ)

Execute_Transaction(T,TSᵢ):
  UseOfService(TSᵢ) = UseOfService(TSᵢ) + 1
  Control of T is given to TSᵢ
  Check_Suspension(TSᵢ)

Request_Use_Of_Service(TSᵢ):
  RequestedTS = RequestedTS ⋃ TSᵢ
  For ∀ TS | TS ∈ InCompatible(TSᵢ,ActiveTS) do
    Suspend(TS) = true

Check_Suspension(TSᵢ):
  If InCompatible(TSᵢ,RequestedTS) ≠ ∅ Then
    Suspend(TSᵢ) = true
```

Terminating a transaction may result in deactivation of a transaction service. When deactivating a suspended service TS, requested services, incompatible with TS, may possibly be activated, and suspension of TS may subsequently be ended. Activation of requested services is handled by the *Requested_Service_Activation* module, while the *Resume_Service* module ends service suspension.

```
at Termination of T:
  UseOfService(TSᵢ) = UseOfService(TSᵢ) - 1
  If UseOfService(TSᵢ) = 0 Then
    ActiveTS = ActiveTS - TSᵢ
    If Suspend(TSᵢ) Then
      Requested_Service_Activation

Requested_Service_Activation:
  For ∀ TS | TS ∈ RequestedTS AND InCompatible(TS,ActiveTS) = ∅
    do
    ActiveTS = ActiveTS ⋃ TS
    UseOfService(TS) = number of T in WaitingQ(TS)
    TS is given control over every T in WaitingQ(TS)
    RequestedTS = RequestedTS - TS
    Check_Suspension(TS)
    Resume_Service

Resume_Service:
  For ∀ TS | Suspend(TS) AND TS ∉ ActiveTS AND
    InCompatible(TS,RequestedTS) = ∅ do
    Suspend(TS) = false
    If WaitingQ(TS) ≠ empty Then
      Request_Use_Of_Service(TS)
```

4.3   Default Transaction Service Activation Algorithm

The *Default transaction service activation (DefaultTSS) algorithm* allows definition of a default transaction service. As the default service is given priority
over other services, a default service is typically useful if a majority of transactions need the same service, or if a particularly important service should always
be available. The default service is always kept active (i.e. included in the set
ActiveTS) even if it does not control any executing transactions, and is thus
always ready to accept management responsibilities for new transactions. The
TSsynchronizer will also, when a default service is defined, allow multiple active
transaction services.

The below algorithm allows a default service to be activated, changed and
deactivated. Depending on the ChangeMode used in the algorithm, the default
service can either be used immediately or there will be a graceful activation of the
new default service. Choosing an immediate activation will result in the abort of
every transaction using incompatible services. With graceful activation, the new
default service is not available until every incompatible service has completed
currently executing transactions and is subsequently deactivated. Deactivation
of the default service is handled by the module *Deactivate_Default*.

As the default service is continuously active, incompatible services can not be
activated and are thus unavailable until the default service is changed. Services
incompatible with the default service, *DefaultTS*, are put into *quarantine* at
the time when *DefaultTS* is requested, and will stay there until the default
service is changed or deactivated. To quarantine a service means that the service
can not be activated until the quarantine is ended. If an active service is put
into quarantine, concurrently executed transactions are allowed to finish before
the service is deactivated. We use the set *Quarantine* to represent every service
in quarantine, i.e. every $TS \in Incompatible(DefaultTS, AllTS)$, where $AllTS$
represents every service available in the TSenvironment.

```
Change_Default_Service(NewTS, ChangeMode):
  Quarantine = Incompatible (NewTS, AllTS)
  If NewTS ∈ ActiveTS
    If UseOfService(DefaultTS) = 0
      ActiveTS = ActiveTS - DefaultTS
    DefaultTS = NewTS
  Else If NewTS ∉ ActiveTS AND InCompatible(NewTS, ActiveTS) = ∅
    Activate_Default(NewTS)
  Else If NewTS ∉ ActiveTS AND InCompatible(NewTS, ActiveTS)
    ≠ ∅
    If ChangeMode = graceful
      Wait until InCompatible(NewTS, ActiveTS) = ∅
      Activate_Default(NewTS)
    Else If ChangeMode = immediate
      Abort every transaction T using
          TS ∈ InCompatible(NewTS, ActiveTS)
      Activate_Default(NewTS)
```

Activate_Default(NewTS):
```
ActiveTS = ActiveTS ⋃ NewTS
If UseOfService(DefaultTS) = 0
    ActiveTS = ActiveTS - DefaultTS
DefaultTS = NewTS
```

Deactivate_Default:
```
If UseOfService(DefaultTS) = 0
    ActiveTS = ActiveTS - DefaultTS
DefaultTS = ' '
Quarantine = ∅
```

When using a default service, the *Synch_Trans_Service* module from the BasicTSS algorithm must be reconsidered. We now assume that every service incompatible with DefaultTS is in *Quarantine*, and cannot be used by any transaction. If transaction service TS_i is in *Quarantine*, it can not be activated and an error report is returned to the application. Transaction T must either be tried re-executed with a different transaction service, or the default service must be changed or deactivated. Also at termination of T a minor modification is needed since the default service should not be deactivated when no transactions are using the service.

Synch_Trans_Service(TS_i, T):
```
If TSᵢ ∈ Quarantine Then
    Service TSᵢ is incompatible with the Default service and can
    not be accepted.
    Transaction T is returned to the application with an error
    report
Else If TSᵢ ∈ ActiveTS
    UseOfService(TSᵢ) = UseOfService(TSᵢ) + 1
    Control of T is given to TSᵢ
Else If InCompatible(TSᵢ,ActiveTS) = ∅
    Activate_Service(TSᵢ,T)
Else If DefaultTS ∉ InCompatible(TSᵢ,ActiveTS)
    Wait until InCompatible(TSᵢ,ActiveTS) = ∅
    Activate_Service(TSᵢ,T)
```

at Termination of T:
```
UseOfService(TSᵢ) = UseOfService(TSᵢ) - 1
If UseOfService(TSᵢ) = 0 AND TSᵢ ≠ DefaultTS Then
    ActiveTS = ActiveTS - TSᵢ
```

4.4   Discussion

We have presented three algorithms that show how the TSsynchronizer can control concurrent use of different services. BasicTSS and AlternateTSS are alternative synchronization algorithms that activate a transaction service when requested for the execution of a transaction, while the DefaultTSS algorithm allows activation of a default transaction service. Transaction service synchronization is an important part of a flexible transactional environment where different services can be deployed and where a transaction can be controlled by the service guaranteeing the most suited transactional properties.

Not surprisingly, synchronizing incompatible services represents the challenging part of these algorithms. Incompatible transaction services control transaction executions according to conflicting rules, and must thus be synchronized in order to avoid inconsistencies. In the above algorithms, incompatible services are not allowed to be concurrently active. When requesting an inactive service TS_i, incompatible active services must first be returned to an inactive state before TS_i can be activated. Such a switch between services may force transactions either to postpone their execution or abort, and will inevitably effect transaction response time and system throughput.

We need to test our service synchronization algorithms to *i)* evaluate the flexibility achieved by allowing concurrent transaction services, and to *ii)* see how response time and throughput are effected. Depending on the outcome of this, we may need to reconsider our algorithms in order to improve functionality and, if necessary, reduce negative effects on system performance. In the future, the following issues may be addressed.

- To increase concurrency among transaction services and reduce the number of switches between services, we will consider alternative algorithms where synchronization of incompatible services is done differently. We may for instance allow incompatible services to be concurrently active if they control transactions operating on different underlying systems.
- It may further be necessary or beneficial to change transaction service for an executing transaction. This may be triggered by changes in the required execution guarantees, for instance caused by changes in available resources or an unexpected transaction execution progress (such as a lengthy transaction execution). To allow this form of flexibility, new synchronization algorithms are needed.
- For the algorithms described in this paper, we assume centralized control over service activation. In environments where the cooperating nodes are highly autonomous, we need a different approach. Cooperating nodes may for instance use negotiation to agree on the activation of a specific transaction service.

Our work on algorithms for the TSsynchronizer has shown that synchronization of transaction services can be done differently. In this paper we have presented three rather simple algorithms, that each could be used by the TSsynchronizer. The choice of algorithm will depend on requested behaviour for the TSsynchronizer, which again may depend on the properties of the application. This indicates that the behaviour of the TSsynchronizer should be flexible, and may vary between applications and possibly also during the lifetime of an application. The requirement for TSsynchronizer flexibility suggests that the behaviour of the TSsynchronizer may itself be the subject of reflection. This will be further investigated.

5   Conclusion

To support the needs for a highly flexible transaction service, we have presented a transaction service framework, called *TSenvironment*, in which different transaction services can be deployed, and from where a suitable transaction service can be chosen for the execution of a transaction. As a component of this framework, we have described a *transaction service manager* that *i)* allows deployment of new or modified transaction services and *ii)* controls concurrent use of available services. Varying and dynamically changing transactional requirements within the application will thus be supported. We have also presented different algorithms for transaction service synchronization. Service synchronization is needed to guarantee correctness when transaction services with different transactional properties are concurrently active.

In section 4.4, we described our plans regarding further work on service synchronization. Additionally, the work towards a reflective transactional system involves a number of issues that will be addressed in future work of this project. The functionality of the TSmanager must be further studied, including component deployment, service specification and assembly, and inspection and modification of behaviour in the TSenvironement.

To facilitate support for adaptive transactional executions in middleware systems, we plan to incorporate the TSenvironment framework in a middleware platform. At the current stage of the project, we find the OpenORB platform [25] suited for this purpose. OpenORB is a reflective, component-based middleware platform composed of a number of interacting component frameworks supporting different services, such as communication and resource management. Our adaptive TSenvironment framework may be included as a new component framework within OpenORB. The work of incorporating the TSenvironment framework in the OpenORB platform is currently under way.

References

1. Ramamritham, K. and Chrysanthis, P.K. Executive briefing: Advances in concurrency control and transaction processing, IEEE Computer Society Press, Los Alamitos, California, 1997.
2. Maes, P., Concepts and Experiments in Computational Reflection, in Proceedings of OOPSLA'87, pp. 147–155, ACM, October 1987.
3. Smith, B.C., Procedural Reflection in Programming Languages, PhD Thesis, MIT, MIT Computer Science Technical Report 272, Cambridge, Mass., 1982.
4. Szyperski, C., Component Software: Beyond Object-Oriented Programming, Addison-Wesley, 1998.
5. Andersen, A., Blair, G., Goebel, V., Karlsen, R., Stabell-Kulø, T., Yu, W., Arctic Beans, Configurable and Re-configurable Enterprise Component Architectures, IFIP/ACM International Conference on Distributed Systems Platforms, Middleware 2001, Heidelberg, Germany, November 12–16, 2001. Also IEEE Distributed Systems Online, Volume 2, No. 7, 2001, http://dsonline.computer.org.
6. Kiczales, G., des Rivieres, J., Bobrow, D., The Art of the Metaobject Protocol, MIT Press, 1991.

7. Karlsen, R., Jakobsen, A.B., Transaction Service Management - An approach towards a reflective transactional service, Proc. of the 2nd Workshop on Reflective and Adaptive Middleware, Rio de Janeiro, Brazil, 2003.

8. Yokote, Y., The Apertos Reflective Operating System: The Concept and Its Implementation, in Proc. of the Conference on Object-Oriented Programming Systems, Languages, and Applications (OOPSLA), October 1992.

9. Stroud, R., Transparency and reflection in Distributed Systems, ACM Operating Systems Review, 22(2), April 1993.

10. Blair, G., Coulson, G., Robin, P., Papathomas, M., An Architecture for Next Generation Middleware, Proc. of the IFIP International Conference on Distributed Systems Platforms and Open Distributed Processing: Middleware'98, The Lake District, U.K., 15–18 September 1998.

11. Barga, R., Pu, C., Reflection on a Legacy Transaction Processing Monitor, in Proc. of the Reflection'96 conference, San Francisco, California, April 1996.

12. Wu, Z. Reflective Java and A Reflective Component-Based Transaction Architecture, OOPSLA workshop, 1998.

13. Zarras, A., Issarny, V., A Framework for Systematic Synthesis of Transactional Middleware, in Porc. of Middleware'98, IFIP, Chapman-Hall, September, 1998.

14. Ramampiaro, H., Nygård, M., CAGISTrans: Providing Adaptable Transactional Support for Cooperative Work, in Proc. of the 6th INFORMS conference on Information Systems and Technology (CIST2001), Florida, 2001.

15. Prochazka, M., Advanced Transactions in Enterprise JavaBeans, in Lecture Notes in Computer Science 1999, Springer Verlag, 2000.

16. Chrysanthis, P., Ramamritham, K., Synthesis of Extended Transaction Models Using ACTA, ACM Transactions on Database Systems, 19(3), 1994.

17. The Open Group, Distributed Transaction Processing: Reference Model, Version 3, 1996.

18. OMG, Object Transaction Service specification, v1.2, OMG White Paper, 2002.

19. Sun Microsystems Inc., Java Transaction Service (JTS), Version 1.0, 1999.

20. Lampson, B.W., Atomic Transactions, in Distributed Systems: Architecture and Implementation - An Advanced Course, Lecture notes in Computer Science, Vol. 105, B.W. Lampson (ed), Springer-Verlag, New York, 1981.

21. Garcia-Molina, H., Salem, K., SAGAS, Proc. of ACM SIGMOD International Conference on Management of Data, ACM Press, New York, 1987.

22. Elmagarmid, A.K., et.al., A Multidatabase Transaction Model for InterBase, Proc. of International Conference on Very Large Databases, 1990.

23. Dunham, M.H., Helal, A., Balakrishnan, s., A Mobile Transaction Model that Captures Both the Data and Movement Behaviour, Mobile Networks and Applications, vol. 2, 1997.

24. Abbott, R.J., Garcia-Molina, H., Scheduling real-time transactions: a performance evaluation, ACM Transactions on Database Systems, Vol. 17, No. 3, 1992.

25. Blair, G.S., et. al., The Design and Implementation of Open ORB version 2, IEEE Distributed Systems Online Journal, vol. 2, No. 6, 2001.

From Distributed Objects to Hierarchical Grid Components

Françoise Baude, Denis Caromel, and Matthieu Morel

INRIA Sophia Antipolis, CNRS - I3S - Univ. Nice Sophia-Antipolis
2004, Route des Lucioles, BP 93
F-06902 Sophia-Antipolis Cedex - France
{Francoise.Baude,Denis.Caromel,Matthieu.Morel}@sophia.inria.fr

Abstract. We propose a parallel and distributed component framework for building Grid applications, adapted to the hierarchical, highly distributed, highly heterogeneous nature of Grids. This framework is based on ProActive, a middleware (programming model and environment) for object oriented parallel, mobile, and distributed computing. We have extended ProActive by implementing a hierarchical and dynamic component model, named Fractal, so as to master the complexity of composition, deployment, re-usability, and efficiency of grid applications. This defines a concept of Grid components, that can be parallel, made of several activities, and distributed. These components communicate using typed one-to-one or collective invocations.

Keywords: Active objects, components, hierarchical components, grid computing, deployment, dynamic configuration, group communications, ADL.

1 Introduction

In this article, we present a contribution to the problem of software reuse and integration for distributed and parallel object-oriented applications. We especially target grid-computing. Our approach takes the form of a programming and deployment framework featuring parallel, mobile and distributed components, so our application domains also target mobile and ubiquitous distributed computing on the Internet (where high performance, high availability, ease of use, etc., are of importance).

For Grid applications development, there is indeed a need also to smoothly, seamlessly and dynamically integrate and deploy autonomous software, and for this provide a *glue* in the form of a software bus. In this sense, we essentially address the second group of Grid programmers such as defined in [1]: first group of users are end users who program pre-packaged Grid applications by using a simple graphical or Web interface; the second group of grid programmers are those that know how to build Grid applications by composing them from existing application "components"; the third group consists of the researchers that build the individual components.

R. Meersman et al. (Eds.): CoopIS/DOA/ODBASE 2003, LNCS 2888, pp. 1226–1242, 2003.
© Springer-Verlag Berlin Heidelberg 2003

We share the goal of providing a component-based high-performance computing solution with several projects such as: CCA [1] with the CCAT/XCAT toolkit [2] and Ccaffeine framework, Parallel CORBA objects [3] and GridCCM [4]. But, to our knowledge, our contribution is the first framework featuring *hierarchical* distributed components. This clearly helps in mastering the complexity of composition, deployment, re-usability required when programming and running large-scale distributed applications.

We propose a parallel and distributed component framework for building meta-computing applications, that we think is well adapted to the hierarchical, highly distributed, highly heterogeneous nature of grid-computing. This framework is based on ProActive, a Java-based middleware (programming model and environment) for object oriented parallel, mobile and distributed computing. ProActive has proven to be relevant for grid computing [5] especially due to its deployment and monitoring aspects [6] and its efficient and typed collective communications [7]. We have succeeded in defining a component model for ProActive, with the implementation of the Fractal component model [8,9], mainly taking advantage of its hierarchical approach to component programming.

Fractal is a general software composition model, implemented as a framework that supports component-based programming, including hierarchical components (type) definition, configuration, composition and administration. Fractal is an appropriate basis for the construction of highly flexible, highly dynamic, heterogeneous distributed environments. Indeed, a system administrator, a system integrator or an application developer may need to dynamically construct a system or service out of existing components, whether in response to failures, as part of the continuous evolution of a running system, or just to introduce new applications in a running system (a direct generalization of the dynamic binding used in standard distributed client-server applications). Nevertheless, the requirements raised by distributed environments are not specifically addressed by the Fractal model. Not because this is not an issue, but, because, according to the Fractal specification, a primitive or hierarchical fractal component *may be* a parallel and distributed software. So, our work also yields to a new implementation of the Fractal model that explicitly provides parallel and distributed Fractal components.

The main achievement of this work is to design and implement a concept of *Grid Components*. Grid components are recursively formed of either sequential, parallel and/or distributed sub-components, that may wrap legacy code if needed, that may be deployed but further reconfigured and moved – for example to tackle fault-tolerance, load-balancing, adaptability to changing environmental conditions.

Below is a typical scenario illustrating the usefulness of our work. Assume a complex grid software be formed of several services, say of other software (a parallel and distributed solver, a graphical 3D renderer, etc). The design of such a software is very much simplified if it can be considered as a hierarchical composition (recursive assembly and binding): the solver is itself a component composed of several components, each encompassing a piece of the computation; the whole software is seen as a single component formed of the solver and the renderer. From the outside, the usage of this software is as simple as invoking a functional service of a component (e.g. call *solve-and-render*). Once deployed and running on a grid, assume that due to load balancing purposes, this software needs to be relocated. Some of the on-going computations may just be moved (the solver for instance), alas others depending on specific peripherals that may not be present at the new location (the renderer for instance) may be terminated and replaced by a new instance adapted to the target environment and offering the same service. As the solver is itself a hierarchical component formed of several sub-components, each encompassing an activity, we trigger the migration of the solver as a whole, without having to explicitly move each of its sub-components, while references towards mobile components remain valid. And once the new graphical renderer is launched, we re-bind the software, so as it now uses this new instance.

This paper is organized as follows: after an introduction on parallel and distributed programming with ProActive, and on the Fractal component model, the principles and design of the proposed parallel and distributed component model are presented. The implementation and an example are described in section 4, while section 5 makes a comparison with related work before concluding.

2   Context

2.1   Distribution, Parallelism, Mobility, and Deployment with ProActive

The ProActive middleware is a 100% Java library (LGPL) [10] aiming to achieve seamless programming for concurrent, parallel, distributed and mobile computing. The main features regarding the programming model are:

- a uniform *active object* programming pattern
- remotely accessible objects, via method invocation
- asynchronous communications with automatic synchronization (automatic futures for results of remote method calls). Note that asynchronicity enables to use one-way calls for transmitting events.
- group communications, which enable to trigger method calls on a distributed group of active objects of the same compatible type, with a dynamic generation of groups of results. It has been shown in [7] that this group communication mechanism, plus a few synchronization operations (WaitAll, WaitOne, etc), provides quite similar patterns for collective operations such as those available in e.g. MPI, but in a language centric approach. Here is an example:

```
//Object 'a' of class A is an active remote object
V v = a.foo(param);
// remotely calls foo on object a

v.bar();
// automatically blocks on v.bar()
// until the result in v gets available.
```

```
// ag is a group of active objects,
// of types compatible with A
V v = ag.foo(param);
// calls foo on each group member
// with some optimisation at serialization time
// V is automatically built as a group of results
v.bar();
// executes as soon as individual results
// of foo calls return
```

– migration (mobile computations): An active object with its pending requests (method calls), its futures, its passive (mandatory non-shared) objects may migrate from JVMs to JVMs. The migration may be initiated from outside through any public method but it is the responsibility of the active object to execute the migration (weak migration). Automatic, transparent (and optimized) forwarding of requests and replies provide location transparency, as remote references towards active mobile objects remain valid.

We are faced with the common difficulties in deployment regarding launching a ProActive application in its environment. We succeed in completely avoid scripting for configuration, getting computing resources, etc. ProActive provides, as a key approach to the deployment problem, an abstraction from the source code such as to gain in flexibility [6] as follows (see figure 8 for an example):

– XML Deployment Descriptors. Active objects are remotely created on JVMs, but *virtual nodes* are manipulated inside the program, instead of URLs of JVMs. The *mapping* of virtual nodes to effective JVMs is managed externally through those descriptors. Descriptors also permit to define how to launch JVMs.
– Interfaces with various protocols: rsh, ssh, LSF, Globus, Jini, RMIregistry enable to effectively launch, register or discover JVMs according to the needs specified in the descriptor.
– Graphical visualization and monitoring of any ongoing ProActive application is possible through a ProActive application called *IC2D* (Interactive Control and Debugging of Distribution). In particular, IC2D enables to migrate executing tasks by a graphical drag-and-drop, and to create additional JVMs.

2.2   The Fractal Component Model

The Fractal component model provides an homogeneous vision of software systems structure with a few but well defined concepts such as component, controller, content, interface, binding. It also exhibits distinguishing features that have proven useful for the present work: it is recursive – components structure is auto-similar at any arbitrary level (hence the name 'Fractal'); it is completely reflexive, i.e., it provides introspection and inter-cession capabilities on components structure. These features allow for a uniform management of both the so-called business and technical components (which is not the case in industrial component frameworks such as EJB [11] or CCM [12] which only deal with business components).

A Fractal component is formed out of two parts: a *controller* and a *content*. The content of a component is composed of (a finite number of) other components, which are under the control of the controller of the enclosing component. This allows for hierarchic components, in the sense that components may be nested at any arbitrary level. Fractal distinguishes *primitive* components (typically associated to a Java class implementing functional services) and *composite* components that only serve to build hierarchies of components, but without implementing themselves functional services.

A component can interact with its environment through *operations* at identified access points, called *interfaces*. As usual, interfaces can be of two sorts: *client* and *server*. A server interface can receive operation invocations (and return operation results of two-way operations), while a client interface emits operations. A *binding* is a connection between components, and more precisely between a client and a server interface. The Fractal model comprises bindings for composite and primitive components. Bindings on client ports of primitive components are typically implemented as language-level bindings (e.g. through type compatible variable affectations of interface references). The type of a binding might be a *collective* one or a *single* one (as default). In case of a collective one, a component may need, for achieving its functional work, to use (thus be bound to) a collection of components, instead of to a single component, all offering the needed interface.

A component controller embodies the control behavior associated with a particular component. Of importance is the following control: suspend (stop) and resume activities of the components in its content. Stopping then resuming is mandatory in order to dynamically change the binding between components or the inclusion of components. The important fact is that all such non-functional calls (stopping, resuming, binding, etc) propagates recursively to each internal component. This prevents the user manually triggering the same call on each sub-sub-...-sub component.

3   From Active Objects to Parallel, Distributed, and Hierarchical Components

3.1   Evaluation of the Needs

A component must be aware of parallelism and distribution as we aim at building a grid-enabled application by hierarchical composition; indeed, we need a glue to couple codes that probably are parallel and distributed codes as they require high performance computing resources. Thus components should be able to encompass more than one activity and be deployed on parallel and distributed infrastructures. Such requirements for a component are summarized by the concept we have named *Grid Component*.

Figure 1 summarizes the three different cases for the structure of a Grid component. For a composite built up as a collection of components providing common services, (fig. 1 c)) *collective communications* are essential, for ease of programming and efficiency purposes.

As general requirements, because we target high performance grid computing, it is very important to efficiently implement point-to-point and group method invocations, manage the deployment complexity of those components distributed all over the grid and possibly debug, monitor and reconfigure those running components – across the world.

3.2   ProActive Components

In the sequel, we describe the component framework we have designed and implemented using both Fractal and ProActive. It enables to couple parallel and distributed codes directly programmed using the Java ProActive library. A synthetic definition of what is a ProActive component is given below.

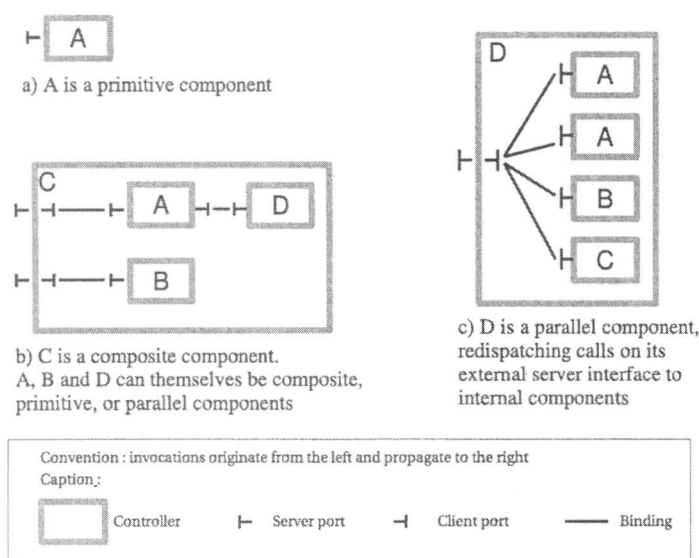

Fig. 1. The various basic architectures for a Grid component

Definition of a ProActive component:

- It is formed from one (or several) Active Objects, executing on one (or several) JVM
- It provides a set of server ports (Java Interfaces)
- It possibly defines a set of client ports (Java attributes if the component is primitive)
- It can be of three different types :
    1. primitive : defined with Java code implementing provided server interfaces, and specifying the mechanism of client bindings.
    2. composite : containing other components.
    3. parallel : also a composite, but redispatching calls to its external server interfaces towards its inner components.
- It communicates with other components through 1-to-1 or group communications.

ProActive components can be configured using:

- an XML descriptor (defining use/provide ports, containment and bindings in an Architecture Description Language style)
- the notion of virtual node, capturing the deployment capacities and needs

---

Deployment of ProActive Components. Components are a way to globally manipulate distributed and running activities, and in this context, obviously, the concept of *virtual node* is a very important abstraction. The additional need regarding the ones already solved by the deployment of active objects, is to be able to *compose virtual nodes*: a composite component is defined through a number of sub-components that already define their proper usage and mapping of virtual nodes. What should the mapping of the composite be ? For instance on fig. 2, when grouping two components in a new composite one, assume that each of the two sub-components, named respectively A and B, requires to be deployed respectively on VNa (further associated to 3 JVMs through the deployment descriptor) and the same for VNb (3 other JVMs). The question is how to define the mapping of the new composite ? Either distributed mapping is required (see fig. 2 a)) meaning that VNa and VNb must respectively launch different JVMs (a total of 6); or, a co-allocated mapping (see fig. 2 b)) where we try to co-locate as much as possible one activity acting on behalf of sub-component A and one activity acting on behalf of sub-component B within the composite C (on the example, only 3 JVMs need to be used).

Composition of virtual nodes is thus a mean to control the distribution of composite components.

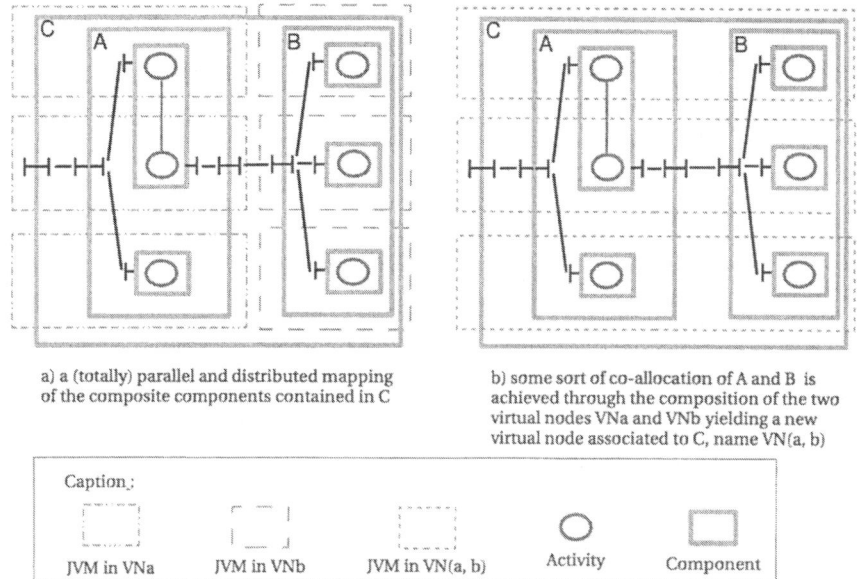

a) a (totally) parallel and distributed mapping of the composite components contained in C

b) some sort of co-allocation of A and B is achieved through the composition of the two virtual nodes VNa and VNb yielding a new virtual node associated to C, name VN(a, b)

Caption :

| JVM in VNa | JVM in VNb | JVM in VN(a, b) | Activity | Component |

Fig. 2. Components versus Activities and JVMs

4   Implementation and Example

Fractal, along with the specification of a component model, also defines an API in Java. There is a reference implementation, called Julia, and we propose a new implementation, based on ProActive (thus providing all services offered by the Fractal library).

4.1   Meta-object Protocol

ProActive is based on a Meta-Object Protocol (MOP)(Figure 3), that allows to add many aspects on top of standard Java objects, such as asynchronism and mobility. Active objects are referenced through stubs, and the communication with them is done in the same manner, would they actually be remote or local.

The same idea is used to manage components: we just add a set of meta-objects in charge of the component aspect (Figure 4). Of course, the standard ProActive stub (that gives a representation of type A on the figure) is not used here, as we manipulate components. In Fractal, a reference on a component is of type ComponentIdentity, so we provide a new stub (that we call representative), of type ComponentIdentity, that references the actual component. All standard Fractal operations can then be performed on the component.

In our implementation, because we make use of the MOP's facilities, all components are constituted of one active object (at least), are they composite or primitive. Of course, if the component is a composite, and if it contains other

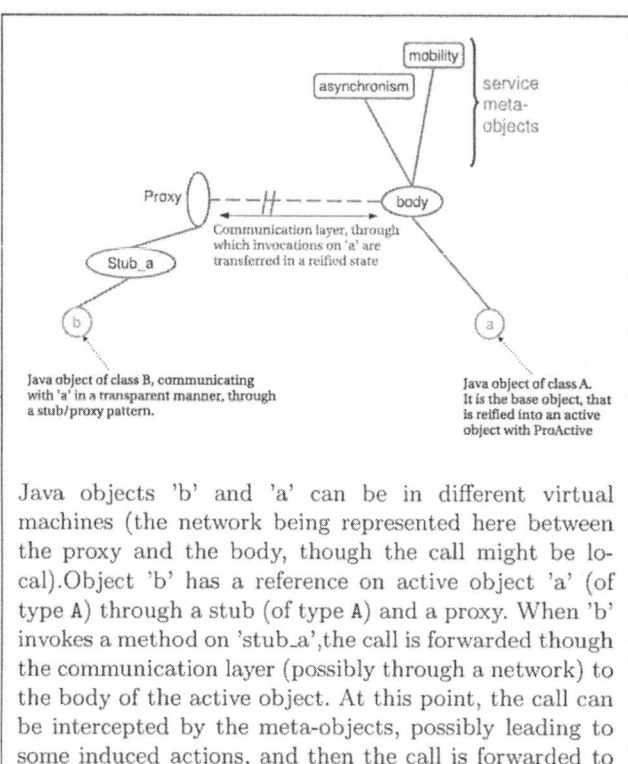

Java objects 'b' and 'a' can be in different virtual machines (the network being represented here between the proxy and the body, though the call might be local).Object 'b' has a reference on active object 'a' (of type A) through a stub (of type A) and a proxy. When 'b' invokes a method on 'stub_a',the call is forwarded though the communication layer (possibly through a network) to the body of the active object. At this point, the call can be intercepted by the meta-objects, possibly leading to some induced actions, and then the call is forwarded to the base object 'a'.

Fig. 3. ProActive's Meta-Object Protocol.

components, then we can say it is constituted of several active objects. Also, if the component is primitive, but the programmer of this component has put some code within it for creating new active objects, the component is again constituted of several active objects.

4.2 Integration within ProActive

To integrate the component management operations into the ProActive library, we just make use of the extensible architecture of the library. This way, components stay fully compatible with standard active objects and as such, inherit from the features active objects have: mobility, security, deployment, etc.

A particular point for the integration of Fractal and ProActive to succeed is the management of component requests besides functional requests. Reified method calls, when they arrive in the body, are directed towards the queue of requests. We assume FIFO is the processing policy. The processing of the requests in the queue is dependent on the nature of this request, and corresponds to the following algorithm :

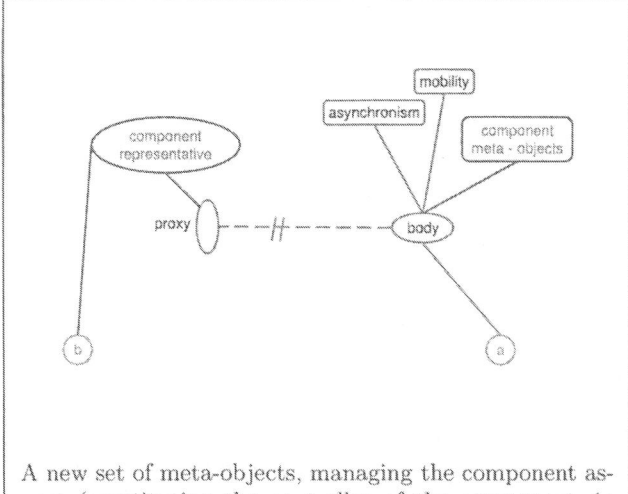

A new set of meta-objects, managing the component aspect (constituting the controller of the component, in the Fractal terminology), is added to the active object 'a', and 'b' can manipulate the component based on 'a' through a specific stub, called *component representative*, of type `ComponentIdentity`. If the component is primitive, 'a' contains the functional code of the component.

Fig. 4. Component meta-objects and component representative.

```
loop
  if componentLifeCycle.isStarted()
      get next request
      // all requests are served
  else if componentLifeCycle.isStopped()
      get next component controller request
      // only component requests are served
  ;
  if gotten request is a comp. life cycle request
      if startFc --> set started = true ;
      if stopFc --> set started = false ;
  ;
;
```

Note that, in the stopped state, only controller requests are served. This means that a standard ProActive call, originating from a standard ProActive stub, will not be processed in the "stopped" state (but it will stay in the queue).

4.3 Collective Ports, Group Communications, and Parallel Components

The implementation of collective ports is based on the ProActive groups API (cf. [7]). According to the Fractal specification, this type of interfaces only has sense on client interface, that would like to be bound to several server interfaces. Besides, one server interface can always be accessed by several client interfaces, the calls being processed sequentially. Specifying a server interface as "collective" wouldn't change its behavior.

The ProActive groups API allowing group communication in a transparent manner, the implementation of the collective interfaces slightly differs from the Fractal specification: instead of creating one new interface with an extended name for each member of the collection, we just use one interface (that is actually a group). Collective bindings are then performed transparently as if they were multiple sequential bindings on the same interface. Using a collective server interface will then imply using the ProActive group API formalism, including the possibility to choose between *scattering* and *broadcasting* of the calls [7]. A feature is that unbinding operations on a collective interface will result in the removal of all the bindings of the collection.

Furthermore, because we target largely distributed and parallel applications, we introduce a new type of component : *parallel components* (Figure 1 c)). These components are composite components, as they encapsulate other components. Their specificity relies in the behavior of their external server interfaces. These interfaces are connectable through a group proxy to the internal components' interfaces of the same type. This means that a call to the parallel component will be dispatched and forwarded to a set of internal components, that will process the requests in a parallel manner (see figure 5 a)).

4.4   Example

We present hereby an example of a component system built using our component model implementation.

Consider the following music diffusion system : a cd-player reads music files from a cd, and transmits them to a set of speakers situated in different rooms. Those speakers can convert music files into music we can listen to. They are incorporated in a parallel component, thus providing a single access interface to them (instead of connecting the cd player's output to each of the speakers).

Figure 6 gives an overview of the system, and represents the component model.

The system can be configured using the ADL (Architecture Description Language) that we provide for the components (Figure 7, coupled with the deployment descriptor, describing the physical infrastructure (Figure 8)).

When using the ADL, the configuration of the components is read from the descriptors, and the components are automatically instantiated, assembled and bound. Figure 9 shows an example of code used to manipulate the components, including instantiation, control and functional operations.

5   Related Work

We compare with closest related work in spirit, i.e. high-performance computing with composition of software components.

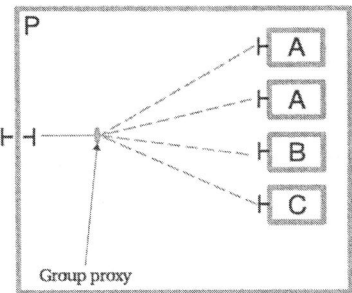

a) group communication inside a parallel component P : the incoming calls on the server interface are dispatched to the inner components.

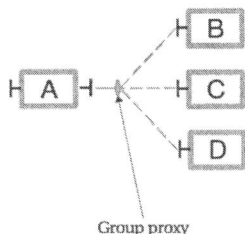

b) group communication as the implementation of a collective client port of A

Fig. 5. Group communications allowing collective bindings and parallel components

CCA. The Common Component Architecture [1] is an initiative to define minimal specification for scientific components, targeting parallel and distributed infrastructures. Ideas are drawn from CCM for the sake of defining components by provide/use ports, calls/events through the usage of a Scientific IDL (SIDL). A toolkit of the CCA specification, called CCAT [2], provides a framework for applications defined by binding CCA-enabled components, in which all services (directory, registry, creation, connection, event) are themselves CCA components (wrapping external services). An instance of this framework, XCAT, permits to describe a component and its deployment using an XML document, which looks very similar to what we have also defined and implemented for ProActive components. In this XML-oriented implementation of CCA, the communication protocol used to implement the remote procedure call between a uses port method invocation and the connected provides port remote objects is based on SOAP. The main drawback of CCA is that the composition model is not related to any specific underlying distributed object oriented model so that the user lacks a clear and precise model of the composition (which is as important as having a clear and precise programming model).

Corba Parallel Objects. The Parallel Corba model [3] targets the coupling of objects whose execution model is parallel (in practice, a parallel object is incar-

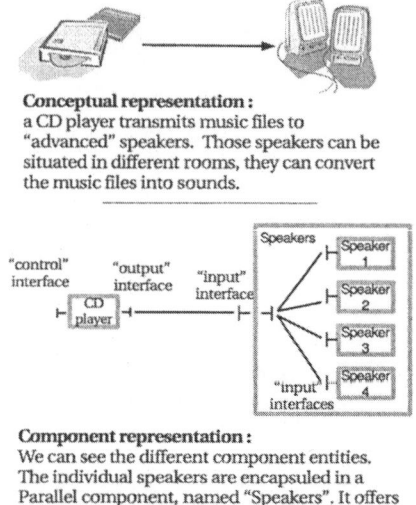

Conceptual representation:
a CD player transmits music files to
"advanced" speakers. Those speakers can be
situated in different rooms, they can convert
the music files into sounds.

Component representation:
We can see the different component entities.
The individual speakers are encapsuled in a
Parallel component, named "Speakers". It offers
a server interface of the same type and name
("input") than the its inner components. This
way, the music is dispatched in a parallel
manner to the speakers.

Fig. 6. A music diffusion system based on components

nated by a collection of sequential objects, and the execution model is SPMD; thus invoking a method on a parallel object invokes the corresponding method on all the objects of the collection, by scattering and redistributing arguments if needed). An implementation, PaCO++, achieves portability through the usage of standard CORBA IDL for object interactions. Notice that parallel and distribution issues are separated, as CORBA is only used to couple distributed codes, and parallel computations are usually managed with MPI. This is obviously an obstacle to easy grid computing.

GridCCM. GridCCM [4], a Parallel Corba component model, is a natural extension of PaCO++ motivated by the fact that a code coupling application can be seen as an assembly of components; however, most software component models (except PaCO++) only support sequential component. In order to have transparency in the assembly of components, a design choice was to make effective communications between parallel components be hidden to the application designer, by introducing collective ports that look like to be ordinary single-point ports. We propose the same sort of facility: ProActive components may also be built as parallel components by providing and using collective interfaces.

None of those approaches define hierarchical components as we have presented here. Moreover, we can encompass both parallel components in an SPMD style, or more generally parallel and distributed components following an MIMD execution model. We emphasize that we provide a unique infrastructure for functional and parallel calls and for component management, which is an alternative

```
COMPONENTS DESCRIPTOR
  Primitive–component  "cd–player"
    implementation = "CdPlayer"
    // name of the Java class with the functional code of the cd player
    VN = Node–player  //see deployment descriptor
    provides
        interface "control"
          signature = soundssystem.PlayerFacade
    requires
        interface "output"
          signature = soundssystem.Output
  Parallel–component  "speakers"
    VN = Node–speakers
    // the parallel component is just a facade to the real speakers
    provides
        interface "input"
          signature = soundssystem.Input

    contains
        primitive–component  "speaker"
          implementation = "Speaker"
          // functional code of the speaker
          VN = Node–speaker (cyclic)  // see deployment descriptor
          // deployment descriptor will specify the location of
          // the instances (thus their number)
          provides
            interface "input"
                 signature = soundssystem.Input
        Bindings
          // bindings to inner components are automatic for parallel
          // components between server interfaces of the same name
Bindings
// between client and server interfaces of the components
bind "cd–player.output" to "speakers.input"
```

Fig. 7. Using the ADL to describe a component system (format is converted from XML)

to what is for instance done in GridCCM [4] (MPI, openMP, etc.,) for functional and parallel codes, and Corba for component management – binding, deployment, life-cycle management, . . .).

6 Conclusion and Perspectives

We have successfully defined and implemented a component framework for ProActive, by applying the Fractal component model, mainly taking advantage of its hierarchical approach to component programming.

This defines a concept of what we have called *Grid components*. Grid components are formed of parallel and distributed active objects, features mobility, typed one-to-one or collective service invocations and a flexible deployment model. They also features flexibility and dynamicity at the component definition level.

We are working on the design of generic wrappers written in ProActive whose aim is to encapsulate legacy parallel code (usually Fortran-MPI or C-MPI codes).

We are also working on GUI-based tools to help the end-user to manipulate grid component based applications. Those tools will extend the IC2D monitor, which already helps in dynamically changing the deployment defined by deployment descriptors (cf. figure 8): acquire new JVMs, drag-and-drop active objects on the grid. We will provide *interactive* dynamic manipulation and monitoring

```
DEPLOYMENT DESCRIPTOR
VirtualNodes  // names of the virtual nodes
        VirtualNode name = "Node–player"
        VirtualNode name = "Node–speakers"
        VirtualNode name = "Node–speaker" – cyclic
        // cyclic: i.e. there will actually be several JVMs
Deployment  // what is behind the names of the virtual nodes
        mapping
        // correspondance between the names of the VNs and the JVMs
                Node–player ––> JVM1
                Node–speakers ––> JVM1
                Node–speaker ––> [JVM2, JVM3, JVM4]
                // 1 VN can be mapped onto a set of JVMs

        JVMs
                JVM1 created by process "linuxJVM"
                JVM2 created by process "rsh–computer1"
                JVM3 created by process "rsh–computer2"
                JVM4 created by process "globus–computer1"

Infrastructure
// how and where the JVMs specified above are created
        process–definition "linuxJVM"
        // this process creates a JVM on the current host
                JVMProcess class=JVMNodeProcess
        process–definition "rsh–computer1"
        // this process establishes an rsh connection
        // and starts a JVM on the remote host
        // (using the previously defined process "linuxJVM"
                rshProcess class=RSHProcess host="computer1"
                // computer1 could be in room1
                processReference = "linuxJVM"
        process–definition "rsh–computer2"
                rshProcess class=RSHProcess host="computer2"
                // computer2 could be in room2
                processReference = "linuxJVM"
        process–definition "globus–computer1"
                globusProcess class=GlobusGramProcess host="globus1"
                // globus1 could be in a room abroad
                processReference = "linuxJVM"
```

Fig. 8. Using the deployment descriptor to describe the physical infrastructure of a component system (format is converted from XML)

```
// CREATE THE COMPONENTS (for example speakers and cd_player)
ComponentIdentity speakers =
ProActive.newActiveComponent(speakers_parameters);
ComponentIdentity cd_player =
ProActive.newActiveComponent(cd_player_parameters);
// If the ADL is used, components instances can be retreived
// through the ComponentsLoader class :
// ComponentIdentity speakers =
// ComponentsLoader.getComponent("speakers");

// BIND THE COMPONENTS (Using the BindingController)
// (this is automatically done when using the ADL)
((BindingController)cd_player
.getFcInterface(BindingController.BINDING_CONTROLLER))
.bindFc(« output », speakers.getFcInterface(« input »));

// START THE LIFE CYCLE OF THE COMPONENTS
// (ENABLE THE COMPONENTS), using the LifeCycleController
((LifeCycleController)speakers
.getFcInterface(LifeCycleController.LIFECYCLE_CONTROLLER))
.startFc();
// this call is recursive, as the component contains other
// components (it also starts the inner components)

((LifeCycleController)cd_player
.getFcInterface(LifeCycleController.LIFECYCLE_CONTROLLER))
.startFc();

// INVOKE SOME ACTIONS ON FUNCTIONAL INTERFACES
// invoking a method of the Input interface
((Input)speakers
.getFcInterface(«input»))
.newMusic (music.mp3);

// invoking a method of the PlayerFacade interface
((PlayerFacade)cd_player
.getFcInterface(« control »))
.play();
```

Fig. 9. Using the API to manipulate components

of the components (besides what can be done by programming as exemplified by figure 9). For instance, it might be useful to generate an ADL such as the one on figure 7, and subsequently dynamically modify the description of the component application. Such tools could be integrated with computing portals and grid infrastructure middleware for resource brokering (ICENI [13], GridT [14], etc.), such as to build dedicated Problem Solving Environments [15].

We also investigate the following optimization: have functional method calls (either single or collective) bypass each inner composite component of a hierarchical component, so as to directly reach target primitive components – that are the only ones to serve functional service invocations. There is a non-trivial coherency problem to solve due to the concurrency of component management method calls (in particular, re-binding calls) towards encapsulating composite components.

Acknowledgments. This work was supported by the Incentive Concerted Action "GRID-RMI" (ACI GRID) of the French Ministry of Research and by the RNTL Arcad project funded by the French government.

References

1. Gannon, D., Bramley, R., Fox, G., Smallen, S., Rossi, A., Ananthakrishnan, R., Bertrand, F., Chiu, K., Farrellee, M., Govindaraju, M., Krishnan, S., Ramakrishnan, L., Simmhan, Y., Slominski, A., Ma, Y., Olariu, C., Rey-Cenvaz, N.: Programming the Grid: Distributed Software Components, P2P and Grid Web Services for Scientific Applications. Cluster Computing **5** (2002)
2. Bramley, R., Chin, K., Gannon, D., Govindaraju, M., Mukhi, N., Temko, B., Yochuri, M.: A Component-Based Services Architecture for Building Distributed Applications. In: 9th IEEE International Symposium on High Performance Distributed Computing Conference. (2000)
3. Denis, A., Pérez, C., Priol, T.: Achieving portable and efficient parallel corba objects. Concurrency and Computation: Practice and Experience (2003) To appear.
4. Denis, A., Pérez, C., Priol, T., Ribes, A.: Padico: A component-based software infrastructure for grid computing. In: 17th International Parallel and Distributed Processing Symposium (IPDPS2003), Nice, France, IEEE Computer Society (2003)
5. Caromel, D., Klauser, W., Vayssiere, J.: Towards seamless computing and metacomputing in java. Concurrency Practice and Experience **10** (1998) 1043–1061
6. Baude, F., Caromel, D., Huet, F., Mestre, L., Vayssière, J.: Interactive and Descriptor-based Deployment of Object-Oriented Grid Applications. In: 11th IEEE International Symposium on High Performance Distributed Computing. (2002) 93–102
7. Baduel, L., Baude, F., Caromel, D.: Efficient, flexible, and typed group communications in java. In: Joint ACM Java Grande - ISCOPE 2002 Conference, Seattle, ACM Press (2002) 28–36 ISBN 1-58113-559-8.
8. Bruneton, E., Coupaye, T., Stefani, J.: Recursive and dynamic software composition with sharing. Proceedings of the 7th ECOOP International Workshop on Component-Oriented Programming (WCOP'02) (2002)
9. Fractal. (http://fractal.objectweb.org)

10. ProActive web site. (http://www.inria.fr/oasis/ProActive/)
11. Sun Microsystems: Enterprise Java Beans Specification 2.0 (1998)
    http://java.sun.com/products/ejb/docs.html.
12. OMG: Corba 3.0 new components chapter (2001) Document ptc/2001-11-03.
13. Furmento, N., Mayer, A., McGough, S., Newhouse, S., Field, T., Darlington, J.:
    ICENI: Optimisation of Component Applications within a Grid Environment. Par-
    allel Computing **28** (2002)
14. Godakhale, A., Natarajan, B.: Composing and Deploying Grid Middleware Web
    Services Using Model Driven Architecture. In: CoopIS/DOA/ODBASE. Number
    2519 in LNCS (2002) 633–649
15. Rice, J., Boisvert, R.: From Scientific Libraries to Problem-Solving Environments.
    IEEE Computational Science and Engineering (1996) 44–53

Re-factoring Middleware Systems: A Case Study

Charles Zhang and Hans-Arno Jacobsen

Department of Electrical and Computer Engineering
and Department of Computer Science
University of Toronto
10 King's College Circle
Toronto, Ontario, Canada
{czhang,jacobsen}@eecg.toronto.edu

Abstract. Aspect oriented programming brings us new design perspectives since it permits the superimpositions of multiple abstraction models on top of one another. It is a very powerful technique in separating and simplifying design concerns. In this paper, we provide detailed descriptions of our aspect oriented re-factoring of ORBacus, an industrial strength CORBA implementation. The re-factored features are the dynamic programming interface, support for portable interceptors, invocations of local objects. Their associated IDL-level re-factorization is addressed by an aspect-aware IDL compiler. In addition, we present the quantification for the changes in terms of both the structural complexity and the runtime performance. The aspect oriented re-factorization proves that AOP is capable of composing non-trivial functionality of middleware in a superimposing manner. The final "woven" system is able to correctly provide both the fundamental functionality and the "aspectized" functionality with negligible overhead and leaner architecture. Furthermore, the "aspectized" feature can be configured in and out during compile-time, which greatly enhances the configurability of the architecture.

1 Introduction

In recent years, the adoption of middleware systems such as Web Services, .NET, J2EE and CORBA are no longer limited to traditional enterprise computing platforms. A very large family of emerging application domains, such as control platforms, smart devices, and networking equipments, require middleware to support special computational characteristics such as real-time, stringent resource constraints, high availability, and high performance. For example, middleware systems are used on the Cisco ONS 15454 optical transport platform to manage hardware customizations and communications among the management software and hardware drivers [14]. Middleware is being used as the software bus for subunits in the submarine combat control systems by the US Navy [4].

The fast broadening of the application spectrum has brought many difficult challenges to the design of middleware. We observe that one of the most prominent problems is that the architecture of middleware constantly struggles

R. Meersman et al. (Eds.): CoopIS/DOA/ODBASE 2003, LNCS 2888, pp. 1243–1262, 2003.

between two conflicting goals: generality and specialization. Generality means vendors desire to support as many application domains as possible by incorporating a large set of features in their middleware implementations. As direct consequence, these systems usually require large memory spaces and abundant computing resources. For example, ORBacus [15], one of the Java implementations of CORBA [8], requires around 7 megabytes of memory[1]. The C-based CORBA implementation ORBit [7] requires at least 2MB of memory space. Therefore, it is very expensive to deploy these types of middleware systems on many handheld devices or wireless devices. This is because, for example, commercial handheld devices typically support memory size of a few mega-bytes with limited processor power. [2]. The computation resource in most cell phones is even more constrained[3].

To accommodate these computing environments with stringent resource constraints and special runtime requirements, middleware architects often choose to specialize the architecture of middleware in order to optimize its performance for domain specific characteristics such as real time, small memory space, high availability, and high performance. As a result, for the same technology, there often exist multiple specifications, various branches of code bases, and different implementations. Each of these implementations require a tremendous amount of effort to develop and to maintain. It is a challenge for the vendor to ensure that the distributed computing properties are consistent across many different versions of the same technology. It is also a challenge for users of middleware to well understand the differences and, although not always possible, to match specific implementations with their specific needs.

Recent research such as OpenCOM [12] and DynamicTAO [10] mainly aim at improving the configurability and the adaptability of middleware by introducing new software engineering techniques like component based architecture and reflection. Astley et al. [3] achieve middleware customization through techniques based on separation of communication styles from protocols and a framework for protocol composition. LegORB [13] and Universally Interoperable Core (UIC)[4] are middleware platforms designed for hand-held devices, which allow for interoperability with standard platforms. Both offer static and dynamic configuration and aim to maintain a small memory footprint by only offering the functionality an application actually needs. The QuO project at BBN Technologies constitutes a framework supporting the development of distributed applications with QoS requirements (see [11] for an example). QuO supports a number of description languages, referred to as Quality Description Languages (QDL). The QDLs are used to specify client-side QoS needs, regions of possible level of QoS, system

---

[1] This includes the JVM memory footprint. Classes of ORBacus take more than 4MB of memory. This is estimated by comparing the size of ORBacus runtime with a simple Java program.

[2] The new Palm M515 devices support 8M of memory and operate at 33MHz. http://www.palm.com/products/palmm515/m515ds.pdf

[3] Cypress corporation predicts in 1999 that newer cell phones would have SDRAM of 4M. See *MoBL: The New Mobile SRAM. Cypress Whitepaper*

[4] http://www.ubi-core.com/

conditions that need to be monitored, certain behavior desired by clients, and QoS conditions [11]. Further extensions of these languages are envisioned to also be able to define available system resources and their status. Loyall *et al.* [11] interpret these different description languages as aspect languages that are processed by a code generator to assemble a runtime environment supporting the desired and expected quality of service by client and server in a distributed application. Zinky *et al.* [18] further elaborate on the issue of adaptive middleware code that cross-cuts the platform's functional decomposition. It is illustrated that aspect orientation could be used to manage the QoS of a connection in a distributed application. The QuO approach to specifying QoS guarantees is very powerful. However, the focus in the QuO project lies on managing communication QoS, which are important aspects for distributed applications, but QuO dose not address the problem of re-factoring a legacy middleware platform to make it configurable and customizable for a particular application domain or even application, which is the focus of our work.

Our approach differs from the afore described work as we believe that it is more concrete and effective to study the benefit of applying AOP to the legacy architecture of middleware. This is because, as AOP claims, conventional decomposition methods cannot modularize crosscutting concerns and, therefore, cause a considerable degree of logic tangling and concern scattering. Following this theoretical conjecture, we first provided quantification of aspects in legacy middleware systems [16,17]. We proved, through the method of aspect mining and aspect oriented re-factorization, that concern crosscutting is an inherent problem in CORBA-based middleware systems implemented by conventional means. In this paper, we complement our previous work by presenting an architectural view of this aspect oriented re-factorization work. We describe, in UML diagrams and code examples, how a number of non-trivial internal features of middleware are captured in a separate set of aspect modules. We also present a prototype of the aspect-aware interface definition language (IDL) compiler, which performs the aspect oriented re-factorization at the stub/skeleton generation stage.

The rest of the paper is organized as follows: Section 2 introduces the new language features of AspectJ [1], the aspect oriented language we use to perform the re-factoring. Section 3 presents a detailed description of building four major CORBA features using AspectJ for the ORBacus implementation. It also includes the evaluation, which reflects both architectural changes and the performance effects of the aspect oriented implementations. In contrast to [16], we, here, present aggregated results to quantify the total sum of changes and to illustrate the benefit of our approach in a different perspective.

2 Aspect Oriented Programming and AspectJ

Aspect oriented programming offers an alternative design paradigm, which achieves a very high degree of *separation of concerns* in software development. "Aspects tend not to be units of the system's functional decomposition, but rather be properties that affect the performance or semantics of the components in systemic ways." [9] Examples of such properties include security, reliability, manageability, and more [5]. The existence of aspects is attributed to handling crosscutting concerns using the traditional "vertical" decomposition paradigms. AOP overcomes the limitations of traditional programming paradigms by providing language level facilities to modularize these systematic properties as separate development activities. The AOP compiler is capable of producing the final system by merging the aspect modules and the primary functionalities together. We employ the following AOP artifacts to address problems in the middleware design.

Component Language. A component language is used for performing the primary decomposition. It can be any regular programming languages such as Java or C.

Aspect Language. The aspect language defines logic units that can be used to compose aspects into modules. Representative aspect languages are AspectJ [1] and Hyper/J [2]. We can use these languages to implement crosscutting concerns.

Aspect Weaver. The responsibility of an aspect weaver is to instrument the component program with aspect programs to produce a final system. In the context of middleware architecture, the implementations of both the core functionality of middleware and the features as aspects can be defined separately and coexist in the final "woven" system.

There are a number of aspect-oriented languages. Hyper/J supports multi-dimensional programming by allowing programmers to compose the system differently according to specific concerns in Java. The HyperJ compiler performs bytecode transformations to generate different final systems according to extraction specifications. Each extraction is analogously termed as "hyperslicing". AspectJ [1], designed as an extension of the Java language, is a mature aspect oriented programming language. AspectJ provides "pointcut" constructs to designate a collection of interception points in the execution flow of software systems. AspectJ also provides method-like constructs called advices, such as "before", "after", and "proceed". These constructs can contain normal Java code, which gets executed before, after, or in place of the interception points designated by the "piontcut" constructs. It also contains *inter-type declarations*, also called *introductions*, which are used to declare new members (fields, methods, and constructors) in other types. In the later sections, we illustrate in detail how these special constructs can be used to re-factor crosscutting concerns in middleware systems.

3   Aspect Oriented Re-factorization of CORBA

We have chosen CORBA as our case study because CORBA has been addressing middleware concerns for over a decade. Its architecture reflects distinct evolution cycles in the domain of middleware and can be treated as an excellent example of traditional decomposition approaches. CORBA is a long term standardization effort by OMG[5]. We use the ORBacus CORBA code base as our case study. ORBacus is an industrial-strength and open source CORBA implementation. The version used for the re-factoring is 4.1.1. It follows the Open Connector Interface (OCI) architectural model, which provides further standardization of the internal structures of the Orb.

In this section we use a number of software engineering metrics to track the changes resulting from re-factoring the ORBacus code base with aspects. We present the detailed re-factoring of the following ORBacus features: dynamic programming interface, support for portable interceptors, and invocation of local servers. To support the re-factoring at the IDL and stub layer, we describe an AOP-based design of an aspect-aware IDL compiler. We then present the quantification as the result of factoring out specific features from the ORBacus implementation. We also discuss the limitations of our aspect-oriented implementation.

3.1   Quantification Metrics

Metrics are measures for the quality of software designs. We think it is appropriate to use a combination of metrics to address various properties of the "aspectized" architecture, including both the structural metrics, which directly reflect the cost of development and maintenance, and the runtime metrics, which reflect the cost of adopting the technology. The structural metrics include cyclomatic complexity, size, weight of class, and coupling between classes. Cyclomatic complexity is an index which measures the complexity of the control flow in a program. The size measures the number of lines of executable code. The weight of class refers to the number of methods in a class definition. The coupling metric measures the number of references to other classes in a particular class. please refer to [16] for a detailed discussion and the collection method of these metrics. To measure the response time of the broker, we divide the total time for the roundtrip of a request into four intervals: **Interval A:** Client-side marshalling **Interval B:** Server-side unmarshalling and dispatching. **Interval C:** Server-side marshalling.**Interval D:** Client-side unmarshalling.It is necessary for the aspect oriented re-factoring to at least preserve the response time of the broker. In the case of having crosscutting features factored out, AOP re-factorization is expected to decrease the processing time due to the simplification of program logic.

3.2   AOP Based Performance Measurement

Each of the four intervals in the traversal of the middleware stack requires measurements taken at many different points in the execution path of ORBacus. To avoid changing the ORBacus code for these different measurements, we write the timing code in Java and define four sets of pointcuts in AspectJ. To obtain high-resolution time, we use a simple C-based timing tool written in Java Native

---

[5] Object Management Group. http://www.omg.org

Interfaces. Since the instrumentation code for time measurement is nicely captured in one module, it also becomes convenient to perform more advanced statistical analysis of the response time. The inserted calls to aspect methods incur slight performance overhead in the order of a few microseconds. This overhead is eliminated when performing comparative analysis. To verify the correctness of the re-factorization, we adopted the demonstration code, which is a part of the standard ORBacus source distribution as test cases as well as for taking performance measurements. The re-factored Orb is transparent to the test programs. The stack traversal intervals are measured in microseconds and computed as the average of 100,000 remote invocations on a Pentium III 1GHz Linux workstation. Each remote invocation involves an integer message sent from the client process to the server. The server also responds with an integer message.

3.3   Code Transformation

As the first step in the re-factorization, we need to identify, before re-factorization, the presence of a particular crosscutting property in two forms, the *implementation structure* of the property and the crosscutting structure for that property with the primary decomposition model. Therefore, the tangled code is transformed into three class groupings in the AOP implementation, namely primary classes, aspect implementation classes, and the weaving classes. The transformation is illustrated by Figure 1, where the outside box on the left depicts that the original implementation is one monolithic entity. The primary model and the aspect model coexist in a single structure with parts intersecting among each other. The package diagrams on the right presents a clear division of structures. The importance of such division is that it allows all three components to be designed, tested and evolved with unprecedented independence and freedom. We use the package diagrams in Figure 1 to illustrate the hierarchical structure and the major types of relationship between aspect packages and the component program, using the dynamic programming interface as an example.

3.3.1 Dynamic Programming Interface. A dynamic programming model allows an application to be designed without prior knowledge of the interface

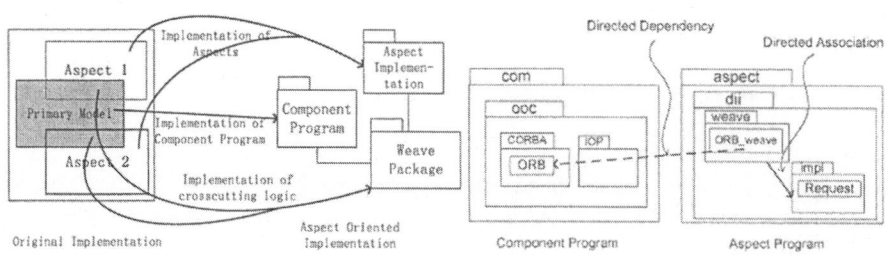

Fig. 1. (1) Code transformation for re-factoring. (2) Package organization for re-factorizat

definitions of the invoked objects. Instead, invocations on a remote interface can be composed during runtime. In middleware platforms, where the primary programming model is static, the support for the dynamic programming model crosscuts the entire architecture. Our AOP based re-factoring of the dynamic programming model consists of two parts, the client-side Dynamic Invocation Interface (DII) and the server-side Dynamic Skeleton Interface (DSI).

Dynamic Invocation Interface (DII). The client-side facility for the dynamic programming model is supported through the implementations of the interface `org.omg.CORBA.Request` and `MultiRequestSender`. Those two class types are taken out of the original implementation and grouped under the aspect implementation package for DII. We then identify, in the primary decomposition model, the places where operations of classes need to acquire or to exploit the knowledge of these class types. These places are the crosscutting points of the DII aspect. In AspectJ, these crosscutting points can be implemented as *"join-points"* instead. *Special note on UML:* Since UML has yet no direct support for AOP notions, we model an "aspect" as a regular class. We model an `advice` as a regular class method. We model "Introduction" constructs as regular attributes and methods. Their names are prefixed with the names of the classes within which these attributes and methods are declared. Due to the special construct of `advice`, most UML tools would generate some oddities on the diagram. Figure 2 presents the UML diagram of the aspect implementation of the DII. As a concrete mapping of Figure 1, the AOP implementation involves three packages. The primary program package on the left represents the original implementation of the ORB objects with the logic of the DII removed. The DII code is placed in the package on the right as the aspect implementation. The package organization of these classes is left intact. The package in the middle of the diagram includes the "weaving" modules which define how the aspect implementation of the DII interacts with the primary program.

The "weaving" modules in the UML diagram shows that the aspectization of the DII involves four classes in the Orb, namely, `ORB_impl`, `ORBInstance`, `DowncallStub` and `Delegate`. To interpret the diagram for the `aspect.dii.weave` package, we use the aspect module `ORBDII` as an example. In the aspect module `ORBDII`, an extra field `MultiRequestSender` and an ad-

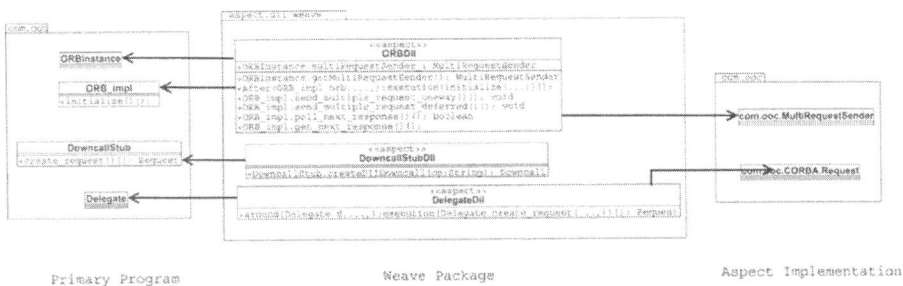

Fig. 2. UML Diagram of The DII Aspect Implementation

ditional method `getMultiRequestSender` are added to the class `ORBInstance` to support the sending of multiple DII requests. Extra code is executed after the execution of the `initialize` method of the `ORB_impl` class to perform DII specific initializations during the ORB start-up time. Four DII related methods are also declared in the class `ORB_impl` to support DII operations. In other aspect modules, we use the "*inter-type declarations*" to inject the downcall creation logic for dynamically composed downcalls. We use "**around**" to change the behavior of the request creation in the `Delegate` class.

Figure 3 shows a major fragment of the aspect module ORBDII responsible for sending multiple DII requests. In this code snippet, lines 7-12 declare a new attribute and a new method to support multiple DII request sending in class `ORBInstance`. Lines 14-19 create the runtime instance of the new attribute `multiRequestSender_` "after" the initialization work of `ORB_impl` finishes. Lines 21-28 enable the DII multiple request sending capability of `ORB_impl` by adding new application programming interface (API) send-_multiple_requests_oneway.

Dynamic Skeleton Interface (DSI). The server side facility for the dynamic programming model is supported through the ORBacus implementations of the OMG interfaces including `ServerRequest` and `DynamicImplemenation`. We first remove these two class types and group them under the aspect implementation package. Figure 4 presents the organization of the classes for the AOP implementation of DSI.

As in the case of DII, the "`aspect.dsi.weave`" package defines how DSI implementation is added back to the regular ORB implementations. This package identifies the crosscutting points which are implemented as follows:

1. We used the "*around*" construct to replace the request dispatching call with an alternative implementation which dispatches client requests to a dynamic server implementation.
2. ORBacus prohibits the direct invocations for DSI server implementations. We use the "*around*" construct to check whether an invocation is towards a dynamic implementation preceding the normal invocation process in order to prevent direct invocation.

To illustrate how DSI is implemented, we present the complete AspectJ code in figure 5 for weaving the checking logic into the class `ActiveObjectOnlyStrategy`, an activity described previously in the second item.

3.3.2 Invocation of Collocated Objects. The key abstraction provided by middleware systems is the transparency of the location of server objects. Location transparency allows remote services to be invoked in the same fashion as calling a method on an object while performing marshalling and unmarshalling behind the scene. Some CORBA implementations optimize the calling process to avoid unnecessary marshal/unmarshal work in the case where server objects

```
package aspect.dii.weave;                                              1
//imports are omitted                                                  2
privileged aspect ORBDII                                              3
{                                                                     4
    //introduce a new field multirequest sender in ORBInstance.This field is    5
    //initialized by ORB_Impl,which is executed before ORBInstance    6
    private MultiRequestSender ORBInstance.multiRequestSender_;        7
                                                                      8
    public MultiRequestSender ORBInstance.getMultiRequestSender()      9
    {                                                                10
        return multiRequestSender_;                                  11
    }                                                                12
                                                                     13
    after(ORB_impl orb,org.omg.CORBA.StringSeqHolder args,..,):      14
    execution(private void initialize(org.omg.CORBA.StringSeqHolder,...,    15
    String, int, java.util.Properties, int, int, int))               16
    &&target(orb)&&args(//omitted){                                  17
        orb.orbInstance_.multiRequestSender_= new MultiRequestSender();    18
    }                                                                19
                                                                     20
    public synchronized void                                         21
    ORB_impl.send_multiple_requests_oneway(Request[] requests){      22
     if(destroy_) throw                                              23
     new org.omg.CORBA.OBJECT_NOT_EXIST("ORB is destroyed");         24
     com.ooc.OB.MultiRequestSender multi =                           25
      this.orbInstance_.getMultiRequestSender();                     26
     multi.sendMultipleRequestsOneway(requests);                     27
    }                                                                28
}                                                                    29
```

Fig. 3. DII: Multiple request sending

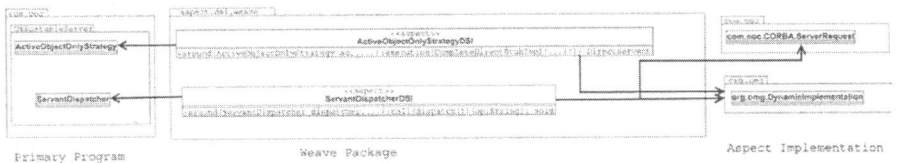

Primary Program   Weave Package   Aspect Implementation

Fig. 4. UML Diagram of The DSI Aspect Implementation

are deployed or migrated into the same process as the client. In ORBacus, the optimization logic is an integral part of the request processing process, which is designed primarily for making remote invocations. We believe the optimization for in-process server objects in ORBacus is logically orthogonal to its remote invocation mechanism. Therefore, we identify the optimization for local invocations as an aspect of ORBacus implementation of CORBA.

```
package aspect.dsi.weave;                                              1
privileged aspect ActiveObjectOnlyStrategyDSI                          2
{                                                                      3
  DirectServant around( ActiveObjectOnlyStrategy ao, ...,)             4
  : execution(protected DirectServant ActiveObjectOnlyStrategy.        5
  completeDirectStubImpl( org.omg.PortableServer.POA, ...))            6
  &&target(ao)&&args(...)                                              7
  {                                                                    8
   if(servant instanceof org.omg.PortableServer.DynamicImplementation){  9
     return null;                                                      10
   }                                                                   11
   return proceed(ao,poa,rawoid,servant,policies);                     12
  }                                                                    13
}                                                                      14
```

Fig. 5. Dynamic Skeleton Interface

In ORBacus terms, in-process objects are referred to as collocated objects. To distinguish between normal remote invocation calls and calls to collocated servers, ORBacus uses *CollocatedClient* and *CollocatedServer* to handle corresponding request processing for the client and server respectively. We completely decouple these class types from the ORBacus source and moved them into the aspect package.

In ORBacus, the collocation invocation is mainly implemented in the object initialization phase for both the client and the server. We present the AOP implementation of local server invocation in the UML diagram in Figure 6.

The mechanism of collocation invocation is implemented by the `aspect.collo.weave` package which includes the following actions:

1. The *"around"* construct in `ClientManagerCo` weaves into the class `Client-Manager` the client-side logic of checking whether the object reference is pointing to a collocated server. If yes, a different communication model is set up to avoid marshalling and network operations.
2. The `ServerManagerCo` aspect first adds a new attribute of type `Collocated-Server` to the class `ServerManager`. The "after" construct creates the run-

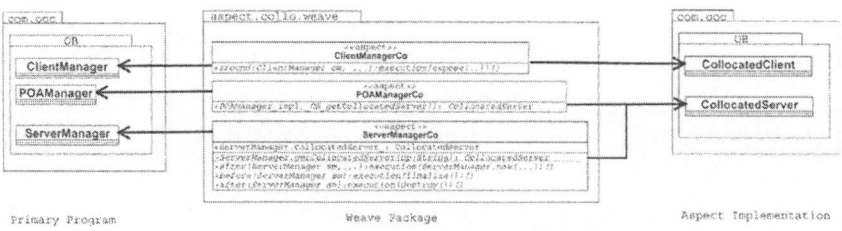

Fig. 6. UML Diagram of Aspect Implementation for Collocated Invocations

time instance of the `CollocatedServer` after the constructor of `Server-Manager` is executed. The second "after" advice disposes the `Collocated-Server`. The "before" construct verifies the validity of the `Collocated-Server` instance.

3. The `POAManagerCo` aspect first adds a method to allow the access to the `CollocatedServers`.

Figure 7 presents the AspectJ code of `POAManagerCo`. Lines 5-9 declare one attribute and the accessor for that attribute in the class `ServerManager`. Lines 11-14 enforce some condition checking before the `finalize` method is invoked. Lines 16-20 create the runtime instance of the collocated server and add it to the list of servers. Lines 22-25 destroy the runtime instance for garbage collection as an additional step after the `destroy` method in the base implementation finishes execution.

3.3.3 Support for Portable Interceptors Portable Interceptors are hooks into the Orb through which CORBA services can intercept various stages during

```
package aspect.collocation.weave;                                        1
import com.ooc.OB.*;                                                     2
privileged aspect ServerManagerCo                                       3
{                                                                        4
 private CollocatedServer ServerManager.collocatedServer_;              5
 public synchronized CollocatedServer                                   6
ServerManager.getCollocatedServer(){                                    7
  return collocatedServer_;                                             8
 }                                                                       9
                                                                        10
before(ServerManager sm):execution( * ServerManager.finalize()         11
  throws Throwable)&&target(sm){                                        12
  Assert._OB_assert(sm.collocatedServer_ == null);                     13
 }                                                                      14
                                                                        15
after(ServerManager sm,...): execution(ServerManager.new(...))         16
&&target(sm)&&args(...){                                                17
   sm.collocatedServer_ = new CollocatedServer(oaInterface, concModel); 18
   sm.allServers_.addElement(sm.collocatedServer_);                    19
 }                                                                      20
                                                                        21
after(ServerManager sm):execution(public synchronized void destroy()) 22
&&target(sm){                                                           23
   sm.collocatedServer_ = null;                                        24
 }                                                                      25
}                                                                       26
```

Fig. 7. ServerManager Collocation Invocation

the request process. They are observer [6] style entities. Interceptors allow a third party to plug in additional Orb functionalities such as transaction support and security.

In ORBacus, the functionality of portable interceptors is implemented through three categories of classes. They include the classes related to implementing the interceptor interfaces defined by the OMG. They also include ORBacus specific interceptor initialization classes and request processing classes that support portable interceptors. We separated classes in these three categories from ORBacus and grouped them under the aspect implementation package. Figure 8 presents the UML diagram for the portable interceptor implementation as aspect programs. The crosscutting points where the primary ORB model tangles with support for portable interceptors correspond to the standardized behaviour of portable interceptor. That is, an ORB implementation must allow interceptions made to the client request process, the server request process and the creation process of server objects. Since the "weaving" implementation of the portable interceptor suppport is rather complex, we present a summary of our AOP implementations as follows:

1. The portable interceptors can intercept the request sending process before it starts. Therefore, in ORBacus, the request sending process, i.e., the downcall creation process, needs to check if any client request interceptors are registered. If so, a downcall object is initialized with the portable interceptor information. Instead of letting ORBacus perform the checking regardless of whether portable interceptors are used or not, we moved the code segments into the aspect program in a "around" construct. As the result, the "aspectized" ORBacus only performs necessary checks if a portable interceptor is required for a particular application.

2. A similar situation occurs in the server-side request dispatching process, e.g., the upcall creation process. We moved the checking and upcall creation code into the aspect implementation. That makes the server request processing

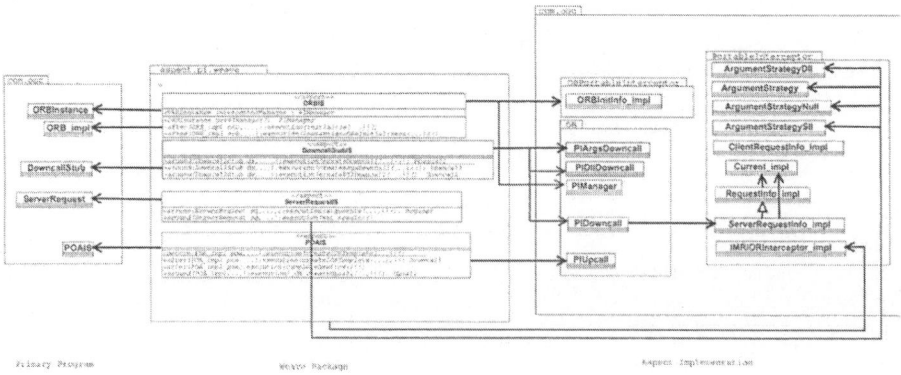

Fig. 8. UML Diagram of Portable Interceptor Support Aspect Implementation

leaner and more precise. That is, it needs to reference and to handle portable interceptors only when it is necessary.

3. The portable object adaptor (POA) plays a key role in the process of object creation. It needs to notify all the interceptors if there are interceptors registered for intercepting the object creation process. Consequently, the POA code needs to have extra control paths in order to support that requirement. We moved that checking logic into the aspect code and implemented the same logic via the "*after*" construct. That is, following the completion of object creation, the checking code is executed only if the support for portable interceptors is required.

4. The ORB also contains the initialization code for loading portable interceptors and registering them with the ORB. We moved the corresponding code into the aspect implementation such that, if the interceptor support is not needed, it is no longer necessary for the ORB to perform the extra initialization procedures.

We present two code snippets since the implementation of portable interceptor support is more complex than previous cases. Figure 9 is part of the POA related implementation of interceptor support. As defined in the OMG specification, compliant ORB implementations must notify interceptors of the object creation time. Lines 3-9 notify the portable interceptor manager "before" creating the internet object reference (IOR). The `after` advice notifies the manager when IOR is created (lines 11-16).

```
package aspect.pi.weave;                                              ·1
privileged aspect POAIS{                                              2
  before(POA_impl poa,IORInfo_impl iorInfoImpl):                     3
  execution(private void POA_impl.                                   4
  createIORTemplate(com.ooc.PortableInterceptor.IORInfo_impl))       5
  &&target(poa)&&args(iorInfoImpl){                                  6
    com.ooc.OB.PIManager piManager = poa.orbInstance_.getPIManager();  7
    piManager.establishComponents(poa.iorInfo_);                     8
  }                                                                  9
                                                                    10
  after(POA_impl poa,...):execution(private void POA_impl.          11
  createIORTemplate(com.ooc.PortableInterceptor.IORInfo_impl))      12
  &&target(poa)&&args(iorInfoImpl){                                 13
    com.ooc.OB.PIManager piManager = poa.orbInstance_.getPIManager();  14
    piManager.componentsEstablished(poa.iorInfo_);                  15
  }                                                                 16
}                                                                   17
```

Fig. 9. POA Portable Interceptor Support

Figure 10 adds the support for portable interceptors to the class ORB. Firstly, the aspect code adds the new attribute PIManager and the corresponding accessor to the class ORB(Lines 5 - 8). PIManager is responsible for managing the interceptors registered in the ORB. Lines 13-15 create the runtime instance of PIManager as the first task after the ORB finishes initialization. Lines 18-24 instantiate a codeset interceptor and register it with the manager. Lines 26-38 invoke customized ORBInitializers after the normal initialization of ORB finishes. The last line (line 39) notifies all the interceptors registered with PIManager of the event that the ORB has been initialized.

3.4 Aspect-Aware IDL Compiler

Our re-factoring work not only resolve the crosscutting of the internal architecture, but also aims at simplifying the user's view of the Orb by developing the aspect-aware IDL compiler. This is because certain CORBA features, such as the dynamic programming interface and the collocated server invocation, require special treatment and support in the CORBA API, i.e., the standardized IDL definitions and the associated language mappings. The complete re-factorization of these features must include the associated API code. This is because even if these features are not required by particular applications, the associated API code still contributes to the complexity of the overall API set and consumes computing resources.

In this case study, we explore the functionality of the aspect-aware IDL compiler by implementing two additional tasks as compared to the ordinary stub compilers during the language translation. These tasks are *API splitting* and *Local Invocation Optimization*. Both features require modifications to the IDL compiler code in a crosscutting manner and can therefore be implemented using AspectJ. Our implementation is experimental and based on the JacORB IDL compiler since the source of ORBacus IDL compiler is not part of the open source distribution. The implementation consists of the following modifications added to JacORB compiler using AspectJ:

1. Two additional compiler options are added. The "-split" argument is followed by a subset of original IDL definitions, which corresponds to the features that are already factored out. This tells the compiler to generate these IDL definitions as AspectJ modules consisting of "inter-type declarations"s. At the same time, it skips the same API defined in the original IDL definition. In this way, we do not change the original IDL definition. The "-local" argument is designed to eliminate parts of the generated stub code deciding if the optimization of collocated invocations are needed. These additional compiler options are added in an "after" advice, which parses the command line arguments and sets the corresponding flags in the parser.
2. The stub code for the original IDL definition is split into two sets of modules, the standard language mapping and AspectJ modules. This is done through three steps: 1. The parser first reads the IDL definitions following the "-split" switch and stores the declarations of the interfaces and methods; 2.

An "around" advice is defined to replace the code generation method in the IDL compiler. It checks if this particular interface needs to be split by doing a lookup from the storage. If the interface contains operations supporting the "aspectized" feature, a separate print stream is set up for generating the AspectJ code. Upon the completion of code generation for the interface, the print stream generates the enclosing AspectJ symbols if necessary; 3. Before generating the stub code for methods, a "before" advice uses the

```
package aspect.pi.weave;                                                1
privileged aspect ORBIS{                                                2
//introduce a new field PIManager in ORBInstance. This field is initialized by   3
//ORB_Impl, which is executed before ORBInstance                        4
private PIManager ORBInstance.interceptorManager_=null;                 5
public PIManager ORBInstance.getPIManager(){                            6
  return interceptorManager_;                                          7
}                                                                       8
                                                                        9
after(ORB_impl orb, ...,):execution(private void                       10
initialize(StringSeqHolder, String, ...))&&target(orb)&&args(...)      11
{                                                                       12
   PIManager piManager = new PIManager(orb);                           13
   piManager.setORBInstance(orb.orbInstance_);                         14
   orb.orbInstance_.interceptorManager_=piManager;                     15
   // Initialize Portable Interceptors - this must be done after installing the OCI   16
   //plug-ins to allow an ORBInitializer or interceptor to make a remote invocation   17
   try{                                                                18
     piManager.addIORInterceptor(new com.ooc.OB.                       19
        CodeSetIORInterceptor_impl(nativeCs, nativeWcs),false);        20
   }                                                                   21
   catch(DuplicateName ex){                                           22
      com.ooc.OB.Assert._OB_assert(false);                           23
   }                                                                   24
   //set up ORBInitInfo                                               25
   if(!orb.orbInitializers_.isEmpty()){                              26
   com.ooc.OBPortableInterceptor.ORBInitInfo_impl info =             27
   new com.ooc.OBPortableInterceptor.ORBInitInfo_impl(...);          28
   java.util.Enumeration e = orb.orbInitializers_.elements();        29
   while(e.hasMoreElements()){                                        30
     ((ORBInitializer)e.nextElement()).pre_init(info);               31
   }                                                                  32
   e = orb.orbInitializers_.elements();                              33
   while(e.hasMoreElements()){                                        34
     ((ORBInitializer)e.nextElement()).post_init(info);              35
   }                                                                  36
   info._OB_destroy();                                                37
   }                                                                  38
   piManager.setupComplete();                                         39
}                                                                      40
```

Fig. 10. ORB Portable Interceptor Support

alternative output stream set up earlier if the method is to be translated into AspectJ "inter-type declaration"s. Figure 11 illustrates a simple usage of this feature. The original IDL definitions contain two methods, where the underlined method supports a re-factored feature. This method is re-defined using IDL syntax in a separate file and read by the compiler following the "-split" option. The generated Java language mapping as well as the AspectJ code is shown at the bottom of the figure.

3. The "-local" switch is to tell our compiler to simplify the control logic of the stub code if the feature of optimizing for invoking collocated servers is not needed. In our current implementation, using the switch will eliminate the conditional statements in the stub code, which checks if the remote server is actually located in-process. This is done by replacing the original translation code with our own methods defined in a "around" advice.

Our IDL compiler implementation has the following properties: 1. We achieve the maximum reuse of existing code as no modifications is made to the original IDL compiler code. 2. New compiler features can be added and removed very easily as they are all implemented in AspectJ. In addition, since these features are implemented in separate aspect modules, they can be independently added or removed without affecting others. 3. Existing IDL language features are sufficient for our compiler to generate "aspectized" code. No aspect oriented extension are needed to support the "aspectization" at the IDL definition level.

Our implementation introduces some overhead to the compilation process because we need to check, for every method, whether the AspectJ code needs to be generated. Testing shows a lookup from storage of interfaces which are to be generated in the aspect code takes around 20 microseconds. The overhead is therefore not noticeable even compiling a very large set of IDL files.

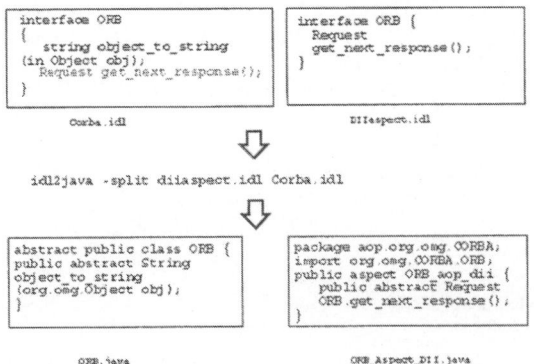

Fig. 11. Aspect-aware IDL Compiler

3.5   Re-factorization Results

Table 1 presents the measurements of both the structural metrics and the runtime metrics for the AOP re-factoring of dynamic programming interface, portable interceptor support, collocation invocation. The structural metrics are collected on the ORBacus implementation prior to and after the AOP re-factoring. Table 1 reports the accumulated reductions for every re-factored features. The data indicates that, through the aspect oriented re-factorization, we reduce the size of ORBacus by more than two thousand lines and around 70 references to other class types. The structure of ORBacus becomes less complex with features taken out and still capable of supporting transparent remote invocations with improved response time to the original implementation. Table 1 also reports the runtime interval measurements for the four segments of the ORBacus stack traversal. The response time is measured using the original implementation, the "woven" implementation(re-combined), and the implementation with features factored out(re-factored). The runtime performance of the three Orbs is largely equivalent. The sizes are in lines of executing code; weight is in number of methods; interval is in micro-seconds. Other metrics are indexes, see earlier section for an interpretation.

Table 1. Metric Matrix for the re-factorization of DII, DSI, Portable Interceptor, Collocation Invocation, and overall assessment (CCN - Cyclomatic Complexity Number.)

	Structural Metrics				Interval			
	CCN	*Size*	*Weight*	*Coupling*	*A*	*B*	*C*	*D*
Dynamic Invocation Interface								
Original	25.4	2000	200	203.35	105	125	37	59
Re-factored	23.8	1490	188.35	196.55	108	124	35	59
Dynamic Skeleton Interface								
Original	7.28	369	18.66	28	79	126	43	8
Re-factored	6.92	262	18.66	27	76	119	41	9
Portable Interceptor Support								
Original	24.66	4218	160.8	208.5	78	118	42	8
Re-factored	24.0	2909	160.2	194.28	79	122	42	9
Collocation Invocation								
Original	15.66	638	33.99	63	79	126	43	8
Re-factored	15.00	435	32.01	57.99	76	126	41	7
Overall								
Original	105	7320	412.5	528.25	76	126	37	9
Re-factored	101	4899	400	458.25	76	123	37	9
Re-combined	n/a	n/a	n/a	n/a	74	123	37	8

3.6   Limitations

During our aspect oriented re-factoring of ORBacus, we have also realized some limitations in our approach due to insufficient research in the area, overwhelming programming effort and limitations in the tool support.

1. We did not completely factor out class types such as Any and NVList, which are used widely for other purpose in addition to the dynamic programming interface, such as the request context passing. While failing to factor these types out does not prevent us from evaluating the aspect oriented approach, we defer the work until future research when it is necessary to exactly quantify the aspect of dynamic programming interface.
2. Our re-factorization of the CORBA features in the generated stub code and API code is not complete. Our aspect-aware IDL compiler is of a prototype nature and needs to be extended. This is due to the fact that new aspects of CORBA are still being discovered. The role and the features of the aspect-aware IDL compiler ought to be thoroughly analyzed. We defer this discussion to future work. As the consequence, the user code is still able to use the corresponding OMG interfaces for a feature that is possibly factored out. The Orb throws exceptions during runtime to flag that these features do not exist.
3. We decided not to collect the memory usage due to the fact that our "aspectization" experiment is conducted on the Java platform. We do not have an accurate memory profiling tool that allows us to the monitor memory usages of the application objects. Also the expense of running the full JVM makes the memory improvements achieved by our AOP re-factoring almost trivial.

4   Conclusion

We believe that adaptability and configurability are essential characteristics of middleware substrates. Those two qualities require a very high level of modularity in the middleware architecture. Traditional software architectural approaches exhibit serious limitations in preserving the modularity in the process of establishing decomposition models for crosscutting design concerns. Those limitations correspond to the scattering phenomena in the code. The aspect oriented programming approach has brought new perspectives to software decomposition techniques. The concept of aspect allows us to compose, with respect to the primary decomposition model, the most appropriate solution for each design requirement. By weaving the aspects together, we are able to improve the modularity of final systems in the dimension of aspects.

To better approximate the benefit of designing middleware with AOP, we use AspectJ to re-factor a number of aspects. The implementations which exist in multiple places of the original code are grouped within a few aspect units. The successful re-factorization shows that middleware systems are able to provide the fundamental services with certain pervasive features factored out or factored in. Aspect oriented re-factorization has shown its superb capability of loading and unloading pervasive features of the system, which is not possible in legacy implementations. The "woven" system transparently supports these re-factored features. The runtime performance is equivalent to the original implementation.

In the light of our experimentation, we are very optimistic that aspect oriented programming will show more promises in conquering the complexity of middleware architecture. In our future work, we will try to gain more experience in terms of applying aspect oriented development methodologies. We are exploring various techniques to help us define horizontal decomposition procedures more concretely. We will eventually use all these experience to design a fully aspect oriented middleware platform.

References

1. AspectJ. URL: http://www.eclipse.org/aspectj.
2. Hyper/J. URL: http://www.alphaworks.ibm.com/tech/hyperj.
3. M. Astley, D.C. Sturman, and G. A. Agha. Customizable Middleware for Modular Software. *ACM Communications*, May 2001.
4. Louis DiPalma and Robert Kelly. Applying CORBA in a contemporary embedded military combat system. OMG's Second Workshop on Real-time And Embedded Distributed Object Computing, June 2001.
5. Robert Filman. Achieving ilities.
   http://ic.arc.nasa.gov/~filman/text/oif/wcsa-achieving-ilities.pdf.
6. Erich Gamma, Richard Helm, Ralph Johnson, and John Vlissides. *Design Patterns*. Addison-Wesley, 1995.
7. Gnome. ORBit.
   URL: http://www.gnome.org/projects/ORBit2/.
8. Object Management Group. The common object request broker: Architecture and specification. December 2001.
9. G. Kiczales. Aspect-oriented programming. *ACM Computing Surveys (CSUR)*, 28(4), 1996.
10. Fabio Kon, Manual Roman, Ping Liu, Jina Mao, Tomonori Yamane, Luiz Claudio Magalhaes, and Roy H. Campell. Monitoring, Security, and Dynamic Configuration with the dynamicTAO Reflective ORB. *IFIP/ACM International Conference on Distributed Systems Platforms and Open Distributed Processing*, 2000.
11. Joseph P. Loyall, David E. Bakken, Richard E. Schantz, John A. Zinky, David A. Karr, Rodrigo Vanegas, and Kenneth R. Anderson. QoS aspect languages and their runtime integration. In *Fourth Workshop on Languages, Compilers, and Run-time Systems for Scalable Computers. Lecture Notes in Computer Science, Vol. 1511, Springer-Verlag*, Pittsburgh, Pennsylvania, USA, May 28–30, 1998.
12. Clarke M., Blair G., Coulson G., and Parlavantzas N. An efficient component model for the construction of adaptive middleware. *IFIP / ACM International Conference on Distributed Systems Platforms (Middleware'2001)*, November 2001.
13. M. Rom, D. Mickunas, F. Kon, and R. H. Campbell. LegORB and Ubiquitous Corba. In *IFIP/ACM Middleware'2000 Workshop on Reflective Middleware*, pages 1–2, Palisades, NY, USA, 2000.
14. Cisco Systems. Cisco ons 15327 - sonet multiservice platform.
    URL: http://www.cisco.com/univercd/cc/td/doc/pcat/15327.htm.
15. Iona Technologies. ORBacus.
    URL: http://www.iona.com/products/orbacus_home.htm.

16. Charles Zhang and Hans-Arno Jacobsen. Quantifying Aspects in Middleware Platforms. In *2nd International Conference on Aspect Oriented Systems and Design*, pages 130–139, Boston, MA, March 2003.
17. Charles Zhang and Hans-Arno Jacobsen. Re-factoring middleware with aspects. *IEEE Transactions on Parallel and Distributed Systems*, 2003. (accepted for publication).
18. John Zinky, Joe Loyall, Partha Pal, Richard Shapiro, Richard Schantz, James Megquier, Michael Atighetchi, Craig Rodrigues, and David Karr. An AOP challenge problem: Managing QoS on iteractions between distributed objects. In *White Paper for ECOOP 2000 Workshop on Aspects & Dimensions of Concerns*, April 2000.

Dynamic Placement Using Ants for Object Based Simulations

Cyrille Bertelle, Antoine Dutot, Frédéric Guinand, and Damien Olivier

Laboratoire d'Informatique du Havre
Université du Havre
25 rue Philippe Lebon
76600 Le Havre
Antoine.Dutot@univ-lehavre.fr

Abstract. A distributed application may be considered as a set of interacting entities continuously evolving. Such application can be modeled as a graph with one-to-one mappings between vertices and entities and between edges and communications. Performances depend directly on a good load balancing of the entities between available computing devices and on the minimization of the impact of the communications between them. However, both objectives are contradictory and good performances are achieved if and only if a good tradeoff is found. Our method for finding such a tradeoff is new and based on colored ant colonies. Each computing resource is associated to one ant colony characterized by a color, allowing an implicit consideration of the load balancing constraint. Then, using colored pheromones, ants are just seeking for communicating structures. The method operates on graphs which structural and numerical parameters may change dynamically during the execution.

Keywords: Ant algorithms, dynamic graph, clustering, auto-organization, distributed applications.

1   Introduction

In distributed application, often a very large number of entities are used to represent a complex system. The dynamics of such systems discourages a static distribution made upstream, before application execution. As the system evolves communications between entities change. Communications and entities may appear or disappear, creating organizations. As a consequence, an entity location that was correct at the beginning, can severely impact performance two hundred time steps after. Therefore we need an anytime distribution method that advices the application on better locations for each entity preserving load-balancing between computing resources, but ensuring that entities that communicate heavily are close together (ideally on the same processing resource).

In this paper, a method based on the Ant System[6] is described that advises on a possible better location of some entities according to the tradeoff between load balancing and minimization of communications overhead.

The Paper is organized as follows. Section 2 provides some background about ant algorithms and some of their applications. Section 3 details the graph representing the

R. Meersman et al. (Eds.): CoopIS/DOA/ODBASE 2003, LNCS 2888, pp. 1263–1274, 2003.

distributed application. Operating on this graph, our colored ant system is described in section 4. Finally, our implementation is discussed in section 5 and illustrated by some experiments, before we conclude with further expected improvements and perspectives for this system.

2   Ant Algorithms

Ant algorithms are a class of meta-heuristics based on a population of agents exhibiting a cooperative behaviour[10]. Ants continuously forage their territories to find food[8] visiting paths, creating bridges, constructing nests, etc.

This form of self-organization appears from interactions that can be either direct (e.g. mandibular, visual) or indirect. Indirect communications arise from individuals changing the environment and other responding to these changes: this is called *stigmergy*[1].

For example, ants perform such indirect communications using chemical signals called *pheromones*. The larger the quantity of pheromones on a path, the larger the number of ants visiting this path. As pheromones evaporate, long paths tend to have less pheromone than short ones, and therefore are less used than others (binary bridge experiment).

Such an approach is robust and well supports parameter changes in the problem. Besides, it is intrinsically distributed and scalable. It uses only local informations (required for a continuously changing environment), and find near-optimal solutions. Ant algorithms has been applied successfully to various combinatorial optimization problems like the Travelling Salesman Problem[5] or routing in networks[3,11], but also to DNA sequencing[1], graph partitioning[9], coloring[4] and clustering[7].

3   Dynamic Communication Graph

3.1   Model

We model the application by a graph $G = (\mathcal{V}, \mathcal{E})$ where $\mathcal{V}$ is a set of vertices representing entities of the application and $\mathcal{E} = \mathcal{V} \times \mathcal{V}$ is a set of edges $e = (v_i, v_j)$ representing communications between entities represented by vertices v_i and v_j. Communications direction being without effect on the ant algorithm, edges are undirected. Edges are labeled by weights representing communication volumes (and possibly more attributes). Each vertex is assigned to an initial processing resource at start. No assumption is made about this initial mapping.

We distinguish two different kinds of communications. On the one hand communications occurring between entities located on the same computing resource are supposed negligible. On the other hand, communications between entities located on distinct computing devices, called *actual communications*, constitute the source of the communication overhead. Our goal is to reduce the impact of actual communications by identifying clusters of highly communicating entities in order to map all entities belonging to one

---

[1] PP. Grassé, in Insectes Sociaux, 6, (1959), p. 41–80, introduced this notion to describe termite building activity.

cluster on the same computing resource. Of course, one trivial solution is obtained by mapping all entities on only one computing resource. In order to avoid this, we use several colored ant colonies that produce colored clusters, each color corresponding to one computing resource.

3.2 Dealing with a Dynamic Environment

As said above, the graph represents the application as it runs, it is therefore dynamic at several levels:

- weights change continuously;
- edges, that is communications, can appear and disappear at any time;
- vertices, that is entities, can appear and disappear at any time.
- processing resources can appear or disappear and change power at any time.

These changes in both topology and valuation are one of the major motivation for using ant algorithms.

Indeed, a monotonic approach is one way to achieve clustering on a graph. It consists in regularly applying a computation on a frozen copy of the dynamic graph, then trying to use this information, though the real graph is still evolving. This approach is problematic: the graph can have changed during computation and results may not be usable any more, creating discrepancies between the real application state and calculated migration hints. Furthermore, it is not incremental, each time the algorithm is performed anew.

Another way is to use an anytime algorithm. The dynamic graph is considered as a changing environment for computing entities that travel on the graph, taking into account the changes as they appear, and storing the solution directly in the graph, as an effect of their evolution. Ant algorithms are well suited for that task as it has been shown in[6]. Moreover this approach is implicitly distributed and results can be stored directly in the graph.

4   Colored Ant System

As shown above, we model large scale distributed applications by a dynamic graph $G = (\mathcal{V}, \mathcal{E})$. The ant algorithm is used to detect clusters of highly communicating entities. To solve load balancing problems we introduce *colored ants* and *colored pheromones* that correspond to available processing resources. To suit our algorithm we extend our graph definition:

Definition 1 (Dynamic Communication Colored Graph). *A dynamic communication colored graph is a weighted undirected graph* $G = (\mathcal{V}, \mathcal{E}, \mathcal{C})$ *such that:*

- $\mathcal{C}$ *is a set of p colors where p is the number of processing resources of the distributed system.*
- $\mathcal{V}$ *is the set of vertices. Each vertex has a color belonging to* $\mathcal{C}$.
- $\mathcal{E}$ *is the set of edges. Each edge is labelled with a weight. A weight* $w(u, v) \in \mathbb{N}^+$ *associated with an edge* $(u, v) \in \mathcal{V} \times \mathcal{V}$ *corresponds to the importance of communications between the couple of entities corresponding to vertices u and v.*

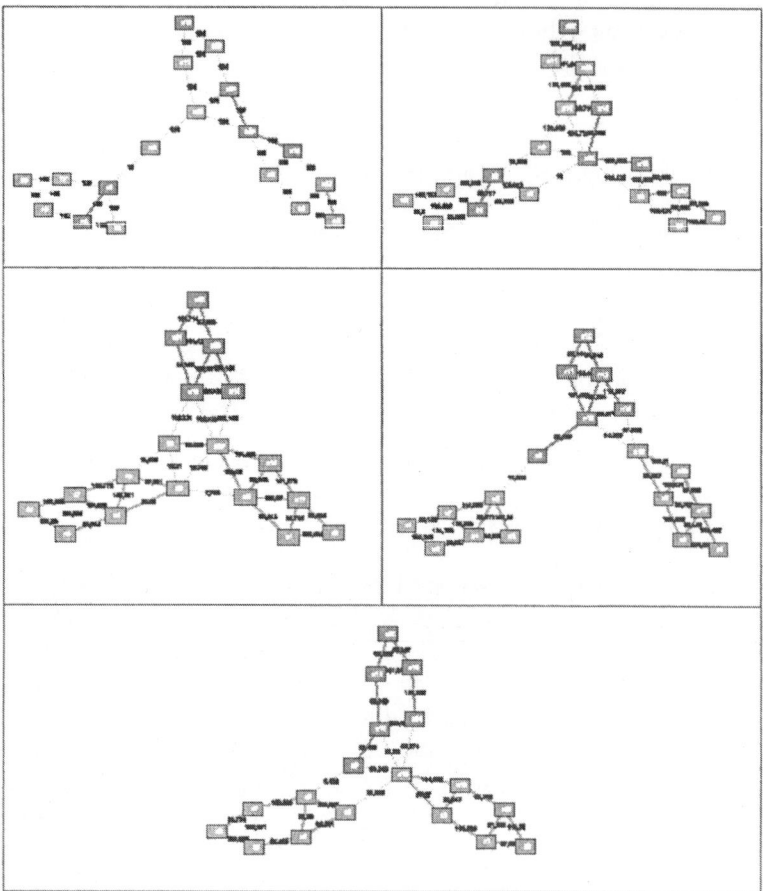

Fig. 1. Example of a dynamic communication graph at five stages of its evolution

The figure 1 shows an example of a dynamic communication colored graph at several steps of its evolution. The proposed method changes the color of vertices if this change can improve communications or processing resource load. The algorithm tries to color vertices of highly communicating clusters with the same colors. Therefore a vertex may change color several times, depending on the variations of data exchange between entities.

4.1   The Colored Ant Algorithm

Our algorithm is inspired by the Ant System[6]. We consider a dynamic communication colored graph $G = (\mathcal{V}, \mathcal{E}, \mathcal{C})$.

- Each processing resource is assigned to a color. Each vertex gets its initial color from the processing resource where it appears. For each processing resource, ants are allocated as explained in section 4.3.
- The algorithm is based on an iterative process. Between steps $t - 1$ and t, each ant crosses one edge and reaches a new vertex. During its move, it drops pheromone of its color on the crossed edge. Moreover, each ant has the ability to remember one or more vertices it comes from.

We define the following elements:

- The quantity of pheromone of color c dropped by one ant x on the edge (u, v), between the steps $t - 1$ and t is noted $\Delta_x^{(t)}(u, v, c)$.
- The quantity of pheromone of color c dropped by the ants when they cross edge (u, v) between steps $t - 1$ and t is noted:

$$\Delta^{(t)}(u, v, c) = \sum_{x \in \mathcal{F}} \Delta_x^{(t)}(u, v, c) \tag{1}$$

- The total quantity of pheromone of all colors dropped by ants on edge (u, v) between steps $t - 1$ and t is noted:

$$\Delta^{(t)}(u, v) = \sum_{c \in \mathcal{C}} \Delta^{(t)}(u, v, c) \tag{2}$$

- If $\Delta^{(t)}(u, v) \neq 0$, the rate of pheromone of color c on the edge (u, v) between the steps $t - 1$ and t is noted

$$K_c^{(t)}(u, v) = \frac{\Delta^{(t)}(u, v, c)}{\Delta^{(t)}(u, v)} \tag{3}$$

This rate verifies $K_c^{(t)}(u, v) \in [0, 1]$.

- The current quantity of pheromone of color c present on the edge (u, v) at step t is denoted by $\tau^{(t)}(u, v, c)$. Its initial value (when $t = 0$) is 0 and then is computed following the recurrent equation:

$$\tau^{(t)}(u, v, c) = \rho \tau^{(t-1)}(u, v, c) + \Delta^{(t)}(u, v, c)$$

Due to evaporation, we define the persistence of the pheromones on an edge: $\rho \in [0, 1]$.

- At this stage of the algorithm, we have computed the current quantity of pheromone, $\tau^{(t)}(u, v, c)$ classically, as a reinforcement factor for clustering formation based on colored paths. We need now to take into account the load balancing in this auto-organization process. For this purpose, we need to balance this reinforcement factor whith $K_c^{(t)}(u, v)$, the relative importance of considered color with regard to all other colors. This corrected reinforcement factor is noted:

$$\omega^{(t)}(u, v, c) = K_c^{(t)}(u, v) \tau^{(t)}(u, v, c)$$

Unfortunaly, this corrected reinforcement factor can generate an unstable process. So we prefer to use a delay-based relative importance of considered color with regard to all other colors. For a time range $q \in \mathbb{N}^+$, we define:

$$K_c^{(t,q)}(u,v) = \sum_{s=t-q}^{t} K_c^{(s)}(u,v).\tag{4}$$

According to this definition, we compute the new corrected reinforcement factor :

$$\Omega^{(t)}(u,v,c) = K_c^{(t,q)}(u,v)\tau^{(t)}(u,v,c)\tag{5}$$

- Let us define $p(u,v_k,c)$ the probability for one arbitrary ant of color c, on the vertex u, to walk over the edge (u,v_k) whose weight is noted $w(u,v_k)$.
  - At the initial step $(t=0)$,

$$p(u,v_k,c) = \frac{w(u,v_k)}{\sum\limits_{v \in \mathcal{V}_u} w(u,v)}\tag{6}$$

- After the initial step $(t \neq 0)$,

$$p(u,v_k,c) = \frac{(\Omega^{(t)}(u,v_k,c))^{\alpha}(w(u,v_k))^{\beta}}{\sum\limits_{v_q \in \mathcal{V}_u}(\Omega^{(t)}(u,v_q,c))^{\alpha}(w(u,v_q))^{\beta}}\tag{7}$$

Where $\mathcal{V}_u$ is the set of vertices adjacent to u.

The relative values of α and β give the weighting between pheromone factor and weights. We will see later that this weighting is a major factor in the way the algorithm achieves its goals.

The choice of the next edge crossed by an ant depends on the previous probabilities. However, to avoid the ant moves to oscillate between two vertices, we introduce in the formula a penalisation factor $\eta \in [0,1]$. Given $\mathcal{W}_x$ the set of the last vertices visited ant x with $|\mathcal{W}_x| < M$, the new probability formula for the specific ant x is:

$$p_x(u,v_k,c) = \frac{(\Omega^{(t)}(u,v_k,c))^{\alpha}(w(u,v_k))^{\beta}\eta_{x,k}}{\sum\limits_{v_q \in \mathcal{V}_u}(\Omega^{(t)}(u,v_q,c))^{\alpha}(w(u,v_q))^{\beta}\eta_{x,q}}\tag{8}$$

Where

$$\eta_{x,q} = \begin{cases} 1 \text{ if } v_q \notin \mathcal{W}_x \\ \eta \text{ if } v_q \in \mathcal{W}_x \end{cases}\tag{9}$$

- The color of a vertex u, noted $\xi(u)$ is obtained from the main color of its incident arcs:

$$\xi(u) = \arg\max_{c \in C} \sum_{u \in \mathcal{V}_u} \tau^{(t)}(u,v,c)\tag{10}$$

4.2   Solution Quality

It is necessary to have a measure of the quality of the solution, to know if we improve the obtained solution. There are two aspects to take into account :

- The global costs of communications;
- The load-balancing of the application.

They are antagonist. So, in order to evaluate our solution we first defined two quality criterions r_1 and r_2. The first criterion r_1 identifies between two solutions which has proportionally less actual communications. Thus we compute actual communication costs, noted a, by summing actual communications on the graph (between entities located on distinct processing resources). Then we compute a ratio r_1 among the total volume of communications, noted s, on the graph and we have:

$$r_1 = a/s$$

The more r_1 is close to 0, the more actual communications are low, as expected. The second criterion r_2 considers the load-balancing. For each color c, we have v_c the number of vertices having color c and p_c the power of processing resource affected to c as defined in section 4.3. Then we have:

$$r_2 = \frac{min\mathcal{K}}{max\mathcal{K}} \quad \text{where} \quad \mathcal{K} = \left\{ \frac{v_c}{p_c}; c \in C \right\}$$

The more r_2 is close to 1, the better the load-balancing. For example, we obtain on the two graphs (Figure 1) $r_1 = 0.15$, $r_2 = 1.0$ for $t = 0$ (first graph) and $r_1 = 0.88$, $r_2 = 1.0$ for $t = 300$ (last graph).

These criterions are used to compare different solutions obtained during the computation, essentially to verify if we improve the solution during the steps. These criterions, enable us to store the best solution obtained so far.

We use also these criterions to compare communication graphs where clusters are already identified. For these graphs colors allocations are randomly shuffled. Then the algorithm tries to find the original allocation on the graph as a solution, or a solution where the criterions are closest.

4.3   Dynamic Aspects

As described above, the algorithm does not specify how it handles dynamic aspects of the graph. We indeed also need to define what happens when:

- an edge appears or disappears;
- a vertex appears or disappears;
- a processing resource appears or disappears.

We need to maintain a given level of population for the algorithm to work. When there are too few ants, evaporation makes pheromones disappear and the algorithm becomes a variant of a greedy algorithm. If there are many ants, pheromones take a too large part and the system efficiency decreases.

Furthermore, the population must take into account the number of entities to distribute and the number of processing resources. A graph with twenty entities will not need as many ants as a graph with three thousand entities.

Therefore ant allocation strategy is:

- When an entity e appears, we allocate $floor(N*p_c)*|\mathcal{C}|$ ants, with N an integer constant greater than 1 and p_c a number $\in \mathbb{R}^+$ representing the power of the processing resource characterized by color c. We place these ants on the vertex corresponding to e. This ensures that each processing resource has a number of ants dependant of its power and that the number of ants is related to the number of entities. Colors are assigned uniformly to this set of ants.
- In the same way, when an entity disappears, we remove randomly $floor(N*p_c)*|\mathcal{C}|$ ants, not necessarily on the vertex that disappear. Remaining ants that are on disappearing vertex and that are not removed die and hatch on a new vertex as explained in section 4.4.
- When an edge disappears we merrily do nothing. Indeed this only affects ants on the possible path they can follow. Identically, when an edge appears, we do nothing, ants can potentially use it immediately.
- when a processing resource of color $c \in C$ appears, we allocate $N*p_c*|\mathcal{V}|$ ants of the new color c, that we spread over the graph uniformly.
- When the processing resource disappears, all ants of its color simply die.
- When the power of the processing resource of color c changes between steps $t-1$ and t (because it is more or less available) we make Δ_{ants} ants die or hatch (according to the sign of Δ_{ants}). Let $\mathcal{F}(\mathcal{C})$ be the set of ants of color $\mathcal{C}$, we compute the difference:
$$\Delta_{ants} = |\mathcal{F}(\mathcal{C}|) - (N*p_c^{(t)}*|\mathcal{V}|).$$

4.4 Further Improvements

Furthermore, the algorithm as stated above has several problems, mostly due to dynamics, but not only, we need to improve what happen if:

- the graph becomes a not connected graph?
- we find local minima, ants running across some preferred edges and not others, stigmergy increasing the process over and over?

To tackle these problems, we add some death and hatching mechanisms. Again, we want to maintain a stable level of population to avoid problems cited in section 4.3. Therefore, we choosed to make one hatch for one death. The goal is to perturb the ants repartition that is generating small stable clusters which are the result of local minima. Furthermore this procedure makes senses since our algorithm runs continuously not to find a static solution as the standard Ant System, but to provide anytime solutions to a continuously changing environment. In order to do that we try to determine when an ant is at the wrong location and unable to leave it by itself. If we detect such a case, we kill the ant and make a new one hatch at a selected position (always to keep population constant).

The algorithm is modified to detect such cases.

1. We define the following elements:
   - $\tau^{(t)}(u, c)$ is the quantity of pheromone of color c dropped on all edges connected to vertex u:

$$\tau^{(t)}(u, c) = \sum_{v_q \in \mathcal{V}_u} \tau^{(t)}(u, v_q, c) \qquad (11)$$

   - $\tau^{(t)}(u)$ is the quantity of pheromone of all colors dropped on all edges connected to vertex u:

$$\tau^{(t)}(u) = \sum_{c \in \mathcal{C}} \tau^{(t)}(u, c) \qquad (12)$$

   - $\varphi_c(u) \in [0, 1]$:

$$\varphi_c(u) = \frac{\tau^{(t)}(u, c)}{\tau^{(t)}(u)} \qquad (13)$$

     the relative importance of pheromones of color c compared to pheromones of all colors on edges leading to vertex u.

2. Then, at each step, before the ant chooses an arc to cross (equations 6 and 8), we must choose weither the ant will die or not. We determine this using a threshold parameter $\phi \in [0, 1]$ for an ant of color c on vertex u:
   - if $\varphi_c(u) < \phi$ we make the ant die and create a new ant choosing a new location for it as follows: we select randomly a set $\mathcal{V}_n$ of n vertices. Let $|\mathcal{F}(v)|$ be the number of ants on vertex v. Then we select a vertex u in $\mathcal{V}_n$ using:

$$u = \arg \min_{v \in \mathcal{V}_n} (|\mathcal{F}(v)|) \qquad (14)$$

     and make the new ant hatch on it.
   - else, we proceed as specified in the original algorithm choosing a new edge using probablities (equation 6 and following).

This mechanism brings several advantages. First this eliminate problems tied to disconnected graphs, as shown in figure 2. In this figure, the graph oscillates between a configuration where it is made of four non connected subgraphs (where ants could otherwise stay blocked), and a grid configuration. The first stage shows the initial configuration. The second is taken 30 steps after, clusters have formed with a very high level of death and hatching. At the third stage, the graph changes and becomes a grid. twenty steps after clusters reappear according to communication in the grid. In the fourth stage, as the graph changes anew, some parts of the grid clusters tend to remain.

This mechanism, while keeping population constant, allows to avoid local minima, small stable clusters inside others.

Finally, this procedure does not need a global system to observe the distributed application, all can be done locally (since hatching is random).

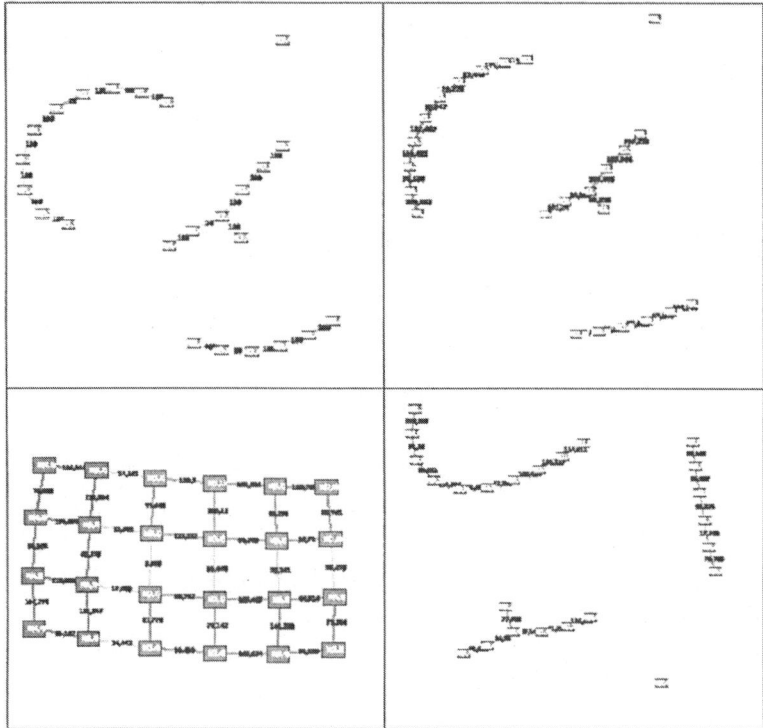

Fig. 2. Example of a disconnected dynamic graph

5   Implementation and Experimentation

Here are several experiments we made with two dynamic graphs. For these tests, we used program that simulate the application by creating a graph and then applying events to it. Events are the appearance or disappearance of an edge, a vertex or a processing resource, but also functions that change weights on edges.

In the following figures, the graph representation is as follows. Vertices are rectangles. Edges are shown with a pie chart in the middle that indicates relative levels of pheromones with the maximum pheromone level numbered. Vertices are labeled by their name at the top with under at the left the total number of ants they host and at the right a pie chart indicating the relative number of ants of each color present on this vertex.

The first experiment, already shown in figure 1 and detailed in figure 4.4 is a small graph (18 vertices), where three main communication clusters appear. These clusters are linked at the center by low communication edges that appear and disappear. Inside the clusters some edges also appear and disappear. For this experiment we used parameters $\alpha = 1.0$, $\beta = 4.0$, $\rho = 0.8$ $\phi = 0.3$, $\eta = 0.0001$, $N = 10$ and $|\mathcal{W}_x| = 4$ vertices. These parameters will be the same for all other experiments excepted when noted.

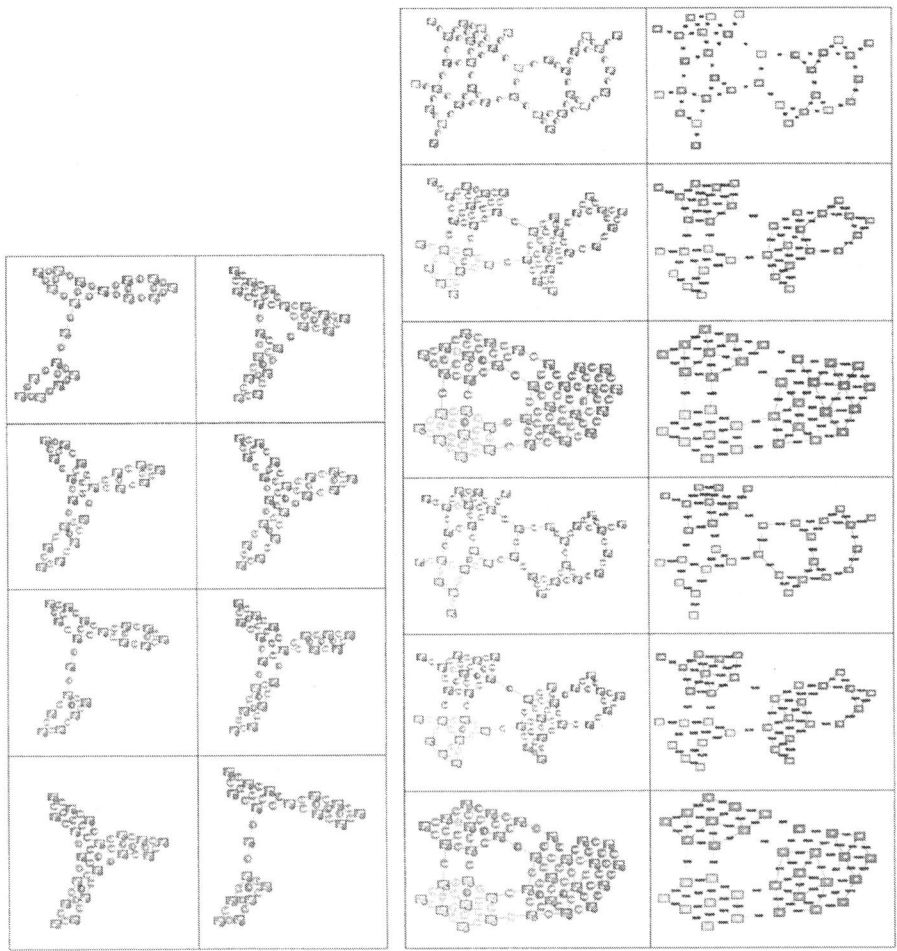

Fig. 3. Experiment 1   **Fig. 4.** Experiment 2

The second experiment used a bigger graph (32 vertices) that continuously switch between three configurations. Figure 4.4 shows two views for each snapshot of the graph. The first one, in the first column, shows all informations as explained above, the second only shows cluster relevant informations and may be easier to follow. Six snapshots of the graph are presented and show that clusters remains stable across reconfigurations.

6   Conclusion

In this paper we have presented a variant of the Ant System called Colored Ant System that offers advices for entity migration in a distributed system taking care of the load and communication balancing. We have described a base colored ant algorithm, observed its behaviour with dynamic graphs and provided methods to handle them. We have shown several experiments with different graphs of this system.

We develop actually an heuristic layer allowing to handle some constraints tied to the application, like entities that cannot migrate (e.g. bound to a database), but also informations peculiar to the application.

This work takes place within the context of aquatic ecosystem models[2], where we are faced to a very large number of heterogeneous auto-organizing entities, from fluids representatives to living creatures presenting a peculiar behaviour.

References

1. C. Bertelle, A. Dutot, F. Guinand, and D. Olivier. Dimants: a distributed multi-castes ant system for dna sequencing by hybridization. In *NETTAB 2002*, pages 1–7, AAMAS 2002 Conf, Bologna (Italy), July 15th 2002.
2. C. Bertelle, V. Jay, and D. Olivier. Distributed multi-agents systems used for dynamic aquatic simulations. In D.P.F. M ller, editor, *ESS'2000 Congress*, pages 504–508, Hambourg, September 2000.
3. G. Di Caro and M. Dorigo. Antnet: A mobile agents approach to adaptive routing. Technical report, IRIDIA, Université libre de Bruxelles, Belgium, 1997.
4. D. Costa and A. Hertz. Ant can colour graphs. *Journal of Operation Research Society*, (48): 105–128, 1997.
5. M. Dorigo and L.M. Gambardella. Ant colony system: A cooperative learning approach to the traveling salesman problem. *IEEE Transactions on Evolutionary Computation*, 1(1): 53–66, 1997.
6. M. Dorigo, V. Maniezzo, and A. Colorni. The ant system: optimization by a colony of cooperating agents. *IEEE Trans. Systems Man Cybernet.*, 26: 29–41, 1996.
7. B. Faieta and E. Lumer. Diversity and adaptation in populations of clustering ants. In *Conference on Simulation of Adaptive Behaviour*, Brighton, 1994.
8. D.M. Gordon. The expandable network of ant exploration. *Animal Behaviour*, 50: 995–1007, 1995.
9. P. Kuntz, P. Layzell, and D. Snyers. A colony of ant-like agents for partitioning in vlsi technology. In *Fourth European Conference on Artificial Life*, pages 417–424, Cambridge, MA: MIT Press, 1997.
10. C.G. Langton, editor. *Artificial Life*. Addison Wesley, 1987.
11. T. White. Routing with swarm intelligence. Technical Report SCE-97-15, 1997.

Developing Adaptive Distributed Applications: A Framework Overview and Experimental Results

Francisco José da Silva e Silva[1], Markus Endler[2], and Fabio Kon[3]

[1] Federal University of Maranhão
Av dos Portugueses, s/n, Campus do Bacanga
65085-580 São Luis - MA, Brazil
fssilva@deinf.ufma.br
[2] PUC-Rio
Rua Marquês de São Vicente, 225, Gávea
22453-900 Rio de Janeiro - RJ, Brazil
endler@inf.puc-rio.br
[3] University of São Paulo
Rua do Matão, 1010, Cidade Universitária
05508-090 São Paulo - SP, Brazil
kon@ime.usp.br

Abstract. Building self-adaptive applications is a complex and challenging task. Developers must consider several issues in addition to the implementation of the application-specific functionalities. These issues include the selection of which environment elements must be monitored for detecting when adaptations should take place, how to perform the monitoring, which software adaptations should be carried out, and when should they take place.

Our work aims at reducing the complexity of building adaptive distributed applications. To achieve this, we developed an object-oriented framework that provides a set of integrated tools for monitoring resource usage and component interactions, detecting composite events, and reconfiguring distributed applications.

This paper describes the framework model and how it was used to incorporate adaptive mechanisms to a distributed information service for mobile users. It also presents several results obtained through the execution of a set of simulated scenarios. The results indicate that, besides detecting resource availability fluctuations, it is also important to monitor the interactions between application components, looking for patterns that indicate the necessity to perform dynamic adaptation. We drive conclusions about the applicability of using the framework for the design and implementation of adaptive distributed applications.

1 Introduction

Self-adaptive software is able to modify its own behavior at runtime to adapt to changes in its execution environment for optimizing its performance and availability in different environmental situations. [17,7]. Adaptation is particularly

R. Meersman et al. (Eds.): CoopIS/DOA/ODBASE 2003, LNCS 2888, pp. 1275–1291, 2003.

useful for distributed, mobile, and ubiquitous systems because of the dynamic nature of these environments. This dynamism can be observed in form of variations in resource availability or error rates, in frequent disconnections, reconfigurations of hardware and software, and device mobility [20,14].

Dynamic adaptation requires software to monitor its execution environment to detect when a significant change has happened and then to reconfigure itself to adapt to this change. The developer of an adaptive application must take into account several issues besides the implementation of the application functionalities. These include the selection of which resources elements should be monitored, how to perform the monitoring, how to detect relevant environmental changes, which software adaptations should be carried out and when should they take place. All those issues make the development of adaptive software a complex and challenging task.

Our work aims at addressing the complexity of building adaptive distributed applications and systems by presenting a framework that provides a set of integrated tools for monitoring, detecting complex events, and reconfiguring distributed applications dynamically.

This paper gives an overview of the framework model, and focuses on our experience on using the framework to add adaptive mechanisms to a prototype implementation of an information service for mobile users. It also describes several experimental results obtained through the execution of the adaptive distributed application on a set of simulated scenarios, which shall clarify the benefits of our approach. With this experience, we collected evidence that, besides detecting variations in resource availability, it is also important to monitor the interactions among application components, searching for patterns that indicate the necessity to perform dynamic adaptation.

Specific details about the framework architecture are described elsewhere [6, 5]; in this paper we give a short description of the framework model and then focus on experimental results and on the evaluation of the framework usability.

2   Framework Model

Our framework model satisfies the following design requirements.

- The framework should be **generic** so as to be usable for the development of a wide range of distributed applications.
- It should promote a clear **separation of concerns** between the application's functional code and the adaptation-specific code.
- It should support the development of highly distributed applications, which implies in providing mechanisms to **coordinate reconfiguration actions** between distributed components.
- Framework components should be **flexible and extensible**, in order to accommodate specific applications needs.
- Framework components shared between applications at runtime must **support concurrent execution** of adaptive applications.

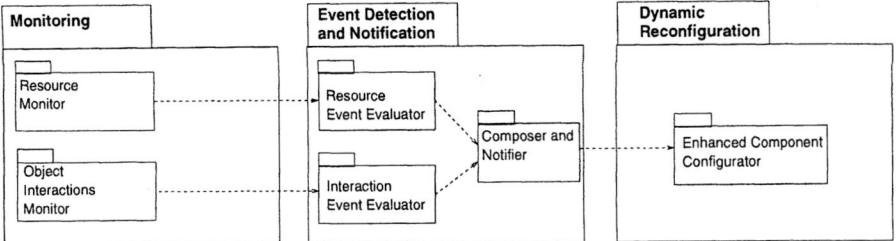

Fig. 1. Framework UML Package Diagram

- Framework components must provide a **management interface** to allow the user to configure and customize its execution parameters.

Figure 1 shows the framework UML package diagram [3], which is composed of three high-level packages. The `Monitoring` package is responsible for monitoring the application execution environment. The data collected by the components of this package are saved in persistent storage or sent directly to the `Event Detection and Notification` package. The latter is responsible for analyzing these data and determining the occurrence of relevant events which are of interest for adaptation decision-making. These events are then sent to the `Dynamic Reconfiguration` package, which is responsible for applying the required reconfiguration actions to adapt the system.

The framework is composed of a collection of CORBA objects and services. Our implementation comprises 21,852 lines of Java code and uses JacORB [22] as the CORBA ORB. The framework is available for download as open-source software at `http://www.ime.usp.br/~sidam/software/AdaptationFramework`.

2.1 Monitoring Package

The main goal of monitoring is to collect sufficient data to keep track of the state of the execution environment (e.g. the network nodes and links) in which the application is running. Analysis of these data will determine when reconfiguration is required and which are the reconfiguration actions that should be applied to adapt the application to the recent changes in the environment.

Monitoring Distributed Resources. The `Resource Monitor` sub-package monitors the status of distributed resources that normally corresponds to physical resources such as memory, CPU, disk, and network links, but it can also monitor software parameters, such as the number of open threads in a server object.

Monitoring is based on *Monitoring Parameters* [23] which correspond to specific aspects of a distributed resource to be monitored. For instance, for each host one can monitor the amount of main memory available, or the percentage of processor utilization. For each network link we can monitor the available bandwidth and latency.

Every Monitoring Parameter has a set of associated operation ranges, which are defined by the framework user. For example, one could use the following operation ranges for monitoring percentage of processor utilization: [0%, 10%), [10%, 25%), [25%, 50%), [50%, 75%), and [75%, 100%].

To implement such monitoring functionality, we use *Resource Monitoring Objects (RMO)*. Each RMO monitors a specific Monitoring Parameter and notifies the Event Detection package whenever there is a change of the operation range of the parameter being monitored.

An example of an application that uses monitoring of distributed resources to adapt its behavior to improve its performance, could be a Web server that converts color images to black-and-white if the available bandwidth to the client drops bellow a given operation range. If the bandwidth drops even more, the client could simply omit the figures.

Monitoring Interactions among Application Components. The Object Interactions Monitor sub-package uses software components called *Interceptors*, which are inserted into the object invocation path, in order to monitor the interactions between the components that comprise the distributed application. Using interceptors, the framework can extract useful information from each method invocation and record it (in persistent storage) for later analysis by the Event Detection and Notification package. Furthermore, each invocation can be time-stamped and one can measure the delay between the method invocation and the receipt of the response.

Interceptors can store different kinds of information from each method invocation, such as the name of the called method, the request timestamp, the IP of the machines that were executing the client and server objects, and the invocation completion time. Besides this generic information, in several cases, it is also useful to store application-specific data, such as method in/out arguments. Our Interceptor implementation can be extended in order to incorporate application-specific needs in this way.

Normally, it is not necessary to monitor the interactions corresponding to all methods of each application component interface. This would impose a heavy overhead on application execution. Thus, the framework allows the user to specify which application methods must be monitored and the overhead imposed to other methods is minimized.

As an example where interaction monitoring is necessary, consider an distributed information service for mobile users. Interceptors could store the physical location of the clients when performing requests and the system could use this information to determine a better distribution of data in order to minimize response time to clients.

2.2   Event Detection and Notification Package

The Event Detection and Notification packages are used to detect relevant changes on the environment state, based on the analysis of the data collected by the Monitoring package. Our framework follows an event-driven approach to notify applications about relevant environmental changes. The framework provides support for two types of events: *Resource Events*, which are triggered when there is a significant change on the state of the distributed resources being monitored; and *Interaction Events*, which are triggered depending on the patterns discovered by the analysis of the data collected by the Object Interactions Monitor sub-package.

Since each adaptive application has interest on a particular set of events and this package works as a stand-alone service in the distributed system, a major requirement for this package is the ability to extend and modify dynamically the set of events that can be detected. This is done by allowing the user to provide new event definitions that are dynamically loaded into the system by using reflective Java mechanisms [13]. We also allow the replacement of event definitions without interrupting the event detection service.

Resource Event Evaluation. As described in Section 2.1, a Resource Monitoring Object notifies a component of the Resource Event Evaluation subpackage (called Resource Manager) whenever there is a change on the operation range of the parameter being monitored. The Resource Manager keeps the last value informed by all RMOs instantiated on the environment, obtaining a global view of the state of the distributed resources.

The evaluation of a resource event is based on a boolean expression provided by the user as part of the event definition. The expression is composed of one or more Monitoring Parameters, as illustrated in the following expression: (cpu_use > 4 AND memory_available < 2). This expression evaluates to true when, in a host, the operation range for the percentage of processor utilization is greater than 4 and the operation range that describes the availability of main memory is bellow 2. In order to trigger event notification, the corresponding boolean expression must stay true during a user-specified time. This avoids the generation of an event when a temporary situation, such as a peak in CPU usage, occurs.

Interaction Event Evaluation. As described in Section 2.1, the data collected by the interception of method invocations is kept in persistent storage. The Interaction Event Evaluator sub-package periodically searches these data, looking for patterns that indicate some abnormal or undesired situation, or simply a change in application behavior.

The detection of interaction events is performed by *Evaluators*. Each Evaluator is responsible for the detection of an specific type of interaction event. The framework provides an abstract class, called Evaluator, that implements the basic functionality of an Evaluator.

For each application-specific interaction event, the developer of an adaptive application must implement a subclass of Evaluator, overriding two methods:

user_evaluation_code(), that reads the persistent storage and searches for a pattern of interest; and clean_database(), responsible for removing analyzed data from the persistent storage. user_evaluation_code() must return an object of type EventNotification when the pattern is found.

A component of the framework, the Interaction Manager, is responsible for the execution of Evaluators, each of which is executed in an independent thread. The Interaction Manager executes the user_evaluation_code() method in a periodicity defined by the user as part of the interaction event definition. It also allows dynamic loading and replacement of Evaluators using Java reflection mechanisms [13].

Event Notification. The framework uses the CORBA Event Service [19] to define an event channel used to notify the occurrence of resource and interaction events. This channel uses a push approach, where the Resource and Interaction Managers are registered as event producers and components of adaptive applications responsible for carrying out dynamic reconfiguration are registered as consumers.

2.3   Dynamic Reconfiguration Package

The main goal of the Dynamic Reconfiguration package is to determine which adaptive action(s) should be performed when a significant change on the environmental state occurs and to support the application of those actions in a safe and consistent way.

In order to provide the required mechanism to trigger the reconfiguration, we extended the functionality of the Component Configurator [16,15], which defines an architecture for reconfiguring distributed applications. In this architecture, each application component has a corresponding Component Configurator object. The Component Configurator keeps track of the dynamic dependencies between the component and other system or application components. By maintaining an explicit representation of those dependencies, it is possible to guarantee runtime consistency.

Component Configurators are also responsible for disseminating events across inter-dependent components. Examples of common events are the failure or migration of a component, internal reconfiguration, or replacement of the component implementation. The rationale is that those events affect all the dependent components. This communication mechanism is used in order to coordinate reconfiguration actions between the application components.

The Component Configurator is the place where programmers insert the code to deal with these configuration-related events. This provides a clear separation of concerns between the application functional code and the code that supports application reconfiguration.

We extended the original component configurator architecture with an environment-aware thread that registers itself with the notification channel provided by the Event Detection and Notification package. This thread receives the notification of events that indicate relevant environmental changes. Depending on the type of the event, it executes the appropriate actions required to adapt the application to the new environment state, using the Component Configurators to coordinate reconfiguration actions between the application components. The framework organizes the code that treats each environment event as a set of strategies, using the Strategy Pattern [12].

3   Experimental Results

Our framework was developed within the scope of the SIDAM research project [10], which aims at studying problems related to the design and implementation of decentralized information systems for mobile users. The SIDAM reference application is a distributed information service disseminating information about traffic conditions in a large metropolitan area. Generation, storage, and query of traffic information is fully decentralized and clients are mobile. In this case, adaptation becomes essential for achieving high service availability, dynamic load balancing, and short response times for clients.

We used the SIDAM application as a use case in order to validate the facilities provided by our framework. This section gives a brief overview of the SIDAM application and describes the experimental results we obtained.

3.1   The SIDAM Application

The SIDAM reference application is a distributed information service disseminating road traffic information for a metropolis such as São Paulo or New York. In order to keep the size of the information base and the corresponding queries manageable, the SIDAM application logically divides the city into micro-regions (a few blocks), which are the atomic units to which a piece of traffic information can be associated. Traffic data of a micro-region is stored at *Information Servers*, each of which can hold data from one or more micro-regions. Information servers reside at fixed hosts that are connected to each other through a reliable wired overlay network.

Traffic information can be queried and updated by mobile users, which may be either common citizens requiring information about the traffic situation in a specific part of a city or staff from the Traffic Engineering Department feeding the system with data about the observed traffic conditions. The mobile network is infra-structured, and hence all communications to and from a mobile host are intermediated by some base stations [1].

3.2   Simulated Scenarios

We have evaluated the benefit of using our framework through the execution of the adaptation-instrumented SIDAM application in several simulated scenarios in order to validate the gain of performance when interactions among application components are also monitored. For each simulated scenario we varied the amount of requests originated from each city region as well as the frequency by which this pattern changed.

A hypothetic city was divided into four regions: North, South, West and East. The simulations were performed in an Ethernet local area network with 10 Mbps, having the communication costs (e. g. latencies) between computers belonging to different regions simulated by adding communication delays as described on Table 1. The SIDAM application components as well as the framework components were instantiated in several nodes, as would happen in the real scenario. Each node of the network consisted of a Pentium II with 400 MHz, 128 MB of RAM, running Linux 2.4.18.

Table 1. Communication cost between city regions in milliseconds

	North	South	West	East
North	-	20	8	10
South	20	-	10	8
West	8	10	-	15
East	10	8	15	-

We used the framework to intercept calls to the `queryInfo()` method, provided by the Information Servers. This method returns the traffic situation in a specific city region. By analyzing the monitored data, we could determine the amount of requests directed to each Information Server grouped according to the city region where the mobile clients were when the request was made. The system then uses this knowledge to choose a better distribution of the Information Servers across the network of fixed hosts. The main form of adaptation done by the SIDAM application is just a relocation of Information Servers to a host which is closer to most of its current clients, aiming at reducing the overall access latency. This is advantageous in a network suffering from significant variations of the access pattern, such it is the case in a network with mobile users.

In order to simplify the analysis of the collected data, we used just one Information Server in our tests, but our implementation does not restrict the number of Information Servers that can be instantiated.

First Scenario. The first simulated scenario is composed of two phases. In the first one, the majority of accesses (50%) is performed by clients located in the South region, while the North, East, and West regions are responsible for 10%, 20%, and 20% of the queries, respectively. After performing a fixed number of `queryInfo` calls, we switched to the second phase, changing the access pattern to one in which clients located in a different region (e.g. West) become responsible for 70% of the accesses. All the other regions accounted for only 10% of the queries. As expected, the adaptive SIDAM application reacts to such a change by migrating the Information Server to a host "close to" the West region, which in fact, reduces the mean response time of the queries, because the communication overhead is reduced.

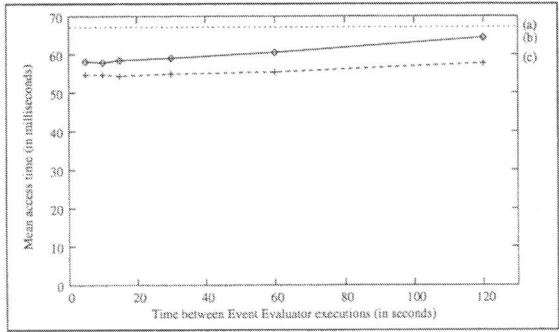

Fig. 2. First Scenario

We performed several experiments with this scenario, changing the execution frequency of the Evaluator responsible for detecting changes of the access pattern. Figure 2 shows the results we obtained. The x axis indicates the frequency of the Evaluator execution while the y axis represents the mean response time spent by the Information Server.

At Figure 2, the solid line (b) shows the results obtained with 600 queries, while the dotted line (c) shows the results when we executed 1,200 queries. The dotted horizontal line (a) indicates the mean response time obtained when executing the non-adaptive version of the SIDAM application.

The results show that the best adaptation is obtained with a frequent event evaluation.

The graph on Figure 3 shows the access time for each of the 600 queries performed when executing the non-adaptive version of the SIDAM application. For the majority of queries, the access time remained between 50 and 100 milliseconds, most of them around 75 milliseconds.

Figure 4 illustrates a similar graph, obtained with the execution of the adaptive SIDAM application. As seen, the adaptive version of the SIDAM application reduced the access time of most of the queries to a value around 50 milliseconds.

These results indicate clearly that, in this scenario, adaptation enhances application performance significantly.

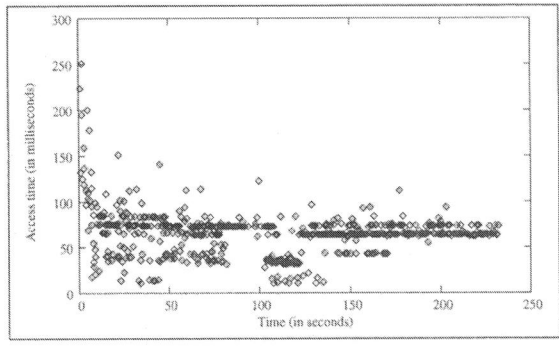

Fig. 3. First Scenario: Non-Adaptive SIDAM Application

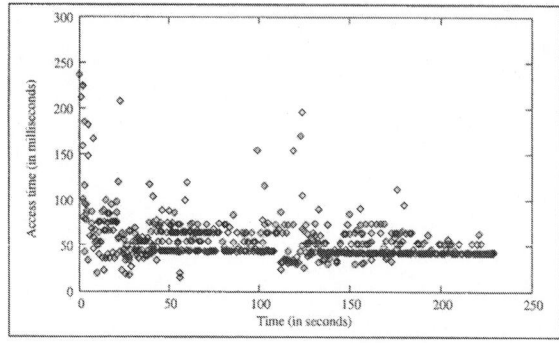

Fig. 4. First Scenario: Adaptive SIDAM Application

Second Scenario. The second scenario was chosen to tests a situation where the amount of accesses performed from each region is approximately the same. This scenario is also composed of two phases. In the first one, each city region generates the same amount of requests. Then, the access pattern changes to a situation where the clients located at one region (South) become responsible for 40% of the requests, while each of the other regions generate only 20% of the total amount of requests. During this second phase, the adaptive application migrates the Information Server to the south, but only a little gain is obtained, as shown by Figure 5.

Third Scenario. The third scenario illustrates a situation where the access pattern changes with high frequency. Each access pattern is kept only for a short time, approximately 1 minute and consist of a fixed number of requests originated from a single region. We have then switched back and forth between two such patterns (origin: South and North).

During our tests we realized the importance of adjusting the parameter which determines the frequency in which the Evaluator analyses the data collected by

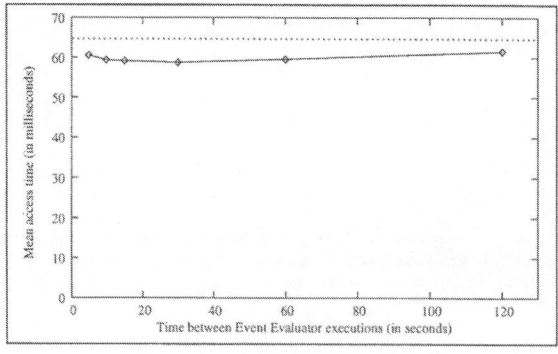

Fig. 5. Second Scenario

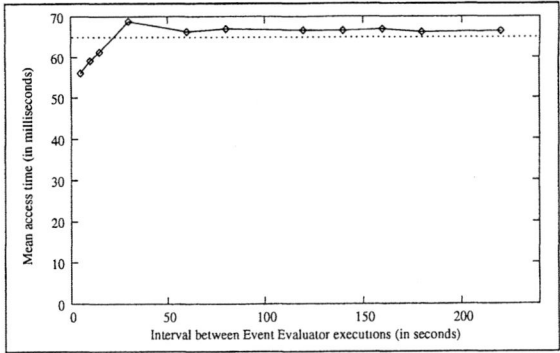

Fig. 6. Third Scenario

the monitoring package. If the parameter value is close to the rate in which the environment changes, the adaptive application can show worse performance than the non-adaptive implementation, as shown in figure 6. This happens because shortly after the application reconfigures itself to adapt to a certain pattern, this pattern is changed to a new one, and hence the application becomes more busy with reconfiguration than with serving client requests. On the other side, if the parameter value is too high (comparing to the rate in which the environment changes), the response times become closer to the non-adaptive ones. This is shown in Figure 6, where the access times of the adaptive application were only less then the non-adaptive application when there was a high frequency of event evaluations.

Table 2. Communication cost between city regions in milliseconds

	North	South	West	East
North	-	100	100	100
South	100	-	100	100
West	100	100	-	100
East	100	100	100	-

Forth Scenario. This scenario demonstrates a situation where the adaptive mechanisms promote a very significant gain of performance to the application. In a first phase, the majority of accesses (90%) is performed by clients located in one region (North). After 600 accesses, the access pattern is changed to one in which clients located in a different region (e.g. South) become responsible for 90% of the accesses. In this second step we also perform 600 access. For this scenario, we defined different communication costs for clients issuing requests from each of the regions, illustrated on Table 2.

Figure 7 shows the results we obtained. The use of the non-adaptive version of the application resulted in a mean response time 132,92% greater than the

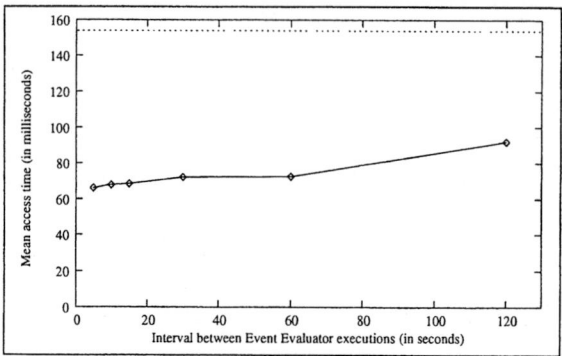

Fig. 7. Forth Scenario

adaptive one when the interval between the evaluation of the access pattern was set to 5 seconds.

3.3   Experience on Using the Framework

The experiments with the four scenarios aimed at identifying the situation in which dynamic adaptation triggered by detection of unbalanced access patterns can bring performance gains. The main focus of our experiments were not the design and evaluation of monitoring and adaptation strategies tailored for a specific application such as the SIDAM, but rather the validation of the framework usability for building adaptive distributed applications.

In fact, the experience of using our framework for incorporating adaptive behavior into a non-trivial application such as the SIDAM information service turned out to be a very positive one, since we could validate the requirements established for its architecture, described in Section 2. The major benefits observed were:

- The framework simplified the requirement and architectural analysis by defining a clear separation between the aspects related to environment monitoring, detection of environmental changes, and dynamic application reconfiguration;
- System design was also simplified, since the framework "suggests" the components in charge of performing each of the above tasks, defining the collaboration model between them trough well defined interfaces. In that manner, the framework achieves the goal of enabling *design reuse*;
- The framework enabled intense *code reuse* through the reuse of its components, minimizing the effort on programming;
- The framework showed to be very flexible, letting the developer customize the aspects related to monitoring, event detection, and reconfiguration considering specific application needs;
- The framework promoted a clear separation of concerns between the application functional code and the code related to dynamic reconfiguration;

- The framework successfully provided the adequate mechanisms necessary to reconfigure an application composed of several components spread throughout a distributed system.

Despite the fact that the framework eases the construction of adaptive distributed applications, it does not address some other issues related to the development of adaptive applications, such as:

- What is the goal when incorporating adaptation: performance gains, fault tolerance or optimizing resource consumption, etc ?
- Under which circumstances does adaptation lead to significant gains considering its costs?
- Which environment variables must be monitored ?

These questions can only be answered after considering the specific adaptive application to be constructed. The framework role is to provide the basic structure of the mechanisms and their interactions that are necessary to implement the functionality defined in response to the above questions, facilitating the analysis and design of the solution.

4   Related Work

Fox et al. [11] address the problem of adapting client/server applications, such as Web browsing, to variations in network bandwidth and the properties of client devices. Adaptation is achieved via data-type-specific lossy compression. Compression is performed by *distillers* that preserve most of the semantic content of the data object. A proxy, placed between the client and the server, retrieves content from Internet servers on the client's behalf, determines the high-level types of the various components (e.g., images, text runs), and determines which distillation engine should be employed to adapt the data to the current bandwidth availability and client device type.

Fox et al. focus their work on applications composed of a client and a server, where a proxy is placed between them. We followed a more generic approach, considering the case of applications composed of several components spread over a network. Fox's proxy adaptation is based on data-type-specific transformations. We believe that other adaptation mechanisms, such as switching to different algorithms as the environment changes, and component reconfiguration, migration, and replication, are complementary changes which are able to deal with a wider range of adaptive applications. Our framework follows a more flexible approach, allowing a choice of the form of adaptation that best suit the application.

Odyssey [18] addresses the problem of providing information access to mobile computers. Their approach is different from Fox's proxies, but uses the same principle of adjusting the data stream according to the environment status.Odyssey is implemented as a set of extensions to the NetBSD operating system, and each application is responsible for deciding how to exploit available resources by selecting the fidelity level of the transmitted data. As with Fox et al., an Odyssey application is divided in client and server components, and the adaptation mechanism allows only to choose between different versions of the data (fidelity levels) so as to be compatible with the resource availability.

Chang and Karamcheti [4] describe an adaptation framework which eliminates the need for adaptation specific decisions to be explicitly programmed into the application. The framework is based on two components: a *tunability interface* and a *virtual execution environment*. The tunability interface provides language support to express availability of multiple execution paths for the application, and the means by which the application execution can be monitored and influenced (by switching to a different path). A driver script repeatedly executes the application in virtual environments, obtaining application behavior profiles. The execution system uses this profile information for adaptation decisions at run time to choose the appropriate execution path that the application must take in order to satisfy user-defined preferences, such as transmission time. All execution paths (algorithms) are coded into a single, monolithic executable, together with monitoring and steering agents. We believe that this approach is not well suited for highly distributed applications since, in this case, one must consider resource availability and application specific load in multiple nodes in order to determine the most suitable adaptation action.

The next two systems, developed at PUC-Rio and BBN respectively, are the ones that share the most similarities with our work.

Moura et al. [8] present an infrastructure that simplifies the development of adaptive distributed applications through a set of mechanisms that allow applications to dynamically select the components that best suit their requirements, to verify whether the system is satisfying these requirements, and to eventually react to variations in the nonfunctional properties of the used services. They use the CORBA Trading Service [19] to support dynamic component selection an have implemented an extensible monitoring facility that supports monitoring of dynamically defined requirements. Moura et al. does not address the problem of how to coordinate reconfiguration actions between application components, an important aspect of highly distributed adaptive applications.

The Quality Objects (QuO) [2,21] project offers a framework for creating applications that adapt to different Quality of Service (QoS) guarantees offered by the resources. QuO provides tools that allows the developer to specify the level of service that the application desires, the behavior alternatives and strategies for adapting to changing levels of service, and to measure and control system resources. QuO also lacks a mechanism to coordinate reconfiguration actions between distributed application components. QuO, as well as the other research projects described in this section, does not explore the analysis of the interactions between application components as a clue to determine when adaptation should be triggered.

5   Conclusions

Incorporating adaptive behavior into a distributed application is a complex task. We address this complexity through the use of object oriented technology by providing a framework that simplifies the development of adaptive distributed applications.

A key point of our work is the support for detecting environmental changes based not only on resource availability but also on changes in the interaction pattern among application components. To demonstrate the use of the framework, we implemented a concrete case study: a distributed service to disseminate traffic information. We have also collected several experimental results by executing a set of simulated scenarios. The results indicate the benefits of using the data collected by the monitoring of the interactions performed by the application components as a way to discover when adaptation must be triggered.

The framework tools that provide the mechanisms for performing resource and interaction monitoring and for detecting environmental changes are extensible, allowing the application developer to accommodate specific application needs.

Other important aspect of our approach is the mechanism to coordinate reconfiguration actions between distributed components, simplifying the development of distributed adaptive applications. The mechanism is based in an extension of the Component Configurator architecture and provides a clear separation of concerns between the application functional code and the adaptation code.

As future work, we intend to provide the support for network monitoring by integrating the framework to the ReMoS [9] system. We also intend for apply the framework to the development of a wider range of distributed adaptive applications and use this experience to build extended framework components, tailored to specific application domains.

Acknowledgments. The authors would like to thank FAPESP (State of São Paulo Research Foundation), sponsor of the SIDAM project. Francisco José da Silva e Silva would like to thank his sponsors, CAPES (Brazilian Federal Agency for Post-Graduate Education), Federal University of Maranhão and FAPEMA (State of Maranhão Research Foundation).

References

1. B. R. Badrinath, A. Bakre, T. Imielinski, and R. Marantz. Handling mobile clients: A case for indirect interaction. In *1993. In Proceedings of the Fourth Workshop on Workstation Operating Systems*, Napa, California, October 1993.
2. BBN Technologies. *QuO ToolKit User's Guide, release 3.0.10*, April 2002. http://quo.bbn.com/.
3. Grady Booch, James Rumbaugh, and Ivar Jacobson. *The Unified Modeling Language User Guide*. Addison Wesley, 1999.
4. Fangzhe Chang and Vijay Karamcheti. Automatic configuration and run-time adaptation of distributed applications. In IEEE Computer Society, editor, *Ninth IEEE International Symposium on High Performance Distributed Computing*, pages 11–20, Pittsburg, Pennsylvania, August 2000.
5. Francisco José da Silva e Silva. *Adaptacão Dinâmica de Sistemas Distribuídos*. PhD thesis, Universidade de São Paulo, February 2003.

6. Francisco José da Silva e Silva, Markus Endler, and Fabio Kon. A framework for building adaptive distributed applications. In *2nd Workshop on Reflective and Adaptive Distributed Middleware. International Middleware Conference*, pages 110–114, Rio de Janeiro, Brazil, june 2003. ACM, IFIP, USENIX, Pontifícia Universidade Católica do Rio de Janeiro.

7. DARPA. Self adaptative software, 1998. BAA 98-12 Proposer Information Pamphlet.

8. Ana Lúcia de Moura, Cristina Ururahy, Renato Cerqueira, and Noemi Rodriguez. Dynamic support for distributed auto-adaptive applications. In *Proceedings of AOPDCS - Workshop on Aspect Oriented Programming for Distributed Computing Systems (held in conjunction with IEEE ICDCS 2002)*, pages 451–456, Vienna, Austria, July 2002.

9. Peter Dinda, Thomas Gross, Roger Karrer, Bruce Lowekamp, Nancy Miller, Peter Steenkiste, and Dean Sutherland. The architecture of the Remos system. In *10th IEEE Symposium on High-Performance Distributed Computing (HPDC'10)*, San Francisco, August 2001. IEEE.

10. M. Endler, D.M. da Silva, F. Silva e Silva, R.A. da Rocha, and M.A. de Moura. Project SIDAM: Overview and Preliminary Results. In *Anais do 2o. Workshop de Comunicação sem Fio (WCSF), Belo Horizonte*, May 2000.

11. A. Fox, S. Gribble, Y. Chawathe, and E. Brewer. Adapting to network and client variation using active proxies: Lessons and perspectives. *special issue of IEEE Personal Communications on Adaptation*, 5(4), August 1998.

12. Erich Gamma, Richard Helm, John Vlissides, and Ralph Johnson. *Design Patterns: Elements of Reusable Object Oriented Software*. Addison-Wesley, 1994.

13. Dale Green. *The Reflection API*. Sun Microsystems, available at http://java.sun.com/docs/books/tutorial/reflect, 2002.

14. Abdelsalam Helal, Bert Haskell, Jeffery L. Carter, Richard Brice, Darrell Woelk, and Marek Rusinkiewicz. *Any Time, Anywhere Computing*. Kluwer Academic Publishers, 1999.

15. Fabio Kon. *Automatic Configuration of Component-Based Distributed Systems*. PhD thesis, Department of Computer Science, University of Illinois at Urbana-Champaign, May 2000.

16. Fabio Kon and Roy H. Campbell. Dependence management in component-based distributed systems. *IEEE Concurrency*, 8(1): 26–36, January/March 2000.

17. Alex C. Meng. On evaluating self-adaptive software. In Paul Robertson, Howard E. Shrobe, and Robert Laddaga, editors, *IWSAS 2000: International Workshop on Self-Adaptive Software*, volume 1936 of *Lecture Notes in Computer Science*, pages 65–74, Oxford, England, April 2000. Springer.

18. B. D. Noble and M. Satyanarayanan. Experience with adaptive mobile applications in odyssey. *Mobile Networks and Applications*, 4(4): 245–254, 1999. Kluwer.

19. OMG - Object Management Group. *The Common Object Request Broker: Architecture and Specification*, November 2002. version 3.0.1.

20. Evaggelia Pitoura and George Samaras. *Data Management for Mobile Computing*. Kluwer Academic Publisher, 1998.

21. Vanegas R, Zinky JA, Loyall JP, Karr DA, Schantz RE, and Bakken DE. Quo's runtime support for quality of service in distributed objects. In *Proceedings of the IFIP International Conference on Distributed Systems Platforms and Open Distributed Processing (Middleware'98)*, The Lake District, England, September 1998.

22. Software Engineering and Systems Software Group at Freie Universität Berlin and Xtradyne Technologies AG. *JacORB Programming Guide*, August 2002. http://jacorb.inf.fu-berlin.de.
23. P. Sudame and B. Badrinath. On providing support for protocol adaptation in mobile wireless networks. Technical report, Department of Computer Science, Rutgers Universit, June 1997.
http://www.cs.rutgers.edu/pub/technical-reports/dcstr -333.ps.Z.

Separating the Concerns of Distributed Deployment and Dynamic Composition in Internet Application Systems

Stefan Paal[1], Reiner Kammüller[2], and Bernd Freisleben[3]

[1] Fraunhofer Institute for Media Communication
Schloss Birlinghoven, D-53754 Sankt Augustin, Germany
stefan.paal@imk.fraunhofer.de
[2] Department of Electrical Engineering and Computer Science, University of Siegen
Hölderlinstr. 3, D-57068 Siegen, Germany
kammueller@pd.et-inf.uni-siegen.de
[3] Department of Mathematics and Computer Science, University of Marburg
Hans-Meerwein-Strasse, D-35032 Marburg, Germany
freisleb@informatik.uni-marburg.de

Abstract. The Internet is currently evolving from a *global information network* into a *distributed application system*. For example, some Internet applications are based on executing remote services which have been previously installed on possibly multiple Internet nodes, whereas parts of other Internet applications are dynamically moved from several remote nodes to be executed on a single node. In this paper, we focus on the related problem of how the parts of an Internet application that have been independently deployed on multiple Internet nodes can be transparently located, seamlessly retrieved and dynamically composed on a particular node by request. We propose a novel deployment and composition approach using so called *modules* and *module federations* and show how to separate the logical application composition from the physical module deployment. The realization of our proposal in Java and C++ is presented and the use of the approach in ongoing research projects is demonstrated.

1 Introduction

Originally, the Internet was supposed to interconnect spatially distributed computing nodes and serve as a *communication* medium to exchange data among them. However, during its evolution, the Internet slowly turned into an *interconnection* medium that was used by some Internet applications to link Internet nodes on the application level. Each Internet node hosting a web server became part of a certain kind of *service federation*, namely the WWW, and users got the illusion of a *global information network* in which all participating nodes are seamlessly linked together and the web browser is a universal interface to this network [1]. With the advent of *web services* [2] in recent years, Internet nodes offer customized services which can be remotely accessed similar to web servers [3]. The invention of web services also promoted new kinds of Internet application systems, so called *application servers,* which are able to host custom Internet applications instead of fixed applications. Moreover, today various Internet applications are distributed and interact across multiple nodes, as in the

R. Meersman et al. (Eds.): CoopIS/DOA/ODBASE 2003, LNCS 2888, pp. 1292–1311, 2003.
© Springer-Verlag Berlin Heidelberg 2003

case of the *grid computing paradigm*. From this point of view, the Internet finally turned into a *cross-platform application environment* and the Internet nodes have become part of *distributed Internet application systems* [4, 5]. In the depicted contexts, Internet applications are typically statically deployed and appropriately configured on each node by the site administrator. However, it is neither always possible nor desired to deploy and setup an application in advance on the node where it is to be executed. Thus, an application is not longer installed on each node but rather deployed into an application repository. From there, it is automatically downloaded onto the target node and appropriately configured before the application is started, as e.g. in *Sun Java Web Start* [6] or *Netx* [7]. In other scenarios, applications are not longer deployed in terms of a single executable but are dynamically composed of smaller parts like libraries or components, as e.g. in the case of *Sun Enterprise Java Beans (EJB)* [8]. Furthermore, similar to orchestrating web services at runtime (which, however, typically remain on the remote node) [9], an Internet application may also be flexibly composed by downloading services from different providers dynamically to perform additional tasks on a single node as in the case of *Jtrix* [10]. Finally, already running applications may want to travel across various nodes (such as software *agents*) or they have to migrate from one host to another. While migration itself already raises many questions regarding saving and restoring object states and application contexts, a major problem is *code mobility* in terms of deploying, configuring and composing an application [11].

To summarize, there are scenarios where Internet applications have to be arbitrarily deployed and executed across various Internet nodes. This leads to a particular need for dynamically locating, retrieving and installing an application from and on certain nodes by request. Moreover, an application itself may be composed of smaller parts, which also touches a major problem in *component-based software engineering (CBSE)*, namely the negotiation and gluing of unknown and originally incompatible components [12]. However, while this indeed is an important issue in an open world scenario, we think that Internet applications are not typically composed of unknown and inherently insecure code fragments but rather of familiar and trustable elements. Thus, in the following we explicitly assume that the composition of related Internet applications is characterized by *selecting* an appropriate component out of a group of compatible components and not by *gluing* possible incompatible components. Therefore, the focus of the approach presented in this paper is the clear separation of component deployment, platform configuration and application composition. We propose a novel deployment and composition approach using so called *modules* and show how they can be used to separate the deployment configuration of the current Internet node from the composition configuration of the Internet application. Along with that we introduce remote module repositories and organize them in so called *module federations* which enable to transparently deploy and query modules in a distributed application system and to dynamically retrieve them from various remote nodes by request.

The paper is organized as follows. In section 2, we discuss the features and requirements of distributed Internet application systems regarding deployment and composition issues and consider existing solutions. Section 3 presents our approach to separating the deployment and composition configuration and illustrates its realization in Java and C++. The application of the approach is demonstrated in section 4. Finally, section 5 concludes the paper and outlines areas for further research.

2   Distributed Internet Application Systems

In this section, we address two of the fundamental problems concerning code mobility, namely deployment and composition of Internet applications.

2.1   Deployment

A basic task of software development is the deployment of an application. In a single managed runtime environment an application can be deployed in a simple manner, but in a distributed Internet application system with multiple involved and independently managed nodes the deployment task is more complex. In this context, we define a *module* as a deployable unit which may contain different code resources and can be separately distributed. The following issues have to be addressed with respect to deployment in distributed Internet application systems.

Managing Different Variants. A module typically exists in different variants, e.g. debug or release version, single-thread or multi-thread capability and so on. We assume that an appropriate module variant is selected matching given attributes. Furthermore, it is likely in a distributed Internet application system that every variant is retrieved concurrently by possibly different nodes. Consequently, a basic feature is the deployment of the same module in different variants and its simultaneous use and provision.

Distributed Deployment. An application on a standalone platform can only retrieve locally deployed modules which typically do not vanish. In contrast, an Internet application has to retrieve modules from remote module repositories which may disappear by chance or turn inaccessible due to network errors or shutdowns. Thus, a module has to be distributable across different module repositories from where it can be transparently retrieved and dynamically deployed on the requesting node without the explicit involvement of the user.

Distributed Updates. Another issue is the evolution of applications and their constituent modules. While a missing module can be easily detected by the requesting Internet application system, it is usually not possible to determine whether somewhere a newer variant is available without issuing a query. Hence, collaborating module repositories should be automatically updated after a new variant has been released.

2.2   Composition

Another basic concern is composition which is typically tightly coupled with deployment. While deployment has to deal with the *separation* of an application, composition is about *assembling* an application. It is usually performed during runtime and relies on the deployed modules. The following issues must be considered regarding composition in distributed Internet application systems.

Separation of Deployment and Composition. A major advantage of composable applications is their ability to arrange the real composition after the actual development has been finished. A particular problem of composition within distributed Internet application systems is the diversity and permanent change of component deployment due to the large range of changing system and network constellations. Thus, the composition process should be configurable independent of the current deployment scenario and the hosting Internet node.

Dynamic Composition. While the location of deployed modules on a single Internet node can be easily tracked and resolved, this is not always possible when each module has been deployed on a different Internet node. The related issue is about how modules can be transparently queried and retrieved. Furthermore, after an appropriate module has been located it has to be dynamically retrieved, which may happen in different ways. However, the application should be able to transparently request and access each module in the same way independent of its location.

Multi-composition System. As mentioned in the introduction, application servers are supposed to host more than one application concurrently. In this scenario, different applications may refer to the same modules. Thus, the composition process has to support *multi-composition,* sharing the same modules and components with several applications. In turn, there are modules which have to be used exclusively by each application, e.g. because of security reasons. Consequently, the composition process should be customizable with respect to sharing and shielding components.

2.3   Related Work

After having highlighted the special concerns of deployment and composition in distributed Internet application systems, in the following we examine various approaches along with related work regarding these issues.

Native Runtime Environments. As mentioned above, deployment is an essential part of application installation and subsequent dynamic composition. For example, Microsoft Windows dynamically deploys components using *Dynamic Link Libraries (DLL)* and UNIX derivates like Linux use *Shared Libraries,* respectively. While they allow encapsulating various components, they have to be packaged in particular files and typically installed in certain paths. Consequently, they require applications to know the physical location of the DLL or the shared library, as illustrated in fig. 1.

```
HINSTANCE hInst = LoadLibrary("c:\sdk\components.dll");
```

Fig. 1. Loading a dynamic link library in MS Windows

Apart from using unique filenames, there is no native versioning support in MS Windows, since the loader distinguishes DLLs by their module names and prevents to load another DLL using the identical module name into the same address space. Moreover, the application can not inspect or query for DLLs matching certain properties without loading them first into memory. And even then, only the basic information can be reviewed, such as module name or particular function entry points. There is no support for revealing the contained components or other resources, simply because DLLs are not primarily intended to carry queryable components but library functions which can be addressed by their well-known name, as shown in fig. 2 for `MyFunc`.

```
typedef bool (*MYFUNC)(void*);
MYFUNC mf = (MYFUNC) GetProcAddress(hInst, "MyFunc");
```

Fig. 2. Retrieving a library function from a MS Windows DLL

Regarding lookup and loading, the native library loader can only retrieve libraries which have been deployed on the local machine. There is typically no support to query remote module repositories for requested libraries. On the other hand, MS Windows DLLs and UNIX shared libraries can be easily deployed by simply copying them into the appropriate directory where the loader is looking for them by file name. As a result, the native development and runtime support for dynamic deployment and composition of components is limited by the constraints mentioned above. Instead, developers have created workarounds like well-known plugin directories to look for components or special configuration files where the location and properties of components can be queried. But these are proprietary approaches and can not be easily ported to other application scenarios.

Virtual Runtime Environments. Besides *native runtime environments* which are inherently bound to certain operating systems like MS Windows or Linux, there are *virtual runtime environments* used in Sun Java or MS .NET [13, 14]. They are particular suited for Internet applications in that they enable the same application executable to be run on different platforms without re-compilation. Regarding dynamic deployment and composition in Java, it differs from the native approach used for C programs in MS Windows and Linux. The fundamental difference is the granularity of loading components. While components of C programs have to be encapsulated in a DLL or a shared library and can only be retrieved together, Java classes can be separately loaded from *Java Archives* provided that the archives and classes are configured in the CLASSPATH, as shown in fig. 3 for the class `mypack.MyClass`.

```
Class c = Class.forName("mypack.MyClass");
mypack.MyClass o = (mypack.MyClass) c.newInstance();
```

Fig. 3. Loading a single class in Java

A variant is the use of a custom class loader which mainly extends the way how classes are located and loaded but not how they are selected, e.g. by given version or vendor properties [15]. Another approach is MS .NET whose dynamic deployment and composition capabilities heavily rely on so called *assemblies*. They represent an improvement over DLLs in that they contain additional metadata and a manifest file which specify further details of the assembly like version number, vendor etc. While the versioning information is evaluated by the *assembly resolver* only for *shared assemblies* stored in a global directory, *private assemblies* are exclusively used by one application and are stored in the path of the application installation directory. Similar to a DLL, an assembly can be easily loaded during runtime, as shown in fig. 4 for `myassembly.dll`. Via the static method `Load` of the class `Assembly` an assembly is dynamically loaded and assigned to the application. The example in fig. 4 also illustrates the use of reflection with `GetTypes` to inspect the content of the assembly.

```
Assembly a = Assembly.Load("myassembly.dll");
Type[] types = a.GetTypes();
```

Fig. 4. Loading an assembly in MS .NET

While virtual runtime environments represent an abstract execution layer on top of the actual platform environment, they still rely on the underlying deployment constraints, such as system environment settings in Java or a well-known directory as in MS .NET. Thus, they are not designed to support distributed deployment and composition scenarios across several and differently configured platforms.

Frameworks. Native and virtual runtime environments are often extended with particular frameworks which add special features regarding dynamic composition, whereas deployment is rarely supported further [16]. Well-known examples with particular composition support are *Sun EJB, CORBA Components*, or *Apache Avalon* [8, 17, 18]. They introduce component models which allow composing applications from independently developed components for different purposes but still rely on the inherent deployment scheme of the underlying runtime environment. Thus, regarding distributed Internet application systems, they are supposed to be primarily used on a single platform and are not designed for cross-platform application environments. However, there is also support for special deployment features in selected application scenarios. As an example, web applications can be easily deployed using so called *Web Archives* [19]. The corresponding Java Servlet Engine dynamically configures an appropriate application environment and instantiates the web application. But once deployed, the web application will not be updated if a newer version replaces the former archive. Furthermore, the web archive approach is only applicable when the entire application can be packaged within a single file but not if it is to be composed and completed with other, external components. Another example is *Sun Java Web Start* [6]; it eases the deployment of *Java Applets* in that it organizes downloaded Java archives on the client side in a locally managed cache. Each time an applet is to be started, Java Web Start compares the cached version with the server version and downloads the applet only if there is a newer version on the server. However, it relies on Java archives and thus it inherits the same problems as mentioned above. Moreover, while it is a good starting point for distributed Internet application systems, it is not able to directly communicate with JAR repositories but by downloading and evaluating a *Java Native Launch Protocol (JNLP)* configuration file from a web server. And it does also not allow a customer to dynamically change the provided configuration of a JNLP application. Finally, there are related frameworks and approaches dealing with composition by refactoring legacy code using *Aspect-Oriented Programming (AOP)*. However, their objectives are different in that they focus on increasing the modularity and configurability of legacy code by using AOP to single out orthogonal features and compose them into aspects [20]. Moreover, due to AOP which is typically applied during compile time, these frameworks are often limited regarding distributed deployment and dynamic composition configuration during runtime.

Application Servers. While a framework typically extends a native application runtime and/or development environment with special features and is usually deployed along with the application itself, this is not feasible for all kinds of extensions. As an example, for concurrently managing *multi-applications* like web applications or web services a so called *application server* is needed. It is started before the actual applications are loaded and then launches each application and service as part of the same process. Related applications are developed using a certain application model and can be solely executed in the target application environment provided by the application server; examples are *Jtrix, Apache Avalon, Jakarta Tomcat, Sun ONE, JBOSS* [10, 18, 19, 21, 22]. While the application server approach is feasible for managing multiple applications and an enhanced runtime environment, it is typically still limited to a single platform architecture and a certain application model. Moreover, due to their orientation towards well-defined server-side scenarios with fixed system configurations, application server approaches have not been designed to be configured on the fly for the dynamic composition of new applications or services. Thus, the composition process is limited to components previously installed and known on the target platform and can not dynamically include custom modules provided by remote users on other Internet nodes. An interesting approach in this direction is provided by Jtrix which is not fixed to a single host but targets *code mobility* across multiple platforms. It propagates so called *netlets* which represent a certain kind of Java service. They can be dynamically retrieved from a remote repository and instantiated on the current platform as well as migrated and spread across different nodes. In this sense, Jtrix represents a particular cross-node application server with respect to nomadic services but therefore it only supports service-based deployment and composition, respectively.

In summary, there are particular requirements regarding deployment and composition in distributed Internet application systems. Although there are existing approaches and solutions which address some of them, deployment and composition are basically supposed to be employed in a single Internet application system, in particular application scenarios or fixed system configurations, respectively. Thus, they lack basic support for transparent retrieval of locally and remotely managed components, sharing and shielding of loaded components and distributed synchronization of deployed components.

3   Module Federations

In the following, our approach to deployment and composition using so called *modules* and *module federations* is presented along with its features and its realization in Java and C++.

3.1   Conceptual Approach

According to the requirements of distributed Internet application systems described above, first of all the *logical composition* of application systems should be separated from the *physical deployment* aspects of the involved Internet platforms. For this purpose, we introduce so called *modules* which are special assemblies of components and represent virtual deployable units with well-known resources, unique module ids and property tags. They can be logically retrieved and transparently resolved across different physical deployment scenarios given the module id. Internet applications do not longer work directly with the deployed units of the native approach, e.g. Java archives or MS Windows DLL, but they refer to modules for their composition requests. From this point of view, modules enable the separately configurable *virtual deployment* on top of the *physical deployment,* as illustrated in fig. 5.

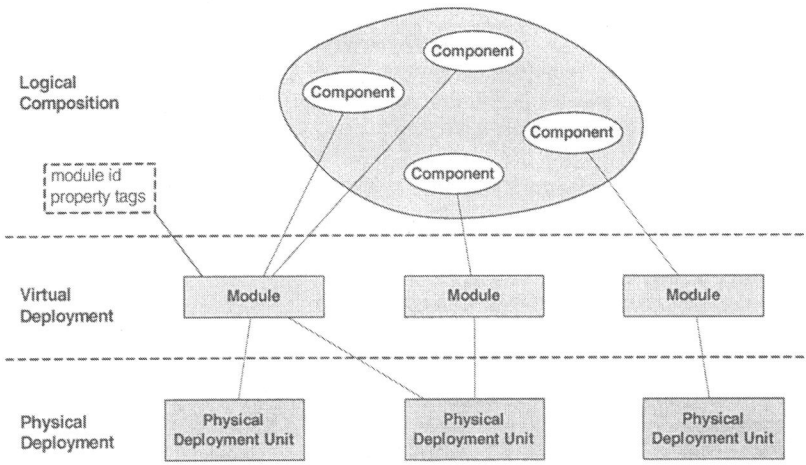

Fig. 5. Physical Deployment, Virtual Deployment and Logical Composition using Modules

A module is acting as a mediator between the physical deployment units and the logical components. It shields the application system and its composition requests from the currently underlying host platform and its configuration scenario. In contrast to native libraries and other deployment units, modules are managed within so called *module repositories* which do not have to be located on the same platform but can be remotely found, queried and managed, as shown in fig 6. A *module controller* on platform AS handles the module loading requests received from the hosted applications and transparently retrieves the module from a possible remote module repository. This is particularly suitable for distributed and decentrally organized system configurations like peer-to-peer networks or mobile scenarios.

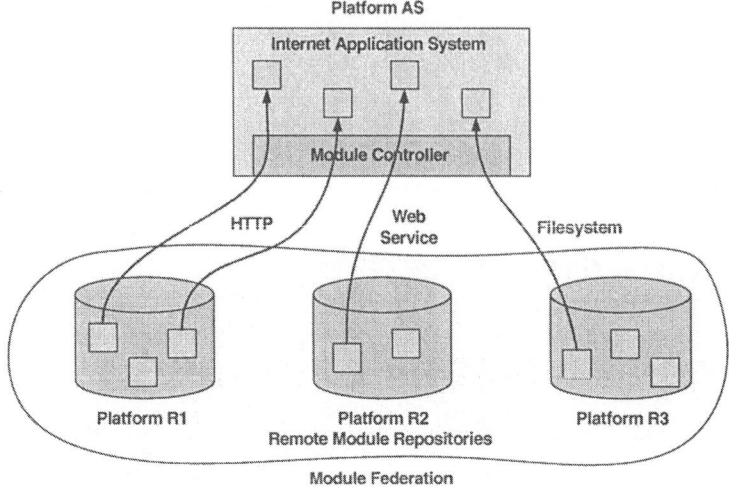

Fig. 6. Module repositories and module federation

Moreover, module repositories can be organized in so called *module federations* for sharing and synchronizing modules across distributed Internet platforms, as also shown in fig. 6. While there are various options to manage a federation, its nodes and the distributed resources [23], our approach does neither rely on a particular organization nor communication protocol as long as there is an appropriate plugin to enable the module controller to interact with the federation or a single repository and shield the logical application composition from the physical module deployment. As an example, the discovery of available module repositories could be managed by manually edited local configuration files, well-known directory services or peer-to-peer approaches. Some repositories may provide network access to their modules over HTTP whereas others may use web services and SOAP. Furthermore, the localization of a module can be performed by querying each module repository one-by-one or by a lookup in a central directory service based on LDAP where each module has been registered previously. In effect, the federation hides the physical deployment of modules across various remote nodes, and once a module has been deployed into the federation, each Internet application system can transparently query and retrieve this module. From this point of view, a module federation represents a group of well-known, trusted and collaborative module repositories which finally behave like a single virtual module repository. Due to the introduction of modules which act as mediators between *deployment constraints* of the involved platforms and *composition constraints* of the concerned application systems, the approach is especially suitable for flexible application systems and variable platform scenarios. It is not bound to a certain programming language feature or operating system and is open to package different kinds of components like classes, binary resources or programming libraries and to dynamically deploy them into module repositories by request.

3.2   Features

The main features and benefits of the proposed conceptual approach regarding deployment and composition in distributed Internet application systems are as follows.

Custom Component Packaging. An important issue concerning component deployment is the custom packaging into deployable units. While the native deployment items like DLLs or Java archives originally lack support for registering, describing and retrieving single components, a module provides options to arbitrarily manage and assemble components within a deployment unit.

Queryable Description. While deployment units are typically addressed using absolute filenames or well-known identifiers, there are often different variants which can only be selected by evaluating custom properties like e.g. versioning information. Thus, remote module repositories can be queried for appropriate modules and components without actually downloading the module.

Transparent Handling of Variants and Dependencies. A component is often used in conjunction with other components. The result is a dependency graph between components and deployment units, often across different variants. Our approach hides the dependency handling from the application in that it provides a uniform way to retrieve modules and contained resources without bothering the developer to manually resolve possible module dependencies.

Distributed Module Repositories. A frequent constraint of current Internet application systems is their limitation to be composable only of locally deployed components. Our approach uses module repositories which can be locally or remotely found and supports the transparent sharing of a deployed module. Thus, a developer does not have to update every involved Internet application system but must only deploy the module once into a single module repository.

Dynamic Deployment and Composition. In native application scenarios, deployment units like Java archives or MS Windows DLLs have to be deployed by the site administrator before the application can be started. In contrast, our modules can be dynamically deployed into a module repository and retrieved by each application in the module federation without customizing the current host platform.

Module Handler. Native deployment units have only limited support for managing the unit during runtime. For example, there is basically no central initialization of the Java archive when a contained Java class or component is accessed the first time. Our approach comes with a module handler which provides a uniform API for accessing the contained resources and tracks their usage.

Shared and Shielded Module Instances. A single application system can easily track down which modules have already been loaded and will not load the same module more than once. On the other hand, Internet application systems are often dealing with concurrently loaded services. We ensure that shared modules are only loaded and instantiated once. Subsequent requests return the same module instance and allow the reuse of resources across concurrently hosted applications.

3.3 Realization

As mentioned above, our conceptual approach is neither bound to a certain programming language feature nor operating system. Thus, in the following we describe the realization of the approach in an exemplary fashion for Java and C++ for MS Windows. We will primarily focus on how to work with modules regarding development, deployment, composition and configuration issues. The tasks of how to implement and synchronize a federation are not covered in detail since they have been already addressed in other works [23]. In fact, the interaction with the module federation and the participating nodes is actually performed by module controller plugins which hide the details of discovering module repositories, querying modules and downloading them onto the requesting Internet node.

Java Implementation. In contrast to MS Windows or Linux runtime environments, the Java Virtual Machine (JVM) does not couple a physical deployable unit one-by-one with logical composable entities. Each Java class within a deployed Java archive can be independently retrieved and used for composition without addressing the other classes in the same archive. However, this is not valid for MS Windows DLLs or shared libraries of Linux which have to be completely loaded for retrieving a contained component. Thus, the basic question for realizing the approach in Java is how to define the required classes of a Java module when there is no option to group classes logically but only physically. We have addressed this problem in previous work by introducing so called *class collections* [24], as shown in fig. 7.

```
<collection name="sun-jaf" id="sun-jaf">
 <variant> <property name="release" value="1.0.1"/>
  <file location="/sdk/sun-jaf-1.0.1/activation.jar">
    <package name="com/sun/activation/.*"/>
    <package name="javax/activation/.*"/> </file>
 </variant> </collection>
```

Fig. 7. Grouping Java classes using class collections

Each collection definition contains a unique id that can be used to refer to this collection like *sun-jaf* in fig. 7. The subsection can then define different variants of the collection with various properties which are later also used to select a particular variant among several variants. Finally, the location of the JAR file where the contained classes can be found is given in conjunction with class name patterns that specify which classes can be loaded from the JAR files. To evaluate the collection configuration, the system class loader of the JVM is replaced by a custom class loader which checks each class loading request and determines the right class according to the configuration file. The module configuration in turn uses class collections to specify the required classes when the module is about to be used, as shown in fig. 8.

```
<module name="texteditor" id="{A9D52EF1}"
        handler="de.fraunhofer.texteditor.CModule">
<property property name="vendor" value="Fraunhofer" />
<dependency>
  <module id="{2E6210AA}"/><module id="{D181334A}"/>
</dependency> <collection id="texteditor">
  <property name="release" value="1.0.0" />
</collection> <collection id="apache-xerces">
  <property name="release" value="2.4.0" />
</collection> </module>
```

Fig. 8. Module deployment using class collections

The module `texteditor` is marked with a *globally unique identifier (GUID)* and defined to use a collection `texteditor` and `apache-xerces` with the given properties. As a result, the module configuration does not longer rely on Java archives or has to specify exactly which classes are needed. Instead, the class collections shield the composition of the module from the actual deployment of the required classes. The attribute `handler` points to a class which represents the module handler of the current module, e.g. performing the initialization or providing access to its resources. Furthermore, the module may also define properties like `vendor` which can be used to query this module. Finally, the `dependency` section indicates which modules have to be loaded by the module controller before the current module can be used.

After the physical deployment of modules, we have to define the logical composition, configuration and management of loaded modules. What will happen when the same module is requested in two different variants by two applications hosted within the same JVM? Or how can an application determine whether the module to be retrieved is already loaded and initialized or not? The first question is targeting a basic problem of the original class loader approach of Java which does not allow loading two classes having the same *fully-qualified class name (FQCN)* by the same class loader [25]. Thus, in order to support the composition of modules in different variants within the same JVM, we have to use and manage several class loaders. This problem has been also addressed by our previous work introducing so called *class spaces* [26]. They enable developers and administrators of Internet application systems to configure exactly which Java classes and class collections are shared across or shielded from other concurrently loaded applications. The class space approach is used as the basis to specify which modules are shared and which are shielded by introducing so called *module spaces* as shown in fig 9. There is one module space `shared` and two child module spaces `shielded-1` and `shielded-2`. While the module space `shared` is configured to load two modules which are shared across `shared`, `shielded-1` and `shielded-2`, the latter two are organized to hold only one module which is not seen by any other module space.

```
<modulespaces> <space id="shared" parent="application">
  <module id="{36242453}"/> <module id="{BE441538}"/>
</space>
<space id="shielded-1" parent="shared">
```

```
<module id="{A9D52EF1}"/>
  <property name="vendor" value="FhG" /> </module>
</space>
<space id="shielded-2" parent="shared">
 <module id="{2EBF97FD}" /> </space>
</modulespaces/>
```

Fig. 9. Module sharing and shielding using module spaces

In case a shared module is to be requested a second time, it is not loaded again but its reference is returned to the caller without initializing the module twice. In general, the module spaces are organized in a hierarchical structure where modules in a child module space can only share the modules on the path to the root space. In turn, the modules located in other module spaces are shielded. In effect, our module management completely hides the issues of lookup, loading and initializing modules from the application, as depicted in fig 10. The application can simply request a module by specifying the related module id modId1 and will get a reference to it.

```
CModuleId modId1 = new CModuleId("{657B3CA5 }");
IModule mod1 = getModuleManager().openModule(modId1);
```

Fig. 10. Requesting a module in Java

The module requestor can also pass additional parameters describing the desired module like a property list, or the related module space is accordingly configured with properties like e.g. vendor, as already shown in fig. 9. The module resolver plugin evaluates these additional parameters before loading the module and tries to resolve an appropriate module. However, there are also other resolving approaches, such as *semantic trading* as used in [27], which evaluate particular aspects like module behavior and the current composition context. For this purpose, additional resolver plugins can be included in our approach that model the related resolving scheme.

After the module has been successfully loaded, it will be initialized using the method init within the module handler object. This method is called only once and can be used to setup the module, e.g. register contained resources or request other required modules like mod2 as shown in fig. 11. In turn, when the last user of the module has released its reference, a corresponding method exit is called which can be used to release acquired modules or to cleanup other resources.

```
public void init() {
  registerResource("{B5C91A0B}", new CMyResource());
  IModule mod2 = openModule("{CDACCCD7}"); }
```

Fig. 11. Initializing a module

The next step for the module requestor is to access the contained resources and components. For this purpose, each module exposes a particular module handler interface which can be used to query a module for well-known resources by unique identifiers. As already described above, we do not want to address the dynamic negotiation, adaptation and gluing of arbitrary components, e.g. by using contracts to describe the interface semantics [28]. Rather, we want to support the transparent deployment and composition of already collaborative and suitable components which are distributed and managed on remote Internet platforms. Thus, if a requested module has been found and loaded, there is no longer the question whether and how the contained components will fit but only how to get a reference and to access them, as shown in fig. 12. A component within the module is requested by openResource given the corresponding resource id which has also been previously used to register the resource and as depicted above.

```
IResource res = mod1.openResource("{B5C91A0B}");
```

Fig. 12. Accessing a certain resource within a module

Finally, the module approach has been implemented in Java in conjunction with class collections and class spaces [26]. It offers developers of components, configurators of applications and administrators of Internet platforms a unique way to separately define physical deployment, logical composition and configuration of Java components. Along with the distributed management of modules within module federations it represents a transparent foundation of composable distributed Internet application systems written in Java.

C++ Implementation. Applications compiled into platform-dependent executables as in the case of C++ programs can not be directly transferred to arbitrary platforms like with Java. At least the source code must be compiled for different platform architectures, although the basic programming strategy may remain the same. Therefore, while we limit the discussion in the following to the realization with C++ and MS Windows, our approach has also been implemented for Linux environments in a similar way. In MS Windows, the deployment strategy of dynamically loadable components mainly relies on DLLs which can be independently deployed and easily incorporated into an application. Basically, there are two ways. The first automatically retrieves the DLL before an application is loaded. If the DLL can not be located and loaded, the application is not started. Using DLLs in this way is the simplest option for developers because there is no need to change the program code compared to linking an application against static libraries. However, the administrator of the hosting Internet platform or the application itself can not adjust the resolution strategy or loading process. The required DLL must be in the path of the application, otherwise the DLL loader will not be able to find the DLL. The second way is more dynamic. The application itself can request a certain DLL during runtime and dynamically specify an arbitrary file location as long as the DLL is stored somewhere on a mounted file system. In contrast to a Java archive, a DLL represents more or less a closed deployment unit. It does not allow inspecting or retrieving parts of it as in the case of loading a single Java class out of a Java archive. Everything contained in the DLL will be always deployed and retrieved completely in an all or nothing fashion. However, this also greatly supports the packaging of a module within a DLL. As an example, fig. 13 shows a configuration file used by a module repository which defines a module that is tagged with the property vendor. There is no need for an additional class collection configuration file as in the case of Java archives. But similarly, instead of relying on the physical deployment unit DLL and its possible varying location on different platforms, an application can virtually request modules by issuing an `openModule` to the module controller with the related module id. The module controller will then load the configured DLL and initialize the contained module similar to the Java implementation showed above.

```
<module id="{A9D52EF1}">
 <property name="vendor" value="Fraunhofer"/>
 <dll id="teditor" loc="http://crossware.org/teditor"/>
</module>
```

Fig. 13. Module deployment using MS Windows DLLs

In addition, we again use *module spaces* like in the Java implementation and are able to define shared and shielded modules similar to the discussion above. After all, a module has to be initialized when it is loaded the first time. In contrast to Java, there are several ways how modules can be used in MS Windows applications. They may be part of a static library linked with the application, they are implicitly loaded with a DLL when the application is started or they are explicitly loaded by an application on request. Either way, an Internet application system with different loaded applications has to ensure that each module is only loaded and initialized once. But in contrast to Java, there is a problem referencing a particular class out of a DLL. There is no way to get access to single classes but only to exported functions, as described above in fig. 2. However, the module management must know which modules are contained within the DLL and how to get a reference to them. To solve this problem, each module is automatically registered to the module controller when the DLL is loaded. For static libraries, static methods are used to do that when the application is started. For implicitly and explicitly loaded DLLs, the corresponding DLL initialization function `DLLMain` is used to register all contained modules, as shown in fig. 14.

```
BOOL WINAPI DllMain(HINSTANCE hinstDLL, DWORD fdwRea-
son, LPVOID lpvReserved){
 m1=GetModuleManager()->RegisterModule(&Tools::Module);
 m2=GetModuleManager()->RegisterModule(&Edit::Module);}
```

Fig. 14. Registering of modules packaged within the same DLL

In effect, each module is registered and only initialized once in a similar way to the Java realization. The differences between modules contained in static libraries, implicitly or explicitly loaded DLLs are hidden from the caller and therefore a common API can be used to request a module, as shown in fig. 15.

```
CModuleId modId1 = new CModuleId("{AA9C391B}");
IModule mod1 = GetModuleManager ()->OpenModule(modId1);
```

Fig. 15. Requesting a module in C++

After getting a reference to the module controller, the desired module is requested by `OpenModule` passing the related module id `modId1` or eventually further parameters which may be evaluated by certain module resolver plugins as already described for the Java implementation. Whenever the module controller is called to retrieve a module, it transparently loads and initializes the module and returns a reference to it. In case the module has been previously loaded, it directly returns the related object reference. This way, if a module originally requested by the application needs also other modules, they are resolved without explicit intervention of the application. The module manager also pays attention that the same module is not loaded twice within the same module space and that it is not initialized repeatedly.

3.4   Discussion

The presented proposal has been implemented using Java and C++ with MS Windows and Linux, having had in mind to introduce a common, *platform- and programming language independent approach* to distributed software deployment and dynamic application composition. As a result, the actual underlying deployment and composition strategy is completely hidden and its configuration is separated. Modules containing components and other deployed resources can be transparently retrieved and are automatically instantiated. In contrast to native, deployment dependent composition approaches like MS Windows DLLs or Java archives, the developer can focus on the business logic and dynamically request a certain component or resource without considering how and where the resources have been actually packaged and deployed. In effect, the tasks of composition and deployment are cleanly separated among developers and deployers of modules and administrators of an Internet application system, respectively. With respect to existing source code, the approach can be seamlessly added and used without introducing a particular packaging or deployment strategy as in the case of Java servlets or a heavy-weight composition framework like Sun Enterprise Java Beans (EJB). Instead, it is built upon native packaging approaches like Java archives and MS Windows DLLs in conjunction with particular module loaders and configuration files that can be extended to support different resolving schemes. In addition, it requires only small changes of the source code of how components are retrieved and accessed. Furthermore, the presented approach allows customers to logically compose an application on their own and is not limited to existing native deployment units like Java archives and predefined composition configuration as in the case of JNLP-based approaches. Another important point is runtime performance. In comparison to native approaches like the original Java classloader or DLL loader of MS Windows, the realizations in Java and C++ reveal overhead only for the localization of an appropriate module matching the module request and loading it from a possibly remote module repository. This depends heavily on the actual application scenario and represents the cost for a highly configurable and distributed component deployment. However, the loading time can be reduced by installing a local module repository which is caching retrieved modules or is automatically synchronized by the module federation. Finally, the actual access on a component within an already loaded module and subsequent composition remain as fast as with the original approach.

4   Application of the Approach

In the following, we depict the application of our approach on *cross-platform computing* [29] where several Internet nodes are grouped to create a multi-platform application environment. Each node is capable to host an arbitrary application which in turn is dynamically composed of components deployed by various developers within a so called *platform federation*. We use this concept in the ongoing research project *CAT* [30] for the development of the Java-based open community platform *netzspannung.org*. Each member of the platform is encouraged to develop new components for the system and to offer them to other members by deploying the related modules into provided distributed module repositories as shown in fig. 16.

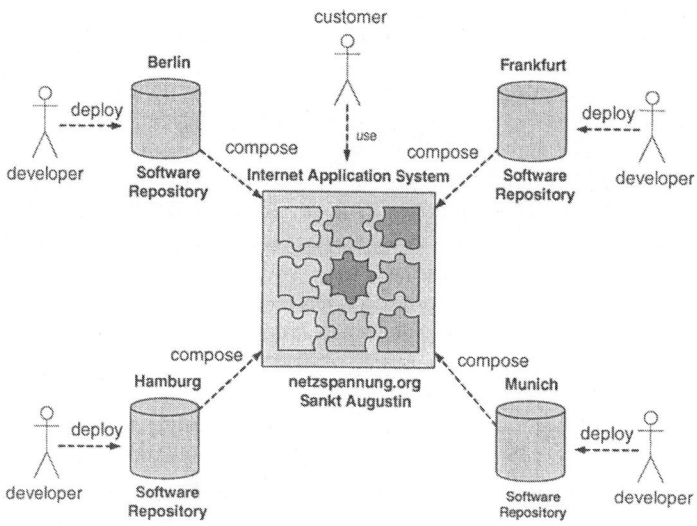

Fig. 16. Dynamic deployment and composition in netzspannung.org

A developer who wants to add a new component to the system first has to add a module handler to his/her project and implement the `init` method as described in section 3.3. There, (s)he registers and initializes all components, resources and objects to be accessible using the module handler. Next, after having packaged all related Java classes in JAR files, (s)he runs a provided tool `collection` to automatically create a collection configuration file of the related JAR files indicating the concrete classes that can be found in there. In this file (s)he also adds configuration lines to specify which third-party Java classes are also needed. Then, (s)he manually creates a module configuration file listing the class of the module handler, constraints of the module and the required class collections, as shown in fig. 8. Finally, the developer uses a helper tool `mddeploy` to upload the JAR files, the collection and module configuration files to a participating module repository. As a result, the configuration files can be used to inspect the module as well as the constraints of the underlying JAR files without actually downloading them from the repository, as described in section 3.3 and in [26]. In case a module represents a new application to be published on netzspannung.org, it must be registered with its module id in the application list of the site configuration by the administrator. Consequently, when the application is to be started, the corresponding module id is taken from the application list and the platform module controller is querying the module repositories for the related module. It automatically resolves the specified dependencies, downloads the module code and uses the information in the module configuration to find the class of the module handler for initialization. Finally, the module is initialized and in turn can request further required modules. This way, each module is loaded one-by-one and the application finally gets composed without knowing from where and how the modules are retrieved. In effect, a customer is able to start each application on the platform and gets the illusion that everything has been deployed on a single host instead of different nodes. Based on the *netzspannung.org* platform (which is operational since about two years) and its module repositories we are currently conducting a further research project called AWAKE [31] which deals with knowledge management via the Internet. Besides particular server-side components, an important part is the client-side user interface for accessing the knowledge space of AWAKE and working with different views. For that, we developed a so called *Internet Application Workbench* which provides a desktop-like GUI and works with modules retrieved from remote module repositories similar to the *netzspannung.org* platform. However, the underlying module framework is not pre-installed but dynamically established on the client-side using Sun Java Web Start. But in contrast to pure JNLP-based approaches like *Object Component Desktop* [32], the actual subsequent composition of an application is not performed using a JNLP file, but can be individually customized by the customer choosing modules from different providers and module repositories.

5   Conclusions

In this paper, we have investigated distributed Internet application systems with respect to their functional requirements to deployment and composition. We have argued that existing solutions lack transparent support for distributed deployment and dynamic composition of remotely located and managed components. Consequently, we have presented a novel solution for solving these problems by introducing so called modules and module federations. Their realizations in Java and C++ for MS Windows were described, and the suitability of our proposal was demonstrated by presenting its application in ongoing research projects. As a result of our approach, different deployment scenarios are hidden from the application and can be easily tackled during runtime using particular composition and deployment configuration files. In effect, the Internet is turned into a distributed Internet application system where each node can be equally used to host applications which are dynamically composed of remotely managed components. Although we are already using the approach in different projects and public installations like netzspannung.org, we are still investigating how to extend existing and include new features. A basic problem of the current deployment strategy is the lack of authentication when a new member is registering to become part of a module federation. Currently, each module repository must be configured to trust the new module repository and its managed modules. The same is valid for a new developer who wants to deploy a module on a new module repository. Another issue concerns access and composition control and whether a particular component can be used or combined with other components in a certain Internet application system. In this context, the presented approach could be also employed to open a new business model for software leasing, which could be called *feature leasing* of composable applications. Depending on the leasing contract, a customer may be able to use only selected features, and the application is only composed with the requested functionalities. Moreover, thinking of client side applications whose components have been downloaded over the Internet, updated components may be only retrieved and installed after upgrading the leasing contract. The resolution of modules is currently performed by resolver plugins matching property lists. However, we are already working on the implementation of plugins for more flexible semantic-based module trading. Finally, the concept of the presented approach is not limited to Java or Linux. Basically, it could also be used to realize a similar module strategy for MS .NET. However, as long as MS .NET is not available for a platform type different than MS Windows, its application is limited and typically not feasible in a heterogeneous network environment like the Internet.

Acknowledgements. The presented approach has been applied in the ongoing research projects CAT and AWAKE which are financially supported by the German Ministry of Education and Research (BMBF). The projects are conducted by the research group MARS of the Fraunhofer Institute for Media Communication, Sankt Augustin in cooperation with the University of Siegen and the University of Marburg, Germany. Special thanks go to Monika Fleischmann, Wolfgang Strauss, Jasminko Novak and Daniel Pfuhl.

References

1. Schatz, B. R. The Interspace: Concept Navigation Across Distributed Communities. IEEE Computer. Vol. 35, Nr. 1. pp. 54–62. IEEE 2002.
2. Vaughan-Nichols, S. J. Web Services: Beyond the Hype. IEEE Computer. Vol. 6, Nr. 2. pp. 18–21. IEEE 2002.
3. Vinoski, S. Web Services Interaction Models – Putting the "Web" into Web Services. IEEE Internet Computing. Vol. 6, Nr. 4. pp. 90–92. IEEE 2002.
4. Milenkovic, M., Robinson, S. H., Knauerhase, R. C., Barkai, D., Garg, S., Tewari, V., Anderson, T. A., Bouwman, M. Toward Internet Distributed Computing. IEEE Computer. Vol. 7, Nr. 5. pp. 38–46. IEEE 2003.
5. Lawton, G. Distributed Net Applications Create Virtual Supercomputers. IEEE Computer. Vol. 33, Nr. 6. pp. 16–20. IEEE 2000.
6. Srinivas, R. N. Java Web Start to the Rescue. JavaWorld. IDG 2001. Nr. 7. http://www.javaworld.com/javaworld/jw-07-2001/jw-0706-webstart_p.html
7. Netx. http://jnlp.sourceforge.net/netx
8. Monson-Haefel, R. Enterprise Java Beans. O'Reilly & Associates. 2000.
9. Vinoski, S. Web Services Interaction Models – Current Practice. Internet Computing. Vol. 6, Nr. 3. pp. 89–91. IEEE 2002.
10. Silver, N. Jtrix: Web Services beyond SOAP. JavaWorld. IDG 2002. Nr. 5. http://www.javaworld.com/javaworld/jw-05-2002/jw-0503-jtrix_p.html
11. Fugetta, A. Picco, G. P., Vigna, G. Understanding Code Mobility. IEEE Transactions on Software Engineering. Vol. 24, Nr. 5. pp. 342–361. IEEE 1998.

12. Ning, J. Q. Component-Based Software Engineering (CBSE). Proc. of the 5th Intl. Symposium on Assessment of Software Tools (SAST). pp. 34–43. IEEE 1997.
13. Eckel, B. Thinking in Java. Prentice Hall. 2002.
14. Prosise, J. Programming Microsoft .NET. Microsoft Press. 2002.
15. Gong, L. Secure Java Class Loading. IEEE Internet Computing, Vol. 2, Nr. 6. pp. 56–61. IEEE 1998.
16. Fayad, M. E., Schmidt, D. C., Johnson, R. E. Implementing Application Frameworks: Object-Oriented Frameworks at Work. John Wiley & Sons. 1999.
17. Marvic, R., Merle, P., Geib, J.-M. Towards a Dynamic CORBA Component Platform. Proc. of 2nd International Symposium on Distributed Objects and Applications (DOA). Antwerpen, Belgium. pp. 305–314. IEEE 2000.
18. Apache Server Framework Avalon. http://jakarta.apache.org/avalon/framework/index.html
19. Goodwill, J. Apache Jakarta Tomcat. APress. 2001.
20. Zhang, C., Jacobsen, H.-A. Quantifying Aspects in Middleware Platforms. Proc. of the 2nd International Conference on Aspect-Oriented Software Development (AOSD). pp. 130–139. ACM 2003.
21. Watson, M. Sun One Services (Professional Middleware). Hungry Minds. 2002.
22. JBOSS Application Server. http://www.jboss.org
23. Lestideau, V., Belkhatir, N., Cunin, P.-Y. Towards Automated Software Component Configuration and Deployment. Proc. of the 8th Intl. Conference on Information Systems Analysis and Synthesis. IIIS 2002.
24. Paal, S., Kammüller, R., Freisleben, B. Java Class Deployment with Class Collections. Proc. of the 3rd International Conference for Objects, Components, Architectures, Services and Applications for a Networked World (NODE). Erfurt, Germany. pp. 144–158. 2002.
25. Liang, S., Bracha, G. Dynamic Class Loading In The Java Virtual Machine. Proc. of the Conference on Object-Oriented Programming, Systems, Languages, and Applications (OOPSLA). pp. 36–44. Canada 1998.
26. Paal, S., Kammüller, R., Freisleben, B. Customizable Deployment, Composition and Hosting of Distributed Java Applications. Proc. of 4th Intl. Symposium on Distributed Objects and Applications (DOA). LNCS 2519. Irvine, USA. pp. 845-865. Springer 2002.
27. Bernard, G., Kebbal, D. Component Search Service and Deployment of Distributed Applications. Proc. of 3rd Intl. Symposium on Distributed Objects and Applications (DOA). pp. 125–135. IEEE 2001.
28. Crnkovic, I., Hnich, B., Jonsson, T., Kiziltan, Z. Specification, Implementation, and Deployment of Components. Communications of the ACM. Vol. 45, Nr. 10. pp. 35–40. ACM 2002.
29. Cusumano, M. A., Yoffie, D. B. What Netscape learned from Cross-Platform Software Development. Communications of the ACM. Vol. 42, Nr. 10. pp. 72–78. ACM 1999.
30. Fleischmann, M., Strauss, W., Novak, J., Paal, S., Müller, B., Blome, G., Peranovic, P., Seibert, C., Schneider, M. netzspannung.org – An Internet Media Lab for Knowledge Discovery in Mixed Realities. In Proc. of 1st Conference on Artistic, Cultural and Scientific Aspects of Experimental Media Spaces (CAST01). St. Augustin, Germany. pp. 121–129. Fraunhofer 2001.
31. AWAKE - Networked Awareness for Knowledge Discovery. Fraunhofer Institute for Media Communication. St. Augustin, Germany. 2003. http://awake.imk.fraunhofer.de
32. Object Component Desktop. http://ocd.sourceforge.net

Method-Based Caching in Multi-tiered Server Applications

Daniel Pfeifer and Hannes Jakschitsch

Institute for Program Structures and Data Organisation (IPD)
Universität Karlsruhe, Germany
{pfeifer,s_jaksch}@ira.uka.de

Abstract. In recent years, application server technology has become very popular for building complex but mission-critical systems such as Web-based E-Commerce applications. However, the resulting solutions tend to suffer from serious performance and scalability bottlenecks, because of their distributed nature and their various software layers. This paper deals with the problem by presenting an approach about transparently caching results of a service interface's read-only methods on the client side. Cache consistency is provided by a descriptive cache invalidation model which may be specified by an application programmer. As the cache layer is transparent to the server as well as to the client code, it can be integrated with relatively low effort even in systems that have already been implemented.

Experimental results show that the approach is very effective in improving a server's response times and its transactional throughput. Roughly speaking, the overhead for cache maintenance is small when compared to the cost for method invocations on the server side. The cache's performance improvements are dominated by the fraction of read method invocations and the cache hit rate. Our experiments are based on a realistic four-tier E-commerce Web site scenario and site user behaviour is emulated in an authentic way. By inserting our cache, the maximum user request throughput of the web application could be more than doubled while its response time (such as perceived by a web client) was kept at a very low level.

Moreover, the cache can be smoothly integrated with traditional caching strategies acting on other system tiers (e.g. caching of dynamic Web pages on a Web server). The presented approach as well as the related implementation are not restricted to application server scenarios but may be applied to any kind of interface-based software layers.

1 Introduction

In recent years, application server technology has become very popular for building complex but mission-critical systems. One the of most important standards in this context is the Java 2 Enterprise Edition platform by Sun (J2EE), including Java's Remote Method Invocation (RMI), Enterprise Java Beans (EJB) and Java Server Pages (JSP) as major building blocks. A common use case for

R. Meersman et al. (Eds.): CoopIS/DOA/ODBASE 2003, LNCS 2888, pp. 1312–1332, 2003.

this technology is the development of database-driven e-business Web sites and Web applications in general. Although the resulting systems tend to have a clean architecture of well separated components, they often suffer from serious performance and scalability problems. A major reason for this is that total system functionality is distributed amongst various software layers (or tiers) on potentially different machines (e.g. a Web server, an application server and a database server).

Industry and research have developed mechanisms to overcome these problems by stating design patterns and implementation tricks as well as providing sophisticated data caching techniques. On the one hand, design patterns have mostly focused on the design and the interfaces of components residing at an (e.g. EJB-based) application server. Caching techniques, on the other hand, have only dealt with the top and the bottom tiers of Web applications: *Web caches* usually cache entire Web pages (or at least fragments of pages) such as served by a related Web application. *Application data caches* store data that is sent to an application server as a result of database queries. In contrast, the approach of this paper increases system performance by *caching results of method calls* as they occur for example when invoking application server methods from a Web server. The related *method cache* caches method call results on the application server's client side (which is a Web server for the case of Web applications). Thus, it differs from conventional caches who deal with caching attribute values of data objects.

In order to maintain cache consistency, we expect an application developer to create a so called *cache model*. The cache model states read-write dependencies between the methods exposed by the application server. Results of methods that only read data at the application server side (no state changes) may be cached and will be available for potential cache hits. Write-methods (which may change application server states) are always delegated to the application server. As opposed to conventional software components, a part of the classes representing a method cache are automatically *generated* from the cache model. This way, the cache implements the interface classes exposed by the application server. The generated classes may be used on the system's client side. Still, it remains transparent to the client code that it actually invokes methods from the method cache rather than from the application server itself.

The rest of this paper is organized as follows: Section 2 highlights the overall architecture of a method cache differentiating runtime and generation time aspects. Section 3 formally introduces cache models which help to provide cache consistency. It also gives a sample cache model such as processed by our implementation. Section 4 discusses further issues of method caching, e.g. cache size and cache bypassing. Experiments concerning the overall cache performance are presented in Section 5. We then compare our contribution with related work and explain how a method cache can be integrated in a modern Web application architecture (Section 6). The paper closes with a conclusion and an outlook on future work.

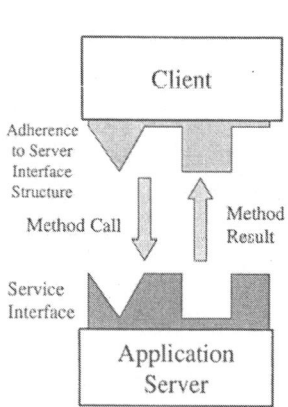

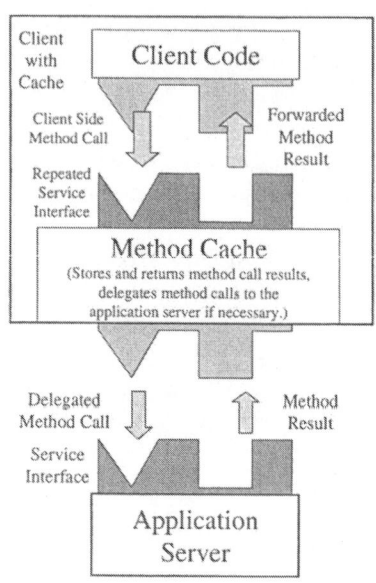

Fig. 1. Abstract interaction scheme for application server and client.

Fig. 2. Interaction of application server and client when using a method cache.

2   General Cache Architecture

This section highlights the general architecture of the method cache system and how it integrates into application server systems. We distinguish between runtime aspects, that relate to the time when the cache is actually used, and generation time aspects.

2.1   Runtime Aspects

Figure 1 gives an illustration of an application server system's client and server part: The application server component exposes an object-oriented interface consisting of a set of abstract classes which hold a set of abstract methods. The client knows about these classes, their methods, and the related invocation protocols. It invokes the methods exposed by the server and receives the corresponding results. The server internally keeps implementation code for executing those methods.

Depending on a system's overall architecture, the calls may be remote or in process. Furthermore, one can distinguish between method implementations that *never* alter the internal state of the application server (or its dependent subsystems) and methods that potentially do. In this paper, we will refer to them as *read methods* and *write methods* respectively.

Figure 2 shows how the system's abstract structure is changed when introducing a *method cache*. The latter is located in between the client and server and exactly repeats the server's service interface. Method calls from the client that formerly addressed the application server are now received by the cache component. The cache component performs different actions depending on whether the called method is a read or a write method.[1] If it is a read method, the component tries to look up a cached method result that has been stored in the cache during a former method call. In order to guarantee the result's correctness the original call must have been performed on an identical application server object and a list of equal method arguments.[2] Hence, a method's signature, its arguments and the invocation-object act as a cache key. If the key's lookup succeeds, there is a cache hit and the stored result is immediately returned to the client. Otherwise the call is delegated to the application server. The result from the application server is then cached and associated with the cache key. Eventually the result is returned to the client.

In case of a write method's invocation, the cache must invalidate all cached read method results that potentially depend on the state-altering effects of the write method call at the application server. The related cache entries are determined by the argument values of the method call and the related cache model. After the entries are deleted from the cache, the write method call is delegated to the application server and the result is propagated to the client.

2.2   Generation Time Aspects

At generation time, a generator tool takes the service interface structure and a related cache model as its input and writes out source files for generated cache classes. After the latter ones have been compiled, they can be used in the cache's runtime environment. The service interface is provided as a set of compiled Java interfaces whose method structure is accessed through the Java Reflection API. The cache model is represented by an XML file whose formal semantics will be discussed in Section 3.

3   Cache Invalidation

In order to guarantee the validity of cached method results, we have designed a structure for specifying cache models. In general, a cache model expresses under what circumstances a cache value must be invalidated because it might not be consistent with the state on the application server side anymore. As our cache strategy is based on methods whose implementations and data dependencies are unknown and potentially difficult (or impossible) to automatically analyze, we expect an application programmer to provide abstract information about data dependencies of methods as part of a cache model.

---

[1] The method's type (read or write) is determined by means of a related cache model whose structure is described in Section 3.

[2] Equality tests for method arguments can be customized. By default, they are based on standard comparison methods for the respective programming language (e.g. `java.lang.Object.equals()` for Java).

This section formally introduces the kind of method dependencies which must be taken into account. Then the semantics and the qualities of the corresponding cache models are discussed. We give a short example on how those models are realized in our system. Lastly, we discuss the data structures and interfaces that are required to efficiently realize our invalidation approach in practice.

3.1   Method Dependencies

In this section, we give a simple but abstract definition of service interfaces and read-write dependencies. In order to focus on aspects that are relevant for cache models, we have avoided many details such as method signatures, method implementations or a related type system.

Definition 1: Let $S = \{s_1, s_2, \ldots\}$ be a countable set of server states and $P = \{p_1, p_2, \ldots\}$ be a countable set of potential method arguments or results. A *service interface* is a finite set of methods $M = \{m_1, \ldots, m_n\}$, where an m_i is a computable function $m_i : S \times P \to S \times P, (s_{bef}, p_{arg}) \mapsto (s_{aft}, p_{res})$.

In other words, a method maps an initial server state (s_{bef}) to a resulting server state (s_{aft}), while accepting a set of arguments (p_{arg}) and returning a result (p_{res}).

Definition 2: A *read method* is a method $m_i \in M$ such that $\forall s \in S, \forall p \in P : \exists p' \in P : m_i(s, p) = (s, p')$. A *write method* $m_j \in M$ is a method which is not a read method.

Definition 3: A *dependency* $dep(m_i, p_k, m_j, p_l)$ exists iff m_i is a read method and $\exists s, s' \in S : \exists p_l', p_k', p_k'' \in P : m_j(s, p_l) = (s', p_l') \wedge m_i(s, p_k) = (s, p_k') \wedge m_i(s', p_k) = (s', p_k'')$
$\wedge p_k' \neq p_k''$.

So, a read method invocation (m_i, p_k) depends on a write method invocation (m_j, p_l), if and only if the write method invocation alters the read method invocation's result for some server state. As read methods don't change server states, there are no dependencies between read methods.

3.2   Cache Models

Cache models must enable dependencies of method calls to be determined on the client side. Unfortunately, computing those dependencies on the client side, would involve a simulation or an execution of the related service method calls in the same place. This cannot be done because the related computation would be too expensive and, also, it would corrupt the entire approach of a client server system. Instead, the formalism proposed below allows for *estimating* a method call's read-write dependencies on the client side. This is done by abstracting from the actual read-write dependencies and replacing them by so-called *model dependencies*.

The central structure for defining model dependencies is a collection of *abstract indexes*. Abstract indexes are sets which help to model invalidation dependencies between read and write methods. If a read and a write method call access the same elements of the same index, it is taken as an indication of a potential dependency between the two calls. At cache runtime, the read method call's cached result will be invalidated, if the write method call writes the corresponding index element. The indexes are abstract in a sense that they may but do not have to represent real data dependencies such as caused by a service method's implementations. Thus, their major purpose is to provide for a consistent but light-weight invalidation policy of cached read method results on the client side.

The number of indexes and the way their elements are accessed must be defined by the cache model designer: For every service method the designer has to specify a set of indexes and a corresponding number of so called *index functions*. An index function's argument is based on the arguments (and the result) of a service method call and an index function's result represents an index element. The cache model designer also declares whether a service method is a read or a write method. When a service method is invoked on the client side, its arguments are well known and the respective index functions can be evaluated. The evaluations just return the index elements which are needed for tracking invalidation dependencies between read and write method calls. The following definitions formalize the related concepts:

Definition 4: Let $IFun$ be a finite set of computable index functions, where each element $f \in IFun$ has the following signature: $f : P \to \mathbb{N}$. Then, a *cache model mod* is a function $mod : M \to \{r, w\} \times \wp(\{1, \ldots, k\} \times (IFun \cup \{\texttt{all}\}))$ (M as in Definition 1).[3]

Here, the number of indexes is represented by k. A function $f \in IFun$ states what index elements are accessed by a method call (m, p) (with $m \in M$ and $p \in P$). In order to keep the model simple, a method call may either access a single index element or all elements of an index. The latter case is indicated by the special function $\texttt{all}$. The values r and w express whether a method performs read or write access.

Definition 5: A *model read method* is a method $m \in M$ where: $mod(m)(p) = (r, ifs)$ with some index function set $ifs \in \wp(\{1, \ldots, k\} \times (IFun \cup \{\texttt{all}\}))$. Otherwise it is a *model write method*. Furthermore, $mrm(mod)$ represents the set of model read methods for the cache model *mod*. More formally: $mrm(mod) = \{m \in M \mid mod(m).1 = r\}$[4]

Definition 6: A *model dependency* $moddep(m, p, m', p')$ exists iff m is a model read method such that $mod(m) = (r, ifs)$, m' is a model write method such that $mod(m') = (w, ifs)$ and $\exists i \in \{1, \ldots, k\} : \exists f, f' \in IFun \cup \texttt{all} : (i, f) \in ifs \wedge (i, f') \in ifs' \wedge (f = \texttt{all} \vee f' = \texttt{all} \vee f(p) = f'(p'))$.

The following model is called the *trivial model* mod_{triv} (for a given M) as it assumes that every method is a model write method: $k := 0, \forall m \in M : m \mapsto (w, \emptyset)$. All model dependencies for a model *mod* form a relation $moddep \subseteq M \times P \times M \times P$. For the trivial model we have $moddep_{triv} = \emptyset$ and also $mrm(mod_{triv}) = \emptyset$.

---

[3] $\wp(x)$ specifies the powerset of a set x.

[4] .1 denotes the selection of the first element of an n-tuple.

Definition 7: A cache model is *correct* iff every model read method is a read method and $\forall m, m' \in M, \forall p, p' \in P : m \in mrm(mod) \Rightarrow (dep(m, p, m', p') \Rightarrow moddep(m, p, m', p'))$.

Correctness only requires that dependencies are indicated by model dependencies for those methods who are model read methods. However, a cache model may cause a "false alarm" and invalidate a cached method result, although the corresponding method invocation on the server would still return the same value. For example, one may declare a read method as a model write method and state model dependencies between this read method and other read methods. Obviously, mod_{triv} is a correct cache model because it contains no model read methods at all.

Lemma (Correctness of Cache Results): Let $m \in M$ be a model read method and seq be a sequence of (consecutive) method invocations of the following form: $seq = (m(s, p) \mapsto (s, res) = (s_{j_1}, res), m_{l_1}(s_{j_1}, p_{m_1}) \mapsto (s_{j_2}, p'_{m_1}), m_{l_2}(s_{j_2}, p_{m_2}) \mapsto (s_{j_3}, p'_{m_2}), \ldots,$
$m_{l_n}(s_{j_n}, p_{m_n}) \mapsto (s', p'_{m_n}), m(s', p) \mapsto (s', res'))$. Then, if mod is a correct model for M and $\forall k \in \{1, \ldots, n\} : \neg moddep(m, p, m_{l_k}, p_{m_k})$ then $res = res'$. (The related proof is straight forward by induction on n.)

Definition 8: Let mod_1 and mod_2 be two correct cache models for the same set of methods M and $moddep_1$, $moddep_2$ the respective model dependencies. Then, mod_1 is *more precise* than mod_2 iff $mrm(mod_2)$ is a proper subset of $mrm(mod_1)$ or, both sets of model read methods are equal and $moddep_1$ is a proper subset of $moddep_2$. More formally: $mrm(mod_2) \subsetneq mrm(mod_1) \vee (mrm(mod_1) = mrm(mod_2) \wedge moddep_1 \subsetneq moddep_2)$.

According to this definition, if the two cache models mod_1 and mod_2 hold the same set of model read methods, mod_1 is more precise because it better models when method calls are independent of each other. On the other hand, if mod_1 contains more model read methods than mod_2, it is more precise than mod_2, since it allows for a larger set of methods to be cached. Note that for correct cache models, the number of model read methods ranges from zero (for the trivial model) to the total number read methods of M. Precision is a semi-ordered relation. Obviously, the trivial model is a lower bound for precision. dep from Definition 3 is the unique upper bound for precision and, in general, it is different from any correct cache model for a given service interface. A useful cache model should be more precise than the trivial model. However, if a cache model is too precise, it might become expensive to compute the related dependencies.

3.3   Example

This section demonstrates how the proposed cache models are realized in practice. In essence, the presented implementation corresponds to the formalism from above. One important difference is that abstract indexes can be named and are not just represented by numbers (such as in Definition 4). Moreover, elements of abstract indexes are now represented by Java objects instead of natural numbers.

The Java pseudo code in Figure 3 represents an extract of a service interface for subscribers holding a list of subscriptions. Here, a subscriber is identified by an ID while the subscription is identified by the corresponding document title. For a subscriber new subscriptions may be added, or existing ones removed. The list of subscribers may be retrieved from a subscription. Also, one may read the list of subscriptions for a certain subscriber.

```
public interface Subscription {
  String getTitle();
  Vector getSubscriberList();
}

public interface Subscriber {
  String getID();
  Vector getSubscriptionList();
  void addSubscription(String title);
  void removeSubscription(String title);
}
```

Fig. 3. Java interface pseudo code for a subscription service.

An XML-based cache model that deals with the given service interface is presented in Figure 4. It defines two indexes named `Subscription` and `Subscriber` (Lines 2 and 3), which correspond to index numbers $k = 1$ and $k = 2$.

Every interface method is annotated with mappings that correspond to elements of function *mod* from Definition 4. E.g. every interface method (identified by its name) is declared as either a read or a write method (attribute `access`). The `model`-tag states on what indexes the corresponding method acts (attribute `index`). The attribute values for `ifun` specify index functions as Java code fragments. A method may read or write all elements of an index (specified by `ifun="all"`) or just a single element. In the latter case the corresponding element is computed at runtime by executing a Java expression which must be stated as `ifun`'s attribute value. The expression must be functional and may refer to the annotated method's `this`-object (by using the keyword `$this$`), its result (by using the keyword `$result$`) or its parameter variables. (The latter two options are not demonstrated in the example.) As mentioned before, index elements may be arbitrary Java objects that result from the expression's evaluation. In the example below `$this$.getID()` is used to specify elements of the `Subscriber`-index as ID-Strings. The use of objects instead of natural numbers is sufficient because index elements only need to be checked for equality (see Definition 6). At cache generation time, the code fragments will be embedded in the generated cache classes.

In the following paragraph, the model's correctness is briefly discussed on an intuitive level: basically, the two given indexes represent the list of `Subscriber` and `Subscription` objects that exist on the server side (Lines 2 and 3). As those objects are uniquely identified by their ID or their respec-

```
1    <cachemodel>
2     <index name="Subscription"/>
3     <index name="Subscriber"/>
4
5     <interface name="Subscription">
6      <method name="getTitle" access="r" >
7       <model index="Subscription" ifun="$this$.getTitle()"/>
8      </method>
9      <method name="getSubscriberList" access="r"
10              mapstrategy="collection" containedclass="Subscriber">
11      <model index="Subscriber" ifun="all"/>
12      </method>
13     </interface>
14
15     <interface name="Subscriber">
16      <method name="getID" access="r">
17       <model index="Subscriber" ifun="$this$.getID()"/>
18      </method>
19      <method name="getSubscriptionList" access="r"
20              mapstrategy="collection" containedclass="Subscription">
21       <model index="Subscriber" ifun="$this$.getID()"/>
22      </method>
23      <method name="addSubscription" access="w">
24       <model index="Subscriber" ifun="$this$.getID()"/>
25      </method>
26      <method name="removeSubscription" access="w">
27       <model index="Subscriber" ifun="$this$.getID()"/>
28      </method>
29     </interface>
30    </cachemodel>
```

Fig. 4. Cache model for the subscription service in XML.

tive title, the applied index functions $this$.getID() and $this$.getTitle() simply return those values. The model tries to reflect changes that occur on the extent of the Subscriber and the Subscription class: e.g., the annotation for method addSubscription() states that adding a subscription writes the subscriber object from which addSubscription() was invoked (Lines 23, 24). The result of method getSubscriberList() changes, if the corresponding Subscription-object is added to or removed from a Subscriber using addSubscription() or removeSubscription(). As this could happen to any subscriber, getSubscriberList() is invalidated whenever a subscriber is written (Lines 23 and 26). Note that every subscription list object is considered as a component of a subscriber object and the list object's state forms a part of a corresponding subscriber object's state.The use of the attributes mapstrategy and containedclass will be explained in Section 4.1.

4   Further Issues of Method-Caching and Their Solution

This section discusses a list of important challenges and problems that occur when implementing a method-based cache.

4.1   Mapping of Result Objects

Once a cache is working for a service interface class, the client using the cache should not get direct access to the corresponding application server objects but act on related cache proxy objects instead. Direct access of application server objects by the client might harm the cache's consistency and leads to bad system performance due to the cache being bypassed. A problem in this context arises when service methods invoked by the client return (handles to) application server objects as results. In this case, the cache has to detect the returned value and map it to a proxy object, which is eventually returned to the client. However, this strategy fails if the returned application server objects are wrapped in runtime objects that should not be cached, e.g. arrays or lists. In this case, the cache needs to create copies of runtime objects in which all references to application server objects are replaced by references to proxy objects. E.g. the method `Subscriber.getSubscriptionList()` from Section 3.3 returns a `Vector` of application server objects with type `Subscription`. The cache maps the method's result to a `Vector` of corresponding proxy objects and passes it on to the client code. It recognizes the required mapping strategy by means of the attributes `mapstrategy` and `containedclass` in the cache model's XML file.

4.2   Correctness of Cache Models

An important issue is to assert the correctness of a cache model and, with it, the cache's returned results. We have implemented a special "correctness check" mode for the cache, in which it runs as usual, but, in case of a cache hit, it also delegates a corresponding method call to the application server. After that, the result coming from the cache's store and the result returned from the application server are tested for equality. If they differ, the cache model is incorrect and must be reworked. If, on the other hand, no inconsistencies can be detected for a set of typical test cases, there is strong evidence that the cache model is correct. Still, the approach does not guarantee the cache model's correctness.[5]

As part of our prototype, we have developed a tool that is used to observe a method cache's behaviour. It allows for connecting to a client's cache at runtime and presents the cache's profile and correctness data which is collected during cache operation. Further, profiling and correctness checks may be turned on and off on a per method basis via the tool's user interface. The tool may also assist a developer in finding out whether the applied cache model is reasonably precise (according to Definition 8). If the cache model is too imprecise, the stored cache results might have to be invalidated too often which leads to poor cache hit rates. The related inefficiencies can be detected by observing cache hit rates and invalidation rates at cache runtime. Based on the corresponding results, the developer may adjust the cache model to improve the its precision.

---

[5] Another more theoretical option would be to prove cache model correctness by analyzing the related method implementations. However, this task cannot be (well) automated and is extremely difficult to handle for a typical application programmer.

4.3   Cache Bypassing

Cache bypassing is any event that changes the application server's state without notifying the cache. The proposed cache concept clearly faces the bypassing problem for reasons, which are discussed next. As in classical client server scenarios, there might be more than one client invoking service methods at a given application server.

A solution to this situation is an extension of the cache component and the application server such that a client's cache must register at the application server when starting up. If the application server encounters a write method invocation from a certain client, it notifies all registered caches of the event, so that they can handle related invalidations. A drawback of this solution is that it is invasive since the application server system or at least some contained components must be adapted.

A second solution is to place the cache right in front of the application server. Then, the cost of potentially performing remote method calls by the client cannot be avoided. However for a cache hit, one still saves all computation costs that otherwise would arise inside the application server. If there is more than one application server, e.g. a cluster of servers, this approach requires communication between the server for exchanging invalidation methods. We are currently working on a client side solution where the clients exchange invalidation messages by communicating with a central *invalidation server*. The invalidation server receives invalidation messages from any client and forwards them to all other clients that potentially need the invalidation messages. We assume that this method is efficient since the messages are short and the related communication protocol is simple.[6] The described mechanism is well applicable to Web application scenarios where there is a fixed but relatively low number of clients (represented by servlet-enabled Web servers).

Another problem occurs if a subsystem of the application server (e.g. an underlying database) potentially changes its state but the application server is not (immediately) notified about the change. In this case, the subsystem should be customized so that it notifies the application server which in turn may trigger notifications of client-side caches: e.g. if an application server accesses a relational database, some other process might perform updates on that database too. Database triggers may then be used to notify the application server of the changes. It is important to note that related invalidation message must refer to the invalidation model instead of the changed server state itself.

Obviously, a time-out-based approach can also be followed to solve this problem. Method results are then automatically invalidated after a certain time limit has been exceeded. However, the time-out strategy has the potential of delivering stale results whenever an application server state changes before a related cached method result times out. Finally, method caching can also be turned off specifically for those methods to which it does not well apply. A good example for this is a method returning the current time.

---

[6] A related message is just a tuple of the form (*index number, index element*) (see Definition 4 in Section 4).

4.4   Cache Size

Controlling cache size is a topic that has been extensively dealt with in the literature. For the sake of completeness, we would like to mention that standard cache replacement strategies such as LRU, LFU or LRD can also be used for the method cache. For our current prototype, we have implemented replacement strategies based on LRU and LFU. Experimental results show that the performance loss of LRU replacement is minor when compared to an ideal "no replacement" strategy (see also Section 5).

5   Performance Experiments

This section discusses experimental results from the usage of a method cache in a realistic E-commerce Web site scenario.

5.1   Experimental Setup

In order to drive our experiments we relied on RUBiS v1.2 [20], a performance test suite for application server systems developed at Rice University. RUBiS authentically models an auction Web site based on eBay.com. The Web site is implemented several times with different implementation variants. Among others, RUBiS comprises three variants based on EJB and Java servlet technology. Persistent user data, which is typical for an auction Web site, is stored in a relational database whose size and structure is comparable to the one used at eBay.com.[7]

The test load on a running RUBiS Web site is generated through a set of HTTP client emulators, modelling typical page access patterns of Web site users. To accomplish this, the emulators run on separate machines and create HTTP requests for a certain number of virtual users, where each user's behaviour is emulated individually. Internally, the clients model user behaviour by means of a state engine. A transition from one user state to the next is chosen randomly based on a given probability table. The resulting URLs are potentially parametrized and cover the entire Web site's functionality such as browsing, logging in, bidding, adding items etc. The load on the auction Web site can then be varied by changing the number of virtual users on the client emulators. About 15% of the resulting requests produce write access on the server side (in other words, updates on the underlying database). According to [5] this is accurately reflects the read-write mix at eBay.com and is quite typical for user access patters of Web applications in general.

For our experiments, we chose to use an EJB variant from RUBiS, which is entirely based on stateless session beans, as it is the best performing EJB variant according to [5]. We tested it both with and without a method cache, while keeping other hard- and software settings fixed. In order to develop the cache model,

---

[7] The research group behind RUBiS compares scalability and other criteria of different applications server architectures. For further information, please refer to [5,4]

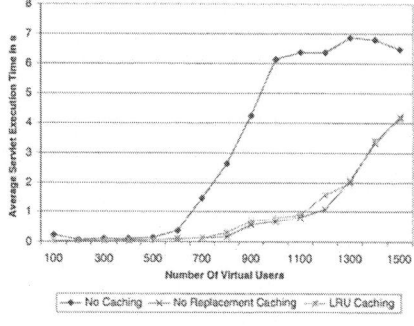
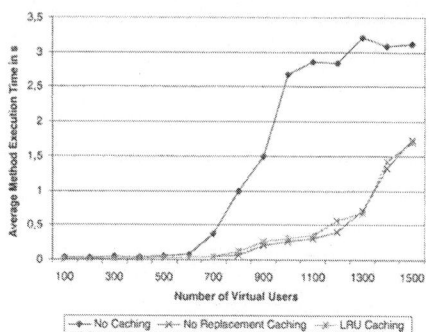

Fig. 5. Average servlet execution time in seconds as a function of the number of virtual users.

Fig. 6. Average method execution time in seconds as a function of the number of virtual users.

35 service methods had to be considered for model dependencies and thereof, 30 were considered as read methods. Furthermore, ten abstract indexes were defined according to Section 3. Before starting any performance experiments, we checked the correctness of the cache model according to Section 4.2. The experiments were performed in a closed network with 6 PCs running under MS Windows XP. One machine acted as the Web server hosting Tomcat v4.0.3 and another machine represented the application server with JBoss v2.4.6. Thus, invocation of bean methods happened over the network using Java's Remote Method Invocation facility (RMI). The Java Developer's Kit (J2SDK) v1.4 from Sun was used as the related Java environment. The Java Virtual Machines (JVMs) for the respective server processes were started with an initial and maximum heap size of 256MB. Apart from this, the JVM's default parameters were used. A separate machine acted as the database server, running the auction site's database under MySQL v3.23.38-max. The database's file size is about 1 GB. It contains 1 million user entries, 33000 items for sale and around 10 auction bids per item. (For further details about the database see [5]). Moreover, three machines acted as client emulators. All machines had the same hardware configuration: a 1.2 GHz Pentium 4 Processor, 512 MB RAM, and a standard PC hard disk drive. By monitoring the related system resources, we ensured that neither network bandwidth nor process load on the client emulator machines represented a potential bottleneck for the experiments.

5.2   Results

Figure 5 shows the average servlet execution times as a function of the number virtual users that hit the site in parallel from the client emulators. The average values are based on all servlet executions that were performed during a run. Every data point represents a run of 5 minutes with a ramp up time of 1 minute. Servlet execution was timed by inserting code for measuring system time right

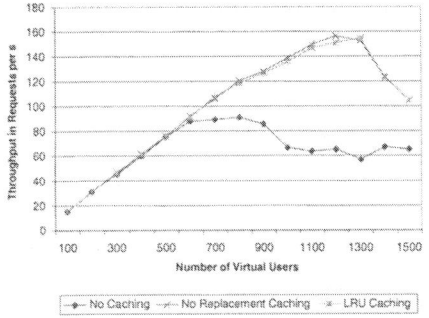
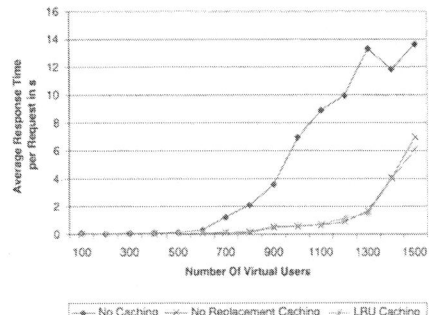

Fig. 7. Throughput in requests per second on the client emulator side as a function of the number of virtual users.

Fig. 8. Average response time per request on the client emulator side as a function of the number of virtual users for the RMI variant.

before and right after the code for the respective servlet execution. In addition to the ramp up time, we granted the Web site a warm-up-phase of 4 minutes when running it with the method cache. The warm-up-phase is required to fill the cache with an initial set of method results, so that the cache hit rate remains constant for a related run. When using the method cache we tried an LRU as well as a no replacement strategy. For LRU the maximum cache size was set to 2000 entries. This means that no more than 2000 method results were stored in the method cache at any point of time. As one can see, the execution times increase with the load of virtual users. However, the average execution times when using the cache remain considerably lower than the corresponding times without the cache. E.g. at a load of 1100 virtual users, the average execution time with the cache is still under 1 second for either variant while it is over 10 seconds when not using the cache.

Figure 6 illustrates the average method execution times of EJB method calls as a function of the number virtual users. Obviously, the execution time gain is very significant due to the savings related to time-consuming RMI calls. Figure 7 presents the throughput in requests per second on the side of the client emulators. The corresponding data was recorded during the kind of runs that have been described above. Figure 8 shows the average response times for HTTP requests on the client emulator side. Here, the performance improvements of using method caching are striking: E.g. at a load of 1100 clients caching requires over 6 seconds in order to serve a page while it needs less than 1 second when using the method cache.

For all performance measures we have presented, the LRU replacement strategy performs about as good an "ideal" no replacement strategy. Note that for very long lasting runs of the client emulators the performance of the no replacement strategy slowly degrades. The reason for this is that the JVM heap space is exhausted by storing more and more method results. As the JVM runs short on

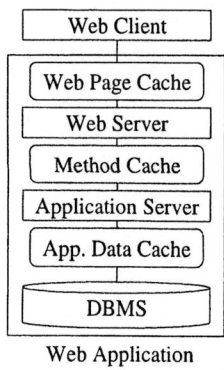

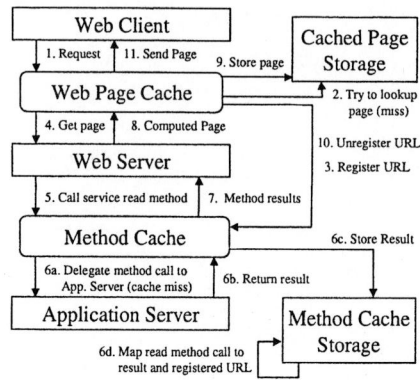

Fig. 9. Common tiers of Web application architectures and related options for caching.

Fig. 10. Execution steps of an integrated Web cache and method cache at a Web page miss.

memory, a lot of CPU time is consumed by garbage collections and eventually the system runs out of memory. Still, the described effects did not affect the data points from above, since the related test runs only last for a few minutes.

Table 1 depicts the average cache hit rate after 10000 method calls when using LRU caching. The hit rate was observed for different LRU cache sizes ranging from a maximum of 30 to 4000 cachable method results. It is interesting that even small cache sizes result in long term hit rates of over 50%. By increasing the cache size the long term hit rate could be raised of up to almost 80%.

6 Our Contribution in Respect to Related Work

6.1 Web Application Caching

In the last two years, research as well as industry has made various efforts to improve the performance of Web applications by means of caching. It is beyond the scope of this paper to discuss all the related approaches in detail (please refer to [16] and [12]). Instead we will compare our approach against existing systems on a more general level and briefly discuss the advantages and disadvantages.

Figure 9 shows the tiers of a typical Web application architecture and highlights where caches potentially come into play:

– Application data caching happens somewhere in between the database and the application server tier. If it is done right in the front of the database

Table 1. Average cache hit rate after 10000 EJB method calls produced by the emulator clients when using the LRU replacement strategy.

LRU Cache Size	30	60	125	250	500	1000	2000	4000
Hit Rate in %	53	62	67	69	71	73	76	78

([7,13,22]), abstractions of database queries are associated with query results in the cache. In case of a cache hit, the query result is immediately returned by the cache as opposed to running the database query engine. At the application server side, application data is cached either programmatically through runtime objects whose structure has been designed by the application developer ([11,15]) or it is controlled by an object-relational mapping framework ([9,17,19]).

– Web page caching usually occurs in front of a servlet- or script-enabled Web server. Beyond the simple task of caching static pages, there are also many approaches for caching dynamically generated Web pages ([1,18,21,23]).

– In contrast, the method cache is inserted at the "backend" of a servlet- or script-enabled Web server from where application server calls are initiated. To the best of our knowledge our approach is the first one enabling caching at this position.

One major question that all dynamic Web caching strategies must deal with is when and how to invalidate cache content. Related solutions are discussed below:

In [3,12] and [14] URLs of dynamic pages on the Web server side are associated with dependent SQL queries on the database level. If a database change affects a corresponding query, the related pages in the cache are invalidated. In [3, 12] dependencies between queries and URLs are automatically detected through sniffing along the communication paths of a Web application's tiers. A general flaw of this URL to SQL query mapping strategy is that it does not account for states from intermediate tiers such as an application server. Although such states might be relevant for dynamic page generation, they can only contribute to a related invalidation policy if they are reflected in the database state. A good example for this problem are stateful session beans from EJB. Clearly, our approach does not encounter this problem as it explicitly deals with application server states.

Other cache strategies for dynamic Web page caching require a developer to provide explicit dependencies between URLs of pages to be cached and URLs of other pages that invalidate the cached ones ([18]). Much as in our approach, the dependencies are declared as abstract named events that may be parametrized. An event parameter usually represents a request parameter of the cached page's URL. Often, server-side page generation scripts or database systems may also invalidate a cached page by invoking invalidation functions of the Web cache's API ([1,21,23]).[8] Unfortunately these strategies are invasive which means that application code (e.g. page generation scripts) has to be changed. Finally, time out-based invalidation policies such as discussed in Section 4.3 are adopted by most dynamic Web caches.

An explicit fragmentation of dynamic Web pages via annotations in page generation scripts helps to separate static or less dynamic aspects of a page from parts that change more frequently ([6,8]). Also, dependencies such as described

---

[8] Typical examples for server-side script languages are Active Server Pages (ASP) and Java Server Pages (JSP).

in the previous paragraph can then be applied to page fragments instead of entire pages. In this respect, our approach enables an even more fined grained fragmentation as it treats dependencies on a level where page scripts invoke service methods from the application server. A great benefit, is that explicit page fragmentation annotations (such as supported by [8]) may then become obsolete. However, when just using the method cache, the corresponding page generation scripts still have to be executed at every page access as only the results of service methods being invoked by the script code will be cached. In the next section, we discuss how page generation can be avoided by integrating dynamic Web page caches with our approach.

6.2   Integration of Web Page Caches

The presented method-based cache can very well improve URL based caching strategies for dynamic Web pages. The basic idea is that invalidation information which is provided by the method cache can not only be used to invalidate method results but also to invalidate cached Web pages. This way, no further invalidation policy is required for the related dynamic web page cache.

Figure 10 illustrates how a dynamic page access is processed in a related system architecture: first, a Web client's HTTP request with the URL of a queried page reaches the Web page cache (1). We assume that the corresponding page is not (yet) cached (2). In order to facilitate integration of the two caches, the Web page cache registers the requested URL at the method cache (3). Then the request is delegated to the Web server (4). A servlet or script runs to generate the requested page and, as an effect, service methods are called from inside the servlet or script code (5). The method cache receives the related method calls and, as usual, either returns cached method results or delegates the calls to the application server (6a). Moreover, it attaches every newly cached or looked up method result with the URL that has been registered in step (3). Hence, besides mapping read method calls to corresponding method results, the method cache now also maps method calls to URLs from dymamic pages whose generation caused those calls (6d). After the page generation has been completed (7, 8), the page is cached inside the Web cache (9). Finally the Web cache unregisters the URL from the method cache (10) and sends the generated page to the Web client (11).

Assuming that no state for generating Web pages is kept at the Web server, a cached page only needs to be invalidated if one of the service method results that were computed during page generation becomes invalid. As the URLs of pages depending on certain service method calls are stored by the method cache at step 5, consistent page invalidation is straight forward: if the method cache invalidates a read method result, it takes all URLs associated with it (at step (6d)) and triggers invalidation of the related pages at the Web cache. If a page computation invokes a model write method (see Section 3), the corresponding page is not cachable, since it (potentially) has side effects at the application server: E.g., in an E-commerce scenarios, this typically happens when users add an article to a shopping cart or submit an order.

6.3   Other Related Approaches

Our approach is heavily influenced by the concept of function materialization as first presented in [10]. In the following, we will briefly highlight the assumptions made in [10] and explain why the related technique cannot be applied in context of service interfaces. In their paper, the authors discuss the *precomputation* of function results (or in our terms read method results) for a given set of objects which is stored in an object-oriented database. They assume that a function's parameter list is relatively short and that the corresponding parameter types are restricted to persistent object types. Since the number of objects in the database is finite, the set of argument combinations for a function is also finite when considering a certain database state. Thus, precomputation of all potential function values may be possible. Further, a precomputed function exclusively operates on database objects, so that its result depends on database states *only*. This enables an automated extraction of potential data dependencies between functions by analyzing on the functions' implementations code. Unfortunately, none of the related assumptions apply to the case of application server scenarios. The dependencies between method implementations may be arbitrarily complex and in general they cannot be automatically analyzed. Also, the set of objects involved in method calls is usually not known until method execution time.

A rather simple approach to method result caching could be found as part of the Torque framework in the Apache DB Project ([2]). In order to cache data of business objects, Torque allows for caching attributes as well a method results. In the Torque framework, the support for method result caching is quite basic as only manager classes for storing and retrieving method call results are offered. The actual code for accessing the cache and transparently delegating method calls must be written by hand. Also, there is no concept of automatically generating a transparent layer of cache classes that implement a set service interfaces such as in our approach. Furthermore, an invalidation strategy must be manually implemented for every cachable service method by following an event notification design pattern. Hence, there is no generic invalidation model which allows for expressing invalidation dependencies on a descriptive level and in a central place.

7   Conclusion and Future Work

This paper has presented the concept of a method cache — an approach for caching results of method-based service interfaces on the client side of an application server system. A typical use case is a Web application whose performance needs to be improved. As our experimental results show, the overall throughput of a realistic system can be considerably increased and its response time extremely reduced when using a method cache. Furthermore, the presented approach is applicable to real world programming languages and development standards such as Java and EJB-based application servers. Still, method cache access is almost seamless to the client code as well as to the server because the cache implements the application server's service interface. This allows for integrating a method cache even in late cycles of project development. The fact that we tested the method cache on the basis of an existing Web application is good demonstration of this feature. Moreover, the chosen Web application is explicitly designed as a benchmarking system for Web-based E-commerce applications (see [20]). For this reason, we believe that the related results are representative for a potential commercial deployment.

It should be stressed that the concept of a method cache is not restricted to application server systems: even the implemented prototype can be applied to any software component that is abstracted by a set of method-based Java interfaces. Obviously, it can be realized for middleware technologies other than EJB such as CORBA, Microsoft DCOM or SOAP.

A cache model, which must be developed by an application programmer, ensures that cached method results are consistent with the state of an underlying software system. Based on our experience, we believe that developing such a cache model is a manageable task for a reasonably qualified developer and that it can be done at low cost. We also presented tool for testing the correctness of cache models by comparing cache results and actual method call results from the server at runtime.

In the context of Web application systems, we have suggested a way to integrate a typical front tier Web cache with a method cache: basically, the dependencies for invalidating method results on the method cache level are reused for triggering invalidation of cached Web pages. In order to enable this integration, only two features are required on the Web cache-side: a mechanism for programmatically invalidating cached pages and allowance for observing URLs which are accessed via the Web cache (see Section 6.2). Due to the integration, conventional invalidation techniques for dynamic Web cache systems become obsolete. The Web application as a whole is then based on a two-level cache strategy, where level one caches entire Web pages and level two caches results of service method calls. The caching feature is still transparent to the application code and from a programming and maintenance point of view the invalidation policy for the caches is located in a single document (the cache model XML file from Section 3.3).

In the terms of aspect oriented programming (AOP), the presented caching feature may be considered as a separate concern. In essence, the cache model can be regarded as an aspect language to define the cross cutting points of the caching aspect with the rest of the application. The cache class generator then represents an aspect weaver.

Examining the performance impact of the integration of a Web page cache and the method cache will be part of our future work. Furthermore, we are in the process of implementing and studying consistency protocols for multiple client-side method caches (see Section 4.3).

References

1. J. Anton, L. Jacobs, Y. Liu, J. Parker, Z. Zeng, and T. Zhong. Web caching for database applications with oracle Web cache. In *Proceedings of the ACM SIGMOD Conference*, Madison, Wisconsin, USA, June 2002. ACM Press.
2. Apache Group. The Torque framework of the Apache DB project. http://db.apache.org/torque.
3. K. S. Candan, W.-S. Li, Q. Luo, W.-P. Hsiung, and D. Agrawal. Enabling dynamic content caching for database-driven web sites. In *Proceedings of the ACM SIGMOD Conference*, Santa Barbara, California, USA, May 2001. ACM Press.
4. E. Cecchet, A. Chanda, S. Elnikety, J. Marguerite, and W. Zwaenepoel. A comparison of software architecturs for E-business applications. Technical Report TR02-389, Rice University, 2001.
5. E. Cecchet, J. Marguerite, and W. Zwaenepoel. Performance and scalability of EJB applications. In *Proceedings of the OOPSLA Conference*, Seattle, Washington, USA, November 2002. ACM Press.
6. A. Datta, K. Dutta, H. Thomas, and D. VanderMeer. A comparative study of alternative middle tier caching solutions to support dynamic Web content acceleration. In *Proceedings of the 27th VLDB Conference*, Rome, Italy, August 2001. Morgan Kaufmann.
7. L. Degenaro, A. Iyengar, I. Lipkind, and I. Rouvellou. A middleware system which intelligently caches query results. In *Middleware*, pages 24–44, 2000.
8. ESI – edge side includes, 2002. http://www.esi.org.
9. Excelon. Javlin – the EJB data cache manager, 2002. http://www.exln.com/products/javlin.
10. A. Kemper, C. Kilger, and G. Moerkotte. Function materialization in object bases. In *Proceedings of the ACM SIGMOD Conference*, Denver, Colorado, USA, May 1991. ACM Press.
11. S. Kounev and A. Buchmann. Improving data access of J2EE applications by exploiting asynchronous messaging and caching services. In *Proceedings of the 28th VLDB Conference*, Hong Kong, China, August 2002. Morgan Kaufmann.
12. W.-S. Li, W.-P. Hsiung, D. V. Kalshnikov, R. Sion, O. Po, D. Agrawal, and K. S. Candan. Issues and evaluations of caching solutions for web application acceleration. In *Proceedings of the 28th VLDB Conference*, Hong Kong, China, August 2002. Morgan Kaufmann.
13. Q. Luo, S. Krishnamurthy, C. Mohan, H. Pirahesh, H. Woo, B. G. Lindsay, and J. F. Naughton. Middle tier database caching for E-business. In *Proceedings of the ACM SIGMOD Conference*, Madison, Wisconsin, USA, June 2002. ACM Press.
14. Q. Luo and J. F. Naughton. Form based proxy caching for database-backed Web sites. In *Proceedings of the 27th VLDB Conference*, Rome, Italy, August 2001. Morgan Kaufmann.
15. F. Marinescu. *EJB Design Patterns*. Wiley, USA, 2002.
16. C. Mohan. Chaching technologies for Web applications, 2001. Tutorial at VLDB Conference 2001, Rome, Italy, http://www.almaden.ibm.com/u/mohan/Caching_VLDB2001.pdf.
17. EJB performance analysis, 2000. http://objectbridge.sourceforge.net/performance/ejb-performance-analysis.html.
18. Persistence Software. Dynamai – a technical white paper, 2001. http://www.persistence.com/products.
19. Persistence Software. Persistence benchmark – extreme EJB performance with PowerTier, 2001. http://www.persistence.com/products.

20. The RUBiS project, 2002. http://rubis.objectweb.org.
21. Spider Software. Accelarting content delivery: The challenges of dynamic content, white paper, 2001. http://www.spidercache.com.
22. Times Ten Team. Mid-tier caching: The TimesTen approach. In *Proceedings of the ACM SIGMOD Conference*, Madison, Wisconsin, USA, June 2002. ACM Press.
23. XCache Technologies. XCache – a dynamic content Web cache. http://www.xcache.com.

DLS: A CORBA Service for Dynamic Loading of Code

Rüdiger Kapitza[1] and Franz J. Hauck[2]

[1]Dept. of Comp. Science, Informatik 4, University of Erlangen-Nürnberg, Germany
rrkapitz@cs.fau.de
[2]Distributed Systems Lab, University of Ulm, Germany
hauck@informatik.uni-ulm.de

Abstract. Dynamic loading of code is needed when rarely used code should be loaded on demand or when the code to be loaded is not known in advance. In distributed systems it can also be used for code distribution. At the extreme, programming concepts as mobile agents and intelligent proxies rely heavily on dynamic code loading. We focus on the CORBA middleware architecture, which does currently not support code loading. Therefore, we specify a CORBA Dynamic Loading Service (DLS) that allows for transparent loading of code modules into a local CORBA environment, regardless of the used programming language and operating system. We also present an implementation of DLS which is able to identify the code implementation that fits best for the current environment. The selection can not only be based on programming language and processor architecture, etc. but also on versions of available libraries and on locally executed and application-specific compatibility tests. In the end, DLS can be used to implement a generic CORBA life cycle service and intelligent-proxy extensions to CORBA.

1 Introduction

Applications will need to dynamically load additional code at run-time if that code is not already bound to the local execution environment. Code modules may be rarely used and the application did not want to load it at start-up time (e.g., the plug-in modules of a Web browser). Other code modules may not be known at compile- or even at start-up-time. This is often the case for distributed applications that have numerous, independently running application parts. Newly developed code should be executed by already running execution environments. Additionally, for some wide-area distributed applications it is simply not feasible to install and load all code modules at every node of the system as they will only be used by a few of the nodes. As code usage often depends on the users' interaction with the distributed application those few nodes may not be known in advance.

In this paper, we focus on CORBA an object-based middleware standard for distributed applications [10]. In CORBA, applications are built from distributed objects which can be developed in a variety of programming languages. A so-called language mapping takes care of interoperability between distributed objects written in different languages. CORBA objects can transparently interact with each other across different address spaces and execution environments. CORBA provides distribution transparency–i.e. there is no distinction between the interaction of local and remote objects–

R. Meersman et al. (Eds.): CoopIS/DOA/ODBASE 2003, LNCS 2888, pp. 1333–1350, 2003.

and location transparency–i.e. it is not necessary to know the object's location for a successful interaction. The implementation of transparent object interaction is based on a standardized protocol (IIOP, Internet Inter-Orb Protocol), a standardized representation of object references (IOR, Interoperable Object Reference), and the automatic code generation of proxy objects (stubs) and server side code (skeletons) from a language-independent description of object interfaces (written in IDL, Interface Definition Language).

With respect to dynamic loading of code, CORBA does not provide any support. An application may interact with CORBA objects that were not known at start-up time. Only the object reference to such objects has to be handed over to or retrieved by that application. However, there is no support for loading of code that was not known at start-up time or is rarely used. Application programmers have to rely on mechanisms provided by the underlying language used to develop CORBA objects. As every language has more or less support for dynamic code loading the mechanisms to be used are rather different. The language-independent programming model of CORBA is compromised at that respect. Thus, CORBA applications using dynamic code loading are hardly portable. Even worse, modern programming paradigms as mobile agents, mobile objects and intelligent proxies require that previously unknown code has to be loaded into the local environment in order to host an agent or an object, or to bind to special objects. Unfortunately the loading mechanisms are different for every language that may be used. Even for the same language there may be different mechanisms due to differences in the underlying operating systems.

We present DLS, a CORBA service for dynamic loading of code. Like other CORBA services it appears as a pseudo CORBA object that has a well-defined interface. This interface can be mapped to any programming language supported by CORBA. The language-specific code-loading mechanisms finally used by the service are hidden from its users. Thus, DLS can also be used as a generic base mechanism for implementing mobile CORBA objects, mobile agents and intelligent proxies.

Beside the service definition, we will outline an implementation of DLS. This implementation does not only use the code loading mechanisms of a specific programming language, but also identifies the code implementation that fits best for the current execution environment. The code selection does not only rely on language, processor architecture and operating system but also takes locally executed tests into account. For certain languages and environments it is possible to load code written in one of a variety of programming languages (e.g., in Java we can load Java code as well as native code written in C or C++). Code written in different languages may expose different properties (e.g., efficiency, memory usage, precision to name a few) that can be taken into account for code selection.

Security issues are beyond the scope of this paper. Dynamic loading of code always involves security considerations, and we assume that standard security mechanisms as code signing and a public-key infrastructure can be used for securing DLS. However, our implementation does not yet make direct use of such techniques.

This paper is organized as follows: Section 2 will discuss code loading in general. In Section 3, we present DLS as a generic and language-independent CORBA service. Section 4 introduces our current implementation of DLS based on and integrated into the *JacORB* open source CORBA implementation [2]. Section 5 briefly describes how DLS can be used to implement mobile objects, mobile agents, and intelligent proxies. In Section 6, DLS is compared to related work. Finally, Section 7 gives our conclusions.

2 Dynamic Loading of Code

Almost every modern programming language provides mechanisms to dynamically load and execute code on demand, e.g., languages like Java and Perl have built-in support for dynamic code loading. Other languages like C and C++ can only load code with support by the underlying operating system, which provide mechanisms like dynamic link loaders and shared libraries. Languages with built-in support rely on a naming scheme for loadable modules.

Java loads code on the class level. A compiled Java class is represented in a standardized format and can be loaded on any platform by any Java Virtual Machine. The hierarchical class name identifies the code to be loaded. The class name is usually made unique by integrating an Internet domain name. With the concept of class loaders, Java also supports remote loading of code including security measures as code-signature verification and trusted code sources. Perl loads code in source form and compiles it at run-time. A naming convention for Perl modules identifies the source file in well-defined directories.

C and C++ programs need to use system calls to the operating system to load and bind new code. Those calls depend of course on the type of operating system used. Also C and C++ code is usually compiled for a special processor architecture, for an operating system and, due to alignment and calling conventions, even for a specific compiler family. Thus, the loaded code does not only depend on the programming language but also on the environment it is going to be executed. The loaded code typically has to be accessible as a shared library file in the file system and the loading program has to know the corresponding file name. Java and Perl can also load compiled C and C++ code (so-called native code) in form of shared libraries. These languages provide corresponding operations to access the loading mechanisms of the operating system. Naming conventions take care that the file name of a shared library can finally be determined.

To summarize, the code loading facilities of programming languages can be used to load code on demand in order to load code only when needed. Loading of unknown code that may be even dynamically loaded from the network is not directly supported by most languages. First the code has to be downloaded into a local file, and second can be loaded into the local execution environment. Java is an exception as it can transparently load code from other hosts using specialized so-called class loaders.

By viewing the loading of code from the perspective of the loading program we can identify two essential requirements: the dynamically loaded code should have a certain functionality, and it should be executable in the local environment. The latter is entirely neglected in current languages as it is assumed that the code is executable and prepared to run on the designated platform. This is entirely different if we move to CORBA or distributed systems in general. Even if we anticipate a certain programming language it will not be clear whether a certain shared library file will do its job on the local platform except it was exactly built for it. This is especially true if the code was loaded from the network. If a CORBA application is distributed over multiple hosts and furthermore assumed that all parts are written in the same language, it may be necessary to provide different shared library files for the same functionality for the different execution environments used (e.g., Windows XP and Linux). If a CORBA application is written in different languages it may be necessary to provide different code packages written in different languages such that the same functionality can be dynamically loaded into the different execution environments.

This scenario implies that naming of code is handled on the level of functionality and not on the level of file names. Assuming, we have a naming scheme for function-alities, the mapping of a name to a suitable implementation of a specific code func-tionality depends on a set of criteria:

- instruction set (of a certain processor architecture or interpreter)
- operating system (assumed semantics of calls into the operating systems)
- compiler family (alignment and calling conventions)
- code format (how is the code written to file)

Of course some of the criteria may collapse, e.g., for Java there is currently only one possible format, the Java class file. However, the selection of implementations may be more complicated: The loaded code may depend on other code already installed or to be loaded into the local environment. It may even depend on a certain version of that other code. This is also true for a distributed system of nodes with same processor type, same operating system and using the same programming language. The code to be loaded may rely on additional properties of the execution environment. As an ex-ample consider a Java program that may want to load a class for fast graphical ren-dering. The same functionality may be provided by three different loadable code packages:

- a native library written in C++ and assembler using MMX processor instructions.
- a native library written in C++ and
- a class written entirely in Java

Ideally, the system should test whether it is possible to load the first variant as it will be the fastest. If this cannot be done, e.g., the local processor does not support MMX instructions or as the code is not available for the current operating system, the pro-gram will try to load the second alternative that is less fast but never the less quite ef-ficient. If this fails too, the third alternative will be loaded. As this implementation is written in Java it will work everywhere.

It is very hard to program this loading strategy into a local application as it requires explicit knowledge about all the alternatives and about their requirements. It is impos-sible to integrate at all if the code and its alternative implementations are not known at compile time. In fact, we would like to have some service that is asked to load code with certain functionality. This service is searching for the best implementation of the required functionality and loads it into the local execution environment.

3 Dynamic Loading Service

We present DLS, a CORBA service for dynamic loading of code. The task of DLS is to load code on request. Code is referred to by a symbolic name. The symbolic name does not include any information about availability of code for a specific platform, compiler or language. Instead the symbolic name just identifies the semantics of the code's functionality which in turn may be implemented in different variants, e.g., for certain platforms, compilers and languages.

As DLS is part of CORBA, we decided to represent the newly loaded code as a CORBA object. We do not require that this object is activated at some object adaptor.

So, it may not be accessible from remote sites. On the other hand, it is possible to activate it, e.g., by passing its reference via a POA[1] using the implicit activation policy or by explicit activation.

Usually this code object comes to life as a side effect of a request to DLS. However, DLS may decide to re-use code objects that have already been requested. On the other hand, DLS may create a new object when the implementation of the code was updated, e.g., for bug fixing. Furthermore we anticipate that the code object is rather stateless. In fact, it may have state, but it should not matter whether DLS creates a new code object or re-uses an existing one if they both are representations of the same functionality, and have the same symbolic name respectively. A typical application is to use the code object as a factory for CORBA objects and values, or for other objects of the language environment. Therefore, we refer to the loaded code object in the following as "factory" object.

The service itself is represented by a pseudo CORBA object. This object is always local to the current execution environment similar to the POA. An object reference to the service object can be retrieved by invoking `resolve_initial_references` at the ORB object. The reference must be named by the string `DynamicLoading-Service`. The DLS pseudo object has a very simple interface that allows clients to dynamically request for new code. A single method named `getFactory()` receives a symbolic name refering to a certain functionality and conforming to the Interoperable Naming Specification [12]. Such a name consists of a sequence of name components. Each name component consists of two attibutes `kind` and `id`. The `id` attribute is an identifier. The `kind` attribute is useful for partitioning the keyspace. The `getFactory()` method is actually provided as two methods, one accepting a sequence of name components and the other accepting a stringified version of such a sequence (cf. section about stringified names in [12]). A naming convention similar to that used to composed Java class names may be deployed. However, it is beyond the scope of this paper to standardize the usage of the key space. The service will now, entirely hidden from the client, retrieve a corresponding code implementation that fits best into the current execution environment. After having loaded the new code it is converted into a CORBA object. A local reference is created and passed back to the caller.

The caller has to know the precise type of the factory object to narrow the reference for further use. Otherwise, the client may want to deploy the dynamic invocation interface (DII) to access and use the factory. We anticipate that for a large group of applications a simple pre-defined factory interface will do. Only in cases where special parameters for object creation are needed object-specific factories are to be defined.

If the requested functionality could not be loaded due to some failure an exception is thrown and no object reference is returned. There can be a variety of reasons why a loading request may fail. One reason may be that the name is not connected to any implementation. In this case an exception named `NotFound` is thrown. Another reason may be that the service is currently not available due to network or service-internal problems. In this case an exception named `ServiceNotAvailable` is thrown. All other reasons imply that the service was not able to find a code implementation that fits into the current execution environment. In this case an exception named `PlatformNotSupported` is thrown.

---

[1] POA = Portable Object Adapter.

The **PlatformNotSupported** exception is augmented by a reason field that gives a hint why the selection of a suitable implementation failed. We do not anticipate that this hint is of any use for the application program. In very most cases, the application will have to resign and live with not having loaded the code if that is possible, otherwise quit. However, we included the hint as it allows the application to print an error message that may be interpreted at least by system programmers to solve the problem. The different failure reasons are:

- There is an implementation but not in the right code format (**format**).
- There is an implementation in the right code format but it has the wrong format version (**format_version**).
- There is an implementation that could be loaded but it contains code for the wrong platform (**mach**).
- There is a loadable implementation for the current platform but it has the wrong byte order (**byte_order**)[2].
- There is a loadable and runnable implementation but it contains code with wrong alignment and addressing scheme (**address**).
- There is a suitable implementation but it uses system calls of another operating system (**os**).
- There is a suitable implementation for the current operating system but the required version of the operating system is not compatible (**os_version**).
- There is a suitable implementation for the current system but it depends on an ORB from another Vendor (**orb**).
- There is a suitable implementation for the current system but the required version of the ORB is not compatible (**orb_version**).
- There is a suitable implementation for the current system but it requires additional libraries that are not available (**lib**).
- There is a suitable implementation for the current system that requires additional libraries; those are available but not in the right version (**lib_version**).
- There is a suitable implementation but additional tests executed by the code have failed to confirm compatibility of the code (**other**).

The order of the reasons described above implies the order of compatibility checks made by a DLS implementation. If an error message occurs apparently none of the available code implementations has passed all compatibility checks. The error message presents the most specific incompatibility that lets the last available code implementation fail to pass the compatibility checks.

Fig. 3.1 presents the IDL definitions of DLS including exceptions. A typical scenario of using DLS in a Java-based execution environment is shown in Fig. 3.2. First, the initial reference to the DLS pseudo object has to be retrieved. Second, the reference has to be converted in a reference to the **DynamicLoader** interface using a CORBA narrow operation. Third, the **getFactory()** method of the service can be called with a name structure referring a certain functionality. In the example code the name consists of two kind-id pairs to specify the needed factory interface and the interface of the objects returned by the factory. However in particular environments dif-

---

[2] This error can occur especially for interpreted languages that can store intermediate code in different byte order.

ferent kind fields may be appropriate. Finally, the returned reference has to be converted to the interface type of the factory by another narrow operation.

```
#include <CosNaming.idl>

module dls {

    typedef CosNaming::Name Name;

    enum PlatformNotSupportedReason {
            format, format_version, mach, byteorder, address, os,
            os_version,orb,orb_version, lib, lib_version, other
    };

    exception PlatformNotSupported {
            PlatformNotSupportedReason reason;
            string reason_message;
    };

    exception NotFound{};
    exception ServiceNotAvailable{};

    interface DynamicLoader{
            Object getFactory( in Name symname )
                    raises( NotFound, ServiceNotAvailable,
                                    PlatformNotSupported );
            Object getFactory( in wstring stringifiedsymname )
                    raises( NotFound, ServiceNotAvailable,
                                    PlatformNotSupported );
    };

};
```

Fig. 3.1. Interface Description of the Dynamic Loading Service

```
import org.omg.CosNaming.NameComponent;

org.omg.CORBA.Object o=
    orb.resolve_initial_references("DynamicLoadingService")

dls.DynamicLoader dl = dls.DynamicLoaderHelper.narrow(o);

NameComponent name[] = {
        new NameComponent("NativeHelloFac","factoryInterface"),
        new NameComponent("NativeHello","objectInterface")
    };

org.omg.CORBA.Object o = dl.getFactory(name);

NativeHelloFac factory = NativeHelloFacHelper.narrow(o);
```

Fig. 3.2. Scenario of Usage from a Java-Based Environment

4 Example Implementation

We built an implementation of a CORBA dynamic loading service that enables an application to request and integrate new functionalities implemented in Java and native code written in C or C++. Our service implementation is built on top of *JacORB* an open source Java-based ORB [2]. However, our DLS implementation is hardly ORB-dependent and thus easily portable to any other Java-based ORB.

The DLS pseudo object that can be received from the ORB object is always local to the current execution environment. This is necessary as the local environment somehow has to integrate the code to be loaded. However, not all components of a DLS implementation need to be local. Some components can be shared by many DLS pseudo objects, and execution environments respectively. The design of our DLS implementation is modular and as system and language independent as possible. Since the dynamic loading of code takes place at runtime, speed is a major concern. The current implementation takes this into account and effectively chooses and loads the right instance of implementation.

4.1 Architecture

Our DLS implementation is split into three parts: the *dynamic loader*, the *code registry* and the *code server*. The *dynamic loader* is the local representative of the DLS service. Its interface is exposed by the DLS pseudo object that can be retrieved from the ORB. The task of the dynamic loader is to select a suitable code implementation, load it and return a reference to the factory object to the calling application. The code registry knows of all loadable functionalities and their implementations. It helps in pre-selecting implementations that can run in the requesting environment. The code server stores code implementations and delivers the one that was finally selected by the dynamic loader. Code server and code registry are built in such a way that only the dynamic loader contains language- and platform-specific parts. Thus, code server and registry can be reused by many execution environments. In fact, these components can even reside on different nodes. Fig. 4.1 shows a setting with three different nodes hosting the three different parts of our DLS implementation.

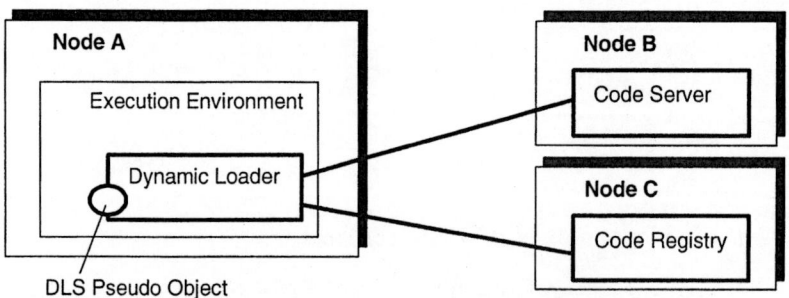

Fig. 4.1. The Architecture of the DLS Implementation

The *dynamic loader* is a core component of the DLS implementation. It is responsible for the coordination of the code-loading process. It receives requests for new functionalities via the `getFactory()` method. Each request is forwarded to the code registry augmented with the local system parameters. System parameters include all the static properties about the local execution environment that are potential selectors for implementations, e.g., processor architecture, byte order, operating system, addressing scheme. In our implementation, those values are supplied by the Java runtime environment via system properties. In general, system parameters can be dynamically computed or pre-configured by system administrators.

The *code registry* maintains a database of code descriptions. For each functionality a description entry is stored together with a name conforming to the Interoperable Naming Specification mentioned above. A new functionality and the associated implementations (further called *implementation instances*) can be registered with such a name. When a dynamic loader wants to load code the code registry will get a name and will have to find a registred name with equal id and kind values and then return the corresponding description in the database. If it cannot find a description to a given name an `NotFound` exception will be thrown and eventually forwarded to the client application. Thus, the implementation of a code registry is comparable to that of a CORBA naming service.

A found description entry contains information about all the loadable instances implementing the functionality, including their dependencies, requirements and locations. Internally the description entry is represented in XML. It is described in more detail in Section 4.2. According to the system parameters passed by the calling dynamic loader, the code registry filters the description entry and returns only information about those implementation instances that are able to run in the calling execution environment. If there is no matching code implementation a `PlatformNotSupported` exception is raised and eventually forwarded to the application.

Since the code registry is not directly involved in code loading it does not necessarily need to be local to the requesting execution environment. Instead it could be located anywhere in a distributed system. In our implementation the code registry is implemented as an ordinary CORBA object that is initially known to each dynamic loader[3]. The code registry object is accessed by standard CORBA remote invocations.

From the code registry, the dynamic loader gets a description entry stripped to a sub-set of the available implementation instances. The deployment of these instances may depend on several conditions that cannot easily be expressed and communicated to the code registry. Those conditions may be

• availability checks of local libraries and

• results of dynamically running and instance-specific tests on the local environment. Thus, the dynamic loader will check each of the instances for compatibility with the local environment. This process is described in more detail in Section 4.3. The decision to integrate a simple pre-selection into the registry and the more specific selection into the dynamic loader was mainly taken due to performance considerations. Passing all necessary information to the registry for a pure registry-based selection on one hand and passing the description of all instances to the dynamic loader for a pure load-based selection on the other hand are both wasting bandwidth.

---

[3] We anticipate that the code registry is registered with the naming service under a well-known name and can thus be retrieved by dynamic loaders. Alternatively the IOR of the code registry may be configured with the ORB.

After having selected a suitable implementation instance the corresponding code will be loaded. Usually the code is provided by traditional Web- and FTP-based servers that act as what we call a *code server*. However, there may be other servers accessible by different protocols. As long as they somehow allow to retrieve a code file they can also be used as code servers. There can be a whole set of code servers in a distributed system. The description entry just stores a suitable URL to the file on the code server. After loading the code, the dynamic loader will create the corresponding factory object and return it to the application.

4.2 XML-Based Description of Implementation Instances

As the code registry shall be language and platform independent we decided to represent description entries of functionalities as XML-based text. Also the filtered description entry returned from the code registry to the dynamic loader is represented as XML text. Alternatively we could have defined a complex data structure in CORBA IDL. However, we decided to pass XML text as it is the native form of the stored descriptions. Converting XML into an IDL data structure would add some additional parsing overhead.

The code registry usually has to manage the data of several implementation instances per given functionality. These instances represent independent entities of code which could implement the functionality in different programming languages and for different platforms. Thus, the structure of a description entry represented in XML is preserved by the root tag `functionality` which includes a name tag and an arbitrary number of `instance` tags. The name tag identifies the functionality and includes a least one `name-comp` tag which has an attribute kind and id. An instance tag includes all necessary information about the instance's requirements and the location of the corresponding code.

The basic requirements are enclosed by the tag `systemparams`. Those are the machine architecture, byte order, address length and the implementation languages of the code. We distinguish between a primary and a secondary language environment. The primary language environment is the one that is used for the factory object to be created. The secondary language environment could be used for additional code written in a different language. In our current implementation Java is always the primary language environment. The secondary language environment can be a C or C++ environment running native code. Both environments are specified using the tags `primary-language` and `secondary-language`. There must be a `primary-language` tag per `instance` tag. Additionally, there could be several secondary-language tags.

The code of an implementation instance sometimes relies on other code modules which have to be locally available at the hosting execution environment. These extended requirements are described inside of a `depend` tag. This tag can enclose tags of type `resource` which describe code modules which the instance of implementation relies on. Optionally there can be `version` and `version-range` tags inside the `resource` tag that specify what versions of a code module are required. Finally an instance of implementation could have additional specific requirements. To check if these requirements are fulfilled a compatibility test could be specified with the `test` tag. Such a compatibility test is comparable to a very simple instance of an implementation and could include almost the same tags as a instance tag.

After the requirements the code location is specified using tag **code**. This tag can include an arbitrary number of **location** tags that describe the location of a code module and how to access it. Multiple location tags describe alternative locations for fault tolerance and availability. Additional the **code** tag could include one or more **checksum** tags. A **checksum** tag has an attribute type which specifies the name of checksum algorithm and encloses the checksum over the code element. A Dynamic Loader can validate the code element through the checksum. This way a Dynamic Loader has only to trust in the Code Registry and not all code providing servers. The last tag of an instance description is the **factory** tag. It specifies how the factory object can be accessed inside the loaded code. The way how this is done depends on the primary language environment. For the Java language, the factory tag refers to the class name of the factory object that needs to be created.

```
<functionality>
    <name>
            <name-comp kind="factoryInterface" id="NativeHelloFac"/>
            <name-comp kind="objectInterface" id="NativeHello"/>
    </name>
    <instance>
            <sysparams>
                    <primary-language name="java" format="bytecode">
                            <version value="1.3"/>
                    </primary-language>
                    <secondary-language name="C/C++" format="elf">
                    </secondary-language>
                    <mach address="32" byteorder="little" name="x86"/>
                    <os name="linux">
                            <versionrange min="2.2.3" max="2.3.1" />
                    </os>
            </sysparams>
            <depend>
                    <resource format="elf" type="lib" name="libxml.so">
                            <major-version><version value="2.2.10"/>
                            </major-version>
                    </resource>
            </depend>
            <test>
                    <code><location format="..." type="jar" url="..."/>
                    </code>
                    <factory name="hello.Test"/>
             </test>
            <code><checksum type="sha1">2af5169acc5371fa76...</checksum>
                    <location format="bytecode" type="jar" url="..."/>
            </code>
            <code><location format="elf" type="lib" url="..."/>
            </code>
            <factory name="hello.HelloFactoryImpl"/>
    </instance>
</functionality>
```

Fig. 4.2. Example Description of a Functionality

Fig. 4-2 shows an example description of a functionality called with the stringified name **NativeHelloFac.factoryInterface/NativeHello.objectInterface**. This functionality has only one instance of implementation. The code of this functionality consists of two elements a Java archive and a shared library. The shared library relies on an x86 processor and Linux as operating system. Additionally the instance specifies a test which ensures that a special requirement is fulfilled by the execution environment (e.g., a certain output device is present).

4.3   Code Selection and Loading

If the code registry returns one or more instances of implementation, the dynamic loader will have to check local dependencies and extended requirements. First the dynamic loader will check whether all code modules that the preselected instances of implementation rely on are locally available and have the required version. Our DLS implementation supports several types of dependent code modules. As the service is implemented in Java, dependent modules may contain Java program code. So, dependent code modules can be single class files or entire *Java Archives* (JARs). Whether a certain class is locally available can be easily verified by trying to load the class through the system class loader. If this fails the class is not available. Testing the availability of a Java archive needs a different procedure. The Java execution environment lists all archives and directories which are accessible to the Java language environment in the system property `java.class.path`. For checking whether a JAR file is available the dynamic loader has to search for the name in the class-path property. Most JARs contain a *Manifest* file in which all important information about the JAR is stored. This includes the version information of the JAR so that the required version can be checked.

Another type of dependent code supported by our DLS implementation is code implemented as shared library. If a Java program wants to call a native method using the Java Native Interface (JNI) [7] it will first have to load the library by using the static method `System.loadLibrary()`. The Java runtime environment completes the library name with the operating-system–dependent name extensions and tries to load it via the system loader. The system loader has to know where the libraries could be located. This information is supplied by the system property `java.library.path`. To determine if a shared library is locally available the dynamic loader only has to check if a file with the library name is available. This is done by checking all directories included in the `java.library.path` for the needed library. To determine whether the needed library is available in the expected version is highly dependent on the operating system. On Unix-based systems the version information is encoded into the file name. So, the dynamic loader has only to check for the according file. All Windows versions support the Dynamic Linking Library format (DLL). This format includes special fields which contain the version information. Thus, the dynamic loader has first to check if the library is locally available and then read the version information of the library.

If the code dependencies are solved the dynamic loader has to check the special requirements of an instance of implementation if there are any. This is done by executing the tests described by the instance of implementation. But before this is possible the code dependencies of the test must be checked and the code of the test has to be loaded from the specified code server. This is a similar process as the loading of an implementation instance. Test implementation instances have a generic test interface including a default method `testRequirement()` that is invoked for executing the actual test. If the test method returns true the processing of the instance of implementation continues otherwise a `PlatformNotSupported` exception is thrown with reason `other`.

If all requirements of an instance of implementation are fulfilled the program code is loaded. In the current implementation the Java code can be loaded by the class `URLclassLoader` of the Java Standard Library which offers a simple interface to retrieve Java byte code from HTTP or FTP servers. The retrieval of native libraries is a bit more complicated. The code has to be stored in a local directory which is listed in the system property `java.library.path` so that the Java runtime environment can dynamically load these libraries. After all code modules are loaded the factory can be instantiated and returned to the calling application.

Of course every step of the processing of an instance may detect errors. If as an end result no implementation instance passes all checks, a final exception is thrown to the calling application. As the exception signals the reason why the last instance failed to pass the checks the exception is most valuable to the application developer or system administrator.

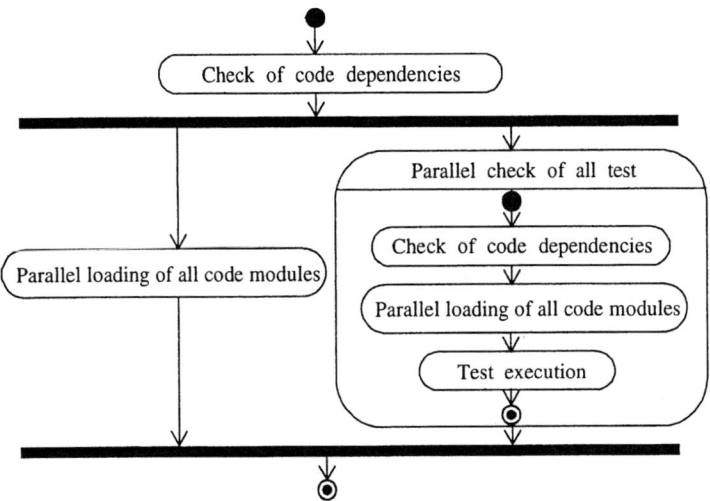

Fig. 4.3. Parallel Processing Model

All the processing could be done in a sequence of single steps, but this is rather time consuming. Since the dynamic loading of code takes place at runtime and speed is a major concern we implemented a parallel processing model. If an application requests a new functionality and the code registry returns one ore more instances of implementation to the dynamic loader the processing of instances executes concurrently. First the code requirements get checked. This could be done quite fast so we need no concurrent execution. The next steps are the checking of special requirements and the loading of code. As the transfer of different code modules from different code servers could be quite time consuming this is done concurrently. If a tests fails or a code server is not accessible all parallel and depending activities are stopped. Already transferred code will be deleted. Fig. 4.3 shows the concurrent execution of code loading and test execution of a single instance.

4.4   Alternative Implementation Architectures

Unlike the presented DLS implementation, CORBA Naming [12] or Trading Object Services [13] could be used to implement parts of the DLS.

A first alternative could define a dedicated CORBA object per functionality and register that object at a Naming Service. If a local *dynamic loader* receives a request it could silently forward the request to the Naming Service which returns the object representing the functionality. This object should have a management interface and a query interface. The management interface enables all kind of management operations for implementation descriptions. The query interface enables the *dynamic loader* to ask for an appropriate implementation. Similar to the current implementation the query interface could only provide a pre-selection. The final selection has to be made by the *dynamic loader* because a remote CORBA Object is not able to check for locally available libraries or execute implementation-specific tests on the local machine.

A second alternative could define dedicated CORBA objects per implementation code of a functionality and register them at a Trading Object Service. Implementations of functionalities provide the same type of service, i.e., they provide the same object interface and the same set of properties. In our case the name of the functionality plus implementation-specific requirements like CPU type, byte order, file format, etc. are provided as property values. If a local *dynamic loader* receives a request the DLS augments it with the system specific properties, forwards it to the Trading Object Service, and discovers service objects that match the given property values of the local environment. The service interface could be fairly simple since it has only to provide informations about the additional requirements of the code, informations about tests and the code elements (e.g., URLs) of the actual functionality. As in the first alternative, a final selection has to be made locally.

With the first alternative the local DLS gets one result object that helps to find the right implementation; with the second alternative the Trading Service returns a bunch of result objects that have to be finally checked for compatibility with the local environment. In both cases the implementations need a local *dynamic loader* to finally select the loadable code and to actually load it. The *dynamic loader* is very similar as in our current implementation. Both alternatives also need an additional CORBA object representing either a functionality or an implementation of it. Those CORBA objects have to be hosted and managed somewhere. However, using CORBA services in a large DLS implementation may improve scalability so that we will consider using them in a second example implementation.

5   Applications of DLS

This section will briefly outline possible applications of DLS. We will first focus on mobile CORBA objects that can also be used to implement mobile agent. Then, we will look at smart proxy implementations.

5.1 CORBA Lifecycle Service

The OMG defined the so-called lifecycle service for the CORBA architecture. This service specifies how CORBA objects can be created, destroyed, copied and moved [11]. Usually it is up to the vendor of a CORBA implementation how the lifecycle service is supported. We claim that with using DLS the CORBA lifecycle service can more or less have a generic implementation. For brevity we just demonstrate how creation and migration of objects can be implemented with DLS as a basic mechanism.

The lifecycle's abstract model of creation is that there is a factory object which provides specialized operations to create and initialize new CORBA objects of the desired type. The new object will reside on the same node as the factory. A requesting program must possess an object reference of a factory and issue an appropriated request on the factory. A factory object in the context of the lifecycle service is comparable in function and implementation to a factory returned by the DLS.

The interaction model of the lifecycle service assumes that the factory object is instantiated before the requirement of a new Object on the target machine arises. As mentioned in the introduction, the requirement for a certain functionality could not always be foreseen and the same applies for the remote creation of objects. Thus, a DLS-based implementation of the lifecycle service can create the needed factories on demand.

A sketch of a generic lifecycle service based on DLS is the following: Special factory finder objects reside on the same node as an instance of DLS. They have to implement the **FactoryFinder** interface of the CORBA Lifecycle Service specification. A factory finder is responsible to locate factories in a defined scope. This could be a single computer like in this case or group of machines on the local area network. The factory finder is a normal CORBA Object and can be handed over to client programs without problems. The interface of the factory finder provides operations to ask for one or more factories. Normally factories have to be registered at a factory finder. In our case the factory finder forwards the request to the local DLS instance which may provide a factory on demand if a suitable implementation is available. Apart from forwarding requests to the DLS instance the factory finder is responsible for managing the already created factories. This way only a single factory of each type has to be created.

The abstract model of migrating an object is somewhat more complex. The object itself provides a method named **move()** that allows to migrate the object to another node. This node is determined in an abstract fashion. Therefore, a parameter referring to a factory finder is passed to the invocation of **move()**. Like in the previous case the factory finder returns one or more references to suitable factories that can create the desired object. Of course it is possible that a factory finder has a wider scope then our specialized factory finder. One could provide a factory finder which queries our specialized factory finders. The implementation of **move()** now has to select a suitable factory, create a new object, transport the original state to the new object and finally make sure that the new object is accessible with existing object references. The latter is usually done with the help of a implementation repository that authoritatively knows the real communication address of an object. As a last step the old object is deleted.

In both cases, creation and migration, the DLS could be easily integrated into the lifecycle architecture via a specialized factory finder which forwards request to a local DLS instance.

5.2 Intelligent Proxies

In certain cases the client-server style of RPC-based interaction between a local stub and the remote CORBA object is not sufficient for distributed applications. Imagine a CORBA object that provides multimedia data at its interface or a replicated object that has many instances installed in the Internet. A client of these types of objects cannot just use a simple stub but needs a more intelligent piece of local software to receive the multimedia data or invoke methods on many replicas at once. As CORBA does not support this kind of communication some research systems extended CORBA by so-called intelligent or smart proxies. As an example we refer to the Squirrel system [4].

AspectIX is the name of our own CORBA implementation that takes the idea of intelligent proxies to an extreme: all proxies, stubs and servants are considered to be part of a single but fragmented object [3]. As soon as a local *AspectIX* environment receives a previously unknown object reference, a local fragment of that object is installed, usually a stub or smart proxy. As the local environment cannot know the code of all object reference that it will ever use, the code of the local fragment has to be loaded on demand. This is done by using DLS. In *AspectIX* an object reference can include a special *AspectIX* profile[4]. The *AspectIX* profile contains the symbolic name needed by DLS to load the code of the fragment. Additional communication addresses stored in the profile help the newly created local fragment to find the other fragments of the same object and to communicate with them. Inside of the *AspectIX* ORB, e.g., in the `string_to_object` operation, the profiles of an incoming IOR are analyzed. In case of a pure CORBA object a traditional CORBA stub is created. If an *AspectIX* profile is found the corresponding code is loaded, a new fragment is created and initialized with the profile's communication addresses.

6 Related Work

We are not aware of any work that has tried to make dynamic code loading available to CORBA applications in a generic way. However, there are of course systems implementing the CORBA lifecycle service, e.g., the *LocALE* system [9]. LocALE provides a framework for supporting the lifecycle of distributed CORBA objects. Objects can even migrate between heterogeneous platforms. LocALE does not address the problem of code migration instead it assumes that the needed code is already installed at the local system. In fact, our DLS implementation could be integrated into LocALE's lifecycle servers to enable dynamic code loading of even system-dependent code.

The *Plug-In Model* [8] is a system that enables the migration of objects through special factories which are not entirely compatible to the CORBA lifecycle service. A

---

[4] The Interoperable Object Reference (IOR) of a CORBA object may include multiple so-called profiles for different ways to contact an object.

so called plug-in server delivers code to a local factory finder. The factory finder creates a factory from the loaded code. The factory is able to create a new object and to manage the state transfer for a migration. The code of the factory has to be provided as a dynamic link library (DLL). The system is thus restricted to Windows-based platforms. However, the factory may be written in a variety of languages. The plug-in server is comparable to our code server since it provides only the code for a requested factory. The factory finder is comparable to a combination of our code registry and dynamic loader. The Plug-In Model does not offer the possibility to choose between multiple implementations and does not allow the selection of system-dependent code.

Software deployment systems can also be considered as related work, e.g., software package management systems. A simple system is the *Red Hat Package Manager* (RPM) [6] used on Linux platforms. It allows to install, update, and verify software packages. A package provider has to describe the software and its dependencies similarly to our description entries. During the build process of a package the host operating system and the machine architecture is automatically detected and noted in the package. There is no possibility to specify further system requirements like operating system version or the address length. However, the RPM system offers the possibility to specify tests as shell scripts which are executed before the actual install process. Besides, all package managing systems are entirely user driven and only support the static deployment of software.

Another interesting software deployment system is *Java Web Start* which uses the Java Network Launching Protocol [5]. This system describes the code and the requirements of a Java application in a special XML format. So described applications can be installed over the net via the Web Start client. The format is highly Java specific and targeted to install and update software. However it considers the possibility that Java application could make use of native libraries. These libraries are describe in a `nativelib` XML tag and enclosed by a resources tag which could have an attributes `os` and `arch` for the specification of the required operating system and platform architecture. So, system-dependent native libraries can be selected and installed by the Web Start client. The current release lacks the support for dependent resources and for locally executed compatibility tests.

7 Conclusion

We presented the informal specification of DLS, a CORBA service for dynamic loading of code. Our service is platform and language independent. Thus, applications using the service are portable from one CORBA platform to the other as long as the service is available on both platforms. We also outlined a prototype implementation of DLS for a Java-based ORB. This implementation is split into environment- and platform-specific parts (implemented in each execution environment using the service) and sharable parts hosted on one or multiple server nodes. The sharable code registry stores code and variant information, the sharable code server delivers the code. The local and environment-dependent dynamic loader finally selects, downloads and integrates the right code module. Our prototype implementation transparently loads not only Java code but also native code written in C or C++ on either Windows, Linux and Solaris platforms, thus improving even Java's sophisticated standard code loading mechanisms.

Our service is easily configured using XML-based description entries per loadable functionality. Code selection is not only done by matching platform-specific properties (e.g., operating system, processor architecture) but also guided by dynamically loaded and executed test modules that check the compatibility of the local execution environment. This potentially enables all sorts of compatibility tests.

The basic motivation for this research was to support the *AspectIX* ORB that provides a smart proxy-like approach using fragmented objects [1]. However, the DLS service can also be deployed for a generic implementation of the CORBA lifecycle service and for building a mobile agent platform.

Our service implementation needs further improvements. So far we did not integrate any security measures apart from using checksums to ensure the integrity of code modules but use the facilities provided by the underlying language environment. However, for a truly generic service this is not enough. Additionally, techniques for scalability and fault tolerance need to be deployed for our code registry (e.g., caching and replication of code modules).

References

[1]   AspectIX Research Team, Univ. of Ulm, Univ. of Erlangen-Nürnberg. *AspectIX Project Home Page*. http://www.aspectix.org

[2]   G. Brose: JacORB: Implementation and Design of a Java ORB. *Proc. of the IFIP WG 6.1 Int. Working Conf. on Distrib. Appl. and Interoperable Sys.* – DAIS (Sep. 30–Oct. 2, 1997, Cottbus, Germany). Chapman & Hall 1997.

[3]   F. J. Hauck, U. Becker, M. Geier, E. Meier, U. Rastofer, M. Steckermeier: AspectIX: a Quality-Aware, Object-Based Middleware Architecture. *Proc. of the 3rd IFIP Int. Conf. on Distrib. Appl. and Interoperable Sys.* – DAIS (Krakow, Poland, Sep. 17–19, 2001). Kluver, 2001.

[4]   R. Koster, T. Kramp: Structuring QoS-Supporting Services with Smart Proxies. *Proc. of the IFIP/ACM Middleware Conf.* (Pallisades, NY, 3.–7. April 2000). Lecture Notes in Comp. Sci. 1795, Springer, 2000.

[5]   R. W. Schmidt: Java Network Launching Protocol & API Specification (JSR-56). Version 1.0, Home Page,Dec. 2000. http://java.sun.com

[6]   E. C. Edward: *Maximum RPM: taking the Red Hat package manager to the limit*. Red Hat Software, Feb. 1997.

[7]   S. Liang: *Java Native Interface: programmer's guide and specification*. Addison Wesley, June 1999.

[8]   C. Linnhoff-Popien, T. Haustein: Das Plug-In-Modell zur Realisierung mobiler CORBA-Objekte. *Kommunikation in Verteilten Systemen* (KiVS), Informatik aktuell, Springer 1999.

[9]   D. Lopez de Ipina, S.-L. Lo: LocALE: a Location-Aware Lifecycle Environment for Ubiquitous Computing. *Proc. of the 15th Int. Conf. on Information Networking* – ICOIN-15 (Jan. 31–Feb. 2, 2001, Beppu City, Japan).

[10] Object Management Group: *The Common Object Request Broker Architectur and Specification*. Ver. 2.6, OMG Doc. formal/01-12-35, Framingham, MA, Dec. 2001.

[11] Object Management Group: *Life Cycle Service Specification*. Ver. 1.1, OMG Doc, formal/00-06-18, Framingham, MA, April 2002.

[12] Object Management Group: *Naming Service Specification*. OMG Doc, formal/02-09-02, Framingham, MA, Sep. 2002.

[13] Object Management Group: *Trading Object Service*. Ver. 1.0, OMG Doc. formal/00-06-27, Framingham, MA, May 2002.

On the Performance of a CORBA Caching Service over the Wide Internet

Roy Friedman[1] and Roman Vitenberg[2]

[1] Computer Science Department, The Technion, Haifa 32000, Israel
roy@cs.technion.ac.il
[2] Computer Science Department, UCSB, Santa Barbara, CA 93106, USA
romanv@cs.ucsb.edu

Abstract. This paper reports on the performance of Cascade, a caching service for distributed CORBA objects. We deploy Cascade in a widely distributed setting comprising of nine hosts at geographically disperse locations over the Internet. The paper presents and analyzes the obtained experimental results, including service response time and network level characteristics such as throughput. In particular, the paper discusses the speedup factor that the application can gain by using Cascade for various consistency policies and workload characteristics.

Keywords: Object Caching, Performance, CORBA.

1 Introduction

Modern client/server middleware standards, such as CORBA, J2EE, Web Services and .NET, provide location transparent remote method invocation capabilities while carrying the object oriented and component oriented programming styles from sequential programming to distributed environments. These platforms encompass a generic implementation independent architecture for interoperable remote method invocation along with standard services for publishing and locating distributed components as well as binding to them, and enterprise level services like transactions and notification. It is envisioned that the middleware will be used to expose various services over the Internet, typically by employing a protocol like IIOP or SOAP/HTTP over TCP/IP. A potential problem with any such service offered over the Internet is that the Internet is prone to long delays, unpredictable performance, and low availability. Moreover, due to the cost of maintaining connections from servers to clients, Internet-based services are bound to suffer from scalability problems.

To alleviate this problem, we have proposed Cascade, a caching service for Internet wide CORBA based services [7]. A distinguishing feature of Cascade is its ability to cache true CORBA objects, including data and code. That is, since in different applications the logic for manipulating the data is different, then in order to be generic the code has to be cached alongside with the data. Cascade is also designed with the goal of preserving the application programming model

R. Meersman et al. (Eds.): CoopIS/DOA/ODBASE 2003, LNCS 2888, pp. 1351–1368, 2003.

while providing a flexible framework of semantic guarantees and supporting a rich variety of consistency conditions [8]. Furthermore, the service dynamically builds a hierarchy of caches for each cached object/service depending on where client accesses are coming from, which is key to the service scalability.

To assess the performance of Cascade, we deployed the caching service at nine locations across the globe - in Australia, Brazil, Israel, Portugal, Taiwan, the Netherlands, and a few hosts across the US. We tested the system by running artificially created client traces against it and comparing the results to a centralized service. The tests were conducted at different hours of the day and on different days of the week during a period of several months. In this paper we report on the results of these measurements, the optimizations we used, and the lessons learned from our experiments.

We analyze our experimental results and provide explanation of the observed caching service behavior. This analysis is complicated due to many factors that affect the service performance, including numerous application parameters (such as the workload, choice of policies, and cached object size), underlying network characteristics (latency and loss rate), specifics of the TCP implementation, etc. Additionally, the results are substantially affected by the logical topology of the communication infrastructure in Cascade, especially because message latencies and loss rates on different communication paths on the Internet often do not preserve the triangle inequality [1,4,11]. Yet, we have discovered that for most typical settings caching can indeed improve the performance of Internet services by as much as a factor of 50–100 in the case of weak consistency requirements, and a factor of 3–4 for strong conditions. For strong consistency, we have identified the length of update requests as the most salient factor, which has a greater impact on response times than, e.g., the percentage of updates in the workload.

2   A Brief Overview of Cascade Architecture

This section briefly describes Cascade, the caching service we use in this work. It appears here for the sake of completeness. More details about Cascade can be found in [7] and [12].

Cascade is a generic caching service for CORBA objects, supporting caching of full-fledged objects, which include both data and code. Caching objects without code either entails using the pre-defined confined set of possible operations or requires the code to be distributed over all the sites that can potentially keep a cached object copy. In the former case, generality is restricted. In the latter case, caching cannot be deployed in large scale dynamic environments. Cascade allows to distribute object code dynamically upon request. Code caching also enables to preserve the standard CORBA programming model: The application works with the cached copy through the same interface it would have worked with the original object. In addition, all object methods (including updates) can be invoked locally, often eliminating the need to contact the remote object. Cascade is highly configurable with regard to a broad spectrum of application parameters. It allows client applications to fully control many aspects of object caching, by

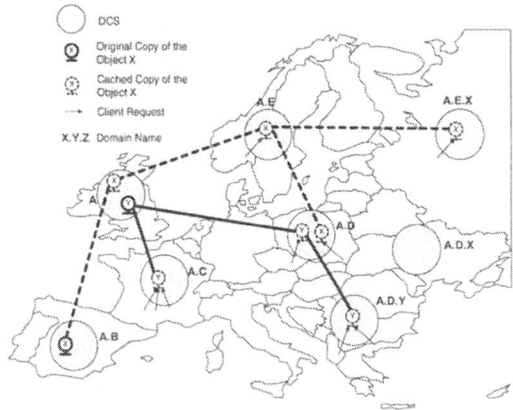

Fig. 1. The Caching Service Architecture

specifying a variety of policies for cache management, consistency maintenance, persistence, security, etc. Cascade is specifically designed to operate over the Internet by employing a dynamically built cache hierarchy.

The caching service is provided by a number of servers, each of which is responsible for a specific *logical* domain. In practice, these domains can correspond to geographical areas. The servers are called *Domain Caching Servers (DCSs)*. Cached copies of each object are organized into a hierarchy. A separate hierarchy is dynamically constructed for each object. The hierarchy construction is driven by client requests. The construction mechanism ensures that for each client, client's local DCS (i.e., the DCS responsible for the client's domain) obtains a copy of the object. In addition, this mechanism attempts to guarantee that the object copy is obtained from the nearest DCS having a copy of this object. This feature dramatically reduces response time and contributes to the scalability of the system. Once the local DCS has an object copy, all client requests for object method invocation go to this DCS, so that the client does not have to communicate to a far server.

The DCS that holds an original object becomes the *root* for this object cache hierarchy. It plays a special role in building the hierarchy and in ensuring consistency of the cached copies. Hierarchies corresponding to each object are superimposed on the DCS infrastructure: Different object hierarchies may overlap or be completely disjoint. Also, overlapping object hierarchies do not necessarily have the same root. For example, in Figure 1 the original copy of the object X is located in the DCS of domain $A.B$. This DCS is the root of the X's hierarchy. The cached copies of X are located in the DCSs of domains A, $A.E$, $A.D$ and $A.E.X$. Note that, in addition to being the holder of the cached copy of X, the DCS of domain A also serves as the root of the object Y hierarchy. Further, the $A.D$'s DCS contains only cached object copies and the $A.D.X$'s DCS does not contain objects at all.

In [7] we discuss the main pros and cons of this hierarchical structure compared with other distributed architectures. Briefly, using a hierarchy allows Cascade to conserve bandwidth, be highly scalable, provide short initial response time, be easy to manage, and simplifies the consistency maintenance.

Cascade is implemented in Java. The considerations of choosing a programming language framework are discussed in [12].

3   Consistency Support in Cascade

When the system concurrently maintains several copies of the same object, it should also guarantee mutual consistency of these copies. Complete description of the consistency framework of Cascade can be found in [8] and [12]. In this section we only briefly outline the most essential features of consistency support that are relevant for the rest of the paper.

All interface methods of an object cached with Cascade are divided into updates that modify the object state and queries that do not. Updates and queries are handled differently by Cascade: We assume that the application invokes queries more frequently than updates. Therefore, the implementation in Cascade propagates update requests to all DCSs in the object hierarchy whereas queries are executed locally, i.e., on the local DCS of the client that invokes the request. This makes executing updates much more expensive compared to queries.

In object oriented client-server middlewares, an object state typically takes much more space than method arguments. Therefore, propagating update requests themselves consumes much less bandwidth compared to propagating object states that result from update invocations. When requests are propagated, they need to be executed at every DCS, whereas propagation of states requires object serialization and deserialization operations. For the prevailing majority of applications, the latter operations consume at least as much server computational resources as executing the requests. Therefore, push based update propagation lends itself to such settings better than state invalidation schemes. In other words, it is more efficient to push update requests to all servers in a hierarchy than to retrieve the entire object state later.

However, in certain cases a request execution can be non-deterministic, i.e., it can produce different results each time the same request is invoked. In particular, it may have some side effects. Such a request should be executed exactly once on one of the servers and it is the resulting state that should be propagated instead of the request. Therefore, Cascade supports both propagating requests and object states and the application has to specify which propagation should be done as part of the policy.

In order to make the caching service as flexible as possible, we support several consistency policies. [8] and [12] describe the Cascade's approach of composeable consistency guarantees in detail. For the sake of discussing Cascade's performance in this paper, it is sufficient to distinguish between strong policies such as sequential consistency and weak policies (e.g., PRAM). In the implementation of strong policies, all update requests first ascend through the hierarchy toward the root DCS. The root of the hierarchy orders the requests in a sequence and propagates ordered requests through the hierarchy toward the leaves. In contrast, the implementation of weak policies applies update requests locally and propagates them through the object hierarchy by using flooding. This shortens the latency of update request and reduces the load imposed on the root DCS. However, different updates may be applied in different order at different DCSs.

Since update propagation may take significant time, especially for strong policies, Cascade supports both blocking and non-blocking updates. For blocking updates, response to the client is delayed until the request is propagated to the root of the hierarchy and back. A non-blocking update request returns immediately but a subsequent query will have to block in order to satisfy the FIFO consistency guarantee.

4   Performance of Cascade in a Wide Area Network

In this section, we describe our experiments with Cascade. We tested the system in a real wide area environment to assess the speedup in terms of service response times (i.e., duration of a remote request invocation) compared with a centralized solution. Furthermore, these tests allowed us to gain insight about network level properties such as throughput. [2] and [3] present the results of running simulations in a local area network with the purpose of evaluating the hit rate and other cache properties. That study is complementary to the results described in this paper.

4.1   The Testing Environment

We ran Cascade on nine hosts at the following geographically disperse locations over the Internet: *MIT*, at the Massachusetts Institute of Technology, Cambridge, MA; *UCSD*, at the University of California San Diego; *AM*, at Vrije University of Amsterdam, Netherlands; *PT*, at the University of Lisbon in Portugal; *TECH*, at the Technion, Haifa, Israel; *HUJI*, at the Hebrew University, Jerusalem, Israel; *SU*, at the Sydney University in Australia; *BR*, at the Federal University of Paraiba in Brazil; and *TW*, at National Taiwan University in Taiwan. The host in Amsterdam runs SunOS operating system on the Sun Sparc architecture. All other hosts run Linux on the Intelx86 architecture, ranging from Pentium II with 128MB of memory to multiprocessor Pentium 4 with 1Gb of memory.

We used the Visibroker ORB in all the tests described in this paper. Recently, we performed testing Cascade with ORBacus and other ORBs. While the absolute values obtained in the new measurements slightly differ, all effects we observed in the tests done with Visibroker apply to other ORBs as well. Furthermore, we run all Java programs with the Sun's implementation of JDK, ranging from JDK 1.2 to JDK 1.4. In Section 2 we briefly discuss the impact of choosing a particular Java implementation on the caching service performance.

In order to track the latency and loss rate of the links connecting these sites, we periodically ran ping from each host to all other hosts, sending a sequence of ping probes once every five minutes. The ping process was monitored by

Table 1. Round trip times (in *ms*) and loss percentage of the links (* denotes links with high variability)

From To	AM	PT	MIT	UCSD	SU	BR	TECH	HUJI	TW
AM		54(97)	141	170	310(376)	367(470)	86(170)	87(170)	334
		0*	0	0	0	6*	1	1	1
PT	55(98)		142	209	311(413)	221	122(193)	124(198)	347(389)
	0*		0	0	2*	6*	1*	1*	1
MIT	145	141		83	227	198(287)	180	190	220
	0	0		0	0	5*	1*	2*	1*
UCSD	167	203	82		178	294	251	255	175
	0	0	0		0	8*	1	2	1
SU	308(376)	357(411)	242	180		449	396	400	296
	2*	2*	0	0		24*	0	0	1
TW	315	341	220	176	293	460	385	391	
	2*	1	1*	1*	1	7*	3*	5*	

a `crontab`. The tests were run for a total of about 150 hours spread over 4 months, during different days of a week and different hours of a day. While ICMP-based ping probes differ in many ways from TCP-based CORBA communication, these measurements provide some intuition about the behavior of the underlying network.

The results are presented in Table 1. This table is not complete: We were unable to run ping measurements between some hosts because of firewalls at some of the locations that filtered out all ICMP communications. In some cases, we were pinging a different host at the same University instead of the host behind the firewall on which Cascade was tested.

The table shows both average round trip times (RTT) in milliseconds and average loss rate in percent. It should be noted that due to the great variability in both characteristics, the average values are not very indicative. This is particularly true for loss rates whose distribution was continuous, i.e., without multiple prominent peaks and base regions. For some links, indicated by an asterisk next to the average loss rate, the distribution was almost uniform, that is, each time we were running a sequence of pings we had a high chance of getting a different value. This effect is especially noticeable for the link from SU to BR where the loss percentage ranged from 10 to 48 depending on the time of the day, day of the week etc. Furthermore, we observed several transient losses of connectivity for short periods of few minutes.

The RTT values were somewhat more persistent. Here, most of the time we observed similar values within a deviation of 3 to 20 percent, depending on the link. However, sometimes the values jumped up drastically and remained high for the duration of few days, most probably because of router or link upgrades. We did not count such infrequent but significant deviations when computing the average but rather wrote them in parenthesis next to the average values in the table. Furthermore, we did not count the periods of these changes when evaluating the response times of an object cached with Cascade, as presented in Section 4.3 below.

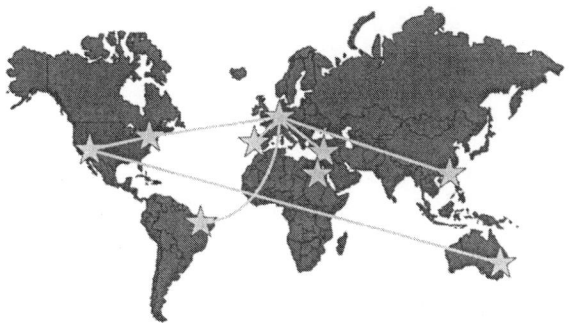

Fig. 2. The experimental hierarchy

This comes in line with research of end-to-end Internet path properties, e.g., in [6,9,11,13]. These works show that end-to-end Internet performance is extremely hard to analyze, predict, and simulate. Another distinguished feature in the Internet is that message latencies on different communication paths often do not preserve the triangle inequality because the routing policies of Internet routers often do not choose an optimal path between two hosts. For example, it follows from the above table that communication from AM to BR would be significantly faster if routed through PT. This phenomenon, in particular, provides a motivation for creating deeper hierarchies because it may prove better to connect new DCSs to intermediate nodes rather than directly to the root of the hierarchy.

4.2   The Experimental Hierarchy

In all our tests, we ran a single DCS on each host. All experiments comprised two steps: a) building the hierarchy, and b) executing requests on the objects. We did not consider object evacuations from the cache; it was the subject of a separate study in [3]. While we ran our experiments with several hierarchies that included the hosts listed above, we observed no significant differences in network level communication properties or in the speedup of object response times compared with the case of a centralized single object.[1] Thus, we chose to present results for one particular hierarchy depicted in Figure 2.

We chose the root of the hierarchy to be at AM because the sum of the distances from AM to all other hosts is smaller than the sum of the distances from most other sites (e.g., from BR to all other hosts). Furthermore, the host in AM is a strong machine that can handle the extra burden of request ordering and processing incurred on a root node. The hosts in the same geographical

---

[1] However, a considerable number of sufficiently large hierarchies should be considered to evaluate the hierarchy construction mechanism and scalability properties. Since coordinating between a large number of hosts in the Internet and managing large hierarchies is difficult, these properties should rather be tested in simulations.

locations were made connected to each other, e.g., HUJI was a child node of TECH. Note that the hierarchy is four level deep, SU being at the 4th level of the hierarchy. Thus, we were able to analyze the impact of a hierarchy depth on latencies and other communication properties.

4.3   Invocation Time Measurements

The main goal of response time tests was to compare request invocation times of an application using a centralized object with the same application using Cascade. Since the root of a hierarchy corresponds to the centralized object location in the original application, we first deployed a centralized object in AM, ran a set of application clients on a set of workloads at the locations in all other domains, and collected the results. Then we constructed the hierarchy described in Section 4.2 with the root in AM and ran the same application clients on the same set of workloads at the same locations.[2] This way, we were able to make a fair comparison of invocation times for the centralized object and for Cascade.

The Test Application and Workload. The implementation of the testbed involved three parts: (a) A sample object whose interface has both update and query methods, the size of an object being a parameter; (b) A mechanism for generating a synthetic workload, i.e., a sequence of update and query requests to be run from all locations. A workload was generated off-line prior to starting each test and made publicly accessible through the Web; (c) A test client application that can be run at any location. This application downloads a workload from the Web in the beginning of the test and then simulates it by invoking requests on either a centralized object or a cached copy.

The application also logs response times on a disk. Furthermore, DCSs also kept a log for their operations including processing times. To reduce the amount of time spent on disk writes and to make it negligible compared to invocation times, only individual operations that took more than five seconds as well as average values and distributions over a considerable period of time were recorded.

The most challenging part was generating adequate workloads because there are very few publicly available traces of CORBA, or other object based distributed systems operating in wide area networks. Note that numerous Web traces and traces for various file systems are of no help since typical sequences of requests for method invocations can fundamentally differ from requests for Web document or file data retrieval. When we started our experiments, we were trying to distribute all requests between different domains by using various distributions (e.g., Pareto, Zipf etc.). Fortunately, we found out that the exact type of distribution has very little impact on performance. Thus, in all our runs described below, requests were distributed uniformly over the nine origin domains. Based on our initial experiments, we concluded that among all workload

---

[2] Interhost times within a domain were small, up to 10 milliseconds for the requests that were used in the experiments.

parameters it was a) percentage of updates, b) request length, and c) request production rate, that had the strongest influence on invocation times. The percentage of updates and request length were ranging from 10% to 20% and from 10B to 15KB (not including IIOP and TCP headers), respectively. Since we wanted to separate the study of network latencies and behavior from the study of a load on Cascade servers, we ran these tests under a moderate request production rate (10 requests per second from each domain). Moreover, our object implementation was relatively lightweight: An execution of each method took few milliseconds, which matches the request execution times for a web server, a file server, or information retrieval systems but does not consider objects providing computational services. The size of the object was ranging from few bytes to about 100KB.

Factors Contributing to Invocation Times. Since Cascade is a complex multilayered system, there are many factors that affect the service operation. In addition to the environmental settings, cached object implementation and application workload discussed above, there are also internal Cascade parameters (e.g., thread pool tuning) and policies defined by the application for the cached object.

In particular, the choice of consistency policy substantially affects invocation times. For weak consistency policies, all operations are executed on a local DCS without being blocked on costly request transfer between DCSs. In our experiments, each invocation took 5 to 20 milliseconds in this case, depending on the host where the DCS runs and the exact environment settings. On the other hand, a remote invocation on a single centralized object can take up to 400–500 milliseconds for slow WAN links as can be seen from Table 1 and results presented below in the next section. Thus, for applications with weak consistency requirements, the service time can be reduced by a factor of 20–100 by employing caching solutions such as Cascade. This speedup does not depend on the percentage of updates in the workload. Furthermore, it increases for long requests that enlarge request transfer and service response times for a centralized object but have much less effect when requests are invoked on and replies are returned from a nearby cached copy. Thus, the most interesting situation for performance analysis is when the application requires a strong consistency policy. Below we consider only this case.

Another object policy that strongly affects invocation times is the type of propagation done by the consistency implementation, by requests or by objects. Since the object implementation used in the test was not computationally heavy and the state of the object was longer than update requests, which is consistent with most object based distributed applications, propagating requests proved to be considerably more lightweight than propagating object states. The difference was especially prominent for large objects: We found out that the object size plays a very important role for object propagation while having almost no significance when requests are propagated.

In many aspects, propagating object states for large objects is similar to propagating update requests for long requests because both lead to intensive

Table 2. Factors contributing to response time

Factor	Marshaling	Interceptors	In queues and execution	Network latency
Percentage	< 1%	< 1%	6%	93%

communication between DCSs. However, propagation by objects requires object serialization and deserialization that may be relatively heavy operations in Java, depending on the platform, Java implementation etc. On the other hand, when objects are propagated, Cascade performs data merges and replacements (a detailed description of these mechanisms is given in [12]) thereby substantially reducing the amount of propagated data. This tradeoff becomes particularly interesting for higher request production rates when both effects have strong impact on the service performance. Our experiments suggest that when object states and requests are of comparable size, propagating objects can turn slightly more efficient when DCSs run on powerful server machines. However, the difference was not very significant. While all performance results that appear below mention only the effect of request lengths, they can also indicate the influence of an object size for object state propagation.

It should be noted that the length of request results (i.e., the return values of an invocation) is much less important than the length of the request itself (i.e., the size of input parameters). This is because requests themselves are disseminated between all DCSs in a hierarchy while invocation results are only returned to the client that invoked the request.[3]

Table 2 shows a typical distribution of time between the operations that constitute a request invocation. This distribution corresponds to the case when an update request is invoked on a local DCS, propagated to the root, ordered and applied by the root, and the results are propagated back to the local DCS. Another situation covered by this distribution is when a query request is invoked on a local DCS, and this query request has to block until a previously issued update request arrives. All operations performed by the ORB (i.e., marshaling, request interception and dispatching, etc.) were taking less than one percent of the total time in all our tests. The overhead of processing the request by Cascade (that includes the time when the request is pending in various queues) and the proper object execution were typically taking 3 to 8 percent, depending on the factors we described above throughout this section. The network latency constituted most of the overall invocation times, just as we expected.

Typically, request processing time at a DCS was 2 to 25 milliseconds. Most of this time went to serialization/deserialization operations for object propagation, garbage collection, synchronization between Java threads (in particular, monitor contention), and waiting while these operations are performed for preceding requests. The distribution of time between these operations as well as the absolute duration values strongly depended both on the computational resources of

---

[3] To be precise, when a request is executed only once on the root DCS, returned values are also transferred between the root DCS and the DCS that accepted the client request.

Table 3. Parameters describing the test configuration

Samples/graph	Period	ConsPol	Prop	Blocking	ObjSize	ReqSize	UpdRate
> 10,000,000	4 mon	Strong	Updates	Q or U	70B–100KB	10B–15KB	10%–20%

the DCS host (i.e., the amount of memory and CPU speed) and the particular implementation of JVM. For example, serializing a 10KB object takes about one millisecond with JDK 1.4 on Pentium IV with 1Gb of memory but up to few dozens of milliseconds with JDK 1.2 on Pentium II with 128MB of memory. It is well known that the garbage collection mechanism was substantially improved in JDK 1.3. At the same time, it is somewhat surprising that the implementation of a JVM has at least the same effect on efficiency of serialization and monitor contention as the platform settings. For example, we initially ran a DCS at MIT with JDK 1.2 and contention on Java monitors for some workload was about 10 milliseconds per request, which was more than on other hosts with exactly the same JDK implementation. When we replaced JDK 1.2 with 1.3, the monitor contention times for the same workload dropped to just a couple of milliseconds per request. In some cases, we observed an improvement in monitor contention times following a Linux upgrade to a newer version.

Results of Response Time Tests. We now present the results of running over a hundred of tests, each test containing 100,000 invocation requests. These tests were conducted at different hours of the day and different days of the week during a period of about four months. Table 3 summarizes the main parameters used throughout the experiments.

As described above, each test included a workload consisting of both update and query requests that originated from all locations. In general, the invocation times measured by the client reflected the patterns of changes in network latency as described in Section 4.1. In particular, the standard deviation of response times was as high as 30 percent.

Response Times for Short Requests. Figure 3 (a) shows five distributions of response times as measured at MIT for the tests with short requests (about 100B long, including IIOP and TCP headers). Recall that the MIT node is at the second level in the hierarchy and it was directly connected to the root at AM. Update requests in this experiment were blocking, i.e., response to the client was delayed until the request is propagated to the root, ordered and received back. The first distribution refers to the case of a centralized object, when there is no difference for update and query requests. All other distributions describe response times when using Cascade. The second and the third distributions refer to the workload in which 10 percent of all requests were updates. They describe invocation times for queries and updates, respectively. The fourth and fifth distributions also refer to queries and updates but when update requests constitute 20 percent of the workload.

We can see that virtually 100 percent of query requests have invocation times of 0 to 20 milliseconds, independently of the number of update requests in the

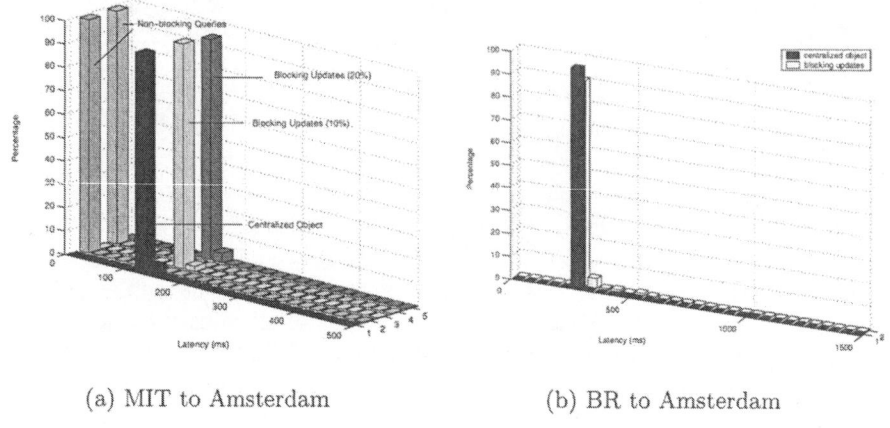

(a) MIT to Amsterdam   (b) BR to Amsterdam

Fig. 3. Invocation time histogram for 100B requests

workload. The distributions for update requests and for the centralized object were slightly more heavy tailed but still more than 90 percent of invocations fall in the same 20 millisecond time interval. These three distributions appear almost identical. Thus, we can conclude that for short requests, each individual update invocation takes about the same time independently of the percent of updates in the workload. Furthermore, the response time for an update is always the same, whether for a centralized object or for an object cached with Cascade.

Figure 3 (b) shows analogous distributions measured at BR. BR is at the same level in the hierarchy as MIT but the link from BR to AM is more lossy. Here only distributions for a centralized object and for update requests with Cascade are presented. Again, the distributions are almost identical but the distribution for a cached object is slightly more heavytailed. This indicates that the loss rate on the link has a bit stronger negative effect in the case of Cascade than in the case of a centralized object.

Response Times for Long Requests. Response times for long update requests are presented in Figure 4 (a). The two distributions are for workloads with 10 and 20 percent of update requests, respectively. These distributions are fundamentally different from the corresponding ones for short requests. Not only they are quite heavytailed but we can clearly see two distinctive peaks (in fact, there is another peak in the interval above 1 second but this peak is small and not so prominent as the first two). This is due to message losses on the link: for a long request, there is a high probability that at least one TCP packet belonging to this request gets lost. Such a packet loss causes a severe increase in the invocation time for the request. The second peak corresponds to the case when a request execution is delayed by a single segment retransmission. The third peak is due to multiple packet losses. Note that if two consecutive packets are lost, TCP can detect

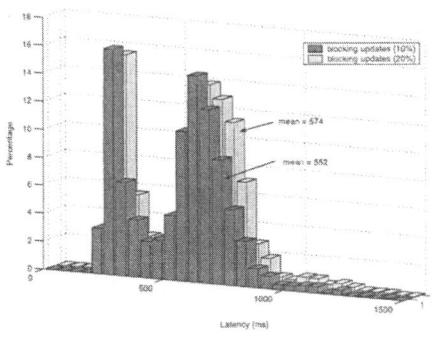

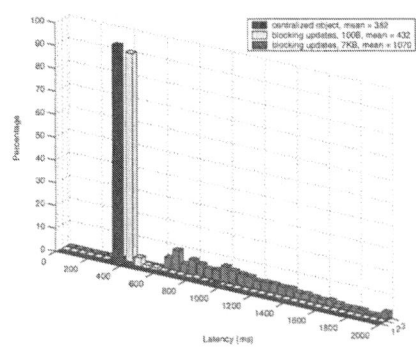

(a) Response times for long updates   (b) Effect of the hierarchy depth

Fig. 4. Influence of different factors on response times for update requests

this and retransmit the packets at the same time, so that the invocation time increases by only one packet retransmission period. This explains why the second peak is almost as big as the first one while the third peak is substantially smaller.

In addition, we can see that percentage of updates in the workload has small but noticeable effect for long requests, unlike for short ones. Specifically, the distribution for 20 percent is slightly more heavytailed and its average is 20 millisecond higher compared with the distribution for 10 percent. The reason for this is an increased amount of communication, which causes more packet losses and out of order arrivals as shown in Section 4.4.

Impact of the Hierarchy Depth. We also tried to investigate how invocation times with Cascade are affected by the location of the DCS in the hierarchy. Figure 4 (b) depicts the histogram of update invocation times for SU, which is at the deepest (fourth) level in the hierarchy, being connected to AM by two intermediate nodes. The three presented distributions correspond to the cases of a centralized object, short update requests with Cascade, and long update requests, respectively. We can see that the distribution for short requests has a very distinct peak interval into which over 90 percent of invocations fall. This is only a bit less than the percent of invocations that fall into the peak interval for a centralized object. The exact location of these two peaks relatively to each other is determined by how efficient the constructed hierarchy is. For our hierarchy, the path to the root through UCSB and MIT was slightly longer than the path of a direct connection to AM. In addition, processing at each node adds some 5 to 20 milliseconds to the overall invocation time, once for the propagation to the root once for the backward propagation.

However, the distribution for long requests was drastically different: It was almost uniform. As in the case of other distributions, the most influential com-

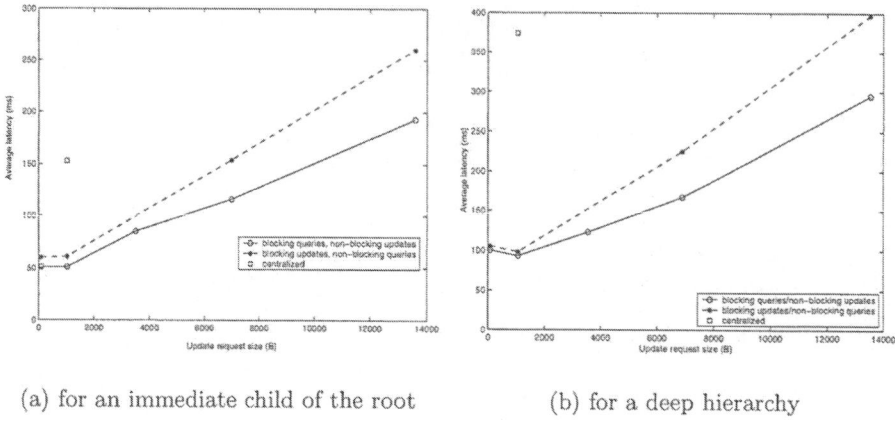

(a) for an immediate child of the root   (b) for a deep hierarchy

Fig. 5. Average invocation time as a function of update request size

ponent of an invocation time was the network latency. The network latency for each of the three links on the path from SU to AM had a distribution similar to the one presented in Figure 4 (a) but with different peak locations. When these three distributions are superimposed on each other to contribute to the invocation times at SU, the resulting distribution is significantly more heavy-tailed. The practical implication of this fact is that for applications with long update requests, it is important to keep the hierarchy depth small, even when placing a node deeper into the hierarchy would not make its distance to the root (computed as the sum of latencies in the intermediate links) longer.

Comparison between the Centralized Object and Cascade Communication. Figure 5 (a) shows the dependency of the average request invocation time with Cascade on the update request size. The presented results are for a workload with 20 percent of updates and for the link from MIT to AM. Note that unlike all graphs presented earlier in this section, this figure makes no distinction between update and query requests, i.e., each point here represents an average time over all requests in the test.

The two displayed curves correspond to blocking and non-blocking updates. For blocking updates, response to the client is delayed until the request is propagated to the root of the hierarchy and back. A non-blocking update request returns immediately but a subsequent query will have to block in order to satisfy the FIFO consistency guarantee. In addition, the figure shows the average invocation time for a centralized object, which changes very slowly as the request size increases.

As we would expect, using non-blocking update requests is more efficient than blocking because it allows for a pipelining between propagating a previously issued update request and handling of a subsequent query. The dependency on the size of update requests is almost linear in the both cases. This dependency turned out very similar for a workload with 10 percent of updates but the slope of the curve was about twice smaller.

Clearly, the curves are quite steep. This steepness is due to the fact that requests are pushed through the hierarchy resulting in a lot of packets being sent in a bursty fashion. The communication for a centralized object is much more regular as described in Section 4.4. Therefore, the curve for the centralized case is much less steep. While the advantage of using Cascade is very prominent for short requests, the curves intersect at some point. Thus, starting from a certain request size, the invocation time for Cascade can become worse than the invocation time for a centralized object. The location of the intersection point depends on many factors but especially on the percentage of update requests in the workload.

Fortunately, in many applications update requests are short and most data is transferred in response to query requests. For example, in the typical Cascade application such as Yellow Pages, an update request typically contains the new values of only few fields. At the same time, a query request may retrieve a lot of information. This gives a definite advantage to the caching solution of Cascade over a centralized object. In such settings, we can expect a 3–4 times speedup in the mean response time when using strong consistency, as implied by the ratio of invocations times for update requests up to 1KB in Figure 5.

Finally, Figure 5 (b) presents analogous dependencies for the SU location, which is at the fourth level in the hierarchy. The results here are very similar to those for the MIT location. The advantage of Cascade for short update requests is even more prominent. However, the curves for Cascade are even steeper because of the way in which latency distributions for intermediate links are superimposed on each other.

4.4   Assessing Network Level Properties of the Communication

To gain deeper insight about the pattern and properties of DCS-to-DCS communication in the Internet, we monitored the TCP packets sent at the network level. Since such monitoring requires administrative privileges, we could do it only at TECH where we had such permissions. Specifically, we ran the tcpdump program to collect information about all packets that were sent or received by the DCS running at TECH. Then, we used the tcptrace program [10] to process the collected statistics and present it in a comprehensible form. In this section, we present the most interesting characteristics of the communication. Complete description of this analysis can be found in [12].

First of all, all hosts where the DCSs ran supported MTU discovery. Therefore, both the average and maximal allowed segment sizes were about 1420B.

We also analyzed the "activity" on the connection, i.e., all sent, received, and acknowledged packets. As we intuitively expected, the pattern of communication between DCSs in Cascade is more irregular compared with the alternating request-reply messages in the case of a centralized object. This irregularity is partly responsible for a bigger number of retransmissions and packets arriving out of order. This analysis also allowed us to conclude that the buffer space on the receiver's side was not a problem in these tests.

In addition, we considered the amount of outstanding data, i.e., the number of unacknowledged bytes. This characteristic can give some approximate idea of the congestion window (as estimated by TCP). The amount of the outstanding data was bigger and with much stronger variation for the communication in Cascade compared with the centralized object. This goes in line with irregularity of the communication pattern in Cascade that renders the communication more prone to packet losses and packets arriving out of order. Note, however, that amount of outstanding data does not necessarily indicate the real available capacity of the links: If the communication is not very intensive, the congestion window will not grow beyond the required size.

Finally, Figures 6 (a) and (b) show throughput measurements for the centralized object and Cascade communication, respectively. Of course, these measurements were done on the same workload (20 percent of update requests that were 7KB long). Note that while the DCS at TECH has a child DCS at HUJI, these results take into account only the communication between TECH and AM. This makes a fair comparison because we also do not take into account the requests sent from HUJI to the centralized object.

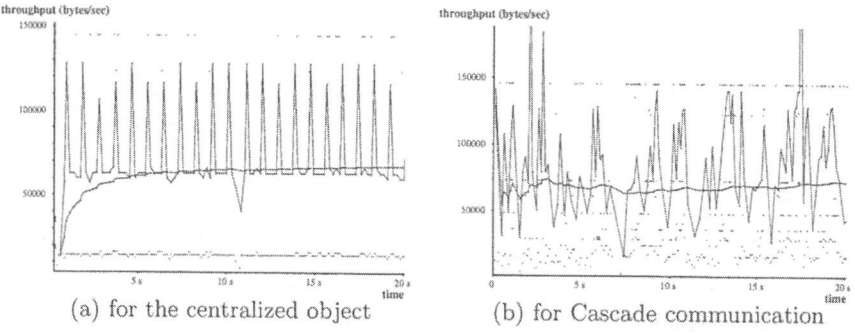

(a) for the centralized object   (b) for Cascade communication

Fig. 6. Throughput graphs

The dots in these graphs represent "instantaneous throughput", which is defined as the size of the segment divided by the time elapsed since the previous segment arrived. Due to clock granularity, there tends to be a lot of banding in these points. The zigzag line is an average of the previous ten dots. The smoother line is the average throughput over the life of the connection to that point (i.e., the total number of bytes divided by the total number of seconds).

We can see that the average throughput for the centralized object and for Cascade communication is almost the same in these particular experiments but the pattern for Cascade is more irregular. In general the comparison is not quite straightforward. For a centralized object, all requests travel forth and back over WAN links, whereas only update requests are propagated by Cascade. On the other hand, every request in Cascade is flooded through the hierarchy, i.e., sent over multiple links compared with a single link for a centralized object. This flooding propagation may result in an intensive communication, especially for large hierarchies with high fan-out number of nodes. Note, however, that this effect is mitigated by using flow control optimizations in Cascade (see [12] for a detailed discussion on this subject). Yet, its impact may be significant when the workload contains a high percent of update requests that are produced at high rate.

5   Conclusions

We have presented our experiments with running Cascade over the Internet and compared the response times of the application that uses the caching service with those of the centralized version. In particular, we have shown that for applications with weak consistency requirements, the service time can be reduced by a factor of 20–100 by employing caching solutions such as Cascade.

For strong consistency conditions, we can hope for an improvement factor of 3–4 as long as update requests are short and not very frequent. Yet, the advantage of using Cascade becomes less prominent for long and intensive update requests because Cascade pushes updates through the hierarchy resulting in higher bandwidth consumption compared with the communication to and from the centralized object. Thus, starting from a certain update request size, the invocation time for Cascade can become worse than the invocation time for a centralized object. The exact size when it occurs depends on a great number of factors that we have discussed throughout the paper, notably on the amount of available network bandwidth. Taking into account that in modern networks, bandwidth increases with a steady rate while latency remains approximately constant, we expect Cascade to become beneficial for application with longer and longer update requests as time goes by. Furthermore, we continue exploring the end-to-end TCP behavior and various flow control techniques to make handling long requests more efficient.

We would like to point out that while this study was made in the context of the CORBA architecture, we believe that many of its lessons are applicable to any TCP/IP based middleware, and in particular to the emerging Web Services standard. When considering all major existing distributed middleware standards, as far as remote method invocation is concerned, all of them share more or less the same pattern. In particular, a client request is passed to some local stub or proxy, which encapsulates the request in some high level protocol header, and then the request is transmitted over a TCP/IP connection to the server machine. In the server machine, the request is picked by the middleware, the high level protocol headers are stripped, and the request is invoked on the target object or service. The reply that is generated then follows a reverse path. The main functionality of CASCADE lies in this exact common path between all these middlewares, and the main sources of efficiency and inefficiency are related to this type of communication pattern rather than to the specific IIOP protocol headers, the way requests and responses are represented on the network, or the particular way CORBA locates objects. Thus, while CASCADE itself is not immediately portable to other middleware platforms, we believe that the results of this performance study are highly applicable to any of them.

Acknowledgements. Gregory Chockler participated in the original design of the Cascade system. He and David Breitgand contributed many valuable suggestions towards devising a realistic testbed. The following people kindly allowed us to use the computing resources of their labs for testing Cascade in the Internet: Francisco Brasiliero, Danny Dolev, Alan Fekete, Yuh-Jzer Joung, Idit Keidar, Keith Marzullo, Luis Rodrigues, and Maarten van Steen.

References

1. D. Andersen, H. Balakrishnan, F. Kaashoek, and R. Morris. Resilient Overlay Networks. In *ACM SIGOPS Symposium on Operating Systems Principles (SOSP)*, Oct. 2001.
2. H. Atzmohn, R. Friedman, and R. Vitenberg. Replacement Policies for a Distributed Object Caching Service. In *Symposium on Distributed Objects and Applications*, Oct. 2002.
3. H. Atzmon. Replacement Policies for Internet Wide Caching of Distributed Objects. MSc Thesis, Technion, 2002.
4. O. Bakr and I. Keidar. Evaluating the Running Time of a Communication Round over the Internet. In *ACM Symposium on Principles of Distributed Computing (PODC)*, pages 243–252, July 2002.
5. L. Brakmo and L. Peterson. TCP Vegas: End to End Congestion Avoidance on a Global Internet. *IEEE Journal of Selected Areas in Communication*, 13(8): 1465–1480, Oct. 1995.
6. B. Chandra, M. Dahlin, L. Gao, and A. Nayate. End-to-end WAN Service Availability. In *Third Usenix Symposium on Internet Technologies and Systems (USITS01)*, Mar. 2001.
7. G. Chockler, D. Dolev, R. Friedman, and R. Vitenberg. Implementing a Caching Service for Distributed CORBA Objects. In *Proceedings of Middleware '00*, Apr. 2000. The Best Conference Paper award.
8. G. Chockler, R. Friedman, and R. Vitenberg. Consistency Conditions for a CORBA Caching Service. In *Proc. of the 14th International Symposium on Distributed Computing (DISC)*, pages 374–388, Oct. 2000.
9. S. Floyd and V. Paxson. Difficulties in Simulating The Internet. *IEEE/ACM Transanctions on Networking*, 9(4): 392–403, Aug. 2001.
10. S. Ostermann. *tcptrace*. http://www.tcptrace.org/.
11. S. Savage, A. Collins, E. Hoffman, J. Snell, and T. Anderson. The End-to-End Effects of Internet Path Selection. In *ACM SIGCOMM*, pages 289–299, Sept. 1999.
12. R. Vitenberg. *Internet-Wide Caching of Distributed Objects*. PhD thesis, The Technion, 2002.
13. Y. Zhang, N. Duffield, V. Paxson, and S. Shenker. On The Constancy of Internet Path Properties. In *ACM SIGCOMM Internet Measurement Workshop*, Nov. 2001.

Semi-automatic Parallelization of Java Applications

Pascal A. Felber

Institut EURECOM
06904 Sophia Antipolis, France
felber@eurecom.fr

Abstract. Some types of time-consuming computations are naturally parallelizable. To take advantage of parallel processing, however, applications must be explicitly programmed to use specific libraries that share the workload among multiple (generally distributed) processors. In this paper, we present a set of Java tools that allow us to parallelize some types of computationally-intensive Java applications *a posteriori*, even when the source code of these applications is not available. Our tools operate using techniques based on bytecode transformation, code migration, and distributed parallel method executions.

1 Introduction

Motivations. The Java language is widely considered as inadequate for computationally-intensive tasks. The obvious reason lies in the "poor" performance of Java programs, which run significantly slower than their C or Fortran counterparts. There are a number of reasons, however, why Java may be used for such applications.

First, Java is easy to learn, safe, and scalable to complex programming problems. Its popularity and wide adoption have attracted significant interest from the scientific and engineering community and led to the development of tools and libraries adapted to high performance and parallel computing [1,2,3].

More importantly, Java's processor and operating system independence make it possible to deploy distributed parallel applications on heterogeneous platforms and harness the processing power of idle workstations in the Internet. This has the potential to extend the reach of parallel distributed applications far beyond specialized clusters of homogeneous machines traditionally used for high-performance computing.

Finally, Just-In-Time (JIT) compilers that translate Java bytecode into native instructions have made significant advances to improve performance, and modern JIT compilers have been estimated to reach up to two thirds of the speed of C code [4]. IBM's Ninja project has also demonstrated that, when compiling Java applications specifically for parallel architectures, one can achieve between 80 and 100% of the performance of highly optimized Fortran code [5]. Combined with quasi-static techniques [6,7], Java code can be as efficient as C or Fortran code.

R. Meersman et al. (Eds.): CoopIS/DOA/ODBASE 2003, LNCS 2888, pp. 1369–1383, 2003.

Overview and Contributions. The goal of the work presented in this paper is to provide mechanisms to seamlessly parallelize some kinds of Java applications and execute them on distributed processors, without requiring the application programmer to explicitly use dedicated message-passing libraries. These mechanisms can be applied to code that has not been programmed with parallelization in mind and whose source is not available. Parallelism is implemented at the coarse level of method invocations, by transforming a computationally-intensive operation into a set of shorter equivalent operations executed on multiple machines. Transformations are performed according to simple "rewriting" rules specified by the application deployer.

Our parallelization mechanisms consist of two major components: (1) a wrapper generator that instruments Java bytecode at load time and effectively wraps selected methods with user-specifier filters; and (2) a parallelization engine that instantiates application classes on multiple processes, dispatches method invocations to these processes, and finally collects and aggregate replies. Although the program does not need to be modified, some rewriting rules need to be specified by the application deployer. Parallelization is therefore transparent to the application, but not completely automatic (hence *semi-automatic*).

We would like to emphasize that our techniques can only be used with *some types* of Java applications with loosely-synchronous tasks. The focus and contributions of this work are less on raw speed or features, which may be better achieved using C and dedicated message-passing libraries, than on transparency and applicability of our parallelization techniques to legacy Java code. They provide an easy way to harness the processing power of idle workstation to increase the performance of applications with no built-in support for parallel processing.

To the best of our knowledge, this work is the first to address the problem of automatic parallelization of Java applications by instrumenting bytecode and transparently executing computationally-intensive programs on distributed processors.

Related Work. Automatic parallelization of a program is generally achieved using parallel compilers that generate code optimized for parallel architectures [8, 9]. In the context of the Java programming language, javar [10] is a source code transformation engine that makes implicit loop parallelism and multi-way recursive methods explicit by means of the multi-threading mechanism provided by the Java virtual machine. The resulting code can execute faster on parallel machines that run multiple threads on separate processors. Javab [11] performs essentially the same transformations, but on the program's bytecode rather than its source code. JOIE [12] is another toolkit for Java bytecode transformations, but it has been designed to modify the behavior of the code rather than optimizing its execution for a given target environment. IBM's Ninja project [5] includes a prototype Java compiler that performs high order loop transformations and parallelization completely automatically, resulting in runtime performance similar to Fortran code in a variety of benchmarks.

The development of parallel applications targeted for execution on distributed processors traditionally requires parallelism to be dealt with explicitly. These applications are traditionally implemented using specialized message-passing libraries such as PVM [13] and MPI [14], which manage communications between sets of collaborating processes executing on multiple machines. PVM and MPI have mappings for several programming languages, and have recently been extended to support Java [15,16]. Although powerful and robust, theses message-passing libraries are also complex to program, even in their Java incarnation. JavaParty [17] simplifies this process by introducing language constructs for the development of distributed and parallel Java applications, but the programmer still needs to deal explicitly with parallelism. COPS [18] goes one step further by using parallel design patterns to automatically generate the structural code necessary for a Java application to run in parallel.

Organization. The rest of this paper is organized as follows. Section 2 presents an overview of our Java parallelization framework. Section 3 describes the wrapper generator used to transparently instrument Java bytecode and intercept selected method invocations. Section 4 presents the parallelization engine responsible for managing communications between distributed processors. Section 5 illustrates our tools using a concrete example, and Section 6 elaborates on their performance. Finally, Section 7 concludes the paper.

2   Program Parallelization

There are several approaches to make a program execute faster using parallel processing. For instance, a multi-threaded program can benefit from parallel architectures by having each thread run on a distinct processor. In this paper, we focus on coarse-grain parallelization, where multiple *distributed* computers work together to perform time-consuming computations. As the time necessary for communication between collaborating computers is not negligible, this approach works well when computations require significant processor resources, in the order of seconds, and each processor can compute its share independently of other processors (loose synchronization).

Several types of applications can benefit from distributed parallel processing. For instance, complex database queries can be executed by having each processor looking through part of the data, or executing part of the query. Complex computations, such as cryptographic key discovery, or synthesis image generation, can also be parallelized by having each processor explore part of the space of input values (using "divide-and-conquer" algorithms).

The idea underlying our Java application parallelization framework is to instrument the classes responsible for time-consuming computations, instantiate them on multiple machines, and re-direct the invocations to computationally-intensive methods to all the instances for parallel execution. Method interception is achieved by the means of a wrapper generator toolkit, which constitutes the

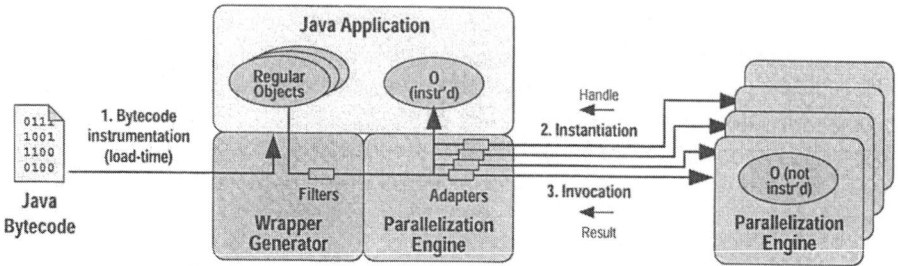

Fig. 1. Semi-automatic Parallelization of a Java Application.

lowest layer of our parallelization framework. At the next level, the Java parallelization engine takes care of load sharing and communication with distributed processors. Finally, the deployer has to provide application-specific adapters that essentially define "rewriting rules" for splitting requests and merging replies. The overall system architecture is shown in Fig. 1.

Rewriting rules are application-specific. They specify for each application how a computationally-intensive request can be split into multiple simple sub-requests that can execute in parallel. In addition, they specify how the results of these individual sub-requests can be combined to produce the complete result expected from the initial request. A typical rule for the computation of a synthesis image would rewrite request arguments and assign non-overlapping areas of the image to each target processor; the results from each processor would later be combined into a single image by appending them in the right sequence.

Our approach is transparent to the application being parallelized, as it does not require source-code modifications, but it is not fully automatic, in the sense that the application deployer has to specify the rewriting rules. All the information pertaining to the rewriting rules, the classes to instrument, the addresses of the distributed processors, etc. are specified using Java properties and configuration files.

3   The Java Wrapper Generator

We have developed a tool, called the Java Wrapper Generator (JWG), which uses load-time reflection to transparently insert pre- and post-filters to any method from a Java class. These generic filters allow developers to add crosscutting functionality to compiled Java code and extend it with various features, such as debugging, profiling, proxying, runtime validation, security, or aspect-oriented extensions. In this section, we briefly present the major features of our wrapper generator, used by the parallelization engine to add parallel distributed behavior to sequential centralized Java programs.

3.1   Filters

The Java wrapper generator allows Java developers to transparently insert pre- and post-filters to any method of a Java class. Filters are custom classes written by the user and attached to specific methods at the time the class is loaded by the Java virtual machine, by instrumenting the bytecode (1. in Fig. 1). It is therefore not necessary to access the source code of the Java class.

Pre- and post-filters can be installed at the following levels, from the most to the least specialized: an *instance method* filter applies to a specific method of a given instance; an *instance* filter applies to all methods of a given instance; a *class method* filter applies to a specific method of a given class; a *class* filter applies to all methods of a given class; and finally, a *global* filter applies to all methods of all classes. Upon invocation of an instrumented method, the wrapper generator runtime searches all installed filters in decreasing order of specialization, until it finds a valid filter. If no filter is found, then no filtering takes place.

Pre-filters are invoked at the beginning of each instrumented method. In the special case of constructors, pre-filters are invoked after the call to the constructor of the superclass or the class itself, i.e., after the constructor of the `Object` base class has been called. Pre-filters receive as parameters the target object (for non-static methods) or class (for static methods), and the method name, signature, and arguments. A pre-filter can modify the values of the method arguments, but the number and types of the arguments must remain consistent with the method's signature. A pre-filter can terminate in three different manners: (1) the filtered method continues normally after execution of the filter (normal termination); (2) the filtered method terminates immediately with the return value provided by the filter, which must be of a type consistent with the method signature (short-circuit); and (3) the filtered method terminates immediately by throwing the exception provided by the filter, which must be consistent with the exceptions declared by the method (exceptional termination).

Post-filters are invoked at the end of each instrumented method. They are also invoked upon abrupt completion (`return` statement in the middle of a method) or when an exception occurs during method execution. Post-filters receive as parameters the target object (for non-static methods) or class (for static methods), the method name, signature, and arguments, and the return value or exception resulting from the method's execution. A post-filter can modify the arguments (which may be used to return data to the caller) and the return value or exception. In addition, a return value can be replaced by an exception, and vice versa, as long as the type of the return value or exception remains consistent with the method's signature.

The association of filters with specific classes, objects and methods can be performed declaratively (via a configuration file) or programmatically. Furthermore, the wrapper generator provides a simple API to dynamically install and remove filters during program execution.

3.2   Bytecode Instrumentation

Bytecode instrumentation is performed using the BCEL bytecode engineering library [19] and a custom "class loader", with overrides the default behavior of the Java class loading mechanism. The code of selected methods is modified to include calls to user-specified pre- and post-filters. The functionality added to the bytecode is minimal: it includes parameter transformation (simple types are transformed in their equivalent object types), filter invocation, and exception and result management. Additional logic is implemented in regular Java libraries.

The names of the classes and methods to be instrumented can be specified at deployment time via a configuration file. Although instrumented methods can have no filter attached to them, unmodified code executes faster and it is therefore desirable to restrict the scope of instrumentation to only those classes that need it. Methods that are not instrumented during class loading are not filterable.

4   The Java Parallelization Engine

The Java parallelization engine builds on top of the wrapper generator described in the previous section. It is responsible for sharing the workload and managing communication with the distributed processors.

4.1   Architectural Overview

The parallelization engine consists of two major components (see Fig. 1). A client-side library that attaches itself transparently to the application being parallelized, and a server-side daemon program that provides its processing power to the application. Both of these components are independent of the target application. Application-specific functionality is specifies by the means of "adapters", which act as the glue that binds the client-side parallelization engine and the target application.

Although we could have re-used specialized toolkits such as PVM [13] and MPI [14] to implement the parallelization engine and handle our communications, we have rather chosen to develop lightweight mechanisms adapted to our specific requirements. Server applications, also called "workers", listen to incoming TCP connections from parallelized clients. (Note that we could have used Java RMI instead, but raw TCP has less overhead and makes it easier to quickly detect and recover from worker failures.) Each worker can service multiple clients concurrently, using Java's multi-threading features. Once a connection is established between a client and a worker, the client can send requests to be processed by the worker. There are three types of requests: object creation, object invocation, and object deletion. These requests control all interactions between the parallelized Java program and the remote processors utilized by the parallelization engine.

4.2 Distributed Invocations

The parallelization engine filters the constructors of each parallelized object, and issues a remote object creation request to multiple workers when such a constructor is called (2. in Fig. 1). The bytecode of the classes to instantiate (or alternatively a URL/URI to that bytecode) is sent together with the creation request, which leads to the instantiation of a non-instrumented copy of the object in each worker process. The worker returns a handle—a string identifying the object in the server process—to the client; this handle is subsequently used in client requests to identify objects on the server. The parallelization engine transparently keeps track of the object handles associated with each parallelized object at each worker. An instrumented copy of the object is also created locally; this copy can be used for serving requests that do not need to be parallelized.

Regular invocations to a parallelized object are also intercepted by the parallelization engine. The method invocation is first passed to an adapter for rewriting (to be described shortly), and then sent to each worker along with the handle of the object on that worker (3. in Fig. 1). Once the request has been processed by each worker, replies are sent to the client, combined using the adapters, and returned to the invoker.

Finally, when a parallelized object is no longer needed and its `finalize` method is called, the parallelization engine sends a deletion request to each worker along with the handle of the object to delete. All objects and resources allocated for a given client are also automatically reclaimed when the connection to that client is closed.

4.3 Adapters

Adapters are regular Java objects that implement the `Adapter` interface. They implement a `split` method, which takes the original request targeted to the non-parallelized version of an object, and transforms it into a request to be sent to a single worker in the parallel version of the program. Likewise, the `join` method combines the replies sent back by individual workers into a single reply returned to the original program. Both the `split` and `join` methods are given the total number of workers, as well as the index of the worker concerned by the current request/reply; this information enables adapters to deterministically determine which part of the request must be processed by each worker. For instance, given n workers, the workload can be split into n equals parts, with the worker at index i being responsible for the ith part. It is also possible to configure the parallelization engine to call each worker multiple times in the context of a given client invocation, and to implement more dynamic scheduling algorithms, such as guided self scheduling [20].

The parallelization engine creates one adapter per worker. An adapter is assigned to a single worker during its lifetime, and is guaranteed that each invocation to `join` directly follows the matching invocation to `split`. These properties enable adapter objects to maintain consistent state information about the workers they are responsible for.

The `split` method is given information about the method being invoked, as well as its parameters. A simple rewriting rule would change the arguments to specify the part of the workload affected to a given worker. An adapter may have to consistently rewrite the arguments of several methods, including the constructor of the parallelized object, to ultimately achieve the desired partial computation.

The `join` method is given information about the target method, the parameters that were received as part of the non-parallel invocation, and the results from the execution on the worker. A typical rewriting rule would copy the relevant portion of the data received from the worker into the parameters/return value associated with the original invocation. Examples of `join` and `split` method implementations are given in the next section, in Listing 1.2.

4.4 Failures

When the client application fails, all TCP connections with the workers are closed and the resources associated to that client are automatically reclaimed. When one of the worker fails, the client runtime will transparently re-submit the partial request assigned to that worker to another worker. Optionally, it can also recursively split and share the aborted partial request among all non-failed workers. By default, no new connections are opened at runtime and failed workers are not replaced during the lifetime of the client. This does not pose a problem in practice as the lifetime of clients is generally much shorter than that of the workers and failures are expected to be rare events. In addition, clients can initially connect to a larger number of workers that they actually need, to account for possible failures.

4.5 Limitations

As previously discusses, one of the major contributions of our work lies in the automatic parallelization of binary Java applications. The steps involved in the parallelization process are the discovery of the classes and methods to parallelize, the specification of rewriting rules in the form of adapter objects, and the deployment of the parallelized application with multiple worker processes.

Because of its transparency feature, our parallelization framework has several limitations. First, it only applies to applications that are naturally parallelizable, and for which the gain of parallelization exceeds its cost. Note that this is also true of distributed parallel application deployed with specialized message-passing libraries such as PVM [13] and MPI [14]. Our transparency goals also limit our scope to applications that can be parallelized by intercepting and rewriting selected invocations. This is more often the case with well-engineered object-oriented applications, which have a modular structure and encapsulate functionality (e.g., compute-intensive tasks) inside objects with a well-defined interface.

Programs that have a complex structure, for instance because they extensively use callbacks or exchange complex objects that are not serializable as part of invocation arguments, may also not be parallelizable without modifications to their source code. Note again that such program would also need major reengineering to be deployed on top of PVM or MPI. Finally, classes that use native libraries and are not written in 100% pure Java cannot be instrumented by the wrapper generator.

5 Example

In this section, we illustrate the use of our framework by showing the steps necessary to parallelize a computationally-intensive Java program that generates fractal images.

5.1 The Mandelbrot Set

An example of an time-consuming, easily-parallelizable application is the computation of the Mandelbrot set. The Mandelbrot set is a fractal structure defined in the complex plane by the following equation: $z_n = (z_{n-1})^2 + z_0$. The set itself is the area where $\lim_{n\to\infty} z_n < \infty$.

It is demonstrated that if $|z_i| > 4$, then z_n will eventually reach ∞. An approximation of the set can be computed by iterating the formula. Points where $|z_i| > 2$ are not part of the set, and the remaining points *may* be part of the set. The resulting set is traditionally displayed in a two-dimensional picture.

This computation is time-consuming: for each point the formula is iterated until $|z_i| > 2$, or a constant number of iterations have been performed. Because the adherence of each point to the set is determined only by the point's position, the computation is easy to parallelize.

5.2 The Application

We have taken an existing Mandelbrot application written in Java [21]. Roughly-speaking, this application consists of several classes responsible for the graphical user interface, and a `MandelComputer` class responsible for computing a region of the Mandelbrot set. The application has been programmed with no parallelism in mind: the computation of the complete region displayed on the screen is performed by a single instance of the `MandelComputer` class.

```
1  public class MandelComputer {
2      public MandelComputer(int w, int h /* ... */);
3      public final void computeRegion(short[] buf, int l, int w, int t, int h);
4  }
```

Listing 1.1. Structure of the class responsible for the computation of the Mandelbrot set. This class will be instrumented for parallelization.

Although the actual parallelization of a Java application does not require access to its source code, one needs to understand enough of the application structure to determine which classes and methods to instrument and how to define the rewriting rules. To that end, one can use `javap`, a tool provided with Sun's Java compiler that lists the signatures of the methods defined in a class file. Note that it can be difficult to understand the actual semantics of the methods and their parameters when source code is not available, without adequate documentation or a decompiler. The structure of the `MandelComputer` class is shown in Listing 1.1 (for the sake of clarity, we have slightly modified the method signatures).

A `MandelComputer` object is instantiated with a given width and height, as well as parameters such as the maximal number of iterations. Once instantiated, the object computes a region of the Mandelbrot set upon invocation of its `computeRegion`. The top-left corner, the width, and the height of the region are given as parameters. The result of the computation is stored in an array, also handed as parameter to the method.

5.3   The Adapter

Once the classes to parallelize have been defined, one needs to write the adapter object responsible for the rewriting of the requests and replies sent to and received from individual workers. Listing 1.2 shows the code of the adapter for our Mandelbrot application. Note that this code has less that 40 lines.

In the **split** method, we only rewrite the parameters for invocations to `computeRegion`.[1] This is achieved by splitting the area into horizontal bands of equal sizes, with each worker being responsible for one such band. Arguments are modified to update the new coordinates of the top of the band, its height, as well as to provide a properly-dimensioned array for storing the computed data. For performance reasons, we also store the location in the full region where the band assigned to the current worker will be stored; this index will not have to be re-computed in the `join` method.

In the `join` method, we simply copy the data computed by the worker at the right position in the array originally provided by the client application.

5.4   Deployment

Deployment of the parallelized application merely consists of starting multiple workers on distributed processors, and launching the Mandelbrot application. The addresses of the workers, the maximum number of workers to use, the name of the adapter classes, and the name of classes and methods to filter, are all specified using configuration files and Java properties.

As bytecode modification is performed using a custom class loader, the Java application must be started using a special launcher program that makes sure

---

[1] Note that, for space efficiency, we could also have rewritten the arguments of the constructor to reduce the dimensions of the Mandelbrot set instantiated on each worker. However, this strategy would require non-trivial changes to the rewriting rules for `computeRegion`.

that the application classes are effectively loaded by our class loader. This is achieved by invoking the Java application as follows:

    java [properties...] jwg.Launcher Mandelbrot [arguments...]

Other than instrumenting the bytecode, this command has virtually the same effect as invoking directly the Java application using the following command:

    java [properties...] Mandelbrot [arguments...]

6 Performance Evaluation

6.1 Experimental Setup

We have run tests with the Mandelbrot program on a set of 18 identical Sun Ultra 10 workstation, with a 440 MHz processor and 256 MB of memory, running Solaris 2.8. We have computed images with a resolution of 720×512 pixels and

```
1   public class MandelAdapter implements Adapter {
2
3       int idx_;   // Start index for this worker in returned array
4
5       public void split(int id, int nb,
6                       String classname, String method, String signature,
7                       Object[] args)
8       {
9           if(method.equals("<init>")) {
10              // MandelComputer(int w, int h, ...)
11              // May rewrite constructor (not required for this application)
12          } else if(method.equals("computeRegion")) {
13              // computeRegion(short[] buf, int l, int w, int t, int h)
14              int w = ((Integer)args[2]).intValue();
15              int h = ((Integer)args[4]).intValue();
16              int t = id * h / nb;
17              idx_ = t * w;  // Pre-compute index since we have t and w anyway
18              h = (id == nb - 1 ? h - t : ((id + 1) * h / nb) - t);
19              args[0] = new short[w * h];
20              args[3] = new Integer(t);
21              args[4] = new Integer(h);
22          }
23      }
24
25      public void join(int id, int nb,
26                      String classname, String method, String signature,
27                      Object[] in_args, Object in_result,
28                      Object[] out_args, ResultHolder out_result)
29      {
30          if(method.equals("computeRegion")) {
31              // computeRegion(short[] buf, int l, int w, int t, int h)
32              short[] dst = (short[])out_args[0];
33              short[] src = (short[])in_args[0];
34              int idx = idx_;  // Index has been pre-computed in split()
35              for(int i = 0; i < src.length; i++)
36                  dst[idx++] = src[i];
37          }
38      }
39  }
```

Listing 1.2. Adapter object for parallelizing the Mandelbrot application.

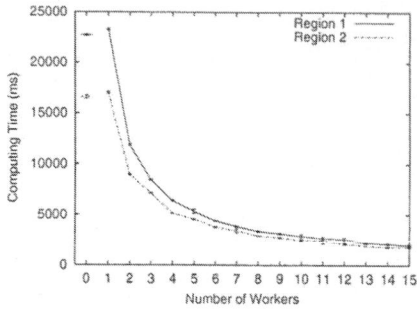

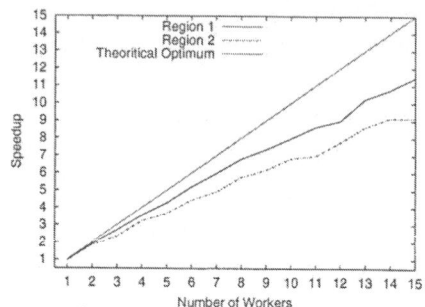

Fig. 2. Performance improvements with parallel processing.

Fig. 3. Speedup factor with parallel processing.

up to 1200 iterations for two distinct regions of the Mandelbrot set. We have run experiments with the non-instrumented application (centralized), and with semi-automatic parallelization using from 1 to 15 worker processors. Each worker was running on a separate machnie, in its own Java virtual machine (version 1.4.1). For each configuration, we have run the program 12 times on random subsets of the workstations and taken the mean of the measurements.

6.2   The Gain of Parallelization

The computation times as a function of the number of workers are shown in Fig. 2 (error bars correspond to the 95% confidence intervals). The value for 0 worker corresponds to the execution of the non-parallelized version of the program. The graph clearly shows that performance increases as a function of the logarithm of the number of workers.

We have also computed the speedup factor gained from parallelization, in comparison with the non-parallelized version of the program. The speedup, shown in Fig. 3, remains within 25% of the optimum for the first region, and within 35% for the second region. Two main reasons prevent the speedup to remain closer to the optimum. First, the time necessary for communications, and for request and reply rewriting is not negligible and must be accounted for. Second, our program splits the Mandelbrot set in equal regions sent to each worker; as some regions require more computations than others, the load is not distributed equally and speedup cannot be maximized. In our experiments, the second region appears to be more affected by this problem as its speedup is smaller than for the first region.

6.3   The Cost of Parallelization

The overhead of the parallelization framework can be observed in Fig. 2 as the difference between the non-parallelized version of the program and the parallel version with 1 worker. In our tests, this cost was 501 *ms* on average. It can be broken down into the cost of method interception, the cost of request and reply processing, and the cost of remote invocation. These various sources of overhead are detailed in Table 4.

Method interception	$< 1 \ \mu s$
Request processing	288 ms
Reply processing	44 ms
Remote invocation	169 ms
Total cost	501 ms

Fig. 4. Cost of Parallelization

Method interception only introduces a small performance overhead. In our experiments, adding empty pre- and post-filters to a method costs less that 1 μs with a JIT compiler. In addition to processing overhead, instrumented classes also incur a size penalty due to the extra code added during instrumentation. For our Mandelbrot application, the size of the MandelComputer class grows from 1,702 to 2,646 bytes with two instrumented methods, i.e., an increase of less than 1 kB. If only a fraction of the classes of an application are instrumented, we can safely ignore both the time and space penalty of method interception.

Request processing is clearly the most expensive operation during parallelization, because it includes the creation of one thread per worker,[2] in addition to the rewriting and marshaling of the request. Reply processing is significantly cheaper, as it only includes the cost of unmarshaling and rewriting. Finally, the cost of remote invocation, which includes both the round-trip communication time and the data un/marshaling on the server, also adds non-negligible overhead to the parallelized application.

Despite the overhead introduced by the parallelization process, it appears clearly that the performance improvements resulting from parallelization well exceed its cost, even when using as few as two workers. Other applications that can be parallelized using a divide-and-conquer strategy should exhibit similar performance gains.

7 Conclusions

In this paper, we have presented mechanisms to parallelize certain types of Java applications, without modifications to their source code. Once parallelized, applications execute their time-consuming computations on multiple distributed processors.

Bytecode is first instrumented by our Java wrapper generator, which controls the flow of Java applications by inserting filters in selected methods. At runtime,

---

[2] Thread creation is a costly operation in Java. As an obvious improvement, we could avoid the cost of thread creation by using a pool of threads.

invocations to instrumented methods are intercepted by the Java parallelization engine, which is responsible for rewriting the requests, sharing the workload among multiple workers, and aggregating the return values. A small piece of code—called an adapter—must be provided to the parallelization framework for handling application-specific request and reply transformations.

We have illustrated our mechanisms with an existing Java application that computes regions of the Mandelbrot set, and we have evaluated the performance of the resulting parallelized application. Experimental results demonstrate that the speedup of parallelization increases almost linearly with the number of processors, while its cost remains reasonably small.

The major contribution of this work lies in the semi-automatic parallelization and distributed deployment of legacy Java code. Our parallelization framework provide an easy way to harness the processing power of idle, heterogeneous workstation on the Internet to increase the performance of applications with no built-in support for parallel processing.

References

1. Fox, G., ed.: Special Issue on Java for Computational Science and Engineering–Simulation and Modeling II. Volume 9 (11) of Concurrency: Practice and Experience. John Wiley & Sohn Ltd. (1997)
2. Fox, G., ed.: Special Issue on Java for High-performance Network Computing. Volume 10 (11–13) of Concurrency: Practice and Experience. John Wiley & Sohn Ltd. (1998)
3. Lobosco, M., de Amorim, C., Loques, O.: Java for High-performance Network-based Computing: A Survey. Concurrency: Practice and Experience **14** (2002) 1–31
4. Hsieh, C.H., Gyllenhaal, J., Hwu, W.M.: Java Bytecode to Native Code Translation: The Caffeine Prototype and Preliminary Results. In: Proceedings of the 29th International Symposium on Microarchitectures. (1996)
5. Artigas, P., Gupta, M., Midkiff, S., Moreira, J.: Automatic Loop Transformations and Parallelization for Java. In: Proceedings of the International Conference on Supercomputing (ICS 2000). (2000) 1–10
6. Serrano, M., Bordawekar, R., Midkiff, S., Gupta, M.: Quicksilver: A Quasi-Static Compiler for Java. In: Proceedings of the ACM Conference on Object-Oriented Programming, Systems, Languages, and Applications (OOPSLA). (2000) 66–82
7. Yu, D., Shao, Z., Trifonov, V.: Supporting Binary Compatibility with Static Compilation. In: Proceedings of the 2nd Java Virtual Machine Research and Technology Symposium (JVM'02). (2002) 165–180
8. Polychronopoulos, C.: Parallel Programming and Compilers. Kluwer (1988)
9. Wolfe, M.: High Performance Compilers for Parallel Computers. Addison-Wesley (1996)
10. Bik, A., Gannon, D.: Automatically Exploiting Implicit Parallelism in Java. Concurrency: Practice and Experience **9** (1997) 579–619
11. Bik, A., Gannon, D.: JAVAB–A Prototype Bytecode Parallelization Tool. Technical Report TR489, Indiana University (1997)
12. Cohen, G., Chase, J., Kaminsky, D.: Automatic Program Transformation with JOIE. In: Proceedings of the 1998 USENIX Annual Technical Conference. (1998)

13. Sunderam, V.: PVM: A Framework for Parallel Distributed Computing. Concurrency: Practice and Experience **2** (1990) 315–339
14. Hempel, R.: The MPI standard for message passing. In Gentzsch, W., Harms, U., eds.: High-Performance Computing and Networking, International Conference and Exhibition, Proceedings, Volume II: Networking and Tools. Volume 797 of Lecture Notes in Computer Science., Springer-Verlag (1994) 247–252
15. Yalamanchilli, N., Cohen, W.: Communication Performance of Java-Based Parallel Virtual Machines. Concurrency: Practice and Experience **10** (1998) 315–339
16. Baker, M., Carpenter, D., Fox, G., Ko, S., Lim, S.: mpiJava: An Object-Oriented Java interface to MPI. In: Proceedings of the 1st Java Workshop at the 13th IPPS & 10th SPDP Conference. Lecture Notes in Computer Science, Springer-Verlag (1999)
17. Philippsen, M., Zenger, M.: JavaParty: Transparent remote objects in Java. Concurrency: Practice and Experience **9** (1997) 1225–1242
18. MacDonald, S.: From Patterns to Frameworks to Parallel Programs. PhD thesis, University of Alberta (2002)
19. The Apache Software Foundation: BCEL: Byte Code Engineering Library. http://jakarta.apache.org/bcel (2003)
20. Polychronopoulos, C., Kuck, D.: Guided Self Scheduling. IEEE Transactions on Computers **36** (1987) 1425–1439
21. Ziring, N.: JManEx: Java Mandelbrot Explorer. http://users.erols.com/ziring/mandel.html (2001)

Transparent Integration of CORBA and the .NET Framework*

Johann Oberleitner and Thomas Gschwind

Distributed Systems Group
Technische Universität Wien
Argentinierstraße 8/E1841
A-1040 Wien, Austria
{joe,tom}@infosys.tuwien.ac.at

Abstract. A large number of distributed object programming technologies exist today ranging from CORBA and RMI to Microsoft's .NET platform. Programmers face a difficult choice when they have to decide for either technology. To some degree this problem has been lessened by the introduction of RMI over IIOP which supports the interoperability between RMI and CORBA. In this paper, we present our solution that enables the transparent integration of CORBA into the .NET framework and also allows these distributed object systems to communicate with each other. The contribution of this paper is threefold: first, we present how .NET's remoting technology can be extended, second, we present how this extension mechanism can be used to add CORBA interoperability to the .NET framework, and finally we evaluate the performance of our approach.

1   Introduction

CORBA [1] is a well-established tool for building distributed applications that target multiple system platforms or multiple programming languages. Hence, CORBA implementations are available for a large number of systems and language mappings for many programming languages are available. Even Java RMI has been extended with RMI-over-IIOP which allows the use of CORBA's IIOP protocol [2].

However, Microsoft does not support CORBA and tries to boost their own distribution standard, the Distributed Component Object Model (DCOM) [3]. Microsoft's .NET framework [4,5] provides a new technology to build distributed systems similar to Java RMI. Not completely unexpected, this new remoting technology does not contain support for CORBA. It ships with two different transport protocols that can be used: a binary transport protocol based on TCP and another protocol that uses XML and SOAP [6].

One approach to access CORBA from .NET is to use .NET's P/Invoke mechanism to call native code that resides in DLLs [7]. Hence, a CORBA ORB can

---

* We gratefully acknowledge the financial support provided by the European Union as part of the EASYCOMP project (IST-1999-14151).

R. Meersman et al. (Eds.): CoopIS/DOA/ODBASE 2003, LNCS 2888, pp. 1384–1401, 2003.

be accessed that resides in the DLL. However, this approach has several limitations: each call leads to a transition between .NET managed code and the DLL's unmanaged code which may be forbidden because it compromises security and system safety.

Although future CORBA standards may require that they can communicate with SOAP [8] this is not the case today. Furthermore, not every feature supported by CORBA is provided by actual SOAP implementations or is not fully standardized. Hence, it seems that it is difficult to combine CORBA objects and .NET applications with SOAP. The standard solution to still access CORBA is to develop a CORBA ORB for .NET. This approach, however has several weaknesses. First, it requires a major development effort to implement a CORBA ORB. Second, it requires existing .NET code to be adapted to use language mappings for a .NET programming language. Third, it restricts the client to interact only with CORBA objects.

However, Microsoft let open a backdoor for integrating CORBA into .NET. Its .NET Remoting framework supports various extensibility points. We have supplemented this remoting framework with support for the IIOP transport protocol. Using this extension, CORBA services can be used from within .NET in a way similar to the approach taken by RMI over IIOP.

This paper is structured as follows. In section 2 we discuss the .NET remoting infrastructure. Section 3 provides information about IIOP that we use as communication protocol. On the basis of these two sections, we present the implementation of our IIOP channel and its integration into the .NET framework in section 4. Implementing CORBA support mechanisms are explained in section 5 We evaluate the performance of our approach in section 6. In section 7, we present future work and consider related work in section 8. Finally, we draw our conclusions in section 9.

2   .NET Remoting

Microsoft's .NET initiative builds on the .NET Framework as its development platform. This platform consists of the Common Language Runtime (CLR) as the Virtual Machine and the Framework Class Library (FCL) [4] for .NET.

The framework provides not only classes for low-level communication primitives such as sockets or eases interoperability with Microsoft COM+ but also includes yet another RPC like intercommunication technology. This technology, .NET Remoting, however, has the advantage that it supports hooks for each individual communication layer in the client-server communication path. As we will show, these hooks allow developers to turn remotely accessible .NET classes into classes accessible via any communication channel in a transparent way [5,9].

2.1   Implementing a .NET Remoting Application

We illustrate a .NET communication path with a simple calculator application built with the C# program language. The ICalculator interface (figure 1) de-

```
public interface ICalculator {
  double Sum(double x, double y);
}
```

Fig. 1. Calculator Interface

clares a method for adding two numbers and returning the result. This interface is used on both sides of the communication, the server and the client.

.NET objects reside inside application domains. Such a domain isolates objects from other application domains. Objects of one domain can't directly access data or execute code of another application domain [9].

The `CalculatorImpl` class (figure 2) implements the `ICalculator` interface and the required functionality. `CalculatorImpl` is a regular C# class apart from that this class inherits from `MarshalByRefObject`. Usually all .NET classes inherit `Object` implicitly. When a .NET class explicitly inherits from `MarshalByRefObject` it denotes its capability for being accessible across application domains.

In addition to the calculator interface and the implementation class the server requires also a main program. This program has two tasks: first it registers all classes that are exposed by this server, and second it must not terminate as long as it shall support client requests. Our example uses a console .NET application. We simply wait until the user presses any key on the console. It is also possible to use Microsoft's Internet Information Server (IIS) to host remoting applications. The registration of the classes is done with a .NET configuration file (figure 3). Microsoft's .NET framework uses XML based configuration files that can be deployed in the installation directory. Alternatively, a programmatic registration is possible.

The client has to register all .NET classes that it wants to access with .NET Remoting. This can be done programmatically or with a remoting section in a configuration file similar to that of the server configuration file.

```
public class CalculatorImpl: MarshalByRefObject, ICalculator {
  public CalculatorImpl () {}
  public double Sum (double x, double y) { return x+y; }
}

public class CalculatorServer {
  public static void Main (string[] args) {
    RemotingConfiguration.Configure ("Server.exe.config");
    System.Console.ReadLine ();
  }
}
```

Fig. 2. Calculator Server

```
<configuration>
  <system.runtime.remoting> <application name="CalculatorServer">
      <service> <wellknown mode="Singleton"
          type="CalculatorImpl,_Calculator"
          objectUri="Calculator.soap"/> </service>
    </application> </system.runtime.remoting>
</configuration>
```

Fig. 3. Server Configuration File

```
public static void Main (string[] args) {
    RemotingConfiguration.Configure ("Client.exe.config");
    WellKnownClientTypeEntry[] clientEntries =
      RemotingConfiguration.
          GetRegisteredWellKnownClientTypes();

    ICalculator calculator =
      (ICalculator) Activator.GetObject (
          typeof (ICalculator),
          clientEntries[0].ObjectUrl  );

    double sum = calculator.Sum (5.0, 7.0);
}
```

Fig. 4. Calculator Client

The client code (figure 4) loads the registration file and uses `Activator.GetObject` to return an instance of a class that implements the `ICalculator` interface. When .NET remoting is used this class is a proxy that invokes the remoting chain on the client. Subsequently, the client calls this proxy and calculates the sum of x and y.

2.2   .NET Remoting Architecture

Figure 5 illustrates the client communication path of .NET Remoting. We start in the client application with the call of the `Sum` method (bullet 1 in the figure). With this call the .NET Remoting infrastructure creates a so-called *Transparent Proxy* (2) on the fly [9]. This transparent proxy has exactly the same interface as the type parameter provided as first argument to the `GetObject` method. In our case the transparent proxy provides the same methods as the `ICalculator` interface. Calls to the transparent proxy lead to the creation of a message object. This message object contains the name of the method, the argument values, the argument signature, etc. The message object is of particular importance in the .NET remoting infrastructure because it provides a dictionary data structure and hence, provides a common data structure for all elements in the communication chain. The message object allows that new data can be added to it similar to hash table data structures.

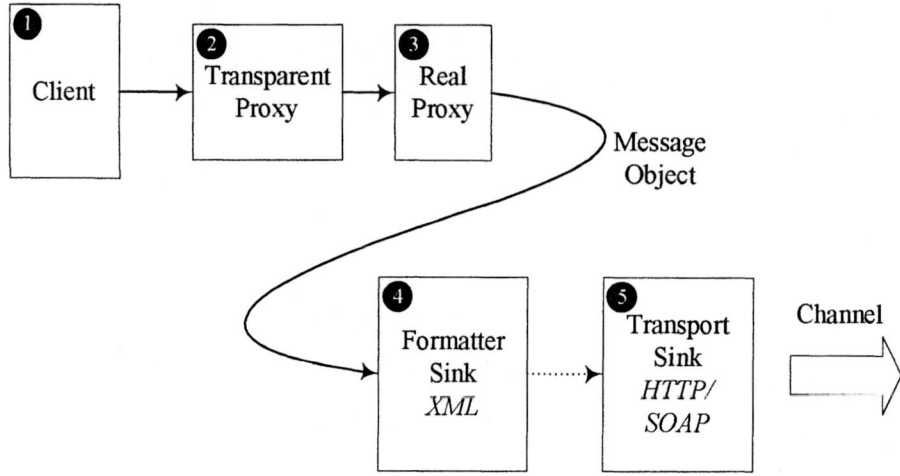

Fig. 5. .NET Remoting Communication Flow - Client

The transparent proxy forwards the message object to the second proxy involved, the *Real Proxy* (3). This real proxy uses this constructed message object for further processing. .NET Remoting does not allow developers to provide their own transparent proxy. However, the real proxy can be extended or replaced by a custom proxy.

The predefined real proxy forwards the message to several *sink chains*. Each sink in these chains has to process the message, potentially add or replace data in the message dictionary, and forward the message object to its successor in the chain. Processing can be done synchronously, or asynchronously. Asynchronous processing completes after the request message has been forwarded to the next sink and the sink gets notified when the response message has arrived. More interesting for our purpose is the channel sink chain. It is entered at the *client formatter sink* (4). Its purpose is to extract data from the message object and create the data representation for the tranportation channel. The sink serializes method name, method arguments, etc. to a request stream. This stream is forwarded to the next element of the channel sink chain.

The remaining channel sinks process the request stream. The last sink in this chain, the *transport sink* (5) uses this data and puts it onto a communication channel. What this communication channel might be is entirely up to the developer. As for the other sinks described before .NET Remoting allows the exchange of the channel sinks, hence other channels can be used with .NET Remoting.

Figure 6 illustrates the server side of the communication. The channel-specific message arrives in the server-side channel's transport sink (bullet 1). This transport sink takes off the message from the channel, creates a request stream and forwards it to the next sink in channel sink chain. The *server formatter sink* (2) creates the server-side .NET message object. The responsibility of the server formatter sink is to fill the message dictionary with data to allow the .NET runtime call the proper method.

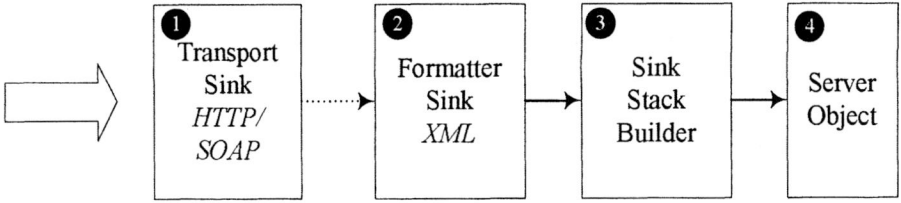

Fig. 6. .NET Remoting Communication Flow - server

The message is processed by all sinks on the server and finally reaches the predefined *stack builder sink* (3). This sink is the counterpart of the transparent proxy at the client side. It uses the message object to set up the stackframe for the method call in question and invokes the remote object's method (4).

After this method call has been accomplished, throwing an exception or not, the whole communication flow is reverted. The stack builder sink creates a return method message object and puts return values and outgoing parameters to the message. The server formatter sink creates a response message that the server-side transport sink puts onto the physical communication channel. The client-side transport sink receives the response data and forwards it up through the channel sink chain to the client formatter channel sink. This sink creates a return method message object that is forwarded to the message sink chain. Finally, the real-proxy and the transparent proxy are reached with the return value and optional out parameters of the initial remote object method request.

.NET Remoting allows developers to build their own sinks and register them to be used with the remoting framework. It is also possible to add new sinks between existing sinks. While channel sinks are used to support new communication media, context sinks are used to support logging, transactions or security mechanisms [9].

3   IIOP

ORB interoperability among CORBA ORBs is based on the *General Inter-ORB Protocol (GIOP)* [1,10]. Based on GIOP is the *Internet Inter-ORB Protocol (IIOP)*. The GIOP specification consists of different elements [1]:

Common Data Representation (CDR). CDR denotes rules for transforming OMG IDL data types into a representation that can be transfered on a communication medium. CDR specifies how IDL data types are represented as bytes.

Message Formats. GIOP uses 8 different message types that are used to communicate between CORBA ORBs. The format of each of these messages is exactly specified.

Transport Assumptions. General assumptions about the network transport layer are specified that may be used to transfer GIOP messages [1].

IIOP is a specialization of GIOP for the TCP/IP protocol and adds TCP/IP specific issues to the specification.

3.1   Common Data Representation

The CDR specification describes how each of the IDL data types is represented in a byte stream. Primitive data types are aligned on their natural boundary [1]. This means that a 4-byte unsigned integer always starts at an offset that is a multiple of 4. Constructed types are not aligned in general, but their members are. For instance an IDL *struct* contains a 2-byte and a 4-byte integer in this order. The whole struct is aligned on an offset that is a multiple of 2 (due to the 2-byte short). The 4-byte integer starts at the next offset that is a multiple of 4. Hence, an alignment padding of 2 byte has to be inserted.

Object references may reference other hosts and hence need to contain transport specific addressing information. So no general-purpose interoperable format for object references has been defined. IIOP provides a specific format for Interoperable Object References (IOR) which are described in section 3.3.

3.2   Messages

GIOP uses only a small number of message types for communication (see table 1). All of these message types have the same *message header* that contains the magic byte sequence *'GIOP'* for identification, a GIOP version number, message flags, one of the 8 message types, and the message size. The message header is followed by a message type specific header. Depending on the type of the message a message body can follow this header. Table 1 shows the different messages. Message specific headers can address particular objects, i.e. the header of the *Request* message carries an object key and an operation string to identify the target object and the operation to invoke. Corresponding request/response messages are identified with a numeric request id.

3.3   Interoperable Object References

To provide transparent access to objects at arbitrary locations *Interoperable Object References (IOR)* [1,10] have been introduced. Each IOR contains the type-id string identifying the object's IDL type and a set of profiles that contain all information needed to send a request. Of particular interest is the profile for IIOP. It contains a version number, a host string that identifies the Internet host, the TCP/IP port number, and an object key. This object key contains target specific information to distinguish among different objects.

IORs use CDR representation and are converted to hex-coded strings [1]. This is not very convenient for users. Hence, alternative representations have been introduced that allow the use of an URL schema for identifying objects. For instance, the URL *corbaloc:iiop:1.1@myHost:3456/ObjectKey* can be used instead of IORs.

Table 1. GIOP Message

Message Type	Sender	Purpose	Content of Message Body
Request	Client	initiate an operation on the target	input parameters
Reply	Server	response to a request message	return value & output parameters
CancelRequest	Client	cancels a previous request	-
LocateRequest	Client	queries if the server accepts a request	-
LocateReply	Server	response to LocateRequest	IOR for new target
CloseConnection	Server	inform client that server intends to close connection	-
MessageError	Both	indicates that message version or type are unknown	-
Fragment	Both	continues a request or reply message	see above

4   CORBA Support for .NET Remoting

This section describes how we used the .NET Remoting extension mechanisms to allow .NET clients to transparently access CORBA objects and to allow CORBA clients to access .NET objects.

When designing the CORBA support we had two different goals in mind:

1. Enable the use of CORBA communication for existing .NET Remoting applications. This means that these applications shall be able to not only use the predefined Remoting communication protocols, TCP or HTTP, but shall also work together with or our own communication channel that supports IIOP. In the best case only a small amount of code, potentially only the Remoting configuration file, shall be modified.
2. Conforming to the CORBA specification [1]. In particular, it is required that CORBA clients and CORBA servants can be accessed transparently.

These two goals, however, conflict with each other. For instance, CORBA interfaces implicitly inherit the CORBA Object type. This type provides support for various methods for exporting IORs or accessing the interface repository. It is possible to build an interface for this type and let the corresponding .NET interfaces extend this interface to let clients use it. However, the server implementation would have to implement this interface, too. But this implementation might be useless for the other communication channels, TCP and HTTP.

Although it is always possible to build a full-fledged ORB from basic communication primitives we decided to focus on the first goal, support .NET Remoting, and realize as much as possible of the second goal.

We have extended the .NET Remoting architecture by replacing transport sinks and formatter sinks as presented in section 2. The main difficulty of this approach was to allow .NET clients and servers communicate using the IIOP and convert the corresponding calls to and from the message objects.

4.1   Configuration

To replace transport sinks on either side of a communication, a so-called .NET Remoting channel has to be implemented. This channel consists of two parts, a client channel and a server channel. The primary task of these channels is to extract channel-specific data from the configuration files and register the appropriate sink chains. The channel can be registered in .NET configuration files by providing a reference to the implementation class.

4.2   .NET Language Mapping

To allow .NET applications to work with existing CORBA applications it was necessary to define those parts of a language mapping that map CORBA IDL data types to .NET data types. In general this mapping has similarities to the Java Langage Mapping [11].

Fortunately, .NET has a richer type system and hence, the mapping of basic IDL types to the corresponding .NET types can be done in a straight forward way.

Table 2 shows how we mapped constructed types. An IDL struct is mapped to a .NET struct and public fields for each of the initial struct's members. Exceptions are transformed similar to structs but inherit from a .NET exception class to conform to syntax conventions of .NET. Both, IDL arrays and sequences are mapped to .NET arrays. IDL arrays have a fixed length. When arrays are marshaled into CDR the length is not transmitted. Hence, it is necessary that this length is available for unmarshaling. We have implemented an `ArrayLength` custom attribute that can be applied to the declaration of such an array. Sequences can have a dynamic length and have a length attribute that is marshaled. Enums and strings are mapped as expected.

Interfaces are realized with .NET interfaces. Operations are mapped to .NET methods. In language mappings for Java [11] or C++ [12,10] IDL attributes are mapped to a pair of accessor and modifier methods. .NET supports so-called *properties* that model data access by such accessors and modifiers. Programming languages such as C# or VisualBasic.NET can then provide a syntax equivalent to a field access. Since properties can be declared also in interfaces we use such properties to represent attributes.

The mapping of the operation parameters is done in a straightforward way. Unlike Java that does not support out parameters or reference parameters we have been able to map parameter direction attributes to .NET constructs.

CORBA object references are mapped to the object data type of .NET. However, when used within a remote operation it is only allowed that this object is a proxy representation for a remote object. When a .NET object reference has to be marshaled information about its target location is extracted. This information is then converted to the CDR representation of a CORBA object reference. When a CORBA object reference is demarshaled an `ObjRef` instance has to be created with appropriate information about the communication channel and target. We have extended the `ObjRef` class to simplify marshaling to and

Table 2. Mapping for Constructed IDL Types

IDL Type	.NET Type	Comment
struct	.NET struct	public fields
exception	exception class	extends System.ApplicationException
arrays	.NET array	custom attribute denotes fixed length
sequence	.NET array	
enum	.NET enum	automatically treated as integer
string	System.String	
object reference	System.ObjRef	
interface	.NET interfaces	Attributes realized as .NET properties
operation	.NET method	
attribute	.NET property	

unmarshaling from CDR format. When clients encounter an instance of `ObjRef` the transparent proxy is used on method calls instead.

We currently do not support all types that may be defined with CORBA IDL files. In the future, however, we plan to support more types.

4.3   CORBA Support for .NET Clients

As already explained above we realize the access of CORBA servers from .NET clients with customized channel sinks that realize IIOP communication. Client-side configuration provides IORs as parameters to IIOP servers. When the client application makes a call to a type registered for using IIOP the remoting framework calls into the channel and provides the IOR url as parameter. The connection information is extracted from the IOR and the channel sink chain is created.

When a client makes a call to an interface that is accessed via our IIOP channel, the communication is initiated as described in section 2. After some steps the client formatter sink's `SyncProcessMessage` method is called with a message object that describes the call that shall be executed on the remote object. The sink formatter object extracts the type of the target interface, the operation's name, its signature, and the method arguments from the message dictionary. The client formatter sink creates a new request stream and marshals all in arguments and all inout arguments to this stream. Marshaling converts the arguments into the CDR. Since, there is no support for CDR in .NET, we had to write our own classes for marshaling and unmarshaling .NET objects into CDR and back. Interestingly, the information that is delivered to us with the message dictionary does not suffice to support marshaling for the different kinds of parameters, in-going, out-going, or both. It was necessary to use .NET reflection to lookup the type and method to find out if a parameter is marked as a .NET out parameter or as a .NET reference parameter (inout).

We faced one difficulty in the marshaling task: CORBA relies on the *receiver makes it right* principle. This means it is allowed that clients send requests in CDR using either Little Endian or Big Endian byte order. Our IIOP support must deal with both formats. However, .NET supports only the use of Little Endian within data streams quite well. Big Endian, however, was not supported by stream classes. Hence, we had to build our own stream classes that deal with Big Endian, as well.

After the data had been put onto the request stream the next channel sink's `ProcessMessage` is called. In our case this is just the transport sink. It uses the information retrieved from the IOR and opens a client socket connection. An IIOP *request message* is created that contains the IOR object key and the data stored in the request stream. This request message is sent to the target CORBA ORB. After this send action, an IIOP *reply message* is received from the same socket, and in case that the reply is valid and no error code has been received, put into a response stream.

After leaving the transport sink's `ProcessMessage` the formatter sink processes the response stream. It creates a *return message* object that is the counterpart of the request message. Depending on the outcome of the remote call the return message's dictionary is filled with two different kinds of data. In the successful case the dictionary takes the return value, and out-going parameters. These parameters have to be unmarshaled from the response stream. In the other case, when an exception occurred during the remote call, only the exception element is filled with an exception object constructed from the IIOP reply message.

In both cases, the return message is returned up to the sinks, until it reaches the real proxy and the transparent proxy. In case that no exception has been stored in the dicitionary the method call is finished and its return values and `out` as well as `ref` parameters are updated. In the other case an exception has been stored in the dictionary and will be propagated to the client.

4.4   .NET Classes as CORBA Servants

In addition to using .NET applications as clients we also allow .NET classes to be used as CORBA servants. Similar to the client we have built IIOP channel support for the server-side. As for the client registering the IIOP channel for the server can be done with configuration files.

Clients need IORs to use CORBA objects. To create these IOR we have built a class that can create an IOR based on the wellknown service description. This class can be used in the server main class, or applied directly on the remote configuration file.

When the server's main class is started the channel is created, and the server channel class instantiated. Similar to the client channel, server transport sink and server formatter sink are created and chained together. However, the order of the chain is reversed. The server channel class has to to start and stop listening on a predefined socket endpoint. We initiate a server-side socket for listening on *localhost* and on the port specified in the configuration file. A background thread is created that's working routine starts in the server transport sink.

The background thread uses an infinite loop until an incoming socket message arrives. The data is received and put into a stream. When the message is an IIOP request message it is forwarded to the `ProcessMessage` method of the next sink, the server formatter sink. This sink reverses the operations done on the client side: it unmarshals the request stream and creates the message object. It has to fill the message dictionary with appropriate values: the type name, the assembly, and the object URI are extracted from the object key. The method name is extracted from the request message's operation field. Reflection has to be used to get the argument types. These types are provided as a message dictionary entry and are also necessary to direct unmarshaling of the argument values that are stored in another dictionary entry. After creating this message it is forwarded to the next sink's `ProcessMessage` method. Internally, this forwarding ends up in calling the method of the object instance declared in the configuration file with the proper parameters. The control flow continues after the call to `ProcessMessage` has ended. It returns a response message that contains another dictionary. In case an exception occurred it has an exception entry that denotes the exception thrown. Otherwise the response message's dictionary contains a return value entry and outgoing argument entries. In any case, a reply message is generated. Finally, the transport sink sends this reply message to the ingoing socket as answer to the previous request.

5   Implementing CORBA Support Mechanisms

Just implementing an IIOP channel provides interoperability between CORBA and .NET. This is fine to let .NET clients access CORBA servers and it is also possible to let CORBA clients built with Java or C++ to access .NET servers. However, a variety of support mechanisms exist for CORBA that eases application development. We have implemented some of these mechanisms also for our interoperability solution.

5.1   Name Service

A name service [13,10] stores mappings of readable names to object references. Once such a mapping has been stored, clients can make lookups into the name service. This has the advantage that clients no longer need the IOR of the CORBA objects they want to use. Instead they can query the name service if an object is bound to a particular name.

   We have built a rudimentary implementation of such a name service that can be started in the main method of the server class. It binds each wellknown service stored in the .NET Remoting configuration files to a name. This simplifies the use of .NET Remoting classes with CORBA clients.

   Since the name service is a remotable class clients can access the name service via the IIOP channel. Our implementation currently supports only bind and resolve methods.

5.2   Interface Repository

The interface repository [1, ch.10] stores informations about objects. The repository can be used to find out about the operations and attributes an interface contains, and the parameters of these operations. It contains a tree of objects that implement interfaces for navigating the contained elements. We have implemented a subset of the Interface Repository. When a CORBA client calls the get_interface operation on an object reference our server formatter sink intercepts this call, dynamically creates an object that is returned as result for get_interface. .NET reflection is used to fill this object.

One problem occurred using the get_interface in .NET clients. To use this method the client has to use an interface that contains this method. However, it makes no sense for servers to implement this method, since it is already provided by the server formatter sink. One solution we found was that the client registers and casts the remote object to an interface that extends the original interface with the get_interface.

6 Evaluation

We have done a couple of performance tests to see if our IIOP channel is competitive enough to be used in distributed systems.

6.1 .NET Remoting Environments

The .NET framework includes already the support for two different communication channels: the TCP channel that uses a proprietary protocol with a binary representation, the HTTP channel that uses SOAP and an XML based message format. We have complemented these channels with our IIOP channel.

We have evaluated each of these communication channels under different data transmission scenarios concerning the parameters to be marshaled or unmarshaled. We have declared a C# interface that defines a couple of methods. Our server class implements this interface. Since we wanted to test only the performance of the communication and marshaling/demarshaling process the methods do not contain any functionality beyond storing incoming parameters in instance fields or returning one of these fields as method return value.

The ping method just calls the remote server. The sendString method sends strings. The sendPerson method sends a C# struct that stores several string and integer values and a nested address struct that itself has strings and integers. sendObjRef and getObjRef are of particular importance because object references can be marshaled across a channel and rematerialize as proxy objects. We wanted to see how expensive marshaling of object references is.

Since the .NET Remoting architecture allows the exchange of channels by modifying just the configuration files we have been able to use the same client and the same server for all three channels without modification of the source code. The client called each of the interface's methods multiple times with different input parameters. To eliminate measurement deviations each call was repeated 100 times. Each such measurement was then repeated two times and the median of the three values was selected. We have executed two complete tests: one with the client and server on the same Pentium-III, with 667 Mhz and 256 MB, and

Microsoft Windows XP Professional. This test used the loopback adapter. For the other test the same host was used as the server. The client host was an AMD with 550 Mhz, 256 MB and Microsoft Windows 2000 as operating system connected by a 10 Mbit LAN. Table 3 shows the measurements for six method calls.

Table 3. Remoting Channel Performance Comparison (values in ms)

Test-set	TCP	HTTP	IIOP	TCP	HTTP	IIOP
		lookback			LAN	
ping	110	751	250	170	951	220
sendString len=50	110	731	250	160	1011	230
sendString len=5000	200	951	371	691	1502	751
sendPerson count=10	270	1512	451	361	2343	561
sendObjRef	300	941	531	391	1312	651
getObjRef	320	951	501	391	1242	661

The numbers show that our IIOP channel is not as fast as the TCP channel provided by Microsoft. This is valid for both, the single host and the dual host setting. However, the numbers show also that the IIOP channel performs much faster than the HTTP/SOAP channel. Interestingly, some of the tests that use only small messages performed faster in the LAN than on the loopback adapter which we assume is due the fact that client and server have to share the same CPU.

We believe that two different reasons are responsible that our IIOP channel never performed better than the TCP channel. First, we have only a non-optimized version of our channel. Another reason might be that the TCP channel is really well-integrated into the .NET Remoting framework.

We have also measured the overhead of each protocol concerning the raw size of the data transmitted. Table 4 compares this for each of the three channels. The payload denotes the pure content without administrative data such as string length or method name. The remaining columns show the size of the data in bytes that is transmitted in one complete request and response message. The values in the braces show the value relative to the payload. The numbers for the protocol overhead show that IIOP in general is quite effective. For small payloads IIOP can be more effective than Microsoft's TCP channel protocol.

6.2   Heterogeneous Environments

We also wanted to see how the channel performs when communicating with CORBA clients and CORBA servers. We have built an IDL file for the test interface described above and built corresponding client and server classes for the Java based JacORB CORBA ORB [14].

We applied the same tests as above. We tested each combination of .NET client and JacORB client with .NET server and JacORB server. Table 5 shows

Table 4. Protocol Overhead (values in bytes)

Test-set	Payload	TCP	HTTP	IIOP
ping	0	255	1648	116
sendString len=50	50	317 (6.34)	1724 (34.48)	159 (3.18)
sendString len=5000	5000	5268 (1.05)	6675 (1.34)	5109 (1.02)
sendPerson count=10	620	827 (1.33)	4410 (7.11)	1085 (1.75)
sendObjRef	-	793	2356	328
getObjRef	-	844	2489	324

the results. The first value in each column denotes the setting where both client and server were on the same host. The second value denotes the measured times for the LAN.

Table 5. IIOP C/S Performance Comparison (values in ms)

Test-set	.NET client		JacORB client	
	.NET server	JacORB server	.NET server	JacORB server
ping	250 220	270 250	210 240	170 220
sendString len=50	255 230	260 260	231 260	171 300
sendString len=5000	370 751	391 781	440 892	440 881
sendPerson count=10	451 561	370 841	300 431	140 291
sendObjRef	531 651	501 601	411 460	300 261
getObjRef	500 661	551 631	400 411	250 361

In general, the combination of the JacORB server with the JacORB client was the fastest. However, when looking at the LAN setting several test cases showed that the performance of our IIOP channel is close to the JacORB combination, especially when strings are involved. However, the last three rows in the table show that structs and object references do not perform as good as the *ping* or the *sendstring* operations. The use of object references in parameters or return values lead to the creation of proxy objects. It might be the case that this is the reason for the poor performance of the IIOP channel when object references are involved.

The performance numbers obtained in this section are starting points for further work on our ORB. We currently use reflection in each method request. Caching the information that we obtain from reflection might lead to better performance results.

7   Limitations and Future Work

Our IIOP channel suffers from a couple of implementation limitations so far. The most serious limitation is that we have not built a complete mapping for all IDL data types [1]. In the future we want to support the complete set of IDL data types. We plan to integrate full support for *unions* and the *fixed decimal* data type. Our support for the polymorphic *any* type is only rudimentary today. This data type is used in various object services such as the CORBA event service, and in the CORBA's *Dynamic Invocation Interface*. The difficulty in integrating these types is not the mapping of types to C# but the implementation of the marshaling and demarshaling operations.

Recent CORBA specifications define *value types*, too. These types can have interfaces as other CORBA objects do, but when provided as arguments to operations their whole content is marshaled into CDR. .NET serializable types are similar to these value types. The .NET framework includes already several classes to deal with object graph serialization. It might be possible to implement IDL value types with .NET serializable formatters and object graph serialization.

At the current level of the implementation we have to convert IDL files to .NET interfaces manually. We plan to write an IDL parser that generates .NET interfaces automatically and vice-versa. Compiler frameworks such as ANTLR [15] include already grammar definitions for OMG IDL. Since ANTLR supports the generation of C# compilers this might be a convenient choice.

We have built a very simple naming service for our .NET servers. Not all operations defined by the name server IDL file are yet implemented. However, since the name service has only a small set of operations it might be possible to build a complete name service.

Other services such as the CORBA notification service [16] or the event service [17,10] may be interesting, too. The ultimate goal is to provide support for the CORBA Component Model (CCM) [18]. At least client-side support of CCM shall be possible.

8 Related Work

.NET Remoting is a distribution technology that is more flexible and extensible than Microsoft DCOM/COM+. One would expect that Microsoft provides a channel implementation for the DCOM protocol to allow .NET applications and components to work together with distributed COM+ components. Interestingly, this is not the case. Microsoft supports interoperability of COM and .NET components with proxy mechanisms built into the Common Language Runtime [7]. One proxy, the Runtime Callable Wrapper (RCW), is responsible for mediating calls from .NET to COM. The other proxy, the COM Callable Wrapper (CCW) is responsible for mediating calls from COM to .NET. This allows the use and the implementation of COM components and COM interfaces with any .NET compliant programming language. An addition to this support is the use of COM+ services with .NET classes. The support for these enterprise services in .NET is referred to as *COM+ Interop* [7]. This enables the use of COM+ provided object pooling and automatic transactions with .NET.

Several chapters of the CORBA specification [1] are devoted to an Interworking Architecture for CORBA and Microsoft's COM. This architecture describes how objects and interfaces of one distribution environment can be transparently mapped to the other one. Furthermore, the specification explains how object identity and object lifecycle can be handled. There are mappings for the whole type system of COM and mappings for a restricted type system used by *Automation* aware components. The later are used by scripting languages such as VBScript. Today only few ORBs support this interworking architecture and the integration is not as transparent as the interoperability support for .NET and COM, and our IIOP channel.

Remote Method Invocation (RMI) is already provided by the Java Development Kit (JDK) since version 1.1. The initial release of RMI provided simple remoting capabilities similar to .NET Remoting. To construct an RMI capable Java class one has to declare a Java interface that extends the empty `Remote` interface. The implementation class has to implement this interface and extend the `UnicastRemoteObject` class. Instances of this implementation class can be registered in the RMI registry and can be looked up by clients. RMI differs conceptually in several points. RMI allows the use of custom socket classes for RMI communication comparable to .NET Remoting's transport sinks. However, it is not possible to hook into the call mechanism of RMI in the same flexible way as for .NET. RMI-over-IIOP has been introduced [2]. This allows the use of IIOP for RMI communication and allows CORBA servers or CORBA clients to communicate with their RMI counterparts. Obviously, RMI-over-IIOP has similarities to our approach of interoperability support for CORBA and .NET.

Our approach of integrating CORBA/IIOP into .NET is not the only existing one. IIOP.NET [19] and Remoting CORBA [20] also provide support for integrating .NET and CORBA. Due to the limited documentation available the differences to our approach is unclear. Based on the webpages it seems that they have fewer support mechanisms. IIOP.NET supports CORBA value types but has no support for arrays.

9   Conclusions

Microsoft's .NET Remoting provides a new tool for distributed system design and implementation. .NET Remoting does not only allow the construction of distributed systems with the Microsoft provided communication channels that use either a proprietary protocol based on TCP or the use of HTTP/SOAP but support the integration of new transport mechanisms into their framework.

We have leveraged this extension mechanisms to build a new communication channel that supports CORBA's IIOP protocol. We hooked into .NET Remoting's channel sink chain and replaced two different sinks on, both, the client and the server. We provided our own formatter sink to marshal and unmarshal data to the Common Data Representation (CDR) used with IIOP and a transport sink to put this data onto a socket or receive data from a socket. This allows the use of CORBA servers directly from .NET applications and the use of .NET server classes with any computing system that supports CORBA and the IIOP protocol. For .NET Remoting applications our approach allows to be used in addition to the TCP or the HTTP channel. The transition to another protocol is as simple as modifying a configuration file. Nothing has to be changed within the source code.

The performance evaluation we have done shows that the approach is promising. Although our IIOP channel is not optimized yet, it performs always better than the HTTP/SOAP channel provided by Microsoft. When used in combination with a Java CORBA ORB our test cases show the IIOP channel can perform better than a CORBA ORB.

In the future we plan to provide better IDL data type support and add new CORBA object services to complement our IIOP channel for .NET Remoting.

References

1. Object Management Group: The Common Object Request Broker: Architecture and Specification. 3.0.2 edn. (2002)
2. Schaaf, M., Maurer, F.: Integrating Java and CORBA: A programmer's perspective. IEEE Internet Computing 5 (2001) 72–78
3. Eddon, G., Eddon, H.: Inside Distributed COM. Microsoft Press (1998)
4. Richter, J.: Applied Microsoft .NET Framework Programming. Microsoft Press (2002)
5. Hoffman, K., Gabriel, J., Gosnell, D., Hasan, J., Holm, C., Musters, E., Narkiewickz, J., Schenken, J., Thangarathinam, T., Wylie, S., Ortiz, J.: Processional .NET Framework. Wrox Press (2001)
6. Box, D., et al.: Simple Object Access Protocol (SOAP) 1.1. W3C. (2000)
7. Troelson, A.: COM and .NET Interoperability. APress (2002)
8. Object Management Group: CORBA-WSDL/SOAP Interworking. (2003)
9. McLean, S., Naftel, J., Williams, K.: Microsoft .NET Remoting. Microsoft Press (2003)
10. Henning, M., Vinoski, S.: Advanced CORBA Programming with C++. Addison Wesley Longman, Inc. (1999)
11. Object Management Group: IDL To Java Language Mapping Specification. 1.2 edn. (2002)
12. Object Management Group: C++ Language Mapping Specification. (1999)
13. Object Management Group: Naming Service Specification. 1.2 edn. (2002)
14. Brose, G.: Jacorb: Implementation and design of a java orb. In: Proceedings of the DAIS'97, IFIP WG 6.1 Internation Working Conference on Distributed Applications and Systems, Chapman & Hall (1997)
15. Schaps, G.L.: Compiler construction with ANTLR and Java. Dr. Dobb's Journal (1999)
16. Object Management Group: Notification Service Specification. 1.0.1 edn. (2002)
17. Object Management Group: Event Service Specification. 1.1 edn. (2001)
18. Siegel, J.: CORBA 3: Fundamentals and Programming. Second edn. John Wiley & Sons, Inc. (2000)
19. IIOP.NET: (http://iiop-net.sourceforge.net/)
20. Remoting CORBA: (http://remoting-corba.sourceforge.net/)

Can Aspects Be Injected? Experience with Replication and Protection

Sara Bouchenak[1], Fabienne Boyer[1], Noel De Palma[2], and Daniel Hagimont[3]

[1] Université Joseph Fourier
[2] INPG (Grenoble Institute of Technology, France)
[3] INRIA (French National Institute for Research in Computer Science and Control)
INRIA – Sardes Research Group
655, avenue de l'Europe, 38334 Montbonnot St Martin France
{Sara.Bouchenak,Fabienne.Boyer,Noel.Depalma,Daniel.Hagimont}
@inria.fr

Abstract. Separation of concerns, which allows programming the nun-functional aspects of an application in a more or less orthogonal manner from the functional code, is be-coming a general trend in software development. The most widely used architectural pattern for implementing aspects involves indirection objects, raising a performance overhead at execution time. Thus, it appears as being an attractive challenge to be able to inject the code of aspects within the business components of an application in order to avoid indirection objects. With regard to two aspects (replication and protection), this paper replies to the following question: being given the code of an aspect as with an indi-rection-based implementation, is it possible to use a generic (aspect-independent) tool which would automatically inject this code within the application components ? The results show that this injection process is feasible and can be automated through the handling of a specific injection pattern.

1 Introduction

A general trend in software development is to separate, as long as possible, the development of different *aspects* of an application in order to improve the quality of the software which is easier to maintain. This principle of aspect separation has been addressed in several contexts, such as the AoP domain (Aspect-Oriented Programming]) 0 and the component based programming research community. In the last case, this lead to the development of middleware environments such as CCM 0 and EJB 0, where aspects are described separately from applications' business code, and associated at runtime with applications through configurable objects (containers) that link aspects to business components.

Whatever the context is, most implementations rely on *indirection objects* for the implementation of aspects. These objects capture the interactions between the appli-

R. Meersman et al. (Eds.): CoopIS/DOA/ODBASE 2003, LNCS 2888, pp. 1402–1420, 2003.
© Springer-Verlag Berlin Heidelberg 2003

cation components and allow executing additional treatments during these interactions. However, they generate a performance overhead at execution time, which may become significant for applications which involve a large number of interactions between components.

This paper examines the feasibility of injecting the code of aspects within the business components of an application in order to avoid indirection objects. A main goal of our work is to let the aspect programming model stay unchanged. The proposed injection process is thus applied to the code of an aspect programmed as with an indirection-based implementation. With regard to an experimentation performed with two aspects (replication and protection), the contribution of this paper is to reply to the following question : being given the code of an aspect as with an indirection-based implementation, is it feasible to automatically inject this code within the application components ?

In a previous work on aspects, we implemented two prototypes, managing respectively replicated and protected components through indirection objects [3][4]. In order to improve the performance of the applications, we implemented a new version of each prototype, based on aspect-injection. These new prototypes were however implemented in an aspect-specific manner. The proposition that is made in this paper corresponds to the lessons learned from these experiments, which have shown that it is possible to implement a generic injector which takes as input the classes of the indirection objects managing an aspect.

The rest of the paper is organized as follows. The following section presents the basic principle of the injection process. Sections 3 and 4 respectively describe our experiments with the replication and protection aspects. Section 5 summarises the lessons learned from the presented experiments. The performance aspect is treated in in section 6. Finally, in Section 7 we describe the related work and in section 8 we present our conclusions.

2 Approach

In the indirection-based implementation of aspects, several successive indirection objects[1] may be involved, forming a chain between an invoking object and an invoked object. In the rest of the paper, we respectively use *caller* for the invoker object and *callee* for the invoked object. These terms are also used to denote a *potential* caller (an object having a reference to another object) or a *potential* callee.

In a general framework, two indirection objects are involved: the first one, associated with the caller, which we call the Client Indirection Object (CIO) and the second, associated with the callee, called the Server Indirection Object (SIO)[2], as shown in Figure 1. In more complex frameworks, the cardinality of the CIO or SIO may vary from 0 (either the CIO or the SIO may be absent) to n (an aspect may involve multiple CIO and SIO, as for the protection aspect considered further in this paper).

---

[1] The term object may refer to simple Java objects as well as components.
[2] CIO and SIO can be considered as stub and skeleton.

The CIO and SIO capture interactions between objects and respectively allow the association of aspect-related code with the caller and callee objects. The general idea that we have experimented is to inject the aspect-related code within the code of the application.

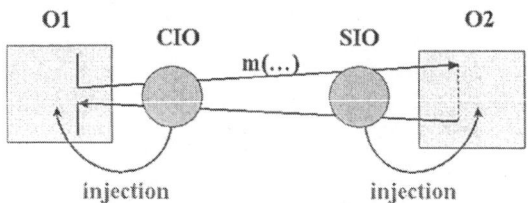

Fig. 1. Principle of aspect injection

Code injection techniques that we experimented apply at the level of Java byte-code. In the rest of the paper, and for clarity purpose, we will illustrate our experiments through Java source code.

3 Replication Aspect

The Javanaise replication service 0 0 that we designed and implemented previously, is taken as reference. The Javanaise objects are transparently replicated, so that the application developer can program as in a centralized setting. (S)he only has to specify the access modes associated with its application's objects, i.e., read/write modes of the business (i.e. application-specific) methods. This is done through a Java-based extended IDL (Interface Description Language). Javanaise ensures the consistency of the replicated objects, which are brought on demand on the requesting nodes and are cached until invalidated by the coherency protocol.

The implementation of Javanaise using indirection objects is presented in 3.1 while the injection-based implementation is described in 3.2.

3.1 Indirection-Based Implementation of Replication

Javanaise has been implemented on top of Java and relies on indirection objects. For each object reference, a pair of indirection objects (*CIO* and *SIO*) is transparently inserted between the callee (the object identified by the reference) and the caller (the object that contains the reference). This transparency is ensured by the fact that the caller views the CIO as being the callee (the CIO implements the same interface as the callee).

The Object1 and Object2 classes given in Figure 2, illustrate a sample program where an object *o1* calls a method *foo* which itself calls a method *m* on an object *o2*. In a centralized and non-replicated environment, the caller *o1* would directly reference the callee *o2*. When implementing replication using indirection objects, and in the case the callee *o2* is replicable, the caller *o1* references a CIO which itself references a SIO that references the callee *o2*.

```
class Object1 implements Itf1 {          class Object2 implements Itf2 {
    Itf2 o2;                                  void m(Itf3 o3) {
    Itf3 o3;                                      // Code of m
    void foo() {                                  ...
                                              }
        ...                                   ...
        o2.m(o3);                         }
        ...
    }
    public static void main(String[] args) {
        Object1 o1 = new Object1();       interface Itf2 {
        o1.foo();                             void m();          read
    }                                         ...
}                                         }
```

Fig. 2. A sample program with replicated objects

Let's focus on the call of the method *m* by the object *o1* on the object *o2*. The associated CIO and SIO are implemented as illustrated by Figure 3 :

- *o2_CIO* manages the *dynamic binding* to the callee *o2*. It contains the unique identifier of *o2* (*id_o2* in *o2_CIO*'s code), and a reference to the associated SIO (*o2* in *o2_CIO*'s code). If this reference is null, it means that it is the first time that *o1* accesses *o2*. In this case, a copy of *o2* is fetched, either locally if *o2* is already cached or remotely from a Javanaise server using *o2*'s unique identifier.

- *o2_SIO* manages the *synchronization*, i.e., invalidation and update, of an *o2* replica. It contains the unique identifier of *o2* (*id_o2* in *o2_SIO*'s code), and a reference to a local replica (*o2* in *o2_SIO*'s code). According to the access modes specified in the object's interface, the methods of a replicated object are bracketed with *lock_read/lock_write* and *unlock_read/unlock_write* calls. The full explanation of the protocol can be found in 0.

This implementation using indirection objects significantly increases the number of method calls. In the given example, the call of method *m* from *o1* to *o2* is transformed into three method calls: first *o1* calls method *m* on *o2_CIO*, then *o2_CIO* calls method *m* on *o2_SIO*, and finally *o2_SIO* calls the effective method *m* on *o2*.

3.2   Injection-Based Implementation of Replication

In this section, we detail how we used code injection to implement more efficiently the replication service. The basic idea is to inject the CIO (resp. the SIO) within the caller (resp. callee) object.

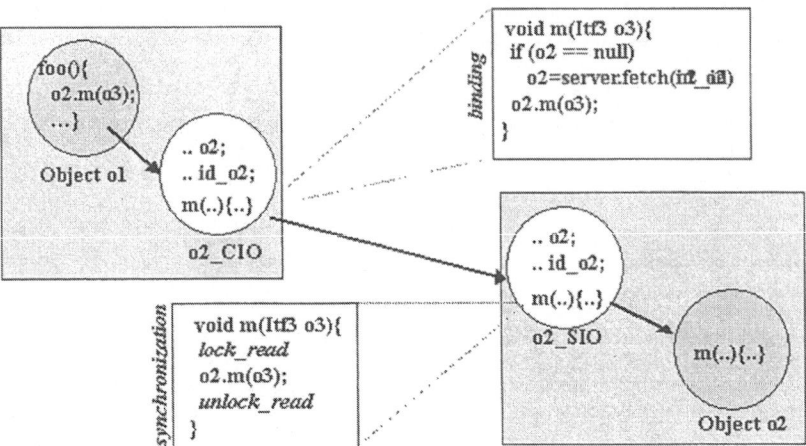

Fig. 3. The invocation of O2 by O1 is performed on a local replica of O2

Injection of CIO into a Caller Object

Injecting the CIO in the caller object implies to inject both the CIO's code and the CIO's data within the caller's class.

The CIO implements the methods defined in the interface of the callee object. It forwards the invocations of each method towards the SIO of the callee object, but it executes some pre and post treatments. These treatments are injected in the caller before and after the concerned invocations. In the *o1* object for example, the code that checks the binding to *o2* is injected before any call on *o2* (see Figure 4).

Injection of the CIO's data is difficult, because these data are strongly coupled with the reference of the callee object. Any reference manipulation should keep into account the CIO's data in a way that ensures that these operations provide the same semantic than with an indirection-based implementation. With regard to the operations that can be performed on a reference (assignment, transfer as parameter and comparison), there are two aspects to consider to manage the CIO's data :

- this data should follow the reference when transmitted from one object to another,
- the consistency of this data with regard to the reference should be ensured.

The first aspect is required to provide the semantic of the indirection-based implementation, in which a receiver of a reference obtain a way to access the CIO's data associated with the reference. Each time an object reference is transferred as a method parameter or as a result, some code should be injected to transfer, as additional parameters, the CIO's data associated with the reference.[3] This may be performed by

---

[3] In fact, the receiver of a reference has at least to be able to retrieve the CIO's data associated with the received reference. The most simple way to perform this is to transfer a copy of these data along with the reference, which is possible in the most common cases because the CIO's data size is often small.these data along with the reference, which is possible in the most common cases because the CIO's data size is often small.

modifying the signature of the business methods of the application objects. In the case of object *o2*, the signature of the business method *m* has been modified in order to include the data *(id_o3)* associated with the received reference to *o3* (see Figure 4).

In the same way, each time an object reference is assigned, some code should be injected to assign accordingly the CIO's data associated with the reference. In the case of *o1*, the CIO's data associated with the *o2* reference are composed of the unique identifier of *o2* (see the declaration of *id_o2* in Figure 4). Any assignment of the *o2* reference should also raise the according assignment of the *id_o2* data.

The management of reference comparison depends on the application programming model, which may allow or disallow the direct comparison of references (through the use of the == operator). For centralized applications, direct comparison may be authorized. In this case, the injection process does not perturb this model because it also permits a direct comparison between object references.

In the case only indirect comparisons are authorized by the programming model, through the use of a specific method defined in the CIO's code (such as the *equals()* method), then the injection process operates as for any CIO's method, by expanding the *equals()* invocation in the code of the application.

Injection of SIO into a Callee Object

SIO injection implies the injection of both the SIO's data and the SIO's code within the associated callee object replica.

The injection of the SIO's data is more or less straightforward. In the case of the o2 object, both the declaration of id_o2 (unique identifier of o2) and of the lock field (for the synchronisation of o2) of the SIO have to be injected in o2's class.

As for the CIO objects, the SIO's code is mainly composed of methods which perform actions before and after calling the effective business methods on the callee. The injection of the SIO's code consists in placing this code at the right place in the callee (see figure 5).

Finally, in accordance with the injection of CIO objects, the signatures of the business methods of a callee object may have to be modified in order to take into account the transfer of the CIOs data. Practically, in the case of *o2*, the signature of the business method *m* has changed in order to take the identifier associated with the received reference of *o3*.

The experience on using the code injection techniques described in this section has shown that injection is feasible in the case of replicated distributed objects. The main injection pattern which has been highlighted by this experience is the need to manage *data strongly coupled with object references*, in a way that ensures that these data follow the reference all along its road. In the present case, these data correspond to the CIO's data which are composed of the unique identifier of the object identified by a reference.

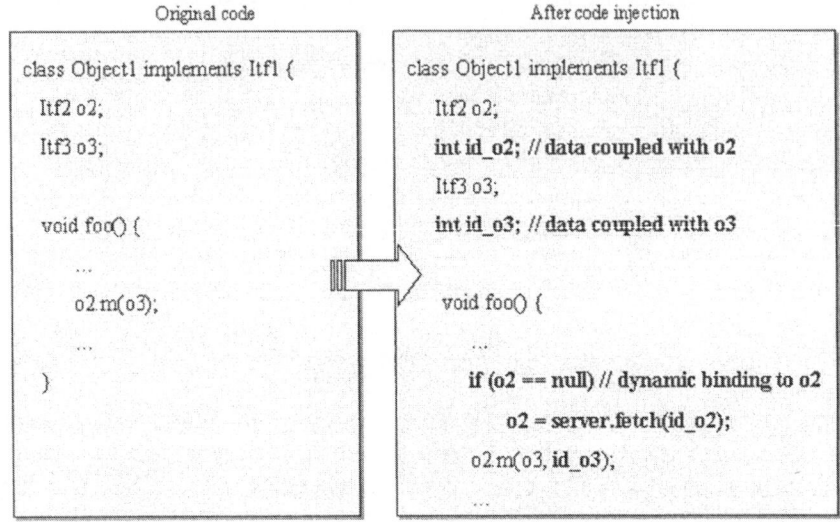

Fig. 4. Injection of the CIO in the case of the sample program of Figure 3

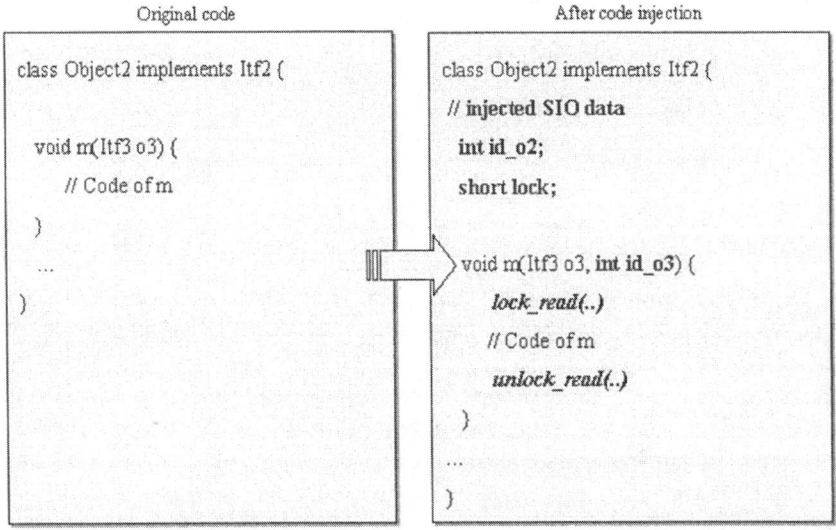

Fig. 5. Injection of the SIO in the case of the sample program of Figure 3

4 Protection Aspect

The second aspect that we addressed is protection, which purpose is to control interactions between mutually suspicious objects. We take as reference a protection model
that we proposed in a previous work, based on *hidden software capabilities* 0.

4.1 The Considered Capability-Based Protection Ayspect

The protection of a given application is expressed in an extended Interface Definition
Language (IDL) through the concept of *views* which are restrictions of Java interfaces. A view specifies a set of authorized methods. A *not* before a method declaration means that the method is not permitted. When an object reference is passed as
parameter in a view, the programmer can specify the view to be passed with the reference using the key-word *pass*. If no view is specified, it means that no restriction is
applied to this reference.

Let's consider the example of a printing service that allows a client to print out a
file; this service provides a *print* operation for printing a text, and an *init* operation,
for resetting the underlying printer. Figure 6 shows the protection views related to the
printer example. The *Printer_client_view* view represents the protection policy from
the client point of view: it specifies that the view *Text_server_view2* must be associated with the text parameter when the *print* method is invoked. The
Text_server_view2 view only authorizes *read* operations on texts, because a client
allows a printer to read the text but not to modify it.

Similarly, *Printer_server_view1* and *Printer_server_view2* represents the protection policies from the printer point of view. The printer protects itself with the
Printer_server_view2 when the caller is a client. This view prevents clients from
calling the *init* method on printers because only administrators are allowed to reset the
printer. On the other side, the printer uses the *Printer_server_view1* to protect itself
when the caller is an administrator.

During the execution, the protection views are managed through *capabilities*. A
capability is an object reference coupled with the identification of the views controlling its use. In order to be allowed to invoke a particular method on an object, an
application must own a capability to that object with the required access rights.

More precisely, a capability identifies two protection views : the client view and
the server view. The client view defines the caller protection while the server view
defines the callee protection, being given that the caller is the application owning the
reference. With the Printer example, a client may own a capability on a printer identifying respectively *Printer_client_view* and *Printer_server_view1* for the client and
server views.

Client protection	Printer protection

view **Printer_client_view**
implements Printer_itf {
  void init();
  void print(Text_itf text **pass**
                 Text_server_view2);
}
 	
view **Text_server_view1**
implements Text_itf {
  String read();
  void write(String s);
}
 	
view **Text_server_view2**
implements Text_itf {
  String read();
  void **not** write(String s);
}
	view **Printer_server_view1**
	implements Printer_itf {
	  void init();
	  void print(Text_itf text);
	}
	
	view **Printer_server_view2**
	implements Printer_itf {
	  void **not** init();
	  void print(Text_itf text);
	}
	
	view **Text_client_view**
	implements Text_itf {
	  String read();
	  void write(String s);
	}

Fig. 6. The Printer views

A capability can be passed from an application to another application (through method invocation). The views associated with the capability may be redefined, according to the definition of the protection in the extended IDL.

In the printing example, when the *Client* calls the *print* method on the *Printer* object, a read-only capability (*Text_capacity*) on the *Text* object is passed from the *Client* to the *Printer* according to the *Printer_client_view* view (see step 1 in Figure 7). The client and server protection views associated with this capability are respectively *Text_client_view* and *Text_server_view2*. This capability allows the *Printer* object to read the content of the text (see step 2 in Figure 7).

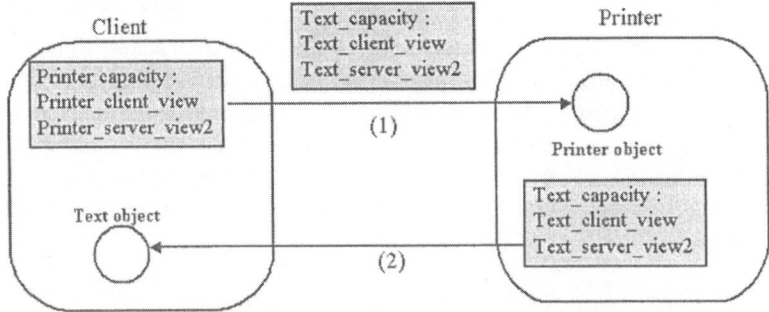

Fig. 7. Protection in the printing example

4.2 Indirection-Based Implementation of Protection

The indirection-based implementation of the protection model presented above relies on indirection objects which raise an exception when an unauthorized method is called, while forwarding an invocation to the callee object in the other case.

This implementation uses both CIO and SIO indirection objects as described in section 0. CIO and SIO respectively implement a client protection view and a server protection view.

When a caller invokes a method on a callee, both the CIO and the SIO associated with the invoked reference control the parameters which are transferred according to the IDL views. An outgoing object reference may be replaced by a SIO reference. Conversely, an ingoing reference may be replaced by a CIO reference.

In the case of the printer application, when a *Client* object invokes a *Printer* object, it passes a reference to a *Text* object as a parameter of the *print* method. The CIO of the Client (of class *Printer_client_view*) replaces the reference of the Text object with a reference to a SIO object of class *Text_server_view* according to the definition of the IDL views. Figure 8 shows the code of the indirection objects used in the printer example.

4.3 Injection-Based Implementation of Protection

In this section, we show how code injection has been used to implement the capability-based access control model without indirection objects. There is a major difference with the previous experiment on replicated objects, which makes the protection experiment complementary with the previous one: being given the class of a callee object, both the CIO and the SIO classes were unique with the replication aspect, while they can be multiple with the protection aspect.

```
public class Printer_server_view1
implements Printer_itf (
  Printer_itf printer; // ref. of the callee object

  public void init() ( printer.init();)

  public void print(Text_itf text) {
    printer.print(text);
  }}
```

```
public class Printer_server_view2
implements Printer_itf (
  Printer_itf printer; // ref. of the callee object

  public void init() (Exception !!!)

  public void print(Text_itf text) {
    printer.print(text);
  }}
```

```
public class Printer_client_view
implements Printer_itf (

  Printer_itf printer; // ref of the printer SIO

  public void init() {
    printer.init();
  }

  public void print(Text_itf text) {
    Text_reader_view text_SIO =
      new Text_reader_view2 (text);
    printer.print(text_SIO);
  }
}
```

Fig. 8. Code of some indirection objects used in the printer example

As illustrated in Figure 9, being given the Printer class, there exists at least two SIO classes implementing two different views of the printer: *Printer_server _view1*(for administrators) and *Printer_server_view2* (for clients), and two CIO classes*: Printer_client_view* and *Printer_adm_view* (although not shown in the Figure 9, a same caller object could use both CIO classes in the case it interacts with different printers with different roles).

The two main principles that have been applied to deal with the multiplicity of CIO/SIO classes are the following (the details of injection are given subsequently):

(1) to inject in any *callee* object (resp. *caller* object) the code of all the possible SIO classes (resp. CIO classes), being given that a CIO code has to be executed on a caller side while a SIO code has to be executed on a callee side.

(2) to associate to any object reference, the information that will allow to select, during a method invocation, both the right CIO and SIO code to execute. In Figure 9, this principle results in associating with the Printer reference used within the Client, the *indexes* that allow identifying CIO Printer_client_view and SIO Printer_server_view1 for the calls made from the Client to the Printer. *These indexes are considered as data strongly coupled with object references[4].*

Injection of CIO into a Caller Object

As for the replication aspect, the CIO mainly implements the methods defined in the interface of the callee object. Within a caller object, the injection process has to expand the invocations of these methods by their corresponding CIO code. Because multiple CIO can be injected within a caller, the selection of the right CIO code to execute is performed by injecting a *switch* statement applied on the indexes that are associated with the reference of the callee object.

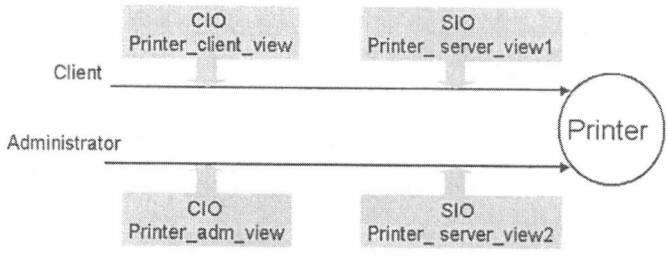

Fig. 9. Basic architecture for protection management

Injection of SIO into a Callee Object

As for CIO, injecting several SIO within a callee object requires the indexing mechanism which allows to select the right code to execute on a given method invocation. During a particular method invocation, the index of the SIO code to execute should be received as a parameter of the method invocation. In the case of the printer example (Figure 10), the parameter *printer_SIO* has been added to the interface of the *print*

---

[4] In the case of replication, both the CIO and SIO were unique for a given couple of interacting objects. Thus, there was no need for using CIO/SIO indexes.

method. According to the value of this parameter, the printer checks that the access rights grant access to the invoked *print* method.

Data Strongly Coupled with Object References

In the case of the indirection-based implementation of protection, an object reference identifies a CIO object, which itself contains a reference to a SIO object through which the invocations should cross. CIO as well as SIO objects do not contain additional data. Thus the data strongly coupled with an object reference are limited to the indexes of both the CIO and SIO code. The management of these data takes into account the following kinds of operations on references: invocation, assignment, transfer as parameter and comparison.

Concerning object invocation, the data strongly coupled with an object reference may be divided into two parts : the data used at caller side and the data used at callee side[5]. In the present case, the caller-side data are composed of the CIO index, and the callee-side data of the SIO index. During an invocation, the SIO index has indeed to be known at the callee side in order to select the right SIO code to execute. To keep the semantic of an indirection-based implementation of protection, the callee-side data have to be transferred to the callee each time the callee is invoked. Thus, for any invocation on a protected object, code injection should add as a new parameter the index of the SIO to use at the callee side (either index of SIO printer_server_view1 or of SIO printer_server_view2 in Figure 11). The injection process modifies the signatures of the business methods of the application objects to take into account this additional parameter.

```
class Printer implements Printer_itf {
  ...
  /**
  * Print method
  * @param    printer_SIO : the SIO to use for the printer
  * @param    text : the reference of the Text object to print
  * @param    text_index : the CIO/SIO to use when invoking the text
  */
  public void print (short printer_SIO, Text_itf text, short text_index[]) {

    // Check the availability of the print method according to printer_SIO
    if (printer_SIO!= ... ) { // raise an exception !!! }

    // Associate CIO to ingoing references according to printer_SIO
    ...

    // Transfer the SIO index to use at the callee side
    text.read(text_index[SIO]);
    return;
  }}
```

Fig. 10. Code of the server after protection injection

---

[5] This distinction was not introduced in the case of the replication aspect, because the data strongly coupled with object references were only composed of data used at callee side.

About reference assignment, each time a reference is assigned in the application's code, code should be injected to assign accordingly the data coupled with the references (CIO/SIO indexes). In the case of the printer reference contained in the *Client* class as shown in Figure 10, any assignment of *printer* should also raise the assignment of the *printer_index* variable (which include both CIO and SIO indexes).

In the same way, each time a reference is transferred as a method parameter or as a result, the CIO/SIO indexes associated with the reference should also be transferred. This is once again performed by modifying the signature of the business methods of the application objects. In the case of the *Client* class, the signature of the business method *print* has changed in order to transfer the indexes *(text_index)* associated with the reference *text*.

Finally, concerning reference comparison, the protection programming model only authorises indirect comparison of object references, through calls to an *equals()* method provided by CIO objects. The injection process operates as for any other CIO method, by expanding the method's code within the caller object.

```
public class Client {

public static void main(String args[]) {

    Printer_itf printer;
    // index of the CIO/SIO views to use when invoking the printer
    short printer_index[2];

    Text_itf text;
    // index of the CIO/SIO views to use when invoking the text
    short text_index[2];

    ...

    // Invoke print method
    // the management of outgoing references depends on the
    // current CIO view associated to the printer
    switch (printer_index[CIO]) {

        ...
        text_index[SIO] = Text_itf.Text_server_view2;
        ...
    }
    printer.print(printer_index[SIO], text, text_index);         ←
    }
}
```

Fig. 11. Code of the client after protection injection

This section has described a way to inject a protection aspect within the objects of an application. A way to manage the multiplicity of CIO/SIO classes is firstly to inject the whole collection of CIO code (resp. SIO code) within the corresponding application objects[6], and secondly to use indexes to allow the selection of the right code to execute during a particular method invocation. We consider CIO/SIO indexes as data strongly coupled with object references. Moreover, in the protection example, these data include both a caller-side and a callee-side parts. The callee-side part has to be transferred to the callee when the reference to which it is coupled is invoked.

5 Lessons Learned

The lessons learned from the injection experience which is described in this paper are firstly a list of injection patterns that should be implemented by a generic aspect-injector tool :

–   Define additional data and methods within a class.

– Add instructions at the beginning and at the end of a particular method definition.

– Add instructions before and after a particular method invocation.

– Modify the signature of a method (add parameters).

– Enhance the components references with aspect-related data (detailed just after).

The highlighting of the last injection pattern, that we call the *extended reference injection pattern*, is the first main result of our experience. It allows to associate with a reference, the data that allows to manipulate the referenced component according to a given aspect. These aspect-specific data are associated with references in a way that provides the same semantic as if they were part of references.

Providing this pattern implies to inject the convenient code to ensure that for any extended reference transferred as parameter or as result of a method invocation, the whole extended reference content is transferred. Similarly, reference assignment and comparison should consider the whole extended reference content.

Concerning the invocations that are performed on an extended reference, we distinguish between two kinds of data composing the reference: the data used at caller side and those used at the callee side. An injector tool providing the extended reference pattern should inject the convenient code to ensure that the caller-side (resp. callee-side) data are actually present at the caller (resp. callee) side during an invocation.

The way to ensure the previous properties is to modify, by injection, the components interfaces. On a method invocation, the *data of the invoked reference, which are used at callee side,* have to be transferred to the callee as additional parameters. Moreover, for any reference transferred as parameter (or as result), the transfer of the whole extended reference content also involves additional method parameters.

---

[6] This is possible because both the size and the number of CIO/SIO classes associated with a given component is often small.

The following table illustrates the use of the extended reference injection pattern, by detailing the composition of an extended reference according to the composition of the indirection objects used for a given aspect. The index parts (CIO index and SIO index) are required as soon as there are multiple classes of CIO/SIO that can be associated with a given component. It should be noted that the SIO's data do not appear in this table because they can be injected within the callee object.

Table 1. Extended reference content

Data used at caller side	Data used at callee side
CIO data	
CIO index	SIO index

In the case of the replication aspect, the extended reference was only composed of data used at caller side, because of the uniqueness of the SIO indirection object (only one SIO object can be associated with a duplicated object). This uniqueness has allowed to avoid the use of SIO index.

The other result of our experience is the fact that, for the considered aspects, their injection can be automated in the sense that it can be performed by a generic (aspect independent) injector tool. Being given the classes of both the CIO and SIO indirection objects managing a given aspect, an injector tool should be able to automatically determine the composition of the extended reference, as shown by the previous table. The injection process may then be entirely driven by the classes of the indirection objects and the extended reference composition.

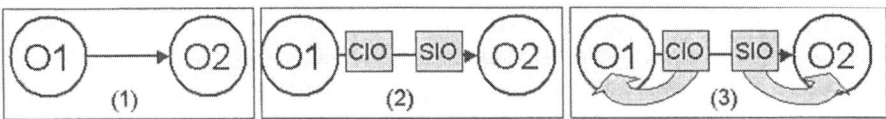

Fig. 12. Basic schemes for performance evaluation

6 Performance Evaluation

This section provides the performance evaluation results in the case of a basic method invocation scheme illustrated in Figure 12.

In this scheme, object *o1* invokes a method *m()* on object *o2*. We consider the case where method *m()* does not take any parameter and the case where it takes a reference to another object *o3* as parameter. The code of method *m()* is empty. The measurements have been done under three conditions:

- on Java (JDK1.3) without integration of any aspect (case 1 in Figure 12).
- with the aspects (replication[7] and protection[8]) implemented with indirection objects (case 2 in Figure 12).
- with the aspects implemented with code injection (case 3 in Figure 12).

The following table presents the resulting performance figures using a 1Gh Pentium processor with 256 Mo of RAM. These results are given for 100 millions of iterations over the method call. We detail each case in the following.

	Protection		Replication		Java
	Indir.	Inject.	Indir.	Inject.	
Method m()	6458 ms	3354 ms - 48%	13889 ms	7591 ms -45%	1552 ms
Method m(o3)	14400 ms	3565 ms -75%	16022 ms	8453 ms -47%	1713 ms

Protection
In the case of a single method call with no parameter, the speedup is 48%. This speedup is explained because two indirection calls are avoided. In the case of a method call with a reference parameter, the speedup is 75%. In the version based on indirection objects, when a protected object reference (to *o3*) is transmitted as parameter, the SIO associated to the transmitted reference has to be instantiated. In the injection version, the indirection objects do not have to be instantiated since the protection code is embedded in the caller and callee objects (however we have to pass new parameters to implement the capability transfer).

Replication
In the case of a single method call with no parameter, the speedup is near 45%. Like for the capability experimentation, this speedup is explained because we avoid two indirection calls. In the case of a method call with a reference parameter, the speedup is about the same (47%). The contrast with the protection aspect is explained because with the replication aspect, the indirection objects are shared by the application components (only one CIO is created per object duplica).

The implementation of the replication service has a higher cost than the implementation of the protection service, because the replication service requires costly synchronization operations.

---

[7] In case of the replication aspect, the measurements were performed after the callee object has been replicated on the local machine.

[8] In the case of the protection aspect, four views were used (two client views and two server views).

7 Related Work

In the domain of component-based middleware such as EBJ 0 or CCM 0, the integration of non-functional properties such as security, transactions or persistence generally relies on indirection objects which allow capturing the interactions between components, and therefore to reify invocations. In the context of AoP 0 [10], the focus has rather been on the definition of language support for programming aspects (e.g., AspectJ 0). The integration often relies on extra method calls (on aspect objects) which are injected in the code of the applications before, after or at entry of business method calls. Some optimizations are performed to reduce the performance overhead. In particular, AspectJ inlines some calls to aspect methods, but this is performed for limited cases only (statically known final methods in particular). In the same way, the JIT uses techniques that, in some cases, expand the called code in the calling code (In-lining). As soon as an aspect involve either indirection objects containing data, or multiple indirection objects, such inlining techniques are no longer sufficient. Indeed, in these cases, injecting aspects imply to modify the signatures of the business methods of the application components, as synthesized in 5.

Our proposal should be considered as complementary with the solutions proposed either by tools such as Aspect/J, or environments such as EJB or CCM. The injection process that we propose is indeed applied on the classes of the indirection objects, *after* these have been generated by these tools or environment.

Another point that should be considered is the domain of reflexive environments, which instrument and reify applications' behaviour during execution 0. Such environments may be used for managing aspects 0. However, these environments usually use additional objects at runtime (meta-objects), leading to the same observation as the one we addressed in this paper.

From a technical point of view, many different projects have experimented with Java bytecode transformation tools such as Javassist 0 or BCEL [17], in order to inject additional code in applications' functional code. The Software Fault Isolation technique 0 injects binary code that verifies that a component does not address the memory region allocated to another component. Software fault isolation allows component confinement without having to manage components in separate address spaces, which would be costly due to address space boundaries crossings. Other projects uses binary transformation techniques with different objectives, considering applications resource control 0, distribution 0, and thread migration 0.

8 Conclusion and Perspectives

Separation of aspects is promoted by several domains, such as component-based environments and AoP languages and runtime supports. Resulting software is easier to build, reuse and adapt. The main motivation of these environments is to provide programmers with the flexibility of integrating orthogonal aspects into their applications. But this flexibility may be obtained to the detriment of performance, as the implementation of aspects through indirection objects incurs an overhead on applications.

In this paper, we experimented a complementary approach: we investigated the issue of combining the flexibility of separation of aspects with efficiency. In the proposed approach, rather than implementing aspects using indirection objects, code injection techniques are used in order to optimise the integration of aspects into applications' code. One main objective of our work was to let the aspect programming model stay unchanged. This implies that the injection process be applied to the code of aspects programmed as with the indirection-based implementation.

Relying on an experimentation performed with two main aspects (replication and protection), this paper has the following results.

1. Being given the code of an aspect as with the indirection-based implementation, it is it feasible to use a generic (aspect-independent) injector which automatically injects the aspect code within the application components.

2. Aspects, even complex, can be injected with a benefit on the execution performances.

3. The injection process uses a specific injection pattern that we called *extended reference*. It basically allows to enhance usual object references with strongly coupled data accompanying references all along their road.

There are two important issues that we plan to address in a future work. Firstly, the injection of multiple aspects within an application has to be studied. Secondly, the monitoring and the instrumentation of an aspect-injected application becomes complex, because the code of aspects is distributed all over the application's components rather than localized within indirection objects. The identification of the code specific to the management of aspects becomes more difficult and should be helped by the provision of suitable monitoring features.

Another issue to investigate is dynamic aspect integration 00. Managing aspects in indirection objects provides a means to dynamically add/remove aspects. Injecting aspects in the business code of the application makes it more difficult to dynamically modify aspects, since it may modify the structure of the application objects. We are currently working on the possibilities of making the components of an application evolve dynamically, by capturing (serializing) their state and rebuilding (de-serializing) a new version of their state with the newly integrated aspects. Such flexibility could be provided by implementing primitives which capture (serialize) the state of the application's objects and rebuild (de-serialize) a new version of these objects with the new integrated aspects. This is also a perspective to our work.

References

[1]   W. Binder, J. Hulaas, A. Villazón, R. Vidal. Portable Resource Control in Java: The J-SEAL2 Approach, ACM Conference on Object-Oriented Programming, Systems, Languages, and Applications (OOPSLA'2001), October 2001.

[2]   S. Chiba. Javassist - A Reflection-based Programming Wizard for Java, ACM OOPSLA'98 Workshop on Reflective Programming in C++ and Java, October 1998.

[3]   D. Hagimont, J. Mossière, X. Rousset de Pina, F. Saunier. Hidden Software Capabilities, Sixteenth International Conference on Distributed Computing Systems (ICDCS), May 1996.

[4]   D. Hagimont, D. Louvegnies. Javanaise: Distributed Shared Objects for Internet Cooperative Applications, IFIP International Conference on Distributed Systems Platforms and Open Distributed Processing (Middleware'98), September 1998.

[5]   D. Hagimont, F. Boyer. A Configurable RMI Mechanism for Sharing Distributed Java Objects, IEEE Internet Computing, Volume 5, number 1, January 2001.

[6]   G. Kiczales, J. Lamping, A. Menhdhekar, C. Maeda, C. Lopes, J.-M. Loingtier, J. Irwin. Aspect-Oriented Programming. European Conference for Object-Oriented Programming (ECOOP '97), Jyväskylä, Finland, June 1997.

[7]   M. O. Killijian, J. C. Ruiz, J. C. Fabre. Portable Serialization of CORBA Objects: a Reflective Approach. 17th ACM Conference on Object-Oriented Programming, Systems, Languages, and Applications (OOPSLA'2002), Seattle, WA, USA, November 2002.

[8]   Object Management Group, CORBA Components: Joint Revised Submission, OMG TC Document orbos/99-08, August 1999.

[9]   R. Pawlak, L. Duchien, G. Florin. An automatic aspect weaver with a reflective programming language. 2nd International Conference on Meta-Level Architectures and Reflection (Reflection'99), Saint-Malo, France, June 1999.

[10] A. Popovici, T. Gross, G. Alonso. Dynamic weaving for aspect-oriented programming. 1st Aspect Oriented Software Development (AOSD'02), Enshede, The Netherlands, April 2002.

[11] T. Sakamoto, T. Sekiguchi, A. Yonezawa, Bytecode Transformation for Portable Thread Migration in Java, International Symposium on Mobile Agents (MA'2000), September 2000.

[12] B. Smith Reflection and Semantics in a Procedural Language. Technical Rapport, Laboratory for Computer Science, Massachussets Institute of Technology, 1982.

[13] Sun Microsystems, Enterprise Java Beans Specifications, Version 2.0, 2001.

[14] M. Tatsubori, T. Sasaki, S. Chiba, K. Itano. A Bytecode Translator for Distributed Execution of "Legacy" Java Software. European Conference on Object-Oriented Programming (ECOOP'2001), Budapest, Hungary, June 2001.

[15] R. Wahbe, S. Lucco, T. Anderson, S. Graham, Efficient Software-Based Fault Isolation, 14th ACM Symposium on Operating System Principles (SOSP'93), pp. 203–216, December 1993.

[16] Charles Zhang, Hans-Arno. Jacobsen, Quantifying Aspects in Middleware Platforms, Conference on Aspect-oriented software development (AOSD'03), pp. 130–139, Boston, Massachusetts, March 2003.

[17] BCEL, 2002. http://bcel.sourceforge.net/

Analysing Mailboxes of Asynchronous Communicating Components

Jean-Claude Royer and Michael Xu

Equipe LOAC, Ecole des Mines de Nantes, 4, rue Alfred Kastler – BP 20722,
F-44307 Nantes Cedex 3
Jean-Claude.Royer@emn.fr, Kaiye.Xu@eleve.emn.fr

Abstract. Asynchronous communications are prominent in distributed and mobile systems. Often concurrent systems consider an abstract point of view with synchronous communications. However it seems more realistic and finer to consider asynchronous communicating systems, since it provides a more primitive communication protocol and maximize the concurrency. Several languages and models have been defined using this communication mode: agent, actor, mobile computation, and so on. Here we reconsider a previous component model with full data types and synchronous communications with an asynchronous flavour. The dynamic behaviour of a component is represented as a structured symbolic transition system with mailboxes. We also present an algorithm devoted to an analysis of the dynamic behaviour of the system. This algorithm decides if the system has bound mailboxes and computes the reachable mailbox contents of the system. The component model and the algorithm are illustrated on a flight system reservation.

Keywords: Asynchronous Communication, Component, Architecture, Dynamic Behaviour, Unbound or Bound Mailbox

1 Introduction

Architectures and components [25,16,15,21,35,6,2,27] are nowadays technologies in software development. They promote software architectures based on communicating software entities. In this domain previous experiences are the actor model [4,3,18], concurrent object-oriented programming [10,9], mobile computation [33] and the multi-agent systems [34]. Actors and agents are rather based on asynchronous message sending while often components and objects promote synchronous communications or Remote Procedure Calls. Nevertheless there are few examples of object-oriented languages with asynchronous call, for instance ProActive [1] and Piccola [2].

In the context of distributed computing, asynchronism of communications should be the default policy, especially in wide area networks. [23] presents a comprehensive discussion about distributed computing and its main characteristics. We may note that some applications like news or mail are naturally asynchronous. Asynchronous communications are simpler and more primitive than

R. Meersman et al. (Eds.): CoopIS/DOA/ODBASE 2003, LNCS 2888, pp. 1421–1438, 2003.

synchronous one, even if each one can simulate the other. Asynchronism is the choice done by several theoretical approaches but less often by real platforms, for example client-server has generally synchronous communications. Many infrastructures or component languages have basically synchronous communications: EJB, CORBA, RMI [16], this is also true with several classic models and languages like ADA, CCS, CSP or LOTOS. Asynchronous communications are less constraining from a concurrency point of view but the emitter does not know if a message will be received by the receiver. Other important facts with asynchronism are the impossibility to differentiate a slow component from a stopped one and the impact of failures. Thus it implies more complex descriptions, we need to cope with more errors and it produces complex dynamic behaviours. On the other hand this communication mode is simpler to implement. To the contrary synchronous communications are more time consuming, more abstract and produce simpler dynamic behaviours.

There are already several language categories which use asynchronous communications: some concurrent object-oriented languages, some component languages, actor languages and multi-agent systems. We think that this use will grow conjointly with the emergence of distributed applications and distributed languages. For example EJB 2.0 and CORBA have introduced some forms of asynchronism. Thus there is a need to provide analytic tools to study or understand behavioural problems with asynchronous communications. The ability to compute the global dynamic behaviour of such system and to reason about it are important both at the specification level and at the coding/testing level. Here we focus on asynchronous communications with safe communications, without real time aspect and process failure. One classic way to simulate asynchronism in a synchronous context is to use buffers which memorize messages between emitters and receivers. It introduces two kinds of entity: the components and the buffers. Furthermore the resulting dynamic behaviour is complex and it requires a similar analysis technique than for pure asynchronism. So we prefer to use native asynchronism with buffers inside components. It is much more uniform and simpler to implement in a distributed context.

In this paper we introduce a component model with asynchronous communications. It is based on some previous experiences with synchronous communications. This model defines interfaces and protocols for components, it also introduces architecture and communication schemes. We illustrate some graphical notations with a simple example of flight reservation. Our purpose is to study the global behaviour of such a system. We assume that sent messages always arrive to the receiver, in other words we have reliable or safe communications. Message lost are out of the scope of our study, see [29] for a related study. We provide means to have a look at the dynamic behaviour and to help designers to detect problems. We briefly describe a data structure for structured state and transition systems with mailboxes to code the global dynamic behaviour of such systems. From this and using the technique of [30,5] it is possible to prove properties on the system. Here we are rather interested in some specific mailbox analysis. There is a need to know the size of the mailboxes and if there are bound or not. Such informations are important for semantics reasons but also for optimisations ones. We propose a general algorithm to decide if the system is bound or not and which builds a complete simulation of the behaviour.

The paper is organised as follows. Section 2 presents the principles of the model, some notations for behavioural aspects and an example. Section 3 shows how to compute the global behaviour of such a system. It also describes our algorithm which calculates a view of the dynamic behaviour taking into account the contents of the mailboxes. Finally, related work is discussed and a conclusion finishes this presentation.

2   The Asynchronous Model

Our current work is based on some previous experiences about architectures and components. This work is rather at the specification level, since we are firstly interested in designing good architectures. The KORRIGAN model [12,11] is devoted to the structured formal specification of mixed systems through a model based on a hierarchy of views. It allows one to specify in a uniform and structured way both data types and behaviours using Symbolic Transitions Systems (or STS) and algebraic specifications. Symbolic Transition Systems are finite state machines with guards and variables in addition to traditional labels. The main interest with these systems is that (i) they avoid state explosion problems, and (ii) they define equivalence classes (one per state) and hence strongly relate the behavioural and the algebraic representations of a data type. STS may be related to Statecharts [17] but they are simpler and stricter on the semantic side. KORRIGAN is relevant to describe reusable components, architectures and communication schemes. The Graphic Abstract data Type model [31] improves the KORRIGAN model on specification method and verification. It proposes a general way to prove properties for the system which is also successful to prove temporal logic properties. The technique [30,5] uses the synchronous product of STS and first-order logic to write temporal properties.

In this paper we reused some principles coming from our previous work: component, architecture, symbolic state machine and the synchronous product. Note that in our previous work we take into account full description of component and system with abstract data types. But here we are mainly interested in behavioural descriptions and we avoid full data type descriptions. However sometimes we need guards in the state machine descriptions.

As an example we model a simple example with four concurrent components, a previous version with synchronous communications is [28]. This is a part of a flight seat reservation system with a component for the seat reservation, one for simulating the bank, one for the flight company and a last one for the client. The client gives its account number when he requests a seat to the counter. The counter asks the company to know if there is a seat. This may fail or succeed, in this last case the seat reservation orders the price to the bank. The order may fail or if it succeeds then the counter prints a ticket and the company books the reservation.

2.1   Component Principles

Strictly speaking we model types of component rather than components but this has no consequence on our current discussion. Another common choice is to consider atomic components and to define complex components as an architecture of asynchronously communicating subcomponents.

Asynchronous communication distinguishes message sending and its execution. If `op` is an operation call we note `>op` the message sending and `op>` its execution. The emitter does not memorize messages; this is done by the receiver in a specific buffer. This buffer acts as an asynchronous channel but it is part of the component as for an actor. This buffer or message queue contains the messages received by a component, it will be called a *mailbox* since no specific strategy is privileged. Sometimes operation may be executed but no receipt is needed: we call them autonomous operations and simply note them `op`. An `op` *autonomous operation* is an action which does not need a receipt to be executed. It takes into account the fact that a component may know sufficient information to trigger this action. A *receipt*, noted `>op`, denotes the receipt of a message in the mailbox. A specific guard [not fullMailBox] is used to ensure that the mailbox is not full. An *action*, `op>`, means an operation which will be triggered when the component receives the corresponding message receipt (`>op`). The fact that the component received the message is denoted by the guard [&op]. Message sending is done during the execution of an operation. The notation `op>` stands for the usual provided service and `>op` for the required service of many other component languages.

Graphically a component is a box with *input pins* corresponding to message receipts and *output pins* corresponding to message sending. Input pins (resp. output pins) are put on the left of the component (resp. on the right). An autonomous operation has only a right output pin, other operations have a left input pin (receipt) and a right output pin (action and sending). For example the bank is represented in the left part of Fig. 1. There is an operation for message receipt `>order` with two arguments: the account number of the client (`?i:Ident`) and the price of the ticket (`?p:Real`). The operations `fail` and `success` are autonomous. The different pins may be (or may not be) connected in a given architecture, it expresses the receipt of messages (on the left) or message sending (on the right).

The previous figure describes the interface part of the bank, we also take interest in the dynamic behaviours or protocols. Such a protocol is represented in the right part of Fig. 1. Note that each state has transition loops for message receipts, `>order` in the bank example. A sender does not block except if the buffer is full and nothing else is possible, this is also true for the receiver except if the message buffer is empty and without autonomous operation. Here we avoid the descriptions of the other components, see [32] for more details.

2.2   The Architecture Example

One key issue in designing good architectures is to separate the communications from the component to get more reusability. This has several consequences: to

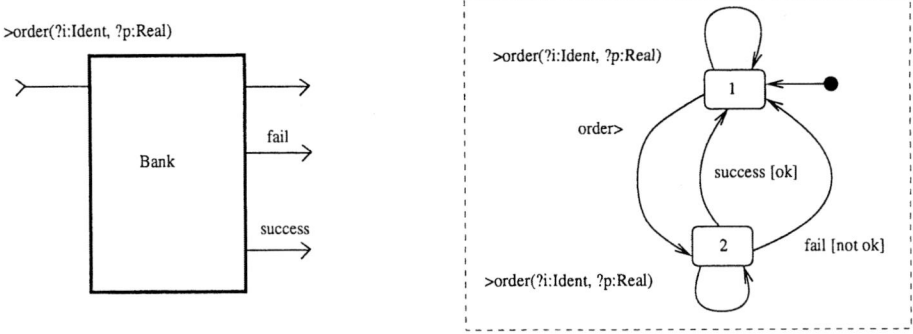

Fig. 1. The Bank Component and Its Dynamic Behaviour

have a local naming of operation per component and to define a glue language to denote communications in the architecture. Figure 2 represents the architecture of our flight reservation system. A message transmission is graphically denoted by a thin line from an output pin to an input pin. For example in Figure 2 the line from the checkPlace port of Company to the price port of Counter means that the checkPlace action sends a price message. Some pins like request> and book> for the company, fail for the counter or order> for the bank are not connected since they do not send messages in this configuration.

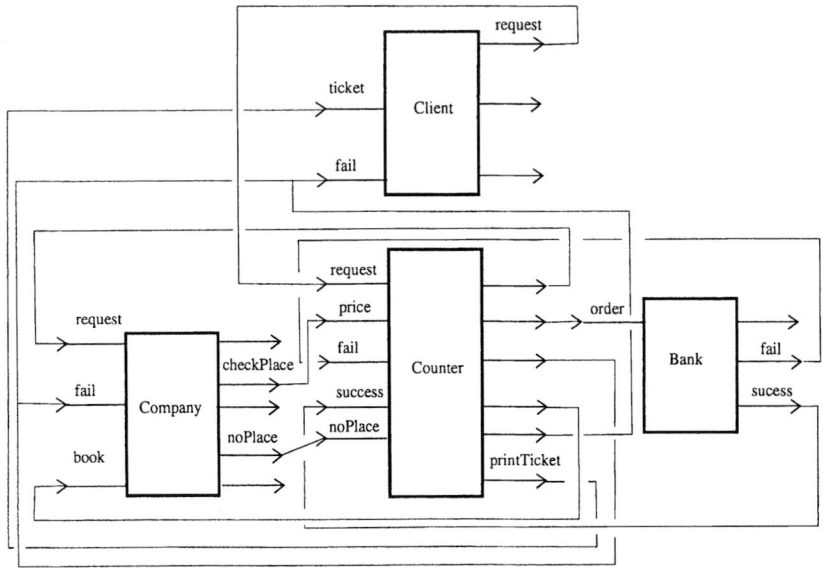

Fig. 2. The System Architecture

To simplify the figures we avoid the effective arguments and the guards of messages. Such an architecture may be transformed into a component, however nested components are not required in this example.

2.3   Communication Schemes

We provide some other communicating schemes. To *broadcast* a message a link is drawn from the emitter pin to the destination pins. *Multiple inputs* is done by linking one input pin with several output pins, it obviously denotes exclusive communications. In some cases we need to send messages, under some conditions, it is *conditional communication.* For example an advanced design of our architecture may connect the output pin request of the company to the input pins fail and success of the counter component. In this case we add the guards [noPlace] and [place] to control the exclusivity of the communication links. An architecture may mixed these different schemes, provided that some rules are checked. The use of guards on links provides dynamicity in communications which is an important feature of distributed computing. For instance in our example, guards in communications allows us to get a stable architecture relatively to the number of clients. The current behaviour of the counter serializes the client requests but it is possible to change it and to allow request interleaving.

2.4   Discussion and Implementation

We first briefly comment some other possible choices about our model. One first choice was to explicit receipt and action/emission. A finer approach would be to distinguish receipt, action and emission. In fact we think that emission or receipt need to be associated with action else we cannot get a right model where events result from some activities related to the components. Another point is about the association of receipts and actions in the dynamic behaviour. We have at least three main possibilities. The first is to sequentialize the message receipt >op and its execution op>, but this blocks the sender as with synchronous communication. A less blocking policy is to have a receipt loop on each source state for op>. A more liberal than the latter one, which is used here, is to receive a message in each state. Notes that these choices change neither our overall model nor our algorithms, it only impacts the dynamic behaviour of the atomic components.

We assume here safe communication but unsafe ones may be simply simulated by emission transition without synchronisation and reception. We have also an approach which provides synchronous communications without difficulty in a uniform context. Lastly, it is possible to take into account non-determinism in communication by the use of guards.

We implemented the flight reservation system in ProActive [1] which is an asynchronous language based on JAVA. Every atomic component is mapped to a ProActive component composed of an active object and some internal passive objects. An input pin of a component is easily transformed into a public method of the active objects with the correct name, type and parameters. For the output pin of a component we have to implement its actions and the message emissions.

For the action part, the output pin is mapped to the public method of the corresponding active object. The message sending from an output pin to an input pin is translated into a method call inside the process of the ProActive component associated to the receiver. These experimentations confirm the feasibility and the simplicity of such an implementation and give us a first view of translation rules from our component model to the ProActive language.

3   To Analyse the Global Behaviour

As explained in the introduction asynchronism generates more complex descriptions and behaviours. Generally a synchronous model does not work if it is embedded in an asynchronous communication framework, it must be redesigned carefully. It is often mandatory to provide a failure associated to each business action, for example in some previous designs we avoid `fail` for the company and for the client. Our analysis shows some wrong results (deadlocks, unbound buffers, ...) but it was definitively not prominent in the architectural design. Another example of problem was the occurrence of a deadlock in a bus controller due to a wrong choice in the buffer strategy. Thus once the components and the architecture have been designed, the problem is to get some confidence in the global behaviour. We present in this section one way to compute the global behaviour of the architecture and an example of analysis.

3.1   The Concurrent and Communicating Product

We first compute the global protocol from the component protocols and the architecture. There are several ways to express concurrency, synchronisation and communication. Mainly there are: process algebra expression, temporal logic formula or state machine. Our semantics of concurrency is based on the synchronous product of STS associated to the components. The synchronous product originating from [8] has been adapted to our STS [31]. Each state of the product of STS is a compound state which has two or more inner states corresponding to the component states. The transitions of the product are also compound in the way depicted in Fig. 3. To take into account the fact that a component may act asynchronously, we use a special nil transition noted -. A message sending, from the `foo` output pin to the `bar` input pin, is represented as a synchronisation between the emitter when it triggers `foo>` and the (buffer) receiver when it triggers `>bar`. The message is received in the mailbox of the receiver and asynchronously executed by the receiver. Thus the message sendings of the architecture are translated into synchronisations and expressed by the so-called *synchronous vector*.

One example of synchronisation concerns the emission of the `>price` message to the `counter` by the `checkPlace>` operation of the `company`. During this communication the first and the fourth component (the client and the bank) do nothing. This is a structured transition (- `checkPlace>` `>price` -) which starts from a structured state CL2, C2, C2 B1, which means `client` in state

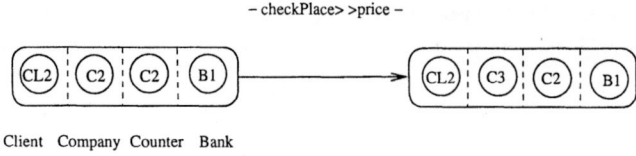

Fig. 3. Communication Representation

1, company in state 2, counter in state 2 and bank in state 1. In this example
(- checkPlace> >price -) is an element of the synchronous vector. The draw-
ing of the global behaviour, in a real case study, becomes too complex, but it can
be automatically computed from the component protocols and the architecture.

The synchronous vector collects the tuples of operation which are allowed to
synchronize. The general conformance rule is one output pin and one or more
input pins, and if an input pin receives more than one message a guard must
guaranty the exclusivity of the messages. There are several possible synchronisation rules to handle operations not in the synchronous vector (as in LOTOS
or CCS for example). Here we choose the same as in LOTOS [20] since we do
not have other synchronisation or communication.

From the architecture we built the synchronous vector with the following
rules. Basically a communication link from the output pin foo> to input pin
>bar leads to a tuple with foo> and >bar at the right place and - elsewhere.
Broadcasting simply extends this principle to more than one input pin. Multiple
inputs express a quantification over output pins, it is translated into several
broadcasting communications, one for each output pin. It must result in a legal
synchronous vector, we assume that guards on multiple inputs are exclusive. A
conditional communication is considered as multiple communication links with
guards.

3.2   Some Remarks

The global product is a symbolic machine however it may be complex. This is
partly due to the complex nature of asynchronous model. We obtain a system
with 48 states and 296 transitions from our architecture which has a rather small
size. The similar example with synchronous communication mode, see [28], has
nearly 10 states and 15 transitions. However we must precisely compare it with a
synchronous system simulating asynchronous communication. A quick analysis
shows that the number of states and transitions would be nearly the same. This
increases the need for analytic tools, preferably automatic tools.

Once we get the global behaviour it is a structured STS and it is not really adequate for tools like classic model-checkers. However several transformations may
be done to get a labelled transition system, see [30] for example. The general idea
is to simulate the STS choosing some limits for data types. Here we rather partially evaluate the guards, we only consider the [&op] and [not fullMailBox]
guards and the contents of mailboxes. The [&op] means that there is at least

one `>op` message in the mailbox and [not `fullMailBox`] checks if the mailbox if full or not. In our example it is obvious that some actions cannot be triggered since the corresponding message has not been received. Another interesting fact is about the size of the mailboxes, it must be bound or not.

We think that it is better to define several dedicated algorithms to increase the reusability by allowing the composition of analyses. A first algorithm, called the `width` algorithm, produces a simulation of the system taking into account fixed capacity mailboxes. To handle unbound mailboxes is more subtle, this is the goal of the `bound` algorithm. To have both, fixed capacity mailboxes and unbound mailboxes, may be done in two ways. The first is to process the `split` algorithm after a `bound` analysis. The `split` algorithm duplicates the states with fixed capacity mailboxes and the edges starting from these states. The second way is to define a specific algorithm mixing the `bound` and the `split` algorithms. Since the most original algorithm is the `bound` one we avoid a comprehensive discussion about the `width` and the `split` algorithms.

3.3   The Bound Analysis

We have designed a `bound` algorithm which is able to simulate the behaviour coping with unbound mailboxes. The algorithm searches in the dynamic system and computes the states with their mailbox contents. When a mailbox has a possible infinite contents a star is put to avoid the construction of an infinite set of states. We have experimented several examples and the different experimentations are based on dictionaries which memorizes the number of received messages.

The Data Structures. We briefly give a look at the data structures used to represent the dynamic behaviour of our systems. These data structures are described with a UML class diagram in Fig. 4, but we avoid some specialisations and constraints to do not overload too much the diagram. Simple states are simply identifiers, we have also structured states, both are organised along a composite pattern. A simple transition is a source state, a target state, a label plus various parameters, we also structured them along a composite pattern manner. The `ATransition` class describes three kinds of transition labels: `autonomous` (A), `receipt` (R) and `action/emission` (E). These transitions have mailboxes in their source and target states. A labelled transition system is a set of simple states, and a list of simple transitions. A structured system is compound from structured states and structured transitions. The `AGATSystem` class defines structured labelled systems where transitions are compound from `ATransition` instances. The `AGATSystem` class is used to represent the dynamic behaviour of our architecture and it is the input and the output data structure of the `bound` algorithm. The input `AGATSystem` results from the synchronous product, as described in Section 3.1, and has empty mailboxes. It seems possible to have a general `Mailbox` class which may be specialised to code any specific buffer strategy. However our actual algorithm only deals with dictionaries of the number of received messages.

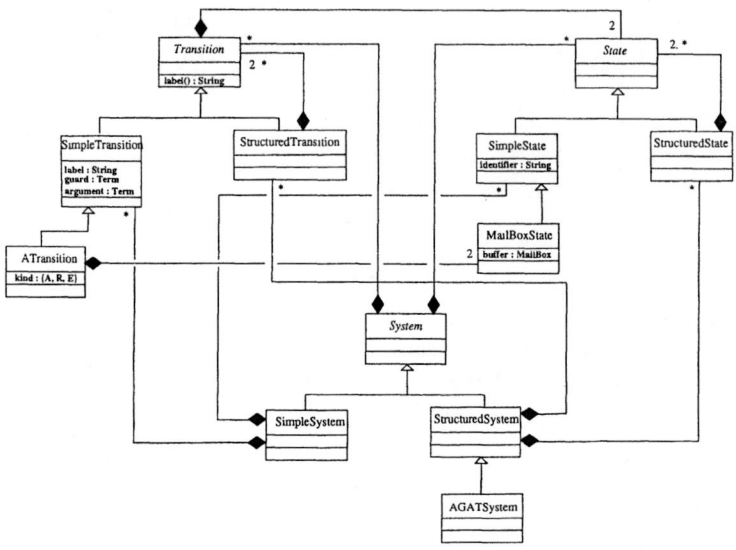

Fig. 4. The UML Class Diagram for Structured STS

The Algorithm. The goal of the bound algorithm is to compute the complete simulation of a structured system and to put * when the mailbox capacity becomes unbound. In the algorithm page 1431: [,] are lists, (,) tuples, and <- assignments. The algorithm takes as input a self:AGATSystem and produces another AGATSytem instance with the labels of the input system and the contents of the mailboxes. Mailboxes are dictionaries counting the number of received messages, it may contain star which represents an infinite number of messages. A mailbox overlaps another one if the former has the same values except some stars. The algorithm ensures the following invariant: *for all label of self, and for all reachable mailbox contents, it exists a single output state with the same state label and a mailbox which is the same or an overlapping one.* In other words it computes a finite accessibility graph associated to the input system. Basically this algorithm visits the state, the listState contains the new states to visit. The history and listHistory are variables used to detect cycles in the input system. The history variable denotes the list of visited states from the initial one to currentState. newState denotes a reachable label with a new mailbox contents. There are four exclusive cases. (i) newState already exists in the current result or it exists an overlapping state (overlap function); in this case we simply add a new transition. (ii) newState exists in history but with a lesser mailbox contents (superior function), in this case we have a cycle and we must propagate stars in the graph. propagateStar propagates stars and also rebuilds the graph since to add stars may collapse several existing states. (iii) if there is no cycle there may be existing states in the current result which are overlapped by newState. In this case we consider one of them and we propagate stars and collapse states as in the previous case. (iv) the last case is the simplest since it adds the new state and a new transition in the resulting graph.

```
BEGIN
listState <- [initial of self]                          # list of states to visit
historyList <- [[ ]]
history <- [ ]
newAGAT <- init the resulting AGAT
WHILE listState != empty DO                              # main loop on states to visit
  currentState <- first listState                       # current state of newAGAT
  stateLabel <- identifier(currentState)
  mailbox <- buffer(currentState)
  history <- add currentState in historyList.pop()
  listNeighbours <- neighbours of stateLabel in self
  WHILE listNeighbours != empty DO                       # visit the neighbours
      transition <- listNeighbours.pop()                # of the currentState
      IF transition is possible from mailbox THEN
          newMailBox <- apply transition to mailbox
          target <- target(transition)
          label <- label(transition)
          newState <- createState(target, newMailBox)
          IF newState already exists in newAGAT          # the state already exists
             THEN
             newAGAT.addTransition(label, currentState, newState)
          ELSE
             config <- find the mailbox <= newMailBox
                                    in history           # uses the superior function
          IF config exists
             THEN
             indices <- newMailBox.dicoIndices(config)
             newAGAT.addTransition(label, currentState, config)
             removeStates <- newAGAT.propagateStar(newState, indices)
             removeStates from history, listHistory, listState
          ELSE
             config <- newAGAT.findInf(newState)         # finds  an overlapped state
             IF  config exists
                 THEN
                 newAGAT.addTransition(label, currentState, config)
                 config.copyNotOmega(newTable)
                 removeStates <- newAGAT.propagateStar(newState, newTable.findOmega())
                 removeStates from history, listHistory, listState
                 IF not config in listState
                     THEN
                     add newState in listState
                     add newState in historyList
                 ENDIF
             ELSE
                 newAGAT.addState(newState)                   # simple addition
                 newAGAT.addTransition(label, currentState, newState)
                 add newState in listState
                 add newState in historyList
             ENDIF                                        # overlapped config exists
          ENDIF                                           # config exists in history
      ENDIF                                               # newState exist
      ENDIF                                               # transition
      remove currentState from listState
  ENDWHILE                                                # listNeighbours
ENDWHILE
END
```

Careful attention must be paid in already existing states and loops which complicates a little the management of histories. This algorithm needs to define several operations to compare mailboxes, mainly the overlap and the superior functions.

- overlap(d1, d2): d1 != d2 and for all msg, d1[msg] = * or d1[msg] = d2[msg]
- superior(d1, d2): d1 != d2 and for all msg, d1[msg] => d2[msg]

where d[msg] is the number of received messages of name msg in the d dictionary.

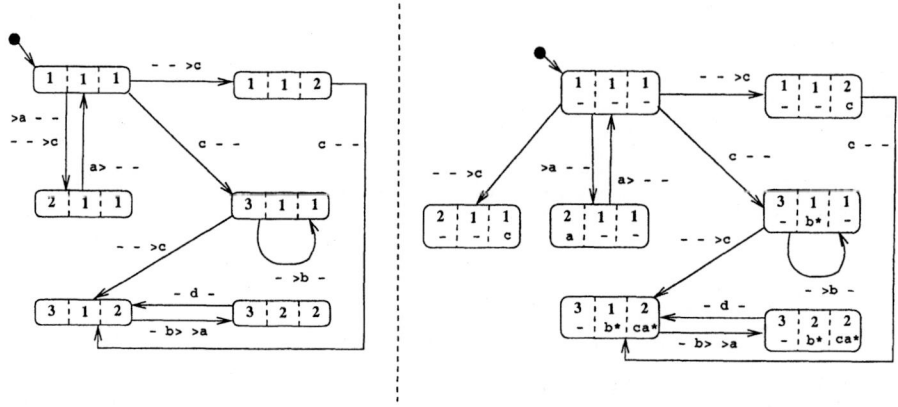

Fig. 5. A Fictitious AGATSystem Example and its Resulting Analysis

Application Examples. We have processed several examples of protocols, communication patterns, and some simple applications. The bound algorithm gives some relevant informations about the dynamic behaviour and helps to improve architectural design.

A fictitious example is described in Fig. 5 and the result shows the mailbox contents which are dictionaries of the number of received messages. It demonstrates a deadlock in state $(2,1,1)$ after the receipt of a c message on the third component. States $(3,1,1)$, $(3,1,2)$ and $(3,2,2)$ have stars in their mailboxes since they are parts of cycles in the graph (a loop and a 2-states cycle) which accumulate receipts. Figure 6 shows the simulation of the flight reservation system with dictionaries of messages. In this figure a state is labelled by the state labels of the components and each line describes the content of the mailbox component. Now the system is reduced to 22 states and 31 transitions and represents the global behaviour of the system in a more concise form. It also shows that we can optimise the data structure for buffers since we have at most two messages in each buffer. In this example the result is simpler in terms of state and transition, that is not always the case. However the bound algorithm simplifies the global behaviour in the sense that it removes some impossible transitions and it provides a compact description for infinite mailboxes.

Note that in this simulation we have only one client, then it is important to extend it to any number of clients. Of course it is possible to compute this simulation when the maximum number of client is known. For example with 3 clients we get a global system with 192 states and 2048 transitions, the bound analysis gives a result with 1174 states and 3809 transitions. But if the maximum number of clients is not known our current approach is not able to compute the global behaviour of the system. In this case one solution is to extend our symbolic machines to take into account n-ary state and transition. Another way would be to use an algebraic or a temporal logic description of the dynamic behaviour. This is a point which needs future researches.

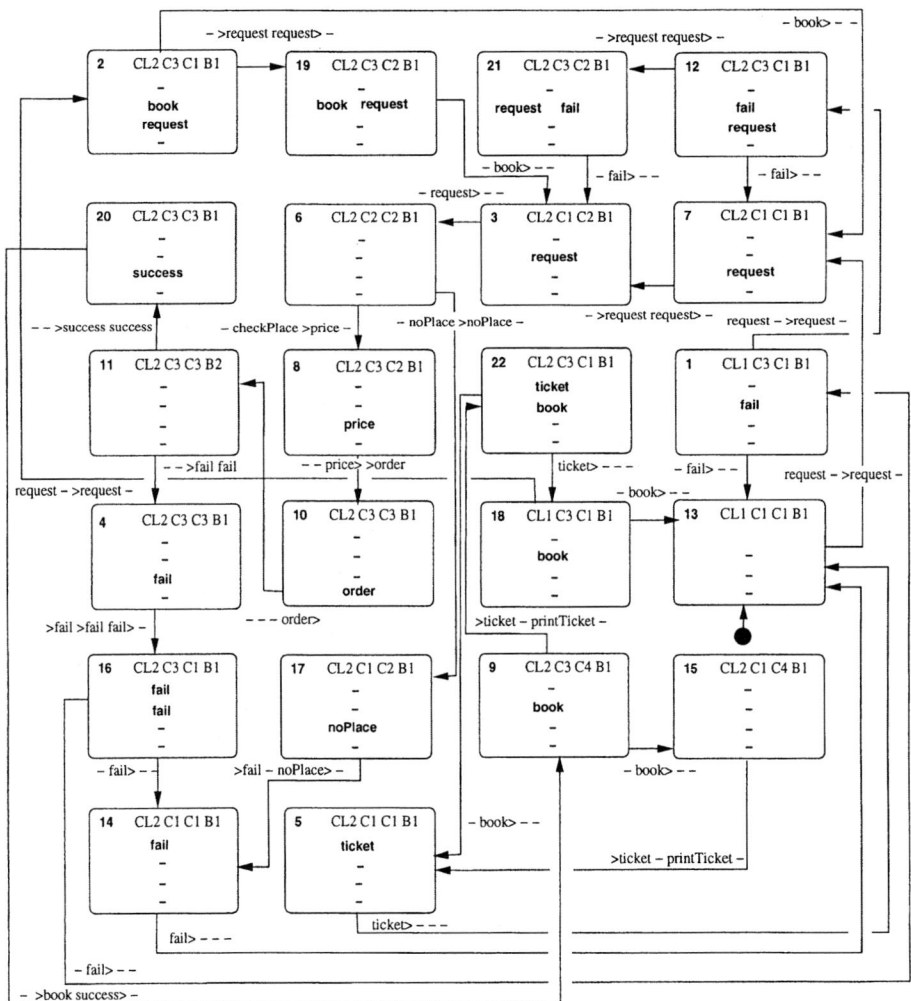

Fig. 6. The Dynamic Behaviour: Client × Company × Counter × Bank

The datas and the algorithm have been implemented in PYTHON [24] and also in JAVA. Two different versions of the algorithm (a breadth-first and a depth-first traversal) have been checked. We are currently proving the algorithm and analysing its complexity. At first glance the space complexity is the size of the resulting graph which is $O(n \times m \times (max + 1)^{\#msg})$, where n is the maximum number of edges, m the number of states of the input system, max is the maximum capacity of the bound mailboxes and $\#msg$ the number of operation receipts. The time complexity is lesser than $O(n \times m^2 \times (max + 1)^{2\#msg})$. We expect to improve efficiency, one related and feasible optimisation is to compute directly this analysis from the architecture without calculating explicitly the global product as in [19].

4   Related Work

Of course some analysis may be conducted using Petri Net tools, model-checkers, or other automata related tools. Generally our systems are not adequate for this and a preliminary translation is needed. However the main reason to try another way is that we have structured systems with data types and guards. Thus we need a powerful approach taking into account the full description of the system. From this powerful approach it seems relevant to propose more specific but automatic tools. Our approach computes all the mailbox contents without hypothesis on the arrival rate of events. To the contrary queuing networks and various stochastic techniques are able to calculate the average size of buffers coping with message probabilities.

Our component and architecture description is related to architectural description languages (ADL), see [25] for a good survey. We have atomic and complex components with interfaces and dynamic behaviours. Our approach gives a way to specify mixed systems *i.e.* with both full data types and dynamic behaviours. Here we only present a graphical representation of the architectural description language, this is not generally sufficient for automatic processing and full code generation. A main difference is the use of asynchronous communications while most of the time ADLs promotes synchronous communications.

In [14] the authors proposes rewriting logic as an executable specification formalism for protocols. Rewriting logic is able to model object-oriented message passing, various concurrency mode and reflective aspects. They use the Maude rewrite engine to analyse all configurations of a system. However, as with model-checking, this works well if the system configuration is finite. The authors improve this with the narrowing technique which allows to start the analysis with several initial states. We have a less flexible approach which may be embedded into rewriting logic. But it is also more readable and close to programming practice. In this context we have also experimented the use of provers (LP [30] and PVS [5]) and an extension of the CTL* logic with data types.

At this stage it is interesting to compare our approach with WRIGHT [7,6]. WRIGHT is a formal architectural description language with first class components and connectors. A component has a set of ports and a behaviour part. A connector defines a set of roles and a glue specification. Roles are expected to describe the local behaviour of the interacting parts. The glue describes how the local activities of the different parts are coordinated. The semantics of these constructions is defined by a translation into CSP. This has the advantages to get effective model checking for CSP and related work about behavioural re-finement. However, most of these verifications are limited by the state explosion problem and consider simple data types. WRIGHT proposes a deep analysis about automatic checking for architectural languages. It allows connector consistency, configuror consistency, and attachment consistency using mainly techniques to prove deadlock freedom and behavioural refinement. We improve readability by graphic notations, this is important for large scale applications. In our approach we consider both dynamic and functional properties not only dynamic properties with restricted data types. This is a first important difference but others are the use of symbolic transitions systems and asynchronous communications.

The use of Petri Net and the reachability/coverability algorithms [26] may solve our mailbox contents analysis, but it needs, at least, a translation into the Petri Net world. Our algorithm is different on several point: we have abstract buffers (not only marks), we have a complete simulation (all the states of the result are reachable), and we do not compute a tree but directly the reachability graph. We have an algorithm, limited to our special case, which represents the reachability graph, even if the system is not bound, using stars as in the coverability algorithm.

Our current work is dedicated to the analysis of mailboxes in an asynchronous communicating context. It may help to detect some specific deadlocks but there are advanced work in this context [19,22]. The former presents a technique us-ing the CHAM formalism and operating at the architectural level. One of the major contributions is to prove deadlock freedom of a system without building a complete finite-state of it. [22] consider various synchronisation primitives and threading policies current in todays middlewares. They propose UML stereo-types with formal semantics using a process algebra. The deadlock detection is based on model-checking.

Model checking is a technique to verify automatically temporal properties of finite state systems. Tool examples are CADP, MEC, VIS, see [8,13] for more details. Model checking is useful to quickly prove deadlock or other related properties. The state explosion problem of model checking can be limited by using BDD coding. This technique is called *symbolic model checking*, although it does not address the worst-case complexity of the problem. In practice it is useful and allows the verification of very big systems with more than one million of states. It is possible to compute the set of the reachable states which verify some properties like: one >op must always occur before an op>. But it is more difficult to cope with guards like [not fullMailBox].

In [29] the authors propose a notion of stuckness, that is to eliminate pro-grams waiting to receive or trying to send messages in vain. That is a more formal but complementary work in the context of unsafe communications.

5   Conclusion

We provide an approach to design component and architecture with asyn-chronous communications and dynamic behaviours. To handle asynchronous communications we distinguish emission and receipt operations rather than the use of specific buffers to memorize messages. Our approach provides a uniform and formal way to express synchronous and asynchronous communications, it seems readable and close to software engineer practices. We show how to compute the global behaviour of an architecture and to represent it without lost of information. We propose an algorithm which simulates such a dynamic system and computes the reachable configurations of the mailboxes. The algorithm is able to decide if a mailbox has a bound size or not. The result may be used to verify the dynamic behaviour but also to optimise the architecture deployment. This also may be used as a general framework for other class of systems like actors, multi-agent, synchronous communication, or channel based communications. We have done sensible choices which are not too constraining and our current model is able to cope easily with extensions to unsafe and non-determinism of communications. This approach may be generalised on the mailbox policy.

One trend of future researches is to extend our approach to cope with other analysis, for example with guards in communications. Another one is to consider a variable number of components. These are important features to fit with more realistic systems.

References

1. ProActive. http://www-sop.inria.fr/oasis/ProActive/.
2. Franz Achermann and Oscar Nierstrasz. Applications = Components + Scripts – A Tour of Piccola. In Mehmet Aksit, editor, *Software Architectures and Component Technology*, pages 261–292. Kluwer, 2001.
3. Gul Agha. Concurrent Object-Oriented Programming. *Communication of the ACM*, 33(9):125–141, September 1990.
4. Gul Agha and Carl Hewitt. Concurrent programming using actors: Exploiting large-scale parallelism. In S. N. Maheshwari, editor, *Foundations of Software Technology and Theoretical Computer Science*, volume 206 of *Lecture Notes in Computer Science*, pages 19–40. Springer-Verlag, Berlin-Heidelberg-New York, 1985.
5. Michel Allemand and Jean-Claude Royer. Mixed Formal Specification with PVS. In *Proceedings of the 15th IPDPS 2002 Symposium, FMPPTA*. IEEE Computer Society, 2002.
6. Robert Allen, Remi Douence, and David Garlan. Specifying and Analyzing Dynamic Software Architectures. In *Proceedings of the 1998 Conference on Fundamental Approaches to Software Engineering (FASE'98)*, volume 1382 of *Lecture Notes in Computer Science*, pages 21–37. Springer-Verlag, 1998.
7. Robert Allen and David Garlan. A formal basis for architectural connection. *ACM Transactions on Software Engineering and Methodology*, 6(3):213–249, July 1997.
8. André Arnold. *Finite Transition Systems*. International Series in Computer Science. Prentice-Hall, 1994. ISBN 0-13-092990-5.
9. Denis Caromel. Object Based Concurrency: Ten Language Features to Achieve Reuse. In *Workshop on Object Based Concurrency and Reuse*, Utrecht, the Netherlands, June 1992. ECOOP'92.
10. Denis Caromel. Toward a method of object-oriented concurrent programming. *Communications of the ACM*, 36(9):90–102, September 1993.

11. Christine Choppy, Pascal Poizat, and Jean-Claude Royer. Formal Specification of Mixed Components with Korrigan. In *Proceedings of the 8th Asia-Pacific Software Engineering Conference, APSEC'2001*, pages 169–176. IEEE, 2001.
12. Christine Choppy, Pascal Poizat, and Jean-Claude Royer. Specification of Mixed Systems in KORRIGAN with the Support of a UML-Inspired Graphical Notation. In Heinrich Hussmann, editor, *Fundamental Approaches to Software Engineering. 4th International Conference, FASE 2001*, volume 2029 of *LNCS*, pages 124–139. Springer, 2001.
13. Edmund M. Clarke, Orna Grumberg, and David E. Long. Verification tools for finite-state concurrent systems. In *A Decade of concurrency – Reflections and Perspectives*, volume 603 of *Lecture Notes in Computer Science*. Springer Verlag, 1994.
14. Grit Denker, José Meseguer, and Carolyn L. Talcott. Protocol specification and analysis in Maude. In N. Heintze and J. Wing, editors, *Proceedings of Workshop on Formal Methods and Security Protocols, June 25, 1998, Indianapolis, Indiana*, 1998. http://www.cs.bell-labs.com/who/nch/fmsp/index.html.
15. Wolfgang Emmerich. Distributed component technologies and their software engineering implications. In *Proceedings of the 24th Conference on Software Engeneering (ICSE 02)*, pages 537–546. ACM Press, 2002.
16. Wolfgang Emmerich and Nima Kaveh. F2: Component technologies: Java beans, COM, CORBA, RMI, EJB and the CORBA component model. In Volker Gruhn, editor, *Proceedings of the Joint 8th European Software Engeneering Conference and 9th ACM SIGSOFT Symposium on the Foundation of Software Engeneering (ESEC/FSE-01)*, volume 26, 5 of *SOFTWARE ENGINEERING NOTES*, pages 311–312. ACM Press, 2001.
17. David Harel. Statecharts: A visual formulation for complex systems. *Science of Computer Programming*, 8(3):231–274, June 1987.
18. Kohei Honda and Mario Tokoro. An object calculus for synchronous communication. In Pierre America, editor, *European Conference on Object Oriented Programming (ECOOP'91)*, volume 512 of *Lecture Notes in Computer Science*, Geneva, Switzerland, 1991. Springer-Verlag.
19. Paola Inverardi, Alexander L. Wolf, and Daniel Yankelevich. Static checking of system behaviors using derived component assumptions. *ACM Transactions on Software Engineering and Methodology*, 9(3):239–272, July 2000.
20. ISO/IEC. LOTOS: A Formal Description Technique based on the Temporal Ordering of Observational Behaviour. ISO/IEC 8807, International Organization for Standardization, 1989.
21. Michael Jackson and Pamela Zave. Distributed feature composition: A virtual architecture for telecommunications services. *IEEE Transactions on Software Engineering*, 24(10):831–847, October 1998.
22. Nima Kaveh and Wolfgang Emmerich. Deadlock detection in distributed object systems. In Volker Gruhn, editor, *Proceedings of the Joint 8th European Software Engeneering Conference and 9th ACM SIGSOFT Symposium on the Foundation of Software Engeneering (ESEC/FSE-01)*, volume 26, 5 of *SOFTWARE ENGINEERING NOTES*, pages 44–51, New York, September 10–14 2001. ACM Press.
23. Leslie Lamport and Nancy Lynch. *Distributed Computing: Models and Methods*, pages 1156–1199. Elsevier Science Publishers, 1990.
24. Mark Lutz. *Programming Python*. O'Reilly & Associates, 1996.
25. Nenad Medvidovic and Richard N. Taylor. A classification and comparison framework for software architecture description languages. *IEEE Transactions on Software Engineering*, 26(1):70–93, 2000.

26. T. Murata. Petri nets: properties, analysis, and applications. *Proceedings of the IEEE*, 77(4):541–580, April 1989.
27. OMG. CORBA Component Model Specification, v3.0. Technical report, Object Management Group, 2002. www.omg.org/technology/documents/.
28. Liang Peng, Annya Romanczuk, and Jean-Claude Royer. A Translation of UML Components into Formal Specifications. In Theo D'Hondt, editor, *TOOLS East Europe 2002*, pp. 60–75. Kluwer Academic Publishers, 2003. ISBN: 1-4020-7428-X.
29. Sriram K. Rajamani and Jakob Rehof. Conformance checking for models of asynchronous message passing software. *Lecture Notes in Computer Science*, 2404:166–179, 2002.
30. Jean-Claude Royer. Formal Specification and Temporal Proof Techniques for Mixed Systems. In *Proceedings of the 15th IPDPS 2001 Symposium, FMPPTA*, San Francisco, USA, 2001. IEEE Computer Society.
31. Jean-Claude Royer. The GAT Approach to Specify Mixed Systems. *Informatica*, 27(1):89–103, 2003.
32. Jean-Claude Royer and Michael Xu. Analysing Mailboxes of Asynchronous Communicating Components. Technical Report 03-09, Ecoles des Mines de Nantes, 2003. http://www.emn.fr/x-info/jroyer.
33. T. Thorn. Programming languages for mobile code. *ACM Computing Surveys*, 29(3):213–239, September 1997.
34. Mike Wooldridge and P. Ciancarini. Agent-Oriented Software Engineering: The State of the Art. In P. Ciancarini and M. Wooldridge, editors, *First Int. Workshop on Agent-Oriented Software Engineering*, volume 1957 of *Lecture Notes in Computer Science*, pages 1–28. Springer-Verlag, Berlin, 2000.
35. Pamela Zave and Michael Jackson. A component-based approach to telecommunication software. *IEEE Software*, 15(5):70–78, 1998.

TUPI: Transformation from PIM to IDL

Teresa Nascimento, Thais Batista, and Nélio Cacho

Federal University of Rio Grande do Norte (UFRN)
Informatics Department (DIMAp)
Campus Universitario – Lagoa Nova
59072-970 – Natal-RN – Brazil
{teresa,thais}@ufrnet.br, neliocacho@ig.com.br

Abstract. In this work we present a tool that performs a transformation from a PIM (Platform Independent Model) to a PSM (Platform Specific Model) - expressed in CORBA IDL – according to the MDA (Model-Driven Architecture) specification. This tool, named TUPI (Transformation from PIM to IDL) is based on XML (eXtensible Markup Language). It receives a XMI (XML Metadata Interchange Format) file that contains a textual description of the application PIM model and makes a transformation, using conversion rules, to the IDL language. ArgoUML is used as a support tool to construct the PIM model and to produce the XMI file. PIM follows the syntax proposed by the UML profile to EDOC. The conversion rules (the PIM-IDL mapping) are described in XSLT (eXtensible StyleSheet Language Transformation) – a XML standard language to transformations. These rules are processed by TUPI to produce the CORBA IDL application description corresponding to the application PIM model.

1 Introduction

Middleware platforms have an important role in component-based development, providing an useful framework to the development of distributed applications. OMG (Object Management Group) has published specifications of middleware platforms and also has published a specification of a standard to support all systems lifecycle: MDA (Model Driven Architecture) [5]. MDA is a language, vendor and middleware independent approach that uses UML (Unified Modeling Language) [3] to build systems models.

System development using MDA separates the structure and behavior specification from the details of how the system uses the resources of the platform in which it will be executed. Thus, MDA allows to specify the system independently of the target platform - this specification is called PIM (Platform Independent Model). When a platform is chosen, the PIM model should be transformed into a particular platform model - this other specification is called PSM (Platform Specific Model).

This approach allows a single model to be mapped into multiple platforms models. It also allows the integration of different applications via the relationship

R. Meersman et al. (Eds.): CoopIS/DOA/ODBASE 2003, LNCS 2888, pp. 1439–1453, 2003.
© Springer-Verlag Berlin Heidelberg 2003

among their models. Since new platforms and technologies are always emerging, the use of MDA makes feasible the adaptation of the system to a new scenario.

In this work we present a tool - TUPI (Transformation from PIM to IDL) [1] - that does an automatic transformation from a PIM to the corresponding specification in CORBA IDL [10]. TUPI implements a conversion algorithm that does such transformation. The transformation is based on XML (eXtensible Markup Language) [2]. TUPI receives as input a XMI (XML Metadata Interchange Format) [7] file that contains the meta-model description of the PIM model. ArgoUML [9] is used to produce the PIM model. The PIM model follows the syntax proposed by the UML profile for EDOC [6]. The PIM-PSM conversion rules are described in XSLT (eXtensible StyleSheet Language Transformations) [11] and they produce a specific model to the CORBA platform represented in IDL (Interface Definition Language). The details of the mapping is the main focus of this work.

Without the support offered by an automatic tool such as TUPI, the mapping from a PIM model into the corresponding PSM is an error-prone task.

This paper is organized as follows. Section 2 briefly describes MDA and CORBA. Section 3 presents the mapping from PIM into CORBA IDL. Section 4 presents TUPI architecture and implementation. Section 5 contains a case study implemented using TUPI. Section 6 presents the final remarks.

2   MDA and CORBA

2.1   Model-Driven Architecture

MDA is an UML-based software modeling approach that defines guidelines to systems specifications, separating the system functionality specification from the specification of the implementation of that functionality in a specific platform.

The syntax of MDA is represented by UML diagrams and its semantics is represented by the OCL (Object Constraint Language) formal language.

MDA separates system models to create a coherent structure of these models and to represent the viewpoints of a system. A viewpoint is an abstraction to focus on a set of architectural concepts and structures. This architecture of models is essentially defined by three models: a computation independent model (CIM), a platform independent model (PIM) and a platform specific model (PSM).

CIM is a model of the computation independent viewpoint, that focuses on the system requirements. This model, also called domain model or business model, depicts the domain perspective, presenting the expected behavior of the system. It does not present details of the system structure.

PIM is a model of the platform independent viewpoint, that focuses on the system functionality, regardless the runtime platform. This model describes the computational components and their interactions that are the solution for the problem specified by the CIM model, in a platform-independent way.

PSM is a model of the platform specific viewpoint. It focuses on how the solutions presented by the platform independent viewpoint are implemented in a specific platform.

PSM is derived from PIM applying a model transformation. Figure 1 illustrates the MDA pattern and the transformation from a PIM to a PSM.

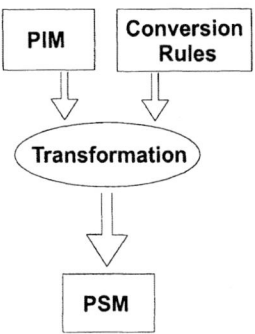

Fig. 1. MDA pattern

Figure 1 shows that the PIM model and the conversion rules are combined in the transformation phase to produce the PSM model. There are some types of PIM-PSM mapping in MDA:

- *Model Type mapping*: this mapping is a transformation of a model built using PIM language specific types to another one that uses specific types of the PSM language;
- *Model Instance mapping*: this mapping consists basically in identifying PIM elements that will be transformed into PSM particular concepts (the marks), given a chosen platform;
- *Combined Type and Instance mappings*: some mappings consist of a combination of the techniques described above.

2.2   Common Object Request Broker Architecture

CORBA (Common Object Request Broker Architecture) is a standard proposed by OMG that allows interoperability between applications in heterogeneous and distributed environment. CORBA determines the separation between object interface and object implementation. Object interface is described using the *Interface Definition Language (IDL)*. Object implementation can be done using a programming language with a binding to CORBA.

CORBA architecture is composed by a set of functional blocks that use the communication support of ORB (Obj ect Request Broker) - the element that coordinates the interaction between objects intercepting the client invocations and directing them to the appropriated server.

3   PIM-PSM Mapping

This section presents the mapping proposed by TUPI to transform a PIM into a PSM to the CORBA platform. This mapping is a *Model Type mapping*: the PIM specific types are transformed into specific types of the PSM model.

The types used to build the PIM model are specified in the UML profile for EDOC [6]. This profile aims to simplify the development of component based EDOC systems. It offers a modeling framework based on UML and in conformance with MDA. A sub-profile of this profile – ECA *(the Enterprise Collaboration Architecture)* – defines a concise structure to the definition o f PIMs, as proposed by the MDA.

The transformed PSM is expressed in IDL (Interface Definition Language) - the language used to describe the interface of CORBA objects.

3.1   PIM Syntax

The EDOC ECA specification defines a set of entities used to specify PIMs. The main elements are: ProcessComponent and Ports. A *ProcessComponent* represents a component that performs actions – it "does something".

ProcessComponents may have *PropertyDefinitions*. A *PropertyDefinition* defines a configuration parameter of the component, which can be set when the component is used.

The communication contract between *ProcessComponents* is realized via *Ports*. Therefore, a *Process Component* defines a set of ports. A *Port* defines a point of interaction between *ProcessComponents* and it is owned by these components. *FlowPorts, ProtocolPorts, MultiPorts and OperationPorts* are subtypes of *Port*. *Ports* have an important property named *direction*. This property can assume two values. The first is *initiates*, used when the port initiates the conversation sending the first message. The second one is *responds*, used when the port responds to the initial message in order to continue the conversation. The simplest form of a port is the *FlowPort*, which may send or receive a single data type. More complex interactions between components use a *ProtocolPort*, which refers to a *Protocol* - a complete "conversation" between components. A *Protocol* may optionally define who are the *InitiatingRole* and the *Responding-Role* of the conversation. A *MultiPort* is a grouping of ports whose actions are tied together. Information must be available on all sub-ports of the MultiPort for some action to occur within an attached component. An *OperationPort* defines a port that does a typical request/response operation and it allows *ProcessComponents* to represent both document-oriented (*FlowPort*) and method-oriented (*OperationPort*) subsystems. An *OperationPort* must contain exactly one Flow-Port with the direction set to "responds" and exactly one FlowPort with the direction set to "initiates".

These entities are modeled in UML as stereotypes of classes. For example, a *FlowPort* is modeled as a <FlowPort> stereotype of class. Some entities have a different representation. Data types manipulated by ports are modeled as a <Composite Data> stereotype of class. According to the EDOC ECA specification, a *Classifier* must be used to represent a *ProcessComponent*. In UML, a *Classifier* is the superclass of *Class, DataType, and Interface* - in this work we use class representation to model a *ProcessComponent* stereotyped as <ProcessComponent>.

An *OperationPort* is represented by an operation of the class (ProcessComponent or Protocol) that represents the owner of the port. The *FlowPort* that initiates the conversation will be the signature of the operation with each attribute of the port as a parameter of the operation. The *FlowPort* that have the property direction set to "responds" will be a return value for the operation. A *PropertyDefinition* is represented by an attribute of the *Protocol* class.

Ownerships are represented by an UML aggregation. In this way, a *Port* aggregates its *ProcessComponent or Protocol. MultiPort* aggregates its ports. Protocol aggregates its roles, *InitiatingRole or RespondingRole. ProtocolPorts* inherits the *Protocol* - using a UML generalization.

3.2   PSM Syntax

The entities that compose the syntax of IDL are: modules, interfaces, operations, attributes and exceptions.

Module is the element that groups another elements. An interface defines a set of operations provided by an object and its attributes. The declaration of attributes initiates with the keyword *attribute*. Attributes types can be: basic, built, templates or interfaces.

Figure 2 shows a piece of code that illustrates an example of an IDL interface with attributes and an operation.

```
module ServiceApp{
   interface User{

    //Attributes
      readonly attribute long code;
      attribute User spouse;
      attribute string phone;
      readonly attribute float credit;

    //Operations
      void EnhanceCredit(in float newCredit);
   };
```

Fig. 2. IDL Description

3.3   EDOC ECA PIM-IDL PSM Mapping

Basically, all entities of EDOC ECA specification are transformed by TUPI into an IDL interface, except *OperationPort* and *PropertyDefinition*. *OperationPorts*, as in the PIM model, are transformed into operations of the interface generated to their owner with the same signature, parameters and return value. *PropertyDefinitions* are transformed into attributes of the interface generated to their owner component, with the same type and initial values, if they are present.

PIM ports are transformed into IDL interfaces. The UML classes attributes and operations are mapped into attributes and operations of the IDL interface that represents the port. For each *FlowPort* of a multiple port a new interface is generated. For each sub-port of a protocol a new interface is generated. The *direction* property of a *FlowPort* - represented in UML as a taggedvalue of the class associated to the port - is transformed into an operation of the IDL interface of the port. The operation has no returned type. If the property value is "initiates", the operation is named *initiates* and has the *out* parameter that is of the same type of the data type manipulated by the port. Otherwise, if the property value is "responds", the operation is named *responds* and has the *in* parameter that is of the same type of the data type manipulated by the port. The data type manipulated by the port is mapped into an interface and each port that uses it includes an attribute of its type.

Table 1. EDOC ECA – IDL Mapping

EDOC ECA Element	IDL Element
ProcessComponent	interface with an attribute of the type of each port that it contains
PropertyDefinition	attribute of the interface of its owner component
FlowPort	interface + attribute of the interface of its owner component
FlowPort Direction	operation (initiates or responds) of the interface of the port
FlowPort Data Type	interface + an attribute of the interface of each port that uses it
MultiPort	interface + attribute of the interface of its owner component + atribute of this interface to each subport
OperationPort	operation of the interface of its owner component
Protocol	interface
ProtocolPort	interface with an attribute of the type of the protocol that it is connected
InitiatingRole / RespondingRole	interface with an attribute of each protocol port + attribute of the protocol interface that it participates

Protocols are also transformed into interfaces. *ProtocolPorts* are also transformed into IDL interfaces and contains an attribute of the type of the protocol that it is connnected. The UML class that represents the protocol roles *InitiatingRole* and *RespondingRole* are transformed into IDL interfaces with an attribute of the type of each ProtocolPort.

ProcessComponents are mapped into IDL interfaces. Each interface has an attribute of the type of each port that it contains. The UML attributes and operations are mapped into attributes and operations of the IDL interface that represents the component.

The UML classes relationships are mapped as follows. Aggregations are mapped into attributes. A port *Port1* associated to a component *Component1* produces an IDL interface named *Port1* and other IDL interface named *Component1*. The aggregation between two classes is transformed into an attribute of type *Port1* of the *Component1* interface. This transformation is done for ports of any type aggregated to a component, except the *OperationPort*. All sub-ports of a port are attributes of the owner IDL interface. The roles associated to a protocol that was transformed into interfaces are mapped into attributes of the protocol.

Table 1 presents a table that contains the summary of the mapping proposed by TUPI to PIM-PSM.

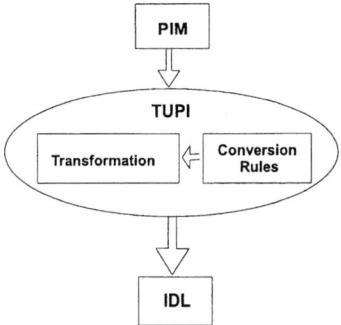

Fig. 3. TUPI Architecture

4   TUPI

The transformation done by TUPI follows the MDA pattern, as shown in Figure 3.

Initially the PIM model is built following the syntax of EDOC ECA specification. TUPI uses a modified version of ArgoUML to build the PIM model. ArgoUML was chosen because it is open source and it supports XMI (*XML Metadata Interchange*). XMI offers a standard format to import/export models. TUPI uses the UML model produced using ArgoUML and generates a textual representation of this model following the XMI standard. Thus, the conversion done by TUPI translates the XMI file elements - PIM elements - into IDL language elements according to the mapping described in section 3.3.

In order to do transformations based on XMI it is necessary to manipulate the structured data stored in a XMI document. In this work we adopt a XML transformation standard language - XSLT (*eXtensible StyleSheet Language*

Transformation). XSLT is a simple language used to declare the transformation rules that will be used to transform a XML document into another format. In this way, XSLT is used to specify the actions that should be executed when a given element is found in the input file.

In this work the XSLT language is used to create the conversion rules of the EDOC ECA-IDL mapping. The conversion rules basically indicate the IDL elements that should be generated when a given PIM element is found in the XMI file. A conversion software, developed in Java, receives as input a XMI file that contains the PIM description and produces the PSM in IDL using XSLT rules.

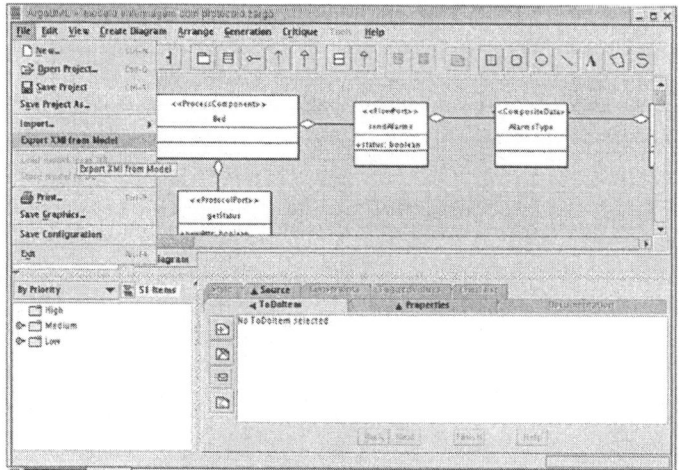

Fig. 4. Modified ArgoUML interface

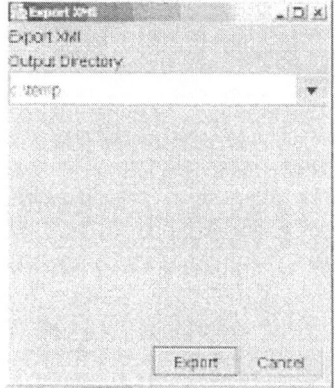

Fig. 5. XMI File Path Input Window

4.1   Producing the Metamodel

In order to support the creation of XMI files used by TUPI, ArgoUML has been modified. The modified version of ArgoUML is used in PIM modeling and also to obtain the PIM metamodel. Figure 4 illustrates an snapshot of the modified ArgoUML including the menu option to create XMI files.

When the menu "Export XMI from Model" is selected, a window is shown (Figure 5) to receive the complete path where the XMI file should be stored.

When the option "Export" is selected, an object of *ArgoUML XMIWriter* class is instantiated. This class produces a XMI output file. In the next step, the *gen()* method is invoked. This method writes in the specified file the XMI document corresponding to the PIM model. The next step realized by TUPI is to convert the metamodel into IDL interfaces.

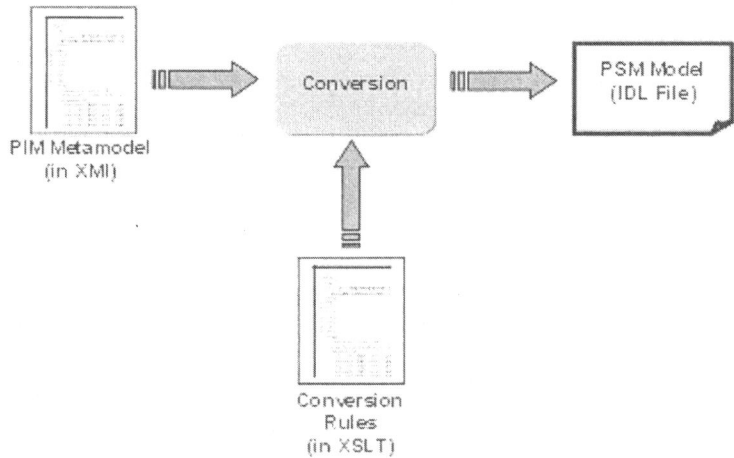

Fig. 6. TUPI Functionality

4.2   Converting the Metamodel in IDL

Figure 6 shows the functionality of TUPI to do the PIM-IDL transformation.

The conversion rules used in the PIM-IDL mapping are in the Conversion Rules module and are written in XSLT. This module analyses each element of the metamodel and determines the corresponding output. When the Conversion program is executed, a transformation module, implemented in Java, is invoked to start the conversion process. This module uses XML Java packages to implement the transformation of XML documents.

The basic idea of the transformations represented in XSLT is to determine a rule to each entity specified in the XMI file. We present now some XSLT rules defined by TUPI.

The rule illustrated in Figure 7 refers to the conversion of the *Founda-tion. Core. Class* XMI element that represents the PIM UML classes. This rule basically produces the interface signature that is composed by: the keyword *interface*, the interface name obtained in *Foundation. Core.ModelElement.name* (line 3), and the representation of their supertypes (applying the rule in line 4). The rule in line 7 executes the rules selected to the interface that is being analyzed.

```
1. <xsl:template match="Foundation.Core.Class">
2.   <xsl:text>interface </xsl:text>
3.   <xsl:value-of select="Foundation.Core.ModelElement.name"/>
4.   <xsl:call-template name="generalizacoes">
5.   </xsl:call-template>
6.   <xsl:text>{</xsl:text>
7.   <xsl:apply-templates>
8.   <xsl:text>};</xsl:text>
9. </xsl:template>
```

Fig. 7. Rules to Interface Signature

Figure 8 shows the rules to produce the attributes. In XMI they are *Founda-tion. Core.Attribute* elements. The reference of the attribute type is stored in the variable *tipo_atributo*. Line 4 contains the instruction that generates the class name or the data type name whose reference is stored in *tipo_atributo*.

```
1. <xsl:template match="Foundation.Core.Attribute">
2.   <xsl:text>attribute </xsl:text>
3.   <xsl:variable name = 'tipo_atributo' select=
4.   "Foundation.Core.StructuralFeature.type//@xmi.idref"/>
5.   <xsl:value-of select=" Foundation.Core.Class |
6.   Foundation.Core.DataType [@xmi.id = $tipo_atributo]"/>
7.   <xsl:value-of select = "Foundation.Core.ModelElement.name"/>
8.   <xsl:text>;</xsl:text>
9. </xsl:template>
```

Fig. 8. Rules to Attribute

Figure 9 shows how the operations are generated. From line 1 to line 4 the operation type is composed. Next, in line 5, the operation name is generated.

Figure 10 shows other rules that analyses the operation parameters. A XSLT loop instruction, *xsl:for-each*, analyses the parameters. Initially the parameter type is generated (in line 12) and next the parameter name is generated.

Figure 11 shows the instruction that generates ”,” after each parameter, if it is not the last parameter of the operation.

```
1. <xsl:template match="Foundation.Core.Operation">
2.   <xsl:variable name = 'tipo_operacao' select =
3.   "Foundation.Core.Parameter.type//@xmi.idref[../Foundation.Core.
Parameter/Foundation.Core.Parameter.kind/@xmi.value='return']"
/>
4.   <xsl:value-of select="Foundation.Core.Class |
Foundation.Core.DataType [@xmi.id = $tipo_operacao]"/>
5.   <xsl:value-of select="Foundation.Core.ModelElement.name"/>
```

Fig. 9. Rules to Operations

```
6.  <xsl:text> ( </xsl:text>
7.  <xsl:for-each select="Foundation.Core.Parameter
8.  [Foundation.Core.Parameter.kind/@xmi.value != 'return']">
9.  <xsl:value-of select="Foundation.Core.Parameter.kind/
10. @xmi.value"/>
11. <xsl:variable name = 'parameter_type' select=
12. "Foundation.Core.StructuralFeature.type//@xmi.idref"/>
13. <xsl:value-of select=" Foundation.Core.Class |
14.    Foundation.Core.DataType [@xmi.id = $parameter_type] "/>
15.    <xsl:value-of select=
16. "Foundation.Core.ModelElement.name"/>
17. </xsl:for-each>
```

Fig. 10. Rules to Operations – parameters

```
1. <xsl:if test="last() != position()">
2.   <xsl:text>, </xsl:text>
3. </xsl:if>
```

Fig. 11. Rules to Operations – parameters sequence

To the other entities, a set of similar rules is analyzed by the conversion module. This module produces the result of the PIM-IDL mapping corresponding to the input metamodel.

5   Case Study – The Patient Monitoring System

As a case study to test TUPI we model the Patient Monitoring System (PMSys) [4]. The system is composed by three components: *Bed, DataLog* and *Nurse*. The Bed component continuously checks vital information of a patient. When a vital data is out of range, an alarm message is emitted. The Nurse component receives messages emitted by the Bed components. The DataLog component records patient history.

The *Bed* component has two ports: *sendAlarms* and *getStatus*. The *DataLog* component has *sendData* and *getHistory* ports. The *Nurse* component has three ports: *sendHistory, sendQuery* and *getAlarms*.

In the PIM model two types of ports are used to express the relationship between the components: FlowPort and ProtocolPort. A FlowPort is used to connect the Bed and the Nurse components. A ProtocolPort is used to connect the Bed and the DataLog components and also to connect the DataLog and the Nurse components.

Figure 12 shows a part of the PMSys PIM model. It shows that FlowPorts are used to connect the Bed component to the Nurse component.

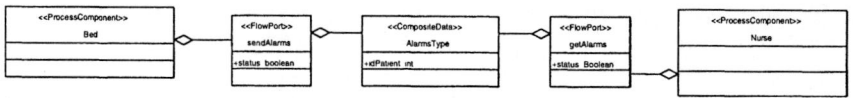

Fig. 12. FlowPort in PMSys

```
interface Bed{
    attribute sendAlarms att1;
        . . .
};
interface sendAlarms{
    attribute boolean status;
    void initiates (out AlarmsType value);
    attribute AlarmsType att2;
};
interface AlarmsType{
    attribute int IdPatient;
};
interface getAlarms{
    attribute Boolean status;
    void responds (in AlarmsType value);
    attribute AlarmsType att3;
};
interface Nurse{
    attribute getAlarms att4;
        . . .
};
```

Fig. 13. CORBA IDL code – Bed and Nurse

TUPI generates the corresponding CORBA IDL code (the PSM model). In this work we describe only some pieces of the IDL code produced by TUPI. Figure 13 shows the IDL description, generated by TUPI, corresponding to the PIM model illustrated in Figure 12 .

In the Bed interface and also in the Nurse interface only one attribute is included. The binding between the Bed and Nurse components is done by the sendAlarms and getAlarms interfaces. Such interfaces define *initiates* and *responds* methods and share the AlarmsType interface.

Figure 14 illustrates the use of a ProtocolPort to connect the Nurse and DataLog components. Figure 15 shows the mapping done by TUPI from the PIM model to CORBA IDL. The IDL contains only attributes to represent the functionality of the PIM ProtocolPort.

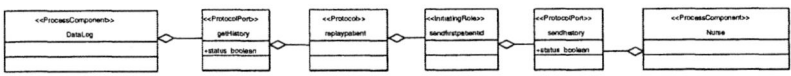

Fig. 14. ProtocolPort in PMSys

```
interface Nurse{
     attribute sendhistory att1;
          . . .
};
interface DataLog{
     attribute getHistory att2;
          . . .
};
interface getHistory{
     attribute boolean status;
     attribute replaypatient att3;
};
interface replaypatient{
     attribute sendfirstpatientid att4;
};
interface sendfirstpatientid{
     attribute sendhistory att5;
};
interface sendhistory{
     attribute boolean status;
};
```

Fig. 15. CORBA IDL code – DataLog and Nurse

Analyzing this case study we conclude that a lot of IDL code is produced. This is neither a limitation of the proposed TUPI's converting rules nor of the automatic mapping done by TUPI. This occurs due to the limitation of the CORBA IDL that does not address interconnection between components. Thus, the mapping of PIM models of other applications to CORBA IDL will present the same problem because the concept of ports - presented in PSM - does not have a corresponding concept in CORBA IDL.

6   Final Remarks

TUPI is an instantiation of the MDA approach to the automatic transformation from a platform independent model to a platform specific model. It generates interface definitions described in CORBA IDL. Although TUPI does not generate implementation code, the IDL description is an important part of the CORBA-based development. The interface definition is the basis for programmers to produce the implementation code.

The main challenge of implementing tools such as TUPI is to define the mapping algorithm. IDL is a declarative language with the concepts of interfaces, attributes and operations. These concepts should be used to represent all types of a PIM.

The case study illustrated in section 5 shows that the CORBA object model has some limitations that difficulties the mapping PIM-IDL. CORBA IDL has few constructions and UML has much more concepts. Therefore, some UML concepts, such as ports, are not directly supported by CORBA IDL.

Due to this limitation of CORBA IDL, that difficulties the mapping from architectural languages (such as UML) into CORBA, the CORBA CCM model defined a extension of CORBA IDL that includes concepts that are similar to those of architectural languages. In order to follow this improvement, TUPI is being extended to support the mapping from PIM to IDL CCM.

As a future work we intend to develop a mapping to other specific platforms such as EJB and COM.

TUPI is available for download at www.lcc.ufrn.br/ teresa/tupi/Tupi.html

References

1. Batista, T., Nascimento, T.: A tool to convert a PIM model into a CORBA IDL Specification. Abstract published at MDA Implementers Workshop. OMG, Orlando – FL (2003)
2. Birbek, M.: Professional XML (Programmer to Programmer). 2nd Edition. Wrox Press Inc. (2001)
3. Booch, G., Rumbaugh, J., Jacobson, I.: The Unified Modeling Language User Guide. Addison-Wesley. (1999)
4. Kramer, J., Magee, J. Dynamic Configuration for Distributed Systems. IEEE Transactions on Software Engineering, SE-11(4), (1985) 424–435
5. Miller, J., Mukerji, J.: Model-Driven Architecture – MDA. OMG. ormsc/2001-07-01. (2001) Available at www.omg.org/mda
6. OMG: UML Profile for Enterprise Distributed Object Computing Specification (EDOC). OMG Document ad/01-08-18, (2001).
7. OMG: XML Model Interchange (XMI) OMG Document ad/98-10-05, (1998).
8. Peltier, M., Belaunde, M.: From EDOC Components to CCM Components: A precise mapping specification. Lecture Notes in Computer Science (LNCS) 2306. (2002)

9. Ramirez, A., Vanpeperstraete, P., Rueckert, A., Odutola, K., Bennett, J., Tolke, L.: ArgoUML – a Tutorial and Reference Description (2000). Available at argouml.tigris.org/

10. Tari, Z., Bukhres, O.: Fundamentals of Distributed Object Systems – The CORBA perspective. John Wiley & Sons. (2001)

11. W3C: XSL Transformations Specification W3C. (1999). Available at www.w3.org/TR/xslt

Active Data

Richard Arthur, Virginia DiDomizio, and Louis Hoebel

GE Global Research Center, 1 Research Circle, Niskayuna, NY 12309
{Arthurr,DiDomizio,Hoebel}@research.ge.com

Abstract. In complex domains, certain problem-specific decompositions provide advantages over monolithic designs by enabling comprehension and specification of the design. In this paper we present an intuitive and tractable approach to reasoning over large and complex data sets. Our approach is based on Active Data, i.e., data as atomic objects that actively interact with environments. We describe our intuition about how this bottom-up approach improves designs confronting computational and conceptual complexity. We describe an application of the base Active Data concepts within the air traffic flow management domain and discuss implementation in this domain.

1 Introduction

Large and complex systems present at least two challenges in trying to apply advanced information systems to the underlying data. First is the computational complexity and related performance impacts of applying polynomial and, even worse, factorial or exponential algorithms to the reasoning process. We use reasoning here in its broadest sense to include such computational sub-disciplines as data mining, computed data updates, cognition and understanding as well as decision-making. The second challenge is that discovery and explanation for humans for decision-making or just simple understanding is a non-trivial task encompassing consideration of user interfaces (presentation), circumscription (domain of explanation and computation), human cognition, relevance and confidence of the reasoning and result. In many complex systems, the act of specification itself may be infeasible in creating the governing logic, exceptions, and design.

Data are widely distributed and come in a myriad of formats. Information changes with time, yet lives on in archives. Humans touch information and mix in opinion, perspective, and nuance of free text. Sources vary in confidence and bias. Storage can be unreliable, prioritized for availability, or require special access. Messages can be repeated, obfuscated, fabricated, and contradictory. Sources for query are created and removed. Data are now being generated at an exponentially increasing rate [14]. In short, data are becoming intractable to digest and store, and more importantly human users require sophisticated tools for querying systems for the information they need.

As an example, we consider flow and congestion detection in the Air Traffic Management (ATM) domain. The complexity includes the number of flights per day (1000's), the number of potential intersections of flight trajectories as well as the

R. Meersman et al. (Eds.): CoopIS/DOA/ODBASE 2003, LNCS 2888, pp. 1454–1470, 2003.
© Springer-Verlag Berlin Heidelberg 2003

number of airports (100's) and the interaction and complexity of the ground-based operations, which includes scheduling of crews and equipment and gate constraints. The domain, in its entirety, includes several NP hard problems. Our examples will focus on just flight routing (the filed flight plan) and identification of congestion in air sectors for flights en-route from origin to destination.

Our approach to this problem is a bottom-up or data-driven approach. We avoid the top-down issues of central control and circumscription of action and explanation as these are both too hard to design and too costly computationally. The small and simple data approach provides an uncomplicated means of circumscription of what data sets are relevant (and considered) for both computation and explanation of results. The issues to consider are (1) whether the hidden complexity transfers to the approach we proposed and (2) what problem types are amenable to a general (monolithic or agent-based) approach as well as our Active Data approach.

2 Architecture, Data, and Agents

An agent architecture typically refers to design by functional decomposition (as opposed to a traditional monolithic design). That is, small, specialized, encapsulated programs (agents) provide services to other agents within a medium whereby a community is formed. Within the community, various agent types facilitate exchange such that they form the functional equivalence of the traditional monolithic system.

Agents provide explicit functionality like providing a weather report given a postal code, or provide a transient service like extracting precipitation information from a weather report agent and calculating a visibility code for a map-generation agent. Agents may post requests and capabilities to a global "blackboard" or communicate peer-to-peer. In either case, world-rules govern the basic allocation of resources, inter-agent communication, etc. Communication can be based on a language such as KQML[1] or a formal knowledge specification such as KIF[2]. Note that neither provides an architecture specification or a paradigm of action, control or reasoning. In any case, an internal representation and reasoning system for each domain may be required.

Active Data (AD) is an abstraction of an Agent Architecture, whereby the community is composed not of functional elements, but data elements. Notions may be introduced to the community and characterized. AD are then evaluated in the context of a problem space. Within the problem space, data have a context by which to essentially ponder their existence and carry out behaviors such as:

- Aggregating / abstracting based upon peer-data
- Combining with other data
- Alerting other data or known consumers
- Discovery of new information or information gaps
- Self-archival (or deletion)

---

[1] http://www.cs.umbc.edu/kqml
[2] http://www.cs.umbc.edu/kif

- Self-replication when "forking" conceptually
- Self-update with newer or higher fidelity information
- Resolution of conflicting information, self-repetition, etc.
- Manage exceptions / preferences per world-rules

The base instincts will be to validate truth, improve confidence and detail, and to inhabit an appropriate level of storage. Through such activity, we hypothesize improved storage efficiency, identification of gaps, repetition, and consolidation, leading to potential discoveries through the data themselves.

Additionally, Active Data will self-evaluate in a global context as expressed through constraints and values. Constraints may be based upon resource limitations (e.g. a telescope may be pointed at only one place at a time), temporal limitations (e.g. a package requires 3-5 days for delivery), or similar. Tuple representations and transformation grammars may be applied to guide enforcement of the constraints and evaluation [8].

Active Data differs from a high level definition of agents [4], in that agents have a design objective. AD has no objectives, goals or intentions. It does not have beliefs but does have a primitive notion of behavior. AD is immutable at the atomic level with respect to its data value and its (lack of) meaning. On the other hand, characterizing attributes such as Hyperdata (q.v.) of AD can be extremely dynamic.

Table 1. Active Data, Agents, and ATM comparisons

Type or *domain*	Attribute (w/computation and controls)	Environment interactions
Agents	Goals, intentions, beliefs (with methods on self)	Agent behaviors
Active Data	Data (value, immutable)	Data behaviors
Air Traffic Management	Trajectory (graph nodes, w/constraint propagation)	Sections; calculate times/distances

AD and Agents may share certain methods and behaviors, i.e., interfaces and interactions with the environment. The data (value) of AD can come from acts of composition, extraction, abstraction, etc. AD values are not transformable; it may only be deleted, stored or archived after it is removed from active memory. In Table 1 we look at the Agent and AD types and how AD is instantiated in the domain space of Air Traffic Management.

ATM trajectories are updated by constraint propagation (along the graph that represents the air space trajectory). Reasoning is done by the sector over the associated set of trajectory nodes. The ATM atomic Active Data element is the trajectory node associated with a particular sector.

We propose to infuse the data itself with the ability to monitor sources, make new connections, and finally to alert users and environments of new, interesting, relevant information. The activation of data will push many of the tasks of data amalgamation from the user or central-style reasoning system to the data itself. Data in the active system will be responsible for maintaining a constant level of search, propagation and integration. Additionally, data will be capable of some understanding of its relative importance, and will thus move itself to cold storage (if it is no longer needed) or will place alerts (if it is pertinent to a current query) as appropriate. This data-centric approach, where actions are pushed to individual data elements, is in contrast to other currently recognized approaches, e.g., Active Database Management Systems (ADBMS). Whereas in an ADBMS the system must behave at a base level as a DBMS[1] thus following database constructs, data locations, and query formats; our system releases each individual fact into the operating system, data interact according to people's initial profiles, and learn new queries as they form new connections. Additionally, the only similar data constructs are the initialized wrappers around each fact, our system does not require that each fact contain the same kind or amount of information.

2.1 Architecture

In order to accomplish the challenging goal of imbuing data with such capabilities, it is necessary to first create an environment in which ecology of data might exist. This backplane should be transparent to both the data and the users of the system, much as an operating system is transparent to the users of office applications. We first introduce some concepts.

2.1.1   Terms and Definitions

- *Active Data*: Data are the raw materials for all systems professing to act on information, knowledge or intelligence. Often we characterize data as a 'material' that must be gathered, mined, transmitted, analyzed, etc. that is – playing a passive role in the system. Systems, programs, crawlers, agents, and engines are terms for the entities that actively use CPU cycles to make things happen to and from the data. In the case of AD, we instead look to imbue these traditionally passive participants with the basic capabilities to survive in an ecosystem (*behaviors*):
  - o *Activity*: ability to gain resources (CPU, memory, bandwidth)
  - o *Communication*: ability to interact with other data
  - o *Mobility*: ability to change system and storage location

  While we do not literally mean to consider delegation in a strict sense – carried out by functional methods on an object – we pose the question of a conceptual model where this delegation is possible as a means of reducing complexity in managing vast, heterogeneous, multidimensional, multi-ontology data stores.

- *Metadata*: Meta is a prefix that in most information technology usages means "an underlying definition or description." Thus, metadata is a definition or description of data.[3] Typically, metadata is defined within a product or community to describe certain relevant and objective characteristics such as source, size (e.g., Kb or number of elements), or location.

---

[3] http://searchdatabase.techtarget.com/sDefinition/0,,sid13_gci212555,00.html

- *Hyperdata*: Unlike metadata, Hyperdata describe dimensional attributes of data beyond the objective. Examples may relate to your perspective of the data source's trustworthiness or bias, or belief to which you feel the data is true, fully detailed, or exposed as common knowledge. Note the changes in Hyperdata over time can be of particular interest.

- *Notion*: To refer to an absolutely generic *thing*, we use the term Notion. It is not a Fact, as it may not be true. It is not an Entity, as it may be an idea or collection. A Notion is quite simply a node in our model, which may correspond to any concept we like – true or false, singular or plural, general or specific. Examples of top-level notions include:

  o *Assumption*: A Notion of posed truth. E.g. *Flight 1234 is on time.*
  o *Goal*: A Notion of directional interest. E.g. *Least risky investment.*
  o *Hypothesis*: A Notion of explanation. E.g. *Rover ate the homework.*
  o *Event*: A Notion of occurrence. E.g. *Flight 1234 arrived at 1:10pm.*

- *Ontology*: An ontology is a specification of a conceptualization. That is, an ontology is a description (like a formal specification of a program) of the concepts and relationships that can exist for an agent or a community of agents.[4] Historically, ontologies have been the goal of large standards bodies seeking extensive, detailed models for problem spaces requiring a common taxonomy of vocabulary to allow matching, aggregation and abstraction.

2.2 Active Data Characteristics

As we delegate to the data, it should no longer need to be a simple row in a database return, or a simple noun phrase match in an online article with some static metadata attached. The data itself can take on many characteristics as it traverses the system. As a piece of Active Data moves about the system seeking validation or additional relevant information, information is gathered along several axes: truth, confidence, level of detail, public exposure, cache level/storage location, missing information, complementary information, refuting information, and time.

- *Complementary Information* – Information that supports the piece of Active Data. AD is trying to tell a complete story. Any information that it can identify that supports it is useful.

- *Refuting Information* – Information that refutes the piece of Active Data. Necessarily, the data will encounter information that refutes it. This does not mean it immediately discounts the original assumption. Instead, it might factor this refuting information into the total confidence value.

- *Missing Information* – Data that would make the story Active Data are compiling more complete for the user. Given that the AD is piecing together a complete story around this one fact for the user, the AD system can know what kind of information is missing from the complete data set, and could search appropriately.

---

[4] http://www-ksl.stanford.edu/kst/what-is-an-ontology.html

- *Truth* – Based on complementary, refuting, and missing information, how true or false the data believes itself to be. Independent of Confidence, Truth ranges from [-1,1] –1 is False, 1 is True. One can have a high confidence in a notion being false.

- *Confidence* – The degree to which the data is certain of its truth-value. This may be based upon history with the source, corroboration, and subjective measures. E.g. [0,1] 0 is uncertain, 1 is absolute confidence.

- *Cache Level/Storage Location* – Based on the users' profiles in the system, as well as the truth and confidence values, the Active Data will store itself in the appropriate cache system. Additionally, if the AD is false or not useful, it may destroy itself.

- *Time* – Each of the data elements have relevance over some period of time. Often the most interesting observations can be gathered from changes in these elements.

Given this more complete view of data, more complete query answers can be generated. Sources users have never explicitly queried can be included in the response, and sources that have low accuracy can be noted as such. Users will have a more complete view of the total data set.

Some problem characteristics that lend themselves to this paradigm include the data being:

- free of context, or context-introspective
- environment-aware
- locally representative and autonomous
- describable with a simple ontology
- composable into answers
- infeasible to comprehend or specify management in a monolithic paradigm
- opportunistic in forming relationships, aggregations, and value
- pruned from undesirable computations

2.3 Operating System for Data

A necessary construct to enable the abstraction of Active Data will be to codify and implement a control structure by which the elements will be managed. Operating systems reside between computer hardware and applications for two main purposes: to simplify implementation of applications and to efficiently use the hardware resources. That is, there are numerous tedious activities common to all applications that can be pushed into the background and effectively taken for granted by merit of running in the environment. Additionally, resources such as CPU cycles, memory, storage, and bandwidth require allocation control to fully exploit their capacity.

An operating system includes four Management Systems whose functions have important roles in an AD architecture:

- *Activity Manager* – provides resource scheduling for processes
  E.g., Start/End/Suspend/Resume/Abort
- *Communications Manager* – handles interoperations and communications between distinct processes or devices
  E.g.,, Open/Close/Send/Receive/Block/Confirm
- *Storage Manager* – interfaces between process memory and permanent file or structured storage
  E.g., Create/Insert/Free/Lock/Commit/Rollback/Query
- *Security Manager* – protects process boundaries and data access as well as assigns identity and role context
  E.g.,Authenticate/Authorize/Role/Virtual Machine

It is important to distinguish that abstractions of these services are taken for granted so that the designer of an Active Data system, like an application developer, has pervasive access to such capabilities.

These design features of an operating system will have direct parallels in the Active Data paradigm, where data:

- Are managed like processes (or threads)
- Manage persistent storage
- Communicate with each other
- Provide mechanisms for data integrity and access control.

The envisioned architecture should draw upon the rich past experience in the field of systems engineering.

In fact, Active Data should lend itself much more powerfully to a system based upon parallel, distributed, or peer-to-peer architectures in that there are highly delegated activities with very small barriers to start-up. Further, such a paradigm shift to handling individual data items as processes on such a fine level of granularity may require developing new methods of computing.

In Fig. 1 we can see a potential architecture for Active Data. Raw Data entering the system would be encapsulated to include requisite metadata and hyperdata. The data wrapper includes basic facts (date and time of collection, source, size, etc.) and preliminary conclusions (e.g., trust level of source, belief in accuracy, ontology-based classification). At this point, the marked-up data is released into the operating system where, over time, more basic facts are added and more definitive conclusions are drawn. Users would specify points of interest by *subscription* – these could be conceptual, spatio-temporal, etc. Then data would be activated by a Resource Scheduler based upon priorities presented by these points of interest.

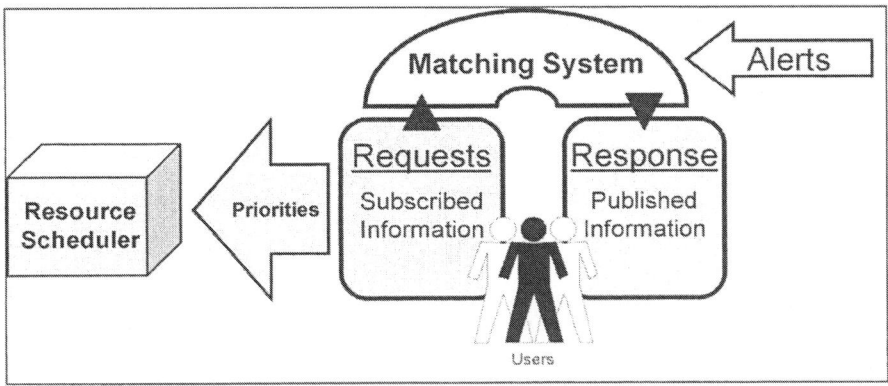

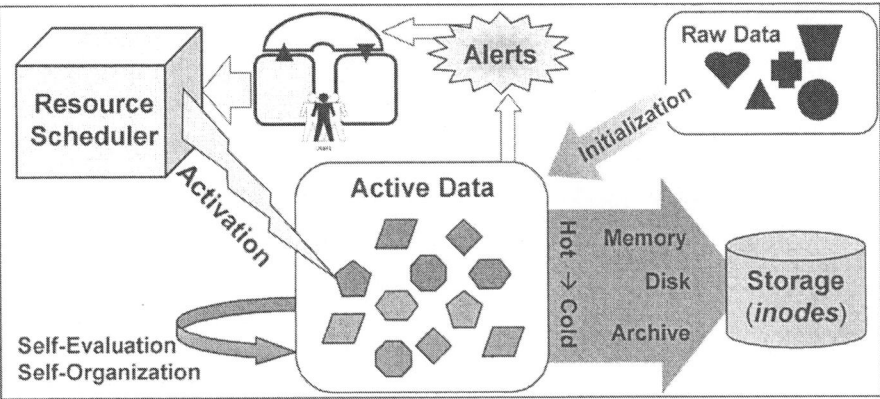

Fig. 1. Active Data Lifecycle: User Perspective (top) and Combined Operating System Perspective (bottom)

Activation would result in tasks such as those seen in Fig. 2. For example:

- *Resolution* would result from repeated, redundant or conflicting data.
- Two or more Active Data could result in a *Hypothesis, Aggregated* Notion, etc. Potentially creating new data (Aggregation) from multiple sources or suggesting potential actions and conclusions (Hypothesis) from single, multiple or context-sensitive sources.

These sorts of self-organizing and self-evaluation activities are driven by the priorities in the Resource Scheduler. In seeking other Active Data with which to compare, activate, etc., we introduce the concept of N-Dimensional Nearness (Figure3). As data moves through the operating system and new facts are generated and certainties are updated, data items are either reinforced as true and important, or are discredited. Once a data item has gained enough certainty to believe it has high relevance, it alerts the appropriate user. Conversely, if data is not queried, finds no matching or supporting data, or is proven false, the data will remove itself from the operating system, archiving itself to cold storage.

Self-evaluation will typically involve update to the hyperdata such as confidence, level of detail, or recency.

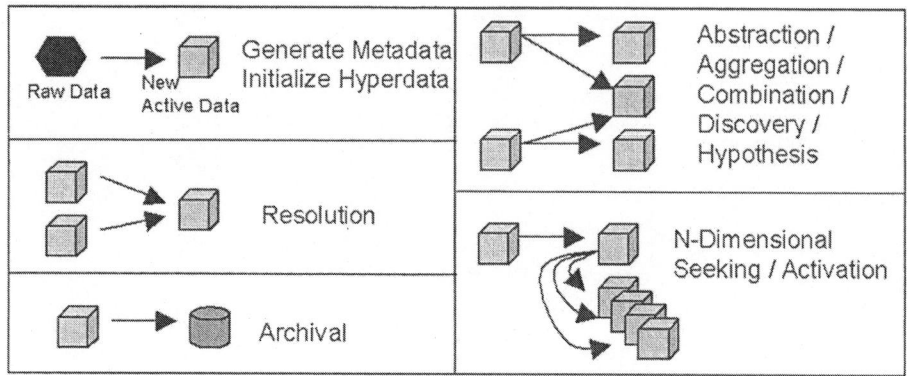

Fig. 2. Active Data Activities

An example of Resolution is in Fig. 2 would be a duplicate news report on election results from CNN and MSNBC. An aggregation may count instances such as "two flights were delayed 16-Oct-2002." An inferred hypothesis might be "The US President is in Paris" - based upon "Air Force One arrived in Paris" and "The US President is on Air Force One." The labels of these activities are not intended to have special or distinct meaning, but rather characterize a group of similar activities.

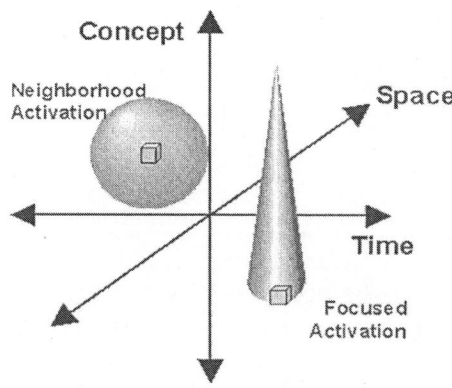

Fig. 3. N-Dimensional Nearness - Space, Time, and N Conceptual Dimensions.

Fig. 3 depicts a simplification of N-dimensional criteria. As the Resource Scheduler activates AD, these must then consider other AD in the contexts of these dimensions, whether intervals in time, spatial position, or in some sort of ontological categorization. A nearest neighbor search may manifest as a symmetrical range query (or

"Neighborhood Activation") or as a directional query across interval constraints in specified dimensions ("Focused Activation"). This abstraction allows us to explore Computational Geometry techniques as a mechanism for Activation [17].

While Neighborhood Activation will typically be abstract in nature due to multi-dimensionality, examples of Focused Activation might address one or more intervals such as:

Temporal: 8-10am, on Tuesdays, before 1990

Spatial: on I-95, in Bologna, near the Danube

or Conceptual: Military Operations, Fuel Stations

2.4 Multi-participant Model

When the domain must consider data sources such as free text news articles, data may be composed of opinions as well as factual statement. Additionally, systems built to manage data in the context of competitive edge may require deeper understanding of deliberate manipulation by the sources of data.

Truth is often independent of perception, yet perceptions can be important information in decision-making. The field of Game Theory addresses the interaction of decision-makers, based upon behavioral expectations and understanding their strategy. In the real world, we often do not have perfect information among the participants, nor will participants always act rationally, but some fundamentals in competitive behavior still apply, and in the context of data (active or not), the decision-maker with the newest, most accurate, most detailed data has the advantage.

This is particularly true when inferring or aggregating information based upon connections with proprietary information – producing a "window of opportunity" during which one participant possesses a superior position.   To evaluate such an opportunity, perception and awareness hyperdata need to be considered in the context of the data set. This means deduce information about what other participants know, whether they know you know or compounded again with confidence and detail over time. Clearly, already vast sums of data now include components that make things even more vast.

Active Data solves problems by making the data itself take on the characteristics of the participants and evaluate relative distance from an equilibrium position. Nash's Non-cooperative Equilibrium refers to a state where all participants are mutually satisfied with their expected result [16]. Applying these Game Theoretic approaches, we can impose a mathematical control to activate data to self-evaluate toward a steady state. In the absence of perfect information by all parties, a scoring distance could be formulated which would allow us to assess whether tactical advantage might be achieved, with appropriate notification to the human decision-maker.

We intend to measure the stability of such a system experimentally and address governing functions to manage equilibrium.

3 Active Data in Air Traffic Management

As was described above, Active Data has several key characteristics, including mobility, self-awareness, and operating system-like allocation ability. In this section, we describe how we can apply some of these AD characteristics to an Air Traffic Management (ATM) system. We are currently implementing some of these AD ideas within an ATM prototype system.

3.1 Air Traffic Management – Problem Description

Despite the drop in air traffic since September 11, 2001, it is predicted that by 2020, air traffic will not only return to its previous levels, but will, in fact, double[5].

The ATM problem, due to its size, complexity, and distributed nature, is not amenable to a centralized control solution. The current ATM system will be required to handle new security guidelines as well as this increase in flights. The US Federal Aviation Administration (FAA) and the Federal government have concluded that the current ATM will not be capable of handling this volume. The proposed new ATM system will address "...the four most troublesome airspace issues today: the rate of arrivals and departures; en route congestion; local weather; and en route severe weather."[6] In this paper, we present how Active Data would play into helping alleviate congestion before planes even depart.

The FAA has several goals in mind as it controls air traffic. Some of the factors to consider include: safety, volume, efficiency, and congestion management. These criteria are propagated to the airlines as each airline schedules flights to meet its passengers' requirements. Airlines themselves impose further requirements on their air traffic. For example, they want to deliver the maximum number of passengers safely to their destination along preferred trajectories. This entire set of requirements is further bounded by the space through which trajectories are flown.

Air space in North America is divided into zones, and then further divided into three-dimensional areas called sectors. Planes fly through sectors as they follow their flight plans. Flight plans are requested before take-off and contain waypoints the airplane will fly through en route to its destination. (See Fig. 4.)

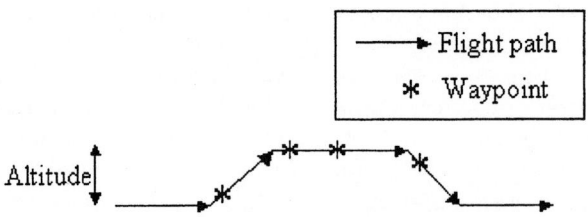

Fig. 4. Depiction of a typical flight path. The departure airport is Albany, NY, and the arrival airport is Memphis, TN. Waypoints between the endpoints are shown as asterisks.

---

[5] http://www.boeing.com/atm/background/longview.html
[6] http://www.aviationnow.com/content/ncof/ncf-n27.htm

Individual sectors have entry and exit points that planes must use as they come into or leave that air space. As can be imagined, each sector has properties such as open or closed air space, wind speed, and current weather conditions. (See Figure 5.)

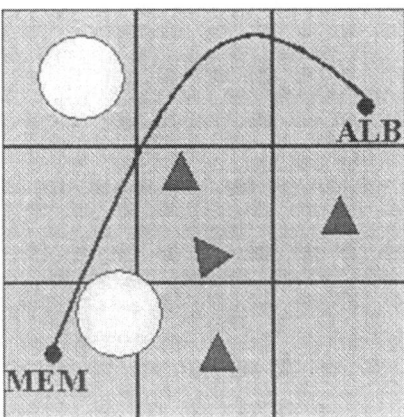

Fig. 5. The flight path in Figure 4 laid out over the different sectors. Each shaded square represents an individual sector. The black triangles represent flights currently en route (which may contribute to congestion in the individual sectors). The lightly shaded circles represent severe weather conditions in individual sectors and are typical of neighborhood activation, while the flight path is typical of focused activation.

Not only can the interior sector properties change over time, but also the sector boundaries themselves can change over time. Additionally, at any given time, flight plans must consider flights currently en route to their destinations. Based on these facts, rules about congestion are determined, a threshold number of planes are allowed through this air space, and flight plans are approved or adjusted.

The goal of our system is to take the current state of air traffic at a specific time (e.g., planes en route at 06:00 EST), and using historical flight data and current sector definitions, predict congestion in the next 4 hour time window, thus enabling congestion avoidance.

There are several factors to consider in determining congestion:

- The physical state of the air space (e.g., physical boundaries of the sector, or the location of closed zones within a sector)
- The changing condition of weather in an air space
- Flights currently en route
- Scheduled flights that requested and been added to routes through sectors

When scheduling a flight, there are several things to look at as well:

- Potential flight paths
- Weather impacts
- Other delays that flight will encounter

Given the number of sectors, and the individual conditions each sector manages, a central controller for ATM would have to maintain a vast amount of information and reason globally for each flight. The question is not simply "what flights will be in this sector?" Instead, the question involves understanding the potential delays for every other flight that may be in that sector (due to weather, or take-off delays or previous aircraft delays) as well as anything that may occur in that sector within the next four hours. This involves thousands of flights over all of the sectors, and requires a tremendous amount of reasoning every time the system checks for congestion. For example, consider delays by one flight in its first sector. This adds unusual delays to all of its following sectors, impacting every flight that will be in those sectors, and so on over the length of the delays that extend from there. This is obviously an unwieldy amount of data about which to reason centrally.

If we move to the Active Data architecture, however, most of the propagated effects of this information can be resolved locally. Thus, rather than manage this information from a central controller, the AD model will push the information and decision-making processes to the individual sectors, cutting down on the number of comparisons.

4 ATM Architecture

In considering the ATM system and congestion management, we have several types of objects:

Sectors
Sectors have boundaries as well as information about the physical space within the boundaries (weather or closed air space). Additionally, sectors contain information about flights currently en route to their destination and flights that have been assigned to fly through that sector within the upcoming four-hour window. Finally, sectors have definitions of congestion for their air space. These definitions may be simply a number of allowable flights, or may involve more complicated algorithms where weather and closed airspaces are included.

Subsectors
Sectors are divided into smaller components called subsectors. These portions of sectors have two properties: first they are the smallest unit at which congestion is defined, and second each sector is completely covered by non-overlapping subsectors.

Airplanes
Airplanes have requested and proposed flight information (such as departure time, arrival time, altitude, and air speed) as well as a representation of a proposed trajectory, or flight path.

Trajectories
Each flight path is described as a series of waypoints. An airplane requests a specific set of waypoints in its proposed flight plan, beginning with the departure airport, and

finishing with the destination airport. Straight-line segments join the waypoints. These segments may be wholly contained in a subsector or may cross two or more subsectors.

The main idea is to understand at what times there will be pieces of trajectories causing congestion in specific subsectors and sectors. In solving this problem, the smallest particle of data with which the system will deal is the amount of time a plane will be in a subsector. Below, we describe how aspects of solving the ATM congestion problem are simplified through using key attributes of Active Data. One can look at this as a non-cooperating zero sum game with each airline (flight) playing a strategy to get preferences (rewards) as it travels a preferred sector route.

Mobility
Perhaps the most obvious application of Active Data in ATM is mobility. While the objects are physically moving through the air space, here the active data interacts with the appropriate data in the AD operating system. These data are moving through the n-dimensional data space interacting with other data in its activation neighborhood (a sector) or within its focused activation area (a flight path).

A central question for the ATM system is this:

Is there congestion if this specific flight with this specific trajectory is added?

To answer this question, there are several actions the system and the data must take. The trajectory identifies which sectors and subsectors lie along its path as well as what times the aircraft will be within that subsector (focused activation). It is these time and space intersections of the flight plan within each sector that will be the AD. It is the job of each of these atomic pieces of data to operate appropriately within the context of the Sector (neighborhood activation) i.e., they must meet the weather constraints, not cause congestion, and not fly through restricted air space.

There are three possible cases for a trajectory segment to add itself to a subsector.

Case 1 – No Congestion. The trajectory path doesn't cause congestion and it adds itself to the subsector. In this case, the Active Data remains in that subsector, waiting for other flights to appear. If, as time passes, there is a case where congestion is caused by another trajectory segment, the set of AD reason together or bargain as described in the case below. Once the flight is en route, the AD moves itself to the en route queue, and finally removes itself from the system when the flight is complete. For example, in the figure below, Sector S has not yet reached its congestion-threshold. (It currently contains four trajectory segments, and given the restricted airspace and weather conditions, it can handle six trajectory segments.) Thus, when flight 3412 adds itself to Sector S, the AD, subsector, and Sector continue normal operations.

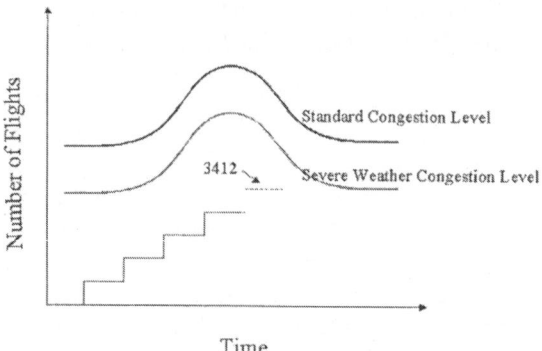

Fig. 6. Illustration of a sector where the congestion levels for both calm weather and severe storms have not been reached. The sector is able to add flight 3412 to the set of allowable flights.

Case 2 – Congestion is Reached. If a segment of the trajectory causes congestion, the AD works with other segments in that Sector context to identify the best solution. (Re-routing the newest addition to the sector may not be the preferred solution.) Once the re-routing plan is determined, the affected trajectory segments remove themselves from their current context and insert themselves into the new subsector. As illustrated in Fig. 7 below, Sector S is now congested – it contains 6 trajectory segments belonging to 6 independent airline flight paths. At this point, a trajectory attempts to add itself to Sector S, and the congestion threshold is exceeded. Each of the trajectory segments work together at this point to localize the perturbation to the ATM system. That is, we would prefer to localize the changes to flight plans and trajectories. Each trajectory segment investigates its preferred paths, the least global set of changes that is acceptable to the Sector contexts is identified, and the trajectory segments move themselves to the appropriate subsector environments.

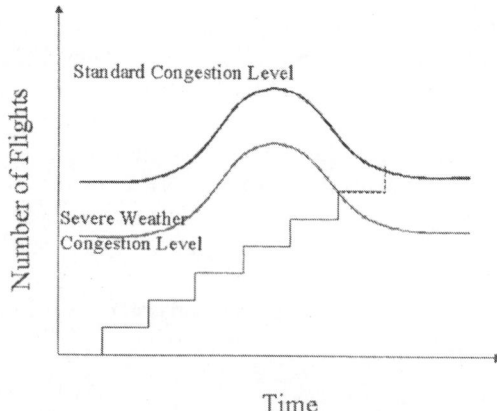

Fig. 7. Illustration of a sector where the congestion levels for both calm weather and severe storms have not been reached. The sector is not able to add flight 3412 to the set of allowable flights.

Case 3 – Context Constraint Violated. Congestion being reached within a subsector is merely a specific example of a Sector's constraints being violated. For example, weather or closed or restricted airspace may generate the need for segments to re-evaluate their appropriate subsector placement. Again, the Active Data segments within that Sector work to understand the optimal solution.

Self-Reasoning and Introspection

Another key attribute of Active Data is self-reasoning. As was discussed previously, AD is aware of its surrounding context, and is able to operate within that context. One example of this would be trajectory segments' reacting to weather conditions. Once a segment of the airplane trajectory is placed within a subsector, it must remain aware of the flow of weather in the system.

Weather conditions are represented in each subsector as a set of conditions in that three-dimensional volume. Air speed, storm conditions, and turbulence are examples of what is tracked. Obviously, severe weather storms follow their own trajectories through a series of subsectors. Trajectory segments reason not only about their current subsector's weather, but watch to see the path of a storm, and self-adjust their path as severe weather moves about the system.

4.1 Liveliness

As discussed previously, data has three main levels of existence in the AD system: hot, cold, and archived. Hot data is actively querying and interacting with its environment, cold data remains in memory, but is not actively queried during decisioning, and archived data needs to be retrieved to be included in the decision process. In the ATM problem, sectors are most interested in the flights that are nearest to departing, or the weather that is shortly going to affect the sector's capacity. A sector interested in understanding its immediate congestion characteristics would receive alerts from the hot data, or data concerning flights in an immediate timeframe. As the time window moves forward, the operating system will activate cold data, thus allowing querying to continue focusing on the most time-relevant data. Finally, as flights reach their destinations, they are archived.

5 Summary

We have introduced the concept of Active Data, a decentralized concept for a bottom-up approach to reasoning in large complex heterogeneous data environments. We have characterized Active Data and we have shown the basic differences to Agents. We believe this proactive approach leads to further research to address performance, security and subsequent considerations, all of which is beyond the scope of this paper. We also described an application domain, Air Traffic Management. Finally, we presented our initial implementation work in applying Active Data to that domain for prediction of air space congestion.

References

1. ACT-NET Consortium. The Active Database Management System Manifest: A Rule-base of ADBMS Features. *ACM Sigmod Record, 25(3)*, 40–49. 1996
2. Anderson, B.; Shasha, D. Persistent Linda: Linda + transactions + query processing. In J.P. Banatre and D. Le Metayer, editors, Research Directions in High-Level Parallel Programming Languages, number 57 in LNCS, pages 93–109. Springer, 1991.
3. Arthur, R.; Deitsch, A.; Stillman, J. Tachyon: A Constraint-Based Temporal Reasoning Model and Its Implementation. SIGART Bulletin 4:3, July 1993
4. Bradshaw, J. Software Agents . Cambridge, MA: The MIT Press , 1997.
5. Brooks, R. 1986. A Robust Layered Control System for a Mobile Robot. IEEE Journal of Robotics and Automation 2 (1): 14–23.
6. Brooks, R. Intelligence without representation. In Proceedings of the Workshop on the Foundations of Artificial Intelligence, June 1987.
7. Brooks, R. Intelligence without reason. In Proc. of IJCAI-91. Morgan Kaufmann, San Mateo, 1991.
8. Carriero, N.; Gelernter, D. Linda in Context, Comm. of the ACM, Vol 32, No. 4, 1989.
9. DiDomizio, V., Project Rainbow: Universal Querying of Distributed Databases, Thesis Rensselaer Polytechnic Institute , Troy NY 1998
10. DiDomizio, V.; Dixon III, W.; Epter, S.; Hoebel, L.; Oksoy, O.; Stillman, J.; Corman, J, inventors; Lockheed Martin Corporation, assignee. Method and system for universal querying of distributed databases. U.S patent 6,523,028. 2003 February 18. 21 p. Int. Cl7 G06F 17/30; A45T 9/11.
11. DiDomizio, V.; Dixon III, W.; Oksoy, O.; Lockheed Martin Corporation, Bethesda, MD, Method and system for importing database information,
    U.S patent 6,424,358 2002 July 23. 25 p. Int. Cl7 G06F 17/30.
12. Forrest, S. Emergent Computation. MIT Press, Cambridge, MA, 1991.
13. Forrest, S.; Mitchell, M. Relative Building Block Fitness and the Building Block Hypothesis. In Whitely, L. D., editor, Foundations of Genetic Algorithms 2. San Mateo: Morgan Kaufmann, 1993.
14. Hawking, S., The Universe in a Nutshell, Bantam Books, 2001.
15. Hofmeyr S.; Forrest, S. Architecture for an Artificial Immune System, submitted to Evolutionary Computation. 2000.
16. Nash, J. Non-cooperative games. Annals of Mathematics, 54: 286–295, 1951.
17. Preparata, F.; Shamos, M. Computational Geometry: An Introduction. Springer-Verlag, 19911

What Must (Not) Be Available Where?

Felix Bübl

imphar AG, Berlin, Germany
felix.buebl@imphar.com

Abstract. Arranging the distribution of data, objects or components is a critical task that can ultimately affect the performance, integrity and reliability of distributed system. This paper suggests to write down *what must (not) be available where* in order to reveal conflicting distribution requirements and to detect problems early on. Distribution requirements are expressed via a new notion of constraints: a context-based constraint (CoCon) can indirectly select its constrained elements according to their context. The context of an element characterizes the situation in which this element resides and is annotated via metadata. CoCons facilitate checking the compliance of a system or a model with distribution requirements during (re-)design, during (re-)configuration or at runtime. This paper focuses on validating UML models for compliance with distribution CoCons in order to take distribution requirements into account right from start of the development process.

1 Introduction

1.1 Recording Distribution Decisions

Up to now the rationale for distribution decisions is barely recorded during the design and development of software system. Instead, distribution is typically taken into account during implementation or deployment and is expressed directly in configuration files or in source code. But, the context for which a software system was designed changes continuously throughout its lifetime. In order to prevent the violation of distribution requirements when adapting a systems to new requirements, the distribution requirements must be written down. By using a formal language for expressing distribution requirements, a system can automatically be checked for whether it complies with these distribution requirements.

After distributed applications became popular and sophisticated in the 80s, over 100 *programming languages* specifically for *implementing* distributed applications were invented according to [2]. But hardly anyone took distribution into consideration already on the *design* level. In order to reveal conflicting distribution decisions and to detect problems early on, they should be written down and considered already in the model. Fixing them during implementation is much more expensive. Moreover, distribution requirements should be expressed in an *artefact-independent* way: it should be possible to check the system's *model* as well as its *source code* or its *configuration files* for compliance with distribution

R. Meersman et al. (Eds.): CoopIS/DOA/ODBASE 2003, LNCS 2888, pp. 1471–1487, 2003.

requirements without restating the distribution requirements for each artefact type. Artefact-independent expressions can be considered throughout the lifetime of a distributed system – they enable software development tools to detect the violation of distribution requirements automatically during (re-)design, (re-)configuration or at runtime.

This paper proposes to specify distribution requirements via constraints. For instance, one distribution constraint can express which element must (not) be allocated to which computer. An element can be an *object*, *data*, or *component*. This paper focuses on components. When applying the approach discussed here during modelling, please read 'element' as *model element* throughout the paper. However, keeping track of each individual elements becomes increasingly difficult if the number of components or computers grows. In large-scale systems, it is not practical to specify distribution constraint relating to individual components or individual computers. Instead, it must be possible to specify constraints relating to possibly large groups of elements. Furthermore, this difficulty increases if the components or computers involved change frequently. In complex or frequently changing system, it is too expensive to write down which individual component must (not) reside on which individual computer. Therefore, this paper suggest to express distribution requirements in an *adaptive* way: a new specification technique is presented that defines what must (not) be available where according to the components's or the computer's context.

1.2   Example: Availability Requirement

The following availability requirement is used as an example in this paper: *All components needed in the workflow 'Create Report' must be allocated to all computers belonging to the 'Controlling' department.* Due to this requirement, any computer of the controlling department can access all the components needed in the workflow Create Report even if the network fails. Hence, the availability of the workflow Create Report is ensured on these computers. But, which system elements should be checked for whether they are (not) allocated to which computers? How can the system be checked for compliance with this requirement? The answers start in the next section.

1.3   The Paper in Brief

This paper suggests defining distribution requirements via Context-Based Constraints (CoCons). Their basic concept introduced in [5] can be explained in just a few sentences.

1. The system elements, e.g. components or computers, are annotated with formatted metadata called 'context properties'. A context property describes its element's context. As defined in section 2, context is any information that can be used to characterize the situation of an element.
2. Only those elements whose context property values fit the CoCon's context condition must fulfil the constraint. Up to now, constraints do not indirectly

select their constrained elements according to their context properties as explained in section 3.

3. A CoCons refers to *two* sets of elements. It relates each element x of one set to each element y of the other set and defines a condition $C(x, y)$ on each pair of related elements. If one set contains components and the other set contains computers then this condition on a pair of related elements can state that 'x must be allocated to y' as discussed in section 4.

When adapting a systems to new, altered or deleted requirements, existing distribution requirements should not unintentionally be violated. Two different kinds of automatically detectable CoCon violations are discussed in this paper:

- An **inter-CoCon conflict** occurs if one CoCon contradicts another CoCon as discussed in section 5.
- An **illegal artefact element conflict** occurs if a artefact element does not comply with a CoCon's predicate on how it must (not) relate to another artefact element. As an example, checking the compliance of UML deployment diagrams with distribution requirements is discussed in section 6.

2 Context Properties

2.1 What Is Context?

This paper focuses on the context of software system elements. It uses context for one specific purpose explained in previous section: it refers to context of software system elements in order to distinguish those elements that reside in the same context from other elements that don't.

The context models used in software engineering typically focus on internal context of software systems as explained next. A software system consists of artefacts, like source code files, configuration files, or models. One artefact can consist of several elements. An **internal element** is contained in at least one of the system's artefacts. For example, the name of a component, the name of a method, or the name of a method's parameter are internal elements. On the contrary, an **external element** is not contained in any of the system's artefacts. An **internal context** of a software system element refers to other internal elements. It does not refer to external elements.

For example, the 'context of a component' is defined as 'the required interfaces and the acceptable execution platforms' of components in [23]. This is an internal notion of context because it only refers to internal elements: other components or containers are defined as context of a component. Likewise, the context of an Enterprise Java Bean is defined as 'an object that allows an enterprise bean (EJB) to invoke container services and to obtain information about the caller of a client-invoked method'. Once more, the context of a component (the EJB) only refers to other internal elements: both the container and the calling component are system elements. This paper proposes also to take external contexts into account. It suggests to select constrained elements according to their context regardless whether their context is part of the system or not.

Context is defined in [11] as 'any information that can be used to characterize the situation of an entity'. This definition needs a precise definition of 'situation'. In situation calculus ([10]), **situation** is defined as structured part of the reality that an agent manages to pick out and/or to individuate. This definition suits well for this paper because context is used here for distinguishing those elements that are involved in a requirement from the other elements that don't. A context is not a situation, for a situation (of situation calculus) is the complete state of the world at a given instant. A single context, however, is necessarily partial and approximate. It cannot *completely* define the situations. Instead, it only characterizes the situation.

Section 2.2 will present a syntax and informal semantics for expressing (situational) context of software elements.

2.2   Context Properties: Formatted Metadata Describing Elements

The context of an element can be expressed as metadata. 'Metadata' is typically defined as 'data about data'. According to [1], the attribute-value pair model is the commonly used format for defining metadata today. As well, the context of a system element is epressed in the simple attribute-value syntax here: a **context property** consists of a name and a set of values.

First, this section defines a textual syntax of context properties via BNF rules. Afterwards, it informally explains the semantics of context properties.

The standard technique for defining the syntax of a language is the Backus-Naur Form (BNF), where "::=" stands for the definition, "Text" for a nonterminal symbol and "**TEXT**" for a terminal symbol. Square brackets surround [optional items], curly brackets surround {items that can repeat} zero or more times, and a vertical line '|' separates alternatives. The following syntax is used for assigning values of one context property to an element:

ConPropValues ::= ContextPropertyName ['(' ElementName ')'] ':'
    ContextPropertyValue {',' ContextPropertyValue}

A context property **name** (called ContextPropertyName in the syntax definition given above) groups context property values.

For instance, the values of the context property 'Workflow' reflect the most frequent workflows in which the associated element is used. Only the names of the workflows used most often are taken into account for requirement specification here. In this case, the name of the context property is 'Workflow'. The BNF rule ContextPropertyValue defines the **valid values** of one context property name. For instance, the four values allowed for Workflow can be   ContextPropertyValue := 'New Contract' | 'Delete Contract' | 'Create Report' | 'Split Contract'. A subset of the valid values can be associated with a single element for each context property name. These values describe how or where this element is used – they describe the context (as discussed in section 2.1) of this element. The context property name stays the same when associating its values with several elements, while its values might vary for each element.

2.3 Research Related to Context Properties

Many notations for writing down metadata as attribute-value pairs exist and can be used for expressing the context of elements. For example, tagged values ([15]) can be used to express context properties in UML.

As summarized in [20], a concept similar to context properties was discussed in the 90ties: database objects are annotated via intensional description called 'semantic values' ([21,19]) in order to identify those objects in different databases that are semantically related. Likewise, context properties are annotated to elements in order to determine the relevant element(s). However, the semantic value approach has a different purpose and, thus, a different notion of *relevant*: the purpose of semantic values is to identify semantically related objects in order to resolve schema heterogeneity among them. On the contrary, context properties are not annotated in order to identify those database objects in heterogeneous databases that correspond to each other. Instead, context properties are annotated to elements in order to identify those elements that are involved in a certain requirement as explained in the next section. The application of semantical values differs from the application of context properties. Still, the concepts are similar because they both can denote elements residing in the same context.

Another concept similar to context properties are 'domains' introduced in [22]. They provide a means of grouping objects to which policies apply. In contrast to context properties, a domain does not consist of a name and corresponding values. Instead, a domain consists of one single term. Domains are a unit of management similar to file directories in operating systems, and provide hierarchical structuring of objects. As well as any other metadata concept, domains can be used to express the context of elements. Section 3.1 will explain that context can be expressed with any metadata concept as long as a query language for the other metadata concept exists.

A context property groups elements that share a context. Existing grouping mechanisms like inheritance, stereotypes or packages are not used because the values of a context property associated with one element might vary in different configurations or even change at runtime. An element is not supposed to change its stereotype, its inheritance, or its package at runtime. Context properties are a simple mechanism for grouping otherwise possibly unassociated elements - even across different views, artefact types, or platforms. The primary benefit of enriching elements with context properties is revealed in the next section, where they assist in identifying those elements that are involved in a requirement.

3   Context-Based Constraints (CoCons)

3.1   Indirect Selection of Constrained Elements

This section presents a new notion constraints that can indirectly select the constrained elements when expressing which component must (not) be available at which computers. A **context-based constraint** (CoCon) can indirectly select the constrained elements according to their context property values. It expresses a condition on how its constrained elements must be related to each other. This condition is called **CoCon-predicate** here. Different types of CoCon-predicates exist. A 'CoCon-predicate type' is abbreviated as **CoCon type** here. Hence, 'CoCon type' is a synonym for 'CoCon-predicate'. The Context-Based Constraint Language **CCL** introduced in [4] consists of 21 different types of CoCons. This paper, however, discusses only those CoCon types of CCL that define distribution requirements.

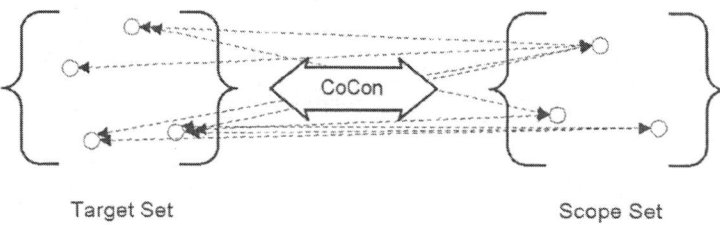

Target Set   Scope Set

Fig. 1. A CoCon Relates any Element of the 'Target Set' with any Element of the 'Scope Set'

Figure 1 illustrates that a CoCon relates each element of one set to each element of the other set and expresses a CoCon-predicate (depicted as dotted arrows) for each *pair* of related elements. The two sets related by a CoCon are called 'target set' and 'scope set'. Both target set elements and scope set elements of a CoCon can either directly or indirectly be selected. Indirect selection is the key concept of context-based constraints. A CoCon can *indirectly* select set elements via a **context condition** that defines, which context property values an element must (not) have in order to be constrained by the CoCon. If the context property values of an element comply with the CoCon's context condition then the CoCon constrains this element: in that case, this element must fulfil the CoCon-predicate in relation to other constrained elements. In section 1.2, the target set elements are selected via the following context condition: "*All components whose context property 'Workflow' has the value 'Create Report'*". These target set elements are anonymous. They are not directly named or associated, but described indirectly according to their context property values. If no element fulfils the context condition, the set is empty. This simply means that the CoCon actually does not apply to any element at all.

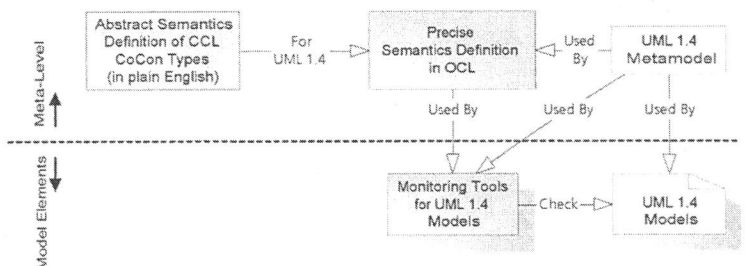

Fig. 2. Two-Step Approach for Defining the Semantics of CoCons

The same set of elements can both be selected directly and indirectly. For example, the direct selection '$component_1$, $component_4$ and $component_7$' can describe the same components as *All components whose context property 'Workflow' has the value 'Create Report'*. However, the indirect selection *automatically* adapts to changed elements or context changes, while the direct selection doesn't. For instance, eventually a new component will be managed by the system that was not managed yet when writing down the CoCon. The new component $component_{31}$ is not selected by the direct selection given above. On the contrary, the indirect selection will automatically apply to $component_{31}$ as soon as $component_{31}$'s context property 'Workflow' has the value 'Create Contract'. The indirect selection statement must not be adapted if system elements or their contexts change. Instead, the indirectly selected elements are identified by evaluating the context condition each time when the system is checked for whether it complies with the CoCon.

The concept of CoCons is independent of the *context property data schema*. A simple and flat attribute-value schema for context properties has been introduced in section 2. Of course, more expressive data schemata for storing the context properties of one element, e.g. hierarchical, relational, or object-oriented schemata, can be used. The *query language* used to specify the context condition depends on the context properties data schema. If the context properties of each artefact element are stored in a relational schema then a relational query language, e.g. SQL, can be used to express context conditions. If the context properties are, e.g., stored in a hierarchical XML schema then a query language for XML document can be used, e.g. XQuery. However, this paper focuses on the non-hierarchical, non-relational, non-object-oriented data schema for context properties defined in section 2.

3.2 Two-Step Approach for Defining CoCon Type Semantics

This section discusses *how to* formally define the CoCon semantics.

CoCons can be applied to artefacts at different development levels, e.g. models at design level or component instances at runtime. Different artefact types or different versions of the same artefact type can be used at each development level. For instance, UML 1.4 models or other specification techniques can be used at the design level. Figure 2 illustrates the two-step approach for defining semantics of CoCon types for the artefact type 'UML 1.4 models':

- The **artefact-type-independent semantics definition of a CoCon type** does not refer to specific properties of an individual artefact type as discussed in section 3.3.
- The **artefact-type-specific semantics definition** of a CoCon type refers to a metamodel of a specific artefact type in order to define the semantics in terms and constructs of this metamodel in a formal or semi-formal language. For example, which concepts express ACCESSIBLE TO in UML 1.4 models? Section 6 will discuss which UML model elements must (not) be associated in which way with which other UML model elements in order to comply with ACCESSIBLE TO CoCons.

3.3   Formalization of Context-Based Constraints

Instead, CoCons are a limited version of predicate logic as described next. A CoCon expresses a condition on how its constrained elements must be related to each other. This condition is called CoCon-predicate. Each element of the target set must relate to each element of the scope set as defined by the polyadic CoCon-predicate. The CoCon semantics can be expressed via the following predicate logic formula:

$$\forall x, y : T(x) \wedge S(y) \rightarrow C(x, y)$$

The CoCon-predicate is defined via a (polyadic) relation $C(x, y)$, like x MUST BE ACCESSIBLE TO y. On the contrary, $T(x)$ and $S(y)$ are monadic predicates on a different level. They define the context condition and are specified via a query language. $T(x)$ represents the target set context condition, and $S(y)$ represents the scope set context condition. The variable x holds all elements in the target set, and the variable y hold all elements in the scope set. In order to represent a CoCon, $T(x)$ must define a condition on the context property values of x, and $S(y)$ must define a condition on the context property values of y.

Each CoCon-predicate $C(x, y)$ can be combined with the CoCon-predicate operation NOT or ONLY:

- NOT negates the relation $C(x, y)$ as follows: $\forall x, y : T(x) \wedge S(y) \rightarrow \neg C(x, y)$
- ONLY is mapped to two propositions:
  - $\forall x, y : T(x) \wedge \neg S(y) \rightarrow \neg C(x, y)$
  - $\forall x, y : T(x) \wedge S(y) \rightarrow C(x, y)$

3.4   Research Related to Context-Based Constraints

The key concept of CoCons is the indirect selection of constrained elements. Any unknown element becomes involved in a context-based constraint simply by having the matching context property value(s). Hence, the constrained elements can change without modifying the CoCon specification. The indirect selection of constrained elements is particularly helpful in *highly dynamic systems or models*. Every new, changed or removed element is automatically constrained by a CoCon due to the element's context property values.

A recent and interesting access control policy approach can indirecly select the constrained network elements: the Ponder language for specifying management and security policies is defined in [9]. Three differences between CoCons and Ponder exist. First, CoCons don't have operational semantics, while Ponder has. Second, Ponder does not address distribution requirements, while CoCons do. And finally, Ponder is based on the domain concept discussed in section 2.3. Similar to context conditions, Ponder uses domain scope expression ([24]) for selecting elements according to their domain. A domain, however, consists of a single name, while context properties consist of a name and values.

4   Distribution CoCons

4.1   The Notion of Distribution CoCons

Distribution CoCons determine whether the target set elements have to be available at the CoCon's scope elements or not. The target set of a distribution CoCon can contain any element type that can be contained in other elements, such as 'components' can be contained in 'containers'. As well, the scope set of distribution CoCons can contain any element type that can contain the other element type of the target set. However, nothing but 'components' in the target sets and 'computers' in the scope sets of distribution CoCons are discussed here.

4.2   Distribution CoCon Types

This section proposes several CoCon types for expressing distribution requirements. Each CoCon type can be combined with the CoCon-predicate operation 'NOT' or 'ONLY' after the keyword MUST. For example, the CoCon type ALLOCATED TO can either state that certain elements MUST BE ALLOCATED TO other elements, or that they MUST NOT BE ALLOCATED TO other elements, or that they MUST ONLY BE ALLOCATED TO other elements. The abbreviation '(NOT | ONLY)' is used to refer to all three possible CoCon-predicate operations of one CoCon type in the next sections.

A (NOT | ONLY) ALLOCATED TO CoCon defines that the components in its target set must (NOT | ONLY) be deployed on the containers or the computers in its scope set.

Replication is well known in distributed databases and can also be realised with some middleware platforms. In this paper, the term 'a component is replicated' means that the component's state is serialized and the resulting data is copied. The following CoCon types handle replication:

A (NOT | ONLY) **SYNCHRONOUSLY REPLICATED TO** CoCon defines that the components in its target set must (NOT | ONLY) be synchronously replicated from where they are allocated to – specified via ALLOCATED TO CoCons – to the elements in its scope set.

A (NOT | ONLY) **ASYNCHRONOUSLY REPLICATED TO** CoCon defines that the components in its target set must (NOT | ONLY) be asynchronously replicated from their allocation – their allocation is specified via ALLOCATED TO CoCons – to the elements in its scope set.

4.3   Examples for Using Distribution CoCons

The 'availability' requirement introduced in section 1.2 can be written down via CCL as follows:

ALL COMPONENTS WHERE 'Workflow' CONTAINS 'Create Report' MUST BE ALLOCATED TO ALL COMPUTERS WHERE 'Operational Area' CONTAINS 'Controlling' .

The values of the context property 'Operational Area' describe, in which department(s) or domain(s) the associated element is used. It provides an organisational perspective.

4.4   Related Research on Distribution and Network Policies

One way in which we cope with large and complex systems is to abstract away some of the detail, considering them at an architectural level as composition of interacting objects. To this end, the variously termed *Coordination, Configuration and Architectural Description Languages* facilitate description, comprehension and reasoning at that level, providing a clean separations of concerns and facilitating reuse. According to [13], in the search to provide sufficient detail for reasoning, analysis or construction, many approaches are in danger of obscuring the essential structural aspect of the architecture, thereby losing the benefit of abstraction. On the contrary, CoCons stay on an abstract level in order to keep it simple.

Aspect-oriented languages supplement programming languages with properties that address design decisions. According to [12], these properties are called *aspects* and are incorporated into the source code. Most aspect-oriented languages do not deal with expressing design decisions in during *design*. D^2AL ([3]) differs from the other aspect oriented languages in that it is based on the system model, not on its implementation. Objects that interact heavily must be located together. D^2AL groups collaborating objects that are directly linked via associations. It describes in textual language in which manner these objects interact which are connected via these associations. This does not work for objects that are not directly linked like 'all objects needed in the 'Create Report' workflow.

Darwin (or 'δarwin') is a *configuration language* for distributed systems described in [16] that, likewise, expresses the architecture explicit by specifying the associations between objects. However, there may be a reason for allocating objects together even if they do not collaborate at all. For instance, it may be necessary to cluster all objects needed in a certain workflow regardless whether they invoke each other or not. Distribution CoCons allocate objects together because of shared context instead of direct collaboration. They define a context-specific cluster. Distribution CoCons assist in grouping related objects into **subject-specific clusters** and define how to allocate or replicate the whole cluster.

Recent work by both researchers ([7]) and practitioners ([18]) has investigated how to model non-functional requirements and to express them in a form that is measurable or testable. Non-functional requirements (also known as quality requirements) are generally more difficult to express in a measurable way, making them more difficult to analyse. They are also known as the 'ilities' and have defied a clear characterisation for decades. In particular, they tend to be properties of a system as a whole, and hence cannot be verified for individual system elements. The distribution CoCon types introducesd here specify non-functional requirements. Via the two-step semantics definition, these CoCon types can clearly express 'ilities'. They are particulary helpful in expressing crosscutting ilities that apply to more than one system element, because one CoCon can select several involved elements according to their context property values.

5   Detectable Conflicts of Distribution CoCons

If distribution requirements CoCons contradict each other then an tool interpreting the CoCons will not be able to perform an action appropriately because one CoCon negates the effect of the other. Thus, it is important to have a means of detecting and resolving any conflicts that arise. A conflict between constraints arises if they express opposite conditions on the same elements. This section defines **inter-CoCon conflict detection constraints** (short: **inter-CoCon constraints**). First, three general inter-CoCon constraints are presented that apply to each of the distribution CoCon types defined in section 4.2. In predicate logic, each of these CoCon types can be expressed as $C(x, y)$. The first inter-CoCon constraint can apply if one CoCon has a NOT operation, while another CoCon of the same CoCon type hasn't.

General Inter-CoCon Constraint 1: The two CoCons $\forall x, y : T_1(x) \wedge S_1(y) \rightarrow C(x, y)$ and $\forall x, y : T_2(x) \wedge S_2(y) \rightarrow \neg C(x, y)$ contradict each other if $\exists x, y : T_1(x) \wedge T_2(x) \wedge S_1(y) \wedge S_2(y)$.

If $C(x, y)$ is defined as x MUST BE ALLOCATED TO y CoCon-predicate then this general inter-CoCon constraint states that no element x must both be ALLOCATED TO and NOT ALLOCATED TO any y. For instance, the following privacy policy informing forbids to manage personal data on web servers: ALL COMPONENTS WHERE 'Handles Personal Data' CONTAINS 'True' MUST NOT BE ALLOCATED TO ALL COMPUTERS WHERE 'Installed Software' CONTAINS 'Web Server'. According to the general inter-CoCon constraint, this privacy policy contradicts the availability-policy presented in section 1.2 if a web server is installed on any computer used by the controlling department.

The next two inter-CoCon constraints take the CoCon type operation ONLY into account. The semantics of the operation ONLY are defined in section 3.3.

The following inter-CoCon constraint applies if one CoCon without CoCon type operation contradicts another CoCon with the CoCon type operation ONLY:

General Inter-CoCon Constraint 2: The two CoCons

- $\forall x, y : T_1(x) \wedge S_1(y) \to C(x, y)$ and
- $\forall x, y : T_2(x) \wedge \neg S_2(y) \to \neg C(x, y)$
  $\forall x, y : T_2(x) \wedge S_2(y) \to C(x, y)$

contradict each other if $\exists x, y : T_1(x) \wedge T_2(x) \wedge S_1(y) \wedge \neg S_2(y)$.

The following inter-CoCon constraint applies if one CoCon with the CoCon type operation ONLY contradicts another CoCon with the CoCon type operation ONLY:

General Inter-CoCon Constraint 3: The two CoCons

- $\forall x, y : T_1(x) \wedge \neg S_1(y) \to \neg C(x, y)$
  $\forall x, y : T_1(x) \wedge S_1(y) \to C(x, y)$ and
- $\forall x, y : T_2(x) \wedge \neg S_2(y) \to \neg C(x, y)$
  $\forall x, y : T_2(x) \wedge S_2(y) \to C(x, y)$

contradict each other if $\exists x, y : T_1(x) \wedge T_2(x) \wedge ((\neg S_1(y) \wedge S_2(y)) \vee (S_1(y) \wedge \neg S_2(y)))$.

Besides the general inter-CoCon conflict detection constraints, *CoCon-type specific* inter-CoCon conflicts exist as listed next. The elements e_i and e_k are target or scope set elements of distribution CoCons with $i \neq k$. An inter-CoCon conflict exists if any of the following inter-CoCon constraints is violated:

1. No element e_i may be both NOT ALLOCATED TO e_k and SYNCHRONOUSLY REPLICATED TO e_k.
2. No element e_i may be both NOT ALLOCATED TO e_k and ASYNCHRONOUSLY REPLICATED TO e_k.
3. No element e_i may be both ALLOCATED TO e_k and SYNCHRONOUSLY REPLICATED TO e_k.
4. No element e_i may be both ALLOCATED TO e_k and ASYNCHRONOUSLY REPLICATED TO e_k.
5. No element e_i may be both SYNCHRONOUSLY REPLICATED TO e_k and ASYNCHRONOUSLY REPLICATED TO e_k.

Inter-CoCon conflicts can be handled by assigning a different priority to each CoCon – only the CoCon with the highest priority applies. If this Co-Con is invalid because its scope or target set is empty then the next CoCon with the second-highest priority applies. This section has demonstrated that conflicting CoCons automatically can be detected by checking the constrained elements (identified via context conditions) if they violate one of the inter-CoCon constraints defined above. Hence, the conflicting distribution requirements can automatically be detected. This is a major benefit of CoCons.

6   The CoCon Type Semantics for UML

Software tools can support software designers in monitoring the artefacts of a development process for compliance with distribution CoCons if the artefact-specific semantics of the distribution CoCon types are defined. This paper focuses on checking UML models for compliance with distribution CoCons. Hence, this section defines the artefact-type-specific semantics of the ALLOCATED TO CoCon type for UML 1.4 models via OCL.

In UML, deployment diagrams show the configuration of software components. Software component instances represent run-time manifestations of software code units. A deployment diagram is a graph of nodes connected by communication associations. An arrow (= dependency) or the nesting of a component symbol within a node symbol maps specified the deployment of a component at a node. As illustrated in the UML deployment diagram shown in figure 3, the component type 'ContractManagement' is deployed on the computer type 'Laptop'. According to the CoCon in section 4.3, 'ContractManagement' must not be allocated to the 'Laptop' because this computer belongs to the controlling department.

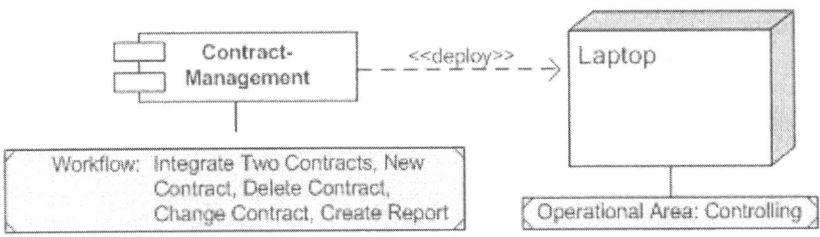

Fig. 3. A Deployment Diagram Showing a Component Type that violates the Availability Requirement of Section 4.3

The ALLOCATED TO CoCon given in section 4.3 can be translated into the two following OCL expressions. The first OCL expression referts to component *types* that are allocated to nodes via deployment associations:

```
context node inv:
        self.taggedvalue -> select(tv | tv.dataValue =
        "Controlling")
        .type -> select(td | td.name = "Operational Area")
        -> notEmpty()
implies self.deployedComponent
        -> select(c | c.oclIsTypeOf(component))
        self.taggedvalue->select(tv | tv.dataValue = "Create
        Report")
        .type -> select(td | td.name = "Workflow")
        -> notEmpty()
```

This OCL statement states that a nodes having the tagged value 'Operational Àrea: Controlling' must (= NotEmpty() in OCL) contain those components having the tagged value 'Workflow: Create Report'. This OCL expression only addresses component types and node types. Nevertheless, distribution also applies to component *instances* and node *instances*. The following OCL expression maps the availability policy to component instances that reside on node instances:.

```
context nodeinstance inv:
        self.taggedvalue -> select(tv | tv.dataValue =
        "Controlling")
        .type -> select(td | td.name = "Operational Area")
        -> notEmpty()
implies self.resident
        -> select(c | c.oclIsTypeOf(componentinstance))
        self.taggedvalue->select(tv | tv.dataValue = "Create
        Report")
        .type -> select(td | td.name = "Workflow")
        -> notEmpty()
```

In case of ALLOCATED TO CoCons, the artefact-type-*independent* semantics definition consists of five words: 'x must be allocated to y'. On the contrary, the corresponding artefact-type-specific OCL listing is about much longer because it considers a lot more details. CCL stays on the artefact-type-independent, abstract level. OCL, however, is too close to programming for expressing requirements at this abstraction level. The effort of writing down a requirement in the minutest details is unsuitable if the details are not important. The designer can ignore many details by expressing the same requirement via CCL instead of OCL. Moreover, it is easier to adapted the short artefact-type-independent CCL expression instead of changing all the OCL expressions if the corresponding requirement changes.

As a proof of concept implementation, the 'CCL plugin' for the open source CASE tool ArgoUML has been implemented and is available for download at http://ccl-plugin.berlios.de/. It integrates the verification of distribution CoCons into the Design Critiques ([17]) mechanism of ArgoUML. However, it only prototypically demonstrates how to verify UML models for compliance with distribution CoCons. It needs to be improved before using it in production.

7   Conclusion

This paper presents an approach for declaratively defining distribution requirements: context-based *constraints* (CoCons) define what must (not) be allocated to what according to the current context of components and documents.

7.1   Availability versus Load Balance

This paper focuses on availability. However, availability and load balanceare contradicting distribution goals. Availability is optimal if every element is allocated to every computer, because each computer can still access each element even if the network or other computers of the system have crashed. However, this optimal availability causes bad load balance, because each modification of an element must be replicated to every other computer of the system. Typically, the limits of hardware performance and network bandwidth don't allow optimal availability. Instead, a reasonable trade of between availability and load balance must be achieved by clustering *related* data. Those elements that are related should be allocated to the computers where they are needed. This paper suggests improving availabilty by grouping related objects into *subject-specific* clusters and allocating or replicating the whole cluster via CoCons to the computer(s) where it must be available.

In order to detect conflicts between availability and load balance early, the system load should be considered already in the model. A system load estimations can either be a result of approximation based on common sense and experience, of a simulation as suggested by [14], or of (maybe prototypical) runtime metrics. Automatically detecting conflicts between system load and distribution CoCons is a topic of future research, though.

7.2   Limitations of Distribution CoCons

The context of components or computers can be expressed via metadata. Taking only the metadata of an element into account bears some risks. It must be ensured that the context property values are always up-to date. The following approaches can improve the quality of context property values:

- If the metadata is extracted newly from its element each time when checking a context condition and if the extraction mechanism works correctly then the metadata always is correct and up-to-date. Moreover, the extraction mechanism ensures that metadata is available at all.
- Contradicting context property values can automatically be prevented via value-binding CoCons as explained in [4].
- Additional Metadata can be automatically derived from already existing metadata via belongs-to relations as explained in [4].

Within one system, only one ontology for metadata should be used. For instance, the workflow 'Create Report' should have exactly this name in every part of the system, even if different companies manufacture or use its parts. Otherwise, string matching gets complex when checking a context condition. If more than one ontology for metadata is used, correspondences between heterogeneous context property values can be expressed via constraint or correspondence techniques, like value-binding CoCons ([4]) or Model Correspondence Assertions ([6]). However, not every vocabulary problem can be solved via engineering techniques. These techniques can reduce the heterogeneity, but they cannot overcome it completely. Hence, the need for a controlled ontology remains the key limitation of CoCons.

7.3   Benefits of Distribution CoCons

Context properties can dynamically group elements. They facilitate handling of overlapping or varying groups of elements that share a context even across different element types or systems. Hence, one distribution requirements definition affecting several unrelated elements that even may not be managed by the same platform can now be expressed via one constraint. Context properties allow *subject-specific clusters* to be concentrated on. For instance, all components belonging to workflow 'X' may form a cluster. Other concepts for considering metadata exist, but none of them writes down constrains that reflect this metadata.

Requirements specification should serve as a document understood by designers, programmers and customers. CoCons can be specified in easily comprehensible, straightforward language. In complex domains, no one architect has all the knowledge needed to control a system. Instead, most complex systems are maintained by teams of stakeholders providing some of the necessary knowledge and their own goals and priorities. This 'thin spread of application domain knowledge' has been identified by [8] as a general problem in software development. Even the person who specifies distribution requirements via CoCons does not have to have the complete knowledge of the components and computers involved due to the *indirect* association of CoCons to the components and computers involved. It can be unknown what exactly must (not) be allocated where when writing down the distribution requirements.

Distribution requirements can change often. The key concept for improving the adaptability of distribution requirements definition is indirection — the constrained elements can be indirectly selected according to their metadata. The metadata can be easily adapted whenever the context of a component or computer changes. Furthermore, each deleted, modified or additional component or computer can be automatically considered and any resulting conflicts can automatically be identified. CoCons automatically adapt to changed contexts, components or computers.

References

1. Thomas Baker. A grammar of dublin core. *D-Lib Magazine*, 6(10):47–60, October 2000.
2. Henri E. Bal, Jennifer G. Steiner, and Andrew S. Tanenbaum. Programming languages for distributed computing systems. *ACM Computing Surveys*, 21(3):261–322, 1989.
3. Ulrich Becker. D2AL – a design-based distribution aspect language. Technical Report TR-I4-98-07 of the Friedrich-Alexander University Erlangen-Nürnberg, 1998.
4. Felix Bübl. The context-based constraint language CCL for components. Technical Report 2002-20, Technical University Berlin, Germany, available at www.CoCons.org, October2002.
5. Felix Bübl. Introducing context-based constraints. In Herbert Weber and Ralf-Detlef Kutsche, editors, *Fundamental Approaches to Software Engineering (FASE '02)*, Grenoble, France, volume 2306 of LNCS, pages 249–263, Berlin, April 2002. Springer.

6. Susanne Busse. Modellkorrespondenzen für die kontinuierliche Entwicklung mediatorbasierter Informationssysteme. PhD Thesis, Technical University Berlin, Germany, Logos Verlag, 2002.
7. Lawrence Chung, Brian A. Nixon, Eric Yu, and John Mylopoulos. *Non-Functional Requirements in Software Engineering.* Kluwer Academic, Boston, 2000.
8. Bill Curtis, Herb Krasner, and Neil Iscoe. A field study of the software design process for large systems. *Communications of the ACM*, 31(11):1268–1287, 1988.
9. Nicodemos Damianou. A policy framework for management of distributed systems. PhD Thesis, Imperial College, London, UK, 2002.
10. Keith Devlin. *Logic and Information.* Cambridge University Press, New York, 1991.
11. Anind K. Dey. Understanding and using context. *Personal and Ubiquitous Computing Journal*, 5(1):4–7, 2001.
12. Gregor Kiczales, John Lamping, Anurag Mendhekar, Chris Maeda, Cristina Videira Lopes, Jean-Marc Loingtier, and John Irwin. Aspect-oriented programming. In Mehmet Aksit and Satoshi Matsuoka, editors, *European Conference on Object-Oriented Programming ECOOP*, volume 1241 of LNCS, pages 220–242, Berlin, 1997. Springer.
13. Jeff Kramer and Jeff Magee. Exposing the skeleton in the coordination closet. In *Coordination 97*, Berlin, pages 18–31, 1997.
14. Miguel de Miguel, Thomas Lambolais, Sophie Piekarec, Stéphane Betgé-Brezetz, and Jérôme Pequery. Automatic generation of simulation models for the evaluation of performance and reliability of architectures specified in UML. In Wolfgang Emmerich and Stefan Tai, editors, *Engineering Distributed Objects (EDO 2000)*, volume 1999 of LNCS, pages 82–100, Berlin, 2000. Springer.
15. OMG. UML specification v1.4, September 2001.
16. Matthias Radestock and Susan Eisenbach. Semantics of a higher-order coordination language. In *Coordination 96*, 1996.
17. Jason E. Robbins and David F. Redmiles. Software architecture critics in the argo design environment. *Knowledge-Based Systems. Special issue: The Best of IUI'98*, 5(1):47–60, 1998.
18. Suzanne Robertson and James Robertson. *Mastering the Requirements Process.* Addison-Wesley, 1999.
19. Edward Sciore, Michael Siegel, and Arnon Rosenthal. Context interchange using meta-attributes. In *Proc. of the 1st International Conference on Information and Knowledge Management*, pages 377–386, 1992.
20. Edward Sciore, Michael Siegel, and Arnon Rosenthal. Using semantic values to falilitate interoperability among heterogeneous information systems. *ACM Transactions on Database Systems (TODS)*, 19(2):254–290, 1994.
21. Amit P. Sheth and Sunit K. Gala. Attribute relationships: An impediment in automating schema integration. In *Proc. of the Workshop on Heterogeneous Database Systems (Chicago, Ill., USA)*, December 1989.
22. Morris Sloman and Kevin P. Twidle. Domains: A framework for structuring management policy. In Morris Sloman, editor, *Chapter 16 in Network and Distributed Systems Management*, pages 433–453, 1994.
23. Clemens Szyperski. *Component Software – Beyond Object-Oriented Programming.* Addison-Wesley, Reading, 1997.
24. Nicholas Yialelis. Domain-based security for distributed object systems. PhD Thesis, Imperial College, London, UK, 1996.

A CORBA-Based Transaction System for the Wireless Communication Environment

Tarcisio da Rocha and Maria Beatriz Felgar de Toledo

Computing Institute, State University of Campinas (UNICAMP)
PO Box 6176, 13083-970, Campinas, SP, Brazil
{tarcisio.rocha,beatriz}@ic.unicamp.br
http://www.ic.unicamp.br

Abstract. This paper introduces a transaction system for the wireless communication environment. Its main feature is providing flexibility and collaborative adaptation. In this type of adaptation the underlying system and applications have different responsibilities. The system is responsible for monitoring resources and notifying transactions about changes in the environment. Transactions can then react properly to these changes. Two aspects are considered: isolation level and operation mode. Moreover, the paper describes the architecture and a prototype based on CORBA.

Keywords: Transaction System, Collaborative Adaptation, Mobile Computing, Wireless Communication, CORBA.

1 Introduction

Advances in the development of portable computing devices and wireless communication technologies have made possible the appearance of mobile computing. Thus, the portable devices can participate in distributed computing while moving.

Although attractive, the mobile environment has a set of restrictions [6, 9, 18] that are not tackled by traditional distributed systems. Among these restrictions we can mention low network bandwidth, high cost of communication in wireless networks, low capacity of the battery in portable devices, larger probability of communication failures and unpredictable disconnections.

There is a spectrum of models [8, 12] for overcoming the obstacles of mobile computing. In the first extreme, *laissez-faire adaptation models*, each application on the client is solely responsible for its own adaptation. While this laissez-faire approach avoids the need for system support, it lacks a central arbitrator to resolve incompatible resource demands of different applications and to enforce limits on resource usage. In the other extreme, *application-transparent adaptation models*, the underlying system is fully responsible for making adaptation decisions for applications. The drawback of this approach is that there may be situations where the adaptation performed by the system is inadequate for some applications. Between these

R. Meersman et al. (Eds.): CoopIS/DOA/ODBASE 2003, LNCS 2888, pp. 1488–1503, 2003.
© Springer-Verlag Berlin Heidelberg 2003

two extremes there is the *application-aware adaptation*. One way to realize the application-aware adaptation is through the collaboration between the system and individual applications. The system monitors resource levels, notifies applications of relevant changes, and enforces resource allocation decisions. Each application independently decides how to better adapt when notified.

In this paper, we present an adaptable transaction system for the wireless communication environment. This adaptation is based on the collaboration of transactions and the underlying system. The underlying system is responsible for resource monitoring and notification of transactions about the significant changes in the environment. When receiving a notification, the transaction can decide the appropriate reactions to the changes. Two possible actions of adaptation are provided to transactions: the change of transactional parameters such as the *isolation level* and/or the *operation mode*.

This article is structured as follows. Section 2 presents related work. The model and a discussion of isolation levels and operation modes are presented in Section 3. The architecture is described in Section 4. Section 5 presents relevant characteristics of the CORBA-based implemented prototype and Section 6 finishes the paper with conclusions.

2 Related Work

Coda [10] is a file system that provides application-transparent adaptation for applications facing network failures. The Coda project introduces the concept of disconnected operation that allows applications to use cached replicas during disconnection. Upon reconnection the locally updated data are propagated back to servers. Later, Coda was extended to overcome the problems of the wireless environment [11] and also to provide transaction support [19]. However, the transaction model provided by Coda only ensures the *isolation* property.

Unlike Coda, Odyssey [12] is based on collaborative adaptation between the applications and the underlying system. In this type of adaptation, the system monitors resources of the environment, notifies applications when changes happen and provides adaptation mechanisms; the application, when notified, decides the best way to react to changes. However the Odyssey project does not provide transactions. Approaches similar to Odyssey were used in the Prayer system [20] and the Cadmium project [21].

Many transaction models for the wireless communication environment are discussed in the literature. [4] provides an axiomatic definition for new transaction models called co-transactions and reporting transactions to model the interaction between a mobile client and the fixed network. Kangaroo Transactions [5] incorporates the hopping property to transactions allowing them to hop from one base station to another as the mobile client moves through cells. However, these models do not provide support for basic problems of the wireless communication such as low bandwidth and disconnected operation.

ProMotion [15] is a transaction system that supports transaction processing in a mobile environment. It is based on compacts. A compact encapsulates access methods, state information and local management information. Transactions may be executed disconnected over local data stored as compacts. [14] presents two types of transactions: weak transactions that may be executed with a certain level of inconsistency and strict transactions which execute over consistent data only.

The model proposed in this paper integrates the collaborative adaptation concept present in Odyssey and transaction management. Its main goal is allowing transactions to react to changes in environment. Moreover it provides flexibility for a large range of applications in the mobile environment allowing them to choose the required isolation level. As [15], it provides several consistency levels to attend the demands of the wide range of applications in the wireless environments.

3   The Adaptable Transaction Model

Traditionally, transactions can be defined as a sequence of read and write operations, executed between a *begin* and an *end* operations. These transactions satisfy the ACID properties, that is, each transaction is *atomic* when all or none of its operations are executed, *consistent* when its execution maintains consistency constraints, *isolated* when it does not observe partial results from any other transaction, and *durable* if its results become permanent after commitment. Although successfully applied in traditional environments, the ACID properties may be too strong in an environment were applications are generally long and subject to the restrictions of the wireless medium.

The transactional system proposed in this paper relaxes the ACID properties of the traditional model in order to provide the required flexibility for applications in wireless environments. For that, it uses the successfully adaptation concept introduced by the Odyssey project. Each transaction can specify the necessary resources for its execution and adapt in case some resource is out of the required bounds. Thus, the system provides resource monitoring and notifications when there is a significant variation in any resource of interest. A transaction, when notified, can adapt executing contingency actions. These contingency actions may consist of transaction aborts or changes in transaction attributes such as isolation level and operation mode. These adaptation parameters are discussed in 3.1 and 3.2 respectively.

3.1   Isolation Levels

The concept of isolation levels (or consistency levels) was initially introduced in [7] becoming the basis for ANSI SQL-92 [2]. The highest level of isolation (or consistency level) is achieved with serialization [3]. Considering that not all transactions require serializability, we use isolation levels lower than serialization to improve concurrency and performance.

In our model, a two-phase locking concurrency control was adopted [3] and isolation levels are ensured through short or long locks (see Table 1). The definition of isolation levels based on short and long locks is showed in [1] [22].

Table 1. ANSI isolation levels based on locks

Isolation Level	Read lock	Write lock
Level 0	None	Short write lock
Level 1 = UNCOMMITTED_READ	None	Long write lock
Level 2 = COMMITTED_READ	Short read lock	Long write lock
Level 3 = SERIALIZABILITY	Long read lock	Long write lock

Level 0 isolation offers the lowest isolation level and allows the phenomena called lost update, on the other hand it causes the lowest overhead and lock contention. With Level 1 dirty data may be accessed. This level may be entirely satisfactory for gathering statistical information from a large database when exact results are not required. For a transaction with Level 2, it is assured that every item read is clean. However, no guarantee is made that subsequent access to the same item will yield the same values. Level 3 offers the utmost isolation level, but causes the highest overhead and lock contention. In this isolation level, the user sees the logical equivalent of a single user system. Every read item is clean, and subsequent reads yield the same values.

A transaction in the proposed system specifies at its beginning the isolation level under which the operations on its participant objects should be executed (see line 5 of the Example 1). Isolation levels may be changed during transaction execution (see line 10 of the Example 1). A transaction can use this mechanism to execute groups of operations with different isolation levels improving concurrency and providing a greater flexibility with respect to consistency.

Example 1. Specification and change of the isolation level

```
1    MyAtomicAction act; //Transaction Specification
2    ObjectA objA;
3    ObjectB objB;
4
5    act.Begin(SERIALIZABILITY); //Begins the transaction
6                                //with isolation level 3.
7        objA.operation1();
8        objB.operation2();
9        ...
10       act.setIsolationLevel(UNCOMMITTED_READ); //Changes
11                                                //level.
11       objA.operation3();
12   act.End(); // Ends the transaction
```

3.2   Operation Modes

Another adaptation parameter that can be specified in the beginning of a transaction and modified during its execution is the operation mode. The operation modes considered are three: *remote*, *local-remote* and *local*.

When a transaction opts for the *remote* operation mode, all operations on objects are executed in the remote machine where the object is located. The access to remote objects will be subject to *two-phase locking* and will obey the isolation level of the transaction. This approach is suitable when the mobile machine is connected or when objects are too large to be transferred to local cache.

A transaction may instead opt for the *local-remote* operation mode. In this mode, a copy of the remote object is transferred to the local cache and operations are executed on the local copy. To maintain the consistency between the local copy in the cache and the remote copy in the fixed network, the remote object will be locked. But the operations are executed on the local copy. Only at the end of the transaction, the remote object is updated and the corresponding lock released. This approach is suitable when network bandwidth is low because communication is reduced.

In the *local* operation mode, a copy of the remote object is transferred to the local cache and operations are executed locally. However, with this operation mode the remote object will not be locked by the requesting transaction. After transaction commitment and when the mobile machine is connected, a validation is performed. Basically, this validation consists of checking if the local objects accessed by the validating transaction are consistent with the corresponding remote objects. If this is false, the transaction will be aborted and its local results will be discarded. Otherwise, the results of the transaction are transferred to the remote hosts where objects are located. This approach is suitable when the probability of disconnections is high.

The operation mode of a transaction, like its isolation level, is a parameter that can be specified in the beginning of the transaction and changed during its execution (see Example 2).

Example 2. Specification and change of the operation mode of a transaction

```
1   MyAtomicAction act; // Transaction Specification
2   ObjectA objA;
3   ObjectB objB;
4   // Begins the transaction with isolation level 1 and
5   // operation mode REMOTE
6   act.Begin(UNCOMMITTED_READ, REMOTE);
7     objA.operation1();
8     objB.operation2();
9     ...
10    act.setOperatioMode(LOCAL); // Changes operation mode
11    objA.operation3();
12 act.End(); // Ends the transaction
```

4 Architecture

The basic architecture of the developed prototype is shown in Figure 1. Each mobile host in our system has one or more transactions that can access local and remote objects, a resource monitor, a commit queue, an object store, and a cache manager. Each fixed host has an object store that stores objects that can be accessed by remote transactions. Each component is described below.

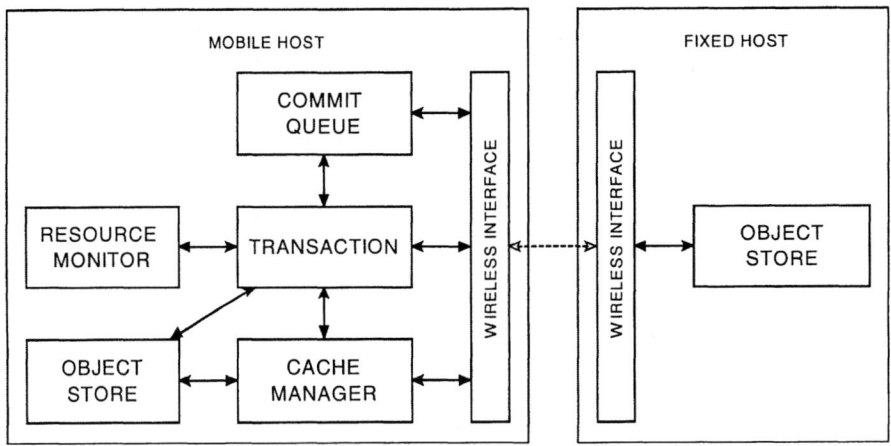

Fig. 1. Architecture of the prototype

4.1 Resource Monitor

The Resource Monitor (RM) is responsible for monitoring resources on behalf of transactions. The RM can aggregate one or more monitoring modules responsible for one specific resource. New monitoring modules can be implemented and added to the RM modules using the operation `addMonitor`. Examples of resources that can be monitored are the following:

1. communication bandwidth between the mobile unit and the fixed network;
2. energy level of the mobile unit;
3. disk space of the mobile unit;
4. communication cost;
5. network latence;

Each transaction may request monitoring of one or more resources using the operation `request` in the RM interface. The operation takes a resource descriptor identifying a resource to be monitored and specifying a *window of tolerance* (lower and upper bounds) on its availability. This operation expresses the transaction requirement to be notified if the availability of the resource gets outside the window.

In this case, the Resource Monitor notifies the correspondent transaction calling the operation notify in the transaction interface. Then, the notified transaction may execute adaptation actions to react accordingly to the notified changes.

The operation notify has two parameters. The first parameter is the resource identifier, which identifies the resource whose availability has changed. The second parameter gives the new availability.

4.2   Cache Manager

The Cache Manager (CM) is responsible for the management of objects in the mobile machine. It provides operations such as: transfer of remote state of objects to the local cache; removal of an object from the cache; version check between local and remote copies.

The CM operations are especially useful in the prefetching process when the mobile unit is preparing for disconnection. The process generally transfers copies of remote objects to the cache of the mobile machine. Upon disconnection, a transaction can continue execution using the objects in the local cache. Later, they should be validated against remote copies and, if the validation is successful, their new states will be transferred back to the remote machines.

4.3   Object Store

Once a transaction commits, the final states of the its participant objects should be made permanent. The Object Store provides appropriate mechanisms to store object state into secondary memory and to retrieve object state from secondary memory. Objects stored on the object store are passive and they must be made active before accessed by a running transaction.

The life cycle of a persistent object is [13]:

1. The object is initially in its passive state with its state stored on the Object Store.
2. When a transaction invokes an operation on that object, it is activated if it is not active yet (its state is recovered from the Object Store to primary memory) passing to the active state.
3. When the object is not used for some time, it is deactivated (its state is saved into the Object Store) going back to the passive state.

An instance of Object Store exists in each fixed server of the network where objects can be manipulated by transactions. Each mobile machine should also have one instance of the Object Store to make local objects persistent.

4.4   Commit Queue

When a transaction executes under the *local* or *local-remote* operation modes the operations are executed on local copies. This characteristic allows the transactions to continue to execute even if the local machine is disconnected. However, commitment requires reconnection in order to process validation and later propagation of results. If the mobile unit is disconnected in the commit phase, the transaction will delegate all responsibility of its commits to the Commit Queue (CQ) and the transaction will enter in the *pending* state. Thus, the CQ will commit or abort the transaction.

The CQ will execute the following steps:

1. It verifies when the connection is established.
2. It executes the commit for each queued transaction.
3. If the commit is successful, it sends a commit notification to the pending transaction that may now finish its execution.
4. If the commit fails, it aborts the operations of the corresponding transaction and send an abort notification to the transaction

These steps are executed for each transaction in the queue and constitute an idempotent operation that can be reinitiated after a failure.

4.5   Transaction Managers

A transaction manager is defined as an `AtomicAction` (see Example 3). The `Begin` and `End` operations are delimiters of a transaction. The operation `Begin` starts the execution of the transaction. This operation can have the execution parameters: isolation level and operation mode. If these parameters are not specified, the transaction will execute with isolation level 3 (`SERIALIZABILITY`) and operation mode *remote* as default.

The operation `End` executes the *two-phase commit* [3] protocol terminating a transaction with an abort or commit. By issuing a commit, the transaction terminates normally and all of its effects will be made permanent. By issuing an abort, the transaction terminates abnormally and all of its effects will be undone.

The isolation level and operation mode are adaptation parameters that can be changed during the execution of the transaction through the operations `setIsolationLevel` and `setOperationMode` respectively.

Each transaction in our model can have an independent adaptation policy. The transaction programmer can define this adaptation policy by implementing the abstract operation `notify`. The RM calls this operation when it discovers that the availability of a resource is outside of the specified bounds. The adaptation policy will implement the reaction to this change.

For example, if the bandwidth is too low or the cost of communication is high, the transaction can change its operation mode from remote to local. If the level of energy in the mobile machine is low, the application can save energy by changing its operation mode to local or can decide to abort an on-going transaction. If a machine is out of disk space, the application could choose the remote operation mode to save disk space necessary to store local objects persistently.

Example 3. The AtomicAction abstract class

```
1   abstract class AtomicAction{
2       int Begin();
3       int Begin(int isolationLevel, int operationMode);
4       int End();
5       int Abort();
6       ...
7       int setIsolationLevel(int isolationLevel);
8       int setOperationMode(int operationMode);
9       ...
10      abstract void notify (String requestId,
11                            String monitorId,
12                            int resourceLevel);
13  }
```

5 Implemented Prototype

The model was fully implemented using Java and CORBA. In the implemented prototype, we used the J2SE 1.4 (Java 2 Platform, Standard Edition) [16] and JavaIDL (CORBA implementation of the Sun Microsystems) [17]. The choice for Java was motivated by its property to be multiplatform. This is an important aspect in a mobile system, where a mobile client access services and data from various machines.

The CORBA was chosen because it provides transparent remote object access, making the development of distributed applications easier. Furthermore, it is a relatively stable technology and has been used successfully in many contexts.

The components of the architecture such as the Cache Manager, the Object Store, the Resource Monitor and the objects that the transactions manipulate are implemented as CORBA servers. The transactions are CORBA clients that access these components and objects.

We chose JavaIDL because it is freely obtained in the site of Sun integrated in the J2SE 1.4.1 and supplies a group of services used in the prototype such as:

Portable Interceptors. Provides hooks, or interception points, through which ORB services can intercept the normal flow of execution of the ORB.

Servant Activators. Servant activator allows the activation of servants on demand when an inactive object receives a request.

Persistent Naming Service. Provides persistence for naming contexts across service shutdowns and startups, and is recoverable in the event of a service failure.

Portable Interceptors were used to intercept and to add a context to the operations of transactions on remote objects. The interceptor in the mobile machine adds to the remote request the identifier of the transaction that requests the operation. Thus, the identifier can be retrieved on the remote object server and used by the lock manager for concurrence control purposes. The servant activators were used to improve efficiency and to save memory. With the use of servant activators the servers do not need to load all objects when they start up. The persistent naming service allows the naming contexts to be recovered in event of failures in the mobile machine.

5.1 Local Cache

Objects necessary for a transaction execution when disconnected should be explicitly chosen by the user and the Cache Manager will be responsible for transferring these objects to the local cache prior to disconnection.

5.2 Disconnections

There are two kinds of disconnections that can occur in mobile machines: planned disconnections and unexpected disconnections. In the first case the mobile machine can be prepared for disconnection.

In case of unexpected disconnection, the actions taken will be different depending on the type of operation mode of an affected transaction. For transactions executing in the *local* operation mode the transaction will continue to execute normally. If the connection is not reestablished until the commit phase, the transaction will delegate the commit process to the Commit Queue and will enter a *pending* state. It will stay in this state retaining all its locks until the commit queue can propagate the transaction results.

For transactions executing in the *local-remote* operation mode the transaction can opt for:

1. Aborting.
2. Changing the operation mode to *local* and continuing execution using the cached copies only.

For transactions in the *remote* operation mode, the transactions will be aborted by the system.

5.3 Lock Collector

Transactions executing in the *remote* or *local-remote* operation mode will acquire locks over objects in the fixed network. Upon a disconnection these locks may never be released. To avoid this, there will be a Lock Collector (LC) responsible for releasing locks that would never be released by some astray transaction.

The Lock Collector (LC) releases the lost locks with the following algorithm:

1. When one transaction *A* wants to access an object *O* locked by other transaction *B* with one lock *L*, the LC sends one message to the transaction B and waits for a response.
2. If transaction B does not respond, L is considered a *lost lock*. Thus the LC releases the lock *L*.
3. If transaction B responds, L is not considered a lost lock and will be kept.

A deadline may be associated with every lock. Thus, the locks are only released by the LC after expiration of the associated deadline.

5.4 Validation Protocol

Transactions can execute in the operation mode *local*. For that, the Cache Manager copies remote object states to the cache of the mobile machine. However, as the remote objects are not locked, inconsistency can happen between the remote objects and its copies in the cache.

To guarantee consistency, it is necessary a version number. When an object state is copied to the cache of a machine, its version number is also copied. The version number will only be incremented after the transaction that updates it commits.

Thus, a transaction *Tr* in the operation mode *local* will only be committed if it passes by the validation protocol. Basically, this protocol will verify if the local objects accessed by the validating transaction are consistent taking into account the transaction isolation level. For each object, the local version number is checked against the remote version number. The object is consistent if the version numbers are equal or if the object was just read by a transaction with a weak isolation level (less than 2).

The validation protocol will be executed in the commit phase of each transaction that executes in the operation mode LOCAL. If all objects of a transaction pass the validation, the validation process returns true. If at least an object is inconsistent or had its lock broken by the LC, the validation process fails and the transaction will be aborted.

The validation protocol will also be executed when a transaction changes its operation mode from LOCAL to LOCAL-REMOTE or from LOCAL to REMOTE because the operation mode REMOTE and LOCAL-REMOTE requires the remote copy to be consistent. The validation will happen when the transaction enters a new operation mode for all objects involved in the transaction.

5.5 Recovery and Persistence

A transaction has recovery and persistence mechanisms. The recovery mechanism wipes out the effects of partially completed transactions. That is, it ensures that the objects do not reflect the results of such transactions. The recovery mechanism is related with the *atomicity* property. The persistence mechanism ensures that the results of transactions that do commit are never lost.

For ensuring recovery, the transaction saves the initial state[1] of each object in recovery records. These recovery records are stored in persistent memory until the end of the transaction. If the transaction ends successfully (commits), the final results are made permanent and the recovery records are discarded. If the transaction fails or

---

[1] The initial state is the state of the object before modifications by the transaction.

aborts, the state of objects manipulated by the transaction are restored with the initial states stored in the recovery records.

For ensuring persistence, the two-phase commit protocol saves the state of all objects manipulated by a transaction in the persistent memory during the prepare-phase of the two-phase commit protocol. Only after saving these objects the transaction is considered committed. If for some reason one or more objects cannot be made persistent, the transaction will abort.

5.6 Concurrency Control

The Lock Managers (LM) implement the *two-phase locking* mechanism [3]. The available operations are SetLock e ReleaseLock (see Example 4). The operation setLock locks an object with a specific lock and must be called before any other operation on the object. The operation releaseLock releases a lock on the object.

Example 4. The class LockManager

```
1   class LockManager{
2       int setLock(Lock lock);
3       int releaseLock(String lockId);
4       ...
5   }
```

The Example 5 presents an object C that uses the concurrency control operations.

Example 5. Using the operation setLock

```
1   class C extends LockManager{
2       ...
3       void operation_1{
4           if (setLock(new Lock(WRITE) == GRANTED)){
5               // Executes a write operation
6           }
7       }
8   }
```

If the operation setLock is called within the scope of a transaction (between the Begin and End operations) the lock will obey the transaction isolation level and will be released automatically by the transaction. Otherwise, if the operation setLock is called outside of the scope of a transaction, the programmer will be responsible for releasing the lock using the operation releaseLock.

The parameter of the operation setLock is an instance of the class Lock (see Example 6). The lock modes implemented by the system are: the read mode and the write mode. The operation conflictsWith verifies if the lock conflicts with other lock. The operation modifiesObject verifies if the lock allows modifications in the locked object. Table 2 shows the conflict relation between lock modes.

Example 6. The class Lock

```
1   class Lock{
2        // Constructor
3        Lock(short lockMode);
4        // Operations
5        boolean conflictsWith(Lock otherLock);
6        boolean modifiesObject();
7        ...
8   }
```

Table 2. Conflicts between lock modes

	READ	**WRITE**
READ	compatible	incompatible
WRITE	incompatible	incompatible

5.7 Example of Use

To illustrate the use of the proposed system, we will consider Example 7 where a transaction MyAtomicAction in the mobile machine executes a set of operations on remote objects objA and objB. The adaptation policy for MyAtomicAction is implemented within the operation notify. If the bandwidth level is less than 10000bps the transaction will change the operation mode and isolation level for LOCAL and UNCOMMITTED_READ respectively.

Example 7. Defining the adaptation policy

```
1   class MyAtomicAction extends AtomicAction{
2
3       void notify (String monitorId, int resourceLevel){
4           // Adaptation policy
5           if (monitorId == "BandwidthMonitor"){
6               if (resourceLevel < 10000 ){
7                   setOperationMode(LOCAL);
8                   setIsolationLevel(UNCOMMITTED_READ)
9               }
10          }
11      }
12  }
```

MyAtomicAction begins the execution with the isolation level SERIALIZABILITY and operation mode REMOTE (Example 8). MyAtomicAction requests the RM bandwidth monitoring. With this request the transaction expresses the need to be notified if the availability of the bandwidth strays outside the window of tolerance. This window of tolerance is specified as the parameter resourceDescriptor.

As MyAtomicAction begins with the REMOTE operation mode, the operations on objects objA and objB will be invoked on the remote copies of the objects.

Example 8. Using an adaptive transaction

```
1   MyAtomicAction act; // Transaction definition
2   ObjectA objA;
3   ObjectB objB;
4
5   act.Begin(SERIALIZABILITY, REMOTE);
6     resourceMonitor.request(act, resourceDescriptor);
7     objA.operation1();
8     objB.operation2();
9     ...
11    objA.operation3();
12  act.End(); // Ends the transaction
```

If during the execution of the transaction, the bandwidth level strays outside the specified window of tolerance, the RM will call the operation `notify` of `MyAtomicAction`. Thus, the adaptation policy of `MyAtomicAction` will be executed. The transaction will then be executed with uncommitted-read isolation level and local operation mode.

6 Conclusions

This paper presents a transactional system for the wireless computing environment, which provides features for adaptation and greater flexibility. It is flexible as it allows a transaction to specify at its beginning two execution parameters: the operation mode and the isolation level. Moreover, these parameters can be changed during transaction execution. This flexibility is required to meet the needs of the wide range of applications in the mobile environment. With respect to adaptation, the model provides *application-aware adaption* in which the underlying system is responsible for resource monitoring and notification of transactions about significant changes in the environment. When receiving a notification, the transaction can decide the appropriate reactions to the change. The contingency actions may consist of transaction aborts or changes in the transaction execution parameters.

The novel aspect of the proposed model is the integration of the adaptation idea to transaction management making it more flexible for the demands of the mobile environment.

Moreover, the model was validated by the development of a prototype written in Java and using the Java IDL-ORB as the communication platform.

Acknowledgments. We would like to thank the CNPq (National Council for Scientific and Technological Development) for the financial support of our research.

References

1. Adya, A.: "Weak Consistency: A Generalized Theory and Optimistic Implementations for Distributed Transactions", Massachusetts Institute of Technology, PhD Thesis, March (1997).
2. ANSI X3.135-1992: "American National Standard for Information Systems – Database Languages – SQL", November (1992)
3. Bernstein, P. A., Hadzilacos, V. and Goodman, N.: "Concurrence Control and Recovery in Database Systems", Addison Wesley (1987)
4. Chrysanthis, P. K.: "Transaction Processing in a Mobile Computing Environment", Workshop on Advances in Parallel and Distributed Systems, 77–82 (1993)
5. Dunham, M. H. and Helal, A.: "A Mobile Transaction Model that Captures Both the Data and the Movement Behavior", ACM-Baltzer Journal on Mobile Networks and Applications, 149–161 (1997)
6. Forman, G. H. and Zahorjan, J.: "The Challenges of Mobile Computing", IEEE Computer, Vol. 27, April (1994)
7. Gray, J., Lorie, R., Putzolu, G. and Traiger, I.: "Granularity of Locks and Degrees of Consistency in a Shared Database", Modeling in Database Management Systems, Amsterdam: Elsevier North-Holland (1976)
8. Jing, J., Helal, A. and Elmagarmid, A.: "Client-Server Computing in Mobile Environments", ACM Computing Surveys (CSUR), Vol. 31, No. 2, June, (1999)
9. Katz, R. H.: "Adaptation and Mobility in Wireless Information Systems", IEEE Personal Communications, Vol. 1, No. 1 (1995)
10. Kistler, J. J. and Satyanarayanan, M.: "Disconnected Operation in Coda File System", ACM Symposium on Operating Systems and Principles, Vol. 10, No. 1, February (1992)
11. Mummert, L. B., Ebling, M. R. and Satyanarayanan, M.: "Exploring Weak Connectivity for Mobile File Access", 15th ACM Symposium on Operation Systems Principles, Colorado, December (1995)
12. Noble, B. D.: "Mobile Data Access", Carnegie Mellon University, PhD Thesis (1998)
13. Parrington, G. D., Shrivastava, S. K., Wheater, S. M. and Little, M. C.: "The Design and Implementation of Arjuna", USENIX Computing Systems Journal, Vol. 8, No. 3 (1995)
14. Pitoura, E. and Bhargava, B.: "Maintaining Consistency of Data in Mobile Distributed Environment", 15th Int. Conference on Distributed Computer Systems (1995)
15. Walborn, G. D. and Chrysanthis, P. K.: "Transaction Processing in PRO-MOTION", 14th ACM Annual Symposium on Applied Computing (1999)
16. J2SE 1.4: "Java2 Platform, Standard Edition", http://java.sun.com/j2se/1.4/index.html, (2003)
17. CORBA: "CORBA Technology and Java Platform" http://java.sun.com/j2ee/corba/, (2003)
18. Imielinski, T. and Badrinath, B. R.: "Mobile Wireless Computing: Challenges in Data Management", Communications of ACM, Vol. 37, No. 10, October (1994)
19. Lu, Q. and Satyanaranyanan M.: "Isolation-only transactions for mobile computing", ACM Operating Systems Review, 28(3) (1994)

20. Dwyer, D., and Bharghavan, V.: "A Mobility-Aware System for Partially Connected Operation", Operating Systems Review, Vol. 31, N° 1 (1997)
21. Baggio, A.: "Design and Early Implementation of the Cadmium Mobile and Disconnectable Middleware Support", Rapport de Recherche, n° 3515, INRIA, October (1998)
22. Astrahan, M. M. et al.: "System R: Relational Approach to Database Management", ACMTransactions on Database Systems, 97–137, June (1976)
23. Telecom Wireless CORBA. In http://www.omg.org/cgi-bin/apps/doclist.pl, (2001)

Experiences with the Active Collections Framework

Rajendra K. Raj

Rochester Institute of Technology
Department of Computer Science
102 Lomb Memorial Drive
Rochester, NY 14623–5608, USA
rkr@cs.rit.edu

Abstract. With increased intra- and inter-enterprise collaboration, consistent near-real-time sharing of operational enterprise data is a major problem faced by large enterprises. Shareable enterprise data is typically stored in persistent data stores such as relational database systems, and enterprise-wide applications continually create, retrieve, update, or delete this data. The Active Collections Framework (ACF) was developed as a simple yet effective approach to address this problem by unifying application access to both enterprise data and subsequent data changes through the Active Collection concept. This paper describes practical experiences with ACF to illustrate its strengths and weaknesses in building distributed enterprise applications.

1 Introduction

An enterprise typically is an organization of people or entities that share some common goals or objectives. Enterprises may vary in size and shape—large and small, commercial and non-commercial, and local and global. Despite these differences, most modern enterprises use software applications to address common needs such as customer/client management, information sharing, and asset/resource tracking and management. Operational enterprise applications are distributed transactional applications that work together to support seamless information flow throughout the enterprise. In recent years, enterprise applications have been built using approaches such as DCE, CORBA, J2EE, .NET, and Web Services. These approaches use different kinds of middleware [1] that focus on how best to amalgamate functionality or services. This paper focuses on operational, not decision support, enterprise applications.

Given early lessons on integrated distributed computing as a research student on the Eden project [2], recently reaffirmed by Fowler's First Law of Distributed Object Design: Don't distribute your objects [3], the author was looking for techniques that minimized the use of distributed objects to improve the performance of such enterprise applications. To this end, we made several observations about enterprise applications. First, enterprise applications typically involve data that is persistent across different runs of individual applications. Second, enterprise

R. Meersman et al. (Eds.): CoopIS/DOA/ODBASE 2003, LNCS 2888, pp. 1504–1520, 2003.
© Springer-Verlag Berlin Heidelberg 2003

data typically lives for several years. Third, users and enterprise applications concurrently share this data, i.e., they perform create, retrieve, update, and delete (CRUD) operations on this data. Fourth, an early problem identified with enterprise-wide sharing of data (that was not designed to be shared) highlights dissonance in the data, both structural (one application's *employee* may be another application's *serf*) and semantic (one application's employee may be required to be a *current* employee while another application's employee could either be a *current* and *former* employee). Problems of data dissonance appear to make data integration difficult and usually motivate the use of distributed objects and services in building enterprise applications.

Despite the apparent problems with data integration, we decided to place enterprise data at the center of enterprise applications. Data dissonance was handled by first massaging the data to a standard form, similar to but not necessarily same as a data warehouse or data mart schema, i.e., applications are exposed to neither raw database schema nor raw data. At the same time, to support CRUD and data sharing across all applications, we developed the Active Collection Framework (ACF) [4], which synthesizes efforts in research areas such as object-oriented frameworks, distributed event and notification mechanisms, and active databases. ACF is an object-oriented framework for distributed transactional applications whose usage metaphor is that of an *active database* [5], as illustrated in Fig. 1. To support the *database* metaphor, our framework hid distribution behind the database. To support the *active* metaphor, the framework required applications to view changes to existing data as events of interest. Other requirements included local and wide area support, and a simple API for programmers of differing abilities to construct enterprise applications.

Several generations of ACF were built to support global mission-critical financial applications successfully in a high-paced setting of a global financial services company [4], and work on ACF is continuing in an academic setting [6]. This paper summarizes some of our practical experiences with ACF in industry and academia. We begin with an overview of ACF, and section 3 describes our experiences with and lessons learned from building and using ACF. Section 4 describes some of the related work in this area.

2   The Active Collection Framework

ACF was designed to facilitate the rapid design and development of distributed applications that need to share enterprise data in near-real-time. Like many frameworks, ACF provides partially specified client-extensible concepts and fully specified services to aid in the development of distributed transactional applications.

2.1   ACF Concepts

As discussed below, the two main concepts in ACF are those of ACF objects and Active collections.

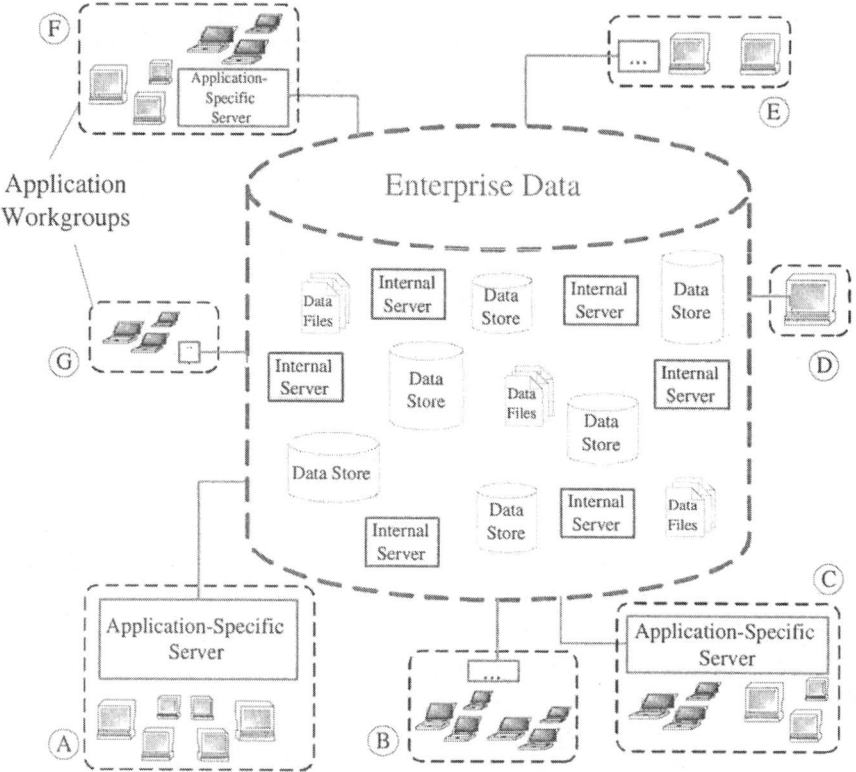

Fig. 1. Enterprise Applications using the Active Database Metaphor

ACF objects. ACF objects are essentially object representations of data stored in the underlying relational data store[1]. The ACF approach to object-relational mapping is similar to that of Ambler's [7]. In the simplest case, instance variables of a simple ACF object typically correspond to fields in a single row in a relational database table, with the table itself corresponding to the object's class. For example, in a human resources application, an employee object may have its data attributes (e.g., employee id, name, and address) represented as columns in a row of a relational table, say Employee, which represents all employees. More complex ACF objects can be composed with corresponding changes to type and numbers of required relational tables. While no limits are placed on ACF object complexity, performance considerations usually impose simplicity to ensure efficient CRUD operations.

---

[1] The paper treats data stores as being only relational databases to reflect our experiences with ACF implementations. In general, ACF data stores can be object databases, flat files, XML documents, or data streams, but we have not investigated these different data stores in depth.

ACF objects are instances of subclasses of ACFObject, and inherit behavior from ACFObject, which provides methods for each object to store and retrieve itself using ACF services. Each application can provide additional domain behavior within subclasses of ACFObject used in the application.

Active Collections. Active collections are ACF's technique to integrate access to both data and data changes. Informally defined, an active collection is a collection of objects whose membership is specified by a predicate (query) on enterprise data. The collection is active in the sense that its contents change as enterprise data changes. New objects enter the collection when they satisfy the query, and existing objects leave the collection when they no longer satisfy the query. Active collections unify the use of the same query for both data selection and data changes; this leads to a useful abstraction that can be applied to simplify the construction of near-real-time transactional distributed applications.

While predicates underlying active collections may be arbitrarily dynamic, they usually tend to be simpler and static in order to make them understandable and performant. From a pragmatic consideration, complex ACF queries can lead to prohibitive limits on performance because these queries need to be applied on the data store as well as on data on the network. Queries for active collection membership are typically expressible in a subset of a query language such as SQL. As data changes, objects change, and so do active collections, whose members get removed, added, or modified. An active collection is loosely dependent on each of its objects; in Observer pattern terminology, the active collection is the observer and each object in the collection is a subject.

ACF provides an assurance to keep each client's active collections up-to-date as long as the collections are being used. Clients specify the degree of commitment required, with weaker commitments allowing for better performance but with looser consistency, and vice versa. In programming terms, the client requests the construction of an active collection by specifying a query to ACF, along with specific parameters to establish: (a) synchronous or asynchronous notification of the initial active collection as needed, (b) when change notification is to be received: at specified times, specified intervals of time, or whenever a data change event takes place, and (c) a list of dependents for the active collection. ACF evaluates the query, and then creates and returns the active collection to the client as specified.

2.2   Client and Web API

ACF's client API provides standard operations for (a) creating, modifying or deleting ACF objects and (b) retrieving ACF objects in the form of active collections. We have experimented with a web API but the use of the http protocol makes truly active notifications infeasible [6]. For full ACF functionality, clients must use a client API written in a supported language: in the past, Smalltalk-80, C++, and Java were supported in different ACF implementations.

The data-centric view promoted by ACF requires all CRUD operations to be supported:

1. Creation: Clients create new ACF objects and store them on the data store within the context of an ACF transaction. For a transaction that commits, ACF inserts the required data in the data store. Failed transactions are reported to the issuing client program, along with likely causes for failure.
2. Retrieval: To retrieve ACF objects, the client requests ACF to create an active collection, which handles both data retrieval from the data stores and subsequent data changes during run-time.
3. Updating and deleting: Modifications or deletions to existing objects are similar to creation: instead of creating ACF objects, the client program first retrieves existing objects into new active collections, and then modifies or deletes these objects in the context of a transaction.

To build an application using ACF, application developers need to perform two major tasks: (a) develop appropriate client tier applications, and (b) develop object implementations (behavior) for application extensions to ACF classes. ACF permits its application developers to focus on their business problem domain, not low-level infrastructural issues of data access, event handling, and distribution.

2.3   ACF Services

At a logical level, the ACF Service monitors all changes made to the data store by all applications. For each data change, it re-evaluates the previously registered active collection queries. When ACF detects a data change that both satisfies an active collection query and impacts its (the collection's) contents, the ACF Service updates the collection with the specific data change: addition or removal of an item, or an update to an existing member. This is similar to publish-subscribe mechanisms used for distributed events, but our focus is on managing and reacting to data changes. Subsequently, the collection notifies its dependents, if any, and changes propagate consistently throughout the client application. All re-evaluations performed by ACF are event-based and processed in the order in which data changes are received. The physical ACF implementation optimizes the logical description where possible, e.g., minimizes use of the underlying (slower) data store.

Client applications in the top tier interact with ACF using a proprietary client API to the middle tier, as depicted in Fig. 2. The ACF server manages (1) queries underlying active collections, (2) subsequent notifications to issuing clients, and (3) vagaries of underlying data stores. The data tier is assumed to consist predominantly of relational databases.

Additional details about ACF may be found available in earlier documents [4,6].

3   Experiences and Lessons Learned

ACF has been successfully used in the financial domain to build a diverse mix of applications including high-speed trading systems, performance monitoring of

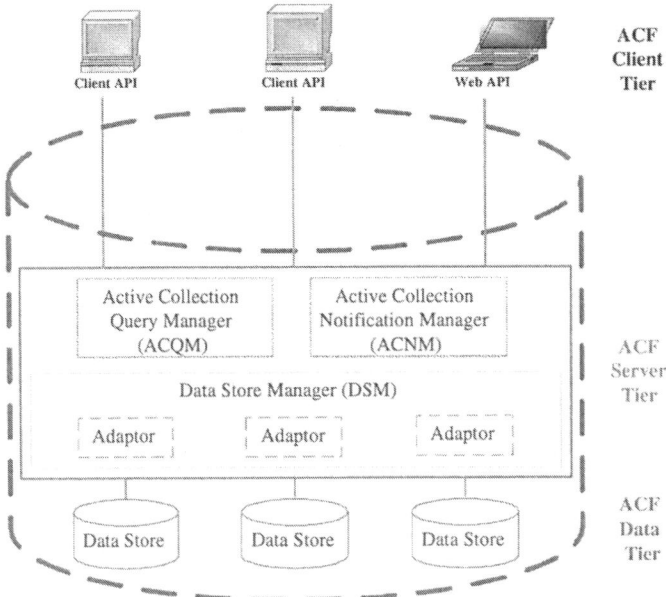

Fig. 2. Logical Architecture of ACF

stock portfolios, and near-real-time risk management systems for bond traders. Despite its origins in the financial domain, ACF is a general object-oriented framework to facilitate the construction of distributed applications in different domains. Several generations of ACF (Smalltalk-80 through C++ to Java) were built to address our errors and omissions, as well as the changing needs of the enterprise. ACF was originally built using proprietary technologies and later with CORBA in an industrial setting. At present, ACF is being re-designed and re-implemented using messaging and other "open" products in a university setting.

This section describes practical experiences with ACF and lessons learned. Although ACF uses an active database metaphor, we believe several lessons are applicable to others building distributed applications. While several experiences are closely related, we categorized them into separate subsections for ease of explanation.

3.1   Data Standardization

For ACF to be used, it is essential that enterprise-wide applications that want to share operational data have agreed on representation and usage of the common data. While a canonical representation for operational data is useful, our experience has been that such standardization was not required. More importanatly, ACF's application developers had to agree on how to organize and inter-relate data, and when and how often to share data among applications. ACF's object-relational mapping was sufficiently flexible that it supported the creation of objects in different object-oriented languages, e.g., Smalltalk-80, C++, and Java, from the same data representation, and also supported objects of different classes within each object-oriented language. This allowed different applications to be written by different application developers in the programming language of their choice.

On the database system side, ACF was designed to utilize DBMS features such as views and materialized views to accommodate any representation differences. Also, because it was targeted for operational data, not warehoused data, ACF was not concerned with tracking canonical historical data where schema standardization, integration, and evolution are (harder) problems that must be solved. Our practical experience has been that with sufficient impetus from senior enterprise management, operational data differences can easily be addressed; without such impetus, we have observed that it is difficult to get data designers and application developers come to closure on data representation and sharing.

A major lesson learned in this context was that a substantial portion of the work needed to build distributed applications with operational data integration is completed when applications agree on the format and pattern of data sharing. In the case of ACF, its simple client API did permit data, once structured, to be shared in multiple formats.

3.2   Client Issues

The *active* nature of ACF requires change notifications to be pushed to clients when their active collections have changed. Our basic approach was to provide a "fat client" API to push notifications using callbacks, and we successfully implemented such client APIs in Smalltalk-80, C++, Java, as well as a CORBA (specifically, Orbix) client. When we moved to web clients, the http protocol prevented active change notification so we relied on an adapted polling technique [6].

Although one of the prime motivators for ACF was the need to support active notifications, our experience after building several applications with ACF was that few applications truly require such active notifications implemented within ACF. That is, while the active metaphor should be preserved in the client API, a polling-based internal implementation of ACF would have been sufficient for many applications. A polling-based approach was adapted for implementing wide-area scalability as discussed in Section 3.5. A fairly common reason for enterprise applications not utilizing fully active notifications was simply that many applications had been originally designed to check for changes periodically, e.g., hourly or daily, and extra effort would have been required on the part of both application developers (to modify their applications) and application users (to adapt to a more flexible mode of operation). On the other hand, active notifications were a boon in situations where changes were highly unpredictable but required immediate action on the part of applications or their users. Regardless of actual need, providing an active client API was found to be simplify application development.

From a client programming language perspective, in each of the languages used, a traditional inheritance from ACFObject approach was used to implement general ACF objects, which was acceptable for developing new applications. When third party or legacy applications needed to use ACF, however, such an inheritance-based technique was simply not usable. In several of these situations, the use of mixins (or STL in C++) was more appropriate and used. The real issue here was that the business application model needed to be tightly coupled to the ACF approach to make effective use of active notifications. Part of this coupling made sense because ACF offers features not offered by any other framework; we believe this is no different than the use of other mechanisms to handle distributed events, which also impose similar coupling.

By requiring *a priori* agreement on data and integration models, ACF makes it easier to achieve language and platform independence. Because ACF objects are data-centric, not behavior-centric, objects created in one language are similar to objects created in another, i.e., sharing data between clients written in Smalltalk-80 or C++ is simplified. For example, in a foreign exchange financial application, programs written in Smalltalk-80 were being replaced by programs written in C++; "data" objects created in the former Smalltalk-80 applications could be used from the database system as "data" objects in the C++ applications. Moreover, during parallel production testing of the Smalltalk-80 and C++ applications, the old and new applications could (and did) use the same database system, which alleviated testing requirements considerably.

On the client side, our experience was that ACF was not sufficiently flexible. As a result, we have begun investigating the use of SOAP-like messaging to achieve transport and application semantics independence.

3.3   Container Managed Persistence (CMP)

The adaptors to different data stores, as depicted in Fig. 2, were initially custom-crafted for the ACF server so any support for automated development of these adaptors would have simplified ACF server development. Additionally, initial ACF versions required the addition of two fields to each relational table used to store, instantiate, and share ACF objects: (1) a unique object identifier and (2) a version number (or timestamp). Unique identification of objects was essential for flexible and consistent caching of objects for efficient sharing. Versioning was required to support an optimistic concurrency control scheme to enhance distributed system performance. As we gained experience with ACF's usage, subsequent versions of ACF were modified to eliminate the requirement for these fields. We dropped the unique object identifier in favor of a unique (preferably non-composite) key in the database table(s) corresponding to each ACF object. We also made the version number optional to allow ACF support legacy and third-party data better: when a versioning mechanism was available, ACF could continue to provide optimistic concurrency control. Our experience with ACF has convinced us that these two fields are necessary for creating performant distributed applications, but as expected, there are trade-offs between flexibility and performance.

Some problems encountered with ACF are similar to problems faced by Enterprise JavaBeans (EJB) [8] developers in the context of entity beans. Transparent CMP leads to database schemas that are hard to maintain and evolve, whether in EJB or in ACF. The data and middle tiers are tightly coupled due to mapping between database tables and objects instantiated in the middle tier. In ACF, however, the objects are really cached representations of data stored in the database, and ACF middleware can be optimized to make use of the underlying database system effectively: ACF supports aggregated object retrieval and storage (e.g., retrieving all required employee objects in one trip to the database system), as well as demand-driven object retrieval (e.g., retrieving employee objects only when actually needed). The lesson learned here was that any middleware should flexibly utilize the full power of the underlying database systems.

3.4   Performance

With the experience of several generations of ACF implemented and ACF applications deployed, we have learned that performance and scalability are not easily grafted on to existing distributed applications, but must be designed into the system from the beginning.

Asynchrony is the *modus operandi* in ACF. Initial and ongoing notifications as a result of the creation and modification of active collections are done using asynchronous callbacks. Asynchronous messaging typically provides flexibility and improves the performance of distributed applications [3], although asynchrony imposes the need for application developers to write correct concurrent programs. We initially provided synchronous messaging from client to ACF server tiers both to register new active collections and make changes to existing objects. We used synchrony in these contexts due to our initial prejudices: we believed it was easier for applications to treat these two kinds of activities synchronously because we felt that these activities were under direct application control, i.e., the application could decide when to create a new collection or to make a change to an existing object. The lesson learned here is that there is really no compelling reason for synchrony to be imposed here: ACF can and should provide a uniform asynchronous model for these activities.

As a result of working with ACF applications, we have learned that separate optimization of database and distributed system performance is not guaranteed to yield optimal performance: system optimizations must be done jointly. While we have developed simple heuristics (e.g., reduce the number of round trips to the database system) on improving overall ACF application performance, we are currently leaning toward using automated tools such as those developed by Tiwary [9]. Overall system performance can also be improved via data and server partitioning as discussed in the context of scalability in the next subsection.

ACF, by default, uses optimistic concurrency control based on our observations for various kinds of financial applications. With over 6 years of running different ACF applications, we found that rollbacks due to concurrency conflicts were needed only twice; on each occasion, an application developer was running some tests by running code in a debugger. Based on this experience, we believe that extending ACF to provide pessimistic concurrency control is not a high priority.

3.5   Scalability

As ACF became more accepted within the enterprise, more applications and more diverse kinds of applications began using ACF. We considered this to be a "good problem" for ACF as it allowed us to explore whether different scaling options developed for ACF actually worked as designed. Scalability was approached in ACF using the standard approaches: scaling up, scaling out, and scaling down.

Scale up refers to the ability to continue to grow within a single instance of the typical ACF configuration and continue to provide required service levels as load increases. Scale up, when it works, is usually the easiest approach because changes typically are accomplished by hardware upgrades, with few changes to the software environment. Testing is needed only to ensure whether the overall system performs as required. Because scale up reaches its limits at some point, a more flexible approach to scalability is usually needed. Our experience with ACF's scaling up was that it provided a sufficient degree of scale up, as would any other distributed frameworks, and there were no noteworthy differences.

Scale out is accomplished by adding instances to the ACF configuration to provide required service levels, and scale out can be applied independently at each tier. Choices available for ACF scale out included load sharing (by duplicating servers) and partitioning (by functionality, workgroup, or geography). We had designed ACF for scale out right from the beginning, and ACF uses partitioning in two ways as discussed below.

First, as depicted in Fig. 3, a federated approach allows a new ACF server at a higher level to connect two partitioned AC servers; here, the users may be partitioned into groups via natural workgroups (e.g., employees by department) or by functionality (e.g., employees who work on different accounts by account number range), or by geography (e.g., employees who work on each given floor), with each group served with adequate performance by their own ACF server. The higher level ACF server is used to provide sharing at a higher level among different groups. Our experience was that this approach worked well within each local area setting.

Second, as depicted in Fig. 4, when geographical partitioning spans a wide-area network, an alternative partitioning was needed so that there could be increased logging between the two local-area networks to support robust failure recovery. In this scheme, a polling technique (cf. Section 3.2) was used to perform notification across the wide-area network within the ACF server infrastructure, although the client interfaces on each end continued to use the active metaphor. ACF users found the hidden polling acceptable because the overall wide-area performance of ACF was kept down to a fraction of a minute. The lesson here was that the databases needed to be replicated across the wide-area network to guarantee local performance, with performance penalties imposed only on

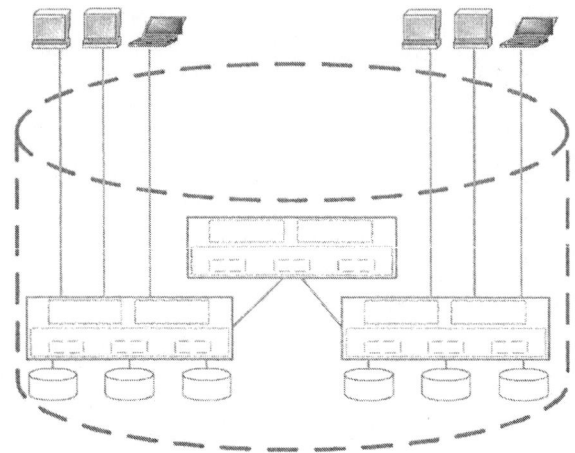

Fig. 3. ACF Local Area Partitioning (Federated Scheme)

wide-area data sharing. We also learned that when data was shared across the wide-area, primary data ownership for changing each given piece of data had to be assigned to one side to reduce data conflicts. For example, in a trading application between London and New York, all London-originated trades were primarily owned by London, and trades originating in New York trades were owned within New York. During common trading hours, New York traders avoided modifying London trades and vice versa to minimize data conflicts due to the increased window size for optimistic concurrency control imposed by wide-area database system replication.

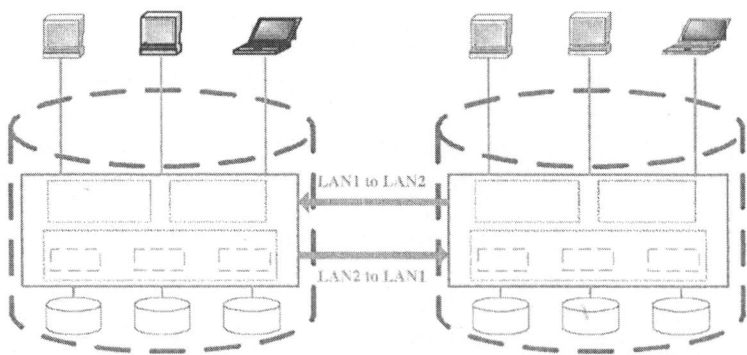

Fig. 4. ACF Wide-Area Partitioning (Replication Scheme)

Scale down refers to the ability to support clients who need less or who cannot (or need not) pay for full ACF functionality. Because the ACF "fat client" API is designed to communicate with a "virtual" ACF database, it can also work directly with a data store without requiring ACF middleware. This permitted ACF to be scaled down to support active collections without requiring the ACF middleware. For example, if the client labeled D in Fig. 1 needed to be scaled down, the client could be connected to a separate database system using the ACF client API to take care of application needs. More importantly, such scale down could be brought about without requiring client application programming changes.

3.6   Failure and Recovery

Our experience was that ACF provided a graceful approach to recovery from failures at the client and middle tiers.

1. Application client process failures: First, note that ACF application clients are really servers for each application workgroup. If an application client process fails, the application is responsible for recovery of any application logic. ACF guidelines and code provided to applications permitted graceful recovery using the inherent power of active collections to permit clients transparently recover application state from the underlying data store. For example, assume an application had set up an active collection to keep track of the number of employees assigned to a specific project in Hawaii, and then the application client crashed. While the application client was down, assume that two new employees, Jane Doe and John Smith, get assigned to the same project. Subsequently when the application client re-starts and re-registers the same active collection using the classes provided by ACF, the client process will automatically be notified of the two new employees in Hawaii due to the active properties of the registered collection.

2. ACF server failures: When an ACF server fails, ACF code within application clients uses "wait to reconnect" logic. When the ACF server restarts, application clients immediately reconnect and re-register the previously created active collections with the ACF server, thus automatically permitting ACF clients to get notified of what changes occurred during ACF server downtime. This transparency is possible because ACF clients and servers jointly share the required knowledge about the active collections held by the application clients.

   Is the ACF server a stateless or stateful server? The server typically maintains information about active collections registered by each client; our experience has been that the state maintained by the ACF server is fairly small under most application conditions. Moreover, if needed to, ACF could store this state on the database to facilitate recovery on failure, which could make the ACF server essentially stateless.

3. Data tier failures: Any failure at the database tier is considered to be a severe failure due to the lack of access to shared enterprise data. When the data tier is down, application clients get notified of the failure. The safest recovery option requires the restarting of the database server. An alternative

approach would be to introduce redundancy at the database tier so that the ACF components could hot backup to the redundant database server. While we have experimented with the hot backup, our experience has been that treating database tier failures as catastrophic failures has not been onerous; in fact, because ACF regards the database tier as the repository of "truth," we believe this approach avoids overall data corruption.

3.7   Messages and Message Formats

Messages between ACF clients and the ACF server use a proprietary, compact, self-defining format to improve the performance of change notifications. Early versions shipped entire (since ACF objects are data-centric, this really means all of the data) objects that had changed, but we found that shipping such big objects led to performance degradation. Later versions of ACF shipped only data changes to each object, which yielded substantial performance improvements, both within local-area and wide-area contexts. Of course, wide-area shipping object changes can be done only if the original object is also available in its entirety at the remote database system, i.e., some modifications to the ACF wide-area infrastructure had to be made.

Lessons learned from ACF messages can be applied to the use of XML in Web Services and other application settings to define interfaces and to format messages. As Baker [10] points out, claimed advantages of XML messages being both textual (non-binary) and self-describing should not be overstated. Because messages in XML, as opposed to binary, are open and standard, application programmers can easily write code to create or understand messages. There are, however, distinct drawbacks. First, an inherent assumption is that there is no message dissonance (disagreement on message structure) between sender and receiver, similar to the lack of data dissonance discussed earlier. Second, verbosity of typical XML messages leads to increased bandwidth requirements, and increased processor time for message marshalling/unmarshalling, both at sender and receiver. Protocols for efficient message transfer and encoding/decoding may be required in time-critical applications, but in other situations, simplified software development and maintenance due to XML, may make the price worth paying. While we have found the message format used by ACF to be convenient, it is not flexible to inter-operate with non-ACF applications. In our current work with ACF, we are experimenting with simpler self-describing textual formats (XML-based and otherwise), and the use of SOAP, but are trying to retain the simplicity of ACF's message format where possible.

3.8   Miscellany

ACF originally worked under closed world semantics, i.e., ACF applications had to live in their own world, and could not share data with non-ACF applications, and vice versa. It was simpler to use closed world semantics both to ensure the validity of active collections and to prevent performance degradation of client notification. Techniques developed for wide-area scale out, discussed in Section 3.5, were easily adaptable for integrating non-ACF applications into the ACF fold but at the expense of requiring components of the wide area infrastructure such as the logging subsystem. We are currently exploring simpler performant techniques to achieve the same degree of openness.

In most production settings, there often is some middleware dark matter [11]: in the case of ACF, which relies on the cleanness of data, we experienced several cases of undocumented or poorly documented software applications typically written using a non-standard (for the given enterprise) mechanism such as Perl or VBA scripts. These applications needed to be integrated belatedly on a case-by-case basis.

Security is critical to many enterprise applications, but current implementations of ACF pay insufficient attention to it primarily because we worked on the assumption that all applications within an enterprise could be trusted. The current reliance, however, on security mechanisms provided by the underlying database systems was found to be insufficient. As with performance, we now believe that applications should be built with security in mind, and we are currently exploring techniques to enhance security within ACF.

4   Related Work

This section outlines some related work in the different areas that ACF synthesizes. The overall approach of focusing on a common API for all enterprise data is similar to the solution suggested by products such as Sybase's Open Server [12]. Open Server provides the tools and interfaces needed to create custom servers that can implement a variety of enterprise data solutions: connect to other relational databases, perform calculations, or even implement parts of the ACF server functionality. Work in federated databases provides some of the motivation for implementing ACF [13].

Active collections derive from two distinct areas of research: active monitoring of information change within databases, and event management in distributed computing. Database systems traditionally tended to be passive, i.e., when a query is made to a database system, the result of the query reflects the state of the database at that specific instant of time. Active databases [5] were proposed to monitor changes in database state by providing rules or triggers for monitoring database state changes. Mechanisms provided by most commercial database systems such as DB2 or Oracle are typically triggers or alerts that are often restricted to single tables. Triggers have been generalized as active queries [14], which may be defined on views, multiple tables, and nested within other active queries. Continuous queries [15] were proposed for monitoring insertions of new records into databases, and subsequently generalized as continual queries [16] to permit monitoring of updates and deletions too. Bhide et al. [17] explore coherency criteria for maintaining stock portfolio changes when using continuous queries. The queries that create ACF's active collections represent a generalization of continual queries as a convenient programming paradigm for use in the context of distributed enterprise application development.

Events and notification are often used in distributed applications [18]. Earlier event management systems were large-grained and static, and so did not provide the fine-grained flexibility required in ACF. ACF's publish-subscribe engine within ACF's query and notification handling has similarities to distributed event handling [19], e.g., efficient multi-stage filtering [20] and composite event handling [21].

Data stores, especially database systems, play a central role in ACF's approach. Recent publish-subscribe work reported by Jin and Strom [22] uses relational subscriptions for events and uses stateful middleware to improve reliability, but the focus is on improved event handling rather than on overall enterprise application development. The Oracle AQ product [23] uses the database system for improving reliability by storing messages on queues and databases as needed. The recent impetus in building data stream management systems is likely to lead to developments in treating data changes as events [24,25]. ACF's focus is on the construction of transactional distributed applications in an overall sense, not on solving subsets of the continual query or distributed event management problems in their own right.

Results of the above-related work may be utilized within corresponding subsets of ACF for our ongoing work. Also, the use of standards-based approaches in distributed application development is now commonplace, with J2EE, .NET, and Web Services being the current dominant approaches. Of course, each of these approaches provides features that correspond to some subset of ACF, for example, the CMP features of J2EE as discussed in Section 3.3.

5   Final Remarks

This paper described several of our practical experiences with and lessons learned from the Active Collections Framework, which attempts to solve the problem of developing reliable distributed applications by focusing on the sharing of enterprise operational data. Active collections simplify application design and development by unifying access to data and changes to data. The ACF model has been implemented in several versions in industry and academia and has been found to be useful in building a variety of financial software applications.

Our overall experience with distributed enterprise application development, using ACF as well as other approaches based on CORBA and J2EE, has convinced us that the hallmark of a good framework for distributed enterprise application is one that imposes the least burden on the programmer, i.e., one that gets out of the programmer's way! While ACF has provided a flexible foundation on which to build transactional distributed applications, it nevertheless imposes its own requirements on the programmer, and so we are exploring different techniques to reduce ACF's onus on the application developer.

Acknowledgements. Association with several computing professionals at Morgan Stanley, where ACF was originally developed, and several graduate students at RIT led to the experiences with ACF reported here. Special thanks are due to Kevin F. Brown, who jointly designed and implemented the initial versions of ACF; to Sumanth Vepa, who helped to generalize ACF concepts and use them in non-financial settings; and to Bhaskar Gopalan, who re-implemented ACF at RIT.

References

1. Bernstein, P.A.: Middleware: A Model for Distributed System Services. Communications of the ACM **39** (1996) 86–98
2. Black, A.P.: Supporting Distributed Applications: Experience with Eden. In: Proc. of the 10th ACM Symposium on Operating Systems Principles. (1985)
3. Fowler, M., Rice, D., Foemmel, M., Hieatt, E., Mee, R., Stafford, R.: Patterns of Enterprise Application Architecture. Addison Wesley (2002)
4. Raj, R.K.: The Active Collection Framework. ACM SIGAPP Applied Computing Review: Special Issue on Distributed Computing **7** (1999) 9–13
5. Widom, J., Ceri, S., eds.: Active Database Systems: Triggers and Rules For Advanced Database Processing. Morgan Kaufmann (1996)
6. Gopalan, B.: Implementing the Active Collections Framework. MS Project Report, Department of Computer Science, Rochester Institute of Technology, Rochester, NY (2003)
7. Ambler, S.W.: The Fundamentals of Mapping Objects to Relational Databases (2003) http://www.agiledata.org/essays/mappingObjects.html.
8. Sun Microsystems: Java 2 Platform Enterprise, Edition (J2EE), v1.4 (2003) http://java.sun.com/j2ee/.
9. Tiwary, A., Pardyak, P.: Evaluating Transaction System Performance and Scalability Using Real Workloads. In: Proc. of the 9th Intl. Workshop on High Performance Transaction Systems (HPTS), Pacific Grove, CA (2001)
10. Baker, S.: Web Services and CORBA. In: Proc. of the Intl. Conference on Distributed Objects and Applications (DOA 2002), Springer-Verlag, LNCS 2519 (2002) 618–632
11. Vinoski, S.: Internet Computing: Toward Integration – Middleware "Dark Matter". IEEE Distributed Systems Online **3** (2002)
12. Sybase Corporation: Open Server Server-Library/C Reference Manual (2001)
13. Conrad, S., Eaglestone, B., Hasselbring, W., Roantree, M., Saltor, F., Schonhoff, M., Strassler, M., Vermeer, M.: Research Issues in Federated Database Systems. SIGMOD Record **26** (1997) 54–56
14. Schreier, U., Pirahesh, H., Agrawal, R., Mohan, C.: Alert: An Architecture for transforming a Passive DBMS into an Active DBMS. In: Proc. of the International Conference on Very Large Data Bases, Barcelona, Spain (1991) 469–478
15. Terry, D., Goldberg, D., Nichols, D., Oki, B.: Continuous Queries over Append-Only Databases. In: Proc. of the ACM-SIGMOD Intl. Conference on Management of Data. (1992) 321–330
16. Liu, L., Pu, C., Tang, W., Buttler, D., Biggs, J., Zhou, T., Benningho, P., Han, W.: CQ: A Personalized Update Monitoring Toolkit. In: Proc. of the ACM-SIGMOD Intl. Conference on Management of Data. (1998)
17. Bhide, M., Ramamritham, K., Shenoy, P.: Efficiently Maintaining Stock Portfolios Up-To-Date On The Web. In: Proc. of the 12th Intl. Workshop on Research Issues in Data Engineering: Engineering e-Commerce/e-Business Systems (RIDE'02), San Jose, CA (2002)

18. Object Management Group: Notification Service Specification (2002)
19. DEBS'02: Proceedings of the Intl. Workshop on Distributed Event-Based Systems (2002)
20. Handurukande, S., Eugster, P.T., Felber, P., Guerraoui, R.: Event Systems: How to Have One's Cake and Eat It Too. In: Proc. of the Intl. Workshop on Distributed Event-Based Systems (DEBS'02). (2002)
21. Pietzuch, P.R., Shand, B., Bacon, J.: A Framework for Event Composition in Distributed Systems. In: Proc. of Middleware 2003, ACM/IFIP/USENIX International Middleware Conference, Rio de Janeiro, Brazil (2003)
22. Jin, Y., Strom, R.: Relational Subscription Middleware for Internet-Scale Publish-Subscribe. In: Proc. of the 2nd Intl. Workshop on Distributed Event-Based Systems (DEBS'03), San Diego, CA (2003)
23. Gawlick, D., Mishra, S.: Information Sharing With the Oracle Database. In: Proc. of the 2nd Intl. Workshop on Distributed Event-Based Systems (DEBS'03), San Diego, CA (2003)
24. Ding, L., Rundensteiner, E.A., Heineman, G.T.: MJoin: A Metadata-Aware Stream Join Operator. In: Proc. of the 2nd Intl. Workshop on Distributed Event-Based Systems (DEBS'03), San Diego, CA (2003) 618–632
25. SWiM'03: Stream Winter Meeting (2003) http://telegraph.cs.berkeley.edu/swim.

Porting OMTTs to CORBA

Raul Silaghi[1], Alfred Strohmeier[1], and Jörg Kienzle[2]

[1] Software Engineering Laboratory
Swiss Federal Institute of Technology in Lausanne
CH-1015 Lausanne EPFL, Switzerland
{Raul.Silaghi,Alfred.Strohmeier}@epfl.ch
[2] School of Computer Science
McGill University
Montreal, QC H3A 2A7, Canada
Joerg.Kienzle@mcgill.ca

Abstract. The Common Object Request Broker Architecture standardizes a platform- and programming-language-independent distributed object computing environment. It also provides a standard for several distributed services. The Object Transaction Service provides an object-oriented framework for distributed transaction processing, especially for Online Transaction Processing in business applications. The current CORBA OTS allows multi-threading inside a transaction, leaving, however, thread coordination to the application programmer, which can be dangerous. Based on the Open Multithreaded Transaction model, we present in this paper the design of a Thread Syn-chronization Coordinator, *ThreadSyncCoordinator*, which provides the desired thread control inside a multithreaded transaction. A blocking commit protocol ensures that once in a transaction, a thread cannot leave before the outcome of the transaction has been determined, guaranteeing the ACID properties for multi-threaded transactions. We also show how the *ThreadSyncCoordinator* can be used to design and implement complex applications, e.g., an Online Auction System, in an elegant way.

Keywords: CORBA, Object Transaction Service, OMTTs, Transactions, Concurrency.

1 Introduction

Online Transaction Processing is the foundation of the world's business computing. It is the system that ensures that the last two seats on flight LX 1754 to Catania (Sicily) are assigned, *together*, to a honeymooning couple; that the balance printed on your ATM ticket in Taipei *exactly* matches the balance in the bank's central datastore in Zürich; or that the last discovered ancient sarcophagus is promised to only *one* museum. Moreover, this reliability is accomplished even in the face of (non-catastrophic) failure of hardware and software around the system.

Transactions are an important programming paradigm that simplify the construction of reliable business applications. Initially deployed in commercial applications to

R. Meersman et al. (Eds.): CoopIS/DOA/ODBASE 2003, LNCS 2888, pp. 1521–1542, 2003.

protect data in centralized databases [1], the transaction concept has been extended to the broader context of distributed data and distributed computation. Nowadays, it is widely accepted that transactions are key to constructing reliable distributed enterprise applications, ensuring the correct handling of interrelated and concurrent updates of data and providing fault tolerance in the presence of failures.

A transaction is a unit of work comprised of several operations made on one or several shared system resources (also referred to as *transactional objects*), governed by the ACID properties: *Atomicity, Consistency, Isolation,* and *Durability* [1]. Once a new transaction is started, all update operations on transactional objects are done on behalf of that transaction. At any time during the execution of the transaction, it can *abort*, which means that the state of the system is restored (i.e., *rolled back*) to the state at the beginning of the transaction. Once a transaction has completed successfully (referred to as *committed*), the effects become permanent and visible to the outside world.

Along with the Common Object Request Broker Architecture (CORBA), the Object Management Group defined a set of standard object services. One of these services is the Object Transaction Service (OTS), which provides an object-oriented framework for distributed transaction processing. Besides the fact that the OTS supports flat and nested transactions, it also allows multithreading inside a transaction, leaving, however, thread coordination inside the transaction to the app-lication programmer. Unfortunately, this can be dangerous. For example, a thread can decide to leave the transaction and perform some other operations before the outcome of the transaction has been determined, or a thread can roll back the transaction without notifying the other threads. In the OTS model, threads do not actually "join" a transaction, because the transaction support is not aware of concurrency. Instead, they get associated a *transaction context*, which makes them act on behalf of that transaction. Since transaction contexts can be passed around, a thread might get associated a transaction context even if it is already working within the scope of another transaction. In this case, the previous transaction context associated with the thread is simply discarded. Using such a model, it is very hard to guarantee the ACID properties for multithreaded transactions.

In order to overcome this drawback, we considered the Open Multithreaded Transaction (OMTT) model for controlling and structuring not only accesses to objects, as usual in transaction systems, but also threads taking part in transactions. Based on this model, we designed a Thread Synchronization Coordinator, *ThreadSyncCoordinator*, that sits between the individual client threads and the CORBA OTS, providing safe thread control inside a multithreaded transaction. With the help of this object, client threads are able to explicitly join an ongoing transaction, and get access to the shared transactional resources. A blocking commit protocol ensures that once in a transaction, a thread cannot leave before the outcome of the transaction has been determined. Events are used to signal all participant threads in a multithreaded transaction to vote on the outcome of the transaction.

The outline of the rest of this paper is as follows: Section 2 provides an overview of the CORBA Object Transaction Service, introducing the major components and interfaces, the different application programming models, and the problems related to multithreaded transactions. Section 3 describes briefly the Open Multithreaded Transaction model. Section 4 presents the design of the Thread Synchronization Coordinator that implements the OMTT model on top of CORBA OTS; some issues related to the proposed design are also discussed in this section. Section 5 shows how the Thread Synchronization Coordinator can be used to design and implement an Online Auction System in an elegant way, and Section 6 draws some conclusions.

2   The CORBA Object Transaction Service

In this section, we provide a brief introduction to the Common Object Request Broker Architecture with a special emphasis on the Object Transaction Service and the way it provides transaction support to application developers. Towards the end, we highlight the major problems in the current CORBA OTS with respect to multithreaded transactions.

The *Object Request Broker* (ORB) is a software component that mediates the transfer of messages between distributed objects, hiding the underlying complexity of network communications from developers. The architecture and the specifications of the ORB are defined by the Object Management Group (OMG) [2] in the Common Object Request Broker Architecture (CORBA) [3]. The CORBA standard enables transparent interoperability between applications in heterogeneous distributed environments. Due to its Interface Definition Language (IDL), CORBA allows the construction of complex applications in the form of a set of interacting software components that may communicate across the boundaries of networks, using different programming languages and operating systems. According to the standard, ORB implementations for different languages and platforms can work together using the Internet Inter-ORB Protocol (IIOP).

Object Services are a collection of basic services for using and implementing objects. These services are required to construct distributed applications, and are independent of application domains. They should be designed to do one thing *well*, and they should only be as complicated as they need to be. Not all services have to be provided by a CORBA vendor; however, the most important ones, such as Naming, Event, Notification, *Transaction*, Concurrency, Persistence, and Security, usually are.

2.1   The Object Transaction Service

Transaction processing systems have become ubiquitous and are the basis for all facets of commercial applications that rely on concurrent access to shared data. The *transaction paradigm* has been an integral part in designing reliable distributed applications. The *object computing paradigm* has been proven to increase productivity and improve quality in an application development that purports the reuse of components and distributed computing. Amalgamation of these paradigms successfully addresses the business requirements of commercial transaction processing systems.

OMG's CORBA Object Transaction Service (OTS) [4] provides transactional semantics to the distributed objects world. It enables multiple objects that are distributed over a network to participate in a single global transaction. A distributed application can use the IDL interfaces provided by the OTS to perform transactional work involving these distributed objects. While the ORB handles the complexity of network communication between distributed objects, the OTS provides a good framework to implement critical applications in distributed environments by providing transactional integrity.

2.1.1   Transaction Service Architecture

Figure 1 illustrates the major components and interfaces defined by the Transaction Service. The *transaction originator* is an arbitrary program that begins a transaction. The *recoverable server* implements an object with recoverable state that is invoked within the scope of the transaction, either directly by the transaction originator, or indirectly through one or more transactional objects.

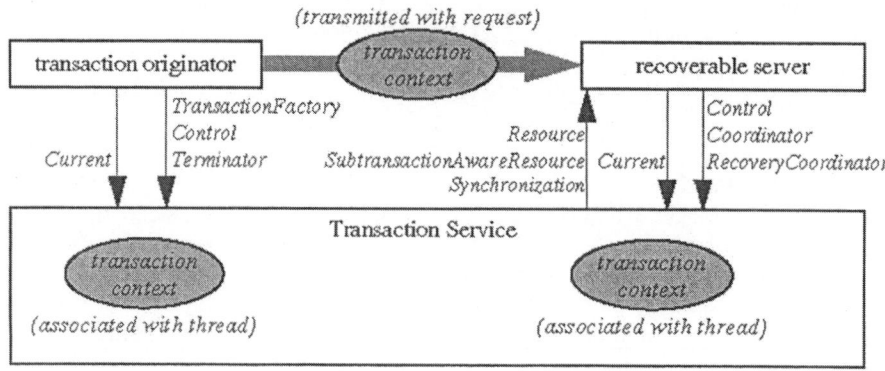

Fig. 1. Major Components and Interfaces of the Transaction Service [4]

The transaction originator issues a request to a *TransactionFactory* to create a new top-level transaction. The factory returns a *Control* object specific to the new transaction. From the developer's point of view, a *Control* object is the transaction representation at the application level. However, the *Control* does not directly support management of the transaction. Instead, it provides access to a *Terminator* and a *Coordinator*. Typically, it is the transaction originator that uses the *Terminator* to commit or rollback the transaction; however, this is not a constraint. Any thread that gains possession of a *Control* object, e.g., as a result of parameter passing, can get its *Terminator* object and invoke one of the two operations to end the corresponding transaction. The *Coordinator* can also be used to create subtransactions and to test relationships between transactions; however, its main purpose is to serve recoverable servers, which register *Resources* with the *Coordinator*. Each *Resource* implements the two-phase commit (2PC) protocol which is driven by the Transaction Service. A recoverable server may also register a *Synchronization* with the *Coordinator*. The *Synchronization* implements a dependent object protocol driven by the Transaction Service. A *SubtransactionAwareResource*, which tracks the com-pletion of subtransactions, can also be registered with a recoverable server. A *Re-source* uses a *RecoveryCoordinator* in certain failure cases to determine the out-come of the transaction and to coordinate the recovery process with the Transaction Service.

To simplify coding, most applications use the *Current* pseudo object, which provides access to an implicit per-thread transaction context. More details about the transaction context, and the ways to deal with transaction management and transaction context propagation are presented in the next section.

2.1.2   Issues Related to the Transaction Context

A transaction can involve multiple objects performing multiple requests. The scope of a transaction is defined by a *transaction context* that is shared by the participating objects. As part of the environment of each ORB-aware thread, the ORB maintains such a transaction context. The transaction context associated with a thread is either null (indicating that the thread has no associated transaction), or it refers to a specific transaction. A client thread can then issue requests and these requests will implicitly be associated with the client thread's transaction, i.e., they share the client thread's transaction context. It is permitted for multiple threads to be associated with the same transaction at the same time, in the same execution environment or in multiple execution environments, as it is presented in section 2.1.3.

When nested transactions are used, the transaction context remembers the *stack of nested transactions* started within a particular execution environment (e.g., process), so that when a subtransaction ends, the transaction context of the thread is restored to the context in effect when the subtransaction was begun. However, when the transaction context is passed between execution environments, the received context refers only to one particular transaction, not a stack of transactions.

The Transaction Service allows a client program to manage a transaction indirectly or directly. *Indirect* context management implies that the application program uses the `Current` object to associate the transaction context with the application thread of control. *Direct* context management implies that the application program manipulates itself the *Control* object and the other objects associated with the transaction. With these two models in place for managing transactions, propagating the transaction context can happen in two different ways, implicitly or explicitly. With *implicit* propagation, the transaction context associated with the client thread is passed on to the transactional objects without the client's intervention. With *explicit* propagation, the application passes the transaction context to trans-actional objects as explicit parameters in the method invocation. A client may use either form of context management and may control the propagation of the transaction context by using either method of transaction context propagation. This provides us with four *application programming models* that a client can use to communicate with transactional objects: indirect context management with implicit propagation, direct context management with explicit propagation, indirect context management with explicit propagation, and direct context management with implicit propagation.

The two most used application programming models, indirect/implicit and direct/explicit, are illustrated in Figure 2 a, and Figure 2 b, respectively, by means of short code snippets. Please notice the number of Transaction Service interfaces used in each approach, and the number of parameters in each request involving transactional objects. As a final remark, all interfaces defined by the Transaction Service specification [4] are located in the `CosTransactions` module.

```
CORBA.ORB orb = CORBA.ORB.init(...);      CORBA.ORB orb = CORBA.ORB.init(...);
CosTransactions.Current tx_crt =          CosTransactions.TransactionFactory f =
  CosTransactions.CurrentHelper.            CosTransactions.
    narrow(                                   TransactionFactoryHelper.narrow(
      orb.resolve_initial_references(           orb.resolve_initial_references(
        "TransactionCurrent"));                   "TransactionFactory"));
...                                       ...
tx_crt.begin();                           CosTransactions.Control control =
...                                         f.create(0);
...                                       ...
zürichAccount.deposit(amount);            zürichAccount.deposit(amount,
...                                                            control);
...                                       ...
tx_crt.commit(false);                     CosTransactions.Terminator t =
...                                         control.get_terminator();
                                          t.commit(false);
                                          ...
```

           a. Indirect and Implicit   b. Direct and Explicit

                       Fig. 2. Application Programming Models

2.1.3   OTS Support for Multithreaded Transactions

Using the OTS, a transactional application is not restricted to a single thread within a transaction. To allow multiple threads to participate in a transaction, a reference to the transaction Control must be passed to any thread that wills to join the transaction. If the direct/explicit application programming model is used, then this is enough. If the indirect/implicit model is used, then the threads still have to set their implicit transaction context by calling CosTransactions.Current.resume and passing the Control object as input parameter.

Thus, OTS actually allows multiple threads to access transactional objects on behalf of the same transaction, but without paying special attention to this additional form of cooperative concurrency. Figure 3 depicts such an OTS multithreaded transaction. One thread, here Thread C, starts a transaction T1. Other threads will eventually learn about the transaction's Control object and will be able to access transactional objects on behalf of T1. The OTS does not restrict the behavior of these threads in any way. They can spawn new threads, or terminate within the transaction. Any thread can commit or roll back the transaction T1 at any time, here Thread B, and the transaction will be committed or rolled back regardless of what the other participating threads might have voted. Thread exit from a transaction is not coordinated.

As seen in Figure 3, the OTS model is quite general and flexible, and may be suitable for many business applications. However, it leaves thread coordination inside a trans-action to the application programmer, and this can be error-prone. For example, a thread can decide to leave the transaction and perform some other operations before the outcome of the transaction has been determined, like Thread A in Figure 3. If this thread makes further use of any information that has been computed inside T1, e.g., modifies other transactional objects accordingly, then this might lead to information smuggling if T1 gets rolled back later on. Another unpredictable outcome might arise when a thread rolls back T1 without notifying the other threads. It might even happen that a thread gets associated with a new transaction context (Control object) although it is already working on behalf of another transaction. In Figure 3, for example, Thread B′ switches directly from T1 to

T2. A thread might also forget to vote on the outcome of a transaction, for instance because an exception has caused the program to skip over the commit statement. As a result, the transaction will hold resources for a potentially unlimited amount of time. Finally, transactional objects might not be aware of intra-transaction concurrency either. If they do not provide mutual exclusion for update operations, concurrent execution of operations might corrupt their state.

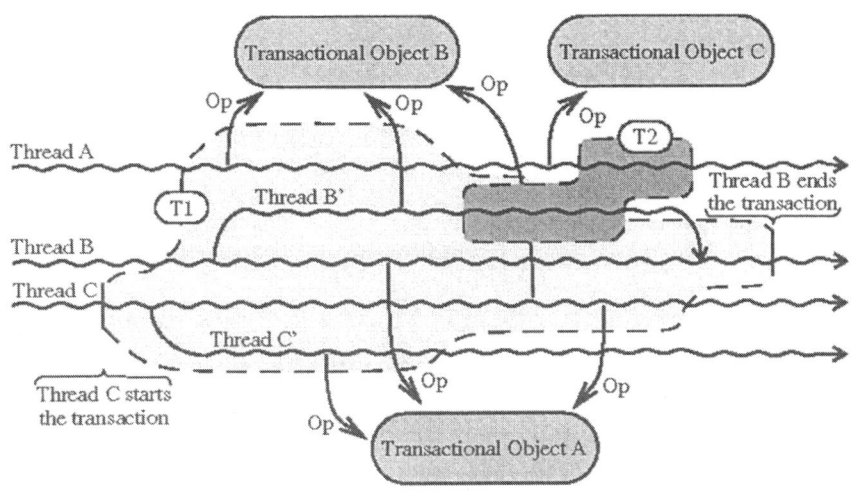

Fig. 3. Multithreaded Transaction in CORBA OTS

It seems obvious that the CORBA OTS does not really integrate concurrency and transactions; one might better say that concurrency and transactions coexist. The main drawback of this model is that there is no real transaction border, making it hard to guarantee the ACID properties for multithreaded transactions.

3   The Open Multithreaded Transaction Model

In this section we provide a brief overview of the Open Multithreaded Transaction model, stressing out mainly the rules imposed by OMTTs for controlling and structuring not only accesses to objects, as usual in transaction systems, but also threads taking part in transactions.

Open Multithreaded Transactions (OMTTs), first introduced in [5] and then fully described in [6], form an advanced transaction model that allows several threads to enter the same transaction in order to perform a joint activity. It provides a flexible way of manipulating threads executing inside a transaction by allowing them to be forked and terminated, but it restricts their behavior when necessary in order to guarantee correctness of transaction nesting and enforcement of the ACID properties.

Any thread can create an open multithreaded transaction becoming its first *joined participant*. The newly created transaction is said to be *Open*, and as long as it remains as such, other threads are allowed to *join* it, thus becoming joined participants of the transaction as well. A thread can join an open multithreaded transaction if and only if it does not participate in any other transaction. Otherwise, information local to a thread could be passed between transactions that should normally be isolated. Open multithreaded transactions can be *nested*. A participant of a transaction that starts a new transaction creates a nested transaction. Joined participant threads may spawn new threads which automatically become *spawned participants* of the innermost transaction in which the spawning thread participates. Any participant can decide to *close* the transaction at any time. Once the transaction is *Closed*, no new client threads can join the transaction anymore; however, a joined participant can still spawn new threads. All participants *finish* their work inside an open multithreaded transaction by voting on the transaction outcome. The only possible votes are *commit* or *rollback*. In order for a transaction to commit, all its participants must have voted *commit*. If any of the participants votes *rollback*, the transaction is rolled back. Participants are not allowed to leave the transaction (they are *blocked*) until its outcome has been determined. This means that all participant threads of a *committing* open multithreaded transaction exit synchronously. This rule prevents information smuggling by not allowing threads to make use of, or to reveal uncommitted information to the outside world. If a transaction is *rolled back*, the participants may exit asynchronously.

Figure 4 shows two open multithreaded transactions: T1 and T1.1. Thread C creates the transaction T1, and threads A, B, and D join it. Threads A, B, C, and D are therefore *joined participants* of the multithreaded transaction T1. Inside T1 thread C forks a new thread C' (a *spawned participant*), which performs some work inside the transaction and then terminates. Thread B also forks a new thread, thread B'. B and B' perform a *nested transaction* T1.1 inside of T1. B' is a spawned participant of T1, but a joined participant of T1.1. In this example, all participants of T1 vote commit. The joined participants A, C, and D are therefore *blocked* until the last participant, here thread B, has finished its work and given its vote.

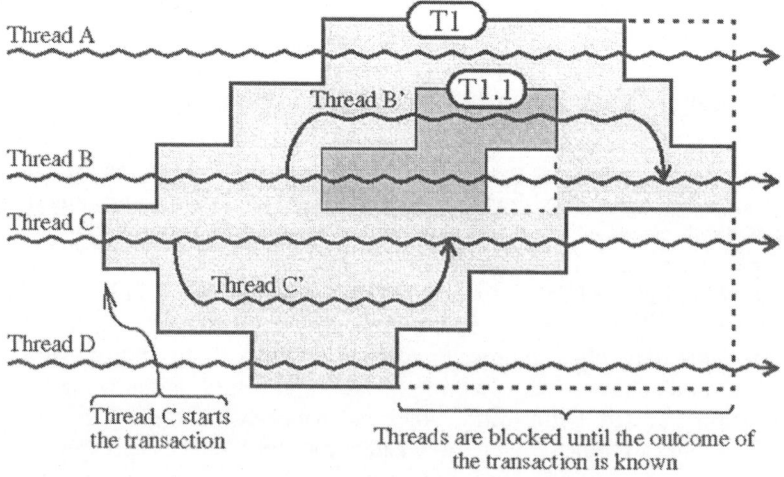

Fig. 4. An Open Multithreaded Transaction

Even though the OMTT model incorporates several other features, such as disciplined exception handling adapted to nested transactions, we consider they go beyond the purpose of this paper and they will not be addressed here.

OPTIMA (OPen Transaction Integration for Multithreaded Applications) [7] is the name of an object-oriented framework that provides the necessary run-time support for OMTTs. A prototype of the OPTIMA framework has been implemented for the concurrent object-oriented programming language Ada 95. It has been realized in form of a library based on standard Ada only. This makes the approach useful for all settings and platforms which have standard Ada compilers. Based on the features offered by Ada 95, procedural, object-based, and object-oriented interfaces for the transaction framework have been implemented.

4   Porting OMTTs to CORBA

In order to overcome the problems that might appear in CORBA multithreaded transactions, as presented in section 2.1.3, we will present in this section the design of a Thread Synchronization Coordinator, *ThreadSyncCoordinator*, that implements the behavior of OMTTs on top of CORBA OTS. The *ThreadSyncCoordinator* sits between the individual client threads and the CORBA OTS, allowing several threads to explicitly *join* the same transaction in order to perform a joint activity on some shared transactional resources. Moreover, thread control is improved inside a transaction, by enforcing a *blocking commit protocol*, which ensures that once in a transaction, a thread cannot leave before the outcome of the transaction has been determined. With the help of the *ThreadSyncCoordinator* we make sure that the rules imposed by OMTTs, as described in section 3, are respected by the participating threads, so that we can ensure that the ACID properties for CORBA multithreaded transactions are met.

4.1   The Design of the Thread Synchronization Coordinator

The design of the Thread Synchronization Coordinator is shown in Figure 5 by means of a class diagram compliant with the Unified Modeling Language (UML) [8] notation. Although not complete, the diagram shows all classes, attributes, and operations referred to in the sequel of this section. Design patterns [9], [10] were used in order to maximize modularity and flexibility.

A ThreadSyncCoordinator has attributes for:

- transaction management: the attribute enclosedControl links it to a COR-
  BA OTS Control object;
- thread management: the attribute status, indicating the status of the multithreaded transaction, the attribute participantThreads, yielding the list
  of all threads participating in the multithreaded transaction together with some
  associated information concerning their vote, and the attribute maxParti-
  cipants, representing the maximum number of participants in the multithreaded transaction.

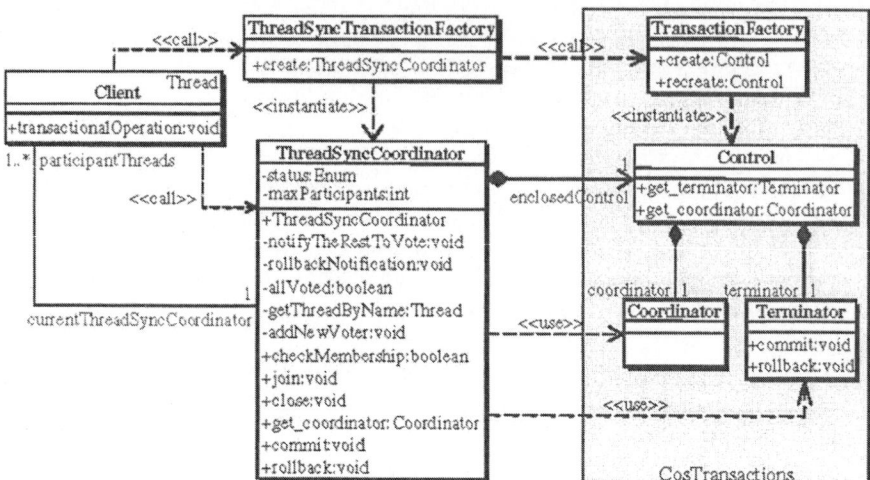

Fig. 5. Design of the Thread Sychronization Coordinator

A `ThreadSyncCoordinator` makes visible to the clients four operations: `join`, `close`, `commit`, and `rollback`. The creation of a `ThreadSyncCoordinator` is handled following the Factory design pattern by the `ThreadSyncTransactionFactory`, which provides one operation to the client, i.e., `create`.

The sequence diagram presented in Figure 6 illustrates that we use the current facilities offered by the CORBA OTS, and only enhance them with thread synchronization when dealing with multithreaded transactions.

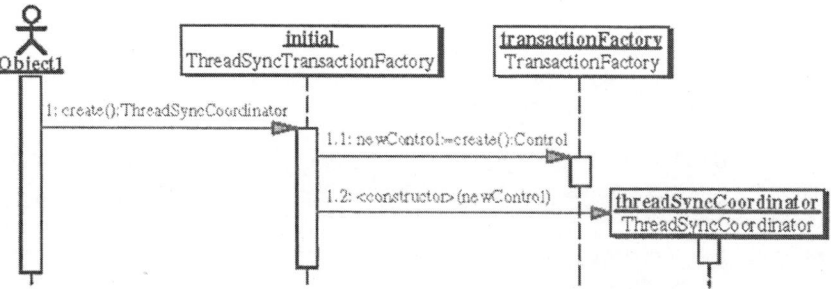

Fig. 6. Creating `ThreadSynCoordinator` Object Instances

The `ThreadSyncTransactionFactory` acts like a proxy for the `TransactionFactory` provided by the CORBA OTS. However, unlike in the Proxy design pattern, the client is still allowed to use the CORBA OTS support directly (by connecting to the `TransactionFactory` and obtaining `Control` objects), if s/he does not plan to have multithreaded transactions, or if s/he does not care about the blocking commit protocol for multithreaded transactions.

By invoking the `TransactionFactory` of the CORBA OTS, we get a COR-BA OTS `Control` object, which is further passed to the constructor of the

ThreadSyncCoordinator. This Control object, which is encapsulated inside the ThreadSyncCoordinator, will be used to interact with the transaction support offered by the CORBA OTS. Even if we will require to pass around the ThreadSyncCoordinator object, so that other threads can join it and participate in the same multithreaded transaction, we will use the encapsulated Control object for registering multiple Resources with the same transaction, and thus, make use of the CORBA OTS two-phase commit protocol for transaction completion. A multithreaded transaction with thread synchronization inside is actually mapped to a normal CORBA transaction with an explicit external thread control mechanism. Our ThreadSyncCoordinator is just a *wrapper* for the CORBA OTS Control object, providing it with additional functionality, i.e., join, close, commit, and rollback, for better management of threads that participate in the same transaction (corresponding to the encapsulated Control object), for forcing them to vote on the outcome of the transaction, for blocking them to leave before the outcome of the transaction has been determined, and for ensuring in this way that the ACID properties are met for multithreaded transactions as well.

We are not going to enter into concrete implementation details for any of the presented classes or methods, but we will use small code snippets to point out some important aspects that the implementor should follow in order to get the intended functionality. Moreover, we consider that the names of the methods presented in the class diagram are sufficiently eloquent to give the implementor a good hint about their purpose.

4.1.1   Joining and Closing a Multithreaded Transaction

Like in the current CORBA OTS model, where transactions are modeled by using Control objects at the application level, multithreaded transactions with thread synchronization are modeled by using ThreadSyncCoordinator objects.

A thread can join a ThreadSyncCoordinator object, and implicitly the corresponding multithreaded transaction, by simply calling the join method and providing its name, e.g., Thread.currentThread().getName() in Java (the Thread class does not implement Serializable, so we can only send its name). In order to achieve this, the client thread has to learn (at run-time) or to know (statically) the identity of the ThreadSyncCoordinator it wishes to join. Moreover, the multithreaded transaction needs to be in the *Open* status. Only threads that have already joined the ThreadSyncCoordinator are allowed to invoke operations on transactional objects on behalf of the enclosing multithreaded transaction.

Only participant threads of a multithreaded transaction are allowed to close the transaction by calling the close method. By closing a multithreaded transaction we are blocking any further joins from other threads. This feature has been introduced for two reasons:

- There might be static systems in which one of the participants (most probably the creating thread) knows how many participants are needed to successfully complete the transaction. In that case, it can specify the number of participants during creation of the ThreadSyncCoordinator object. As soon as this number of participants is reached, the ThreadSyncCoordinator object automatically closes.

- In dynamic systems, i.e., systems where at transaction creation time the number of participants is not known, there is a potential *livelock*, even though all participants behave correctly. In order to successfully commit a multithreaded transaction, all participants must vote commit. However, new participants can arrive at any time. This might lead to the situation where all current participants have decided to commit, but before they can do so, a new participant arrives. It will take some time for this participant to realize that all the work inside this transaction has already been completed. Once it has, it also commits. But during this time, a new participant might have arrived, and so on. In order to prevent this from happening, the transaction must be closed at some point. For some applications, it makes sense to close the transaction as soon as one of the participants has voted commit. Other applications might want to leave the decision to a participant that plays a special role (like the *seller* in the auction system example presented in section).

A discussion could be opened here on the operations that should be allowed inside a closed multithreaded transaction: whether the participants should be allowed to continue to invoke operations on transactional objects, or they should be constrained to vote on the outcome of the transaction, i.e., the only operations allowed would be commit or rollback. We considered the first approach in our implementation.

4.1.2   Committing or Rolling Back a Multithreaded Transaction

In order to implement synchronous exit, the ThreadSyncCoordinator must have a means to suspend the execution of its participants. In Java this is done using the wait() method. As shown in Figure 7, the ThreadSyncCoordinator object suspends a client thread when it votes commit and when there are still other participants working on behalf of the transaction. Successively, all participant threads will go to sleep in ①, waiting for the last voting thread. The last participant, which will take the then branch, triggers the final commit of the multithreaded transaction by getting the Terminator object of the enclosed Control and calling the COR-BA OTS commit on this Terminator, and then wakes up the sleeping threads by calling notifyAll() on the object that was considered for synchro-nization, in our case the ThreadSyncCoordinator. The CORBA OTS two-phase commit proto-col will ensure a synchronous update of the changes made to different transactional objects on behalf of the committing multithreaded transaction.

A similar approach is used for implementing the rollback operation, except the fact that the blocking protocol is not needed anymore. Once a client thread votes rollback, all the participant threads may exit asynchronously, and changes made to transactional objects on behalf of the multithreaded transaction will be undone by the CORBA OTS two-phase commit protocol.

Both the commit and rollback operations begin with a first check of the rights the client thread has within the current ThreadSyncCoordinator. Only participant threads are allowed to commit or to roll back the enclosing multithreaded transaction. Also, events ([11], or its evolved successor [12]) are used to signal all participant threads in a multithreaded transaction to vote on the outcome of the transaction once a client thread has voted commit, or to just let them know that the multithreaded transaction has rolled back. Of course, if the client does not want to complicate the structure of his or her application by using events, we can imagine that a fixed "reasonable" timeout, decided on a per-application basis, could be set for allowing all the other participants to vote.

```
public void commit(                    public void rollback(
    String clientThread) {                 String clientThread) {

if (! checkMembership(                  if (! checkMembership(
clientThread)) return;                  clientThread)) return;

synchronized (this) {                   synchronized (this) {

 addNewVoter(clientThread);              Terminator terminator =
                                           enclosedControl.get_terminator();
 if (allVoted()) {                       terminator.rollback();
 Terminator terminator =
  enclosedControl.get_terminator();      rollbackNotification();
 terminator.commit();
                                         this.notifyAll();
 this.notifyAll();
                                        } // end synchronized
 } else {
 notifyTheRestToVote();                 return;
                                        }
 wait(); ①
 }

} // end synchronized

return;
}
```

Fig. 7. `ThreadSyncCoordinator's` `commit` and `rollback` Operations

An obvious problem that has not been discussed yet are *deserters*, i.e., threads participating in a multithreaded transaction that suddenly disappear without voting on the outcome of the transaction. This can happen if a thread is explicitly killed, or when the process of a participant thread dies incidentally. This special cases are treated as errors, and will cause the multithreaded transaction to roll back, ensuring the all-or-nothing semantics of transactions.

4.2   Discussion

In this paper, we focused only on the blocking commit protocol, which ensures that once in a transaction, a thread cannot leave before the outcome of the transaction has been determined. However, other important issues are still to be addressed. One of the most important probably is concerning concurrency within the same transaction. Since the OMG's Concurrency Control Service [13] does not address this issue (providing only two ways to acquire locks: on behalf of a transaction, or on behalf of the current thread, but the thread must be executing *outside* the scope of a trans-action), it becomes the job of the transactional objects to provide additional concurrency control mechanisms (e.g., *synchronized* methods in Java) for preventing corruption of their state when accessed within a multithreaded transaction.

For the time being, the `ThreadSyncTransactionFactory` and the `ThreadSyncCoordinator` are implemented as stand alone CORBA objects. A potential client has to use the Naming Service [14] to locate them, and only then s/he can make use of their services. Ideally, the provided functionality could be integrated in the future versions of the CORBA OTS specification, so that ORB vendors will have to implement it (if they want to be compliant with the specification) and provide it directly to the application developers.

The chosen name, i.e., Thread Synchronization Coordinator, was very much influenced by the interface and the functionality that is provided to the client. Even though we use a `Factory`, explicit propagation, and encapsulate a CORBA OTS `Control`, the functionality of the `ThreadSyncCoordinator` object is not at all similar to the one provided by a CORBA OTS `Control`. It is not the responsibility of the application programmer to get the `Terminator` and to `commit` the transaction on the CORBA OTS. Instead, the interface is much closer to the CORBA OTS `Current` interface, providing operations like `commit`, `rollback`, and even `begin` in a slightly different way. However, the transaction context propagation is not performed implicitly, which is the case with the CORBA OTS `Current`. Finally, the CORBA OTS `Coordinator` came the closest to the functionality provided. Just as the OTS `Coordinator` is used for registering `Resources` so they participate in the two-phase commit protocol when a transaction ends, the `ThreadSyncCoordinator` allows threads to join (it can be seen as a registration as well) a multithreaded transaction, providing them with a blocking commit protocol until the outcome of the transaction has been determined.

As already shown in Figure 4, nested transactions and spawned threads are also supported within OMTTs, and their use is clearly illustrated in the implementation of the Online Auction System presented in section 5.2. For this, additional information is kept with the `ThreadSyncCoordinator`. For example, the transaction hierarchy, i.e., a list of subtransactions and a reference to the parent transaction, is managed by the `ThreadSyncCoordinator` as well. The blocking commit protocol is enforced at each level of nesting by different `ThreadSyncCoordinator` objects, one for each multithreaded transaction. We also make a difference between *joined* and *spawned* participants, and their role in committing a multithreaded transaction. Two additional rules restrict thread behavior inside and outside of a multithreaded transaction: a thread created inside an open multithreaded transaction must also terminate inside the transaction; and, a thread created outside of an open multithreaded transaction is not allowed to terminate inside the transaction.

The identity of the calling thread, its *name*, needs to be sent as a parameter every time for at least one of the following reasons. First of all, we might need it for updating our local information about the threads participating in the enclosing multithreaded transaction, like in the case of `join`. Second of all, we might need it for validation purposes, like in the case of `close`, `commit`, and `rollback`. Everytime a client thread invokes an operation on a `ThreadSyncCoordinator` we must ensure that it had joined it previously. Another reason, which is more technical this time, is related to the fact that the thread identity changes when making distributed calls. Client requests are executed in some sort of *TCP-Connection* threads, which have nothing in common with the calling client threads. Moreover, attention must be paid when using Graphical User Interface elements on the client, since all Java GUI interactions are handled inside a special thread, i.e., the *AWT-EventQueue-0*.

The `create` operation provided by the `ThreadSyncTransactionFactory` does not take any parameter, which means that a thread can create as many `ThreadSyncCoordinator` objects as it wants. In order to participate in a multithreaded transaction, a client thread has to explicitly join one of these `Thread-`

`SyncCoordinator` objects. Moreover, in order to be compliant with the OMTT model, it must be ensured that a client thread can join *only one* `Thread-SyncCoordinator`, and thus participate in *only one* multithreaded transaction. Since this check cannot be done at the `ThreadSyncCoordinator` level (it is not natural for a `ThreadSyncCoordinator` to know about all the others `Thread-SyncCoordinators` currently existing in the system), it has to be done at a higher level, where the developer decides to keep track of all ongoing multithreaded transactions (like the `AuctionManager` in the auction system example presented in section 5.3).

A similar functionality could be implemented on top of the CORBA OTS `Current`, so that application developers familiar with the indirect/implicit application programming model can use the benefits of multithreaded transactions without worrying about thread control inside a transaction.

5 Online Auction System Implementation Using Enhanced CORBA Multithreaded Transactions

An Online Auction System is an example of an inherently dynamic, distributed, and concurrent application, with multiple auctions going on and with clients participating in several auctions at the same time. As a consequence, the auction system becomes an excellent case study for testing the performance of new transaction models, in our case CORBA multithreaded transactions with thread control provided by `Thread-SyncCoordinator` objects.

5.1 Online Auction System Case Study Description

The informal description of the auction system presented in this section is inspired by the auction service example presented in [15], which in turn is based on auction systems found on various internet sites, e.g., www.ebay.com or www.ubid.com.

The auction system runs on a set of computers connected via a network. Clients access the auction system from one of these computers and are allowed to buy and sell items by means of auctions. Different types of auctions may be imagined, like *English, Dutch, 1st Price, 2nd Price*. In the *English* auction, which will be considered in this case study, the item for sale is put up for auction starting at a relatively low minimum price. Bidders are then allowed to place their bids until the auction closes. Sometimes, the duration of the auction is fixed in advance, e.g., 30 days, or, alternatively, a time-out value, which resets with every new bid, can be associated with the auction.

After a first *registration* phase, the user becomes a *member* of the auction system. Then, s/he has to *log on* to the system for each session in order to use the services provided. All members must deposit a certain amount of money to an account under control of the auction system. Once logged, the member may choose from one of the following possibilities: start a new auction, browse the current auctions, participate in one or several ongoing auctions by placing bids, or deposit or withdraw money from his or her account. Each bid is validated in order to ensure that the bidder has sufficient funds, that a bidder does not place bids in his or her own auction, and that the new bid is higher than the current highest bid.

If the auction closes and at least one valid bid has been made, then the auction ends successfully and the participant having placed the highest bid wins the auction. The money is withdrawn from the account of the winning participant and deposited on the account of the seller, minus a commission, which is deposited on the account of the auction system for the provided services.

If an auction closes, and no participant has placed a valid bid, then the auction was unsuccessful and no charge is required for the provided services.

The auction system must be able to tolerate failures. Crashes of any of the host computers must not corrupt the state of the auction system, e.g., money transfer from one account to the other should not be executed partially.

5.2   Enhanced CORBA Multithreaded Transactions: An Elegant Match

The auction system is an example of a dynamic system with cooperative and competitive concurrency. Concurrency originates from the multiple connected members, who may each participate in or initiate multiple auctions simultaneously. Inside an auction, the members cooperate by bidding for the item on sale. On the outside, concurrent auctions compete for external resources, such as the user accounts.

The number of participants in an auction is not fixed in advance. Therefore, auctions must also be dynamic, allowing members to join ongoing auctions at any time.

And, at last, the most important requirement for auctions is to be fault-tolerant. All-or-nothing semantics must be strictly adhered to. Either there is a winner, and the money has been transferred from the account of the winning bidder to the seller account and the commission has been deposited on the auction system account, or the auction was unsuccessful, in which case the balances of the involved accounts remain untouched.

All these requirements can be met if an individual auction is encapsulated inside a multithreaded transaction, and if the enclosing `ThreadSyncCoordinator` object is provided to the other participants, so that they can join the multithreaded transaction. A graphical illustration of an *English auction* is shown in Figure 8.

Since the OMTT model requires a thread to be participant in *only one* multithreaded transaction, every member must spawn a new thread that will act on his or her behalf inside one particular auction. In this way, the original member thread can continue its work and maybe spawn other threads to join other multithreaded transactions. As a result, a member can participate in several auctions simultaneously.

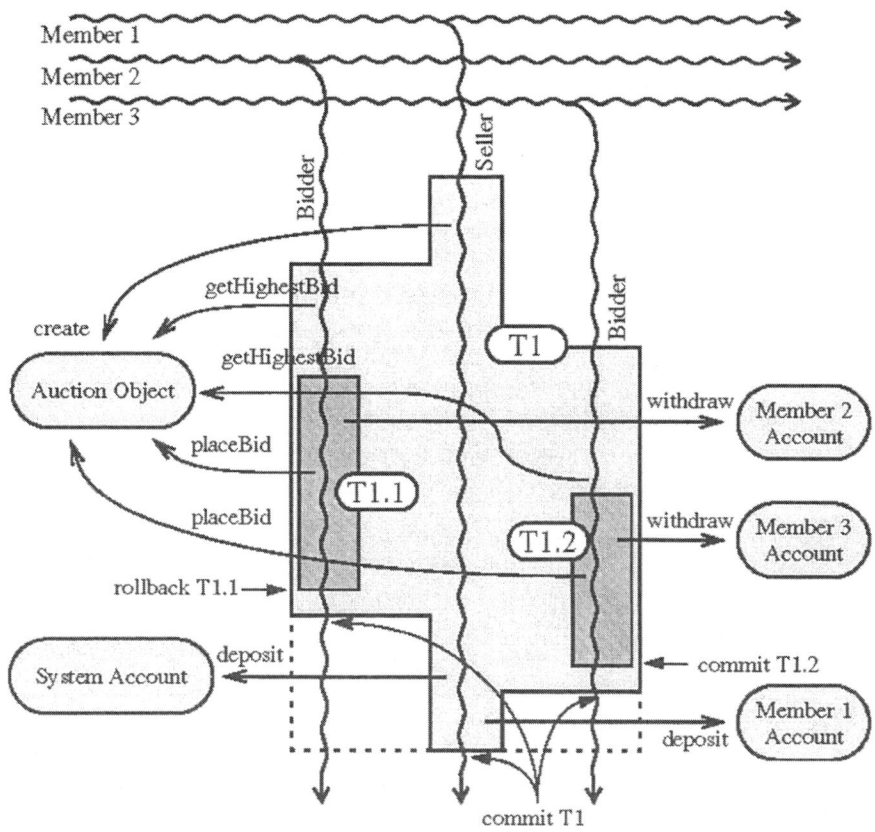

Fig. 8. The English Auction Multithreaded Transaction

In Figure 8, member 1 starts a new auction, creating a new *seller* thread. Once the item form has been completed, the `create` method is invoked, which creates a new `ThreadSyncCoordinator` object, and together with it, a new CORBA multithreaded transaction, here named T1, is started. Only then, the client auction with the provided parameters is created and automatically added to the list of current auctions. In our example, member 2 decides to participate. A new *bidder* thread is created, which joins the multithreaded transaction T1 (using, of course, the `Thread-SyncCoordinator` object). It queries the amount of the current bid by invoking the `getHighestBid` method on the auction object. Before placing the bid, a new `ThreadSyncCoordinator` object is created, and together with it, a new CORBA multithreaded subtransaction, here named T1.1, is started. Within the subtransaction, the required amount of money is withdrawn from the account of member 2. Since there is enough money on the account, the withdrawal completes successfully and the bid is announced to the `Auction` object by calling `placeBid`. Please notice that at this point, member 2 has not yet voted on the outcome of the subtransaction T1.1, which means that it can still be either committed or rolled back later on.

In the meantime, member 3 joins the auction, spawning also a *bidder* thread, which joins the multithreaded transaction T1. After consulting the current bid, member 3 decides to overbid member 2. Again, a subtransaction is started, here named T1.2, and the required amount of money is withdrawn from the account of member 3. The new bid is announced to the Auction object by calling placeBid. Once the bidder thread of member 2 gets to know this, it consequently roll(s)back the subtransaction T1.1 (by talking to its corresponding ThreadSyncCoordinator object), which in turn rolls back the withdrawal performed on the account of member 2. The money returned to the account of member 2 can now be used again for placing new bids.

In the example shown in Figure 8, no other bidders enter the auction, nor does member 2 try to overbid member 3. The bidder thread of member 2 has therefore completed its work inside the auction, and commits the global transaction T1. Since the blocking commit protocol is enforced by the associated ThreadSync-Coordinator, the bidder thread of member 2 will be blocked until the outcome of the multithreaded transaction is determined, i.e., until the other two participating threads give their vote.

Once the auction closes, the bidder thread of member 3 gets to know that it has won the auction. It then commits the subtransaction T1.2, which confirms the previous withdrawal. It also commits the global transaction T1. The *seller* thread in the meantime deposits two percent of the amount of the final bid on the account of the auction system as a commission, deposits 98% of the amount of the final bid on the account of member 1, and finally also commits T1.

Only now that all participants have voted commit, the ThreadSyncCoordinator will invoke the CORBA OTS commit and will let the two-phase commit protocol make the changes made on behalf of T1 persistent, i.e., the creation of the auction object, the bidding, the withdrawal from the account of member 3 (inherited from subtransaction T1.2), the deposit on the auction system account, and the deposit on the account of member 1.

5.3   Online Auction System Design and Implementation

Figure 9 presents a UML class diagram describing our design of the auction system that was previously presented in section 5.1. Inside the auction system, it is the task of the AuctionManager to create auctions, to associate auctions with multithreaded transactions, and to keep track of the current ongoing multithreaded transactions. It is its responsibility to check whether a client thread has already joined a transaction, e.g., joinedSomewhere(), and to block it from joining other transactions. However, it is the responsibility of the ThreadSyncCoordinator to check if a client thread has previously joined it or not, and thus to accept or refuse operations called by a client inside the multithreaded transaction (in our case, operations on Auction objects).

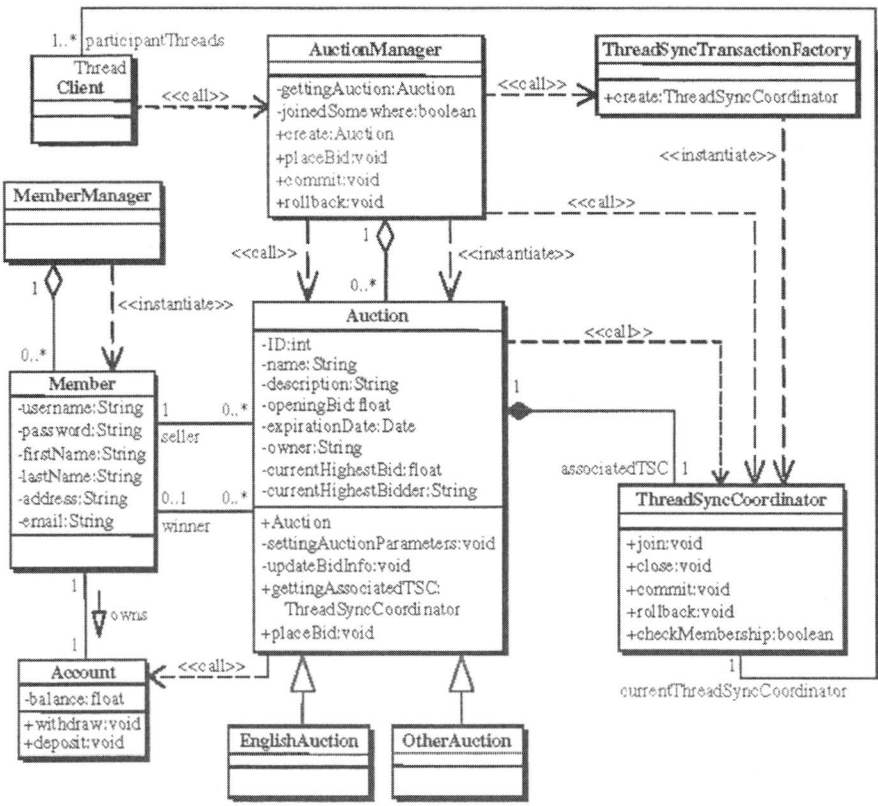

Fig. 9. The Design of the Online Auction System

Two UML collaboration diagrams show briefly how an Auction is actually created (Fig. 10) and how client bids are handled by the auction system (Fig. 11). The String in the method signatures represent the client thread's identity, i.e., its name, further referred as clientThread in the diagrams. Besides all the checkings that are done at different levels, please notice that the constructor of an Auction takes as parameter one ThreadSyncCoordinator object, which will handle thread coordination for that particular Auction.

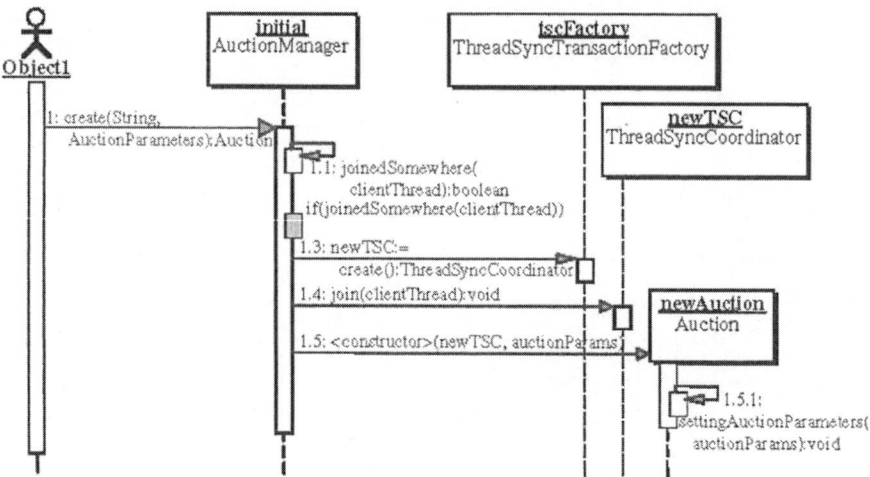

Fig. 10. Creating an Auction insinde the Auction Sytem

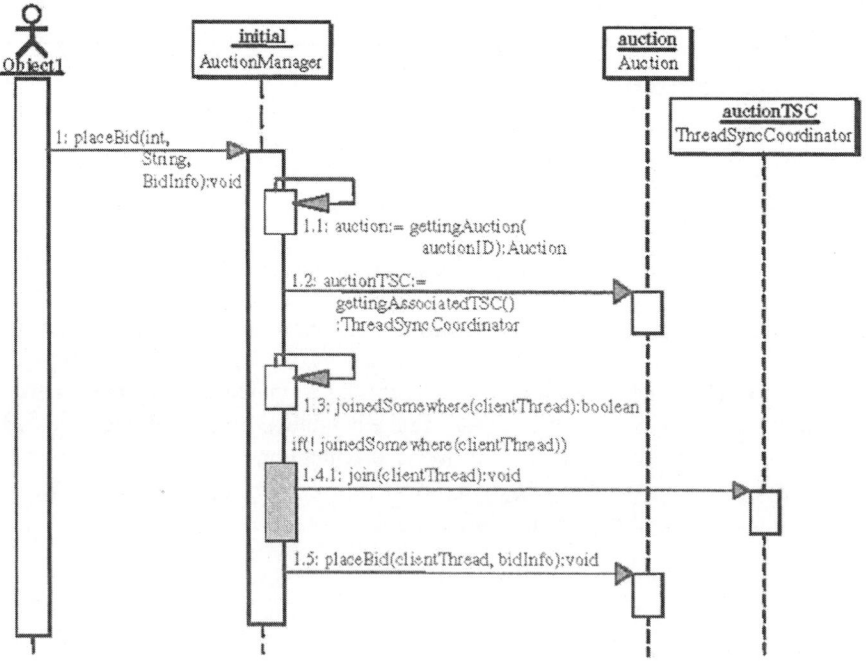

Fig. 11. Placing a bid in a Auction

The shaded rectangles in Figure 10 and Figure 11 indicate then branches of if statements. The then branch in Figure 10 does not contain anything, which indicates a return to the calling object. So, the diagram should be read as: if the client thread is already a member somewhere else, then `return`, because it is not allowed to create another multithreaded transaction.

One should also notice that the client thread is forced by the `AuctionManager` to join the `ThreadSyncCoordinator` associated with the `Auction` it wants to bid in (Fig. 11 , operation 1.4.1).

6 Conclusions

Allowing application developers to use multithreading inside a transaction can be dangerous when there is no support for thread coordination inside the transaction. Threads can decide to leave the transaction and perform some other operations before the outcome of the transaction has been determined, or a thread can get associated a new transaction context while already acting on behalf of another transaction. This freedom makes it very hard for application developers to guarantee the ACID properties for multithreaded transactions.

In order to overcome this drawback, we considered the Open Multithreaded Transaction model, which, based on a few rules, constrains the participating threads to behave in a disciplined way, so that we can guarantee that the ACID properties are met for multithreaded transactions as well. Further on, the OMTT model was ported to CORBA by implementing a Thread Synchronization Coordinator, *ThreadSync-Coordinator*, that sits between the individual client threads and the CORBA OTS, providing the desired thread control inside a CORBA multithreaded transaction. Thanks to the *ThreadSyncCoordinator*, client threads are now able to explicitly join a transaction, and get access to the shared transactional resources, simulating somehow that the transaction support is aware of concurrency. A blocking commit protocol ensures that once in a transaction, a thread cannot leave before the outcome of the transaction has been determined. Events are used to signal all participant threads in a multithreaded transaction to vote on the outcome of the transaction.

Implementing the Online Auction System has shown how the complexity of a dynamic, distributed, and concurrent application can be reduced by structuring it using enhanced CORBA multithreaded transactions with thread control provided by the *ThreadSyncCoordinator*.

References

[1] Gray, J.; Reuter, A.: *Transaction Processing: Concepts and Techniques*. Morgan Kaufmann Publishers, 1993.
[2] Object Management Group, Inc.: http://www.omg.org/
[3] Object Management Group, Inc.: *The Common Object Request Broker: Architecture and Specification*, v3.0, July 2002.
[4] Object Management Group, Inc.: *Transaction Service Specification*, v1.3, September 2002.
[5] Kienzle, J.; Romanovsky, A.; Strohmeier, A.: *Open Multithreaded Transactions: Keeping Threads and Exceptions under Control*. Proceedings of the 6th International Workshop on Object-Oriented Real-Time Dependable Systems, Universita di Roma La Sapienza, Roma, Italy, January 8-10, 2001. IEEE Computer Society Press, 2001, pp. 209–217.

[6]   Kienzle, J.: *Open Multithreaded Transactions: A Transaction Model for Concurrent Object-Oriented Programming*. Ph.D. Thesis #2393, Swiss Federal Institute of Technology, Lausanne, Switzerland, April 2001.

[7]   Kienzle, J.; Jiménez-Peris, R.; Romanovsky, A.; Patiño-Martinez, M.: *Transaction Support for Ada*. Proceedings of the 6th International Conference on Reliable Software Technologies, Ada-Europe, Leuven, Belgium, May 14–18, 2001. LNCS Vol. **2043**, Springer Verlag, 2001, pp. 290 – 304.

[8]   Object Management Group, Inc.: *Unified Modeling Language Specification*, v1.5, March 2003.

[9]   Gamma, E.; Helm, R.; Johnson, R.; Vlissides, J.: *Design Patterns: Elements of Reusable Object-Oriented Software*. Addison-Wesley, 1995.

[10]   Metsker, S. J.: *Design Patterns: Java^{TM} Workbook*. Addison-Wesley, 2002.

[11]   Object Management Group, Inc.: *Event Service Specification*, v1.1, March 2001.

[12]   Object Management Group, Inc.: *Notification Service Specification*, v1.0.1, August 2002.

[13]   Object Management Group, Inc.: *Concurrency Service Specification*, v1.0, April 2000.

[14]   Object Management Group, Inc.: *Naming Service Specification*, v1.2, September 2002.

[15]   Vachon, J.: *COALA: A Design Language for Reliable Distributed Systems*. Ph.D. Thesis #2302, Swiss Federal Institute of Technology, Lausanne, Switzerland, December 2000.

[16]   Silaghi, R.; Strohmeier, A.: *Critical Evaluation of the EJB Transaction Model*. Proceedings of the 2nd International Workshop on scientiFic engIneering of Distributed Java applIcations, FIDJI, Luxembourg-Kirchberg, Luxembourg, November 28-29, 2002. LNCS Vol. **2604**, Springer-Verlag, 2003, pp.15–29. An extended version is also available as Technical Report, EPFL-IC-LGL N° IC/2002/069, September 2002.

[17]   Siegel, J.: *CORBA 3 Fundamentals and Programming, Second Edition. Includes New CORBA Component Model and Persistence Service*. John Wiley & Sons, 2000.

Author Index

Lecture Notes in Computer Science

For information about Vols. 1–2806
please contact your bookseller or Springer-Verlag